Tikal Report No. 20A

EXCAVATIONS IN RESIDENTIAL AREAS OF TIKAL: NON-ELITE GROUPS WITHOUT SHRINES: THE EXCAVATIONS

University Museum Monographs 139

Tikal Report No. 20A

EXCAVATIONS IN RESIDENTIAL AREAS OF TIKAL: NON-ELITE GROUPS WITHOUT SHRINES: THE EXCAVATIONS

William A. Haviland

Series Editors

William A. Haviland

Christopher Jones

Published by

UNIVERSITY OF PENNSYLVANIA MUSEUM

of Archaeology and Anthropology

Philadelphia

2014

LIBRARY OF CONGRESS CATALOGING-IN-PUBLICATION DATA

Haviland, William A.
Excavations in residential areas of Tikal. Non-elite groups without shrines : the excavations / William A. Haviland.
  pages cm. -- (University museum monographs ; 139) (Tikal reports ; 20A)
Includes bibliographical references.
ISBN 978-1-934536-70-4 (hardcover : acid-free paper) -- ISBN 1-934536-70-9 (hardcover : acid-free paper)
1. Tikal Site (Guatemala) 2. Excavations (Archaeology)--Guatemala. 3. Mayas--Guatemala--Antiquities. I. Becker, Marshall Joseph.
Excavations in residential areas of Tikal. Groups with shrines. II. Title. III. Title: Non-elite groups without shrines.
F1435.1.T5H38 2014
972.81'01--dc23

                              2014013663

© 2014 by the University of Pennsylvania Museum of Archaeology and Anthropology
Philadelphia, PA
All rights reserved. Published 2014

Published for the University of Pennsylvania Museum of Archaeology and Anthropology by the University of Pennsylvania Press.

Printed in the United States of America on acid-free paper.

DEDICATION

To the memory of William R. Coe, a driving force in the Tikal Project and a strong supporter of housemound excavations before they were fashionable. For that, and many a stimulating discussion about the nature of Tikal society, my profound gratitude.

Table of Contents

Tables

Illustrations

I

Introduction

This is the second of three accounts of excavation in small, presumably residential structures of Tikal. As such, it constitutes a sequel to TR. 19, which details work done in Gp. 4F-1 and 2. Those were the first two small-structure groups excavated at Tikal, and much of the discussion here builds on data presented in TR. 19. Hence, the reader of this report will find it helpful to be familiar with the preceding one. Further background to small-structure excavations at Tikal is given in TR. 12 (pp. 26–32).

This report is concerned with the following six questions:

1. How typical of small-structure groups in use after AD 550 are Gp. 4F-1 and 4F-2 (Haviland 1963:44)?

2. Do small-structure groups in use in Preclassic and Early Classic times differ from those in use after AD 550 (Haviland 1963:537)?

3. Do data appear in excavation to supplement those from Gp. 4F-1 and 4F-2, which surely suggest that most small structures were, in fact, houses (Haviland 1963:44)?

4. Small structures normally occur in groups of two or more, arranged around the edges of plazas or higher supporting platforms. Groups 4F-1 and 2 themselves are actually composed of some five or six such plaza-structure units. Where such groups exist, were all structures contemporary, and did they function as a unit (Haviland 1963:44–45)?

5. As an extension of the above, can it be assumed that all the small structures on the Tikal site map represent a true picture of Tikal at one point in time, presumably the Late Classic, or were some structures in use before others? Are there likely to be a number of small-structure ruins that may be discovered only through excavation (Haviland 1963:45)?

6. If these small structures were indeed houses, what do their arrangement, architecture, associated burials, and other special deposits and artifacts suggest about the people who lived in them, and the way their society was organized (Haviland 1963:45, 537)?

To deal with these questions, in 1961 and 1963 I carried out excavations in 43 structures in 16 groups, located in all quadrangles of the 9 km² site map (TR. 11), save the Bejucal and Inscriptions Quadrangles. The first season (Op. 67 and 68) served as the basis for my doctoral dissertation (Haviland 1963). Thoroughly revised, this, with the second season of excavation (Op. 67 and 68), serves as the core of this report. This has been expanded to cover a variety of other excavations, however, which contribute to the solution of some or all of the questions just stated. These other excavations are all listed in Table 1.1, which also indicates their potential relevance to those questions. In short, TR. 20 deals with all investigations, of whatever sort, of small structures at Tikal, except for those discussed in TR. 21. The latter is focused specifically on small- to medium-sized structures in groups that include temples on the E.

The inclusion of data on so many groups imposes organizational problems. Hence, the presentation cannot precisely duplicate that of TR. 19, even though it continues its discussions. To make this report manageable, I have divided it into two parts, of which this (TR. 20A) is the first. It lays out the excavation data for each group or locus and is comparable to part II and Appendix A of TR. 19. The presentation is organized according to the quadrangle sheets of TR. 11 on which the groups and loci appear. This approach has the advantage of giving the reader some feeling of the relative thoroughness (or lack thereof) with which the small structures of various parts of the central nine square kilometers have been sampled. For each quadrangle, those groups excavated beyond mere test pitting are discussed first, in numerical and alphabetical order. Following this, those groups that have been only minimally tested are discussed, in the same order. The report concludes with descriptions of the burials and other special deposits encountered in the various groups. These correspond to the descriptions of similar deposits in parts V and VI of TR. 19. This makes it easy for those interested solely in special deposits, as one does not need to search for them in the excavation data. Conversely, tables in these sections enable readers to quickly relate specific groups to the special deposits they produced.

The intent in TR. 20A is to present basic data, keeping analysis and interpretation to a minimum. Although they cannot be avoided altogether, analysis, interpretation, and synthesis are the purpose of TR. 20B. In that volume will be found analysis of architecture, burials, other special deposits, and artifactual material (comparable to parts IV, the discussion sections of V and VI, and VII of TR. 19). For the most part, the general problems of analysis are discussed in the appropriate sections of TR. 19, although some further issues are raised here. The concluding section of TR. 20B attempts to pull together the data to address questions posed in this introduction.

Another issue relates to the fact that many data are drawn from a diversity of research programs. In particular, this poses problems of analysis. Dennis E. Puleston's chultun program, for example, was concerned primarily with the form and function of chultuns, and so (understandably) minimal attention was devoted to the investigation of nearby standing architecture, or the procurement of samples of occupation debris associated with specific structures. T. Patrick Culbert's ceramic test-pit program only aimed to procure ceramic samples, so again minimal attention was usually devoted to architecture and the relationship of artifactual material to specific structures.

Yet another problem is that some of the excavations were, frankly, salvage jobs (e.g., Str. 4C-34; 5C-56), and so there are frequent gaps in the data. The point is that all of this affects the comparability of data from one group to another. The reader should be aware of this problem at the outset, though I shall raise it again in TR. 20B.

A final problem relates to the date of preparation of this manuscript. A fundamentally complete draft was finished in 1972. Since that time, additional data have become available, requiring insertions and revisions. I have worked such material in as best I could, and revised where necessary to ensure consistency. In the process, I have cited some of the literature on the Maya that has become available since 1972. I have made no attempt, however, to "cover" this post–1972 literature. The intent has been to understand Tikal in its own terms; comparisons with other Maya sites may then follow.

As in TR. 19, I have adhered to Tikal terminology (TR. 12:47–48, 61–63); deviations (and they are only partial) are those spelled out in TR. 19 (pp. 3–4) for *bench, interior platform, plaza,* and *platform.* At various points where chronology is under discussion, the reader will encounter various dates stated as AD or BC. These are at best

approximations; dating here is almost wholly dependent on ceramics, and when dates are given, they are those that apply to the various ceramic complexes at Tikal (see TR. 27A:xiv). Problems of dating are also discussed in TR. 20B.

As many people had a hand in the excavations of Gp. 4F-1 and 4F-2, so too did many people have a hand in these. In 1961, I had as my field assistant Dennis E. Puleston. He was not only an ideal assistant, but he stepped into the breach and successfully wrapped up field operations when I became seriously ill. I have always been grateful to him for that. In 1963, my field assistant was Edward Crocker, who also served me well. Those responsible for other excavations included here are Marshall J. Becker, Bennett Bronson, William R. Coe, T. Patrick Culbert, Robert E. Fry, Christopher Jones, Carlos Rudi Larios V, and Puleston (Table 1.1). Each has been assisted by various field assistants too numerous to list here, but who are credited elsewhere in the appropriate Tikal Reports. In working up the excavations of others for inclusion in this report, I have tried not to do violence to their views, and I have from time to time been pulled back from various shaky interpretive limbs by their comments. Even at that, we have not always seen "eye to eye," but I regard this in a positive, rather than negative light. Perhaps, in such cases, a dispassionate reader can straighten us all out, and provide new leads to follow.

Special thanks are due a number of people who have always been willing discussants of the problems of small-structure excavations, and interpretation of those excavations. In particular, I have always found the thoughts of William R. Coe, Marshall J. Becker, Christopher Jones, Peter D. Harrison, and Dennis E. Puleston invaluable to my own thinking. I have profited as well from various exchanges of views with Wendy Ashmore, Arlen and Diane Chase, Annabel Ford, William T. Sanders, Gordon R. Willey, and Evon Z. Vogt. Our views have not always been the same, but for this very reason, I have found their comments particularly helpful.

As director of the Tikal Project, William R. Coe was always an avid backer of small-structure excavations, as was Edwin Shook before him. T. Patrick Culbert and Hattula Moholy-Nagy have been extraordinarily helpful to me where sherds and artifacts are involved. Jennifer B. Quick and Christopher Jones are due a vote of thanks for having satisfied a sometimes insatiable appetite for material from the Tikal files in Philadelphia. Jane Homiller, who drafted all plan and section drawings, has my thanks for her expertise and patience. To Janis Campbell, one of my students, go my thanks for an endless amount of proofreading. Barbara Hayden, who was responsible for data entry, editing, and other aspects of book production, also deserves my thanks. My wife, Anita, too, deserves special thanks for having put up with my seemingly endless involvement with Tikal.

The assembly of the final report was assisted financially from several sources. Two summer research fellowships from the University of Vermont assisted, as did small grants from the Tikal Project itself. A large shot in the arm came in the form of a fellowship from the American Council of Learned Societies. I could not have done without any of their help.

TABLE 1.1 (Part 1)
Excavations in Small Structure Groups Reported in Tikal Report No. 20
(Excepting Op. 24, 38C, 39D, 67, 68, and 72A)

Group or Locus	Operation	Excavator in Charge	Contribution Relevant to Problem					
			1	2	3	4	5	6
1D-1	13C,P	Fry					X	
1D-2	146J	Fry					X	
1D-3	146K	Fry					X	
1D-4	136A	Fry					X	
1D-5	136B	Fry					X	
1D-6	136F	Fry					X	
1D-7	136E	Fry					X	
1D-8	136D	Fry					X	
1E-1	146G,H	Fry					X	
2B-1	66W	Puleston	X				X	
2C-1	58F-H	Culbert					X	
2C-2	58A-E	Culbert					X	
"Ch.2E-2"	72F	Puleston					X	
2F-1	118A-E	Bronson		X			X	
Ch.2F-5	16A	Puleston					X	
2F/G: "Vacant Terrain"	69A,B;1P; 118A	Bronson/ Culbert					X	
2G-3	1P	Culbert					X	
Str.2G-48	1P	Culbert					X	
3C-2	57G,H	Culbert					X	
3C-3	57B	Culbert					X	
3C-4	57C-F,I-K	Culbert					X	
3D-4	59L-N	Culbert					X	
3D-5	59C,D	Culbert					X	
3D-6	59A,B,E	Culbert					X	
3D-7	59F	Culbert					X	
3D-8	59O-T	Culbert					X	
3D-9	125A-C	Bronson					X	
3E-1	60A,B	Culbert					X	
Ch.3F-4,5	72L,M	Puleston					X	
4C-1	55F-J	Culbert					X	
4C-2	55E	Culbert					X	
4C-3	55B	Culbert					X	
4C-4	55D	Culbert					X	
4C-5	55C	Culbert					X	
4C-6	55A	Culbert					X	
Str.4C-34	140A	Larios					X	
4D-3	71S	Culbert					X	
4D-4	62A-D	Culbert					X	
4F-4	71P	Culbert					X	
4F-5	72K	Puleston					X	
4F-6	24B	Coe					X	
4F-7	72J	Puleston					X	
4G-2	71D	Culbert					X	
4G-3	103C	Culbert					X	
Ch.4G-2	72N	Puleston					X	
5B-3	66O	Puleston					X	
5C-3	121A,B	Bronson		X			X	
5C-4	54A	Culbert					X	
5C-5	54C	Culbert					X	
5C-6	54B,D	Culbert					X	
Ch.5C-6	66L	Puleston					X	
Str.5C-56	26A-H;49A,B;	Jones/	X	X	X		X	X

TABLE 1.1 (Part 2)
Excavations in Small Structure Groups Reported in Tikal Report No. 20
(Excepting Op. 24, 38C, 39D, 67, 68, and 72A)

Group or Locus	Operation	Excavator in Charge	Contribution Relevant to Problem					
			1	2	3	4	5	6
	66A	Puleston						
5D-1	76A,B;77A,B	Coe	X		X	X	X	X
5E-1	71T	Culbert					X	
5E-2	63B	Culbert					X	
5E-3	71U	Culbert					X	
5E-4	63E,F;71G,I	Culbert					X	
5F-1	71F,L,M	Culbert		X	X		X	
5F-2	119A,B	Bronson		X	X	X	X	X
5F-3	71N	Culbert					X	
5F-4	119F	Bronson					X	
5G-3	101A	Culbert					X	
5G-4	102A	Culbert					X	
6B-3	66N	Puleston					X	
6C-2	70E	Becker	X				X	
6C-5	66F-H	Puleston	X	X	X	X	X	X
6C-6	38B	Culbert					X	
6C-7	37X	Culbert					X	
6C-8	37S;38D	Culbert					X	
6C-9	38E	Culbert					X	
6C-10	38A	Culbert					X	
Str.6C-60	66D,E	Puleston		X	X	X	X	X
6D-1	37R	Culbert					X	
6D-2	37U,Z	Culbert					X	
6D-3	37A,F,G	Culbert					X	
6D-4	37B-E	Culbert					X	
6D-5	1Q	Culbert					X	
6D-6	37T,V,W,Y	Culbert					X	
6E-3	35M	Culbert					X	
6E-4	35A	Culbert					X	
6E-5	35Ñ,R	Culbert					X	
6E-6	35I,S,T	Culbert					X	
6E-7	35J	Culbert					X	
6E-8	1Q	Culbert					X	
6E-9	35H,U	Culbert					X	
6E-10	35N-P	Culbert					X	
6E-11	35E	Culbert					X	
6E-12	35G,L,V,W	Culbert					X	
6E-13	35D	Culbert					X	
6E-14	35C	Culbert					X	
6E: "Vacant Terrain"	1Q	Culbert					X	
Str.6F-62	72D;103B	Puleston					X	
7B-1	39E	Culbert					X	
7C-3	39A	Culbert					X	
7C-4	39C	Culbert					X	
7C-5	39B	Culbert					X	
Str.7C-62	39F-H	Culbert		X	X		X	X
7E-1	36A	Culbert					X	
7E-2	36N	Culbert					X	
7E-3	36B,C,F-H,U-X	Culbert					X	
7E-4	36D,O	Culbert					X	
7E-5	36R,S	Culbert					X	
7E-6	36P,Q,T	Culbert					X	
7F-2	66Y,Z;103A	Puleston/ Culbert					X	
7G-1	72C	Puleston					X	

Excavations

1. Excavations in the Bejucal Quadrangle

Introduction

The small-structure groups of this quadrangle are among the least investigated at Tikal. The only intensive excavations were carried out in Gp. 2B-1 (this report) and Gp. 3C-1 (TR. 21). Even these were limited in scope. Eighteen test pits were dug in five additional groups. The 231 structures mapped in this quadrangle are arranged in groups that, from inspection of the map, total about 56 in all. Therefore, the sample takes in 13% of these.

Group 2B-1

Group 2B-1 is located on the site map (TR. 11) at 2B:S135 E337. It occupies a knoll above the 217 m contour. To the N, E, and S the elevation drops markedly; to the W the drop is slight, after which the terrain rises steadily higher. *Bajo* is just 100 m to the E. The area evidently was not densely built up, but the isolated Str. 2B-5 is only 55 m to the NE, while Str. 2B-10 and 11 are an equal distance to the S. From here, other groups of small structures extend in a line to the SE.

As mapped by H. M. Gregerson, the group consists of four structures: 2B-6, 7, 8, and 9, arranged on the four sides of a plaza. All are similar in size, although Str. 2B-8 is slightly smaller, and 2B-6 slightly larger, than the other two. On the fringes of the group are six chultuns (Ch. 2B-9, 10, 11, 13, 14, and 16). A seventh, Ch. 2B-15, is located beneath the end of Str. 2B-7. Excavations by Puleston in 1963 sought to investigate the relationship between this chultun and the structure.

STRUCTURE 2B-7-2ND

This seems to have been a rectangular platform, perhaps a foundation for a building of pole-and-thatch, with a small, centrally placed, interior platform (Fig. 1a and 3). For its construction, four stages are proposed: CS. 4 for demolition of earlier construction (see below). Then, as CS. 3, the main platform was built. For this, a wall of a single line of masonry was laid directly on bedrock. Now badly ruined for the most part, this wall is represented on the E only by a line of rubble. On the N, it was partially razed when Str. 2B-7-1st was built. Along the E end of the S wall, where bedrock is high, a vertical face was quarried in line with the wall so as to provide for a level plaza in front. Within the wall, the Maya dumped a mixed fill of earth, some trash, and a few stones.

As CS. 2, a small platform (Fig. 1a, 3a:1) was built on the fill of CS. 3. Mound configuration and excavated exposures suggest axial placement. With a wall of two lines of masonry facing rubble hearting, its fill differs from that for CS. 3 in that it includes many more stones. A floor (U. 1) was laid over the main platform, turning up to the exterior of the axial platform. Although the floor is now badly preserved, traces of its small stone foundation were found up to the E end of the structure. The small platform was probably paved as well, but of this no trace survives.

Construction Stage 1 is proposed for a building of perishable materials on the main platform, with the small axial platform inside. No positive evidence for such a building was found, but this is scarcely surprising in view of poor preservation and the presence of later disturbance (see 2B-7-1st). Nor were any corners searched for postholes. Since similar structures at Tikal are known to have supported such buildings (e.g., Str. 4F-3-2nd-B, 4F-5-A; TR. 19:118), the assumption that this one did is reasonable. Its main posts would have been set in place probably during CS. 3, with completion after the floors were laid.

STRUCTURE 2B-7-1ST

At some time, Str. 2B-7 was extensively altered. This began with partial demolition of 7-2nd, and construction of a raised area on the E end. A similar change may have altered the W end, a possibility that was not investigated.

For all this construction, three stages are proposed (see Fig. 1b, 3).

Construction Stage 3 is defined for partial demolition of the earlier structure. Immediately E of the (presumed) interior platform, the N wall of the main platform was torn out. Obviously, this would have required destruction here of any wall of pole-and-thatch. The masonry wall was replaced, as CS. 2, by a new one (U. 2). Built on bedrock of a single course of rectangular slabs, it is not in good alignment with the other walls, for it is oriented to magnetic, rather than true, E-W. Its top is some 0.15 m higher than the old U. 1, but about 0.25 m below the surface of the interior platform.

Unit 2 was not followed all the way around the E end of the structure, but there seems little doubt that U. 3, another wall, is part of the same construction. Unit 3 abuts the front of the interior platform 1.20 m from its SE corner. It rests on U. 1, runs S to the front wall of the main platform, then E along the top of this. Apparently, U. 1 continued in use as floor at the center of the structure. From this, one steps up to a higher level on the E, of which U. 2 and 3 are the walls. There was a further step up to the interior platform. No pavement survives for this new construction, but one undoubtedly was provided.

On the assumption that a new pole-and-thatch building was erected, a final construction stage (1) is proposed.

STRUCTURE 2B-SUB.1

Evidence exists for construction unrelated to either Str. 2B-7-2nd or 1st. This consists of eight postholes in bedrock (Table 2.1 and Fig. 2a, 3:U. 4 through 11) and a floor remnant (Fig. 2a, 3b:U. 12). Some of the postholes are beneath Str. 2B-7-2nd, and obviously earlier. Other postholes outside the walls could be later, earlier, or both.

Of the postholes, U. 4 and 7 form a straight line, very roughly E-W, beneath the SE portion of Str. 2B-7. It seems a safe assumption that they pertain to one wall of a building, which may be called Str. 2B-Sub.1, since it seems unrelated to Str. 2B-7-2nd. That it was the S wall is suggested by the remnant of floor U. 12, to the N. This remnant, just NE of the orifice of Ch. 2B-15, lies directly on bedrock, and was later covered by fill for Str. 2B-7-2nd.

The overall form and dimensions of Sub.1 are unknown. Unit 4 cannot mark the SW corner of the building, for no other holes for posts of a W wall were found in the trench. Units 8, 9, and 10 do not seem related to the structure, for they are located S of the line of U. 4–7. The missing E and W walls of Sub.1 should have run N from that line. Unit 11 might be a posthole from the back wall, for if one draws a line through it parallel to the presumed front wall, a structure 3.50 m in width is indicated. This is comparable to the 3.72 m width of Str. 2B-7-2nd. If U. 11 does indeed mark the N wall of 2B-Sub.1, then one

would expect to find another posthole about 2 m W of U. 11, just outside the area excavated. This compares with an interval of 0.80 m between U. 4 and 5, 1.26 m. between U. 5 and 6, and 1.40 m between U. 6 and 7. Given such variable spacing of posts, a 2-m interval between two of those for the rear wall cannot be ruled out.

CHULTUN 2B-15

DESCRIPTION

Access to the chultun (Fig. 2b, 3b) was through a manhole-like orifice, which was open at the time of its discovery. The orifice rim is stepped on the W side only. The neck beneath flares markedly downward into Chm. 1; this flare was probably not so marked prior to collapse from the ceiling. The antechamber is unusual, in that it is represented by little more than three steps cut from the bedrock. Moreover, its depth and breadth are unusual (Table 2.2). Access would have been difficult without a ladder, unless there were footholds in the wall of the neck and antechamber. None were seen, but they might have been obliterated by erosion. Overall, apart from its width, the antechamber by itself resembles a bottle-shaped pit.

The upper portion of Chm. 2 had collapsed, but its shape can be reconstructed with confidence. It was rectangular in plan, with walls meeting in well-defined corners. The walls rise quite vertically, with a marked break from the floor. In contrast, the ceiling was not clearly demarcated from the walls. Instead, the latter curved into a dome-shaped ceiling, necessary for stability, given the soft consistency of the marl beneath the bedrock crust. Had the ceiling been flat and clearly demarcated from the walls, there would not be nearly so much debris from its collapse in the chultun.

DISCUSSION

The chultun as found contained much debris, but it seems clear that it was essentially empty upon abandonment. Together on the floor of Chm. 2 were a number of large, well-preserved sherds with sharp, rather than worn, breaks. These likely represent vessels that were broken in the chultun. Along with the sherds were a few pieces of limestone and the broken stone cover for the chultun. Over this lay earth of a white color that progressively becomes darker towards the top. Mixed in were rodent, bird, peccary and jaguar bones. The color of the fill, in addition to clear evidence of ceiling collapse, leaves no doubt about its origin. The bones indicate that the ceiling collapse occurred over time, rather than in one event. Meanwhile, some animals used (or fell into) the chultun, and some outside material washed in.

Of prime interest is the relationship of the chultun to the overlying structure. Of significance here is a substantial mound of earth that overlies Str. 2B-7:U. 1 and 3, as well as the area immediately S. This mound (Str. 2B-7:U. 13) consists of white earth near the top, with darker earth near the bottom. A reasonable explanation for this deposit is that it is spoil from the construction of the chultun. If the chultun was constructed through the structure platform, as implied by the position of U. 13 over the wall and floor, the fill of the platform had first to be removed. Hence, the dark material at the bottom of U. 13 would be this fill, while the lighter material would be marl from construction of the chultun proper, as this would have been thrown on top. There can be no doubt that construction of Ch. 2B-15 followed that of Str. 2B-7-1st.

This raises the question as to why the chultun was dug through a structure platform. To attempt an answer, two unique features must be kept in mind: 1) the spoil was left heaped around, which would have served as a funnel for rainwater into the chultun; 2) there was no sill to keep water out of the deep inner chamber. By contrast, all indications are that it was desirable to keep rainwater out of chultuns (TR. 32). Perhaps the chultun was never finished, and the builders intended to remove the spoil heap. This is unlikely, for the broken vessels in the chultun suggest that it was used after construction. More likely, some sort of pole-and-thatch outbuilding was erected over the orifice, which would have eliminated the water problem entirely. That building may have been Str. 2B-7-1st, or it could have been a structure of which Str. 2B-7:U. 8, 9, and 10 are the only surviving traces. If indeed any or all of these postholes do relate to such a structure, it is difficult to visualize how. Further excavation would be needed to clarify matters.

POSSIBLE EARLY ACTIVITY

Quarrying activity is evident from a cut 0.54 m in depth E of Str. 2B-7. Its temporal relation to the structure is unknown, although there are two other cuts in bedrock, one of them N of the structure, and the other beneath it. These consist of grooves that might have been attempts at quarrying contemporary with that to the E. If so, then the quarrying preceded construction of Str. 2B-7-2nd. This, however, is tenuous.

SHERDS AND ARTIFACTS

Lot groups defined for the structures and chultun excavated in Gp. 2B-1 are presented in Table 2.3, while content appears in Tables 2.4 and 2.5.

CONSTRUCTION FILL

None of the material from fills was sealed, but LG. 1 from Str. 2B-7-2nd seems relatively uncontaminated. This includes the earliest material excavated, with some Cauac and Ik, but mostly Manik sherds. On the assumption that

most of the fill for 7-2nd was drawn from nearby, it is likely that the Manik material pertains to the preceding Str. 2B-Sub.1. Lot Group 2 is probably fill for Str. 2B-7-2nd for the most part, and the ceramics are similar to those from LG. 1. Noteworthy is a mano fragment, a household item possibly associated with use of one of the three structures here.

MATERIAL ABOVE LIVING LEVELS

Lot Groups 3a and 3b include material in this category. Although there may be some debris from use of Str. 2B-7-1st, it is clear that much is disturbed fill. This is certainly true of LG. 3b, material removed for construction of the chultun. The ceramic material (not plentiful) in both lot groups is virtually identical to that in LG. 1 and 2.

Lot Group 4, from the surface, clearly contains some late occupation debris, as indicated by the presence of Imix sherds. Of interest, therefore, is the presence of a mano fragment, along with a few other purely utilitarian artifacts.

CHULTUN

As noted, the chultun was filled with debris from the collapse of its ceiling, along with debris that washed in, mostly fill of Str. 2B-7-1st and 2nd. On the floor, however, were the sherds of late Ik vessels that appear to have been broken when the chultun was in use. They should help date its use. Most, if not all, of the animal bones should postdate the use of the chultun.

TIME SPANS

Stratigraphy permits definition of the time spans in Tables 2.6, 2.7, and 2.8 for the structures and chultun, and their correlation in Table 2.9. Presumably, excavation of other elements of Gp. 2B-1 would require revision of these group time spans.

Sherds found in and around the structure and chultun make it clear that Str. 2B-7-2nd was constructed after the appearance of Ik ceramics, which are present in all fill samples. Since they are outnumbered by Manik sherds, and

TABLE 2.1
Structure 2B-7: Posthole Dimensions (meters)

Feature	Diameter	Depth
Unit 4	0.11	0.20
Unit 5	0.07	0.09
Unit 6	0.18	0.18
Unit 7	0.17	0.06
Unit 8	0.12	0.10
Unit 9	0.22	0.14
Unit 10	0.19	0.20
Unit 11	0.10	0.06

since Ch. 2B-15 seems to have been constructed while Ik ceramics were still in use, Str. 2B-7-2nd quite likely dates not long after Ik ceramics first appeared, around AD 550. The abundance of Manik sherds suggests construction of Str. 2B-Sub.1 while they were in vogue. The presence of a few Cauac pieces suggests a Late Preclassic occupation somewhere in the vicinity, perhaps elsewhere in Gp. 2B-1.

Some late Ik ceramic vessels were apparently left in situ in Ch. 2B-15, after which the chultun was abandoned. A scattering of Imix sherds on the surface, however, indicates use of the group while such ceramics were in vogue.

Construction of the chultun clearly followed that of Str. 2B-7-1st, and there is no hint of Imix ceramics in fill of the latter. Apparently, Str. 2B-7-2nd, 1st, and Ch. 2B-15 all succeeded one another at this locus during the 150 years or so of Ik ceramic production, with the chultun being abandoned by the time Imix ceramics made their appearance. Even so, Gp. 2B-1 was not abandoned completely until some time later. It is impossible to state just when this was without further excavation. Clearly, it was after AD 700, but surely by AD 869, for no Eznab ceramics were found.

TABLE 2.2
Chultun 2B-15: Average Dimensions (meters)

Feature	Length	Width	Height	Diameter Minimum	Diameter Maximum
Neck	---	---	1.32	0.45	0.45
Lip step	---	0.10	0.05	---	---
Chm. 1	0.95	2.14	---	---	---
Chm. 2	2.26	2.80	2.22	---	---
Top step	0.20	1.30?	0.18	---	---
Step 2	0.38	1.60	0.30	---	---
Bottom step	0.20	2.20	0.60	---	---

TABLE 2.3
Group 2B-1: Lot Groups

Feature	Lot Group	Lot	Provenience	Ceramic Evaluation
Str. 2B-7 (Op. 66W)	1	3,9	Fill, Str. 2B-7-2nd, unsealed	Ik, Manik, some Cauac
	2	4,6,7	Fill, Str. 2B-7-1st and 2nd, unsealed	Mostly Manik, some Ik
	3a	8	Outside structure walls, surface to bedrock	Ik and/or Imix; some Manik
	3b	2,5	Spoil from chultun excavation (Str. 2B-7:U. 13)	Manik and probable Ik and/or Imix
	4	1	Surface	Ik, Imix and Manik
Ch. 2B-15 (Op. 66W)	1	10-12	Fill of chultun	Ik

TABLE 2.4
Structure 2B-7: Artifacts by Lot Group

Study Category	Object	Lot Group				
		1	2	3a	3b	4
Pottery Vessels	Sherds per cubic meter (lbs)	Not recorded, but small				
Other Pottery Artifacts	Unclassifiable formed object			1		
Flaked Chert Artifacts	Core					1
	Ovate biface		1			1
	Unclassifiable biface		1			
	Thin biface	1				
	Flakes, used	2				
	Flakes, unmodified	1	6			1
Flaked Obsidian Artifacts	Prismatic blade		1			
Ground, Pecked, and Polished Stone Artifacts	Manos		1	1		1

TABLE 2.5
Chultun 2B-15: Artifacts By Lot Group

Study Category	Object	Lot Group 1
Pottery Vessels	Sherds per cubic meter (lbs)	Not recorded
Flaked Chert Artifacts	Flake, unmodified	1
Shell and Bone Artifacts	Bone, unmodified	5

TABLE 2.6
Structure 2B-7: Time Spans

Time Span	Architectural Development	Construction Stage	Unit	Descriptive Data	Lot Group	Ceramics in Vogue
1				Abandonment and ruin of entire group		Imix
2				Abandonment of locus and ruin of structure, continued activity elsewhere in the group		
3				Continued use of locus, perhaps as outbuilding	4	
4			8?,9? 10?,13?	Partial or complete demolition of 1st; possible construction of outbuilding	3b	
5				Use		
6	Str. 2B-7-1st	1		Reconstruction of building of perishable materials	2	
		2	2,3	Construction of raised area at E end of platform		
		3		Partial demolition of Str. 2nd		Ik
7				Use	3a	
8	Str. 2B-7-2nd	1		Construction of building of perishable materials		
		2	1	Construction of small interior platform		
		3		Construction of main platform	1	
		4		Demolition of Str. 2B-Sub.1		

TABLE 2.7
Structure 2B-Sub.1: Time Spans

Time Span	Architectural Development	Construction Stage	Unit	Descriptive Data	Lot Group	Ceramics in Vogue
1				Demolition of structure		
2				Use; possible quarrying activity		----------
3	Str. 2B-Sub.1		4-7; 11,12	Earliest activity: construction of Sub.1; possible quarrying activity		Manik

TABLE 2.8
Chultun 2B-15: Time Spans

Time Span	Architectural Development	Construction Stage	Descriptive Data	Lot Group	Ceramics in Vogue
1			Abandonment with subsequent collapse of ceiling		----------
				1	Imix
2			Use of chultun		----------
3	Ch. 2B-15	1	Construction of Chm.2		Ik
		2	Construction of orifice, neck, and Chm. 1		

TABLE 2.9
Group 2B-1: Time Spans

Group Time Span	Str. 2B-7 (Table 2.6)	Str. 2B-Sub.1 (Table 2.7)	Ch. 2B-15 (Table 2.8)
1	1		
2	2		1
3	3		2
4	4		3
5	5		
6	6		
7	7		
8	8	1	
9		2	
10		3	

TABLE 2.10
Test Pit Locations: Bejucal Quadrangle

Group	Test Pit	Location
2C-1	58F	SW corner of group
	58G	Midden, behind Str. 2C-15
	58H	Plaza in front of Str. 2C-16
2C-2	58A	Center of platform for Str. 2C-24 through 28
	58B	NW corner of Str. 2C-24
	58C	Behind Str. 5C-27
	58D	Behind Str. 5C-24
	58E	Behind Str. 5C-25
3C-2	57G	Plaza in front of Str. 3C-9
	57H	Plaza in front of Str. 3C-7
3C-3	57B	Plaza of Str. 3C-11 and 12
3C-4	57C	Between Str. 3C-46 and 51
	57D	Between Str. 3C-45 and 46
	57E	Plaza in front of Str. 3C-52 through 55
	57F	Between Str. 3C-50 and 54
	57I	Plaza in front of Str. 3C-56 through 58
	57J	Off E end, Str. 3C-62
	57K	Between Str. 3C-60 and 62

Group 2C-1

This group, comprised of Str. 2C-15 through 21, is located in the SW corner of Sq. 2C. Structures 2C-15, 16, 17, and 21 are arranged on the four edges of a large plaza, with Str. 2C-18, 19, and 20 on the edges of a smaller one just E of Str. 2C-17. All appear to be ruins of small rectangular platforms suitable for house foundations. Three test pits (Table 2.10) were excavated in and around the larger plaza.

The ceramic data (Table 2.11) suggest that there was a Late Preclassic occupation here, but none during Early Classic times. The visible construction probably all postdates AD 550, and occupation of the group lasted relatively late, until after the appearance of Eznab ceramics. The presence of an obvious midden behind Str. 2C-15 suggests that the occupation was of a residential nature. Lack of a break in this midden between Imix and Eznab material implies continuous occupation, rather than a late reoccupation of the locus.

Group 2C-2

This group, including Str. 2C-22 through 28 with Str. 3C-1, might almost be considered as two. Five of the structures are arranged on the four edges of a raised platform. The other three are arranged on three sides of a lower plaza just W of Str. 2C-24, about 20 m S of Gp. 2C-1. Structures 2C-22 and 24 appear to have been small range-type structures, the latter with some kind of construction off its back. Structure 2C-26 might have been a small shrine located E of the group (TR. 21). The other structures appear to have been small- to medium-sized rectangular platforms, suitable for house foundations. Four out of five test pits (Table 2.10) were located in and around the raised platform. The other (Op. 58D), located behind Str. 2C-24, might pertain to either subgroup.

The ceramic samples overall were small, but seem clearly to indicate continuous occupation of this locus from Late Preclassic times through the time when Imix ceramics were in vogue (Table 2.11).

TABLE 2.11
Ceramic Evaluation: Bejucal Test Pits

Group	Lot	Provenience	Ceramics
2C-1	58F/1	0-20 cm	Ik and/or Imix through Eznab
	58F/2	20-40 cm	Late Preclassic; Ik and/or Imix
	58G/1-3	Midden	Imix and Eznab
	58H/1	0-20 cm	Late Imix, possible Eznab
	58H/2	20-40 cm	Late Preclassic; Ik and/or Imix
	58H/3	40-60 cm	Late Preclassic
2C-2	58A/1	0-20 cm	Ik and/or Imix, possible Manik
	58A/2	20-40 cm	Probable Late Preclassic through Late Classic
	58A/3	40-60 cm	Mostly Late Preclassic
	58B/1	0-20 cm	Ik and/or Imix
	58B/2	20-40 cm	Ik, possible Imix
	58C/1	0-20 cm	Ik and/or Imix
	58C/2	20-40 cm	Ik and/or Imix
	58D/1	0-20 cm	Imix
	58E/1	0-20 cm	Ik and/or Imix, possible Manik
	58E/2	20-40 cm	Ik and/or Imix; Manik
	58E/3	40-60 cm	?
3C-2	57G/1	0-20 cm	Ik and/or Imix; Manik; 1 Late Preclassic
	57H/1	0-30 cm	Ik and/or Imix
3C-3	57B/1	0-20 cm	Ik and/or Imix
3C-4	57C/1	0-20 cm	Ik and/or Imix
3C-4	57C/2	20-40 cm	Ik and/or Imix; Manik
	57D/1	0-20 cm	Mostly Ik and/or Imix
	57E/1	0-20 cm	Ik and/or Imix?
	57E/2	20-40 cm	Ik and/or Imix; Manik
	57E/3	40-60 cm	?
	57F/1	0-20 cm	Ik and/or Imix; possible Eznab
	57F/2	20-40 cm	Ik and/or Imix; including Ik
	57F/3	40-60 cm	Ik and/or Imix; possible Manik
	57F/4	60-80 cm	Ik and/or Imix; Manik
	57I/1	0-20 cm	Ik and/or Imix; Manik; 1 Chuen
	57I/2	20-40 cm	Mostly Ik and/or Imix
	57J/1	0-35 cm	Ik and/or Imix; Manik
	57K/1	0-20 cm	Ik and/or Imix; including Imix
	57K/2	20-40 cm	Ik and/or Imix; Eznab
	57K/3	40-55 cm	Ik and/or Imix; Eznab

Group 3C-2

Located in the NW corner of Sq. 3C, this group includes Str. 3C-5 through 10. Like Gp. 2C-2, it is composed of two subgroups. The northernmost appears to be made up of a small range-type structure on the N edge of a plaza, with two small rectangular platforms, possible house foundations, on the W side. On the S side is Str. 3C-8, a medium-sized rectangular structure that separates the two subgoups. South of this is a plaza with small, rectangular structures, perhaps house platforms, on the W and S sides. Two test pits sampled both subgroups (Table 2.10).

The ceramic data (Table 2.11) point to an occupation of the S subgroup that began when Manik ceramics were in vogue. Had it begun in Preclassic times, more than a single such sherd would have been found. The northern subgroup apparently was constructed after AD 550, with no earlier occupation. Group 3C-2 was abandoned by the time of Eznab ceramic production.

Group 3C-3

This group includes Str. 3C-11 and 12, and is 1.30 m SE of Gp. 3C-2 and 70 m W of Gp. 3C-1 (TR. 21). The two structures appear to be low rectangular platforms that could have been house foundations. They are arranged on the N and W sides of an apparent plaza area, into which a single test pit was sunk (Table 2.10). The small ceramic sample (Table 2.11) indicates that the group was built and occupied between AD 550 and 869.

Group 3C-4

Complex Gp. 3C-4 consists of a number of plaza-structure units. It is located near the SE corner of Sq. 3C, just N of Gp. 4C-1. Its 21 structures (3C-42 through 62) include apparently medium-sized, range-type structures as well as low rectangular platforms (possible house platforms), and at least one small temple-type structure that faces W (Str. 3C-46).

Seven test pits (Table 2.10) were sunk in various parts of the group. The results (Table 2.11) indicate an initial occupation when Manik ceramics were in vogue. A single identifiable Preclassic sherd found is best regarded as a stray, and does not necessarily indicate Preclassic occupation, which appears to have been continuous until some time after the appearance of Eznab ceramics, when the group was abandoned. The Eznab occupation may have been limited in spatial extent, for such ceramics come from at most two test pits. This may simply be the result of a short duration of the occupation, however, coupled with the fact that fill was primarily sampled in the test pits, rather than late occupation debris.

2. Excavations in the North Zone Quadrangle

Introduction

Knowledge of small structures in the North Zone Quadrangle is only slightly better than in the case of the Bejucal Quadrangle. Intensive excavations were confined to Gp. 3D-3 and 3D-9 (see below), along with Str. 3D-126 (TR. 21). Of these, Gp. 3D-3 is the best known. There was also excavation of the feature that appears on the map

as Ch. 2E-2, which might be associated with an unknown structure or structures. Besides these, a total of 17 test pits were dug in 6 different groups of small structures, in Sq. 3D and 3E. If all the structures of the North Zone proper are ignored, there remain 232, arranged in 62 groups. Of these, there is information (however scanty) on 16%.

Group 3D-3

Group 3D-3 is located in Sq. 3D of the Tikal site map (TR. 11), S20 E175. As mapped in 1960, the group includes three structures, 3D-8, 9, and 10 (Fig. 7), arranged around the W, N, and S sides, respectively, of Plat. 3D-5. The terrain on which this group sits is low, and projects slightly out into bajo, towards which the ground slopes down on the NW. This bajo is only about 20 m from the group itself. Excavations by Haviland in August 1963 tested all three structures for final plan and sequence.

STRUCTURE 3D-8

This structure was in such an extraordinarily poor state of preservation that little could be learned of it, although its NE and SE corners were located, and a trench was dug through it (Fig. 4). The trench was dug first, through what appeared from surface indications to be the axis. Not until later did we discover that it was off-center, our initial mistake being a direct result of the poor preservation of the structure.

The Maya's first action (CS. 4) was to prepare a base surface on which to build. For this, apparently the existing earth (represented by U. 1) was leveled and packed. Unit 2, a light-colored stratum, is this packed surface, and it probably served as an informal floor behind the structure after it was built.

Dark in color and devoid of cultural material, U. 1 overlay unmodified bedrock in some places, and a layer of brown earth (U. 4) in others. The reason why this soil was not disturbed much when Str. 3D-8 was constructed is that bedrock is lower here than anywhere else in Gp. 3D-3, and bajo is not far distant. Removal of this earth would have meant that the structure would be quite low in relation to the other two, and there would have been the added risk of occasional floods.

Once the base surface was prepared, the area serving as Plat. 3D-5 was built up (as CS. 3) to a height of about 0.70 m above the base surface. For this, a gray earth fill (U. 3) was dumped over U. 1 and the E end of U. 2.

With the surface of Plat. 3D-5 built up, the walls of Str. 3D-8 were constructed (as CS. 2). The front wall, of a single course of masonry, was built above U. 3. A plaza floor, running E, may have been in union with the base of this wall. At present, there is no trace of such a floor, a likely consequence of poor preservation here, but an equivalent floor does survive in front of Str. 3D-9 (Fig. 5, Str. 3D-9:U. 1).

The rear wall of Str. 3D-8 is now badly preserved, but seems to have consisted of two or three courses of masonry resting on fill a few centimeters thick over U. 2. Presumably, the same is true of the end walls, but their depth was not investigated. Given the position of the rear wall relative to U. 2, the construction of the walls and the dumping of earth fill within them must have taken place concurrent with one another. Had the fill been placed after the walls were built, then the rear wall would rest directly on U. 2. Conversely, the entire fill could not have been deposited without walls to contain it. No pavement survives for the platform, but one probably existed. Its absence now is easily explained by exceptionally poor preservation.

A final stage (CS. 1) is allowed for construction of a building of perishable materials on the platform, although there is no direct evidence for this. Since some small platforms supported such buildings, however, this may have done so as well.

STRUCTURE 3D-9-2ND

The structure seems originally to have been a one-level platform (Fig. 5). Since some other such platforms supported buildings of pole-and-thatch, perhaps this one did also, a possibility that was not investigated. On the assumption that this was the case, however, Str. 3D-9-2nd was probably built in three construction stages, as was Str. 3D-8. First, the base surface was prepared (CS. 3), and then platform walls were set, with mixed earth and trash placed within their perimeter (CS. 2). A plaster floor (U. 1) for the plaza turned up to the base of the front wall. No pavement for the platform itself was found, but this does not preclude its one-time existence, as there was little overburden to offer protection. Finally, the building itself would have been constructed (CS. 1), although corner posts were no doubt set in an earlier stage of construction.

The area behind the structure probably was not paved. A stony layer (U. 2) that runs up to the back wall seems to mark the occupation level here.

STRUCTURE 3D-9-1ST

A separate architectural development is proposed for the upper platform level, as its fill is quite different from that for the lower level (Fig. 5b). Generally, where two-level platforms were built as a single architectural entity, the fills of the two levels did not differ to this degree. Here, the walls of the upper level platform have been destroyed over the centuries, but the distinctive fill of stone rubble (U. 3) testifies to its one-time existence. The floor that probably once existed has also been de-

stroyed, as it was virtually at what is now ground level of the ruin mound.

Given the later construction of an upper platform level, any building of perishable material already in existence must have been extensively rebuilt. Thus, three construction stages might be defined: one for partial or total dismantling of the building (CS. 3), one for construction of the new platform on the original lower level (CS. 2), and one for total or partial reconstruction of the building (CS. 1).

STRUCTURE 3D-10-2ND

This structure occupies the most commanding position in the group, and seems to have been the largest of the three. Since bedrock here is higher than elsewhere in the vicinity, preparation of a base surface for Str. 3D-10 required its alteration (CS. 4). Specifically, it was quarried in such a way as to conform to the outline of the NE corner of the structure (Fig. 6a:1), although this particular operation may have followed, rather than preceded, construction of U. 4 (see below). Once the construction was completed, the level surface of bedrock evidently served as an occupation surface behind the structure.

Assembly of this structure (Fig. 6) differed in a fundamental way from that of most two-level platforms at Tikal. Here, a main platform was constructed (as CS. 3), to which a lower level was then added (CS. 2, below). Placement of the walls of the main portion of the structure and the fill operation seem to have taken place simultaneously. The front wall is represented by U. 2, which is based on bedrock. The back wall, however, was set in the structure fill itself (U. 1). This back wall, constructed of inner and outer face-stones, with rubble between, has well-cut outer stones based on a thin stratum of fill over bedrock. The inner stones, which are rougher, were placed after more fill had been dumped inside the outer wall stones.

Following construction of the main portion of the platform, an extension to the N wall was added (CS. 2). That this was an integral portion of 2nd seems indicated by the basic similarity of fills, as well as by the fact that a high step up of about 0.50 m would have been required without the addition. The wall of the addition, U. 4, is based partly on bedrock, and partly on earth fill. It contains a compact earth fill (U. 3) of a slightly lighter color than U. 1.

Worth pointing out is that the walls of the finished Str. 3D-10-2nd platform are notable for their apparently poor alignment. This does not seem to be the result of post-abandonment destruction. Rather, the walls were placed in such a way that they are not at all parallel, with one end of the structure considerably wider than the other. The overall impression is one of sloppy construction.

Presumably, a building of perishable materials was constructed on this platform, although direct evidence is lacking. This is the basis for CS. 1, although the main posts would probably have been set in the course of Stages 2 and 3. No floors were found anywhere in the excavation of Str. 3D-10. A plaster floor for Plat. 3D-5 undoubtedly once existed, for such a floor was identified by Str. 3D-9 (Fig. 5). In the case of Str. 3D-10, it has been destroyed by the elements, as is probably true for floors on the structure itself.

STRUCTURE 3D-10-1ST

Evidence for this final architectural development is extremely tenuous. It consists of U. 5 (Fig. 6), a well-cut masonry block that was found above U. 1 on the E side of the trench through the structure. This, with some rubble along the back wall, suggests that another platform level, or perhaps an interior platform, was added to the original structure. The fill seems to have been quite different from U. 1. If a whole new platform level were added, it would probably have required three construction stages, as in the case of Str. 3D-9. The addition of no more than an interior platform might or might not have involved such extensive reconstruction.

SHERDS AND ARTIFACTS

Lot groups defined for the structures of Gp. 3D-3 are presented in Table 2.12, with content given in Tables 2.13–2.15.

CONSTRUCTION FILL

Almost all cultural material from Gp. 3D-3 falls in this category. Because structures were so poorly preserved, sealed lots are a rarity. It is likely that most surface material, except for Str. 3D-8:LG. 2, derives from fill. Much of the trash used as fill in Gp. 3D-3 in all probability was taken from nearby sources, such as refuse originating around Str. 3D-5 through 7, or 3D-11 through 13. The later architectural developments of Str. 3D-9 and 10 may have been drawn from trash associated with their earlier versions.

MATERIAL ABOVE LIVING LEVELS

Only Str. 3D-8:LG. 2 clearly includes occupational material of midden quality. Even so, this is surely mixed with refuse eroded from structure fill (especially Lots 10 and 18). Structure 3D-10:LG. 1b contains material from above the floor of Plat. 3D-5, which probably explains why some of the content is later than that in LG. 1a (structure fill). This later material should pertain to occupation of Str. 3D-10.

TABLE 2.12
Group 3D-3: Lot Groups
(All Operation 67E)

Feature	Lot Group	Lots	Provenience	Ceramic Evaluation
Str. 3D-8	1a	6	Fill of U. 3	Imix, some Ik and Manik
	1b	5,9,13-15	Unsealed fill	Imix, some Ik and Manik
	2	4,10,18	Outside structure, surface to base of walls	Heavy Imix, some Ik, and Manik
Str. 3D-9	1	12	Unsealed fill of 2nd	Imix and/or Ik
	2	11	Fill of 1st	Ik and Imix
Str. 3D-10	1a	7,8,17	Sealed fill of 2nd (U. 1)	Ik, some Manik
	1b	1,2	Unsealed fill of 2nd (U. 1)	Ik and Imix
	2	3,16	Unsealed fill of 1st	Imix, Ik and Manik

TABLE 2.13
Structure 3D-8: Artifacts by Lot Group

Study Category	Object	Lot Groups 1a	1b	2
Pottery Vessels	Sherds per cubic meter (lbs)	Not recorded		
Other Pottery Artifacts	Figurines		1	1
	Miscellaneous modeled sherds (censer fragments?)		1	1
Flaked Chert Artifacts	Ovate bifaces			2
	Flake, used		1	
	Flakes, unused	2		
Ground, Pecked, and Polished Stone Artifacts	Mano	1		
	Metates	1		1
	MS. 66 (TR. 33A:90, fig. 64y)			1

TABLE 2.14
Structure 3D-9: Artifacts by Lot Group

Study Category	Object	Lot Groups 1	2
Pottery Vessels	Sherds per cubic meter (lbs)	Not recorded	
Flaked Chert Artifacts	Ovate biface		1
Ground, Pecked, and Polished Stone Artifacts	Manos		2
	Rubbing Stone		1

TABLE 2.15
Structure 3D-10: Artifacts by Lot Group

Study Category	Object	Lot Group 1a	1b	2
Pottery Vessels	Sherds per cubic meter (lbs)	Not recorded		
Flaked Chert Artifacts	Elongate bifaces			2
	Unclassifiable bifaces	2		1
	Flakes, unused		1	7
Flaked Obsidian Artifacts	Prismatic blade core			1
Ground, Pecked, and Polished Stone Artifacts	Manos	1		3
	Metates			5
	Rubbing stone			1
Shell and Bone Artifacts	Bone	1		

TIME SPANS

Tables 2.16–2.18 list the time spans defined on the basis of the sequences outlined above. Table 2.19 is an attempt to integrate these into time spans for Gp. 3D-3 as a whole. This is somewhat difficult, given uneven ceramic samples from the group. The evidence is firm that Str. 3D-8 was built and occupied after the appearance of Imix ceramics (Table 2.12), and the same seems true of 3D-9-1st. Structure 3D-10-2nd is dated by Ik ceramics, and 1st seems to have been in use when Imix ceramics were in vogue (LG. 1b and 2; see Table 2.12). It seems a reasonable hypothesis, then, to equate the final versions of 3D-9 and 10 with construction of Str. 3D-8 (Fig. 7). Structures 3D-9-2nd and 10-2nd were probably contemporary.

On this basis, activity in 3D-3 may probably be bracketed between the dates of AD 550 and 869. No post-Imix ceramics were identified, and the very few Manik sherds probably were present in fill brought in from a neighboring group.

TABLE 2.16
Structure 3D-8: Time Spans

Time Span	Architectural Development	Construction Stage	Unit	Descriptive Data	Lot Group	Ceramics in Vogue
1				Abandonment and collapse		— — — — —
2				Use	2	
3	Str. 3D-8	1		Construction of building of perishable materials	1b	Imix
		2		Construction of platform		
		3	3	Placement of fill to raise plaza level and provide base surface for front wall of structure	1a	
		4	2	Preparation of base surface		
4			1,4	Original accumulation of earth		— — — — —

TABLE 2.17
Structure 3D-9: Time Spans

Time Span	Architectural Development	Construction Stage	Descriptive Data	Lot Group	Ceramics in Vogue
1			Abandonment and and collapse	2	
2			Use		
3	Str. 3D-9-1st	1	Reconstruction of building		Imix
		2	Construction of upper platform level		
		3	Partial demolition of 2nd		
4			Use		
5	Str. 3D-9-2nd	1	Construction of building of perishable materials	1	Ik?
		2	Construction of platform		
		3	Preparation of base surface		

TABLE 2.18
Structure 3D-10: Time Spans

Time Span	Architectural Development	Construction Stage	Unit	Descriptive Data	Lot Group		Ceramics in Vogue
1				Abandonment and collapse	2		----------
2				Use			
3	Str. 3D-10-1st		5	Construction of final structure, possibly in three stages			Imix
4				Use			----------
5	Str. 3D-10-2nd	1		Construction of building of perishable materials			Ik
		2	3,4	N addition to platform			
		3	1,2	Construction of main platform	1a	1b	
		4		Preparation of base surface			

TABLE 2.19
Group 3D-3: Time Spans

Group Time Span	Str. 3D-8 (Table 2.16)	Str. 3D-9 (Table 2.17)	Str. 3D-10 (Table 2.18)
1	1	1	1
2	2	2	2
3	3	3	3
4	4	4	4
5	5	5	

Group 3D-9

Group 3D-9 is located on the Tikal site map (TR. 11) at 3D:S100 E400. The nearest construction is Str. 3D-31, 20 m NE, but the North Zone proper is only 75 m to the S. The terrain here slopes steeply down to the NW, and the soil is quite thin.

As mapped, the "group" appears to consist of a single structure, 3D-32, set on a broad, natural terrace on the hillside. A brief excavation by Bronson in 1966, however, revealed that the terrace is artificial. Apparently, a square platform was constructed, raised on its downhill edges. On this were built not one, but two structures. On the E side is the mapped Str. 3D-32, on the W side the unmapped 3D-127 (Fig. 8, 9). Both appear, on the basis of very limited information, to be low platforms suitable for house foundations.

STRUCTURE 3D-127

Little can be said about this structure, since only a single wall stone, and a bit of fill, were exposed by excavation (Fig. 9). The W wall is represented by a well-cut masonry block (U. 1), based on the plaza fill (Plat. 3D-3:U. 2), and parallel to the plaza wall (Plat. 3D-3:U. 1). East of the wall is a stony fill that also rests on Plat. 3D-3:U. 2, and extends as high as the wall. This fill was later cut into for some reason, and a pile of nearby sterile earth and stones was placed in the resulting hole. To the W, and again on plaza fill, is a thick layer of buff-colored soil that is rich in cultural material. This, evidently, is primary trash that was tossed from the structure, and this layer extends W of the plaza. There is little doubt, therefore, that there was a structure here, hence the new structure number.

PLATFORM 3D-3

This is the plaza on which Str. 3D-32 and 127 are based. Its approximate size is indicated on the site map (TR. 11:Sq. 3D) by the 29 m contour line, which runs W from Str. 3D-32, and then S. Only a very small portion of the W side was actually excavated (Fig. 8, 9). Unit 1 is a section of the W wall of the plaza, and consists of two courses of roughly shaped masonry, based on bedrock. There is probably a third course that has since collapsed. Behind the wall is fill of blue to tan soil (U. 2) that slopes upward to the E. This is the plaza fill, which undoubtedly was leveled off and, perhaps, paved with plaster. The wall of Str. 3D-127 was based on U. 2, and very probably was contemporary with construction of the plaza. There is no trace of an actual occupation surface beneath the structure. West of the plaza wall is a deposit of trash, apparently associated with use of this structure.

Lot Groups for Gp. 3D-9 are defined in Table 2.20, with objects recovered in Table 2.21.

CONSTRUCTION FILL

Platform 3D-3:LG. 1 is the only material from fill. Mixed together here are plaza fill, structural fill, and material from an intrusive pit into Str. 3D-127. The ceramics cannot therefore be used to date construction.

MATERIAL ABOVE LIVING LEVELS

In this category is material W of the structure and plaza, which is divided into Plat. 3D-3:LG. 2A, 2B, and 2C. The distinction between 2A and 2B is purely arbitrary, for both appear to be parts of a primary midden immediately W of the construction. Undoubtedly, though, there is contamination from the fill of the badly eroded platform and structure, most severe in the case of LG. 2B. In the test pits to the W (and also N and S of LG. 2A and 2B), which constitute LG. 2C, there is a steady drop-off in quantities of sherds and artifacts as one moves away from Gp. 3D-9 (measured in terms of sherd counts in Table 2.22; sherd weights were not recorded for Op. 125). This drop-off culminates in Test Pits 7, 14, 23, 28, and 33 (shown in Fig. 8). It seems a safe assumption that the material in the pits E of the five just listed derives from Gp. 3D-9. The test pits are far enough removed that one might expect that most of the material in them was refuse discarded occasionally by those who made use of the structures of the group. Yet the ceramic evaluation of this material (Table 2.20) might seem to refute this. Still, the occurrence of Manik through Imix sherds is explicable if the group was occupied from some time in Early Classic through Late Classic times. Beyond this, though, it is impossible to correlate specific items with specific structures in the group.

The material in LG. 2A, 2B, and 2C, therefore, appears to date the period of use of Gp. 3D-9. Further, the material in LG. 2C should afford a general idea of the function of the structures. Lot Groups 2A and 2B should give more specific clues to the function of Str. 3D-127.

OTHER SOURCES

Lot Group 3, from the surface, is probably a mixture of fill and occupation debris. Since there are less mixed samples of fill on the one hand, and potential occupation debris on the other, LG. 3 is not particularly useful. Further material, though, comes from test pits N, S, and W of LG. 2C. For the most part, sherd counts in those pits just beyond LG. 2C show higher frequencies, and there is no way to be sure how much of the material was discarded by the occupants of Gp. 3D-9, as opposed to those of two groups to the W. There is, consequently, no discussion of these test pits here.

The content of the various test pits is given in Table 2.23. Most measure 2 m², and go to bedrock. Where bedrock is close to the surface, a single object lot has been defined for the particular pit. Where bedrock is deeper, multiple lots have been defined, with Lot 1 always uppermost (surface and topsoil) and others below. Hence, the stratigraphic position of the lots is indicated by the lot numbers. At the NW corner of the test area, some test pits were enlarged, and others dug nearby. All material from these excavations has been lumped as Op. 125C.

South of LG. 2C, sherd frequencies drop off to the E and W of Test Pits 16, 9, and 4. This suggests, but by no means proves, that there was a frequently used route of travel between Gp. 3D-9 and one to the S that includes Str. 3D-51 and 52. Similarly, relatively high sherd counts in Test Pit 29 and the Op. 125C test pits suggest a route leading to Str. 3D-20 and 21. The high sherd counts along these routes would be explained as the result of those traversing them occasionally dropping litter along the way.

TABLE 2.20
Group 3D-9: Lot Groups

Feature	Lot	Lot Group	Provenience Evaluation	Ceramic
Plat. 3D-3	1	125B/6	Platform and structure fill, unsealed	Some Manik, mostly Ik, possible Imix
	2A	125B/4,5	W of the structure and platform, top to base of wall	Manik, some Ik and/or Imix
	2B	125B/2,3	Above LG. 2A	Some Manik, Ik, Imix
	2C	125A7/1,2;125A13/ 1,2;125A14/1; 125A19/ 1,2,3;125A20/1; 125A21/1;125A22/1, 2;125A23/1;125A25/ 1,2;125A26/1;125A 27/1;125A28/1;125A 31/1;125A32/1;125A 33/1,2	Test pits W of 2A	Manik, Ik and Imix
	3	125B/1	Surface over platform and structure	Ik and Imix

TABLE 2.21
Platform 3D-3: Artifacts by Lot Group

Study Category	Object	Lot Groups				
		1	2a	2b	2c	3
Pottery Vessels	Sherds per cubic meter (lbs)	Weights not recorded				
Other Pottery Artifacts	Figurines			1		1
	Centrally perforated sherd			1		
	Unperforated shaped sherds	1		3		
	Unclassifiable formed objects					1
Flaked Chert Artifacts	Ovate bifaces	1			1	
	Elongate bifaces	1	1			
	Thin bifaces		1	2		
	Irregular retouched flakes		1		1	
	Blades				2	
	Used flakes	1		8	3	
	Unused flakes	3	4	13	6	1
Flaked Obsidian Artifacts	Core			1		
	Irregular retouched flake					1
	Prismatic blades	3	2	6	4	
	Unused flake			1		
Ground, Pecked and Polished Stone Artifacts	Manos		1	3		
	Metate			1		
	Hammer stone					1
	Unclassifiable artifacts	1				
Shell and Bone Artifacts	Shell, L-shaped object			1		
	Shell, unmodified	1		1		

TABLE 2.22
Numbers of Sherds in Test Pits of
Platform 3D-3: Lot Group 2C
(See for Locations Fig. 8)

Test Pit	Number of Sherds
7	0
13	28
14	0
19	283
20	2
21	99
22	67
23	4
25	197
26	65
27	61
28	24
31	112
32	55
33	50

TABLE 2.23 (Part 1)
Test Pit Contents West of Group 3D-9

Test Pit	Operation/Lot	Contents
1	125A1/1	68 sherds Unclassifiable chert biface
	125A1/2	112 Sherds Chert ovate biface 5 Unmodified flint flakes Obsidian prismatic blade
	125A/3	11 Sherds
2	125A2/1	————————
3	125A3/1	23 Sherds Unmodified chert flake
	125A3/2	25 Sherds
4	125A4/1	154 Sherds Unclassifiable chert biface Chert blade Used chert flake Unmodified chert flake
5	125A/1	9 Sherds Slate or shale fragment
	125A/2	6 Sherds
6	125A6/1	11 Sherds
	125A6/2	4 Sherds
8	125A8/1	21 Sherds
9	125A9/1	80 Sherds Chert flake 2 Unmodified chert flakes
10	125A10/1	35 Sherds
	125A10/2	17 Sherds
11	125A11/1	21 Sherds
	125A11/2	3 Sherds
12	125A12/1	15 Sherds
15	125A15/1	38 Sherds
	125A15/2	17 Sherds

TABLE 2.23 (Part 2)
Test Pit Contents West of Group 3D-9

Test Pit	Operation/Lot	Contents
16	125A16/1	9 Sherds
		Unmodified chert flakes
	125A16/2	26 Sherds
		Unmodified chert flakes
	125A16/3	54 Sherds
17	125A17/1	21 Sherds
	125A17/2	24 Sherds
		2 Unmodified chert flakes
18	125A18/1	9 Sherds
24	125A24/1	4 Sherds
29	125A29/1	47 Sherds
	125A29/2	34 Sherds
	125A29/3	2 Sherds
30	125A30/1	30 Sherds
34	125A34/1	93 Sherds
	125A34/2	98 Sherds
	125A34/3	8 Sherds
35	125A35/1	11 Sherds
	125A35/2	14 Sherds
	125A35/3	69 Sherds
		Centrally perforated sherd
		5 Unmodified chert flakes
	125A35/4	10 Sherds
36	125A36/1	60 Sherds
	125A36/2	158 Sherds
		Chert flake core
		3 Unmodified chert flakes
		Metate
Op. 125C	125C1/1	Sherds (Number not recorded)
		Chert thin biface
		Obsidian prismatic blade

TIME SPANS

Whether or not either structure was ever modified is not known. Since Str. 3D-32 was not excavated, it is not possible to define group time spans, except in a very tentative manner. They have been defined for Plat. 3D-3 (Table 2.25), Str. 3D-127 (Table 2.24), and the locus as a whole (Table 2.26). They are of necessity rather gross; future excavation might reveal architectural sequences for the structure and plaza.

Construction of both features (TS. 3) seems to date from the period when Ik ceramics were in vogue (AD 550–700). These ceramics occur in such abundance in fill that it is probable that they had been in use for some time. Moreover, Ik sherds are not as abundant in occupation debris as are those from Imix vessels. The few Manik sherds, therefore, probably were present in fill that was procured from some nearby group, and do not indicate an Early Classic occupation of Gp. 3D-9. There is no Eznab or later material, so abandonment (at the start of TS. 1) was surely by AD 869, which dates the end of the Imix Ceramic Complex. It is assumed here that a pit, dug in Str. 3D-127, was excavated at the time of abandonment, since there is no other evidence for post-abandonment activity.

TABLE 2.24
Structure 3D-127: Time Spans

Time Span	Architectural Development	Unit	Descriptive Data	Lot Groups	Ceramics in Vogue
1			Abandonment; digging of hole; collapse		
2			Use	Plat. 3D-3: 2a,b; 3	Imix
3	Str. 3D-127	1	Construction	Plat. 3D-3:1	Ik

TABLE 2.25
Platform 3D-3: Time Spans

Time Span	Architectural Development	Unit	Descriptive Data	Lot Groups	Ceramics in Vogue
1			Abandonment and ruin		
2			Use	2a,b;3	
3	Plat. 3D-3	1,2	Construction	1	Imix Ik

TABLE 2.26
Tentative Time Spans, Group 3D-9

Group Time Span	Structure 3D-127 (Table 2.24)	Platform 3D-3 (Table 2.25)
1	1	1
2	2	2
3	3	3

Group 3D-4

Group 3D-4 includes Str. 3D-55 through 62; Ch. 3D-3 is probably a part of it as well. The structures, with two exceptions, are arranged around the edges of a raised platform located off the NW corner of the North Zone. Those two exceptions are Str. 3D-61 and 62, which project out from the W wall of the platform. These, along with 3D-59, appear to be low rectangular platforms that could have supported buildings of perishable materials. Structures 3D-56, 57, and 58 resemble small temples that

face W, typical of family shrines (TR. 21). Structure 3D-55 appears to have been a small range-type building. The feature labeled "Str. 3D-60" probably is a wall for the supporting platform of the group, rather than a structure.

The three test pits (Table 2.27) were all located in the platform of the group, and so probably sample redeposited fill for the most part, rather than late occupation material. The data (Table 2.28) suggest initial construction when Manik ceramics were in vogue. Occupation certainly continued after AD 550, and probably into the period between AD 700 and 869.

Group 3D-5

Included here are Str. 3D-63, 64, and 65, located 140 m W of the North Zone. The three structures are arranged on the N, E, and S sides of the plaza. A chultun (3D-5) is located in front of the S structure. All three structures appear to be small-to-medium rectangular platforms that could well have served as house foundations.

Two test pits (Table 2.27) sampled both plaza fill, and possible occupation debris behind one of the structures. The latter seems also to contain a large amount of washed-out fill, however. The ceramic data (Table 2.28) indicate occupation in Early Classic times, extending well beyond AD 550, possibly as late as AD 869. An initial Late Preclassic occupation is possible but dubious.

Group 3D-6

Group 3D-6 is located immediately W of the twin pyramid Gp. 3D-1, with St. 30, dated 9.13.0.0.0 (TR. 33A:62). It includes Str. 3D-88 through 97, arranged around the four sides of two plazas. At least two of these buildings were probably small range-type structures, and the rest were likely low rectangular platforms for the support of buildings of perishable materials.

Three test pits (Table 2.27) appear to have sampled both construction fill and occupation debris. Unfortunately, most of the ceramic samples were quite small. However, the data (Table 2.28) indicate that occupation was entirely after AD 550, probably postdating 9.13.0.0.0, unless earlier material was completely collected for use as construction fill in the neighboring twin pyramid group. This is unlikely, however, for earlier material survived in Gp. 3D-7, despite the construction nearby of two twin pyramid groups (see below). Group 3D-6 was abandoned some time after the appearance of Eznab ceramics.

Group 3D-7

This group, including Str. 3D-101 through 106, is located immediately N of the twin pyramid Gp. 3D-1 (which, as just noted, includes St. 30, dated 9.13.0.0.0), and W of the twin pyramid Gp. 3D-2 (which includes St. 20, dated 9.16.0.0.0; TR. 33A:45). The six structures are arranged on the four sides of a plaza. One appears to have been a small ritual structure, and faces W in the manner of household shrines (TR. 21). The others look like small rectangular platforms, most of which could have served as house foundations.

A single test pit (Table 2.27), which produced very small ceramic samples, was sunk into what is probably collapsed structure fill, and perhaps mixed with intermittent occupation trash. Obviously, conclusions based on such a sample must be tentative, but the data (Table 2.28) do seem to indicate an occupation from Late Preclassic into the period between AD 550 and 869.

Group 3D-8

This complex is located just S of the junction of the Maler and Maudslay Causeways. It consists of Str. 3D-108 through 120, arranged on the edges of five plazas. The majority of the buildings look as if they were medium-to-large range-type structures, with a few small rectangular platforms that perhaps supported buildings of perishable materials.

Six test pits here (Table 2.27) for the most part sampled construction fill, and produced rather small samples. A slight amount of late occupation debris may be included in Op. 59R, and 59T/1. The data (Table 2.28) imply an occupation lasting over a period when Manik, Ik, and Imix ceramics were in use. A terminal Classic reoccupation, or possibly abandonment at the time of Gp. 3D-8 cannot be ruled out, but is dubious. An initial Late Preclassic occupation is possible, but again doubtful on the evidence of only two sherds that could simply have been strays in the original construction fill.

Group 3E-1

This group, located just off the NE corner of the North Zone, includes Str. 3E-41 through 52 and Str. 3D-38 on the W. These are arranged on the edges of one large-sized, one medium-sized, and one small-sized plaza, except for Str. 3D-52, which projects out from the E wall of Str. 3D-51. Four of the structures could be fair-sized range-type structures, while two others might be very small temples. The others are small- to medium-sized rectangular platforms that could have supported buildings of perishable material. On one of the range-type structures (3E-48) was found a metate made from a reworked altar fragment (MS. 81; TR. 33A:9 and fig. 65k,l).

Two test pits (Table 2.27) sampled construction fill, with perhaps occupation debris in Op. 60A. The small fill sample of Op. 60B (Table 2.28) indicates that initial construction possibly was during the time of Manik ceramic production, though this is not conclusive. The larger 60A sample demonstrates that abandonment took place sometime after the appearance of Imix ceramics.

"Chultun 2E-2"

This small basin was incorrectly mapped as a chultun by Carr in 1960. Though it has coordinates of S311 and E305 on the site map (TR. 11), Carr gives the coordinates as S315, E305 in his field notes. The basin was completely excavated by Puleston in 1963. It was chosen for investigation because of the unusual shape of what was thought to be its orifice. Carr compared it to a pear, complete with a little cut representing the stem. It was given special mention in TR. 11 (p. 11) as one of the few chultuns with an orifice that was not circular.

The basin consists of little more than a slightly oval pit 0.50 m deep. The pear-shape ascribed to it by Carr is an illusion created by a slight flatness of the SE side and a small cut he saw as the stem. The bottom of the pit is fairly flat and the sides are near vertical. The SE wall even undercuts a little, and it is easy to see how this made it look like a chultun. There are two shallow cuts in the surface around the rim. The one on the W side is about 0.15

m deep with two squared corners; that on the SE side was smaller and only 3 cm deep.

The basin would not be mentioned here, except that it is very similar to two basins near Ch. 6C-7 (discussed in this report). The latter are associated with Str. 6C-62 and 63. Therefore, it is suggested that a similar structure, unmarked by any visible ruin, exists near "Ch. 2E-2," as the nearest evident ruin is more than 50 m away. Since the basins associated with Str. 6C-62 and 63 seem to have been inside the structures, it is possible that this one was as well. No ceramics were discovered, thus there is no clue to the date of any possible structures. Based on use of the basins near Ch. 6C-7 when Ik, if not Imix, ceramics were in vogue, one might speculate that this example was also contemporary.

TABLE 2.27
Test Pit Locations: North Zone Quadrangle

Group	Test Pit	Location
3D-4	59L	Plaza in front of Str. 3D-58
	59M	Plaza in front of Str. 3D-57
	59N	W edge of plaza
3D-5	59C	Plaza in front of Str. 3D-63, 64, 65
	59D	Behind Str. 3D-63
3D-6	59A	SW corner, Str. 3D-92
	59B	Corner juncture of Str. 3D-94, 95
	59E	Behind Str. 3D-97
3D-7	59F	Behind Str. 3D-103
3D-8	59O	Main plaza of group
	59P	Behind Str. 3D-118
	59Q	Edge of plaza between Str. 3D-117 and 118
	59R	Juncture of Str. 3D-118 and 119
	59S	End of Str. 3D-112
	59T	Plaza in front of Str. 3D-116
3E-1	60A	In front of Str. 3E-49
	60B	Plaza behind Str. 3E-48
	72F	"Ch. 2E-2"

TABLE 2.28
Ceramic Evaluations: North Zone Test Pits

Group	Lot	Provenience	Ceramics
3D-4	59L/1	0-20 cm	Ik, possible Imix
	59L/2	20-40 cm	Ik and/or Imix; possibly Manik
	59L/3	40-60 cm	Ik and/or Imix; Manik
	59L/4	60-80 cm	?
	59M/1	0-20 cm	Ik, possibly Imix
	59M/2	20-40 cm	Ik and/or Imix; Manik
	59N/1	Not given	Ik and/or Imix; Manik
3D-5	59C/1	0-20 cm	Ik and/or Imix
	59C/2	20-40 cm	Ik and/or Imix
	59C/3	40-60 cm	Ik and/or Imix; Manik
	59C/4	60-80 cm	Ik and/or Imix; Manik
	59D/1	0-20 cm	Ik and/or Imix; Manik
	59D/2	20-40 cm	Ik and/or Imix; mostly Manik; possibly Late Preclassic
3D-6	59A/1	0-20 cm	Ik and/or Imix
	59A/2	20-40 cm	Ik and/or Imix; Eznab
	59A/3	40-60 cm	Ik and/or Imix
	59B/1	0-35 cm	Ik and/or Imix
	59E/1	0-20 cm	Imix and/or Eznab
	59E/2	20-40 cm	Ik and/or Imix; Eznab
3D-7	59F/1	0-20 cm	Ik and/or Imix
	59F/2	20-40 cm	Manik; possible Ik and/or Imix
	59F/3	40-60 cm	Late Preclassic; Manik; possible Ik and/or Imix
	59F/4	60-80 cm	Late Preclassic
3D-8	59O/1	0-20	Mostly Ik and/or Imix
	59O/2	20-40	Ik and/or Imix; possible Manik
	59O/3	40-60 cm	Ik and/or Imix; Manik
	59O/4	60-80 cm	Ik and/or Imix; Manik; 1 possible Late Preclassic
	59P/1	0-20 cm	Ik and/or Imix; some Manik
	59Q/1	0-20 cm	Possible Ik and/or Imix
	59Q/2	20-50 cm	Ik and/or Imix; Manik; 1 possible Late Preclassic
	59R/1	0-30 cm	Ik and/or Imix; Manik; 1 possible Early Postclassic
	59S/1	0-20 cm	Ik and/or Imix
	59T/1	0-20 cm	Ik and/or Imix, including Imix
	59T/2	20-40 cm	Ik and/or Imix; Manik
	59T/3	40-70 cm	Ik and/or Imix; Manik
3E-1	60A/1	0-50 cm	Ik and/or Imix, including Imix
	60B/1	0-20 cm	Ik and/or Imix; Manik

3. Excavations in the Encanto Quadrangle

Introduction

Unlike those of the Bejucal and North Zone Quadrangles, the small structures of the Encanto Quadrangle have received considerable attention. Five of the groups were a part of the 1961 excavations (Gp. 2G-1, 2G-2, 3F-1, 3F-2, 3G-1, this report). In 1963, two other groups were investigated: Gp. 3F-3 (this report), and Gp. 3G-2 (TR. 21). Two more groups were sampled by surface collection, and one test pit. Together, these give a sample of material from 19% of the 45 groups mapped in all four squares of the Encanto Quadrangle.

Considerable attention was also given to terrain on which no structure ruins are visible. This led to discovery of four unmapped structures and a large, low platform. In addition, excavation of Ch. 2F-5, excavations around Ch. 2F-3, 6, 16, and 17, extensive surface collections in Sq. 2F and 2G above the 195 m contour, and one test pit enlarge the sample of material from "vacant terrain."

Group 2F-1

In April and July 1966, Bronson tested an extensive area of Sq. 2F for possible structures. A raised saddle between two low hills, this area lies some 60 m N of St. 27. The nearest visible construction is 60 m to the SW (Str. 2F-9 through 13), although there are six mapped chultuns (Ch. 2F-1 through 6). The terrain is well suited for houses (despite the lack of visible surface features suggestive of structures) and the chultuns might indicate one-time habitation. In order to search for evidence of this, an area of 5,000 m^2 was tested (Fig. 10). A line of pits was dug from Ch. 2F-6 N to a point just behind Ch. 2F-3. A second line was dug N from a point between Ch. 2F-4 and 2F-5, to one beyond Ch. 2F-4. Remains of construction were found at two locations, and were investigated further. Since these constructions are only 10 m apart, it seems warranted to consider them as parts of a single group (2F-1) that also includes Ch. 2F-4. In addition to the remains of Gp. 2F-1, two new chultuns (2F-16 and 17) were discovered.

PLATFORM 2F-1-3RD AND STRUCTURE 2F-30

Poor preservation, poor quality of construction, and limited exposure make this construction hard to interpret (see Fig. 11). Most of the architectural components seem to be parts of a low platform (Plat. 2F-1), but a single wall (U. 5 of Plat. 2F-1-3rd) seems to be part of a structure, Str.

2F-30. The earliest construction appears to have been a platform 22 m long, 14.5 m wide, and 0.04 m high. Surviving are four walls and a tough packed layer of small stones. This layer (U. 1), only a few centimeters thick, lies directly on bedrock (Fig. 12). Its surface is quite level, and probably served as an occupation surface. On the W, U. 1 abuts the base of U. 2, a freestanding wall of unshaped masonry also built on bedrock. Both U. 1 and 2 seem contemporary; U. 1, on the N and S, has the same stratigraphic relationship to U. 3 and 4, two other walls built on bedrock and similar in construction to U. 2. None of these walls were followed in their entirety. They were exposed at a number of points, however, and there seems little doubt that U. 1 was limited on the W, and at least most of the N and S, by a wall some 0.12 m high. None of these walls were particularly straight, nor do they meet at right angles.

On the E side of U. 1, things are less clear. It appears that there was a large inset in the NE corner of U. 1. The S wall of this inset (Fig. 11:U. 5) runs E from a point 9.50 m S of U. 3 and 10.20 m E of U. 2. This wall bears the same stratigraphic relationship to U. 1 and bedrock as U. 2, 3, and 4. At its W end, it turns a good right angle to run N, but seems to have been destroyed here at a later time. The same seems true 2.50 m E of the corner. How far the wall originally ran to the E is therefore unknown. Since U. 1 runs E of the excavation, U. 5 probably did as well.

Four facts lead to the belief that U. 5 represents the SW corner of a structure for which U. 1 served as a platform: 1) although similar in construction to U. 2, 3, and 4, its exposed face (S and W) was dressed to give a "finished" appearance; 2) the corner is closer to a right angle than those of the presumed platform; 3) the wall seems to be laid out in a straighter line than at least U. 2; 4) the inset in the platform suggests the existence here of something of significance such as a building. For this the designation Str. 2F-30 is proposed.

There may have been other structures associated with Plat. 2F-1-3rd, particularly to the SE (an area not excavated).

PLATFORM 2F-1-2ND AND 1ST

Platform 2F-1 was altered on at least one occasion, and probably two. In the absence of complete excavation, it is impossible to be sure just how many renovations there really were. On the basis of present information, the following reconstruction seems plausible:

Structure 2F-30 was largely razed, and a new wall (U. 6) was built across the N of the platform, 6 m S of U. 3 (Fig. 11). This wall was not followed in its entirety, but was exposed in three trenches. It was built of rubble and cut stone, and rests directly on U. 1 W of the old Str. 2F-30. East of this it had collapsed in part, but clearly rested on bedrock, which had been stripped of fill for Str. 2F-30.

Following this operation, fill was dumped inside the walls where U. 2 and 6 meet, and SW of U. 5. The fill was largely of small stones and rubble (Fig. 12:U. 7, 8, and 9), perhaps much of it drawn from the old Str. 2F-30. Similar fill (U. 10) was placed S of U. 7. Otherwise, fill consisted of a light-colored earth that was relatively free of stones. Lines of stones (Fig. 11:U. 12–16) demarcate the various different fill operations. Once these operations were complete, a plaster floor (U. 11) was laid over the fill, at the same elevation as the tops of the platform walls. This pavement is now poorly preserved, and in most instances destroyed. The best exposure was directly off the corner of U. 5 (which the floor must have covered). Overall, Plat. 2F-1-2nd measured ca. 16 by 14.50 m, and stood 0.28 m high.

The situation N of U. 6 (Fig. 11) is unclear. This area may have been filled also, but if so, why was U. 6 constructed? Most likely, this filling took place as an even later operation, and is therefore the basis of a final architectural development for the platform. This restored its original horizontal dimensions, while retaining the height of 2nd.

Presumably, a structure (or structures) stood on Plat. 2F-1-1st and 2nd, although no evidence for such was found. This scarcely rules out their one-time existence, for the poor state of preservation, the rather shoddy construction, and our limited exposure might explain the lack of evidence. Moreover, the structures might have been built wholly of pole-and-thatch.

STRUCTURE 2F-31-2ND AND 1ST

The earliest version of this structure was probably built in three stages. First (CS. 3), Str. 2F-Sub.1-1st (see below) was partly demolished. The building that stood on this platform was removed, along with the front walls of the two upper platform levels.

Second (CS. 2), the platform of 2F-31 was constructed. A W wall (Fig. 13 and 14:U. 1) was built on the floor of Str. 2F-Sub.1-1st. This consists of two courses of roughly rectangular blocks. The E wall (Fig. 13 and 14:U. 2) was built of cut masonry blocks placed in part on top of the E wall of Sub.1-1st. To the N (Fig. 13 and 15), two steps (U. 3, 4) seem to have been constructed as earth fill was dumped within the walls to the level of their tops. Much of this fill appears to have been drawn from trash and fill from Str. 2F-Sub.1-1st and 2nd. The surface on top of the platform looks to have been of packed, limy earth.

The third stage (CS. 1) is proposed for fabrication of a building of perishable materials. No traces of postholes for such an edifice were found, scarcely surprising given the limited excavation. The main posts for such a building would probably have been set in place during CS. 2. North of the structure (Fig. 15), a hard, limy earth surface served as an informal occupation floor. To the W and E, surfaces identified with Str. 2F-Sub.1-1st continued in use.

Although the evidence is scant, it appears that Str. 2F-31 was given increased width. A new E wall (Fig. 13 and 14:U. 5) was constructed 2 m from the original wall. Now badly collapsed, its fill has spilled into Ch. 2F-4 nearby. It was constructed on the surface Str. 2F-Sub.1:U. 9 (see below).

At some point, the area W of 2F-31 was filled to the level of the structure itself. Possibly, this was purposeful, but more probably it is a natural accumulation that followed abandonment of the structure. Following this, there was intermittent activity in the area.

STRUCTURE 2F-SUB.1-2ND AND 1ST

Little is known of Str. 2F-Sub.1-2nd, as excavation was limited to a trench 1 m in width (Fig. 13). Apparently, it was a square or rectangular building with freestanding masonry walls (Fig. 14). To begin construction, bedrock was stripped clear (CS. 3). The one exception may be U. 1 (Fig. 14), a layer of stony fill in a low area of bedrock to the W. As CS. 2, the building walls were then set directly on bedrock. Our excavations exposed a small portion of the doorway and W wall just to the N (Fig. 14:U. 3). The rear (E) wall was later torn out, but its location could be seen. The W wall, 0.88 m thick, was built of large masonry blocks. Following construction of the walls, a layer of packed, limy material about 0.15 m thick was laid (as CS. 1) within the walls and on through the doorway to the W. This layer, U. 2, served as the occupation surface. It is not known whether the masonry walls of the building were full height, or whether they were dwarf walls for upper works of pole-and-thatch.

Eventually 2F-Sub.1 was altered, at which time the existing structure was largely razed. In this process, its E wall was demolished. In its place was put a line of burned, limestone rubble. A new W wall (U. 4) was built on U. 2, 6.10 m W of U. 3 (Fig. 13 and 14). This, too, consists of limestone rubble. Behind it, over U. 2, was dumped an earth fill (U. 5). This runs E to the old U. 3 (Fig. 14), which was extended S by more limestone rubble (U. 6). Unit 6 continues N, on the W side of U. 3, and U. 5 abuts this.

Over U. 5 is another layer of earth fill (Fig. 14), on which the plaster Fl. 1 was laid. This runs 3 m E of U. 4, turns up, and after a break continues E at a higher level to turn up to U. 6. Apparently, this is the remnant of a floor for a three-level platform. It must have run E from the top of U. 6 to U. 7, the burned limestone rubble that replaced the rear wall of Str. 2F-Sub.1-2nd, to form the third level.

There is some evidence for a building of perishable materials on top of this platform. This is U. 8, a single round hole, 10 cm in diameter and 6 cm deep, in U. 2 just behind U. 4. It appears to be a posthole.

The construction of Str. 2F-Sub.1-1st may be summed up in five construction stages. Demolition of Sub.1-2nd defines CS. 5. This was probably followed by the placement of U. 6 and 7, with an earth fill between to help stabilize them (CS. 4). Unit 4 and the U. 5 fill followed (CS. 3). All of these rubble walls must have been finished off with a coat of plaster, probably when Fl. 1 was laid (CS. 2). By this time, the main posts of a building had to be in place, but the building was most likely completed as CS. 1.

Behind Str. 2F-Sub.1-1st is a thin layer of earth and stone, U. 9 (Fig. 14). This abuts U. 7, and represents an informal occupation surface. It may have accumulated naturally, but more probably was purposely placed. This is suggested by the lack of sherds as recent as those in the fill of the structure, to be expected if it was redeposited material from Sub.1-2nd. It was kept from spilling into Ch. 2F-4 by rubble around the chultun orifice. Unit 10 is a similar layer W of U. 4, and probably has a similar origin.

CHULTUN 2F-4

The orifice of Ch. 2F-4 is located in the long trench (Fig. 13 and 14) through Str. 2F-31 and Sub.1, 2.20 m E of 31-1st. The manhole-like orifice was provided with a stepped lip to receive a round stone cover, now absent. On the W side, rubble appears to have been placed on bedrock. This would have prevented Str. 2F-Sub.1:U. 9 from spilling into the chultun, which, as found, was filled with earth to within 0.50 m of the lip. As this was not excavated, nothing more can be said of the chultun (Table 2.29).

TABLE 2.29
Chultun 2F-4: Average Dimensions (meters)

	Diameter Minimum	Diameter Maximum	Depth
Neck	0.60	0.60	0.46
Lip Step	--	0.70	0.12

SHERDS AND ARTIFACTS

Lot groups for Gp. 2F-1 are defined in Table 2.30, with sherd and artifact distributions in Tables 2.31–2.34.

CONSTRUCTION FILL

In no instances were lots found wholly sealed by intact plaster floors. Nonetheless, LG. 1 and 2a, from Plat. 2F-1-3rd and 2nd, seem relatively free of contamination from more recent material. By contrast, LG. 2b and 3, from Plat. 2F-1-2nd and 1st, do appear to be mixed with more recent material. Although the sherds in LG. 1 are indeterminate as to ceramic complex, it is probable that Plat. 2F-1-3rd was constructed just prior to the appearance of Chuen pottery. This would account for the Tzec sherds both in LG.

4a (W of the platform) and 2a. In the former, the sherds were redeposited from initial occupation of the platform and Str. 2F-30. In the latter, the Tzec sherds might derive from demolition of Str. 2F-30 when Plat. 2F-1-2nd was built.

Platform 2F-1-2nd clearly was built sometime after the appearance of Chuen ceramics, since such sherds are plentiful in LG. 2a and 2b. A few possible Cauac pieces in LG. 2a suggest construction at about the time such ceramics made their appearance. Sherds in LG. 3 do not permit dating of Plat. 2F-1-1st, but on the basis of evidence presented below, it still was within Preclassic times.

The situation for Str. 2F-Sub.1 is clear. The fill of Sub.1-2nd in LG. 1 contains only Preclassic sherds. Lots from the fill of Sub.1-1st (LG. 2) consistently include pieces of Manik, as well as Preclassic pottery. These early sherds, and those in LG. 3 (a deposit W of the structure), probably derive largely from 2F-Sub.1-2nd.

Lot Group 1 from the fill of Str. 2F-31-2nd contains many pieces of Preclassic pottery, but also consistent quantities of Manik sherds in all lots. The Preclassic material, as in the case of LG. 2 from Str. 2F-Sub.1, undoubtedly is redeposited from Str. 2F-Sub.1-2nd. Tzec sherds in LG. 2 from 2F-31-1st fill clearly indicate that much of this was drawn from trash around Plat. 2F-1.

MATERIAL ABOVE LIVING LEVELS

In Gp. 2F-1, it is clear that much occupation refuse was eventually redeposited as construction fill. Platform 2F-1:LG. 4a, however, represents a deposit of habitation debris that accumulated W of the platform after construction of Plat. 2F-1-3rd. It includes sherds from Tzec and Chuen vessels, plus one Ik and two Manik sherds. This suggests abandonment in Preclassic times, with later intermittent Classic activity. The same is suggested by surface LG. 4b, which probably is a mixture of root-disturbed fill, a scatter of occupation debris (the Cauac sherds), and some from intermittent later activity (Manik sherds), discarded by the occupants of Str. 2F-Sub.1-1st and 2F-31.

Undisturbed deposits of occupation trash from Str. 2F-Sub.1 are lacking. Many of the Preclassic (particularly Cauac) sherds in Str. 2F-31:LG. 1 and 2, however, may have come from such deposits. Some, of course, may also have come from trash near Plat. 2F-1. Middens are likewise lacking in the case of Str. 2F-31. Some occupation material may be included in LG. 3, which also includes fill material (Cimi sherds next to the structure wall), as well as post-occupation material (a few Ik sherds).

OTHER SOURCES

Eight test pits and trenches, primarily S and W of Gp. 2F-1, constitute the other sources of sherds and artifacts (LG. 5). These are located in Fig. 10 and their contents listed in Table 2.34.

TABLE 2.30
Group 2F-1: Lot Groups

Feature	Lot Group	Lots	Provenience	Ceramic Evaluation
Str. 2F-31	1	Op. 118B/2D Op. 118D/5,11	Fill of 2nd, unsealed	Tzec, Cauac, Manik
	2	Op. 118D/14, 15	Fill of 1st, with material E of structure	Tzec, Cauac
	3	Op. 118B/2C Op. 118D/4	W of structure	Preclassic (including Cimi), Manik, Ik
	4	Op. 118B/2A,2B Op. 118D/1,2,3	Surface	Chuen, Manik, Ik, possible Imix
Str. 2F-Sub.1	1	Op. 118D/10	Fill of 2nd, partial seal	Preclassic
	2	Op. 118D/6, 7,8,12,13	Fill of 1st, partial seal	Preclassic (including Tzec), Manik
	3	Op. 118D/9	Fill, U. 10	Preclassic
Plat. 2F-1	1	Op. 118E/7, 18,21	Fill of 3rd	Preclassic
	2a	Op. 118E/16, 17,20,22,23, 25	Unmixed fill of 2nd	Tzec, mostly Chuen, some Cauac
	2b	Op. 118E/2,3, 5,10-12,15, 19,24	Fill of 2nd, with some later material	Preclassic (including (Chuen, Cimi) 1 possible Imix
	3	Op. 118E/6	Fill of 2nd, with some later material	Preclassic
	4a	Op. 118E/13	W of Plat. 2F-1	Tzec, mostly Chuen, 2 Manik, 1 Ik
	4b	Op. 118E/1,4, 9,14	Surface	Tzec, Cauac, some Manik
Gp. 2F-1	5	Op. 118A/3A-C; 4A-H; 5A,B;6A, B;7A,B. Op. 118B/1; Op. 118C/1	Test pits around 2F-1	

TABLE 2.31
Platform 2F-1: Artifacts by Lot Groups

Study Category	Object	Lot Group					
		1	2a	2b	3	4a	4b
Pottery Vessels	Sherds per cubic meter (lbs)	Not recorded					
Other Pottery Artifacts	Figurines			1			1
Flaked Chert Artifacts	Flake cores			2	1		
	Ovate bifaces		1	2		1	1
	Irregular biface						1
	Unclassifiable biface					1	
	Thin biface						1
	Irregular, retouched flakes	1	1	1		1	
	Point-retouched flake			1			1
	Used flakes	4	14	47	9	9	28
	Unused flakes	2	10	16	1	4	3
	Unclassifiable artifact					1	
	Nodule			1			
Flaked Obsidian Artifacts	Prismatic blades			1			2
	Used flake						1
Ground, Pecked, and Polished Stone Artifacts	Mano					1	
	Celt			1			
Shell and Bone Artifacts	Shell, unworked						1

TABLE 2.32
Structure 2F-31: Artifacts by Lot Group

Study Category	Object	Lot Group			
		1	2	3	4
Pottery Vessels	Sherds per cubic meter (lbs)	8.82	4.11	5.24	3.02
Other Pottery Artifacts	Censer		1		
	Perforated worked sherd		1		
Flaked Chert Artifacts	Flake cores				4
	Thin bifaces			2	
	Used flakes	10	3	8	28
	Unused flakes	2	3	2	6
Flaked Obsidian Artifacts	Core				1
	Prismatic blade				1
Ground, Pecked, and Polished Stone Artifacts	Metate			1	
	Rubbing stone			1	

TABLE 2.33
Structure 2F-Sub.1: Artifacts by Lot Group

Study Category	Object	Lot Group		
		1	2	3
Pottery Vessels	Sherds per cubic meter (lbs)	.42	2.93	.64
Other Pottery Artifacts	Figurine	1		
Flaked Chert Artifacts	Used flakes		4	
	Unused flakes		3	
Ground, Pecked, and Polished Stone Artifacts	Rubbing Stone		1	
Shell and Bone Artifacts	Bone, animal, unworked		several	

TIME SPANS

The time spans for Plat. 2F-1 are presented in Table 2.35. None are defined for Str. 2F-30, since so little is known about it. Time spans for Str. 2F-31 and 2F-Sub.1 are in Tables 2.36 and 2.37, with group time spans in Table 2.38. Ceramic data (Table 2.30) suggest that Plat. 2F-1-3rd was constructed just prior to the advent of Chuen ceramic production (Plat. 2F-1:TS. 8). Platform 2F-1-2nd may barely postdate the appearance of Cauac ceramics (TS. 6), whereas Plat. 2F-1-1st was apparently abandoned when Cauac ceramics were still in use (TS. 2). Since later sherds are so rare, they may be taken to indicate intermittent later activity in the area, prior to the final abandonment of Tikal, and this is the basis for TS. 2.

Structure 2F-Sub.1-2nd may have been built as a replacement for an earlier structure associated with Plat. 2F-1. Our suggestion is that TS. 5 of this structure was built when Cauac ceramics were in vogue, on the basis of the Preclassic sherds in its fill and Manik sherds in the fill of 2F-Sub.1-1st. An earlier date of construction is unlikely. Preclassic ceramics (including Cimi) in the fill of Str. 2F-31-2nd may have been discarded by the users of Str.

2F-Sub.1-2nd. Tentatively, Str. 2F-Sub.1:TS. 5 is correlated with TS. 4 of Plat. 2F-1 (as Gp. TS. 11), which should date well along in the interval when Cauac ceramics were in vogue.

Structure 2F-Sub.1-1st clearly postdates the appearance of Manik ceramics. By this time (Gp. TS. 8), Ch. 2F-4 was surely in use. This is signaled by rubble apparently intended to prevent earth from spilling into the chultun from an informal occupation surface associated with Str. 2F-Sub.1-1st.

The correlation of Str. 2F-Sub.1:TS. 1 with Str. 2F-31:TS. 6 (Gp. TS. 6) is on the basis of stratigraphy, and is dated by Manik ceramics. Structure 2F-31-1st was certainly abandoned by a time no later than just after the appearance of Ik ceramics, if not earlier.

In terms of absolute dates, the occupation of Plat. 2F-1 (Gp. TS. 14) began just before 350 BC (the beginning of Chuen ceramic production). It ended (Gp. TS. 8) sometime after AD 1, surely by AD 150 (the dates for the Cauac Ceramic Complex). By this time Str. 2F-Sub.1-2nd was built; it certainly was in existence before AD 250. The structures were surely abandoned just after AD 550 (the appearance of Ik ceramics and the end of Gp. TS. 2).

TABLE 2.34
Sherds and Artifacts from Group 2F-1: Lot Group 5
(See Fig. 10 for Locations)

Test Pit	Operation/ Lot	Provenience	Contents
3	118A/3A	Topsoil	2 lb 6 oz sherds 1 irregular, retouched chert flake 2 used chert flakes
	118A/3B	Subsoil, W part pit	2 lb 14 oz sherds 3 used chert flakes 1 unused chert flake
	118A/3C	Subsoil, E part pit	1 lb 8 oz sherds 1 chert flake core 2 ovate bifaces 1 used chert flake 2 unused chert flakes
4	118A/4A	Topsoil, S 25 m^2 of pit	3 lb 4 oz sherds 1 unclassifiable biface 2 used chert flakes 1 unused chert flake
	118A/4B	Subsoil, below 4A, except for NW 3m^2	7 lb 6 oz sherds 12 used chert flakes 1 unused chert flake 1 obsidian prismatic blade
	118A/4C	Below 4A, NW 3m^2	2 lb 6 oz sherds 2 used chert flakes 3 unused chert flakes
	118A/4D	Mouth of Ch. 2F-16	1 lb 1 oz sherds 1 obsidian prismatic blade
	118A/4E	NE extension of pit	5 lbs sherds 1 unclassifiable biface 38 used chert flakes 14 unused chert flakes 3 obsidian prismatic blades
	118A/4F	NW extension of pit, topsoil	2 lb 4 oz sherds 3 used chert flakes 1 unused chert flake
	118A/4G	NW extension pit, subsoil	2 lbs 7 oz sherds 5 used chert flakes 1 unused chert flake
	118A/4H	NE extension of pit	3 lb 6 oz sherds 5 used chert flakes 3 unused chert flakes
5	118A/5A	Topsoil	1 lb 7 oz sherds
	118A/5B	Subsoil	1 lb 7 oz sherds 1 irregular, retouched chert flake 2 used chert flakes
6	118A/6A	Topsoil	1 lb 10 oz sherds 1 unused chert flake
	118A/6B	Subsoil	4 lb 7 oz sherds 11 used chert flakes
7	118A/7A	Topsoil	2 lb 3 oz sherds 2 used chert flakes 1 unused chert flake
	118A/7B	Subsoil	2 lb 5 oz sherds 3 used chert flakes 1 unused chert flake
8	118B/1	Entire trench	2 lb 4 oz sherds 3 used chert flakes
9	118C/1	Mouth, Ch. 2F-3	1 lb 1 oz sherds 1 pottery figurine 1 used chert flake 1 chert nodule

TABLE 2.35
Platform 2F-1: Time Spans

Time Span	Architectural Development	Unit	Descriptive Data	Lot Group			Ceramics in Vogue
1			Total abandonment of area with forest growth				
2			Abandonment with intermittent later activity				Cimi-Ik
3			Use		4b		
4	Plat. 2F-1-1st	17	Final modification				Cauac
5			Use				
6	Plat. 2F-1-2nd	6-16	First modification	2a	2b		
7			Use with Str. 2F-30			4a	Chuen
8	Plat. 2F-1-3rd	1-5	First construction at locus	1			Tzec

TABLE 2.36
Structure 2F-31: Time Spans

Time Span	Architectural Development	Construction Stage	Unit	Descriptive Data	Lot Group	Ceramics in Vogue
1				Total abandonment of area with forest growth		
2				Abandonment with inter-mittent later activity	3,4	Ik
3				Use		
4	Str. 2F-31-1st	None defined	5	Renovation	2	
5				Use		
6	Str. 2F-31-2nd	1		Construction of building of perishable materials	1	Manik
		2	1-4	Construction of building platform		
		3		Partial demolition of Str. 2F-Sub.1-1st		

TABLE 2.37
Structure 2F-Sub.1: Time Span

Time Span	Architectural Development	Construction Stage	Unit	Floor	Descriptive Data	Lot Group	Ceramics in Vogue
1					Abandonment		
2					Use		
3	Str. 2F-Sub.1-1st	1			Construction of building of perishable materials		Manik
		2	9?10?	1	Walls and floor plastered		
		3	4,5,8		Construction of W wall		
		4	6,7		Construction of E wall and wall for 2nd platform level		
		5			Demolition of 2nd		
4					Use		(Cimi)
5	Str. 2F-Sub.1-2nd	1	2		Construction of floor		Cauac
		2	3		Construction of building		
		3	1		Preparation of base surface		

TABLE 2.38
Group 2F-1: Time Spans

Group Time Spans	Platform 2F-1 (Table 2.35)	Structure 2F-31 (Table 2.36)	Structure 2F-Sub.1 (Table 2.37)
1	1	1	
2		2	
3		3	
4		4	
5		5	
6		6	1
7			2
8			3
9	2		
10	3		4
11	4		5
12	5		
13	6		
14	7		
15	8		

Group 2G-1

Group 2G-1 is located in Sq. 2G of the Tikal site map (TR. 11) at S430 E210. As mapped in 1960, the group includes five structures and one chultun: Str. 2G-56 through 60 and Ch. 2G-5. The five structures are arranged around the four sides of a plaza, Plat. 2G-1 (Fig. 27). Structure 2G-56 sits on the W side of the plaza, S of the end of 2G-57, and its NE corner is superimposed on the SW corner of that structure. Chultun 2G-5 is located about 10 m SE of the corner of the plaza. One other chultun (Ch. 2G-11) and one other structure (2G-Sub.1) were discovered during excavations beneath Str. 2G-59.

The terrain occupied by this group is low and slopes down to bajo, 40 m to the E. Structures 2G-56 and 57 are built on higher ground, about 3 m above the level of the bajo.

The group was excavated in February 1961 by Haviland as Op. 24C and D to test the chultuns and all five structures for final plan and sequence. In addition, resistivity and magnetic surveys were run S and E of the group by R. E. Linnington. The results of these were inconclusive.

STRUCTURE 2G-56-B

Excavation revealed this to be a two-level rectangular platform, probably for the support of a pole-and-thatch building (Fig. 16, 17a). The first stage in its construction (CS. 4) was to prepare a surface on which to build. To accomplish this, the area was filled and leveled. Unit 2, a stratum of gray, compact material with a large inclusion of small stones, is the fill for this operation; it overlies U. 1, a sterile stratum that represents the original ground surface. Units 3 and 4 are tamped areas on U. 2, on which the platform walls were set.

Clearly distinguishable from U. 2 is the structure fill itself, placed as CS. 3. Retained by one-course masonry walls, this brown fill contains abundant sherds and flecks of charcoal. The S end wall of Str. 2G-57 abuts the front wall of 56, while the N wall end of the latter abuts the back wall of 57. Structure 2G-56 seems to be the later of the two, and a block was probably removed from the corner of 57 to permit construction of the front wall of 56.

Units 5 and 6, areas of light-colored tamped earth, are the pause-line on which the upper platform level was built (as CS. 2). Unit 7 is the front wall of this, and U. 8 is the inner face of the back wall (its outer portion has collapsed). One course high, these walls were built of two masonry veneers with stone rubble hearting between. The substantial area enclosed by this masonry was filled with a brown earth that cannot be distinguished from the fill of CS. 3. The exposed area of the top of the lower platform level in front of the upper level was paved with plaster averaging 3 cm in thickness. This floor, of which U. 9 is a remnant, was laid directly on the fill of CS. 2. It apparently was in union with U. 7, though actual evidence for this no longer survives. Construction Stage 2 terminated with the laying of a floor directly on the fill of the upper platform level, of which U. 10 is a fragment.

It is assumed that a pole-and-thatch building was constructed on the platform of Str. 2G-56 (see TR. 20B). A final CS. 1 is proposed for this, although the main supporting posts for such a building would probably have been set in place in the course of CS. 3.

STRUCTURE 2G-56-A

In its final form, Str. 2G-56 consisted of a two-level platform, with a smaller platform, rectangular in shape, situated on the axis of the upper platform level. It must have been a later addition, as it was built on the floor of CS. 2. Unit 11 (Fig. 16) is the wall of this platform. As with U. 7 and 8, U. 11 is one course high and constructed of two veneers with rubble hearting. The area within was filled with brown earth similar to that used for the rest of the building. A floor probably covered the new platform, although no traces of one survive.

STRUCTURE 2G-57-2ND

In its original form, Str. 2G-57 was a one-level platform, probably the foundation for a pole-and-thatch building (see TR. 20B). The front wall was built on a compact stratum of gray earth (Fig. 17b:U. 1). A floor was laid from the top of this front wall W at least as far as U. 3 (Fig. 16 and 17b). Unit 2 (Fig. 16) is a surviving portion of this original pavement. Unit 3 is a line of stones beneath the back wall of the final structure, evidently all that remains of the back wall of this original platform. Unit 4, however, a burned floor fragment at the same level as U. 2 and W of this wall (Fig. 16), may be a fragment of the floor. Unit 3, in that case, would be associated with the final construction.

Unit 5, a fragmentary pavement in front of the E wall of the platform (Fig. 17b), may be part of the plaza floor that served Str. 2G-57-2nd. Or, it may be part of a later floor associated with the final structure. That it is the only plaza floor found suggests its contemporaneity with the original platform.

Although positive evidence is lacking, the assumption is that the platform of Str. 2G-57-2nd was built as a single construction stage (CS. 2), after which a building of perishable materials (CS. 1) took form above it.

STRUCTURE 2G-57-1ST

Modification of 2G-57 saw the addition of an upper platform level and at least one interior platform (Fig. 16, 17b). To begin (CS. 3), height of the back wall (U. 7) was raised and the second level was built on top of the original platform. The front wall of this second level (U. 6) is now badly preserved, but a line of rubble marks its location. It was apparently placed directly on the surface of U. 2, the original floor. New pavement was probably laid in front of this upper platform, though no trace of it survives. Nor can any trace of a floor be found for the upper platform, though one probably was provided.

The next stage (CS. 2) was construction of at least one apparently small (interior?) platform (U. 3). Located S of the front-rear axis, it is not known whether a similar feature was built on the N part of the structure. The two walls for the sides rest on a thin stratum of earth above U. 2, the earlier floor. The front wall is the same as that of the upper platform. No floor traces can be found on this interior platform, though pavement probably existed. A final CS. 1 is assumed for erection of a new building upon the platform.

STRUCTURE 2G-58-3RD

Structure 2G-58, on the N edge of Plat. 2G-1, was built against a rise in bedrock (Fig. 18, 19). As originally constructed, this was a three-level, rectangular platform, on which a pole-and-thatch building may have been erected (TR. 20B).

Work began (as CS. 4) by leveling bedrock to the approximate level of Plat. 2G-1, up to a point at which bedrock was originally about 0.30 m above the probable plaza level. Here, a vertical face was cut, forming the first of three platform levels. Bedrock at the top of this cut is now level, probably naturally, rising only 0.20 m in four meters. On this surface, the walls of the structure itself were built.

As CS. 3, the first course of masonry for the back, and undoubtedly the end walls, was put in place along with a row of blocks for a second platform level in front. This second level is about 1 m N of the lower "step" just quarried. None of the construction is directly on the bedrock, but rather rests on a layer of earth and small stones. This leveled the surface, filling in any small dips in bedrock. Unit 1, a light-colored layer of packed earth, is the pause-line on the top of fill for this stage of construction.

Another course of masonry raised the platform to the desired height for its third level (CS. 2). No remains of the front wall for this can now be seen, but its existence is required by the height of the platform floor. The position of this final "step" has been reconstructed on the basis of the relative positions of the front walls of the lower two. Construction ended with the laying of pavement, U. 2, over the top of the platform.

A building of perishable materials is assumed as part of Str. 2G-58-3rd. A final CS. 1 is proposed for this, although the main supporting posts must have been placed during earlier construction.

STRUCTURE 2G-58-2ND

Evidence for this architectural development consists of a floor remnant only, U. 3 (Fig. 18, 19), which survives over the rear portion of the structure. It was laid directly on the surface of U. 2. Since U. 3 survives near the rear wall of the structure, it is assumed that it was laid at a time when there was no building wall in the way; otherwise, it is unlikely that the floor would have reached the rear wall of the platform. What is implied, then, is a major renovation of the structure. Presumably, the building wall of Str. 2G-58-3rd (if indeed there was such a building) was dismantled (CS. 3), a new floor was laid (CS. 2), and a new building wall put up (CS. 1). The main posts for the building need not have been disturbed.

STRUCTURE 2G-58-1ST

The possible existence of a third architectural development may be indicated by U. 4, a few stones placed on the back portion of U. 3. Badly broken, the stones gave no indication of their purpose; they may have served to raise the level of the platform surface. Alternatively, they may represent a freestanding base-wall. In either case, a major renovation of the structure similar to that of 58-2nd is suggested.

STRUCTURE 2G-59-5TH

Structure 2G-59 is the most complex structure in the group, and five architectural developments are known. An even earlier structure is represented by postholes in bedrock (see below). The form of 59-5th is not well known. It is represented by U. 1, a low platform about 0.20 m high, which later evolved as the E platform of Str. 2G-59-1st, 2nd, and 3rd. Its floor is U. 2 (Fig. 24), a plaster pavement 2 cm thick. This lies directly on earth fill. The walls are unknown; probably they were torn out in a later renovation. Very little of U. 2 was exposed during excavation, and its relationship to other construction features is unknown.

STRUCTURE 2G-59-4TH

The next architectural development is somewhat better known than 5th. The original U. 1 platform, now modified, was the primary element. Its original walls were probably torn out, and new ones built. The new N wall was constructed of unshaped stones, though in the S wall

(Fig. 24:U. 3) well-cut masonry blocks were used. The N wall was set on a layer of earth 8 cm thick, the S wall directly on bedrock. A layer of packed white earth (U. 4) that overlies U. 2 probably is a pause-line of this operation. Unit 5 (Fig. 20 and 24), a floor 3 to 4 cm thick, was laid on a thin earth fill over this light layer. It turns down over the N wall, and covers the tops of the stones of the S wall. To the W, the floor turns up to a row of stones 0.29 m high, which is designated U. 6 (Fig. 20). The western edge of U. 6 meets U. 7, a floor surface that at one time probably covered its top. The extent of U. 7 is not known; it could be an early plaza floor. Units 8 and 9 (Fig. 23b), two floor fragments beneath Plat. 2G-1:Fl. 2, are probably pieces of the same early floor.

STRUCTURE 2G-59-3RD

As in the preceding architectural development, a basic remodeling of the existing platform was carried out. Now, however, U. 1 was no longer the primary element of construction, but an adjunct of a structure built on its W side. Little of the structure itself survived subsequent building activity. A smaller platform was added to the N (see Fig. 20, 23, and 173a).

The remodeling of U. 1, now the E platform of a structure represented by U. 13, saw the raising of its floor level at least 0.33 m above that of old U. 5. An entire new N wall (U. 10) was built, on an earth fill 5 cm below the level of the top of U. 3 to the S. Since the N wall of the earlier platform ran more truly E-W than the newer one, the western end of the latter rests on U. 5. A new S wall (U. 11) was constructed on the surface of U. 5, directly over the older wall. The platform was then filled with brown earth, as was the area N of the platform, so that the fill came to the level of the second course of masonry (about 0.36 m above bedrock). No trace of summit pavement survives for this platform, though it probably existed. Burial 55 might have been placed in the platform fill at this time, though this is doubtful.

At the W end of this platform, a masonry wall (U. 13) likely represents the E wall of an otherwise unknown structure. Built on the surface of U. 5, it is located 8 cm E of U. 6. The other walls of this structure were apparently torn out in the course of later construction. Burial 58 intruded through U. 7 and seems related to U. 13.

North of the E platform and U. 13 structure, a small platform (U. 15) was built. This was constructed largely on the fill that was deposited after renovation of U. 1. A wall 0.61 m long (U. 14) joins this N platform to U. 1. Unit 14 is one course of masonry, behind which is an informal surface of tamped earth level with the top of U. 6. The S wall of U. 15 rests on this tamped earth surface, as well as the N end of U. 6; the W wall rests on U. 7. The N wall rests on U. 9, and the other wall was built on the earth fill N of U. 13. A plaster floor (U. 16) covers the earth fill of U. 15, as well as the S and E walls, but abuts the tops of the stones of the N and W walls. Tamped earth remains exposed between the N and E platforms W of U. 14.

Platform 2G-1:Fl. 2 turns up to the W wall of U. 15. This pavement could be followed 0.40 m W of the front wall of the final structure. To the S it could be followed to a point in line with the S wall of U. 15. The end wall of U. 13 was probably located here or, less likely, 0.50 m farther S, in line with the N wall of the E platform.

STRUCTURE 2G-59-2ND

This development saw the major portion of the U. 13 structure razed, a new structure built, and the E platform remodeled (Fig. 21, 23, 24). The N portion of this new construction is well preserved beneath the final structure, although nothing remains of the S portion. Work on Str. 2G-59-2nd commenced with the removal of the fill N of the E platform that was associated with 59-3rd. A cut in bedrock 0.57 m deep was made to receive Bu. 54 prior to construction above it. Building then began by putting in place platform walls. The back wall, N of the earlier construction, consists of at least five courses of masonry, based on older fill averaging 10 cm in thickness over the underlying bedrock. This wall abuts the N wall of U. 15 at right angles. The surviving southern portion of the new wall continues in a straight line, and was built on U. 16. It cannot now be followed past the S edge of U. 15.

The front wall was based on fill indistinguishable from that within the N portion of the structure. This fill was placed at the start of construction. The wall base is 0.27 m above bedrock, in line with the W wall of U. 15, penetrating Fl. 2 of the plaza. The W wall of U. 15 was utilized as part of the lower course of masonry. The wall can now be followed 0.50 m S of the S wall of U. 15; the earlier structure represented by U. 13 was largely destroyed to permit its construction. The quantity of large stones used in the fill of the S portion of 59-2nd suggests that the torn-out masonry of 3rd was the source of some of this fill.

Remains of a stairway still survive, built against the front wall of the structure, although portions have been torn out to permit the placement of later burials. Two steps were built on Fl. 2 of the plaza, with plaster patches turning up to the bottom step. The major part of Fl. 2 apparently continued to serve with this new structure. These stair remains survive only along the N portion of the structure, with their S end 2.24 m from the N end wall. Quite possibly, another stairway to the S balanced this northern one, as in the reconstruction (Fig. 21). Total destruction in that area, however, makes this hypothetical. At any rate, at least 2.86 m of the building front was without stairs.

The structure fill is brown earth that contained PD. 64 and five burials (Bu. 9, 50, 52, 56, 57), besides Bu. 54. As mentioned, the fill of the southern portion contained many large masonry blocks.

During the time when 59-2nd was under construction, the E platform was greatly enlarged. This was accomplished by building four new walls (U. 17-20) some distance out from those of the E platform of 59-3rd. The N wall incorporated the portion of U. 15 not buried beneath the new structure. When U. 15 was built, however, it rested on a fill some 0.30 m thick, while the new wall used the same surface as the back wall of 59-2nd. For this reason, where U. 17 meets the back structure wall, it is one course high, whereas for the rest of its extent, it is several courses high. The E and S walls of the platform were set on bedrock. At the W end of the S wall, a short wall running E in line with U. 13 forms a western boundary S of the structure. The fill between the early and late walls contains a great quantity of irregular stones. Burial 55, referred to previously, could have been placed at this time. No remains of pavement on top of the platform survive, though one undoubtedly existed.

To sum up the construction of 2nd, four stages may be defined. The first (CS. 4) consisted of demolition of a large portion of 3rd and preparation of a base surface on which to build. Burial 54 was interred at this time. Construction of the structure walls defines CS. 3, with the stairs added as CS. 2. The final CS. 1 is inferred for a building of perishable materials on the main platform. The E platform may have been remodeled in the course of CS. 3 or any time thereafter.

STRUCTURE 2G-59-1ST

Assembly of Str. 2G-59 in its final form (Fig. 22–24) saw again the partial demolition of earlier construction. This final structure took the form of a two-level platform, with its long axis running N-S. The E platform retained the form it had with 59-2nd.

The wall of the first level of 1st is located 1.20 m W of the stairs of its predecessor. Of a single course of masonry, this was built on the surface of Plat. 2G-1:Fl. 2. Floor 1 of this plaza, visible by the SW corner, is in union with this masonry. East of the short axis, front wall masonry is now missing for a distance of 0.92 m. The good preservation of the other blocks in this vicinity suggests that this masonry was robbed subsequent to abandonment.

The W wall of the upper platform level is badly preserved; it was placed on fill just above the surface of the first step of 59-2nd. The already existing masonry of 2nd was utilized for the E wall, with new stonework extending this wall 3.08 m to the N. The masonry for this newer addition is in a different style than that used in 2nd. One result of the lengthening to the N was the inclusion of Str.

2G-Sub.1 in the fill of 1st. The N end of this final structure has collapsed, but apparently it incorporated the N wall of Sub.1.

The S wall was built on earth fill a few centimeters above U. 7. Platform 2G-1:Fl. 2 had been ripped out in this area, along with Str. 2G-59-2nd. The wall extends E to U. 13, where it joins the short W wall (U. 20) of the E platform.

The fill of a large portion of 59-1st consists of surviving portions of 59-2nd and Sub.1. The rest is a brown earth similar to that in the earlier structure. Several burials were placed in this final fill, or dug into the earlier structure. They included Bu. 49, 50, 52, 63, 56, and 60. Burial 59, E of the structure and N of the E platform, should perhaps also be considered in this group; Bu. 55, referred to before, may also be contemporary. While some interments may have been placed at the time of construction, others were surely later, possibly even postdating occupation. These possibilities are discussed in connection with the individual burials in section III ("Special Deposits").

No surface pavement was found on either the structure or its E platform; there is no reason to doubt, however, that a pavement once existed.

Four stages may be defined for the construction of Str. 2G-59-1st: CS. 4, partial demolition of 2nd and platform Fl. 2; CS. 3, construction of the lower platform level; CS. 2, construction of the upper platform level; CS. 1, inferred for a building of perishable materials.

STRUCTURE 2G-60-2ND

Structure 2G-60, on the S side of Plat. 2G-1, grew as two architectural developments. Of the first, little is known, as its remains were exposed only in the trench excavated through the short axis of 2G-60. These consist of a floor and wall beneath the front part of 60-1st. The floor (U. 1) can be seen in the E portion of the axial trench (Fig. 25), S to the line of the back wall. Unit 1 is probably part of a plaza floor, and turns up to a wall (Fig. 25:U. 2) that runs N-S. Only 1.10 m of this wall was exposed in excavation, and it may perhaps be the end wall of an earlier structure, Str. 2G-60-2nd.

STRUCTURE 2G-60-1ST

The final structure may have been a two-level building platform (Fig. 25), and as such was undoubtedly built in three construction stages. The front wall, in the E portion of the axial trench, was built (on U. 1) of a row of stone blocks one course high. The back wall rests on earth fill at the level of U. 1 and, like the front wall, was of one course of masonry. These walls, with their fill, define CS. 3.

Construction Stage 2 is suggested by U. 3 and 4, broken stones that indicate the one-time presence of an upper platform level. Unit 3 forms a line parallel to the front

wall, and U. 4 is a single block. These two features rest on the fill of the lower platform. The upper platform level is reconstructed as running the length of the basal platform, a common pattern of small-structure construction (TR. 20B). The possibility exists that U. 3 and 4 could represent a small platform of less length than the structure itself.

No plaster floors survive for the structure, though these presumably existed at one time. On the plaza in front, a level of compact pebbles at the elevation of the base of the front wall (also the elevation of U. 1), probably marks the disintegrated plaza surface.

A final construction stage, CS. 1, is proposed for a building of perishable materials on the platform.

STRUCTURE 2G-SUB.1

This diminutive platform was built 0.54 m N of Str. 2G-59-2nd (Fig. 21). Its N wall later served as part of the N wall for Str. 59-1st. The structure was obviously in use along with 59-2nd, for both were based on the same surface, and both were built over by 59-1st. Essentially square, 2G-Sub.1 may have had steps along its front. The N, S, and E walls are of two courses of masonry.

CHULTUN 2G-5

DESCRIPTION

In plan (Fig. 26), this chultun is like many others at Tikal (TR. 32). To construct it, the Maya dug a circular, manhole-like orifice into bedrock (CS. 2). This was extended downward as a neck, widening out into the antechamber. The maximum diameter of the chamber itself is greatest near the floor (Table 2.39). Together with neck and orifice, it has the form of a bottle-shaped pit. The rim of the orifice shows evidence that it was stepped, so that a stone cover would fit tightly in place.

Upon completion of the antechamber, a lateral chamber was dug to the N (as CS. 1). The entrance to this is restricted on both sides. Elliptical in plan, the maximum diameter of Chm. 2 (Table 2.39) is in an E-W direction, with its floor 0.20 m below that of the antechamber. The walls are essentially continuous with the ceiling to produce an overall dome shape.

DISCUSSION

A moderate amount of heavily weathered sherds, as well as the major portion of the stone cover, were found as the chultun was cleaned out. The latter was near the bottom of the antechamber in loose earth. This loose earth did not completely fill the chultun, indicating that it was left empty by the Maya. When this chultun was abandoned the cover must have been left in place. The material inside, including the sherds, represents earth that washed in after the stone cover broke and fell in.

TABLE 2.39
Chultun 2G-5: Average Dimensions (meters)

Feature	Height	Length	Width	Maximum Diameter	Minimum Diameter
Neck	0.40	--	--	0.66	0.63
Chm. 1	0.80	1.16	0.86	--	--
Entrance	0.84	0.24	0.93	--	--
Chm. 2	0.98	2.61	1.91	--	--

CHULTUN 2G-11

DESCRIPTION

This chultun was discovered during excavation of Str. 2G-59 immediately N of the NW corner of Str. 2G-59:U. 15 (Fig. 20), and was covered by Str. 2G-59-2nd (Fig. 23, section A-A'). The chultun consists of a single chamber cut into bedrock, and has the form of a bottle-shaped pit. The round, simple orifice (at 0.54 m) is narrower than the greatest diameter of the chamber (0.89 m), which was near its bottom. Depth of the neck is 0.26 m and depth of the chamber is 0.74 m.

The chultun was filled with a compact, gray earth that contained a moderate quantity of sherds, some of them well preserved. At the bottom was a sterile layer 8 cm thick that probably accumulated naturally during the time the chultun was in use. On this was a large masonry block that measures 0.48 by 0.50 m and is 0.14 m thick. This may be a portion of a stone cover that, when the decision was made to fill the chultun, was worked to a size small enough to be dropped inside.

DISCUSSION

There is no doubt that this chultun was purposely filled, but the time of its filling is not clear. Possibly this was contemporary with construction of Str. 2G-59-3rd, when the area N of that structure was filled (see Str. 2G-59-3rd). If not, a shaft would have been needed to keep this fill from falling in. Since this particular area was cleared to bedrock for construction of Str. 2G-59-2nd, any such arrangement would have been destroyed at that time. If the chultun was in use with Str. 2G-59-3rd, surely was filled prior to construction of 59-2nd.

The time of original construction of this chultun is also a matter for speculation. It might predate Str. 2G-59-5th, or it might have been dug at any time thereafter. Since the earth overlying bedrock in this area was not thick when 59-5th and 4th were built, the chultun might logically have been associated with one or both of these features.

POSSIBLE EARLY ACTIVITY

Bedrock was found to have been quarried to some extent, where exposed during excavation through the short axis of Str. 2G-59. The principle area of this quarrying is located beneath the front wall of the final structure. Here, a series of cuts created a pit some 0.40 m deep with stepped sides. This quarrying probably was related to construction at this locus, possibly for an Early Classic structure. Two other features were found in bedrock beneath the final structure (aside from the pits for Bu. 49, 54, and Ch. 2G-11). These are two apparent postholes, U. 21 and 22 (Fig. 20), located in the floor of the cut for Bu. 49. Unit 21 has a diameter of 0.16 m, U. 22 of 0.18 m; both are 0.15 m deep. Evidently they relate to construction predating Str. 2G-59-2nd. For what it is worth, a line drawn through both is parallel to the wall of U. 13 (Fig. 20), but the location of U. 15 makes it improbable that the U. 13 structure extended this far N.

The presence of a large quantity of Manik sherds in the fills of Str. 2G-59 (Table 2.40) suggests that an Early Classic structure may once have stood here prior to construction of Str. 2G-59-5th. If so, these two postholes might well have pertained to that structure.

RESISTIVITY AND MAGNETIC SURVEY

As part of the investigation of Gp. 2G-1, a traverse was cleared to a position just W of Str. 3G-1 in the next group to the S. The traverse was a strip 4 m wide running from Ch. 2G-5; specifically, between 34 and 38 m E of Datum 24C (Fig. 27), and for a distance of 78 m magnetic S of the same datum. A ceramic sample from Str. 3G-1 (see Gp. 3G-1, this report) suggests that the structure was roughly contemporary with Gp. 2G-1 (see discussion of Gp. 3G-1). R. E. Linnington surveyed this traverse with resistivity (Geohm) and magnetic (Proton Magnetometer) equipment. His purpose was to gain an idea of the area between two groups, and to see if any features existed that might suggest the former presence of structures erected without benefit of masonry substructures, which would warrant further investigation.

A second traverse was cleared for Linnington 6 m in width, running between 0 to 6 m N of Datum 24C. This traverse ran a distance of 60 m magnetic E from a point 36 m E of Datum 24C. The purpose of this study was to test the area E of Gp. 2G-1 a short distance into bajo to see if this was an area of trash disposal.

The results of this work were not encouraging, although a more extensive test in the future might be worthwhile. Only slight changes in the reading occurred, but the total variation was considered too small by Linnington to be significant. His conclusions are as follows:

> The results from the house mound areas, as well as the results from other parts of Tikal appeared to show that magnetic methods are not of very great value. In particular it appears that under jungle conditions either the soil does not attain the levels of magnetic intensity found under moderate agricultural conditions, or the variations that may have been expected are destroyed by extensive mixing of soil constituents by the jungle vegetation. It is thus unlikely that magnetic methods will help in the problem of invisible house mounds.
>
> Resistivity methods are also likely to be of little value as any slight variations produced by archaeological features are likely to be completely hidden by larger scale effects of moisture variation caused by the vegetation cover.

SHERDS AND ARTIFACTS

Lot groups defined for the constituent structures and chultuns of Gp. 2G-1 are presented in Table 2.40, with content given in Tables 2.41–2.45.

STRATA UNDERLYING CONSTRUCTION

Material in this category comes from Str. 2G-56:U. 2, 2G-57:U. 1, and 2G-60:U. 6. All three structures are based on the surfaces of these strata. In the case of 2G-57, U. 1 overlies bedrock, and forms a base surface for the front structure wall alone. Unit 2 of Str. 2G-56 and U. 6 of 2G-60 both overlie deeper strata with no cultural material. All three strata might be either deposits that predate construction, purposeful fill to provide level building surfaces, or as modification, by scraping and filling, of original surfaces. As ceramic analysis demonstrates the contemporaneity of Str. 2G-56:U. 2 and Str. 2G-60:U. 6 with overlying structure fills, it seems most likely that these are purposeful fills. Moreover, cultural material was abundant in both. Structure 2G-57:U. 1 is problematical. It does not contain much cultural material. This and its proximity to bedrock, plus the fact that Str. 2G-57 may predate 2G-56, suggest that this stratum was a remnant of the original surface of the area.

CONSTRUCTION FILL

Sherds and artifacts were generally abundant in the fills of all structures, but were most abundant in that of 2G-56. Since this structure seems to postdate several others in Gp. 2G-1, it seems a safe assumption that much of this material was drawn from nearby trash deposits that accumulated during earlier occupation of the group. Such deposits would certainly have been the most readily available sources of material for construction fill, not only for this structure, but also for the latest architectural developments of Str. 2G-59. Such use would explain as well why deep midden deposits do not seem to exist in Gp. 2G-1.

Generally, ceramic appraisals for the lot groups from the structure fills are not specific. Form frequencies suggest that the ceramics belong to the late Ik Complex, but a few elements diagnostic of Imix are included, which cannot be explained as a result of mixture with later occupation debris. Apparently this fill was derived from dumps that contained Ik ceramics, but construction dates from a time when pottery of the Imix Complex, or more probably the Ik-Imix transition, was in vogue. Even though the affiliation of fill ceramics is not absolutely clear, a consideration of burial vessels and architectural sequence permits minimal dating of activity in Gp. 2G-1.

Chultun 5G-11 was purposely filled prior to construction of Str. 2G-59-2nd, probably at the time of 3rd. The material in the chultun is therefore included in one lot group associated with Str. 2G-59 (LG. 3), and it is most likely to be contemporary with LG. 2a and 2b of that structure.

MATERIAL ABOVE LIVING LEVELS

Lot groups above living levels around structures should contain any occupation trash to be found, but erosion has been extensive in the case of most structures, so that contamination from fill is inevitable. Sherd fits between Str. 2G-57:LG. 2a and Str. 2G-56:LG. 3a; Str. 2G-58:LG. 2 and 3; and Str. 2G-59:LG. 5a and 6d demonstrate this. Assessment of the degree of contamination must be made in the case of every structure.

Although the Maya seem to have tolerated considerable refuse strewn over plaza surfaces while a group was in use, here, any material in front of a structure is suspected of being in large part washed-out fill, unless proven otherwise. That there was a good deal of fill contamination is indicated by the fact that some surface lots contain more cultural material than lots directly on living levels. The same comments apply to material above living levels on a structure itself. In most cases, floors are now so broken up that surface material consists almost wholly of fill that has been uprooted. Hence, surface lots are considered fill unless proven otherwise. In the case of Str.

2G-56 and 57, fragments of vessels scattered in LG. 3a and 4 of 56, and LG. 3b and 4b of 57, are one indication that late material was left scattered around the structure floors, probably when the group was abandoned. Ceramic analysis confirms this interpretation. The large size of some sherds in Str. 2G-59:LG. 5b suggests that some of this deposit is occupation debris.

As expected, the best deposits of cultural material associated with the occupation of Gp. 2G-1 are located behind the structures. Although sherd weights appear low in most of the relevant lot groups, this is largely a factor of inclusion of surface lots in the tabulation. Surface lots in these instances generally show a low sherd weight in relation to lot volume, while lots directly on living levels show a very high sherd weight relative to lot volume. This debris appears to have been more plentiful in Gp. 2G-1 than in a number of other groups investigated for this study (especially Op. 24).

CHULTUN 2G-5

The material inside this chultun probably washed in after abandonment. Objects from LG. 2 should therefore be contemporary with those lot groups from Gp. 2G-1 that contain occupation material, and material dating from abandonment. Lot Group 1, the material from the surface around the orifice, should be the same. The ultimate derivation of the few sherds and one artifact in these lot groups is a problem; they could have been discarded by the occupants of any of the structures in Gp. 2G-1.

OTHER SOURCES

Twelve burials (nos. 49–60) and one problematical deposit (64), from in and around Str. 2G-59, constitute the only other sources of sherds and artifacts from Gp. 2G-1.

TIME SPANS

Tables 2.46–2.51 summarize sequences discussed above in terms of time spans. These are correlated as group time spans in Table 2.52. Since specific archaeological features were not traced from structure to structure (with the exception of Str. 2G-56 and 57), correlation has had to depend upon seriation of architectural characteristics and artifacts. This has been difficult, since it seems apparent that the architectural developments of the various structures were restricted to such a brief period of time that there has not been much change in artifact inventories. Nonetheless, a probable sequence of 13 group time spans may be formulated. These are based largely on ceramic evidence (Table 2.40), as summarized below.

Structure 2G-59-4th dates no earlier than a time when Ik ceramics were produced. Burial 58 suggests that ceramics of this complex (TR. 25A:fig. 42b) were still in

vogue when 2G-59-3rd was built, and the fill samples do not contradict this. Construction of 2G-59-2nd clearly took place after the appearance of ceramics of the Ik-Imix transition, but probably not long after, judging from the ceramics of Bu. 54 (TR. 25A:fig. 52b). The final construction took place when early Imix ceramics were still in use.

It is difficult to say when Str. 2G-59-5th was built, but it was probably no earlier than the era of Ik pottery production. Considerable numbers of Manik sherds in the fills of 2G-59 and 58 indicate a probable Early Classic occupation of this locus, however. Perhaps Str. 2G-59:U. 21 and 22, two postholes, are all that remain of a late Early Classic structure (2G-59-6th?).

Structure 2G-57-2nd is thought to date to the period of Ik pottery use, although the fill ceramics are of little help. This dating seems probable in view of an occupation of Str. 2G-59 when Ik ceramics were in vogue, and the likelihood that Str. 2G-56, which was built no earlier than the appearance of Ik-Imix transitional pottery, postdates Str. 2G-57-2nd.

The fill of Str. 2G-58-3rd did not provide good ceramic samples, and all that may be said with certainty is that its appearance dates from sometime between AD 550 and 869. The sherds of LG. 1a do suggest that late Ik ceramics were in vogue at the time. If so, construction of 3rd may have been more or less contemporary with that of 2G-57-2nd, that of 58-2nd with 56-B, and that of 58-1st with 56-A. Also plausible, even though unproven, is correlation of the two modifications of Str. 2G-56 with those of 2G-60.

What is obvious is that there was construction at the locus of Str. 2G-59 before there was construction at the locus of any other structure in Gp. 2G-1. Ceramics of the Ik-Imix transition were in vogue by the time 59-2nd was built, as they were when 56-B was built. Both 59-1st and 56-A were built when Imix ceramics were in vogue. The time spans for these structures may, therefore, be equated. Assuming the proposed correlations between Str. 2G-56, 60, 58-2nd and 1st, the time spans for these structures may also be fit into this scheme. Structure 2G-57 and 58-3rd are more of a problem. Apparently, ceramics of the Ik Complex were being produced when the earliest architectural versions of these structures were built, with later ceramics in use when the structures were renovated. Time span 5 of Str. 2G-57 and 7 of 58, therefore, may be equated with TS. 7 of 2G-59 (Gp. TS. 7). Time span 3 of Str. 2G-57, on the other hand, might actually be placed in Gp. TS. 3 or 5.

It is difficult to say when Gp. 2G-1 was abandoned. All the material above living levels was contaminated to some degree by fill. But some vessels, coarse jars in particular, seem to suggest that abandonment was probably after the appearance of late Imix ceramics. Monochrome

TABLE 2.40 (Part 1)
Group 2G-1: Lot Groups

Feature	Lot Group	Lot	Provenience	Ceramic Evaluation
Str. 2G-56 (Op. 24C)	1a	29,30	Fill of CS. 4 or early Imix	Ik-Imix transition
	1b	13	Fill of CS. 4, mixed with later material	Ik or Imix
	2a	24,41	Partially sealed fill of CS. 3	Ik-Imix transition or early Imix
	2b	40	Unsealed fill of CS. 2	Ik-Imix transition or early Imix
	2c	37	Unsealed fill of 56-A	Ik-Imix transition or early Imix
	3a	2,4,5,42	E of structure, surface to base of wall	Imix
	3b	1,6	W of structure, surface to base of wall	Imix
	3c	8	W of structure, surface to U. 1	Early and late Imix
	4	3,7,16, 21, 36	Surface of structure to floor levels	Early and late Imix
Str. 2G-57 (Op. 24C)	1	20	Unsealed fill of Plat. 2G-1	?
	2a	49,58	Partially sealed fill of 2nd	Ik and/or Imix
	2b	52,92	Unsealed fill of 1st	Ik and/or Imix
	2c	25	Unsealed fill of 1st: U. 8	?
	3a	26,34, 35,65	W of structure, surface to base of wall	Late Imix
	3b	11,12,14	E of structure, surface to base of wall	Imix
Str. 2G-57	4a	43	On floor, lower platform level	Manik, Ik and Imix
	4b	19,44,50, 66	Surface of structure to floor levels	Imix

TABLE 2.40 (Part 2)
Group 2G-1: Lot Groups

Feature	Lot Group	Lots	Provenience	Ceramic Evaluation
Str. 2G-58 (Op. 24C)	1a	80-83	Partially sealed fill of 3rd	Manik, late Ik or early Imix
	1b	72	Unsealed fill of 1st	Manik, Ik and/or Imix
	2a	59,61, 73-75	N of structure, surface to base of wall	Imix
	2b	57,77	S of structure, surface to base of wall	Manik, Ik and late Imix
	3	60,76, 79,109	Surface of structure to floor levels	Manik, Ik and Imix
Str. 2G-59 and Sub.1 (Op. 24C)	1	136	Sealed fill of 4th	Ik and/or Imix
	2a	110,129	Partially sealed fill of 3rd	Manik, Ik and/or Imix
	2b	64,121, 139,140	Unsealed fill (U. 1) of 3rd	Manik and Ik
	3	113,115- 117,123	Ch. 2G-11, unsealed	Ik and Imix
	4a	71,78, 111,124, 125	Unsealed fill of 2nd	Manik, Ik, and Ik-Imix transition?
	4b	28,38,39, 56,62,85, 87,89	Unsealed fill (U. 1) of 2nd	Manik, Ik, and Ik-Imix transition?
	4c	23,27,63, 84,86,88	Surface of U. 1 to floor level	Manik, Ik, and Ik-transition?
	4d	47,48	Unsealed fill of Str. 2G-Sub.1	Ik-Imix transition?
	5a	33,67,68, 103,134, 145	Unsealed fill of 1st	Manik, Ik and Ik-Imix transition or early Imix
	5b	10,90, 112,144	Surface of structure to floor level	Manik, Ik, and Ik-Imix transition or early Imix
	5c	130,131	Partially sealed fill of Plat. 2G-1:Fl. 1	Imix

TABLE 2.40 (Part 3)
Group 2G-1: Lot Groups

Feature	Lot Group	Lots	Provenience	Ceramic Evaluation
	6a	9,22,31, 32	W of structure, surface to base of wall	Manik, Ik and early Imix
	6b	45,46, 132,133	N of structure, surface to base of wall	Late Imix
	6c	101,102, 126	S of structure, surface to base of wall	Manik, Ik and Imix
	6d	18,54,55, 91,128	E of structure, N of U. 1, top to base of wall	Manik, Ik and Imix
	6e	15,17, 51,53	Above LG. 6d	Manik, Ik and Imix
	6f	100,122	N and S of U. 1, surface to base of wall	Early Imix
Str. 2G-60 (Op. 24C)	1	105-7, 118, 119	Strata beneath construction (U. 5, 6)	Manik, Ik and Ik-Imix transition or early Imix
	2	108,120	Unsealed fill of 1st	Ik-Imix transition or early Imix
	3a	95-97, 142	S of structure, surface to base of wall	Imix
	3b	99	N of structure, surface to base of wall	Imix
	4	98	Surface of structure to floor levels	Ik-Imix transition or early Imix
Ch. 2G-5 (Op. 24D)	1	1	Surface around orifice	Imix
	2	2-4	Chultun fill	Imix
Ch. 2G-11 (see Str. 2G-59: LG. 3)				

TABLE 2.41
Structure 2G-56: Artifacts by Lot Group

Study Category	Object	Lot Group								
		1a	1b	2a	2b	2c	3a	3b	3c	4
Pottery Vessels	Sherds per cubic meter (lbs)	25	11.6	40	14.6	74.2	15.5	12.8	15.5	
Other Pottery Artifacts	Figurines	1		3	1	1		1		
	Centrally perforated sherd			1						
	Eccentrically perforated sherd	1		1						
	Pellet				1					
	Unclassifiable formed objects	3		2					1	1
Flaked Chert Artifacts	Flake cores	1					1			1
	Ovate bifaces			3			5	1		
	Elongate bifaces			1	1			1		
	Bifacial core tool fragment					2				
	Thin bifaces			4						
	Irregular retouched flakes					2	1	1		
	Blades			2			3			2
	Used flakes	3		1	1			2		3
	Unmodified flakes	22	3	41	11	14	51	8	3	26
	Unmodified, fire-spalled flakes	9		2	2	1	6			7
Flaked Obsidian Artifacts	Prismatic blades	2		4	1	1	4	1		1
Ground, Pecked, and Polished Stone Artifacts	Manos	1		2				1		
	Metates			1	1	1				
	Hammer stone							1		
	Celt			1						
Shell and Bone Artifacts	Shell	2								
	Bone			4						

TABLE 2.42
Structure 2G-57: Distribution of Artifacts by Lot Group

Study Category	Object	Lot Group							
		1a	2a	2b	2c	3a	3b	4a	4b
Pottery Vessels	Sherds per cubic meter (lbs)	1.1	7.9	7.0	5.7	9.5	7.3	--	5.7
Other Pottery Artifacts	Figurines					2	2		
	Perforated modeled disc						1		
	Censer					1			
Flaked Chert Artifacts	Flake core		1						
	Ovate biface						1		
	Thin biface					1			
	Irregular retouched flake				1				
	Used flake		1			1			
	Unmodified flakes			7	6	3	8	5	3
	Unmodified, fire-spalled flakes	1	2	2	2		1		
Flaked Obsidian Artifacts	Prismatic blades				3	1	2	2	4
	Nodule					1			
Ground, Pecked, and Polished Stone Artifacts	Mano					1			
	Metate						1		
	Hammer stone			1					
	Unclassifiable artifact					1			

TABLE 2.43
Structure 2G-58: Artifacts by Lot Group

Study Category	Object	Lot Group				
		1a	1b	2a	2b	3
Pottery Vessels	Sherds per cubic meter (lbs)	2.8	115	6.2	11.4	5.5
Other Pottery Artifacts	Figurines			2		
	Centrally perforated sherd			1		
	Unclassifiable formed object			1		
Flaked Chert Artifacts	Ovate biface			1		1
	Elongate biface	1				
	Thin bifaces			2		
	Irregular retouched flake					1
	Blades			1	1	
	Unused flakes	1		2		1
	Unmodified flakes	3	1	29	3	6
	Unmodified, fire-spalled flakes	1		2	1	
Flaked Obsidian Artifacts	Prismatic blades			1	1	2
	Unclassifiable object (red and black streaked)			1		
Ground, Pecked, and Polished Stone Artifacts	Metates			1	1	
	Hammer stones			2		
	Ground pebble	1				
Bone and Shell Artifacts	Shell			2		
	Bone				1	6

TABLE 2.44
Structure 2G-59: Artifacts by Lot Group

Study Category	Object	Lot Groups																
		1	2a	2b	3	4a	4b	4c	4d	5a	5b	5c	6a	6b	6c	6d	6e	6f
Pottery Vessels	Sherds per cubic cubic meter (lbs)	3.3	3.2	14		22.3	8	5.3	11.3	7.3	5.6	3.5	14.7	8.3	8.2	10.7	4	5.6
Other Pottery Artifacts	Figurines			7		1							2					
	Centrally perforated sherds																	
	Eccentrically perforated sherd												1					
	Censers		1									1		1				
	Unclassifiable formed objects			2		1		3		1	1	1	1	1	1			
Flaked Chert Artifacts	Flake cores	1		1			1			1			1					
	Ovate bifaces		1	3		4	1	2	1	2	2			2	3			
	Elongate biface													1			1	
	Thin bifaces		4				1	1		1						1		
	Irregular, retouched flakes		2				3									1		
	Point-retouched flakes	1					1						2					
	Blades	1					2				1		1					
	Flakes, used	2		2		1	1	1		1						1		1
	Flakes, unmodified		7	42	1	58	33	102	28	51	15	2	43	27	6	52	12	18
	Flakes, unmodified fire-spalled	4		7	1	10	18	9	2	7	2		14	3	1	2	3	10
Flaked Obsidian Artifacts	Thin bifaces	2		2						1								
	Prismatic blades	6		6		3	4	1		5	2	1		4	1	6	1	1
Ground, Pecked, and Polished Stone Artifacts	Manos		1		1	1	2	1		2	1		1		1	2	1	
	Metates			3			3	3			1					2		
	Rubbing stone											1						
	Hammer stones									1								
	Ground pebbles					2												
	Metallic mosaic element								1						1	1	1	
	Unclassifiable artifacts										1			1				
Shell and Bone Artifacts	Shell										1		1					
	Bone			6		1	4		5		4		3			1		

TABLE 2.45
Structure 2G-60: Artifacts by Lot Group

Study Category	Object	Lot Group 1	2	3a	3b	4
Pottery Vessels	Sherds per cubic meter (lbs)	10.2	4.15	21	8.7	17.7
Other Pottery Artifacts	Incomplete perforated sherd					1
Flaked Chert Artifacts	Ovate bifaces	2	1		1	1
	Elongate bifaces	1	1	1		
	Thin biface	1				
	Irregular retouched flake	1				
	Blades	1	1			
	Unmodified flakes	7	6	13	3	5
	Unmodified, fire-spalled flakes	2	1	1		4
Flaked Obsidian Artifacts	Prismatic blades	3		3		2
Ground, Pecked, and Polished Stone Artifacts	Mano			1		
	Metate					1
	Unclassifiable artifact					1
Shell and Bone Artifacts	Shell	1				

TABLE 2.46
Structure 2G-56: Time Spans

Time Span	Architectural Development	Construction Stage	Unit	Descriptive Data	Lot Group		Ceramics in Vogue
1				Abandonment and collapse	3a 3b	1b	----------
2				Use	3c		(late)
3	Str. 2G-56-A	None defined	11	Modification	2c		Imix (early)
4				Use			----------
		1		Construction of building of perishable materials	4		
		2	5-10	Construction of upper platform level	2b		
5	Str. 2G-56-B	3		Construction of lower platform level	2a		Ik-Imix
		4	2-4	Preparation of base surface	1a	1b	
6			1	Preconstruction activity			---------- Ik

TABLE 2.47
Structure 2G-57: Time Spans

Time Span	Architectural Development	Construction Stage	Unit	Descriptive Data	Lot Group	Ceramics in Vogue
1				Abandonment and collapse	3a,3b,4a,4b	Imix
2				Use		
3	Str. 2G-57-1st	1		Construction of building of perishable materials		Ik-Imix
		2	8	Construction of interior platform(s)	2c	
		3	6,7	Construction of upper platform level	2b	
4				Use		
5	Str. 2G-57-2nd	1		Construction of building of perishable materials		
		2	1,2; 3-5?	Construction of building platform	1,2a	Ik

TABLE 2.48
Structure 2G-58: Time Spans

Time Span	Architectural Development	Construction Stage	Unit	Descriptive Data	Lot Group	Ceramics in Vogue
1				Abandonment and collapse		
2				Use		Imix
3	Str. 2G-58-1st	None defined	4	Apparent renovation		
4				Use		
5	Str. 2G-58-2nd	1		Reconstruction of building		Ik-Imix transition
		2	3	Laying of new floor		
		3		Partial demolition of building		
6				Use		
7	Str. 2G-58-3rd	1		Construction of building of perishable materials		Ik
		2		Construction of upper platform level		
		3	1,2	Construction of middle platform level	1a,b 3	
		4		Preparation of bedrock and formation of lower platform level		

TABLE 2.49
Structure 2G-59: Time Spans
(includes Chultun 2G-11)

Time Span	Architectural Development	Construction Stage	Unit	Special Deposits: Burial	Special Deposits: Problematical Deposit	Descriptive Data	Lot Group	Ceramics in Vogue
1				53,55? 59?,60		Abandonment and collapse		(late)
2						Use	6a-f	
3	Str. 2G-59-1st	1				Construction of building of perishable materials		Imix
		2		50?		Construction of upper platform level	5b	
		3		52		Construction of lower platform level: Plat. 2G-1:Fl. 1 laid	5a,c	(early)
		4		49,56		Partial demolition of 2nd		
4						Use		
5	Str. 2G-59-2nd	1				Construction of building of perishable materials		
		2	17-20			Construction of stairs, probable alteration of E platform	4b,c	
		3		57		Construction of principal platform walls	4a	Ik-Imix
		4		54	64	Demolition of major portion of 3rd; probable construction of Str.2G-Sub.1	4d	
6						Use		
7	Str. 2G-59-3rd	None defined	10-16	58		Renovation of U. 1 platform as E Platform for principal structure; Plat. 2G-1:Fl. 2 laid; Ch. 2G-11 possibly filled	2a,b,3?	Ik
8						Use		
9	Str. 2G-59-4th	None defined	3-9			Renovation of U.1, Ch.2G-11 still in use	1	
10						Use of 5th and Ch.2G-11		
11	Str. 2G-59-5th	None defined	2			Construction of U. 1; possible construction of Ch. 2G-11		
12						Use of earliest construction		
13	Str. 2G-59-6th?		21,22			Earliest probable construction at locus; possible construction of Ch.2G-11		Manik

TABLE 2.50
Structure 2G-60: Time Spans

Time Span	Architectural Development	Construction Stage	Unit	Descriptive Data	Lot Group	Ceramics in Vogue
1				Abandonment and collapse	3a,b	(late)
2				Use		
3	Str. 2G-60-1st	1		Construction of building of perishable materials	4	
		2	3,4	Construction of upper platform level		
		3		Construction of lower platform level	2	Imix (early)
4				Use		
5	Str. 2G-60-2nd	None defined	1,2,6	Earliest construction	1	Ik-Imix
6			5	Preconstruction activity		Ik

TABLE 2.51
Chultun 2G-5: Time Spans

Time Span	Architectural Development	Construction Stage	Descriptive Data	Lot Group	Ceramics in Vogue
1			Abandonment and accumulation of debris	1, 2	
2			Use		Imix
3		1	Construction of Chm. 2		
		2	Construction of antechamber		Ik

TABLE 2.52
Group 2G-1: Time Spans

Group Time Spans	Str. 2G-56 (Table 2.46)	Str. 2G-57 (Table 2.47)	Str. 2G-58 (Table 2.48)	Str. 2G-59 (Table 2.49)	Str. 2G-60 (Table 2.50)	Ch. 2G-5 (Table 2.51)
1	1	1	1	1	1	1
2	2		2	2	2	
3	3		3	3	3	
4	4	2	4	4	4	
5	5	3	5	5	5	
6	6	4	6	6	6	2
7		5	7	7		3
8				8		
9				9		
10				10		
11				11		
13				13		

red bowls suggest the same. Although there is late occupation material from only three structures (Gp. TS. 2), there is no reason to assume that these were used for any significant length of time after the other two were abandoned.

The position of Ch. 2G-5 in this scheme is problematical. Cultural material within the chultun was generally contemporary with material from Gp. 2G-1 occupation contexts. This no doubt arose from the fact that Ch. 2G-5:LG. 2 derived from some of this trash that washed down into the chambers. The implication is that the chultun was left open when Gp. 2G-1 was abandoned, and did not fill up before that time. This, and the proximity of the chultun to the group, suggests that it was in use while the group was occupied. The time of construction is unknown. It could have been later than some of the construction in Gp. 2G-1, but probably no earlier. No Manik sherds were found around the chultun, and it is hard to imagine a chultun existing in isolation. Although this is speculative, it is just possible that the chultun was constructed when Ch. 2G-11 was filled (Gp. TS. 7).

To sum up, activity in Gp. 2G-1 may be bracketed between a date slightly earlier than AD 550 on the one hand, and AD 869 on the other.

Group 2G-2

INTRODUCTION

Group 2G-2 is in Sq. 2G of the site map (TR. 11): S180 E300. As mapped by H. M. Gregerson in 1960, it includes three structures, 2G-13, 14, and 15. One of these, 2G-15, is of such small size that Gregerson, in his field notes, considered the possibility that its mound might cover a monument rather than a structure. As it turned out, it had a complex sequence. One chultun, 2G-10, was discovered during excavation of Str. 2G-14. The group occupies the top of a prominent hill, not far from several other mounds. The hillside falls steeply to the W to bajo, which separates this group from Gp. 2G-1 and others to the W. To the S, a slightly lower ridge extends into the bajo, and several structures are located along it. To the N and E are more groups, among them what appear to be substantial range-type structures.

Two structures and the chultun of Gp. 2G-2 were excavated as Op. 24E and F in March 1961 by Haviland. Structure 2G-14, located on the W side of a plaza, revealed a sequence of two architectural developments and one subsequent modification. Investigation of supposedly diminutive Str. 2G-15 revealed a more complex sequence of rebuilding, and led to discovery of another structure, 2G-Sub.2.

STRUCTURE 2G-14-2ND

This structure (Fig. 28, 29) quite likely was a one-level rectangular platform that probably served as a foundation for a building of pole-and-thatch (TR. 20B). It was built on the surface of U. 1 and 2 (see below). Unit 4, a small floor fragment, is a remnant of the platform surface. The lower portion of U. 3, composed of a vertical arrangement of rough stones, is a remnant of the back wall, the facing stones possibly having been removed at a later time. Two well-cut masonry blocks in the top of U. 3 probably relate to Str. 2G-14-1st-B. Given the limited exposure of Str. 2G-14-2nd (in a 2-m wide trench), nothing more can be said of it.

STRUCTURE 2G-14-1ST-B

This structure (Fig. 28, 29) saw enlargement of 2nd, with an upper level and small interior platform built on its top. As CS. 3, work began with the ripping out of the E wall of Str. 2G-14-2nd with new fill for 1st packed in against the existing fill. Apparently, construction of the new E portion of 1st followed immediately on the destruction of the old wall, or the fill of 2nd would have slumped at least a bit. The new E wall served as the riser for a lower platform level, the pavement of which is represented by U. 5. The elevation of this floor was a bit lower than the old one for 14-2nd. The wall for this lower platform level rests directly on U. 2, with the eastern portion of that early pavement possibly surviving in use over the plaza to the E.

As CS. 2, the E wall for a second platform level was placed just W of the probable location of the earlier E wall of 2nd. No trace of pavement for this second platform now survives. A projection to the W from the top of this wall, however, indicates that the floor must have abutted a two-course wall of well-cut masonry blocks that forms the upper portion of U. 3. The similarity of this masonry to that of the two other E walls of 14-1st-B, and its difference from that of the rest of U. 3 below, identified this upper portion as a part of the new 1st-B construction. It could represent the E wall of a third platform level or the E wall of a small platform positioned midway along the rear of the structure. The latter is more probable, on the basis of what is known of the succeeding 1st-A.

The back wall of the final structure survives as U. 7, a new one-course wall of masonry. Given the height of U. 3, U. 7 must have consisted of more than this one course. The absence of additional masonry is easily explained as the result of collapse down the steep slope W of Str. 2G-14. Unit 7 was built on an earth fill, the height of which

in relation to the steep slope down to the W suggests that there must have been yet another wall to the W, creating at least one terrace. No such wall can now be seen, but again, collapse down the slope may be the reason.

Precisely how U. 7 and the upper part of U. 3 fit in the sequence of construction stages for 14-1st-B is not known. At least the bottom part of U. 7 must have been built no later than CS. 3. Perhaps all of it, with the top of U. 3, may have been built as part of CS. 2, with U. 7 being completed afterwards.

Although no positive evidence exists, it is likely that a building of perishable materials stood on the platform of Str. 2G-14-1st-B. A final construction stage (no. 1) is allowed for this.

STRUCTURE 2G-14-1ST-A

This final modification of 2G-14 saw enlargement of a rear, axially placed platform, the original front wall of which was the upper part of U. 3. Unit 6 (Fig. 28, 29), a square arrangement of stones, is all that now remains of the wall of this platform.

STRUCTURE 2G-15-3RD

This seems to have been a low platform on which a pole-and-thatch building may have stood (Fig. 30a, 31). It is represented by U. 1, a piece of construction built on a floor associated with the already existing Str. 2G-Sub.2-2nd (see below). Unit 1 survives as two walls that form the NW corner of the structure. They were constructed of blocks of masonry two courses in height. The floor on which they rest, which served Str. 2G-Sub.2-2nd, may have continued in use with this new construction, or a new floor may have been laid of which no trace survives. Structure 2G-Sub.2-2nd surely continued in use with 15-3rd.

STRUCTURE 2G-15-2ND

An enlargement of 3rd (Fig. 30b, 31) is represented by U. 2, a relatively complete N wall, as well as portions of E and W walls. These were built of well-cut masonry blocks three courses high, so as to bury U. 1 within the fill of the new platform. Between U. 2 and Str. 2G-Sub.2-1st to the N, a plaster floor (U. 3) was laid that turns up to U. 2.

STRUCTURE 2G-15-1ST

For construction of the final structure, U. 2 along with Str. 2G-Sub.2-1st were partially razed. A new platform, with its long axis oriented N-S, was then erected over what was left of these earlier edifices (Fig. 30c, 31). This final platform was in a very poor state of preservation, as a large Ramon tree was growing on top of it; all that is known is that it has a rectangular shape, and must once have been at least 0.55 m in height. The E wall of the preceding structure was apparently utilized as part of the corresponding wall of the final one. There may have been a step on the W side of the axis, for five stones, probably originally associated with 15-2nd, are so situated as to suggest that they survived in use as part of a step. If so, they would have formed the basis of a step centered precisely on the axis, with a distance of exactly 2 m from either stair end to either corner of the structure. The step itself would have been 0.56 m deep. An entrance to 15-1st would be expected on its W side, as Str. 2G-14-1st across the plaza opened to the E. Unfortunately, destruction is so extensive in the area that the possibility exists that the plaza floor associated with Str. 2G-15-1st covered the stones in question. The hypothesis that they were part of a step is favored, however, for the height of the platform would seem to require one. A plaza floor, U. 4, turns up to the northern portion of Str. 2G-15-1st.

STRUCTURE 2G-SUB.2-3RD

This earliest architecture at the locus of Str. 2G-15 is little known, but probably was a platform for a pole-and-thatch building (Fig. 31). Attesting to its one-time existence are two floors, an apparent posthole, and a distinctive fill. The floors are U. 1 and 2; U. 2 ends 1.70 m S of Datum 24E, and U. 1 begins 6.50 m S of Datum 24E to run farther S. Unit 1, about 3 cm thick, rests on a foundation of small pebbles that lie on earth fill. Unit 2, about the same thickness, ends at a stone by a possible posthole (U. 4). South of this hole, U. 3, a fill of large stones, rises to 0.50 m above the floor level. This same stratum can be followed beneath the surface of U. 2, and forms the foundation for that floor. Unit 3 clearly represents the fill of an otherwise unknown structure associated with U. 2. The posthole, U. 4, suggests that the structure may have been partially built of perishable materials.

Unit 1, which falls within 2 cm of the same elevation as U. 2, undoubtedly is part of the same floor as U. 2 S of the structure, represented by U. 3.

STRUCTURE 2G-SUB.2-2ND-A AND B

Evidence for this structure (Fig. 30a, 31) consists of a floor, U. 5, that overlies U. 1 by 9 cm. Unit 5, 2 cm in thickness, was laid on a foundation of small stones. Its position suggests some degree of renovation of the structure represented by U. 3.

Unit 6 is a floor that lies on a foundation of pebbles directly above U. 5. Its position only 4 cm above the latter floor does not suggest major renovation of U. 3, but neither does it rule it out. Unit 6 defines Str. 2G-Sub.2-2nd-A, while U. 5 and 7 define Sub.2-2nd-B. Unit 7 is a floor by the NW corner of the later Str. 2G-15-3rd, at the same elevation as U. 5, and undoubtedly is a part of the same floor.

STRUCTURE 2G-SUB.2-1ST

The remains of this structure consist of its S and W walls (Fig. 30b, 31). The S wall was built at the same time as Str. 2G-15-2nd, 0.45 m to the N. It was assembled of two courses of masonry covered by a thick coat of hard plaster. Although the masonry itself is vertical, the plaster coat produces a considerable batter. The earlier structure, of which U. 3 is a part, was razed to permit construction of Sub.2-1st, and only some of its fill survived. The floor (Str. 2G-15 U. 3) between Str. 2G-15-2nd and 2G-Sub.2-1st turns up to the latter structure. North of Sub.2, another floor remnant (U. 8) probably is a portion of the same pavement, as its elevation is the same.

PLATFORM 2G-2

Little attention was devoted to the plaza of Gp. 2G-2, save elements in close proximity to the structures investigated. Hence, separate floor and unit numerations apart from those of structures were not defined. Already discussed are Str. 2G-15:U. 3, 4 and Str. 2G-Sub.2:U. 1, 2, and 5-8; all are floor remnants near and beneath those structures. Here, Str. 2G-14:U. 1 and 2 (already mentioned in the write-up of that structure) are given further discussion. These are two floor surfaces beneath that structure. Unit 1, the westernmost surface, lies directly on a gray earth fill, without benefit of any special foundation material. Unit 2, at the same level, was laid on a special foundation of small stones. Both surfaces may have been two parts of a single floor, though the presence of a foundation in the case of U. 2 alone suggests that U. 1 may have been a later extension of it. Both floors are at the level of Plat. 2G-2, and the E part of U. 2 may have continued to serve as part of a plaza floor associated with Str. 2G-14-1st-B. Originally, the two pavements may have been laid before any structure was built on the W edge of the plaza.

CHULTUN 2G-10

Description

Chultun 2G-10 was discovered hidden under Str. 2G-14 during excavation. It consists of five bedrock chambers, clustered around Or. 1 (Fig. 32 and Table 2.53). This leads through an unusually long neck into Chm. 2. A stepped rim once allowed a stone cover to fit snugly in place, but there is now no trace of such a cover. Two other orifices gave access at one time to this chultun. One of these, Or. 2, still has its stone cover in place. The neck from this orifice, considerably shorter than the first neck, opens into Chm. 3. The other orifice, slightly larger and a bit more irregular in shape than the others, opens into Chm. 5.

The chambers are all approximately dome-shaped to varying degrees, and are of varying depths. Chamber 1 is the smallest, located just S of Or. 1. There is a small hole in the E wall into Chm. 4, and another to the W suggests that there may be another chultun to be found there.

Chamber 2 is much larger than Chm. 1, and extends N of Or. 1. An entrance on the E, restricted only on the S wall but nowhere else, leads to Chm. 3, into which Neck 2 leads. Chamber 3 almost has the appearance of a passage between Chm. 2 and 4. It opens, to the S, into Chm. 4, the deepest of all. There is no sill or other restriction in this entrance.

Chamber 5, the one with the highest floor, opens into the S side of Chm. 4 through an entrance restricted on the sides and floor. The most notable thing about Chm. 5 is its cramped space; it is less than 1 m from floor to ceiling. As found, the entrance between Chm. 4 and 5 was blocked by a stone slab 0.56 square and 0.20 m thick.

DISCUSSION

When discovered, the entire chultun was filled with compact earth indistinguishable from the lower fill of the construction above. This fill contained an abundance of cultural material, particularly sherds, along with considerable ash. Numerous interlot fits between sherds from all levels and all chambers, and the lack of distinct depositional strata, demonstrate that the chultun was purposely filled all at once. This was just prior to construction of Str. 2G-14:U. 2 (Fig. 29). The nature of the fill, the large size of the sherds, and the sharp nature of the breaks on these, all point to the source as a nearby midden. Had the material been carried any distance, the sherds would have been smaller with greater wear on their edges.

Given the above, a very real problem is the presence of the entrance block between Chm. 4 and 5. Clearly, it was not placed there to retain fill in Chm. 5 while Chm. 4 remained in use. The most likely explanation is that it is associated with Bu. 63, which was placed in Chm. 5 at the time it was filled. The burial was probably put in place and the chamber was then filled and sealed. Immediately following this, the rest of the chultun was filled up.

A further problem with this chultun is the presence of so many orifices. Of those chultuns dealt with in this report that have more than one orifice, there is good reason to suppose that only one of these openings was functional at a given time. That may have been the case here, for the presence of a cover on Or. 2, but not Or. 1, suggests that Or. 2 alone was in use at the time of abandonment. On the other hand, in the case of chultuns filled through a single orifice (see Ch. 2F-5 and 6E-7, this report), the inner chambers are not normally so full as they are here. This might suggest that fill was dumped through both Or. 1 and 2. Alternatively, when the decision to fill was made, a long unused orifice may have been reopened to facilitate operations.

When Or. 3 is considered, there are further problems. Its larger size and irregularity suggest that it is not a conventional orifice, but a cut into the ceiling of Chm. 5 made for the placement of Bu. 63. Arguing against this, the burial could have been put in place from Chm. 4 without going to this trouble. Furthermore, the elevation of the floor of Chm. 5 relative to that of Chm. 4, and the

TABLE 2.53
Chultun 2G-10: Average Dimensions (meters)

Feature	Length	Width	Height	Minimum Diameter	Maximum Diameter
Orifice 1	-	-	0.70*	0.36	0.36
Orifice 2	-	-	0.30*	0.50	0.50
Orifice 3	-	-	1.00*	0.75	1.14
Chamber 1	1.12	0.79	1.00	-	-
Chamber 2	2.15	1.60	0.80	-	-
Chamber 3	1.60	0.80	1.20	-	-
Chamber 4	2.00	1.58	1.48	-	-
Chamber 5	1.19	0.90	0.90	-	-
Entrance 1-2	0.15	0.42	0.75	-	-
Entrance 2-3	0.10	0.82	0.80	-	-
Entrance 3-4	-	0.80	1.04	-	-
Entrance 4-5	0.16	0.84	0.59	-	-
Sill 4-5	-	-	0.28	-	-

*Neck Height

presence of a sill, suggest that Chm. 5 served as an ante-chamber. Perhaps, then, the size and irregularity of Or. 3 are the result of damage inflicted at the time the chultun was abandoned.

Related to the problem of the multiple orifices are the multiple chambers. The sherds from the chultun indicate that it was probably filled around AD 700 (Table 2.54). Further, there is no evidence that any architecture of Gp. 2G-2 predates ca. AD 550, although there were a few Pre-classic sherds in the chultun. Of those chultuns dealt with in this report, those with more than three chambers were all built in Preclassic times. Those built in Early Classic times never have more than three chambers, and those built in the Intermediate or Late Classic periods generally have even fewer. Although there is an outside chance that Ch. 2G-10 was built in Preclassic times, it seems more likely, based on when it was filled, that it was built to serve with the early architecture of Gp. 2G-2, between AD 550 and 700. Taking all these points into consideration, then, it seems likely that Ch. 2G-10 began as one or two sep-arate smaller chultuns. It is impossible to be sure about this, and all that can be done is to suggest some possible alternative interpretations:

1. The original chultun consisted of Chm. 3 and 4, served by Or. 2. Because of lack of a sill, water seeped through the orifice and into Chm. 4, so this orifice was abandoned, and a new one (Or. 1) was built farther away, with new chambers to connect to the old. This still was not satisfactory, so Or. 1 was abandoned, and Or. 3 with Chm. 5 were built. This time, a high sill was placed be-tween the antechamber and the rest of the chultun.

2. The original chultun consisted of Chm. 3 and 4, with Or. 2. Later, a second chultun, consisting of Chm. 1 and 2 with Or. 1, was begun, but it broke into the ante-chamber of the original chultun and so its orifice (no. 2) was closed up. Later, because of a water problem, Or. 1 was abandoned, and Chm. 5 with Or. 3 were built.

3. Two chultuns were built, one consisting of Chm. 4 and 5 with Or. 3, and one consisting of Chm. 1 and 2 with Or. 1. Orifice 2 was intended to replace one or the other of these, but its construction accidentally broke into the other chultun, thus joining them.

4. The original chultun consisted of Chm. 3 and 4 with Or. 2. A second, "dumbbell-type" chultun was built next to it, accidentally breaking into the antechamber of the first. Orifice 2, then, was abandoned. Later, probably because of water problems, a new orifice and antecham-ber (Or. 3 and Chm. 5) were provided, and Or. 1 was abandoned.

To sum up, all that can be said is that the chultun probably was modified one or more times after its initial construction to result in Ch. 2G-10 as it was at the time of abandonment. The precise nature of that modification

(or modifications) remains unknown; there are good argu-ments both for and against the hypothetical sequences of modifications outlined above.

SHERDS AND ARTIFACTS

Lot groups for Gp. 2G-2 are defined in Table 2.54, with content given in Tables 2.55–2.57.

CONSTRUCTION FILL

The earliest material from Gp. 2G-2 comes from this source. In only a few instances was fill sealed beneath ac-tual pavement; thus there is a large chance for contam-ination in most fill lots. Since preservation of all of the structures is poor, it is probable that material over their surfaces is largely rooted-out fill. To add to this problem, sherds in particular are in most cases not plentiful, so that appraisals are somewhat problematical.

Worthy of special note is the material in Ch. 2G-10, which appears to be redeposited from a midden. If the conclusions are correct concerning the time of construc-tion and use of the chultun (see below), it is quite possible that much, if not all, the fill was originally trash discarded by the occupants of Str. 2G-Sub.2.

MATERIAL ABOVE LIVING LEVELS

Material in this category is scarce in the case of Str. 2G-14. Its LG. 3, which might have contained some oc-cupation debris, looks to be structure collapse. What little material there is in LG. 4 may have been occupation trash.

A good sample of sherds and artifacts was collected from around Str. 2G-15. Although the structure is bad-ly destroyed, causing contamination of material found around it, both LG. 4a and 4b appear to be largely occupa-tion trash. Lot Group 4c may be more mixed. The greatest accumulation of sherds is to the E of the structure, and the greatest accumulation of artifacts to the W.

TIME SPANS

Time spans defined for Str. 2G-14, 15, 2G-Sub.2 and Ch. 2G-10 are listed in Tables 2.58–2.61. Those for the latter two structures are easily correlated in a one-to-one manner on the basis of architectural associations, if the assumption is made that Sub.2-2nd, already in exis-tence, was modified when 15-3rd was built. This assump-tion seems reasonable given the close proximity of the two structures. Moreover, it is known that Sub.2-1st and 15-2nd were constructed, used, and abandoned simulta-neously.

Correlation of these time spans with those for Str. 2G-14 is difficult, given the erratic nature of the ceramic samples from the group (Table 2.54), and so those given must be regarded with caution. Briefly, the ceramic evi-dence indicates that Ch. 2G-10 was filled probably soon

TABLE 2.54
Group 2G-2: Lot Groups

Feature	Lot Group	Lots	Provenience Evaluation	Ceramic
Str. 2G-14 (Op. 24E)	1a	16,23	Fill, sealed by U. 2	Ik and/or Imix
	1b	15	Fill, sealed by U. 1	Ik and/or Imix
	2a	20	Unsealed fill of 1st and 2nd	Ik and/or Imix
	2b	14,21	Unsealed fill of 1st	Ik and/or Imix
	2c	33	Unsealed fill of 1st, 2nd, and U. 2	Ik and/or Imix
	3	7,9	W of structure, surface to bedrock	Early Imix
	4	10	E of structure, surface to base of wall	Imix
	5	2,6,8	Surface over structure floor levels	Early Imix
Str. 2G-15 (includes Str. 2G-Sub.2; Op. 24E)	1	34	Unsealed fill of Sub.2-3rd	?
	2a	32	Unsealed fill of 15-2nd and Sub.2-1st	Ik and/or Imix
	2b	22,29	Unsealed fill of 15-2nd	Imix or Ik-Imix transition
	3	11,12,18,31	Unsealed fill of 15-1st	Imix or Ik-Imix transition
	4a	1,4,17,30	N of structure, surface to base of wall	Late Imix
	4b	3,25,27	W of structure, surface to base of wall	Late Imix
	4c	13,19,24	E of structure, surface to base of wall	Early, late Imix
	5	5,26,28	Surface over structure to floor level	Imix or Ik-Imix transition
Ch. 2G-10 (Op. 24F)	1	All lots	Fill	Ik, a few Ik-Imix transition, a few Cauac

TABLE 2.55
Structure 2G-14: Artifacts by Lot Group

Study Category	Object	Lot Group 1a	1b	2a	2b	2c	3	4	5
Pottery Vessels	Sherds per cubic meter (lbs)	4.28	2.4	10.3	4.3	2.8	6.7	8.4	3.58
Other Pottery Artifacts	Figurine						1		
	Centrally perforated sherd						1		
	Miniature vessel					1			
	Censer						1		
Flaked Chert Artifacts	Flake core	1							1
	Ovate bifaces							1	1
	Elongate biface					1			
	Irregular, retouched flake					1			
	Blade						1		
	Used flakes	1			2		2	1	1
	Unmodified flakes	1		6	8	10	7	15	9
	Unmodified, fire-spalled flakes				1	1	7	2	1
Flaked Obsidian Artifacts	Flake core (green)	1							
	Irregular, retouched								
	Prismatic blades	1			1		2		1
Ground, Pecked and Polished Stone Artifacts	Manos					1			1
	Metates							1	1

TABLE 2.56
Structure 2G-15: Artifacts by Lot Group

Study Category	Object	Lot Group							
		1	2a	2b	3	4a	4b	4c	5
Pottery Vessels	Sherds per cubic meter(lbs)	-	.2	2.4	5.0	6.0	6.7	11.9	4.07
Other Pottery Artifacts	Figurines				1		1		
	Candelero						1		
	Unclassifiable object								1
Flaked Chert Artifacts	Flake cores					1	1		
	Ovate bifaces					1	3		1
	Elongate biface								1
	Irregular retouched flakes					1	1		
	Point-retouched flake								1
	Blade								1
	Used flakes					5	1		1
	Unmodified flakes		18	15		31	29	10	26
	Unmodified, fire-spalled flakes			3		7	8		5
Flaked Obsidian Artifacts	Flake core (green)			1					
	Thin biface (green)						1		
	Prismatic blades			1			2		1
Ground, Pecked, and Polished Stone Artifacts	Mano							1	
	Metate						1		
	Hammer stones						1	1	2
	Spindle whorl						1		
	Barkbeater	1							
	Unclassifiable artifact				1	1			
Shell and Bone Artifacts	Bone				1				

TABLE 2.57
Chultun 2G-10: Artifacts by Lot Group

Study Category	Object	Lot Group 1
Pottery Vessels	Sherds per cubic meter (lbs)	Not calculated
Other Pottery Artifacts	Drum	1
Flaked Chert Artifacts	Elongate biface	1
	Point-retouched flake	1
	Rounded, retouched flake	1
	Unmodified flakes	19
Flaked Obsidian Artifacts	Nodule (green)	1
Ground, Pecked, and Polished Stone Artifacts	Metates	2
	Rubbing stone	1
	Hammer stones	3
	Celts	3
Shell and Bone Artifacts	Bone, animal, unmodified	45

TABLE 2.58
Structure 2G-14: Time Spans

Time Span	Architectural Development	Construction Stage	Unit	Special Deposits: Burial	Descriptive Data	Lot Group	Ceramics in Vogue
1					Abandonment and collapse		----
2					Use	4	
3	Str.2G-14-1st-A	None defined	6		Modification	2a 2b	
4					Use		
5	Str.2G-14-1st-B	1			Construction of building of perishable materials		
		2	3 (upper part)? 5		Construction of upper platform level		(late)
		3	7		2nd partially razed; construction of lower platform level	2a 2b 2c 3	Imix
6					Use		
7	Str.2G-14-2nd	1			Construction of building of perishable materials		
		2	3 (lower part) 4		Construction of platform	2a 2c 3	(early)
8					Use of earliest construction		
9	None defined	None defined	1,2	63	Earliest construction at this locus (plaza floor?)	1a 1b 5	Ik-Imix

TABLE 2.59
Structure 2G-15: Time Spans

Time Span	Architectural Development	Unit	Descriptive Data	Lot Group		Ceramics in Vogue
1			Abandonment and collapse			– – – – – – – – –
2			Use	4a 4b	4c	(late)
3	Str. 2G-15-1st	4	Construction, with incorporation of portions of 15-2nd	3, 5		Imix
4			Use			(early)
5	Str. 2G-15-2nd	2,3	Construction	2a, 2b		Ik-Imix
6			Use			– – – – – – – – –
7	Str. 2G-15-3rd	1	Original construction on plaza floors associated with Str. 2G-Sub.2-2nd			Ik

TABLE 2.60
Structure 2G-Sub.2: Time Spans

Time Span	Architectural Development	Unit	Descriptive Data	Str. 2G-15: Lot Group	Ceramics in Vogue
1			Abandonment		Imix (early)
2			Use		– – – – – – –
3	Str.2G-Sub.2-1st	8	2G-Sub.2-2nd razed, construction of final structure	2a	Ik-Imix
4			Use		– – – – – – –
5	Str.2G-Sub.2-2nd-A	6	Presumed modification		
6			Use		
7	Str.2G-Sub.2-2nd-B	5,7	Presumed renovation		Ik
8			Use		
9	Str.2G-Sub.2-3rd	1-4	Earliest construction	1	

TABLE 2.61
Chultun 2G-10: Time Spans

Time Span	Architectural Development	Special Deposits: Burial	Descriptive Data	Lot Group	Ceramics in Vogue
1		63	Chultun abandoned and filled	1	Ik-Imix
2			Use, with possible modifications		
3	Ch. G-10		Original construction		Ik

TABLE 2.62
Group 2G-2: Time Spans

Group Time Span	Structure 2G-14 (Table 2.58)	Structure 2G-15 (Table 2.59)	Structure 2G-Sub.2 (Table 2.60)	Chultun 2G-10 (Table 2.61)
1	1	1		
2	2			
3	3			
4	4	2		
5	5	3	1	
6	6			
7	7			
8	8	4	2	
9	9	5	3	1
10		6	4	
11		7	5	
12			6	
13			7	
14			8	2
15			9	3

after the appearance of ceramics of the Ik-Imix transition, which serves then as a lower limit date on the floors (Str. 2G-14:U. 1 and 2) that overlie the chultun. Similarly, Str. 2G-15-2nd seems at the earliest to date from a time when such pottery was in use.

Structures 2G-14-2nd and 1st seem to date from a time when ceramics of the Imix Complex were in vogue, with the latter possibly late. Given the time of construction of 2G-15-2nd, the last architectural development of this structure probably took place when Imix ceramics were present, and so would seem to correlate with TS. 5 or 7 of 2G-14.

These correlations, then, suggest that 14 time spans for Gp. 2G-2 may be defined (Table 2.62). It is unlikely that any construction at this locus predates the appearance of Ik ceramics, for no Manik sherds were found. The earliest development of Str. 2G-Sub.2 probably dates to the time of Ik ceramic manufacture. One can only guess as to when the earliest version of Ch. 2G-10 was constructed, but there is evidence that it was no earlier than TS. 9 of Str. 2G-Sub.2. Certainly, its use does not seem to have been closely associated with Str. 2G-15, for it was filled during much of the time when one or another version of that structure was in use. One might therefore hazard a guess that the chultun was constructed at about the same time as Str. 2G-Sub.2-3rd.

Evidence for the time of abandonment of Gp. 2G-2 is not clear on account of poor preservation. Monochrome red bowls and fine vessels around Str. 2G-15 suggest a later element than most of the material around 2G-14, however, and point to affiliation with the late Imix Complex. Given the dating of 14-1st, it appears that both structures remained in use during late Imix ceramic production.

To sum up, then, activity in Gp. 2G-2 may be bracketed between the approximate dates of AD 550 and 869, which mark the appearance of Ik and the disappearance of late Imix ceramics, respectively.

Structure 2G-61 Locus

INTRODUCTION

In March 1961, Haviland conducted excavations as Op. 24G in the vicinity of Ch. 2G-1, 2G-2, and 2G-3, which are located together at S395 E54 in Sq. 2G of the Tikal site map (TR. 11). These excavations were the first at Tikal that sought to find traces of one or more small structures in an area where there were no visible surface features from which to predict their presence. Excavated at the same time was Ch. 2G-2/3 as Op. 24H; two years later Puleston returned to excavate Ch. 2G-1 (Op. 66C). The terrain here is essentially flat, but does slope downward almost imperceptibly to the SE. The nearest

apparent construction is Gp. 2G-3, 50 m to the E. Stela 27, excavated by Haviland in 1959 (TR. 8), is 90 m to the W. The chultuns as found were almost entirely covered by forest debris (Fig. 175b). After an area 50 by 60 m was completely cleared of bush around the chultuns, no trace of any construction was noted (Fig. 175a). Stripping the soil to bedrock over an area 10 m N-S and 28 m E-W, however, revealed the presence of Str. 2G-61 and 2G-62. Selective test trenches extending up to 20 m N-S and 44 m E-W did not disclose further construction.

STRUCTURE 2G-61

This large, low platform (Fig. 34–36) was built over a high area of bedrock that the Maya had quarried both to its E and W (Qu. 2G-1 and 2). The N wall (Fig. 175c), constructed of a single course of roughly shaped stones 0.17 m high, rests on a thin layer of gray earth that overlies bedrock. The similarly constructed W wall (Fig. 175d) was built on a thin layer of gray earth, directly over the quarried edge of bedrock. The line of this wall runs by the E edge of Or. 1 of Ch. 2G-1.

The S structure wall is represented by stone rubble that terminates in an E-W line. The location of the SE corner is clearly indicated by rubble, but no other traces of the E wall were found. A projection from the corner indicates that the E wall, like the W one, was positioned on the high bedrock, and followed a quarried bedrock face (Qu. 2G-1).

Four remnants of plaster pavement have survived. Units 1, 2, and 3, which are surely parts of a single floor, rest on a foundation of small stones. Unit 4, located farther S than U. 1–3, is 0.42 m lower than U. 3; hence it is probable that there was a step up to a higher platform level to the N. Where the S wall of this upper level was positioned is unknown, but was no farther N of the S wall than 2.10 m. Here, the stone fill rises to a level higher than the surface of U. 4.

Unit 5 is a step that was built against the N portion of the W wall of the structure. It was constructed of rough stones on a stratum of gray earth (Qu. 2G-2:U. 1), the top of which was the ancient outside living surface.

STRUCTURE 2G-62

Located 6.40 m W of Str. 2G-61 (Fig. 34) is a small hole in bedrock, 0.20 m in diameter (Str. 2G-62:U. 1). In line with this to the NW, at intervals of 2.44 m, are two smaller holes (Fig. 34:U. 2 and 3 of 2G-62). The sizes of U. 1, 2, and 3, as well as the regularity of their spacing and linear arrangement, suggest that they are postholes of a small pole-and-thatch building that once stood here. Unit 4, a fourth hole (not shown in Fig. 34) is located 5.70 m to the SW in the proper position for the corner post of the western wall, if U. 3 was the NE corner post.

This find makes it virtually certain that a pole-and-thatch building once stood here. Although designated as Str. 2G-62, nothing is known of its architecture, other than that perishable materials were used. Originally, the building could have been based upon a masonry building platform, which was later destroyed. This may have been the case, as four things suggest that Str. 2G-62 was abandoned by the time Str. 2G-61 was built. First, there is no trace of a tamped earth floor surface of the sort one might expect a structure built entirely of pole-and-thatch to have had. Second, the quantity of occupation trash steadily decreases to the W of Str. 2G-61 (see Fig. 40). But if Str. 2G-62 was occupied simultaneously with 61, one would expect at least a slight increase in the quantity of debris near it. By contrast, had 62 been previously abandoned, associated trash would have been scraped away by the builders of 61. Third, the discovery of some quantity of Chuen sherds suggests an occupation of the general area prior to construction of Str. 2G-61 (dated by Cauac ceramics). Fourth, Ch. 2G-2 was in use prior to construction of 61 (see below); in which case, one would expect that the chultun was situated near to some other structure. Structure 2G-62 is the only known candidate for such a structure.

CHULTUN 2G-1

This five-chambered chultun (Fig. 37, 38, and Table 2.63) was served by two orifices, but both probably were not in use simultaneously (see discussion below). The chambers are in a rough cruciform arrangement, with the last chamber the deepest. Chamber 1 was entered from above through Or. 1, which was discovered with a round stone cover partially in place (Fig. 176a). The rim of the orifice was stepped on its S and E sides. Neck 1 extends downward from this orifice into the center of the ceiling below. The neck is unusual for its depth and straightness, although a slight flare is visible on the W side near the bottom. The chamber itself is roughly circular and almost continuous with Chm. 2 to the W. Chamber 3 opens into the other side (see below). Chamber 1 was found filled to a depth of 0.75 m with a conical pile of gray earth (U. 1) that overlies a thin stratum of hard-packed gray earth of a slightly lighter shade (U. 2).

At one time, Chm. 2 could be entered from Chm. 1, or directly through Or. 2. This latter opening does not appear on the site map (TR. 11), and was discovered only in the course of excavation. It had been sealed at some point by a stone cover, which was broken, probably by roots, subsequent to abandonment. A pile of unshaped stones was placed above this. The rim is stepped, although the step does not run all the way around the orifice.

Chamber 2, as found, was partially filled with the same deposit of earth as Chm. 1 (U. 1). Here, it is somewhat shallower and lighter in color. Beneath it is the same thin layer of hard-packed gray earth (U. 2). The floor is slightly higher than that of Chm. 1, the entrance to which is very slightly narrowed on the side.

Chamber 3 is entered from Chm. 1 through a restricted entrance with an unusually high floor sill. It gives access to the deeper Chm. 4 and 5 beyond. The space is roughly circular, but in the upper NW the walls and ceiling meet in a distinct corner. The floor level is 0.20–0.30 m lower than that of Chm. 1. The ceiling gives evidence of having lost considerable material as a result of collapse of the limestone. Chamber 3 was found partially filled with material similar to that in Chm. 2 (U. 1). In addition, a masonry block was found in the NW corner that measures 0.40 by 0.25 by 0.13 m. The central portion of the block across the short axis is quite smooth and worn down, as if by friction.

Chamber 4, the smallest room in the chultun, is entered from the N end of Chm. 3 through a small, rounded, restricted entrance. It was found partially filled with a continuation of the material from Chm. 3 (U. 1), here much lighter in color. It also contained a limestone ball with a diameter of 0.22–0.26 m (TR. 27B:fig. 115a). On two opposite sides of this are shallow, cup-like depressions 2.5 cm in depth and 8 cm in diameter.

TABLE 2.63
Chultun 2G-1: Average Dimensions (meters)

Feature	Length	Width	Height	Minimum Diameter	Maximum Diameter
Neck 1	-	-	0.75	0.40	0.46
Neck 2	-	-	0.36	0.45	-
Stone Cover 1	-	-	0.10	0.50	0.50
Stone Cover 2	-	-	Broken	-	-
Chamber 1	-	-	1.00	1.80	1.80
Chamber 2	-	-	0.80	1.00	1.80
Chamber 3	2.50	1.90	1.10	-	-
Chamber 4	2.10	1.40	0.90	-	-
Chamber 5	-	-	1.00	1.80	1.80
Entrance 1-2	-	1.52	0.94	-	-
Entrance 1-3	-	0.80	0.54	-	-
Sill 1-3	-	-	0.30	-	-
Entrance 3-4	-	0.50	0.52	-	-
Sill 3-4	-	-	0.18	-	-
Entrance 3-5	-	0.70	-	-	-

Chamber 5 is entered from the S end of Chm. 3 through a large unrestricted entrance. Its floor is some 1.50 m below that of Chm. 3. Chamber 5 also contained a stratum of the same gray fill as found in the rest of the chultun (U. 1). Here it lay, however, above a stratum of darker gray earth (U. 3), 0.40–0.50 m thick, in which were packed many unshaped stones 0.10–0.25 m in diameter, as well as several large sherds and three unworked animal bone fragments. This in turn overlay a stratum of fine, gray, siltlike material 0.15 m in thickness (U. 4). Beneath this was gray earth that contained small, scattered pieces of carbon (U. 5).

Orifice 2 was clearly sealed in preference for the deep and more awkward Or. 1, but just why is not clear. Certainly, Or. 2 was much easier to access. Perhaps a structure was built above Or. 2, but no evidence for this could be detected. Three peculiarities of the chultun suggest a possible explanation. The first is the absence (perhaps through destruction) of a sill between Chm. 1 and 2; the second is the low elevation of the bedrock surface at Or. 2 relative to the surrounding area; the third is the presence of silt (U. 4) in Chm. 5. The situation at the orifice is such that undesirable rainwater could readily have entered the chultun. In the absence of a sill, there is nothing to prevent this water from running into other portions of the chultun (Chm. 1). Given water in sufficient quantity, it could have spilled over into other chambers in spite of the high sill in the entrance to Chm. 3. Indeed, the very prominence of this sill suggests that the Maya themselves anticipated such a problem. In spite of this, however, the silt in Chm. 5 suggests that water nonetheless did spill into the rest of the chultun. To deal with this problem once and for all, the Maya may have sealed off the original orifice and then dug a new one. Perhaps the material of U. 5 was put in place at this time.

A clue that Or. 1 was a later addition to the chultun is the extreme depth and narrowness of its neck. Moreover, the slight slant of the neck towards Chm. 2 suggests that workmen were groping for the cavity that they knew was below. Finally, excavations of other Tikal chultuns suggest that a functional chultun did not require more than one orifice (TR. 32).

One might argue that Chm. 3–5 were dug at the time of construction of Or. 1. In favor of this is the presence of sills between Chm. 2 and 3, and 3 and 4. There is no sill between Chm. 1 and 2. Moreover, if these two chambers are taken alone, with Or. 2, one has a common type of Tikal chultun with small antechamber and larger inner chamber. This proposition is unlikely, though, on the basis of the silt in Chm. 5, which seems to have been deposited by water. With Or. 2 closed, it would be difficult to account for the presence of this silt, unless the chamber was in existence when flooding through Or. 2 was a prob-

lem. Moreover, the sherds in U. 3 suggest long usage of Chm. 5 prior to the final period of use of the chultun. Unit 3, on the basis of ceramic evidence, seems to have been put in place at about the time that Str. 2G-61 was built. The existence of the deposit (U. 5) beneath the silt suggests usage for a period of time before this event. Finally, perhaps little importance should be assigned to the absence of a sill between two chambers, and the presence of one between others. The missing sill might have been worn down through use, or perhaps was purposely destroyed when Or. 1 was built so that Chm. 1 and 2 became almost a single entity.

None of the chambers was completely filled, in marked contrast with Ch. 2G-2, which had been purposely filled by the Maya (see below). That Ch. 2G-1 was not deliberately filled, with such fill later settling into deeper chambers, is indicated by comparison with Ch. 5C-8, 6E-6, and 6E-7, where this occurred (discussed in this report, Str. 5C-56 locus and Gp. 6E-1). In these three examples, there was a more prominent mound of earth beneath the orifice than in this case. Moreover, the bulk of U. 1 in the deeper chambers of Ch. 2G-1 seems to have fallen from the ceiling, rather than the slump of fill from Chm. 2. Chultun 2G-1 was therefore probably used by the occupants of Str. 2G-61, a conclusion that is consistent with evidence from ceramic analysis (see below).

The gray fill of Chm. 1 and 2 probably represents material that washed into the chultun beneath the edges of the loosely placed stone cover on Or. 1. Against this notion, it might be argued that the stone cover was firmly in place until moved by the tree root that was found growing into the chultun. It might also be argued, however, that the tree root grew here precisely because there was already a slight opening. Further, the material in Chm. 1 and 2 might have washed in only during the last century or so.

When the chultun was excavated, it was found to be occupied by over a dozen bats, who undoubtedly also contributed to the fill in the chambers. The whiter nature of the U. 1 fill in the deeper chambers most probably was because it consisted almost entirely of material that had fallen from the ceiling. The harder packed U. 2 beneath these deposits, and U. 5 in Chm. 5, probably represent an accumulation of material packed down while the chultun was in use. It is perhaps noteworthy that a similar deposit was not found in Chm. 3.

CHULTUN 2G-2/2G-3

DESCRIPTION

Chultun 2G-2 and 3 are in reality the two end chambers of a single three-chamber chultun (Fig. 36, 39, and Table 2.64). Chamber 1 is entered through a manhole-like opening (Or. 1; "Ch. 2G-3" on the site map). To the E, the chamber opens into the quarried area E of, and below, the wall of Str. 2G-61 (Qu. 2G-1). This quarry was filled with packed small stones and earth. The quarry likely postdates the chultun, for it would have been easier to pack in the small stones after the chultun had been filled. The fact that the quarry stops on the surface in a straight line at the wall of Str. 2G-61, but was undercut somewhat, suggests that those who quarried it intentionally avoided damage to Str. 2G-61. Moreover, there would have been little reason to fill the quarry had the structure not been in use at the time. Therefore, either the structure was already in existence, or was in the process of construction at the time of the quarrying. Since the chultun was filled when the overlying structure was built, the quarry appears to have penetrated to the end of the already filled chultun, and was subsequently filled with stones.

Chamber 2 is large and dome-shaped, with walls continuous with the ceiling. Its floor is 0.15 m below that of Chm. 1 and 0.20 m below that of Chm. 3. The entrance from Chm. 1 to 2 is slightly constricted. Another entrance, more constricted, gives access to Chm. 3 (see above). The chamber was filled with earth and large masonry blocks, and a rectangular stone slab blocked the entrance to Chm. 2. The stone cover, purposely battered to a size small enough to be dropped inside, was found in the fill of the chamber.

Discussion

Three things reveal that this chultun was purposely filled. First, the stone cover of Or. 2 had been worked to a size smaller than the opening and dropped inside, an action that may have occurred in the case of Ch. 2G-11 (this report, see Gp. 2G-1). Second, the chultun was found full of compact earth to within 0.30 m of the bedrock surface. In those chultuns that most clearly were filled by the Maya (e.g., Ch. 2G-10, 2G-11, and 3G-5, this report), they were completely full of fairly compact earth. This situation contrasts with those chultuns that were abandoned unfilled (e.g., Ch. 2G-5, 3F-6, 5C-5, and 7C-3, this report), and were found only partially full of loose earth. In the present case, an inadequate job of filling, combined with scant protection from an overlying structure, would account very well for the settling of the chultun fill. Finally, only one chultun investigated at Tikal (Ch. 2B-15 in Gp. 2B-1, this report) has been found to be located beneath a structure that had clearly not been purposely filled. These data, and those that pertain to the fill for Qu. 2G-1 to the E, clearly indicate that the construction and use of Ch. 2G-2 preceded construction of Str. 2G-61.

The chultun does not seem to have been filled all at once. Chamber 3, with its orifice, in relation to the rest of the chultun (excepting Or. 1), has the appearance of a typical Tikal chultun antechamber. This, and the fact that its fill differs from that in the rest of the chultun, suggests that Chm. 3 was filled through its orifice, and a new means of access to the rest of the chultun was provided (Or. 1). The entrance block between Chm. 2 and 3 prevented the fill from spilling out into the rest of the chultun. Why this should have been done is a mystery. Perhaps it was easier to take whatever was put in the chultun in and out through the new orifice, which was more centrally located. Since Tikal chultuns normally have but one orifice, Or. 2 would have been closed off.

These conclusions permit definition of two architectural developments for the chultun: 2G-2-2nd (Or. 2 with Chm. 2 and 3, and perhaps Chm. 1) and 2G-2-1st (the new Or. 1, along with Chm. 1 and 2). After a period of use of 1st, the rest of the chultun was filled, probably when Str. 2G-61 was built above it.

QUARRIES 2G-1, 2G-2, AND 2G-3

At some time bedrock was quarried extensively in the vicinity of Str. 2G-61 (Fig. 34). Cut faces may be noted near its E and W walls. Quarry 2G-1, to the E, is the deepest, reaching a depth of 1.90 m below the bedrock surface (Fig. 36, 39). It opens into the E end of Ch. 2G-2. For reasons already discussed, Qu. 2G-1 was dug either at the time of construction of Str. 2G-61 or during its occupation, and postdates the use of the chultun (see its discussion). The quarry was then filled with small stones and earth almost to the original level of the bedrock surface, probably while the structure was still in use.

Quarry 2G-2 is located just W of Str. 2G-61, and extends to a point 6.4 m W of Str. 2G-61:U. 5 (Fig. 34, 36). This area was quarried only to a depth of 0.50 m, and was partially filled prior to construction of Str. 2G-61:U. 5; the latter rests on the surface of this fill (U. 1). West of this quarry, bedrock may have been exposed during occupation of Str. 2G-61.

TABLE 2.64
Chultun 2G-2: Average Dimensions (meters)

Feature	Length	Width	Height	Minimum Diameter	Maximum Diameter
Neck 1	-	-	0.80	0.63	0.63
Neck 2	-	-	0.60	0.55	0.55
Chamber 1	2.20	1.10	1.25	-	-
Chamber 2	2.70	2.10	1.30	-	-
Chamber 3	2.16	1.15	1.00	-	-
Entrance 1-2	0.14	1.24	1.12	-	-
Entrance 2-3	0.20	0.62	0.94	-	-

Quarry 2G-3, 0.76 m deep, is located about 4 m N of Str. 2G-61 (Fig. 35). It might have been contemporary with occupation of the structure, or it could have been created earlier. In any case, it, too, was partially filled after the quarrying. Bedrock between this quarry and the structure was largely exposed while the structure was in use.

DISCUSSION

Perhaps Qu. 2G-2 supplied stone for use in Str. 2G-61. It seems to have been of a size sufficient for this purpose, and it probably predates construction of the platform. The other quarries are a problem, for it is obvious that they would have provided more than just the stone needed for Str. 2G-61. The largest building in the vicinity is more than 200 m to the W. This is a small, Late Classic, range-type structure to judge from its masonry. Presumably, stone could have been found nearer at hand for its construction. Moreover, if Qu. 2G-1 postdated use of Str. 2G-61, there would have been no need to end one face of the quarry in line with the E wall of that structure so as not to destroy it, nor to fill the quarry. The most logical hypothesis is that this area was quarried while Str. 2G-61 was in use. Therefore, the quarrying would have been contemporaneous with the Late Preclassic and Early Classic activity in the area. This is consistent with evidence for extensive occupation of the area N, S, and W of Str. 2G-61 at precisely this time.

POSSIBLE 19TH-CENTURY ACTIVITY

Quarry 2G-2:U. 2 is a cluster of burned stones 2 m W of U. 5 that lie on U. 1, the ancient living surface (Fig. 34). The significance of these stones is not known. Burning was apparent in several instances in Op. 24G. Some of the wall stones of Str. 2G-61 were scorched and carbon, as well as fire-spalled chert, was prominent everywhere. One explanation for this activity is that this was a milpa area when Tikal was inhabited sometime between 1850 and 1880 (TR. 37). C. L. Lundell (pers. comm.), who studied the vegetation of Tikal, believed that the forest around Str. 2G-61 was secondary, perhaps 50 to 75 years old. The abundance of carbon is unusual, but incomplete burning of green wood could account for it. Finally, Han Gregerson, while mapping 370 m NE of Str. 2G-61, discovered *ollas*, glass bottles, an axe head, and a machete of the type associated with the 1850–1880 settlement (TR. 37).

SHERDS AND ARTIFACTS

Definition of lot groups for Str. 2G-61 and proximate features is in Table 2.65. For distribution of sherds and artifacts, see Tables 2.66–2.68.

CONSTRUCTION FILL

In no case are floor remnants sufficiently extensive to seal material in structure fill, hence the possibility of con-

tamination is ever present. Fill lots, however, have been divided to isolate those where contamination is minimal from others where contamination is more likely. Cultural material is generally abundant in the fill and is overwhelmingly Preclassic. Construction seems to be dated by ceramics of the Cauac Complex, in spite of a greater frequency of Chuen sherds, for this is consistent with ceramics from LG. 6, which imply an occupation that lasted perhaps just into Early Classic times. The presence of so many Chuen sherds makes sense if the fill was drawn from trash associated with the apparently earlier Str. 2G-62.

MATERIAL ABOVE LIVING LEVELS

This includes refuse from around the walls of Str. 2G-61, and from some distance beyond, above what appear to be the ancient occupation surfaces. The material from surface lots also belongs in this category, but the object lots have been tabulated separately, since they are more prone to contamination from intermittent later activity. Many of the sherds and artifacts are probably occupation debris that accumulated around Str. 2G-61 in the course of time. In view of the poor preservation of the structure, however, there is probably a fair amount of contamination from its fill. This factor varies with provenience, and is the basis for some of the groupings of lots. Material in the vicinity of Str. 2G-62 has been kept separate.

Generally, cultural material is abundant in all these lot groups, but quantities are always greater near to Str. 2G-61 than at a distance (Fig. 40). Thus, almost all the sherds and artifacts likely pertain to use of Str. 2G-61, with none referable to Str. 2G-62.

Material above the floor level of Str. 2G-61 itself presents a problem, for one would not expect much accumulation of refuse on a structure floor. Probably most of the objects in LG. 5a and 5b have been turned up from the structure fill by tree roots and erosion. In fact, the ceramics are comparable to those from the structure fill except for a slightly higher percentage of Ik and/or Imix sherds.

Objects worthy of special note are the few sherds from Ik and/or Imix vessels, three Intermediate or Late Classic figurine fragments, and a subtriangular biface, another possible Intermediate or Late Classic object (TR. 27B:18 and fig. 45d). These were scattered above Str. 2G-61 and to the N, E, and W. They confirm intermittent activity in the area after abandonment of 2G-61. Group 2G-3 (this report), was in use in Late Classic times, and is located a mere 50 m to the E.

Abundant in lots above living level are numerous carbon samples, as well as pieces of fire-spalled chert. As discussed above, this suggests presence of a milpa when Tikal was occupied between AD 1850 and 1880.

SURFACE MATERIAL

Material from the top 0.20 m was kept separate from deeper lots, for the chance of late contamination is greater. The surface material is generally interpreted as occupation debris that has been turned up by roots and erosion, except directly above the structure, where it was probably uprooted from the fill.

CHULTUNS

Material from Ch. 2G-1 was collected as Op. 66C. Generally, material in LG. 2a, 2b, and perhaps 3 should pertain to use of the chultun, as should two objects from LG. 4b found in Chm. 3 and 4. The rest in LG. 4a and 4b probably washed into the chultun after its abandonment; if so, it most likely derives from the extensive trash deposits W of Str. 2G-61 (Str. 2G-61:LG. 6C), with some admixture of structure fill.

Material from Ch. 2G-2 was collected as Op. 24H. It represents purposeful fill, and could be contemporary with the fill of Str. 2G-61 or earlier. If occupation of Str. 2G-62 was contemporary with use of the chultun, as seems likely, then the most probable source for the chultun fill would be trash from that structure (for an analogous situation, see Ch. 5C-8, this report).

OTHER SOURCES

Material from Qu. 2G-1 is purposeful fill, and is later in time than the fill of Str. 2G-61, for reasons already outlined. The fill of Qu. 2G-2 contains early material, quite possibly trash associated with Str. 2G-62, for the filling preceded construction of Str. 2G-61. In this connection, trash from Str. 2G-62 should have been the most likely source of fill for Str. 2G-61 and Ch. 2G-2.

Quarry 2G-3 presents a problem, for it is not surely known if it was deliberately filled, or whether material slowly accumulated over the years. The former is thought most likely. The cultural material is no earlier than that in fill of Str. 2G-61.

TABLE 2.65
Structure 2G-61 Locus: Lot Groups

Feature	Lot Group	Lots	Provenience	Ceramic Evaluation
Str. 2G-61 (Op. 24G)	1a	59-63,66,67, 73-77,81,105, 106	Partially sealed fill of Str. 2G-61	Much Chuen, some Cauac, 4 Ik and/or Imix
	1b	2,3,94	Unsealed fill of Str. 2G-61	Chuen
	2	5	Fill of Qu. 2G-1	Chuen, Cauac, Cimi, a few Manik and Ik and/or Imix
	3	72,89,98, 101	Fill of Qu. 2G-2 (U. 1)	Chuen
	4	35,40,41	Fill, Qu. 2G-3	Chuen and Cauac
	5a	65,78,80	Surface, Str. 2G-61, above floor fragments	Chuen, Cauac
	5b	8,9,13,14, 39,79,82,92, 93	Surface, Str. 2G-61, above projected floor levels	Chuen, Cauac, a few Manik and Ik and/or Imix
	6a	7,22,25,34, 36,44,47,48, 50,54,55,85, 103,104	Outside Str. 2G-61, top to base of walls, minimum possibility of contamination from fill	Much Preclassic, some Manik, Ik, and/or Imix
	6b	4,43,51,57, 58,68,69,70, 71,91	Outside Str. 2G-61, top to base of walls, maximum possibility of contamination from fill	Much Preclassic some Manik, 11 Ik and/or Imix
	6c	46,52,64	W of Str. 2G-61, top to base of wall, minimum possibility of contamination	Much Preclassic, 3 Ik and/or Imix
	6d	37,38,84,87, 95,102	Same vertical limits as 6c in area of Str. 2G-62	Much Preclassic, some Manik, 3 Ik and/or Imix
	6e	96,99,100	Same vertical limits as 6C, W of 6d	Preclassic
	6f	12	Test trench NE of Str. 2G-61	Preclassic
	7a	1	Surface, E of Str. 2G-61	Preclassic and Manik
	7b	10,15,27,28, 42,45,49	Surface, up to 7 m W of Str. 2G-61	Preclassic, 1 Manik, 2 Ik and/or Imix
	7c	16-19,29,53, 56,83,86,90	Surface, W of LG. 6c	Preclassic, 6 Ik and/or Imix
	7d	6,11,20,21, 23,24,26,30-33	Surface, N of Str. 2G-61	Preclassic, 4 Ik and/or Imix
	8	107	Lost provenience	Chuen, Cauac
Ch. 2G-1 (Op. 66C)	1	2,3	Surface to bedrock around Or. 2	Preclassic, some Manik and Ik and/or Imix
	2a	4	Chm. 1 and 2: U. 2	Preclassic
	2b	9	Chm. 5: U. 5	No data
	3	7,8	Chm. 5: U. 3	Chuen, probable Cauac and Cimi
	4a	1	Chm. 1: U. 1	Late Preclassic
	4b	5,6	Chm. 3 and 4: U. 1	No data
Ch. 2G-2 (Op. 24H)	1	All lots	Fill	Preclassic

TABLE 2.66
Structure 2G-61: Artifacts by Lot Group

Study Category	Object	1a	1b	2	3	4	5a	5b	6a	6b	6c	6d	6e	6f	7a	7b	7c	7d	8
Pottery Vessels	Sherds per cubic meter (lbs)	3.16	1.92	4.50	1.75	14.93	3.24	5.43	5.21	6.46	3.76	1.99	1.17	4.40	2.03	2.63	1.51	2.62	-
Other Pottery Artifacts	Figurines					1				1								1	
	Centrally perforated sherds								1	1									
	Unclassifiable formed objects	1		2				5		1		1				1		1	1
Flaked Chert Artifacts	Flake cores	4																	
	Ovate bifaces	1			1	1		11	1	2			1		1	1	1	1	
	Elongate bifaces							2	3	4	1	1					1		
	Rectangular/oval bifaces							1	1	1									
	Subtriangular biface								1										
	Irregular retouched flakes	14	2		5	1		12	11	5		10				3	2	5	
	Point-retouched flake							1			1								
	Rounded retouched flake	1							1										
	Blades	2				1		2	1	1						1	1		
	Used flakes	4			1		1	1	5	2						1	1		
	Unmodified flakes	127	16	24	12	28	26	176	114	119	24	60	1	5	9	25	37	20	6
	Unmodified fire-spalled flakes	76	9	16	5	17		65	52	40		22			7	8	13	3	
Flaked Obsidian Artifacts	Prismatic blades	5			2		2	6	8	3	1	2		1		3	3	3	
Ground, Pecked, and Polished Stone Artifacts	Manos	2		1				1	1							1	1		
	Metates	1						3	1								1		
	Rubbing stones	1		1						1		1				1			1
	Hammer stones	4						4		3		3							
	Celt									1									
	Bark beaters						1												
	Ground pebble							1											1
	Unclassified artifacts							1	1			1	1					1	
Shell and Bone Artifacts	Shell	2								1		1				4	5		
	Bone	34									3						2		

TABLE 2.67
Chultun 2G-1: Artifacts by Lot Groups

Study Category	Object	Lot Groups					
		1	2a	2b	3	4a	4b
Pottery Vessels	Sherds per cubic meter (lbs)	2.63?	.02	?	?	.40	.03
Flaked Chert Artifacts	Used flakes	2			1	2	
	Unused flakes	7				9	
Ground, Pecked, and Polished Stone Artifacts	Unclassifiable artifact					1	
Shell and Bone Artifacts	Bone, animal, unworked			3	2		

TABLE 2.68
Chultun 2G-2: Artifacts by Lot Group

Study Category	Object	Lot Group 1
Pottery Vessels	Sherds per cubic meter (lbs)	.93
Flaked Chert Artifacts	Irregular, retouched flakes	2
	Flakes, unmodified	3
	Flake, unmodified, fire-spalled	1
Flaked Obsidian Artifacts	Prismatic blade	1
Ground, Pecked, and Polished Stone Artifacts	Mano	1
Shell and Bone Artifacts	Bone, animal, unworked	24

TIME SPANS

Time spans for Str. 2G-61 and associated features are presented in Tables 2.69 through 2.75 and correlated in Table 2.76. With respect to the latter, there is little doubt about content of Locus TS. 1–3. These are based on evidence for apparent milpa activity that took place between known dates (1850–1880). The rationale for the other correlations appears in the sections of excavation data for the individual structures, quarries, and chultuns. The general ceramic situation, on which so much of the overall correlations depend, is reviewed here.

Structure 2G-61 was apparently built when Cauac ceramics were in use (Table 2.65). Occupation spanned the time when Cimi ceramics (which are not found in the fill) were in vogue, and probably lasted just into Early Classic times. Since Manik sherds are present only in very small quantities, an extended Early Classic occupation is unlikely. This is an important point in view of the presence nearby of an Early Classic monument (St. 27; TR. 8).

Structure 2G-62 was probably occupied when Chuen pottery was in use based on the large quantity of Chuen sherds in the fill of Str. 2G-61, as well as in the fill of Qu. 2G-2 (Table 2.65). It is doubtful that so many sherds predating construction of Str. 2G-61 would be found in the area, had there not been an earlier occupation nearby. Unfortunately, there are so few sherds from the fill of Ch. 2G-2 that it is not known if the ceramics are comparable to those from the fill of Str. 2G-61, but there is no reason to suppose otherwise.

There is reason to believe that the fill of Qu. 2G-2 was trash associated with occupation of Str. 2G-62, for the sherds are earlier than those in the fill of Str. 2G-61, which includes some Cauac sherds (Table 2.65). The fill of Qu. 2G-1, on the other hand, seems slightly later than Str. 2G-61 fill. It contains Cimi sherds, as well as several from Manik vessels. The quarry was probably dug towards the end of occupation of the structure, an interpretation consistent with the excavation data (the few Ik and/or Imix sherds are probably from late contamination). The most likely source of this material would have been occupation debris from Str. 2G-61.

Quarry 2G-3 was no later than Qu. 2G-1, and might even have been contemporary with construction of Str. 2G-61. Certainly, it could not have been earlier.

Chultun 2G-1 evidently was in use at the same time as Str. 2G-61, but there is no evidence as to when it was dug. Perhaps the stones in Chm. 5 (U. 3, Fig. 38) were put in place when Str. 2G-61 was built, for LG. 3 contains both Chuen and Cauac sherds (Table 2.65). If so, the original chultun may have predated Str. 2G-61. The sherds in U. 1 (LG. 4a and 4b) are from Cimi vessels, expectable if the chultun filled up some time after abandonment. Cimi ceramics were in use when Str. 2G-61 was occupied, and its occupants left a good deal of occupation trash around Or. 2 of the chultun. Some of this could easily have washed in over the years.

The light scatter of Ik and/or Imix sherds in the area (Table 2.65) does not indicate an occupation of Str. 2G-61 at that time. Rather, they suggest intermittent activity in the area, for they are found generally in surface lots or those other lots most susceptible to disturbance by the elements.

To sum up, the earliest activity was the construction of Ch. 2G-2 and Str. 2G-62. The supposition that these were contemporary events rests on the assumption that the chultun was used by the occupants of Str. 2G-62, with which the general ceramic situation is consistent.

There is virtually no doubt that when Str. 2G-61 was built, Ch. 2G-2 was filled. Whether it was filled at the time of construction, or somewhat earlier, is not surely known, but the former seems most likely. Structure 2G-62 was certainly demolished by this time, and on the basis of the assumptions already made, it was probably demolished when Ch. 2G-2 was filled. Given the probable association of Ch. 2G-2 and Str. 2G-62, it is tempting to see Str. 2G-61 and Ch. 2G-1 as replacements for the earlier structure and chultun. In the case of the chultun, however, the ceramic data seem to contradict this, and so it is not certain when it was constructed. The possibility that stone for Str. 2G-61 was quarried in Qu. 2G-2 was raised in discussion of the quarry. If so, then quarrying at this locus would correlate with construction of Str. 2G-61. Quarrying here can be no later than this time, and although it could be earlier, this seems less likely.

In preceding discussion, the suggestion was made that Qu. 2G-1 was cut after construction of Str. 2G-61, and this is confirmed by ceramic analysis. The quarry clearly was filled during the time when the structure was in use.

Use of Str. 2G-61 is the basis for TS. 5 of Str. 2G-62 and Qu. 2G-2. Hence, there is no problem with their correlation. Subsequent to abandonment of Str. 2G-61, sporadic finds of Ik and/or Imix sherds, figurine fragments, and a subtriangular biface indicate post-abandonment activity. The basis for the correlation of TS. 1, 2, and 3 has already been discussed.

Thus far, nothing has been said with respect to Qu. 2G-3 (aside from correlation of the three latest time spans). It is not known exactly when it was quarried, but it could have been contemporary with that of the extensive Qu. 2G-1. If Qu. 2G-3 was purposely filled, a point on which there is certainty, then this supposition is even more reasonable.

In terms of absolute dates, activity at this locus seems to have been underway between 350 BC and AD 1 (dates for the Chuen Ceramic Complex). The appearance of

Cauac ceramics is dated about AD 1 and Str. 2G-61 might have been built not far from this time. The appearance of Manik ceramics is dated about 250 AD, and it was probably shortly thereafter that Str. 2G-61 was finally abandoned. Whether occupation was continuous throughout this time is impossible to say, but there is no specific evidence for any abandonment and reoccupation. On the other hand, it is a bit surprising that only two burials (62 and 64) were found for a total period of occupation estimated on the order of 600 years, more or less (ca. 250 alone for Str. 2G-61). It is quite possible that more excavation would reveal more burials in the vicinity. It should also be noted that such a long period of use implies that Str. 2G-61 underwent renovations from time to time, of which no evidence survives. This lack of evidence is not surprising, however, in view of the simplicity of the structure, as well as its poor state of preservation. If there was any break in occupation, it was probably between the filling of Ch. 2G-2 and construction of Str. 2G-61.

TABLE 2.69
Structure 2G-61: Time Spans

Time Span	Architectural Development	Unit	Special Deposits: Burial	Descriptive Data	Lot Group		Ceramics in Vogue
1				Recent forest growth and deposition			
2				Milpa activity: AD 1850-1880			
3				Total abandonment of area with forest growth			
4			64?	Abandonment, with intermittent later activities			Ik-Imix
							Manik
5			64?	Use	6a,6b 6c,6e	7a,7b 7c,7d	Cimi
6	Str. 2G-61	1-5	62	Construction	3,1a,1b	5a,5b	Cauac

TABLE 2.70
Structure 2G-62: Time Spans

Time Span	Architectural Development	Unit	Descriptive Data	Str. 2G-61: Lot Group	Ceramics in Vogue
1			Recent forest growth and deposition		
2			Milpa activity; AD 1850-1880		
3			Total abandonment of area with forest growth		
4			Intermittent later activity		Ik-Imix
5			Activity associated with use of Str. 2G-61	6d	Manik
6			Destruction		Cimi Cauac
7			Use		Chuen
8	Str. 2G-62	1-4	Construction		

TABLE 2.71
Chultun 2G-1: Time Spans

Time Span	Architectural Development	Construction Stage	Chamber	Unit	Descriptive Data	Lot Group	Ceramics in Vogue
1				1	Accumulation of fill after abandonment	4a, 4b 1	Manik
2				2	Use	2a	Cimi
3	Ch. 2G-1-1st	1-3 (exact order unknown)		3	Or. 2 sealed, Or. 1 constructed; fill placed in Chm. 5	3	Cauac
4				4	Ch. 2G-1-2nd flooded		
5				5	Use	2b	
6	Ch. 2G-1-2nd	1	4 or 5		Construction of one inner chamber		Chuen
		2	4 or 5		Construction of one inner chamber		
		3	3		Construction of 3rd chamber		
		4	2		Construction of 2nd chamber		
		5	1		Construction of Or. 2 and antechamber		

TABLE 2.72
Chultun 2G-2: Time Spans

Time Span	Architectural Development	Construction Stage	Chamber	Special Deposits: Burial	Descriptive Data	Lot Group	Ceramics in Vogue
1			62		Chultun abandoned and filled	1	Cauac
2					Use		– – – – –
3	Ch. 2G-2-1st	1			Or. 2 and Chm. 3 filled		
		2	1?		Construction of Or. 1 and perhaps one new chamber		Chuen
4					Use		
5	Ch. 2G-2-2nd	1	1?, 2		Construction of inner chamber(s)		
		2	3		Construction of Or. 1 and antechamber		

TABLE 2.73
Quarry 2G-1: Time Spans

Time Span	Descriptive Data	Structure 2G-61: Lot Group	Ceramics in Vogue
1	Recent forest growth and deposition deposition		
2	Milpa activity: AD 1850-1880		
3	Total abandonment of area with forest growth		
4	Intermittent later activity		Ik-Imix
5	Activity associated with use of Str. 2G-61		Manik
6	Filling of quarry	2	Cimi
7	Actual quarrying activity		Cauac

TABLE 2.74
Quarry 2G-2: Time Spans

Time Span	Unit	Descriptive Data	Structure 2G-61: Lot Group	Ceramics in Vogue
1		Recent forest growth and deposition		
2	2	Milpa activity: AD 1850-1880		
3		Total abandonment of area with forest growth		
4		Intermittent later activity		Ik-Imix
				Manik
5		Activity associated with use of Str. 2G-61	6c	Cimi
6	1	Filling of quarry	3	
7		Actual quarrying activity		Cauac

TABLE 2.75
Quarry 2G-3: Time Spans

Time Span	Descriptive Data	Structure 2G-61: Lot Group	Ceramics in Vogue
1	Recent forest growth and deposition		
2	Milpa activity: AD 1850-1880		
3	Total abandonment of area with forest growth		
4	Intermittent later activity		Ik-Imix
5	Filling? and activity associated with use of Str. 2G-61	4	Manik
6	Actual quarrying activity		Cimi / Cauac

TABLE 2.76
Correlation of the Time Spans for All Features of Structure 2G-61 Locus

Locus Time Span	Str. 2G-61 (Table 2.69)	Str. 2G-62 (Table 2.70)	Ch. 2G-1 (Table 2.71)	Ch. 2G-2 (Table 2.72)	Qu. 2G-1 (Table 2.73)	Qu. 2G-2 (Table 2.74)	Qu. 2G-3 (Table 2.75)
1	1	1			1	1	1
2	2	2			2	2	2
3	3	3			3	3	3
4	4	4	1		4	4	4
					5		
5					6		5
6					7		6
7	5	5	2			5	
						6	
8	6	6	3	1		7	
9			4	2			
			5				
10			6	3			
11		7		4			
12		8		5			

Group 3F-1

INTRODUCTION

Group 3F-1 is located on the Tikal site map (TR. 11) at 3F S243, E245; included are two structures, 3F-24 and 25, which face each other across a plaza, Plat. 3F-1. The E and W ends of the plaza are open (Fig. 45). Chultun 3F-6 is located 4.90 m from the NW corner of Str. 3F-24. The group is situated on a ridge that extends to the N; to the S, and on either side, the ground slopes downward more or less steeply. Several other groups are located along this ridge, one of which, 55 m to the NE, includes a range-type structure (Gp. 3F-3, this report). Many quarries are noted on the map on the slopes of the ridge. Both structures were investigated by Haviland in 1961 (as Op. 24R) in order to discover the plans of final architectural developments, to test for sequence, and to sample both fill and occupation material. The chultun was excavated at the same time by Puleston as Op. 24S.

STRUCTURE 3F-24-3RD

In its earliest known form, the structure was a one-level platform that may have supported a building of pole-and-thatch (Fig. 41). The front wall of the platform is represented by U. 1, built directly on bedrock. The basal course of U. 2 probably served as the back wall. A floor (U. 3) survives at the level of the top of both U. 1 and the basal course of U. 2. It runs beneath U. 4, a wall for 24-2nd, and so it is interpreted as the remains of a plaster surface for 24-3rd. Its destruction 1.70 m N of U. 1 probably is the result of later placement of Bu. 66.

Fill below U. 3 is a very tough marl. Since the bones of Bu. 65 were found firmly embedded in this marl, this interment can be clearly linked to the construction of 24-3rd. Presumably, this took place in two stages: CS. 2 for the platform and CS. 1 for a building. There is, though, no clear evidence that this was so. Interestingly, the platform itself has a somewhat sloppy look about it; based on very limited exposure of the W wall and what is presumed to be the E wall, the end walls were not closely parallel.

STRUCTURE 3F-24-2ND

The first known major modification of 3F-24 was construction of a second platform level (Fig. 41). Since this involved alteration of the rear and end walls, any building that was a part of 24-3rd had to be at least partly razed. This, then, defines CS. 3.

Construction of the new upper platform level defines CS. 2. Unit 4, the new front wall, was built directly on the old U. 3. The height of U. 2 and the two end walls were presumably augmented to match the height of U. 4. Following placement of Bu. 66 and earth fill for the platform,

a floor (U. 5) was laid over the new platform level. Burial 66 is sealed by this pavement. In front of U. 4, over the lower platform level, the absence of any evidence for floor renovation implies that the exposed portion of U. 3 continued to serve 24-2nd.

Construction Stage 1 is proposed for the rebuilding of a pole-and-thatch building on the new two-level platform. There is, though, no positive evidence for or against the existence of such a building.

STRUCTURE 3F-24-1ST

The final renovation of 3F-24 saw the addition of yet another platform, this on top of the second platform level (Fig. 41). Presumably, three construction stages were involved just as in the construction of 2nd (at least, there is nothing to rule this out). Unit 6 is the front of the new upper platform; it survives today as a line of rubble resting directly on U. 5, which may have continued to serve (with U. 3) in front of the new platform level. No pavement survives on top of the upper platform. Given the poor condition of U. 6, no traces of such a floor would be expected, though one probably once existed.

STRUCTURE 3F-25-2ND

In its original form, Str. 3F-25 was a one-level building platform (Fig. 42, 43, 176b) capped by a plaster floor (U. 1). Its walls were built on an earth fill, overlying unmodified bedrock. Unit 2, pavement N of the structure, appears to have been a plaza floor in union with the base of the front wall of the structure (U. 3 and 4). Unit 5, a wall running N from the structure, abuts its NW corner. This wall was probably contemporary with Str. 3F-25-2nd, but was built after the platform itself had been completed; it forms the W retaining wall of Plat. 3F-1.

Three postholes (U. 8, 9, 10, and Table 2.77) in bedrock just inside the front wall of 25-2nd indicate that a building of perishable materials was a part of this structure. Unit 8 is just inside the NW corner, U. 9 is on the axis, and U. 10 is halfway between the axis and the NE corner. Although no posthole was found in that corner, a pole obviously must have been placed there. Bedrock was low here, and the fill of the platform would have been of sufficient depth to support a pole by itself. The spacing between U. 9 and 10 and the NE corner is a standard 3.34 m. Assuming the presence of a post 3.34 m W of U. 9 (unexcavated), this spacing would be standard for five front poles. Of interest is the fact that U. 9 is positioned on the axis, which means that a doorway would have had to be on one side of the axis, unless the front portion of the platform was a roofed porch. In that case, the actual wall would have enclosed the back portion of 2nd (and later, the upper portion of 25-1st; see below). Construction of the building must have constituted a distinct final stage

TABLE 2.77
Structure 3F-25: Posthole Dimensions
(meters)

Posthole	Diameter	Depth
Unit 8	0.20	0.12
Unit 9	0.13	0.11
Unit 10	0.16	0.06
Unit 11	0.49 (S)	0.16 (S)
	0.20 (N)	0.12 (N)

(CS. 1), although the main supporting posts would have been placed during construction of the platform (CS. 2).

STRUCTURE 3F-25-1ST

This is represented by a wall (U. 6), a floor (U. 7), and the rim of an upper course of masonry for the back wall above the level of U. 1 (Fig. 42, 43). These reveal that an upper level was added to the original building platform, the walls of which survive for the most part as lines of rubble. This new platform level was built on the surface of U. 1, which apparently continued in use in front of the new platform level. There is no evidence for any sort of replacement of that floor. The new platform was surfaced by U. 7.

This modification must have required at least partial demolition of the building for 25-2nd, which would then have been repaired. On this basis, three construction stages may be defined for Str. 3F-25-1st: CS. 3 for the demolition, CS. 2 for construction of the upper platform level, and CS. 1 for repair of the building.

CHULTUN 3F-6

DESCRIPTION

The plan of this chultun (Fig. 44a) is essentially the same as that of Ch. 2G-5 (Fig. 26). An irregular rounded orifice, located about 4.90 m NW of Str. 3F-24, opens into an antechamber, with a larger chamber (No. 2) to one side (Table 2.78). Obviously, the orifice and the antechamber had to be constructed (as CS. 2) before the inner chamber could be dug out (as CS. 1). As discovered, the orifice was partially closed by a stone cover of irregular shape. This had been moved by a large tree root that had entered the neck of the chultun (Fig. 176c). The orifice shows no evidence of a stepped rim. The neck, narrowest at the top, widens out into the ceiling of the antechamber (Fig. 44b). The walls of the chamber are more or less continuous with those of the neck.

Once the antechamber was completed, an entrance was dug (to begin CS. 1) for a large inner chamber. This was restricted above and on both sides, but there is now no sign of a sill. Perhaps one was constructed, but was worn away over the years as the chultun was used. Beyond the entrance, Chm. 2 was constructed in a dome-shape, with the walls continuous with the ceiling. The greatest area is near floor level. The floor itself is 0.45 m below that of the antechamber. In plan, Chm. 2 is best described as ovoid.

DISCUSSION

As found, both chambers were partially filled with a loose, brown earth containing very few sherds (Fig. 44b). On the floor was PD. 65, consisting of five whole pottery vessels (Fig. 176d, 177a). These appear to have been abandoned in situ empty, but later filled as earth washed in. This process was facilitated by the tree root that pushed aside the stone cover. The chultun was not deliberately filled; this was clearly indicated by the looseness of the earth, and by the considerable open space that remained in the chambers.

POSSIBLE EARLY ACTIVITY

Bedrock, wherever exposed, was extensively quarried in this area, an observation of interest in view of the many quarried areas noted on the site map in this vicinity. This quarrying is apparent in the several cut grooves and basins where blocks were apparently once removed. Whether it significantly predated construction at this locus, or was related to that construction, is not known.

Five postholes (U. 7–11) can be seen in bedrock in front of Str. 3F-24 (Fig. 41 and Table 2.79). Units 7, 10, and 11, 0.70, 0.50, and 0.50 m S of U. 1, respectively, form an E-W line. Units 8 and 9, 0.50 m apart, are a mere 0.30 m S of U. 1. The alignment of U. 7, 10, and 11 suggests

TABLE 2.78
Chultun 3F-6: Average Dimensions (meters)

Feature	Length Diameter	Width Diameter	Height	Maximum	Minimum
Stone Cover	0.80	0.50	0.28	-	-
Orifice	-	-	-	0.42	0.44
Neck	0.93	0.42	0.47	-	-
Chm. 1	1.35	1.13	0.52	-	-
Chm. 2	2.28	1.70	1.08	-	-
Entrance	-	0.70	0.51	-	-

that a building wall of perishable materials once stood here. One possibility is that the wall relates to Str. 3F-24-3rd, 2nd, and 1st. More likely, it relates to an earlier 24-4th. Although building walls associated with one-level rectangular platforms, such as 24-3rd is thought to have been, were sometimes built in front of the platform wall (cf. Str. 4F-47-2nd in Gp. 4F-3, this report), this was not likely the case here. The great width of the structure places it securely within the category of those with building walls placed on the building platform, not in front of it (TR. 20B). Consistent with this, burials associated with small structures that were not shrines normally have a terminal relationship to construction (TR. 20B). Yet, Bu. 65 was interred when 24-3rd was built. This suggests that 3rd was preceded by an earlier structure. This hypothesis gains credence from the existence of considerable quantities of sherds earlier than those in use when 24-3rd and 25-2nd were built. This earlier material is mixed in lots with later sherds. A likely source for it is trash, redeposited from the debris of a structure that was eventually razed for new construction.

For these reasons, the one-time existence of a structure earlier than 3F-24-3rd, at the same locus, seems all but certain. Since its postholes are in line with the walls of the later structure, and since Bu. 65 seems to have a terminal relationship to it, a logical continuity of architectural developments is implied. The designation Str. 3F-24-4th, therefore, seems appropriate. Since it consisted either wholly or in part of a building of perishable materials, subsequent architectural developments of Str. 3F-24 likely included similar buildings.

Units 8 and 9 are a problem, but they do appear to have a purposeful position vis-à-vis U. 7, 10, and 11. Perhaps they mark some sort of entry way.

A remaining, enigmatic feature is Str. 3F-25:U. 11. This hole in bedrock is located 3.30 m N of Str. 3F-25 (Fig. 42), immediately W of U. 5. In appearance, it sug-

gests a double posthole. As a guess, it may relate to building activity that preceded 3F-25-2nd.

SHERDS AND ARTIFACTS

Lot Groups defined for Gp. 3F-1 are listed in Table 2.80, with content in Tables 2.81 and 2.82.

CONSTRUCTION FILL

This contains the earliest material from Gp. 3F-1. Most fill lots from Str. 3F-25 are sealed beneath plaster floors, but in the case of 3F-24, this is true only for LG. 1a. Sherds are not especially abundant in the fills of 24, but good samples were obtained from 25.

MATERIAL ABOVE LIVING LEVELS

Evidence suggests that Str. 3F-24:LG. 2a–c, and 3, as well as 3F-25:LG. 3, 4, and 5 are largely made up of occupation debris. Any fill contamination appears to be minimal. Most of the actual material comes from areas W of the buildings. Sherds, however, are not especially abundant anywhere. There is little in the artifact inventory of either structure to suggest any functional difference.

CHULTUN 3F-6

Problematical Deposit 65 was found in this chultun, and is discussed below (section III). Since the chultun fill was washed in by natural processes, any sherds and artifacts (aside from PD. 65) should be contemporary with those that lay around in the group. In fact, no artifacts, and practically no sherds, were found.

OTHER SOURCES

Burial 66 constitutes the only other source of cultural material from Gp. 3F-1. Neither Bu. 65 or 67 contained pottery vessels or other artifacts. All three burials are discussed later in section III of this report.

TABLE 2.79
Structure 3F-24-4th: Posthole
Dimensions (meters)

Posthole	Diameter	Depth
Unit 7	0.20	0.21
Unit 8	0.06	0.07
Unit 9	0.11	0.15
Unit 10	0.15	0.22
Unit 11	0.10	0.11

TABLE 2.80
Group 3F-1: Lot Groups

Feature	Lot Groups	Lot	Provenience	Ceramic Evaluation
Str, 3F-24 (Op. 24R)	1a	13	Sealed fill of 24-3rd	No data
	1b	12,14,17,18	Partially sealed fill of 2nd	Ik-Imix transition
	1c	9	Surface N of structure	Ik and/or Imix
	2a	15,23,24	S of structure, surface to base of wall	Early and late Imix
	2b	25,26	W of structure, surface to base of wall	Late Imix
	2c	11	N of structure, base of wall to bedrock	Early and late Imix
	3	10	Surface over structure, above floor levels	Late Imix
Str. 3F-25 (Op. 24R)	1	4,5,21,22, 29,30	Partially sealed fill of 2nd	Ik-Imix transition
	2	3,8	Partially sealed fill of 1st	Ik-Imix transition or early Imix
	3	7,19,20	W of structure, surface to bedrock	Late Imix
	4	6	S of structure, surface to bedrock	Early and late Imix
	5	1,2,28	Surface of structure, above floor levels	Early and late Imix
Ch. 3F-6 (Op. 24S)	1	1-3	Chultun fill	No data

TABLE 2.81
Structure 3F-24: Artifacts by Lot Group

Study Category	Object	Lot Group						
		1a	1b	1c	2a	2b	2c	3
Pottery Vessels	Sherds per cubic meter (lbs)	1.4	1.0	3.6	2.2	5.0	3.2	1.5
Flaked Chert Artifacts	Flake cores		1	1	1	1		1
	Ovate bifaces					2		
	Thin biface			1				
	Point-retouched flake					1		
	Rounded, retouched flake					1		
	Used flakes				1	8		
	Unmodified flakes	1	3	8	5	12		8
	Unmodified, fire-spalled flakes	1	2	2	3	3		1
Flaked Obsidian Artifacts	Prismatic blades	1	1			3		
Ground, Pecked, and Polished Stone Artifacts	Mano							1
	Rubbing stone				1			
	Whetstone				1			
	Hammer stone					1		
	Jade bead	1						

TABLE 2.82
Structure 3F-25: Artifacts by Lot Group

Study Category	Object	Lot Group				
		1	2	3	4	5
Pottery Vessels	Sherds per cubic meter (lbs)	.7	2.7	6.4	4.0	1.3
Other Pottery Artifacts	Figurines			2		
	Unclassifiable formed object			1		
Flaked Chert Artifacts	Flake cores			3	1	1
	Ovate bifaces			2		3
	Elongate biface					1
	Irregular, retouched flake			1		
	Blades			1		1
	Used flakes	4		6	2	2
	Unmodified flakes	9	3	13	4	4
	Unmodified, fire-spalled flakes	3	1	6		
Flaked Obsidian Artifacts	Prismatic blades		2	13	1	3
	Used flake		1			
Ground, Pecked, and Polished Stone Artifacts	Rubbing stone			1		
	Celt			1		

TIME SPANS

Time spans for the structures and chultun are listed in Tables 2.83, 2.84, and 2.85; those for Gp. 3F-1 as a whole are listed in Table 2.86. Eight have been defined, but because elements of construction were not physically followed from one structure to the other, reliance must be placed on analysis of ceramics for purposes of correlation. These data are summarized here (see also Table 2.80).

Structure 3F-24-2nd is securely dated to a time close to that which dates the appearance of early Imix ceramics. This is indicated by the presence of Imix pottery in Bu. 66, ceramics characteristic of the Ik-Imix transition in the fill, and the likelihood that early Imix vessels were still in vogue when 3F-24-1st was built. Structure 3F-24-3rd is equated with 25-2nd, although this is somewhat arbitrary in the absence of firm data. Nevertheless, this interpretation is reasonable given the dating of 24-2nd and 25-2nd (see below). Early Imix ceramics may still have been in vogue when 24-1st was built, given the presence of late Imix sherds in the least mixed deposit of occupation material (LG. 2b), and the presence of early and late Imix sherds in deposits of occupation refuse most likely to have been contaminated by disintegration of 24-1st (LG. 2a and 3).

Structure 3F-25-2nd dates from the time of the Ik-Imix transition, for although vessel form frequencies in its fill are characteristic of the Ik Complex, a few vessels diagnostic of the later transition are represented. These do not seem to be the result of contamination, but rather, of mixture of ceramics from different sources used for fill. Structure 3F-25-1st probably dates from when early Imix pottery was in use, and might be contemporary with either 24-1st or 2nd.

Several sherds from Preclassic vessels were found in fills of both structures. Their presence suggests the possibility of an early occupation at this locus. They might just as well be explained as material brought in from elsewhere, as debris to be used for construction fill, perhaps from Gp. 3F-3 (this report). More important, abundant Ik sherds in the fill of Str. 3F-25 suggest occupation of the group between AD 550 and 700. So plentiful are these broken pieces that the most likely source would have been trash in the immediate vicinity at the time of construction. A possible source is the postulated Str. 3F-24-4th.

Occupation of Gp. 3F-1 clearly continued after the appearance of late Imix ceramics. Sherds from such vessels are present in some quantity in Str. 3F-25:LG. 3 and Str. 3F-24:LG. 2b. They are also present in the otherwise more mixed lot groups from above living levels.

The place of Ch. 3F-6 in this scheme is a problem. Problematical Deposit 65 indicates that it was in use in Postclassic times. There is no evidence for a contemporaneous occupation of the two structures. Yet, the proximity of the chultun and structures suggests that they were associated. Since its form is typical of many Tikal chultuns of Classic times (TR. 32), it seems likely that it was in use with Str. 3F-24 and 25. Problematical Deposit 65, therefore, would represent a reuse of the chultun after it and the structures had been abandoned for a hundred years or so. It is not known exactly when the chultun was constructed, but this was probably no earlier than the construction of Str. 3F-24-4th, for it is difficult to imagine the placement of a chultun where no structures existed. It is assumed here that the chultun and this structure were contemporary, although this cannot be proven. On the other hand, the chultun could have been constructed anytime thereafter, but before the group was abandoned. Thus, the chultun time spans "float" in terms of those for the group, except for TS. 1, 2, and 3. Group TS. 2 is defined on the basis of reuse of the chultun, and the chultun was certainly in use during Gp. TS. 4.

To sum up, all the activity at this locus (discounting possible Preclassic activity) seems to fall between AD 550 and AD 869, with a brief episode after AD 950.

TABLE 2.83
Structure 3F-24: Time Spans

Time Span	Architectural Development	Construction Stage	Unit	Special Deposits: Burial	Descriptive Data	Lot Group	Ceramics in Vogue
1					Abandonment and collapse		(late)
2					Use	2a,b 2c,3	
3	Str.3F-24-1st	1			Construction of building of perishable materials		Imix
		2	6		Construction of upper platform level		
		3			Partial demolition of existing building		
4					Use	1c	
5	Str.3F-24-2nd	1			Construction of building of perishable materials		
		2	4,5		Construction of 2nd platform level	1b	
		3		66	Partial demolition of existing building		(early)
6					Use		
7	Str.3F-24-3rd	1			Construction of building of perishable materials		Ik-Imix
		2	1-3		Construction of platform	1a	
		3		65	Demolition of 4th		
8					Use		Ik
9	Str.3F-24-4th	7-11			Earliest construction		

TABLE 2.84
Structure 3F-25: Time Spans

Time Span	Architectural Development	Construction Stage	Unit	Special Deposits: Burial	Descriptive Data	Lot Group	Ceramics in Vogue
1				67?	Abandonment and collapse		----------
2					Use	3-5	(late)
3	Str.3F-25-1st	1			Construction of building of perishable materials		
		2	6-7		Construction of upper platform level	2	Imix
		3		67?	Demolition of existing building		(early)
4					Use		----------
5	Str. 3F-25-2nd	1	1-5, 8-10, 11?		Construction of building of perishable materials		Ik-Imix
		2			Construction of platform	1	

TABLE 2.85
Chultun 3F-6: Time Spans

Time Span	Architectural Development	Construction Stage	Special Deposits: Problematical Deposit	Descriptive Data	Lot Group	Ceramics in Vogue
1				Abandonment and accumulation of fill	1	----------
2			65	Reuse		Caban
3				Abandonment		----------
4				Use		Ik? through Imix
5	Ch. 3F-6	1		Construction of Chm. 2		----------
		2		Construction of Chm. 1		Ik?

TABLE 2.86
Group 3F-1: Time Spans

Group Time Span	Structure 3F-24 (Table 2.83)	Structure 3F-25 (Table 2.84)	Chultun 3F-6 (Table 2.85)
1			1
2			2
3	1	1	3
4	2	3	
5	6-3	4-3	
6	7	5	
7	8		4?
8	9		5?

Group 3F-2

INTRODUCTION

Located on the Tikal site map (TR. 11) at 3F S320 E335, this group is 48 m S of Gp. 3F-1. Four structures were mapped in 1960: 3F-26, 27, 28, and 29, arranged around the four sides of Plat. 3F-2. Excavation reveals that "Str. 3F-28" is not a structure at all, but the S edge of the plaza (see Fig. 52). The group is the southernmost on the ridge on which previously discussed Gp. 3F-1 also was built. Here, the ridge, after sloping gradually, drops sharply to the S, E, and W.

Group 3F-2 was investigated by Haviland in May 1961. Two of the three structures were tested for final plan and sequence, while 3F-27 was tested for sequence alone. The ephemeral "Str. 3F-28" was also investigated. Finally, magnetic and resistivity surveys were conducted by R. E. Linnington, but as was the case with such surveys near Gp. 2G-1, these were inconclusive.

STRUCTURE 3F-26-3RD

Located on the N edge of the group plaza, very little is known about this structure (Fig. 46, 47). The only element that can surely be attributed to it is U. 1, a plaster floor, and probably Plat. 3F-2:U. 4, an early plaza pavement. The S edge of U. 1 is positioned directly over a vertically quarried bedrock face, which evidently served as a front step. The plaza floor ends at a second bedrock cut, with its surface continued by the horizontal surface of bedrock up to the step of the structure. The original extent of U. 1 is unknown, as later activity resulted in its partial demolition. In spite of this, fill beneath the projected level of the floor is relatively uncontaminated by more recent cultural material. This could mean that the fill was undisturbed and that it sealed Bu. 69, which was placed on bedrock. More likely though, the burial was intruded, and the old fill that had been dug out in the process was thrown back in on top. This interpretation better accounts for the destruction of U. 1, for such destruction would not have been required for any new construction feature overlying 26-3rd. The reuse of the old fill would be logical; when the grave was dug, earth would have been piled up nearby, and easily pushed back in subsequent to the interment.

The N limit of the fill beneath U. 1 suggests that the position of the N wall of 26-3rd was the same as for succeeding architectural developments. The lateral extent of 3rd is unknown. Given such scanty information, no construction stages have been defined.

STRUCTURE 3F-26-2ND

Following abandonment of the earlier structure and interment of two burials (Bu. 68 and 69), a higher platform was built (Fig. 46, 47). Unit 2, the front of this new platform, was placed directly above the bedrock face of the original structure, on the surface of U. 1. Unit 3, 1.20 m S of U. 2, is the front of either a lower platform level, or a step to provide access to the platform. This second alternative seems more probable since no traces of this wall are present near the SW corner. Thus, the structure would have been somewhat like Str. 2G-15-1st (see Gp. 2G-2). Unit 4 is a fragment of pavement that apparently ran from the top of U. 3 to the base of U. 2. Platform 3F-2:U. 12, the latest surviving plaza floor at this locus, turns up to the base of U. 3.

The rear of 26-2nd probably consisted of U. 6 and 7, a fill wall and outer veneer wall respectively. Unit 7 is based on bedrock, in line with a vertically quarried bedrock face. Units 6 and 7 both rise higher than the projected level of the U. 5 pavement. This, and the projection of U. 8 (a pause-line) above the end of U. 5, suggests that the floor ended at the wall of a small platform, or an upper platform level, that was later demolished.

Excavation off the W end exposed a wall, U. 9, at the correct elevation to be interpreted as the end wall linked with U. 2 and 7. This was built on bedrock and also over the coverstones of Bu. 68, revealing that its construction postdates the burial. Unit 10, a remnant of floor at the elevation of the top of U. 9, undoubtedly is part of the same pavement as U. 5.

Given the above information, it is possible to suggest the following sequence of construction stages: CS. 4 for extensive demolition of 26-3rd; CS. 3 for construction of the new platform base; CS. 2 for construction of an upper platform level (of unknown size); and CS. 1 for construction of a building of perishable materials (the main posts of which would have been set as part of CS. 3). The definition of this final stage is based solely on lack of negative evidence and knowledge that such buildings did stand on similar platforms elsewhere at Tikal (TR. 20B).

STRUCTURE 3F-26-1ST

The final development of this structure saw its partial demolition (including the upper platform) as CS. 4. A new upper platform level was then constructed (CS. 3), the front wall of which survives as U. 11 (Fig. 46, 47). This was built directly on the earlier floor which, given lack of evidence to the contrary, probably continued in use in front of U. 11. Unit 12, a line of rubble, indicates the location of the W end wall (Fig. 46). Evidently, this new platform level ran the length of the structure.

Preservation of 1st is not good, and this probably explains the lack of any trace of a paved surface on the U. 11–12 platform. Unit 13 (Fig. 46, 47), another line of rubble, suggests that another small platform, or perhaps a freestanding wall similar to that of Str. 4F-21 (in Gp. 4F-3, this report) was built on the U. 11–12 platform. For this, CS. 2 is proposed. Again it is presumed (in the absence of evidence to the contrary) that a final CS. 1 consisted of the reconstruction of a pole-and-thatch building.

Structure 3F-26:U. 4 and Plat. 3F-2:U. 12 continued in use with Str. 3F-26-1st.

STRUCTURE 3F-27

On the Encanto Quadrangle map of TR. 11, this structure on the E edge of Plat. 3F-2 is depicted as square, in the manner of household shrines (TR. 21). After being cleared of vegetation, however, it is apparent that in plan it was rectangular, rather than square; hence Gp. 3F-2 is not an example of "Plaza Plan 2." In a trench through its E-W axis, a one-level platform is represented by two badly preserved walls, U. 1 and 2, and a floor fragment, U. 3 (Fig. 48). The elevation of the floor is slightly higher than the surviving walls, but undoubtedly it ended on their tops. To the E, three floor remnants, U. 4, 5, and 6, represent a single pavement laid behind 27 at the same elevation as the plaza floor in front. One of these remnants (U. 4) appears to have been in union with U. 2. Probably, the slope immediately behind the structure was terraced, and these surviving bits of plaster are all that remain of the terrace pavement. It is not known if a new plaza floor was laid in front of the platform; Plat. 3F-2:U. 6 may have continued to serve, with some minor patches.

Construction of Str. 3F-27 likely took place in two or three stages. First, fill was dumped E of the original plaza wall (CS. 3). Once the surface of this area was level with the plaza, the platform itself was built (CS. 2). Finally, a building of perishable materials was probably erected on the platform (CS. 1). There is no direct evidence for this, but no effort was made to look for postholes in the corners of the structure. Since there is sufficient fill so that main posts would not have had to penetrate bedrock, such effort would probably have been profitless. Since some other similar platforms at Tikal supported buildings of this nature (TR. 20B), it is likely that this one did also. For reasons given in TR. 20B, it is thought that the front building wall was located W of the front platform wall. Burial 70, located beneath a portion of the plaza in front of the structure platform, may have been under a floor enclosed by the building walls. Root destruction obliterated evidence as to whether this interment was intrusive (see its discussion). Because it is on the axis of the structure, however, it was definitely oriented to it, and probably was so placed either during construction, when the building was occupied, or even upon its abandonment.

STRUCTURE 3F-29-2ND

Positioned on the W side of the plaza, this was a rectangular platform of one level that probably supported a pole-and-thatch building, as the succeeding Str. 3F-29-1st surely did (Fig. 49). This platform is represented by two walls, U. 1 and 2. Unit 2 (the western wall) is based on bedrock in line with a vertically quarried face, except in the N end of the trench where it rests on fill. Unit 1 rests on a thin layer of fill. Possibly this wall was plastered to bedrock 0.10 m. below. The bedrock surface is near plaza level. Unit 3, a floor remnant, probably is all that is left of platform pavement. Unit 4, a plaster surface near the SW corner (U. 5), could be a piece of the same floor. The back portion of this corner rests on bedrock; the end portion rests on a layer of marl. Platform 3F-2:U. 8, a low wall that abuts the end of the structure, continues the line of the back wall and represents a plaza retaining wall.

Construction of 29-2nd must have taken place in two or three stages, with the last (CS. 1) for erection on the platform of a pole-and-thatch building. Evidence for such a building is indirect, and rests in part on the probable presence of one for 1st (discussed below). One of the postholes (Fig. 49a:U. 9) for 1st penetrated bedrock just inside U. 2, the W platform wall that served both 1st and 2nd. To dig the hole when 1st was built inevitably would have disturbed U. 2 and the fill inside it, but no trace of such disturbance was seen. Therefore, it must be coeval with construction of 2nd. No counterpart of U. 9 was seen inside U. 2, where a hole would seem to be required by the height of the bedrock and thinness of fill above it. Such a hole (Fig. 49a:U. 10) does exist for 1st, just inside its front wall. This raises the distinct possibility that U. 10, like U. 9, was reused from 2nd, and that the roofed space of 2nd incorporated the plaza surface immediately in front of its platform.

STRUCTURE 3F-29-1ST

Modification of the original structure saw a widening of its platform, its front being placed 1.32 m to the E (Fig. 49). Unit 7 is a portion of this new wall. It is based on U. 8, a white marl stratum that must have been fill of Plat. 3F-2. That the new architecture was a true building platform is indicated by two postholes, U. 9 and 10 (Table 2.87), located N of the front-rear axis just inside U. 2 and 7. As noted above, at least one of these, and likely both, continued in use from 2nd.

To sum up construction of 1st, it would have begun with partial demolition of the earlier building (CS. 3). Then, the platform could have been enlarged (CS. 2), following which the new building would have been erected (CS. 1).

TABLE 2.87
Structure 3F-29: Posthole
Dimensions (meters)

Posthole	Diameter	Depth
Unit 6	0.17	0.06
Unit 9	0.20	0.24
Unit 10	0.27	0.20

STRUCTURE 3F-SUB.1

At the locus of Str. 3F-26, six postholes were found in bedrock, U. 14 through 19 (Fig. 46 and Table 2.88). Three of these, U. 14, 16, and 17 form a line, but one outside the walls of all known developments of Str. 3F-26. Units 16 and 14 are spaced 1.97 m apart. Units 14, 16, and 17 may belong to a single structure, since not only are they in line, but they are similar enough in size to suggest the common pattern in small structures at Tikal: the spacing of the major poles of a building at regular intervals (TR. 19:118 and TR. 20B). If two other postholes exist between U. 16 and 17 (an area not excavated), the five holes would all conform to the same 1.97 m spacing.

There are two possible interpretations of these postholes: one is that they relate to a building of perishable materials erected on the known architectural developments of Str. 3F-26, as once suggested by Puleston (1974); the other is that they relate to a building of perishable materials that predates 26-3rd. The first is improbable, and the second most likely, on several accounts. First, the alignment of U. 14, 16, and 17 is not the same as the masonry walls of Str. 3F-26 in any of its known forms. Second, although some one-level platforms (such as 26-2nd may have been) had building walls located in front of their platform walls (cf. Str. 3F-29-2nd and 4F-47-2nd), 26-3rd seems to have been too wide for this to have been probable. Third, the presence of several Manik sherds in plaza fill, as well as in the other structure fills, suggests the one-time presence at this locus of a structure that later furnished fill for the later Classic ones.

It is, therefore, all but certain that Str. 3F-26-3rd was preceded by an even earlier structure at this locus, built perhaps towards the end of Early Classic times. Because its alignment differs from that of 26, it is designated as Str. 3F-Sub.1. Unit 18 probably relates to the same structure, as a small pole next to a large one is a pattern that has been noted elsewhere at Tikal (e.g., Str. 4F-3; TR. 19:7 and fig. 5). Unit 19, however, does not seem to belong to the same building.

That the earliest structure at the locus of 3F-26 consisted in part of a building of perishable materials suggests that the later architectural developments of 26 did as well. Definite proof is lacking, however.

PLATFORM 3F-2-2ND

On the site map (TR. 11), a low mound is shown on the S side of Gp. 3F-2, labeled "Str. 3F-28." Test excavations, however, revealed that this was not a structure at all, but rather the S edge of the Plaza (Fig. 50, 51). The earliest architectural development at this locus is represented by U. 1, 2, and 3. Unit 1 is an amorphous mass of pebbles 22

TABLE 2.88
Structure 3F-Sub.1: Posthole
Dimensions (meters)

Posthole	Diameter	Depth
3F-26: U. 14	0.24	0.15
3F-26: U. 15	0.23	0.16
3F-26: U. 16	0.17	0.12
3F-26: U. 17	0.22	0.30
3F-26: U. 18	0.14	0.16
3F-26: U. 19	0.07	0.16

m S of Datum 24T-W. These form a level 0.20 m beneath the surface, at datum 216.60 m, the elevation of the plaza floor by Str. 3F-27 (Fig. 48). Only 0.18 m above bedrock, it is probable that plaza pavement in this area was about at this elevation. Units 2 and 3 are two masses of small rubble S of U. 1 that are arranged in definite E-W lines. If one assumes that the floor of Plat. 3F-2 was at the 216.60 m elevation (from its location at Str. 3F-27 and U. 1), then it is apparent that the tops of U. 2 and 3 would have been covered. On the other hand, if these features were the remains of a structure, the plaza floor would have to have been extremely low in relation to its level elsewhere. Therefore, it seems most reasonable to identify U. 2 and 3 as either fill-retaining walls or badly ruined finish walls for the plaza. Since only two plaza floors are known, because the sherd material in fill behind U. 2 and 3 seems essentially the same, and because the features themselves are so irregular, U. 2 and 3 are identified as fill-retaining walls. A finished retaining wall, later destroyed, must have been placed just S of U. 3, as ceramic analysis shows that fill between U. 3 and 10 was clearly a later addition.

The only surely surviving portion of the original plaza pavement is U. 4, in front of Str. 3F-26-3rd (Fig. 46, 47). This ends on the N at a bedrock cut, with its surface continued up to the structure by the level top of bedrock. To the E, U. 5, the fragment of a floor buried beneath fill of Str. 3F-27 (Fig. 48), probably is part of the floor for Plat. 3F-2-2nd. This is at the same elevation as the top of a retaining wall (U. 7) that runs N and S. West of Str. 3F-27 is U. 6, another floor remnant at the same elevation as U. 5, and possibly a part of the same pavement.

Farther W, bedrock E of Str. 3F-29-2nd is at about the same elevation as the plaza pavement (Fig. 49). Its level surface probably served as part of this floor, as was also the case S of Str. 3F-26-3rd. Unit 8, a low wall that abuts the end of 29-2nd and continues the N-S line of its back wall, represents the plaza retaining wall. Unit 9, a wall that abuts U. 8 and runs W, remains unexplained. Unit 13, a floor remnant, probably served Plat. 3F-2-1st and 2nd.

PLATFORM 3F-2-1ST

This is represented at the S end of the plaza by U. 10 (Fig. 50, 51), a feature even more amorphous than U. 2 and 3. Unit 10 is a line of rubble that apparently is all that survives of a broken-up plaza wall that ran E-W. The sherds from its fill are clearly later than those in fill of U. 2 and 3.

Excavation of a 2-m square, 30 m S and 13 m E of Datum 24T-W (Fig. 50), revealed a line of masonry oriented to a line a few degrees from magnetic N-S (U. 11). This is probably an end wall of the plaza. Otherwise, the continuation of the S end wall of the plaza (U. 10) to a point in line with Str. 3F-27 would have required a major amount of fill and an end wall quite high, since bedrock dips steeply in this area. That the top of U. 11 as found is lower than U. 10 to the E is easily explained by the fact that at this corner, the walls would have been higher than elsewhere, and thus more prone to collapse. Therefore, it would seem that the plaza was not a true rectangle, but had an inset in its SE corner.

The only surviving portions of plaza floor for 1st are U. 12 and 13. Unit 12 (Fig. 46, 47) overlies U. 4 and turns up to Str. 3F-26:U. 3, a part of 26-2nd. The fill of this structure contains late Imix sherds, as does fill for U. 10. Although no physical link between U. 10 and 12 can be demonstrated, it is likely that they were contemporary. Unit 13 (Fig. 49a) is a floor remnant S of Str. 3F-29, presumed to have served Plat. 3F-2-1st as well as 2nd.

It is not known if U. 12 was a local grading floor, or whether a whole new pavement was laid across the plaza. No surviving floor was found near Str. 3F-29, and no renovation of the plaza associated with Str. 3F-27 was noted.

QUARRYING ACTIVITY

As was true in Gp. 3F-1, there had been much quarrying of bedrock. South of U. 4, this left several grooves about 8 cm in depth. The blocks removed may have been used in early Gp. 3F-2 construction. As already noted, vertically shaped faces of bedrock were incorporated into Str. 3F-26-3rd. In the case of Str. 3F-29, the building platform was constructed on a high, table-like area of bedrock that has quarried faces on its E and W sides (Fig. 49). Perhaps the stone removed was used in the construction of 29-2nd. Near the S end of the structure, bedrock seems to have been completely quarried away (U. 11); perhaps there was once a chultun here that was later filled in with earth and then covered with a layer of marl, 6 cm thick. Time did not permit excavation of this feature. Unit 6, an apparent posthole just S of the structure (Table 2.87), may relate to a building earlier than 29-2nd, contemporary with 3F-Sub.1.

RESISTIVITY AND MAGNETIC SURVEY

In addition to excavation, Linnington carried out magnetic (Proton magnetometer) and resistivity (Goehm) surveys. To investigate features revealed by these surveys, a test trench was dug by the SW corner of Str. 3F-29. These, though, failed to turn up anything significant. Linnington sums up his work in Gp. 3F-2:

> The resistivity survey showed a fair degree of variation in the values of measured resistance over the mounds and court of this group. However, little or no correlation was possible between this observed variation and the results of the excavations. The observed resistance variation would seem to be mainly caused by moisture variations in the top soil, which was often very scanty, the largest variations corresponding fairly accurately to areas of extensive tree development.
>
> The magnetic survey showed little variation, none of which was of sufficient size to be considered significant. No correlation with excavated features occurred.

SHERDS AND ARTIFACTS

Definitions of lot groups for Gp. 3F-2 are given in Table 2.89, with content in Tables 2.90–2.93.

CONSTRUCTION FILL

In this category is the earliest material from this group. In the case of Str. 3F-26, stratigraphy permits division of fill into three basic groups (LG. 1, 2a–c, and 3). Ceramic analysis supports the validity of this separation in so far as material in LG. 1 is earlier than that in 2a. The surface material also seems to be uprooted fill (LG. 5).

Fill from the other construction has also been subdivided, but in no case are floor seals complete.

MATERIAL ABOVE LIVING LEVELS

All of these lot groups, presumed to contain whatever undisturbed occupation debris remained to be found, are probably contaminated by fill material, this being greatest in the case of Str. 3F-27:LG. 2. The best deposit of potential occupation trash is located around the SW corner of Str. 3F-29 (LG. 3b). A second prime source is S of Plat. 3F-2 (LG. 3a,b). The high frequency of decorated sherds from the last two lot groups suggests an affinity with material around Str. 3F-26. Here, also, the frequency of decorated sherds is high. Perhaps much of the deposit S of the plaza derives from the same source as that around Str. 3F-26.

OTHER SOURCES

Burials 68 and 70 constitute the only other sources of artifacts from Gp. 3F-2 (Bu. 69 was devoid of material other than the skeleton).

TABLE 2.89
Group 3F-2: Lot Groups

Feature	Lot Group	Lots	Provenience	Ceramic Evaluation
Str. 3F-26 (Op. 24T)	1	15,16,19,20	Partially sealed fill of 3rd	Early Imix
	2a	7-9,12,13	Partially sealed fill of 2nd	Late Imix
	2b	14,17	Unsealed fill of 2nd: rear wall (U. 6 and 7)	Ik and/or Imix
	2c	24	Fill, Bu. 68	Ik and/or Imix
	3	10,11	Fill, 26-1st	Ik and/or Imix
	4a	3,4,18	N of structure	Late Imix
	4b	22,23,25,26-28	W of structure	Late Imix
	5	1,2,21	Surface of structure, above floor levels	Imix
Str. 3F-27 (Op. 24W)	1	2,4,6	Fill	Imix
	2	1,3	Surface of structure, above floor levels	Imix
Str. 3F-29 (Op. 24U)	1	5	Partially sealed fill of 2nd	Ik and/or Imix
	2	3,4	Partially sealed fill of 1st	?
	3a	6,7	W of structure	Late Imix
	3b	11-13	S of structure, surface to base of wall	Late Imix
	4	1,10	Surface of structure, above living level	Imix
Plat. 3F-2	1a	24V/9,10	Unsealed fill of 2nd, N of U. 2	Ik-Imix transition or Imix
	1b	24V/4,7	Fill of 2nd, between U. 2 and 3, unsealed	Early Imix
	1c	24T/6	Fill of 2nd, sealed by U. 4	No data
	1d	24W/5,7	Fill of 2nd, partially sealed by U. 5 and 6	Ik-Imix transition or early Imix
	1e	24U/2,8,9	Unsealed fill of 2nd, E of Str. 3F-29	Ik and/or Imix
	2a	24V/3,6,8	Unsealed fill of 1st, between U. 3 and 10	Late Imix
	2b	24T/5	Fill of 1st, sealed by U. 12	No data
	3a	24V/2,5,11,12	S of Plat. 3F-2	Late Imix
	3b	24V/13,14	In SE inset in Plat. 3F-2	Late Imix
	4	24V/1	Surface, S end of plaza, above living level	Ik-Imix transition or Imix

TABLE 2.90
Structure 3F-26: Artifacts by Lot Group

Study Category	Object	Lot Group							
		1	2a	2b	2c	3	4a	4b	5
Pottery Vessels	Sherds per cubic meter (lbs)	8.8	4.5	3.3	--	1.5	.4	6.9	2.0
Other Pottery Artifacts	Figurine	1							
	Centrally perforated sherd	1							
	Candelero			1					
	Miniature vessel	1*							
	Pellet	1							
Flaked Chert Artifacts	Flake core	1							
	Ovate bifaces	1	1						
	Elongate bifaces		1						
	Rectangular/oval biface							2	1
	Thin biface	1							
	Point-retouched flake							1	
	Blade	1							
	Used flakes	13	1	1		2	1	18	1
	Unmodified flakes	23	1	1		1		15	2
	Unmodified, fire-spalled flakes	3	2					4	2
	Unmodified nodules	5						2	
Flaked Obsidian Artifacts	Thin biface (green)				1				
	Prismatic blades								2
	Umodified flake								1
Ground, Pecked, and Polished Stone Artifacts	Metates							1	1
	Whetstones							2	
	Hammer stones	3							
	Spindle whorl	1							
Shell and Bone Artifacts	Shell								1
	Bone, worked	1							

*Illustrated as fig. 97c in TR. 25A, but incorrectly attributed to Bu. 69.

TABLE 2.91
Structure 3F-27: Artifacts by Lot Group

Study Category	Object	Lot Groups	
		1	2
Pottery Vessels	Sherds per cubic meter (lbs)	1.0	1.2
Flaked Chert Artifacts	Flake cores	2	
	Used flakes	5	7
	Unmodified flakes	5	6
	Unmodified, fire-spalled flake	1	
	Unmodified nodules	2	2
Flaked Obsidian Artifacts	Thin biface	1	
Ground, Pecked, and Polished Stone Artifacts	Metates	1	3
	Hammer stones	1	7

TABLE 2.92
Structure 3F-29: Artifacts by Lot Group

Study Category	Object	Lot Group				
		1	2	3a	3b	4
Pottery Vessels	Sherds per cubic meter (lbs)	.3	3.3	1.1	11.3	2.3
Pottery Artifacts	Figurine					1
Flaked Chert Artifacts	Flake cores			1	1	1
	Ovate bifaces	1	1	1		3
	Irregular, retouched flakes	1	1			
	Point-retouched flake				1	
	Rounded, retouched flake				1	
	Blade					1
	Used flakes	3	1	1	21	2
	Unmodified flakes	2	1	3	14	6
	Unmodified, fire-spalled flakes	2		1	2	4
	Unmodified nodules	2				1
Flaked Obsidian Artifacts	Thin biface				1	
	Prismatic blades				3	
Ground, Pecked, and Polished Stone Artifacts	Mano			1		
	Hammer stone					1

TABLE 2.93
Platform 3F-2: Artifacts by Lot Group

Study Category	Object	Lot Group									
		1a	1b	1c	1d	1e	2a	2b	3a	3b	4
Pottery Vessels	Sherds per cubic meter (lbs)	1.5	3.3	1.7	2.6	.3	12.7	--	2.7	4.3	2.3
Other Pottery Artifacts	Figurines								2	1	
Flaked Chert Artifacts	Flake cores					2					
	Ovate bifaces					1	1		1		
	Elongate bifaces					1	1		1		
	Irregular, retouched flake	2			1						
	Point-retouched flakes						2				
	Blades	1			1				1	1	
	Used flakes	1	1		1	3	19		8	2	8
	Unmodified flakes	1	1		3	1	9	1	7	2	9
	Unmodified flakes, fire-spalled							1			
	Unmodified nodules				3		2				
Flaked Obsidian Artifacts	Prismatic blades					2	2				
Ground, Pecked, and Polished Stone Artifacts	Mano				1						
	Metate				1						
	Hammer stone									1	
	Unclassifiable	1									

TIME SPANS

Time spans for Gp. 3F-2 are defined in Table 2.99, with those for each feature listed in Tables 2.94 through 2.98. Although architectural elements were not followed from one structure to another, certain time span equivalents are suggested by the interpretation given data from Plat. 3F-2. On this basis, with ceramics as a cross check, nine time spans have been defined that provide a reasonably clear picture of the development of the group.

The evidence clearly indicates that Str. 3F-26-3rd was built no earlier than the time when early Imix pottery was in use (see Table 2.89). Platform 3F-2-2nd seems to be contemporary. Construction of Str. 3F-26-2nd and 1st date from the time of late Imix production, as does Plat. 3F-2-1st (Table 2.89). The floor of the latter is associated with Str. 3F-26-2nd.

Evidence from Str. 3F-27 is not as clear as desired, and ceramics indicate only a general contemporaneity with other construction in Gp. 3F-2 (Table 2.89). Since it is positioned above earlier plaza construction, it is most logical to consider 27 as no earlier than Str. 3F-26-2nd and Plat. 3F-2-1st, a time of late Imix pottery production.

Structure 3F-29 also presents problems. Since a sequence of two structures must be accounted for, the inclination is to date the earliest to the time of early Imix pottery use; the latest to the time of late Imix ceramics. This cannot be proven nor disproven at the moment, but at least the general contemporaneity of 3F-29 with the other structures of Gp. 3F-2 is clear (Table 2.89).

A fairly large number of Manik sherds (not noted in Table 2.89) occur in various lots from fill of Plat. 3F-2, and in the fills of the structures. It is not known if these derive from an Early Classic occupation of this locus. Perhaps they were associated with the occupation of the postulated 3F-Sub.1, a structure succeeded by 26-3rd near the time when Imix ceramics came into production. Without more extensive excavation, one can do no more than pose this problem.

Occupation debris from Gp. 3F-2 generally provides samples of late Imix ceramics (Table 2.89), and the group probably was abandoned after late Imix pottery had been in use for some time. In terms of provisional date approximations, then, activity in this group would be bracketed between a date prior to AD 550, and AD 869. All of the definable architectural developments, probably excepting Str. 3F-Sub.1, seem to date no earlier than AD 700.

TABLE 2.94
Structure 3F-26: Time Spans

Time Span	Architectural Development	Construction	Unit	Special Deposits: Burial	Descriptive Data	Lot Group	Ceramics in Vogue
1					Abandonment and collapse	4a,b	---------
2					Use		
3	Str. 3F-26-1st	1			Construction of building of perishable materials		
		2	11-13		Modification of platform	3	
		3			Demolition of existing building		
4					Use	5	
5	Str. 3F-26-2nd	1			Construction of building of perishable materials		(late)
		2	2-10		Construction of new platform	2a,b	
		3		68,69	Demolition of existing structure	2c	
6					Use		Imix
7	Str. 3F-26-3rd	1			Construction of building of perishable materials		
		2	1		Construction of platform		(early)
		3			Demolition of existing Str. 3F-Sub.1		

TABLE 2.95
Structure 3F-27: Time Spans

Time Span	Architectural Development	Construction Stage	Unit	Special Deposits: Burial	Descriptive Data	Lot Group	Ceramics in Vogue
1				70?	Abandonment and collapse	2	---------
2					Use of structure		
3	Str. 3F-27	1			Construction of building of perishable materials		Imix
		2	1-6		Construction of platform	1	(late)
		3			Area E of plaza filled		

TABLE 2.96
Structure 3F-29: Time Spans

Time Span	Architectural Development	Construction Stage	Unit	Descriptive Data	Lot Group	Ceramics in Vogue
1				Abandonment and collapse	3a,b	
2				Use		
3	Str. 3F-29-1st	1		Construction of building of perishable materials		(late?)
		2	7	Modification of platform	2	
		3		Demolition of existing building	4	
4				Use		Imix
5	Str. 3F-29-2nd	1		Construction of building of perishable materials		(early?)
		2	1-5, 8-10	Construction of platform	1	
		3		Preparation of base surface, perhaps with quarrying of bedrock		
6			6?, 11?	Earlier activity at this locus		

TABLE 2.97
Structure 3F-Sub.1: Time Spans

Time Span	Architectural Development	Unit	Descriptive Data	Lot Group	Ceramics in Vogue
1			Demolition for construction of Str. 3F-26-3rd		Early Imix
2			Use		Ik?
3		Str.3F-26:U.14-19	Construction		Manik

TABLE 2.98
Platform 3F-2: Time Spans

Time Spans	Architectural Development	Unit	Descriptive Data	Lot Group	Ceramics in Vogue
1			Abandonment; ruin of plaza		
2			Use	3a,b	(late)
3	Plat. 3F-2-1st	10-13	Modification of plaza	2a,b	Imix
4			Use		
5	Plat. 3F-2-2nd	1-9	Construction of plaza	1a-e	(early)

TABLE 2.99
Group 3F-2: Time Spans

Group Time Span	Str. 3F-26 (Table 2.94)	Str. 3F-27 (Table 2.95)	Str. 3F-29 (Table 2.96)	Str. 3F-Sub.1 (Table 2.97)	Plat. 3F-2 (Table 2.98)
1	1	1	1		1
2	2				
3	3				
4	4	2	2		2
5	5	3	3		3
6	6		4		4
7	7		5	1	5
8			6	2	
9				3	

Group 3F-3

INTRODUCTION

The location of this group in Sq. 3F of the Tikal site map (TR. 11) is S185 E296. It occupies the highest point on the same ridge on which previously discussed Gp. 3F-1 and 2 are located, with 3F-1 only 55 m to the SW, and 3F-2 108 m in the same direction. As mapped in 1960, Gp. 3F-3 includes five structures. The largest, 3F-12, is located on the N edge of Plat. 3F-3, and faces the smaller

Str. 3F-15 across the plaza. Structure 3F-11 is located on the W edge of the plaza, and faces two small, apparently square structures on the other side: 3F-13 and 14.

Interest in Gp. 3F-3 was prompted by its proximity to other groups on this ridge that collectively seemed to resemble Gp. 4F-1 and 4F-2 (TR. 19). These latter groups, composed of 17 structures in all, are located on a high spot of land, and are separated from other such groups by empty space on all sides. One of the structures, 4E-31, is quite distinctive. A small range-type structure, it seems to have served a special function as indicated by the presence of an axially placed dedicatory cached offering, along with five contemporaneous burials flanking the front-rear axis. Similarly, Gp. 3F-3 is one of eight groups (including Gp. 3F-1 and 3F-2), with a total of about twenty-three small structures, situated together on this ridge. These eight are closer to one another than to other such groups, even though they happen to be spread out a bit more than is the case with Gp. 4F-1 and 4F-2. One structure among them, 3F-12, stands out from the rest, and before excavation appeared to be a small range-type structure comparable to Str. 4E-31. Curiosity prompted Haviland to seek confirmation of its architectural resemblance to Str. 4E-31, and to see whether or not it, too, contained caches and burials. In August of 1963, it was excavated sufficiently (as Op. 67F) to reconstruct its final plan and to test its front-rear axis for sequence and the presence of special deposits. Concurrently, Str. 3F-13 and 14 were investigated (as Op. 67G).

STRUCTURE 3F-12-2ND

The original structure at this locus seems to have taken the form of a two-level (building?) platform. Its remains were seen only in a trench through the front-rear axis of the final structure (Fig. 54), so its lateral extent is unknown. Surely attributable to it are U. 1 and 2. Unit 1 is a wall that runs E-W beneath the floor of the supplementary platform of 3F-12-1st, and is probably the front wall of the original structure. Unit 2 is the lowest floor beneath the interior platform of the final structure. It was laid on the same fill of mixed earth, stones, and cultural debris that is contained by U. 1 to the S. Since the floor is 0.77 m higher than the base of U. 1, a front step would have been required for access, or else the platform must have had two levels. In support of this, U. 3, a wall that later formed the front of the building platform for 3F-12-1st, seems to represent the front of an upper level for the earlier structure. Not only does it appear to contain the fill for 2nd, but the room floor of 1st abuts the wall 4 cm from its top. In fact, the top of U. 3 is at exactly the same elevation as the surface of U. 2. That pavement, therefore, probably extended S to the top of U. 3. Later, the southern 1.72 m of pavement was ripped out in the course of construction of the new architectural development.

Unit 2 also appears to have run farther to the N at one time, for the inner face of the rear wall of the final building partially rests on it. It is suspected, without actual proof, that the back wall of 2nd was composed in part of a quarried bedrock face that was later buried just inside the rear wall of the supplementary platform for 1st. This face runs E-W in line with U. 1 and 3, but the possibility exists that it served 1st-C alone. If it was part of 2nd, U. 2 would have been torn out here at the time of construction of the back building wall for 1st.

The apparent reuse of U. 3 as the front wall for the building platform of the final structure suggests a high degree of architectural continuity between Str. 3F-12-1st and 2nd, in spite of the great apparent difference between a range-type structure and a two-level platform. Given such continuity, perhaps a building of perishable material was erected on the upper level of the early structure, while the surface of the lower level constituted an open porch. This is suggested by the form of the final structure, with its open supplementary platform (or "porch") in front of the actual building. In other words, Str. 3F-12-2nd might be visualized as a kind of pole-and-thatch range-type structure. No trace of postholes for such a building was found, but given our very limited exposure of 2nd, and the fact that the crucial portions of the structure were later ripped out, this scarcely constitutes proof to the contrary.

STRUCTURE 3F-12-1ST

Construction of Str. 3F-12-1st-C may be divided into at least three main stages. The first (CS. 3) saw extensive demolition of 2nd. As indicated above, the building (assuming one existed), the back wall, and most of the floors were destroyed. Disturbance of its fills, however, was minimal.

Once the earlier structure was sufficiently razed, new walls for a building of three rooms were constructed (as CS. 2) on the remains (Fig. 53, 54). These are of inner and outer masonry veneers with hearting of rubble. The front wall is set back from the face of U. 3, on which the front veneer rests, to form a plinth of 2 cm. Unit 3 served as the front wall of the building platform, as perhaps it had done for the earlier structure. Whether the plinth was carried around to the rear of the structure is not known. It may have been, but not enough remains of the rear wall to be certain. Only the basal course of the outer masonry for this wall survives. It was based on bedrock, 0.10 m S of the quarried face noted in discussion of 2nd. The inner face for this rear wall is based at a higher level, in part on U. 2 and also on fill. It is assumed that the vault of the building was constructed as part of CS. 2, although its collapse is complete.

Inside the center room in the front wall, on either side of the doorway, are four holes (U. 14–17). The bottom ones on either side, 0.29 m above the floor, are square in shape. The upper ones, 1.06 m above the floor, are round. The upper E hole has a smaller, round hole opening into it from below.

Once the building walls were complete, a low interior platform apparently was built (CS. 1). Its walls no longer remain, but its floor surface (U. 4) does. This is only 0.20 m above the room floor, which terminates at a line of stones beneath a later wall (U. 6). The room floor also turns up to the building walls.

At some point in this construction sequence, 1st-C was provided with a supplementary platform. Exactly when this happened is a question, for the building does not sit on the supplementary platform in the usual sense. Rather, it rests on remains of 2nd that were incorporated into the new supplementary platform. Earth was dumped behind a wall, long since destroyed by the elements, located somewhere about 2.20 m S of U. 1. The riser for a step survives 0.30 m S of this, suggesting the approximate location of the front of the supplementary platform.

The rear of the supplementary platform may have been the quarried bedrock face that has already been mentioned. If so, the face may have been quarried at this time, though more probably it served as part of the rear wall for 2nd. In its latest form, the rear of the supplementary platform consisted of a wall (U. 5) located 0.10 m N of the bedrock face. This could have been constructed as part of 1st-C, or as part of a later modification of 1st. The first is most probable, for it would have maintained the symmetry of the structure.

Unit 7 is a remnant of the pavement over the supplementary platform. It turns up to U. 3, covers U. 1, and was laid directly on the earth fill of the supplementary platform.

STRUCTURE 3F-12-1ST-B

After a period of use, Str. 3F-12 underwent modification, as the level of the interior platform was raised some 0.14 m. The floor, laid on a thin fill of small stones, survives as U. 8. Nothing more is known about this platform, except that its size was probably the same as that of its predecessor.

STRUCTURE 3F-12-1ST-A

The final modification again involved the interior platform. This time, the old front wall was torn out and replaced with a new one (U. 6, Fig. 53, 54). This consists of a course of vertically set masonry blocks, arranged so that the central portion is outset. These are based on the stones to which the floor of the room originally ran, and against U. 4 and 8 with their fills. The building floor was patched to turn up to U. 6. On top of the vertical slabs was a second course of masonry blocks, laid on their flat surfaces so as to project 3 cm beyond the face of the lower masonry. Unit 6 abuts the end walls of the room.

On the surface of this new interior platform were constructed two dividing walls (U. 10 and 11), similar in position to those found in Str. 4E-31 (TR. 19:fig. 2) and 4E-50 (this report). The lateral faces of these are in line with the outset in U. 6. Not known is how high these walls once stood, or whether they had medial shelves as in Str. 4E-50. Units 10 and 11 abut the back wall of the room with their fronts in line with the face of the top masonry course of U. 6. Pavement for the interior platform (U. 9),

laid on a thin fill of small stones, turns up to U. 10 and 11. A small round hole (U. 12) in U. 9 is a puzzle, but suggests that a post for an unknown purpose was set in this floor.

STRUCTURE 3F-13

Since only the W portion of its S wall was excavated, little can be said about 3F-13. To judge from its ruin, it was square, and seems to have been built against the E end of the front of Str. 3F-12-1st, as may Str. 3F-11 on the W (Fig. 53). The E wall of 13 seems to have been located E of the end wall of the supplementary platform for 12-1st. The N wall may have been in line with the S wall of the supplementary platform of 12-1st, or somewhat farther N so that the structures overlapped.

The S wall of 13 was built of masonry blocks much like those used in Str. 12-1st and 3F-14. It was based on Str. 3F-14:U. 1 (Fig. 55), with its top at the same elevation as the surface of the supplementary platform of 12-1st. Implied is a continuous surface over the two structures. In fact, 3F-13 may have been no more than an open platform, really an adjunct of 3F-12, but more excavation would be required to confirm this.

STRUCTURE 3F-14

The walls of this square structure (Fig. 53) are of a single course of masonry that sits on gray earth (Fig. 55:U. 1). Curiously, this masonry survives only in the N wall, portions of the E wall, and the E end of the S wall. This suggests that masonry was robbed at a later date for some unknown purpose. A dark fill of earth and trash is contained within the walls. No trace of summit pavement survives, but one probably existed. Nor are there any traces of postholes, but this is scarcely surprising. The earth fill is more than sufficient to have supported posts for a building without their penetrating bedrock. Thus, Str. 3F-14 may have consisted in part of a building of perishable materials. On this assumption, a single stage (CS. 2) may be defined for construction of the platform, and another (CS. 1) for a building.

Unit 1, on which 3F-14 was built, was the original ground level. It overlies bedrock, and contains no cultural material. No burial or other special deposit was placed in it beneath the front-rear axis of the structure. Presumably, plaster pavement covered this layer outside the structure walls, but traces of this have long since vanished.

POSSIBLE EARLY ACTIVITY

Enigmatic U. 13 is a wall of a single course of roughly dressed masonry that abuts U. 1 of Str. 3F-12 (Fig. 53). Excavation followed it S for a distance of 1 m, but what happened to it after that is not known. It may have been contemporary with, or earlier than, U. 1. It was buried by 3F-12-1st-C.

In the trench through the axis of Str. 3F-12, bedrock was found to have been extensively quarried. Of particular note is a deep hole in which PD. 109 was found. The hole itself surely predates construction of U. 13, and could predate PD. 109 (see its discussion in section III of this report).

It is not known if the quarrying beneath fill of 3F-12-2nd was carried out at the same time as the pit. Possibly it relates to construction of 12-2nd, as may the vertical quarried face beneath the rear wall of 3F-12 that has already been discussed.

SHERDS AND ARTIFACTS

Lot groups defined for Gp. 3F-3 are listed in Table 2.100, with content in Tables 2.101–103.

CONSTRUCTION FILL

Most of the sherds and artifacts recovered from Gp. 3F-1 fall into this category, and generally material was not abundant. The earliest, on stratigraphic grounds, should be in Str. 3F-12:1a and 1b. Since most of the floors of 3F-12-2nd were eventually ripped out, however, there is the chance that a few later sherds found their way into LG. 1b. Structure 3F-12:LG. 2b, 3, and 4 would be expected to contain some material from earlier occupation of Gp. 3F-3. The same is true of LG. 2a, from the pit in which PD. 109 was found. This pit must have been filled when 12-2nd was in use. The two Manik vessels in PD. 109 probably date construction of 2nd and the possible Ik sherds were likely introduced when 1st-C was built.

MATERIAL ABOVE LIVING LEVELS

Here, Str. 3F-12:LG. 5b and 5c, and probably 5a, contain a scatter of material from late usage of the group (including Eznab ceramics). Some earlier occupation refuse may also be included in these lot groups, as well as in Str. 3F-13:LG. 1, but this last is surely mixed with fill material from structure collapse. Lot Group 2, around the walls of Str. 3F-14, is of midden quality; sherds are from Imix and Eznab vessels. This appears to be relatively uncontaminated from structure collapse.

OTHER SOURCES

As noted above, PD. 109 was found on the front-rear axis of 3F-12.

TABLE 2.100
Group 3F-3: Lot Groups

Feature	Lot Group	Lots	Provenience	Ceramic Evaluation
Str. 3F-12 (Op. 67F)	1a	15	Sealed fill of 2nd	One Preclassic, much Manik, possible Ik and/or Imix
	1b	6,10,11	Partially sealed fill of 2nd	Preclassic, Manik, some Imix
	2a	1,7,8	Unsealed fill of 1st-C	Preclassic including Cimi; Manik, possible Ik
	2b	14	Sealed fill of 1st-C	No data
	3	13	Sealed fill of 1st-B	No data
	4	12	Sealed fill of 1st-A	No data
	5a	3,5	Directly on floor surface in Rm. 2	Ik and/or Imix
	5b	2	Directly on floor of supplementary platform	Eznab
	5c	4	N of structure	Imix and/or Eznab
Str. 3F-13 (Op. 67G)	1	2	S of structure, surface to base of wall	Imix and Eznab
Str. 3F-14 (Op. 67G)	1	4	Unsealed fill	Ik and Imix
	2	1,3,5	Outside structure, surface to base of wall	Ik, much Imix, Eznab

TABLE 2.101
Structure 3F-12: Artifacts by Lot Group

Study Category	Object	Lot Groups								
		1a	1b	2a	2b	3	4	5a	5b	5c
Pottery Vessels	Sherds	Not calculated								
Flaked Chert Artifacts	Ovate biface			1						
	Unused flakes			3						
Ground, Pecked, and Polished Stone Artifacts	Metate			1						
	Rubbing stone			1						
	Hammer stone			1						

TABLE 2.102
Structure 3F-13: Artifacts by Lot Group

Study Category	Object	Lot Group 1
Pottery Vessels	Sherds	Not calculated
Flaked Chert Artifacts	Rectangular biface	1
Ground, Pecked, and Polished Stone Artifacts	Mano	1

TABLE 2.103
Structure 3F-14: Artifacts by Lot Group

Study Category	Object	Lot Group	1	2
Pottery Vessels	Sherds	Not calculated		
Other Pottery Artifacts	Figurines		1	1
	Miscellaneous modeled sherd			1
Flaked Chert Artifacts	Elongate bifaces		2	
	Unclassifiable bifaces		1	1
	Retouched flakes		2	
	Used flakes			3
	Unused flakes		4	4
	Unused core		1	
Flaked Obsidian Artifacts	Prismatic blade			1
Ground, Pecked, and Polished Stone Artifacts	Hammer stone		1	1
	Unclassifiable artifact			1
Shell and Bone Artifacts	Bone		5	

TABLE 2.104
Structure 3F-12: Time Spans

Time Span	Architectural Development	Construction Stage	Unit	Special Deposits: Problematical Deposit	Descriptive Data	Lot Group	Ceramics in Vogue
1					Abandonment and collapse		
2					Use	5a-c	Eznab
3	Str. 3F-12-1st-A	1	9-12		Construction of dividing walls and floor	4	
		2	6		Construction of new wall for interior platform		
		3			Destruction of original wall for interior platform		
4					Use		
5	Str. 3F-12-1st-B	None defined	8		Interior platform raised	3	Imix
6					Use		
7	Str. 3F-12-1st-C	1	4,5?,7?		Construction of interior platform and perhaps supplementary platform	2b	
		2	14-17		Construction of building		
		3			Partial demolition of 2nd		
8					Use		Ik
9	Str. 3F-12-2nd	1?			Construction of building of perishable materials?		
		2	1-3,13?		Construction of platform	1a b	Ik or Manik
		3?		109?	Preparation of base-surface, including quarrying beneath structure?		
10					Earliest activity		Cimi-Manik

TIME SPANS

Time spans are defined for Str. 3F-12, 13, and 14 in Tables 2.104, 2.105, and 2.106. Table 2.107 is an attempt to combine these into group time spans. These are somewhat tentative, for two structures were not even tested. Assumed is that construction of Str. 3F-13 and 14 was contemporary, and there seems no reason to doubt this. Structure 3F-13 probably was not constructed earlier than 3F-12-1st-C, nor was Str. 3F-14, to judge from the fill ceramics (Table 2.100). They might, however, have been built somewhat later.

Group TS. 12 is based on the presence in some quantity of Late Preclassic and Manik sherds in construction fills (Table 2.100); they indicate an occupation of the locus prior to construction of Str. 3F-12-2nd. It is doubtful that many sherds were brought from some place far removed, for presumably fill material would have been drawn from a nearby source. Perhaps some of the bedrock was quarried during this time span.

Group TS. 11 is defined by construction of Str. 3F-12-2nd, which dates from late Early Classic times (PD. 109 and Table 2.100; Imix sherds in Str. 3F-12:LG. 1b are clearly intruded).

Final abandonment of the group took place after appearance of Eznab ceramics, which were found around both Str. 3F-12 and 14 (Table 2.100). Whether or not any of the other structures were abandoned prior to the appearance of such ceramics is not known. In Gp. 4F-1, the similar (to 3F-12-1st) Str. 4E-31 seems to have been converted to residential use after the other less substantial dwellings were deserted (TR. 19:56). Although proof is lacking, Str. 3F-12 may have undergone a similar conversion from nonresidential to residential use. To learn more of this final occupation, excavation of the other structures of Gp. 3F-3 would be necessary.

This final period of occupation took place in Gp. TS. 3, which is formally based on evidence of masonry robbing from Str. 4F-14. Obviously, this structure was abandoned by this time.

In summary, people seem to have been living in the vicinity of Gp. 3F-3 by about AD 150, as a rough approximation, when Cimi ceramics were in use. The area was probably continuously utilized until slightly after AD 869, when Eznab ceramics were present. The earliest known construction, however, dates somewhere between AD 250 and 550, when Manik ceramics were in vogue.

TABLE 2.105
Structure 3F-13: Time Spans

Time Span	Architectural Development	Unit	Descriptive Data	Lot Group	Ceramics in Vogue
1			Abandonment and collapse		--------- Eznab
2			Use	1	---------
3	Str. 3F-13		Construction		Imix
4		1	Earlier activity		--------- Ik

TABLE 2.106
Structure 3F-14: Time Spans

Time Span	Architectural Development	Construction Stage	Unit	Descriptive Data	Lot Group	Ceramics in Vogue
1				Total abandonment and ruin		----------
2				Abandonment and robbing of masonry		Eznab
3				Use	2	----------
4	Str. 3F-14	1		Construction of building of perishable materials		Imix
		2		Construction of platform	1	
5			1	Earlier activity		----------
						Ik

TABLE 2.107
Group 3F-3: Time Spans

Group Time Span	Structure 3F-12 (Table 2.104)	Structure 3F-13 (Table 2.105)	Structure 3F-14 (Table 2.106)
1	1		
2			1
3		1	2
4	2		
5	3		
6	4		
7	5		
8	6	2	3
9	7	3	4
10	8		
11	9	4	5
12	10		

Group 3G-1

INTRODUCTION

Located in Sq. 3G of the Tikal site map (TR. 11) at S3 E253, Gp. 3G-1 (as mapped in 1960) included five structures, arranged around the four sides of a plaza. The terrain here is identical to that occupied by Gp. 2G-1, the next group to the N. About 10 m due E is the bajo.

Of the five structures in this group, only 3G-1, on the W edge of the plaza, was tested (as Op. 24X) for sequence. This was carried out in May 1961 by Haviland in connection with the previously discussed resistivity and magnetic survey that ran S from Ch. 2G-5 (in Gp. 2G-1) to a point W of Str. 3G-1. In the course of excavation, a chultun (3G-5) was discovered beneath the structure. This was excavated by Puleston in the summer of 1963 as Op. 72A.

STRUCTURE 3G-1-3RD

Five construction stages may be defined for the earliest structure at this locus (Fig. 56, 57). They are known solely on the basis of architecture seen in a trench excavated through the mid-point of the ruin mound. Construction Stage 5 is defined for the filling of Ch. 3G-5 (see its discussion below). Rubble was dumped above the chutun to cover the orifice. The very edges of this rubble rest on Str. 3G-1:U. 1, the top of which probably was the ground surface when the chultun was in use.

Once the chultun was filled, the level of the plaza was built up (CS. 4). Evidence for this operation consists of a light-colored fill of earth and trash that covers U. 1 and some of the rubble over the chultun. A wall to retain this fill to the W must have been built, to be ripped out later when Str. 3G-1-2nd was built. The fill is capped by a thin stratum of packed clay (U. 2), a pause-line marking the end of this construction stage.

Following preparation of the plaza level, the rear wall must have been built up higher, as more earth fill was put in place. This consists of dark earth containing some trash, which rests on U. 2. This operation defines CS. 3.

The next step (CS. 2) saw completion of a two-level platform. A front wall was built on the fill for CS. 4, and a fill of light earth and trash was dumped behind it, against the fill for CS. 3. The wall for the upper platform level was built on this, and fill operations were completed. Plaster pavements were then laid over the fill. One of these, U. 3, runs from the top of the front wall and turns up to the base of the upper platform wall. The other, U. 4, runs from the top of this wall to the back of the structure.

The assumption is that a building of perishable materials was constructed on the platform. Evidence for this was not sought in excavation, on the presumption that a search would be fruitless. The fill was sufficiently deep so that posts would not have penetrated bedrock. Moreover, plaster floors in small structures at Tikal through which posts did penetrate have almost invariably been destroyed by tree roots in the crucial areas. Since some other platforms of this sort did support such buildings (TR. 20B), however, it seems reasonable that this one also did. A stage (CS. 1) is allowed for its erection, though the main posts must have been set in the course of earlier stages.

STRUCTURE 3G-1-2ND

After a period of use, Str. 3G-1 underwent alterations that may be divided into a sequence of four construction stages (Fig. 56, 57). As CS. 4, the back wall of 3rd was torn out. If a building did stand on the platform, this too must have been demolished.

Construction Stage 3 saw erection of a new rear wall. Where this survives N of the chultun, its base is on bedrock, and two courses of masonry survive. Earth fill was placed behind it, against the surviving fill of the earlier structure. This back wall must have risen to an elevation 0.30 m above the upper floor of 3rd, requiring a third course of masonry. In the upper portion, the wall seems to have consisted of two veneers: an outer face that was a continuation upward of the two lower courses based ultimately on bedrock, and an inner one based on the new fill, at the level of U. 4, and just above the location of the earlier wall that had been ripped out. The presumed upper course of the outer veneer no longer survives, but the inner one, of less well-dressed masonry, does (U. 5). The one-time existence of the third course of outer veneer is indicated by the quantity of collapsed fill. This was too great to have spilled from behind the lower two courses alone, W of the structure, above U. 1. Rather, this fill must also have been placed as hearting between U. 5 and a third course of outer veneer masonry.

Following construction of the new rear wall, two walls were laid on the surface of U. 4 (CS. 2). One of these, U. 6, runs E from U. 5. The other, U. 7, runs S from U. 6. A floor remnant, U. 8, abuts and turns up to the base of U. 7. It probably is a patch on U. 4, which may have continued in use E of U. 7. A logical interpretation of these remains, given their limited exposure (the trench through the middle of the mound) is that U. 7 is the front wall of a third platform level. Unit 6, which rises 0.20 m higher than U. 7, is the S wall of a small, interior platform that projects above, and in front of, the upper platform level.

A final CS. 1 is allowed for construction of a new building of perishable materials on the platform. The poles for the back wall of this would have been set between U. 5 and the outer veneer of the back wall. It is not known if the floors continued over this area, for none at all now survive.

TABLE 2.108
Chultun 3G-5: Average Dimensions (meters)

	Length	Width	Height	Minimum Diameter	Maximum Diameter
Orifice	---	---	1.00***	1.00*	1.28**
Chamber 1	---	---	0.80	---	1.10
Chamber 2	---	---	0.89	1.25	1.40
Chamber 3	---	---	0.90	1.12	1.12
Entrance 1-2	---	0.50	0.42		
Entrance 2-3	---	0.55	0.38		

*at step
**at surface
***neck height (to step)

STRUCTURE 3G-1-1ST

Eventually, the front wall of the upper platform of 3G-1 was moved eastward, so that its second platform level became more like a step (Fig. 56, 57). The new front wall for this upper level, U. 9, was built on U. 4, 0.32 m W of the front wall for the upper level of the original structure. Pavement for this new upper level must have been at the same elevation as that associated with U. 7. The interior platform, of which U. 6 is thought to be a portion, must have continued in use. Its front would have been in line with U. 9.

Again, there is no direct evidence for a building on this platform. If one existed on the earlier platform, this may have continued in use, probably with some renovation. Therefore, at least two construction stages seem appropriate for this final structure: CS. 2 for reconstruction of the platform, and CS. 1 for renovation of the building.

CHULTUN 3G-5

DESCRIPTION

The orifice of Ch. 3G-5 (Fig. 58) is located beneath the rear portion of Str. 3G-1 (Fig. 56, 57). Round in shape, it has a deeply stepped rim. No stone cover can now be found. Below the step, the neck flares downward into a small, circular antechamber from which two chambers open, one to the N and one to the S. The one to the N (Chm. 3) is the larger of the two. Both take the form of domes with good level floors that meet the walls at right angles. The entrances to both chambers are restricted on the sides, but have no sills. It may be noted that the excavator, who was of average stature (by North American standards), found it most awkward to enter the cramped chambers (see Table 2.108 for dimensions).

DISCUSSION

It is obvious that the first step in construction was to dig out the orifice and antechamber, and that one of the lateral chambers had to be dug out before the other. Hence, three construction stages were involved, but it is impossible to positively assign construction of the particular lateral chambers to either CS. 2 or 1, except arbitrarily (as in Table 2.113). Structure 3G-1:U. 1 apparently represents the occupation surface in use when the chultun was dug.

Except for air spaces in the upper portions of Chm. 2 and 3, the chultun was found to be completely full of a mixture of light gray soil, numerous stones, and some cultural material. A thin layer of dark earth covered the fill surfaces in the air spaces. This was apparently deposited by the decay of rootlets, which had worked their way down through the limestone. Many such rootlets could be observed hanging from the ceilings of both inner chambers. All in all, it is certain that this chultun was deliberately filled, probably to permit construction of Str. 3G-1-3rd. The situation is similar to Ch. 2G-2, 2G-10, and 2G-11 (this report), all of which were purposely filled, but stands in marked contrast to Ch. 2G-1, 2G-5, and 3F-6 (this report), none of which were purposely filled. The presence of PD. 214 is noted elsewhere (this report, section III).

SHERDS AND ARTIFACTS

Lot groups for the structure and chultun are presented in Table 2.109, with distribution of sherds and artifacts in Tables 2.110 and 2.111.

CONSTRUCTION FILL

The structure furnished a classic case of reverse stratigraphy. The fills of 3rd (LG. 1a and 1b) consistent-

TABLE 2.109
Group 3G-1: Lot Groups

Feature	Lot Group	Lot	Provenience	Ceramic Evaluation
Str.3G-1 (Op. 24X)	1a	13	Partially sealed fill of 3rd, CS. 4	Ik
	1b	8,11,12	Partially sealed fill of 3rd, CS. 2 and 3	Manik and Ik
	1c	5,15	Unsealed fill of 2nd, CS. 2 and 3	Imix
	1d	7	Unsealed fill of 1st, CS. 2	Imix?
	1e	6,9	Mixed fill of 1st and 2nd	Ik
	1f	4	Mixed fill of U. 1 and Str. 3G-1-2nd	Imix
	2	10	Directly on structure floor (U. 3)	Imix
	3a	1	E of structure, surface to base of wall	Ik and/or Imix
	3b	2,3	W of structure, surface to base of wall	Ik and/or Imix
Ch. 3G-5	1	24X/14	Chultun orifice	Ik
	2	72A/1-6; 8,9	Fill of chultun	Ik and Imix

ly contain pieces of Ik pottery vessels. At first, this appears to make sense, for sherds from later architectural developments appear referable to the Imix Complex (LG. 1c, 1d, 1f). Although much of the pottery from Ch. 3G-5 pertains to the Ik Complex, on the floors of Chm. 2 and 3 Imix sherds were found. These cannot be explained as the result of intrusion. The situation becomes comprehensible only if it is assumed that existing trash deposits, probably from Gp. 3G-1 coeval with use of the chultun, were recycled as fill. This illustrates the difficulty of dating a structure on the basis of a single test pit into fill; in this case, a test pit would have suggested that Str. 3G-1 was in existence at a time when Ik ceramics were still in use.

Also noteworthy is a sherd fit between LG. 1b (fill of 3rd) and 1d (fill of 1st). This illustrates the way earlier material could be used in later fills.

MATERIAL ABOVE LIVING LEVELS

Around Str. 3G-1 such material is not abundant. Moreover, in all cases it appears to be mixed with debris that washed out of the structure fill. This is indicated not only by stratigraphy, but it is verified in the case of LG. 1d (fill) and 2 (on-floor) by sherd fits. It does appear as if LG. 2 includes sherds from a vessel that probably was broken upon abandonment of the structure.

OTHER SOURCES

The one other source of cultural material from Gp. 3G-1 is PD. 214.

TABLE 2.110
Structure 3G-1: Artifacts by Lot Group

Study Category	Object	Lot Group								
		1a	1b	1c	1d	1e	1f	2	3a	3b
Pottery Vessels	Sherds per cubic meter (lbs)	.61	3.38	6.98	3.51	3.29	10.83	15.94	1.30	1.89
Other Pottery Artifacts	Figurine									1
	Centrally perforated sherd									1
	Unclassifiable formed objects		1		1					
Flaked Chert Artifacts	Subtriangular bifaces	1								
	Unclassifiable bifaces			1		1				
	Thin biface			1						
	Point-retouched flakes	2								
	Blades	1				1				
	Used flakes	4	8		3	3	2	1		
	Unmodified flakes	3	18	1	7	3	2	3	1	7
	Unmodified, fire-spalled flakes	1				1			1	1
	Unmodified cores	1	1	1						
Flaked Obsidian Artifacts	Prismatic blades	1	2	1				1		
Ground, Pecked, and Polished Stone Artifacts	Metates		1							1
	Rubbing stone					1				
	Hammer stone									
	Unclassifiable artifacts		1	1				1	1	
Shell and Bone Artifacts	Bone		1							
	Shell			1						

TABLE 2.111
Chultun 3G-5: Artifacts by Lot Group

Study Category	Object	Lot Group	
		1	2
Pottery Vessels	Sherds per cubic meter (lbs)	27.68	
Other Pottery Artifacts	Figurine		1
Flaked Chert Artifacts	Flake cores		3
	Subtriangular bifaces	2	
	Irregular biface		1
	Used flakes	4	1
	Unmodified flakes	7	1
	Unclassifiable artifact	1	
Flaked Obsidian Artifacts	Prismatic blade		1
Ground, Pecked, and Polished Stone Artifacts	Rubbing stone		1
	Hammer stone		1
Shell and Bone Artifacts	Bone, animal, unmodified		144

TIME SPANS

Time spans are defined for Str. 3G-1 and Ch. 3G-5 in Tables 2.112 and 2.113. As should be apparent from what has been said thus far, these time spans are readily correlated (see Table 2.114). Obviously, these group time spans should be thought of as tentative. If the other four structures of Gp. 3G-1 are ever excavated, these will undoubtedly have to be redefined.

To sum up the sequence and dates, Ch. 3G-5 seems to have been in use up to the time when Imix ceramic production began. This is when the chultun was filled, and Str. 3G-1-3rd built above it. Interestingly, most of the sherds in this fill are from Ik vessels (Table 2.109). The filling of the chultun and construction above it would unhesitatingly be dated to the time such ceramics were in use, were it not for the presence of Imix sherds on the floor of the chultun.

Just when the chultun was constructed cannot be said. It could have been just prior to the appearance of Ik ceramics, for Manik sherds are known from the fill of Str. 3G-1 (Table 2.109). These at least open the possibility that there was a late Early Classic occupation of Gp. 3G-1, to which the chultun initially related. It is doubtful that the chultun is any older, for one would not expect to find a chultun in an area devoid of structures.

As noted, Str. 3G-1-3rd was built just after the appearance of Imix ceramics. It underwent two subsequent modifications, and was ultimately abandoned prior to the appearance of Eznab ceramics. Consequently, activity at this locus was underway shortly before AD 550, and ended by AD 869, the dates for the beginning of the Ik Complex and the end of the Imix Complex, respectively. It is assumed, but without definite proof, that these dates apply to all of Gp. 3G-1.

TABLE 2.112
Structure 3G-1: Time Spans

Time Span	Architectural Development	Construction Stage	Unit	Descriptive Data	Lot Group			Ceramics in Vogue
1				Abandonment and collapse				
2				Use	2a			(late)
		1		Construction or renovation of building of perishable materials				
3	Str. 3G-1-1st	2	9	Modification of platform				
4				Use		1e		(late)
		1		Construction of building of perishable materials				
5	Str. 3G-1-2nd	2	6,7	Construction of upper platform level and interior platform	1c			
		3	5	Construction of rear wall	1f		3b	Imix
		4		Partial demolition of 3rd				
6				Use				
		1		Construction of building of perishable materials				
		2	3,4	Completion of two-level platform	1b			
7	Str. 3G-1-3rd	3		First fill operation				(early)
		4	2	Preparation of base surface	1a			
		5		Ch. 3G-5 filled				
8			1	Earliest activity				Ik Manik?

TABLE 2.113
Chultun 3G-5: Time Spans

Time Span	Architectural Development	Construction Stage	Special Deposits: Problematical Deposit	Descriptive Data	Lot Group	Ceramics in Vogue
1			214	Chultun filled and abandoned	1,2	Imix (early)
2				Use		Ik
3	Ch. 3G-5	1		Construction of Ch. 2 or 3		Manik?
		2		Construction of Ch. 2 or 3		
		3		Construction of orifice and antechamber		

Chultun 2F-5

INTRODUCTION

Located in Sq. 2F of the site map (TR. 11) at S320 E440, this chultun is 70 m N of St. 27 (TR. 8:163), about 35 m S of Gp. 2F-1, and 25 m NE of Ch. 2F-6 (Fig. 10). Topographically, the area is well suited for habitation, although there are no visible structure ruins anywhere nearby. Since two tests by similar chultuns (2F-4 and 2G-1) nearby both disclosed traces of construction (Gp. 2F-1 and Str. 2G-61, in this report), it is virtually certain that a search would reveal traces of construction near Ch. 2F-5. It seems likely that much of a surface collection of sherds from near Ch. 2F-6, as well as sherds and artifacts of test pits 1 and 2 N of that chultun (Fig. 10) pertain to a structure, or group of structures, with which Ch. 2F-5 was associated.

The chultun (Fig. 59 and Table 2.115) was completely excavated (as Op. 16A) by Alexandre Nicouline, a visitor to Tikal in 1958. It was revisited by Puleston in 1963, whose interpretation is followed here.

DESCRIPTION

The antechamber for this chultun is oval in plan. Its concave walls and ceiling are all clearly differentiated from one another, even though the juncture of floor and walls, and walls with ceiling, are rounded rather than sharply cut right angles. The chamber floor slopes slightly to the NW, away from Chm. 2, so that small amounts of water that may have entered the chultun would not have

TABLE 2.114
Group 3G-1: Tentative Group Time Spans

Group Time Spans	Structure 3G-1 (Table 2.112)	Chultun 3G-5 (Table 2.113)
1	1	
2	2	
3	3	
4	4	
5	5	
6	6	
7	7	1
8		2
9	8	3

flowed into the deeper inner chambers. Perhaps this was done to compensate for the lack of a sill in the opening to Chm. 2.

Chamber 1 is entered from above through Or. 1, the only one for this chultun. A neck with vertical sides leads down from this manhole-like opening in the bedrock crust, flaring slightly where it opens into the approximate center of the ceiling of Chm. 1. The rim is not stepped,

TABLE 2.115
Chultun 2F-5: Average Dimensions (meters)

	Length	Width	Height	Minimum Diameter	Maximum Diameter
Orifice	---	---	1.30*	0.42	0.42
Chamber 1	---	---	0.90	1.60	2.00
Chamber 2	---	---	1.15	1.00	1.70
Chamber 3	---	---	1.25	1.08	1.60
Chamber 4	---	---	1.10	1.27	1.90
Chamber 5	---	---	0.90	1.03	1.12
Entrance 1-2	---	1.11	0.85	---	---
Entrance 2-3	---	0.60	0.80	---	---
Entrance 2-5	---	0.88	0.90	---	---
Entrance 3-4	---	1.39	0.87	---	---

*Neck height

and no stone cover was found for this chultun. Rubble may have been placed around the orifice to prevent soil (now ca. 0.50 m deep) from spilling into the opening, but this has not been verified.

As found, Chm. 1 was nearly full of detritus. At the top is a layer of humus and roots (U. 1) blocking the entrance to Chm. 2. Beneath this, the color of the soil lightens, with this continuing down to floor level (U. 3). White marl less than 5 cm thick (U. 9) can be seen where the ceiling of the entrance to Chm. 2 slightly overhangs the floor of Chm. 1. A few sherds and artifacts seem to have been included in U. 3.

Chamber 2, located SE of Chm. 1, is entered from this chamber through a wide entrance only slightly restricted on the sides. As already noted, there is no sill. Moreover, the SW part of the entrance floor was cut back into the floor of Chm. 1, forming a nearly square step (U. 7) leading to the lower floor of Chm. 2. The shape of the chamber is difficult to describe; it seems more or less circular. The walls are clearly demarcated from floor and ceiling, but as in Chm. 1, all surfaces are concave, and the points of juncture are rounded. The floor of the chamber slopes down towards Chm. 5.

As found, Chm. 2 was about half filled. The top 0.10 m of this fill consists of light-colored earth and limestone (U. 2). Beneath this is a continuation of U. 3 from Chm. 1. Lower still, on the floor, is a 5 cm stratum of white marl (U. 9) that covers a number of large sherds scattered on the floor. The largest pieces were on U. 7, with a large jar neck close by on the floor of Chm. 2.

From the S side of Chm. 2, an opening restricted on the sides leads into roughly circular Chm. 3. On the floor of this opening is a masonry sill (U. 8) that is 0.15 m high. Its effective height, though, is increased since the floor of

Chm. 2 is 0.22 m lower than that of Chm. 3 in the entrance. The ceiling of this cavity is also higher than the ceiling of Chm. 2. As in Chm. 1 and 2, walls, ceiling, and floor are all clearly demarcated from one another, but with rounded points of juncture.

As found, Chm. 3 was probably about half filled with continuations of U. 2, 3, and 9. Unfortunately, the excavator's field notes do not describe this deposit.

In plan, Chm. 4 is larger than all but Chm. 1, but the surprisingly low ceiling gives it a considerably smaller volume than Chm. 2. Access is through a wide entrance, only slightly narrowed on its sides, from the W end of Chm. 3. The floor slopes markedly downward to the W from the floor of Chm. 3. By contrast to Chm. 1, 2, and 3, walls, floors, and ceiling are not clearly demarcated from one another.

The excavator's field notes report little about the contents of this cavity, other than that it produced a few sherds and a piece of obsidian (a prismatic blade?). It is assumed that U. 2, 3, and 9 continued into this chamber.

Small, round Chm. 5 adjoins the SE portion of Chm. 2. Its entrance is only slightly restricted on the sides. The floor of Chm. 5 is 0.35 m below that of Chm. 2, which slopes down slightly towards it, and there is no sill. The floor itself is unusually level. In section, Chm. 5 shows no clear demarcation between walls and ceiling.

This cavity was found almost completely full. Units 2, 3, and 9 apparently continued in from Chm. 2. Unit 9, the white marl, continues across the chamber at the level of the floor of Chm. 2. Beneath this is U. 4, a deposit 0.10 to 0.15 m thick, containing minute particles of carbon. At the bottom of U. 4, large pot sherds were found lying on a stratum of irregular stones (U. 5) that the excavator reports were in two layers. Beneath U. 5, on the floor of the chamber, is a deposit of fine, silty earth (U. 6), 0.10 m thick, again with minute carbon particles.

DISCUSSION

This chultun is thought to have been deliberately filled upon abandonment. In this view, the material of which U. 3 is composed was dumped into the orifice, until it reached ground level. Filled in this way, little of this material would have found its way into the inner chambers. As time passed, though, there would have been a tendency for this deposit to slump gradually into inner chambers (see Ch. 6E-7, this report, for a particularly clear example of this). The process quite likely would have accelerated with time; as the U. 3 material continued to settle, it would have been replaced by decaying leaves and humus (now represented by U. 1, which quite clearly is more recent). The looser consistency of this would permit more water to enter the chultun, washing more of the fill into deeper chambers.

Consistent with this interpretation are the positions of U. 1 and 3 and the large amount of fill (on the order of 5 cubic meters). Along with this fill, there is no evidence for significant slumping of surface material around the orifice, such as might be expected had there been considerable washing of this material into the chultun. Moreover, the available evidence suggests that the ceramics from the chultun do not duplicate surface deposits near the orifice, as would be expected had the material washed in. Finally, the lack of a stone cover may be significant. The chultun quite likely was abandoned long before Tikal was deserted (see below), in which case an open chultun would have been a hazard. Dogs, children, or people in general could have fallen in, with disastrous results. Given the absence of a stone cover, purposeful fill seems likely. The cover may even have been included in the fill in fragmentary form, and so was not recognized by the excavator. While examples of empty, open chultuns are known prior to abandonment of Tikal (i.e., Ch. 6C-7, this report), they probably are not as common as abandoned chultuns closed off in some manner (e.g., Ch. 2G-1, 4F-2, 4F-4, 4G-2, 5C-6, 5F-5, 6C-6, 6C-9, 6C-10, 6E-6, 6E-7; all in this report).

There is no mystery about U. 2; it clearly derives from minor ceiling collapse, with some fill admixture. Small pieces of ceiling probably fell from time to time as U. 3 was settling into the deeper portions of the chultun. A distinct, visible stratum, however, would not be distinguishable until the settling was virtually complete, with fairly level surfaces. Unit 3, it may be noted, does contain a number of pieces of limestone.

Unit 9, the thin layer of marl seen in Chm. 2 and part of Chm. 1, seems to consist in part of occupation debris, as indicated by the large sherds, and pre-fill flaking from the ceiling. Its whiteness indicates little contamination by drift from outside, so presumably it accumulated while the chultun was still protected by a stone cover. Puleston saw this as evidence that the chultun was abandoned with its stone cover in place, to be filled much later, perhaps after a century or so. The most likely time of filling in his view would be in the Early Classic period. Haviland, on the other hand, sees no reason why the Early Classic Maya would have opened an already closed, abandoned chultun to fill it; this would have been unnecessary work. Moreover, evidence discussed below indicates that water did get into the chultun while it was in use. Hence one may ask why water did not seep in following abandonment, if the chultun were left empty with the same stone cover in place around which water

had previously leaked in. Consequently, Haviland would see the filling as connected with abandonment. Perhaps the problem would be resolved by extensive excavation of the immediate vicinity.

Units 4, 5, and 6 are obviously of a different nature, and predate U. 9. Units 4 and 6 both appear to be water-borne deposits, from the excavator's description. The stones of U. 5 bring to mind the stones placed in a deep chamber of Ch. 2G-1 (this report), which are thought to have facilitated water drainage. Apparently water did run into this chultun (lack of sills between Chm. 1, 2, and 3 has already been noted), collecting in the deep Chm. 5. At some point, stones were placed on the accumulating silt to facilitate drainage, or perhaps to reduce the amount of standing water after flooding. Following this, more silt accumulated, finally being covered by U. 9. The large sherds in U. 4 indicate that water was not the only thing to collect in Chm. 5, some occupation debris did as well.

The problem with water, coupled with other features of this chultun, suggest some further points. The ceiling of Chm. 3 was constructed in such a way so that water seeping along the ceiling of Chm. 2 would have dripped down prior to entering Chm. 3. Since the sill between Chm. 2 and 3 is of masonry, and not of quarried bedrock as is more usual, the inference is that it was a later addition to the entrance between the two rooms. This suggests that water running into this chamber was a problem that had to be corrected. Yet, it is hard to see how water could have done this, given the presence of the much deeper Chm. 5. A solution to this dilemma, of course, is to interpret Chm. 5 as a later addition to the chultun. In keeping with this, the walls and ceiling of Chm. 5 are not demarcated from one another as they are in Chm. 1, 2, and 3. This could be because Chm. 5 was not part of the same construction. In this respect, Chm. 4 and 5 resemble one another.

Putting this all together, the following scenario seems reasonable. As originally constructed (Ch. 2F-5-2nd), the chultun consisted of an antechamber (Chm. 1) and two deeper chambers (Chm. 2 and 3). Thus, it was constructed in three stages, for Chm. 2 could not be dug until Chm. 1 was essentially complete, or 3 before 2. Flooding was not expected to be a problem, and so no sills were constructed. The slope of the floor of Chm. 1 away from the entrance to Chm. 2 was expected to be sufficient to handle any water problems, or this may have been the first of a number of modifications of the chultun.

The predictions of the designers of the chultun apparently went awry, for a serious water problem did develop. To cope with this, alterations were made that produced Ch. 2F-5-1st-B. Chamber 2 was "written off" as a dry chamber, and Chm. 5 was added to drain off the water that ran through it. To insure that Chm. 3 remained dry, a sill in its entrance was also constructed. Alternatively, perhaps the sill was constructed first, but was insufficient to handle the water problem. Finally, Chm. 4 was constructed as a "dry" replacement for the "wet" Chm. 2. Perhaps as part of these alterations, the ceiling of Chm. 3 was altered so as to be higher than that of Chm. 2, to guard against water dripping into it. Two or three construction stages might be defined for these alternations, but since their precise sequence is not known, such stages have not been defined.

After some use of the modified chultun, U. 5 was placed in Chm. 5, probably to promote better drainage (Ch. 2F-5-1st-A). No other purposeful modifications of the chultun are known.

SHERDS AND ARTIFACTS

Lot groups for Ch. 2F-5 are defined in Table 2.116, with content listed in Table 2.117.

CHULTUN FILL

There is little to say about the sherds and artifacts. First, all the chultun contents were lumped together into one lot (now LG. 1). Second, all the material was subsequently lost. The excavator's field notes speak of a number of large sherds found lying on or near the floor of the chultun, especially U. 7, and on or near U. 5. This sounds very much like miscellaneous occupation debris. Unit 3 produced a few very small sherds, and a few pieces of chert and obsidian artifacts. These probably washed into the chultun from the nearby ground surface. Prior to their loss, the sherds were examined by R. E. W. Adams in 1958, who identified them as "Chicanel appearing pottery." Undoubtedly, the chultun was constructed and used when Cauac and/or Chuen pottery was in vogue. Just when it was filled remains a problem. Adams's evaluation suggests the presence of nothing later than Preclassic sherds. Yet Classic sherds are consistently present in collections made nearby (see below).

OTHER SOURCES

No sherds or artifacts have been collected in the immediate vicinity of Ch. 2F-5. Chultun 2F-5, however, is a mere 25 m NE of another chultun, 2F-6. This, in turn, is 17 m S of Ch. 2F-17, and this chultun is 27 m from Ch. 2F-5. It is possible, although conjectural, that these chultuns all relate to a single group of structures for which there is now no visible surface indication. Certainly, they are close enough to one another (see Fig. 10) for this to

be the case. The other possibility is that Ch. 2F-5 was associated with a structure or structures to the E. At any rate, collections of sherds and artifacts have been made by the other two chultuns, and because these collections may say something about structures related to Ch. 2F-5, they are treated here as lot groups of it (LG. 2, 3, and 4). If Adams's evaluation of LG. 1 is correct, these lot groups contain consistently later material, even though Preclassic sherds are abundant. The material is probably a scatter of occupation debris.

TIME SPANS

The above discussion results in definition of TS. 8–3 in Table 2.118. The material in LG. 1 (Table 2.116), composed of occupation debris as well as fill, reasonably indicates that the chultun was built and used in Preclassic times—just how early is not clear. Although the earliest construction in nearby Gp. 2F-1 came a bit before 350 BC, when Chuen ceramics appeared, there is nothing to indicate activity nearer Ch. 2F-5 prior to that date (Table 2.116).

Just when the chultun was abandoned is not clear (TS. 2). So far as is known, none of the sherds in LG. 1 postdate the Late Preclassic. This, though, need mean no more than that material used to fill the chultun contained no later sherds, and those included in the fill could have been quite old at the time. In fact, LG. 2–4 (Table 2.116) indicate an occupation nearby into Early Classic times (the few Ik and/or Imix sherds may only indicate that people passed by occasionally after abandonment, as they did near Str. 2G-61). On the other hand, Preclassic sherds in occupation debris no earlier than TS. 3, beneath the fill, suggest abandonment before the appearance of Manik ceramics (ca. AD 250). On the basis of LG. 2, 3, and 4, therefore, Ch. 2F-5 was abandoned before any potentially related structure or structures. Alternatively, it is unrelated to the material to the W, and a structure or structures E of Ch. 2F-5 were also abandoned in Preclassic times. If the former sequence is accurate, Ch. 2F-6 and 17 could have replaced Ch. 2F-5. If the latter, they could be equally old. Only further excavation could resolve these matters.

Chultun 2F-5 may not have been filled upon abandonment, but rather after passage of considerable time. This was the view of Puleston, and it would require that TS. 2 be divided into two time spans. As outlined above, however, there are problems with this interpretation. Because of these, and because no post-Preclassic sherds are known from the chultun itself, the interpretation followed here is that the chultun was filled upon abandonment. Thus, TS. 1 covers subsequent settling of that fill.

TABLE 2.116
Chultun 2F-5: Lot Groups

Lot Group	Lot	Provenience	Ceramic Evaluation
1	Op. 16A (lost)	Chultun fill	Preclassic
2	118A/1A	Test pit covering 25 m^2 3.50 m S and 21.50 m W of Ch. 2F-5 (2 m N of Ch. 2F-6). Surface to bedrock	Classic?
3	118A/2A-C	Test pit covering 43 m^2 4.25 m N and and 25 m W of Ch. 2F-5, surface to bedrock above Ch. 2F-17	Mostly Preclassic (Chuen, Cauac); a few Manik and Ik and/or Imix
4	1P/7	Surface collection E of Ch. 4F-6	Late Preclassic, Manik, some Ik and/or Imix

TABLE 2.117
Chultun 2F-5: Artifacts by Lot Group

Study Category	Object	Lot Group			
		1*	2	3	4
Pottery Vessels	Sherds per cubic meters (lbs)	?	.20	.57	?
Flaked Chert Artifacts	Flake core			1	
	Ovate bifaces			2	
	Elongate biface			1	
	Used flakes			10	
	Unused flakes			2	
Flaked Obsidian Artifacts	Prismatic blades			8	
Ground, Pecked, and Polished Stone Artifacts	Manos			2	
	Hammer stone			1	

*Material lost

TABLE 2.118
Chultun 2F-5: Time Spans

Time Span	Architectural Development	Construction Stage	Chamber	Unit	Descriptive Data	Lot Group	Ceramics in Vogue
1				1,2	Settling of fill into deeper chambers and buildup of humus in neck	2-4	Imix
							Ik
							Manik
2				3,9?	Chultun abandoned and purposely filled (perhaps with a substantial period of time between)	1	Cauac?
3				4,9?	Use		
4	Ch. 2F-5-1st-A	1		5	Final modification of chultun		
5				6	Use		
6	Ch. 2F-5-1st-B	None defined	4,5	8	Construction of new chambers and sill		
7					Use		
8	Ch. 2F-5-2nd	1	3		Construction of second inner chamber		Chuen?
		2	2	7	Construction of first inner chamber		
		3	1		Construction of antechamber		

Chultuns 3F-4 and 3F-5

These chultuns are located together in Sq. 3F of the site map at S215 E266 (Ch. 3F-4) and S220 E265 (Ch. 3F-5). They are on the same ridge as Gp. 3F-1, 2, and 3 (this report); Gp. 3F-1 is 18 m SW, and Gp. 3F-3 is 34 m NE of these chultuns. Their positions alone do not necessarily indicate the nearby presence of unmapped structures, for they could easily have been used by people living in either Gp. 3F-1 or 3. Chultun 3F-4 was partially excavated as

Op. 72L, and Ch. 3F-5 almost wholly excavated as Op. 72M by Puleston in 1965.

CHULTUN 3F-4

DESCRIPTION

Excavations (Fig. 60a,b) were sufficient to show that this chultun falls somewhere between the classic "bottle-shaped" and cylindrical (TR. 32). The unusually large orifice, nearly circular, was not provided with a stepped rim, nor was any stone cover found. Below the orifice, the neck is nearly vertical to a point approximately 0.60 m below the surface. At this point, where bedrock is softer than it is above, the sides begin to flare out. This flare is related both to erosion and the way the chultun was constructed. One possible posthole was noted on the surface just E of the orifice (not shown in Fig. 60a). For average dimensions, see Table 2.119.

DISCUSSION

As it was not excavated all the way to the floor, one cannot be certain if the chultun fill is just like that in the similarly shaped, nearby Ch. 3F-5 (see below). Nor is it known whether or not the chultun was purposely filled. The presence of just a few sherds in fill excavated to a depth of 0.90 m at least rules out purposeful fill from convenient trash deposits, as were used in the case of Ch. 2G-10 (in Gp. 2G-2, this report). In the absence of any indications to the contrary, it is assumed that this chultun was used for the same purposes as Ch. 3F-5 (see below).

CHULTUN 3F-5

DESCRIPTION

This chultun is virtually identical to Ch. 3F-4 (Fig. 60c,d and Table 2.120). Again, there is no evidence of a stepped rim, or stone cover. The orifice is unusually large, opening into a neck that is not clearly distinguishable from the chamber itself. Although the lower part of the chultun is now extensively eroded, the walls do appear to have bowed out slightly, providing a roughly oval chamber slightly larger than the neck. In the floor of the chamber is a small oval pit (U. 1), slightly W of the center of the floor.

DISCUSSION

As found, Ch. 3F-5 was filled with earth. At the top, it consists of humus, but this grades down into gray, limestone-flecked soil to yellowish-brown earth below. The fill probably is the result of erosion of the sides of the chultun, coupled with earth washed in from the ground surface. If this happened, one would expect to find leaf-mold near the top, and the limy material concentrated towards the bottom.

Beneath the fill is a stratum of very fine soil (U. 2), brownish gray in color, quite different from the deposit above. Most likely, this represents silting up of the chultun prior to any marked erosion of the walls or washing in of humus. This possibly took place in whole or in part when the chultun was in use. Consistent with this, U. 2 includes a relatively large number of sherds, not like those from the debris above U. 2. Since these are well mixed into the stratum, they can best be explained as the result of occupation debris being trampled into U. 2 during use of the chultun. After a period of time, the chultun walls began to erode, and humus had built up sufficiently to begin to wash into the chultun. This interpretation is favored, given the lack of a sharp break between U. 2 and the debris above.

There is some question as to whether or not this

TABLE 2.119
Chultun 3F-4: Average Dimensions (meters)

Feature	Length	Width	Height	Minimum Diameter	Maximum Diameter
Neck	-----	-----	0.60	0.74	0.80
Chamber	1.40	1.20	?	---	----

TABLE 2.120
Chultun 3F-5: Average Dimensions (meters)

Feature	Length	Width	Height	Minimum Diameter	Maximum Diameter
Neck	----	----	0.60	0.72	0.78
Chamber	1.50	1.10	2.10	---	---
Unit 1	0.56	0.49	0.12	---	---

chultun (and Ch. 3F-4) was ever provided with a cover. The large size of the orifice, which would have required a very large (and heavy) stone cover, lack of a stepped rim, and the presence of silt in the chultun hints that it was uncovered. On the other hand, some sort of roofed shelter could have kept water out of the chultun until after abandonment. Note that there was a posthole on the surface near the orifice of the very similar Ch. 3F-4.

The function of U. 1 remains enigmatic. It seems much too small to have been an effective drain.

SHERDS AND ARTIFACTS

Lot groups for the two chultuns are defined in Table 2.121, with content in Tables 2.122 and 2.123.

FILL

This material, not abundant in any case, appears for the most part to have washed into the chultuns from the surrounding area. Given this, the temporal mixture displayed by the sherds is scarcely surprising. Presumably,

TABLE 2.121
Chultuns 3F-4 and 3F-5: Lot Groups

Feature	Lot Group	Lot	Provenience	Ceramic Evaluation
Ch. 3F-4 (Op. 72L)	1	None	Surface around orifice	No data
	2	1,2	Chultun fill	Ik and/or Imix, possible Preclassic
Ch. 3F-5 (Op. 72M)	1	None	Surface around orifice	No data
	2	1-3	Chultun fill down to U. 2	Manik, Ik, and Imix
	3	4	In U. 2	Imix

TABLE 2.122
Chultun 3F-4: Artifacts by Lot Group

Study Category	Object	Lot Group	
		1	2
Pottery Vessels	Sherds per cubic meter (lbs)	few	.5

TABLE 2.123
Chultun 3F-5: Artifacts by Lot Group

Study Category	Object	Lot Group		
		1	2	3
Pottery Vessels	Sherds per cubic meter (lbs)	--	.7	2.0
Chert Flaked Artifacts	Unmodified flakes		2	
Flaked Obsidian Artifacts	Prismatic blade		1	

they represent periodic cast-offs by the occupants of a number of different structures in the area, including those of Gp. 3F-1 and 3.

As noted above, the material from Ch. 3F-5:U. 2 may have been left in the chultun upon abandonment. Consistent with this, the sherds (LG. 3) are not temporally mixed as are those above. They are also more abundant, suggesting a different derivation. These sherds, then, should help date the chultun, and might also help indicate something about the people who used it.

SURFACE MATERIAL

No cultural material was found in the very small excavations around the chultuns. This is not surprising, given the small quantities of material in the chultuns (excepting Ch. 3F-5:LG. 3), and given the interpretation of the origin of that material.

TIME SPANS

Time spans for these chultuns are listed in Tables 2.124 and 2.125. There is little to say about them. The similarity of shape might suggest their contemporaneity, but this is tenuous. They might be of the same shape because they served the same function, but one could have been a replacement for the other. The Imix sherds over the floor of 3F-5, in a silty deposit (Table 2.121), probably date the use of this chultun. Since the rest of the sherds likely washed in from the surrounding area, they may have nothing to do with the time of construction or use of the chultuns. Worth noting here is that Preclassic sherds (as probably occur in Ch. 3F-4) are found in Gp. 3F-1, Early Classic sherds (as found in Ch. 3F-5) in Gp. 3F-3, and Ik and/or Imix sherds (both chultuns) in both groups.

TABLE 2.124
Chultun 3F-4: Time Spans

Time Span	Descriptive Data	Lot Group	Ceramics in Vogue
1	Chultun filled, probably naturally	1,2	
2	Use		?
3	Construction		

TABLE 2.125
Chultun 3F-5: Time Spans

Time Span	Unit	Descriptive Data	Lot Group	Ceramics in Vogue
1	2	Natural filling of chultun following abandonment	1,2	
2		Use	3	Imix
3	1	Construction		?

Group 2G-3

Group 2G-3 is located about 30 m NW of Gp. 2G-1 and 50 m E of Ch. 2G-1 and 2G-2 (Table 2.126). Included are six structures, 2G-50 through 55, all but two of which are situated on a raised platform. Structure 2G-50, the largest, appears to be a small, range-type building. Small, square Str. 2G-52 and 53 might perhaps have been household shrines (TR. 21). The other structures seem to be small rectangular platforms, suitable for house foundations.

A single surface collection (Table 2.127) produced a large number of sherds, as well as chert chipping waste. The material could be domestic refuse (TR. 20B). The ceramic data indicate an occupation between AD 550 and 869. An absence of Manik sherds reflects a lack of earlier occupation, and two Preclassic sherds probably relate to heavy Preclassic occupation to the E (see below).

STRUCTURE 2G-48

This small structure sits alone on the W edge of a small plaza 120 m N of Ch. 2G-1 and 2G-2. It has the appearance of a rectangular platform, comparable to known house foundations at Tikal. A surface collection that produced numerous sherds probably consists for the most part of rooted-out structure fill. A test pit (Table 2.126) was dug to the W of the structure, and appears to have sampled a trash deposit, with perhaps some fill admixture. The ceramic data (Table 2.127) indicate an occupation that began when Ik ceramics were present, and lasted through the time when Imix ceramics were in vogue. A small amount of Chuen and Manik material in Level 2 of the test pit appears to be somewhat out of context, and probably is redeposited fill. This earlier ceramic material may well have come originally from the Preclassic and Early Classic occupation to the S and W.

"VACANT TERRAIN"

The remaining surface collections and test pit from the Encanto Quadrangle (Table 2.126) are best discussed together. The surface collections may be expected to be biased somewhat on the late side, since earlier material tends to be deeper. Therefore, it seems significant that Preclassic sherds are so prominent in the collections. Thus, the ceramic data (Table 2.127) suggest a heavy Preclassic occupation around Ch. 2F-2, 4, and perhaps 2F-3, as well as in the area N and S of Ch. 2G-1 and 2. Indeed, this has been verified in two instances by the discovery of Str. 2G-61, 62, and Gp. 2F-1. The remains of other structures would probably be found in proximity to Ch. 2F-2 through 2F-6. By analogy with Str. 2G-61 and 62, this occupation probably began in the era of Chuen ceramic production, although occupation of Gp. 2F-1 began slightly earlier. This gains some slight support by the presence of Chuen ceramics in two surface lots (1P/9 and 1P/15).

As in the case of Str. 2G-61, the occupation appears to have lasted into Early Classic times. Manik ceramics are not as widespread as Preclassic ceramics, but are found NW of Str. 2G-61 and beyond St. 27, SE as far as Gp. 2G-1, and N almost to Str. 2G-48. There was probable abandonment of most early structures and associated chultuns part way through Early Classic times (as in the case of Str. 2G-61), followed by the first occupation of some of the visible mound groups, such as Gp. 2G-1.

Ik and/or Imix ceramic material, although heavy around visible structures, appears to be light where there are no visible ruins. Such sherds found in these instances are probably analogous to those from around Str. 2G-61.

TABLE 2.126
Locations of Test Pits and Surface Collections:
Encanto Quadrangle

Group	Collection	Location
2G-3	1P/2	W of Str. 2G-48
——	1P/12	Str. 2G-48
——	69B	W of Str. 2G-48 (test pit)
——	1P/8	by Ch. 2F-3
——	1P/9	by Ch. 2F-4
——	1P/15	by Ch. 2F-2
——	1P/10	Sq. 2G: 208 m N, 24 m E
——	1P/11	Sq. 2G: 206 m N, 107 m E
——	1P/20	Sq. 2G: 198 m N, 62 m E
——	1P/3	Sq. 2G: 144 m N, 30 m E
——	69A	Sq. 2G: 124 m N, 64 m E
——	1P/1	Sq. 2G: 124 m N, 84 m E
——	1P/4	Sq. 2G: 54 m N, 88 m E

TABLE 2.127
Ceramic Evaluation: Encanto Test Pits and Surface Collections

Group	Lot	Provenience	Ceramics
2G-3	1P/2	Surface	Ik, Imix, 2 possible Late preclassic
___	1P/12	Surface	Late Preclassic, Ik, Imix
___	69B/1		Imix; some Ik
___	69B/2		Ik-Imix transition, some Manik, 1 Chuen
___	69B/3		Mostly Ik
___	1P/8	Surface	Mostly Ik and/or Imix
___	1P/9	Surface	Late Preclassic, including possible Chuen
___	1P/15	Surface	Late Preclassic, including Chuen
___			Late Preclassic; Manik; Ik and/or Imix
___	1P/10	Surface	Late Preclassic
___	1P/11	Surface	Late Preclassic; Manik; Ik and/or Imix
___	1P/20	Surface	Late Preclassic
___	1P/3	Surface	Late Preclassic; Manik; Ik and/or Imix
___	69A/1	0-38 cm	?
___	69A/2	38-52 cm	Late Preclassic
___	1P/1	Surface	Manik; Ik and/or Imix
___	1P/4	Surface	Mostly Preclassic

4. Excavations in the Temple IV Quadrangle

Introduction

Architecturally, the mapped small structures of this quadrangle are known only for Gp. 5B-2 (below). With respect to chronology, there is somewhat more information. A total of 13 test pits sampled material from 9 different groups of small structures. In addition, excavation of Ch. 5B-11 provided some information on Gp. 5B-3. The 118 mapped small structures of this quadrangle are arranged into groups that total about 39 in all, and so the sample is 28% of these.

Much attention in this quadrangle was devoted to terrain on which no structure ruins were visible. The result was discovery of Gp. 5C-3, S of Temple IV, and Str. 5C-56 and 57 by Ch. 5C-5. One other chultun (5C-6) may be associated with similar structures.

Group 5B-2

Group 5B-2 is located in Sq. 5B of the site map (TR. 11) at S57 E470. As mapped in 1959, it includes two structures: 5B-6 on the N side of a plaza (Plat. 5B-2), and 5B-7 on the W side of the plaza. The terrain here slopes downward slightly to the W. A mere 80 m to the E, on higher ground, sits Temple IV (Str. 5C-4). Excavations by Haviland as Op. 67L in July 1963 sought data on final plan (Fig. 64) and sequence for both structures.

STRUCTURE 5B-6-2ND

Construction began (CS. 4) as fill of dark gray earth (U. 1) was piled up on the exposed surface of bedrock (Fig. 61b). The first course of masonry for the N wall was set in place concurrently on U. 1, which had reached a depth of some 0.20 m. More fill was dumped S of the wall until it reached the level of the top of the masonry. The fill continued at this level S of what was to be the location of the front wall of the structure, revealing that the level for Plat. 5B-2 was built up at the same time these operations took place.

The next step (CS. 3) was to build the back wall higher, although none of this masonry has survived the ravages of time. Apparently it served to retain a fill of small pebbles that extended S into the plaza. Unit 2 (Fig. 61b), a deposit of marl in this fill, marks the pause-line for this stage. It is close to the elevation of the plaza surface, and it was above this level, apparently, that the structure itself was built.

As the fill was built up, a S wall for the structure was assembled on it, and more fill was dumped behind this (CS. 2). Finally, a floor (Fl. 1 of 2nd) was laid over it. A plaza floor (Str. 5B-6:U. 3) was laid on the same fill in front of the structure, to turn up to the platform wall (see Fig. 61).

A final stage (CS. 1) is assumed for construction of a building of perishable materials. There is no direct evidence for this, but the corners were not searched for post-holes. Since the fill is so deep above bedrock, experience indicates that it would be unlikely for evidence of post-holes to have survived, although it is known that some similar platforms did support buildings of perishable materials (TR. 20B).

STRUCTURE 5B-6-1ST

Eventually, an upper level was added to the platform (Fig. 61). This would have required at least partial demolition of any existing building, and it is this that defines CS. 3. A front wall was then built on the floor of 2nd for the upper level, at which time the height of the rear wall must have been increased. The old pavement may have continued in use in front of the upper level. Another floor that no longer survives must have paved over the earth fill of the upper level (CS. 2). Finally, it is assumed that a building of perishable materials was rebuilt (CS. 1).

STRUCTURE 5B-7-2ND

Construction of the earliest version of this structure (Fig. 62, 63) may be divided into at least four stages. The earliest (CS. 4) saw assembly of the lowest course of what was to be the W wall. This was set directly on bedrock, about 0.80 m E of a vertically quarried bedrock face. East of the masonry, a fill was dumped (U. 1) that consists of small pebbles quite similar to those used for CS. 2 of Str. 5B-6-2nd. The excavations penetrated only the top of this layer, which appears to continue into the plaza.

As CS. 3, the back wall was increased in height. A fill of gray earth, containing some small stones and trash, was dumped on top of U. 1. This fill, too, continues out into the plaza. Units 2 and 3, pause-lines from this operation, are close in elevation to that of the plaza floor. Thus, fill was built up to the plaza level, at which point the structure itself was erected.

The structure platform was built as CS. 2. A floor (U. 4) abuts the front wall and served as a plaza surface. Structure 5B-7-2nd:Fl. 1 was laid over the platform fill (which was of the same material used for CS. 3). This abuts a line of stones 0.34 m inside the back wall. These apparently represent the inner face of a low masonry dwarf wall along the back of the structure. The presence of such a dwarf wall implies that there was an upper wall of perishable materials, and that a building was based on the platform. Construction of this building defines CS. 1.

STRUCTURE 5B-7-1ST-B

Eventually Str. 5B-7, like 5B-6, was converted to a two-level building platform (Fig. 62, 63). The existing building must have been extensively demolished, and the rear wall increased in height. A front wall, badly preserved, was placed directly on the floor for 2nd. A fill of earth, trash, and stones was placed within the walls, and presumably paved over by a floor, no trace of which survives. The older floor may have continued in use in front of the upper platform level. Finally, the building must have been rebuilt. All of these operations would have taken place as a sequence of three construction stages.

STRUCTURE 5B-7-1ST-A

The significance of U. 5 (Fig. 62) is not known. This is a wall that runs E-W in the S side of the trench excavated through the front-rear axis of the structure. It was built on the level of floor for 2nd (this no longer survives here), and it abuts the front of the wall for the upper platform level. Presumably it represents some sort of modification of 1st, but without more excavation this must be taken as tentative.

QUARRYING ACTIVITY

A bedrock quarry was discovered during excavation W of Str. 5B-7. About 0.80 m W of the structure is a vertically quarried face (Fig. 62 and 63:6) that is 0.57 m high in the N side of the axial trench. In the S side, however, this continues down 1.97 m into a pit. A portion of this pit was excavated in 0.20-m levels. Its upper part was filled with gray earth, the lower 0.90 m with darker earth, containing many large blocks of masonry similar to a block found in the N part of the axial trench. Problematical Deposit 110 was in the very bottom of the pit. The pit seems to have been filled all at one time, as sherds from the top are no later than those at the bottom.

It seems that the vertical quarried face was exposed when Str. 5B-7 was in use, though probably the pit itself was filled. Bedrock E of the face is quite level, and the face itself parallels the structure wall. Perhaps the face was quarried concurrent with construction of 5B-7. More likely, though, it was connected with nearby construction of the huge Str. 5C-4. For this, existing structures may have been razed (see "Time Spans," below). Structure 5B-7 was built soon afterward, for apparently there had been no accumulation of debris over the bedrock surfaces. If this is correct, 5B-7 capitalized on the prior existence of the N-S quarried bedrock face.

SHERDS AND ARTIFACTS

Table 2.128 defines lot groups for Gp. 5B-2, while content is given in Tables 2.129 and 2.130.

CONSTRUCTION FILL

Here, the only fully sealed deposit is Str. 5B-7:LG. 1a, from fill of 2nd. Other fill lots are only partially sealed at best, so contamination from later material is always a possibility. Nonetheless, this does not appear to be much of a problem, for there is fair consistency of samples from one source to another.

One feature of almost all fill lot groups is the inclusion of numerous Manik sherds that predate known construction here. These sherds were not brought from any great distance, to judge from the material in the quarry behind Str. 5B-7 (see below). Evidently, trash and fill from an earlier structure (or structures) that had been razed was reused in the later construction. Similarly, trash from occupation of Str. 5B-6-2nd and 7-2nd may well have been the source of fill for the later versions of these structures. The sherds and artifacts do not differ significantly in character from those in Str. 5B-6:LG. 3 or 5B-7:LG. 4, both from above living levels, and both of which contain a mixture of Manik and Imix sherds.

MATERIAL ABOVE LIVING LEVELS

In Gp. 5B-2, Str. 5B-6:LG. 3 and 5B-7:LG. 4 are most likely to include late occupation debris. Comparison with material from the structure fills, however, indicates that both are heavily contaminated by material that spilled from the structure platforms as masonry collapsed.

TABLE 2.128
Group 5B-2: Lot Groups

Feature	Lot Group	Lot	Provenience	Ceramic Evaluation
Str. 5B-6 (Op. 67L)	1a	5,21, 22	Partially sealed fill of 2nd	Manik and Imix
	1b	3	Unsealed fill of 2nd	Manik and Imix
	2	4	Unsealed fill of 1st	Imix
	3	2	N of structure, surface to base of wall	Manik and Ik and/or Imix
Str. 5B-7 (Op. 67L)	1a	24	Sealed fill of 2nd	Manik and Imix
	1b	1	Unsealed fill of 2nd and 1st	Manik and Imix
	2	6,7,23	Unsealed fill of 1st	Much Manik, some Imix
	3a	10-14	Upper fill, pit W of structure	Eb, Chuen or Cauac, middle Manik
	3b	15-20	Lower 0.90 m of pit W of structure	Middle Manik
	4	8,9	W of structure, surface to bedrock	Manik and Imix

TABLE 2.129
Structure 5B-6: Artifacts by Lot Group

Study Category	Object	Lot Group 1a	1b	2	3
Pottery Vessels	Sherds per cubic meter (lbs)	Not recorded			
Other Pottery Artifacts	Figurine	1			
Flaked Chert Artifacts	Elongate biface				1
	Thin bifaces	1	1		
	Unidentifiable bifaces	3			
	Retouched flake		1		
	Used flakes	3			
	Unused flake	1			
Flaked Obsidian Artifacts	Thin biface	1			
	Prismatic blade	1			
	Used flake	1			
Ground, Pecked, and Polished Stone Artifacts	Manos	2			
	Metate	1			
	Rubbing stone			1	
	Hammer stones		1		1
	Unmodified pumice	1			
Shell and Bone Artifacts	Worked bone, gouge?	1			
	Unworked bone	1			

TABLE 2.130
Structure 5B-7: Artifacts by Lot Group

Study Category	Object	Lot Group 1a	1b	2	3a	3b	4
Pottery Vessels	Sherds per cubic meter(lbs)	Not recorded					
Other Pottery Artifacts	Figurines		2				1
Flaked Chert Artifacts	Elongate biface					1	
	Thin biface		1				
	Used flakes		1			1	2
	Unused flakes		3		3	6	4
Flaked Obsidian Artifacts	Thin bifaces	1	1				
	Prismatic blade		1				
	Used flake		1				
Ground, Pecked and Polished Stone Artifacts	Metate						1
	Rubbing Stone		1				
Shell and Bone Artifacts	Unworked animal bone						1
	Unworked human longbone scrap						1

OTHER SOURCES

Material from the deep quarry behind Str. 5B-7 was subdivided into LG. 3a and 3b, but there is no real difference between them. The abundant sherds are all middle Manik, except for a few Cauac, Chuen, and Eb pieces. Evidently, the quarry was filled all at once, undoubtedly with material from nearby, which must have been from the use of structures now unknown. Masonry blocks in the quarry are probably from the walls of these structures. For other content, see PD. 110 (section III).

TIME SPANS

Stratigraphy, combined with the ceramic information contained in Table 2.128, allows definition of the time spans of Tables 2.131 and 2.132; these are correlated in Table 2.133. That both Str. 5B-6-2nd and 5B-7-2nd were built at the same time is clearly evident (Gp. TS. 7). Both were built on bedrock as part of the same operation that produced a raised plaza surface in front of the structures. Traces of no more than a single plaza floor can be found in front of each structure, implying that there was but a single pavement that turned up to both. The sequence of construction stages is the same for each structure, and the fill material of 7-2nd:CS. 4 is identical to, and was probably drawn from the same source, as that for CS. 2 and 3 of 6-2nd. Finally, sherd material from the fills of both

structures is contemporaneous (Table 2.128).

Both structures seem to have been abandoned at about the same time. This (along with their original, contemporaneous construction) suggests that Str. 5B-7 underwent major alteration at about the same time as did 5B-6 (Gp. TS. 5). This latter structure seems not to have been altered again, whereas 5B-7 probably underwent one more minor alteration (Gp. TS. 3 and Fig. 64). Unfortunately, there is no way to verify this proposed correlation of 6-1st with 7-1st-B, for the total use-span of Gp. 5B-2 was not long, nor are there really good ceramic samples from the late fills. Nevertheless, this scheme seems reasonable. Group TS. 9 is defined for the quarrying behind Str. 5B-7. This clearly preceded 7-2nd by some time, or one would expect to find at least a few late Manik or Ik sherds here as in the structure fill. The abundance of Manik sherds implies that earlier structures once stood at this locus, but were razed, perhaps to permit extensive quarrying.

To sum up, then, the known architecture of Gp. 5B-2 dates from sometime after about AD 700 (when Imix ceramic production began). The group was abandoned by about AD 869, prior to appearance of Eznab ceramics. There seems to have been an earlier occupation of the locus sometime between AD 250 and 550, the dates for the Manik Ceramic Complex. The Preclassic sherds are so few in number that an earlier occupation is not necessarily indicated.

TABLE 2.131
Structure 5B-6: Time Spans

Time Span	Architectural Development	Construction Stage	Floor	Unit	Descriptive Data	Lot Group		Ceramics in Vogue
1					Abandonment and collapse			
2					Use		3	
3	Str.5B-6-1st	1			Reconstruction of building of perishable materials		2	
		2			Construction of upper platform level			
		3			Partial or total demolition of existing building			
4					Use			Imix
5	Str.5B-6-2nd	1			Construction of building of perishable materials	1a, 1b		
		2	1	3	Construction of platform			
		3		2	Fill raised to plaza level			
		4			First fill operation			
6					Hiatus			Ik
7					Early activity			Manik

TABLE 2.132
Structure 5B-7: Time Spans

Time Span	Architectural Development	Construction Stage	Floor	Unit	Special Deposits: Problematical Deposit	Descriptive Data	Lot Group		Ceramics in Vogue
1						Abandonment and collapse		4	
2						Use			
3	Str. 5B-7-1st-A	None defined				Modification of 1st			
4						Use			
5	Str. 5B-7-1st-B	1				Construction of building of perishable materials			
		2				Construction of upper platform level	1b	2	Imix
		3				Partial or total demolition of existing building			
6						Use			
7	Str. 5B-7-2nd	1				Construction of building of perishable materials			
		2	2	4		Construction of platform	1a	3a,3b	
		3		2,3		Fill raised to plaza level			
		4		1		First fill operation			
									Ik
8						Hiatus			
9					110	Quarrying			
10						Early activity			Manik

TABLE 2.133
Group 5B-2: Time Spans

Group Time Span	Structure 5B-6 (Table 2.131)	Structure 5B-7 (Table 2.132)
1	1	1
2		2
3		3
4	2	4
5	3	5
6	4	6
7	5	7
8	6	8
9		9
10	7	10

Group 5C-3

Group 5C-3 is known only from a single platform (Plat. 5C-4), and its large size suggests that one or more contemporary structures were built upon it. In support of this are a few slim bits of evidence for the existence of two such structures. Consequently, a formal group designation is used here.

The group is located in Sq. 5C of the site map (TR. 11), at S450 E140, or about 330 m S of Temple IV (Str. 5C-4). There is absolutely no visible structure ruin or chultun in the area. The nearest visible ruin is Str. 5C-55, some 85 m E; the nearest chultun, 5C-6, is 135 m N. Yet the terrain seems well suited for ancient habitation. The ground is high, well drained, and slopes gently down to the S. In 1966, Bronson chose an area of 5,000 m² (extending down into Sq. 6c) in which to dig a number of test pits. A grid of 10 m intervals was set up and 66 pits were dug (as Op. 121A) at the intersections of grid lines (Fig. 65). In four of these pits, poorly preserved plaster fragments were found. Therefore, the excavations were expanded (as Op. 121B) to seek other traces of construction. It was not possible, however, to clear enough of the construction to reveal complete details of plan.

PLATFORM 5C-4-2ND

Four units (U. 1 through 4) are assigned to this architectural development (Fig. 66, 67), although U. 4 may

have been built earlier than the others. Unit 1 is a linear arrangement of poorly cut stones based in a loose, red-brown earth fill (U. 2). Since this fill rises to the same elevation as the top of U. 1 on its N side, U. 1 is interpreted as the S wall for a platform (Table 2.134), with U. 2 serving as fill N of the wall, and an unpaved occupation surface to the S. Units 1 and 2 are, therefore, contemporary; the area was filled to the desired level, the wall masonry set in place, and more fill dumped behind it.

Unit 1 runs a total distance of 22 m E-W. Its W end is unknown, but the eastern one turns an approximate right angle to extend N. The wall was not followed farther by excavation. The fill, U. 2, lies in part on bedrock, in part on light, tan-colored silt in low areas of bedrock, and in part on hard, dark-colored silt. About 3.50 m N of U. 1, the dark-colored silt rises to the same elevation as U. 2, which ends here. The break is indistinct, but it looks as if U. 2 was laid up against the older stratum, which seems to have been sufficiently high so that artificial fill was not needed.

Unit 3 is a wall that was seen in excavation by the W end of U. 1. This, again, appears as a line of stones, which runs N an unknown distance from the E-W wall. It may have been associated with a structure built near the end of Plat. 5C-4-2nd.

Unit 4 is a mass of masonry about 7 m W, and 6.50 m N, of the E and S walls of Plat. 5C-4-2nd. It rests on the surface of the hard, dark silt against which U. 2 was dumped, just N of U. 2. Thus it probably was in use with U. 1, though the possibility exists that it was built before U. 1 and 2 and, therefore, Plat. 5C-4-2nd. Like U. 3 it may also be the remnant of a structure.

PLATFORM 5C-4-1ST

Platform 5C-4 was modified so as to increase its extent at least on the E and S (Table 2.134). The walls for this new platform are U. 5 and 6 (the E wall; Fig. 66, 67). It was constructed of two courses, probably in a manner similar to U. 6 (see below). It rests on a fill of earth and stones. A brown earth fill was placed behind it, and plaster Fl. 1 was laid across the top.

Unit 6 was seen in only one trench at the W end of the excavation. It was constructed of a lower course of stretcher stones, and an upper course of headers. Behind is the same brown fill as that behind U. 5, and it is covered by the same Fl. 1. There is no doubt, then, that this represents the W end of the platform.

Fragments of Fl. 1 can be followed E for a distance of close to 50 m and perhaps farther (not known is where the eastern end of the platform lies). To the N, Fl. 1 can be seen in one place to turn up to high bedrock some 12.50 m from the S wall. This would seem to represent the width of Plat. 5C-4-1st. The floor covered the earlier U. 1,

TABLE 2.134
Platform 5C-4: Average Dimensions (meters)

Feature	Length	Width	Height
Platform 5C-4-2nd	?	?	0.12
Platform 5C-4-1st	?	14	0.30

3, and 4, and was laid around U. 7, which is possibly a wall. Its stones are in the vicinity of U. 4, suggesting that, if U. 4 represents the remains of a structure, U. 7 represents its modification.

Unit 8 is a line of stones near the W end of the platform, on Fl. 1. It probably is part of a wall, and suggests renovation of a structure represented earlier by U. 3. This interpretation is tentative, however, in view of the scant evidence available.

QUARRYING ACTIVITY

Clearing to bedrock almost everywhere in the test area revealed that it had been quarried. Some of this preceded construction of Plat. 5C-4, since this was undisturbed above quarry marks in some places. Towards the W, however, U. 1 and 5 were removed by the Maya and there is evidence of quarrying. Here the structure was obviously disturbed by the activities of quarrymen.

SHERDS AND ARTIFACTS

Table 2.135 lists lot groups for Plat. 5C-4, with distribution of sherds and artifacts in Table 2.136.

CONSTRUCTION FILL

In the present instance, cultural material is almost nonexistent. This is not surprising in the case of LG. 1, for there may not have been readily available trash to use as fill for the earliest construction. It is somewhat surprising in the case of LG. 2, as the most likely source of fill in this case should be earliest occupation material.

MATERIAL ABOVE LIVING LEVELS

The only apparent undisturbed deposit is LG. 3a, which on stratigraphic grounds relates to Plat. 5C-4-1st. This deposit shows a number of deposition lines illustrating how it accumulated as refuse was thrown or swept from the platform. Sherds are somewhat more abundant here than in any other lot group (though still not plentiful). All (except one Tzec sherd) derive from Manik pottery.

SURFACE AND OTHER MATERIAL

As indicated above, some quarrying was carried out following abandonment of Plat. 5C-4. In the process,

structure fill was disturbed, later elements might have found their way into the fill, and this may explain the few Ik or Imix sherds in LG. 5. Lot Group 4, on the other hand, clearly seems to be disturbed fill.

Sixty-two test pits were dug S and E of Gp. 5C-3. These are illustrated in Fig. 65, and their contents are listed below (Table 2.137). Unfortunately, sherd weights were not recorded. Bronson's field notes report an average of 30–40 sherds per cubic meter throughout the test area. Generally, frequencies were lower in proximity to Plat. 5C-4. They were greatest in Test Pit 54 from which were taken approximately 800 sherds. Given this abundance, with the similarity of the sherds to those in LG. 3a of Plat. 5C-4, and the location of the pit only 18 m from the platform, there is a good possibility that Test Pit 54 samples a deposit of occupation debris from the platform. Because of this, the material is assigned to a Lot Group (3b) of Plat. 5C-4.

TIME SPANS

Although the sequence of activities here is reasonably clear-cut (Table 2.138), dating the time spans is somewhat problematical, since the sherd samples are so small. Platform 5C-4-2nd, however (TS. 6), surely is a Preclassic construction, and Manik ceramics were surely in vogue when 5C-4-1st was in use (TS. 3; see also Table 2.135). The fill for 5C-4-1st contains probable Cauac and Manik sherds (Table 2.135). It is probable, then, that Plat. 5C-4-2nd is Late Preclassic, and that the Cauac sherds are redeposited from an original association with the earliest platform. With a fair measure of confidence, therefore, one may say that there was construction at this locus some time after AD 1 when Cauac pottery production began. Platform 5C-4-1st had been abandoned by AD 550 (when Ik ceramics replaced Manik). In the face of only one known renovation of the platform, 550 years seems much too long for its use. Therefore, it is probable that original construction dates from late Cauac times, with abandonment quite some time before the end of Manik times.

Late quarrying (TS. 2) probably was between AD 550 and 869, on the basis of the few Ik and/or Imix sherds.

TABLE 2.135
Platform 5C-4: Lot Groups

Lot Groups	Lot	Provenience	Ceramic Evaluation
1	121B/14,16,19	Unsealed fill of 2nd	Preclassic
2	121A63/1;121A64/1; 121A65/1,2; 121A66/1;121B/11-13,15,17,18,20	Partially sealed fill of 1st	Preclassic (Cauac?), possible Manik
3a	121B/8-10	S of platform	Manik
3b	121A54/1-9	Test Pit 54 (Fig. 65)	Manik
4	121B/22-24	Late quarry	Manik? possible Preclassic
5	121B/1,3,4	Surface over and around platform	Preclassic, Manik, Ik and/or Imix
6	121B/2,5,6,7,19,21	Fill and other material mixed	Preclassic, Manik

TABLE 2.136
Platform 5C-4: Artifacts by Lot Group

Study Category	Object	Lot Group						
		1	2	3a	3b	4	5	6
Pottery Vessels	Sherds per cubic meter (lbs)	Not recorded						
Other Pottery Artifacts	Miscellaneous modeled object						1	
Flaked Chert Artifacts	Unidentified biface				1			
	Point-retouched flake	1						
	Irregular, retouched flake						1	
	Used flakes	3	1		7	2	6	
	Unused flakes	1			4	1	2	
Flaked Obsidian Artifacts	Prismatic blades	2	1			1		1
	Retouched flake						1	
	Used flakes				1		1	
Ground, Pecked, and Polished Stone Artifacts	Mano						1	
Shell and Bone Artifacts	Bone, unidentified				6			
	Bone, human				10			

TABLE 2.137 (Part 1)
Content of Test Pits in and near Group 5C-3, as located in Fig. 65

Test Pit	Operation/Lot	Provenience	Contents
1	121A1/1	Topsoil	Sherds
	121A1/2	Subsoil	Sherds
			Unmodified shell
2	121A2/1	Topsoil	Sherds
3	121A3/1	Topsoil	Sherds
	121A3/2	Subsoil	Sherds
			Figurine
	121A3/3	Below 121A3/2	Sherds
4	121A4/1	Topsoil	----
	121A4/2	Subsoil	Sherds
			Mano
5	121A5/1	Topsoil	Sherds
6	121A6/1	Topsoil and subsoil	Sherds
7	121A7/1	Topsoil	Sherds
	121A7/2	Subsoil	Sherds
	121A7/3	Below 121A7/2	Sherds
8	121A8/1	Topsoil	Sherds
9	121A9/1	Topsoil and subsoil	Sherds
10	121A10/1	Topsoil	----
11	121A11/1	Topsoil	Sherds
12	212A12/1	Topsoil	Sherds
			Cut animal bone
			2 unmodified animal bones
13	121A13/1	Topsoil	Sherds
			Used chert flakes
			Unused chert flake
			Obsidian prismatic blade
			Unmodified animal bone
	121A13/2	Subsoil	Sherds
			Chert thin biface
			Irregular retouched chert flake
			3 used chert flakes
			3 shell fan handles
			1 shell tinkler
			1 unworked shell
	121A13/3	Below 121A13/2	Sherds
14	121A14/1	Topsoil	Sherds
			Used chert flake
	121A14/2	Subsoil	Sherds
	121A14/3	Below 121A14/2	Sherds
			Used chert flake
15	121A15/1	Topsoil	Sherds
			Used chert flake
	121A15/2	Subsoil	Sherds
			Obsidian thin biface
			Human skull fragment, unmodified
16	121A16/1	Topsoil	----
17	121A17/1	Topsoil	Sherds
18	121A18/1	Topsoil	Sherds

Test Pit	Operation/Lot	Provenience	Contents
19	121A19/1	Topsoil	Sherds
	121A19/2	Subsoil	Sherds
			Green obsidian
			Prismatic blade
20	121A20/1	Topsoil	Sherds
	121A20/2	Subsoil	Sherds
21	121A21/1	Topsoil	Sherds
	121A21/2	Subsoil	Sherds
22	121A22/1	Topsoil	Sherds
			Green obsidian (prismatic blade?)
23	121A23/1	Topsoil	Sherds
24	121A24/1	Topsoil	Sherds
			Obsidian (prismatic blade?)
25	121A25/1	Topsoil	Sherds
	121A25/2	Subsoil	Sherds
			Used chert flake
			Unused chert flake
	121A25/3	Beneath 121A25/2	Sherds
26	121A26/1	Topsoil and first stratum below	Sherds
			Figurine
			Obsidian prismatic blade
	121A26/2	Second stratum below topsoil	Sherds
			Used chert flakes
	121A26/3	Topsoil	Sherds
	121A26/4	First stratum below topsoil	Sherds
	121A26/5	Second stratum below topsoil	Sherds
			Human bone
	121A26/6	Third stratum below topsoil; over bedrock	Sherds
			Human bone
27	121A27/1	Topsoil	Sherds
28	121A28/1	Topsoil	Sherds
			Obsidian prismatic blade
	121A28/2	Subsoil	Sherds
29	121A29/1	Topsoil	Sherds
30	121A30/1	Topsoil	Sherds
31	121A31/1	Topsoil	Sherds
			Obsidian prismatic blade
			Charred animal bone
	121A31/2	Subsoil	Sherds
32	121A32/1	Topsoil	Sherds
33	121A33/1	Topsoil	Sherds
34	121A34/1	Topsoil	Sherds
35	121A35/1	Topsoil	-----
36	121A36/1	Topsoil	Sherds
37	121A37/1	Topsoil	Sherds
38	121A38/1	Topsoil	Sherds
	121A38/2	Subsoil	Sherds
39	121A39/1	Topsoil	Sherds
40	121A40/1	Topsoil	Sherds
41	121A41/1	Topsoil	Sherds
			Irregular, retouched chert flake
42	121A42/1	Topsoil	Sherds
	121A42/2	Subsoil	Sherds
43	121A43/1	Topsoil	Sherds
			Used chert flake
44	121A44/1	Topsoil	Sherds
45	121A45/1	Topsoil	Sherds
46	121A46/1	Topsoil	Sherd
			Unmodified chert flake

TABLE 2.137 (Part 3)
Content of Test Pits in and near Group 5C-3, as located in Fig. 65

Test Pit	Operation/Lot	Provenience	Contents
47	121A47/1	Topsoil	Sherds
			Used chert flake
48	121A48/1	Topsoil	Sherds
49	121A49/1	Topsoil	Sherds
			Unused chert flake
			2 obsidian prismatic blades
	121A49/2	Subsoil	Sherds
50	121A50/1	Topsoil	Sherds
51	121A51/1	Topsoil	Sherds
52	121A52/1	Topsoil	Sherds
			Chert (flake?)
			2 obsidian (prismatic blades?)
53	121A53/1	Topsoil	----
54	See Plat. 5C-2: Lot Group 3b (TR. 22A: table 72)		
55	121A55/1	Subsoil	Sherds
56	121A56/1	Topsoil	Sherds
	121A56/2	Subsoil	Sherds
			Used chert flake
57	121A57/1	Topsoil	Sherds
			Obsidian prismatic blade
58	121A58/1	Topsoil	Sherds
59	121A59/1	Topsoil	Sherds
60	121A60/1	Topsoil	Sherds
61	121A61/1	Topsoil	Sherds
	121A61/2	Subsoil	Sherds
62	121A62/1	Topsoil	Sherds

TABLE 2.138
Platform 5C-4: Time Spans

Time Span	Architectural Development	Unit	Floor	Descriptive Data	Lot Group	Ceramics in Vogue
1				Total abandonment of area and forest growth		----------
2				Quarrying and other intermittent activity following abandonment	4 5	Ik and Imix?
3				Use	3	Manik
4	Plat. 5C-4-1st	5-8	1	Enlargement of platform	2	----------
5				Use		
6	Plat. 5C-4-2nd	1-4		Construction of platform	1	Cauac?
7				Early quarrying		

Structure 5C-56 Locus

In September 1961, excavations were undertaken by Alfonso Mora and (in 1962) by Christopher Jones around Ch. 5C-5, located at S305 E280 in Sq. 5C of the Tikal site map (TR. 11). This spot was selected by the Tikal Project as the site of a quarry for stone to be used for consolidation and reconstruction of major buildings at the epicenter of the site. In the course of this work, a new chultun, 5C-8, was discovered when stone cutters accidentally broke through into its E chamber. This chultun contained the first good sample of Cimi ceramics found at Tikal, and so it was completely excavated (as Op. 26A–G). The area above it was investigated (as Op. 49A) to see if traces of any structures could be found, despite absence of any surface indication that architecture existed here. The remains of at least two structures (5C-56 and 57) were found (Fig. 68). Finally, Ch. 5C-5 was excavated (as Op. 66A) by Haviland in June 1963.

The two structures and chultuns, along with Ch. 5C-4, are located together on a prominent knoll. From this, the land slopes downward considerably to the N and S, but less so to the W. To the E, after a very slight dip, it rises towards the "Mundo Perdido" group that includes Str. 5C-49, a large temple. The edge of the plaza for the temple is the nearest construction, and it lies 40 m distant.

STRUCTURE 5C-56-2ND

Unfortunately, little is known about this or the succeeding architectural development, as the quarrymen of the Tikal Project removed the E portion of the structure. Its long axis, however, seems to have been laid out in a roughly E-W line. The original structure was represented by portions of three walls, and by its rubble fill (Fig. 68, 69). Unit 1 is a section of an E-W wall that is based on very thin earth fill over bedrock. It is in union with a plaster floor to the S (Plat. 5C-6:U. 1) that turns up to the base of the wall. North of U. 1 is a fill of rubble and earth, its top 0.20 m below that of U. 1. It is probable, but not certain, that the fill originally came to the top of the wall and was covered by a plaster floor. To the W, the fill is contained by U. 2, apparently the structure end wall. Unit 3 contains the fill to the N, and is a portion of the back wall. North of the walls, there is no apparent formal living surface.

Nothing more is known of 5C-56-2nd. It may well have been a rectangular, one-level platform with a building of pole-and-thatch. No positive evidence was found for this, but in view of the extent of destruction, this is scarcely surprising. Moreover, the fill in the surviving corners is of sufficient depth to have supported poles without the necessity of their being set in bedrock. The structure may also have been modified on the three occasions when the plaza S of U. 1 was altered prior to construction of Str. 5C-56-1st.

STRUCTURE 5C-56-1ST

At some point, the front of 5C-56 was extended 2.20 m to the S (Fig. 68, 69). Unit 4 is what remains of the new S wall; it stands only 0.12 m high above Plat. 5C-6:U. 4, but must originally have been higher. This is shown by the height of U. 5, the W wall of the new addition; this survives to the same height as the original S wall, U. 1. A floor that no longer survives probably ran from the top of U. 4 and 5, covering the older U. 1.

Unit 5 was built 0.30 m W of the W wall for 56-2nd (U. 2), so the new S addition extends a full 0.75 m farther in that direction. On the N side of this extension, a single masonry block was placed in line with U. 1 to form the wall.

Structure 5C-56-1st, like its predecessor, may have been topped by a building of pole-and-thatch. Again, there is no evidence one way or the other. Platform 5C-6:U. 5 turns up to the S wall of the structure.

STRUCTURE 5C-57

The existence of this structure is indicated by a series of five postholes in bedrock; no other remains survive. Units 1 through 12 are postholes (Fig. 68 and Table 2.139) found around Ch. 5C-5. Three of these (U. 1, 2, and 3) form a SE-NW line and are separated by regular intervals of 1.25 m. About 1.50 m SW of the two end holes, U. 1 and 3, are two others (U. 4 and 5). The regularity of their spacing, and the fact that they seem (with U. 1–3) to form the end of a rectangle, suggest that these five holes were for the posts of a rectangular building of perishable materials. Units 1–3 would have been for the posts of the NE end wall, U. 4 and 5 for posts of the SE and NW side walls. No postholes were found for the SW end of the structure. Bedrock is low in that area, however, whereas it is high where U. 1–5 were found. Therefore, postholes would not be expected to the W. It may even be that after the structure was abandoned, the SW bedrock was quarried away, which would have destroyed any postholes. All that can be said is that the structure must have run at least 3.25 m NE-SW, and it may have been even longer; its width was 2.70 m.

Whether or not the building stood on a platform is not known for certain. The overall situation here, however, is reminiscent of Str. 2G-61 and 2G-62 (this report). In this case, five things suggest that Str. 5C-57 was abandoned by the time 5C-56 was built. First, there is no evidence for a tamped earth floor as might be expected for a building constructed wholly of perishable materials. Second, there are no obvious trash deposits associated with the structure. This suggests that such trash was scraped away, in the course of which the walls of a building platform might have been removed as well. Third, there is no known instance at Tikal where a structure was built over a chultun, unless the chultun had been filled or sealed first (see Ch. 2G-2, 2G-10, 2G-11, 3G-5, 6E-6, and 6E-7, this report). Chultun 5C-5 was not sealed, suggesting that the structure predates the chultun. If so, any structure walls of masonry (if these existed) would probably have been removed when the chultun was constructed. Fourth, a quantity of Cimi sherds was found in Ch. 5C-8. These could derive from occupation of the nearby Str. 5C-57. Moreover, the blocks of masonry that were found in the chultun (see below) might have come from the walls of the building platform of that structure. Finally, Ch. 5C-8 was in use prior to construction of Str. 5C-56. Another chultun, 5C-5, seems to have been constructed to serve that structure, and there is evidence that bedrock was quarried at that time all around its orifice (see the discussion of this feature). This certainly would have required destruction of some of the masonry walls of Str. 5C-57. One would expect that some structure was located near Ch. 5C-8 when it was in use, and 5C-57 seems to have been that structure. It may well have consisted in part of a building platform.

TABLE 2.139
Structure 5C-57: Posthole Dimensions (meters)

Feature	Diameter
Unit 1	0.14
Unit 2	0.12
Unit 3	0.16
Unit 4	0.12
Unit 5	0.12
Unit 6	0.14
Unit 7	0.12
Unit 8	0.12
Unit 9	0.13
Unit 10	0.13
Unit 11	0.18
Unit 12	0.13
Unit 13	0.11
Unit 14	0.13

PLATFORM 5C-6

Platform 5C-6 is the level area S and W of Str. 5C-56. At the time 56-2nd was built, a floor was laid to the S of it. This is Plat. 5C-6:U. 1 (Fig. 68, 69a), and it defines Plat. 5C-6-E. It was laid over a fill of earth and small pebbles, and is in union with Str. 5C-56:U. 1. Although the floor is now broken above the orifice of Ch. 5C-8, this appears to have been a late occurrence. Originally, the orifice of

the chultun was filled with rubble and the floor sealed it.

West of Str. 5C-56, the floor runs up to the quarried face of the high bedrock around the opening to Ch. 5C-5 (see below). The surface continues S of this, however, and the limits of the plaza, aside from Str. 5C-56, are not known. The side extent of the surface suggests that other contemporary structures may have been located to the W, S, or (less likely) E. The present excavations were too limited to explore this possibility.

The original floor of the plaza had a considerable slope down towards the S, in part perhaps the result of rather thick fill that may have settled. Whatever the cause, a new grading floor, U. 2 (Fig. 68, 69a), was apparently laid to compensate for the slump. This defines Plat. 5C-6-D. Unit 2 was laid on a fill of pebbles and earth similar to that for U. 1, progressively thicker to the S. To the N, this pavement tapers to meet the surface of U. 1, 3.30 m S of Str. 5C-56-2nd.

The next modification of the plaza, 5C-6-C, is defined on the basis of U. 3 (Fig. 69a). This is a second grading surface that joins that of U. 1 only 0.45 m S of Str. 5C-56-2nd. It, too, was laid on a fill of pebbles and earth, which becomes thicker to the S.

Unit 4 (Fig. 69a) testifies to a third renovation of the plaza surface, 5C-6-B. This, too, is a grading floor, laid directly on the surface of U. 3. It tapers to meet the surface of this preceding pavement about 1.10 m S of Str. 5C-56-2nd.

When Str. 5C-56-1st was built, there was a final modification of the plaza (5C-6-A). Unit 4, the final grading floor in front of the earlier structure, was torn out S of 5C-56-1st. Then, a new floor (Fig. 68, 69a:U. 5) was laid to turn up to the face of 56-1st. Little of this pavement survives, so its extent is not known. Unit 5 might be part of a plaza-wide floor, since destroyed, or it might be a local patch that joined the surface of U. 3 or 4 farther S.

CHULTUN 5C-5

DESCRIPTION

This is a common type of Tikal chultun, with two main chambers opening from two opposite sides of a smaller antechamber (Fig. 69b,c). A round orifice gives access to the antechamber from above. The rim of this orifice is not stepped; the chamber itself is roughly circular. Two chambers open from the antechamber, Chm. 2 to the N and Chm. 3 to the S, the former being the smaller of the two (Table 2.140). Both are essentially dome-shaped, with their floors at a level lower than that of the antechamber. The entrances to the rooms are restricted at the sides. A small hole in the N wall of Chm. 2 opens to the surface of the quarried bedrock face 1.60 m N of the orifice.

To state the obvious, the first step in construction was to dig out the orifice and antechamber, and one of the lateral chambers had to be dug before the other. Hence, three construction stages were involved, but it is impossible to say which of the side chambers was the first to be constructed.

It is evident that this chultun was left open upon its abandonment. In this respect it may be contrasted with Ch. 3G-5 (this report), one very similar in plan, but which was purposely filled. As found, material in Ch. 5C-5 at no point reached a depth of more than 0.60 m. The surface of this deposit sloped downward into the inner chambers from below the orifice. It was of loose consistency, composed of earth mixed with material that had fallen from the ceiling. This gave a light color in particular to the fill in Chm. 2. A sprinkling of cultural material was found near floor level.

Given that Ch. 5C-5 was never deliberately filled, it is evident that Str. 5C-57 predates it. There is no case at Tikal where a structure was built over a chultun without it having been sealed in some manner (cf. Ch. 2G-2, 2G-10, 2G-11, 3G-5, 5C-8, this report). The structure may have been destroyed at the time the chultun was built, or even earlier.

As remarked elsewhere, the orifice of the chultun opens in the center of a bedrock platform that rises above Plat. 5C-6. It is evident from this that surface water could not have run into the chultun. The surrounding bedrock was possibly quarried to produce this platform at the time the chultun was constructed. It was not quarried after U. 1 of the plaza was laid. Because the chultun orifice is so well centered, however, it is unlikely, although not impossible, that quarrying preceded construction of the chultun by any great amount of time.

DESCRIPTION

The orifice of this multi-chambered chultun (Fig. 70, 71, 178a, and Table 2.141) is round, manhole-like, and leads through a neck that flares downward into the ceiling of Chm. 1. In plan, this is rounded, with a relatively level floor that turns sharply upward to near-vertical walls. These in turn are quite distinct from the slightly concave ceiling. Chamber 1 opens into Chm. 2 to the E and Chm. 3 to the W.

Chamber 1 was filled to the ceiling with earth and trash much like that in Chm. 2 and 3. An air space of 0.50 m in the neck separated this fill from a layer of stones in the orifice itself. Above the orifice was fill for the floors of Plat. 5C-4. The significance of this fill is discussed below.

Chamber 2 was accidentally broken into by Tikal Project stone cutters, in 1961, which is how this previously unknown chultun was discovered. A constricted entrance leads into it from Chm. 1 to the W. Its floor is at a slightly lower level, but otherwise the space is comparable in size, shape, and presence of differentiated walls and ceiling, to Chm. 1. As found, it was filled to a depth of about 0.60 m by material comparable to, and continuous with, that in Chm. 1.

The largest chamber of the chultun, Chm. 3 has a floor some 0.40 m lower than that of Chm. 1. A slightly restricted entrance, with a sill, gives access to Chm. 3 from Chm. 1 to the E. In turn, entrances lead from Chm. 3 into Chm. 4, 5, and 6 (Fig. 178a). Chambers 7, 9, and 10 open into the floor of Chm. 3. In plan, the space is roughly rounded. Its floor is quite level, the walls are nearly vertical, and the roughly concave ceiling is distinct from the walls.

Chamber 3 contained fill to a depth of about 0.50 m. This consisted of earth and trash, including carbon and

TABLE 2.140
Chultun 5C-5: Average Dimensions (meters)

Feature	Length	Width	Height	Minimum Diameter	Maximum Diameter
Neck	---	---	0.84	0.48	1.06
Chm. 1	1.30	1.06	---	---	---
Chm. 2	---	---	1.08	1.70	2.00
Chm. 3	---	---	1.22	1.92	2.50
Entrance 1-2	0.22	0.40	0.62	---	2.50
Entrance 1-3	0.13	1.36	0.76	---	---

scattered fragments of burned bone. It was continuous with the material in Chm. 1, and its most likely source was a domestic midden (see below). In addition, there were several masonry blocks in the fill, some of which may have served as entrance blocks to other rooms (see Chm. 6). Below all this was U. 7, a deposit of water-laid clay similar to U. 2 in Chm. 10. The significance of all this is discussed below.

Access to Chm. 4 is through an entrance from the W end of Chm. 3. It is restricted on the sides, and has a sill. The cavity itself is roughly round in plan. Walls, ceiling, and floor all are clearly differentiated, but all tend to have slightly concave surfaces. Chamber 4 was found filled to a depth of 0.60 m. It contained fragments of bones, both human and animal, as well as many sherds, charcoal, earth, and stones. The bones appear to have been scattered at random. The sherds were abundant, especially near the entrance where most of the large stones were. The sherds are of midden quality, and several of them fit together. No whole pots are represented, however. Many of the stones are large, some have been burned, and one of them partially blocked the entrance.

Chamber 5 opens into the S wall of Chm. 3. Its entrance, an unusually long one, is narrowed on the sides, and a large sill is present. Floor level is 0.25 m below that of Chm. 3. Since the sill is so large, there is a step cut from bedrock down to the floor. In size, shape, and plan, this space is very like Chm. 4. Walls, ceiling, and floor are all clearly distinguishable from one another.

Chamber 5 was eventually filled to a depth of about 0.60 m near its entrance, but only about 0.16 m near the back. This fill was much like that from Chm. 4, and contained several sherds as well as some large blocks of masonry.

Chamber 6 opens into the N wall of Chm. 3. It is very similar to 4 and 5 in plan, size, and shape, and presence of a restricted entrance with sill. Several blocks of masonry were found in the entrance. The fill found inside differs fundamentally from that in the rest of the chultun. Virtually devoid of cultural material, it consisted of thin layers of white lime and gray soil. Some stones were also present.

Chamber 7 is entered through an orifice, around which is a sill, in the NE floor area of Chm. 3. The situation might almost be described as a chultun within a chultun. The floor of Chm. 7 is 0.90 m below that of Chm. 3. It has the shape of a rough dome, circular in plan. A further entrance gives access to Chm. 8, to the N. When found, this Chm. 7 was completely filled with earth and trash, in which were sherds from bowls and jars, stones, and bones.

Chamber 8 opens northwards and downwards from Chm. 7. It is rounded to rectangular in plan, and quite irregular in section. Its walls are essentially continuous with the ceiling. As found, the slightly restricted entrance was blocked by stones that appeared to have plaster on their inner faces.

On the S side of the entrance to Chm. 3 from Chm. 1 is Chm. 9, in many respects a smaller version of Chm. 7 on the other side of the same entrance. Chamber 9 is similar to 7 in that it is entered through a hole in the floor of Chm. 3, is round in plan, and is roughly dome-shaped. Its floor is 0.80 m below that of Chm. 3. As in Chm. 7, a raised sill is present around the orifice. Chamber 9 was found filled with earth and sherds similar to material in Chm. 3. A large block of masonry found below the orifice may have sealed it at one time.

Chamber 10, located in the N portion of the floor of Chm. 3, has the form of a roughly oval, bottle-shaped pit, and it was filled by six distinct strata. The lowest of these, U. 1, was a brown earth about 0.15 m in thickness. Above were banded layers of apparently water-laid clay (U. 2). Over this was a layer of brown dirt, U. 3, full of burned bones and charcoal. This was covered in turn by U. 4, a loose sandy earth, yellow in color. Over this was a loose brown earth, U. 5, with stones. In the S half of the space, U. 5 came to the level of the floor in Chm. 3. In the N half, it was covered by U. 6, a lime deposit. Of special note are many human remains from above the clay deposit (see PD. 72).

DISCUSSION

This chultun seems to have been purposely filled at one time. This is indicated first by the arrangement of material throughout the chultun. The top of the fill was highest in Chm. 1 below the orifice. From here, it sloped off into Chm. 2 and 3 on either side. It did not fill the neck, expectable if most of the fill was simply dumped through the orifice. In that case, the inner chambers would not have been completely filled, and the fill would have tended to settle down into them (see Ch. 6E-6 and 6E-7, this report, for similar situations). The stones that plugged the orifice did not fall, for they were sufficiently wedged in place. They did settle enough so that the plaza floors above apparently cracked, however. This allowed roots to enter later on, and these destroyed the floors directly over the orifice.

The settling process would have been helped along if the innermost chambers of the chultun were originally blocked by stones that later were pushed down by the pressure of the fill. That this happened is suggested by the blocks of masonry found in and near the entrances of Chm. 4, 5, 6, 8, and 9. One of these was still in situ in the entrance to Chm. 6. The rest were positioned in a manner consistent with their collapse into the chambers. The fill would then have settled rather quickly into the

TABLE 2.141
Chultun 5C-8: Average Dimensions (meters)

Feature	Length	Width	Height	Minimum Diameter	Maximum Diameter
Neck	---	---	---	0.44	0.57
Chm. 1	---	---	0.80	1.64	---
Chm. 2	---	---	0.99	1.62	1.82
Chm. 3	---	---	1.30	2.44	2.62
Chm. 4	---	---	1.18	1.86	2.02
Chm. 5	---	---	1.10	1.84	2.15
Chm. 6	---	---	1.24	1.62	1.95
Chm. 7	---	---	1.04	1.60	1.60
Chm. 8	---	---	0.60	0.56	0.82
Chm. 9	---	---	0.70	0.92	1.10
Chm. 10	1.50	1.40	0.90	---	---
Entrance 1-2	0.20	0.64	?	---	---
Entrance 1-3	0.10	1.36	0.37	---	---
Entrance 3-4	0.10	0.74	0.53	---	---
Entrance 3-5	0.36	0.64	0.50	---	---
Entrance 3-6	0.30	1.16	0.92	---	---
Entrance 3-7	---	---	0.26	0.52	0.54
Entrance 3-9	---	---	0.30	0.60	0.60
Entrance 3-10	0.90	0.50	0.16	---	---
Entrance 7-8	0.10	0.48	0.50	---	---

lower empty spaces. Chambers 7 and 9 were apparently totally filled, and the masonry from Chm. 7 settled into the deeper Chm. 8, as would be expected. The other spaces were partially filled, and large items, such as sherds, were caught amongst the masonry blocks. Again, this is what one would expect under this scenario.

There are other facts consistent with this interpretation. Not only was fill highest beneath the orifice, but also it was lowest in Chm. 4 and 5 (Chm. 6 was an exception, this to be explained below). Furthermore, there were a great number of cases where a sherd found in one chamber fit one from another. Such fits interlace material from all chambers. This reveals that the fill came primarily from one source, most likely at one time.

Not all of the fill may be explained in the above manner. For example, the character of fill in Chm. 6 suggests that it consisted in large part of material removed when Chm. 10 was dug, mixed with bat dung (noteworthy is that the latter chamber is located in front of the entrance to Chm. 6). For its part, Chm. 10 was deliberately filled as a special operation. The lowest stratum here was sealed by the clays of U. 2. This shows that at one time water entered the chultun. Unit 7, a similar deposit of clay on the floor of Chm. 3, is undoubtedly contemporary. Unit 7 did not cover the fill of Chm. 10. Above U. 2, U. 3 through 6 were purposely placed (PD.

72). Since there is no sill around its entrance, as there are for Chm. 7 and 9, Chm. 10 along with Chm. 3 shows the water-deposited clay. In Chm. 3, this ran up to the block of masonry in the entrance to Chm. 6. The masonry was therefore set in place before water got into the chultun.

Given all this information, the sequence of events when the chultun was filled may be reconstructed as follows. First, Chm. 4, 5, 6, 7, and 9 were sealed by masonry so as to minimize the amount of fill needed. Chamber 10 was also dug at this time, just before Chm. 6 was sealed. A bit of trash seems to have been carried in, and is represented by U. 1, the basal stratum in Chm. 10. Then, water got into the chultun, perhaps because the orifice was no longer protected in any way, as it might have been when the chultun was in use. It is unfortunate for this hypothesis that it was not noted by the excavator whether clay was deposited in Chm. 1. Next, human remains were placed in Chm. 10, which was then filled up. Finally, trash was dumped through the chultun orifice to complete the job of filling.

The character of the fill in the chultun raises the question as to its ultimate derivation. It seems clearly to have come from a domestic situation, as revealed by numerous utilitarian artifacts and sherds from utilitarian vessels. Moreover, there was abundant charcoal and bone material, as well as burned stones and even the remains of corn and beans. This certainly suggests a household midden (TR. 19:99–100). The human bones in Chm. 10 (PD. 72) might have come from a household burial. Overall, it looks as if a house was completely razed, and its masonry, fill, and nearby trash were all dumped into the chultun. Such extensive demolition very likely would have led to disturbance of a primary burial, which then had to be reinterred. Alternatively, the death of a household head may have prompted his two-stage burial and destruction of his house. In either case, this would account for all the elements present in the fill of Ch. 5C-8: trash, masonry, and human bones.

The most likely structure to have been demolished would have been Str. 5C-57. Certainly, the trash in the chultun was not carried any great distance, for many of the sherds are of large size, with sharp breaks, and some pots are represented by several sherds. Had it been carried far, it would have been broken and crushed to a much greater extent. It would also probably have been more mixed. Structure 5C-57 not only was close by, but also could have been in use at the same time as the chultun. Consistent is that both the structure and chultun were in use prior to construction of Str. 5C-56.

Not certainly known is whether or not the chultun represents just a single architectural development (excluding for the moment Chm. 10). The single orifice suggests that it was, as does the essential symmetry of the arrangement of chambers around No. 3. Moreover, Chm. 1, 2, 4, 5, and 6 all are similar in shape. Chambers 7 and 9, entered through the floor of Chm. 3, are also quite similar to one another, though they differ somewhat from the other spaces. The fact that Chm. 2 was built off of Chm. 1, however, might suggest that it was a later addition. The deep chambers might also have been later additions, but the raised sills around their orifices suggest otherwise.

Even if only a single architectural development is recognized for the whole chultun, it is not known how many construction stages were involved. Once Chm. 1 and 3 were built, the rest could have been completed in a single stage given enough workers. There were certainly at least three stages to construction; there may have been as many as nine.

Alteration of Bedrock

Considerable quarrying beneath the plaza took place at some time, especially in the vicinity of Str. 5C-57. This runs over to the W wall of Str. 5C-56, near which a partially quarried block can be seen. Apparently, the Maya removed the bedrock surface over a large area before construction of Plat. 5C-6-E, possibly to provide building blocks. In contrast, bedrock was deliberately left around the orifice of Ch. 5C-5, thereby producing a kind of raised platform. This might suggest that the chultun was already in existence, or was constructed at the same time. Some of the quarrying does run beneath the area where the walls of Str. 5C-57 stood. Since the quarrying evidently postdates use of that structure, it would require that any building platform wall that existed be removed.

Other alterations of bedrock consist of postholes (Fig. 66 and Table 2.139). Those marking walls of Str. 5C-57 (U. 1–5) have already been discussed, the others (Str. 5C-57:U. 6–12) remain enigmatic. They fall inside, or just barely outside, those walls. Perhaps they were associated with that structure. Otherwise, some or all of them might relate to one or more earlier or later structures, or even a shelter over the orifice of Ch. 5C-5. Their arrangement forms no detectable pattern, but then other related postholes might remain to be found beyond the excavation limits. Units 13 and 14 are two other postholes 2.25 m E of Str. 5C-57. Even farther away is Str. 5C-56:U. 6, just N of that structure, and possibly related to it. In any event, the occurrence of three holes at such a distance lends credence to the idea that U. 7–12 were not associated with Str. 5C-57.

SHERDS AND ARTIFACTS

Defined in Table 2.142 are the lot groups for this locus; with artifacts listed in Tables 2.143–2.146.

Construction Fill

Fill samples were obtained from Str. 5C-56-1st (LG. 1) and Plat. 5C-6-E (LG. 1). In neither case was the sample sealed, but contamination appears to be minimal. The material from all lot groups of Ch. 5C-8 should date construction of Str. 5C-56-2nd, as its filling evidently served to prepare for construction of this structure with its plaza.

Material Above Living Level

Here, such material is contained in Str. 5C-56:LG. 2. It appears to be extensively mixed with fill that has eroded from 5C-56, however. Since the material comes from above the plaza surface, the part that is not fill should relate to final use of the structure.

Because Str. 5C-57 was thoroughly demolished, it is obvious that any related occupation material has been disturbed. As noted in discussion of Ch. 5C-8, such material, undoubtedly mixed with structure fill, seems to have been used to fill this chultun.

Chultuns

The cultural material inside Ch. 5C-5 seems to have washed in after abandonment, and is in part contemporary with material in LG. 2 around Str. 5C-56. The material in Ch. 5C-8 (including PD. 72), on the other hand, was purposeful fill. As just noted, it should include trash from occupation of Str. 5C-57.

TABLE 2.142
Structure 5C-56 Locus: Lot Groups

Feature	Lot Group	Lot	Provenience	Ceramic Evaluation
Str. 5C-56 (Op. 49A)	1	2	Unsealed fill of 1st	Ik
	2	4	W of structure, to level of plaza floor	Ik and Imix
Plat. 5C-6 (Op. 49A)	1	3	Partially sealed fill of 5C-1-E	Manik and Ik
	2	5	Unknown	No data
Ch. 5C-5 (Op. 66A)	1	1-5	Fill, Chm. 1	Preclassic, Manik, Ik and/or Imix
	2	6	Fill, Chm. 2	No data
Ch. 5C-8	1	26C/1	Fill, Chm. 1	Cimi, some Ik
	2	26A/1	Fill, Chm. 2	Cimi, some Ik
	3	26B/1	Fill, Chm. 3	Cimi, Manik, some Ik
	4	26E/1-6	Fill, Chm. 4	Cimi
	5	26D/1-5	Fill, Chm. 5	Cimi
	6	26F/1,2	Fill, Chm. 6	Cimi
	7	26B/4-8	Fill, Chm. 7	Eb or Tzec, Manik, some Ik
	8	26B/9,10	Fill, Chm. 8	
	9	26B/2	Fill, Chm. 9	?
	10	26B/3; 26H/1-3	Fill, Chm. 10 (excludes PD. 72)	Manik
	11	26G/1,2; 49A/1	Unknown	Cimi and Manik, 1 possible Ik and/or Imix

TABLE 2.143
Structure 5C-56: Artifacts by Lot Group

Study Category	Object	1	2
Pottery Vessels	Sherds	weights not recorded	
Other Pottery Artifacts	Figurines	2	12
	Censer		1
Flaked Chert Artifacts	Flake cores	3	1
	Ovate bifaces	3	6
	Elongate bifaces		7
	Rectangular/oval biface	1	
	Irregular biface	1	
	Unclassifiable bifaces		2
	Irregular retouched flake		1
	Point-retouched flake		1
	Blades	1	1
	Used flakes	53	76
	Unused flakes	5	61
	Nodules	1	12
Flaked Obsidian Artifacts	Thin bifaces	1	2
	Prismatic blades	1	35
	Used flake		1
Ground, Pecked, and Polished Stone Artifacts	Metates	4	2
	Hammer stones	1	3
	Rubbing stone	1	
	Spindle whorl	1	
Shell and Bone Artifacts	Shell, tinklers		2
	Shell, ring		1
	Shell, bead		1
	Shell, cut fragments		2
	Unmodified shells	1	1
	Bone, animal, unmodified	3	2
	Bone, cut		1
	Bone, human, unmodified		14

TABLE 2.144
Platform 5C-6: Artifacts by Lot Group

Study Category	Object	Lot Group 1	2
Pottery Vessels	Sherds	weights not recorded	
Other Pottery Artifacts	Pendant		1
Flaked Chert Artifacts	Elongate biface	1	
	Irregular, retouched flake	1	
	Used flake	1	

TABLE 2.145
Chultun 5C-5: Artifacts by Lot Group

Study Category	Object	Lot Group 1	2
Pottery Vessels			
Flaked Chert Artifacts	Blade	1	
	Unused flake	1	
Ground, Pecked, and Polished Stone Artifacts	Metates	3	
	Jade bead		1

TABLE 2.146
Chultun 5C-8: Artifacts by Lot Group

Study Category	Object	Lot Group										
		1	2	3	4	5	6	7	8	9	10	11
Pottery Vessels	Sherds	weights not recorded										
Other Pottery Artifacts	Figurines		1	1				4				1
	Miniature vessel				1							
	Censer									1		
	Pellet	1										
	Bead	1										
	Centrally perforated sherd			1								
	Unclassifiable formed object			1								
Flaked Chert Artifacts	Flake cores			3				6	1		7	
	Ovate bifaces	3		4					1			1
	Elongate bifaces	1			2							
	Irregular bifaces	2				1			1			1
	Unclassifiable bifaces			1		1		2				
	Irregular, retouched flakes	1		4				2				
	Point-retouched flakes			1		1				1		
	Blade			1								
	Used flakes	1		15		3		4				33
	Unmodified flakes	1			3	4		24	2		22	1
Flaked Obsidian Artifacts	Thin bifaces	2	1									
	Prismatic blades	9	4	1		2		15	1	3	3	2
	Used flakes	3						2				
	Unmodified flakes				1			7		1	1	
Ground, Pecked, and Polished Stone Artifacts	Manos			2		1						
	Metates	1						2		1	1	1
	Rubbing stone				1							
	Grind stone							1				
	Hammer stones			1		1				1	1	
	Celt										1	
	Jade bead										1	
Shell and Bone Artifacts	Shell, unmodified	1	1	1	4			4		1	2	2
	Shell, worked										5	1
	Bone, animal, unworked	1+	9+	12	15		1	34+		14+	59	
	Bone, animal, rasp	1									1	
	Bone, animal, pin		1									
	Bone, animal, needle or pin points	2										
	Bone, animal, perforated tooth										1	
	Bone, animal, worked	2	2					11				
	Bone, human, worked							1				
	Bone, human, unworked	13+	8					7+	1+	12	12+	

TIME SPANS

Time spans for these structures, chultuns, and plaza are presented in Tables 2.147 through 2.151, and are correlated in Table 2.152. The rationale for most of the correlations appears in the sections of excavation data for the individual features. The ceramic data (Table 2.142) conform to the sequence of events quite well. This may be summarized here.

The earliest activity was construction of Str. 5C-57 and Ch. 5C-8 (as locus TS. 13). The belief that these were coeval events rests on the assumption, consistent with ceramic analysis, that both were in use at the same time, and were abandoned at the same time. Since the fill of Ch. 5C-8 contained a number of Manik sherds (LG. 3, 7, and PD. 72), it may mean that Str. 5C-57 was occupied into Early Classic times. This gains support from evidence that links destruction of Str. 5C-57 to placement of PD. 72 in the chultun, at ca. AD 378 (see discussion of PD. 72, this report).

There is virtually no doubt that the filling of Ch. 5C-8 took place when Str. 5C-56-2nd and Plat. 5C-6-E were built (locus TS. 11). This might appear to have taken place shortly after the appearance of Ik ceramics, since a few sherds were found in the chultun fill (LG. 1, 2, 3, and 7). These sherds appear to have washed in after Str. 5C-56 had collapsed into ruin, however, for all such sherds were restricted to Chm. 1, 2, and 3, and 7 (from which fill had settled into the deeper Chm. 8, allowing fill from Chm. 3 to settle in turn into Chm. 7). The Ik sherds, then, could have fallen through the orifice after the chultun fill had

begun to settle, coming to rest in those chambers nearest to the orifice. It is, therefore, more probable that Str. 5C-56-2nd and Plat. 5C-6-E were built, and the chultun was filled, while Manik ceramics were still in vogue. Consistent is the lack of any debris on the chultun floors, such as might be expected, had it been abandoned for any significant time prior to construction of the overlying features after the appearance of Ik ceramics.

It appears, therefore, as if the platform of Str. 5C-57 was demolished at the time of someone's death, or else a burial was disturbed in the course of demolition and reburied in the chultun (PD. 72). The remains of the structure were used to fill Ch. 5C-8. Immediately following this, the new structure, plaza, and probably Ch. 5C-5 were constructed (locus TS. 11).

Ik ceramics were in use when Str. 5C-56-1st was built (locus TS. 3). Since they are relatively abundant in its fill, they had probably been in production for some time. It is impossible, however, to correlate any particular modifications of Plat. 5C-6 with their appearance. All that is known is that Ik ceramics appeared some time between locus TS. 10 and 4.

Locus TS. 2 covers the final period of use of Str. 5C-56 and its plaza. Apparently, Imix ceramics were in use, for such sherds occur in some quantity in Str. 5C-56:LG. 2.

To sum up, then, there was construction at this locus by about AD 150, when production of Cimi ceramics began. There seems to have been more or less continuous occupation up to at least sometime after AD 700, when Imix ceramics appeared, but not necessarily as late as AD 869.

TABLE 2.147
Structure 5C-56: Time Spans

Time Span	Architectural Development	Unit	Descriptive Data	Lot Group	Ceramics in Vogue
1			Abandonment and collapse		
2			Use	2	Imix
3	Str. 5C-56-1st	4,5	Enlargement	1	
4			Use		Ik
5	Str. 5C-56-2nd	1-3	Construction		Manik
6		6?	Earlier activity		Cimi

TABLE 2.148
Structure 5C-57: Time Spans

Time Span	Architectural Development	Unit	Descriptive Data	Lot Group	Ceramics in Vogue
1			Later activity		– – – – – – – Ik through Imix
2			Destruction to fill Ch. 5C-8		Manik
3			Use	None	– – – – – – –
4	Str. 5C-57	1-5, 6-14?	Construction		Cimi

TABLE 2.149
Platform 5C-6: Time Spans

Time Span	Architectural Development	Unit	Descriptive Data	Lot Group	Ceramics in Vogue
1			Abandonment and ruin		– – – – – – –
2			Use		Imix
3	Plat.5C-6-A	5	Final modification of plaza floor		Ik
4			Use		– – – – – – –
5	Plat. 5C-6-B	4	Third grading floor laid		
6			Use		
7	Plat. 5C-6-C	3	Second grading floor laid	2	Manik or Ik
8			Use		
9	Plat. 5C-6-D	2	First grading floor laid		
10			Use		– – – – – – –
11	Plat. 5C-6-E	1	Construction of plaza, Ch. 5C-8 filled, probable quarrying activity	1	Manik
12			Earlier activity		– – – – – – – Cimi

TABLE 2.150
Chultun 5C-5: Time Spans

Time Span	Architectural Development	Construction Stage	Descriptive Data	Lot Group	Ceramics in Vogue
1			Abandonment and accumulation of debris	1,2	
2			Use		Ik through Imix
3	Ch. 5C-5	1	Construction of Chm. 2 or 3		
		2	Construction of Chm. 2 or 3		
		3	Construction of orifice and antechamber		Manik
4			Earlier activity		Cimi

TABLE 2.151
Chultun 5C-8: Time Spans

Time Spans	Architectural Development	Chamber	Unit	Special Deposits: Problematical Deposit	Descriptive Data	Lot Group	Ceramics in Vogue
1		10	1-7	72	Chultun filled	1-10	Manik
2					Use		
3	Ch. 5C-8	1-9			Construction		Cimi

TABLE 2.152
Correlation of Time Spans for All Features of Structure 5C-56 Locus

Locus Time Span	Str. 5C-56 (Table 2.147)	Str. 5C-57 (Table 2.148)	Plat. 5C-6 (Table 2.149)	Ch. 5C-5 (Table 2.150)	Ch. 5C-8 (Table 2.151)
1	1		1	1	
2	2		2		
3	3		3		
4			4		
5			5		
6			6		
7			7		
8			8		
9			9		
10	4	1	10	2	
11	5	2	11	3	1
12		3			2
13	6	4	12	4	3

TABLE 2.153
Chultun 5B-11: Average Dimensions (meters)

Feature	Length	Width	Height	Minimum Diameter	Maximum Diameter
Neck	---	---	0.58	0.52	0.52
Chm. 1	1.00	1.00	1.14	---	---
Chm. 2	2.08	2.00	1.50	---	---
Passage	---	0.68	0.60	---	---

Group 5B-3

Chultun 5B-11 was discovered and excavated (as Op. 66O) by Puleston in the summer of 1963. Its location is 5B:S237 E37, 6 m N of Str. 5B-15 (TR. 11). This is one of six structures of varying size, the two largest (5B-13 and 17) possibly being small range-type structures. The smallest (5B-18) does not seem large enough to have been a house. The structures are arranged around the four sides of a raised platform, just N of which is one other chultun, 5B-4. The group as a whole is on a high rise above the 250 m contour, with no other visible ruins in the vicinity. Undoubtedly, both chultuns were used by occupants of Gp. 5B-3.

CHULTUN 5B-11

DESCRIPTION

The plan of this chultun is typical of two-chambered Tikal chultuns in general (Fig. 72 and TR. 32). The first step in construction was to cut a round, manhole-like opening through the bedrock crust (CS. 2). This was extended downward as a neck that flares out rapidly to form the walls of the antechamber. This, with the neck above it, resembles a bottle-shaped pit, and is unusual in its shallowness (Table 2.153). No stepping is visible around the rim of the orifice, nor is there any trace of a stone cover.

Upon completion of the antechamber, a lateral chamber (Chm. 2) was dug out to the N. If there was once a sill between the two rooms, there is now no trace of it. Chamber 2 is circular in plan, with its floor 0.80 m below that of Chm. 1. From the floor, the walls flare outward up to a height of about 0.50 m, and then begin to curve inward to form a domed ceiling.

DISCUSSION

The chultun contained, in part, loose earth in which there were a few sherds, but no artifacts. The overall situation is much like that of Ch. 2G-5 (in Gp. 2G-1, this report), and undoubtedly the fill represents a slow, post-abandonment accumulation of washed-in soil, leaves, and such material.

SHERDS AND ARTIFACTS

Lot groups are defined in Table 2.154, with content given in Table 2.155. Inside the chultun (L.G. 1), as noted above, there is very little in the way of cultural material. Lot Group 2, from the surface, contains a bit more. Presumably, the sherds and artifacts in both represent occasional discards by those making use of the structures just S of the chultun.

TIME SPANS

Time spans for Ch. 5B-11 are listed in Table 2.156, and require little comment. Manik and Ik and/or Imix sherds (Table 2.154) indicate that Gp. 5B-3 probably was in use between AD 250 at the earliest (the appearance of Manik ceramics) and AD 869 at the latest (the end of the Imix Complex). The chultun itself could have been constructed at any time between these dates.

TABLE 2.154
Chultun 5B-11: Lot Groups

Lot Group	Lot	Provenience	Ceramic Evaluation
1	660/2-6	Contents of chultun	Probable Ik and/or Imix
2	660/1	Surface to bedrock around orifice	Manik, Ik and/or Imix

TABLE 2.155
Chultun 5B-11: Artifacts by Lot Group

Study Category	Object	Lot Group	
		1	2
Pottery	Sherds per cubic meter (lbs)	2.3	1.1
Flaked Chert Artifacts	Flake core		1
	Ovate biface		1
Flaked Obsidian Artifact	Prismatic blade		1

TABLE 2.156
Chultun 5B-11: Time Spans

Time Span	Construction Stage	Descriptive Data	Lot Groups	Ceramics in Vogue
1		Abandonment and accumulation of fill	1	
2		Use		Imix
				Ik
3	1	Construction of main chamber		Manik?
	2	Construction of ante-chamber and orifice	2	

Chultun 5C-6 Locus

Chultun 5C-6 is located at 5C:S330 E90, and was excavated as Op. 66L by Puleston in the summer of 1963. Although only 20 m SW of Str. 5C-33 and 34 (which are near Gp. 5C-3), the chultun does not seem related to that group. Rather, remnants of plaster floor are suggestive of a plaza for one or more structures, of which there are no visible ruins. The floor seems to postdate the chultun.

CHULTUN 5C-6

DESCRIPTION

This chultun (Fig. 73 and Table 2.157), of the common two-chamber type (TR. 32), was constructed in a series of two stages. First, the orifice, neck and antechamber were dug. In this case, the orifice was deeply stepped,

forming a relatively deep bowl. The stone cover, found in situ, fit down in this basin. The cover stone itself, though slightly squared on two adjacent corners, is round.

Beneath the orifice, the neck flares out almost immediately to form the wall of Chm. 1. In form, this suggests a bottle-shaped pit with round floor.

Following construction of Chm. 1, a passage and large lateral chamber were constructed (CS. 1). The passage, restricted on the sides, is unusually small, making it most difficult for the excavator to get into Chm. 2. There may once have been a sill in this passage, but there is now no sign of one.

Chamber 2 is oval in shape, a bit wider than it is long. The floor tends to slope down towards the back of the room, although this may be the result of overly enthusiastic excavation. The walls of the chamber bow out, but walls, floor, and ceiling are all clearly demarcated from one another.

TABLE 2.157
Chultun 5C-6: Average Dimensions (meters)

	Length	Width	Height	Minimum Diameter	Maximum Diameter
Stone cover	---	---	0.12	0.47	0.47
Neck	---	---	0.64	0.38	0.58
Chm. 1	0.88	0.96	0.94	---	---
Chm. 2	1.60	1.92	0.96	---	---

DISCUSSION

The stone cover of this chultun was found in place, with a number of small stones packed around its edge. Just NE of the orifice, and at an elevation 0.13 m above the stone cover, is a floor remnant (Ch. 5C-6:U. 3). This is at the same elevation as bedrock on all but the E side of the orifice, and lies on fill in a quarried area. The quarry cuts into the bowl-like portion of the orifice, widening out to the E.

To take the relationship between the chultun and quarry first, two possibilities exist. The first is that the chultun predates the quarry. In support of this, it seems unlikely that a chultun would have been excavated half-way over the lip of a quarry. Why, then, would this cut have been made after the construction of the chultun? If those who did the quarrying were simply looking for a vantage point and decided on the lip of a chultun, why did they leave the stone cover in place? They could not have cut into the rim of the orifice by accident, since the ground must have been cleared before quarrying began. Perhaps the cut was designed to minimize the amount of water that trickled into the chultun after a heavy rain. The unusual depth and width of the bowl-like step certainly would have collected water, and this would have nowhere to go except into the chultun. The lack of a sill in the passage below could have made this water troublesome indeed. Once the orifice had been given its basin-like shape, there was no way to remedy the situation other than by cutting an outlet that would drain the bowl and prevent water from collecting there. Where the quarry meets the orifice is a hump in bedrock, U. 1, which could have been intended to facilitate the drainage away from the orifice.

The main problem with this explanation is that the quarry is far more extensive than needed just for drainage. For this reason, the second interpretation seems more plausible. This suggests that the chultun orifice was intentionally located on the edge of an already existing quarry, which then functioned as a drain as outlined above. In other words, an attempt was made to deal with the water problem at the outset, rather than correcting a mistake. This, then, raises the question: Why construct a bowl-like orifice in the first place? The only apparent explanation that comes to mind is that a measure of concealment was desired for the orifice. This would have been afforded by its position in the corner of an abandoned quarry. Why such concealment was desired is yet another mystery.

If the quarry served to keep water from running into the chultun, it is unlikely that the quarry was immediately filled to permit the laying of the floor represented by U. 3. Nor is it likely that the chultun postdates the floor. This would have required a protective shelter over the chultun because of the water problem, and there is no evidence for such a structure. The particular placement of the stone cover in the orifice, with small stones packed in around its edge, suggests that the chultun was sealed off by the Maya. It is reasonable to suppose that this was done in conjunction with the laying of the floor, although it could have been earlier. Beneath the juncture of the orifice and quarry, the lip looks as if it had broken off (U. 2:Fig. 73c). If so, this may have been the reason for abandonment of the chultun. This, however, is speculative.

Nothing more is known of floor U. 3. Given its elevation relative to bedrock nearby, the most likely explanation of U. 3 is that it is the floor of a plaza associated with one or more structures for which there is no visible evidence in the form of a ruin mound.

Chultun 5C-6 was found filled with three strata. At the top was humus and material that had eroded from the ceiling. Beneath this, in Chm. 2, were two deposits. In the W end, sloping down to the E, was black earth, mixed with a few sherds. Over this in the E portion of the chamber, in part beneath the humus and collapse, was a very light-colored earth packed with sherds and a few other artifacts. What this suggests is that, prior to sealing off the chultun, earth was dumped into Chm. 2, forming a slope down from the floor of Chm. 1. On this was dumped material from a midden. Perhaps the dark soil was from the top of an old midden, no longer serving as a dump, with the rest of the material from deeper down in the same deposit. What is surprising is that these operations ceased before the entire chultun was filled up. This appears to reflect a decision to save effort by just sealing the stone cover in place, rather than filling the entire chultun.

BEDROCK "BASIN"

Not mentioned so far is a circular pit, U. 4, cut in bedrock, just NW of the chultun orifice. Unit 4 is about the same size as the orifice, and is 0.10–0.15 m deep. It is very like "Ch. 2E-2" and the two basins associated with Ch. 6C-7 (all this report). Since a number of such basins exist elsewhere, they presumably served a special function, as yet unknown. That they represent chultuns begun but not finished is not very convincing, for why did construction invariably stop so soon after they were begun?

Presumably, U. 4 predates the floor represented by U. 3. Other than this, its chronological relationship to the chultun is unknown.

SHERDS AND ARTIFACTS

Lot Groups for Ch. 5C-6 are listed in Table 2.158, with content in Table 2.159.

CHULTUN FILL

Material in LG. 1A is from a midden that was reused as fill. Presumably, the Maya did not go farther afield than necessary to get the material, so this probably came from a nearby structure, in much the manner that Ch. 5C-8 was filled with material from the nearby Str. 5C-57 (this report). Hence it is probable that the cultural material in Ch. 5C-6:LG. 1a was discarded by those who used both the chultun and the nearby, unknown structure. As a consequence, it should help date use of the chultun, as well as the time of its filling.

Lot Group 1b may be from the same source as 1a. Lot Group 1c, on the other hand, probably represents a mixture, such as one from LG. 2 and 3.

SURFACE MATERIAL

The surface material is subdivided, with some from above the level of floor U. 3 (LG. 3) and some from below (LG. 2). The latter should be floor fill for the most part, the former a mixture of rooted-up floor fill, with late occupation and possible post-occupation material.

TIME SPANS

Time spans for Ch. 5C-6 are listed in Table 2.160. To sum up the sequence, at some time a quarry was excavated and left open (TS. 6). This could have been as early as Preclassic times (LG. 1a and 3:Table 2.158). Later, a chultun was dug with its orifice located in the SW corner of the quarry (TS. 5); this arrangement was either to facilitate excavation or to permit drainage of water away from the bowl-shaped opening. The chultun was probably in use when Manik ceramics were in vogue, as the bulk of the midden sherds used to fill its chambers are of that complex (Table 2.158). A few Ik and/or Imix sherds, however, suggest that the filling postdates slightly the appearance of Ik ceramics. At the time it was filled (TS. 3), the quarry also was filled and leveled for a plaza floor, in use when Ik and/or Imix ceramics were in production.

In terms of dates, all this activity may be bracketed between a date perhaps somewhat prior to AD 250 (when Manik ceramics appear) and AD 869 (the end of the Imix Ceramic Complex), if not slightly earlier. Abandonment could have been up to 100 years prior to the end of the Imix Complex.

TABLE 2.158
Chultun 5C-6: Lot Groups

Lot Group	Lot	Provenience	Ceramic Evaluation
1a	66L/4,6	Chultun fill: reused midden	Manik; possible Preclassic and Ik and/or Imix
1b	66L/5,7	Chultun fill: beneath reused midden	Manik and Ik and/or Imix
1c	66L/2,3	Chultun fill; surface	Manik
2	66L/8,9	Floor fill, partially sealed	No data
3	66L/1	Surface, above floor level	1 Cauac, some Manik, mostly Ik and/or Imix

TABLE 2.159
Chultun 5C-6: Artifacts by Lot Group

Study Category	Object	Lot Group 1a	1b	1c	2	3
Pottery Vessels	Sherds per cubic meter (lbs)	28.3	?	?	3.0	?
Flaked Chert Artifacts	Flake core	1				
	Unclassifiable biface			1		
	Used flake	1				
	Unused flakes	3				1
Flaked Obsidian Artifacts	Prismatic blades	2	2			
Ground, Pecked, and Polished Stone Artifacts	Rubbing stone					1
Shell and Bone Artifacts	Bone, animal, unworked	8	3			

TABLE 2.160
Chultun 5C-6: Time Spans

Time Span	Architectural Development	Construction Stage	Unit	Descriptive Data	Lot Group	Ceramics in Vogue
1				Abandonment, ruin of floor, some recent drift in chultun		----------
2				Use of plaza floor	3	Ik and Imix
3			2?, 3	Chultun abandoned, filled and sealed, plaza floor laid	1a-c, 2	
4				Use		----------
5	Ch. 5C-6	1		Construction of lateral chamber		Manik
		2	1	Construction of orifice and antechamber		
6			4?	Early quarrying activity		---------- Cauac?

Group 4C-1

Group 4C-1, comprised of Str. 4C-5 through 14 (TR. 11), is located in the NE portion of Sq. 4C; just S of Gp. 3C-4 (this report). The ten structures are arranged around the edges of three plazas. The largest of these plazas is in the center, and around it are the largest structures. One of these, 4C-5, appears to have been a small (but large by local standards), range-type structure. The others seem to have been medium-sized rectangular platforms that could have served as house foundations. South of this plaza is a smaller one with three similar medium-to-small rectangular platforms. Three other small rectangular platforms are on a plaza NE of the principal one.

Five test pits (Table 2.161) sampled construction fill in Gp. 4C-1, with perhaps a small amount of late occupation debris in surface lots. The ceramic data (Table 2.162) indicate an occupation that began some time after the appearance of Manik ceramics, and lasted into the time when Imix ceramics were in use.

Group 4C-2

This is located 100 m SW of Gp. 4C-1, and includes Str. 4C-20 through 23 (TR. 11). These four structures are situated on the edges of a single plaza. Structure 4C-22, on the E side, is similar in appearance to known household shrines (TR. 21). The other three seem to have been small rectangular platforms comparable to known house foundations. A single pit (Table 2.161) tested plaza fill in front of 4C-23. The ceramic data (Table 2.162) clearly indicate an occupation that began in Late Preclassic times, and continued through the time when Ik and/or Imix pottery was in vogue.

Group 4C-3

Included here are two structures, 4C-42 and 43, situated on the S and W sides of a plaza (TR. 11). The group is located 70 m SE of Gp. 4C-2 and 50 m W of the Maudslay Causeway. The larger 4C-43 seems to have been a range-type structure of moderate size. Structure 4C-42 apparently was a small rectangular platform comparable to known house foundations. A single test pit (Table 2.161) that sampled plaza fill produced a very small ceramic sample, with nothing really distinctive in the deep lot (Table 2.162). The group was probably built and occupied when Ik and/or Imix ceramics were in use.

Group 4C-4

This is located just E of the Maudslay Causeway about midway between the N and S margins of Sq. 4C. It includes four structures, 4C-35 through 39, arranged on the four edges of a raised platform (TR. 11). All four appear to have been small platforms, three of which were rectangular. The shape of 4C-35 is somewhat indeterminate. The group as a whole seems comparable to known domestic groups at Tikal. A test pit sampled plaza fill (Table 2.161). Unfortunately, this was not deep, and little was recovered in the way of distinctive ceramics (Table 2.162). The group probably was occupied during the time of Ik and/or Imix ceramic production, with the possibility of an earlier initial occupation.

Group 4C-5

Situated W of the Maudslay Causeway, Gp. 4C-5 is 60 m SW of Gp. 4C-3. It includes Str. 4C-44 through 48, arranged around the four edges of a plaza (TR. 11). All but 4C-45 appear to be small-to-medium rectangular platforms that could have served as house foundations. In size and shape, 4C-45 seems comparable to known household shrines (TR. 21), but is located in the NE corner instead of in the center of the E side of the group.

Again, a single test pit sampled plaza fill (Table 2.161), with apparently a mixture of late occupation debris. The data indicate activity that began when Ik and/or Imix ceramics were in vogue (Table 2.162). Final abandonment came sometime after the appearance of Eznab pottery.

Group 4C-6

These four structures, 4C-49 through 52, are situated in the shadow of Temple IV, just N of its base and W of the Maudslay Causeway. All are small rectangular platforms that seem comparable to known house foundations, and are situated on the four sides of a raised supporting platform (TR. 11). A single pit (Table 2.161) sampled the platform fill. Despite small samples, an occupation from Late Preclassic times through the time when Ik and/or Imix ceramics were present is indicated (Table 2.162).

Structure 4C-34 Locus

The sole sources of information about this entity are Bu. 212 and PD. 221, both described in section III of this report. The structure is located 45 m E of Gp. 4C-

4, where the terrain slopes down to the S from the NE. South and W, numerous exposures of bedrock reveal evidence of extensive quarrying. The structure stands all by itself (TR. 11), and appears to be unusually long and wide for its low height.

Portions of Str. 4C-34 were accidentally disturbed in 1986 by Tikal Project quarrying to provide stone for the repair of major architecture. In the course of this, the burial and problematical deposits were exposed, at which point Carlos Rudi Larios V. recorded all available data and supervised removal of both deposits. The only architecture seen by Larios consisted of two tamped surfaces (Fig. 167b and 171c:U. 1 and 2) and a wall (Fig. 171c:U. 3). Units 1 and 2 could be the remains of surfaces for an exceptionally large two-level rectangular platform, or U. 1 could be a plaza surface in front of a normal-sized rectangular platform (represented by U. 2). The wall (U. 3) suggests that an upper platform level was added to the original 4C-34, so that more than one architectural development is represented. The problematical deposit should date the earliest of them.

No time spans have been defined, since so little is known about 4C-34. Thorough excavation would no doubt require extensive redefinition of any time spans defined here. The pottery of the problematical deposit (TR. 25A:fig. 153d) indicates that the earliest known version of 4C-34 postdates the appearance of late Imix pottery. Absence of surely identifiable Eznab sherds indicates abandonment of the hypothetical Str. 4C-34-1st by AD 869. The presence of several Manik sherds in the fill of 34 suggests that there was an earlier predecessor at this locus.

TABLE 2.161
Locations of Test Pits: Temple IV Quadrangle

Group	Test Pit	Location
4C-1	55F	Plaza in front of Str. 4C-13
	55G	Center of Plaza of Str. 4C-12 through 14
	55H	Center of Plaza of Str. 4C-5, 6, 10, 11
	55I	Inside corner, Str. 4C-5 and 6
	55J	Plaza of Str. 4C-7, 8, 9
4C-2	55E	Plaza in front of Str. 4C-23
4C-3	55B	Plaza of Str. 4C-42 and 43
4C-4	55D	Plaza of Str. 4C-34 through 38
4C-5	55C	Plaza of Str. 4C-44 through 48
4C-6	55A	Plaza of Str. 4C-49 through 52
5C-4	54A	Plaza of Str. 5C-29 through 32
5C-5	54C	Plaza of Str. 5C-25 through 28
5C-6	54B,D	Platform of Str. 5C-2 and 3

Group 5C-4

The structures of this group, 5C-29 through 32 (TR. 11), are arranged around the four sides of a plaza 130 m S of Str. 5C-4 (Temple IV). The largest, 5C-29, appears to have been a medium-sized range-type structure. Structure 5C-30 has the form of a household shrine (TR. 21), in keeping with its position on the E edge of the group. The other two structures appear to have been rectangular platforms of medium size, comparable to known house foundations. A single pit (Table 2.161) tested plaza fill, and produced sherd samples that are generally small. The ceramic data (Table 2.162) indicate an occupation that began after the appearance of Manik ceramics, and lasted through the period when Ik and/or Imix ceramics were in vogue.

Group 5C-5

Located immediately N of Gp. 5C-4, this group consists of three structures (5C-25, 26, 27) and a chultun (5C-7). Structures 5C-25 and 27 are situated on the W and N sides respectively of a plaza (TR. 11). The third structure, 5C-26, is off the NW corner of the plaza, behind the other two. All three appear to have been small, rectangular house foundations. The site map shows a possible fourth structure, 5C-28, but this is probably just the SE corner of the group platform.

A test pit (Table 2.161) sampled plaza fill, as well as a deposit of domestic occupation debris of midden quality. The ceramic data (Table 2.162) clearly indicate an initial occupation in Late Preclassic times. This seems to have continued through the time when Imix ceramics were in vogue.

Group 5C-6

Immediately S of Str. 5C-4 (Temple IV) and 80 m NE of Gp. 5C-5 is 5C-6. The nature of its two structures, 5C-2 and 3, is hard to determine on the basis of surface appearance (TR. 11). The smaller of the two, 5C-3, seems to be located behind 5C-2, which is on the W side of a raised platform. A test-pit and backhoe-trench sampled the fill of the supporting platform (Table 2.161). The ceramic data (Table 2.162) indicate an occupation that began in Late Preclassic times and continued through the period when Ik and/or Imix ceramics were in vogue.

TABLE 2.162
Ceramic Evaluation: Temple IV Quadrangle Test Pits

Group	Lot	Provenience	Ceramics
4C-1	55F/1	0-40 cm	Ik and/or Imix and some earlier
	55G/1		Ik and/or Imix; possible Manik
	55G/2		Ik and/or Imix
	55H/1	0-20 cm	Manik and Ik and/or Imix
	55H/2	20-40 cm	Manik through Imix
	55H/3	40-60 cm	Manik and Ik and/or Imix
	55II/1	0-50 cm	Manik and Ik and/or Imix
	55J/1	0-22 cm	Ik and/or Imix
4C-2	55E/1	0-20 cm	Late Preclassic through Ik and/or Imix
	55E/2	20-40 cm	Ik and/or Imix, possible Manik
	55E/3	40-60 cm	Heavy Preclassic
4C-3	55B1	0-20 cm	Probable Ik and/or Imix
	55B/2	20-40 cm	?
4C-4	55D/1	0-20 cm	Ik and/or Imix; possible earlier
4C-5	55C/1	0-20 cm	Ik and/or Imix and Eznab
4C-6	55A/1	0-20 cm	Manik and Ik and/or Imix
	55A/2	20-45 cm	Late Preclassic; Ik and/or Imix
	55A/3	45-60 cm	Manik
	55A/4	60-80 cm	Preclassic
5C-4	54A/1	0-20 cm	Manik and Ik and/or Imix
	54A/2	20-40 cm	Manik and ?
5C-5	54C/1	0-20 cm	Ik and/or Imix
	54C/2	20-45 cm	Mostly Ik and/or Imix; some Manik; possible Late Preclassic
	54C/3	45-60 cm	Ik and/or Imix; possible Manik and Late Preclassic
	54C/4	60-80 cm	Mostly Late Preclassic
	54C/5	Extension 0-80 cm	Mostly Ik and Imix
5C-6	54B/1	0-20 cm	Manik; Ik and/or Imix
	54B/2	20-40 cm	Mostly Ik and/or Imix; some Manik and Late Preclassic
	54B/3	40-60 cm	Mostly Late Preclassic; some Ik and/or Imix
	54B/4	60-80 cm	Fragments of large Preclassic vessel
	54D	Later back-hoe trench	

5. *Excavations in the Great Plaza Quadrangle*

Introduction

Although a large percentage of the structures in the squares of this quadrangle consist of major temples, range-type structures, ballcourts, and related architecture, there are some 30 or so groups of small- to medium-sized structures that might possibly have been houses. Most are in Sq. 4D, 4E, and 5E. The architecture in two groups (4E-1 and 4E-2) was investigated as part of the 1961 program of small-structure excavation. A third group (5D-1) was investigated at a later date. Four other groups were sampled as test pits, so for chronological purposes there is a sample on the order of 23% of potentially non-elite domestic groups of this quadrangle.

Group 4E-1

Located in Sq. 4E of the Tikal site map, Gp. 4E-1 is only 26 m N of Gp. 4E-4, the twin pyramid group that includes St. 22, dated at 9.17.0.0.0 (TR. 4 and 33A). The terrain here is essentially flat, with a slight dip to the NE. To the S, 26 m from the group, the ground rises abruptly 5 m to the level of Gp. 4E-4. Originally, a masonry retaining wall for this group must have stood here to prevent wash-out, though no such wall can now be seen.

Included in Gp. 4E-1 are five structures: 4E-14, 15, 16, 17, and 18. Of these, the first three are arranged on the S and W sides of Plat. 4E-1; the other two are off the E edge of the plaza. In 1961, Haviland excavated Str. 4E-14 and 16, along with some probable monument fragments (MS. 57–62) behind Str. 4E-14 (Op. 24J and K). Test pits were dug on the W side of Str. 4E-15 (Op. 24L) and the N edge of Plat. 4E-1 (Op. 24M).

STRUCTURE 4E-14

Structure 4E-14 is a two-level rectangular platform on the W side of the plaza, behind Str. 4E-15. Knowledge of it comes from limited excavations through its short axis, along 4 m of its W wall, and around MS. 57–62 (Fig. 74, 75, 178b). Four stages may be defined for its construction. First (CS. 4), the two lower courses of the W wall were built on the surface of soft, sterile marl. A pause-line of packed earth (U. 1) overlies fill that was placed inside the wall masonry.

A third course of masonry was added to the W wall as CS. 3, at the same time that an E wall (U. 3, now largely in ruins) was built. Unit 2, a second pause-line, overlies the fill for CS. 3 and marks its end. Then, as the platform

was completed, at least one or possibly two courses of masonry were added to the W wall, and U. 4 was built on the surface of U. 2. This last is the front of an upper platform level. The W wall was given added strength by the addition of an inner wall of rough masonry, U. 5, to help retain the fill. Unit 6, a small floor remnant, slightly above the surviving top of U. 4, marks the elevation of the pavement of the platform. Another floor remnant, U. 7, is in union with the base of U. 4, and evidently ran E to the top of the front wall of the structure. It utilized the U. 2 pause-line as its foundation.

Structure 4E-14 may well have supported some kind of building, for some platforms of similar form surely did (TR. 20B). For this, CS. 1 is defined. Here, the building may have had dwarf walls of masonry that were extended upward by perishable materials. Suggesting this is the large amount of building rubble around the platform. Although no dwarf-walls now survive, there seems to be too much rubble to have come only from collapse of the platform. Of relevance is the fact that at least one other structure in the group, 4E-16, did have dwarf walls.

West of 4E-14 is a layer of gray earth (U. 8), about 0.20 m thick, that overlies the natural marl and conceals the bottom 0.24 m of the W wall. This postdates construction, but it is not known if this was a purposeful deposit, or earth that gradually accumulated over a period of time. The latter interpretation is probable, although it cannot be proven. Miscellaneous Stones 57–62, the six possible monument fragments noted above, rest on the surface of this stratum. They may have been left in their present position about the time of the collapse of the structure, as masonry debris also rests at this level.

STRUCTURE 4E-15

Structure 4E-15 sits on the W edge of Plat. 4E-1, E and somewhat N of Str. 4E-14 (Fig. 80). Its long axis is oriented to a magnetic N-S line. The mound was tested by a trench into the middle of its W side that penetrated as far as the back wall of the structure (Fig. 76). This resulted in collection of a large amount of cultural material that may represent occupation of the structure, as well as some spilled-out fill. Overall plan is unknown, as only a portion of one wall, U. 1, was exposed. This consists of at least two courses of masonry built upon the same natural marl seen beneath Str. 4E-14. Several large blocks that lie to the W probably are collapsed remnants of a third and possible fourth course of U. 1. These stones lie on earth (U. 2) that bears the same relation to this structure as does Str. 4E-14:U. 8.

Unit 3 is a rough stone wall against the fill of the mound, where the upper part of U. 1 has collapsed. It seems to be analogous to Str. 4E-14:U. 5, an inner fill-retaining wall.

The configuration of the ruin mounds of Str. 4E-14 and 15 is similar, although the latter is somewhat larger. The heights of both structures are approximately the same. Structure 4E-15 probably is a multiple-level platform, not unlike 4E-14.

STRUCTURE 4E-16-2ND

In its original form, 4E-16-2nd consisted of a two-level building platform, topped by a building with masonry dwarf walls (Fig. 77, 78). The front platform walls, each of one course, are represented in the axial trench by U. 1 and 2. Unit 1 rests on thin fill above natural marl and U. 9, pavement that turns up to the base of U. 1, is a remnant of the plaza floor. Unit 20 is part of pavement that turns up to the base of U. 2. The building platform represents a single construction stage (CS. 2).

Units 6 and 7 are the inner and outer faces respectively of the rear wall. Unit 7 was placed on a thin gray fill, whereas U. 6 rests on the thick fill of CS. 2. Unit 8, a thin band of light earth behind the top of the lowest course of U. 7, marks a pause level. This lowest course of U. 7, therefore, was a part of CS. 2, while the upper courses pertain to CS. 1. The interior floor, U. 5, turns up to the base of U. 6. Units 3 and 4, remnants of the same floor, continued in use with 16-1st as well as 2nd.

The front wall is represented in the axial trench by U. 12 and 13 (Fig. 78:9), the inner and outer faces of this wall, respectively. The U. 4 floor surface is in union with U. 12. This front wall, the back wall, and the W end wall of central Rm. 1 were all built as a single operation. The end walls of the structure have not been located, but presumably were incorporated into those of the final building, although this has not been verified. If this was the case, then the building must have had at least three rooms, and probably more.

STRUCTURE 4E-16-1ST-B

This modification of 16-2nd saw an addition to the front of the building platform, modification of the platform itself, and addition of interior platforms within the rooms (Fig. 77, 78). Units 10 and 11 are remnants of the front of the N addition to the building platform, and apparently are parts of a broad step that gave access to the platform, which now consisted of just a single level. The W end wall of the step is inset 1.10 m from the W end of the building platform. The position of the front wall of the building platform remained the same as for 2nd, though it was raised to the level of floor U. 3, 4, and 19, which apparently remained in use.

In plan, the building may best be described as of the "range" type. It consists of at least three, but more probably five, rooms arranged in a row. The positions of Rm. 2 and 4 were clearly visible before excavation by high spots in the ruin mound. Although the outer end-walls of Rm. 3 and 5 were not definitely identified, a distance of 3.40 m between the end wall of Rm. 4 and the end wall of the building platform makes the existence of Rm. 3 and 5 more likely than not. The walls of Rm. 1 and 4, the only ones investigated, were original with 2nd. Fallen stones of U. 7 behind the building demonstrate that these masonry dwarf walls projected at least 1.14 m above the surface of U. 5, the original floor, but probably no higher. Wide interior platforms were built against the back wall above U. 4, 5, and 19 in Rm. 1 and 4, and in Rm. 1, the floor (U. 4) was patched to turn up to U. 15, the front of the platform of that room. Unit 14 is a remnant of the floor of this platform.

STRUCTURE 4E-16-1ST-A

A final small-scale modification saw construction of two more small interior platforms, U. 17 and 18, in the ends of Rm. 1. Their walls abut the front and back building walls, as well as the front of the original interior platform. They rest on the surfaces of U. 4 and 14, and were at least 0.20 m higher than the surface of U. 14. No similar interior platforms are apparent in Rm. 4.

PLATFORM 4E-1

In addition to the excavations associated with Str. 4E-14, 15, and 16, Plat. 4E-1 was investigated by a limited exposure of its northern extent (Fig. 79). The goal was to verify existence of a plaza retaining wall as shown on the Tikal site map (TR. 11), and to test for trash deposits near the wall. For this, a trench 2 m wide and 3 m long was opened. Two walls were identified, possibly the elements of a stairway. Unit 1 designates the northernmost wall, which rests directly on natural marl, without doubt the same stratum discussed in connection with Str. 4E-14. Unit 1 was built of a single course of vertically set masonry slabs. In line with their N face, the marl has been cut to a depth of 0.12 m. South of U. 1 is a fill-retaining wall of rough masonry (U. 2), behind which is a fill of gray-brown earth.

Unit 3 is another wall, 0.80 m S of U. 1. Poorly preserved, its masonry rests on the gray-brown fill of U. 1 and 2, at the same elevation as the top of U. 1. Behind (S) of it is a fill of yellow-brown earth. Despite poor preservation, the top of this wall is only 8 cm lower than Str. 4E-16:U. 9, the floor of Plat. 4E-1 associated with 16-2nd.

Two interpretations of the N wall are possible: U. 1 and 3 may be two risers of a stepped wall, or U. 3 may be an early wall with U. 1 the bottom part of a later one. The relative positions of U. 1 and 3 make the first interpretation more plausible.

POSSIBLE EARLY ACTIVITY

In none of the excavations could hard bedrock crust be found. Instead, soft marl underlies the culture-bearing strata. This is sterile, and apparently is entirely natural. Usually one finds hard bedrock crust of varying thickness above such marl. Absence of such crust here suggests that it was consumed by extensive quarrying, a possibility made more plausible by Gp. 4E-4, the construction of which required a large amount of stone (TR. 15). It is logical to assume that masonry and material for fill would have been secured as near as possible to the site of construction in order to minimize problems of transport. Quarrying in the area that was later the site of Gp. 4E-4 would have provided masonry and fill for construction of that group, and incidentally would have served to level the terrain, thereby accentuating the steep rise to the twin-pyramid group from the surrounding area.

Although the possibility that quarrying provided construction material for the buildings and platforms of Gp. 4E-1 cannot be absolutely ruled out, it is doubtful if quarrying would have been as extensive if that had been the case. Certainly, excavation in other groups of small structures commonly reveals some quarrying, but nowhere has there been such extensive removal of the bedrock crust. Therefore, the favored hypothesis is that quarrying here was associated with construction of Gp. 4E-4, the twin pyramid group, and dated at 9.17.0.0.0 by St. 22 (TR. 18).

MISCELLANEOUS STONES 57–62

LOCATION

These possible six monument fragments are located in an apparent haphazard arrangement behind (W of) Str. 4E-14, as shown in Fig. 74. Their positions relative to Datum 24 J-M are given in Table 2.163

All rest on the surface of Str. 4E-14:U. 8, generally on their largest surface, except for MS. 57. The latter roughly resembles the top of a monument in shape, and as such would be in an upright position.

DESCRIPTION

All six are of the same kind of bedded limestone, and show extensive weathering where the edges of the bedding are visible. As for their potential as monument

TABLE 2.163
Locations of Miscellaneous Stones 57-62
Relative to Datum 24J-M

MS 57:	9.94 m	N, 4.22 m E
MS 58:	4.60 m	N, 3.03 m E
MS 59:	6.32 m	N, 2.85 m E
MS 60:	9.57 m	N, 1.64 m E
MS 61:	10.90 m	N, 1.68 E
MS 62:	12.40 m	N, 2.04 m E

fragments, they resemble closely the stone used for Late Classic Tikal monuments (TR. 33A:2).

Since these stones have been badly broken up, little can be said about their original shape. Miscellaneous Stone 57, however, has a top that is curved (unevenly) from side-to-side and front-to-back. Its base suggests that it was broken off a longer piece of stone. Overall, it gives the appearance of a heavily weathered top that has been broken from a stela. Its surviving height is 0.68 m, maximum breadth, 0.90 m (at the break), and its thickness 0.52 m.

The other stones are of amorphous shape, but the two larger (MS. 59 and 61) have two broad, flat surfaces that are parallel and so could derive from broken monuments. Surviving dimensions of MS. 59 are 0.90 m (height); 0.76 m (breadth); and 0.75 m (thickness). Miscellaneous Stone 61 is 0.64 in height, 0.64 m in breadth, and 0.71 m in thickness. Miscellaneous Stones 58, 60, and 62 are all smaller in size.

EXCAVATION DATA

A trench was dug to bedrock from Str. 4E-14 around all of these fragments with the exception of MS. 62. Revealed was that all rest on a deposit that seems to have accumulated while the structure was in use (Str. 4E-14:U. 8). This deposit, thickest near 4E-14 (0.20 m), overlies sterile marl.

DISCUSSION

These stones are likely fragments of one or more monuments. This is supported by the following facts: (1) the stone is the type used in monuments after 9.14.0.0.0 (TR. 33A:2); (2) stones of this size are almost never found lying loose this way in Tikal; (3) the shape of MS. 57 is suggestive of a weathered monument top; (4) the broad surface of MS. 59 and 61 are suggestive of monument surfaces and (5) the stones seem to have been placed here (see below) at a time when it is known that monuments were being moved around and broken at Tikal (TR. 3).

Since the stones do indeed appear to be monument fragments, the question is, how many monuments are represented? A final answer to this cannot be given on account of the broken and weathered condition of the stones. The discrepancy in thickness between MS. 57, on the one hand, and MS. 59 and 61, on the other, suggests that at least two monuments are represented. It is unlikely (though unproven) that each stone is from a separate monument, however. Indeed, MS. 59 and 61 could be pieces of a single one.

The place of origin of the monuments is not known. Given their proximity to twin pyramid groups, with their plain monuments, one might suppose that the fragments were moved from one or more of these locations (TR. 33A:90).

The stones were probably brought to their final resting place in TS. 2 for Str. 4E-14, in a time of Eznab ceramics (see below). The original monuments must have been made in Late Classic times, perhaps not earlier than 9.15.0.0.0 (the presumed date for Twin Pyramid Gp. 4D-1).

SHERDS AND ARTIFACTS

Lot groups for the structures and plaza of Gp. 4E-1 are defined in Table 2.164, with content listed in Tables 2.165–2.168.

CONSTRUCTION FILL

Such material comprises Str. 4E-14:LG. 1 and 4E-16:LG. 1 and 2. Since both structures were built on natural marl, this should be the earliest material from the group. In the case of 4E-14, although four construction stages were defined, there seems no reason to subdivide LG. 1, given that all are parts of a single architectural development. Some material E and W of the walls has also been included as fill, since it comes from debris that obviously is from collapse of the structure and can easily be separated stratigraphically from the occupation refuse that it overlies. Analysis of ceramics does not contradict this, although some minor contamination can be noted from late activities in the group. Also included in LG. 1 is some material found above the level of the floor of the structure, but which also seems to be disturbed fill for the most part. Cultural material is not plentiful in this fill, but an adequate sherd sample was secured for dating purposes.

The situation with respect to Str. 4E-16 is straightforward, as stratigraphy permits segregation of fill from the two architectural developments. In the case of 16-1st, some material in areas of collapse above the structure has been included in LG. 2, where this is felt to be warranted. In the case of 2nd, material is in large part sealed beneath floors. The problem of lag between the accumulation of trash in one area and its later use as construction fill elsewhere is nicely illustrated, in that fill for 1st appears to be earlier (early Imix), than that for 2nd (late Imix). As in the case of Str. 4E-14:LG. 1, cultural material in the fills is not abundant, yet an adequate sherd sample was secured for dating purposes.

MATERIAL ABOVE LIVING LEVELS

There is a general paucity of material from this group as a whole. Sherds are most abundant in back of Str. 4E-15. Some of these are undoubtedly from fill, but several pieces of nearly whole vessels with sharp breaks, and abundant inter-lot fits, suggest a refuse pile, but without any great time depth. It seems most probable that the de-

posit consists of trash dumped in back of the structure while the group was in use.

Sherds are also abundant N of the plaza, suggesting that this area may have served as a periodic dump. Artifacts, however, are scarce here. Both Lots 1 and 2 are essentially similar, with perhaps a large admixture of fill in Lot 1.

As noted, cultural material is not abundant around Str. 4E-14 and 16. In the case of 14, most non-sherd material is in LG. 2a from U. 8. On stratigraphic grounds, this postdates construction, and probably represents debris that accumulated gradually while the structure was in use. Lot Group 2b, farther W, and in proximity to the several probable monument fragments, should be comparable to LG. 2a, but the area is more disturbed. Lot Group 3, from the surface of the mound, seems to be a mixture of post-occupation material with structure fill.

Occupation refuse probably accounts for most of LG. 3a and 3b from Str. 4E-16, as there is little evidence that construction debris is included. Lot Group 4 may include some artifacts left at the time of abandonment, but there must be admixture of fill. The paucity of material associated with this range-type structure is of interest. The same sort of situation pertains to Str. 4E-50, another such structure (in Gp. 4E-2, this report). Since most of the material comes from just off the W end of the structure, there is the possibility that it did not originate from 4E-16, but might have come from elsewhere in the group, possibly Str. 4E-14. Since there is clear evidence in the case of 4E-14 for post-abandonment activity in the group, some of the on-floor material from Str. 4E-16 could pertain to such activity.

TIME SPANS

Time spans for the excavated structures of Gp. 4E-1 are defined in Tables 2.169 through 2.172, and combined into six group time spans in Table 2.173. Since actual floors and walls were not followed from one structure to another, specific correlations between most of their time spans are not possible. Instead, group time spans are based on inference and ceramic data (Table 2.164).

Group TS. 6 provides a base for the group, and is represented everywhere by complete removal of the bedrock crust. This most probably took place at the time of construction of twin-pyramid Gp. 4E-4 in which St. 22 stands. This was followed by construction of Str. 4E-16-2nd (Gp. TS. 5), no earlier than the time of late Imix ceramics.

Not known is how construction of Str. 4E-14 and 15 correlates with the sequence for 4E-16. Both might have been contemporary with 16-2nd. Or, on the basis of the lack of renovation of either structure, plus the location of 15 towards the middle of Plat. 4E-1, it might be that 14 correlates with 16-1st-B, and 15 with 16-1st-A. This is lit-

TABLE 2.164
Group 4E-1: Lot Groups

Feature	Lot Group	Lot	Provenience	Ceramic Evaluation
Str. 4E-14 (Op. 24J)	1	4-6,8-12,14, 16,18,19	Unsealed fill	Late Imix and Eznab
	2a	2,7	W of structure, near base of wall (U. 8)	Late Imix
	2b	13,15,17	W of 2a, around MS. 57-62	Late Imix and Eznab
	3	1,3	Surface, over and around structure	Late Imix and Eznab
Str. 4E-15 (Op. 24L)	1	1-7	W of structure, surface to marl	Late Imix
Str. 4E-16 (Op. 24K)	1	7,9,10,12-14,17,19,22	Partially sealed fill of 2nd	Late Imix
	2	1,3,6,11,16,25	Partially sealed fill of 1st	Early Imix
	3a	18,20,21,23, 24,27,29	W of structure	Late Imix
	3b	4	S of structure	Late Imix
	3c	26	N of structure, surface to base of wall	Late Imix
	4	5,8,15,28	Surface of structure to floor levels	?
Plat. 4E-1 (Op. 24M)	1	1	Surface	Late Imix
	2	2	N of plaza	Late Imix

TABLE 2.165
Structure 4E-14: Artifacts by Lot Group

Study Category	Object	Lot Group 1	2a	2b	3
Pottery Vessels	Sherds per cubic meter (lbs)	.5	1.4	.6	.7
Flaked Chert Artifacts	Flake core			1	
	Ovate biface	1			
	Used flakes	17			
	Unmodified flakes	19		2	1
	Unmodified, fire-spalled flake	1			
Flaked Obsidian Artifacts	Unmodified flake				1
	Nodule (green)	1			
Ground, Pecked, and Polished Stone Artifacts	Rubbing stones	2			

TABLE 2.166
Structure 4E-15: Artifacts by Lot Group

Study Category	Object	Quantity
Pottery Vessels	Sherds per cubic meter (lbs)	18.8
Other Pottery Artifacts	Figurines	7
	Perforated sherd disc	1
	Unclassifiable formed object	5
Flaked Chert Artifacts	Ovate biface	1
	Small point	1
	Irregular, retouched flakes	3
	Used flakes	3
	Unmodified flakes	16
Flaked Obsidian Artifacts	Prismatic blades	3
	Thin biface	1
Ground, Pecked, and Polished Stone Artifacts	Mano	1
	Rubbing stone	1

TABLE 2.167
Structure 4E-16: Artifacts by Lot Group

Study Category	Object	Lot Group 1	2	3a	3b	3c	4
Pottery Vessels	Sherds per cubic meter (lbs)	4.3	3.4	2.6	--	--	1.0
Other Pottery Artifacts	Figurine	1					
	Unclassifiable formed object	1					
Flaked Chert Artifacts	Ovate bifaces	1	1				1
	Thin bifaces	1				1	
	Irregular, retouched flake		1				
	Rounded, retouched flake		1				
	Used flakes	1		1			
	Unmodified flakes	9	17	9			1
	Unmodified, fire-spalled flakes		4	3			
Ground, Pecked, and Polished Stone Artifacts	Manos	1					1

TABLE 2.168
Platform 4E-1: Artifacts from Operation 24M

Study Category	Object	Quantity
Pottery Vessels	Sherds per cubic meter (lbs)	16.1
Flaked Chert Artifacts	Ovate bifaces	3
	Unmodified flake	1
	Unmodified flake, fire-spalled	1

tle more than speculation, however, and so Gp. TS. 5 has been left broadly defined to cover all these events. Group TS. 4, then, covers at least the final period of use of Str. 4E-14 and 15, as well as use of 16-1st-A.

Late activity in Gp. 4E-1 is indicated by Pabellon Modeled-carved sherds, one of which was found near MS. 57. Two others were found on the W slope of collapsed fill from Str. 4E-14, and another was found near its surface. Such sherds are diagnostic of the Eznab Ceramic Complex, whereas general occupation debris in this group contains only late Imix sherds. This, and the position of three of the Eznab sherds above debris from the collapse of 4E-14, seem to indicate that the structure was abandoned probably near the end of the time when Imix ceramics were in vogue, and it had fallen into ruin by the time users of Eznab ceramics appeared in the group. Therefore, reoccupation, rather than continuing late occupation, is indicated. This is the basis of Gp. TS. 2. Since the miscellaneous stones overlie occupation debris, and since one Eznab sherd was found near MS. 57, the movement of these stones to their present resting place was probably connected with this reoccupation.

The undiagnostic nature of material on the floors of Str. 4E-16 is unfortunate, for it is not possible to tell whether or not it pertains to activities of Gp. TS. 2 or 4. It is just possible that users of Eznab ceramics lived in this building, as they did in the case of other small range-type structures such as 3F-12 (in Gp. 3F-3, this report), Str. 4E-31 (TR. 19), and Str. 7F-29 and 7F-32 (TR. 22). That these people actually lived in Gp. 4E-1 seems indicated by the sherd finds already referred to, for it is doubtful if people who were just moving some large stone fragments through would have been carrying pottery along at the time. Moreover, a small point of chert in the debris behind Str. 4E-15 looks to be of a late type, and so may have been lost by those responsible for the Eznab sherds and the miscellaneous stones (TR. 27B:20 and fig. 48a). If so, it also suggests people actually living in the area. Given the collapsed nature of Str. 4E-14 and 15 at the time, 16, which could have been repaired, becomes the most likely place of residence. Another possibility is that they were living in the masonry Str. 4E-37, in Gp. 4E-4 just behind Gp. 4E-1.

In summary, initial construction in Gp. 4E-1 seems to date from some time just after AD 771, the date of St. 22 (TR. 33A:48). The group was abandoned around AD 869, the date for the end of the Imix Ceramic Complex, but was reoccupied briefly after that time.

TABLE 2.169
Structure 4E-14: Time Spans

Time Span	Architectural Development	Construction Stage	Unit	Miscellaneous Stones	Descriptive Data	Lot Group		Ceramics in Vogue
1					Final abandonment			----------
2				57-62	Post-abandonment activity			Eznab
3					Abandonment and collapse			----------
4					Use	2a,b	3	
5	Str. 4E-14	1			Construction of building			Imix
		2	4-7		Construction of upper platform level			
		3	2,3		Construction of lower platform level	1		
		4			Construction of platform base			(Late)
6					Quarrying of bedrock			

TABLE 2.170
Structure 4E-15: Time Spans

Time Span	Architectural Development	Unit	Other Data	Lot Group	Ceramics in Vogue
1			Final abandonment		- - - - - - - - -
2			Post-abandonment activity		Eznab
3			Abandonment and collapse		- - - - - - - - -
4		2	Use		
5	Str. 4E-15	1,3	Construction	1	Imix
6			Quarrying of bedrock		(Late)

TABLE 2.171
Structure 4E-16: Time Spans

Time Span	Architectural Development	Construction Stage	Unit	Descriptive Data	Lot Group	Ceramics in Vogue
1				Abandonment and collapse		- - - - - - - - -
2				Use	3a, 3b	
3	Str. 4E-16-1st-A	None defined	17,18	Final modification of structure	4	
4				Use		
5	Str. 4E-16-1st-B	None defined	10,11, 14-16	First modification of structure	2	Imix
6				Use		
7	Str.4E-16-2nd	1	3,4,6, 12,13	Construction of building	1	
7	Str.4E-16-2nd	2	1,2,7, 8,9,19	Construction of building platform		(Late)
8				Quarrying of bedrock		

TABLE 2.172
Platform 4E-1: Time Spans

Time Span	Architectural Development	Unit	Descriptive Data	Lot Group	Ceramics in Vogue
1			Final abandonment		---------
2			Post abandonment activity		Eznab
3			Abandonment and ruin		---------
4			Use	2	
5	Plat. 4E-1	1-3	Construction	1	Imix
6			Quarrying of bedrock		(Late)

TABLE 2.173
Group 4E-1: Time Spans

Group Time Span	Str. 4E-14 (Table 2.169)	Str. 4E-15 (Table 2.170)	Str. 4E-16 (Table 2.171)	Plat. 4E-1 (Table 2.172)
1	1	1		1
2	2	2		2
3	3	3	1	3
4	4	4	2	
			3	
5			4	
			5	
			6	4
	5?	5?	7	5
6	6	6	8	6

Group 4E-2

Located at 4E-S427 E457 on the Tikal site map, Gp. 4E-2 consists of four structures: 4E-50, 51, 52, and 53, arranged around the four sides of Plat. 4E-2 (Fig. 88). The group is built on the side of a steep hillside; Str. 4E-50, the largest of the four, is built on a slightly sunken shelf into the hillside to the W; Str. 4E-53 is opposite, built on a high terraced area. On the crest of the hill 155 m to the W is a major group (4E-14) of range-type structures that includes Str. 5E-1 and 4E-44 through 48 (the "F Group" of Morley; TR. 23A:21–26 and fig. 14–19). In April 1961, Haviland conducted excavations in all four structures as Op. 24N, P, and Q, with an additional probe in 1963.

STRUCTURE 4E-50-B

This largest and most elaborate structure in Gp. 4E-1 began as a small vaulted range-type structure (see Fig. 81, 82, 178c). Three stages may be defined for its construction, although a fourth, for which there is scant evidence, is a possibility. As the first (CS. 3), the lower level of a two-level building platform was built on the surface of U. 2. Possibly the stair masonry and the lowest course of the veneer walls were laid, or they may have been part of CS. 2. These walls rest on natural bedrock and marl. Units 5, 6, and 7, remnants of a single pause-line, mark the top of the filling operation of CS. 3 beneath the building proper. Unit 7 is a particularly thick layer of packed lime that provided a firm foundation for the front wall of the following stage.

The upper level of the building platform was built as CS. 2 and possibly U. 13 (pavement of the front portion of the lower platform level) was laid. This floor turns up to the front of the upper level. The finished veneer of the entire building platform was surely in place by the end of this stage. Units 8 and 9 are two pause-lines that cap the fill of the platform. Unit 9 was specially leveled and tamped to serve as a foundation for the interior platforms of CS. 1, and for the building floor.

Upon completion of the building platform, a masonry building was erected (CS. 1) that took the form of a single room, probably with three doorways, though this detail has not been verified. An interior platform, built against the back wall, was integral with the building walls, as were two walls built on the interior platform that divide it into three parts. Unit 12, the interior floor, is in union with the front wall of the interior platform, and U. 14, the floor of the interior platform, turns up to the building walls and to U. 16 and 17. Traces of red paint can be seen on U. 14.

Units 16 and 17, the two interior platform dividing walls, each are inset on their medial side, 0.60 m above the surface of the platform, to form shelves 0.30 m deep.

Not known is whether these walls extended all the way to the ceiling.

The ceiling of 50-B was vaulted; this is clearly indicated by the great amount of collapsed building rubble in which were stones with a pronounced bevel. Although included here in CS. 1, the vault may have been built as a fourth construction stage, as it is probable that the building walls may have been allowed to settle prior to construction of the vault. A complete reconstruction of the room in section is not possible, as no evidence of the location of the spring stones survives.

STRUCTURE 4E-50-A

At some time after a period of use, renovations were carried out on the building. Evidence for this consists of U. 15, a second floor on the top of the interior platform, and the secondary N end wall of what then became an axial room. This wall abuts the interior platform and building walls. With the addition of this and presumably a corresponding partition to the S, three rooms were created from the original one, presumably with a doorway opening into the center of each. The doorway into central Rm. 1, and probably the other two, were part of the original construction. The final interior platform floor was laid directly on the original one, turning up to U. 16 and 17, as well as the building walls. Unit 14 had not been prepared in any special way for the laying of U. 15. Traces of red paint were noted on U. 15.

STRUCTURE 4E-51-2ND

This architecture is known only from a trench through the short axis of the structure (Fig. 83). Originally it stood as a one-level platform that could have supported a building of perishable materials. From the configuration of its ruin mound, it probably was rectangular. Its masonry walls enclose a fill of light-colored earth that is capped by a plaster floor (U. 1). Since the ground at this locus slopes markedly down to the N, it had to be built up prior to actual construction of 51-2nd. This, and the information above, suggest three stages in construction: CS. 3 for preparation of the surface on which to build, CS. 2 for assembly of the platform, and CS. 1 for construction of the building. Alternatively, 51-2nd may postdate original construction of Plat. 4E-2. If so, CS. 3 did not exist; the structure would merely have been put up on the existing level surface. Against this is the lack of evidence for a floor beneath the fill of 51-2nd. On the other hand, there may not have been any plaster floor here, if U. 3 (discussion below) was in use prior to construction of 2nd.

STRUCTURE 4E-51-1ST

Evidence for this consists of a single wall, U. 2 (Fig. 83). It was excavated sufficiently to show that it probably extends the length of the structure. Hence, it likely represents the front wall for an upper platform level, and not for a small (interior?) platform. It was built directly on U. 1, with this pavement perhaps continuing in use in front of the new upper level. At least there is no evidence that it was altered or replaced here. No trace of pavement for the new upper platform level could be found, nor was there any trace of a rear wall. This, however, seems the result of the ravages of time.

If it is correct that Str. 4E-51 was converted into a two-level platform, then any building that stood on the platform of 2nd also must have been modified. Consequently, the following stages of construction are proposed: CS. 3 for at least partial removal of the building walls; CS. 2 for construction of the upper platform level; and CS. 1 for reconstruction of the building.

Two features in front of 4E-51 deserve special notice. One is a pit, apparently basin-shaped, which penetrates a grainy, white fill for Plat. 4E-2 to bedrock (Fig. 83b). Only its SE corner was excavated (Fig. 83a). It was filled with small burned stones. Since no traces of a floor for Plat. 4E-2 could be seen here, it is not certain whether the pit was dug prior to construction of a platform surface, or whether it was a later intrusion. An earth oven would leave remains such as these, and Reuben Reina (pers. comm.) has seen earth ovens in use today in some Indian communities on Lake Peten for roasting pig heads on special occasions. The pits measure about 2 m across, and 1 m in depth. Heated stones are placed in the bottom, the pig head is then put in, and covered with more heated stones. Unit 3, while slightly shallower, has the correct lateral dimensions as far as can be judged. Moreover, the stones within the pit are comparable to those used today.

Unit 4 is a deposit of stones W of the front of Str. 4E-51, overlying fill of Plat. 4E-2. These could have been part of fill for a portion of 51 no longer distinguishable otherwise, but it is more probable that they are simply from post-occupational decay of the structure.

STRUCTURE 4E-52

Structure 4E-52 probably was a three-level platform that could have supported a building of perishable material (Fig. 84, 85). Units 1, 2, and 3 are front walls of the three levels; U. 4 is the back. All walls (seen only in a trench through the short axis) were too badly preserved to permit meaningful observations of masonry. Units 1, 2, and 4 each were based on a grainy gray fill, while U. 3 was placed on brown earth used as structure fill. Units 5 and 8 are fragments of the floors of the exposed portions of the first and second platform levels respectively. The fill between U. 2 and 4 is a brown earth with no pause-lines apparent. The fill between U. 1 and 2, however, is of

packed stones, suggesting that this portion of the structure could have been an addition. The second level of the platform defines one construction stage (CS. 4); the third level defines CS. 3, and the front extension (the first level) defines another (CS. 2). Construction Stage 1 is inferred for construction of a building of perishable material, although a search was not made for evidence confirming its existence.

Units 7 and 8 designate two exposures of a grainy gray earth, undoubtedly a single deposit. Units 1 and 2 rest on it, and U. 4 probably does as well. This gray earth overlies unmodified bedrock and probably represents fill that was placed for construction of the level plaza area. This application seems to form the earliest construction phase (CS. 5).

STRUCTURE 4E-53-2ND-A AND B

The original structure at this locus was undoubtedly a one-level platform (built as CS. 2) that could have supported a pole-and-thatch building (built as CS. 1; Fig. 86, 87). Units 1 and 2 are portions of the front wall, while U. 3 and 4 are masonry blocks, apparently fallen from the rear. This rear wall must have rested on a yellow-brown fill that served to raise the low area to approximately the same elevation as Plat. 4E-2 in front (CS. 3). In the axial trench, a floor for Plat. 4E-2 (Str. 4E-53:U. 7) turns up to U. 1. At the N end of 53, two floors (U. 5 and 6) apparently turn up to U. 2. It is probable that U. 5, the lower of the two, is equivalent to U. 7. Unit 6, therefore, would represent a later grading floor to compensate for the slope of Plat. 4E-2 near the end of the platform. Units 8 and 9 are surely remnants of a single pavement that capped the fill of the platform.

STRUCTURE 4E-53-1ST

This consisted of an enlargement of the structure to the W, and the addition of an upper platform level. The line of the original E wall (U. 3 and 4) was preserved, but an upper course must have been added to obtain the desired height for the upper platform surface. This second course, however, was not found in situ. Unit 10, exposed in the middle trench, is a portion of the E wall of the lowest platform level; it extended the platform 2.15 m E of U. 1. This wall seems now to be completely destroyed at the NE corner. Unit 10 sits on the surface of U. 7, the original floor of Plat. 4E-2. Unit 11, the pavement of Plat. 4E-2 that turns up to U. 10, probably is the same surface as U. 7, but the continuity was broken during construction and the turnup is a later patch.

Units 12 and 13 are portions of the W wall of the upper platform level, and rest on fill above the original plaza floor. No floors for the final platform surfaces now survive.

To sum up, construction of 53-1st was probably in four stages: an older building was torn down (CS. 4); the lower platform level was built (CS. 3); followed by the upper platform level (CS. 2); a final stage (CS. 1) is allowed for a new pole-and-thatch building on the platform.

Excavations at the base of the slope E of 4E-53 exposed a sloping, quarried bedrock face, at least 1.80 m high. This had largely been buried by debris, much of which probably had eroded and washed down from Gp. 4E-2 to the W. Contrary to what we hoped to find, there was very little cultural material in this wash. It is not impossible that the quarrying here was related to construction of the structures of Gp. 4E-2.

POSSIBLE EARLY ACTIVITY

Bedrock, where exposed in the trench through the axis of Str. 4E-50, had been modified to a large extent. As shown in Fig. 81 and 82, the naturally rising rock was cut and utilized as a portion of the riser for the lowest step in front of the structure. West of this point, bedrock was cut down to the level of marl that generally underlies the hard crust. At least as far as the back wall of the building platform, this crust was completely removed. Undoubtedly, this quarrying was connected with construction here, and served to provide stone for building as well as to provide a sunken shelf in the high area here on which to build a structure.

Another feature, U. 18, is a pit dug in bedrock in front of the first step of 4E-50, on its axis. This penetrates to 0.70 m below the base of this step. The purpose of the pit is unknown; its axial position is reminiscent of the pit that contains PD. 109 beneath architecturally similar Str. 3F-12, but it contained neither burial nor cached offerings.

Units 1 and 2 designate two strata of earth that overlie marl beneath the rear portion of 4E-50. Ceramic analysis shows that these predate the structure fill. Three interpretations of U. 1 and 2 are possible. One is that they are construction fill that happened to come from an earlier trash deposit than did overlying materials, or they might be an incidental accumulation of material already in place when construction commenced. Finally, they might be the remains of fill for earlier architecture that was largely razed prior to construction of 4E-50-B. A final decision between these alternatives cannot be made, but the second seems least probable. The third seems most likely, for four reasons. First, the fill ceramics from the other three structures of the group are earlier than those in the fill of 4E-50 above U. 1 and 2. This, of course, could merely be the result of coincidental use of early trash for fill in the three structures, but not in 4E-50. This seems unlikely; one would expect contamination of the early fills in such instances by a few later elements, as has been noted in several other small structures at Tikal. One is left to conclude

that 4E-50-B postdates the other structures.

Second, it seems unlikely (but still possible) that two or three structures would be built, without one on the W side of the group. This would mean that the Maya went to considerable trouble to raise the level of the terrain for 4E-53, when they could more easily have built it in the high area where 4E-50 stands. Third, the best source of material to build up the terrain for 4E-53 would have been the high area where 4E-50 now stands. To lower that area and then leave it empty seems odd, though not impossible. Finally, there is U. 18; this pit seems to have served no purpose in relation to Str. 4E-50, but it could have for an earlier structure. Such reasoning is at best circumstantial, but it is suggestive. If such an early structure did stand here, its destruction would define the earliest stage in the construction of 4E-50-B.

SHERDS AND ARTIFACTS

For definition of lot groups, see Table 2.174; for content, see Tables 2.175–2.178.

MATERIAL BENEATH ARCHITECTURE

Included here are Str. 4E-50:LG. 1a and 1b from U. 1, 2, and 18; 4E-51:LG. 1 from U. 3; and 4E-52:LG. 1. Of these, the second is the most problematical; the third appears to be fill, placed to provide a level surface on which to build. Of special note is that sherds from 4E-50:U. 1 and 2 are earlier than those from overlying structure fill. As argued above, this may mean that an earlier structure was razed to permit construction of 4E-50-B, or that U. 1 and 2 came from early occupation debris associated with the other three structures of the group, already in use by the time 4E-50-B was built.

CONSTRUCTION FILL

Little need be said about this. Most surface lots throughout the group seem composed of uprooted fill, a possible exception being Str. 4E-51:LG. 3b. This seems to be material above the floor level of Plat. 4E-2. In some instances, fills of late architectural developments contain fewer sherds and artifacts than earlier fills, but cultural material of all sorts tends to be scant in all structure fills. Ceramic data are really satisfactory only for Str. 4E-50.

MATERIAL ABOVE LIVING LEVELS

In Gp. 4E-2, lots above living levels appear to be contaminated to a minor extent by fill, but lot groups as a whole are marked by a paucity of all cultural material. The most likely place for a dump, at the base of the slope E of Str. 4E-53, produced almost no sherds or artifacts. Still, the four objects found in excavations at this spot are the most from any lot source presumed to contain occupation material. Lot Group 3 of Str. 4E-52 was also expected to contain fair amounts of trash, but in fact does not.

Of particular interest are five artifacts from the small range-type 4E-50. One, a spindle whorl, was found off the end of the structure, and therefore may have washed out of the fill. Mano and metate fragments, however, were found on the floor of the building, as were sherds of a single coarse jar. The latter was apparently left in situ, but later broke when the vault collapsed on it. A neck from a monochrome red jar was found on the front platform floor.

TIME SPANS

Time spans for the structures of Gp. 4E-2 are listed in Tables 2.179 through 2.182 and combined into seven group time spans in Table 2.183. Since actual architectural relationships could not be used to correlate time spans, those for the group rely heavily on ceramic data (Table 2.174). The weakness of this correlation lies in the small size of sherd samples throughout the group.

Group TS. 5 and 6 include the earliest activity here. The particular situation of the group on the hillside called for considerable cutting and filling to construct a level platform on which to build, and it seems likely that after all this effort at least the E and W sides, and perhaps the others, would have supported stru`ctures. This is consistent with the ceramic data, such as they are. While 4E-50-B could have been built no earlier than a time when late Imix ceramics were in vogue, LG. 1a contains earlier sherds. These raise the possibility of an earlier structure at this locus. Ceramics from the fill of Str. 4E-53 preclude its construction earlier than the appearance of transitional Ik-Imix pottery, but more probably when early Imix pottery was in vogue. The same is indicated for 4E-52.

The other group time spans assume all of the structures, save 4E-52, were modified at about the same time.

While such a practice was not always followed by the Maya at Tikal, it was often enough in small-structure groups to be a reasonable assumption. Moreover, it is plausible that renovation of the group platform was carried out when so large a structure as 4E-50-B was built. Since 4E-53-2nd-A really involved renovation of the platform floor in front (rather than alteration of 53 itself), it is logical to equate TS. 5 of 4E-50 with TS. 5 of 4E-53.

Whether or not Str. 4E-51-2nd dates from this time cannot be proven. It might have been in the course of the platform floor renovation that Str. 4E-51:U. 3, a possible earth oven, was eliminated and a structure built here. This makes sense, if 4E-50-B was preceded by some sort of ceremonial structure that was associated with the earth oven. Consequently, the two architectural developments of 4E-51 would be correlated with the two forms of 4E-50. But definitive proof for all this is lacking.

Occupation sherd samples from the final period of use of Gp. 4E-2 (Gp. TS. 2; Fig. 88) are so poor as to be of little use for dating purposes. In view of the time of construction of Str. 4E-50, late Imix Complex ceramics must have been in use. No Eznab ceramics can be identified, so that use of the structures may be presumed to have ceased by AD 869 (the end of the Imix Complex). The first construction dates to around AD 700 (when Imix ceramic production began), despite the presence of a few Manik sherds in fill samples. The latter are so few in number as to indicate that they were probably included in trash brought in from other structures in the neighborhood, to be used as fill. The need for such outside fill seems called for by the amount required to build up the E side of the group platform. This could easily have used up all the material from excavation into the hillside for the W edge of the platform, leaving little debris on hand for use as structure fill.

TABLE 2.174
Group 4E-2: Lot Groups

Feature	Lot Group	Lots	Provenience	Ceramic Evaluation
Str. 4E-50 (Op. 24N)	1a	9	Unsealed fill of CS. 4 (U. 1 and 2)	Ik-Imix transition or Early Imix
	1b	10	Pit (U. 18) in front of stairs	No data
	2	2,5-7, 8,11,13	Sealed fill of building platform	Late Imix
	3	1	Surface over and around structure	Imix
	4	3,4,12	Directly on structure floors, with material S of structure	Imix
Str. 4E-51 (Op. 24Q)	1	3	Fill of stone-filled pit (U. 3)	Ik and/or Imix
	2	7,9	Partially sealed fill of 2nd	Ik and/or Imix
	3a	2	S of structure surface to base of wall	Ik and/or Imix
	3b	1	Surface of structure	Ik and/or Imix
Str. 4E-52 (Op. 24P)	1	4,7	Beneath structure fill	Imix
	2	3,5,9	Partially sealed fill of structure	Imix
	3	6,10	N and S of structure, surface to base of walls	Imix
	4	1,2,8	Surface of structure floor levels	Ik-Imix transition or Early Imix
Str. 4E-53 (Op. 24Q)	1	6,10	Partially sealed fill of 2nd	Ik and/or Imix
	2	5,8, 15,16	Unsealed fill of 1st	Ik and/or Imix
	3	12,13	Base of slope E of structure	Ik and/or Imix
	4	4,14	Surface over and around structure	Ik-Imix transition or Imix

TABLE 2.175
Structure 4E-50: Artifacts by Lot Groups

Study Category	Object	Lot Group				
		1a	1b	2	3	4
Pottery Vessels	Sherds per cubic meter (lbs)	7.1	2.7	2.6	.5	2.3
Other Pottery Artifacts	Figurine			1		
	Spindle whorl					1
Flaked Chert Artifacts	Flake core	2		5	1	
	Thin biface			1		
	Point-retouched flake		1			
	Used flakes			3		
	Unmodified, fire-spalled flakes			2		
Flaked Obsidian Artifacts	Prismatic blades	1		1		
Ground, Pecked, and Polished Stone Artifacts	Manos			1		1
	Metate					1
	Ground pebble				1	

TABLE 2.176
Structure 4E-51: Artifacts by Lot Group

Study Category	Object	Lot Group			
		1	2	3a	3b
Pottery Vessels	Sherds per cubic meter (lbs)	3.3	3.7	4.0	1.1
Flaked Chert Artifacts	Flake cores	1		1	
	Unmodified flakes		2	2	1
Ground, Pecked, and Polished Stone Artifacts	Manos	1			1
	Rubbing stone				1

TABLE 2.177
Structure 4E-52: Artifacts by Lot Group

Study Category	Objects	Lot Group 1	2	3	4
Pottery Vessels	Sherds per cubic meter (lbs)	2.4	8.1	3.0	5.0
Flaked Chert Artifacts	Irregular, retouched flake	1			
	Used flakes		1		6
	Unmodified flakes	4	3	1	14
	Unmodified, fire-spalled flakes		1		1
	Nodules		1		1
Flaked Obsidian Artifacts	Prismatic blade	1			
Ground, Pecked, and Polished Stone Artifacts	Mano			1	
	Metate				1

TABLE 2.178
Structure 4E-53: Artifacts by Lot Group

Study Category	Object	Lot Group 1	2	3	4
Pottery Vessels	Sherds per cubic meter (lbs)	4.2	1.3	.7	.7
Other Pottery Artifacts	Candelero			1	
Flaked Chert Artifacts	Unmodified flake			1	
	Fire-spalled nodule	1			
Flaked Obsidian Artifact	Prismatic blade			1	
Ground, Pecked, and Polished Stone Artifacts	Mano			1	

TABLE 2.179
Structure 4E-50: Time Spans

Time Span	Architectural Development	Construction Stage	Unit	Descriptive Data	Lot Group	Ceramics in Vogue
1				Abandonment and collapse		
2				Use	4	
3	Str. 4E-50-A	None defined	15	Modification of structure		
4				Use		
5	Str. 4E-50-B	1	10-12, 14,16,17	Construction of building	2,3	
		2	8,9,13	Construction of upper level of building platform		
		3	5-7	Construction of lower level of building platform		(Late)
		4		Preparation of base surface		Imix
6			1-4,18	Earlier activity	1a,b	(Early)

TABLE 2.180
Structure 4E-51: Time Spans

Time Span	Architectural Development	Construction Stage	Unit	Descriptive Data	Lot Group	Ceramics in Vogue
1				Abandonment and collapse		
2				Use		
3	Str. 4E-51-1st	1		Construction of building of perishable materials	3a,3b	
		2	2	Construction of upper platform level		
		3		Demolition of existing building		
4				Use		
5	Str. 4E-51-2nd	1		Construction of building of perishable materials	2	(Late) Imix
		2		Construction of platform		
6?			3?	Use of earth oven?	1?	(Early?)
7?				Construction of Plat. 4E-2??		

TABLE 2.181
Structure 4E-52: Time Spans

Time Span	Architectural Development	Construction Stage	Unit	Descriptive Data	Lot Group	Ceramics in Vogue
1				Abandonment and collapse	3	
2				Use		(Late)
3	Str. 4E-52	1		Construction of building of perishable materials		Imix (Early)
		2	1,5	Construction of lowest level in front of platform	2 / 4	
		3	3,4,6	Construction of upper platform level	2	
		4	2	Construction of middle platform level		
		5	7,8	Preparation of base	1	

TABLE 2.182
Structure 4E-53: Time Spans

Time Span	Architectural Development	Construction Stage	Unit	Descriptive Data	Lot Group	Ceramics in Vogue
1				Abandonment and collapse	3	— — — — —
2				Use	3	
3	Str. 4E-53-1st	1		Construction of building of perishable materials		
3	Str. 4E-53-1st	2	12,13	Construction of upper platform level	2	
3	Str. 4E-53-1st	3	10,11	Construction of lower platform level	2	
3	Str. 4E-53-1st	4		Demolition of existing building		
4				Use	4	
5	Str. 4E-53-2nd-A	1		Patching of plaza floor by structure		(Late)
6				Use		Imix
7	Str. 4E-53-2nd-B	1		Construction of building of perishable materials	1	
7	Str. 4E-53-2nd-B	2	1-5; 7-9	Construction of platform	1	(Early)
7	Str. 4E-53-2nd-B	3		Preparation of base surface	1	

TABLE 2.183
Group 4E-2: Time Spans

Group Time Spans	Str. 4E-50 (Table 2.179)	Str. 4E-51 (Table 2.180)	Str. 4E-52 (Table 2.181)	Str. 4E-53 (Table 2.182)
1	1	1	1	1
2	2	2		2
3	3	3		3
4	4	4		4
5	5	5		5
6		6?	2	6
7	6	7?	3	7

Group 5D-1

Located at S32 on the W edge of Sq. 5D of the site map, Gp. 5D-1 is immediately N of the Tozzer Causeway, 70 m N of Temple III (Str. 5D-3), and 90 m W of the West Plaza (see TR. 11). It is this proximity to major architecture at the very heart of Tikal that makes these structures, so small by comparison, of particular interest. There are five buildings, arranged on the edges of a low plaza on the W and a raised platform on the E (Fig. 98). The plaza on the W (Plat. 5D-30) is behind Str. 5C-9, a substantial range-type structure that faces Temple IV (Str. 5C-4), 270 m to the W (TR. 23A:27–28 and fig. 20–22). On the N edge of Plat. 5D-30 is Str. 5C-10. This has not been excavated, but its ruin mound is comparable to that of 5D-6, on the E edge of the plaza. Directly behind this is the raised Plat. 5D-29, with Str. 5D-7 on its W edge. On the N edge of Plat. 5D-29 is Str. 5D-8, and on the E, Str. 5D-9. The latter, unexcavated, is represented by a ruin comparable to that of Str. 5D-8.

The first excavations in Gp. 5D-1 were those of Jones, around St. P36. This lies just NW of the center of Plat. 5D-29. In 1964, Puleston began excavations in Str. 5D-6, 7, and 8 (Op. 76A, B; 77A, B), which were concluded by Coe. Each of these was excavated to bedrock through the front-rear axis, with tests off the N ends of 5D-6 and 7. The excavations in Str. 5D-8 were expanded to secure data for more complete plan reconstruction.

STRUCTURE 5D-6-3RD

This early version of 5D-6 (Fig. 89, 92) was constructed in part over a floor (Plat. 5D-30:U. 1) that seals a rich deposit of Manik sherds, with none later. Hence, it may be that the floor was associated with the little known Str. 5D-7-6th to the E. At any rate, when 5D-6-3rd was built, the western portion of Plat. 5D-30:U. 1 was torn up.

A precise sequence of construction stages for 5D-6-3rd cannot be defined, as excavations were restricted to a trench through its front-rear axis. It seems to have taken the form of a two-level platform, perhaps for support of a pole-and-thatch structure. The E and W walls of the upper platform level are represented by U. 1 and 2, with U. 1 in union with a floor behind it, Plat. 5D-29:U. 9. The E wall and floor both rest on fill 0.21 to 0.23 m above Plat. 5D-30:U. 1. The fill beneath Plat. 5D-29:U. 9, a dark earth, differs from the light-colored earth and rubble of the structure itself. It appears as though the fill for the floor was put down first, and then structure fill was dumped to the W. As this was piled up, U. 1 was put in place to hold it. Unit 2, to the W, was also placed as the depth of platform fill increased. A floor, represented by U. 3, was laid across the top of the platform fill between the tops of U.

1 and 2. Unit 3 is a very distinctive surface—quite hard, with a small, blue stone aggregate. Traces of burning are apparent on this surface.

The front (W) wall of the lower platform level is represented by U. 4. Although no floors now survive in the area, U. 4 appears to have been about 0.45 m high, judging from surviving fills. Pavement must have run from its top eastward to the base of U. 2.

Access to the platform seems to have been by two steps, one narrow and one quite broad (U. 5 and 6). The lower riser, U. 5, is based on a dark earth fill that presumably was provided with a plaster plaza surface. The second riser, U. 6, is 0.16 m E of the back of U. 5. The gap between them undoubtedly was plastered, though this no longer survives. From the top of U. 6, a broad plaster tread must have run to the base of U. 4.

STRUCTURE 5D-6-2ND

Following a period of use, it looks as if the width of the upper platform was almost doubled (Fig. 90, 92). A new E wall (U. 7) was built above the level of Plat. 5D-29:U. 9, which was partially destroyed at this time. Owing to later activity (see below), only a small portion of the fill for this addition survives; it consists of rubble and dark earth, over which plaster pavement (U. 8) was laid. Unit 8 turns down over the top of U. 7 and is continuous with plaster on the wall face. Since this runs to the base of U. 7, Plat. 5D-29:U. 9 may have been patched up here, so that it could continue to service this structure. The evidence no longer survives, however.

Unit 9 is a major floor patch on the older U. 3. It may be associated with the alteration that produced Str. 5D-6-2nd, or it may be a later renovation (see below).

Three stages are assumed for construction of 5D-6-2nd: CS. 3 for partial destruction of a building (if one existed); CS. 2 for construction of U. 7 and 8 (and perhaps 9); and CS. 1 for a new building (if one existed).

STRUCTURE 5D-6-1ST

The final known modification of this structure saw a return to the original width of the upper platform level (Fig. 91, 92). All but the eastern 0.54 m of the addition that constituted 2nd was torn out, so that the old E wall of 3rd (U. 1), with Plat. 5D-29:U. 9, was once again exposed to serve as the rear wall. The surviving 0.54 m of U. 7 and 8, with their fill, was incorporated into a lower step for a raised and expanded portion of Plat. 5D-29 to the E. It is quite likely that 1st had a rear, and perhaps front, dwarf wall. If so, this would lend credence to the idea that a building stood on the upper platform level. The evidence for dwarf walls is indirect; it consists of several masonry blocks in debris behind U. 1, as well as a large quantity of debris above the structure floor. It is hard to account for this stone unless there were once masonry dwarf walls.

Unit 9 has already been mentioned; given reduction in the width of the upper platform level, it is likely that a new dwarf wall was built on the rear of the platform. Such construction would call for floor patching, so U. 9 may have been part of this operation.

To sum up the construction of 1st, three stages may be defined: CS. 3 for partial demolition of 2nd; CS. 2 for a new rear wall and refurbishing of the floor; and CS. 1 for completion, using perishable materials, of a new building.

STRUCTURE 5D-7-6TH

This earliest architectural development of 5D-7 is represented by no surviving architecture at all. Its existence is signaled, though, by the presence of Bu. 169 (Fig. 94), interred while Manik ceramics were in vogue (see its discussion in section III). The burial shows its closest kinship to those elsewhere at Tikal in small-to-medium Early Classic household shrines (TR. 21). Thus one might postulate such a squarish structure, facing W, with this burial on its front-rear axis.

STRUCTURE 5D-7-5TH

Again, a structure is postulated for which there is no surviving architecture. Its presence seems called for on account of the termination of a floor (U. 7) for Plat. 5D-29. This pavement ends about 0.60 m E of Bu. 169, but its fill continues over that grave, feathering out 0.50 m W of its opening (Fig. 94). Given the existence of preceding and succeeding structures at this locus, the best interpretation is that Plat. 5D-27:U. 7 was laid in conjunction with construction of a structure that faced E, the front wall of which stood somewhere between Bu. 169 and the surviving W edge of Plat. 5D-29:U. 7. Presumably, the floor and wall were in union. Nothing more can be said of Str. 5D-7-5th.

STRUCTURE 5D-7-4TH

For this architectural development, a few pieces of construction survive that probably began with the interment of Bu. 171. To accommodate this burial, most of the preceding architecture was razed to the natural marl. The problem is that Bu. 171 contains no objects that would help to verify this reconstruction through its chronology. Fill in the grave does contain Manik sherds, and none later. This fill is continuous, however, with the fill above (Fig. 94:1), in which some Imix sherds were found. Therefore, these sherds must date the burial, which then must postdate Plat. 5D-29:U. 7, hence the postulated Str. 5D-7-5th.

Following the burial, brown earth fill was piled up over it and to the E. As this was done, a fill-retaining wall, U. 1 (Fig. 94), was erected just W of the grave. More fill was dumped W of this, to approximately 0.65 m above the natural marl, and a floor can be seen 0.10 m W of Str. 5D-7:U. 1, indicating that finished masonry for a W structure wall was positioned here against the face of U. 1. How high this structure stood is not known, for no other architecture survives. Since the structure postdates Plat. 5D-29:U. 7, it must have stood at least 1 m above Plat. 5D-29:U. 8. Although the beginning steps in construction are known, a complete series of construction stages cannot be defined.

STRUCTURE 5D-7-3RD

The NW corner of this architectural development was revealed in excavation. Evidently, its axis was positioned to the S of the axis of 6th and 1st. Again, construction commenced with destruction (partial in this case) of preceding architecture and interment of a burial (Fig. 94). A pit was dug through Plat. 5D-29:U. 8 down into the natural marl behind Str. 5D-7-4th. Burial 170 was then interred, at the same time that at least the upper part of Str. 5D-7-4th was demolished. Fill (Fig. 94:2) was then dumped over the burial, and brought up to a level 0.36 m above Plat. 5D-29:U. 8. This was carried eastward over the remains of 4th. The corner of 3rd (Fig. 94:U. 2) was set on this fill, which was then piled up higher on the inside. The height of the structure walls is unknown; the corner presently survives to only 0.22 m. Given the elevation of the preceding Plat. 5D-29:U. 7, Str. 5D-7:U. 2 must have risen at least 0.70 m above Plat. 5D-29:U. 10. The latter is a floor W of U. 2, which accords with its base.

STRUCTURE 5D-7-2ND

The next architectural development is again not well understood. It is represented by a floor surface (Plat. 5D-20:U. 11), laid on a dark fill dumped W of, and over, the partly demolished remains of Str. 5D-7-3rd (Fig. 94). It also covered PD. 124, while containing PD. 126. Because the floor fill appears to continue to the W, the pavement is interpreted as a surface behind the structure. The W wall of the structure was probably not far E of the W wall for 5D-7-1st, in its fill.

STRUCTURE 5D-7-1ST

This is the only version of this structure that is at all well known (Fig. 93, 94). The first step in its creation appears to have been extensive demolition of Str. 5D-7-2nd (CS. 5). Since, to the E, the natural marl was stripped clean for this new project, everything down to the level of Plat. 5D-29:U. 11 was probably demolished. This plaza floor is within 8 cm of the elevation of natural marl to the E. Then, as CS. 4, the structure core was built up of rubble and earth. The E fill-retaining wall for CS. 4 is represented by U. 3; it rests on part of the core fill, and in part on a remnant of fill for Plat. 5D-29:U. 7. The fill behind this wall, up to at least 1.40 m W, rests on the surface of nat-ural marl. There may have been a W retaining wall; this possibility was not investigated. Alternatively, U. 4, the W wall of the structure, may have been built as part of CS. 4. Unit 4 is based on Plat. 5D-29:U. 11, and another floor, Plat. 5D-29:U. 14, abuts and turns up to it.

Construction Stage 3 is defined for assembly of two steps with a front platform surface that abuts U. 3. The top of U. 3 probably served as a riser to the upper plat-form level. The bottom step riser rests on the surface of Plat. 5D-29:U. 7, which may have served Str. 5D-7-2nd through 5th. A new floor that no longer survives proba-bly was laid up to the base of the bottom step (as in the case of Str. 5D-8-2nd). There is no evidence one way or the other whether the lower riser ran the whole length of the structure.

The second riser stone is based on fill 0.14 m W of the first riser. This gap was probably given a plastered sur-face, now long since destroyed. Level with the top of the riser are the badly preserved remains of a floor, U. 5, and this appears to have turned up to U. 3.

Stage 2 is defined for construction of a puzzling fea-ture, U. 6. A floor, U. 7, is in union with the base of U. 6, and seems to have run to the top of retaining wall U. 3. A probe at the N end of the structure shows that U. 6 extends all the way to that end, thus it appears to be a free-standing dwarf wall. Consistent is the veneer masonry on both E and W faces, the lack of floor beneath its fill, and the union of its E wall with U. 7. This rules out the W ve-neer masonry as the E face of an interior platform, which was later given a 0.90 m extension to the E. The problem with the freestanding-wall hypothesis is that a comparable wall in Str. 4F-21 (in Gp. 4F-3, this report) had an opening in it on the structural axis. A similar opening is not indi-cated here (from the configuration of the ruin mound, it is reasonably certain that excavation did expose this axis). Perhaps, though, openings were located off this axis. In support of this, the only remaining hypothesis is to as-sume that U. 6 in toto served as the front wall of a raised platform level, but this seems contradicted by the finished veneer masonry on its W face.

Stage 1 is inferred for construction of a building of perishable materials, the existence of which is suggested by the presence of a dwarf wall, if indeed U. 6 is such a wall.

STRUCTURE 5D-8-C

The initial operation here (CS. 6) was to tear out the existing floor of Plat. 5D-29 where the rear of the new structure was to be built (Fig. 95, 96). A core of earth and rubble fill was then built up to a height of about 1 m over the remaining floor surface (CS. 5). This is held in place by rough masonry retaining walls, of which U. 1 and 2 are the N and S walls respectively. Unit 1 rests on exposed fill for

Plat. 5D-29-6th, just N of the chop-line in the old floor; U. 2 was built on the floor itself.

The next operation (CS. 4) was probably to build up the front platform and steps of the new structure. The bottom step rests directly on the old plaza floor, over which a new one (Plat. 5D-29:U. 15) was laid to turn up to the new steps. A floor encountered in a test at the E end of the structure (Plat. 5D-29:U. 18) has the same el-evation as Plat. 5D-29:U. 15, and is undoubtedly part of the same pavement. Platform 5D-29:U. 19, encountered in a test at the W end of the structure, could be part of the same floor or part of the earlier Plat. 5D-29:U. 1. Its eleva-tion is 0.11 m below that of Plat. 5D-29:U. 15, but the N retaining wall behind Str. 5D-8-C is lower than the floor in front, so at either end of the structure the surrounding floor must have dipped to the N (as did Plat. 5D-29:U. 1). It is doubtful that the lower step to 5D-8 ran the length of the structure. The somewhat comparable step of Str. 4E-16 (Fig. 77) did not.

The second step riser rests in the dark earth fill that was placed behind the bottom riser, which was also brought up to the level of the top of the second riser stone. A gap of 0.16 m separates the front of the upper riser from the back of the lower one. Presumably, this was once plastered over, but no trace of this now survives.

Stage 3 saw completion of the building platform. For this, a two-course wall (U. 3) was built on the dark fill of CS. 4, just S of U. 2. A rear masonry wall (U. 4) was erect-ed on the exposed surface of the fill for Plat. 5D-29-6th, 0.60 m N of U. 1, and fill was dumped between U. 1 and 4. The latter was carried up to the same elevation as U. 3, and a dark earth fill was placed between these walls over the fill of CS. 5. It may have been as part of CS. 3 that pavement (U. 5) was laid over the front, lower portion of the building platform. This floor is laid in union with U. 3, and it must have covered the top of the upper step riser.

As Stage 2, building walls were erected on the upper level of the platform, apparently with their faces aligned with those of the building platform. The general lack of much rubble indicates that these were dwarf walls, proba-bly topped by pole-and-thatch construction in the manner of Str. 4E-16 (in Gp. 4E-1, this report). Construction of this upper zone defines CS. 1.

The building consists of a large central room (Rm. 1) flanked by two slightly smaller ones. Room 1 was entered by a wide doorway that opens into its center; Rm. 2 and 3 were entered by doorways set close to the partitions sep-arating them from Rm. 1. The interior floor, U. 6, is in union with the walls and was likely laid as part of CS. 2.

North of Str. 5D-8-C, a plaster surface (now de-stroyed) must have run out 0.64 m to the top of a retain-ing wall, Plat. 5D-29:U. 5. Although the plaster surface was laid as part of the same operation as Plat. 5D-29:U.

15 and 18, the wall itself may have been constructed originally to serve with Plat. 5D-29:U. 1.

STRUCTURE 5D-8-B

Following a period of use, 5D-8 was altered by construction of interior platforms that filled the rear portion of at least two, and probably all three rooms (Fig. 95, 96), very much like those in Str. 3F-12, 4E-16, and 4E-50 (Fig. 53, 77, 81). The front walls of these "benches" were seen in Rm. 1 and 2 (U. 7 and 8), but Rm. 3 was not excavated. They were built on the original room floors (U. 6 in Rm. 2), and new pavement was laid to turn up to the front (U. 9 in Rm. 2). Undoubtedly, the interior platforms were given plaster surfaces of which no trace now survives. The fill of the platform in Rm. 2 consisted in part of redeposited midden material.

STRUCTURE 5D-8-A

Following another period of use, 5D-8 was provided with a new floor (U. 10), at least in Rm. 1 (Fig. 95, 96). It was laid directly on older U. 9, to turn up to U. 7.

PLATFORM 5D-29-6TH

This is the earliest version of Plat. 5D-29 to which visible architecture may be assigned. Beneath Str. 5D-8 (Fig. 96), it is represented by U. 1 through 5. Unit 1 is a plaster floor that covers a fill of brown earth (U. 2), thicker to the N where the natural marl is deepest. Beneath U. 2 is another stratum of earth (U. 3), also thickest to the N. This lies partly on natural marl, and partly on another stratum of dark earth, U. 4. Both U. 3 and 4 contain nothing more recent than Manik sherds, and the distinction between them is not sharp. Unit 2, on the other hand, is easily distinguished from U. 3, and contains some Ik sherds. Units 3 and 4, then, could represent undisturbed fill from an earlier version of Plat. 5D-29. Or they might be material, redeposited or not, associated with use of Str. 5D-7-6th.

The northern portion of U. 1 was destroyed when Str. 5D-8-C was built. Unit 2 can be seen to run farther N to U. 5, however. Unit 5 appears to be the base of a retaining wall, built on U. 3, probably for U. 1 and 2. Later U. 1 was ripped out, Str. 5D-8-C built, and new plaster was laid from the rear wall of that structure to the top of U. 5. Erosion, however, has destroyed all traces of such a floor.

North of U. 5, at the same level as the base of that wall, is a compacted layer of earth and pebbles (U. 6). This must be the remnant of an informal occupation surface to the N of Gp. 5D-1. It probably served from the time Plat. 5D-29:U. 5 was constructed until the group was abandoned.

At the locus of Str. 5D-7 (Fig. 94), Plat. 5D-29-6th is probably represented by Plat. 5D-29:U. 7. This is a plaster pavement that runs beneath the front step of 5D-7-1st. Its elevation is precisely the same as Plat. 5D-29:U. 1, S of Str. 5D-8. The fill of U. 1 contained Ik sherds, and construction overlying the floor followed the appearance of Imix ceramics. Moreover, the fill of U. 1 overlies strata (U. 3 and 4) that may relate to an Early Classic occupation of the area. The sample of fill from beneath U. 7 is very much smaller than that from beneath U. 1, but it does contain Intermediate (Ik) and/or Late Classic (Imix) sherds, covers the Early Classic Bu. 169, and the succeeding construction postdates the appearance of Imix ceramics. All in all, the evidence supports identification of U. 7 as part of the same floor represented elsewhere by U. 1.

Unit 7 can now be observed to run only 0.20 m W behind the front step of Str. 5D-7-1st. Its fill, however, runs another 1.70 m W, covering the grave of Bu. 169. Two possibilities are suggested: 1) Plat. 5D-29-6th ended about where pavement U. 7 now ends, at the wall of a structure built at the same time as this floor. Later, the structure was completely razed. 2) Plat. 5D-29-6th ran farther W, but was later thoroughly torn up beyond the location of Bu. 169. The former theory is preferred, but there is no real proof either way.

No surface for Plat. 5D-29-6th was encountered in the excavations around St. P36. Based on the elevations of U. 1 and 7, such a surface would have been approximately at the present ground surface level near the stela (Fig. 97c). So presumably it was destroyed by exposure to the elements at this location.

PLATFORM 5D-29-5TH

This architectural development is represented by a floor remnant (U. 8) behind Str. 5D-7-4th (Fig. 94). It seems to have turned up to the rear wall of that structure, with which its fill is continuous. Later, Bu. 170 was intruded through U. 8, so it is not known how far W this floor ran. Excavations immediately W of Bu. 170 might pick up surviving traces of it. It is possible that pavement associated with 5D-6-3rd, which runs E from that structure (Fig. 92), is a portion of the same floor (designated as Plat. 5D-29:U. 9). This is the first of three architectural developments that postdate the appearance of Imix ceramics. Similarly, U. 8 is the first of five architectural developments of Plat. 5D-29 that postdate the appearance of such ceramics. Moreover, Plat. 5D-29:U. 9 at its present easternmost extent is only 0.30 m below the elevation of U. 8 by Bu. 170. Considering that these exposures are separated by some 9 m, this is a small difference. In addition, the surface of U. 9 is very uneven. It does, however, rise slightly from W to E; similarly, U. 8 dips from E to W. All things considered, there is a reasonably good chance that U. 8 and 9 are parts of a single surface of Plat. 5D-29-5th, one that ran from Str. 5D-7-4th to the back of Str. 5D-6-3rd.

Nothing more is known about Plat. 5D-29-5th. In the absence of evidence to the contrary, it is possible that Plat. 5D-29:U. 7 continued in use E of Str. 5D-7-4th.

PLATFORM 5D-29-4TH

This is represented by U. 10, a floor W of Str. 5D-7-3rd (Fig. 94). It is in union with that structure, and their fills are continuous. The floor does not now continue along the N wall of Str. 5D-7-3rd, but this may be the result of the later intrusion of PD. 124. How far W U. 10 ran is an enigma. Nothing that can be remotely connected with it is evident in the excavations behind Str. 5D-6. One possibility is that U. 10 ends on the top of a retaining wall that would be encountered in an eastward extension of the Str. 5D-6 excavation.

Again, nothing more is known of Plat. 5D-29-4th. In the absence of evidence to the contrary, U. 10 is regarded as an addition to the still-utilized U. 7.

PLATFORM 5D-29-3RD

The only positive evidence for this platform is U. 11, a remnant of the floor on which the rear wall of Str. 5D-7-1st sits (Fig. 94). Presumably, U. 11 is associated with Str. 5D-7-2nd. The floor does not now extend very far W of the rear wall of Str. 5D-7-1st. A further projection of its surface correlates well with the top of a rubble fill E of Str. 5D-6, however (Fig. 92). This fill seems to be associated with two steps down to the level of Plat. 5D-49:U. 9. The lower riser of these steps is represented by U. 12. This is on U. 9, and was placed against a surviving bit of fill from Str. 5D-6-2nd (partly demolished at this time). Set back 0.40 m from the face of U. 12, on a floor remnant from Str. 5D-6-2nd (Str. 5D-6:U. 8), are the poorly preserved remains of the second riser (U. 13), built of two courses of masonry. Unit 13 was approximately the same height as U. 12. New plaster, which no longer survives, must have been laid from the top of U. 12 to the base of U. 13. East of U. 13, and the remnant of Str. 7F-6-2nd on which it was built, is a fill of mixed earth, stones, and occasional pieces of masonry. Since this extends down to the surface of the old Plat. 5D-30:U. 1, it is evident that Plat. 5D-29:U. 9, or whatever surface served E of Str. 5D-6-2nd, was demolished along with most of the structure.

In a trench excavated off the N end of Str. 5D-6 (Fig. 91, 97a), a wall, Plat. 5D-29:U. 17, was discovered. A projection of its alignment to the S meets, very nicely, Plat. 5D-29:U. 13. The top of U. 17 is some 0.70 m higher than that of U. 13 where exposed in excavation. The excavations are separated by some 16 m, however, and a dip of between 4 and 5 cm per meter to the S is not unthinkable. For example, Plat. 5D-29:U. 1, beneath Str. 5D-8 (Fig. 96), shows a dip of as much as 9 cm in the space of 1 m. On the other hand, the top of U. 17 is some 1.20 m higher

than the surface of Plat. 5D-29:U. 1, 27 m due E, and U. 1 is thought to have continued in use as part of Plat. 5D-29-3rd. While this may seem at first a major difference, a dip of less than 5 cm per meter would account for it.

PLATFORM 5D-29-2ND

This architecture is thought to be represented by U. 14 and 15 (Fig. 94, 96), although their correlation is not particularly firm. Unit 14 is pavement that overlies the remnant of U. 11 by 6 cm. It abuts and turns up to the rear of Str. 5D-7-1st. Unit 15 is a floor that overlies Plat. 5D-29:U. 1 by 6 cm, and turns up to the front step of Str. 5D-8-C. Structure 5D-8-C was built on the surface of Plat. 5D-29:U. 1. Structure 5D-7-1st was built in part on Plat. 5D-29:U. 7 and in part on Plat. 5D-29:U. 14. Taking all these together, and if Plat. 5D-29:U. 11 represents an addition to Plat. 5D-29:U. 7, which continued to serve with it (as is thought to have been the case with the preceding Plat. 5D-29:U. 10), then it is reasonable to assume that Plat. 5D-29:U. 14, 15, Str. 5D-7-1st, and Str. 5D-8-2nd were all built at the same time, and that U. 15 abutted and turned up to the front step of Str. 5D-7-1st. Unit 15, in front of Str. 5D-7, would have been 0.16 m above the elevation of U. 14, an insignificant difference. This floor was probably torn up all the way to the steps, to provide for the laying of the new floor.

It is assumed that U. 14 ran W to the previously built steps E of Str. 5D-6. Given the destruction of the preceding U. 11 a short distance W of Str. 5D-7, this floor was also probably torn up all the way to the steps, to provide for the laying of the new floor.

PLATFORM 5D-29-1ST

This final architectural development is defined for the construction of stairs at the NW corner, leading down to Plat. 5D-30 at the N end of Str. 5D-6-1st (Fig. 91, 97a). New pavement over the W portion of Plat. 5D-29 probably was associated with this, although the two pieces of architecture are not conclusively proven to be contemporary. The floor is U. 16, and it abuts the W wall of Str. 5D-7-1st (Fig. 93, 94). Its elevation is 0.12 m above U. 14. It could represent a local resurfacing of the platform, but its height above the preceding floor suggests a major architectural modification, rather than minor resurfacing.

The stairs are represented by four risers, the lowest of which is at an elevation only 0.10 m below that of Plat. 5D-29:U. 9, 16 m to the S (Fig. 89, 92). Considering that the level of Plat. 5D-29-3rd was 0.70 m higher here than it was 16 m S, it may be that the surface of Plat. 5D-30, to which these steps led, was comparably higher than that same surface to the S. This suggests that the steps led not to Plat. 5D-29:U. 9, but rather to the surface of Plat. 5D-30, which served in front of Str. 5D-6-1st. This, as well as the location of the steps by the end of that structure, indicates that access to the area behind Str. 5D-6-1st and W of Plat. 5D-29-1st was no longer necessary or desirable.

The steps themselves consist of rectangular blocks set as stretchers, with a gap of 0.20 to 0.25 m between the back of one riser and the front of the next. Presumably, this was coated with plaster that no longer survives. The width of the stairway is not known. The top risers are missing, but a projection on the basis of the known steps leads to a level 0.20 m above that of U. 16 (Fig. 94), some 18 m to the S. The difference is not significant. The possibility exists, though, that the steps were constructed with U. 14, for they were built against a wall (U. 17) associated with Plat. 5D-29-3rd. Tenuous though this may be, on the basis of available evidence, the link with U. 16 is preferred, on the grounds noted above.

PLATFORM 5D-30-2ND

Surviving architecture for this version of Plat. 5D-30 consists of U. 1 (Fig. 92). This is the floor that underlies the fill of Str. 5D-6-3rd. It overlies a fill of hard, packed, medium-brown earth that is especially rich in sherds, suggesting it consists largely of redeposited midden material. Beneath this is natural marl.

The original extent of U. 1 is not known. Its western portion was destroyed when Str. 5D-6-3rd was built, and at some point it was also demolished E of Str. 5D-6-2nd. No attempt was made to follow it to the N or S. The very large sherd sample from beneath produced nothing later than Manik, suggesting an association between U. 1 and Str. 5D-7-6th to the E. This, in turn, raises the possibility that Str. 5D-7-6th faced W onto Plat. 5D-30, rather than E onto Plat. 5D-29, as did its later versions. This would be in keeping with the presence beneath Str. 5D-7-6th of a burial typical of those beneath westward-facing Early Classic shrines.

PLATFORM 5D-30-1ST

Evidence for this platform is indirect. When Str. 5D-6-3rd was constructed, much of Plat. 5D-30:U. 1 was destroyed. Structure 5D-6-3rd was provided with stairs that lead down to a level 0.80 m below the elevation of U. 1. Evidently, a new pavement was laid here, of which there is now no trace (Fig. 92:6). Presumably, this is the surface to which the steps N of Str. 5D-6 from Plat. 5D-29-1st eventually led. Nothing more is known of 30-1st.

POSSIBLE EARLY ACTIVITY

Wherever exposed in the excavations in Gp. 5D-2, no hard bedrock crust was seen. Instead, there is a stratum of packed marl, quite sterile and apparently natural. This is just like the situation in Gp. 4E-1, and may be explained in a similar manner. It is probable that the hard bedrock crust was entirely quarried away for some of the major construction in the vicinity. Just when this may have taken place is not certainly known. A hint is afforded by Str. 5D-7:U. 8 (Fig. 94). This consists of a hollowed-out area in the natural marl just E of Bu. 171. Unit 8 was not thoroughly investigated, so its extent is not known. The best guess is that it is a chultun; if so, it would have been rendered useless once the hard crust had been removed from bedrock above. Thus, it is probable that it was filled and abandoned at about that time. Little of this fill was sampled, but only Preclassic sherds were produced. On this basis, removal of the bedrock crust is thought to predate construction of Str. 5D-7-6th.

STELA P36

LOCATION

The N end is 8.40 m S and 6.60 m E of datum for Op. 76 and 77, about 2.35 m E of Str. 5D-7-1st and 6.90 m S of Str. 5D-8-1st, on Plat. 5D-29 (Fig. 97b,c, 98).

DESCRIPTION

The stone resembles that normally used in monuments before 9.14.0.0.0 at Tikal (TR. 33A:2). Its front and back are parallel to one another, with rounded edges. The sides taper to a bluntly pointed base, but are nearly parallel in the upper half of the monument. Above this, they are rounded over to the broad top. Overall dimensions are 2.44 m maximum length; 0.90 m maximum width; 0.62 m maximum thickness.

EXCAVATION DATA

The monument was found in several fragments, all lying together in earth from 0.05 to 0.20 m above natural marl (Fig. 97d). No floors survive in the area, but based on existing floor remnants in front of Str. 5D-7 and 8 (Fig. 94, 96), pavement would have been near present surface level. This is about 0.16 to 0.40 m higher than the underneath surfaces of the monument fragments.

DISCUSSION

The fragments of the monument were lying in such a way as to indicate that it was broken where found. There is no indication, in the form of a pit, that the monument ever stood here. Nor, according to Tikal standards, would a standing monument be expected in Gp. 5D-2 in Classic times. The monument, therefore, probably did not fall from position and break. Rather, it was brought here from somewhere else, where it was broken by human or (more likely) natural agencies.

The position of the fragments partly below ground surface, as well as the probable level of the platform floors, suggest that the monument was brought here after

Gp. 5D-2 had been abandoned. Otherwise, some trace of those floors would be expected beneath the fragments. In this connection, the presence of probable Eznab ceramic material W of Str. 5D-8 takes on possible significance. It suggests that movement of the monument took place at a time when such ceramics were in use, after abandonment of the structures of Gp. 5D-2.

SEQUENTIAL POSITION

The sequential position of Platform 5D-29 can be found in:TS. 2 (Table 2.193).

SHERDS AND ARTIFACTS

Listed in Table 2.184 are the sources of cultural material from Gp. 5D-1; Tables 2.185–2.189 list content.

MATERIAL UNDERLYING CONSTRUCTION

The only material clearly put in place before known construction is in LG. 1 of Str. 5D-7. This comes from U. 8, thought to be a chultun that was filled at the time the hard bedrock cap was quarried away. A single large Preclassic sherd was the only cultural material recovered from this fill. Preclassic material, however, was found in a number of other lot groups (Str. 5D-7:LG. 3, 5, 7b; Str. 5D-8:LG. 1a, 1b; Plat. 5D-29:LG. 1, 2a, 2b, 2c, 4a). This could be redeposited from a Preclassic occupation associated with the chultun.

CONSTRUCTION FILL

Most of the material in Gp. 5D-1 falls in this category, and for the most part probably derives from earlier occupation here. The least contaminated by later material are Str. 5D-6:LG. 1; Str. 5D-7:LG. 2-5; Str. 5D-8:LG. 1a, 2; Plat. 5D-29:LG. 1, 2a, 4b, 5 (drawn probably from an Intermediate Classic midden); and Plat. 5D-30:LG. 1. The ceramics in these lot groups provide reliable lower-limit dates for the associated architecture. Of particular note are the quantities of Manik sherds in most deposits. Platform 5D-29:LG. 1, 2b, and 4b (a midden-like depos-

it) contain no later material. All this may be redeposited trash and fill associated with Str. 5D-7-6th. Some, however, could be undisturbed debris (in Plat. 5D-29:LG. 1). Painted and modeled stucco fragments in Str. 5D-8:LG. 1a and Plat. 5D-29:LG. 1 and 3 could be from various architectural developments of Str. 5D-7.

MATERIAL ABOVE LIVING LEVELS

Most of this material seems to consist of spilled-out construction fill as indicated by the large number of sherds that predate associated construction. Much of the material in LG. 2 of Str. 5D-6 comes from the higher Plat. 5D-29-3rd to the E (note the high sherd densities in Str. 5D-6:LG. 2 and Plat. 5D-29:LG. 4a and 4b), and a collapsed dwarf wall of the structure to the W. Most of the material in LG. 3 comes from the dwarf wall. Lot Groups 7a and 7b of Str. 5D-7 derive in large part from a destroyed dwarf wall on that structure, along with material from collapse of its back. Structure 5D-8:LG. 3a must consist wholly of fill, for there are no post-Manik sherds in it. Perhaps four pieces of painted, modeled stucco in this lot group fell from the end wall of Str. 5D-8. Lot Group 4, on the other hand, includes much collapsed architecture, and also extends deeply behind the wall of the interior platform of Str. 5D-8-B.

All of this leaves Str. 5D-7:LG. 6 and Str. 5D-8:LG. 3b as the sole sources of probable occupation debris (but see also PD. 124; discussed in section III). The former, which comes from behind the structure, nonetheless contains a significant amount of material earlier than that in use when the structure was built. The latter consists of material that may pertain to a later reoccupation of the group, when Str. 5D-8 could have been used for purposes other than those for which it was originally built.

OTHER SOURCES

Burials 169, 171, and PD. 124, 126 constitute the other sources of cultural material from Gp. 5D-1.

TABLE 2.184
Group 5D-1: Lot Groups

Feature	Lot Group	Lot	Provenience	Ceramic Evaluation
Str.5D-6 (Op.77A)	1	4	Partially sealed of 3rd	Manik; possible Ik
	2	6	Above living level between Str. 5D-6-1st and Plat. 5D-29-3rd	Manik; some probable Ik and/or Imix
	3	1,5	Surface over and around structure	Manik; Ik; Imix
Str.5D-7 (Op.76B)	1	16	Probable chultun E of Bu. 171	Preclassic
	2	5	Unsealed fill of 6th	No data
	3	12,17	Partially sealed fill of 4th	Preclassic (Chuen?); Manik; Ik; Imix
	4	11	Partially sealed fill of 3rd	Ik; probable Imix
	5	2,7	Partially sealed fill of 1st	Preclassic; Manik; Ik; possible Imix
	6	3	W of structure, top of wall to Plat. 5D-29:U. 16	Manik; Ik; probable Imix
	7a	10	Surface, N of structure	No data
	7b	1	Surface to floor levels over, E and W of structure	Preclassic; Manik; Ik and/or Imix
Str.5D-8 (Op.76A)	1a	2,6,7	Partially sealed fill of 8-C	Preclassic; much Manik; Ik and Imix
	1b	9	Unsealed fill of 8-C	Preclassic; Manik; probable Ik and/or Imix
	2	4	Unsealed fill of 8-B	Much Manik; some probable Ik and/or Imix
	3a	8	E of structure, surface to floor level	Manik
	3b	15	W of structure, surface to floor level	Ik and/or Imix probable Eznab
	4	1,3,5	Surface to floor level over, N and S of structure	Manik and Ik and/or Imix
Plat.5D-29	1	76A/ 12,14	U. 3	Preclassic (Cimi); Manik
	2a	76A/ 10,13	Fill of 6th, sealed by U. 1	Preclassic; much Manik; some Ik
	2b	76A/11	Fill of 6th, partially sealed by U. 1	Preclassic; Manik
	2c	76B/6	Fill of 6th, partially sealed by U. 7	Preclassic; Manik; Ik and/or Imix
	3	77A/7	Fill of 5th, partially sealed by U. 9	Manik; Ik; Imix
	4a	77A/2, 3,9,10	Unsealed fill of 3rd	Preclassic; Manik; Ik, probable Imix
	4b	76B/9	Fill of 3rd, partially sealed by U. 11	Manik
	5	76B/4	Fill of 1st, partially sealed by U. 16	Ik; possible Imix
	6	76B/18	Surface	No data
Plat.5D-30	1	8	Fill of 2nd, sealed by U. 1	Manik

TABLE 2.185
Structure 5D-6: Artifacts by Lot Group

Study Category	Object	Lot Group		
		1	2	3
Pottery Vessels	Sherds per cubic meter (lbs)	1.61	2.35	1.34
Other Pottery Artifacts	Censer	1		
Flaked Chert Artifacts	Flake cores			3
	Elongate bifaces			2
	Irregular biface		1	
	Unclassifiable biface			1
	Used flakes	1		3
	Unused flakes			2
	Nodules			2
Flaked Obsidian Artifacts	Prismatic blades	7		4
Ground, Pecked, and Polished Stone Artifacts	Manos	1		1
	Metates	1		2
	Hammer stones	1	1	
	Unclassifiable artifact	1		
Shell and Bone Artifacts	Bone, animal, misc. worked	1		
	Bone, animal, unworked	1		3
	Bone, unworked	1		

TABLE 2.186
Structure 5D-7: Artifacts by Lot Groups

Study Category	Object	Lot Groups							
		1	2	3	4	5	6	7a	7b
Pottery Vessels	Sherds per cubic meter (lbs)	?	--	.02	.06	1.83	3.38	--	1.11
Other Pottery Artifacts	Figurines					1			
	Candelero					1			
Flaked Chert Artifacts	Flake cores			3	1	1			
	Unclassifiable bifaces			1		1	1		
	Irregular retouched flakes		1	4	1	4			1
	Point-retouched flake			1					
	Used flakes		2	7		6	1		
	Unused flakes		2			3	1		8
	Nodules			5		2	3		4
Flaked Obsidian Artifacts	Prismatic blades		1			2	1		1
	Unused flake		1						
Ground, Pecked, and Polished Stone Artifacts	Manos			2		1			
	Metates						2		
	Rubbing stones			2					
	Carved shale (MS-74)					1			
	Unclassifiable artifact		1						
Shell and Bone Artifacts	Shell, unmodified		1						

TABLE 2.187
Structure 5D-8: Artifacts by Lot Group

Study Category	Object	Lot Group					
		1a	1b	2	3a	3b	4
Pottery Vessels	Sherds per cubic meter (lbs)	1.85	1.60	16.20	.06	--	.48
Other Pottery Artifacts	Figurine						1
	Censer						1
	Candelero	1					
Flaked Chert Artifacts	Flake core						1
	Ovate bifaces	2					1
	Elongate biface			1			
	Unclassifiable bifaces						3
	Irregular retouched flakes	2				1	
	Point-retouched flake						1
	Used flakes	1		4			
	Unused flakes	4	1				4
	Nodules	16		2			
Flaked Obsidian Artifacts	Thin bifaces	2					
	Prismatic blades	5	4	3		1	3
Ground, Pecked, and Polished Stone Artifacts	Mano		1				
	Metates						2
	Rubbing stone	1					
	Grinding stone	1					
Shell and Bone Artifacts	Shell, unmodified	2					
	Bone, animal, unmodified	1		1			1
	Bone, unidentified	1					

TABLE 2.188
Platform 5D-29: Artifacts by Lot Group

Study Category	Object	Lot Group								
		1	2a	2b	2c	3	4a	4b	5	6
Pottery Vessels	Sherds per cubic meter (lbs)	5.98	2.72	8.65	2.86	9.76	3.39	2.78	12.76	--
Other Pottery Artifacts	Figurine								1	
	Censer		1							
Flaked Chert Artifacts	Flake cores	1	2	4			2			
	Ovate biface		1							
	Unclassifiable bifaces								3	
	Thin biface					1				
	Irregular retouched flakes	2					1			
	Point-retouched flake							1		
	Used flakes	1	1			3	2	3	1	
	Unused flakes	20						1	1	
	Nodules	25	13			5				
Flaked Obsidian Artifacts	Core		1							
	Nodule					1				
	Prismatic blades	15	2	14	3	3				
	Thin bifaces				1	1				
Ground, Pecked, and Polished Stone Artifacts	Metate					1				
	Rubbing stones						2			
	Hammer stone	1								
	Spindle whorl								1	
	Slate, unmodified				1					
	Unclassifiable artifact									1
Shell and Bone Artifacts	Shell, misc. worked	1 (scarcely altered)								
	Shell, unmodified	1 (fresh clam)			1 (fresh)					
	Bone, animal, unmodified		1				1			
	Bone, unmodified	1					3			

TABLE 2.189
Platform 5D-30: Artifacts by Lot Group

Study Category	Object	Lot Group 1
Pottery Vessels	Sherds per cubic meter (lbs)	1.11
Other Pottery Artifacts	Earspool Miscellaneous worked sherd Unclassifiable artifact	1 1 1
Flaked Chert Artifacts	Thin biface Irregular retouched flakes Used flakes Nodules	1 4 3 7
Flaked Obsidian Artifacts	Core Thin biface Prismatic blades Unused flakes	1 1 5 3
Ground, Pecked, and Polished Stone Artifacts	Unclassifiable artifact	1
Shell and Bone Artifacts	Bone, unmodified	5

TIME SPANS

The time spans for the excavated structures and platforms of Gp. 5D-1 are defined in Tables 2.190 through 2.194. Group time spans are defined in Table 2.195, based both on stratigraphy and ceramic analysis (Table 2.184). Group TS. 20 consists of a number of activities. At some time, the bedrock crust was completely quarried away, leaving natural marl. This is the basis for correlation of the structure and platform time spans included in Gp. TS. 20. This obviously took place before construction of Str. 5D-7-6th (in Gp. TS. 19), but by how much is uncertain. Group TS. 19 is dated by the ceramics of Bu. 169, as well as those in Plat. 5D-30:LG. 1. Evidently, Manik pottery had been in vogue for some time, or there would not be so many Manik sherds in this lot group. At the time the bedrock cap was quarried, what may have been a chultun was filled (Str. 5D-7:U. 8). This fill contained no sherds later than Preclassic. Although the sample is meager, this and the consistent presence of Preclassic sherds in other lot groups suggests some sort of Late Preclassic occupation, probably prior to the quarrying. This could have been at the end of Preclassic times, when substantial construction on the North Acropolis would have required extensive

quarrying. Or, it could have occurred early in the Early Classic period. In any case, given the scanty information available, all this activity (possible construction, use, and abandonment of a chultun, along with the quarrying) is lumped together in a single time span.

Group TS. 17 is defined on the basis of stratigraphy, and dated by Ik ceramics in Plat. 5D-29:LG. 2a. For Gp. TS. 15, however, both ceramic data and stratigraphy are involved. In the text above, reasons were given for supposing that a floor behind (and associated with) Str. 5D-6-3rd and another behind (and associated with) Str. 5D-7-4th are one and the same. Both represent the earliest construction at their loci following the appearance of Imix ceramics (Str. 5D-7:LG. 3; Plat. 5D-29:LG. 3). Hence, construction of Str. 5D-6-3rd and 5D-7-4th can be reasonably associated as contemporary.

Contemporaneity of Str. 5D-6-1st and 5D-7-2nd (Gp. TS. 11) is demonstrated by demolition of 5D-6-2nd for construction of Plat. 5D-29-3rd, associated with Str. 5D-7-2nd. Given this, and the correlation of Str. 5D-6-3rd with 5D-7-4th, a similar relationship between Str. 5D-6-2nd and 5D-7-3rd is highly likely. This is the basis for Gp. TS. 13.

The correlation of Str. 5D-7-1st and 5D-8-C (Gp. TS. 9) is based on three factors: construction of both on the floor of Plat. 5D-29-3rd; association of both with a new floor for Plat. 5D-29, laid 6 cm above the old one; and the use of similar construction methods in both that consisted of building a structure core followed by the addition of a lower platform level, with steps, to its front. This contrasts with the more common procedure of building up multilevel platforms in layers.

The next sure correlation is that of Gp. TS. 3, marking abandonment of the group. This leaves the final modification of Plat. 5D-29 "floating" with respect to the modifications of Str. 5D-8. One might arbitrarily assign the final plaza floor and steps N of Str. 5D-6 to Gp. TS. 7, at which time the interior platforms were added to Str. 5D-8, for this is the larger scale of two modifications of that structure. The platform modifications could have taken place at any other time in Gp. TS. 6 through 4, however.

Group TS. 2 is defined for a brief reoccupation, at a time when Eznab ceramics were in production (Str. 5D-8:LG. 3b). That this was a reoccupation, and not just the end of the Late Classic occupation of this group, is suggested by St. P36. Its fragments lay in earth, below the projected level of the known floors of Plat. 5D-29. Not a single trace of floor survived beneath the fragments. This seems to indicate that the monument was brought here after the floors had been destroyed by the elements; otherwise, the monument would have afforded protection and some slight traces of floor might be expected to have survived. On the whole, the situation seems greatly similar to Gp. 4E-1, where monument fragments were abandoned in the group after collapse of the buildings; these were associated with Eznab ceramics. No one was necessarily living in Gp. 5D-1 (as in Gp. 4E-1) at this time.

Translating all this into dated activity, the earliest could go back somewhat before AD 1, but there was certainly activity here by AD 150 when Cimi ceramics appeared. Group TS. 19, however, is dated by Manik ceramics, so that it postdates AD 250 but predates AD 550, when Ik ceramics made their appearance. Abandonment (Gp. TS. 3) probably occurred at about AD 869, when Imix production ended, with the reoccupation of TS. 2 taking place some time later, but prior to AD 950 (the end of Eznab pottery production).

TABLE 2.190
Structure 5D-6: Time Spans

Time Spans	Architectural Development	Construction Stage	Unit	Descriptive Data	Lot Groups		Ceramics in Vogue
1				Abandonment and collapse			---------
2				Use			
3	Str. 5D-6-1st	1		Completion of building using perishable materials	3	2	
		2	9	Construction of rear dwarf wall and refurbishing of floors			
		3		Demolition of E portion of 2nd			
4				Use			
5	Str. 5D-6-2nd	1		Reconstruction of building			Imix
		2	7,8	Extension to E of upper platform level			
		3		Partial demolition of existing building			
6				Use			
7	Str.5D-6-3rd	None defined	1-6	Construction of original Str. 5D-6	1		

TABLE 2.191
Structure 5D-7: Time Spans

Time Span	Architectural Development	Construction Stage	Unit	Special Deposits: Burial	Problematical Deposit	Descriptive Data	Lot Group	Ceramics in Vogue
1						Abandonment and collapse		
2						Use	6	
3	Str.5D-7-1st	1	6,7			Construction of building of perishable materials	7a,b	
		2	5			Construction of dwarf wall	5	Imix
		3				Construction of steps and lower platform level		
		4	3,4?			Construction of platform core		
		5				Demolition of 2nd		
4						Use		
5	Str.5D-7-2nd	None defined			124?	Construction		
6						Use		
7	Str.5D-7-3rd	None defined	2	170		Construction	4	
8						Use		
9	Str.5D-7-4th	None defined	1	171		Construction	3	
10						Use		
11	Str.5D-7-5th	None defined				Construction		Ik
12						Use		
13	Str.5D-7-6th	None defined		169		Construction	2	Manik
14			8			Earlier activity	1	Preclassic

TABLE 2.192
Structure 5D-8: Time Spans

Time Span	Architectural Development	Construction Stage	Unit	Descriptive Data	Lot Group	Ceramics in Vogue
1				Final abandonment		
2				Intermittent post-abandonment activity	3b	Eznab
3				Abandonment and collapse		
4	Str.5D-8-A			Use		
5	Str.5D-8-A		10	Resurfacing of floor in Rm. 2		
6				Use		
7	Str.5D-8-B		7-9	Interior platforms built; new room floor(s) laid	2	
8				Use		
9	Str.5D-8-C	1		Completion of building of perishable materials	3a,4	Imix
	Str.5D-8-C	2	6	Construction of dwarf-walls		
	Str.5D-8-C	3	3-5	Completion of building platform		
	Str.5D-8-C	4		Construction of front portion of building platform	1a	
	Str.5D-8-C	5	1,2	Construction of building platform core		
	Str.5D-8-C	6		Preparation of locus for building operations		

TABLE 2.193
Platform 5D-29: Time Spans

Time Span	Architectural Development	Unit	Stela	Special Deposits: Problematical Deposit	Descriptive Data	Lot Group		Ceramics in Vogue
1					Final abandonment			---------
2			P36		Post-abandonment activity			Eznab
3					Abandonment and erosion			---------
4					Use			
5	Plat.5D-29-1st	16			Floor renovation and construction of stairway N of Str. 5D-6			
6					Use			
7	Plat.5D-29-2nd	14,15, 18,19			New floor laid over entire(?) platform			
8					Use			Imix
9	Plat.5D-29-3rd	11-13,17		126	Construction of steps between Str. 5D-6 and 5D-7	4a,4b		
10					Use			
11	Plat.5D-29-4th	10			Western portion raised			
12					Use			
13	Plat.5D-29-5th	8,9			Extension to the W	3		
14					Use			---------
15	Plat.5D-29-6th	1-7			First formal platform constructed	1,2a	2b,2c	Ik
16					Hiatus	1,2a	2b,2c	---------
17					Quarrying of bedrock			Manik Preclassic

TABLE 2.194
Platform 5D-30: Time Spans

Time Span	Architectural Development	Unit	Descriptive Data	Lot Group	Ceramics in Vogue
1			Abandonment and erosion		----------
2			Use		
3	Plat. 5D-30-1st		Construction of new surface, lower than Plat. 5D-30-2nd, to serve Str. 5D-6-3rd		Imix
4			Use		---------- Ik
5	Plat. 5D-30-2nd	1	Original plaza constructed	1	---------- Manik
6			Quarrying of bedrock cap		

Group 4D-4

Group 4D-4 is located on high ground along the W side of the Maler Causeway between the two twin pyramid groups 4E-3 and 4D-1 (TR. 18; Complex R and Complex O of TR. 11). Its structures, 4D-35 through 42, are arranged around two plazas. On the S plaza, Str. 4D-35 through 37 appear to have been short-to-long rectangular platforms, possibly for pole-and-thatch buildings. Behind 4D-37, 4D-38 is somewhat higher than the others, and could have been a high platform or small range-type structure. Structure 4D-39, on the S edge of the N plaza, seems to have been a rectangular platform. On the S, W, and N sides of the plaza were medium-sized range-type structures, 4D-40, 41, and 42.

Four test pits were dug in Gp. 4D-4 (Table 2.196). Of these, two (62A,C) tested fill of the N plaza, with some possible later occupation material mixed in. Another (62B) sampled fill of the S plaza, and the fourth (62D) sampled redeposited fill. The ceramic data (Table 2.197) seem to indicate continuous occupation from Late Preclassic times into the period of Imix pottery production. There may have been a late occupation (or reoccupation) after the appearance of Eznab ceramics. Since there is a good deal of major construction nearby, it is not certain that the earliest ceramic material really pertains to structures antecedent to 4D-35 through 42, or to some other construction. To determine this would require considerable excavation.

Group 5E-1

Group 5E-1 is located only 50 m E of the "F Group" of Morley (TR. 11:19), a group of large, range-type buildings (TR. 23A:21–26). Structures 4E-49 and 5E-7 are long, rectangular ones on the N and S edges of the raised platform on which the structures of the group stand. Smaller rectangular (building?) platforms on the W and E sides of the platform are 5E-5 and 6. Behind 5E-5 is what appears to be another long rectangular platform, Str. 5E-4.

Unfortunately, no ceramic information from the one test pit in this group (Table 2.196) can now be located. Given that visible ruins almost always produce Ik and/or Imix ceramics, an Intermediate through Late Classic occupation here is not unreasonable.

Group 5E-2

Located 90 m S of Gp. 5E-1, the map of TR. 11 shows this one to include eight structures. Of these, 5E-16 and 17 are located on the W and N sides of a raised, square platform. Both small, rectangular structures seem similar to known house foundations. South of these is a long, narrow plaza. On its S side are Str. 5E-13, 14, and 15, which actually might be portions of a single long, narrow, range-type structure. Structure 5E-12, probably a small rectangular (house?) platform, is located along the E side of the plaza and the end of 5E-132. Behind the latter

TABLE 2.195
Group 5D-1: Time Spans

Group 5D-1 Time Span	Str. 5D-6 (Table 2.190)	Str. 5D-7 (Table 2.191)	Str. 5D-8 (Table 2.192)	Plat. 5D-29 (Table 2.193)	Plat. 5D-30 (Table 2.194)
1			1	1	
2			2	2	
3	1	1	3	3	1
4			4		
5			5		
6			6	4	
7			7	5	
8		2	8	6	
9		3	9	7	
10	2	4		8	
11	3	5		9	
12	4	6		10	
13	5	7		11	
14	6	8		12	2
15	7	9		13	3
16		10		14	
17		11		15	
18		12			4
19		13		16	5
20		14		17	6

are what might be two rectangular platforms, Str. 5E-10 and 11, one of which seems to have had a subsidiary platform built on the end of one side.

As with Gp. 5E-1, ceramic data for the test pit (Table 2.196) in this group cannot now be located. Again, an occupation when Ik and/or Imix ceramics were in vogue, at least, seems likely, but is speculative.

Group 5E-4

This group is located in the SE portion of Sq. 5E, 40 m N of the Mendez Causeway (TR. 11). It includes Str. 5E-75 through 83. Of these, 5E-81, 82, and 83 are situated on the W, E, and N sides of a small plaza. All three appear similar to ruins of known house foundations. Slightly more substantial are Str. 5E-75 through 78, situated on the edges of a raised platform just S of Str. 5E-81. All of these, save 5E-78, might have been rectangular house foundations. The latter, on the E side of the plaza, seems to resemble in form household shrines (TR. 21). Just E of the raised platform, on a small plaza of their own, are Str. 5E-79 and 80. These, too, could well have been rectangular house foundations.

Five test pits sampled cultural material from this group (Table 2.196). Of these, three sampled fill from the group raised platform, and two sampled potential habitation refuse E and W of this. The ceramic data (Table 2.197) indicate that occupation of this group was primarily Intermediate and Late Classic, while Ik and then Imix ceramics were in use. The very few Manik sherds recovered might have been in debris from some nearby source that was used as fill. Alternatively, the first construction here might date from near the end of Early Classic times. It seems clear, however, that there was no substantial Early Classic occupation of Gp. 5E-4.

TABLE 2.196
Location of Test Pits: Great Plaza Quadrangle

Group	Test Pit	Location
4D-4	62A	Between Str. 4D-39 and 40
	62B	Behind Str. 4D-37
	62C	Plaza in front of Str. 4D-41
	62D	Behind Str. 4D-41
5E-1	71T	Plaza of Str. 4E-49, 5E-4 through 7
5E-2	63B	In front of Str. 5E-13
5E-4	63E	Behind Str. 5E-76
	63F	Plaza in front of Str. 5E-76
	71E	Plaza near juncture of Str. 5E-75 and 76
	71G	Plaza, near 71E test pit
	71I	Between Str. 5E-75 and 79

TABLE 2.197
Ceramic Evaluations: Great Plaza Test Pits

Group	Lot	Provenience	Ceramics
4D-4	62A/1	0-20 cm	Ik and/or Imix
	62A/2	20-40 cm	Ik and/or Imix
	62A/3	40-60 cm	Manik; Ik and/or Imix
	62A/4	60-80 cm	Manik; Ik and/or Imix
	62B/1	0-20 cm	Ik; Imix
	62B/2	20-40 cm	Ik; Imix
	62B/3	40-60 cm	Manik; 1 Cimi
	62C/1	0-20 cm	Ik and/or Imix; possible Eznab
	62D/1	0-20 cm	Mostly late Preclassic; some Manik; possible Ik and/or Imix
	62D/2	20-40 cm	Late Preclassic through Ik and/or Imix
5E-1	71T/		Lost
5E-2	63B/1		Lost
5E-4	63E/1	0-20 cm	Mostly Ik and/or Imix
	63E/2	20-40 cm	Ik and/or Imix and some Manik
	63F/1	0-20 cm	Ik and/or Imix
	63F/2	20-30 cm	Imix
	71E/1	0-45 cm	Ik and/or Imix
	71G/1	0-20	Imix
	71I/1		Ik; Imix
	71I/2		Ik and/or Imix

6. Excavations in the Camp Quadrangle

Introduction

Seven mapped groups in this quadrangle have been more or less intensively excavated: Gp. 4F-1 and 2 (TR. 19), Gp. 4F-3 and 5F-1 (this report), and Gp. 4G-1, 5G-1 and 5G-2 (TR. 21). Burials 45 and 198, Ch. 4F-2 and 4F-4 (this report) and Gp. 5F-5 (TR. 37) provide information of at least chronological significance for four additional groups. Seven test pits in six other groups, as well as the structure that produced Bu. 198, increase this sample to almost 44% of the 48 to 50 structure groups that may be defined for this quadrangle. Finally, an area of seemingly vacant terrain was searched in Sq. 5F, resulting in discovery of Gp. 5F-2 (this report). In Sq. 4G, Ch. 4G-2 may indicate the existence of yet another such group (this report).

Group 4F-3

Group 4F-3 is located on the site map (TR. 11) at 4F:S37 E250. The ground here slopes almost impercepti-

bly down from W to E, with the only nearby group some 25 m to the W. As originally mapped in 1957, Gp. 4F-3 was depicted as consisting of the single Str. 4F-21, but re-survey in 1960 revealed Str. 4F-47. Two others, Str. 4F-48 and 49, were identified only after considerable excavation. The four are arranged around two sides of a plaza (Plat. 4F-6) in an "L" configuration (Fig. 99). In 1961, the four structures were extensively excavated by Haviland.

STRUCTURE 4F-21-2ND

As originally constructed on the N edge of Plat. 4F-6 (Fig. 100, 178d), this structure took the form of a one-level platform with masonry walls and a plaster surface (U. 4). It was probably built in three stages, of which the first (CS. 3) consisted of preparation of the surface on which to build (see below). Following this, the front and end walls were built (CS. 2), standing about 0.30 m in height. The front wall (which was retained in 21-1st) was based on bedrock. Badly ruined, the original back wall appears to have been of two courses of roughly dressed masonry. Plaster floor was laid directly on the earth fill of the platform (see Fig. 101a).

The platform of 2nd likely was topped by a building of perishable materials. No positive evidence of this was found, but given the resemblance of the structure to others that did include such buildings (TR. 20B), a final stage (CS. 1) is allowed for construction of one here.

STRUCTURE 4F-21-1ST

In due course, Str. 4F-21 was widened, and a second level added to its platform (see Fig. 100 and 101a). To begin (CS. 4) any existing building on the original foundation would have been removed. New walls extending the platform to the N (Fig. 101a:3) were then assembled as CS. 3. Completing this stage, walls for an upper level were placed, with the front wall (Fig. 100 and 101a:U. 1) set on the floor that had served the earlier structure. The 1.50 m southern portion of this pavement seems to have continued in use in front of the upper level of the final structure, since no evidence of floor refurbishing can be seen.

Once platform fill was in place, another wall (Fig. 100 and 101a:U. 2) was built on top (CS. 2). Except for a possible opening in the center, this ran almost the length of the structure. Unit 3, a remnant of pavement for the upper platform level, abuts the base of this wall (see Fig. 101a). The other relations of U. 2 could not be determined, but it probably represents a part of a building that otherwise was constructed wholly of perishable materials (TR. 20B). Erection of this building defines CS. 1.

STRUCTURE 4F-47-2ND

On the W side of Plat. 4F-6 is a raised terrace (Plat. 4F-10) on which stands Str. 4F-47. So inconspicuous was the ruin of the structure that it was missed in the original map survey, although it was detected in a second survey carried out in 1960. As originally conceived by the Maya, 4F-47-2nd was a building set on a one-level platform, rectangular in shape. The back and portions of the end walls of this platform were later utilized as part of 47-1st. Postholes (Fig. 102:U. 9 and 10 and Table 2.198), located inside the corners at the back of this platform, bear witness that 47-2nd consisted in part of a building of perishable materials, as did its successor structure. The front wall (Fig. 103:U. 1) was constructed on a layer of hard-packed gray earth (U. 6). Platform 4F-10:Fl. 1 seems to turn up to this wall. The fill of the building platform consists of a brown earth.

On either end of the building platform, two smaller interior platforms were built (Fig. 102:U. 2 and 3). Their fills, however, are primarily of small stones. The masonry of both U. 2 and 3 is now badly broken up, and no traces of a plaster surface can be identified, though both interior platforms presumably were paved. Between them, pavement (Fig. 103:U. 4) was laid over the center portion of the building platform, in union with the walls of U. 2 and 3. This floor is 0.22 m higher than the surface of Plat. 4F-10, and lies directly on the earth fill of the building platform.

As noted, two postholes (U. 9 and 10) in the rear corners signal the presence of a building of perishable materials. Though reused in Str. 4F-47-1st (see below), they must have originated with 2nd. Otherwise, the small stone fills of U. 2 and 3 would have been extensively disturbed, which they were not. Since these rear postholes penetrated bedrock, it would be surprising if holes for the front poles did not do so as well. Yet the only other postholes (Fig. 102 and Table 2.198:U. 7 and 8) are 0.72 m in front of the E wall of 2nd. Although these, like U. 9 and 10, survived in 47-1st, they too may originally have served 2nd. Thus, the pole-and-thatch building of 2nd may have included a portion of the floor of Plat. 4F-10, with the structure platform occupying only the rear portion of the building. It also suggests that Str. 4F-47-1st amounted to an extension of the early platform around the existing building framework, perhaps at the same time as replacement of worn-out thatch.

To sum up, the sequence of construction of Str. 4F-47-2nd:CS. 4 saw preparation of the base surface, including digging holes for the corner posts. Stage 3 consisted of construction of the building platform, and undoubtedly the corner posts for the building were set at this time. The interior platforms were then built, and U. 4 laid, as CS. 2. Stage 1 saw completion of the building.

STRUCTURE 4F-47-1ST

This construction probably began (as CS. 4) with at least partial destruction of the earlier building (existing corner posts were probably retained, otherwise U. 2 and 3 fills would have been disturbed). Then the width of the earlier platform was increased by construction (as CS. 3) of a new front wall (Fig. 102 and 103:4) 0.90 m E of the earlier one, which was largely destroyed in the process. This final E wall, of a single course of large, well-cut masonry blocks, was based on Plat. 4F-10:Fl. 1. A patch, Plat. 4F-10:U. 1 (Fig. 103), turns up to the wall. The rest of the original floor of Plat. 4F-10 continued in use with the final structure.

As CS. 2, a second level was added to the building platform directly on the surface of U. 4 (see Fig. 102 and 103). This runs the length of the final structure, and incorporated U. 2 and 3. The front wall (U. 5) of this upper level is positioned 1.10 m W of the front wall of the lower platform. About 0.20 m of Str. 4F-47:U. 4 survives E of U. 5, which suggests that U. 4 was used as part of a floor in front of the upper platform level. It is possible, however, that a whole new floor, now destroyed, was laid to turn up to U. 5. Any pavement that may have existed on the upper level has been totally destroyed.

Postholes in bedrock (Fig. 102:U. 7–10), just inside the corners of the final masonry walls, show that the platform supported a building of perishable materials. As noted, all four likely originated with 2nd, but continued to serve 1st. As CS. 1, the building was probably largely rebuilt.

STRUCTURE 4F-48

This small, poorly preserved square platform was discovered 1.00 m E of the end of Str. 4F-21 (Fig. 100, 179a). It does not open directly onto Plat. 4F-6, but sits 1.60 m N of the edge of this plaza. There was no clue on the surface that any structure was located here, even after thorough clearing, and it remained for exploratory excavation to reveal its presence.

Virtually all of the wall masonry of the platform is now broken, with the exception of three well-cut blocks in the S wall. The fill within the walls includes a large number of small stones; no trace of overlying floor survives. The platform was built on the same stratum of hard-packed gray earth (Str. 4F-21:U. 6) that underlies Str. 4F-21 (Fig. 101b). The surface of this stratum must have served as an informal floor around the platform. Although no postholes were found that relate to Str. 4F-48, similarity to Str. 4F-49 (see below) suggests a building of pole-and-thatch was once part of it. Thus, three stages of construction may be defined: CS. 3 for preparation of the surface on which to build; CS. 2 for construction of the platform; and CS. 1 for the building.

STRUCTURE 4F-49

This small platform is essentially comparable to Str. 4F-48 in size and relative location; it is based 2.88 m S of Str. 4F-47, at the end of Plat. 4F-10. Platform 4F-10:U. 4 (Fig. 102), a low wall that marks the W side of the terrace S of 4F-47, joins 4F-49 at its NW corner. As with Str. 4F-48, there were no surface features to indicate the presence of this platform. All the wall masonry is now broken, though the surviving rubble preserves the essential outline. The walls apparently were built directly on bedrock, which is close to the surface. The fill was mostly of small stones, with some cultural material included. Excavation of this fill, in two corners only, revealed the presence of two postholes (Fig. 102:U. 1 and 2; Table 2.198). Clearly, this platform supported a building of perishable materials, and its construction can be divided into three stages: CS. 3 for preparation of the base surface; CS. 2 for construction of the platform; and CS. 1 for that of the building.

Behind the structure, bedrock had been quarried superficially, and apparently served afterward as a dump area.

PLATFORM 4F-6

Platform 4F-6 designates the area E of Plat. 4F-10 and S of Str. 4F-21 and 4F-48 (Fig. 99, 100, 102). No trace of pavement remains in any of the areas excavated. The presence of an artificially leveled plaza area, however,

paved or unpaved, is demonstrated by the remains of a stone retaining wall 2 m SE of Str. 4F-48, as well as by the quarrying of bedrock immediately E of Plat. 4F-10 (see below). Platform 4F-6:U. 1 (Fig. 100) designates rubble 1 m S and 1 m E of Str. 4F-48. Although broken and formless, it lies in a line that runs 1.60 m E, then turns a right angle, to run in a line to the S. The northern portion of U. 1, which runs E-W, is directly in line with the S wall of Str. 4F-21. Structure 4F-48 is located 1.60 m N of this line. Unit 1 clearly represents the remains of the NE corner of the plaza. The only burial found in Gp. 4F-3, Bu. 61, was placed just inside the corner of U. 1.

PLATFORM 4F-10

The "terrace" or raised area W of Plat. 4F-6, on which Str. 4F-47 stood, is designated as Plat. 4F-10. For a distance of 7.80 m S of Str. 4F-21, the front wall of the terrace consists largely of the quarried face of bedrock, but this line is continued S for a distance of 3.44 m by a wall of 0.60 m-high masonry (Fig. 102:1). A change in the earth E of this wall near elevation 205.40 m probably marks the level of the surface of Plat. 4F-6, hence the top of the bedrock rises only about 0.40 m higher than the plaza surface. At its northern end, the quarried bedrock wall of the terrace turns a right angle to the E, where it is incorporated into the front wall of Str. 4F-21 (see Fig. 100).

Floor 1 of Plat. 4F-10 was identified immediately in front of Str. 4F-47. This pavement relates to 47-2nd, with the front wall of 47-1st set on it (see Fig. 103). Unit 1, a patch on Fl. 1, turns up to this final structure. Floor 1 could be followed 1.08 m to the E of the final platform wall. Since its level is about 0.70 m above the probable lower plaza surface, it likely did not extend all the way to the front terrace wall, but probably ended in two steps leading down to the plaza. The surviving terrace wall would therefore represent the bottom step of this postulated stairway, while a stratum of gray material that overlies bedrock beneath the terrace suggests that the location of the upper step was 0.80 m W of the lower riser, or perhaps slightly closer.

Unit 3, a floor surface between Str. 4F-47 and 4F-49 (Fig. 102), seems to be a surviving portion of Fl. 1 in this area. It occupies the same relative position to the S wall of Str. 4F-47 as does Fl. 1 to the front of 47-2nd. It must have turned up to Str. 4F-49, although destruction has obliterated actual traces of this. Unit 3 turns up to U. 4 (Fig. 102), a low masonry wall that runs between the two structures. This wall is of well-cut masonry blocks, the tops of which rise 6 cm above the surface of U. 3. West of this wall, the hard-packed gray stratum (Str. 4F-47:U. 6) served as an informal surface.

Unit 5 (Fig. 102:3), the neck of a jar 0.16 m in diameter, penetrates U. 3 in the corner, where U. 4 abuts the

S wall of Str. 4F-47. Evidently, this jar neck was placed at the time the floor was laid, since there is no trace of plaster patches. Its purpose is unknown, though an obvious possibility is that it functioned as a drain.

POSSIBLE EARLY ACTIVITY

Twenty centimeters E of Str. 4F-21 is a posthole in bedrock (U. 5). Seemingly unrelated to 4F-21, it may pertain to an early structure, the one-time existence of which is suggested by the presence of Preclassic ceramic material in U. 6. Another posthole unrelated to the structure above is Str. 4F-48:U. 1 (Fig. 100; Table 2.198). It could relate to the postulated structure represented by 4F-21:U. 5.

Unit 6 of Str. 4F-21 is a layer of hard-packed gray material beneath the back portion of 4F-21 on which the N and E walls of 1st and 2nd were built (Fig. 101). This averages 0.20 m in thickness, but lenses out 1.00 m N of the S retaining wall. It probably represents an occupation level and early debris that was leveled prior to construction of 21-2nd. Evidence for this consists of a number of sherds from Preclassic ceramic vessels in U. 6, which may have come from the structure of which U. 5, and possibly Str. 4F-48:U. 1 (see below) are the only remnants. The surface of U. 6 remained exposed N of Str. 4F-21 during occupation, and served as an informal floor.

Beneath Str. 4F-47 and overlying bedrock is a layer of compact gray earth (Fig. 102:U. 6) that contains some cultural material, including Early Classic sherds. The relatively level top of this stratum was used as the surface on which to construct 4F-47. Behind the structure, the top of U. 6 was left exposed during occupation. Between 4F-47 and 49 it was paved (see Plat. 4F-10). Since cultural material is sparse in this stratum, it may be that earlier construction was not razed to permit construction of Str. 4F-47-2nd.

Beneath Str. 4F-48, bedrock has been quarried to some extent, but elsewhere was not, save in conjunction with construction of Plat. 4F-6 and 10.

SHERDS AND ARTIFACTS

Lot groups for the four structures and platforms of Gp. 4F-3 are specified in Table 2.199, with content listed in Tables 2.200–2.204.

STRATA UNDERLYING CONSTRUCTION

Sources include Str. 4F-21:U. 6, and Str. 4F-47:U. 6. Theoretically, these could be early deposits that predate construction, or fill put in place to provide level surfaces on which to build. A third possibility is that these strata are original earth, modified by scraping and filling for construction. In the case of Str. 4F-47:U. 6, two things favor the last interpretation: first, the sherds do not differ markedly from those within the earliest structure fill,

which would indicate that it was not the leveled remains of earlier occupation trash. Second, cultural material is not plentiful, and what there is may very well be explained as fill material or occupation trash that was trampled into the underlying earth. On the other hand, evidence already discussed suggests that an early structure stood at the locus of Str. 4F-21, so 4F-21:U. 6 may be scraped up occupation debris or fill from that early entity. Cultural material from these strata is included in Str. 4F-48:LG. 1, 4F-47:LG. 1, and 4F-21:LG. 1.

CONSTRUCTION FILL

Generally speaking, plaster floors for all the structures of Gp. 4F-3 are either badly broken up or gone altogether. Therefore, there is always the possibility that what is considered here as fill is contaminated by occupation trash. More likely, however, fill material has been uprooted and washed out, contaminating other lot sources. Fill for Str. 4F-21-2nd and 47-2nd should be relatively free from contamination, as plaster floors beneath later fill are fairly well preserved. Since the latest floors are usually destroyed, in the absence of evidence to the contrary, the assumption is that surface lots over the structures are in reality rooted-out fill, and they are so considered in the analysis (cf. Str. 4F-21:LG. 4; 4F-47:LG. 4; 4F-49:LG. 1). Structure 4F-48:LG. 2 also includes a thin surface stratum.

Platform 4F-6 poses a special problem, since no plaster pavement could be found. The existence of such a floor is postulated, and all material below its probable level is considered as fill (cf. Plat. 4F-6:LG. 1a, 1b). The material from the other lot groups is problematical, but LG. 2b probably is fill that has washed-out of Plat. 4F-10, the height of which in relation to the plaza renders it particularly vulnerable to erosion. Lot Group 2a is undoubtedly occupation trash.

Cultural material in structure fills tends to be most abundant in the latest architectural developments of Str. 4F-21 and 4F-47. Thus the sherds and artifacts from the latest structure fills may be trash from the early occupation of the group. Since sherds are also abundant in the fill of Str. 4F-49, this structure may postdate Str. 4F-47-2nd. Most ceramic samples are poor, however, and their analysis neither supports nor contradicts this idea.

MATERIAL ABOVE LIVING LEVELS

This category includes material around the walls of the structures, but not from the surface above them. Most of this material likely dates from the occupation, and particularly the time of abandonment of the structures, although fill contamination is undoubtedly present. Such contamination probably accounts for a good deal of material above formal floors (cf. Str. 4F-47:LG. 3c and 3d), whereas occupants might have been more tolerant of debris behind their structures. Some sherds and artifacts on plaster floors, however, might represent trash left at the time of abandonment.

Material above living levels is most abundant near Str. 4F-49, with 21 pounds of sherds per cubic meter in the quarried area W of the structure. The next largest deposit of sherds and artifacts is W of the wall that joins Str. 4F-49 to 47, and the quantity steadily decreases to the N, behind 47. This deposit, W of Str. 4F-49 and Plat. 4F-10, is the nearest thing to a midden discovered in the Op. 24 excavations of 1961. The only deposits from that season comparable in respect to concentrations of trash are behind the five structures of Gp. 2G-1, off the end of Str. 3F-29 in Gp. 3F-1, and near Str. 2G-61. Although the sherd concentrations in some of these lots are greater than in the case of Str. 4F-49:LG. 2b, they do not appear to cover so large an area, as far as can be determined from limited excavations.

In comparison with Str. 4F-47 and 49, there is a paucity of cultural debris above living levels near 21 and 48. The largest deposit is located E of Plat. 4F-6 (LG. 2a); the next largest is near the NE corner of Str. 4F-21. Perhaps this difference in quantity has cultural significance, but it is possible that debris was simply kept clear from Str. 4F-21 and 48 to a greater extent than in the case of the other two structures.

TIME SPANS

Time spans for Gp. 4F-3 are listed in Tables 2.205 through 2.210. For the two structures associated with Plat. 4F-10, architectural stratigraphy, in the form of floor turnups and connecting walls, permits one-to-one correlation between the time spans for the three constructions (Table 2.210). For Str. 4F-21, 48, and Plat. 4F-6, such architectural relationships are lacking, and ceramic analysis is little help. There are clues that permit correlations with a high degree of probability, however (see Table 2.211). The existence of Plat. 4F-10 necessitates a plaza area to the E; moreover, the E wall of this terrace merges into the front wall of Str. 4F-21, suggesting that the two features are essentially contemporary. Similarly, the contemporaneity of Plat. 4F-6 and Str. 4F-21-2nd is suggested by the continuation E of the N wall of the plaza, from the end of the S wall of Str. 4F-21-2nd. Structure 4F-48 remains the biggest problem; it could have been constructed later than the other structures. But since Str. 4F-49 is known to be contemporary with 47-2nd, the similar 4F-48 is assumed contemporary with 21-2nd.

The ceramic data do not contradict any of this (Table 2.199). Structures 4F-21-2nd and 47-2nd cannot predate the appearance of transitional Ik-Imix ceramics. Sherds from the fills of Str. 4F-48 and 49 indicate no more than that they postdate the appearance of Ik ceramics. Sherds

from the fill of Plat. 4F-6, though badly mixed, suggest that this plaza does not predate the appearance of ceramics transitional between Ik and Imix.

It is not known if construction of Str. 4F-21-1st and 47-1st took place at precisely the same time, but experience in other small-structure groups indicates a high probability for this. Hence, both are assigned to group TS. 3.

Preconstruction deposits are the basis of group TS. 6 and 7. A good many Preclassic sherds were found in the stratum that underlies Str. 4F-21 and 48 (Str. 4F-21:U. 6). This suggests activity here prior to known construction. Possibly the sherds relate to a structure that survives only as two postholes, Str. 4F-21:U. 5 and Str. 4F-48:U. 1.

Beneath Str. 4F-47, several Manik sherds were found, which may indicate an Early Classic occupation of this locus.

Sherds associated with the period of use of the known structures of Gp. 4F-3 indicate that Imix ceramics (early and late) were in vogue during group TS. 4-2. Group TS. 3, when Str. 4F-21-1st and 47-1st were constructed, might arbitrarily be assigned to the transition from early to late Imix ceramics. There is no evidence for or against this, but it probably is not too far from the truth. The best example of late occupation material is from Str. 4F-49:LG. 2b, and there is certainly no reason to believe that this structure was abandoned later than any of the others.

In summary, there seems to have been some activity in Gp. 4F-3 by the first century AD. This continued into Early Classic times, but the focus of the activity seems to have shifted from the locus of Str. 4F-21 to that of 4F-47. Just prior to AD 700, with the appearance of Ik-Imix transitional ceramics, the four known structures of the group were built. They were abandoned sometime around AD 869 (which dates the end of the Imix Ceramic Complex).

TABLE 2.198
Dimensions of Postholes in Group 4F-3
(meters)

Posthole	Diameter	Depth
Str. 4F-47: U. 7	0.20	0.25
Str. 4F-47: U. 8	0.22	0.32
Str. 4F-47: U. 9	0.24	0.18
Str. 4F-47: U. 10	0.22	0.05
Str. 4F-48: U. 1	0.16	0.20
Str. 4F-49: U. 1	0.22	0.18
Str. 4F-49: U. 2	0.24	0.20

TABLE 2.199
Group 4F-3: Lot Groups

Feature	Lot Group	Lot Group	Provenience	Ceramic Evaluation
Str. 4F-21 (Op. 24A)	1	14,31,34, 47,54	Unsealed stratum beneath construction (U. 6)	Preclassic and Ik and/or Imix
	2a	8,17,30,39, 46,55	Partially sealed fill of 2nd	Ik-Imix transition or Imix
	2b	15,17a,19, 32,35,42, 49,50	Partially sealed fill of 1st	Ik-Imix transition or Imix
	2c	57	Unsealed fill of 1st and 2nd	Ik-Imix transition or Imix
	3a	2,7,16,43	N of structure, surface to base of wall	Imix
	3b	13	E of structure, surface to base of wall	Imix
	3c	59	W of structure, surface to base of wall	Imix
	4	9,10,36,38, 40	Surface of structure to living levels	Ik and/or Imix
Str. 4F-47 (Op. 24A)	1	69,72b	Unsealed stratum beneath construction (U. 6)	Manik and Ik and/or Imix
	2a	68,72a	Sealed fill of 2nd	Ik-Imix transition or Imix
	2b	63,73	Unsealed fill of 1st	Ik-Imix transition or Imix
	2c	29,72	Unsealed fill of 1st and 2nd	Ik-Imix transition or Imix
	3a	48,58	W of structure, surface to base of wall	Imix
	3b	53	W of Plat. 4F-10:U. 4	Imix
	3c	41,44	S of structure, surface to floor of Plat. 4F-10	Early Imix
	3d	25,26,28	E of structure, surface to floor level of Plat. 4F-10	Early Imix
	4	27	Surface of structure to floor levels	Early Imix
Str. 4F-48 (Op. 24A)	1	52	Unsealed stratum beneath construction (Str.4F-21:U.6)	Preclassic and Ik and/or Imix
	2	37,51	Unsealed fill	Ik and/or Imix
	3	45	N, E, and S of structure, surface to base of walls	Ik and/or Imix
Str. 4F-49 (Op. 24A)	1	60	Surface of structure	Ik and/or Imix
	2a	64-66	E and S of structure, to base of walls	Ik and/or Imix
	2b	56,70	W of structure in quarried area	Late Imix
Plat. 4F-6 (Op. 24A)	1a	21,22,24	Unsealed fill, W portion	Ik-Imix transition or Imix
	1b	61, 62	Unsealed fill, NE corner	Ik and/or Imix
	2a	67,71	NE of plaza surface to base of wall	Ik and/or Imix
	2b	1,3,4-6, 11,12,33	S of Str. 4F-21	Ik and/or Imix
	2c	20,23	W portion, above L.G. 1a	Ik and/or Imix

TABLE 2.200
Structure 4F-21: Artifacts by Lot Group

Study Category	Object	Lot Group 1	2a	2b	2c	3a	3b	3c	4
Pottery Vessels	Sherds per cubic meter (lbs)	.5	1.8	2.5	.8	1.8	1.2	2.4	1.5
Other Pottery Artifacts	Figurine						1		
	Eccentrically perforated sherd		1						
	Candelero					1			
	Unclassifiable formed objects				1				1
Flaked Chert Artifacts	Flake cores								2
	Ovate bifaces		1						2
	Elongate biface			1					
	Irregular, retouched flake					1			
	Blades		1	1					
	Used flake	1							
	Unmodified flakes	2	3	51	3	10			47
	Unmodified, fire-spalled flakes	1		1					3
Flaked Obsidian Artifacts	Prismatic blades	2		1		2			5
Ground, Pecked, and Polished Stone Artifacts	Manos					1			1
	Metates					2			

TABLE 2.201
Structure 4F-47: Artifacts by Lot Group

Study Category	Object	Lot Group 1	2a	2b	2c	3a	3b	3c	3d	4
Pottery Vessels	Sherds per cubic meter (lbs)	1.7		1.5	3.0	.7	7.2	4.6	1.7	2.4
Other Pottery Artifacts	Figurines				1		2			
	Eccentrically perforated sherd						1			
	Miniature vessel			1						
	Censer							1		
	Unclassifiable formed objects							4		
Flaked Chert Artifacts	Flake core				1		1			
	Ovate bifaces					1		1	1	
	Elongate biface									1
	Thin bifaces					2				
	Point-retouched flake							1		
	Blades		1		4	1		2	1	
	Used flakes					1	1	2		
	Unmodified flakes	1	3	2	2	40	20	21	17	4
	Unmodified, fire-spalled flakes				1	8	2	4		
Flaked Obsidian Artifacts	Prismatic blades		1	1		2	2	6	2	1
	Unmodified flakes				1	1				
Ground, Pecked, and Polished Stone Artifacts	Pestle						1			
Shell and Bone Artifacts	Bone							1	2	

TABLE 2.202
Structure 4F-48: Artifacts by Lot Group

Study Category	Object	Lot Group		
		1	2	3
Pottery Vessels	Sherds per cubic meter (lbs)	1.9	2.6	1.9
Flaked Chert Artifacts	Flake cores	1	1	
	Ovate biface		1	
	Used flake			1
	Unmodified flakes	8	42	
	Unmodified, fire-spalled flakes	2	14	
Flaked Obsidian Artifacts	Flake core		1	
	Prismatic blades		3	
Ground, Pecked, and Polished Stone Artifacts	Metates		1	1
Shell and Bone Artifacts	Shell		1	

TABLE 2.203
Structure 4F-49: Artifacts by Lot Group

Study Category	Object	Lot Group		
		1	2a	2b
Pottery Vessels	Sherds per cubic meter (lbs)	8.1	--	21.1
Other Pottery Artifacts	Figurines			5
	Centrally perforated sherd			1
	Unclassifiable formed objects			5
Flaked Chert Artifacts	Flake core			1
	Ovate bifaces		1	3
	Elongate biface			1
	Thin biface		1	
	Irregular, retouched flakes		1	3
	Blades	1		2
	Used flake	1	1	
	Unmodified flakes	12	6	42
	Unmodified, fire-spalled flakes	6	1	4
Flaked Obsidian Artifacts	Prismatic blades	3		6
Ground, Pecked, and Polished Stone Artifacts	Manos	2		3
	Metate			1
	Hammer stone		1	

TABLE 2.204
Platform 4F-6: Artifacts by Lot Group

Study Category	Object	Lot Group 1a	1b	2a	2b	2c
Pottery Vessels	Sherds per cubic meter (lbs)	5.8	7.8	4.7	1.0	4.2
Other Pottery Artifacts	Figurines	3		1		1
	Unclassifiable formed objects	1	1	1		1
Flaked Chert Artifacts	Ovate biface	1				
	Irregular, retouched flakes	1				1
	Blades	1			1	1
	Used flake	1				
	Unmodified flakes	38	2		8	22
	Unmodified, fire-spalled flakes	3				1
Flaked Obsidian Artifacts	Blade core	1				
	Thin biface					1
	Prismatic blades	6		2		1
	Unmodified flake	1				
Ground, Pecked, and Polished Stone Artifacts	Manos	1				1
	Metate			1		
	Hammer stone	1				
	Ground pebble	1				
Shell and Bone Artifacts	Shell, unworked	1				
	Bone					1

TABLE 2.205
Structure 4F-21: Time Spans

Time Span	Architectural Development	Construction Stage	Unit	Descriptive Data	Lot Group	Ceramics in Vogue
1				Abandonment and collapse		----------
2				Use	3a,b,c	(Late)
3	Str.4F-21-1st	1		Construction of building		Imix
		2	2,3	Construction of base wall	2b	
		3	1	Construction of lower and upper platform levels	2c,4	
		4		Demolition of existing building		
4				Use		(Early)
5	Str.4F-21-2nd	1		Construction of building of perishable materials		Ik-Imix
		2	4	Construction of platform	2a	
		3		Preparation of surface for construction		
6				Hiatus		Manik-Ik
7			5,6	Early activity	1	Preclassic

TABLE 2.206
Structure 4F-47: Time Spans

Time Span	Architectural Development	Construction Stage	Unit	Descriptive Data	Lot Group	Ceramics in Vogue
1				Abandonment and collapse	3a,b, c,d	(Late)
2				Use		
3	Str.4F-47-1st	1		Construction of building of perishable materials		Imix
		2	5	Construction of upper platform level		
		3		Construction of lower platform level	2b	
		4		Demolition of existing building		
4				Use		(Early)
5	Str.4F-47-2nd	1		Construction of building of perishable materials	2c,4	Ik-Imix transition
		2	2-4	Construction of interior platforms	2a	
		3	1	Construction of building platform		
		4	7,8,9?,10?	Preparation of surface for construction		
6			6	Earlier activity	1	Manik-Ik

TABLE 2.207
Structure 4F-48: Time Spans

Time Span	Architectural Development	Construction Stage	Unit	Descriptive Data	Lot Group	Ceramics in Vogue
1				Abandonment and collapse	3	
2				Use		Imix
3	Str. 4F-48	1		Construction of building of perishable materials	2	Ik-Imix
		2		Construction of platform		
4				Hiatus		Manik-Ik
5			1; Str. 4F-21: U.6	Early activity	1	Preclassic

TABLE 2.208
Structure 4F-49: Time Spans

Time Span	Architectural Development	Construction Stage	Unit	Descriptive Data	Lot Group		Ceramics in Vogue
1				Abandonment and collapse			
2				Use	2b	2a	(Late) Imix (Early)
3	Str. 4F-49	1		Construction of building of perishable materials			Ik-Imix
		2		Construction of platform	1		
		3	1,2	Preparation of surface for construction			

TABLE 2.209
Platform 4F-6: Time Spans

Time Span	Architectural Development	Unit	Special Deposit	Descriptive Data	Lot Group	Ceramics in Vogue
1			Bu. 61?	Abandonment and ruin		
2				Use of plaza	2a	Imix
3	Plat. 4F-6	1		Construction of plaza	1a,b,2b,c	Ik-Imix

TABLE 2.210
Platform 4F-10: Time Spans

Time Span	Architectural Development	Unit	Floor	Descriptive Data	Equivalent Time Spans: Str. 4F-47	Str. 4F-49	Plat. 4F-6
1				Abandonment and ruin	1	1	1
2				Use	2		
3	Plat.4F-10-A	1		Modification	3		
4				Use	4	2	2
5	Plat.4F-10-B	2-4,5	1	Construction	5	3	3
6		Str.4F-47:U.6		Early activity	6		

TABLE 2.211
Group 4F-3: Time Spans

Group Time Span	Str. 4F-21 Time Span (Table 2.205)	Str. 4F-47 Time Span (Table 2.206)	Str. 4F-48 Time Span (Table 2.207)	Str. 4F-49 Time Span (Table 2.208)	Plat. 4F-6 Time Span (Table 2.209)	Plat. 4F-10 Time Span (Table 2.210)
1	1	1	1	1	1	1
2	2	2				2
3	3	3				3
4	4	4	2	2	2	4
5	5	5	3?	3	3	5
6	6	6	4			6
7	7		5			

Group 5F-1

Group 5F-1 is located on a knoll about 220 m S of the Tikal Reservoir at 5F:S60 E474. As mapped by Kent Day in 1964, it consists of two structures, 5F-17 and 18, on the W and N sides of the raised Plat. 5F-1 (Fig. 104). Overall, it resembles more closely Gp. 6E-1 (this report) than is suggested by the site map (TR. 11), which seems to depict Str. 5F-17 erroneously. As part of Culbert's ceramic test program, Edward Sisson and Henry Schwartz dug three test pits in different parts of the group. The discovery of a pure deposit of Tzec ceramics (including a burial) suggested that very early domestic architecture might be found in the fill of the platform, as was the case in Gp. 6E-1. Therefore, expanded excavations were undertaken in 1964 by Kent Day. In the end, although traces of Preclassic architecture were indeed discovered, overall knowledge of the group does not begin to compare with the more detailed understanding of Gp. 6E-1.

STRUCTURE 5F-17

Located on the N edge of Plat. 5F-1, the long axis of the structure is approximately N-S. As originally mapped by Hazard for the site map, the structure is shown too far N, with what appears to be a smaller adjunct attached to its S end. A new plane-table survey by Kent Day in 1964, after thorough clearing of vegetation, suggests that this original depiction probably is not correct. Rather, the structure appears to have been rectangular, with its N wall about 8 m S of Str. 5F-18.

Although the structure was not excavated, Day's map shows a wall at the W end of his test trench through Plat. 5F-1 (Fig. 104:U. 1 of Str. 5F-17). The elevation of this wall is not given, but its position relative to the ruin mound is as expected for the front wall of Str. 5F-17.

STRUCTURE 5F-18

Located on the N edge of Plat. 5F-1, the long axis of this structure runs approximately magnetic E-W. It was investigated by two test pits alone: Op. 71L on the axis in front of the mound, and 71M in its center (Fig. 104). The first was soon abandoned, but the second was excavated to bedrock. Obviously, knowledge of this structure is minimal.

In the 71M test pit is a wall (U. 1) that rests on a white, 0.54-m thick fill (Plat. 5F-1:U. 2) over bedrock (Fig. 105). South of the wall, on top of Plat. 5F-1:U. 2, is a fill of light brown earth (Str. 5F-18:U. 2) that is obviously different from that on which U. 1 sits. This is topped by a badly preserved floor, U. 3, which runs to the top of U. 1, and above it is 0.28 m of topsoil. Other than this, there is little to say about this structure. The surface of the white fill, however, can probably be correlated with the latest occupation surface for Plat. 5F-1 on the E (Plat. 5F-1:U. 1, see Fig. 106). The sherds in the fill are identical; the greater depth of Plat. 5F-1:U. 2 compared with U. 1 is because it was covered here by later construction.

Structure 5F-18:U. 1 probably is the front wall of a rectangular platform built at the same time as Plat. 5F-1:U. 2. It may have been the foundation for a building of perishable materials. Later, the platform was considerably broadened with the construction of U. 3. Two architectural developments might therefore be defined, but on the basis of such scant information, it is best to be cautious.

STRUCTURE 5F-SUB.1

The NE corner of this structure was discovered in the original 1963 test pit into the E edge of Plat. 5F-1 (see below). Its E wall was exposed, along with the collapsed remnants of the N wall and some fill (Fig. 104 and 106). Because of later extensive demolitions, very little is known of the overall architecture of Sub.1. It may have been renovated a number of times, but evidence for this does not survive. The structure was built on bedrock, here about 0.50 m below the surface. Its E wall is 0.30 m high, of well-cut masonry of small size. The N wall, however, seems to have been of larger masonry blocks dressed only on one face. As found, this was completely collapsed. The fill was of earth and cultural debris, later extensively disturbed by modern forest growth.

Nothing more is known of 5F-Sub.1. The only preserved dimension is the length of the E wall (4.90 m); the structure could have been square or rectangular. In text below it is argued that the structure was associated with Plat. 5F-1:U. 7. If so, then the height of this probable platform could have been at least 0.95 m, which would require one or two steps on its W side.

STRUCTURE 5F-SUB.2

This structure, located 4.60 m E of Str. 5F-Sub.1 (Fig. 104) is known from a single wall of rectangular stones not unlike those used in Sub.1. It is based on U. 3 of Plat. 5F-1 (see below) and stands about 0.20 m high. The wall parallels the E wall of Str. 5F-Sub.1, suggesting that the two structures were in simultaneous use.

Since the known wall of 5F-Sub.2 is so close to the presumed location of the retaining wall associated with Plat. 5F-1:U. 1 (Fig. 104:1), it is likely that almost all of Sub.2 was demolished when that later wall was built.

CHULTUN 5F-5

DESCRIPTION

Chultun 5F-5 (Table 2.212) was discovered beneath the fill of Plat. 5F-1, S of Str. 5F-18 and E of 5F-17 (Fig. 104). Its orifice is located at 5F:81.70 S492E. Regrettably, no plan or section drawing exists. Bedrock here is 0.60 m below present ground surface. Access to the chultun is through a single round orifice, which was provided with a deeply stepped lip. A round stone cover was in place, with small pebbles placed between its edge and that of the opening. Over this was a layer of plastered small stones, which sealed the chultun. When the chultun was in use, it was possible to remove the cover easily, as it is slightly smaller than the diameter of the orifice.

From the orifice, a neck opens into the ceiling of Chm. 1. Originally, the ceiling was essentially flat, but now is slightly domed as a consequence of material fallen from it. From this, a mound 0.50 m high accumulated over the floor of the chamber. The walls are nearly vertical, and the form of the chamber is roughly rectangular.

In the E wall of Chm. 1 is a rectangular opening into Chm. 2. There is no sill in this entry, but the sides and ceiling are narrowed. Like the antechamber, Chm. 2 is rectangular in form, with walls meeting one another, as well as ceiling and floor, at right angles. They are nearly perpendicular, and ceiling and floor are quite flat. The ceiling is at the same elevation as that of Chm. 1, but the floor is 0.70 m lower. As found, the floor was covered by a 0.30 m deposit of decayed limestone, in which was PD. 131. Chambers 3 and 4 differ in form from the other two; Chm. 3 is N of Chm. 1, with a rectangular entrance, the top of which is continuous with the ceiling of both chambers. The sides are restricted, and there was a sill that is now largely worn down. Chamber 3 has the form of a half dome placed against Chm. 1, with its floor 0.40 m lower.

Chamber 4 is identical in form to Chm. 3, though somewhat smaller. Access is through an opening in the W side of Chm. 3 that is restricted on all sides. Its floor is 5 cm below that of Chm. 3. Pick marks are quite prominent in the walls and ceiling of Chm. 4.

DISCUSSION

The difference in form between Chm. 1 and 2 on the one hand and 3 and 4 on the other suggests, but

TABLE 2.212
Chultun 5F-5: Average Dimensions (meters)

Feature	Length	Width	Height	Minimum Diameter	Maximum Diameter
Neck	1.00	---	---	0.70	0.55
Cover	---	---	---	0.65	0.65
Chm. 1	1.80	1.00	0.80	---	---
Chm. 2	2.40	2.20	1.55	---	---
Chm. 3	2.00	1.50	1.00	---	---
Chm. 4	1.30	1.00	0.88	---	---
Entrance 1-2	0.30	0.50	0.70	---	---
Entrance 1-3	?	0.70	0.60	---	---
Entrance 3-4	?	0.50	0.63	---	---

by no means proves, that two architectural developments are involved. If the entire chultun was built at one time, it seems odd that the Maya would have taken the trouble to make the rectangular Chm. 1 and 2 so much alike, then made two other chambers rather carelessly by comparison. It seems more probable that the original chultun (2nd) was built in two stages; one for the orifice and antechamber, and one for the inner chamber. Later, two other chambers were added (1st), Chm. 3 as one construction stage, Chm. 4 as another.

The relations of the chultun to Plat. 5F-1 are not clear on the basis of stratigraphy. Surely, the chultun was in use prior to construction of Plat. 5F-1:U. 3 (see below). The presence of Ik sherds beneath the fallen ceiling in Chm. 1 indicates abandonment after the appearance of such ceramics, which was much later than construction of Plat. 5F-1:U. 3. Since that floor may have been as much as 0.20 m above the bedrock near the orifice, there must have been some provision to retain its fill around the orifice (cf. Ch. 6E-6, this report). This was probably destroyed when the chultun was finally sealed.

PLATFORM 5F-1

This is the raised platform on which Str. 5F-17 and 18 were built. In August 1963, Sisson excavated a ceramic test pit 1.5 m square in the platform at 5G:S80 E8, near its E edge, as part of Culbert's ceramic test program. This was subsequently expanded to the N, S, E, and W (Fig. 104). Although very little in the way of surviving architecture was found, it is clear that a complex sequence of renovations must have taken place. Nevertheless, information is insufficient to permit definition of specific architectural developments. Therefore, the features that were uncovered in the excavations are simply described here in reverse order of time.

At approximately 0.20 m below the surface, the excavations continually encountered a thin layer of small stones (Fig. 106 and 107:U. 1). These are particularly prominent in the trench N of Plat. 5F-1:U. 5 (see below), where stone slabs form a flat surface. Evidently, this is all that remains of a platform floor, which dates from the Late Classic period (Table 2.213). Presumably, this correlates with U. 2 (Fig. 105), the platform surface associated with Str. 5F-18. This pavement clearly buried the remains of Str. 5F-Sub.1 and Sub.2.

How far E this floor extended is not known. Probably its edge was about 5.02 m E in Sq. 5G, where the remnant of a wall appears. East of this, there is a midden full of Imix sherds.

At approximately 0.40 m below the surface are the remains of another occupation surface, one on which Str. 5F-Sub.2 was built. Its top is somewhat irregular, dipping to 0.60 m below the surface in the area of U. 5 (where

underlying fill is the deepest) and 0.65 m W of Ch. 5F-5. In the former instance, the deep fill has probably settled; in the latter, a shallow pit may have been dug at one time or perhaps a tree-fall has formed such a pit. This occupation surface (Fig. 106 and 107:U. 3) consists in part of bedrock itself. Where this dips slightly, it was filled with stone that still bears traces of plaster. Where fill is especially deep, U. 3 is marked by a compact level of small stones with traces of plaster, above which roots grow horizontally. These stones were probably a ballast for a plaster surface.

About 3.50 m NE of Str. 5F-Sub.1 is a shallow basin (Fig. 104:U. 4) in U. 3. It is filled with burned cobbles and fine charcoal, and probably was used as a hearth. Beneath U. 3, immediately N and E of Str. 5F-Sub.1, is a deep deposit of earth and cultural material that fills a deep pit in bedrock (Fig. 104 and 106b:U. 5). In the fill was placed Bu. 158. The full dimensions of U. 5 are unknown, and it could be of natural origin. Nevertheless, it brings to mind Qu. 4F-1 in Gp. 4F-1 (TR. 19:36–37 and fig. 17, 18). The abundance of cultural material, and the undisturbed stratigraphy represented, indicates that it is an ancient midden that later was incorporated as platform fill. Cultural material becomes less abundant to the E, away from Str. 5F-Sub.1 (see below).

One meter S of U. 5, and just E of Str. 5F-Sub.1, is a pit that clearly is artificial (Fig. 104 and 106:U. 6). Roughly circular, the top of U. 6 is between 0.50 and 0.60 m below the surface. It was purposely filled with a densely packed fine, ashy soil, with a few stones in which was a heavy concentration of well-preserved sherds. The walls of the pit are nearly vertical to 0.60–0.70 m below the rim, about 0.20–0.25 m long, 0.08–0.10 m wide, and 0.04–0.06 m thick. These continue halfway down into a smaller pit in the floor of the large pit. Beneath the stones, in the small pit, is a fill like that above the stones.

Beneath U. 3 W of Str. 5F-Sub.1 are two features: a floor and Ch. 5F-5. The latter is described above. The floor, U. 7 (Fig. 107), is about 1.15 m below the surface. It was not followed up to Str. 5F-Sub.1. Unit 7 is 6 cm thick and consists of plaster, with an inclusion of small pebbles. It overlies an earth fill over bedrock. On the floor, in the westernmost excavation, is PD. 130.

SHERDS AND ARTIFACTS

For definition of lot groups, see Table 2.213; content is given in Tables 2.214–2.216.

Construction Fill

Most material from Gp. 5F-1 falls into this category, although some fill derives from a large, early midden that was sealed beneath a later platform floor (Str. 5F-Sub.1:LG. 2a–c). This will be discussed separately below.

Most of the other material in fill is likely redeposited from early occupations of Gp. 5F-1.

Lot Group 1 from Str. 5F-18 contains just a few sherds and no artifacts. It is mixed temporally; sherds from Preclassic, Intermediate, and Late Classic vessels are present. The objects in LG. 2 are probably rooted out of the fill. Original construction of 5F-18 is dated by sherds in Plat. 5F-1:LG. 4b, which includes many Preclassic, with some Manik, Ik, and Imix sherds. This mixture is virtually identical to Plat. 5F-1:LG. 4a, from beneath U. 1. On this basis, Plat. 5F-1:U. 1 and 2 are regarded as equivalent (see also below).

The fill sample from Str. 5F-Sub.1 (LG. 1) is badly mixed as a result of subsequent activity. The bulk of the sherds, however, are from Tzec and early Chuen ceramics. The latter probably date the structure, particularly since early Chuen ceramics accumulated against its E wall (see below). As a consequence, later sherds are from activity associated with construction of the final platform floor (U. 1), at which time the structure was partially demolished.

The earliest fill samples from the group platform are LG. 1 and 2. The first is from a pit E of Str. 5F-Sub.1 (Plat. 5F-1:U. 6), beneath Str. 5F-Sub.1:LG. 2a (see below). Therefore, this pit predates the structure. The second is sealed beneath the deep floor, U. 7. The sherds are from Tzec and early Chuen vessels, just as in the fill of Str. 5F-Sub.1. The next platform floor, U. 3, was laid over a fill W of Str. 5F-Sub.1 that includes Chuen and Cauac ceramics, plus a handful of later sherds ascribable to later contamination. The Cauac sherds, therefore, should date the floor. East of Str. 5F-Sub.1, U. 3 was laid directly over a primary midden, the top of which was probably scraped level for the purpose (Str. 5F-Sub.1:LG. 2a, below). The fill for U. 1 has already been discussed.

MATERIAL ABOVE LIVING LEVELS

The earliest material in this category is that E of Str. 5F-Sub.1, which fills a depressed area of bedrock (Str. 5F-Sub.1:LG. 2a–c). At the bottom (LG. 2c) is a deposit up to 0.90 m deep of pure Tzec sherds, with a variety of other bone, stone and shell artifacts. The great abundance of objects, some of them burned (15% of the chert artifacts), and the presence of animal bone and charcoal, all indicate a primary midden. Overlying this is LG. 2b, from which the sherds are transitional between the Tzec and Chuen Complexes. Finally, above this, LG. 2a contains sherds of the early Chuen Complex. All indications are of a steady deposition of material over a long period of time with no break. The only disturbance was of a minor nature for the inhumation of Bu. 158.

There is no doubt that the most recent (top) part of this midden is associated with Str. 5F-Sub.1. The early Chuen material rests in part against its E wall, the deposit is deepest there, and it falls off markedly to the E. Since Sub.1 is dated by early Chuen sherds, it is obvious that an earlier structure, of which we have no knowledge, must have preceded it at this locus. The Tzec material of LG. 2c would derive from this unknown entity. Since logical continuity is implied, the designation Str. 5F-Sub.1-2nd may be used to refer to this hypothetical structure.

Later potential occupation refuse is included in Plat. 5F-1:LG. 5a (surface), 5b (surface plus fill), 6a and 6b (E of the platform). Lot Group 5b is mostly fill, as it goes to bedrock. Lot Group 5a is heavily mixed with material uprooted from beneath U. 1, but much of the Imix material may be occupation debris that lay scattered on the platform surface. Of special note are a number of Caban sherds N of the 1963 test pit. Lot Group 6a is a midden that probably lay just off the E edge of the final platform. The sherds are predominantly of the Imix Complex, with a few of the Eznab Complex, and so contemporary with construction and use of Str. 5F-18. Cimi, Manik, and Ik sherds occur beneath in LG. 6b. This probably is a mixture of early incidental accumulation of trash, as well as fill for Plat. 5F-1:U. 3 (which extended E here), the result of erosion, tree falls, and root growth.

CHULTUN FILL

Very few sherds, and no other artifacts, were taken from the chultun, as it was empty when sealed. A few Ik sherds found beneath the orifice date abandonment of the chultun to a time after the appearance of such ceramics, however. They were covered by debris from ceiling collapse. Problematical Deposit 131 is also from the chultun.

OTHER SOURCES

In addition to PD. 131, other sources of material from Gp. 5F-1 include PD. 108, 130, 140, and Bu. 158.

TABLE 2.213
Group 5F-1: Lot Groups

Feature	Lot Group	Lot	Provenience	Ceramic Evaluation
Str. 5F-18	1	71M/2,3	Partially sealed fill of 1st	Mostly Preclassic; some Ik and/or Imix
	2	71M/1	Surface, above floor level	Ik and/or Imix
Str. 5F-Sub.1	1	71F/27,61	Unsealed fill	Tzec and early Chuen
	2a	71F/3,4,10,11,20, 21,30,31,39,40, 53,54,83,126, 127-130,160	E of structure ca. 0.40-0.80 m below surface	Mostly early Chuen; a few Manik
	2b	71F/5,12,22,32, 41,55,131	E of structure, ca. 0.80-1.00 m below surface	Apparently transitional Tzec-Chuen
	2c	71F/6,7,13-16,23-26,33,42-46,48, 49,56,57,87,133, 149,155,156,161	E of structure, ca. 1.00 m to bedrock	Tzec
Ch. 5F-5	1	71F/163	Fill of Chm. 1	Ik
Plat. 5F-1	1	71F/84,85,87,88, 90,92	Unsealed fill of U. 6	No data
	2	71F/148	Sealed fill of U. 7	Tzec, and early Chuen
	3	71F/72,95,99,101, 104,105,113-115, 117,136,137,140, 147,150,152,157, 159,162	Partially sealed fill of U. 3	Chuen, Cauac, a few Manik
	4a	71F/2,9,19,29,38, 52,60,63,65,67, 69,71,73,76,82,86, 91,94,98,100,111, 124,125,134,135, 142-144,146,151, 158,166	Partially sealed fill of U. 1	Tzec, Chuen, Cauac, Cimi, Manik, Ik and/or Imix
	4b	71M/4	Unsealed fill of U. 2	Preclassic; Manik, Ik, Imix
	5a	71F/1,8,18,28, 37,51,58,59,62, 64,66,68,70,74, 75,77-81,89,93, 96,97,107,121, 122,123,132,138, 139,141,145,153; 71L/1,2	Surface of platform to level of U. 1	Preclassic; Manik, Ik, Imix, a few possible Eznab, Caban
	5b	71F/17,47	Surface to bedrock by Str. 5F-Sub.1	Preclassic; Manik, Ik, and/or Imix
	6a	71F/102,106, 109,112	E edge of platform and beyond: surface to 0.20 m	Preclassic; Manik, Ik, mostly Imix, some Eznab
	6b	71F/103,108,110, 116,118,119,120	E edge of platform and beyond: 0.20 m to bedrock	Preclassic; Manik, Ik, Imix

TABLE 2.214
Structure 5F-18: Artifacts by Lot Group

Study Category	Object	Lot Group	1	2
Pottery Vessels	Sherds per cubic meter (lbs)	No weights recorded		
Flaked Chert Artifacts	Pointed, retouched flake			1
Ground, Pecked, and Polished Stone Artifacts	Mano			1

TABLE 2.215
Structure 5F-Sub.1: Artifacts by Lot Group

Study Category	Object	Lot Group 1	2a	2b	2c
Pottery Vessels	Sherds per cubic meter (lbs)	No weights recorded			
Other Pottery Artifacts	Figurines		1		10
	Centrally perforated sherds				2
Flaked Chert Artifacts	Flake cores	1	1	1	15
	Ovate bifaces	1			3
	Elongate biface			1	
	Irregular biface				1
	Unclassifiable biface				1
	Thin bifaces				2
	Irregular retouched flakes	2			17
	Point-retouched flakes			1	4
	Blades			2	9
	Used flakes		2	22	307
	Unused flakes	4		2	3
	Nodules				11
Flaked Obsidian Artifacts	Prismatic blades			1	17
Ground, Pecked, and Polished Stone Artifacts	Manos				3
	Rubbing stones				4
	Hammer stones				3
	Minor sculpture				1
	Limestone sphere		1		
	Unclassifiable artifact				1
Shell and Bone Artifacts	Shell, Tinkler				1
	Shell, worked				7
	Shell, unworked				20
	Bone, animal?, incised tube				1
	Bone, animal, worked				1
	Bone, animal, unworked				12
	Bone, human, unworked				2

TABLE 2.216
Platform 5F-1: Artifacts by Lot Groups

Study Category	Object	Lot Group								
		1	2	3	4a	4b	5a	5b	6a	6b
Pottery Vessels	Sherds per cubic meter (lbs)	No weights recorded								
Other Pottery Artifacts	Figurines						1	2		
Flaked Chert Artifacts	Flake cores		1		1			2		
	Ovate bifaces	1			2		3			
	Elongate bifaces				3					
	Rectangular/oval biface			1						
	Unclassifiable biface						1			
	Irregular retouched flakes							2		
	Point-retouched flakes							3		
	Used flakes				4		3	29		
	Unused flake							1		
	Nodules							2		
Flaked Obsidian Artifacts	Prismatic blades				1			1		
	Used flake				1					
Ground, Pecked, and Polished Stone Artifacts	Manos		2				2			2
	Metates				1		2		1	
	Rubbing stones		1				1	1		
	Bark beater						1			
	Ground spheres				1		2			
	Unclassifiable artifacts	2		2	2		1			
	Unworked jade				1					
Shell and Bone Artifacts	Shell, worked						1	1		
	Shell, unworked							1		
	Bone, animal, unworked						2	1		

TIME SPANS

Time spans for the features of Gp. 5F-1 are defined in Tables 2.217 through 2.221, with group time spans in Table 2.222. Thorough excavation of the group would no doubt call for revision of these, given the sketchiness of present information. The correlation of time spans rests on ceramic data in Table 2.213. To sum up the sequence: Gp. TS. 13 is defined for the earliest construction. This includes the hypothetical Str. 5F-Sub.1-2nd, and perhaps Ch. 5F-5-2nd as well as a pit E of Str. 5F-Sub.1 (Plat. 5F-1:U. 6). This is all dated by Tzec ceramics, which appeared at Tikal about 600 BC. Their production continued during Gp. TS. 12, the period of use of this construction. The contemporaneity of Str. 5F-Sub.1-1st and the

earliest known floor of Plat. 5F-1 (Gp. TS. 11) is indicated by the close similarity of their fills. Early Chuen ceramics were in production by this time, and continued in use through Gp. TS. 10. During this, the midden E of the structure continued to grow. Platform 5F-1:U. 6 surely was filled sometime in TS. 10.

The next construction for which there is evidence is a new surface for Plat. 5F-1 (Gp. TS. 9). This was constructed after the appearance of Cauac ceramics. Structure 5F-Sub.1 continued in use, but its old midden was buried beneath the new floor. Structure 5F-Sub.2 probably was built at this time, and was the reason for extension of the platform surface to the E. Some provision must have been made to prevent the new floor fill from blocking the entrance to Ch. 5F-5.

Group TS. 8 covers the period of some 500 or so years to the next known construction, during which Cimi, Manik, and Ik ceramics came and went. Since all complexes are represented, occupation was probably continuous. If so, there must have been many alterations to the group, and further excavation would require subdivision of this time span. Alterations that might have occurred during TS. 8 are construction of Ch. 5F-5-1st and its final abandonment. There are no clues as to when this construction took place. In regard to the abandonment, there are a number of Ik sherds found on the floor of the antechamber. The proximity of the chultun to Str. 5F-Sub.1 suggests, however, a functional association of the two. The evidence indicates that the structure was torn down at about the time when Imix ceramics made their appearance (Gp. TS. 7). Such ceramics are present in very small numbers beneath the platform floor that was laid at this time. Therefore, the

Ik sherds in the chultun would not be surprising, if it was abandoned when the structure was destroyed. Moreover, fill for Plat. 5F-1 became quite deep near the chultun, which may have made it difficult to use thereafter. Along with destruction of Str. 5F-Sub.1, abandonment of Ch. 5F-5, and construction of a new platform surface, Str. 5F-Sub.2 was destroyed and Str. 5F-18 (and perhaps Str. 5F-17?) was built as part of Gp. TS. 7. The last construction for which there is evidence is renovation of Str. 5F-18 in Gp. TS. 5. Imix ceramics were still in use, and were accumulating E of Plat. 5F-1 in a small midden. This accumulation continued (Gp. TS. 4) until abandonment. By this time (the start of Gp. TS. 3), Eznab ceramics had made their appearance. At Tikal, this occurred at about AD 869. Since there are so few Eznab sherds, abandonment must have been very soon after this time. There was evidently a reoccupation of the locus by users of Caban ceramics (Gp. TS. 2).

TABLE 2.217
Structure 5F-18: Time Spans

Time Span	Architectural Development	Unit	Descriptive Data	Lot Group		Ceramics in Vogue
1			Abandonment and collapse			Eznab
2			Use of modified structure			- - - - - - - - -
3	Str.5F-18-1st?	2,3	Modification of structure	1	2	
4			Use of original structure			
5	Str.5F-18-2nd?	1	Original structure constructed			Imix

TABLE 2.218
Structure 5F-Sub.1: Time Spans

Time Span	Architectural Development	Descriptive Data	Lot Group		Ceramics in Vogue
1		Destruction			Imix
					- - - - - - - - - - -
2		Use			Cauac, Manik, Ik
					- - - - - - - - - - -
3	Str. 5F-Sub.1-1st	Construction	1	2c	Chuen
					- - - - - - - - - - -
4		Use of earliest structure		2b	
5	Str. 5F-Sub.1-2nd	Presumed early construction at this locus		2a	Tzec

TABLE 2.219
Structure 5F-Sub.2: Time Spans

Time Span	Architectural Development	Descriptive Data	Lot Group	Ceramics in Vogue
1		Destruction	Plat.5F-1:4a	Imix
2		Use		Manik and Ik
3	Str.5F-Sub.2	Construction	Plat.5F-1:3	Cauac

TABLE 2.220
Chultun 5F-5: Time Spans

Time Span	Architectural Development	Construction Stage	Chamber	Special Deposit	Descriptive Data	Lot Group	Ceramics in Vogue
1				PD.131?	Abandonment	1	Imix
2					Continued use		Ik
3	Ch.5F-5-1st	1	4		Enlargement		Manik
		2	3				Cauac
4					Use		Chuen
5	Ch.5F-5-2nd	1	2		Original construction		Tzec?
		2	1				

TABLE 2.221
Platform 5F-1: Time Spans

Time Span	Architectural Development	Unit	Special Deposits: Burial	Problematical Deposit	Descriptive Data	Lot Group	Ceramics in Vogue
1					Final abandonment and ruin		
2					Reoccupation of locus		Caban
3					Abandonment		Eznab
4					Final use	6a	
5	Plat.5F-1-1st?	1,2		PD. 140	Last known modification	4a,b 5b	5a / Imix
6		4?			Continued use		Manik and Ik
7	Plat.5F-1-2nd?	3			First known modification	3,6b	Cauac
8				PD. 130	Use	1	
9	Plat.5F-1-3rd?	7			First of known construction	2	Chuen
10			Bu. 158	PD. 108	Accumulation of trash N of U. 6		Tzec
11		6?					

TABLE 2.222
Group 5F-1: Time Spans

Group Time Span	Str. 5F-18 Time Span (Table 2.217)	Str. 5F-Sub.1 Time Span (Table 2.218)	Str. 5F-Sub.2 Time Span (Table 2.219)	Ch. 5F-1 Time Span (Table 2.220)	Plat. 5F-1 Time Span (Table 2.221)
1					1
2					2
3	1				3
4	2				
5	3				
6	4				4
7	5	1	1	1	5
8			2	2	6
9			3	3?	7
10		2		4	8
11		3			9
12		4			10
13		5		5?	11

Group 5F-2

The location of this group on the Tikal site map (TR. 11; compare TR. 13, fig. 2a) is at 5F:S108 E110. Prior to excavation, there was no indication whatsoever that construction would be found here. The nearest visible ruins are about 22 m SW (Gp. 5F-4, this report), and the nearest chultun is even farther removed. In an area 4,000 m², a grid with 10 m intervals was set up by Bennet Bronson in the spring of 1966. Test pits were dug at the intersections of the grid lines (Fig. 108). Some of these disclosed the remains of construction, and so were extended to reveal more details of the seven structures and supporting platform that were discovered (Fig. 109). Even at that, no really complete plans of the individual structures could be recovered, on account of limitations of both time and labor. It is this construction that is discussed here. Most of the other test pits pertain to a system of drainage leading to the Tikal *aguada*, and so are treated in TR. 23I.

The terrain occupied by Gp. 5F-2 is transitional to bajo. Here, the bedrock dips deeply to the E, where it is covered by a thick deposit of clay. The land surface itself dips more gradually in the same direction. The vegetation reflects the transitional nature of the terrain, and ranges from both dense bajo growth to more open forest. There are no visible structure ruins closer than 200 m in an easterly direction, where the ground again rises.

STRUCTURE 5F-42-3RD

As noted, seven structures are known for this group (see Fig. 109), six of which appear to have been positioned around the centrally located Str. 5F-42. In its earliest form, 5F-42 seems to have been rectangular in shape, but with a rounded N wall (Fig. 109). This is of two courses of well-cut masonry. The front of the upper course is set back 0.30 m from the front of the lower course, and obviously was put in place after some fill had been dumped behind the lower course. This fill consists of a mixture of stones and marl. It rests on a sterile layer of clay, whereas the wall is based on a thin deposit of pebbles and mud over the clay. On either side of the rounded portion of the wall are straight extensions to the corners, each extension roughly 1 m in length.

The E wall of the structure was apparently destroyed at a later time, but it is assumed to have occupied the same position relative to the rounded portion of the N wall as the W wall does. The basal course of the W wall is a continuation of Plat. 5F-2:U. 2 (see below). The S wall must have been destroyed when Str. 5F-42-2nd was built, but may have had a central outset. The covering floor was destroyed at the same time.

The platform probably served as the foundation for a building of perishable materials, of which no trace survives. In terms of construction stages, such a building would define CS. 1; CS. 2 would comprise construction of the platform.

STRUCTURE 5F-42-2ND

Ultimately, Str. 5F-42 was extended to the S; for this, the S wall of the original platform, and also much of the original fill, was torn out. For the new addition, workmen heaped a fill of small stones over the floor of Plat. 5F-2 (Fig. 110:13). Against this, running N over the original platform fill, they dumped a mixture of earth and stones. The new walls (Fig. 109:U. 1–3) were also based on this floor of Plat. 5F-2. Units 1 and 2, the E and W walls, extend the lines of the original platform walls. A plaster floor (Fig. 110:U. 4) covers this new fill over the entire platform surface. Presumably, a new pole-and-thatch building was then constructed, but a search was not made for any evidence of such a building. On the E side, a small projecting platform (U. 5) was part of this construction (Fig. 109).

Given this proposed reconstruction of events, three construction stages are defined: CS. 3 for partial demolition of 42-3rd; CS. 2 for construction of the addition; CS. 1 for reconstruction of the building.

STRUCTURE 5F-42-1ST

A final modification of 5F-42 was to extend at least the S part of its platform some 5 m to the E. Since excavations were limited here, the new E wall (U. 6) was seen only in one trench. It was built on the E wall of the older Str. 5F-Sub.3 (see below). The E wall probably runs the full length of the structure. At least, no trace of the original E wall could be found at the N end, despite deep protective overburden here. Presumably, the reason is that this portion of the wall was torn out when the new U. 6 was built. More excavation (for which there was no time in 1966) could verify this. From the top of U. 6, a floor (U. 7) runs W to join with U. 4.

Again, three construction stages are implied: CS. 3 for partial demolition of 42-2nd; CS. 2 for the actual widening of the platform; and CS. 1 for reconstruction of the building.

STRUCTURE 5F-43

Whether this structure was rectangular or square is unknown, since only its S end was cleared by excavation (Fig. 109). The three known walls are represented by lines of rubble. These rest on Str. 5F-43:U. 1, a packed stratum of earth that overlies Plat. 5F-2:U. 1 and abuts Str. 5F-Sub.3 (see Fig. 111). Structure 5F-43:U. 1 could be an occupation surface contemporary with Plat. 5F-2:U. 4. The fill of 5F-43 is composed of earth, with a cover of small stones; this stone probably served as foundation for pavement, but all traces of plaster have disappeared.

Given this absence, it cannot be stated whether Str. 5F-43 consisted in part of a building of perishable material. The walls seem to have projected above the floor level, however, suggestive of dwarf-walls for a building of pole-and-thatch.

On the basis of this rather sketchy evidence, two construction stages are defined: CS. 2 for construction of the platform, and CS. 1 for the building. Possibly, there was a CS. 3 that consisted of raising the surface of the area E of Str. 5F-Sub.3, where Str. 5F-43 was to be built.

STRUCTURE 5F-44

West of Str. 5F-42 (Fig. 109) is one-level rectangular platform Str. 5F-44, on which a pole-and-thatch structure may have stood. It was built on a thick earth fill (U. 1) that runs to the base of the wall of Str. 5F-42-2nd, and covers earlier walls associated with Str. 5F-42-3rd (Fig. 111). Unit 1 may have been purposely placed as CS. 3.

The walls of the platform were constructed (CS. 2) of large masonry blocks, laid on rubble of small stones. Placed inside these walls was a fill of earth, stones, and trash. This was then covered over by a floor of packed silt and stones. Given the poor state of floor preservation, it was not possible to confirm the presence of a building of perishable materials. Nonetheless, CS. 1 is proposed for its construction.

STRUCTURE 5F-45-2ND

Located S of Str. 5F-42 and 44 (Fig. 109), the wall for this structure rests on sterile clay, and is built of roughly shaped masonry blocks. Platform 5F-2:U. 1 ends in line with its E wall; presumably the floor and structure were in use together. Inside the walls is a fill of earth, stones, and trash. A floor at one time probably covered this, but no traces of pavement survive.

On the assumption that a pole-and-thatch building stood on this platform (for which there is no evidence one way or the other), the following construction stages may be suggested: CS. 3 for preparation of a base surface for construction; CS. 2 for construction of the platform; CS. 1 for construction of the building.

STRUCTURE 5F-45-1ST

For this architectural development there is scant evidence, but it looks as if the length of the original structure was increased some 1.25 m to the N. All traces of construction have vanished on account of excavation by the Maya (in Intermediate or Late Classic times) of a trench. This N addition may also have extended a bit to the W of 45-2nd, for a rubble wall seems to run in that direction from the NW corner of Str. 5F-45-1st (Fig. 109). More excavation would be needed to investigate this possibility.

Given the sketchiness of information, no construction stages have been defined for Str. 5F-45-1st.

STRUCTURE 5F-46-2ND

Directly S of Str. 5F-42 (Fig. 109), Str. 5F-46-2nd was a square to rectangular platform, on which a pole-and-thatch structure was probably built. The walls of this platform were built of well-cut blocks of masonry. The N wall, which runs parallel to the S wall of Str. 5F-42-2nd, was laid in part on Plat. 5F-2:U. 1 and a thin extension of its fill to the S (Fig. 110). Apparently, the floor and structure were contemporary, in spite of the lack of floor abutment as in the case of Str. 5F-45 (above) and Str. 5F-Sub.3 (below), for the floor extends S along the W side of the structure (between it and Str. 5F-45). What is implied by this difference is that Str. 4F-45-2nd and Sub.3 were constructed just before the floor was laid and Str. 5F-46-2nd was built immediately after. The S wall of 46-2nd was laid on natural clay soil. The E wall was not found, probably because there was insufficient overburden to afford protection from the elements. The fill within the walls is of earth, with some stones and cultural material.

What appears to be a small subsidiary platform, U. 1 (interior platform if the structure was roofed), was built on the NW corner of the platform. This could represent a later addition, and indeed its small stone fill differs from that of the main platform. The absence of any floor remnants beneath U. l, however, argues for contemporaneity with the main platform.

In the absence of evidence pro or con, it is supposed that a building of pole-and-thatch was based on the platform. Presumably, construction was carried out in three stages: that of the main platform (CS. 3); that of U. 1 and the laying of plaster floors (of which no traces survive; CS. 2); and that of a building (CS. 1).

STRUCTURE 5F-46-1ST

Precisely what was involved in this construction is not known. It is represented by small stone rubble (Fig. 110:U. 2), not unlike that in Str. 5F-43, with some traces of plaster. This covers the platform of Str. 5F-46-2nd to the level of the top of U. 1. Unit 2 extends 1 m S of the original structure, and a SW corner appears to be well marked. Likewise, a NE corner is evident, but approximately 1.50 m to the E, U. 2 extends about 1.65 m to the N. Farther E, U. 2 terminates in a straight line.

What this probably represents is an enlargement of the original platform. This new platform would have been rectangular in shape, with perhaps a projection from the N wall. Presumably, three stages were involved in this enlargement: at least partial demolition of any building that was a part of 46-2nd (CS. 3); enlargement of the platform (CS. 2); and (presumably) reconstruction of the building (CS. 1).

STRUCTURE 5F-47

This seemingly peculiar construction lies due N of Str. 5F-44 (Fig. 109). Just what is involved is not at all clear. Test trenches reveal that the structure was built on U. 1 (Fig. 112), a thick layer of dark tan earth. This extends to the E, N of Str. 5F-42, which it abuts. Its surface here is packed, smooth, and level. Evidently, this served as an unpaved, outside occupation surface.

The structure is represented by a wall (U. 2), floor fragments (U. 3), and stone rubble (U. 4). Unit 2 begins 3.40 m N of the NE corner of Str. 5F-44. For the first 1.70 m, it consists of masonry blocks, but beyond this, it is composed of plastered small stone rubble. It extends 2 m N, then turns a right angle to run W for 1.65 m, where it terminates. Unit 2 is in part freestanding, plastered on both sides as well as its W end.

West of U. 2 are the remains of U. 3. Although badly broken up, it can be seen laid over U. 1 westward from U. 2. It clearly ran beyond the W end of U. 2, and perhaps a bit N here. A posthole (U. 5) is located 0.35 m S of U. 2, and suggests that a building was erected as part of this structure. The location of U. 5 indicates that the building opened to the S. Unit 4 is located 4 m W of the S end of U. 2. This mass of rubble suggests a part of a S wall of the structure. Aside from these things, nothing more is known of the architecture.

STRUCTURE 5F-SUB.3

This small, probably square structure was built 1.70 m E of the S end of Str. 5F-42-2nd (Fig. 109), and was covered by new construction for Str. 5F-42-1st. Its three well-made walls exposed by excavation seem to have been constructed at the time U. 1 of Plat. 5F-2 was laid (Fig. 111). This floor abuts the walls of the structure, and is based on the same fill on which the structure walls and fill rest. A fill of small stones was placed inside the walls, then covered by a floor. The N extent of this platform is unknown, but would probably be revealed by further excavation. If Feature 1 (below) represents a structure to the N, 5F-Sub.3 could not have extended far in that direction.

There is no evidence one way or the other, but a building of pole-and-thatch could have been built on this platform. If so, then two construction stages could be defined: one for the platform (CS. 2), and one for the building (CS. 1).

PLATFORM 5F-2

Platform 5F-2 is the designation given the occupation surface round about the structures of Gp. 5F-2. The only construction that can be assigned with confidence to it is located between Str. 5F-42, 45, and 46 (Fig. 109). A number of renovations are indicated, but whether these qualify

as architectural developments, or smaller scale modifications, is unknown. The earliest known construction consists of a floor, U. 1 (Fig. 110), and a W retaining wall of two courses, U. 2 and 3 (Fig. 111). The lowest course of the wall (U. 2) rests on natural clay soil, and behind it is construction fill of Str. 5F-42-3rd. On this, with its face in line with the back of U. 2, is the second course of masonry (U. 3). This runs N to the point at which the S end of Str. 5F-42-3rd terminated. From here, U. 3 runs E about 1.50 m, S almost 1 m, and then farther E. At this point, however, the wall was later destroyed. Unit 2, on the other hand, does not swing E but continues N, in line with the NW corner of Str. 5F-42-3rd. Apparently, U. 2 served as the lowest course of the W wall of that structure. Later, Str. 5F-42-2nd was built over U. 3 where this runs E.

The relations of U. 2 and 3 to Str. 5F-45 are not known, for at a later time a pit was dug down through them (Fig. 109). They probably abutted its N wall. Unit 1 does run up to the E wall of the structure.

Elsewhere, U. 1 is associated with Str. 5F-46-2nd. It does not extend all the way to the S wall of this structure, but rather seems to end in association with a wall, U. 7. This runs W from the structure, then swings N to the S wall of Str. 5F-45, a short distance from its SE corner. To the E, U. 1 abuts the S, E, and W walls of Str. 5F-Sub.3, which is contemporary with the floor.

Two subsequent floors can be seen in the excavation between Str. 5F-42 and 5F-46 (Fig. 110). The first of these, U. 4, abuts the wall of Str. 5F-46-2nd and the top of the wall of Str. 5F-42-2nd. It overlies an earth fill. Later, U. 5 was laid directly over this; U. 5 was later covered by a grading floor (U. 6) N of 46-2nd. This floor turns up to the wall of 46-1st.

At some point, perhaps when U. 4 was laid, the area W of U. 2 and 3 was filled and Str. 5F-44-2nd was constructed. There is no trace of a plaster floor here; perhaps the packed surface of this earth served as an occupation surface.

Unit 8 is a line of rubble that runs in part beneath the S end of Str. 5F-46-1st, and W from here. It is a probable S wall for Plat. 5F-2, built when U. 4 was laid, prior to construction of Str. 5F-46-1st.

Miscellaneous Features

Two apparent walls were encountered in excavation that could not be followed for lack of time. Feature 1 designates a short section of wall E of the N wall of Str. 5F-42 (Fig. 109). It could be part of a structure located N of Str. 5F-43. Feature 2 is a line of rubble just E of Str. 5F-46 (Fig. 109), and it could be part of the W wall of a structure S of Str. 5F-43.

At some time the Maya dug a large pit N of Str. 5F-45 (Fig. 109). This penetrates the N end of that structure, as well as the SE corner of Str. 5F-42-1st and 2nd, and Plat.

5F-2:U. 2 and 3. It does not penetrate the natural clay. The reason for this hole is not known, but it postdates use of the structures in the group.

SHERDS AND ARTIFACTS

Lot groups defined for Gp. 5F-2 are presented in Table 2.223, with content given in Tables 2.224–230.

CONSTRUCTION FILL

The earliest material is in LG. 2 from Str. 5F-42-3rd, in which there are several sherds from Cauac vessels. All fill lots, however, contain predominantly Manik sherds. The few Intermediate or Late Classic sherds from Str. 5F-42-2nd (LG. 1), Str. 5F-47 (LG. 1), and Plat. 5F-2:LG. 2 clearly are from later contamination. Presumably, the later fill material relates to the earliest occupation of the group. Hence, much of the material in Str. 5F-47:LG. 1 likely represents material discarded from time to time by occupants of Str. 5F-42. The stratum (Str. 5F-47:U. 1) from which this material comes (this includes Str. 5F-42:LG. 5) is densely packed, with a moderate content of sherds and other artifacts. It overlies the stratum on which Str. 5F-42-3rd is built, and abuts the walls of that structure. What is suggested is occasional discard of broken objects, which were soon trampled. As time passed, the deposit built up gradually in thickness. (This contrasts with a primary midden, where quantities of trash are being discarded almost constantly. Such middens yield great quantities of reasonably well-preserved material.) Structure 5F-44:LG. 1 is from a stratum (Str. 5F-44:U. 1) continuous with Str. 5F-47:U. 1. Hence, the same comments apply to it. Structure 5F-43 LG. 1 (from Str. 4F-43:U. 1) suggests an equivalent situation, with trash from Str. 5F-Sub.3. It could just as well represent purposeful fill, however.

MATERIAL ABOVE LIVING LEVELS

Apart from those situations noted above, potential occupation debris is contained in Str. 5F-43:LG. 3, Str. 5F-44:LG. 3, Str. 5F-45:LG. 2, and Str. 5F-47:LG. 2a and 2b. All of these are contaminated to some degree by collapse of structure fills, as well as activity in the area after abandonment of the group. The latter is indicated by the consistent presence of Intermediate and/or Late Classic sherds, as well as a figurine and a Thul censer fragment, in surface debris (Gp. 5F-2:LG. 1), a few Ik and Imix sherds in most of the lot groups mentioned above, and a fragment of a Thul censer in Str. 5F-44:LG. 3. Least contaminated is Str. 5F-47:LG. 2a, a deposit of trash distinguished from overlying debris, at the base of the structure wall on the ancient exterior occupation surface.

Besides contamination, another problem with potential occupation debris is associating these deposits with the appropriate structure. So far as the lot groups mentioned above are concerned, this is a problem in the case of Str. 5F-44:LG. 3. This comes from the area between that structure and 5F-42; it probably contains material discarded from time to time by those who used both. Since the bulk of the material comes from the excavations next to the wall of Str. 5F-44, however, it is assumed that most originated in it.

The problem of structural association is greatest in the case of material from nearby test pits; hence this material is included in a lot group for Gp. 5F-2 as a whole (Gp. 5F-2:LG. 3). Only those test pits are included that seem directly relevant to Gp. 5F-2, the others are all included in the discussion of the drainage ditches nearby (in TR. 23I). In the case of the five rows of test pits W of the group, sherd quantities in each row drop off markedly in a westerly direction (just as in the case of Str. 2G-61, this report), then increase again. Minimum quantities are found in Pits 5, 12, 16, 21, and 28 (Fig. 108). This suggests that it is valid to consider the material E of these particular pits as related to Gp. 5F-2.

Surface material has been kept separate from other material excavated. This is because surface lots consistently contain much material from intermittent activity following abandonment of the group (see above). Otherwise, much surface debris over the group proper is undoubtedly disturbed fill. This is particularly evident in the case of Str. 5F-43, where LG. 2 (structure fill), includes surface material. Beyond the group, in the various test pits, much surface debris could represent the top of deposits of occupation trash. But since they, too, show late contamination, they are lumped with surface material in general in Gp. 5F-2:LG. 1.

There is one other source of sherds and artifacts from Gp. 5F-2. This is a trench dug by the Maya that, on stratigraphic grounds, postdates the use of the structures. Consistent is the presence of several Imix sherds in Gp. 5F-2:LG. 2, from the pit.

TIME SPANS

Putting together all the data just discussed permits definition of the time spans of Tables 2.231–2.238, and their correlation in Table 2.239. The latter is based primarily on stratigraphy; because the group was clearly built and occupied while Manik ceramics were in use, and sherd samples are too small in most cases to separate early from middle or late Manik, ceramics are of no help. Ik and Imix material relates to post-abandonment activity, probably by occupants of the nearby Str. 5F-4 and associated structures. Perhaps abandonment was after the appearance of Ik ceramics, but if so, it must have been almost immediately thereafter.

The construction attributed to Gp. TS. 12 is securely correlated on the basis of architectural relationships between Plat. 5F-2 and the structures. The case is not quite so clear for Gp. TS. 10, except that logic suggests a correlation between Str. 5F-42-2nd and 5F-45-1st. Structure 5F-42 occupies such a low elevation relative to the surface of Plat. 5F-2 in group TS. 8 that it was probably abandoned then. If so, its modification was probably in Gp. TS. 10.

In Gp. TS. 8, Str. 5F-42 was renovated for the last time. The second floor of Plat. 5F-2 may be correlated with this, since Str. 5F-Sub.3 was abandoned, and along with it the earliest floor of Plat. 5F-2. The same would hold true for Feature 1 if it was a structure. Since Str. 5F-43 occupies the same relative position to 5F-42-1st as does Str. 5F-Sub.3 to 5F-42-2nd, it may be that this structure was a replacement for Sub.3. Moreover, it is built on a deposit that could have served as an occupation surface contemporary with U. 4 of the plaza (see Fig. 111). Struc-

tures 5F-44 and 47 may be contemporary, since they are built on fill W of Str. 5F-42, which could be associated with the increased elevation of Plat. 5F-2 that occurred then. Structure 5F-46-1st is clearly later than this, as it is associated with a late plaza grading floor (see Fig. 110).

To summarize, Gp. 5F-2 was built and used between AD 250 and 550 (the time frame for Manik ceramics). There must have been a lapse of time between the earlier date and the first construction, or Manik ceramics would not be so common in the earliest fills. Indeed, middle Manik ceramics appeared by Gp. TS. 8, if not earlier. Between AD 550 and 869 (which dates the end of Imix ceramics), people passed through the area from time to time, and at one point dug a trench S of the then-ruined Str. 5F-44. Those responsible were probably the occupants of Gp. 5F-4, a short distance to the SW. Finally, all activity in the area ceased.

TABLE 2.223
Group 5F-2: Lot Groups

Feature	Lot Group	Lot	Provenience	Ceramic Evaluation
Str. 5F-42	1	119A19/3,4	Base surface for construction	Manik
	2	119B/37	Unsealed fill of 3rd	Cauac, and Manik
	3	119A13/2; 119B/19,32, 36,41	Partially sealed fill of 2nd	Manik, 1 Ik or Imix
	4	119B/59,60	Partially sealed fill of 1st	Manik and Preclassic
	5	119A/2	Top to base of wall, N of structure	Manik
Str. 5F-43	1	119B/23	Base surface for construction (U. 1)	Manik, 1 Ik or Imix
	2	119B/25	Unsealed fill	Manik, some Ik and/or Imix
	3	119B/26,27	Surface to base of walls, S and W of structure	Manik, 1 Ik or Imix
Str. 5F-44	1	119A14/2,3; 119B/40,43,56	Base surface for construction (U. 1)	Manik
	2	119B/58	Sealed fill	No data
	3	119B/38,39,49, 50,55	Top to base of walls, E of structure	Manik (mostly middle); 1 Imix
Str. 5F-45	1	119B/47,53,54, 62	Unsealed fill of 2nd	1 Cimi, much Manik, small Ik and/or Imix
	2	119B/46	Top to slightly below base of wall, W of structure	Middle Manik
Str. 5F-46	1	119B/35	Fill of 1st and 2nd	Manik
Str. 5F-47	1	119B/4,6,11, 29	Base surface construction (U. 1)	Mostly Manik, (including middle); small Ik and/or Imix
	2a	119B/22	Outside base of E wall, on U. 1	No data
	2b	119A26/2-6; 119B/65-67	N of structure, from 0.20 m below surface to U. 1 and sterile clay	Manik and Ik and/or Imix
Plat. 5F-2	1	119B/63	Fill, sealed by U. 1	No data
	2	119B/42,44,48	Fill, mostly sealed by U. 4	Some Preclassic, Manik, 1 possible Ik or Imix
Gp. 5F-2	1	119A/1;119A2/1; 119A3/1;119A4/1; 119A7/1;119A8/1; 119A9/1;119A10/1; 119A11/1;119A13/1; 119A14/1;119A15/1; 119A19/1;119A20/1; 119A25/1;119A26/1; 119A27/1;119B/1-3, 5,9,10,13-18,20, 21,24,28,30,31, 35,45,57,64	Surface	Manik, Ik and Imix
	2	119B/12,51-53;61	Intrusive trench between Str.5F-44 and 45	1 Cauac, Manik, several Imix
	3	119A2/2;119A8/2, 3;119A9/2,3;119A-10/2,3;119A11/2; 119A15/2-4; 119A25/2; 119A27/2	Test pits S, W, and N of group; 0.20 m below surface and beneath	3 possible Preclassic, much Manik, Ik, Imix

TABLE 2.224
Structure 5F-42: Artifacts by Lot Group

Study Category	Object	Lot Group				
		1	2	3	4	5
Pottery Vessels	Sherd per cubic meter (lbs)	1.85	1.69	2.50	6.76	9.38
Other Pottery Artifacts	Censer			1		
Flaked Chert Artifacts	Ovate biface			1		
	Used flake				1	
	Unused flake			1		
Shell and Bone Artifacts	Bone, animal?, unworked			4		

TABLE 2.225
Structure 5F-43: Artifacts by Lot Group

Study Category	Object	Lot Group		
		1	2	3
Pottery Vessels	Sherd per cubic meter (lbs)	?	1.18	9.38
Flaked Chert Artifacts	Ovate biface			1
	Used flakes			2

TABLE 2.226
Structure 5F-44: Artifacts by Lot Group

Study Category	Object	Lot Group		
		1	2	3
Pottery Vessels	Sherds per cubic meter (lbs)	3.13	?	1.80
Other Pottery Artifacts	Censer			1
Flaked Chert Artifacts	Ovate biface			1
	Used flakes	3		1
	Unused flake			1
Flaked Obsidian Artifacts	Prismatic blades	2		1
Ground, Pecked, and Polished Stone Artifacts	Metates			2

TABLE 2.227
Structure 5F-45: Artifacts by Lot Groups

Study Category	Object	Lot Group	
		1	2
Pottery Vessels	Sherds per cubic meter (lbs)	16.05	3.62
Flaked Chert Artifacts	Irregular retouched flake Used flake		1 1
Shell and Bone Artifacts	Bone, animal, unworked		1

TABLE 2.228
Structure 5F-47: Artifacts by Lot Group

Study Category	Object	Lot Group		
		1	2a	2b
Pottery Vessels	Sherds per cubic meter (lbs)	1.70	22.04	13.21
Other Pottery Artifacts	Figurine		1	
Flaked Chert Artifacts	Flake cores		2	
	Ovate biface		1	
	Elongate biface		1	
	Unclassifiable bifaces		1	1
	Thin biface	1		
	Irregular retouched flake	1		
	Used flakes	1	9	
	Unused flakes		1	2
Flaked Obsidian Artifacts	Prismatic blades	2	5	
	Unused flake		1	
Ground, Pecked, and Polished Stone Artifacts	Manos		3	
	Metates		4	
	Ballgame handstone	1		
Shell and Bone Artifacts	Shell, unworked		1	
	Bone, animal, unworked	2		

TABLE 2.229
Platform 5F-2: Artifacts by Lot Group

Study Category	Objects	Lot Group	
		1	2
Pottery Vessels	Sherds per cubic meter (lbs)	?	2.16

TABLE 2.230
Group 5F-2: Artifacts by Lot Group

Study Category	Objects	Lot Group		
		1	2	3
Pottery Vessels	Sherds per cubic meter (lbs)	5.74	3.46	9.81
Other Pottery Artifacts	Censers	3		
Flaked Chert Artifacts	Flake cores	1		1
	Ovate bifaces	2		
	Unclassifiable biface	1		
	Thin biface	1		
	Irregular retouched flakes	2		
	Point-retouched flake	1		
	Used flakes	34	1	3
	Unused flakes	18		2
	Unclassifiable artifact	1		
Flaked Obsidian Artifacts	Prismatic blades	28		
Ground, Pecked, and Polished Stone Artifacts	Metates	1	1	
	Hammer stone	1		
	Unclassifiable artifacts	2		
Shell and Bone Artifacts	Shell, worked	1		
	Shell, unworked	1		
	Eggshell, unworked	1		
	Bone, animal?, unworked			2

TABLE 2.231
Structure 5F-42: Time Spans

Time Span	Architectural Development	Construction Stage	Unit	Descriptive Data	Lot Group	Ceramics in Vogue
1				Total abandonment of area with forest growth		
2				Abandonment with later intermittent activity		Ik and Imix
3				Use		
4	Str.5F-42-1st	1-3	6,7	Final modification of structure	4	
5				Use		
6	Str.5F-42-2nd	1		Reconstruction of building of perishable materials	3	
		2	1-5	S extension of platform		
		3		Partial demolition of 3rd		
7				Use	5	
8	Str.5F-42-3rd	1		Construction of building of perishable materials	1,2	Manik
		2		Construction of platform		

TABLE 2.232
Structure 5F-43: Time Spans

Time Span	Architectural Development	Construction Stage	Unit	Descriptive Data	Lot Group	Ceramics in Vogue
1				Total abandonment of area with forest growth		
2				Abandonment with later intermittent activity	3	Ik and Imix
3				Use		
4	Str. 5F-43	1		Construction of building of perishable materials		Manik
		2		Construction of platform	2	
		3?	1	Area E of Str. 5F-Sub.3 raised?	1	

TABLE 2.233
Structure 5F-44: Time Spans

Time Span	Architectural Development	Construction Stage	Descriptive Data	Lot Group	Ceramics in Vogue
1			Total abandonment of area with forest growth		
2			Abandonment, with later intermittent activity	3	Ik and Imix
3			Use		
4	Str. 5F-44	1	Construction of building of perishable materials		Manik
		2	Construction of platform	2	
		3	Preparation of base-surface base-surface	1	

TABLE 2.234
Structure 5F-45: Time Spans

Time Span	Architectural Development	Construction Stage	Descriptive Data	Lot Group		Ceramics in Vogue
1			Total abandonment of area with forest growth		2	---------- Ik and Imix ---------- Manik
2			Abandonment with later intermittent activity			
3			Use			
4	Str.5F-45-1st	None defined	Modification of structure			
5			Use			
6	Str.5F-45-2nd	1	Construction of building of perishable materials	1		
		2	Construction of platform			
		3	Preparation of base surface			

TABLE 2.235
Structure 5F-46: Time Spans

Time Span	Architectural Development	Construction Stage	Unit	Descriptive Data	Lot Group	Ceramics in Vogue
1				Total abandonment of area with forest growth	1	---------- Ik and Imix ---------- Manik
2				Abandonment, with later intermittent activity		
3				Use		
4	Str.5F-46-1st	1-3	2	Modification of structure		
5				Use		
6	Str.5F-46-2nd	1		Construction of building of perishable materials		
		2	1	Construction of small "interior" platform		
		3		Construction of main platform		

TABLE 2.236
Structure 5F-47: Time Spans

Time Span	Architectural Development	Unit	Descriptive Data	Lot Group		Ceramics in Vogue
1			Total abandonment of area with forest growth			
2			Abandonment, with later intermittent activity			Ik-Imix
3			Use	2a,b		Manik
4	Str. 5F-47	1-5	Construction	1		

TABLE 2.237
Structure 5F-Sub.3: Time Spans

Time Span	Architectural Development	Construction Stage	Other Data	Ceramics in Vogue
1			Abandonment	
2			Use	
3	Str.5F-Sub.3	1	Construction of building of perishable materials	Manik
		2	Construction of platform	

TABLE 2.238
Platform 5F-2: Time Spans

Time Span	Unit	Descriptive Data	Lot Groups	Ceramics in Vogue
1		Total abandonment of area and forest growth		
2		Abandonment and intermittent later activity		Ik and Imix
3		Final use of Plat. 5F-2		
4	6	Grading floor laid by Str. 5F-46		
5		Use of upper floor		
6	5	Construction of latest floor		
7		Use of second floor		Manik
8	4,8?	Construction of second floor	2	
9		Use of original floor		
10	1-3,7	Construction of Plat. 5F-2	1	

TABLE 2.239
Group 5F-2: Time Spans

Group Time Span	Str.5F-42 Time Span (Table 2.231)	Str.5F-43 Time Span (Table 2.232)	Str.5F-44 Time Span (Table 2.233)	Str.5F-45 Time Span (Table 2.234)	Str.5F-46 Time Span (Table 2.235)	Str.5F-47 Time Span (Table 2.236)	Str.5F-Sub.3 Time Span (Table 2.237)	Plat.5F-2 Time Span (Table 2.238)
1	1	1	1	1	1	1		1
2	2	2	2		2	2		2
3					3			3
4					4			4
5								5
6								6
7	3	3	3			3		7
8	4	4	4	2		4	1	8
9	5			3				
10	6			4				
11	7			5	5		2	9
12	8			6	6		3	10

Group 4F-5

The only available information on this group comes from the excavation of Ch. 4F-4, discovered by Rafael Morales (former Director of the Tikal National Park) and excavated in 1963 and 1965 by Puleston. Its location is 4F:S60 E425, about 10 m S of the plaza for Gp. 4F-5. Its proximity to this group suggests that it functioned as part of it. The group itself, which is 145 m E of Gp. 4F-3 (this report) and 50 m N of Gp. 4F-6 (see below), consists of two structures: 4F-22 and 23, on the W and N sides of a plaza (TR. 11). The overall setup of structures and chultun is not unlike Gp. 7C-1 (this report).

CHULTUN 4F-4

DESCRIPTION

This chultun is of the "bottle-shaped" variety (Fig. 113b,c and Table 2.240), essentially similar to Ch. 2G-11, 6B-2-2nd, 6F-5, and 7F-2 (all this report). The round orifice, now somewhat damaged by erosion, was not provided with a stepped rim, nor is there any sign of a stone cover. From this orifice, the walls of the neck flare out into the chamber itself, with no clear break between neck and chamber. Near the center of the floor is a small, round hole (U. 3), similar to one in Ch. 6F-5. A second hole (U. 4) is directly next to the wall in the NW portion of the floor. Unit 4, though, suggests an intentional deepening of this part of the floor. Because it was not fully excavated, its full extent is unknown.

Excavations around the orifice exposed the surface of bedrock (Fig. 113a) on all but the N side. The slope of bedrock is away from the orifice, although water running in from the N does not appear to have been a problem. Of particular interest is a narrow, vertically walled trough some 0.36 m deep (U. 2), which extends SE from the orifice. This ends in a hole 0.30 m in diameter, of the same depth. The latter suggests a posthole, but no postholes have been seen around small structures at Tikal with such a trough. Since there is no slope to the floor of this feature, it is unlikely that it served as some sort of drain.

East of the orifice, near the limit of excavation, is a cut in bedrock (U. 1) 0.36 m in depth. This could be a quarry, but there appear to be at least two irregularly shaped stones in the bottom. Apparently, the cut continues beneath these. It is possibly part of a grave, but considerations of time prevented its investigation.

TABLE 2.240
Chultuns 4F-4: Average Dimensions (meters)

Feature	Diameter	Height
Orifice	0.55 (reconstructed)	---
Chm. 1	1.45	1.80 (includes neck)
U. 3	?	0.15

DISCUSSION

As found, the chultun contained U. 7 (Fig. 113c), a 0.15 m thick deposit of fine, gray silty material, almost like clay, over the floor. This appears to have accumulated gradually while the chultun was in use (cf., the basal deposit of Ch. 2G-11, this report). Consistent is a 0.10 m layer of dark brown soil, U. 6, deposited on U. 7. The color and consistency of U. 6 suggest a buildup of humus after abandonment of the chultun. Distinct from this is U. 5, a light brown soil with lots of pebbles and sherds that filled the chultun. There is too much of this to have simply washed in, nor would such a distinct difference between U. 5 and 6 be expected. Apparently, the chultun was used, abandoned for a period of time, and later deliberately filled. Why the filling took place is unknown; it may have been to prevent accidents, or a terminal Classic structure may have been built here, to which U. 1 and 2 relate (see below).

SHERDS AND ARTIFACTS

The two lot groups defined for Gp. 4F-5 are given in Table 2.241, with content in Table 2.242. Regrettably, material from LG. 1 was lost. Lot Group 2, however, is another matter. The presence of Eznab sherds reinforces the idea of terminal Classic reoccupation noted above. The Ik and/or Imix sherds present probably represent incidental debris occasionally cast out by the occupants of Gp. 4F-5 (since most visible small-structure ruins date to when such pottery was in vogue, it is likely that Gp. 4F-5 was in use at this time). Presumably, these were the people who built and used the chultun, but further excavation

TABLE 2.241
Group 4F-5: Lot Groups

Feature	Lot Group	Lots	Provenience	Ceramic Evaluation
Ch.4F-4 (Op.72K)	1	1	Deeper chultun fill	Lost
	2	1	Surface around orifice and upper 0.60 m of chultun fill	Ik and/or Imix; possible Eznab

TABLE 2.242
Chultun 4F-4: Artifacts by Lot Group

Study Category	Object	Lot Group	
		1	2
Pottery Vessels	Sherds per cubic meter (lbs)	Not recorded	
Flaked Chert Artifacts	Unused flakes	4	
Ground, Pecked, and Polished Stone Artifacts	Hammer stone	1	

TABLE 2.243
Chultun 4F-4: Time Spans

Time Span	Architectural Development	Unit	Descriptive Data	Lot Group	Ceramics in Vogue
1			Abandonment of locus until modern construction	1	---------
2			Reoccupation of locus; possible interment of burial		
3		1,2,5	Chultun probably filled in conjunction with new construction at locus		Eznab
4		6	Accumulation of soil in chultun following abandonment	2	---------
5		7	Use of chultun, probably with Gp. 4F-5		Ik and/or Imix
6	Ch.4F-4	3,4	Construction of chultun		

would be needed to verify or refute this. For the present, it remains reasonable.

TIME SPANS

Meager though it is, the evidence suggests that Ch. 4F-4 was used and presumably constructed after the appearance of Ik pottery (Tables 2.241, 2.243). It also indicates that the chultun was abandoned for some length of time prior to its being purposely filled. The presence of Eznab sherds in surface debris around the orifice, and the interpretation that the chultun was used in Ik and/or Imix times, combine to suggest that the filling took place when Eznab ceramics were in use. Since the trough breaks the lip of the chultun, this feature probably postdates use of the chultun. This provides reason to suppose that the trough, with its posthole, are associated with the Eznab ceramics and the filling of the chultun. Given this (and the lack of evidence to the contrary), it is proposed that there was terminal Classic occupation at this locus, at which time the chultun was filled and some sort of pole-and-thatch building erected. Possibly, an associated burial is to be found just E of the chultun.

In terms of absolute dates for all this, TS. 5 falls somewhere between AD 550 and 869, the period of Ik and Imix ceramics, with TS. 2 falling somewhere between AD 869 and 950, the dates for Eznab ceramics.

Group 4F-6

The sole source of information about this group is Bu. 45 (section III, this report). As depicted on the site map (TR. 11), the group includes two structures, 4F-26 and 27. Both are comparable to most of the ruins excavated in the course of this study. The layout impresses one as on the sloppy side; the long axis of 4F-27, the westernmost structure, is very close to a true N-S line. Across the plaza, however, 4F-26 does not directly face 27, nor is it parallel to this structure.

A portion of the W wall of Str. 4F-26 was exposed during the building of the Tikal Park administrator's house in 1961. This wall shows the block veneer masonry so common in small, probable domestic structures of the Late Classic period. One meter E of the N end of the structure, Bu. 45 was discovered by Morales, who excavated and recorded it. Interred in a stratum of gray earth, the top of this is 0.50 m beneath the ground surface. About one meter N of the burial, the vault of another skull, probably that of a child, was discovered (but not excavated) in the same stratum. Overall, the placement of these burials relative to Str. 4F-26 is not unusual for a residential situation.

The pottery placed in the grave of Bu. 45 has been identified by Culbert (in TR. 25A:fig. 45d) as Imix, and the overall layout is consistent with household burials of that vintage (TR. 20B). It is fairly certain that Gp. 4F-6 was in use sometime between AD 700 and 869, the dates for the Imix Ceramic Complex. There is no way of knowing, on the basis of present data, whether abandonment preceded the latter date, or whether the group was in use for any period of time prior to the former date. Because of these problems, time spans have not been defined for any features connected with this group.

Group 4F-7

The only available information on this group comes from excavation of Ch. 4F-2. This was carried out by Puleston in 1965 (as Op. 72J) in order to investigate the purpose of a small hole from the ground surface into the ceiling of the chultun. The chultun is located in Sq. 4F of the site map (TR. 11) at S283 E215, right in the center of the group plaza. On the W, N, and E sides of this open space are Str. 4F-33, 34, and 35; the S side is open. All three ruins are similar to those that normally mark the remains of low, rectangular platforms suitable for house foundations.

CHULTUN 4F-2

Chamber 1: The chultun is a peculiar variant of the common two-chambered type (Fig. 114). The antecham-
ber is unusual in that its walls and ceiling are continuous with those of Chm. 2. Its floor, however, is considerably higher, and as originally constructed, it formed a kind of platform. Later, a masonry wall (U. 2) was built against this platform high enough to serve as a sill between Chm. 1 and 2. The height of this sill varies from 0.08 m near its center to 0.34 m elsewhere. Unit 2 was built on a thin stratum of earth (U. 3) on the floor of Chm. 2 out of roughly shaped blocks and small stones. The blocks, averaging about 0.55 m long by 0.25 m wide and 0.22 m thick, were generally placed on their ends. Between the masonry is a loose, dark brown soil. If plaster or mortar were ever used in U. 2, there is no trace of it now.

Chamber 1 is entered from above through the usual sort of chultun orifice. From this, a neck with vertical sides leads into the ceiling, with a clearly demarcated juncture between neck and ceiling. As found, the stone cover was in place over the orifice, though it did not seal it tightly. The N edge of the rim is stepped to receive the stone cover. As found, Chm. 1 was about two-thirds full of a continuation of deposits from Chm. 2 (Fig. 114c); it is described in connection with that chamber.

Chamber 2: The original shape of this chamber is now discernable only near floor level, as collapse is far more extensive than usual in chultuns. From this, and from the amount of debris that has fallen from the ceiling, it appears that Chm. 2 in plan was basically oval, except for the inward "bulge" of Chm. 1 on the SE. As mentioned above, only the higher floor and sill set the antechamber apart from the inner one; there is no other restriction between them. The walls of Chm. 2 seem to have curved inward, starting near floor level, so that walls and ceiling cannot be distinguished from one another. The chamber, therefore, must have been basically like a dome.

A peculiarity of Chm. 2, and the original reason for excavation of the chultun, is the presence of a hole (U. 1) in its present ceiling from the surface. This hole, 0.24 m in diameter and 0.22 m in depth, is located towards the back of the chamber, about 1 m NW of the chultun orifice (Fig. 114a). In section, U. 1 resembles a cup with a large hole in the bottom (Fig. 114c).

As found, Chm. 2 was mostly full of various deposits (Fig. 114c). On the floor itself is U. 3, on which U. 2 was built. This is a stratum of packed gray earth only 4 cm thick at most. Over this, abutting U. 2, is a layer of brownish-gray material (U. 4) only slightly thicker than U. 3. This, in turn, is overlain by U. 5–8, alternating thin layers of gray and brown earth thickest against U. 2. The dark layers match the interstices of the U. 2 masonry. All four strata contain few sherds and artifacts.

Overlying U. 4–8 is an extensive deposit of whitish-gray material (U. 9), which also extends over the floor in Chm. 1. Unit 9 generally slopes down as one moves

NW from Chm. 1. On this, near U. 2, is a lens of darker earth (U. 10). Both U. 9 and 10 are exceedingly rich in cultural material, especially sherds. Indeed, the density of materials here is much greater than in the soil around the chultun orifice. Sherd densities, however, taper off in U. 9 as one moves away from Chm. 1.

Overlying U. 9 and 10 is U. 11, a gray deposit deepest beneath U. 1, and nonexistent in Chm. 1. Over this, but not clearly distinguishable from it, is the dark brown U. 12, which extends into Chm. 1 over U. 9. Generally, its surface drops in elevation moving from U. 1 into Chm. 1.

DISCUSSION

The first problem here is the source of the fill. Units 3 and 4 represent packed debris that accumulated during the time the chultun was in use. Since U. 2 rests on one, but not both, it must have been added to the chultun following a period of use. This is the basis for differentiating between Ch. 4F-3-A and B (see below).

The alternating layers of U. 5–8 probably represent post-abandonment debris. This, at least, is consistent with the paucity of artifactual material within them (some bones probably are from animals that died in the chultun). The light-colored layers may derive primarily from minor ceiling collapse, and the dark layers from silt washing through the interstices of U. 2 from Chm. 1.

Unit 9 probably cannot be explained as material washed into the chultun, for it is richer in sherds and artifacts than the earth around the orifice. Moreover, there is no obvious explanation for why so many objects should have washed in following a period when so few did. It appears, therefore, that midden debris was dumped in through the orifice, filling Chm. 1 and spilling over slightly into Chm. 2. With the passage of time, however, there would have been a tendency for this material to settle, some of it spilling over little by little into the inner chamber (see Ch. 6E-7, this report, for a somewhat similar situation). As this took place, U. 9 in Chm. 2 may have been augmented somewhat by further minor ceiling collapse. This would account for a reduced number of artifacts away from Chm. 1 rather than close to it.

Unit 10 may be explained as a part of the filling operation, mixed a bit with further water-borne sediments that seeped into the chultun.

Units 11 and 12 obviously have a different derivation from U. 9 and 10, for they slope in quite opposite directions. Unit 11 seems to consist mostly of extensive ceiling collapse, particularly near U. 1. Unit 12 is mostly debris that has washed into the chultun through U. 1.

A second problem is the purpose of U. 1. Given the interpretation of the chultun fill, it is doubtful that U. 1 opened into the chultun until after the post-filling collapse of the ceiling of Chm. 2. Consistent is an in-curving of the sides of U. 1 still evident just before it opens into the chamber. This, and the diameter of U. 1 (comparable to known postholes elsewhere), indicates that U. 1 probably is a posthole that did not open originally into the chultun. The best estimate is that about 0.65 m of bedrock once separated the bottom of U. 2 from the ceiling of Chm. 2.

Given this, a reason for the extensive collapse of the ceiling in Chm. 2 may be suggested. Looking at the ceiling as it is now, there is a rough resemblance to a giant conchoidal fracture with U. 1 as the point of impact. Perhaps, then, a post that bore considerable weight was set in U. 1. This created fracture lines in the limestone, which eventually led to collapse at the weak point, the ceiling of Chm. 2. If, as suggested, U. 10 represents post-fill debris in the chultun, then a period of unknown duration separated the filling from the collapse. Moreover, such a period seems required for so much of U. 9 to have spilled over into Chm. 2, as it settled away from the orifice.

Still to be considered is the reason for a heavy, weight-bearing post above the chultun, which is not near any of the visible ruins of Gp. 4F-7. Some of the sherds in U. 9 are from Eznab ceramics. Probably, then, the filling of the chultun took place in terminal Classic times, in connection with construction of some sort of structure above (for a similar situation, see Ch. 4F-4, this report). One of the posts of this structure was set in U. 1, but after some time, the weight in this posthole became too much and the structure of which the post was part collapsed. This could have been the reason for final abandonment of the locus. Or, it may have occurred shortly after abandonment, but still before the structure had fallen into general ruin.

SHERDS AND ARTIFACTS

FILL

There is little to add to the discussion of the fill just given. Lot Group 3 (Table 2.244), from U. 4, contains Imix sherds that date the use of Ch. 4F-2-A. From U. 5–8 (Table 2.244, LG. 4), the small amount of material should be a micro-sample of debris lying about Gp. 4F-7. Since there are a few Tzec sherds, the possibility is raised of a Preclassic occupation of the locus.

Unit 9, as stated, contains Eznab ceramics (Table 2.244:LG. 5a). This is consistent with the previous conclusion that this fill postdates use of Ch. 4F-2-A. Most of the sherds in LG. 5a, though, are from Ik and Imix vessels. They are of midden quality that, with so many animal bones (Table 2.245; some of these bones could be from animals that died in the chultun), suggests that an occupation midden from Gp. 4F-7 was the source. If so, LG. 5a and 6 (from U. 10) should give clues to the purpose of the structures of Gp. 4F-7 (see Table 2.245 for content).

TABLE 2.244
Group 4F-7: Lot Groups

Feature	Lot Group	Lots	Provenience	Ceramic Evaluation
Ch.4F-2 (Op.72J)	1	14	Unsealed U.3	No data
	2	25	Unsealed fill of U. 2	?
	3	13,24	Unsealed U. 4	Imix
	4	11,12, 21-23	Unsealed U. 5-8	Tzec, Imix
	5a	3,8-10, 19,20	Unsealed U. 9	Ik, Imix, Eznab
	5b	7	Unsealed U. 9, 11	Ik, Imix
	6	6	Unsealed U. 10	Imix
	7	5,16	Unsealed U. 11	Possible Ik, Imix
	8	2,4,15	Unsealed U. 12	1 Manik; Imix
	9	1,26	Surface above chultun	Imix

TABLE 2.245
Chultun 4F-2: Artifacts by Lot Group

Study Category		Lot Group									
		1	2	3	4	5a	5b	6	7	8	9
Pottery Vessels	Sherds per cubic meter (lbs)	Not recorded									
Other Pottery Artifacts	Figurines			1		2		1			
	Pellet					1					
Flaked Chert Artifacts	Used flakes					1		1			
	Unused flakes			2	1	13		1	1	2	
Flaked Obsidian Artifacts	Prismatic blade										1
Shell and Bone Artifacts	Bone, animal, unworked				5	44		22	1		23

Lot Group 8, which postdates the chultun ceiling collapse, should be equivalent to LG. 9 (see below). Other fill sources either contain insufficient material (Table 2.244:LG. 1 and 2) or are too mixed (LG. 5b) to be of use.

SURFACE MATERIAL

The material in LG. 9 (Tables 2.244, 2.245) certainly must contain fill from the plaza for Gp. 4F-7, with perhaps some late occupation debris. Since there is no positive indication of the latter, and since the ultimate source of the fill is unknown, the material from LG. 9 (which, in any event, contains only a single artifact other than ceramics) is of no real utility for determining the uses to which the structures of the group were put.

TIME SPANS

The evidence is that Ch. 4F-2 was used, and presumably constructed, sometime after Ik pottery came into production. This is most clear for Ch. 4F-2-A, as Imix sherds were collected from a thin layer of debris that built up against U. 2 (Table 2.244:LG. 3). The presence of just a single Manik sherd, and a few Tzec sherds, in collections that otherwise included nothing earlier than Ik pottery, strongly suggests that the visible ruins do not predate the appearance of such ceramics. The chultun is therefore probably no earlier (and see below).

As was the case with Ch. 4F-4 (this report), the evidence points to abandonment of the chultun for a period of time, following which it was filled. This operation is dated by Eznab ceramics, at which time a pole-and-thatch structure seems to have been built near, or over, the chultun. It was one of the posts of this structure that was responsible for the collapse of the ceiling of the chultun.

Based on these data, the time spans of Table 2.246 have been defined. Of these, TS. 10 must be regarded as tentative. It is based on the presence of a very few Tzec sherds, which could have been brought in from some locale nearby in debris to be used as fill for the plaza of Gp. 4F-7. Later, these sherds happened to wash into the chultun. If, though, they do indicate a Preclassic occupation of the locus of Gp. 4F-7, there surely was a prolonged hiatus before construction of the structures presently known for this group. Given a reasonably adequate ceramic sample, in which only one Manik sherd can be identified, this construction certainly took place no earlier than the time of the appearance of Ik ceramics. Since such ceramics are included in midden-like material from the chultun thought originally to have been trash from the structures of Gp. 4F-7 (LG. 5a), the origin of the group predates the appearance of Imix ceramics. In terms of absolute dates, this puts it after AD 550 but before AD 700, the dates for the Ik Ceramic Complex. This could date TS. 8 of the chultun, but this is not certain.

The chultun, and presumably the group as well, were abandoned no later than AD 869, perhaps slightly before. This date marks the end of the Imix Ceramic Complex, and Imix sherds occur in the occupation debris of TS. 5. The group was then reoccupied, and again abandoned, by AD 950, which dates the end of the Eznab Ceramic Complex (TS. 3 and 2). There is no further evidence of human activity at this locus until someone dropped a Gallo beer bottle into the chultun.

CHULTUN 4G-2

Chultun 4G-2 was discovered in 1963, when its stone cover collapsed beneath the weight of a vehicle passing over top on the road to Remate. Its coordinates are 4G:S286 E200, and the nearest structure (4G-6) lies 37 m distant (see TR. 11). This suggests a possible association between the chultun and a structure or structures for which there is no surface indication in the form of a mound or mounds. For this reason, and because its location in the Remate Road put its future existence in jeopardy, it was excavated as Op. 72N in 1963 by Puleston.

The chultun is an example of the type with an antechamber and larger lateral chamber. It is unusual for the presence of what appeared to be footholds, although they could not have served as such, as well as the "bean-shape" of the lateral chamber. Unfortunately, drawings of the chultun cannot now be found (but see Table 2.247).

Like other chultuns of this type, this one had to be constructed in two stages. First, a manhole-like orifice was cut, and extended downward as the neck. The orifice itself was provided with a shallow stepped rim, so that the stone cover fit snugly in place. The neck itself widens downward, with its walls continuous with those of the antechamber.

The antechamber itself was constructed as the neck was continued downward. With the neck, the overall chamber is bottle-shaped. In the W and SW walls are two notches (U. 1 and 2), which look as though they were intended as foot-holes. They are positioned more or less opposite one another, some 0.55 m above the chamber floor.

Upon completion of the antechamber, an opening was cut into the wall for a lateral chamber (Chm. 2). The opening itself is a very short passage, with a sill that later was worn down. The sides, also, are constricted. The "drip line" at the top of the passage is over the floor of Chm. 1. Hence, any water leakage was prevented from entering the side chamber.

This side chamber has a plan that can best be described as bean-shaped. The floor itself is unusually level, and the verticality of the rear wall is also noteworthy. In comparison to almost all chultuns excavated at Tikal, this one is unusual for the good preservation of the ceiling. In most chultuns, the limestone has either fallen down in

TABLE 2.246
Chultun 4F-2: Time Spans

Time Span	Architectural Development	Unit	Descriptive Data	Lot Group		Ceramics in Vogue
1		11,12	Abandonment of locus (caused by structure and chultun collapse?)		7,8	
2			Use of new construction			Eznab
3		1,9,10	Chultun filled in conjunction with new construction at this locus	5a,6	5b	Eznab
4		5-8	Accumulation of debris in chultun following abandonment	4		
5		4	Continued use	3		Imix
6	Ch.4F-2-A	2	Construction of sill	2	9	
7		3	Use	1		Ik
8	Ch.4F-2-B		Original construction of chultun			
9			Hiatus			Chuen-Manik
10			Possibly early activity at locus			Tzec

TABLE 2.247
Chultun 4G-2: Average Dimensions (meters)

Feature	Length	Width	Height	Maximum Diameter	Minimum Diameter
Stone Cover	---	---	0.11	0.55	0.55
Orifice	---	---	0.04	0.56	0.40
Neck	---	---	0.52	0.40	0.40
Chamber 1	1.00	0.88	1.05	---	---
Chamber 2	1.48	2.25	0.92	---	---

large pieces, or else flaked off gradually, to produce characteristic deposits of white limestone dust on the floors. Here, because of such good preservation, the marks of the tools used for construction of the chultun are still visible on the ceiling. The marks indicate fairly short strokes, much like those produced by the use of an adze-hafted elongate biface in the construction of an experimental chultun (Puleston 1971:328, fig. 2). Here, they were evidently made by someone sitting with his back to the passage, working away from himself.

DISCUSSION

There are two problems in connection with this chultun: 1) the purpose of U. 1 and 2, and 2) its dating. As noted above, U. 1 and 2 look as though they were intended as footholds. The difficulty is that, on the basis of experimentation, it is impossible to use them as such regardless of the angle of approach. Moreover, the depth of the antechamber is not sufficiently great as to require footholds. Perhaps they served to support some sort of cross-bar. The problem with this is that the notches are so shallow, they would not have served to support much weight. Nor is it easy to imagine a reason for such a cross-bar, which would have interfered with access to the chultun.

In the absence of sherds and artifacts, it is impossible to date this chultun. Since others of this form were in use in Classic times, this one probably was also.

One other point is worth making, for it affords a clue (albeit tenuous) to the function of chultuns. This is the very flat surface of the floor in Chm. 2, which would have been apt if materials were stored here in pottery vessels.

SHERDS AND ARTIFACTS

The only material found in this chultun consists of limestone chunks and grayish-white powder, which had fallen from some portions of the ceiling. Not a single sherd or artifact was found.

TIME SPANS

Table 2.248 gives time spans for this chultun. Given the total lack of sherds or artifacts, these cannot be dated, except that the shape of the chultun suggest use in Classic times, sometime between AD 250 and 869.

Group 4F-4

This group consists of two structures, 4F-19 and 20. They are situated on the W and N sides of a raised platform (see TR. 11), and overall the arrangement appears very similar to Gp. 5F-1 and 6E-1 (this report) before excavation. Group 4F-4 is located 20 m SW of Gp. 4F-3, and 80 m NE of Gp. 4F-2.

The single test pit sampled platform fill (Table 2.249). Not unexpectedly, given the overall resemblance to the two groups just mentioned, Preclassic, Early Classic, and Ik and/or Imix sherds are represented (Table 2.250). Therefore, an occupation that began sometime in Preclassic times, and lasted until sometime between AD 700 and 869, is likely.

Group 4G-2

Group 4G-2, located about 140 m E of the Tikal Reservoir, includes Str. 4G-1 and 4G-2, which are situated on a small plaza. Structure 4G-1 is depicted on the map (TR. 11) as a single L-shaped mound on the N and W sides of the plaza. In reality, it likely was two rectangular platforms suitable for house platforms. Structure 4G-2 is a small rectangular mound on the E side of the plaza, which also could be a ruin of a house foundation.

The single test pit (Table 2.249) sampled plaza fill. The ceramic data (Table 2.250) indicate a substantial Early Classic occupation, which continued into Intermediate or Late Classic times.

TABLE 2.248
Chultun 4G-2: Time Spans

Time Span	Architectural Development	Construction Stage	Chamber	Unit	Descriptive Data	Ceramics in Vogue
1					Abandonment, with accumulation of debris on floors	
2					Use	
3	Ch.4G-2	1	2		Construction of chultun	Manik, Ik, and Imix?
		2	1	1,2		

Group 4G-3

This group is located 140 m S of Gp. 4G-2 and includes two structures, 4G-7 and 8. The latter is located on the E side of a plaza (TR. 11), and resembles in form known household shrines (TR. 21). Structure 4G-7, located on the N side of the plaza, is comparable to the ruins of known house foundations.

The single test pit (Table 2.249) sampled the fill of Str. 4G-7, and also exposed a burial (Bu. 189). This contained Imix pottery (TR. 25A:Fig. 61b), and the group obviously had been occupied since sometime in Early Classic times (Table 2.250). An earlier occupation is unlikely, given only one Preclassic sherd. A Postclassic reoccupation is indicated by the Caban sherds on and near the surface.

Group 5F-3

Group 5F-3 is located 100 m W of Gp. 5F-1 (this report), and includes Str. 5F-13 through 16. All appear to have been rectangular platforms of moderate size, comparable to known house foundations (see TR. 11). Structure 5F-13 may have had an accessory platform on the E end of the N side. Structure 5F-13, 15, and 16 seem to be arranged on three sides of a plaza, with the latter structure set off somewhat from the other two. Structure 5F-14 is based partly behind 5F-15 and off the end of 5F-13.

The single test pit (Table 2.249) probably samples a mixture of late occupation debris and plaza fill. An occupation of the group spanning the period between AD 550 and 869 seems reasonably clear, and is represented by both Ik and Imix pottery (Table 2.250). An earlier Preclassic occupation is a possibility, but on the basis of only a few sherds, it is by no means sure. There is no indication at all of an Early Classic occupation.

Group 5F-4

This is a group of structures 25 m SW of Gp. 5F-2 at 5F:S144 E54. It includes Str. 5F-2 and 4, two apparently rectangular platforms that may have served as house foundations. They are arranged on the N edge of a plaza, with a square structure, 5F-3, in front of 5F-2 (TR. 11). On the W side of the plaza is Str. 5F-1, which resembles the ruins of known range-type structures of moderate size. Its NE corner is near the end of Str. 5F-2, and Str. 5F-3 stands in front of its N end. Structures 5F-5 and 6, on the E side of the plaza, look much like Str. 5F-2 and 4. The slightly larger Str. 5F-7 and 8 are on the S side of the plaza.

Two test pits were excavated in Str. 5F-2 (Table 2.249). These sampled structure fill, with per-

haps a scatter of occupation debris. All of the ceramics pertain to the Imix Complex (Table 2.250).

Group 5G-3

This group is located in the NW corner of Sq. 5G (TR. 11), 34 m NE of Gp. 5F-1. It includes three structures, of which 5G-1 appears to have been a rectangular platform comparable to known house foundations. Two walls that were encountered in the excavation suggest that it had two levels. Structures 5G-47 and 48 are in a line S of the W end of 5G-1, and seem to have been much smaller rectangular platforms.

The ceramic test excavation was a trench 4 m long and 1.5 m in width (Table 2.249). Of the length, 2 m were in front of the structure wall and above the living surface (Table 2.250:Lot 1). The other 2 m portion sampled the structure fill (Table 2.250:Lots 2–9). The result of the test was a surprise, for it indicated that the group was probably abandoned by Early Classic times. This is the only instance where visible mounds within the area covered by the 9 km² site map do not show traces of an Intermediate to Late Classic occupation. The sherd samples are quite consistent here; only one non-Preclassic sherd came to light, and that is from a surface lot. Since Gp. 5F-1 had a Classic occupation, a stray find here in Gp. 5G-3 is scarcely surprising. The situation would be analogous to the scatter of later sherds around Str. 2G-61 (this report).

To be more precise about the Preclassic occupation of this group, it may have been limited to the time of Chuen ceramic production. This conclusion, though, is not as firm as that concerning the lack of a Classic occupation.

Group 5G-4

Group 5G-4 is located 110 m E of Gp. 5G-3, and includes Str. 5G-2, 3, and Ch. 5G-1 (TR. 11). Both mounds

TABLE 2.249
Location of Test Pits: Camp Quadrangle

Group	Test Pit	Location
4F-4	71P	Platform in front of Str. 4F-50
4G-2	71D	Center of plaza
4G-3	103C	E end of Str. 4G-7
5F-3	71N	In front of Str. 5F-14, between Str. 5F-13 and 15
5F-4	119F	Str. 5F-2
5G-3	101A	Trench in center of Str. 5G-1
5G-4	102A	Str. 5G-3

are comparable to ruins of known house foundations. Structure 5G-2, the smaller, is on the W edge of a plaza; the other structure is on the N edge. The chultun is just off the SE corner of the plaza.

The single test pit (Table 2.249) sampled fill in and beneath Str. 5G-3. It is not known if late occupation debris was present in Lot 1 (Table 2.250). Since the deepest deposit contains Imix sherds, the group cannot be proven to predate the appearance of such ceramics. Yet, Cauac, Manik, and Ik ceramics occur in sufficient quantities (Table 2.250) that, had they been found in correct stratigraphic sequence, an occupation of the group through the times when all these ceramics were in vogue would be a reasonable assumption. Perhaps all the pre-Imix sherds are redeposited from some other location. The nearest known source, however, is some 150 m away. More likely, the situation is analogous to Gp. 5F-1 (this report), where much of the earlier construction is located S and E of the latest structures. Probably, then, Gp. 5G-4 was occupied while Cauac, Manik, Ik, and Imix ceramics were in vogue.

TABLE 2.250
Ceramic Evaluations: Camp Quadrangle Test Pits

Group	Lot	Provenience	Ceramics
4F-4	71P/1		Preclassic; Manik; Ik and/or Imix
	71P/2		Preclassic; Manik; Ik and/or Imix
4G-2	71D/1		Manik; Ik and/or Imix
	71D/2		Manik; possible Ik and/or Imix
	71D/3		Manik
	71D/4		Manik
4G-3	103C/1	0-20 cm	Ik and/or Imix; Caban
	103C/2	20-40 cm	Manik; Ik; possible Caban
	103C/3	40-60 cm	1 Cauac; Manik
	103C/4	60-80 cm	Manik; Ik and/or Imix
5F-3	71N/1	0-20 cm	Ik and/or Imix
	71N/2	20-40 cm	Preclassic; Ik; Imix
	71N/3	40 cm	No data
	71N/4		?
5F-4	119F/1	0-20 cm	Imix
	119F/2	20 cm-floor	Imix
	119F/3	below floor	Imix
5G-3	101A/1	0-20 cm, S of structure	Preclassic; probable Chuen
	101A/2,5	0-20 cm	Preclassic; 1 possible Ik or Imix
	101A/3,6	20-40 cm	Preclassic; probable Chuen
	101A/4,7	40-60 cm	Preclassic
	101A/8,9	60-80 cm	Preclassic; probable Chuen
5G-4	102A/1	0-20 cm	Preclassic; Manik; Ik and/or Imix
	102A/2	20-40 cm	?
	102A/3	40-60 cm	Preclassic; Manik; Ik
	102A/4	60-80 cm	Manik; Ik and/or Imix
	102A/5	80-100 cm	Cauac; Ik; Imix
	102A/6	100-120 cm	Manik; Ik and/or Imix
	102A/7	120-140 cm	1 Preclassic; Ik; Imix

7. Excavations in the Perdido Quadrangle

Introduction

Several small-structure groups have been investigated in the squares of the Perdido Quadrangle. Groups 6C-1, 6C-2, 7C-1, and 7C-2 (this report) and Gp. 6B-1, 6B-2, and 7C-3 (TR. 21) were subjected to relatively extensive excavations. Besides these groups of mapped structures, vacant terrain was investigated N and E of the Perdido Reservoir (Gp. 6C-5 and Str. 6C-60 locus) and E of Gp. 7C-1 (all this report). Eleven test pit excavations give chronological information for 10 other groups of probable residential structures. Of the approximately 60 groups in the Perdido Quadrangle, close to 28% have been sampled for chronological information.

Group 6C-1

Group 6C-1 is located in Sq. 6C of the Tikal site map (TR. 11) at S278 E342. As mapped in 1960, the group is composed of four structures arranged around each side of a platform (Plat. 6C-1). Structure 6C-44, the smallest of the four, is situated on the S side; 6C-45 on the W; 6C-46 on the N; 6C-47 (the largest) on the E (Fig. 115). The group is built on the side of a hill with a marked slope down to the W. The portion of the platform on which Str. 6C-45 sits, therefore, had to be built up considerably to provide a level surface. The ground also slopes away to a lesser extent from Str. 6C-44 and 46. By contrast, Str. 6C-47 was built on the uphill side of Plat. 6C-1, and elevated above the others. On higher ground 30 m to the E of 6C-47 is Gp. 6C-8 (this report), which includes a fair-sized temple structure.

Of the four structures, Str. 6C-45, 46, and 47 were excavated (as Op. 67A) in 1963 by Haviland for data on plan and sequence. Structure 6C-44 remains untouched.

STRUCTURE 6C-45-8TH-C

The earliest entity at this locus (Fig. 116a), evidently a building platform, seems to have been constructed in a single stage (CS. 2). Its walls rest on the bare surface of bedrock (Fig. 119), which here slopes off to the W; consequently the E wall is not high, and exposed bedrock itself seems to have served as an occupation surface E of the structure. The N wall and a portion of the E one (the only ones exposed by excavation) consist of several irregular courses of masonry blocks, where the level of bedrock drops. A distinctive feature of the wall of this platform is that its NE, and probably SE, corners are

rounded. By contrast, the NW, and presumably the SW, corners are square.

Enclosed by the wall is an apparently undisturbed midden dating to late Early Classic times; it contains Manik III sherds and none more recent. Evidently a building even earlier than 45-8th-C stood somewhere nearby, probably to the E. When the newer structure was built, its walls were constructed around the existing midden so as to make large-scale fill operations unnecessary.

Floor 1 of 6C-45-8th-C was laid over the earlier midden and the top of the wall masonry to the outer faces of the walls. A single posthole (Fig. 116a:U. 1) was seen in the SE portion of the floor, but not near any wall; its purpose is unknown. There are no postholes through the floor along either the E or N walls, which seems peculiar. One of the best domestic middens found at Tikal is located off the N wall, where it was sealed by later construction. This suggests use as a house or associated outbuilding, so it is likely that a building of perishable materials was associated with the platform, despite the absence of visible postholes. The main corner posts for the E wall may have been set just outside the rounded corners, and those for the W wall inside the squared corners. In this W area, the floor is destroyed and the fill is deep, which would account for lack of evidence for posts. Other posts along the walls could simply have rested on the surface of the plaster floor. On the basis of these speculations, a final stage (CS. 1) is defined for construction of a building of perishable materials.

STRUCTURE 6C-45-8TH-B AND A

The floor of Str. 6C-45-8th was renovated twice. Over the western portion, where fill is deep and therefore likely to settle, a grading floor, U. 2, was laid. This served for an unknown length of time before a second grading floor was laid. This floor, U. 3, is slightly thicker than U. 2, and lies directly on it.

STRUCTURE 6C-45-7TH

After an unknown length of time, the walls of 6C-45 were altered (Fig. 116b). A new N wall was built, more rounded than that of the earlier structure. This extended the length of the platform by some 0.80 m. Presumably, a comparable S wall was constructed, so that the platform approached what has been called an "apsidal" shape. The original E and W walls continued in use. The new N wall is of a single course of masonry, built on midden material that had accumulated off the end of the earlier structure. This was probably rearranged a bit, so that the wall sits 0.35 m above bedrock, but between it and the earlier wall the midden is higher. Specifically, some of the midden was probably dug away just where the wall was to be built, and some of this was then dumped on top of an undisturbed midden to the S. This would have been the most economical manner in which to fill the platform extension. The masonry of the new walls is somewhat better dressed than that of the earlier one, which tends to be rather rough. The edges of the new masonry, however, like those of the older, tend to be rounded rather than sharp.

A new floor (Fl. 1 of 45-7th) was laid on the pavement for 45-8th-A. Only the southern portion of the platform was explored, where the floor becomes thicker as it runs S. Perhaps it is really a grading floor, though quite extensive, and the older surface continued to serve on the N end. One cannot be sure of this, but if it did, another surface, long since destroyed, must have covered the area between the walls of Str. 6C-45-8th and 7th.

On the S portion of the platform, Fl. 1 of 7th turns up to the faces of what must be an interior platform (Fig. 116b:U. 4). The masonry for this is based on the floor of 45-8th. Unit 4 is quite narrow, and measures only 0.90 m in a N-S direction. No floor survives on the top of U. 4.

North of U. 4 are six postholes, U. 5–10, with diameters of 0.12, 0.08, 0.18, 0.15, 0.23 and 0.13 m respectively (Fig. 116b). Their purpose is unknown, for they form no recognizable pattern. No postholes can be identified for a building of perishable materials. Nevertheless, it is assumed that such a building did stand on the platform, for the same reasons given with regard to 45-8th. North of the structure is a substantial midden deposit, much like that for the earlier structure. Here, posts could have been located off the rounded corners, as proposed for the earlier structure. Or, since no floor survives in the area, posts may have been located inside the end walls to follow their configuration. Other posts, along the E and W walls, may simply have rested on the floor surface.

To sum up the construction of 6C-45-7th, four stages may be defined. The new end walls were erected as CS. 4; U. 4, and whatever the posts of U. 5–10 were associated with, were built as CS. 3. The floor was laid as CS. 2 and finally the building itself was constructed (Stage 1).

STRUCTURE 6C-45-6TH

At some point, Str. 6C-45-7th was provided with a raised platform on its southern portion. Since this probably involved alteration of the building itself, this is considered as a separate architectural development, rather than a smaller-scale modification of 7th. Alteration of the building defines CS. 1 and 3, while construction of the platform defines CS. 2.

Unit 11 (Fig. 116b) is apparently the face for the raised southern platform; it seems to have run from the E to the W wall of the main platform, without a break. It was built on the surface of Fl. 1 of 7th against the S face of U. 4, which must have continued in use in front of U. 11. The surface of U. 4 is about 0.15 m lower than the top of

U. 11. No floor on the summit of U. 11 survives, though one must have been present when it was in use. North of the wall, a grading floor (U. 12) was laid to turn up to it and U. 4, but there is no comparable pavement on the S side of the wall. This, and the lack of an opening in the wall, clearly indicate that it is not freestanding, but the face for a raised platform.

STRUCTURE 6C-45-5TH

This structure is a radical departure from what went before, even though logical continuity is still implied. Apparently, the preceding structure was abandoned, and the building was either torn down, or it fell into ruin of its own accord. A new, very much smaller, rectangular structure (Fig. 117a) was then put up over the NE corner and some of the N midden of the older structure, the rest of which was then used as a dumping ground. It is possible, however, that the raised S portion of 45-6th survived as some sort of open platform, since one of its walls was reused at a later date (see below).

The front wall of the new structure was built on fill, which averages about 0.30 m. in depth above bedrock. Presumably, pavement for Plat. 6C-1, since destroyed, was laid up to this wall. A portion of this surface, immediately in front of the platform, very likely was included beneath the roof of Str. 6C-45-5th (TR. 20B). Most of the W wall is based on a thin fill over the floor of the preceding structure (see Fig. 119). A pause-line, U. 13, is visible S of the wall and represents the actual informal occupation surface there. This was later covered by a midden. The N wall of the structure rests on the old N midden of 45-6th. The masonry in these walls of 5th is very similar to that used in Str. 6C-45-6th and 7th, but was installed with liberal use of spalls to chink interstices (Fig. 179d).

No pavement survives on this platform, though it is probable that one once existed. Because of its absence, there is no evidence for or against the presence of a building of perishable materials. The existence of a primary midden off the back of the structure, however, suggests that the platform supported a building of some sort. Clearly, the layers in this midden indicate that trash was thrown out the back by users of the structure.

The construction of 6C-45-5th can therefore be summarized in terms of three stages: (1) Some preparation of the base surface (CS. 3) occurred. At the least, the N midden was leveled somewhat, and fill was dumped to build up the plaza surface. Unit 13, the pause-line noted above, marks the top of this fill S of the structure. The building of the preceding structure may have been purposely razed. Burial 146 was probably interred at this time (this report, section III). (2) The walls were built and fill was put in place for the platform (CS. 2). (3) The final stage (CS. 1) is defined for construction of a building of perishable materials, which may have included within it a portion of the plaza in front of the platform.

STRUCTURE 6C-45-4TH-C

The next architectural development saw enlargement of the platform to proportions more characteristic of 45-6th than 5th, even though a rectangular form was retained (Fig. 117b). For this new structure, fill was dumped above the surface of Plat. 6C-1 for Str. 6C-45-5th (CS. 3). New platform walls of large, roughly dressed stone were then erected on this fill, and on the midden associated with the preceding structure (CS. 2). Platform 6C-1:U. 1 (Fig. 119) abuts this platform wall. Fill was placed within these walls, although much of this space was already taken up by 45-5th and its midden.

Unit 11, the old wall for the upper platform level of 45-6th, was rejuvenated by the addition of an upper course of masonry (Fig. 117b). A covering floor (Str. 6C-45-4th:Fl. 2) was laid to the N; it abuts and turns up to U. 11. South of the wall, at the higher level of U. 11, pavement continues to the end of the structure.

The platform probably supported a building of perishable materials (CS. 1). Unfortunately, the floor is now badly damaged near its perimeter, so that postholes cannot be identified. There is evidence that succeeding architectural developments sustained such buildings, and probably the earlier ones did as well. Hence, such a structure is assumed for 45-4th-C.

One posthole (Fig. 117b:U. 15) can be identified in Fl. 2, though it is nowhere near any wall. Its diameter is 0.18 m. The purpose of a post so located, with no others evident, is unknown.

STRUCTURE 6C-45-4TH-B

After a period of use, Fl. 2 was refurbished. A grading floor (Fig. 119:U. 16) was laid N of U. 11 over some of the surface of Fl. 2. No other known alterations took place at this time.

STRUCTURE 6C-45-4TH-A

As a final alteration of 45-4th, a complete new floor (Fl. 1 of 4th) seems to have been laid over the whole platform (Fig. 117b). It turns up to the N face of U. 11, as do earlier floors. South of this wall, a second floor surface can be seen above Fl. 2. This is more likely to have been a portion of Fl. 1, which covers the entire N end of the platform, than of U. 16, which covers only a portion of the N end. The post represented by U. 15 apparently continued to stand.

It is probable that Plat. 6C-1:U. 2 (Fig. 119) was laid up to the E wall of the platform at this time. It lies below Plat. 6C-1:U. 3, which is associated with Str. 6C-45-3rd. It is more likely that a new floor for Plat. 6C-1 would

have been laid when Str. 6C-45-4th was given an entirely new floor, rather than when this surface was partially renovated.

Unit 17 is a hole that seems to have been dug through Fl. 4 and 5, just S of U. 11 (Fig. 117b). It was filled with burned stones and a few burned sherds. Its 0.40 m diameter is larger than most postholes, and its significance is unknown.

STRUCTURE 6C-45-3RD

When Str. 6C-45-4th-A was abandoned, a new structure was erected above its remains (Fig. 118a, 180a). The first step (CS. 3) in this new construction must have been to raze any building that might have stood on the earlier platform. Fill was then dumped on the older floor for a new surface, which was laid in two levels, at least on the N end of the platform (CS. 2). Here, Fl. 1 of 3rd was laid from the top of the outer walls of the earlier structure (which were reused in the new one) up to the base of a N-S wall (U. 18) with which the floor is in union (see Fig. 119). The floor then continues W from the top of U. 18. Most of this upper surface later disappeared in the course of structure collapse.

Unit 18, and the floor, run S for a distance of 6.26 m. At this point, there is an amorphous pile of stones (Fig. 118a). Perhaps U. 18 stopped here, and the lower portion of Fl. 1 continued over the rest of the platform. Thus, the raised level might simply have been a platform on the NW corner of the structure. The mass of stones may be all that remains of masonry from an E-W end wall for this, which had been ripped out in the course of later construction. Less likely, U. 18 may have run the length of the platform. If so, the stones in the piles are not sufficiently abundant to account for all missing masonry.

Platform 6C-1:U. 3 (Fig. 119) probably is the floor associated with 45-3rd in front of the structure. It seems likely that a new surface would have been provided for such an extensive reconstruction, and Plat. 6C-1:U. 3 is the only candidate for such a pavement.

Two postholes, U. 19 and 20 (with diameters of 0.13 and 0.17 m; Fig. 118a), can be seen in Fl. 1. They are only 0.14 m in depth, which seems inadequate for the major poles of a building. Moreover, they are near neither the front wall, nor U. 18. They are, however, just inside the wall of the succeeding structure, and so probably were associated with a building that was part of it. The posts would then have been set to a more adequate depth of 0.36 m. No postholes can be found for 45-3rd, but since the succeeding structure apparently was topped by a building with a pole frame, the earlier one probably was as well. Unfortunately, Fl. 1 is destroyed near the corners where evidence for main posts would be expected.

STRUCTURE 6C-45-2ND

This next-to-last architectural development (Fig. 118b) saw a shift of its front-rear axis about 2 m to the N. To begin, a base surface was prepared for construction; this included demolition of any building that might have stood on the earlier platform, as well as some demolition of platform masonry (CS. 3). The wall for a one-level building platform (Fig. 180a) was then put in place (CS. 2). The E wall (Fig. 119:4) was based on Str. 6C-45-3rd:Fl. 1, and earth fill to the N and S. The N end wall was built 3.67 m beyond that of its predecessor on earth fill, while the S wall was built on earlier fill 0.80 m inside the wall of the earlier platform. The W wall (Fig. 119:5) was built on the old informal living surface 0.60 m in back of the wall of 45-3rd. The masonry for these walls differs from that used in preceding architectural developments, having flatter surfaces and sharper edges.

Platform 6C-1:U. 9 (Fig. 119) is in union with the base of the E wall. Structure 6C-45-2nd:Fl. 1 runs W from just below the top of the wall over a fill of earth and trash. Floor 1 is extremely poorly preserved, but evidence already cited (U. 19 and 20 discussed above) makes it clear that a building of perishable materials stood on this platform. The main posts for this must have been set when the platform was built, but a final construction stage (CS. 1) is defined for completion of the building.

STRUCTURE 6C-45-1ST

The final modification of this structure converted the building platform from one to two levels. A new N-S wall (Fig. 118b and 119:7) was constructed for the face of the upper platform level. It was apparently based on Fl. 1 of 2nd. The masonry is very badly preserved, and is observable only as a straight line of rubble near the surface of the ruin mound. The W wall, and portions of the N and S walls, must have been built up, and a final floor, long since destroyed, laid over the upper level. Indications were that Fl. 1 of 2nd continued to serve in front of the upper wall.

Three construction stages were probably involved in this modification. In order to raise the rear surface, some alteration of the building walls was necessary. There was probably some demolition of the building walls (CS. 3), followed by construction of the upper level (CS. 2). Then, the building walls would have been reassembled (CS. 1).

STRUCTURE 6C-46-3RD

This earliest structure (Fig. 120b) was built upon a fill of compact gray earth, and is associated with an early floor of Plat. 6C-1 (Fig. 121:U. 7). Since 3rd was later almost totally razed, all that was found in excavation was a single N-S wall, probably the E wall of the structure. It is met on the E by Plat. 6C-1:U. 7. The situation here bears resemblance to what occurred in the development of Str. 6C-45. Where 45-2nd involved a considerable shift of the front-rear axis to the N from an earlier structure, here the front-rear axis of 46-2nd was shifted considerably to the E, to about the location of the end wall of 3rd.

West of the end wall of 46-3rd is a fill of gray earth, which contains considerable cultural materials. Other than this, there is no more information on this structure. It is assumed to have been rectangular, and about 2.40 m in breadth.

STRUCTURE 6C-46-2ND

To prepare for the construction of its replacement, the earlier 46-3rd was almost totally destroyed and the area leveled (CS. 4). A new rear retaining wall (Fig. 121:7) was then laid up, S of which the Maya dumped a fill of light-gray earth that includes debris salvaged from the preceding structure, to judge from the cultural material (CS. 3). This fill continues out beyond the excavations to the S into Plat. 6C-1, indicating that the level of the group platform was raised in connection with this construction, as was the case when Str. 6C-45-2nd was constructed. Following this activity, a front platform wall and the front wall for an upper platform level (Fig. 120a and 121:2 and 3) were put in place, and fill operations terminated (CS. 2). Thus, a two-level platform was created, presumably for support of a building of perishable materials. There is no evidence for the existence of such a building, but since one stood on the similar 45-1st nearby, one probably stood on this platform as well. Structure 6C-46-2nd:Fl. 1, which covers the platform, consists of two different levels. The lower surface is in union with the front wall of the upper level, and a projection of its surviving portion comes within 0.10 m of the top of the badly broken front wall for the lower level. The upper surface runs from the top of the front wall for the upper level to the top of the back structure wall (see Fig. 121).

An important problem with respect to this structure is its relation to U. 1, and U. 10 of Plat. 6C-1 (Fig. 120a). For reasons that will be obvious shortly, it is known that the length of 6C-46-2nd was the same as that of the final structure. Platform 6C-1:U. 10, a freestanding wall for Plat. 6C-1 that runs E from 45-2nd, terminates in line with the W end wall of 46-2nd. The evidence is badly destroyed here as a result of erosion and uprooting of trees, but it appears that this wall ends at a small platform (U. 1) that is partially incorporated into Str. 6C-46. No other interpretation makes sense. The walls of U. 1 are indicated by lines of rubble; evidently, this was about the height of the front platform of 46-2nd. In fact, it appears that the front wall of the lower platform level to the E abuts on the E end wall of U. 1, and this small platform projected about 1 m outward into Plat. 6C-1. Aside from these observations, U. 1 is completely enigmatic. If the front platform level of 6C-46 was unroofed, U. 1 may have been a small utility building for the larger structure. Or, perhaps the roof of 6C-46 covered only the rear half of the surface of the lower platform level.

Unit 9 of Plat. 6C-1 (Fig. 121) was in union with the plaza wall. This unit is a remnant of a surface that must have continued up to the front wall of 46-2nd farther E. This is indicated by the fact that the level of the plaza was raised by fill put in place as CS. 3 for the structure (Fig. 121:5).

STRUCTURE 6C-46-1ST

Construction of this final structure commenced when fill was dumped N of the existing structure (CS. 3). A new N retaining wall (Fig. 120a:1) was constructed on this fill, about 0.90 m behind the earlier wall (CS. 2). The space between them was then filled. The new back wall must have been carried to a level 0.24 m above the upper surface of 46-2nd:Fl. 1, for a new wall (Fig. 120a and 121:4) was set upon the surface of that floor for a higher platform level. In front of the new upper level, the older Fl. 1 may have continued in service, for no newer pavement can be found. The old front wall for the second level of 46-2nd continued in service, as did the front wall and the lower level of 46-2nd:Fl. 1. The end walls seem to have incorporated those of the earlier structure. Unit 1 remains an enigma.

This extension of the width of the platform suggests the possibility that the front platform level was unroofed. The two upper levels of the final structure may be compared with other two-level building platforms, which might have been divided into two rooms longitudinally. There is, however, no proof for such a proposition; one may only say that it is reasonable in the light of speculations concerning U. 1, and nothing more.

STRUCTURE 6C-47

This, the most prominent structure in Gp. 6C-1, sits on the W edge of Plat. 6C-1. Its long axis is somewhat off a magnetic N-S line, so that it does not line up well with the other structures (see Fig. 115). A perfect giant of a tree recently grew from the top of the ruin, but had fallen, roots and all, so as to cover most of this structure and 6C-44. As a consequence, excavation consisted of a few probes in the S end (Fig. 122), so information is accordingly limited.

The structure was built directly where bedrock rises abruptly to the E (Fig. 123). Perhaps this is the reason for the peculiar orientation of the structure relative to others. The Maya apparently took advantage of this rise to pro-

duce a platform much higher and more elaborate than any other in this group. Through a combination of modifications of bedrock, construction of wall faces, and deposition of fill, three high steps were built up from the surface of Plat. 6C-1. A burial was placed in the fill of the second step, probably at this time (see Bu. 136). No plaster step treads have survived the ravages of time, but masonry for the first and third step, and a quarried bedrock face for the second, can be observed. The masonry is of well-dressed blocks, with flat faces and sharp edges, such as was not used elsewhere in Gp. 6C-1 prior to construction of Str. 6C-45-2nd and 46-2nd.

Unit 1 is pavement that survives from a front platform surface. This lies directly on an earth fill, and must have run to the top of a low upper course of masonry, no longer present, for the uppermost stair riser. The floor is in union with the base of a wall of an upper platform level. This wall has an outset at the S end; perhaps there was a matching outset on the N, but this is speculative. No pavement survives for this upper level, but the overburden is so thin that it would have offered no protection to such a floor.

Unit 2 is a wall that runs E from the rear platform wall. It does not stand anywhere near as high as the back wall, which must have run N and S from U. 2. The purpose of this wall is not known.

Structure 6C-47 may have consisted in part of a building of perishable materials. The excavations were so limited, however, that they produced no evidence one way or the other. But since the apparently contemporary Str. 6C-45-2nd had such a building, it seems likely that this one did also.

There is no indication from the limited excavation to bedrock beneath the stairs that earlier architecture stood at this locus. The two object lots from this structure produced abundant Manik sherds, however. This may only mean that earlier trash from Gp. 6C-1 was used as fill, not that any earlier construction would be found beneath the platform itself.

PLATFORM 6C-1-6TH

Little may be said with respect to this architectural development, hence it should be regarded as tentative. The only information comes from around Str. 6C-45, where the bare surface of bedrock seems to have served as an outside "pavement" for Str. 6C-45-8th-C through 6th (Fig. 119). Possibly, portions of bedrock were artificially leveled, but this is not certain.

PLATFORM 6C-1-5TH

This architectural development is not defined on the basis of any specific archaeological feature. The fact that the front wall of Str. 6C-45-5th was built 0.32 m above the surface of bedrock (Fig. 119), however, suggests that the level of Plat. 6C-1 was built up and provided with a floor. No trace of this hypothetical floor is known; presumably it was destroyed in the course of later renovations.

PLATFORM 6C-1-4TH

This architectural development is represented by U. 1 and 4, which appear to be remnants of a single pavement. Unit 1 abuts the front wall of Str. 6C-45-4th (Fig. 119), whereas U. 4 is located in the ceramic test pit (see Fig. 115 for location). The equation of these surfaces requires some explanation. In the Op. 38C test pit, and just E of Str. 6C-45-4th, can be noted two sequences of three floors each. The lower floors in each case seal rich deposits of Manik sherds. Again, in both places material above the uppermost floor includes quantities of Manik sherds, and it appears to be the same sort of fill in both areas. It is probable, then, that these are the same three floors, as seen in two different locations. Unit 1, the lowest floor near Str. 6C-45-4th, is 0.14 m higher than U. 4, the lowest floor in the test pit. This is not a significant difference, however, considering the distance between the two exposures (about 8 m). The same holds true for the 0.20 m discrepancy between the uppermost floor at Str. 6C-45-4th (U. 3), and U. 6, the equivalent floor in the test pit.

Aside from the information above, nothing more is known of Plat. 6C-1-4th.

PLATFORM 6C-1-3RD

This development is represented by U. 2 and 5, the second of the three floors seen E of Str. 6C-45-4th (Fig. 117b) and in the test pit, respectively. As noted above, the floor represented by these units was most probably laid when Str. 6C-45-4th-A was built.

PLATFORM 6C-1-2ND

This is represented by U. 3 and 6, the upper floors in front of Str. 6C-45-4th (Fig. 118a) and in the test pit, respectively. It is also likely that U. 7 and 8 (Fig. 120b), a floor and retaining wall, pertain to this development. These latter are located beneath Str. 6C-46, and together seal a fill that includes abundant Manik sherds, as well as PD. 101. Suggested is contemporaneity with one of the three pavements already discussed. Since the earliest architectural development of Str. 6C-46 (3rd) was built at the same time as U. 7, this pavement could equate with the most recent of the three floor surfaces (U. 3 and 6, associated with Str. 6C-45-3rd). Since the fill of the floor (U. 7) overlies sterile strata, the two floors for Plat. 6C-1-3rd and 4th probably never extended to this locality. Otherwise, one would have to assume that U. 7 is part of an earlier floor, and that there was no construction here when

changes were being made to Str. 6C-45-4th as well as the central area of Plat. 6C-1, a less likely possibility.

PLATFORM 6C-1-1ST

The remnants of this entity are U. 9 and 10 (Fig. 118b and 120a). Unit 9 is pavement that covers the front wall for Str. 6C-45-3rd, and is in union with both Str. 6C-45-2nd and U. 10 (Fig. 118 and 120). The latter is a freestanding wall that bounds Plat. 6C-1-1st on the N, between Str. 6C-45 and 6C-46. Unit 9 probably continued in use with 45-1st, but it is impossible to be sure. There is no floor surface between U. 9 and 3, which here cannot be explained as a result of ancient destructive activity. Therefore, it seems clear that the surface represented by U. 3 did in fact serve Str. 6C-45-3rd.

It seems safe to assume that the surface represented by U. 9 once ran up to the front wall of Str. 6C-46-2nd, and concealed the now-razed 46-3rd. This is consistent with the dates for the ceramics in the fills from both structures. Also consistent is that when 6C-46-2nd was built, the level of the surface for Plat. 6C-1 was raised above U. 7 to a height equivalent to that of U. 9, which is above U. 3 near Str. 6C-45. Thus it appears that construction of Str. 6C-45-2nd, 46-2nd, and Plat. 6C-1-1st was synchronous. The floor represented by U. 9 served both these structures, and probably Str. 6C-45-1st, 6C-46-1st, and 6C-47.

SHERDS AND ARTIFACTS

For definition of lot groups, see Table 2.251; content is presented in Tables 2.252–2.255.

CONSTRUCTION FILL

In Gp. 6C-1, the earliest material in this category comes from LG. 1 of Str. 6C-45. This is an undisturbed midden loaded with sherds from late Manik vessels. Other objects in the midden include human bone fragments from two individuals, one of them an adult male. Other fragments of these same individuals are included in LG. 4b (fill of Str. 6C-45-4th). The likelihood is that these bones represent disturbed burials; material from these burials was continually redeposited as architectural developments of Str. 6C-45 were torn down and rebuilt. Lot Group 1 was eventually sealed beneath the earliest known version of 6C-45. The presence of this midden indicates that another structure or structures stood nearby before construction of 45-8th-C. The midden must have been disturbed to some extent when the construction associated with its deposition was torn down, and the new one built. Eventually, some of this early trash was reused again in later construction.

Structure 6C-45:LG. 2 and 4b derive from a primary midden associated with the first four architectural developments of that structure. Portions of this were sealed at various times beneath subsequent construction, and the associated sherds (all late Manik) should provide good dating control for the various architectural developments. Not only are sherds abundant in the deposit, but there is a wide variety of other artifacts, both utilitarian and ornamental. The deposit also contains human bones, probably from earlier disturbed burials (see above), and a heavy inclusion of ash and charcoal. Actual deposition layers may be noted in the portion of the midden behind Str. 6C-45-5th (Fig. 119). One of these, U. 14, is a marked pause-line. These layers all slope down from the back of the structure, as expected if trash was dumped off the back of 6C-45.

Other lot groups require little comment. Manik sherds are abundant in nearly all cases. The sequence from Str. 6C-45 indicates a late Early Classic occupation of the locus, and so Early Classic trash was abundant and easily accessible for use in later construction fill. This makes it difficult to date the later architectural developments, for early material could be continually reused, while contemporary material would not necessarily find its way into fill. This is illustrated in the case of Gp. TS. 7 (Table 2.260). Material from Str. 6C-45-3rd (LG. 5a and 5b) is full of Manik sherds. Only a single Ik sherd comes from this large sample. Since it is from a sealed situation, it provides a lower limit date for this construction. But had a large fill sample not been procured from this structure, it would

undoubtedly be assigned an Early Classic date. Contemporary fills from Plat. 6C-1:LG. 2 contain no sherds more recent than the late Manik Ceramic Complex.

MATERIAL ABOVE LIVING LEVELS

The present case is an unusual one, for minimally disturbed midden deposits were found in association with several architectural developments of Str. 6C-45 (as mentioned above). Structure 6C-45:LG. 2 accumulated during use of 45-8th. Structure 6C-45:LG. 8a accumulated during the occupation of 7th and 6th. Structure 6C-45:LG. 4b accumulated during occupation of 5th. There is also the early midden, over which Str. 6C-45-8th-C was built (LG. 1). As already noted, these are full of the kind of trash to be expected in a midden. Structure 6C-45:LG. 8b comes from outside the walls of the final structure, but probably consists for the most part of material that has been rooted and washed out of the last two architectural developments.

Lot Group 3 from 6C-46 is the only one from that structure that might contain occupation material. The bulk of the sherds, however, pertain to the Manik Complex, indicating that most of it has spilled out of the structure fill. Similarly, LG. 2 from Str. 6C-47 seems to derive almost entirely from its fill, for destruction has been extensive at that locus. The best occupation samples, then, remain those from the early versions of Str. 6C-45.

TABLE 2.251
Group 6C-1: Lot Groups

Feature	Lot Group	Lot	Provenience	Ceramic Evaluation
Str. 6C-45	1	67A/24,54-60	Sealed fill of of 8th	Late Manik
	2	67A/39,40,43	Unsealed fill of 7th	Late Manik
	3	67A/38	Unsealed fill of 5th	Late Manik
	4a	67A/11,17,28	Sealed fill of 4th	Manik, some Preclassic
	4b	67A/18,32-36, 41,51-53	Partially sealed fill of 4th	Late Manik
	5a	67A/14,27,47	Partially sealed fill of 3rd	Manik
	5b	67A/44,50	Sealed fill of 3rd, 4th, and 5th	Late Manik, Ik
	6	67A/13	Partially sealed fill of 2nd	Manik and Ik and/or Imix
	7a	67A/1	Unsealed fill of 1st	Manik, Ik and Imix
	7b	67A/37,48,49	Unsealed fill of 1st and 2nd	Manik
	7c	67A/26,29,31	Unsealed fill of 1st, 2nd, and 3rd	Manik and Ik
	7d	67A/46	Unsealed fill of 1st, 2nd, 3rd and 4th	Manik
	8a	67A/42	Against outside surface of N wall, 6C-45-7th	Manik
	8b	67A/7,19,22	Outside walls of 1st, to base of walls	Manik, Ik, Imix
Str. 6C-46	1a	67A/10,15	Sealed fill of 2nd	Manik
	1b	67A/5,6	Partially sealed fill of 2nd	Manik, Ik, Imix
	2a	67A/2,3	Unsealed fill of 1st	Manik, Ik, much Imix
	2b	67A/25	Unsealed fill of 1st, 2nd, and 3rd	Manik, some Ik and/or Imix
	3	67A/4,12	Outside structure walls to base of walls	Manik, some Ik and/or Imix
Str. 6C-47	1	67A/30	Unsealed fill	Manik, some possible Ik and/or Imix
	2	67A/20	Outside structure walls, to base of walls	Manik, Ik, some Imix
Plat. 6C-1	1a	38C/4-6	Sealed fill of 4th	Manik
	1b	67A/9	Partially sealed fill of 4th	1 Preclassic; Manik; 1 possible Ik
	2	38C/3 67A/16,21	Sealed fill of 2nd	Late Manik
	3a	38C/1,2	Unsealed fill of 1st	Ik and/or Imix
	3b	67A/8	Sealed fill of 1st 1st	Manik and Ik

TABLE 2.252
Structure 6C-45: Artifacts by Lot Group

Study Category	Object	1	2	3	4a	4b	5a	5b	6	7a	7b	7c	7d	8a	8b
Pottery Vessels		Sherds not weighed													
Other Pottery Artifacts	Figurines	2	1			2		1							
	Stamps	1				1		1							
	Censers	4				3		1							
	Centrally perforated sherds	1								1					
	Unperforated sherd discs							1							
	Unclassifiable formed object	1				2									1
Flaked Chert Artifacts	Flake cores	3		1		4			1	2					
	Ovate bifaces	1				2						1			
	Elongate bifaces	1				1				1		1			
	Rectangular/oval bifaces	1				1									
	Irregular biface	1													
	Unclassifiable biface	1													
	Thin bifaces	4				6		2							1
	Irregular, retouched flakes	1		2		5									
	Point-retouched flakes					2									
	Blades		1					1							
	Used flakes	15	1	2		8		3	1	1	2	1	2		1
	Unused flakes	51	7	8		66		27	1	3		1		3	1
Flaked Obsidian Artifacts	Thin bifaces	4		2		3		5				1			
	Prismatic blades	26	5	9		58		25	2	1	6	3			
	Used flakes					2									
	Unused flakes	1				2									
	Unclassifiable artifact					1									
Ground, Pecked, and Polished Stone Artifacts	Manos	1				4									
	Metates					4		1				2	1		1
	Rubbing stones					2									
	Hammer stones	2				1						1			1
	Celt			1		1									
	Beads							2							
	Unmodified slate					1				1					
	Unmodified sandstone				1										
	Painted plaster fragment					1									
	Unclassifiable artifacts	2	1												1
Shell and Bone Artifacts	Shell, tinklers	3				2		3							
	Shell, worked, adornos	1		1											
	Shell, misc. worked	3		3		2									
	Shell, unworked	15	1			8		6							
	Bone, perforators	4				1		2							
	Bone, tube					1					1				
	Bone, perforated disc	1													
	Bone, animal misc. worked	2	1			4		1				4			
	Bone, animal, unworked	477	7	8		136		55			1				
	Bone, human, misc. worked					3		2					2		
	Bone, human, unworked	141	4	7		40		27	1		1		1	3	
	Bone, unidentified, unworked	4		1		56									

TABLE 2.253
Structure 6C-46: Artifacts by Lot Group

Study Category	Object	Lot Group				
		1	1b	2a	2b	3
Pottery Vessels		Sherds not weighed				
Other Pottery Artifacts	Figurine					1
	Censer				1	
Flaked Chert Artifacts	Flake core					1
	Ovate bifaces				3	1
	Elongate biface					1
	Rectangular/oval biface				1	
	Unclassifiable biface	1				
	Used flakes	1	2	2	4	2
	Unused flakes			4	2	1
Flaked Obsidian Artifacts	Thin bifaces			1	2	
	Prismatic blades			4	14	
	Unused flake				1	
Ground, Pecked, and Polished Stone Artifacts	Metates		2			1
	Celt				1	
	Rubbing stones			1	1	
	Unclassifiable artifact					1
Shell and Bone Artifacts	Worked shell				1	
	Bone, human, unworked				3	
	Bone, animal, unworked	6				

TABLE 2.254
Structure 6C-47: Artifacts by Lot Group

Study Category	Object	Lot Group	
		1	2
Pottery Vessels		Sherds not weighed	
Flaked Chert Artifacts	Flake core	1	
	Unclassifiable biface	1	
Flaked Obsidian Artifacts	Prismatic blades	3	
Ground, Pecked, and Polished Stone Artifacts	Manos	2	
	Metate	1	
	Hammer stone	1	
Shell and Bone Artifacts	Bone, human, unworked	4	
	Bone, animal, unworked	1	

TABLE 2.255
Platform 6C-1: Artifacts by Lot Group

Study Category	Object	Lot Group				
		1a	1b	2	3a	3b
Pottery Vessels		Sherds not weighed				
Flaked Chert Artifacts	Ovate bifaces			1		1
	Thin biface			1		
	Unclassifiable artifact				1	
Flaked Obsidian Artifacts	Thin biface				1	
	Prismatic blades			2	3	
Shell and Bone Artifacts	Shell, Tinkler			1		
	Bone, animal, rasp			1		
	Bone, animal, unworked			5		
	Bone, human, unworked			10		

TIME SPANS

Time spans for the structures of Gp. 6C-1, based on the sequence outlined above, are presented in Tables 2.256–2.259. These are combined into group time spans in Table 2.260. Twenty-six of these have been defined, on the basis of the sequence for Str. 6C-45. The time spans for Str. 6C-46 and Plat. 6C-1 are correlated with these on the basis of architectural relationships already discussed, with ceramic analysis (Table 2.251) as a check. It is virtually certain that Str. 6C-45-2nd and 46-2nd were constructed at the same time. Given this, it is reasonable to assume from the Imix ceramics in Str. 6C-45:LG. 7a and Str. 6C-46:LG. 2a that 45-1st and 46-1st are also contemporary. Similarly, it appears that Str. 6C-45-3rd and 46-3rd were built at the same time.

Structure 6C-47 is not connected with the other structures by any remaining architectural feature. The fact that it consists of only one architectural development, however, makes it likely that it is contemporary with one of the later versions of 6C-45. Its masonry is similar to that of the final two developments of 45, but is quite different from that of the third. The abundance of ceramics in LG. 2 characteristic of the Ik Complex suggests contemporaneity of 47 with 45-2nd. This is further implied by the fact that the last large-scale modification of Plat. 6C-1 occurred at this time. Had Str. 6C-47 been built later, further modification of the group platform might be expected. Construction of Str. 6C-47 then may be attributed with a reasonable degree of confidence to Gp. TS. 5.

The earliest activity was at the locus of Str. 6C-45, and is marked by a midden containing late Manik sherds, which on stratigraphic grounds predates Str. 6C-48-8th-C. It is this that defines Group TS. 26. The evidence indicates continuous occupation from that time. This continued until after the appearance of Imix ceramics, which are present in the fills of Str. 6C-45-1st and 46-1st, as well as in deposits of late occupation trash. In terms of absolute dates, this occupation of Gp. 6C-1 began somewhere between AD 378 and 550 (the dates for the Manik III Ceramic Complex); it ended by AD 869, which dates the end of the Imix Ceramic Complex.

TABLE 2.256
Structure 6C-45: Time Spans

Time Span	Architectural Development	Construction Stage	Floor	Unit	Special Deposits: Burial	Descriptive Data	Lot Group	Ceramics in Vogue
1						Abandonment and collapse		-----------
2						Use	8b	
3	Str.6C-45-1st	1				Construction of building of perishable materials		Imix
		2				Construction of upper platform level	7a 7b 7c 7d	
		3				Partial or total demolition of existing building		
4						Use		-----------
5	Str.6C-45-2nd	1				Construction of building of perishable materials		
		2	1	19,20		Construction of building platform	6	
		3				Partial demolition of existing structure and preparation of base surface		Ik
6						Use		
7	Str.6C-45-3rd	1				Construction of building of perishable materials		
		2	1	18		Construction of platform	5a 5b	
		3				Demolition of existing building		
8				17?		Use		-----------
9	Str.6C-45-4th-A	None defined	1			Final renovation of 4th		
10						Use		
11	Str.6C-45-4th-B	None defined		16		First renovation of 45-4th		
12						Use		
13	Str.6C-45-4th-C	1				Construction of building of perishable materials		
		2	2	15		Construction of platform	4a	
		3				Demolition of existing building; new base surface prepared		
14				14		Use of 5th; earlier structure used as dump	4b	
15	Str.6C-45-5th	1				Construction of building of perishable materials		
		2				Construction of platform	3	
		3		13	146	Preparation of base surface		Manik (late)
16						Use		
17	Str.6C-45-6th	1				Construction of building of perishable materials		
		2		11,12		Construction of raised S platform		
		3				Partial demolition of existing building		
18						Use	8a	
19	Str.6C-45-7th	1				Construction of building of perishable materials		Manik (late)
		2	1			Platform floor laid		
		3		4-10		Construction of interior platform		
		4				Construction of platform		
20						Use		
21	Str.6C-45-8th-A	None defined		3		Final renovation of 45-8th		
22						Use	2	
23	Str.6C-45-8th-B	None defined		2		First renovation of 8th		
24						Use		
25	Str.6C-45-8th-C	1				Construction of building of perishable materials		Manik (late)
		2	1	1		Construction of platform		
26						Probable earlier construction with subsequent accumulation of trash	1	

TABLE 2.257
Structure 6C-46: Time Spans

Time Span	Architectural Development	Construction Stage	Floor	Unit	Descriptive Data	Lot Group		Ceramics in Vogue
1					Abandonment and collapse	3		
2					Use			
3	Str.6C-46-1st	1			Construction of building of perishable materials	2a	2b	Imix
		2			Construction of back wall and upper platform level			
		3			Preparation of base surface; existing building razed			
4					Use			- - - - - -
5	Str.6C-46-2nd	1			Construction of building of perishable materials	1a, 1b		
		2	2	1	Completion of platform			
		3			Construction of platform begun			Ik
		4			Demolition of existing structure			
6					Use			
7	Str.6C-46-3rd				Construction of earliest structure			

TABLE 2.258
Structure 6C-47: Time Spans

Time Span	Architectural Development	Unit	Special Deposits: Burial	Descriptive Data	Lot Group		Ceramics in Vogue
1				Abandonment and collapse	2		- - - - - -
2				Use			Imix
3	Str.6C-47	1,2	136	Construction	1		Ik

TABLE 2.259
Platform 6C-1: Time Spans

Time Span	Architectural Development	Unit	Special Deposits: Problematical Deposits	Descriptive Data	Lot Group		Ceramics in Vogue
1				Abandonment and ruin			
2				Use	3a,3b		Imix
3	Plat.6C-1-1st	9,10		Plaza level raised and final floor laid			
4				Use			Ik
5	Plat.6C-1-2nd	3,6-8	101	Extension to N of plaza and new floor laid	2		
6				Use			
7	Plat.6C-1-3rd	2,5		Renovation of plaza floor			
8				Use			
9	Plat.6C-1-4th	1,4		New plaza floor laid	1a,	1b	Manik
10				Use			
11	Plat.6C-1-5th			Construction of first formal plaza surface			
12	Plat.6C-1-6th			Use of bedrock as living surface			(Late)

TABLE 2.260
Group 6C-1: Time Spans

Group Time Span	Str. 6C-45 Time Span (Table 2.256)	Str. 6C-45 Time Span (Table 2.257)	Str. 6C-47 Time Span (Table 2.258)	Plat. 6C-1 Time Span (Table 2.259)
1	1	1	1	1
2	2	2		
3	3	3		
4	4	4	2	2
5	5	5	3	3
6	6	6		4
7	7	7		5
8	8			6
9	9			7
10	10			
11	11			
12	12			8
13	13			9
14	14			10
15	15			11
16	16			
17	17			
18	18			
19	19			12
20	20			
21	21			
22	22			
23	23			
24	24			
25	25			
26	26			
27	27			

Group 6C-2

Group 6C-2 is located at 6C:S400 E73, where the terrain slopes gently down to the W (TR. 11). This is 58 m S of the Perdido Reservoir, and 65 m from the nearest neighboring group to the S. As mapped in 1960, the group consists of three structures arranged on three sides of a plaza (Fig. 124). Two of these, Str. 6C-58 and 59, are clearly rectangular on the basis of their ruin mounds. The third, on the E side of the plaza, appears to be square. Because of this, with its position on the E, this structure (6C-57) was investigated by Becker in 1963 to see if it might be a household shrine. It was actually a one-level rectangular platform, however, with four steps at the front.

STRUCTURE 6C-57

This structure (Fig. 125), for which there is but a single architectural development, seems to have been constructed in four stages. As CS. 4, there was preparation of the surface on which to build. At the time, bedrock was exposed W of a quarried face (see below). East of this face, two sterile layers (U. 1 and 2) overlie bedrock. To raise this surface and level it, the Maya dumped much fill of gray earth (U. 3). This provided a level surface for the platform itself. Farther W, where the stairs and plaza were to be built, more fill was dumped (U. 4). This consisted of a gray-black earth that was ultimately packed down quite hard. Some of the fill was also dumped on the surface of U. 3 where the front platform wall was to be built, so as to raise it a bit higher.

Once the base surface was prepared, the walls and fill for the platform were set in place above it (CS. 3). The two-course masonry walls are well-dressed, but to judge from the maximum height of the fill, as well as the stairs that were built in front, there must have been a third course. This seems to have collapsed sometime after abandonment. The fill is of brown earth, within which are many stones. Burial 145 was found in this fill, but it probably postdates construction (see its discussion in section III, this report). No summit floor was found, but a surface of some sort was obviously present on the platform at one time. Presumably, it was of plaster.

The next step in the construction (CS. 2) seems to have been to provide the platform with steps in front. Four were built of masonry consisting of large riser-tread blocks, square in cross section, separated by a gap that was filled with stone rubble. This masonry is set against the front wall of the platform, the top of which served as the riser for the fourth step. The stairs are centered on the front-rear axis of the structure and U. 5, a plaza floor, was laid on the U. 4 fill in union with the first stair riser.

A final stage (CS. 1) is allowed for construction of a pole-and-thatch building on the platform; since this possibility was not specifically investigated, there is no evidence that such a building was constructed. There are, though, reasons for supposing that most small structures did consist in part of these buildings (TR. 20B). It is assumed that this building would be the last thing completed in construction, as was apparently the case in most instances, although main posts probably would have been set in place in the course of CS. 3.

POSSIBLE EARLIER ACTIVITY

As mentioned above, some quarried bedrock was exposed in excavation. This consists of a vertical face, just below the location of the second stair riser for the structure (Fig. 125b). After quarrying, two layers, one of light brown earth (the lowest, U. 1) and one of gray earth (U. 2), accumulated to the E against the face. Both are devoid of cultural material, and U. 2 was packed quite hard, perhaps in the course of later construction activity. These layers suggest that a period of time separated construction of the platform from the quarrying. The only problem is that there is no accumulation over bedrock to the W. Perhaps this is because the relatively level surface of bedrock there served as a plaza surface for Str. 6C-58 and 59, prior to construction of 6C-57. The presence of considerable cultural material, and the fact that only a single architectural development is represented, suggests that Str. 6C-57 was built later than one or both of the other structures of the group.

SHERDS AND ARTIFACTS

Lot groups defined for Gp. 6C-2 are listed in Table 2.261, with content in Table 2.262.

Construction Fill

Considerable material is included in this category. Since Str. 6C-57 consists of just one architectural development, and there are no other nearby groups of structures, it is more probable that the material was drawn from trash deposits associated with one or both of the other structures in Gp. 6C-2. This gains further support as the pottery (Manik Complex) is, for the most part, earlier than that in use at the time Str. 6C-57 was built.

Material Above Living Levels

Since the upper portion of the structure had collapsed subsequent to abandonment, most material in this category actually consists of fill. There appears to be no occupation debris to consider.

TIME SPANS

Time spans for Str. 6C-57 are defined in Table 2.263. No group time spans have been defined, since no other features in Gp. 6C-2 were excavated. It may be noted, however, that TS. 3 apparently postdates some other construction in the group. Time span 2 could be contemporary with construction and occupation of at least one other structure, since it includes construction of a new plaza floor. This floor seems much too high above the original plaza surface to have been just a grading floor.

Dating of the structure is a problem. A large sample of Manik sherds from undisturbed fill (Table 2.261) suggests that one or more structures in Gp. 6C-2 were built and used while such ceramics were in vogue. Hence,

Gp. 6C-2 seems to have had its beginnings sometime after AD 250 but before AD 550, the dates for the Manik Ceramic Complex. A few Ik and/or Imix sherds in collapsed fill outside its walls suggest that Str. 6C-57 was built sometime after AD 550 (which dates the appearance of Ik ceramics). Lacking any meaningful occupation debris, one can only speculate as to the time of abandonment of the structure and group. In the absence of evidence to the contrary, it is assumed that the group was abandoned by AD 869, which dates the end of the Imix Ceramic Complex.

TABLE 2.261
Group 6C-2: Lot Groups

Feature	Lot Group	Lots	Provenience	Ceramic Evaluation
Str. 6C-57	1	2,4	Unsealed fill	Manik
(Op.70E)	2	1	Surface and outside structure to base of walls	Manik and Ik and/or Imix

TABLE 2.262
Structure 6C-57: Artifacts by Lot Group

Study Category	Object	Lot Group 1	2
Pottery Vessels		Not recorded	
Other Pottery Artifacts	Figurine	1	
	Censers	4	3
Flaked Chert Artifacts	Ovate biface		1
	Used flakes		2
Flaked Obsidian Artifacts	Thin biface	1	
	Prismatic blades	3	
	Flake	1	
Ground, Pecked, and Polished Stone Artifacts	Metates	2	1
	Celt	1	
	Jade flare	1	
Shell and Bone Artifacts	Shell, misc. worked	1	
	Bone, animal, worked	6	
	Bone, human, unworked	1	

TABLE 2.263
Structure 6C-57: Time Spans

Time Span	Architectural Development	Construction Stage	Floor	Unit	Descriptive Data	Lot Group		Ceramics in Vogue
1				145?	Abandonment and ruin			
2				145?	Use			Ik (and Imix?)
3	Str.6C-57	1			Construction of building of perishable materials			
		2	5		Construction of steps			
		3	3,4		Construction of platform	1	2	
		4			Preparation of base surface			
4			1,2		Accumulation of earth; possible use of bedrock to the W as plaza			
5					Quarrying of bedrock			Manik

Group 6C-5

Group 6C-5 is located at 6C:S206 E45. Two chultuns (6C-6 and 7) and a basin cut in bedrock appear on the site map (TR. 11) here, but there is no surface indication of any structures. In 1963, Puleston (as Op. 66F, G, and H) excavated the two chultuns and cleared the surface to bedrock around them in order to search for traces of structures, such as were found around Ch. 6C-9 (this report). Signs were found of at least two structures (6C-62 and 63) near both chultuns, and another chultun (6C-11) was discovered W of Ch. 6C-6.

The terrain occupied by Gp. 6C-5 seems well suited for habitation. North of the chultuns the ground is quite level. To the S and E, the ground drops off to an arroyo that once conveyed water from the "Mundo Perdido" group (Laporte 2003:285) S of Temple III down to the Perdido Reservoir. The nearest mapped group of structures is over 65 m to the NE.

STRUCTURE 6C-62

This structure is defined on the basis of several apparent postholes N and W of the orifice of Ch. 6C-7 (Fig. 126 and Table 2.264). Because it is difficult to identify any clear pattern among them, about all that can be done is to describe them. The form of the structure itself must remain unknown. Units 1 and 2 are holes in bedrock apparently for posts square at the base (like that set in

Str. 6C-61:U. 4, this report). Unit 2 actually consists of two corners; between them bedrock is not cut so deeply. These two "corners" enclose an area just slightly larger than U. 1, and it is hard to imagine these as other than a support for a post (of two vertical members?) that rested on bedrock.

Units 3–9 are round holes in bedrock more comparable to known postholes elsewhere at Tikal. Of these, U. 7 is the largest, suggesting a post comparable in size to those placed in U. 1 and 2. Moreover, it is in line with the latter two units. Its distance from U. 2 is 1.90 m; U. 2 is 1.50 m from U. 1.

Of the other postholes, little need be said, save that U. 5 and 6 are beside one another, and that U. 4 has what looks like a small drain in its E side. This, though, could be a natural crack in the bedrock.

In the same area as the postholes is U. 10, a feature that appears on the site map (TR. 11) as "Basin Cut in Bedrock." Comparable in diameter to the orifice of Ch. 6C-7, it is only 0.22 m deep. The feature is just E of a line between U. 2 and 7. It is quite similar to "Ch. 2E-2" and basins associated with Ch. 5C-6 (all this report) and Str. 6E-63.

The alignment, spacing, and comparability of size of U. 1, 2, and 7 suggest that these held posts for a main wall of Str. 6C-62. This hypothesis would be on firmer ground if U. 7 was also rectangular, but it is not. Still, the hypothesis seems reasonable, even though unproven. If U. 1, 2, and 7 do mark a structure wall, then it extended no farther

S than U. 7, for there are no postholes in the area up to 3.40 m S of U. 7. This would suggest that Str. 6C-62 stood N of Ch. 6C-7.

Unit 7 probably marks the position of a corner of Str. 6C-62, although this is less clear for U. 1. Excavations were extended only 1.40 m N of this posthole, a distance less than that between either U. 1 and 2 or 2 and 7.

Continuing on the assumption that U. 1, 2, and 7 mark a structure wall, the question arises as to whether it was an E or W wall. It was probably a W wall, for no postholes are to be found in a line perpendicular to U. 1, 2, and 7 from U. 7. This means that the U. 10 basin was inside the structure.

Although it is a plausible hypothesis that U. 1, 2, and 7 mark the W wall of the structure, the other postholes remain to be explained. Three possibilities may be suggested: (1) they relate to a different architectural development of Str. 6C-62; (2) they are associated with minor details connected with the structure (table legs and the like); or (3) they relate to a combination of 1 and 2. In keeping with the first possibility, U. 4–8 form a rough semicircle, which could be a remnant of a round W end wall. Such walls are sometimes found in Early Classic structures; the problem is that there is scant evidence here for an Early Classic occupation. On the other hand, this interpretation allows one to argue that U. 7 was originally used in a wall that included round posts, and was later reused in a wall that otherwise included square posts. Another argument against the rounded end wall idea is that it runs too close to the orifice of Ch. 6C-7. Since the latter may postdate the appearance of Ik ceramics, though, the chultun could postdate an Early Classic version of Str. 6C-62.

In keeping with the second possibility suggested above are the diminutive dimensions of the postholes relative to U. 1, 2, and 7, the difficulty in recognizing patterns among them, and their position for the most part inside (just inside, in fact) the hypothetical structure for which U. 1, 2, and 7 mark the W wall.

TABLE 2.264
Posthole and Basin Dimensions: Structure 6C-62 (meters)

Feature	Length	Width	Diameter	Depth
Unit 1	0.27	0.23	---	0.16
Unit 2	0.30	0.28	---	0.03-0.09
Unit 3	---	---	0.07	0.08
Unit 4	---	---	0.16	0.08
Unit 5	---	---	0.11	0.05
Unit 6	---	---	0.11	0.20
Unit 7	---	---	0.22	0.06
Unit 8	---	---	0.12	0.14
Unit 9	---	---	0.16	0.06
Unit 10	---	---	0.55	0.22

In the last analysis, in view of all the considerations above, all that can be said is that the existence of a Str. 6C-62 in the area N of Ch. 6C-7 seems indicated beyond reasonable doubt. Beyond this, nothing is certainly known about that structure.

STRUCTURE 6C-63

The evidence for this structure consists of U. 1 and 2, apparently postholes in bedrock, and U. 3, a basin similar to Str. 6C-62:U. 10 (Fig. 126 and Table 2.265). In the absence of evidence to the contrary, U. 1 and 2 are thought to have supported posts for a structure wall. Their distance from the postholes of Str. 6C-62 makes it reasonably clear that these particular ones do not relate to that structure. Further, the existence of a second basin in bedrock suggests a second structure. If the interpretation is correct that the basin (U. 10) of 6C-62 was located inside the structure, then the position of Str. 6C-63:U. 3 relative to U. 1 and 2 would suggest that these were parts of the S wall. This structure must therefore have been positioned not far W of 62, in approximately the same alignment, with the S wall of Str. 63 about 1 m farther N than the S wall of 62. Since neither U. 1 nor U. 2 is as large as Str. 6C-62:U. 7, it is doubtful that either supported a corner post. Aside from these things, nothing more is known of the structure.

TABLE 2.265
Posthole and Basin Dimensions: Structure 6C-63 (meters)

Feature	Diameter	Depth
Unit 1	0.12	0.20
Unit 2	0.08	0.05
Unit 3	0.40	0.16

MISCELLANEOUS DATA

A line of "chop marks" 0.17 m long was seen on a bedrock ridge, 1.10 m E of Str. 6C-63. The reason for these is unknown; no stone seems to have been quarried here.

CHULTUN 6C-6

DESCRIPTION

The antechamber of this chultun (Table 2.266 and Fig. 127) is roughly circular in plan and very roughly bottle-shaped in section. The neck opens into the center of its ceiling. Unusual is the orifice, which in plan looks almost square. This, though, may be from erosion. The orifice is deeply stepped to allow placement of a stone cover, which was found in place. Below the step, the walls of the neck are nearly vertical.

Chamber 1 was about three-quarters filled by a deposit of fine gray material almost 0.30 m deep over the floor, which blends into a stratum of brown topsoil.

Chamber 2, the largest of the four chambers of the chultun, is entered from the N side of Chm. 1. The entrance is unrestricted, without even a sill. The floor of this chamber is up to 0.40 m below that of the antechamber. In shape, it is oval. In section, the walls are concave, with no clear distinction of walls from ceiling and floor. Chamber 2 was about two-thirds filled with a continuation of the strata from Chm. 1. Sandwiched between them, though, was a stratum of limestone chunks mixed with light-colored earth. Some of this fill has been left unexcavated on the N side of the chamber.

Chamber 3 is entered from the E side of Chm. 2. Irregular in shape and small in size, its floor is 0.20 m below that of Chm. 2. There is no sill in the entrance. The space was partially filled with a continuation of the material in Chm. 2.

Chamber 4 is virtually identical to Chm. 3 in size and shape. It is entered from the SE side of Chm. 1, but, again, there is no sill. The floor of the chamber is up to 0.16 m below that of Chm. 1. In section, the chamber resembles an irregular, open circle, with no clear distinction between floor, walls, and ceiling.

Chamber 4 was almost completely filled, although the nature of that fill was not recorded. A masonry block in the entrance (U. 1) prevented this fill from spilling out into the antechamber (very much like the masonry block to the entrance of Chm. 5 of Ch. 2G-10, this report). Eventually, the debris in the antechamber built up against the outer face of U. 1.

DISCUSSION

Two questions came to mind with respect to this chultun: (1) is a single architectural development represented, or is Chm. 3 a later addition?; (2) was the chultun, or any part of it, purposely filled by the Maya?

In regard to the first question, three possibilities may be suggested for Chm. 3. One is that it was built at the same time as the rest of the chultun, rather than make Chm. 2 so large as to be vulnerable to collapse. This seems unlikely, in view of the larger size of many chultun chambers at Tikal. As a second possibility, the separate chamber reflects some aspect of social organization connected with stored food, if indeed food storage was the function of chultuns (TR. 32).

Not only is this speculative, it does not seem particularly compelling, given the different sizes of the two chambers. The third possibility, and the one preferred here, is that Chm. 3 was added to provide extra space. This is preferred, in spite of a lack of final proof, because Chm. 3 is almost a duplicate of Chm. 4. The latter was purposely filled (see below), while the rest of the chultun remained open. Hence, Chm. 4 was probably a part of the original chultun. Together, Chm. 1, 2, and 4 would be a variant of the not uncommon "dumbbell"-shaped chultun. The sealing off of Chm. 4 later might have necessitated a replacement; hence Chm. 3 was built. It is too bad that the nature of the fill in Chm. 4 was not recorded; had it been marl, such as construction of Chm. 3 would have produced, it would have confirmed the argument.

As already noted, there is no question but what Chm. 4 was filled and sealed off from the rest of the chultun. The reason for abandonment of the chamber may have been a water problem, for its position is such that any rainwater that got into the antechamber would have run into Chm. 4. Another possibility is that Chm. 4 was originally built to serve as a drain to protect Chm. 2, but the water problem was later solved in a different way. This does not seem likely, though, if Chm. 3 was a replacement for Chm. 4.

The rest of the chultun seems to have been filled by natural processes. Sherds were reasonably abundant in the fill of the antechamber, but not elsewhere. They are also abundant in surface material S and E of the orifice. In terms of ceramic complexes represented, the sherds in the chultun for the most part are like those on the surface. Evidently, it was this high sherd-content material that washed into the chultun. Natural filling of the chultun, it may be noted, is consistent with the presence of the in situ stone cover. With this in place, there was no need to fill the chultun, for example, to prevent people from falling in after its abandonment. The erosion of the edges of the orifice permitted material to enter the chultun in spite of the cover. Since erosion over time would

TABLE 2.266
Chultun 6C-6: Average Dimensions (meters)

Feature	Length	Width	Height	Maximum Diameter	Minimum Diameter
Orifice	---	---	---	0.62	0.54
Step	---	---	0.25	---	---
Neck	---	---	0.24	0.59	0.51
Chamber 1	1.20	1.00	1.10	---	---
Chamber 2	1.90	2.20	1.00	---	---
Chamber 3	0.85	1.20	0.80	---	---
Chamber 4	0.90	1.05	0.70	---	---

have gradually enlarged the space through which debris could fall, one would expect more in the way of cultural material in later, rather than earlier, fill levels. This is precisely the case; the sherd content of the lower stratum in Chm. 1 is 2 lbs per cubic meter, which in the upper stratum is 2.8 lbs per cubic meter. Moreover, the soil of the basal stratum is finer than that above. Finally, there is no clear break between them; they blend into one another.

The situation in Chm. 2 is not quite like that in Chm. 1. Here, after some buildup of the fine, silt-like material, there appears to have been some minor ceiling collapse. Following this, there was further accumulation of material from Chm. 1.

To sum up, two architectural developments are defined for this chultun: 6C-6-1st, consisting of Chm. 1, 2, and 3, and 6C-6-2nd, consisting surely of Chm. 1, 2, and 4, but probably not 3.

MISCELLANEOUS DATA

An irregularly shaped area around the orifice of Ch. 6C-6 was excavated to look for traces of construction. The only such evidence was a single posthole (Fig. 127a:U. 2), 0.40 m from the NE edge of the orifice. Its small size (0.12 m diameter, 0.23 m deep), with the lack of other postholes up to 2.50 m N, 1.50 m S, 4.30 m E or 1.90 m W, suggests that it was not part of any major structure. While a fair amount of cultural material was found to the E, this may very well derive from Str. 6C-63, which was no more than 10.65 m E of the chultun orifice, and perhaps was even closer (its W wall was not located). Already noted is the absence of sills in the chultun. Any water that got in could have flowed unimpeded into all the chambers. Perhaps it did not because of the presence of a small shelter, one that would not have required stout, or even deeply seated, posts. Unit 2, then, could relate to such a shelter. The lack of other postholes is understandable in this view. Unfortunately, it is impossible to be sure that such a shelter existed, it merely seems reasonable, given the facts at hand.

There are four areas of quarried bedrock near the orifice (Fig. 127a). Units 3 and 4 appear to be the result of quarrying. The basin-like U. 5 and 6 may also be the result of quarrying, but there is also the possibility that they were planting pits. Just when this alteration of bedrock took

place cannot be determined with certainty. Since U. 5, at least, is covered by debris that includes Manik sherds, the quarrying may not postdate construction of the chultun. It could, of course, be much earlier, but there is no evidence for this.

CHULTUN 6C-7

DESCRIPTION

This chultun (Table 2.267 and Fig. 128a,b) is a variant of the common, two-chambered type. The manhole-like orifice shows no trace of a stepped rim, nor is any stone cover to be found. The walls of the neck, from the orifice to the ceiling of the antechamber, are nearly vertical.

From the antechamber, a minimally constricted passage opens into Chm. 2. This space is unusual in that its floor is at practically the same level as that of Chm. 1. There is, however, a low sill between the chambers. Chamber 2 has the form of a low dome. In the back is a hole, apparently made by an animal that fell into the chultun and tried to burrow its way out. Animal bones found in the chultun may be those of this creature.

Chultun 6C-7 obviously was constructed in two stages: No. 2 for the antechamber and neck, No. 1 for Chm. 2.

DISCUSSION

The small number of sherds and artifacts, the demise of a small animal that fell into the chultun and was trapped, and the nature of the fill levels, all combine to suggest that Ch. 6C-7 was abandoned unfilled by the Maya. The lowest layer in the chultun is a gray soil, with some limestone in it. Above this is a lens of dark brown fill, overlain by another layer of brownish-gray soil. Above the latter is topsoil, thickest beneath the orifice. What is suggested is an alternation between gradual accumulation of drift and partial collapse of the ceiling. Thus, the thin dark lens over the deepest layer is probably old topsoil that was buried by partial ceiling collapse.

CHULTUN 6C-11

DESCRIPTION

Because the antechamber (Table 2.268 and Fig. 128c,d) is notable for its depth, a ladder was used in order to gain access. It is entered through the usual manhole-like orifice, which in this case has no stepped lip. As found, though, a square stone cover was in place over the orifice. Broken into five pieces, it appears to have been shifted slightly to the W, exposing an opening 0.25 by 0.04 m. Around the N edge of the stone were packed stones slightly larger than fist-sized. One of these was a fragment of a metate. A block of masonry, 0.36 by 0.16 m, was placed against the S edge of the cover.

TABLE 2.267
Chultun 6C-7: Average Dimensions (meters)

Feature	Length	Width	Height	Diameter
Neck	---	---	0.35	0.44
Chamber 1	0.90	0.80	1.36	---
Chamber 2	1.85	2.10	1.00	---

The chultun neck is quite deep, flaring markedly downward into the ceiling of Chm. 1. Since the orifice is off-center relative to the chamber, the NW walls of neck and chamber are continuous. East and SE is an expanse of ceiling that curves downward to blend with the walls. In plan, the chamber is rounded; in section, it resembles a bottle-shaped pit. The floor is nearly level, though it slopes up slightly toward the high sill in the entrance to Chm. 2. In the other direction, it slopes down into Chm. 3. As found, Chm. 1 was only partly filled by U. 1, a low, conical deposit of dark earth that contains a number of sherds and a large metate fragment (66H-8). This covered a portion of PD. 231 on the floor of the chamber.

Chamber 2 is considerably smaller than Chm. 1, and nearly spherical in shape. A high sill separates it from Chm. 1 to the S. In addition to the sill, the entrance to Chm. 2 is restricted at the sides.

Chamber 2 was about two-thirds filled. The bulk of this, U. 2, is a darkish earth. Of loose consistency, its upper part contained a few sherds and animal bones. Lower down were some of the remains of PD. 231. These continue down into U. 3, a stratum of compact earth flecked with white. Most of the artifactual material in U. 3 was near the top, perhaps having been trampled into its surface. Beneath U. 3 was the floor of the chamber.

The plan of Chm. 3, which is not so deep as Chm. 2, may be described as something between a circle and a rectangle. In section, it looks almost like a circle, with all surfaces rounded. Its entrance from Chm. 1, to the N, is slightly restricted at the sides, but there is no sill. If water ever entered the antechamber, it would have flowed into Chm. 3.

Chamber 3 was slightly more than half filled. The uppermost stratum of fill, U. 4, contained a few sherds and a piece of cut shell (66H-37). Beneath this, U. 5 contained numerous artifacts associated with PD. 231. Although the consistency of U. 4 and 5 is quite loose, U. 6, on the floor of the chamber, is packed hard and contained few artifacts.

DISCUSSION

Quite apart from PD. 231, discussed elsewhere (section III), there are two things that require consideration

TABLE 2.268
Chultun 6C-11: Average Dimensions (meters)

Feature	Length	Width	Height	Diameter
Cover	0.53	0.53	0.16	---
Neck	---	---	0.62	0.45
Chamber 1	1.76	1.50	1.24	---
Chamber 2	1.35	1.20	0.43	---
Chamber 3	1.45	1.13	0.71	---

here. These concern the origin of the chultun fill, and the history of the chultun prior to its use as a repository for PD. 231.

There are two possible explanations for the chultun fill. The first is that earth was dumped into the chultun to cover the human remains in PD. 231 and perhaps fill the chultun. In favor of this is the quantity of earth fill and the quantity of sherds in it. Though weights were not recorded, sherds were reasonably abundant. A large metate fragment in the upper part of U. 1 in Chm. 1 is consistent, in that it seems too large to have fallen through the opening as seen just prior to excavation.

The second possible explanation is that the chultun was empty when sealed, except for PD. 231, but that material filtered in gradually over the following centuries. In favor of this is the fact that great though the amount of earth may appear in section, it really is not sufficient to have filled Chm. 1, particularly if the recent humus at the top of U. 1 is considered. In addition, the looseness of the fill, especially in Chm. 2, is more like that found in chultuns that were filled naturally, rather than in those filled purposely. Even the numerous sherds and large metate fragment may be accounted for; sherds are reasonably plentiful on the surface in proximity to the orifice. This opening, as discovered, looked carelessly sealed. It is unlikely that the Maya would have been careless about this, particularly given the content of the chultun. Quite likely, the stone cover was displaced by a tree root, such as has been seen elsewhere (e.g., Ch. 2G-1, 3F-6, this report). Hence, a small root would have gotten a foothold in the orifice, and as it grew, it would have pushed the stone cover to one side, perhaps lifting it at the same time. A possible result of this, given uneven pressure from below, would be breakage (the stone cover is broken). Given the later demise of the tree and its root, the pieces of stone would fall back more or less in place. While the stone was elevated, the metate fragment could have fallen in. Note, in this connection, that another metate fragment was found wedged against the cover; this indicates the strong possibility that the metate from U. 1 was once in a similar position. Sherds could have continued to fall in up to the time of discovery.

One further, albeit speculative, point may be made in support of the natural-filling hypothesis. Given the "tomb-like" contents of the chultun, one might argue that it was sealed up without fill, in the usual manner of chamber burials.

Although the above hypothesis reasonably accounts for U. 1, 2, 4, and 5, U. 3 appears to be an exception. Here a number of artifacts were found in white, compact earth, suggesting that they were covered before the bulk of PD. 231 was deposited.

With respect to the earlier history of the chultun, U.

6 (in Chm. 3) looks to be an occupation deposit. Possibly it was made up of "sweepings" from Chm. 1 and material carried in perhaps by water. The presence of a sill between Chm. 1 and 2, and the absence of one between Chm. 1 and 3, suggests that Chm. 2 was the main storage chamber (note, though, water could have dripped in off the ceiling). Chamber 3 could have served to drain water that otherwise might have risen sufficiently to overflow the sill into Chm. 2. Given this, it is possible (but unproven) that two architectural developments are represented here. Chultun 6C-11 may have been either a one-chamber, bottle-shaped chultun, or possibly a two-chamber chultun. In either case, water problems necessitated the addition of a chamber or chambers to form Ch. 6C-11-1st, the chultun as presently preserved.

MISCELLANEOUS DATA

Excavations on the surface around the orifice of this chultun were limited to a 2-m square with the orifice at about its center (Fig. 128c). A rectangle 2 by 4 m was excavated 2 m E of this. No postholes were found, which contrasts with both Ch. 6C-6 and 7. While not conclusive, it strongly suggests that Ch. 6C-11 was associated with Str. 6C-62 and 63 to the E, rather than with an otherwise unknown structure by the chultun.

SHERDS AND ARTIFACTS

Lot Groups for Gp. 6C-5 are defined in Table 2.269, with content given in Tables 2.270–2.273.

CONSTRUCTION FILL

Since no platforms, or parts thereof, were found, there is no material that can be assigned to this category. If structure platforms existed, for which there is no evidence, their fills would be in Str. 6C-62:LG. 1. This material, unfortunately, was lost.

MATERIAL ABOVE LIVING LEVELS

Material in this category constitutes LG. 1a and 1b of Str. 6C-63. These are thought to be associated with that structure, rather than some unknown building closer to Ch. 6C-6, because Str. 6C-63 was no more than 10.65 m E

of this chultun—probably closer since neither of the two presumed postholes for the S wall seems to mark the SE corner. In the case of Str. 6C-61 (this report), a situation comparable to this, trash clearly associated with the structure extends to between 14 and 15 m SE, much farther than the 10.65 m maximum here. Consistent with this, in LG. 1a, material was most abundant to the E (nearer Str. 6C-63) than to the W. Finally, the material in LG. 1b is later than that in 1a. This is expectable, for through time the lateral extent of trash discarded from a structure would be expected to increase. Lot Group 1a and 1b, therefore, should date the period of use of Str. 6C-63. Moreover, the debris should permit inferences about the use of that structure.

CHULTUN FILL

The nature of the fills of Ch. 6C-6 has already been discussed. Since LG. 2 contains no cultural material, it is of no further interest here. Lot Group 1, though, must derive from the trash of Str. 6C-63:LG. 1a and 1b. It is not surprising, therefore, that the sherds are similar. The few Preclassic sherds occur in the one instance, but not the others, probably because the sample is larger. They are few in number, and thus do not necessarily mean that Str. 6C-63 was built in Preclassic times (though this remains an outside possibility). For purposes of discovering the function of Str. 6C-63, Ch. 6C-6:LG. 1 may be combined with Str. 6C-63:LG. 1a and 1b.

The fill of Ch. 6C-7 also seems to have washed in from nearby. Therefore, it should be useful for dating the period of use of Str. 6C-62, as well as providing clues to the use of that structure.

In Ch. 6C-11, U. 3 and 6 (LG. 2 and 3) predate abandonment of the chultun. Unfortunately, they are devoid of cultural material other than that associated with PD. 231. This deposit gives an approximate date for abandonment. All the other material (LG. 4a–c) probably washed in after abandonment. The absence of Ik and/or Imix sherds, such as occur in LG. 1, probably is an illusion. Most of the sherds from the fill of Chm. 1, where Ik and/or Imix material would most probably be found, were never evaluated.

TABLE 2.269
Group 6C-5: Lot Groups

Feature	Lot Group	Lot	Provenience	Ceramic Evaluation
Str.6C-62 (Op. 66F)	1	3	Surface to bedrock, area of Str. 6C-62 and 63	Lost
Str.6C-63 (Op. 66G)	1a	7	Surface to bedrock W of structure, to 0.50 m E of Ch. 6C-6	Manik and Ik and/or Imix
	1b	1	W of LG. 1a	Ik and/or Imix
Ch.6C-6 (Op. 66G)	1	2-5	Fill, Chm. 1-3	Preclassic, Manik, Ik and/or Imix
	2	6	Fill, Chm. 4	No data
Ch.6C-7 (Op. 66F)	1	1,2	Fill	Ik and/or Imix
Ch.6C-11 (Op. 66F)	1		Surface, near orifice	Ik and/or Imix
	2		U. 3	No data
	3	15	U. 6	No data
	4a	13,14	Fill, Chm. 3	1 Preclassic; Manik
	4b	8-10	Fill, Chm. 2	Manik
	4c	2-7	Fill, Chm. 1	Manik (sherds in top 0.40 m not evaluated)

TABLE 2.270
Structure 6C-63: Artifacts by Lot Group

Study Category	Object	Lot Group	1a	1b
Pottery Vessels	Sherds per cubic meter (lbs)		2.20	0.50
Flaked Chert Artifacts	Elongate biface		1	
	Used flakes		4	
	Unused flakes		4	

TABLE 2.271
Chultun 6C-6: Artifacts by Lot Group

Study Category	Object	Lot Group	1	2
Pottery Vessels	Sherds per cubic meter (lbs)		1.89	0
Flaked Chert Artifacts	Unused flake		1	
Shell and Bone Artifacts	Bone, animal, unworked Bone, human, unworked		4 10	

TABLE 2.272
Chultun 6C-7: Artifacts by Lot Group

Study Category	Provenience	Lot Group	1
Pottery Vessels	Sherds per cubic meter (lbs)		.30
Shell and Bone Artifacts	Bone, animal, unworked		1

TABLE 2.273
Chultun 6C-11: Artifacts by Lot Group

Study Category	Object	Lot Groups					
		1	2	3	4a	4b	4c
Pottery Vessels	Sherds per cubic meter	Not weighed: "abundant"					
Flaked Obsidian Artifacts	Prismatic blade	1					
Ground, Pecked, and Polished Stone Artifacts	Mano Metates	1					2
Shell and Bone Artifacts	Shell, cut fragment				1		

TIME SPANS

Time spans for the structures and chultuns of Gp. 6C-5 are presented in Tables 2.274–2.278. Some comments are needed with respect to the structure time spans, for they seem much simpler than they probably were. For Str. 6C-62, there may have been more than one architectural development, to judge from the several postholes at that locus. Hence, more data might permit subdivision of TS. 2. For Str. 6C-63, trash that accumulated while it was in use (Table 2.269:LG. 1a and 1b) indicates construction at an earlier time than Str. 6C-62, but there is no evidence that it was abandoned sooner. Moreover, the identical alignment of the two structures suggests partial contemporaneity. It stands to reason that if Str. 6C-63 was in use for such a long time, it must have been renovated one or more times. Indeed, Ch. 6C-6, which seems associated with the structures, was altered on one occasion. Hence, TS. 2 of Str. 6C-63 might also be subdivided if more data were available.

Time spans for Gp. 6C-5 as a whole are presented in Table 2.279. These correlations rely heavily on the ceramic data in Table 2.269. Also, the proximity of Ch. 6C-7 to Str. 6C-62 suggests an association of these two features. A similar association between Ch. 6C-6 and Str. 6C-63 seems likely. Structure 6C-63 clearly was built before 6C-62, on the basis of sherds discarded by the users of these structures (these, for Str. 6C-62, are in Ch. 6C-7:LG. 1). The correlation of Ch. 6C-6:TS. 3 with Str. 6C-62:TS. 3 is arbitrary; all that is known is that both postdate the start of Str. 6C-63:TS. 2, but predate the end of that time span.

Problems arise when trying to place the time spans of Ch. 6C-11 into this scheme. The ceramic data (Table 2.269:LG. 1 and PD. 231) suggest abandonment of Ch. 6C-11 before the other chultuns. Since the problematical deposit is redeposited from elsewhere, Ik or Imix ceram-ics could have been in vogue. Yet the presumed construction of Ch. 6C-7, after the appearance of such ceramics, opens the possibility that its construction was necessitated by abandonment of Ch. 6C-11. Speculative though this may be, it is the best that can be done on the basis of the available evidence, and so TS. 3 of Ch. 6C-7 is tentatively seen as following TS. 3 of Ch. 6C-11. Given this, TS. 2 of Ch. 6C-11 would fall into Gp. TS. 2 and 3.

The earliest known construction in Gp. 6C-5 is assigned to Gp. TS. 5. Time span 7 of Ch. 6C-11 is assigned to this on the assumptions that no earlier structures are to be found here, and a chultun would not be constructed where no structures existed. The second assumption seems reasonable, but the first is unproven (note the occasional Preclassic ceramics in Table 2.269). Because of these problems, the placement of the time spans of Ch. 6C-11 in those for Gp. 6C-5 must be regarded as provisional.

In terms of dates, Gp. TS. 5 predates AD 550, when Ik ceramic production began at Tikal. There is no hard evidence that it predates AD 250, when Manik ceramics came into use, except for a very few Preclassic sherds in Ch. 6C-6 and 11, which may relate to Str. 6C-63 or an unknown structure. If they do, this does not mean that the start of TS. 5 was significantly earlier than AD 250.

Group TS. 3 postdates AD 550, but it does not follow that TS. 1 began as late as AD 869. Most other small structures occupied in the last century or so of Late Classic times at Tikal have left traces visible before excavation. Moreover, Ik and/or Imix ceramics are not abundant here, although this could be a factor of sample size as much as anything. Finally, there is no proof that any of the sherds are of Imix vessels. On the basis of experience with both "visible" and "invisible" structures at Tikal, it is likely that Gp. 6C-5 was abandoned long before the collapse of Tikal, but it is impossible to be precise about this.

TABLE 2.274
Structure 6C-62: Time Spans

Time Span	Architectural Development	Unit	Descriptive Data	Lot Group	Ceramics in Vogue
1			Abandonment, with subsequent forest growth		– – – – – – – – – –
2			Use	1	Ik and/or Imix
3	Str. 6C-62	1-10	Construction		

TABLE 2.275
Structure 6C-63: Time Spans

Time Span	Architectural Development	Unit	Descriptive Data	Lot Group	Ceramics in Vogue
1			Abandonment, with subsequent forest growth		--------- Imix?
2			Use	1a	Ik ---------
3	Str. 6C-63	1-3	Construction	1b	Manik

TABLE 2.276
Chultun 6C-6: Time Spans

Time Span	Architectural Development	Construction Stage	Descriptive Data	Lot Group	Ceramics in Vogue
1			Abandonment; gradual filling of Chm. 1-3		---------
2			Use	1	Imix?
3	Ch.6C-6-1st	None defined	Chm. 4 filled and sealed; Chm. 3 probably constructed	2	
4			Use		Ik?
5	Ch. 6C-6-2nd	1	Construction of Chm. 2 or 4		
5	Ch. 6C-6-2nd	2	Construction of Chm. 2 or 4		
5	Ch. 6C-6-2nd	3	Construction of antechamber		Manik?

TABLE 2.277
Chultun 6C-7: Time Spans

Time Span	Architectural Development	Construction Stage	Descriptive Data	Lot Group	Ceramics in Vogue
1			Abandonment; gradual filling	1	-----------
2			Use		Ik and/or Imix
3	Ch. 6C-7	1	Construction of Chm. 2		
3	Ch. 6C-7	2	Construction of orifice and Chm. 1		

TABLE 2.278
Chultun 6C-11: Time Spans

Time Span	Architectural Development	Construction Stage	Chamber	Unit	Special Deposits: Problematical Deposit	Descriptive Data	Lot Group	Ceramics in Vogue
1				1,2, 4,5		Total abandonment of locus, followed by displacement of stone cover by tree root	4a 4b 4c	
2						Continued activity in the area	1	Ik; Imix?
3					231	Abandonment of chultun with stone cover in place		
4				3?,6		Use	2?,3	Manik
5	Ch. 6C-11-1st	1,2?	2?,3			Alteration of chultun to cope with water problem		
6				3?		Use	2?	
7	Ch. 6C-11-2nd	1,2?	1,2?			Construction of chultun with one or possibly two chambers		

TABLE 2.279
Group 6C-5: Time Spans

Gp. 6C-5: Time Span	Str. 6C-62: Time Span (Table 2.274)	Str. 6C-63: Time Span (Table 2.275)	Ch. 6C-6: Time Span (Table 2.276)	Ch. 6C-7: Time Span (Table 2.277)	Ch. 6C-11: Time Span (Table 2.278)
1	1	1	1	1	1
2	2		2	2	
3	3		3	3	2
					3
					4
					5
4		2	4		6
5		3	5		7

Structure 6C-60 Locus

In July 1963, Puleston excavated (as Op. 66D and E) an extensive area around Ch. 6C-9, which is located at 6C:S335 E181 (TR. 11). The only feature mapped here is the chultun. Even after thorough clearing of bush, there was absolutely no surface indication of a structure in the vicinity. The excavations, however, turned up traces of at least three structures (6C-60, 61, and Sub.1), along with another chultun (Ch. 6C-10). Since no more than one structure was occupied at any given time, so far as now known, a group has not been defined.

The terrain here is much like that around Gp. 6C-2 (this report), which is 100 m SW. It slopes very gently to the SW. About 80 m to the W is the Perdido Reservoir. One-hundred meters to the E is Gp. 6C-4 (TR. 21); the only other nearby group is 90 m N.

STRUCTURE 6C-60

South and W of Ch. 6C-9, the presence of at least two structures is indicated by a series of 14 postholes in bedrock, along with an alignment of stone rubble (Fig. 129 and Table 2.280). Six of the postholes almost surely relate to a structure designated as 6C-Sub.1 (see below). Of the remaining eight, all but three are arranged in two lines that may be interpreted as marking the N and W walls of another structure designated as 6C-60. The remainder of the postholes cannot be conclusively associated with either structure, but are thought to relate to 6C-Sub.1.

Of those postholes believed to belong to Str. 6C-60, U. 1–4 form an approximate N-S line. These presumably supported posts for the W wall of a building, with a post for the NW corner standing in U. 4. No other postholes are known N of U. 4, which itself is the largest of these four holes, as might be expected for a corner post. Moreover, this interpretation is consistent with the location of a fifth posthole, U. 5, E of U. 4. A line drawn through U. 5 from U. 4 forms an approximate right angle with the supposed W wall.

Apparently these postholes mark the NW portion of Str. 6C-60. It is not known where the NE, SE, and SW corners stood, except that they must fall outside the excavated area. The structure itself was either square or rectangular, and had essentially the same orientation as Str. 6C-61 (see below).

Two other features support the interpretation given above. One is the presence of a midden, only slightly disturbed, immediately W of the presumed W wall. Such a deposit is to be expected just outside a building. The other is the line of rubble, U. 6, which is just outside the presumed N wall, in line with it. The rubble lies in a shallow trench in bedrock, and may have served to level the area outside the structure. Or, it might be all that remains of either a freestanding, or platform, wall. Such a wall, or platform, could have been all but totally demolished at a later time when bedrock was quarried in this area (see below). Unit 6 would have survived only because it was set below the surrounding bedrock surface.

TABLE 2.280
Structure 2G-60: Posthole
Dimensions (meters)

Posthole	Diameter	Depth
Unit 1	0.09	0.08
Unit 2	0.09	0.07
Unit 3	0.06	0.03
Unit 4	0.15	0.16
Unit 5	0.11	0.10

MISCELLANEOUS DATA

Beneath Str. 6C-60 are traces of quarrying (Fig. 129). Near the presumed N corner are narrow cuts that partially outline what resemble potential masonry blocks. One of these is rectangular, the other beveled (as if for a vault stone). Both suggest blocks that were used for construction in Classic times. Structure 6C-Sub.1:U. 8, a posthole, goes through the apparent vault stone, which may be the reason it was not completely quarried.

About 0.80 m to the S are grooves that outline another rectangular block. Another 0.60 m S of this is a quarry 0.30 m deep, from which masonry blocks had actually been removed. A small groove in one side suggests removal of blocks similar to those begun to the N. Further indications of quarrying are noted in connection with Str. 6C-61.

STRUCTURE 6C-61

This structure lies between Ch. 6C-9 and 10, where portions of its architecture may be seen in a trench excavated between the two chultuns (Fig. 129). These consist of three walls (U. 1–3), a posthole (U. 4), and quarried bedrock (U. 5).

Units 1 and 2 are rubble walls that join at an approximate right angle. Unit 1 extends at least 2.40 m W from this junction; U. 2 runs to the N for a distance of 1.70 m. Here, it is met by a wall that runs E approximately 1.60 m. This latter, U. 3, consists of masonry that has one dressed face, on the S side. Unit 2 appears to be constructed of the same sort of masonry, and the rubble of U. 1 could be the broken-up remains of similar masonry. In any case, the dressed face of U. 3 indicates that this and U. 1 are S walls of a low platform, with U. 2 an E wall. That these were not intended to be freestanding is indicated by the lack of a dressed surface on the inside of U. 3 (the best preserved), and the highly uneven surface of bedrock N of the walls. South of them, on the other hand, is a packed gray stratum of earth (U. 6), now severely churned up by tree roots, which could have served as an informal occupation surface at the level of the base of U. 1.

Unit 4, a square hole in bedrock, suggests that the E

end of U. 3 may be another corner of Str. 6C-61. Its dimensions are 0.24 by 0.24 m and it is 0.16 m in depth. In spite of its peculiar shape, this is interpreted as a hole for a post for an E building wall (see Fig. 126 for other examples of apparently square postholes).

The overall extent of Str. 6C-61 remains unknown, but the approximate location of its NW corner may be indicated by U. 5. This consists of two narrow ledges or "steps" cut into the bedrock, approximately 0.10 m wide (down from NW to SE), which make a right angle complementing the juncture of U. 1 and 2. Bedrock W of this apparent corner is about 0.20 m below the elevation of the top of U. 1, so possibly structure walls were positioned just N and W of these "steps," or even between the two "risers." Given less than 0.20 m of overburden above bedrock, such a wall would have been highly vulnerable to destruction, hence the present lack of remains. If such walls existed, then the steps would have been buried beneath structure fill. The "steps" could be explained, therefore, as a result of quarrying building material. Quarrying stopped just inside the area where the structure walls were to be built; outside, bedrock served as an occupation surface. Situations somewhat akin to this have been seen elsewhere at Tikal (see Str. 4F-3 and 5; TR. 19).

A less likely alternative is that the surface of the structure platform sloped down from SE to NW, with the floor abutting the quarried bedrock, to which one then stepped up. This seems unlikely for, given the present height and collapsed condition of U. 1, this would have amounted to a 0.30 m difference or more in the elevation of the two corners. No comparable situations have been found elsewhere at Tikal and, since the first alternative does fit with situations elsewhere at the site, it is the preferred explanation. A good example is the N part of the E wall of Str. 2G-61 (this report), placed in a vulnerable position relative to Qu. 2G-1. No trace of that wall can now be seen.

MISCELLANEOUS DATA

As was true near Str. 6C-60, there is also evidence here of quarrying (Fig. 129). Some or all of this may have been connected with construction of Str. 6C-61. The most likely instance of this is U. 5, already discussed. Further examples might be U. 7 and 8, 9 m and 7 m SE of the structure, respectively. These areas, from which small amounts of stone appear to have been removed, are covered by rubbish associated with Str. 6C-61 (see below). They could, however, predate the structure. Two more extensive quarries, U. 9 and 11, are located just to the SE (U. 9) and beneath the structure (U. 11). The former was filled by a stratum of gray earth, covered by brown earth, over which U. 6 was laid. Both quarries possibly predate the structure. Since good fill samples were not procured for purposes of ceramic dating, it is impossible to be sure.

STRUCTURE 6C-SUB.1

This structure was located 1.60 m W of Ch. 6C-9, its SE corner beneath Str. 6C-60 (Fig. 129). Five postholes seem surely associated with Sub.1 (Table 2.281). Of these, U. 1, 3, 5, and 9 are of roughly the same diameter. Units 1, 3, and 9 are spaced almost exactly 3 m from one another, in an almost straight line. Taken together, these characteristics indicate that these were probably holes to support the main posts of a building wall. That U. 9 held a corner post is consistent with an absence of any other postholes to the N. The possibility that U. 3 held another is indicated by a lack of another posthole 3 m S, as well as by the position of U. 5. A line drawn through U. 5 to U. 3 forms a right angle with the wall discussed above. Consequently, U. 3 and 9 must mark the SE and NE corners of 6C-Sub.1. The structure was either square or rectangular, with the bulk of it falling W of the excavated area. Its alignment seems to have been closer to true N-S or E-W than Str. 6C-60 and 61, which are aligned closer to the magnetic cardinal directions.

Units 2 and 4 are two very small postholes right next to U. 1 and 3. This same pattern of large and small diameter postholes together has been seen elsewhere at Tikal (see TR. 19:fig. 5), so it seems reasonably sure that U. 2 and 4 pertain to Str. 6C-Sub.1. The purpose of such an arrangement of posts is unknown, and it seems strange that two, but not all three, main posts of the E wall were accompanied by smaller posts. Perhaps, though, a small post did accompany that set in U. 9, only it was not set into bedrock.

Unaccounted for are three other postholes, U. 6, 7, and 8. These could have been associated with Str. 6C-60, 61, or with neither structure. It is believed that they are associated with Str. 6C-Sub.1, as U. 6 and 7 are in line with its presumed S wall, even though outside. They fall 0.30 m and 0.36 m outside, respectively, which compares with the 0.30 m distance of U. 8 from the E wall. Moreover, all three holes are of comparable diameter.

TABLE 2.281
Structure 6C-Sub.1: Posthole
Dimensions (meters)

Posthole	Diameter	Depth
Unit 1	0.16	0.16
Unit 2	0.06	0.04
Unit 3	0.16	0.30
Unit 4	0.06	0.30
Unit 5	0.20	0.20
Unit 6	0.09	0.14
Unit 7	0.08	0.12
Unit 8	0.13	0.09
Unit 9	0.13	0.18

As with Str. 2G-60, the overall dimensions of 6C-Sub.1 are unknown. It seems to have measured about 6.70 m in its N-S dimension.

Miscellaneous Data

Beneath Str. 6C-Sub.1 is a large, curved basin in bedrock, 0.70 m deep (Fig. 129:5). It might be related to the quarrying beneath Str. 6C-60, but probably is not. It differs from the latter in depth, lack of vertical sides, and absence of rectangular corners.

CHULTUN 6C-9

Description

Access to this chultun (Fig. 129, 130a,b; Table 2.282) is through an orifice that has only the slightest indication of a step, on the NE side. No stone cover was found. The neck below the orifice is cylindrical, and opens into the ceiling of Chm. 1. This antechamber is circular in plan, and unusually small.

Chamber 2 is entered from the NW through an entrance restricted on both sides, with a low sill (removed during excavation). The chamber roughly resembles a rectangle with rounded corners. The edges where the ceiling and walls, and walls and floor meet, are slightly squared. Of particular interest is a marked sill, which runs the length of the floor. No other chultun has been discovered at Tikal with such a sill.

Discussion

The chultun, as found, was nearly filled with earth and cultural debris. Over the floor was a deposit that includes some sherds but no other artifacts. Over this was a fairly thick stratum, gray-brown in color, full of sherds, chert flakes, pieces of obsidian, and large biface fragments (most artifacts evidently were not recorded, as few are listed in Table 2.287). This was topped by a deposit of brown earth with few artifacts. The basal layer gives the appearance of having slowly accumulated, whereas the overlying deposit has the appearance of purposeful fill, drawn from nearby trash deposits. The near sterility of the upper layer suggests that some earth washed into the chultun after it was filled.

TABLE 2.282
Chultun 6C-9: Average Dimensions (meters)

Feature	Length	Width	Height	Diameter
Neck	---	---	0.52	0.54
Chamber 1	0.76	0.88	1.00	---
Chamber 2	1.92	1.20	1.06	---
Entrance 1-2	---	0.49	0.60	---

CHULTUN 6C-10

DESCRIPTION

This hitherto unmapped chultun was discovered by a workman quite by accident when Ch. 6C-9 was being excavated. Its orifice is located at 6C:S306 E168.

Access to the chultun (Fig. 130c,d) is through the usual manhole-like orifice, which in this case is somewhat oval. The lip is unstepped. Near the orifice, in topsoil, a roughly square stone slab was found that may have served as a stone cover. The neck beneath the orifice flares downward into Chm. 1, which is round in plan. As found, this antechamber was filled to within 0.50 m of the orifice. The upper portion of this deposit consisted of sterile leaf mold and humus, but deeper down there was .6 lbs of sherds and, just above the SW portion of the floor, some miscellaneous human bones.

Access to the lateral Chm. 2 is through a passage, restricted on the sides, and by a sill on the floor. The floor of Chm. 2 is 0.12 m lower than that of Chm. 1. In plan the chamber is roughly square. In the back is a very rough shelf with holes that extend back into the bedrock. These features most probably are the result of post-abandonment burrowing by animals. The chamber was almost completely filled, and from this came just over a pound of sherds. Also included was Bu. 143.

DISCUSSION

Three factors combine to indicate that this chultun was intentionally filled: (1) the presence of the burial (similar to Bu. 62 in Ch. 2G-2 and Bu. 63 in Ch. 2G-10, this report); (2) the relatively large quantity of sherds in the fill (reminiscent of Ch. 2G-10); and (3) the absence of sherds from a 2-m square excavated around the orifice. Clearly, the sherds in the chultun did not just wash in from outside. The neck was not found filled to the brim because of settling of the fill (reminiscent of Ch. 2G-2), perhaps partly associated with decomposition of the corpse in Chm. 2.

SHERDS AND ARTIFACTS

Lot groups for the structures and chultuns at this locus are defined in Table 2.283. Their content is given in Tables 2.284–2.288.

CONSTRUCTION FILL

Fill samples from these excavations generally leave much to be desired. For the structures near Ch. 6C-9, there appears to have been disturbance following abandonment, so undisturbed fill is virtually non-existent. The one exception may be Str. 6C-Sub.1:LG. 1, from the bedrock pit beneath the structure. The sherds from this are all Preclassic, with Chuen the only identifiable ceramic com-

plex represented. This may have been put in place to level the area for Str. 6C-Sub.1.

The only other fill sample is Str. 6C-61:LG. 1, which contained very few sherds. The latter probably do not date this structure, on the basis of identifiable occupation trash (see below). The likelihood is that the fill was drawn from nearby deposits (it virtually duplicates Str. 6C-Sub .1:LG. 1), which could have been quite old by then.

MATERIAL ABOVE LIVING LEVELS

In this category are Str. 6C-60:LG. 1 and 2. The former appears to be a small midden, perhaps slightly disturbed. The whole deposit is located just outside what is thought to have been the N wall of the structure, but falls both inside and outside the S wall for Str. 6C-Sub.1. Clearly, the midden represents trash associated with the use of 6C-60. It contains Cauac sherds and a few utilitarian artifacts.

Lot Group 2, which overlies bedrock elsewhere around Str. 6C-60 and Ch. 6C-9, is mixed. Most of the sherds are Preclassic, primarily Cauac and Cimi. These may come from the midden, as well as other disturbed occupation deposits. The handful of early and later Classic sherds, particularly the early, probably derive from the use of Str. 6C-61 following abandonment of 6C-60. As one moves NW towards 6C-61, the quantity of Manik sherds picks up considerably, and Preclassic sherds drop off in quantity (illustrated graphically in Fig. 132). Structure 6C-61:LG. 2a, immediately NW of Str. 6C-60:LG. 2, is composed almost wholly of Manik sherds. The latter lot group, on the other hand, contains few such sherds. By the SE corner of Str. 6C-61, sherd quantities drop off markedly, to pick up again about 4.50 m to the NW of the structure (LG. 2b). The latter cannot be dated, but presumably, it should duplicate the material in LG. 2a. At any rate, this pattern of deposition is wholly consistent with the presence of a structure, litter from which was being strewn around close by. There can be little doubt that LG. 2a and 2b are trash from Str. 2G-61, and the sherds should date its use.

CHULTUN FILL

Material from Ch. 6C-9 has been subdivided into three lot groups. Lot Group 1a, in the bottom, seems to be debris that gradually accumulated over the floor, possibly while it was in use, but more probably afterwards. All of the sherds appear to be from Cauac vessels. The fill that overlay this (LG. 1b) is similar to LG. 1 of Str. 6C-60, both in abundance and type of material. The ceramics pertain to the Chuen and Cauac Complexes, with possibly a few Manik sherds. Over this (LG. 1c) is a natural accumulation, with Preclassic and Early Classic sherds. Clearly, Early Classic ceramics washed into the chultun from the surrounding area.

As already noted, Ch. 6C-10 was filled on purpose, so this deposit has not been subdivided. The sherds in it are almost all from Preclassic vessels; indeed they may all be. The presence of a few likely Ik and/or Imix sherds makes it possible that the chultun was filled during Intermediate or Late Classic times, but mostly with material from near Str. 6C-60.

TABLE 2.283
Structure 6C-60 Locus: Lot Groups

Feature	Lot Group	Lot	Provenience	Ceramic Evaluation
Str. 6C-60 (Op. 66D)	1	15,16,46	W of structure	Cauac
	2	1-3,6-11, 17,18,20-27,31	Surface to bedrock, structure locus and N	Cauac, Cimi, a few Manik and Ik and/or Imix
Str. 6C-61 (Op. 66D)	1	40,41	Unsealed fill	Preclassic, including Chuen
	2a	32-39,50	Surface to bedrock SE of structure	Manik (including late), a few Preclassic and possible Ik and/or Imix
	2b	42,44	Surface to bedrock NW of structure	?
Str. 6C-Sub.1 (Op. 66D)	1	19	Pit beneath structure locus	Preclassic including Chuen
Ch. 6C-9 (Op. 66D)	1a	12,29,30	On chultun floor	Preclassic (including Cauac)
	1b	4,5,28,60	Fill, above 1a	Chuen, Cauac, possibly Manik
	1c	13,14	Brown earth above 1b	Preclassic and Manik
Ch. 6C-10 (Op. 66E)	1	1	Surface around orifice	No data
	2	2-5	Fill	Preclassic (including Cimi); possible Ik and/or Imix

TABLE 2.284
Structure 6C-60: Artifacts by Lot Group

Study Category	Object	Lot Group	
		1	2
Pottery Vessels	Sherds per cubic meter (lbs)	8.3	1.9
Flaked Chert Artifacts	Ovate bifaces	3	
	Used flakes	2	

TABLE 2.285
Structure 6C-61: Artifacts by Lot Group

Study Category	Object	Lot Group		
		1	2a	2b
Pottery Vessels	Sherds per cubic meter (lbs)	.20	.90*	.40*
Flaked Chert Artifacts	Unused flake		1	
Flaked Obsidian Artifacts	Core		1	
	Prismatic blade		1	
Ground, Pecked, and Polished Stone Artifacts	Mano		1	
	Hammer stone		1	
Shell and Bone Artifacts	Bone, animal, unworked	Miscellaneous		

*see Fig. 132

TABLE 2.286
Structure 6C-Sub.1: Artifacts by Lot Group

Study Category	Object	Lot Group 1
Pottery Vessels	Sherds per cubic meter (lbs)	Not recorded
Flaked Chert Artifacts	Unused flake	1

TABLE 2.287
Chultun 6C-9: Artifacts by Lot Group

Study Category	Object	Lot Group		
		1a	1b	1c
Pottery Vessels	Sherds per cubic meter (lbs)	11.9	8.0	Not recorded
Other Pottery Artifacts	Stamp		1	
Flaked Chert Artifacts	Blade core		1	
	Unclassifiable biface	1		

TABLE 2.288
Chultun 6C-10: Artifacts by Lot Group

Study Category	Object	Lot Group	
		1	2
Pottery Vessels	Sherds per cubic meter (lbs)	0	1.7
Flaked Chert Artifacts	Unused flakes	2	
Shell and Bone Artifacts	Bone, animal, unmodified	6	
	Bone, human, unmodified	Miscellaneous	

TIME SPANS

Time spans for the structures, chultuns, and the locus as a whole are presented in Tables 2.289 through 2.294. The reasoning behind the correlations in Table 2.294 requires comment. The evidence that Str. 6C-Sub.1 preceded Str. 6C-60 in time is as follows. Beneath Str. 6C-Sub.1 is a bedrock pit with a fill that contains Chuen sherds (Str. 6C-Sub.1:LG. 1; Table 2.283). This was not part of the later quarry activity beneath Str. 6C-60, as indicated by its different character, and the presence of Early and Ik and/or Imix sherds over the later quarry. The Chuen fill, then, could well be for Str. 6C-Sub.1. In addition, there is a Cauac midden (Str. 6C-60:LG. 1; Table 2.283), which, as pointed out, can only be associated with Str. 6C-60. It is not known whether or not 6C-60 was specifically intended as a replacement for Str. 6C-Sub.1, but this is a real possibility. In the absence of any clear indication to the contrary, the abandonment of the one structure is correlated with construction of the other (locus TS. 6), although a time gap may have occurred. However, since 6C-Sub.1 apparently was constructed after Chuen ceramics came into vogue (350 BC at Tikal), and Str. 6C-60 was in use while Cauac ceramics were in use, the idea of the one structure as a replacement for the other seems reasonable.

Structure 6C-60 seems to have been abandoned after the appearance of Cimi ceramics (about AD 150 at Tikal), which are present in LG. 2, but at the time of the appearance of Manik ceramics (about AD 250). Manik sherds are found in small numbers only in the area quarried at the locus of Str. 6C-60, and increase in quantity as one approaches Str. 6C-61 (Fig. 132). As already discussed, this material (LG. 2a) dates the use of Str. 6C-61. So again, what is indicated is abandonment of one structure and replacement by another.

Abandonment of Str. 6C-60 marks the start of locus TS. 4. It would appear that a period of time separated this event from construction of Str. 6C-61 (locus TS. 3), though this hiatus may have been brief (a matter, perhaps,

of only a few weeks). This is suggested, first, by the presence of Manik and Ik and/or Imix sherds directly over the quarried area at the locus of Str. 6C-60. The structure was apparently removed so that the quarrying preceded accumulation of trash from Str. 6C-61. Consistent with this, the fill of Ch. 6C-9 contains sherds and artifacts quite similar to those in the midden of Str. 6C-60 (LG. 1). There are, though, a few Manik sherds as well. This suggests that, when the quarrying took place, nearby trash (and probably fill) from this structure was simply scraped into the chultun as bedrock was exposed. The few Manik sherds suggest contemporaneity with construction of Str. 6C-61.

The problem so far as the chultun is concerned develops when LG. 1a, located on its floor, is considered. If it postdates abandonment, then the chultun may have been abandoned before Str. 6C-60. This seems unlikely, though, in view of the hazard posed by an open chultun near a structure in use. More likely, the structure and chultun were in use together and were abandoned together, after which nearby trash from around the structure washed into the open chultun. Nor is it known when the chultun was constructed. This could have been any time prior to locus TS. 5. In size and form, the chultun bears a resemblance to some Early Classic chultuns. This might suggest construction in locus TS. 6, rather than for use with the much older Str. 6C-Sub.1. Overall, the opinion that the chultun was built and used by the occupants of Str. 6C-60 seems reasonable, but in the last analysis the earliest chultun time spans float in relation to locus time spans.

As there are problems with the time spans of Ch. 6C-9, so are there problems with those of Ch. 6C-10. Its position relative to 6C-61 suggests an association with that structure, leading to the hypothesis that, as Str. 6C-61 replaced 6C-60, so Ch. 6C-10 was constructed (in locus TS. 3) to replace Ch. 6C-9. Similarly, as Ch. 6C-9 was filled shortly after abandonment of Str. 60, so Ch. 6C-10 was filled (with the interment of Bu. 143) when Str. 6C-61 was abandoned. The problem with this interpretation is that it is not certain if the presence of material in the fill of Ch. 6C-10 is later than Preclassic. There are a few possible Ik/Imix sherds, however, which could be analogues to the Manik sherds in Ch. 6C-9. Hence, it may be that old debris in the vicinity was used to fill the chultun, but a few sherds from pottery in use at the time were also included. Consistent with this, a few Ik/Imix sherds occur SE of Str. 6C-61 (Str. 6C-60:LG. 2, mostly material from Str. 6C-60, but some from Str. 6C-61; and possibly Str. 6C-61:LG. 2a). So it appears as if this structure was abandoned just after the appearance of Ik ceramics, as Str. 6C-

60 was abandoned near the beginning of Manik ceramic production. Thus the hypothesis that Ch. 6C-10, with Str. 6C-61, was constructed in locus TS. 3, and used in locus TS. 2, seems reasonable, even though it cannot be conclusively proven.

Following from the above, the last identifiable event at this locus was probably the interment of Bu. 143 and filling of Ch. 6C-10, which marks the start of locus TS. 1. This was associated with abandonment of Str. 6C-61, and this took place probably just after AD 550, which dates the appearance of Ik ceramics.

TABLE 2.289
Structure 6C-60: Time Spans

Time Span	Architectural Development	Unit	Descriptive Data	Lot Group		Ceramics in Vogue
1			Total abandonment of area with forest growth			Ik
						- - - - - - - -
2			Abandonment, followed by quarrying and other intermittent activity			Manik
						- - - - - - - -
3			Use	1	2	(Cimi)
						Cauac
4	Str. 6C-60	1-6	Construction			

TABLE 2.290
Structure 6C-61: Time Spans

Time Span	Architectural Development	Unit	Descriptive Data	Lot Group	Ceramics in Vogue
1			Total abandonment of area with forest growth		- - - - - - - - - -
					Ik
2			Use	2a,2b	- - - - - - - - -
					Manik
3	Str. 6C-61	1-6	Construction	1	
					- - - - - - - - - -
4		7-11	Earlier activity, including quarrying		Chuen-Cimi

TABLE 2.291
Structure 6C-Sub.1: Time Spans

Time Span	Architectural Development	Unit	Descriptive Data	Lot Group	Ceramics in Vogue
1			Total abandonment of area with forest growth		
2			Intermittent later activity		Manik, Ik, and Imix
3			Activity associated with use of Str. 6C-60		(Cimi) Cauac
4			Destruction of Sub.1		
5			Use		
6	Str. 6C-Sub.1	1-5; 6-8?	Construction	1	Chuen

TABLE 2.292
Chultun 6C-9: Time Spans

Time Span	Architectural Development	Construction Stage	Descriptive Data	Lot Group	Ceramics in Vogue
1			Accumulation of later fill	1c	
2			Purposeful filling of chultun	1b	Manik
3			Abandonment and accumulation of debris	1a	
4			Use		Cauac (Cimi)
5	Ch. 6C-9	1	Construction of Chm. 2		
		2	Construction of Chm. 1		

TABLE 2.293
Chultun 6C-10: Time Spans

Time Span	Architectural Development	Construction Stage	Special Deposits: Burial	Descriptive Data	Lot Group	Ceramics in Vogue
1				Later slumping of fill		----------
2			143	Chultun purposely filled	2	Ik
3				Use	1	----------
4		1		Construction of Chm. 2		Manik
	Ch. 6C-10	2		Construction of Chm. 1		

TABLE 2.294
Correlation of Time Spans for All Features of Structure 6C-60 Locus

Locus Time Span	Str. 6C-60: Time Span (Table 2.289)	Str. 6C-61: Time Span (Table 2.290)	Str. 6C-Sub.1 Time Span (Table 2.291)	Ch. 6C-9: Time Span (Table 2.292)	Ch. 6C-10: Time Span (Table 2.293)
					1
1	1	1	1		2
2		2		1	3
3		3		2	4
4	2	4	2	3	
5	3		3	4	
6	4		4	5?	
7			5		
8			6		

Group 7C-1

Group 7C-1 is located in Sq. 7C of the Tikal site map (TR. 11), S65 E154. As mapped in 1960, the group bears a strong resemblance to Gp. 4F-3. Two structures, 7C-3 and 4, are arranged around the same two sides of a plaza (Fig. 133), as are Str. 4F-21 and 47 in Gp. 4F-3 (Fig. 99). The group was excavated by Haviland in June 1963 as Op. 67C in order to determine just how close this resemblance actually was, and to see if structures similar to 4F-48 and 49 were located off the ends of the two structures. None were found. Chultun 7C-3, 20 m SE of the group, might be considered part of it and was excavated (as Op. 66B).

The terrain in this area is very much like that occupied by Gp. 6C-2 (this report), which is about 140 m to the N. The ground slopes very gradually down to the W. Just N of the group is an extensively quarried area. About 50 m to the E is an Early Classic habitation site (Str. 7C-62 locus, this report), and another 50 m to the SE is a group that includes some small, apparently range-type structures (Gp. 7C-5, this report). Group 7C-2 (this report) is located 50 m to the W. Another group is only 60 m away to the SW (Gp. 7C-4, this report). The entire area, therefore, was fairly heavily built up.

STRUCTURE 7C-3-2ND

This structure (Fig. 134), on the N edge of the plaza, apparently was built in four main stages. First (CS. 4), two courses of masonry for the rear and end walls were set in place, on bedrock in some places, and on a thin stratum of earth over bedrock in others. The walls were stabilized by gray earth fill, dumped against them on the inside. Then, more fill, of a light brown color, was dumped in place. This fill extends out beneath the plaza area to the S, which means that the plaza was built up at the same time as the structure. Unit 1, a light pause-line, covers this fill, and marks the end of this construction stage.

As CS. 3, more fill was dumped, from the rear wall S out into the plaza area. Unit 2, a light-colored, stony pause-line, marks the end of this stage. It runs N from just below the plaza surface to disappear about 1 m from the back wall. Its level surface indicates that the fill was purposely leveled as the base surface for the plaza floor and the front wall of the building platform.

The one-level platform was completed as CS. 2. The front wall, of a single course of masonry, was erected on U. 2. Brown fill, similar to that of CS. 3 and probably from the same source, was placed inside the walls above U. 2. Structure 7C-3-2nd:Fl. 1, which ranges up to 7 cm in thickness, was then laid from the top of the front wall and over the fill and masonry of the rear wall. A plaza floor (U. 3) was laid over U. 2; it abuts and turns up to the front wall of the structure.

A building of perishable materials was apparently completed as CS. 1. Evidence for the existence of such a building is provided by U. 4, an apparent posthole through the NE corner of Str. 7C-3-2nd:Fl. 1. The floor is in poor shape in that area, probably because roots gained entrance to the hole and then broke up the pavement. But it does appear that there is a definite hole through the surface. The main corner posts must have been set in the course of CS. 3 or 4 for the floor to run up to them. The rest of the building was completed after the floor was laid.

STRUCTURE 7C-3-1ST

After a period of time, the building platform of 2nd was provided with an upper level (Fig. 134). This must have required three construction stages: one (CS. 3) to at least partially dismantle the existing building; another (CS. 2) to build the new level, and a final one (CS. 1) to reconstruct the building.

All the walls for the new platform level are based on the surface of Str. 7C-3-2nd:Fl. 1. The front wall was constructed of two masonry veneers with a hearting of rubble. The inner veneer is not as carefully dressed as was the outer veneer. The other walls are badly broken up, but they may have been constructed in the same manner. A fill of earth and trash was placed within the walls. Structure 7C-3-1st:Fl. 1, which probably consisted of an upper and lower surface, was laid for this new platform level. The lower surface was laid directly on the older floor, in union with the base of the front wall for the upper platform level. Another surface, since disintegrated, must have been laid over the fill of the upper level.

MISCELLANEOUS DATA

East of the structure, bedrock is badly broken up by tree roots. In the axial trench (Fig. 134b), however, the bedrock appears to have been quarried at some time. Whether it was in conjunction with construction at this locus is unknown. Undoubtedly, it was part of the same quarrying operation shown on the map (TR. 11) immediately N of Str. 7C-3. Thus, this quarry predates construction of 7C-3, and is far too extensive just to have provided stone for construction in Gp. 7C-1. The quarrying may have preceded construction by no great amount of time, however.

STRUCTURE 7C-4

The first step in construction (CS. 3) was to build front and end walls for this structure (Fig. 135). These rest on bedrock, which is quite near the surface here. A light-colored fill (U. 1) may have been dumped within these walls, or the natural earth cover of bedrock in the area may simply have been dug away, except where it was

TABLE 2.295
Chultun 7C-3: Average Dimensions (meters)

Feature	Length	Width	Height	Minimum Diameter	Maximum Diameter
Neck	---	---	0.27	0.46	0.46
Chm. 1	---	---	1.04	1.16	1.30
Chm. 2	---	---	1.30	1.54	2.50
Entrance 1-2	0.10	0.67	1.10	---	---

to be enclosed by the structure walls. The latter seems less likely, but U. 1 does continue W beyond the back wall of the structure, which was built upon it. Moreover, cultural material is quite scarce within it, although this is also true of the fill of Str. 7C-3-2nd. A final decision on this point cannot be made.

Once the front and end walls were prepared, an upper platform level was built (as CS. 2). The walls for this platform rest on U. 1. The surface of U. 1 continued to serve as an informal living surface W of the structure. A fill of earth and trash was placed within the walls.

The remains of two floors were discovered in excavation. Floor 1 is represented by a surface over U. 1, in union with the base of the front wall for the upper platform level. A projection of this pavement to the E reaches the top of the front wall of the structure. An upper level of Fl. 1, since disintegrated, must have covered the fill of the upper platform level. Here, there was no overburden after abandonment to protect such a floor from the elements. Unit 2 is a plaza floor, in union with the front wall of the structure. It was laid directly on bedrock, and actually should be assigned to CS. 3.

A final stage (CS. 1) is inferred for completion of a building of perishable materials. No evidence was sought, nor was any found, which would indicate that such a building stood on this platform. Since Str. 7C-3 consisted in part of such a building, it is likely that the same was true of this one.

MISCELLANEOUS DATA

Bedrock was never modified where it was exposed in the axial trench. It had been quarried where the N end wall of the structure is located, however. This was probably part of the same quarrying activity discussed in relation to Str. 7C-3.

In a test pit S of the structure, two round holes were found in bedrock (U. 3 and 4). Unit 4 contained PD. 99, which is discussed in section III of this report. Unit 3 is a smaller hole, 0.10 m deep. Its significance is not known, but perhaps other postholes would be found beyond the excavated area, which would indicate that a small building

stood here. This is speculative without further excavation, but such a structure might have been analogous to Str. 4F-49 or 6E-163 (both this report), but in this case there was no building platform. Another possibility is that U. 3 relates to an otherwise unknown Early Classic structure with which PD. 99 was associated.

CHULTUN 7C-3

DESCRIPTION

The plan of this chultun (Fig. 136a and Table 2.295) is essentially the same as that of Ch. 2G-5, 3F-6 (this report), and a number of other two-chamber chultuns. A round orifice opens through a neck into the ceiling of the antechamber. There is no flare to the sides of the neck. Around the orifice, on the surface of bedrock, is a partial ring of rubble (U. 1) that appears to have served as a rough retaining wall to keep earth from falling into the chultun. The antechamber is round in plan. Its floor turns up to nearly vertical walls, which are differentiated from the ceiling. An entrance to the E gives access to Chm. 2.

Once the orifice, neck, and antechamber were completed (CS. 2), a single lateral chamber was dug out of bedrock to the E. The entrance to this from the antechamber is constricted, with a sill that continues up the sides, at an angle, to the ceiling. The entrance thus resembles a tilted hatchway. Chamber 2 is larger than Chm. 1. Its plan is irregular, but approaches an oval shape. The floor, 0.30 m lower than that of the antechamber, is quite level. The walls rise nearly vertically for a short distance, then arch over to form a domed ceiling.

DISCUSSION

Were the occupants of Gp. 7C-1 using this chultun? Its distance of 20 m from the SE corner of Gp. 7C-1 is twice that of Ch. 2G-5 from Gp. 2G-1. Certainly, it could have been used by the occupants of Gp. 7C-1, but since the chultun is only 25 m from another group of structures to the E, it might perhaps have been used by the occupants of that group. A decision one way or the other is impossible at this point.

When found, Ch. 7C-3 was almost completely filled with brown earth (Fig. 136b). The consistency of this, as well as its arrangement, indicates that it washed into the chultun over the years after abandonment. A few stones in the fill probably were once part of the rubble ring around the orifice.

SHERDS AND ARTIFACTS

Lot groups for Gp. 7C-1 are defined in Table 2.296, with content in Tables 2.297–2.299.

CONSTRUCTION FILL

Sherds and artifacts were present in the fills of Str. 7C-3 (LG. 1) and Str. 7C-4 (LG. 1a and 1b), but not in abundance. Although the majority of the sherds in both cases are from Manik vessels, Ik and/or Imix sherds occur in both instances. Those from Str. 7C-4 are surely referable to the Ik Complex; those from Str. 7C-3 cannot be more specifically identified. Lot Group 2, from Str. 7C-3, contains more cultural material, as one might expect if it originated as trash associated with Str. 7C-3-2nd.

MATERIAL ABOVE LIVING LEVELS

Potential occupation refuse is not abundant from this group, and everywhere there has been contamination from structure collapse. The best deposit is Str. 7C-4:LG. 2b, found just N of that structure. This contains a mixture of utilitarian artifacts, bone, and sherds. The latter are from Imix vessels, and show a high frequency of utilitarian forms. Clearly, this deposit stems from an incidental accumulation of refuse, and should date the use of Str. 7F-4.

Much smaller deposits occur E of Str. 7F-3 (LG. 3b) and S of Str. 7F-4 (LG. 3a).

CHULTUN FILL

As previously noted, the material in the chultun has washed in since abandonment. Not surprisingly, the cultural material is just like that from Gp. 7C-1, which lies uphill from the chultun. The ceramics are a mixture of Early to Late Classic Complexes.

MATERIAL FROM OTHER SOURCES

In the test pit S of Str. 7F-4 (LG. 3b), the material in the earth that covers bedrock to a depth of 0.30 m is quite different from that in the overlying earth, or other material in the group. The sherds are all from Manik vessels. This, the presence of some Manik sherds in the structure fills, and the presence of at least one posthole in the test pit combine to suggest an Early Classic occupation at this locus that predates the known construction.

TIME SPANS

The time spans for the two structures of Gp. 7C-1 are presented in Tables 2.300 and 2.301. These are combined into group time spans in Table 2.303. The crucial correlation here is between TS. 5 of Str. 7C-3 and TS. 3 of Str. 7C-4. Otherwise, the table is clear from the evidence just discussed. Three factors indicate that Str. 7C-3-2nd and 7C-4 were constructed at the same time. First, a single pavement floor was found in front of both structures. This suggests that the plaza never had more than one floor, of which the two portions found are remnants. Second, there is a basic similarity of masonry between the two structures. This has two well-dressed faces, but otherwise tends to be irregular. The masonry for 7C-3-1st differs from this. Finally, there is a fundamental similarity between fills. Unfortunately, the Ik and/or Imix sherds from Str. 7C-3-2nd (Table 2.296) cannot be specifically identified as to complex, but those from Str. 7C-4 appear referable to the Ik Complex, which presumably dates this construction to Gp. TS. 5. It is obvious that the structures continued in use while Imix ceramics were in production (Table 2.296; Str. 7C-4:LG. 2b). Unfortunately, there is no way to tell if 7F-3-1st dates before or after the appearance of such ceramics, though the latter interpretation is perhaps more likely.

Evidence for occupation that preceded construction of 7C-3-2nd and 7C-4 consists of the numerous Manik sherds (Table 2.296) and one or two postholes S of Str. 7C-4. This is the basis for Gp. TS. 6. Apparently, one or more structures stood at this locus, while Manik ceramics were in use. Since next to nothing is known about this earliest occupation, separate time spans for construction and use have not been defined, nor have any formal numbers been given to any proposed early structures.

The time spans of Ch. 7C-3 (Table 2.302) unfortunately cannot be correlated with those for the group, as it is impossible to be sure when the chultun was constructed. During the latter days of the existence of the group, however, it was in use. For lack of any other indication, TS. 3 of the chultun is placed in Gp. TS. 6.

In summary, there seems to have been an occupation at this locus that started between AD 250 and 550, the dates for the Manik Ceramic Complex at Tikal. This probably began nearer the later date, since there is no huge amount of Manik material. Occupation continued at this locus after AD 700, which dates the start of Imix ceramic production, but ended by AD 869, the end of that complex.

TABLE 2.296
Group 7C-1: Lot Groups

Feature	Lot Group	Lot	Provenience	Ceramic Evaluation
Str. 7C-3 (Op. 67C)	1	9	Sealed fill of 2nd	Mostly Manik, some Ik and/or Imix
	2	4	Unsealed fill of 1st	Mostly Manik, some Ik and/or Imix
	3a	1	Surface to floor level over plaza and lower platform level	Ik and/or Imix
	3b	2	Surface to bedrock E of structure	1 Preclassic, Manik, mostly Ik and/or Imix
Str. 7C-4 (Op. 67C)	1a	7	Unsealed fill	Mostly Manik, some Ik and/or Imix
	1b	11	Unsealed fill of U. 1	Manik and Ik
	2a	6	E of structure, surface to floor of plaza	Manik and Ik and/or Imix
	2b	3	N of structure, surface to bedrock	1 Preclassic, some Manik, mostly Imix
	3a	5	S test pit, upper 0.30 m	1 Manik, Ik, and/or Imix
	3b	8	S test pit, lower 0.30 m	Manik
Ch. 7C-3 (Op. 66B)	1	1-11	Chultun fill	Preclassic, Manik, and Ik and/or Imix

TABLE 2.297
Structure 7C-3: Artifacts by Lot Group

Study Category	Object	Lot Groups			
		1	2	3a	3b
Pottery Vessels	Sherds	Not weighed			
Other Pottery Artifacts	Miscellaneous modeled sherd				1
Flaked Chert Artifacts	Irregular, retouched flake			1	
	Point-retouched flake			1	
	Unused flakes			4	3
Flaked Obsidian Artifacts	Prismatic blades			2	1
Shell and Bone Artifacts	Shell, unworked				1
	Bone, animal, worked				1
	Bone, human, unworked				1

TABLE 2.298
Structure 7C-4: Artifacts by Lot Group

Study Category	Object	Lot Groups					
		1a	1b	2a	2b	3a	3b
Pottery Vessels	Sherds	Not weighed					
Other Pottery Artifacts	Censer					1	
	Miscellaneous formed object				1		
Flaked Chert Artifacts	Ovate bifaces				2		1
	Point-retouched flake					1	
	Unused core				1		
	Used flakes				4		
	Unused flakes				17	2	
Flaked Obsidian Artifacts	Unclassifiable biface				1		
	Thin biface (green)				1		
	Prismatic blades	2			8		3
	Retouched flake (green)					1	
Ground, Pecked, and Polished Stone Artifacts	Mano	1					
	Metates		1		1		
	Rubbing stone				1		
	Barkbeater	1					
Shell and Bone Artifacts	Bone, worked				1	1	
	Bone, human, unworked				1		1

TABLE 2.299
Chultun 7C-3: Artifacts by Lot Group

Study Category	Object	Lot Groups 1
Pottery Vessels	Sherds	Not weighed
Flaked Chert Artifacts	Unused flakes	3
	Nodule	1
Flaked Obsidian Artifacts	Prismatic blade	1
Ground, Pecked, and Polished Stone Artifacts	Unclassifiable artifact	1
Shell and Bone Artifacts	Bone, animal, unmodified	12

TABLE 2.300
Structure 7C-3: Time Spans

Time Span	Architectural Development	Construction Stage	Floor	Unit	Descriptive Data	Lot Group		Ceramics in Vogue
1					Abandonment and ruin			
2					Use	3b		
3	Str.7C-3-1st	1			Reconstruction of building of perishable material	2	3a	Imix
		2	1		Construction of upper platform level			
		3			Existing building partially or totally dismantled			
4					Use			
5	Str.7C-3-2nd	1			Construction of building of perishable materials	1		Ik
		2	2	3,4	Completion of building platform			
		3		2	Completion of base surface			
		4		1	Construction of rear and end walls; first fill operations			
6					Earlier activity			Manik

TABLE 2.301
Structure 7C-4: Time Spans

Time Span	Architectural Development	Construction Stage	Floor	Unit	Special Deposits: Problematical Deposit	Descriptive Data	Lot Group		Ceramics in Vogue
1						Abandonment and ruin	2b,3a		
2						Use			Imix
3	Str.7C-4	1				Construction of building of perishable materials		2a	Ik
		2	1			Construction of upper platform level	1a,b		
		3		1,2,3?		Construction of front and end walls, with fill			
4					99	Earlier activity	3b		Manik

TABLE 2.302
Chultun 7C-3: Time Spans

Time Span	Architectural Development	Construction Stage	Descriptive Data	Lot Group	Ceramics in Vogue
1			Abandonment and accumulation of fill	1	
2			Use		Imix
					Ik
3	Ch. 7C-3	1	Construction of inner chamber (Chm. 2)		Manik?
		2	Construction of orifice, neck, and antechamber (Chm. 1)		

TABLE 2.303
Group 7C-1: Time Spans

Group Time Span	Str. 7C-3: Time Span (Table 2.300)	Str. 7C-4: Time Span (Table 2.301)	Ch. 7C-3: Time Span (Table 2.302)
1	1	1	1
2	2		
3	3		
4	4	2	
5	5	3	
6	6	4	2
			3

Group 7C-2

Group 7C-2 is located at 7C:S80 E78, 50 m W of Gp. 7C-1 (this report). Other groups of structures are located 24 m to the S (Gp. 7C-4, this report), and 60 m to the NW. As mapped in 1960 (TR. 11), the group consists of four structures, 7C-5 through 8, arranged around the four sides of a raised platform (Fig. 137). The one on the E, 7C-5, looks slightly larger than the others. The terrain here is a bit lower, but very much like that around Gp. 7C-1.

In June 1963, Haviland tested Str. 7C-7 as Op. 67B, for sequence. A year before this, a test pit (Op. 39D) had been dug in the group platform. Since the structure seems comparable to dozens of others excavated in 1961 and 1963, since the arrangement of structures is so similar to other situations, and since the structure excavated was dated as Late Classic, no further work was deemed necessary here.

STRUCTURE 7C-7-2ND

The earliest structure on the W side of Plat. 7C-2 was a one-level platform suitable for support of a building of perishable materials (Fig. 138). The walls were based on a dark earth fill that contains many pebbles. This fill was apparently placed on the surface of Plat. 7C-2:U. 3 (see below) at the time of construction, for it is continuous with the fill within the structure walls. The fill of the platform was later covered by Str. 7C-7-2nd:Fl. 1, which on the basis of projection of its surviving surface, ran from the tops of the platform walls. Platform 7C-2:U. 4 abuts and turns up to the lower portion of the front platform

wall. This pavement was based on the same fill as that within the structure.

No evidence was sought, and none was found, for the proposition that a building of perishable material stood on this platform. Because this platform is similar to others that did support such buildings, this one probably did as well (see TR. 20B). On this assumption, the platform was built as one stage of construction (No. 2), a building as another (No. 1).

STRUCTURE 7C-7-1ST

After a period of use, the platform was provided with an upper level. The front wall for this was set on the floor of Str. 7C-7-2nd, 1.08 m W of the front structure wall. Nothing more survives of this upper level, because the structure is located on the downhill side of the group, and so was particularly vulnerable to erosion. Presumably, a pavement once covered the upper platform level. Assumed stages involved in the construction of 7C-7-1st are CS. 3 for demolition of the earlier building; CS. 2 for construction of the new platform level; and CS. 1 for construction of a new building.

PLATFORM 7C-2-2ND

The supporting platform for Gp. 7C-2 was investigated beneath Str. 7C-7 and in a test pit towards the center of the platform. The earliest known architectural development for Plat. 7C-2 is represented by a floor remnant, U. 3, on which the fill for Str. 7C-7-2nd was later placed (Fig. 138b). The surface of this floor was burned at one time or another. It is not known how far W the pavement ran, but it does continue E beyond the locus of Str. 7C-7. Apparently, Plat. 7C-2-2nd was in use prior to construction of Str. 7C-7-2nd. Thus, one or more structures were in use in Gp. 7C-2 before any structure was built on the W edge of the supporting platform.

Unit 3 overlies U. 2, a stratum of gray earth and pebbles. This probably is deliberately placed fill for the plaza. It in turn overlies U. 1, a thin stratum of brown earth over bedrock. Unit 1 probably is natural earth that was buried beneath the fill.

PLATFORM 7C-2-1ST

The only thing known about this architectural development is that its floor was raised some 0.26 m in height. This new surface is represented by U. 4 (Fig. 138b), which abuts and turns up to the front wall of Str. 7C-7-2nd. The fill of U. 4 is continuous with that of the structure. Therefore, the construction of the structure and alteration of Plat. 7C-2 were parts of the same overall operation.

SHERDS AND ARTIFACTS

Cultural material recovered from Gp. 7C-2 is listed in Tables 2.305 and 2.306; lot groups are defined in Table 2.304.

CONSTRUCTION FILL

The earliest material is partially sealed by the floor of Plat. 7C-2-2nd, on which the structure was later built (Plat.

7C-2:LG. 1). It is also the best sample, for material is not so plentiful in LG. 1 and 2 from the structure fills. The sherds in these structure lot groups are also indeterminate. Presumably, they derive from trash deposits associated with earlier structures elsewhere in the group with which Plat. 7C-2-2nd was associated. Material in Plat. 7C-2:LG. 1 probably comes from trash in a nearby group.

MATERIAL ABOVE LIVING LEVELS

No middens were found near Str. 7C-7. Perhaps some material, representative of an incidental accumulation from the last use of the structure, might be included in LG. 3a and 3b, in front of, and behind it. Since destruction of the upper platform level is so complete, however, material in these lot groups most likely comes from the fill of Str. 7C-7-1st. Of course, the cultural material, which is primarily of a utilitarian nature, might derive from the occupation of earlier structures in Gp. 7C-2, even Str. 7C-7-2nd.

TIME SPANS

Time spans for Str. 7C-7 are defined in Table 2.307, and those for Plat. 7C-2 in Table 2.308. These are correlated, on the basis of stratigraphy, in Table 2.309. Although this is done in terms of group time spans, undoubtedly these would have to be reformulated if the groups were more thoroughly excavated.

The correlations are on the basis of stratigraphy alone. Group TS. 7 is securely dated to a time following the ap-

TABLE 2.304
Group 7C-2: Lot Groups

Feature	Lot Group	Lot	Provenience	Ceramic Evaluation
Str. 7C-7 (Op. 67B)	1	5	Partially sealed fill of 2nd	Manik, possible Ik and/or Imix
	2	2	Unsealed fill of 1st	Manik, Ik and/or Imix
	3a	3	W of structure	Some Manik, mostly Ik and/or Imix
	3b	1	E of structure, to floor of Plat. 7C-2	Some Manik, mostly Ik and/or Imix
Plat. 7C-2	1	67B/4	Sealed fill of 2nd	Manik, Ik, Imix
	2	39D/2	Unsealed fill of 1st	Manik, Ik and/or Imix
	3	39D/1	Surface to level of floor for 1st, near center of platform	Ik and/or Imix

pearance of Imix ceramics around AD 700 (Table 2.304; Plat. 7C-2:LG. 1). There is no evidence for an occupation after AD 869, which dates the end of the Imix Ceramic Complex. The consistent inclusion of Manik ceramics in all lot groups (Table 2.304) suggests possible activity in the group prior to group TS. 7.

TABLE 2.305
Structure 7C-7: Artifacts by Lot Group

Study Category	Object	Lot Group			
		1	2	3a	3b
Pottery Vessels	Sherds	Not weighed			
Flaked Chert Artifacts	Blade				1
	Unmodified flakes		1		1
Flaked Obsidian Artifacts	Thin biface		1		
	Prismatic blades		1	5	
	Unused flakes			2	
Ground, Pecked, and Polished Stone Artifacts	Mano				1
	Bead	1			
	Burned limestone chunks		2		
	Unclassifiable artifact	1			
Shell and Bone Artifacts	Bone, animal, unworked				1

TABLE 2.306
Platform 7C-2: Artifacts by Lot Groups

Study Category	Object	Lot Group		
		1	2	3
Pottery Vessels				
Flaked Chert Artifacts	Thin biface	1		
	Unused flake	1		
Shell and Bone Artifacts	Bone, worked	1		
	Bone, animal, unworked	1		

TABLE 2.307
Structure 7C-7: Time Spans

Time Span	Architectural Development	Construction Stage	Floor	Descriptive Data	Lot Group	Ceramics in Vogue
1				Abandonment and ruin		
2				Use	3a,b	
3	Str.7C-7-1st	1		Reconstruction of building of perishable materials		
		2		Construction of upper platform level	2	Imix
		3		Demolition of existing building		
4				Use		
5	Str.7C-7-2nd	1		Construction of building of perishable materials		
		2	1	Construction of platform	1	

TABLE 2.308
Platform 7C-2: Time Spans

Time Span	Architectural Development	Unit	Descriptive Data	Lot Group		Ceramics in Vogue
1			Abandonment and ruin			
2			Use		3	
3	Plat. 7C-2-1st	4	Reconstruction of platform	2		Imix
4			Use, with burning of floor			
5	Plat. 7C-2-2nd	2,3	Construction of platform	1		
6		1	Earlier activity			Ik
						Manik

TABLE 2.309
Group 7C-2: Time Spans

Group Time Span	Structure 7C-7: Time Span (Table 2.307)	Platform 7C-2: Time Span (Table 2.308)
1	1	1
2	2	
3	3	
4	4	2
5	5	3
6		4
7		5
8		6

Structure 7C-62 Locus

In the summer of 1963, as part of Culbert's ceramic test pit operation, excavations were undertaken as Op. 39F, G, and H by Sisson approximately 70 m E of Gp. 7C-1. An old *brecha*, surveyed by the Petty Geophysical Company, runs through this area on a true N-S bearing. In the course of the project survey of this area by Gregerson and others (for TR. 11), large numbers of Manik sherds, fragments of bone, and other artifacts were picked up on the brecha at this spot. Yet there is nothing in this area of relatively flat terrain to indicate the presence of structural remains. The nearest chultun (7C-4) to the S is close enough to Gp. 7C-5 (this report) to be considered as probably related to it. Therefore, all this artifactual material seems indicative of the presence of a "hidden" structure; moreover, one which may have been occupied exclusively in Early Classic times.

STRUCTURE 7C-62

The excavations were undertaken primarily to secure a good, unmixed sample of Manik ceramics. At the same time, they were expanded beyond the usual 2-m test pit in order to see if any traces could be found of one or more structures. The extent of the excavations is shown in Fig. 139. A posthole (U. 2), two informal occupation surfaces (U. 1, 3), and an undisturbed midden were found together—a clear indication that at least one structure stood at this locus.

Unit 1 is a stratum of soft, white soil that overlies bedrock or, in deeper areas, sterile clay. The sherd content of U. 1 is minimal. The posthole, U. 2, penetrates U. 1 down to the surface of bedrock. Its depth is 0.30 m, and its diameter is 0.26 m; its location relative to datum 39F-H is S 3.30, W 7.64 (Fig. 139). This is also the area of the heaviest midden concentration. This midden lies on the surface of U. 1; it is not known if it covered U. 2. Approximately 1 m N of U. 2 the midden quantity tapers off abruptly. North of this, some 0.25 m above U. 1 is the packed surface, U. 3. Its maximum northward extent is unknown. It is overlain by topsoil in which is mixed a moderate amount of artifactual material.

Although there are sufficient remains here to indicate the one-time existence of architecture, it is difficult to be sure of the relationship between the various features. It looks as though U. 1 was the original ground surface of the area. Though it does contain some sherds and artifacts, these could be accounted for as the result of trash being tramped into the ground surface.

Unit 3 could be an artificially built-up surface. The fact that its S edge correlates with the N edge of the heaviest midden concentration suggests that this trash was discarded by people occupying a structure with U. 3 as its floor. Also the midden lies on the same surface (U. 1) above which U. 3 was raised.

The relation of U. 2 to U. 3 and the midden is a problem. A reasonable possibility is that one of several posts stood here for a structure of perishable materials that enclosed U. 3. The trash discarded by the occupants of such a structure may have built up around the post inserted in U. 2. The later rotting of the post in a deposit that may have had a high content of organic material would not be expected to leave any visible trace. Hence, it would appear as though the midden overlay an earlier posthole. The trouble with this interpretation is that it requires the structure walls to have been about 1 m beyond the edge of the floor. Perhaps U. 2 related to an early version, and U. 3 to a later one, of Str. 7C-62.

SHERDS AND ARTIFACTS

Lot groups for Str. 7C-62 are defined in Table 2.310, with content listed in Table 2.311.

STRATUM UNDERLYING CONSTRUCTION

Material from the stratum (U. 1) on which Str. 7C-62 was apparently built, and on which its trash rests, is included in LG. 1a, 1b, and probably 1c. The excavator's field notes are not clear on the latter point, but the depth of the object lots, and the quantity of cultural material, are consistent with this interpretation. Because the quantity of material is much less than in LG. 3, 4a, 4b, and 4c, and because not one object appears to predate material in the

latter lot groups, it seems best to regard the sherds and artifacts of LG. 1a–c as part of the same deposits as LG. 3,
4a–c. Given the apparent propensity of the occupants of
Str. 7C-62 to scatter quantities of rubbish around the area,
some would undoubtedly have been tramped into earth.

Construction Fill

As noted above, U. 3 is thought to represent a part
of Str. 7C-62 itself, possibly a renovation of the original
structure. If the latter, a respectable content of sherds
and artifacts would not be unexpected. On the other
hand, lack of a plaster floor suggests that some occupation debris could have been tramped into U. 3. Then,
too, the penetration of tree roots and digging errors, in
the absence of clear walls and a plaster floor, could have
contaminated the fill sample with much occupation debris. In short, it is not at all certain that the sherds and
artifacts in LG. 2 really are fill items. They do not differ
significantly from items from more obvious occupation
deposits.

Material Above Living Levels

Material in this category is included in LG. 3, and 4a–c.
Lot Group 3 is a midden deposit right next to the remains
of Str. 7C-62, and undoubtedly is trash from it. Some items
from this midden are probably included in LG. 1a (from
directly beneath it) and 4a (above it). The latter also extends
over U. 3, where it may consist of material uprooted from
the midden, as well as some trash left in the structure upon
abandonment. The other lot groups, also midden-like in nature, consist of rubbish strewn around the area from time
to time by the occupants of the structure. Two tiny monument fragments from this trash, MS. 70 and 136, are described in TR. 33A (pp. 86, 91, 94; fig. 65i and 57k).

There is no question as to the time of construction and
use of Str. 7C-62. Sherd samples from all lot groups are
excellent for dating purposes, and there is nothing identifiable as earlier or later than late Manik. Moreover, the censer
material from LG. 1a, 3, 4a, 4b, and 5 all belongs in the
Kataan Complex.

TABLE 2.310
Structure 7C-62: Lot Groups

Lot Group	Lot	Provenience	Ceramic Evaluation
1a	39F/5,9,10-12	U. 1	Late Manik
1b	39G/3,7	Test pit S of Str. 7C-62: U. 1	Late Manik
1c	39H/4,5	Test pit SW of Str. 7C-62: 0.60 m to bedrock	Late Manik
2	39F/4	Unsealed fill of U. 1 and below	Late Manik
3	39F/3,8	Immediately S of U. 3, from 0.10 m above the top of U. 3 to U. 1	Late Manik
4a	39F/1,2,6,7	Surface, over and around Str. 7F-62, to level of U. 3 and LG. 3	Late Manik
4b	39G/1,2,4-6	Test pit S of 7C-62: surface to U. 1	Late Manik
4c	39H/1-3	Test pit SW of Str. 7C-62: surface to 0.60 m	Late Manik
5	39F/13	Lost	No data

TABLE 2.311
Structure 7C-62: Artifacts by Lot Group

Study Category	Object	Lot Group								
		1a	1b	1c	2	3	4a	4b	4c	5
Pottery Vessels	Sherds	Weights not recorded								
Other Pottery Artifacts	Figurine					1				
	Censers	4				2	2	1	1	1
Flaked Chert Artifacts	Ovate biface								1	
	Elongate bifaces	2								
	Unclassifiable bifaces	2								
	Thin bifaces	1			1					
	Irregular retouched flakes					2		1		
	Rounded retouched flake					1				
	Used flakes	3			2			3		
	Unused flakes	7	3	1	3	2	2	6	1	
	Nodule						1			
Flaked Obsidian Artifacts	Thin bifaces	1			1					
	Prismatic blades	6			7	5	1	2	1	
Ground, Pecked, and Polished Stone Artifacts	Manos	1			1					
	Metate	1								
	Rubbing stones		1			1				
	Hammer stones			1		1				
	Earplug	1								
	Monument fragments						1	1		
	Unworked slate	1								
	Unclassifiable artifacts							1		1
Shell and Bone Artifacts	Shell, Tinkler					1				
	Shell, pendants	1		1						
	Shell, unworked	1			2					
	Bone, rasp	1								
	Bones, blunted end	5			1			2		
	Bone, animal, misc., worked	2				1				
	Bone, animal, unworked	62	7	2	5	19	6	1	2	
	Bone, human, worked	2								
	Bone, human, unworked	28	2		2	9	6	33	4	
	Bone, unidentified, unworked		2		4					

TABLE 2.312
Structure 7C-62: Time Spans

Time Span	Architectural Development	Unit	Descriptive Data	Ceramics in Vogue
1			Abandonment and ruin	
2		3?	Use, with possible occasional modification of structure	Manik (Late)
3	Str. 7C-62	1,2,3?	Original construction	

TIME SPANS

Given limited data, only the three time spans of Table 2.312 have been defined. Evidently the structure was built, occupied, and abandoned within a fairly restricted span of time, to be abandoned by AD 550, for not one sherd earlier than late Manik has been found in this large sample (Table 2.310). Consistent is that identifiable censer material is referable to the Early Classic Kataan Complex.

Group 6B-3

Group 6B-3 is located on sloping terrain at 6B:S36 E286. Few other structure groups are to be found in this vicinity; the nearest one is 94 m SE. The four structures of the group are based on a plaza that is raised on the S (downhill) side (see TR. 11). Structure 6B-2 extends across the N side of the plaza, and its ruin suggests a low, rectangular platform oriented to magnetic E-W. Just S of its W end, on that side of the plaza, is the smaller, but similar, Str. 6B-1. Directly opposite is what appears to be a small, square structure, 6B-3. South of it is the similar, but larger, Str. 6B-4. The shape and position of the latter two structures are reminiscent of household shrines (TR. 21). The other two resemble known house foundations.

Between Str. 6B-3 and 4 is the feature labeled as Ch. 6B-1. This was discovered by Martinez is 1960 who, in his field notes, indicated that he did not believe it to be a chultun. Complete excavation by Puleston in 1963 (as Op. 66N) proved Martinez to be correct.

"CHULTUN" 6B-1

In actuality, the "chultun" was a pit, roughly rectangular, about 1 m deep (Fig. 140). The longest dimension is N-S, parallel to the slope of the terrain. The N face of the pit undercuts bedrock slightly, but is otherwise vertical. The S side begins as vertical but quickly curves around to slope more gradually to the deepest part of the pit, on the N.

The pit contained a thin stratum of packed gray earth (U. 1) at its bottom. Over this was earth, which ranges from gray-brown at the bottom to dark brown leaf mold at the top. Indications are that the pit, with the exception of U. 1, was filled all at once. This is supported by the basic homogeneity of the material, and the presence of similar sherds and artifacts at all levels. Unit 1 may best be explained as the result of dust packed down by the feet of workmen in the pit. It is devoid of all cultural material.

The purpose of the pit is an enigma. It may be the result of extraction of limestone. Later, it was filled to restore the ground surface. If so, the intention may have been to quarry masonry blocks. The problem with this is that the extent of the pit seems too limited, and it also seems too deep. An alternative is that it served as a source of small, irregular pieces of limestone, such as are sometimes found in fills. This interpretation is problematical because such material could have been secured in some quantity at regular quarries. Finally, the pit may have been intended as a source of *cal*, but the difficulty here is that it does not penetrate much beneath the hard bedrock cap.

It is more probable that the feature was simply a pit. This is particularly suggested by its limited size, neat rectangular shape, and its intentional filling. Taken together, these suggest a planting pit, perhaps for some kind of fruit tree or deeply rooted garden crop.

SHERDS AND ARTIFACTS

Lot groups for Gp. 6B-3 are defined in Table 2.313, with content in Table 2.314. Excavated materials are divided into two lot groups: LG. 2 is the ancient fill for the pit;

LG. 1 the surface material. The latter is a mixture of fill and occupation debris that has washed into the pit from nearby in the group. Sherds in both lot groups are all from Imix vessels. The most abundant other artifacts are some censer fragments (Thul Complex), of interest in view of the proximity of two potentially ceremonial structures.

TIME SPANS

Time spans for "Ch. 6B-1" are listed in Table 2.315, and require little comment. The Imix sherds (Table 2.313) indicate that Gp. 6B-3 was occupied between AD 700 and 869, the dates for the Imix Complex.

TABLE 2.313
Group 6B-3: Lot Groups

Feature	Lot Group	Lot	Provenience	Ceramic Evaluation
Ch. 6B-1	1	1	Surface over and and near pit	Imix
(Op. 66N)	2	2-4	Contents of pit	Imix

TABLE 2.314
"Chultun 6B-1": Artifacts by Lot Group

Study Category	Object	Lot Group 1	2
Pottery Vessels	Sherds per cubic meter (lbs)	11.7	19.0
Other Pottery Artifacts	Censers Worked sherd	several 1	several
Flaked Chert Artifacts	Ovate biface Used flakes		1 4
Flaked Obsidian Artifacts	Prismatic blade		1
Ground, Pecked, and Polished Stone Artifacts	Metate Hammer stone		1 1

TABLE 2.315
"Chultun 6B-1": Time Spans

Time Span	Construction Stage	Unit	Descriptive Data	Lot Group	Ceramics in Vogue
1			Abandonment, accumulation of debris through erosion from Gp. 6B-3	2	
2			Use of pit		
3	1	1	Fill placed in pit	1	Imix
	2		Excavation of pit		

Group 6C-6

Group 6C-6 is located 100 m N, and slightly E, of the extensively excavated Gp. 6C-1 (this report). It is very similar to the latter group in overall size, position of the four structures (TR. 11:Str. 6C-32 and 35), and the size and shape of the ruin mounds.

A single test pit sampled plaza fill (Tables 2.316, 2.317). A floor was encountered at 0.82 m that seals the lower lots (38B/5,6). On the basis of experience in similar groups, a later floor probably existed at one time near the present surface. Lots 38B/1–4 should be the fill for this floor. The ceramic data clearly indicate that the presumed later floor was laid after the appearance of Ik ceramics, possibly even after they were no longer in production. This is suggested on the basis of the large amount of these ceramics in the fill, and because it is impossible to state that Imix ceramics were clearly absent. The floor at 0.82 m clearly was laid while Manik ceramics were in vogue. Given the large quantity of such ceramics, an Early Classic occupation of the locus prior to the laying of this floor is probable. Although evidence for a Preclassic occupation was not found, later excavation by Proyecto Nacional Tikal (their Group 6C-XI) did recover Middle Preclassic material (Laporte 2003:309). Although proof is lacking, the dating of the latest floor suggests that final abandonment of the group was after the appearance of Imix ceramics. A sample of late occupation material would be required to prove this, but such an interpretation is consistent with experience in more extensively excavated groups.

Group 6C-7

This "group" actually consists of only a single structure, Str. 6C-40, located on high ground 100 m E of Gp. 6C-1. The structure (TR. 11) appears to have been a rectangular platform comparable to known house foundations. Reverse stratigraphy in the test pit (Tables 2.316, 2.317) indicates that redeposited fill was sampled, which overlies a scattering of occupation debris or late plaza fill. The structure probably originated in late Early Classic times and was occupied into the period of time when Ik and perhaps Imix ceramics were in vogue.

Group 6C-8

Group 6C-8 includes Str. 6C-48 through 50, which are situated on an L-shaped raised platform 25 m SE of Gp. 6C-1. On the map (TR. 11), Str. 6C-50 in form appears to be a small temple. Investigation by Proyecto Nacional Tikal revealed it to have vaulted chambers with an access stairway, beneath which were several burials and a cache (Laporte 2003:306). West of this, on the N and S edges of the supporting platform, are the other two structures. They appear to be small, narrow, rectangular platforms. The overall situation is suggestive of a residential group of "Plaza Plan 2" (TR. 21).

Two test pits (Table 2.316) sampled construction fill, with a very light mixture of late occupation debris (38D/1 and 2). Four floors were encountered in the supporting platform (Table 2.317), and experience suggests that another existed, probably near the 0.20 m level. The ceramic data indicate a Late Preclassic date for the deepest floor. The next floor up was laid in Early Classic times, and the third from the bottom either in late Early Classic times or very shortly after the appearance of Ik ceramics. All subsequent construction was clearly Intermediate to Late Classic. The group was occupied until sometime between AD 860 and 950, when Eznab ceramics were in vogue (Laporte 2003:306).

Group 6C-9

Group 6C-9 is located 16 m S of Gp. 6C-8. It is shown on the site map (TR. 11) as consisting of Str. 6C-51 through 53, arranged on the E, S, and N sides of a plaza. All three appear to be small, rectangular platforms, which could have served as house foundations.

Ceramic data from a test pit into plaza fill suggest an occupation from Late Preclassic times through the time when Ik and perhaps Imix ceramics were dominant (Tables 2.316 and 2.317). Later excavations in this group by Proyecto Nacional Tikal (their group 6C-XVI) confirmed occupation here from the third century AD until sometime after AD 869, when Eznab ceramics were in use (Laporte 2003:295–300, 306–309 and 310). The surprise of their excavations was discovery of an extraordinarily elaborate complex of Early and Intermediate Classic buildings beneath the relatively simple Late Classic architecture shown on the site map.

Group 6C-10

Group 6C-10 is located near the N edge of Sq. 6C, just off the SW corner of the "Mundo Perdido" group (Laporte 2003). Structures 6C-16 and 18–21 are all arranged around the edges of a raised plaza and all appear to have been rectangular platforms, of small-to-medium size, comparable to known house foundations (see TR. 11). Structure 6C-17, which is similar, is located in the NW corner of the group. Structure 6C-22, also similar, is just off the NE corner.

A single test pit (Table 2.316) sampled fill of the plaza. Unfortunately, the ceramic samples are small, and so are difficult to interpret (Table 2.317). An Intermediate to Late Classic occupation is indicated. Although late Early Classic occupation is a possibility, a more extensive one is unlikely in view of the very few Manik sherds. Moreover, these might have come from a nearby dump associated with the major structures to the NE, which were perhaps drawn on for fill when Gp. 6C-10 was first built. Preclassic occupation is even more dubious than Early Classic.

Group 7B-1

This group is located in the NE corner of Sq. 7B, and includes Str. 7B-1 through 3. Of these, Str. 7B-2 might be a small, range-type structure (see TR. 11). Structure 7B-1, which forms the N arm of an "L" with Str. 7B-2, is very much lower and seems to be a rectangular platform. Structure 7B-3, comparable in size and shape to Str. 7B-1, is parallel to, and just SW of, Str. 7B-2.

A single test pit (Table 2.316) sampled probable plaza fill. The ceramic data (Table 2.317) indicate only an Ik and/or Imix related occupation.

Group 7C-3

This group is in the far NE corner of Sq. 7C. It consists of four structures (7C-25 through 28) arranged on the four sides of a plaza. One may be a temple on the E; the others appear to be small, rectangular platforms (see TR. 11). The overall situation is suggestive of a residential group of "Plaza Plan 2" (TR. 21).

A test pit sampled plaza fill (Table 2.316). The data surely document an Ik to Imix related occupation (Table 2.317). The much smaller amount of earlier ceramics cannot be taken to surely indicate an earlier occupation, but it is a possibility. A late occupation, when Eznab ceramics were dominant, is also a possibility.

Group 7C-4

Group 7C-4 consists of three structures, 7C-9 through 11, and two chultuns, 7C-8 and 9. The three structures are arranged on the N, W, and S sides of a plaza. The N structure seems to be a small range-type structure; the others may be also, or more probably are large, rectangular platforms (see TR. 11). The two chultuns are within the plaza area. The group is located 23 m S of Gp. 7C-2 (this report).

A test pit (Table 2.316) sampled plaza fill. The ceramic sample (Table 2.317) is very small, and indicates a possible Early Classic to Late Classic occupation.

Group 7C-5

Group 7C-5 is located 50 m SE of the extensively excavated Gp. 7C-1 (this report), and about 30 m SE of extensively sampled "Vacant Terrain" (this report). It consists of a large plaza area, on the N and W sides of which are the apparent range-type structures 7C-16 and 18 (see TR. 11). The apparent rectangular platforms, Str. 7C-15 and 17, bound the rest of the W side of the plaza on either end of Str. 7C-16. A third apparent small rectangular platform is located in the center of the S edge of the plaza. Two similar structures are located off the SW corner of the plaza. Finally, 7C-20, a small range-type structure, or a large rectangular platform, is based on the E edge of the platform. A small temple stands just to the N, or perhaps it is simply an extension of Str. 7C-20. Chultun 7C-4, 16 m to the N of Str. 7C-18, may have been associated with the group.

The single test pit (Table 2.316) sampled plaza fill. The ceramic samples (Table 2.317) are extremely poor, but suggest an occupation when Ik and/or Imix ceramics were in vogue. An Early Classic occupation is possible, but not clearly indicated.

TABLE 2.316
Location of Test Pits: Perdido Quadrangle

Group	Test Pit	Location
6C-6	38B	Center of plaza for Str. 6C-32 through 35
6C-7	37X	In front of Str. 6C-40
6C-8	37S	Str. 6C-50
	38D	Center of plaza
6C-9	38E	Plaza for Str. 6C-51 through 53
6C-10	38A	Center of plaza for Str. 6C-16 through 21
7B-1	39E	Plaza for Str. 7B-1 through 3
7C-3	39A	Plaza for Str. 7C-25 through 28
7C-4	39C	Plaza for Str. 7C-9 through 11
7C-5	39B	Plaza for Str. 7C-14 through 20

TABLE 2.317
Ceramic Evaluations: Perdido Quadrangle Test Pits

Group	Lot	Provenience	Ceramics
6C-6	38B/1	0-20 cm	Manik; Ik and/or Imix
	38B/2	20-40 cm	Manik; Ik
	38B/3	40-60 cm	Ik
	38B/4	60-82 cm (floor)	Manik; some possible Ik and/or Imix
	38B/5	82-100 cm	Manik
	38B/6	100-120 cm	Manik
6C-7	37X/1	0-20 cm	Manik
	37X/2	20-40 cm	Ik and/or Imix
6C-8	37S/1	0-40 cm	Ik and/or Imix
	38D/1	0-20 cm	Ik and/or Imix; possible Eznab
	38D/2	20-50 cm (floor)	Ik and/or Imix; Eznab
	38D/3	50-57 cm (floor)	Late Preclassic; Manik; possible Ik and/or Imix
	38D/4	57-85 cm (floor)	Late Preclassic; Manik
	38D/5	85-92 cm (floor)	Late Preclassic
	88D/6	92-103 cm	Preclassic
6C-9	38E/1	0-20 cm	Manik; Ik and/or Imix
	38E/2	20-40 cm	Late Preclassic; Manik
6C-10	38A/1	0-20 cm	Manik and Ik and/or Imix
	38A/2	20-40 cm	Ik and/or Imix; 1 possible Late Preclassic
	38A/3	40-60 cm	? possible Late Preclassic
7B-1	39E/1	0-20 cm	Ik and/or Imix
	39E/2	20-40 cm	Ik and/or Imix
7C-3	39A/1	0-20 cm	Ik and/or Imix; possible Eznab
	39A/2	20-40 cm	Possibly Late Preclassic through Late Classic
	39A/3	40-60 cm	?
7C-4	39C/1	0-15 cm	Possible Manik and Ik and/or Imix
7C-5	39B/1	0-20 cm	?
	39B/2	20-40 cm	Ik and/or Imix; possible Manik

8. Excavations in the Corriental Quadrangle

Introduction

Two of the small-structure groups of this quadrangle have been extensively excavated: Gp. 6E-1 (this report) and Gp. 6E-2 (TR. 23G). Additional information on chronology comes from 51 test pits in another 22 aggregates of small structures in Sq. 6D, 6E, and 7E. Surface collections sample two other groups, as well as "vacant terrain" at four locales. If major structures and their smaller adjuncts are ignored here, some 376 small- to medium-sized structures are mapped on the Corriental Quadrangle. Many of the groups are complex in their composition, and not always easy to separate one from another, but the structures seem to fall into 102 groups. Of these, 25% have at least been sampled.

Group 6E-1

Group 6E-1 is located in Sq. 6E of the Corriental Quadrangle, S156 E48. As mapped by R. F. Carr in 1960 (TR. 11), it consists of two structures, 6E-25 and 26, set on a square platform. The terrain here has a very gradual slope down to the E. On higher ground to the N is the "G Group" of Morley (TR. 11:17), made up of several major range-type structures (see TR. 23A:55–62). Smaller structures are abundant to the S, E, and W. Group 6E-1 was selected for testing in the ceramic survey of 1962 at which time a pit was sunk as Op. 35B in the NW quadrant. This test exposed a sequence of platform floors, revealed the presence of Preclassic pottery, and uncovered previously unknown Ch. 6E-6. Another test pit in the summer of 1963 by Culbert penetrated the center of the platform to bedrock, confirming the floor sequence and the presence of Preclassic ceramics. It was then decided to excavate extensively here in the hope that Preclassic architecture would be found. This was done by Haviland and Culbert in 1963 as Op. 68, with the assistance of Sisson and Crocker (Fig. 180d). In the course of their work, the remains of five other structures were found, and a second chultun was discovered.

STRUCTURE 6E-25-2ND

The earliest construction beneath the westernmost structure is U. 1 (Fig. 145-147), a wall that runs N-S directly beneath the E wall of 25-1st. The base of the wall was not exposed in excavation. Platform 6E-1-3rd:Fl. 1 abuts this wall within 0.11 m of its top (Fig. 150). Platform 6E-1-6th:Fl. 1 does not meet the wall, so the ma-

sonry could have been intruded through it. Since Str. 6E-25:U. 1 extends at least 0.14 m beneath the surface of Plat. 6E-1-3rd:Fl. 1, however, it seems more likely that Plat. 6E-1-6th:Fl. 1 was originally associated with the wall, an association destroyed in the course of later modification of Plat. 6E-1.

Unit 1 is the only real evidence exposed for 6E-25-2nd. Since the wall corresponds so exactly to the location of the front wall of 25-1st, it seems likely that it represents the front wall of a structure of the same size and shape. The back wall of the final structure may also have served the earlier one.

STRUCTURE 6E-25-1ST

Three components of this structure were exposed: the southern half of the E wall, with the SE corner and a portion of the S wall; the northernmost stone of the E wall; and a portion of the W wall (Fig. 148, 149). The E wall, only a single course high, rests on earth fill 0.15 m thick above U. 1 (Fig. 150). Floor 1 of Plat. 6E-1-2nd abuts the base of this wall. Platform 6E-1:U. 18 continues the line of the S wall of the structure to the E, and abuts the base of the front wall. This feature is discussed elsewhere (see Plat. 6E-1). Platform 6E-1:U. 19, a floor S of the structure, abuts both the structure and Plat. 6E-1:U. 18.

In a test trench W of Or. 1 of Ch. 6E-6 is a single block of masonry, in line with the exposed portion of the E wall of Str. 6E-25. No masonry continues this line to the N, so apparently this marks the NE corner of the structure. The overall mound configuration supports this contention. The W wall of the structure was exposed in a test trench 2 m wide. Only its lower course survives, but a slight batter is indicated.

Structure 6E-25-1st is reconstructed as a two-level platform because of the height of its ruin. No other evidence for this was found, but the height of the mound seems inconsistent with a one-level platform. There is insufficient evidence to permit definition of specific construction stages.

STRUCTURE 6E-26-4TH

The existence of this structure is inferred from the condition of Plat. 6E-1-6th:Fl. 1, and the presence of midden material beneath the walls of Str. 6E-26-3rd that postdates fill material from Plat. 6E-1-6th:Fl. 1. The N edge of the floor ends in a straight E-W line (Fig. 145) and then turns a corner 1.00 m E of U. 4 (see below). From this, the line continues S and then E again. North and E of these edges of Plat. 6E-1-6th:Fl. 1, the same level carries on as a pause-line over the top of a thick layer of light-colored fill (Fig. 151; Plat. 6E-1:U. 10).

The logical explanation of these straight edges of the pavement is that the floor ran up to structure walls, which were later removed. The walls could not have belonged to 6E-26-3rd, for its fill contains sherds of the Imix Ceramic Complex, whereas the latest sherds from a large sample sealed beneath Plat. 6E-1-6th:Fl. 1 are of the earlier Ik Complex. No other architectural remains have been found that are assignable to Str. 6E-26-4th, so it is impossible to reconstruct it precisely. Its shape was probably like that of succeeding 26-3rd, as the line of Plat. 6E-1-6th:Fl. 1 suggests the large inset in the SW corner similar to that of 3rd. Moreover, the S walls of the inset for the subsequent structures are in virtually the same location as the E-W line of Plat. 6E-1-6th:Fl. 1.

The location of the N wall of 26-4th is not known for certain, but since the N walls of 26-3rd through 1st all were built as part of the N walls of Plat. 6E-1, it is reasonable to suppose that the one for 26-4th was as well. The N wall of Plat. 6E-1-6th is thought to have been located at about the maximum northward extent of U. 10 (see below). This means that the W end of 4th was about 1.60 m wide, the E end about 2.80 m wide.

If the E end wall of 26-4th projected at all beyond the E wall of Plat. 6E-1-6th, it could not have been by much. This is indicated by undisturbed midden material (68G/6) on which the E wall of Str. 6E-26-3rd was built. The source of this midden, which is full of sherds from Imix vessels (Fig. 181d), must have been 26-4th. Since the E wall of the succeeding architectural development was built on this, the E wall of 4th had to be farther W.

The Imix sherds in the midden of Str. 6E-26-4th, and the Ik sherds beneath the associated floor of Plat. 6E-1-6th, mean that the occupation of Str. 6E-26-4th spanned a time when Ik (probably late) and then early Imix ceramics were in use. This is consistent with material from fill of 26-3rd that indicates a time of construction sometime after Imix ceramics appeared.

Mention must be made here of Plat. 6E-1:U. 9, a posthole in the floor of Plat. 6E-1-6th, 0.50 m S of the N extent of that floor, and 3.20 m W of its E edge (Fig. 145). This feature possibly relates to Str. 6E-26-4th, but if so, it seems surprising that no more postholes have been found, particularly at the NE corner of the floor. Since none have been found, it is dubious that the posthole relates to the structure itself.

STRUCTURE 6E-26-3RD

In contrast to the preceding architectural development, much of this structure remains (Fig. 146). The N and E walls that continued to serve succeeding structures were built at this time. The E wall rests on midden material associated with 6E-26-4th (see above). The back (N) wall is based in part on a floor remnant (Plat. 6E-1:U. 5) that may be related to Plat. 6E-1-9th.

At the SE corner, the wall of the structure turns 90°

and runs W one meter. Here the wall is several courses high. At the one-meter point, there is a slight interruption by a later platform wall (Fig. 148, Plat. 6E-1:U. 14). Beyond this, the line of the wall is continued by Str. 6E-26:U. 1, constructed of a single course, which ends 3.80 m W of the SE corner of the structure. The W portion of U. 1 rests directly on Plat. 6E-1-6th:Fl. 1. To the E, it rests on fill 4 cm thick that overlies Plat. 6E-1:U. 10.

The multiple-course portion of the S wall ends at a point where a N-S platform retaining wall must have stood, as indicated by the diagonal line where the stones end (Fig. 181b). This diagonal line reveals that the platform wall was battered. Later, this wall was razed when the platform was further modified.

Unit 4 designates the N-S wall that forms the E wall of a large inset, at the SW corner of the structure. This rests on Plat. 6E-1-6th:Fl. 1, and with U. 1, forms a corner. The N wall of this inset, U. 5, is represented only by a line of rubble. This runs W, to the W wall that also serves the later structure at this locus.

The fill within these walls is light earth with a moderate amount of cultural material in it. Prior to the actual fill operation, Plat. 6E-1:U. 10 was dug out and Bu. 129 placed in the excavation (CS. 3). Unit 2 (Fig. 151), a pauseline, marks the conclusion of fill operations over the burial itself. After the interment, the main structure fill was placed and the walls completed (CS. 2).

Units 3 and 6 are portions of the floor for Str. 6E-26-3rd. This was laid directly on the earth fill, without benefit of special floor ballast (Fig. 151). Beneath U. 6, U. 7 represents a pause-line.

Correlation with specific floors of Plat. 6E-1 poses certain problems. The walls of Str. 6E-26-3rd rest on the surface of Plat. 6E-1-6th:Fl. 1, but Plat. 6E-1-4th:Fl. 1 is associated with Str. 6E-26-2nd. Perhaps the floor of Plat. 6E-1-6th was patched and continued in use. Otherwise, one must postulate a platform floor for which there is no evidence. Perhaps lack of specific evidence for patching is a result of the extensive renovation that accompanied construction of Str. 6E-26-2nd.

There is little doubt that Str. 6E-26-3rd represents a building platform. No postholes have been found, but this undoubtedly is a factor of preservation. An extensive midden, lying E and N of the structure, attests to the domestic nature of 16-3rd (Table 2.320:68G/4, 68G/5, 68G/13, 68L). Moreover, architectural resemblance to structures where postholes have been found is obvious (cf. Str. 3F-25, 4F-47, both this report). If the walls of the building of 26-3rd followed the outline of the platform walls, the inset suggests the presence of a roofed, but otherwise open "porch" in one corner, a feature sometimes seen in Maya houses (Thompson 1970:17, 18, and pl. 3a). Alternatively, the front building wall was positioned in line with the N edge of the inset, a possibility discussed in connection with 26-2nd-D.

STRUCTURE 6E-26-2ND-D

This development saw the height of the entire platform raised and the addition of a second (upper) level (Fig. 147). To this end, all the building walls of 3rd were razed, and earth fill was placed on U. 3 and 6 (Fig. 151), the floors of the earlier structure (CS. 4). A front wall for the upper platform level was set on the earth fill (CS. 3). Time and the elements have effectively destroyed any floor for the upper platform level, but U. 8, a floor remnant, turns up to its front wall and represents the floor of the lower platform level.

The increased height of the platform necessitated a stairway to give access to the structure (CS. 2). A set of three steps was constructed against the front of the platform. At this time, an earlier burial was apparently disturbed, and then reinterred beneath these steps (see Bu. 152). The stones of the SW corner of the stairway were clearly intruded into Plat. 6E-1-6th:Fl. 1, and a new platform floor, 6E-1-4th:Fl. 1, turns up to the stones. This pavement was later torn up extensively, so that only this one clear association survives. Fortunately, it is sufficient to correlate the structure with construction on Plat. 6E-1.

The front stairway is no more than 2 m in width. It ends at a one-course wall of Plat. 6E-1, which extends S from the structure (Fig. 147, U. 12). At the same time as construction of Str. 6E-26-2nd-D, the earlier E retaining wall of Plat. 6E-1 was completely torn out, and this demolition may have exposed Bu. 152 in its original location (see above). By this time, the midden E of 26-3rd had become so extensive that it was incorporated into Plat. 6E-1. Unit 12, the new N-S wall, seems to be part of a low platform, of which Plat. 6E-1-4th:Fl. 1 is the surface (see Plat. 6E-1).

Construction undoubtedly terminated (CS. 1) with erection of a building of perishable materials on the platform, as before. In this case, the face of the building must have been in line with the rear of the SW corner inset, as entry was clearly from the front, based on the position of the step. In recent Maya houses with a covered corner "porch," a possibility noted for 26-3rd, entrance was usually from the rear of this feature, but here, height of the building platform was too great for this.

STRUCTURE 6E-26-2ND-C

A first modification at 26-2nd seems to have been a consequence of alteration of Plat. 6E-1. A new N-S wall (Plat. 6E-1:U. 14) was constructed 0.60 m E of Plat. 6E-1:U. 12 (see Fig. 148). In conjunction with this, the stairway to Str. 6E-26 was extended the same distance to the E. A new platform floor was then laid (Plat. 6E-1-3rd:Fl. 1).

STRUCTURE 6E-26-2ND-B

This modification was associated with the laying of Plat. 6E-1-2nd:Fl. 1. A projection of the elevation of Plat. 6E-1:U. 21, a portion of this pavement that has been exposed where it turns up to the W wall of the structure, as well as the N and E walls of the inset, indicate that the lowest step leading to the structure was now buried by Fl. 1 (see Fig. 148). Perhaps Bu. 131 was placed in the course of this construction (see Bu. 131 in section III).

STRUCTURE 6E-26-2ND-A

As the last modification of 26-2nd, the E wall of the inset was moved 0.60 m to the W (U. 9). Platform 6E-1:U. 31 (Fig. 149) is a local grading floor laid on Fl. 1 of Plat. 6E-1-2nd in this area. This surface turns up to the new walls of the inset and the W wall of the structure. One feature of this floor is Plat. 6E-1:U. 33, a hole with an olla neck set into it in the corner of the inset. The olla neck makes it unlikely that this is a posthole associated with the structure. Rather, it seems more likely that it served as a drain (for a similar feature, see discussion of Gp. 4F-3).

Despite construction of the new wall, this particular operation is not defined as a new architectural development. The reason is that no change was necessary in the walls of the building itself. For reasons given above, the front wall of the building seems to have been located in line with the N wall of the inset, and a change in the E wall of the inset need not have affected that of the building.

STRUCTURE 6E-26-1ST

The last modification of the structure involved the elimination of the inset in the SW corner (Fig. 149). This is indicated by a regular line of rubble (U. 10), which rests on Plat. 6E-1:U. 31, and seems to square off the structure. The reason for the elimination of the inset at this late date is, of course, unknown. Up to this point, the front wall of the building ran E-W in line with the N wall of the inset, with a small open terrace between it and the steps (as explained above for 26-2nd-D). Alternatively, the "porch" was included beneath the roof, but now it was included within the walls. In either case, the filling of the inset would have provided more interior floor space. Because this modification of the building walls (and the roof?) is connected with the elimination of the inset, it is regarded as an architectural development, rather than a minor architectural modification of 26-2nd.

Because of the alteration of the front wall of the building, as well as the elimination of the old inset, a new pavement would have been necessary for at least the lower platform level. Unit 11, which overlies U. 8, is such a floor (Fig. 151). It is seen as part of this activity, rather than a change in 26-2nd, because of the major alteration of the building itself.

All of this activity probably took place as three construction stages. As CS. 2 or 3, the front of the existing building must have been dismantled. Alteration of the platform, a separate stage, may have preceded or succeeded this. Reconstruction of the building would have taken place as CS. 1.

STRUCTURE 6E-162

This small, square structure is located off the E end of Str. 6E-26 (Fig. 149, 181c). Its N wall seems to consist of a raised portion of the wall of Plat. 6E-1-1st. Its W wall, which faces Str. 6E-26, is well preserved, and rests directly on an underlying midden. The S wall survives as a line of rubble of nearly the same length as the W wall. Platform 6E-1:U. 32, a floor remnant, appears to turn up to this wall. On this pavement was found some charcoal, though not in sufficient quantity to indicate that 162 had burned down. The E wall of the structure has apparently succumbed to erosion of the eastern portion of Plat. 6E-1.

Within the area enclosed by the structure walls is a floor remnant (Fl. 1). Its elevation shows that Fl. 1 once covered the structure from the top of its W wall. Thus, the structure was a platform, perhaps for a building, only as high as the single course of masonry. No postholes have been found, but natural destruction has been extensive. By analogy with Str. 4F-49 (see Gp. 4F-3, this report), it is probable that 6E-162 was topped by a pole-and-thatch building. Its construction probably took place in two stages; one for construction of the platform (CS. 2), and one for construction of the building (CS. 1).

Worth noting here is that several fragments of the greater portion of a single metate were found scattered about at the level of Fl. 1. This strongly suggests that the pieces were left there by the people who had used this building, providing a clue to its function.

STRUCTURE 6E-163

Situated a mere 2.50 m S of Str. 6E-25 is this small, square structure. In contrast to Str. 6E-162 (which is in an analogous position relative to Str. 6E-26), 163 was completely excavated to ground level. There was no probe below the base level, however, so it is not known if there is a sequence of earlier architecture. As in the case of Str. 6E-162, there was no hint of the existence of this structure prior to excavation S of Str. 6E-25.

Only the corners of the N wall of 163 have actually been identified (Fig. 148, 149). These are indicated by three blocks of masonry still in situ, and the terminal line of Plat. 6E-1:U. 19, the floor in this area, which shows a

turnup to the structure. It is clear by both position and size of the N wall that Str. 6E-163 is analogous to 162. Therefore, the structure is reconstructed as a square building platform, only as high as a single course of masonry. On this, constructed as Stage 2, a building of perishable material was raised (as CS. 1).

STRUCTURE 6E-SUB.1-2ND

Structure 6E-Sub.1 is located directly S of 6E-26, beneath several architectural developments that pertain to Plat. 6E-1. Although the walls have been razed almost completely, there is enough information to permit some reconstruction of the structure (Fig. 142).

The first construction at this locus was a square platform, with a step located at the E end of the S wall (somewhat like the later Str. 6E-26-2nd-D through 1st). It is not known if this supported a building of perishable materials; there is no evidence to sustain either possibility. Only the lower course of the E and S platform walls, and the NW corner, have survived subsequent construction at this locus. The step itself was cut down almost to the level of the surrounding floor when the structure was abandoned, so its full height is not known. The structure platform could have been up to 0.67 m high, however, if the known height of the subsequent Sub.1-1st can be used as a guide.

The structure was based on a dark earth fill that is associated with a low wall to the N (see Plat. 6E-1:U. 2). The floor of Plat. 6E-1-10th, which lies on top of this same dark earth, abuts the S wall and the step of the structure. The fill within the walls of Sub.1-2nd has been extensively disturbed by demolition, as well as by intrusion of two later Classic burials. It appears to have been a mixture of earth, stones, and a moderate amount of cultural material.

As noted elsewhere, Str. 6E-Sub.1-2nd apparently stood surrounded by a wide expanse of floor of Plat. 6E-1. It may have stood alone towards the center of the platform (see Plat. 6E-1-10th).

STRUCTURE 6E-SUB.1-1ST

Evidence for this development consists of two masonry blocks, set vertically, in an E-W line, on an earth fill to the S. They are located just S of the reconstructed location of the N wall of Sub.1-2nd, but in a slightly different alignment (Fig. 143 and 151:5). This is roughly at a right angle to the surviving wall of Str. 6E-Sub.2, which suggests that the orientation of Sub.1-1st was shifted slightly from that of Sub.1-2nd, so as to conform to that of Sub.2. Contemporaneity of these two structures is indicated by the association of Sub.2 with the floor of Plat. 6E-1-9th, and the fact that Sub.1-1st projected some 0.40 m above the level of this surface. In this respect, it is worth noting that the base of the wall of Sub.2 was set 0.15 m below contemporary Plat. 6E-1-9th:Fl. 1. Similarly, the base of the wall masonry for Sub.1-1st was set 0.20 m below the projected level of this same floor.

South of the wall, masonry of Sub.1-1st is on earth fill quite distinct from that of Sub.1-2nd, which it overlies. Included in this fill is Bu. 128, the top of which is about 0.11 m below the top of the wall masonry for Sub.1-1st. The ceramics of Bu. 128 pertain to the Cauac Complex, while the latest sherds in fills contemporary with Sub.1-2nd pertain to the Chuen Complex. The same is true of sherds sealed beneath the floor of Plat. 6E-1-9th. This all seems to indicate that Bu. 128 was put in place at the time that Sub.1-1st was built, soon after Cauac Ceramics came into vogue. The Chuen sherds beneath Plat. 6E-1-9th:Fl. 1 (as well as in fill around the burial) probably indicate that trash from Str. 6E-Sub.1-2nd, and perhaps some of its fill, was used extensively in the new construction.

The condition of the walls of Sub.1-2nd, and the uneven surface of its surviving fill, indicate that much of this structure was dismantled prior to construction of Sub.1-1st. The highest surviving part of the original structure is but 0.10 m below the level of Plat. 6E-1-9th:Fl. 1. This suggests that before Sub.1-1st was built, the whole area was roughly leveled to about the height desired for Plat. 6E-1-9th. This served as a base surface for the new construction and, eventually, the pavement for Plat. 6E-1-9th.

To sum up, then, all the evidence is consistent with the razing of Sub.1-2nd and the filling of the surrounding area, as preparation for construction of Sub.1-1st (and Str. 6E-Sub.2), following which Plat. 6E-1-9th:Fl. 1 was laid. Nothing more is known of Sub.1-1st. After its abandonment, it was almost completely destroyed, possibly in the course of construction of the eastern retaining wall of Plat. 6E-1, contemporary with Str. 6E-26-3rd. Any remains of the E portion of Str. 6E-Sub.1-1st would have been in the way of this. Fill for the floor of Plat. 6E-1-6th was dumped against the N face of the surviving masonry, and Intermediate Classic burials were placed immediately to the S. It is assumed that the structure was comparable in size and shape to Sub.1-2nd. It may have consisted in part of a building of perishable materials, but again there is no evidence for one. Although the structure was built at the same time as Plat. 6E-1-9th, it may also have continued in use with Plat. 6E-1-7th, as did Str. 6E-Sub.2. Reasons for this assumption are given elsewhere.

STRUCTURE 6E-SUB.2

Located 2.36 m W of Str. 6E-Sub.1 (Fig. 144), only one wall survived subsequent alterations to Plat. 6E-1. It rests on earth fill, is a single course high, and runs N-S at about 90° to the surviving wall fragment of Str. 6E-Sub.1-1st. It retains a dark earth fill, and Plat. 6E-1-9th:Fl. 1

abuts the W face of the wall. The later Fl. 1 of Plat. 6E-1-7th (Fig. 144) also abuts the wall, within 9 cm of its top. Directly N of the wall, this floor continues to the W, indicating that the northern end of this surviving wall marks the NE corner of the structure.

Other than these facts, nothing is known about 6E-Sub.2. There is no evidence as to whether or not it consisted in part of a building of perishable materials.

STRUCTURE 6E-SUB.3

Located 1.40 m S of Str. 6E-Sub.1, only a very small portion of a single wall for this structure was excavated (Fig. 144:8). Hence, little can be said about it. The surviving wall was set into the floor of Plat. 6E-1-8th, with which it is in union. The floor, though, continues beneath the structure, as is usual in Early Classic construction at Tikal. The wall is one course in height, and runs N-S. Below, reasons are given for supposing that the floors of Plat. 6E-1-7th, 6th, and 4th, were also associated with this structure.

The size and shape of Sub.3 are completely unknown. It is likely that the known masonry was part of its E wall, for midden-like deposits are extensive just to the E (Table 2.320; Plat. 6E-1:LG. 9C). To the W, Early Classic material is also abundant (Table 2.320; Plat. 6E-1:LG. 8C), but here it looks more like redeposited debris characteristic of fill situations. In discussion of Plat. 6E-1-8th, it is suggested that its floor was torn up when that for Plat. 6E-1-7th was laid, except where protected by Str. 6E-Sub.3. If so, then the N wall of Sub.3 must have been positioned about where the floor for Plat. 6E-1-8th now ends on the N. If the floor of Plat. 6E-1-7th ran up to Str. 6E-Sub.3, as supposed, then the known extent of that floor indicates that the structure could not have measured significantly more than 2 m in an E-W direction. Taking all these things together, a reasonable hypothesis is that the structure was rectangular, longest in a N-S direction, and faced W. It is not known if it consisted, in part, of a building of pole-and-thatch.

CHULTUN 6E-6

DESCRIPTION

Chamber 1 may be entered from above through Or. 1 and Neck 1 (Fig. 153 and Table 2.318). A distinctive feature of this neck is the presence of a stepped rim, with the step 0.40 m below the actual orifice. If a stone cover was placed here, it would have been difficult to open. The chamber itself is small, and round in plan. The slightly concave floor turns up to near-vertical walls, which can be distinguished from the domed ceiling. An entrance leads to the NW into Chm. 2. This is restricted at the sides and top, and has a carefully cut sill. Both Chm. 1 and Neck 1 were blocked by earth and rubble fill when found.

Irregularly shaped Chm. 2 is entered through the entrance from Chm. 3, either directly or from Neck 2. Or, before the opening was blocked, it could be entered through the constricted entrance from Chm. 1. The floor is in two levels, with the lowest portion near the entrance from Chm. 1.

A few centimeters of debris covered the floor. Below this was packed earth, with a few Preclassic sherds. Apparently, this lower level represents an incidental accumulation of material, packed down during occupation. The overlying material drifted in over the years after abandonment, from Chm. 1 to the S and Neck 2 to the N.

Unit 1 designates two stone blocks in the western end of Chm. 2. The size and shape of one of these suggests that it once served as a stone cover. Stone covers have also been found placed in Ch. 2G-2 and Ch. 2G-11 (this report), at the time of abandonment. The other block is nondescript.

Chamber 3 is essentially round, with an uneven floor extending to 1.10 m below the sill of the entrance to Chm. 2. Chamber 3 can be entered either from the neighboring Chm. 2, or from Neck 2 that opens into the roof of the constricted entrance between the two chambers. Chamber 3 was absolutely empty when found.

Orifice 2 opens into the chultun between Chm. 2 and 3 by a masonry shaft (Fig. 182a), set above the neck, which penetrates bedrock. Such stone shafts are exceedingly rare at Tikal. Its masonry is well cut, with the individual stones carefully shaped as arcs and then fitted snugly together to retain the surrounding fill. As found, the neck and shaft were filled with large stone blocks. These closed the chultun, and prevented slump of earth fill for later architectural developments of Plat. 6E-1.

DISCUSSION

Although it is not certain when this chultun was constructed, it is fairly certain when it went out of use. Orifice 1 was sealed by Plat. 6E-1-6th:-Fl. 1. A circular opening in this same floor is associated with Or. 2. The top of the shaft masonry is 0.12 m below the surface of the pavement, however. In the vicinity of Str. 6E-Sub.2, Plat. 6E-1-7th:Fl. 1 is exactly 0.12 m below the surface of Plat. 6E-1-6th:Fl. 1. The best explanation is that the shaft was built to serve Plat. 6E-1-7th, along with the floor. Later, the floor for Plat. 6E-1-6th sealed this orifice (and also

Or. 1). Much later still, the slump of the fill in the neck, as some of it sifted down into the empty chultun, caused the floor of Plat. 6E-1-6th (and the floor of Plat. 6E-1-3rd above it) to break up in a circular area above the hole. This did not happen at Or. 1, where the fill was more extensive and compact. Within the chultun, then, the upper stratum in Chm. 2 (68B, Lot 2) probably was fill that filtered in over the centuries, particularly from Neck 2.

Moving back in time, it was noted that the lower stratum (68B, Lot 3) in Chm. 2 was packed down during use of the chultun. Preclassic sherds were found here, suggesting use with Str. 6E-Sub.2.

Another question concerns why Neck 2 was extended by a masonry shaft, when Neck 1 was not. The following explanation seems probable. The chultun, when originally dug, may not have been as extensive as would appear. If one takes Or. 1 and Chm. 1, with the deep part of Chm. 2, this bears some resemblance to a fairly common type of Tikal chultun that consists of orifice and antechamber with one lateral chamber (cf. Ch. 2B-15, 2G-5, 3F-6, 4G-2, 5B-11, 5C-6, 6C-7, 6C-9, 6C-10, 7C-3). Similarly, Or. 2, with Chm. 3 and the shallow portion of Chm. 2, bears a resemblance to another fairly common type of chultun at Tikal. This is the kind with one orifice and antechamber, and two lateral chambers that are entered from opposite sides of the antechamber (cf. Ch. 3G-5, 5C-5, 6C-11, this report). Perhaps, the original chultun was a variant of the two-chambered type, entered through Or. 1 (Ch. 6E-6-2nd). This would have been in use some time before construction of Str. 6E-Sub.2, presumably when Str. 6E-Sub.1 was in use. If Sub.2 compared in size and shape with Sub.1, a reasonable assumption, then it would have covered Or. 1. At this time, the stepped rim may have been cut, a cover placed in the neck, and fill placed above it for the new structure. Or, more likely, perhaps the whole of Chm. 1 was filled and then the structure

TABLE 2.318
Chultun 6E-6: Average Dimensions (meters)

Feature	Length	Width	Height	Minimum Diameter	Maximum Diameter
Neck 1	1.03	---	---	0.43	0.52
Neck 2	0.30	---	---	0.43	0.43
Shaft	0.44	---	---	0.50	0.50
Chamber 1	---	---	0.89	0.98	1.10
Chamber 2 (Deep Portion)	---	---	1.05	1.44	1.52
Chamber 2 (Shallow Portion)	---	---	1.20	2.10	3.07
Chamber 3	---	---	1.41	2.18	2.60
Entrance 1-2	0.67	0.70	0.44	---	---
Entrance 2-3	0.18	0.76	0.40	---	---

built above. A new chultun was then dug, which was to have been a variant of the three-chambered type. This Ch. 6E-6-1st is represented by Or. 2 (which is well out of the way of Str. 6E-Sub.2) with Chm. 2 and 3. Excavations for Chm. 2 broke through the wall of the lateral chamber of the earlier chultun, however. This became a part of the new chultun and continued to be used, for stone blocks against the fill of the antechamber of the earlier chultun prevented this from falling into it. This whole reconstruction is strengthened by the fact that Tikal chultuns normally (but not invariably) have only one orifice, and not two. It also gains support from the fact that in Chm. 1 and the deep part of Chm. 2, the walls, floor, and ceiling were differentiated from one another. This was not so in Chm. 3, or the shallow part of Chm. 2.

If Fl. 1 of Plat. 6E-1-9th (Fig. 143) extended as far as Or. 2, the first three courses of the shaft may have been put in place when that floor was laid (Ch. 6E-6-1st-B). Later, when Fl. 1 of Plat. 6E-1-7th was laid (Fig. 144), the shaft was raised to a height sufficient to retain the fill of this floor (Ch. 6E-6-1st-A). When Str. 6E-Sub.2 was abandoned, Ch. 6E-6-1st was as well.

CHULTUN 6E-7

Description

Chamber 1 is entered from above through Or. 1 and Neck 1 (Fig. 154 and Table 2.319). Because the neck was not excavated, it cannot be described. An entrance, restricted below and on either side, gives access to Chm. 2 to the S. The chamber is essentially round, with an irregular floor.

As found, Chm. 1 was filled with earth and cultural material that overlay a thin stratum of rubble. This fill was retained in the entrance to Chm. 2 by a large rectangular masonry block. The fill contains numerous sherds, most of which are from vessels of the Cauac Ceramic Complex, though some are from Ik vessels. In contrast, the fill in Chm. 2 and 3 contains mostly Ik and Imix sherds, which indicate a different source for the two fills. This suggests that the entrance block that separated the two fills was put there to keep the fill in Chm. 1 from spilling out into the rest of the chultun. Thus, Chm. 1 was probably filled sometime prior to Ch. 3, an interpretation consistent with the absence of Imix sherds in the fill of Chm. 1.

The S end of this chamber joins Chm. 2 in a wide entrance, only slightly restricted on either side. The floor, in contrast to the other chambers, is irregular in level, and as found was covered by a 0.30 m stratum of earth continuous with the fill in Chm. 3. This material is the result of the gradual settling of the fill of Chm. 3 over the years

after abandonment. At its northern extent, this had accumulated against the block in the entrance to Chm. 1.

Chamber 3 is elliptical in shape, and is entered from above through Neck 2. This opens into the ceiling in the western portion of the room. Chamber 3 was filled with a very loose earth. This spilled over into the neighboring chambers to the N and S, which was responsible for a slump in the fill above Or. 2. Prior to excavation, the location of this orifice was indicated by a depression in Plat. 6E-1, S of the SE corner of Str. 6E-26. Carr, in his field notes, correctly interpreted this feature as the result of the fill having slumped onto some sort of open chamber below. What happened was that the Maya dumped the fill of Chm. 3 through Or. 2, placed some masonry on top, and then more earth fill over this. Since Chm. 2 and 4 were not filled beforehand (see below), this fill through the years tended to settle into the neighboring rooms. Consequently, fill from the platform above filtered down into the chultun, resulting in the slump.

Rectangular Chm. 4 is connected to Chm. 3 through a constricted entrance with a carefully shaped sill below and restriction above. Within the chamber were two layers of fill. The lower, 0.20 m thick, contains sherds from vessels of the Ik Ceramic Complex. On this packed layer was U. 1, a rectangular arrangement of amorphously shaped stones. Over both was a loose stratum of dark earth (68Z, Lot 6), continuous with the fill of Chm. 3. Containing sherds from vessels of the Imix Ceramic Complex, it originated from the settling of fill in Chm. 3.

Orifice 2 is a manhole-like cut in bedrock, which opens through Neck 2 into the ceiling of Chm. 3. The neck was filled with rubble, and two well-cut masonry blocks, each 0.40 m long, 0.20 and 0.25 m wide, and 0.12 and 0.16 m thick. These were wedged into the neck on top of the fill of Chm. 3, apparently to prevent slump of earth fill for later architectural developments of Plat. 6E-1. A similar situation was noted in the case of Or. 2 of Ch. 6E-6.

Discussion

In its original form, Ch. 6E-7 probably had but a single entrance, Or. 1. This is suggested by the fact that it, along with Neck 1 and Chm. 1, resembles a typical Tikal chultun orifice, neck and antechamber. Orifice 2, with Neck 2, appears on the other hand to have been a late addition to Chm. 3. This closely resembles Or. 1 of Ch. 2G-1, which apparently was dug later into the ceiling of Chm. 1 of that chultun (see earlier discussion under Str. 2G-61 locus). It also resembles Or. 1 of Ch. 2G-2, which was apparently later dug into the ceiling of that chultun (earlier discussion under Str. 2G-61 locus). Chultun 6E-7-2nd, therefore, had the form of orifice, neck, and antechamber with two or three other chambers arranged in a line to the

TABLE 2.319
Chultun 6E-7: Average Dimensions (meters)

Feature	Length	Width	Height	Maximum Diameter	Maximum Diameter
Neck 1	---	---	?	0.58	0.58
Neck 2	---	---	0.46	0.53	0.57
Chamber 1	---	---	0.92	1.00	1.00
Chamber 2	---	---	0.90	1.40	2.30
Chamber 3	---	---	2.05	2.10	2.90
Chamber 4	1.80	1.40	1.13	---	---
Entrance 1-2	0.30	0.70	0.73	---	---
Entrance 2-3	0.32	1.27	0.70	---	---
Entrance 3-4	0.22	1.20	0.70	---	---
Unit 1	1.25	0.40	0.20	---	---

SW. It is impossible to be sure on this last point, as the difference in shape between square Chm. 4 and the other three might suggest that the latter were parts of the original chultun, with Chm. 4 a later addition. Thus, it could have been a replacement for Chm. 1 when it was closed off. Square or rectangular chambers are rare at Tikal; although two are Preclassic (5F-5, this report, and 5D-6 in TR. 14:673–674); at least one other (2B-15, this report) is Intermediate Classic.

The actual time of construction of the chultun is not known. Perhaps it was when Ch. 6E-6 was altered to serve with Str. 6E-Sub.2; Ch. 6E-7-2nd then could have served with Str. 6E-Sub.1-1st.

After a period of use, Or. 1 and Chm. 1 were sealed, and a new opening (Or. 2) was provided for the chultun. This new Ch. 6E-7-1st-B is roughly similar, in the arrangement of its chambers relative to the orifice, to Ch. 6E-6-1st, as well as a number of others (see Ch. 3G-5, 5C-5, 6C-11, this report). The new orifice was constructed within the area once enclosed by the walls of Str. 6E-Sub.1-1st, and must have been dug after abandonment of Sub.1. Consequently, Ch. 6E-7-1st could have been constructed at the same time as Plat. 6E-1-6th, but no earlier. Supporting this is the fact that Chm. 1 was apparently filled at this time. This was also when Str. 6E-26-4th was constructed. The E wall of the succeeding Str. 6E-26-3rd rests on a midden accumulation, which indicates that a fair-sized accumulation of trash developed around Or. 1 while Str. 6E-26-4th was in use. Rather than worry about keeping this clear, the decision might have been made to simply do away with this opening into the chultun. Trash could then have continued to be dumped E of Str. 6E-26, as indeed it was, without worry that it would spill into, or block, a still useful open chultun. The fill that was used to close this part of the

chultun apparently was derived from an older trash deposit, originally associated with Str. 6E-Sub.1-1st, which would have been available at the time, but probably not later.

This may have been when U. 1, the arrangement of stones in Chm. 4, was laid out. Unit 1, as noted, was built on accumulated debris in that chamber, which served as an occupation surface during the later history of the chultun. This debris contains sherds from vessels characteristic of the Ik Ceramic Complex (Table 2.320). Similar sherds date Plat. 6E-1-6th and the fill of Chm. 1. This suggests contemporaneity of U. 1 and this version of the platform, which was when Or. 2 was constructed. There is no clue whatever as to the function of U. 1.

Chultun 6E-7-1st seems to have been modified after construction of Or. 2. Hence, construction of the orifice and filling of Chm. 1 are assigned to Ch. 6E-7-1st-B, and the final modification to Ch. 6E-7-1st-A. Subsequent to the construction of the E wall of Plat. 6E-1-6th, debris began to accumulate against the face of the wall. This accumulation continued after construction of Plat. 6E-1-5th and Str. 6E-26-3rd. It is represented by Plat. 6E-1:U. 11, which served as an informal occupation surface. Stone rubble was set around Or. 2 on bedrock in order to hold back the surrounding earth of U. 11. Unit 11 itself overlies some of this rubble, which means that its gradual accumulation continued. It is interesting that an actual stone shaft was not constructed for Ch. 6E-7-1st-A similar to that for Ch. 6E-6-1st. Perhaps the reason was that Or. 2 of Ch. 6E-6 was associated with a formal floor surface, while Or. 2 of Ch. 6E-7 was associated with an informal surface.

The final human activity related to the chultun was, of course, the filling of Chm. 3. This operation could have been carried out at a time when trash deposits became too extensive S of the corner of Str. 6E-26. The evidence suggests that this may have been the case at the time of construction of Plat. 6E-1:U. 12 for Plat. 6E-1-4th (see below). Furthermore, when this wall was constructed, the existing E retaining wall of the platform was torn out, which would have created problems so far as the chultun was concerned, for fill would have spilled into the hole. Thus it is probable that Ch. 6E-7 was abandoned at this time.

PLATFORM 6E-1-11TH

The earliest construction of Gp. 6E-1 predates construction of Str. 6E-Sub.1-2nd and associated features. Components included U. 1, a low wall S of Sub.1, which was exposed in excavation for a distance of only 1.60 m, and Plat. 6E-1-11th:Fl. 1, which abuts this wall to the S (Fig. 141). The wall, as it survives, is only 0.10 m high. Since it was later covered by pavement for Plat. 6E-1-10th, it may have been cut down at this time, so the height of the wall when first built is not known. North of the wall is a layer of packed, light-colored earth and pebbles, 0.20 m thick, the surface of which is level with the top of U. 1. This earth extends N as far as the locus of Str. 6E-Sub.1.

The floor extends some 1.90 m S of the wall, and possesses a very hard surface. This pavement, as well as the wall, was constructed on a fill that consists of a mixture of large and small stones, with many sherds. In the western edge of the trench that exposed U. 1 and the floor, bedrock is only 0.17 m below the floor and wall. To the E, the bedrock was at one time extensively quarried to a depth of 0.95 m below the floor.

The significance of Plat. 6E-1-11th:Fl. 1 and U. 1 is unknown. So little of this construction was revealed by excavation that it is not known whether U. 1 is a remnant of a structure or merely some part of the earliest Plat. 6E-1. Unit 1 does not seem to have extended farther W, as excavations did not encounter construction here earlier than Plat. 6E-1-10th:Fl. 1. Perhaps most of the earlier construction was razed when this later floor was laid, which would also explain this. Nowhere else has excavation uncovered features contemporary with Fl. 1 and U. 1 of Plat. 6E-1-11th.

PLATFORM 6E-1-10TH

Components of this architectural development include Plat. 6E-1-10th:Fl. 1, and U. 2-4 (Fig. 142). The floor, a very well-made, hard, thick pavement, covers an extensive platform area S of Str. 6E-Sub.1. It was laid on a small stone ballast with an average thickness of 0.10 m. It abuts the S wall of Str. 6E-Sub.1-2nd, with which it is contemporary. It covers the construction of the previous architectural development, which may have been largely razed to permit this newer floor to be laid.

No traces of Plat. 6E-1-10th:Fl. 1 can be found W of the location of Sub.1-2nd. Since the W wall of that structure was later demolished, it is probable that the floor was as well. That it originally extended farther N is suggested by U. 2, an E-W masonry wall of one course, located beneath the more recent Str. 6E-26. This wall was set into a layer of dark earth, the same layer on which the walls of Sub.1-2nd were based. The top of U. 2 is at an elevation of 223.40 m, only 0.10 m above the surface of Plat. 6E-1-10th:Fl. 1, 8.50 m to the S, an insignificant difference considering the distance involved. Unit 2 seems best interpreted as the N retaining wall for Plat. 6E-1-10th.

Unit 3 is interpreted as a portion of the E retaining wall for Plat. 6E-1-10th. Platform 6E-1-10th:Fl. 1 cannot be followed all the way up to this wall. Its good surface breaks up 4.80 m W of U. 3, but a packed level of white material (U. 4) runs 3.30 m W from the top of this wall. Unit 4 has the same thickness as Plat. 6E-1-10th:Fl. 1, and the western end is only 0.10 m below the E end of that floor. Since U. 4 slopes upwards to the W, and Fl. 1 dips downward to the E, it is probable that U. 4 is a poorly preserved portion of Fl. 1. The gap of 1.80 m between the two may be attributed to later activity, as the earth fill here appears to be continuous with that above the floors, and sherds that postdate their construction are to be found here.

The wall (U. 3) seems to be set on a layer of very hard, packed gray earth. This can be followed E to the wall of the final platform, though the separation between the hard gray and overlying strata is not clear beyond a point 1.00 m from U. 3. No attempt was made to follow the hard-packed gray stratum westward beneath the wall, but there is no reason to assume that it does not continue here. East of U. 3, this stratum may be regarded as an occupation surface beyond Plat. 6E-1-10th.

Granting the propositions just discussed, the following is indicated: Plat. 6E-1-10th:Fl. 1 extended 5.10 m N of Str. 6E-Sub.1-2nd, and 8.40 m to the E. The floor extended more than 4 m to the S, and 2.60 m to the W of the structure. How much farther is not known. Lack of Preclassic ceramics in the trench into the S wall of the platform indicates that at least the Preclassic occupation of Gp. 6E-1 was centered N of this area. In other words, Sub.1-2nd was based on Plat. 6E-1, with a wide expanse of platform surface on all sides. It is impossible to tell if it was the only structure on the platform without further excavation, particularly to the W, but such a possibility cannot be ruled out.

PLATFORM 6E-1-9TH

The next modification of the platform saw an increase of 0.37 m in elevation at the time of construction of Str. 6E-Sub.1-1st and Str. 6E-Sub.2 (Fig. 143). Platform 6E-1-9th:Fl. 1 is the only surviving architecture of the platform that may be assigned to this development. The floor was exposed by excavation E of the surviving wall of 6E-Sub.2, on which it abuts. It can be followed 1.80 m to the E, at which point the floor breaks up. This break seems to be the result of activity connected with the laying of later Plat. 6E-1-2nd:Fl. 1, for the pavements of Plat. 6E-1-3rd-B, 4th, 6th, and 7th break up along the same line as Fl. 1 of 9th. This is indicative of an intrusion that postdates use of the floor of Plat. 6E-1-3rd-B.

Presumably Plat. 6E-1-9th:Fl. 1 at one time abutted Str. 6E-Sub.1-1st to the E, for the surviving stones from the N wall of that structure projected some 0.40 m. above the elevation of Fl. 1. Burial 128, with Cauac ceramics, is interpreted as initial to Str. 6E-Sub.1-1st, as discussed elsewhere (this report, section III). Thus it should date construction of Fl. 1, if it was associated with erection of the structure. In fact, a very small sherd sample sealed beneath Fl. 1 includes sherds no later than the Chuen Ceramic Complex, expectable since trash deposits available for filling operations would have contained many Chuen sherds. There is, then, no inconsistency of the evidence with the interpretation given here of the relation of Plat. 6E-1-9th:Fl. 1 to the Str. 6E-Sub.1-1st.

Retaining walls for Plat. 6E-1 associated with 9th:-Fl. 1 have not been found, so it is impossible to speculate on the overall size of Plat. 6E-1-9th. One feature that might be noted, however, is U. 5, a floor remnant discovered beneath a portion of the back wall of later Str. 6E-26. This cannot be tied physically to any other piece of architecture. Its elevation is 0.17 m lower than that of Plat. 6E-1-9th:Fl. 1. Considering the distance separating U. 5 from the nearest exposure of Fl. 1, this difference is insignificant. It is a fact that U. 5 does not relate to Plat. 6E-1-10th, and it is so much lower than floors for Plat. 6E-1-7th and 8th that it is doubtful if it can be related to construction later than 9th. The only likely alternative is to regard it as a piece of Plat. 6E-1-9th:Fl. 1, which means that 6E-1-9th extended quite far to the N. This is admittedly speculative, but given the available evidence, it seems to be a reasonable explanation.

In the E trench, it seems likely that U. 3 was raised in height to serve with Fl. 1. The evidence for this is not good, but one or both of two occupation surfaces E of U. 3 (U. 6 and 7) are quite possibly related to Plat. 6E-1-9th. Unit 6, the earlier of the two, overlies a hard fill of light-colored earth E of U. 3. Ceramics from this fill (68F/9) are largely Preclassic, with only a few possible Manik sherds. Since the deposit is not sealed, the very small amount of Early Classic material may be the result of contamination of Preclassic fill. The top of this fill abuts the top surviving course of the U. 3 masonry. If U. 3 relates to Plat. 6E-1-10th, and U. 6 is a Preclassic occupation surface that postdates U. 3, then it must relate to Plat. 6E-1-9th.

Above U. 6 is another occupation surface, U. 7 (Fig. 152). This may also relate to Plat. 6E-1-9th, or perhaps 8th. The latter seems more probable, but only because there is no other feature in this trench assignable to that architectural development.

PLATFORM 6E-1-8TH

South of Str. 6E-Sub.1, a very small portion of a wall was uncovered and designated as Str. 6E-Sub.3 (Fig. 144). It was based on a light-colored packed layer (Plat. 6E-1-8th:Fl. 1), 3 cm thick. This in turn covers earth fill

above Plat. 6E-1-10th:Fl. 1. The elevation of portions of the N end of Plat. 6E-1-8th:Fl. 1 is 5 cm below the surface of Plat. 6E-1-7th:Fl. 1 at its nearest exposure. It appears, therefore, that this floor was not laid in this area, but ended at the walls of a structure based on this packed layer. Cultural material from beneath Fl. 1 of 8th includes no sherds later than Early Classic. Platform 6E-1-7th:Fl. 1, to the contrary, seals a few Ik sherds. Since the sample from beneath Fl. 1 of 8th is extensive, it is reasonable to assume that this predates Fl. 1 of 7th. It may be a part of an occupation surface that covered the entire Plat. 6E-1, a logical assumption in view of its elevation 0.15 m above that of the earlier floor for Plat. 6E-1-9th. It is the only occupation surface that can be attributed to Early Classic times, although abundant Manik sherds of midden quality from a variety of proveniences testify to an Early Classic occupation of Gp. 6E-1. Why the occupation surface should not have been a plaster pavement, since those that went before and after were plaster, is unknown. But for the reasons given above, it has been designated as a floor despite this difference.

Since Str. 6E-Sub.1 and Sub.2 continued in use with the subsequent Plat. 6E-1-7th:Fl. 1, they obviously were in use with the surface of Plat. 6E-1-8th. When Fl. 1 of 7th was laid, however, that of 8th seems to have been extensively destroyed, except where protected by Str. 6E-Sub.3. The actual extent of Plat. 6E-1-8th when Fl. 1 was in use is unknown, as so little information pertaining to this architectural development survives. There are clues, however. In the trench into the S face of Plat. 6E-1 is considerable Early Classic debris. Much of this lies to the S of U. 8, the only wall identified in this cut. All lots S of this wall contain Intermediate and Late Classic sherds as well, but the quantity of such material decreases with depth and proximity to the wall. Extensive root damage and erosion in this area has undoubtedly caused contamination of sherds sampled. If allowance is made for this, the picture presented here is that trash began to accumulate S of U. 8 in Early Classic times.

Cultural material from behind the wall itself seems to bear out this interpretation, although again contamination is a serious problem. Material from behind the best-preserved section of the wall (68K/8) includes only one definite Intermediate Classic sherd. This is probably the result of contamination. All the rest of this material is Early Classic, and sherds from the debris on which U. 8 was built are also Early Classic. A reasonable conclusion is that construction of U. 8 was contemporary with Plat. 6E-1-8th:Fl. 1, both of which originated sometime after the beginning of the Early Classic. Although the wall style of U. 8 by itself is not diagnostic, it at least would not be out of place in an Early Classic context, and it differs from the wall style of later Classic construction in Gp. 6E-1.

To the E, the level of Plat. 6E-1-8th:Fl. 1 does not seem to have extended beyond the later location of U. 14. This is suggested by the existence of apparent Early Classic midden material to the E, which was eventually incorporated into the fill of later architectural developments. In the E trench, U. 7 may be the occupation surface beyond the platform. It is the only feature in this trench that can possibly be associated with Plat. 6E-1-8th. The material above U. 7 is in large part comparable to the Early Classic midden material E of the locus of Str. 6E-Sub.3.

PLATFORM 6E-1-7TH

A single floor (Plat. 6E-1-7th:Fl. 1) is the only evidence of this development of Plat. 6E-1 that survives (Fig. 144). This exceptionally thick floor does not have as smooth and hard a surface as the earlier floors of Plat. 6E-1-9th and 10th. Floor 1 of 7th abuts the surviving wall of Str. 6E-Sub.2, and a straight line of termination shows that it also met the N wall of that structure. To the E, Fl. 1 is broken at the same point at which the floor of Plat. 6E-1-9th breaks up. The reason for this damage has been given above.

There is reason to suspect an association of Fl. 1 of 7th with Str. 6E-Sub.1-1st to the E, although a word of caution is in order. The existence at this time of a structure just S of Sub.1 raises the possibility that Sub.1 was replaced by Sub.3. Since a straight projection of the level of Fl. 1 up to the surviving masonry of Sub.1-1st would have met the wall 4 cm from its top, it is possible that a slight slant would have permitted the pavement to cover a now abandoned Sub.1. Arguing against this is the absence within the area of the structure of any floor that can even remotely be linked to Plat. 6E-1-7th:Fl. 1, and the fact that Fl. 1 ends in a reasonably straight line at a point that seems the most probable location for the northern portion of the W wall of Sub.1-1st. Further, the wall of Sub.2 projects a maximum of only 9 cm above the surface of Fl. 1, which compares with an assumed 4 cm in the case of Sub.1-1st. The evidence, therefore, favors continued use of Str. 6E-Sub.1-1st with Plat. 6E-1-7th:Fl. 1.

It is clear that Fl. 1 also served Str. 6E-Sub.3. At its locus, the floor of Plat. 6E-8th survived the wholesale destruction it seems to have been subjected to elsewhere. The elevation of this floor in places is within 5 cm of that of Plat. 6E-1-7th:Fl. 1. The surviving wall of Str. 6E-Sub.3, associated with the floor of Plat. 6E-1-8th, projects above this, so it is obvious that Fl. 1 of 7th never was laid in this area. Evidently, Str. 6E-Sub.3 remained in use; therefore, Fl. 1 must have abutted its walls.

As in the case of the previous architectural development, the extent of Plat. 6E-1 when Fl. 1 of 7th was in use can only be approximated. As noted elsewhere, Fl. 1 may have been associated with the shaft of Ch. 6E-6 (see its discussion). If so, this indicates the minimal extension of Fl. 1 to the W. Floor 1 was not physically followed that far, however. To the S, U. 8 probably continued to serve as the platform retaining wall.

PLATFORM 6E-1-6TH

This development is defined by two components: Plat. 6E-1-6th:Fl. 1 and U. 10. Floor 1 has been traced extensively over Plat. 6E-1 (Fig. 145). A gap of 0.53 m separates this pavement from Str. 6E-25-2nd to the W, but it seems likely that originally the floor abutted that structure, for its wall masonry extends below the level of the floor surface. The floor completely covers Str. 6E-Sub.2, and a projection of its surface indicates that Str. 6E-Sub.1 was also covered. Conceivably, Str. 6E-Sub.3 continued in use, for Fl. 1 would not have covered its standing masonry.

Platform 6E-1-6th:Fl. 1 was traced to both orifices of Ch. 6E-6. As found, it seals Or. 1, but not Or. 2. Here, the top of the masonry of the shaft is in the same position relative to Fl. 1 as is the floor of Plat. 6E-1-7th farther E, which suggests an association with that floor. Further, evidence presented elsewhere suggests that the chultun was abandoned at the same time as Str. 6E-Sub.2 (see discussion of the chultun). The reason for the hole in Plat. 6E-1-6th:Fl. 1 seems to be that the fill in the neck of the chultun slumped, causing the floor above to break up.

The condition of Fl. 1 in the vicinity of Str. 6E-26 has been discussed in conjunction with that structure. It apparently served both Str. 6E-26-4th and Str. 6E-26-3rd. Unit 9, a posthole, is located in the surface of Fl. 1, where this surface forms an inset in the SW corner of Str. 6E-26.

Unit 10 is a layer of light-colored fill that continues the level of Plat. 6E-1-6th:Fl. 1 to the N (Fig. 151). This is the level on which the walls of Str. 6E-26-4th must have been based. It is not known how far N this fill once ran, for in the trench through the axis of 6E-26, the intrusive cut for Bu. 129 seems to have destroyed the evidence. Beneath the burial, however, the light-colored fill continues to a point 0.15 m N of the Gp. 6E-1 baseline, and this may mark the location of the N retaining wall (Fig. 145:11).

The location of the platform retaining wall on the E poses a problem. Floor 1 of 6th apparently continued to serve Plat. 6E-1-5th, about which information does exist in connection with the retaining wall. A similar wall for 6th could not have been located farther E because it would have blocked Or. 2 of Ch. 6E-7, which was constructed at this time (see discussion of Ch. 6E-7). To the W, Str. 6E-25-2nd seems to have served as the limit of Plat. 6E-1. If the W wall of that structure is the same one that served the final structure, then the wall also represents the actual western extent of Plat. 6E-1-6th. To the S, there is no evidence to indicate that U. 8 did not continue to serve as the S retaining wall.

PLATFORM 6E-1-5TH

The components of this development were Plat. 6E-1-6th:Fl. 1, and a now vanished E retaining wall (Fig. 146). The location of this wall, however, is known from Str. 6E-26. The outer walls of 26-3rd included a S wall with a multiple-course portion running only 1 m from the SE corner. The multiple-course wall ends here, but in a diagonal line indicating a corner, from which a wall with a batter ran to the S. This wall quite likely was built when Plat. 6E-1-6th:Fl. 1 was laid; later, it was abutted by the wall of 26-3rd. This structure wall is securely dated, and it postdates Plat. 6E-1-6th:Fl. 1.

East of the location of the platform retaining wall, U. 11, a layer of packed, light-colored earth was noted at an elevation of 223.65 m. This is high enough to have covered what little was left of Str. 6E-Sub.1-2nd, and at about the right elevation to be interpreted as an informal occupation surface at the base of the platform wall. Unit 11 is well defined near Or. 2 of Ch. 6E-7 (Fig. 154), and it can be traced to Str. 6E-26. Its surface meets the S wall of the structure 0.15 m above the wall base. Some of U. 11 may have accumulated both prior to, and after, construction of Str. 6E-26-3rd and Plat. 6E-1-5th.

A shift in the location of the N wall of the platform seems indicated. Part of the N wall involves the new construction of Str. 6E-26-3rd. Where the earlier wall was located is not clear. The W wall of the platform possibly remained the same, which is to say the rear wall of Str. 6E-25-2nd. The location of the S wall is presumably marked by U. 8. Obviously, with large-scale construction in process, coupled with continued use of Plat. 6E-1-6th:Fl. 1, some extensive floor patching would have been necessary. No evidence of this survives, but later major construction may be responsible for obliteration of traces of this patching.

PLATFORM 6E-1-4TH

This architectural development is represented by Plat. 6E-1-4th:Fl. 1 and U. 12 and 13 (Fig. 147). By now, the trash associated with the occupation of Str. 6E-26 had become quite deep to the E of the structure and group platform. The E retaining wall of the platform was no longer needed, and was torn out. In the process an interment may have been disturbed, which was then reburied out of the way beneath the new front step of Str. 6E-26-2nd (Bu. 152).

To replace the older retaining wall, a one-course wall was constructed 0.60 m farther W. Designated U. 12, this was based on packed earth fill, which blends to the W with midden material associated with the occupation of Str. 6E-26-3rd. Perhaps this midden was added to at this time, to bring the area up to a uniform level. Unit 12 runs

2.60 m S from the SE corner of the stairs for Str. 6E-26-2nd-D, then turns an approximate right angle to run westwards. What the wall did then is unknown, for it was later extensively destroyed. It probably turned another angle to run S again, for Plat. 6E-1-4th:Fl. 1, which is interpreted as the surface for this feature, extends to the S in the area where Str. 6E-Sub.2 once stood.

Floor 1 of 4th was identified in an area 2.80 m W of U. 12. It was laid directly on the surface of Fl. 1 of 6th. This floor cannot now be followed as far as its predecessor to the W, but since the floors of 6th and 3rd seem to be associated with Str. 6E-25-2nd, that structure also obviously had to be in use with Plat. 6E-1-4th:Fl. 1. The floor must have later been destroyed, for unknown reasons.

Floor 1 of 4th cannot now be followed to Str. 6E-26, but there is an isolated floor fragment, U. 13, that turns up to the stairs of Str. 6E-26-2nd-D. Unit 13 is interpreted as a surviving fragment of Fl. 1 of 4th, for the following reasons. Stratigraphically, it is in the same relative position with respect to the floor of Plat. 6E-1-6th. Moreover, the elevation of U. 13 is within 1 cm of the nearest exposure of Fl. 1 of 4th. Unit 13, therefore, serves to establish the connection of Str. 6E-26-2nd-D and Plat. 6E-1-4th.

The situation at the locus of Str. 6E-Sub.3 is anything but clear. A level projection of Plat. 6E-1-4th:Fl. 1 to this area would not have covered the standing masonry of the structure. Moreover, U. 12 appears to have avoided this area altogether, running to the N and then W of it. The conclusion from all this is that 6E-Sub.3 continued in use at this time.

PLATFORM 6E-1-3RD-B

This development involved another shift in the location of the E wall, and the laying of a new floor (Fig. 148). Unit 14, which replaced U. 12 as the E wall of the platform, is located in the same position as the E wall of Plat. 6E-1-5th. It consists of a single course of masonry, as did U. 12. The northernmost stone is bonded into the front wall of Str. 6E-26, and serves as part of the E wall of the stairs for 26-2nd-C. Unit 14 runs at least 8 m to the S, perhaps farther, but later construction obscures this.

Although there is no surviving physical connection of a platform floor with U. 14, it seems all but certain that Plat. 6E-1-3rd:Fl. 1 represents such a feature. This hard plaster surface runs from a point 3 m W of U. 14 all the way to Str. 6E-25-2nd, where it abuts the E wall of that structure (Fig. 150). Various later intrusions are responsible for lack of continuity with U. 14, but a projection of the floor surface would have covered the surviving masonry of both U. 12 and Str. 6E-Sub.3, meeting the top of the masonry of U. 14.

Around Or. 2 of Ch. 6E-6, Fl. 1 of Plat. 6E-1-3rd breaks up in an uneven circle. Since the masonry of the neck of the chultun does not project above the level of the floor for Plat. 6E-1-6th (Fig. 153), it is doubtful if the chultun continued in use with Fl. 1 of 3rd. The best explanation seems to be that fill in the neck of the chultun slumped, and Fl. 1, which covered it, collapsed to form an irregular circular break.

Unit 15 designates a curious feature 2.60 m E of Or. 2 of Ch. 6E-6. This is a hole, averaging 0.60 m in diameter, which penetrates Fl. 1 of Plat. 6E-1-3rd and extends to bedrock. There is no indication as to whether U. 15 postdates the laying of Fl. 1. Lack of any masonry around the hole beneath Fl. 1 might favor this, but this is tenuous. Regardless of the time of its formation, the hole does penetrate Fl. 1 and so is best described here. Function is equally an enigma. Perhaps a new chultun was planned, and for this a neck was excavated. The depth to bedrock might have been so great as to render further work on the chultun impossible. In favor of this, the size and shape of the hole may be compared with Or. 2 of Ch. 6E-6. But, it would have been difficult, if not impossible, to excavate the bedrock by lying on Fl. 1 and leaning into the hole.

The relationship of Plat. 6E-1-3rd:Fl. 1 to Str. 6E-25 has already been mentioned. Floor 1 does not survive in the vicinity of Str. 6E-26, but it must have been associated with 26-2nd-C. If the floor is associated with U. 14, as stated above, then this association with the structure is valid, as U. 14 is clearly associated with 26-2nd-C, as noted above.

PLATFORM 6E-1-3RD-A

This modification of the platform consisted of local patching. Specific evidence consists of U. 16, a very tough, dark plaster surface, 4.20 m S of the N wall of the inset in Str. 6E-26 (Fig. 148). Unit 16 is only 3 cm thick, and its edges taper to meet the surface of Plat. 6E-1-3rd:-Fl. 1. To the N, the two surfaces are blended so well that they were at first mistaken for a single surface.

Perhaps Fl. 1 was patched at other places at this time, though there is no specific evidence for this. In any case, no major construction or alteration was undertaken at this time.

PLATFORM 6E-1-2ND

The first activity connected with this modification concerned the existing floors of earlier architectural developments. Holes in a variety of shapes and sizes were dug through Plat. 6E-1-3rd:Fl. 1. These include U. 22 through 29 (Fig. 148). All are deep enough to penetrate the floor of Plat 6E-1-6th. Unit 26, the largest, just off the SW corner of the stairway of Str. 6E-26, contains stone rubble and large masonry blocks that project above Plat. 6E-1-3rd:Fl. 1. Unit 23, to the W, is much smaller, but contains two masonry blocks that are 0.58 m in length. Since the hole

is small, they were placed on end. Unit 25 contains Bu. 161. The other holes are empty. Their purpose, save that for Bu. 161, is a mystery. One may only hazard a guess that they were connected with some sort of ritual, perhaps concerned with the abandonment of existing structures and the erection of new ones.

Considerable architecture connected with this development survives, so that a relatively complete picture of this penultimate platform may be presented (Fig. 148). To the E, U. 14 continued to serve. Four meters S of Str. 6E-26, however, a narrow stairway (U. 17) was built against U. 14 (Fig. 181a). This was based on exposed fill, apparently a midden accumulation that probably sloped down to the E. Hence, each of the surviving three steps is set on a lower level than the others, going from W to E. Only a portion of the lowermost step survives, which reveals that the eastern portion of the stairway was demolished at a later date. Therefore, it is not surely known if there were more than two steps leading up to the platform level. A change in soil coloration suggests the existence of a low step at the base, followed by two rises of 0.30 m to the floor of the platform.

The stairs of U. 17 terminate at an elevation 8 cm above the top of U. 14. Thus, paving higher in elevation than Plat. 6E-1-3rd:Fl. 1 must have served with U. 17. If so, then U. 14 must have been raised the same height elsewhere. Indications are that this pavement was Plat. 6E-1-2nd:Fl. 1 (see below).

Unit 18 is a wall that runs E from the SE corner of Str. 6E-25-1st. It consists of two faces of masonry set 0.50 m apart, with a rubble hearting. The N face was intruded through Plat. 6E-1-6th:Fl. 1, and of necessity through the floors of 4th and 3rd. The S face, which was more carefully finished than the northern, is in line with the S face of the structure. Unit 18 extends E to the S end of U. 14. The top of U. 18 is at the same approximate elevation as the top of U. 14 and 17. Since all evidence indicates that U. 14 served as a retaining wall, U. 18 must also have served as one. The elevation of the top of U. 18 is the same as Plat. 6E-1-2nd:Fl. 1, so that the pavement must have sealed the earth fill N of U. 18, and E of U. 14. South of U. 18, another plaster surface, U. 19, abuts U. 18 near its base, as well as the S wall of Str. 6E-25-1st. Unit 18, therefore, forms a sort of step running from Str. 6E-25-1st to the E edge of the platform, with a lower level on the S and a higher level on the N.

Unit 19 was not followed to the S except around Str. 6E-163, to which it turns up. It is presumed that this floor runs to the top of U. 8, the wall exposed in the trench that runs into the S face of Plat. 6E-1. Only the lower portion of this wall survives, however, and actual evidence for such an assumption is lacking.

North of U. 18, there are three floor fragments to consider. Platform 6E-1-2nd:Fl. 1 itself is defined in front of Str. 6E-25-1st, on which it abuts. This means it is contemporaneous with that structure, and therefore also U. 18. The similar elevation of the top of U. 18 and Fl. 1 has already been noted. Thus it is clear, as noted above, that Fl. 1 covered the area N of U. 18 and E of U. 14. It is therefore not unexpected to find that projection of Fl. 1, with allowance for its obvious dip to the E, comes to within a few centimeters of the top of U. 17.

Unit 20 is a very small floor remnant 7 m S of Str. 6E-26, and 9.40 m E of Str. 6E-25. Its elevation is such that it fits the hypothetical projection of Fl. 1 to U. 17 just discussed above. Unit 21 is a fairly extensive floor remnant in the inset of Str. 6E-26 that turns up to the walls of Str. 6E-26-2nd-B. Its elevation is consistent with that of Fl. 1 and U. 20. Both U. 20 and 21 have in common with Fl. 1 a very poor consistency, as compared with earlier pavements, so that they tend to break up readily into small chunks. This, then, is a further indication that all are parts of the same floor.

PLATFORM 6E-1-1ST

The final modification of Plat. 6E-1 saw an extension of the formal platform area several meters to the E (Fig. 149). Apparently, midden material was so extensive by now E of Str. 6E-26 and the platform that this extension was easily accomplished by incorporation of the midden with only a minimal addition of fill from other sources. The line of the back wall of Str. 6E-26 was carried 7.20 m to the E. Here the wall turns S. This E wall was exposed by excavation at this NE corner, and also by a trench near the middle of the wall (U. 34). In the E trench, an informal floor surface, U. 35, extends E of the base of U. 34. Unit 8 is the only exposure of the S wall, which was originally constructed for Plat. 6E-1-8th. The W wall seems to have been an extension of the back wall of Str. 6E-25.

A problem that pertains to Plat. 6E-1-1st is the means of access, for the floor of this platform is a good 2 m higher than the surrounding terrain. There obviously must have been a stairway somewhere. Since a stairway for 6E-1-2nd (U. 17) was located on the E side of the platform, one might suspect a similar location for the steps to the final platform. In fact, U. 34 does not seem to correspond with a projection of the E wall of the platform from the NE corner. Since U. 34 projects beyond the expected location of the E wall, it becomes the most likely candidate for a portion of a stairway. Moreover, the masonry differs somewhat from that of the NE corner, and suggests a different function. Finally, the slope of the ruin mound in the vicinity of U. 34 is more gradual than in other areas, suggesting that a near-vertical retaining wall did not stand here. Aside from this, nothing is known of the extent of the stairway. A hypothetical reconstruction does, however, indicate that it must have been largely inset.

Units 18 and 19 apparently continued to serve Plat. 6E-1-1st. However, 0.80 m N of the E end of U. 18, there is an alteration. Instead of continuing N as U. 14, the wall turns E again. This new E-W wall, U. 30, is represented by a line of rubble and a very clear corner where it intersects U. 14. Platform 6E-1 seems, therefore, to have had a higher N and lower S portion. The old U. 14, except for a mere 0.80 m extent, was eliminated.

It is doubtful if a whole new floor was laid on the platform. There is no evidence of one, except for U. 31, a surface that overlies closely U. 21 in the inset of Str. 6E-26. Unit 31 turns up to the walls of 6E-26-2nd-A, and quite likely is a local patch connected with modification of 6E-26. Elsewhere, Plat. 6E-1-2nd:Fl. 1 and U. 19 seem to have continued in use. The new portion of Plat. 6E-1 was probably covered by floors that were blended into the eastern edges of Fl. 1 and U. 19. The only survival of such a floor is U. 32, a small fragment that turns up to the S wall of Str. 6E-162.

An interesting feature of U. 31 is a round hole, 0.14 m in diameter, in which the neck of the olla was inserted (U. 33). The presence of the olla neck seems to eliminate the possibility that this is a posthole. A more plausible suggestion would be that it functioned as a drain. An analogous feature was noted in Gp. 4F-3 (this report).

SHERDS AND ARTIFACTS

Lot groups defined for the various structures, chultuns, and supporting platform of Gp. 6E-1 are defined in Table 2.320, with content in Tables 2.321–2.328.

CONSTRUCTION FILL

By far, the greater bulk of cultural material comes from fill situations. The long, apparently continuous sequence, however, opens the possibility that much fill content is refuse from earlier architectural developments of Gp. 6E-1. This gains some support from the incorporation of middens associated with Str. 6E-26 into the fill of Plat. 6E-1-1st. Indeed, much of the cultural material in the various fills is of midden quality. No attempt is made here to discuss all lot groups from fill sources, as there is such a great quantity. Instead, those lot groups of special importance are singled out for attention. These key lot groups are those of importance for dating, and those that may be important as indicators of the material inventory of early users of Gp. 6E-1.

The earliest known material is in LG. 1a and 1b of the platform. Lot Group 1a is sealed by the deepest floor, and should serve to date Plat. 6E-1-11th (and Gp. TS. 27, Table 2.339). The other is not sealed, but includes a large sherd sample of midden quality that is contemporary with LG. 1a. This lot group provides an excellent sample for analysis of the social dimension of ceramics that should pertain to the earliest activity at this locus.

Platform 6E-1:LG. 2c is both sealed by and dates Plat. 6E-1-10th:Fl. 1, and therefore all construction of Gp. TS. 25. Lot Groups 2b and 2d, which theoretically are contemporary, are contaminated by later material. Platform 6E-1:LG. 3a provides a minimum date for construction of Plat. 6E-1-9th:Fl. 1, which seals it, although Bu. 128 probably gives a more precise date (ca. 25 BC; see section III) for this and the following Gp. TS 22 in general (Table 2.339). Lot Group 3d, also fill for Plat. 6E-1-9th:Fl. 1, is contaminated by later material. Lot Group 3a is perhaps of even more import, since the most logical source of its contents would be trash associated with the use of Str. 6E-Sub.1-2nd. This is consistent with the dating of the ceramics, which pertain to the Chuen Complex. An analysis of the ceramics for social dimension is therefore of extreme importance in an attempt to learn the function of Str. 6E-Sub.1-2nd.

Group TS. 21 (Table 2.339) is dated by material from Plat. 6E-1:LG. 4a, which is sealed by Plat. 6E-1-8th:Fl. 1. Lot Groups 4c–g, from the same fill, are contaminated by later material. Again, the most likely source for this deposit is trash associated with the use of architecture that immediately preceded Gp. TS. 21, and again the dating of the material is generally consistent with this interpretation. The greater mixture of such material with earlier fill, however, may be expected to correlate with a greater period of time from the first activity at this locus.

Platform 6E-1:LG. 4b warrants special attention. This comes from the area between Str. 6E-Sub.1 and Sub.3 and to the E, and includes Bu. 138. This material is made up primarily of late Manik sherds of midden quality. The dating indicates an essential contemporaneity with the use of both structures. Thus, the material E of the structures is probably refuse dumped by their occupants. Material between the structures, however, must be accounted for in another way. The excavation data indicates that a pit was dug here below the level of Plat. 6E-1-8th:Fl. 1, which at its deepest point just barely penetrates Plat. 6E-1-10th:Fl. 1. The reason for the pit is not entirely clear. Perhaps it was dug to receive Bu. 138; if so, it is considerably deeper than necessary. Since the fill of the pit is essentially the same material as the trash to the E of the structure, it is very probable that it originally was a part of that deposit. As the closest available material, it would have been logical to use it to fill the hole. If so, LG. 4b becomes significant as debris representative of the Early Classic occupation of Gp. 6E-1, and of importance for analysis of the social dimension of the ceramics. It dates Gp. TS. 20 (Table 2.339).

Platform 6E-1:LG. 5 is a sample sealed by Plat. 6E-1-7th:Fl. 1. Most sherds are of the Manik Complex, but a few Ik sherds are included, and so date the construction of Gp. TS. 19 (Table 2.339). Platform 6E-1:LG. 6,

sealed by Plat. 6E-1-6th:Fl. 1, similarly dates Gp. TS. 17. Group TS. 18 (Table 2.339) is dated by Str. 6E-26:LG. 1a, which is partially sealed but generally uncontaminated. Similarly, Str. 6E-26:LG. 1b, partially sealed in the fill of Str. 6E-26-2nd-D, dates Gp. TS. 13 (Table 2.339). Chultun 6E-7:LG. 1, 2, and 4 may also be referred to this same group time span. These are the fill of Chm. 2, 3, and 4, and probably derive from the same occupation trash as Str. 6E-26:LG. 2b (see below).

Group TS. 7 (Table 2.339) is dated by Plat. 6E-1:LG. 8a, which was partially sealed by Plat. 6E-1-2nd:Fl. 1, but seems uncontaminated. Lot Groups 8b, 8c, and 8d should be contemporary, although Early Classic material was used for the latter, as well as to fill Str. 6E-163 (LG. 1). This may have come from the fill and trash of Str. 6E-Sub.3. Lot Groups 9a and 9d of Plat. 6E-1-1st should date Gp. TS. 5, but sample size is not good.

Aside from the key samples, material from fill context is either too small in quantity to be useful, or else badly mixed. In the last analysis, it would probably be valid to lump together the ceramic material of each ceramic complex, regardless of provenience, for analysis of social dimension, for this follows from the initial proposition that all the material was in use at one time or another in Gp. 6E-1. This procedure is not necessary in most cases, however, as the key lot groups discussed above provide more controlled samples, and they are also of sufficient size.

MATERIAL ABOVE LIVING LEVELS

Here, material that remains in situ with reference to a specific architectural feature will be considered. This excludes all material that has been disturbed for reuse as construction fill, even though the original association of the material may be inferred with a high degree of probability (as discussed above).

The earliest material that might fall in this category is included in Plat. 6E-1:LG. 4g. This is located immediately outside the S wall of the platform, and seems to represent an incidental accumulation of litter that should be essentially contemporaneous with Plat. 6E-1:LG. 4b (already discussed). The one problem is that destruction from natural causes is extensive in this area, so that LG. 4g is undoubtedly mixed with platform fill as well as some later occupation refuse. Therefore, it is not as good a sample for analysis of social dimension as LG. 4b.

Aside from Plat. 6E-1:LG. 4g, the earliest material not disturbed from its original deposition is Str. 6E-26:LG. 2a. This is a concentration of very large sherds, clearly a midden. This lot group dates Gp. TS. 16 (Table 2.339).

Structure 6E-26:LG. 2b represents a further accumulation of the LG. 2a midden. This deposit continued to build up E of Str. 6E-26 (Fig. 181d), and provides an excellent sherd sample for analysis of social dimension. It also dates Gp. TS. 14 (Table 2.339).

Structure 6E-26:LG. 2c–f all represent midden material associated with that structure. These are essentially mixed, with some content as early as 26-3rd. The bulk of the material, however, should pertain to use of 26-2nd and 1st.

Since Str. 6E-25 was not extensively excavated, good deposits of trash were not encountered. Lot Groups 2a and 2b, S and W of the structure, should contain some occupation debris, but they probably also contain much washed-out structure fill.

Both lot groups associated with Str. 6E-162, from above and around it, should contain occupation litter with some fill contamination. Lot Group 1 includes the fragments of a single metate, apparently left in situ on the floor (Fig. 181c). Lot Group 2 contains some charcoal and burned objects around the structure.

Occupation material from Str. 6E-163 ought to be found in LG. 2. The structure was badly weathered, however, and fill contamination is unquestionably great.

Platform 6E-1:LG. 9a, S of, and overlying LG. 4g, may be interpreted as incidental Late Classic litter. Small sample size and mixture, however, cause this to be a relatively unimportant sample.

Both chultuns contained strata that appear to represent an incidental accumulation during use. These are Ch. 6E-6:LG. 3, and Ch. 6E-7:LG. 3. Neither contains a good sherd sample.

OTHER SOURCES

Sherds and artifacts were recovered from three test pits S and E of Plat. 6E-1. Because the material in them could have come from a number of different sources within Gp. 6E-1, this has been placed in lot groups for Gp. 6E-1 as a whole. Subdivision of the contents within these lot groups is minimal. In the Op. 68C test pit, for example, the sherds of the deepest lot differ in no significant way from these of the surface lot. This refuse is probably a mixture of platform fill and litter occasionally dropped off the platform. Material in the other two test pits also probably represents the occasional discard of trash, coupled with the washing down of bits of rubbish from other places. In both pits, material in deep lots is older on the whole than that nearer the surface.

Other sources of cultural material from Gp. 6E-1 are Bu. 128–131, 138, 151–153, and 161.

TABLE 2.320 (Part 1)
Group 6E-1: Lot Groups

Feature	Lot Group	Lot	Provenience	Ceramic Evaluation
Str.6E-25	1a	68H/4	Unsealed eroded fill of 1st	Imix
	1b	68H/5	Unsealed fill of 2nd	Preclassic; Ik
	1c	68N/1-3,5,6	Unsealed, eroded fill of 1st and 2nd	Manik; Ik; and Imix
	2a	68H/6	S of structure to floor (U. 19) of Plat. 6E-1	Manik and Ik and/or Imix and/or Imix
	2b	68N/4	W of structure, to level of wall base level of wall base	Preclassic; Manik; Ik and/or Imix
Str.6E-26	1a	68G/7,11,15,17	Sealed fill of 3rd	Early Imix
	1b	68G/2	Partially sealed fill of 2nd-D	Imix
	2a	68G/6; 68I/45	E of 4th, beneath wall of 3rd	Imix
	2b	68G/4,5	E of 3rd, above 2a	Imix
	2c	68G/1,3	E of 26, above 2b	Some Manik; mostly Imix
	2d	68G/8	W of structure to level of platform floor	Preclassic; Manik; Ik; Imix
	2e	68G/13 68L/1,3	N of structure, above 2f	Imix
	2f	68L/2,4	N of structure, below 2e, to base of wall	Imix
Str.6E-162	1	68G/10	Surface to floor level	Ik and/or Imix
	2	68G/9	Outside structure to level of Plat.6E-1 floor	Ik and/or Imix
Str.6E-163	1	68H/7	Unsealed fill	Manik
	2	68H/9	Outside structure to floor (U. 19) of Plat. 6E-1	Manik; some Imix
Ch.6E-6	1	68B/1	Fill of Neck 2	Preclassic
	2	68B/2	Upper stratum of fill in Chm.2	Preclassic
	3	68B/3	Lower stratum of fill in Chm.2	Preclassic
	4	68B/4	Fill of Neck 1	Preclassic
Ch.6E-7	1	68Z/1-5	Fill of Chm. 3	?
	2	68Z/6	Upper stratum of fill in Chm.4	Imix
	3	68Z/7,12	Lower stratum of fill (U.1) in Chm.4	Ik
	4	68Z/8,9	Fill of Chm. 2	Imix
	5	68Z/10,11	Fill of Chm. 1	Cauac; Ik

TABLE 2.320 (Part 2)
Group 6E-1: Lot Groups

Feature	Lot Group	Lot	Provenience	Ceramic Evaluation
Plat.6E-1	1a	68I/48	Fill of 11th, sealed	Chuen
	1b	68I/47	Quarried area, N of U. 1, sealed by Fl. 1 of 10th	Late Chuen
	2a	68G/14,16	Unsealed dark earth associated with U. 2 (Fig. 142)	Preclassic
	2b	68F/11	Partially sealed fill associated with U. 3 and 4 (Fig. 142)	Manik
	2c	68I/24,25,29,46	Sealed fill of 10th	Late Chuen
	2d	68I/26, 40,41,43	Unsealed fill of Str. 6E-Sub.1	Chuen; Manik; Imix
	3a	68A/6,8,9; 68I/9-11,17,19,21	Sealed fill of 9th	Chuen
	3b	68A/7	Unsealed fill of 9th	Preclassic
	3c	68I/22	Unsealed fill of Str. 6E-Sub.2	Preclassic
	3d	68F/8,9	Partially sealed fill of U. 7 (Fig. 144)	Preclassic; Manik
	4a	68I/20,23,30	Sealed fill of 8th	Cauac; Manik
	4b	68I/7,28,33-35	Between Str.6E-Sub.1 and Sub.3, unsealed	Late Manik
	4c	68I/38	Fill of Str.6E-Sub.1, and material to the S	Preclassic; Manik; Ik
	4d	68K/9,10,16-18	Brown earth beneath U. 8 (Fig. 144)	Manik
	4e	68K/8,12-15	Unsealed fill behind U. 8 (Fig. 144)	Manik; one Ik
	4f	68K/7,11	Unsealed fill behind U. 8 (Fig. 144) and above 4e	Mostly Manik; some Imix
	4g	68K/3-6	S of U. 8 (Fig. 144)	Mostly Manik; some Ik and/or Imix
	5	68A/3-5; 68I/8,15,49	Sealed fill of 7th	Some Preclassic; mostly Manik; some Ik
	6	68G/12; 68I/4	Sealed fill of 6th	Preclassic; Manik; Ik

TABLE 2.320 (Part 3)
Group 6E-1: Lot Groups

Feature	Lot Group	Lot	Provenience	Ceramic Evaluation
Plat.6E-1	7a	68A/2; 68I/2,14	Sealed fill of 3rd-B	Preclassic; Manik; Ik; Imix
	7b	68I/12	Unsealed fill of U. 14 (Fig. 148)	Manik; Ik
	8a	68H/2	Partially sealed fill of 2nd	Imix
	8b	68G/21	Sealed fill of U. 21 (Fig. 148)	No data
	8c	68I/13,16	Partially sealed fill of U. 20 (Fig. 148)	Manik; Imix
	8d	68H/8	Sealed fill of U. 19 (Fig. 148)	Manik
Plat.6E-1	9a	68G/19	Sealed fill of 1st	Manik
	9b	68A/1,10; 68H/1, 3; 68I/1,3,5,6	Surface to level of floor of 1st	Preclassic; Manik; Ik; Imix
	9c	68F/1,2,4-7,10; 68I/18,36,37,44; 68M/1-4	Unsealed fill of 1st	Manik; Ik and Imix
	9d	68F/3	Partially sealed fill of U. 34 (Fig. 152)	Preclassic; Manik and Ik and/or Imix
	9e	68K/1,2	S of LG. 4g	Manik and Ik and/or Imix
Gp. 6E-1	1a	68C/1-6	Test pit 2 m², 1.20 m deep, directly off the mid-point of the S edge of Plat.6E-1	Manik; Ik; and Imix
	1b	68E/1-3	Test pit 2 m², 10 m S of Plat. 6E-1, surface to 0.75 m	Imix
	1c	68E/4,5	Test pit 2 m², 10 m S of Plat. 6E-1, 0.75 m to 1.25 m	Manik and Ik and/or Imix
	2a	68D/1,2	Test pit 2 m², 15 m E of Plat. 6E-1, surface to 0.40 m	?
	2b	68D/3-5	Test pit 2 m², 15 m E of Plat. 6E-1, 0.40 to 1.00 m	Mostly Preclassic; some Manik

TABLE 2.321
Structure 6E-25: Artifacts by Lot Group

Study Category	Object	Lot Group			
		1a	1b	1c	2a
Pottery Vessels	Sherds	Not weighed			
Flaked Chert Artifacts	Used flakes	1		5	2
	Unused flakes			6	1
Flaked Obsidian Artifacts	Prismatic blades			3	
Ground, Pecked, and Polished Stone Artifacts	Metate	1			
Shell and Bone Artifacts	Bone, animal, unworked			3	

EXCAVATIONS IN RESIDENTIAL AREAS OF TIKAL

TABLE 2.322
Structure 6E-26: Artifacts by Lot Group

Study Category	Object	Lot Group							
		1a	1b	2a	2b	2c	2d	2e	2f
Pottery Vessels	Sherds	Not weighed							
Other Pottery Artifacts	Figurines			2	21	4		22	47
	Miniature vessels								2
	Spindle whorls							3	1
	Censers		3		2	1			2
	Perforated worked sherd								1
	Unperforated worked sherds				1				1
	Unclassifiable formed objects	1							1
Flaked Chert Artifacts	Flake cores	1			1			1	
	Ovate bifaces			2	1			1	4
	Elongate bifaces							2	
	Rectangular/oval bifaces		1					1	
	Subtriangular biface							1	
	Unclassifiable biface	1							
	Thin bifaces	1	3		1	1			1
	Irregular, retouched flakes	1	5		2				1
	Point-retouched flakes	1				1		2	1
	Blades				2			1	2
	Used flakes	19	28	1	7	16	1	20	10
	Unused flakes	9		1	1	4	2	9	9
	Nodule					1			
Flaked Obsidian Artifacts	Cores	1	1					1	
	Prismatic blades	7	3		5	4		5	2
	Unused flake				1				
Ground, Pecked, and Polished Stone Artifacts	Manos				2	3			4
	Metates				1	1	1	3	4
	Rubbing stones		1						1
	Hammer stones		1		5	3			1
	Barkbeater							1	
	Jade pendant							1	
	Unclassifiable artifacts	1	1		1			2	1
	Slate		1						
Shell and Bone Artifacts	Shell, peg								1
	Shell, Tinklers								2
	Shell, misc. worked								1
	Shell, unworked	1			1			2	
	Bone, perforator				1				
	Bone, animal, misc. worked					1			8
	Bone, animal, unworked	1	2	2	3+	2		4	9
	Bone, human, unworked	1		3				2+	1
	Bone, unidentified, unworked	1	1						

TABLE 2.323
Structure 6E-162: Artifacts by Lot Group

Study Category	Object	Lot Group	
		1	2
Pottery Vessels	Sherds	Not weighed	
Flaked Chert Artifacts	Ovate or rectangular/oval biface	1	
Ground, Pecked, and Polished Stone Artifacts	Metates	1	1

TABLE 2.324
Structure 6E-163: Artifacts by Lot Group

Study Category	Object	Lot Group	
		1	2
Pottery Vessels	Sherds	Not weighed	
Other Pottery Artifacts	Figurine	1	
Flaked Chert Artifacts	Flake core		1
	Ovate biface		1
	Irregular retouched flake	1	
	Point-retouched flake	1	
	Used flakes	35	3
	Unused flakes	51	12
Flaked Obsidian Artifacts	Prismatic blades	4	1
Ground, Pecked, and Polished Stone Artifacts	Rubbing stone	1	
	Hammer stones	2	
	Unclassifiable artifact	1	
	Slate		1
Shell and Bone Artifacts	Shell, misc. worked	2	

TABLE 2.325
Chultun 6E-6: Artifacts by Lot Group

Study Category	Object	Lot Groups 1	2	3	4
Pottery Vessels	Sherds	Not weighed			
Flaked Chert Artifacts	Elongate biface	1			
	Unused flake	1			

TABLE 2.326
Chultun 6E-7: Artifacts by Lot Group

Study Category	Object	Lot Groups 1	2	3	4	5
Pottery Vessels	Sherds	Not weighed				
Other Pottery Artifacts	Figurines	1		2		
	Miniature palmate stone	1				
Flaked Chert Artifacts	Elongate biface	1				
	Irregular biface				1	
	Used flakes	2			2	
	Unused flakes	1	4	5		
Flaked Obsidian Artifacts	Thin biface			1		
	Prismatic blades		2	2		
Ground, Pecked, and Polished Stone Artifacts	Metates				2	
	Rubbing stones	2				
	Hammer stones	1			1	
	Jade flare	1				
	Unclassifiable artifact				1	
Shell and Bone Artifacts	Shell, unworked	2		1		
	Bone, animal, unworked		22	20		
	Bone, human, unworked		8	4	2	

TABLE 2.327
Platform 6E-1: Artifacts by Lot Group

Study Category	Object	Lot Groups																													
		1a	1b	2a	2b	2c	2d	3a	3b	3c	3d	4a	4b	4c	4d	4e	4f	4g	5	6	7a	7b	8a	8b	8c	8d	9a	9b	9c	9d	9e
Pottery Vessels	Sherds	Not weighed																													
Other Pottery Artifacts	Figurines	1				3							4		1		1	1	4		1				4			1	13		
	Stamps												2												1						
	Pellets							1																	2						
	Centrally perforated sherds													1																	1
	Eccentrically perforated sherd																														
	Unclassifiable formed object							1											2									1			
Flaked Chert Artifacts	Flake cores			1				2										1										1			
	Ovate bifaces					2							2						2						1			3	1		
	Elongate bifaces												2	1														2	1		
	Rectangular/oval bifaces							1					2						1									3	1		
	Irregular bifaces																1											2	1		
	Unclassifiable bifaces							1						1					2									1			
	Thin bifaces	1											1	1					2	3					2			1	2		
	Irregular retouched flakes	1											1						3	4					1			1	3		
	Point-retouched flake														1																
	Rounded retouched flakes							1							1						1										
	Blades														4		1		1	1	1						1	4	4	1	
	Used flakes	2				1	2	14	3	2	2	9	7	2	27		14	6	7	1	5	3			15		1	63	107	2	
	Unused flakes	12			6	11	12	37	9	4	4	42	27	2	230		34	34	52	1	10	4			41		1	270	457	6	
	Nodules							1				1							1												
Flaked Obsidian Artifacts	Cores																	1	1						2				2		
	Thin bifaces											1	2	1	1				1		1							1	1		
	Irregular retouched blades																				1							1			
	Prismatic blades			2				2			1	4	7	1	17		3		5	1	1				16			23	30	1	
	Flakes			1				1					1		1				1									1			
	Nodule																		1												
Ground, Pecked, and Polished Stone Artifacts	Manos	1					1						5		2		1	1	1		1	1			1			4	4		
	Metates	1											7	1	1							1						7	9		
	Rubbing stones	1											1				1								1			1			
	Hammer stones	1										1	2	1			1	1	2		1							1	5		
	Celts and chisels							1					1	1			1														
	Spindle whorl																											1			

TABLE 2.328
Group 6E-1: Artifacts by Lot Group

Study Category	Object	Lot Groups				
		1a	1b	1c	2a	2b
Pottery Vessels	Sherds	Not weighed				
Other Pottery Artifacts	Figurines	2				
Flaked Chert Artifacts	Elongate biface		1			
	Used flakes	3	2			
	Unused flakes	9	4			
Flaked Obsidian Artifacts	Thin biface	1				
	Flake	1				
	Prismatic blades	2				
Ground, Pecked, and Polished Stone Artifacts	Metate					1
	Slate plaque back	1				
Shell and Bone Artifacts	Bone, animal, unworked		3	2		
	Bone, human, unworked	1	1	1		
	Bone, unidenti-fied, unworked	1				

TIME SPANS

Time spans for the structures, chultuns, and platform of Gp. 6E-1 are presented in Tables 2.329 through 2.338, with group time spans in Table 2.339. The basis for the correlations in Table 2.339 is noted in the text above, where architectural relationships are involved. In addition, ceramic analysis has assisted in the correlations (see Table 2.320). Briefly, the history of Gp. 6E-1 may be summarized as follows: the earliest activity took place S of the locus of Str. 6E-Sub.1 (TS. 26 and 27). The nature of this activity is unknown, given the limited exposure of the archaeological remains (Fig. 141). In TS. 25, Str. 6E-Sub.1-2nd came into being, as did (probably) Ch. 6E-6-2nd (Fig. 142). There were modifications of Plat. 6E-6 that accompanied this. During the following period of use (TS. 24) the manufacture of Cauac ceramics began. Some time later, Str. 6E-Sub.1 was modified, and a new structure (6E-Sub.2) was added (TS. 23; Fig. 143). This structure closed off Ch. 6E-6-2nd, and Ch. 6E-6-1st-B was constructed as a replacement, probably to be used by the occupants of Str. 6E-Sub.2. Chultun 6E-7-2nd may have been constructed at the same time, perhaps to be used by the occupants of Str. 6E-Sub.1-1st. All of this

new construction, of course, called for extensive modification of the group platform.

After the above structures and chultuns had been in use for a while (TS. 22), Str. 6E-Sub.3 (Fig. 144) was added to the group (TS. 21). By this time, Manik pottery had come into use. Again, there were modifications of the group platform associated with this construction. There is no evidence that the other two structures, or the chultuns, were modified at this time, though the structures may have been.

The next construction activity occurred in TS. 19. Not known is whether any of the structures were altered at this time, but ceramics of the Ik Complex had appeared, which indicates that TS. 20 was of long duration. Undoubtedly, the platform surface was by now in rather poor shape (Plat. 6E-1-8th:Fl. 1), and perhaps for this reason the platform was provided with a new pavement (Fig. 144). This called for some modification of Ch. 6E-6, so that it could continue in use.

Structure 6E-Sub.1 and Sub.2 were abandoned for good in TS. 17. They were replaced by Str. 6E-25-2nd and 26-4th (Fig. 145). In conjunction with this major change, the group platform was drastically altered. Chultun 6E-

6, which may have served the users of Str. 6E-Sub.2, was closed up. Chultun 6E-7, which may have served the users of Str. 6E-Sub.1-1st, was provided with a new orifice, and the old one was closed up. Structure 6E-Sub.3 very likely was altered at this time, but there is no certainty about this.

Following a period of use of the above structures (TS. 16), during which Imix ceramics made their appearance, Str. 6E-26 and the platform were altered (TS. 15; Fig. 146). It was probably about this time that stone rubble was placed around the orifice of Ch. 6E-7. The other structures apparently continued in use as before. Further modifications of the group platform and Str. 6E-26 took place in TS. 13 (Fig. 147), and it was then that Ch. 6E-7 was filled and abandoned for good.

It was apparently in TS. 11 that Str. 6E-Sub.3 was finally abandoned. Not much is known about that structure, and it is probable that it had been renovated many times before its final abandonment and destruction. The group platform, of course, was altered at this time, which caused certain minor changes to Str. 6E-26.

After further use of the structures of Gp. 6E-1 during TS. 10, the platform was again renovated. This consisted apparently of patches to Plat. 6E-1-3rd:Fl. 1, as there was no large-scale renovation until TS. 7 (Fig. 148). Then, Str. 6E-25 was drastically altered, and Str. 6E-163 was built off its S end. In conjunction with this, the group platform was also altered. It was this alternation that led to further minor changes to Str. 6E-26.

Time span 5 saw the last major modification of the group platform, which caused some further minor changes to Str. 6E-26. The platform was enlarged considerably to the E, and on this was built Str. 6E-162 (Fig. 149). These were used for a while (TS. 4), before Str. 6E-26 underwent its final modification (TS. 3; Fig. 149).

From all appearances, Gp. 6E-1 was in use continuously from a time that spanned the production of late Chuen ceramics to the appearance of late Imix ceramics. In terms of the dates for these ceramic complexes, this would mean that Gp. 6E-1 was first occupied somewhere around 175 BC, and was never abandoned until approximately AD 869.

TABLE 2.329
Structure 6E-25: Time Spans

Time Span	Architectural Development	Unit	Descriptive Data	Lot Group	Ceramics in Vogue
1			Abandonment and collapse		
2			Use	2a,2b	(Late)
3	Str. 6E-25-1st		Construction; probably a two-level platform with building of perishable materials	1a	Imix
4			Use	1c	(Early)
5	Str. 6E-25-2nd	1	Construction of platform, probably of same size as Str. 6E-26-1st, with building of perishable materials	1b	Ik

TABLE 2.330
Structure 6E-26: Time Spans

Time Span	Architectural Development	Construction Stage	Unit	Special Deposits: Burial	Descriptive Data	Lot Group		Ceramics in Vogue
1					Abandonment and collapse			
2					Use			
3	Str.6E-26-1st	1			Construction of building of perishable materials			(Late)
		2,3	10,11		Existing building dismantled and platform made completely rectangular			
4					Use			
5	Str.6E-26-2nd-A	None defined	9		Final modification of 2nd			
6					Use			
7	Str.6E-26-2nd-B	None defined		131	Second modification of 2nd			
8					Use			
9	Str.6E-26-2nd-C	None defined			First modification of 2nd	2c 2d		
10					Use			Imix
11	Str.6E-26-2nd-D	1			Construction of building of perishable materials			
		2		152 (secondary)	Construction of stairway		2e	
		3	8		Construction of upper platform level	1b	2f	
		4			Lower platform level raised			
		5			Existing building demolished			
12					Use	2b		
13	Str.6E-26-3rd	1			Construction of building of perishable materials			(Early)
		2	1,3-7		Construction of platform	1a		
		3	2	129	Existing structure demolished			
14					Use	2a		
15	Str.6E-26-4th	None defined			Earliest construction			Ik

TABLE 2.331
Structure 6E-162: Time Spans

Time Span	Architectural Development	Descriptive Data	Lot Groups	Ceramics in Vogue
1		Abandonment and collapse; metate fragments left	1	
2		Use	2	Imix
3	Str.6E-162	Construction		

TABLE 2.332
Structure 6E-163: Time Spans

Time Span	Architectural Development	Descriptive Data	Lot Groups	Ceramics in Vogue
1		Abandonment and collapse		
2		Use	2	Imix
3	Str. 6E-163	Construction	1	

TABLE 2.333
Structure 6E-Sub.1: Time Spans

Time Span	Architectural Development	Special Deposits: Burial	Descriptive Data	Lot Group	Ceramics in Vogue
1		152 (primary) 153	Destruction for Plat. 6E-1-6th		Ik
2			Use		Manik
3	Str.6E-Sub.1-1st	128	Construction	2d some 4c	Cauac
4			Use		
5	Str.6E-Sub.1-2nd		Construction		Chuen

TABLE 2.334
Structure 6E-Sub.2: Time Spans

Time Span	Architectural Development	Descriptive Data	Lot Group (Plat.6E-1)	Ceramics in Vogue
1		Destruction for Plat.6E-1-6th		Ik
2		Use		Manik
3	Str.6E-Sub.2	Construction	3c	Cauac

TABLE 2.335
Structure 6E-Sub.3: Time Spans

Time Span	Architectural Development	Descriptive Data	Lot Groups (Plat.6E-1)	Ceramics in Vogue
1		Destruction, probably for Plat. 6E-1-3rd-B		
2		Use	in 4b,c; 9c	Imix
				Ik
3	Str. 6E-Sub.3	Construction	some of 8c	Manik

TABLE 2.336
Chultun 6E-6: Time Spans

Time Span	Architectural Development	Construction Stage	Orifice	Chamber	Unit	Destructive Data	Lot Group		Ceramics in Vogue
1						Settling of fill, with breakup of floors for Plat. 6E-1-3rd and -6th over Or.1	2		Imix
2					1	Abandonment; Neck 1 filled and sealed by Plat. 6E-1-6th:Fl. 1	1		
3						Use			Ik
4	Ch.6E-6-1st-A					Extension of shaft for Plat. 6E-1-7th:Fl.1			
5						Use			Manik
6	Ch.6E-6-1st-B	1,2		3,2 (shallow part)		Construction of new chultun; Neck 2 and Ch.3 filled	4	3	Cauac
		3	2						
7						Use			
8	Ch.6E-6-2nd	1		2 (deep part)		Construction, perhaps when Str.6E-Sub.1-2nd was in use			Chuen
		2	1	1					

TABLE 2.337
Chultun 6E-7: Time Spans

Time Span	Architectural Development	Construction Stage	Orifice	Chamber	Unit	Descriptive Data	Lot Group		Ceramics in Vogue
1						Settling of fill, with eventual formation of pit over Or. 1			----------
2						Abandonment; Chm. 3 and Neck 2 filled	1	2,4	Imix
3						Use			
4	Ch.6E-7-1st-A					Rubble to retain U. 11 of Plat. 6E-1 put in place			
5						Use			----------
6	Ch.6E-7-1st-B		2	4?	1	Chm. 1 and Neck 1 filled	5		Ik
7						Use	3		Manik
8	Ch.6E-7-2nd	1		4?		Original construction			----------
		2		3					Cauac
		3		2					
		4	1	1					

TABLE 2.338
Platform 6E-1: Time Spans

Time Span	Architectural Development	Floor	Unit	Special Deposits: Burial	Descriptive Data	Lot Group			Ceramics in Vogue
1					Abandonment and ruin				--------
2					Use	3d (some) 4f (some) 9c			
3	Plat.6E-1-1st		30-35		E extension of platform	9a	9d	2b (some)	(Late)
4					Use				
5	Plat.6E-1-2nd	1	17-29	161	Modification	8a,b 8c,d		9b 9e	
6					Use				
7	Plat.6E-1-3rd-A		16		Modification				Imix
8					Use				
9	Plat.6E-1-3rd-B	1	14,15		Reconstruction of platform	7a		7b	
10					Use				
11	Plat.6E-1-4th	1	12,13		Reconstruction of platform				(Early)
12			11 (part)		Use				
13	Plat.6E-1-5th	1	11 (part)	151	Reconstruction of platform				
14			11 (part)		Use				--------
15	Plat.6E-1-6th	1	9,10	130?	Reconstruction of platform	6			
16					Use				Ik
17	Plat.6E-1-7th	1		130?	Reconstruction of platform	5			
18				138	Use	4b	4g	4f	--------
19	Plat.6E-1-8th	1	7,8		Reconstruction of platform	4a	4d	4e	Manik
20					Use				--------
21	Plat.6E-1-9th	1	5,6		Reconstruction of platform	3a	3b	3d (some)	Cauac
22					Use				--------
23	Plat.6E-1-10th	1	2-4		Reconstruction of platform	2a	2c	2b (some)	
24					Use				Chuen
25	Plat.6E-1-11th	1	1		Original construction	1a	1b		

TABLE 2.339
Group 6E-1: Time Spans

Group Time Span	Str.6E-25 (Table 2.329)	Str.6E-26 (Table 2.330)	Str.6E-162 (Table 2.331)	Str.6E-163 (Table 2.332)	Str.6E-Sub.1 (Table 2.333)	Str.6E-Sub.2 (Table 2.334)	Str.6E-Sub.3 (Table 2.335)	Ch.6E-6 (Table 2.336)	Ch.6E-7 (Table 2.337)	Plat.6E-1 (Table 2.338)
1	1	1	1	1						1
2		2								
3		3								
4		4	2							2
5		5	3							3
6	2	6		2						4
7	3	7		3						5
8										6
9										7
10		8								8
11		9					1			9
12		10							1	10
13		11							2	11
14		12							3	12
15		13							4	13
16	4	14						1	5	14
17	5	15			1	1		2	6	15
18								3		16
19								4		17
20							2			18
21							3			19
22					2	2		5	7	20
23					3	3		6	8	21
24					4			7		22
25					5			8		23
26										24
27										25

Group 7E-3

Group 7E-3 is located about 415 m S of Gp. 6E-1, and in its final form consists of three low, rectangular structures, 7E-8, 9, and 10 (TR. 11), which appear to be house foundations, and 7E-11, which could have been a household shrine (TR. 21). This is located on the SE corner of the raised platform that supports the group. Just N is Str. 7E-10, also on the E side of the supporting platform, with the other two structures on the N and W sides.

Nine test pits were dug by Culbert in Gp. 7E-3 (Table 2.340). Of these, three (Op. 36C, 36U, 36X) sample the fill of the supporting platform, with perhaps a bit of late occupation debris. At approximately 1.00 m below the surface are traces of an early platform floor, on which stands a building (Str. 7E-Sub.1) S of the location of Str. 7E-9.

STRUCTURE 7E-SUB.1

Since only a very small portion of this structure was exposed in excavation, it cannot be described in detail. Known parts (Fig. 155) consist of walls for a supplementary platform (U. 5), a building platform (U. 8), and a building (U. 1, 2, and 4). Another wall, U. 3, may be a building wall or the wall for an interior(?) platform. Finally, two floor surfaces are represented by U. 6 and 7.

The size of the supplementary platform is unknown, but it must have been square or rectangular, on the basis of the one observed corner. Nor is its height known; the top of U. 5 is 0.66 m above bedrock, but unknown is where the base of the wall falls relative to bedrock. Lack of any apparent steps in front of the supplementary platform suggests that the living surface probably was not much lower than about 0.20 m below the top of U. 5. Of course, it may be that steps once existed, but were later torn out.

The face of the building platform for Sub.1 (U. 8) is set back 0.36 m from the face of the supplementary platform. Unfortunately, the excavator did not record what happens to this wall at the corner of U. 1. Running N from the top of U. 8 is a floor, U. 6. Rising above this are the freestanding walls, U. 1, 2, and 4. Together, these enclose a room (Rm. 1) with a doorway opening to the SE. This doorway breaks the SE building wall in its center. How high the building walls stood is unknown; one possibility is that they were dwarf walls that were topped by an upper zone of pole-and-thatch. Alternatively, they may have been full height, supporting a roof of beam and mortar. The structure was not apparently vaulted, as no vault stones were found.

In the floor in the doorway is a channel, 2 cm deep, which opens to the outside. This, and the slant of the floor to the outside, suggest that drainage of water from Rm. 1

was important to the Maya. It is not known how far into the room this channel goes, as excavations to the floor level were confined to the front 0.14 m of Rm. 1. This channel and another peculiarity of Rm. 1—the contrast between 0.18 m thickness of the NE wall (U. 4) and the 0.50–0.60 m thickness of U. 1 and 2—raises the possibility that it was the sweatroom of a building reminiscent of the sweathouse Str. J-17 at Piedras Negras. Consider the following statement by Satterthwaite (1952:52):

> The record shows that while the front and rear walls of the sweat-room of Str. J-17 correspond to the minimum thickness of 72 cm., one side wall was exposed and measured and was only 55 cm. in thickness. Having failed to observe this at more than one point, and suspecting an error, the broken-line reconstruction of Fig. 26 assumes a constant thickness throughout. *We have positive indication that side walls might on occasion be thinner*, but distrust the evidence. (emphasis added).

The "sweathouse hypothesis" will be discussed in some detail in TR. 20B, but pending that, a further observation is worth making here: the narrowness of the doorway (0.76 m) compares with 0.77 m for Piedras Negras sweathouses and 0.76 m for Tikal Str. 5E-22 (TR. 16:76, table 42). In the absence of further excavation, the wall represented by U. 3 is an enigma. It abuts the outside of the SW wall (U. 2) of Rm. 1. From this, it runs at least 1.50 m SW, parallel to the face of the supplementary platform (U. 5). The 2 m between U. 3 and 5 is covered by a portion of the same plaster floor, U. 6, as occurs inside Rm. 1. Unit 3 could represent the rear wall of a second room, shallower than Rm. 1, or it could represent the wall of a platform, an interior platform if this area was roofed. Again, turning to Str. J-17 at Piedras Negras, U. 3 is highly reminiscent of a wall that runs from the NW wall of the sweatroom of that structure (Satterthwaite 1952:fig. 26A), which Satterthwaite (1952:51) suggests is the wall of a "bench." More excavation to determine the extent of U. 3, and to see what lies behind it, would be necessary to settle the matter, but the interior platform hypothesis seems reasonable at this point.

One other feature encountered in the excavation of 7E-Sub.1 is a floor remnant, U. 7. Apparently, the area immediately in front of Sub.1 was filled to the level of the top of U. 8 and provided with a plaster floor. This could represent an alteration of the plaza in front of the structure or, more likely, an enlargement of the platform on which the building itself stood. In this case, one might speak of a Str. 7E-Sub.1-1st and 2nd. In the absence of necessary excavations to shed more light on the subject, however, it seems best to hold in abeyance the definition of architectural developments. For the same reason, it seems premature to define time spans.

SHERDS AND ARTIFACTS

Sources of cultural materials from Gp. 7E-3 are given in Tables 2.340 and 2.341. Ceramics beneath the floor of Str. 7E-Sub.1 indicate construction while Manik pottery was in vogue. Such ceramics are also prominent in lots in and near the structure, probably trash left around the building when it was abandoned and demolished. It was then buried beneath later Classic construction.

Manik material is also abundant in the four test pits near Str. 7E-10 (Op. 36B, 36F, 36V, 36W). Perhaps this is fill derived from the trash of structures associated with Str. 7E-Sub.1. A midden-like deposit of Ik sherds from a nearby test pit in the supporting platform may be trash from Str. 7E-10.

The remaining test pits pertain to Str. 7E-9, and sample a combination of fill and trash. Abundant late Manik material of midden quality in one test pit probably is litter from structures associated with Str. 7E-Sub.1, which was incorporated undisturbed in later fill. Material behind the structure indicates Intermediate and/or Late Classic occupation.

The presence of Preclassic sherds in one test pit probably does not indicate a Preclassic occupation. Present evidence is that Str. 7E-Sub.1 and its associated platform are the earliest construction, so the few Preclassic sherds may have been brought in from some nearby group in debris to use as fill.

Imix sherds are abundant in Gp. 7E-3, and there was probably construction while such ceramics were produced. A few Eznab sherds in the vicinity of Str. 7E-10 indicate abandonment shortly after the appearance of such ceramics.

Group 6D-1

Group 6D-1 (later investigated as Gp. 6C-XII by Proyecto Nacional Tikal; Laporte 2003:309) includes Str. 6D-13, 14, 6C-37, and 38. These are located 23 m S of the major group of structures formerly designated as "C Group" (TR. 11:18) and 12 m W of the Madeira Reservoir. On the W side of a plaza, Str. 6C-37 appears to be the ruin of a rectangular platform comparable to known house foundations. Structure 6C-38, on the S side of the plaza, appears to be a low, square platform. On the N edge of the plaza is the somewhat larger Str. 6D-13, which may be a two-level platform, perhaps for the support of a house built of pole-and-thatch. Structure 6D-14, on the E edge of the group, may be a small vaulted structure.

A single test pit was dug by the corner of Str. 6D-14, and most likely samples disturbed structure fill, with some late occupation material (Table 2.340). An occupation from Early Classic times, lasting until the appearance of Eznab ceramics, is indicated (Table 2.341).

Group 6D-2

This group (later investigated as Gp. 6D-V by Proyecto Nacional Tikal; Laporte 2003:310) consists of seven structures, 6D-18 through 24, all but one of which are arranged around a large plaza. Its location is 80 m E of the Madeira Reservoir. Structures 6D-18, 19, and 21–23 all appear to be small- to medium-sized rectangular platforms that could have served as house foundations (see TR. 11). Structure 6D-18 is located on the S side of the plaza, and Str. 6D-19 is located off the corner of Str. 6D-20. This last, which appears to be a small range-type structure, is located on the W side of the plaza. Structure 6D-21 is N of this, while Str. 6D-22 and 23 occupy the N edge of the plaza. The broad Str. 6D-24 is in the center of the E edge of the plaza, with open space off either end.

Two test pits were dug in plaza fill, one near Str. 6D-21 and the other more towards the center of the plaza (Table 2.340). The samples are adequate to show clearly that the locus was first occupied when Manik ceramics were in vogue (Table 2.341). The occupation continued until sometime after the appearance of Imix, but before the appearance of Eznab ceramics.

Group 6D-3

This complex group is located in the NE portion of Sq. 6D, immediately N of Gp. 6D-4. The separation of these two groups is somewhat arbitrary, except that a single low platform supports the structures of Gp. 6D-3, but not Gp. 6D-4. The eleven structures of which the group seems to be composed, Str. 6D-38 through 49 (47 and 48 are parts of a single structure) are grouped on the edges of three raised plazas. Structures 6D-38 through 41 are located on the small plaza that extends N from the group. Structures 6D-38 and 39 are on the N edge, Str. 6D-41 appears to be off the W edge, while Str. 6D-40 is situated near the center of the plaza. All four appear to be low, rectangular platforms, possible house foundations (TR. 11).

Structures 6D-44 through 46 are located on a plaza that extends E from the core of the group. Again, all appear to be low, rectangular platforms that could have been house foundations. Structure 6D-45, the larger, occupied most of the N edge of the plaza. It faces the smaller Str. 6D-46 in the center of the S edge. Structure 6D-44 separates this plaza from the larger one to the W.

Structures 6D-42, 43, and 47 all seem to be sizeable range-type structures that were probably vaulted. They are located on the W, N, and edges of the larger of the three supporting raised plazas. The smaller Str. 6D-49, which also may have been vaulted, appears to have been built against the SW corner of the group.

Three test pits were dug in the group; two in the larger raised plaza and one in the E plaza (Table 2.340). The samples range from small to medium in size, and consist mostly of fill sherds. An occupation that began after the appearance of Manik ceramics and lasted through the time when Imix ceramics were in vogue is indicated (Table 2.341).

Group 6D-4

Group 6D-4 is located immediately S of 6D-3. The sixteen structures (6D-50 through 66) are arranged, for the most part, around the edges of three irregularly shaped plazas. The smallest of these plazas is in the NE corner of the group. On its W edge is Str. 6D-50, which may be a small, vaulted, range-type structure (see TR. 11). On the N edge is Str. 6D-51, which may be a low, rectangular platform comparable to known house foundations. Chultun 6D-2 is located in the rear slope of the ruin mound of this structure. Structure 6D-53 is a long, low, and narrow structure on the E edge of the plaza, and separates it from the plaza to the E. This structure could conceivably have been a house foundation. Structures 6D-54 and 55 are located on the S edge of the plaza, and may have been the foundations, possibly, for small houses or utility buildings.

East of this plaza is the small arm of a larger plaza, the main portion of which runs to the S. Structure 6D-52, which is comparable to the ruins of known houses, is located on the N edge of this arm of the plaza. It faces the raised platform that supports Str. 6D-61. East of Str. 6D-52 is the comparable Str. 6D-57, which defines the N edge of the main portion of this plaza. On the E edge is the large Str. 6D-58, which is suggestive of a ceremonial structure. It faces 6D-61, which is located on a raised platform to the W. Between the two is the small, square Str. 6D-59, and the three structures together are suggestive of the pattern seen in Gp. 6E-2 (TR. 25A). Structure 6D-60 is a low, narrow, rectangular mound on the plaza edge S of Str. 6D-59.

The raised platform that supports Str. 6D-61 also supports the low, rectangular Str. 6D-62 through 65. Structure 6D-62, the smallest, runs from the rear of Str. 6D-61 to the N end of 6D-63. The latter, a long, narrow structure, is raised above the W edge of the plaza. Similar Str. 6D-65 is on the S edge. The small, rectangular Str. 6D-64 is behind and parallel to 6D-63. Structure 6D-66 has a similar position with respect to 6D-65. Small, rectangular Str. 6D-56 is sandwiched between the end of 6D-63 and the back of 6D-54.

Four test pits sampled the fill of the three plaza areas (Table 2.340). The samples are not large, but do include Manik ceramics of midden quality. The data (Table 2.341) suggest that this locus was possibly occupied in Late Preclassic, and surely by Early Classic times. The occupation apparently continued through to the period of Imix ceramic production.

Group 6D-5

This group appears to be a rather informal cluster of five small structures 40 m W of Gp. 6E-1. Structures 6D-33, 35, and 37 seem to be rectangular platforms that could have been house foundations (see TR. 11). The smaller Str. 6D-34 and 36 may be foundations for houses, or for utility buildings, but this is speculative.

The sherds of this group are from a surface collection E of Str. 6D-35 (Table 2.340). They suggest an occupation spanning the time when Manik and Ik and/or Imix ceramics were in vogue (Table 2.341). This conclusion, however, is quite tentative.

Group 6D-6

Group 6D-6 is located towards the SW corner of Sq. 6D. It consists of Str. 6D-86 through 91. This is the Gp. 6D-XVIII of Proyecto Nacional Tikal (Laporte 2003:295). Structure 6D-86 appears to be small and square, perhaps a shrine (see TR. 21), and is located on the E edge of the group. Structure 6D-87, on the N, may be a small, vaulted, range-type structure, as may 6D-88, which faces 6D-86. South and W of Str. 6D-88 is the similarly aligned 6D-91, apparently a low, rectangular platform comparable to known house foundations. Smaller, but of a similar shape, Str. 6D-90 runs E from the S end of 6D-91. Structure 6D-89 faces 6D-91. A broad, rectangular platform, it could have served as a house foundation (see TR. 11).

Four test pits were dug in Gp. 6D-6 (Table 2.340). Of these, two (37V, 37Y) sample fill material. The other two include probable fill and occupation debris. Although the samples are small for the most part, the dates (Table 2.341) suggest an occupation that began in Late Preclassic times and lasted until after the appearance of Imix, but was prior to the appearance of Eznab ceramics.

Group 6E-3

This small group is located between Gp. 6D-5 and 6E-1 and is composed of three structures (6E-19, 20, 21) arranged on three sides of a plaza. Structure 6E-19 appears to be a small, low rectangular platform (see TR. 11). Structure 6E-20 runs W from the N half of Str. 6E-19. Structure 6E-20 is hard to interpret on the basis of the visible ruin; it might have been a very small temple, from which Str. 6E-21 extends W and then S.

A single test pit (Table 2.340) samples fill for the plaza. The evidence seems to indicate that construction and occupation were limited to Ik and especially Imix times (Table 2.341).

Group 6E-4

Group 6E-4 is located 30 m E of 6E-1, and consists of nine structures of which one, 6E-30, appears to be a small, vaulted, range-type structure (TR. 11). It is situated on the N edge of a plaza. Four rectangular platforms (Str. 6E-29, 32, 34, and 35), of small-to-medium size, are situated on the other edges of the group platform. Similar structures are located behind Str. 6E-32 (6E-31), Str. 6E-34 (6E-33), and Str. 6E-35 (6E-36 and 37). All of these could conceivably have been house foundations.

A test pit samples plaza fill, with perhaps some late occupation material (Table 2.340). The samples are of fair size, and indicate an occupation spanning the time when Ik and Imix ceramics were in vogue (Table 2.341).

Group 6E-5

This small group is located 60 m E of 6E-4, and consists of three structures (6E-38 through 40) arranged on the edges of a plaza. All three appear to be comparable to known foundations for small houses (see TR. 11).

The test pits sample fill, with a mixture of occupation material (Table 2.340). The samples are small, but seem to indicate an occupation limited to Ik and/or Imix and possibly slightly later times (Table 2.341).

Group 6E-6

Group 6E-6 is located 120 m E of 6E-5. At its center is Str. 6E-73, which appears to be the ruin of a temple on the E side of a raised platform. On the S, W, and N sides are the small-to-large Str. 6E-68 through 70. Taken together, the four suggest a domestic group of Plaza Plan 2 (TR. 21). East of the raised platform is a lower plaza, with Str. 6E-72 on the E side and Str. 6E-67 on the S. Both appear to be rectangular platforms that could well have served as house foundations (see TR. 11).

Three test pits sample construction fill, with late occupation material prominent in Op. 35S (Table 2.340). The samples for the most part are good, and indicate that occupation lasted from probably very Late Preclassic through Late Classic times, when Imix ceramics were in vogue (Table 2.341). Possible Eznab material could be from a reoccupation, or simply a continued late occupation of the group.

Group 6E-7

This group, 16 m E of 6E-6, consists of four structures arranged on the edges of a platform, with one other located just off the SW corner. The latter, Str. 6E-60, seems to be a small, rectangular platform. Structures 6E-58 and 59, on the S and W edges of the platform, appear to be medium-sized, vaulted, range-type structures. Structure 6E-57, which is low and square-shaped, projects N from the NE corner of Str. 6E-58. Structure 6F-1, at the E edge of the group, is similar in appearance to Str. 6E-60. Overall, the arrangement is suggestive of a residential group with outbuildings (see TR. 11).

Unfortunately, the single test pit (Table 2.340) produced only two sherds (Table 2.341). It is probably safe to assume an Ik and/or Imix occupation for the group, but nothing more can be said.

Group 6E-8

Group 6E-8 is located 22 m S of 6E-7 and consists of three very small, apparently rectangular platforms (Str. 6E-61 through 63) on the N, W, and S sides of an open plaza (see TR. 11). They could have served as house foundations.

The small surface collection from this group (see Table 2.340) may represent an incidental accumulation of occupation debris. It very clearly indicates an occupation when Ik and Imix ceramics were in vogue (Table 2.341). Possibly, the occupation began in Late Preclassic times.

Group 6E-9

This group may conform to domestic Plaza Plan 2 (TR. 21). The four small structures (6E-81 through 84) are situated on the four sides of a plaza, and the one on the E seems to be square (see TR. 11). The group is located 72 m NW of Gp. 6E-2, and 200 m SE of Gp. 6E-1.

Two test pits (Table 2.340) produced small-to-medium samples of construction fill with perhaps a slight amount of late occupation debris. The occupation seems to have begun after the appearance of Ik ceramics, and to have continued while Imix ceramics were in vogue (Table 2.341).

Group 6E-10

Group 6E-10 is located 156 m S of 6E-1 and 130 m SW of 6E-9. It includes Str. 6E-110 through 117, all of which, excepting Str. 6E-114, might have been house foundations (see TR. 11). Structure 6E-114, square in shape, is suggestive of a small domestic adjunct. The structures are arranged around the four sides of two plaza areas.

Of three test pits (Table 2.340), one (Op. 35N) samples the fill of the W plaza. The other two probably sample incidentally accumulated trash, not all of which necessarily derives from Gp. 6E-10. The data indicate only that construction here dates after the appearance of Ik ceramics, and occupation continued while Imix ceramics were in vogue (Table 2.341). Perhaps it was not abandoned until after the appearance of Eznab ceramics.

Group 6E-11

This group, located halfway between Gp. 6E-9 and 6E-10, includes Str. 6E-118 through 123, all of which look to be comparable to known house foundations (see TR. 11). Five of the structures are arranged around a plaza; two on the N side and one each on the other sides. Structure 6E-118 is located about 7 m behind Str. 6E-110 on the W.

One test pit produced small samples of plaza fill (Table 2.340). Initial construction seems to have taken place after the appearance of Manik ceramics (Table 2.341). Occupation appears to have lasted through the time when Imix ceramics were in production.

Group 6E-12

Group 6E-12 is situated immediately E of 6E-2. Although the separation of the two groups might appear to be somewhat arbitrary, each appears to be a self-contained architectural unit based on its own distinct supporting platform (see TR. 11). Of the ten structures included, all but one appear to be small- to medium-sized rectangular platforms comparable to those known to have supported houses and associated utility buildings. Five of these (Str. 6E-147, and 149 through 152) are arranged along the W and N edges of the supporting platform. A chultun is located just N of Str. 6E-149. Two other structures, 6E-153 and 154, are arranged in an L-shaped configuration just S of the mid-point of the N platform edge. Centered in relation to Str. 6E-147, 149, and 154 is 6E-148, which appears to be a small square structure. The arrangement of these structures is suggestive of a small-scale version of Gp. 6E-2 (TR. 25A). The other two rectangular structures (6E-155 and 156) are located S of Str. 6E-148.

Two test pits (Op. 35G, 35V) sample fill for the plaza on which Str. 6E-148 is built (Table 2.340). It is likely, however, that this is mixed with some late occupation debris. Two other test pits sample a mixture of fill and occupation debris from Str. 6E-152 and 153. The ceramic evaluations (Table 2.341) suggest a continuous occupation that begins in Late Preclassic times and continued through into terminal Classic (Eznab) times. It is, however, possible that the Eznab material represents a reoccupation.

Group 6E-13

This group is located in the SW portion of Sq. 6E. It includes the large, rectangular Str. 6E-99, which defines the W edge of a raised platform. Two short extensions appear to run E from the ends of the structure (similar, perhaps, to Str. 3F-12; Fig. 53). Against the N extension, Str. 6E-98 is built, on the N edge of the group platform. This appears to be a rectangular platform comparable to known house foundations. On the E edge of the group platform sits 6E-100, a rectangular structure of moderate size. The S edge of the group platform is open, but Str. 7E-1 is situated just off the S. This ruin is quite comparable to known house ruins (see TR. 11).

A single test pit was dug in this group (Table 2.340). The small-to-medium samples from it consist of fill for the supporting platform, and indicate an occupation that probably began towards the end of Late Preclassic times (Table 2.341). Perhaps this is when the floor at 1.06 m in the pit was laid. Occupation seems to have continued on through Ik and/or Imix times.

Group 6E-14

Group 6E-14 is located about 76 m E of 6E-13, and about 90 m SE of Gp. 6E-10. It is a small collection of four structures, 6E-102 through 105, arranged asymmetrically on the edges of a low platform. The ruins of all four structures appear comparable to those of known houses (see TR. 11).

A single test pit samples fill for the platform (Table 2.340). The samples are small to medium in size. A burial (Bu. 118, described in section III) and two early floors were encountered in the pit. The ceramic data (Table 2.341) indicate a probable Preclassic date for the deepest floor, and an Early Classic date for the upper floor. Material above this includes both Ik and Imix ceramics. This and the burial ceramics suggest that occupation was continuous through all this span of time.

Group 7E-1

This group is located in the NW corner of Sq. 7E, about 62 m SW of Gp. 6E-13. It consists of three ruins comparable to known house ruins (see TR. 11). Structure 7D-27 is situated on the W side of a plaza, with Str. 7E-3 and 4 on the N and S sides. The slightly raised E side of the plaza is open.

The small sample, from a single test pit (Table 2.340), consists of scattered refuse from behind one of the structures. An Ik and Imix occupation is indicated (Table 2.341). Since fill was not sampled, it is not clear whether or not there was an earlier occupation. The few Preclassic sherds might come from a nearby group, or there may have been a brief early occupation followed by a hiatus. The third and least likely alternative is that occupation was continuous from Late Preclassic times, and that Manik sherds would be found in construction fill.

Group 7E-2

These structures are located 70 m SE of Gp. 7E-1, and 67 m due S of Gp. 6E-13. Included are three small examples, 7E-15 through 17 (the largest). They are arranged asymmetrically on the W, N, and E sides of a slightly raised plaza. The overall appearance (see TR. 11) is suggestive of probable residential groups, particularly Gp. 3F-2 (Fig. 52).

A test pit sampled plaza fill (Table 2.340). Unfortunately, sherd quantities are small. The evidence, however, is for an occupation that probably began towards the end of Early Classic, and lasted through Ik and probably Imix times (Table 2.341).

Group 7E-4

This group is located 17 m E of Gp. 7E-3, and appears to be a residential group of Plaza Plan 2 (TR. 21). Structures 7E-12 and 13, on the W and N sides, seem to be low, rectangular platforms (see TR. 11). Structure 7E-14, on the E side, is apparently a small, square structure.

Two test pits sample plaza fill and a deposit of what may be an incidental accumulation of refuse behind Str. 7E-12 (Table 2.340). The samples are small, but are consistent with an occupation that lasted from Late Preclassic through Ik and probably Imix times (Table 2.341).

Group 7E-5

Group 7E-5 is located 123 m S of 7E-4, and 180 m NW of the Corriental Reservoir. It includes six apparently rectangular structures of small-to-medium size, all of which could have served as house foundations (see TR.

11). Of these, 7E-46 through 48 and 50 are located on the four sides of a plaza. The smaller Str. 7E-45 and 49 are located off the SW and SE corners of the group. This arrangement, along with their smaller size, is at least suggestive of domestic outbuildings.

Both test pits (Table 2.340) sample the plaza fill, but include some late occupation debris. The samples are small, but consistently indicate an occupation that began in Early Classic, and probably continued through Late Classic (Imix) times (Table 2.341). It may have terminated after the appearance of Eznab ceramics, or else there was a late reoccupation.

Group 7E-6

This group, located 64 m SW of Gp. 7E-5, appears to be another residential group of Plaza Plan 2 (TR. 21). The small, square Str. 7E-43 stands on the E edge of a plaza, and the rectangular Str. 7E-42, 44, and 7D-93 stand on the other three sides (TR. 11).

Two test pits sample the plaza fill (Table 2.340). In one of these (Op. 36Q), Bu. 119 (this report, section III) was found. Much of the material is of midden quality, and probably pertains to early domestic occupation of the group. The material in Op. 36T may be a somewhat disturbed incidental accumulation of trash from Gp. 7E-6. The data seem to indicate an occupation that spanned Early and Late Classic (Imix) times (Table 2.341).

"VACANT TERRAIN"

Four surface collections from Sq. 6E (Table 2.340 and 2.341) may be discussed together here. Only one of them (Op. 1Q/2) produced a sizeable sample. The material could have come from Gp. 6E-4, however, which is only 14 m to the N, but a test pit in that group did not produce Manik ceramics. Therefore, it seems probable that Early Classic structures were located here, the ruins of which are no longer visible. Operation 1Q/1 probably stems from the same structures. The scanty nature of the Op. 1Q/4 sample suggests that there are no "hidden" structures here; the material is likely from Gp. 6E-10 to the S. Similarly, the material in Op. 1Q/7 may pertain to nearby groups to the N and W.

TABLE 2.340
Location of Test Pits: Corriental Quadrangle

Group	Test Pit	Location
6D-1	37R	Corner of Str.6D-14
6D-2	37U	Plaza in front of Str.6D-21
	37Z	Plaza between Str.6D-20, 24
6D-3	37A	Plaza for Str. 6D-42 through 49
	37F	Plaza in front of Str.6D-43
	37G	Plaza between Str.6D-45, 46
6D-4	37B	Plaza for Str. 6D-50 through 55
	37C	Plaza for Str. 6D-52 and 53
	37D	Plaza for Str. 6D-62, 63, and 65
	37E	Plaza for Str. 6D-56, 59, 60
6D-5	1Q/8	E of Str. 6D-35
6D-6	37T	Between Str. 6D-83 and 86
	37V	Plaza in front of Str. 6D-87
	37W	Behind Str. 6D-86
	37Y	By plaza wall near Str. 6D-88
6E-3	35M	Plaza for Str. 6E-19, 20, 21
6E-4	35A	Plaza for Str. 6E-29, 30, 32, 34, 35
6E-5	35N	Behind Str. 6E-38
	35R	Plaza for Str. 6E-38, 39, 40
6E-6	35I	Plaza between Str. 6E-69, 73
	35S	Corner of Str. 6E-68
	35T	Plaza behind Str. 6E-73
6E-7	35J	Between Str. 6E-57, 58
6E-8	1Q/5	E of Str. 6E-62
6E-9	35H	Plaza for Str. 6E-81 through 84
	35U	Corner of Str. 6E-83
6E-10	35N	Plaza for Str. 6E-110 through 114
	35O	E of Str. 6E-116
	35P	W of Str. 6E-111
6E-11	35E	Plaza for Str. 6E-119 through 123
6E-12	35G	Plaza between Str. 6E-148, 153
	35L	Juncture of Str. 6E-152, 153
	35V	Plaza between Str. 6E-147, 148
	35W	Corner of Str. 6E-152
6E-13	35D	Plaza for Str. 6E-98, 99, 100
6E-14	35C	Plaza for Str. 6E-102 through 105
7E-1	36A	Behind Str. 7E-4
7E-2	36N	Plaza of Str. 7E-15, 16, 17
7E-3	36B	Corner of Str. 7E-10
	36C	Group platform in front of Str. 7E-10
	36F	Corner of Str. 7E-10, by 7E-11
	36G	Corner of Str. 7E-9
	36H	Behind Str. 7E-9
	36U	Group platform in front of Str. 7E-9
	36V	Rear of Str. 7E-10
	36W	In back of Str. 7E-10
	36X	Center of group platform
7E-4	36D	Behind Str. 7E-12
	36O	Plaza of Str. 7E-12, 13, 14
7E-5	36R	Plaza in front of Str. 7E-47
	36S	Plaza in front of Str. 7E-50
7E-6	36P	Plaza for Str. 7D-93, 7E-42, 43, 44
	36Q	Plaza in front of Str. 7E-42
	36T	20 m N of Str. 7E-44
---	1a/7	6D: 250 m N, 440 m E
---	1Q/1	6E: 276 m N, 92 m E
---	1Q/2	6E: 302 m N, 130 m E
---	1Q/4	6E: 182 m N, 114 m E

TABLE 2.341 (Part 1)
Ceramic Evaluations: Corriental Quadrangle

Group	Lot	Provenience	Ceramics
6D-1	37R/1	0-20 cm	Ik and/or Imix; Eznab
	37R/2	20-40 cm	Manik, Ik, Imix
	37R/3	40-60 cm	Ik and/or Imix; 1 possible Preclassic
	37R/4	60- cm	Manik
6D-2	37U/1	0-20 cm	Possible Ik and/or Imix, Manik
	37U/2	20-40 cm	Ik and/or Imix; possible Manik
	37U/3	40-60 cm	Manik, Ik, Imix
	37U/4	60-80 cm	?
	37U/5	80-100 cm	Manik; possible Ik and/or Imix
	37Z/1	0-20 cm	Manik; possible Ik and/or Imix
	37Z/2	20-40 cm	Manik; possible Ik and/or Imix
	37Z/3	40-60 cm	Manik
6D-3	37A/1	0-20 cm	Ik and/or Imix; possible Manik
	37A/2	20-40 cm	Probable Manik; Ik and/or Imix
	37A/3	40-60 cm	Probable Manik; Ik and/or Imix
	37F/1	0-20 cm	Probable Manik; Ik and/or Imix
	37F/2		Ik, Imix
	37F/3		Mostly Manik; some Ik and/or Imix
	37G/1	0-20 cm	Probable Ik and/or Imix
	37G/2	20-40 cm	Ik and/or Imix; possible Manik
6D-4	37B/1	0-20 cm	Manik; Ik and/or Imix
	37B/2	20-40 cm	Mostly Manik; some Ik and/or Imix
	37B/3	40-60 cm	Manik
	37B/4	60-80 cm	Manik; possible Late Preclassic
	37B/5	80-100 cm	Manik; possible Late Preclassic
	37C/1		Late Manik
	37C/2		Late Manik
	37C/3		Late Manik
	37D/1	0-20 cm	Mostly Ik and/or Imix
	37E/1	0-20 cm	Ik, Imix, probable Manik
	37E/2	20-40 cm	Probable Manik; Ik and/or Imix
	37E/3	40-60 cm	Probable Ik and/or Imix
6D-5	1Q/8	Surface	Mostly Manik; some Ik and/or Imix
6D-6	37T/1	0-40 cm	Late Preclassic; possible Manik; Ik and/or Imix
	37V/1	0-40 cm	Ik and/or Imix; possible Manik
	37W/1	0-20 cm	Ik and/or Imix
	37W/2	20-40 cm	Probable Manik
	37Y/1	0-20 cm	Manik through Imix
	37Y/2	20-40 cm	Ik, Imix, possible Manik
	37Y/3	40-60 cm	Manik; Ik and/or Imix
6E-3	35M/1	0-20 cm	?
	35M/2	20-44 cm	Mostly Imix
6E-4	35A/1	0-20 cm	Ik, Imix
	35A/2	20-40 cm	Ik, Imix
6E-5	35N/1	0-20 cm	Ik and/or Imix
	35R/1	0-40 cm	Ik and/or Imix; possible Eznab
6E-6	35I/1	0-20 cm	Manik through Imix

TABLE 2.341 (Part 2)
Ceramic Evaluations: Corriental Quadrangle

Group	Lot	Provenience	Ceramics
	35I/2	20-40 cm	Manik; mostly Ik and/or Imix
	35I/3	40-60 cm	Manik; Ik and/or Imix
	35I/4	60-80 cm	Late Preclassic; Manik
	35S/1	0-20 cm	Ik and/or Imix; Eznab
	35S/2	20-40 cm	Eznab?
	35S/3	40-60 cm	Late Preclassic through Ik
	35T/1	0-20 cm	Manik through Imix
	35T/2	20-40 cm	Ik, Imix, possible Eznab
	35T/3	40- cm	Probable Manik; Ik and/or Imix
6E-7	35J/1	0-20 cm	Probable Ik and/or Imix
6E-8	1Q/5	Surface	Ik, Imix; possible Late Preclassic and Manik
6E-9	35H/1	0-30 cm	Ik, Imix
	35U/1	0-20 cm	Probable Ik and/or Imix
	35U/2	20-60 cm	Probable Ik and/or Imix
6E-10	35N/1	0-20 cm	Ik, Imix
	35N/2	20-40 cm	Ik, Imix
	35O/1		Imix and ?
	35P/1	0-20 cm	Imix or Eznab
	25P/2	20-40 cm	Probable Preclassic
	25P/3		No sherds
6E-11	35E/1	0-20 cm	Ik and/or Imix
	35E/2	20-40 cm	Ik, Imix; 1 probable Manik
	35E/3	40-60 cm	?
	35E/4	60-80 cm	Manik
	35E/5		?
	35E/6		?
6E-12	35G/1	0-22 cm	Ik and/or Imix; possible Manik
	35G/2	0-20 cm S of lot 1	Imix
	35L/1	0-20 cm	Eznab; possible Manik and Ik and/or Imix
	35L/2	20-40 cm	Eznab; possible Late Preclassic and Manik
	35V/1	0-20 cm	Ik and/or Imix; possible late Preclassic
	35V/2	20-40 cm	Late Preclassic through Imix, possible Eznab
	35V/3	40-60 cm	Manik; some Late Preclassic
	35W/1	0-20 cm	Ik and/or Imix; Eznab
	35W/2		?
6E-13	35D/1	0-20 cm	Ik and/or Imix
	35D/2	20-52 cm	Manik; Ik and/or Imix
	35D/3	52-72 cm	Manik
	35D/4	72-92 cm	No sherds
	35D/5	92-106 cm (floor)	Mostly Manik, some Late Preclassic
	35D/6	106-126 cm	?
6E-14	35C/1	0-22 cm	Ik, Imix
	35C/2	22-165 cm (floor)	Ik, Imix
	35C/3	165-184 cm	Manik; 1 possible Middle Preclassic
	35C/4	184-218 cm	Preclassic
7E-1	36A/1	0-20 cm	Ik, Imix
	36A/2	20-40 cm	Ik and/or Imix
	36A/3	40-60 cm	Ik and/or Imix; a few Late Preclassic
7E-2	36N/1	0-20 cm	Ik and/or Imix
	36N/2	20-40 cm	Probable Manik; Ik and/or Imix
7E-3	36B/1	0-20 cm	Imix; possible Late Preclassic; Manik; Eznab
	36B/2	20-40 cm	Some Late Preclassic; mostly Ik and/or Imix

TABLE 2.341 (Part 3)
Ceramic Evaluations: Corriental Quadrangle

Group	Lot	Provenience	Ceramics
	36C/1	0-20 cm	Manik through Imix
	36C/2	20-40 cm	Ik, some Imix
	36C/3	40-60 cm	Ik (midden)
	36C/4	60-80 cm	Manik; Ik and/or Imix
	36F/1	0-20 cm	Manik and Imix
	36F/2	20-40 cm	Manik; some Ik and/or Imix
	36F/3	40-60 cm	Manik; 1 possible Ik and/or Imix
	36G/1	0-20 cm	Mostly Manik; Ik and/or Imix
	36G/2	20-40 cm	Late Manik
	36G/3	40-60 cm	Late Manik (midden)
	36G/4	60-80 cm	Late Manik
	36H/1	0-20 cm	Mostly Ik and/or Imix
	36H/2	20-60 cm	Mostly Ik and/or Imix; Manik
	36H/3	60-100 cm	Manik
	36U/1,4	0-20 cm	Mostly Ik, some Manik, Imix
	36U/2,5	20-40 cm	Manik, Ik, Imix
	36U/3,6	40-60 cm	Manik, Ik, Imix
	36U/7	60-80 cm	Manik, some Ik
	36U/8,11	80-100 cm (floor)	Manik
	36U/9,12	100-120 cm	Manik
	36U/10,13	120-140 cm	Manik
	36U/14, 15,18,19	0-100 cm	Manik, Ik, Imix
	36U/16,17	Beneath floor, Str.7E-Sub.1	Manik
	36V/1	0-20 cm	Manik and Ik
	36V/2	20-40 cm	No data
	36V/3	40-60 cm	Manik
	36V/4	60-85 cm (fill)	No data
	36V/5	60-85 cm	Manik
	36V/6	85 cm-bedrock	Preclassic and Manik
	36W/1	0-20 cm	Manik; possible Imix
	36W/2	20-40 cm	Manik; possible Imix
	36W/3	40-60 cm	No data
	36X/1	0-20 cm	No data
	36X/2	20-40 cm	Manik; Ik; Imix
	36X/3	40-60 cm	Manik; Ik; Imix
	36X/4	60-80 cm	Manik; Ik; Imix
	36X/5	80-100 cm (floor)	Manik; Ik
	36X/6	100-120 cm	Manik
	36X/7	120 cm-bedrock	Late Manik
7E-4	36D/1	0-20 cm	Ik and/or Imix; possible Manik
	36D/2	20-40 cm	Manik; possible Ik and/or Imix
	36D/3	40-60 cm	Manik
	36D/4	60-80 cm	Late Preclassic
	36O/1	Surface	Mostly Manik; Ik and/or Imix
7E-5	36R/1	0-20 cm	Ik and/or Imix; Eznab
	36R/2	20-40 cm	Manik; Ik and/or Imix
	36R/3	40-60 cm	Manik
	36S/1	0-20 cm	Ik and/or Imix; Eznab
	36S/2	20-40 cm	Manik; possible Ik and/or Imix
	36S/3	40-60 cm	?

TABLE 2.341 (Part 4)
Ceramic Evaluations: Corriental Quadrangle

Group	Lot	Provenience	Ceramics
7E-6	36P/1	0-20 cm	Manik through Imix; perhaps Late Preclassic
	36P/2	20-40 cm	Manik through Imix
	36P/3	40-60 cm	Manik; Ik
	36P/4	60-80 cm	Manik
	36P/5	80-100 cm	Manik
	36P/6	100-120 cm	Manik; 1 possible Ik and/or Imix
	36P/7	120-140 cm	Manik; probable Ik and/or Imix
	36Q/1	0-20 cm	Manik through Imix
	36Q/2	20-40 cm	Manik; Ik
	36Q/3	40-60 cm	Ik
	36Q/4	60-80 cm	Late Manik and Ik
	36Q/5	80-100 cm	Late Manik, some Ik and/or Imix
	36Q/6	100-120 cm	Late Manik; possible Ik and/or Imix
	36T/1	0-20 cm	Ik; Imix; possible Manik
	36T/2	20-40 cm	Manik through Imix
	36T/3	40-60 cm	Imix; some Manik
	36T/4	60-80 cm	Manik through Imix
	36T/5	80-100 cm	Manik; some Ik and/or Imix
---	1Q/7	Surface	Mostly Ik and/or Imix; Manik
	1Q/1	Surface	Some Late Preclassic; much Manik
	1Q/2	Surface	Manik; possible Ik and/or Imix
	1Q/4	Surface	Ik and/or Imix

9. Excavations in the Inscriptions Quadrangle

Introduction

Mapped small structures of the Inscriptions Quadrangle are 268 in number, arranged in what appear to be about 84 groups. Of these, only one has been intensively excavated (Gp. 7F-1; TR. 22). Structure 6F-62, which stands alone, has not been excavated, but the associated Ch. 6F-3 has been, and the related plaza was extensively tested for ceramic samples (this report). Some information on Gp. 7F-2 comes from excavations of Ch. 7F-2 and 9 (this report). The excavation of St. 25 (TR. 3:82) produced sherds that should provide at least minimal chronological data for one other group (Gp. 7F-3, this report). Sherds from Ch. 7G-4 furnish chronological data for the group of which it was a part (Gp. 7G-1, this report). So it is that only about 6% of the potential residential groups of the Inscriptions Quadrangle have been sampled at least for chronological data. Vacant terrain has been sampled at one point, near Ch. 6F-5. The data were not made available for this report.

Structure 6F-62 Locus

Structure 6F-62 is located in Sq. 6F of the Tikal site map (TR. 11) at 6F:S453 E403, about 10 m SE of the platform on which the Temple of the Inscriptions (Str. 6F-27) was built (sometime around AD 766). About 5 m N of 6F-62 is Or. 1 of Ch. 6F-3. The terrain here is well suited to habitation, sloping gently down both to the E and W. A number of other structures are located to the S, E, and W, and the Inscriptions Reservoir is only 220 m distant.

Structure 6F-62 itself has not been excavated, but Ch. 6F-3 was investigated in 1963 by Puleston and some test trenches were dug close by in 1964 for Culbert's ceramic test program (see Fig. 156). These provide some information, for they encountered remains of a plaza (Plat. 6F-1) presumably associated with the structure, as well as associated trash deposits. The structure itself, on the basis of its ruin, probably was a low rectangular platform similar to many that were more intensively excavated for this report.

PLATFORM 6F-1

Platform 6F-1 is the designation given the area N of Str. 6F-62. Little can be said about it, as excavations were not focused here. Rather, an area of 8.28 m² was excavated above Ch. 6F-3 by Puleston, in connection with his investigations of that chultun, and two trenches 6 m long and 0.50 m wide were excavated by Kent Day as part of Culbert's ceramic test program. The excavator's notes do not give the precise locations for these trenches, but a rough field sketch shows that one ran W for about 6 m from the Puleston excavations, and the other ran N from the Puleston excavations. The former, then, probably falls beyond the limits of Plat. 6F-1; much or all of the latter may also.

Virtually nothing is known of Plat. 6F-1. Apparently, traces of plaster floor were noted in excavations above the chultun, but in the confusion at the close of a field season, these traces were not recorded on plan or section. There are two strata in the 0.80 m of earth above the bedrock, however (Fig. 157a,b). The lowermost, Plat. 6F-1:U. 1, is a grayish earth filled with stones. Sherds from this area are all Preclassic, save for a few Caban vessels. Above this is U. 2, dark brown topsoil in which Ik and/or Imix sherds are consistently present.

In the N ceramic test trench, Ik and/or Imix sherds occur in deposits from 0.20 m below surface to bedrock. The same is true in the W test trench.

Burial 218, oriented E-W, is located S of Or. 1 of the chultun (Fig. 156a). One of its covering stones slightly overlaps the rim of the chultun, suggesting an association with the overlying fill beneath which the chultun was buried.

What these few facts suggest is that U. 1 is fill for a plaza surface, of which the plaster fragments are a remnant. This plaza covered the chultun, and probably was used in Intermediate to Late Classic times. The fill itself is probably the rearranged debris from a Preclassic occupation with which Ch. 6F-3 was associated. The Caban sherds could derive from a late, nearby occupation, by which time the slabs over Or. 1 of the chultun had collapsed. On the basis of the Ik and/or Imix sherds in the deep levels of the two test trenches, the plaza was localized to the area directly N of Str. 6F-62. It seems a safe hypothesis that structure and plaza formed a single architectural unit. The burial was not excavated, but the grave is similar to a number of graves of Intermediate and Late Classic residential burials (this report, section III). Probably, then, the burial relates to Plat. 6F-1 and Str. 6F-62.

CHULTUN 6F-3

Description

Chamber 1 is the largest chamber of the chultun (Table 2.342), is roughly oval in plan, but with one end truncated (Fig. 156b). Walls, ceiling, and floor are roughly demarcated from one another, but the junctures are rounded

and all surfaces are concave. Leading into the NW portion of the ceiling of this chamber is Neck 1, with Or. 1 above. The W end of this opening is rounded in normal fashion, and has a stepped rim 0.10 m deep and 0.04 m wide. From the point of maximum diameter, though, the orifice is elongated into a rectangle, becoming slightly wider to the E. On either side of the E end, notches (Fig. 156a and 157a:U. 1) were cut as if to receive a large stone slab or wooden beam set across the end of the orifice. This slab or beam would have been about 0.70 by 0.32 m, and perhaps 0.20 m thick. Just such a stone was discovered, but lodged at an angle. The rest of the orifice, as found, was plugged with stone rubble. The neck, at its western end, is short and flares down into Chm. 1. At its E end, the sides are vertical and form a sharper angle with the ceiling.

Chamber 1 was about half filled (Fig. 157a,b) by strata, U. 3–6. Unit 6, at the top, consists of dark brown soil that abuts U. 2 and 7 (see below). It is deepest beneath Or. 1. Beneath it is U. 5, a deposit of gray soil containing several small stones. It, too, abuts U. 2 and is deepest beneath Or. 1. Both U. 5 and 6 contain sherds and a few artifacts. Unit 4, beneath U. 5, contains neither sherds nor artifacts. It, too, abuts U. 2, but its consistency differs from U. 5 and 6 and it is not deeper beneath Or. 1 than elsewhere. Unit 4 is composed of very fine, yellowish-gray marl, with no stones. Beneath it is U. 3, another deposit, grayish white in color, which contains some small stones. Unit 3 was not packed as one would expect of material accumulated during use of the chultun. It may not have contained cultural material; although sherds were noted on the lot card, there is no notation of quantity, nor could Culbert locate any for evaluation.

Chamber 2, a very small chamber, is round in plan (Fig. 156b), and on the shallow side (similar to the antechamber of Ch. 5G-24). It is separated from Chm. 1, to the W, by a low (0.18 m) but broad (0.80 m) sill (U. 15). To the S, the only separation from Chm. 3 is a bulge in the N wall, and the entrance to Chm. 1 is shared with Chm. 3. This entrance is very much wider than the others in this chultun, though it is slightly restricted on either side. The entrance was completely closed by a wall, U. 2. This was built on U. 15, the broad sill (see Fig. 157a). Quite thick, (0.65 m), U. 2 was composed of small stone masonry and plaster. On the Chm. 1 side, the small stones are carefully placed and extend all the way to the ceiling. On the Chm. 2 side, plaster does not run all the way to the ceiling; apparently, therefore, U. 2 was constructed from the Chm. 1 side. This is not surprising, for there would have been very little working room on the Chm. 2 side.

Opening into the ceiling of Chm. 2 is Neck 2 from Or. 2. The orifice in this case is the usual round opening, with no stepped lip. Nor is a stone cover to be found, the orifice having been left sealed by rubble. The short neck is essentially continuous with the walls of Chm. 2, which are more or less concave.

Chamber 2 and Neck 2 were found completely filled with earth, stones, and abundant cultural material including sherds in a state of preservation normally characteristic of midden situations. The U. 8 fill was prevented from spilling into Chm. 1 by U. 2. In color, U. 8 ranges from brownish gray at the top to light gray at the bottom. There are no distinct strata.

A small third chamber adjoins Chm. 2 to the N. Like Chm. 2, it is circular in plan, and its floor is continuous with that of Chm. 2. As found, the SE corner of U. 2 projects into the center of the chamber. Retained by the wall was a continuation of U. 8 from Chm. 2. This, however, did not quite reach the ceiling of the chamber.

An otherwise small fourth chamber, N of Chm. 1, is elongated into an arc-shaped passage (Fig. 156b). The W end of this opens through a completely unrestricted entrance in the E wall of Chm. 5, 1.10 m above the floor of this chamber (Fig. 157c). At one time, there was an apparently constricted opening at the E end of the S wall of Chm. 4 into the N side of Chm. 1. As found, though, this was completely closed by a plaster and masonry wall, U. 7, reminiscent of U. 2 (Fig. 157b). Opening into the ceiling of Chm. 4 at its E end is Neck 3 with Or. 3. Like the other two, Or. 3 was sealed beneath deep fill. Unlike the other two, this was accomplished by leaving the stone cover in place. The rim is not stepped, and the neck flares downward so that it is not really distinguished from the room walls themselves. Stones in an arc-like arrangement around the orifice, U. 13, probably were placed to hold back surrounding fill. Based on bedrock, this half-ring of stone rises above it 0.14 m.

Chamber 4 was about half full beneath Or. 3, but less so towards its juncture with Chm. 5. The top layer of fill, U. 9, consists of a grainy, grayish-white earth in which were nearly 4 pounds of Cauac sherds in a condition suggestive of a midden. Beneath this was U. 10, a dark brown stratum containing nearly 3 pounds of Cauac sherds in a condition much like those of U. 9. Both U. 9 and 10 abutted U. 7, which prevented U. 9 from spilling out over U. 6 in Chm. 1.

A fifth chamber is oval in plan and rectangular in section, with well-differentiated ceiling, walls, and floor. The points of juncture, however, are rounded. The chamber is quite deep; its floor is 1.10 m below that of Chm. 4 and 0.50 m below that of Chm. 1. It may be entered from Chm. 4 or Chm. 1, both to the E. The entrance from Chm. 1 is constricted, with an unusually high sill (U. 14; 0.45 m), while that from Chm. 4 is not. Chamber 5 contained only U. 11 (Fig. 157c), a loose, shallow layer of marl devoid of cultural material.

A sixth chamber, smaller than 5, is entered from the N end of the latter (Fig. 156b). This entrance is restricted on the sides and on the bottom by a pronounced sill. Walls, ceiling, and floor are all rounded with no marked points of juncture. In plan, the chamber is oval. As found, it contained only U. 12, a deposit identical to U. 11 in Chm. 5 but even shallower.

DISCUSSION

The first problem to be dealt with here concerns the fill in the chultun. Chambers 2 and 3 were surely purposely filled as a single act through Or. 2. The material used for this came from a midden fill of Cauac sherds somewhere in the vicinity. The fill (U. 8) was prevented from falling into Chm. 1 by the U. 2 retaining wall, built in the entrance to that chamber.

The sherds in the fill of Chm. 4 (both U. 9 and 10) virtually duplicate those in Chm. 2 and 3 in terms of ceramic complex represented, condition of sherds, and quantity. This suggests that the fill was drawn from the same source as that in Chm. 2 and 3, in spite of the color differences between U. 9 and 10, with the further suggestion that Chm. 4 was filled not far from the same time as Chm. 2 and 3. Consistent with this, a stone and masonry wall, U. 7, much like U. 2, prevented the fill from falling into Chm. 1 from Chm. 4. Possibly, though, U. 7 was built some time earlier for another purpose, and later came to serve as a retaining wall (see below). It is noteworthy that a stone cover was in place over Or. 3 that leads into Chm. 4. Perhaps this is why the chamber was not completely filled, although Chm. 2 was. No stone cover was in place over Or. 2, which leads into Chm. 2. Because Chm. 4 was not completely filled, such fill as there was did not spill through the unrestricted entrance into Chm. 5.

Chambers 5 and 6 clearly were left empty. Both contained very shallow deposits of marly material (U. 11 and 12) devoid of sherds. This probably represents decomposition of walls and ceiling following abandonment, as neither chamber is markedly packed.

The bottom stratum in Chm. 1, U. 3, does not exactly replicate U. 11 and 12. The overlying U. 4 differs from U. 3 slightly, in that it is a bit more yellow in color and contains no small stones. Quite possibly, both U. 3 and 4 represent precipitation from the ceiling and walls after abandonment. For this reason, it is probable that Chm. 1 was left empty upon abandonment. Other factors that reinforce this interpretation include the fact that the chamber was not completely filled; the fill was deepest (and highest) beneath Or. 1; the upper two strata (U. 5 and 6) become darker toward the top; and the fill postdates stratigraphically U. 2 and 7. Orifice 1 was probably sealed with pieces of rubble and stone upon abandonment, perhaps for construction of Plat. 6F-1, or perhaps earlier. Much later, the slab over the eastern end of the orifice slipped, allowing overlying fill to settle into the chultun, eventually causing the opening noted by Tikal Project surveyors in 1958. This would accord with the presence of Ik and/or Imix sherds in U. 5, for such sherds occur in deposits above Or. 1. Also worth mentioning here, the sherds per cubic meter in U. 5 and 6 are not far different from those around Or. 1.

Given this interpretation, the chultun in its final form (6F-3-1st) must have consisted of Chm. 1, 5, and 6, with Or. 1. Chamber 4, though not completely filled, probably was not a functional part of this chultun. An unusual feature of Ch. 6F-3-1st is the existence of such a large antechamber. Usually, chultun antechambers are smaller than the other chambers. What this suggests is that Or. 1 was constructed after the other two orifices were closed, especially for Ch. 6F-3-1st.

From all the above, we may conclude that an earlier version or versions of Ch. 6F-3 existed. While absolute certainty is not possible, the following reconstruction seems the most economical given the above, and given the other data at hand. As originally constructed, the chultun consisted of Chm. 1, Or. 3 and that part of Chm. 4 directly below the orifice. In other words, Ch. 6F-3-5th was a typical two-chambered chultun, with small antechamber and larger, deeper, lateral storage chamber. Between the two is the expected sill, and the opening between the two chambers (no smaller than those between Chm. 1 and 5, and 4 and 5) was sufficient to permit passage from Chm. 4 directly to Chm. 1.

Two objections may be raised at this point. The first is that Chm. 4, as now seen, does not look like an antechamber for Chm. 1. Since the shape of Chm. 4 is virtually unique by Tikal standards, however, there is no reason to assume that it was originally built as it now appears. Rather, it may have been lengthened later to give access to Chm. 5. Had it been constructed originally to give access to that chamber, it is reasonable to suppose that the orifice would have been closer to Chm. 5. The second objection is relatively minor. This is that Chm. 4 does not flare from Or. 3 in the usual manner of an antechamber for Chm. 1. Yet, there is some flare, and Section B-B' (Fig. 157b) does not look significantly different from a section of an ordinary two-chambered chultun (see Fig. 26, 44, 127, 130, 136) and is less idiosyncratic than some (see Fig. 3, 32).

As can be seen on Section B-B' (Fig. 157b), the S side of the neck beneath Or. 3 is slightly S of the N edge of the sill beneath it. This means that if water seeped beneath the stone cover, some of it would have dripped directly on the sill, rather than onto the floor of Chm. 4. Because of this, water could have run into Chm. 1. Since the inner chambers were intended to be dry, this created a problem. The solution was probably construction of Chm. 5, to create

Ch. 6F-3-4th-B. In support of this is the unusually high sill (U. 14) between Chm. 1 and 5, which suggests that the Maya were going to be absolutely certain that this time they would have a dry chamber. That Chm. 5 predates 2 and 3 will become evident shortly.

Although Chm. 5 provided a dry chamber, there still may have been a water problem. Anyone going into it had to pass through Chm. 1, into which water could still run. In the rainy season particularly, this could have been an unpleasant experience. Because of this, a further alteration was carried out. Chamber 4 was extended W to open directly into Chm. 5, and the old entrance to Chm. 1 was walled up. In support of this, the plan of Chm. 4 as now seen suggests a deliberate attempt to reach the previously constructed one. The new entrance from 4 to 5 is also equivalent in size to the one it replaced from 4 to 1, as well as the one that leads from 1 to 5.

Chultun 6F-3 in its new form (Ch. 6F-3-4th-A), therefore, probably consisted of an enlarged Chm. 4, with Chm. 5 and 1. Since no sill was provided between 4 and 5, the latter now became a "wet" antechamber for the now "dry" Chm. 1.

The next alteration was probably the construction of Chm. 6 (Ch. 6F-3-3rd). That this followed the opening of Chm. 4 into 5 is indicated by the sill between 5 and 6. No sill would have been needed, unless water was entering Chm. 5, and this could only have occurred through Chm. 4. Actually, Chm. 6 could have been constructed quite soon after 4 was lengthened to open into 5.

With Ch. 6F-3-3rd the Maya had a chultun with two dry chambers, but with the same problem as with 4th-B. They had to crawl through the wet, cramped Chm. 4 into the also wet Chm. 5; all in all it may have been even more unpleasant than the earlier crawl from Chm. 4 through 1 to 5. For this reason, perhaps, they chose to abandon Chm. 4 and Or. 3 altogether, and build a new one, Or. 2. They began (CS. 3) by building a new antechamber E of Chm. 1. They constructed the antechamber from below, rather than above, probably because there was more room to work that way. This was Chm. 3, and between the two is the wide sill, U. 15, located well away from where the orifice was to be so that they would not repeat the same seepage problem as with the sill of Ch. 6F-3-5th. Perhaps the sill was made extra wide so that, if they had to, they could remove some of it on the E, if in fact water did drip on it and run into Chm. 1.

Perhaps because it was easier to dig down, rather than up, the new orifice was constructed from above, rather than from below in the new antechamber (CS. 2). To do this, though, the Maya had to plot the location of the new orifice on the surface and this meant taking a complicated series of measurements. They had to measure from Or. 3 into Chm. 5, turn an angle and measure to the entrance to

Chm. 1, then turn another angle and measure to the center of Chm. 3. All of this had to be precisely repeated above ground, a difficult procedure made even more so by the scrambling about below ground necessary in the first place. Given this, accuracy of the plot for Or. 2 would not be expected, and it does not seem to have been achieved. Orifice 2 came down N of Chm. 3, and because of this, it was necessary to construct Chm. 2 below it. This interpretation nicely accounts for the double antechamber (Chm. 2 and 3) with the single sill, floor, and orifice. Note, too, that the gross miscalculation involved here would have been most unlikely were the Maya working from an existing Or. 1, and almost as unlikely working from Or. 3 via the opening from Chm. 4 into 1.

Once the above construction was completed, Or. 3 could be permanently closed off (CS. 1). The Maya began to fill Chm. 4, but evidently changed their minds, and simply sealed the stone cover in place instead. Not only was this easier in terms of the labor involved in filling the whole chamber, it was also easier because a wall did not have to be built to retain the fill where Chm. 4 opens into 5. The dark colored fill on the floor of Chm. 4 could have accumulated during CS. 2 and 3, and the lighter colored fill above was purposely dumped inside. Some of the sherds from this fill could have gotten trampled into the top of the darker earth.

The Maya who used Ch. 6F-3 seem to have had a propensity for miscalculation. In this case, Or. 2 was badly located, for it was on a downhill slope and hence vulnerable to the entrance of runoff rainwater. Given this, U. 13 may have been insufficient to prevent entry of rainwater into Chm. 1. Thus, the old problem returned: one had to scramble from the wet antechamber through Chm. 1, also wet, before reaching the dry Chm. 5 and 6. Probably for

this reason, the offending 2 and 3 were walled off. The similarity of the fill placed in 2 and 3 to that in Chm. 4 suggests that the Maya probably abandoned these shortly after their construction. Figuring that Chm. 1 was a lost cause anyway, a regular orifice was constructed into it, converting it into an antechamber. While water could now seep directly into it, at least U. 14 protected 5 and 6, and access was through a drier, less muddy area than through Or. 2. Hence, Ch. 6F-3-1st-B probably consisted of Chm. 1, 5, and 6, with a manhole-like Or. 1.

This last argument is important with respect to the one remaining problem: the peculiar shape of Or. 1. Its W half indicates that it probably did begin as the usual manhole-like orifice, in this case with a stepped rim for a stone cover. For some reason, this was expanded (creating Ch. 6F-3-1st-A), perhaps the result of an innovative attempt to facilitate entrance and exit and the passage of stored goods in and out. To close the opening, a series of rectangular slabs may have replaced the original stone cover; certainly, the cover was no longer adequate. The notches (U. 1) may have permitted the seating of a more permanent slab at the eastern end of the orifice. A possibility here is that the builders decided that they had gone too far, and so they reduced the length of the orifice with such a slab, flush with the surface of the bedrock, creating what amounted to a bedrock patch. At any rate, the new, enlarged orifice probably allowed more water into Chm. 1 than did the original Or. 1. At first, this seems puzzling, perhaps implying a certain lack of awareness with respect to water problems. If, however, it was no longer important whether or not water leaked into Chm. 1, then there was really nothing to stop the Maya from experimentation with a chultun orifice.

TABLE 2.342
Chultun 6F-3: Average Dimensions (meters)

Features	Length	Width	Height	Diameter
Neck 1	1.00	0.50	0.40	--
Neck 2	--	--	0.20	0.55
Neck 3	--	--	0.06	0.51
Stone Cover	--	--	0.10	0.59
Chamber 1	2.08	2.00	1.36	--
Chamber 2	0.85	0.80	1.00	--
Chamber 3	1.00	0.80	0.90 (est.)	--
Chamber 4	1.64	0.52	1.04	--
Chamber 5	1.90	1.40	1.70	--
Chamber 6	1.70	1.20	0.80	--
Entrance 1-2	0.70	1.10	0.78	--
Entrance 1-4	0.20	?	0.50	--
Entrance 1-5	0.40	0.48	0.56	--
Entrance 4-5	--	0.50	0.60	--
Entrance 5-6	0.15	0.60	0.54	--

SHERDS AND ARTIFACTS

Lot groups defined for Plat. 6F-1 and Ch. 6F-3 are given in Table 2.343, with content in Tables 2.344 and 2.345.

CONSTRUCTION FILL

The only material in this category is in Plat. 6F-1:LG. 1. Since this is unsealed, and since there has been slumping around Or. 1 of Ch. 6F-3, the presence of a few Caban sherds is no problem; they indicate a late reoccupation somewhere in the vicinity. Otherwise, the material ap-

pears to be redeposited from a Preclassic occupation.

MATERIAL ABOVE LIVING LEVELS

In this category are Plat. 6F-1:LG. 2a–2c in which, contrary to LG. 1, Ik and/or Imix material predominates. In the case of LG. 2b and 2c, such sherds are found down to bedrock. The presence of some Preclassic material, however, testifies to contamination from the earlier Preclassic occupation. It is possible, too, that some of LG. 2c derives from the large platform on which Str. 6F-27 (Temple of the Inscriptions) was built.

TABLE 2.343
Structure 6F-62 Locus: Lot Groups

Feature	Lot Group	Lot	Provenience	Ceramic Evaluation
Plat.6F-1	1	72D/2	Unsealed fill of Plat.6F-1	Cauac or Chuen and Caban
	2a	72D/1	Surface above the level of the plaza floor	Mostly Ik and/or Imix, some Preclassic
	2b	103B/7-12	N of plaza, surface to bedrock	Ik and/or Imix (probably Imix); possible Preclassic
	2c	103B/1-6	W of plaza, surface to bedrock	Ik and/or Imix and some Preclassic
Ch.6F-3 (Op.72D)	1a	9-17	Fill of Chm. 2 and 3 (U.8)	Cauac
	1b	8	Deep fill of Chm.4 (U.10)	Cauac
	1c	7	Upper fill of Chm.4 (U.9)	Cauac
	2a	18	Fill of Chm.5 and 6 (U.11, 12)	No data
	2b	6	Deep fill of Chm.1 (U.3)	?
	2c	5	Second layer of fill of Chm. (U.4)	No data
	2d	3,4	Upper fill of Chm.1 (U.5,6)	Chuen, Cauac and Ik and/or Imix

CHULTUN FILL

The chultun fill has already been thoroughly discussed, so little need be said here. Attention may be called to the great quantities of sherds in LG. 1a (U. 8), 1b (U. 10), and 1c (U. 9). These sherds are large, with sharp breaks. These facts, with the presence of much bone and a number of other artifact fragments in LG. 1a especially, and at least one piece of fire-spalled chert in 1b, indicate a nearby midden as the source. This was probably derived from a structure or structures associated with Ch. 6F-3-2nd. The same source may have provided the material in Plat. 6F-1:LG. 1 (see above), and all these together should provide clues to the use of that structure or structures.

One problem in connection with U. 10 (LG. 1b) is its dark color in contrast to the lighter U. 9 (LG. 1c) above, in spite of the identical nature of the sherds in them. This may be explained if some organic earth got into Chm. 4, perhaps because it was left open while Chm. 2 or 3 were under construction. Then, midden debris was dumped in, which, at the bottom, got trampled and mixed into this darker material.

Previously suggested was that U. 5 and 6 (LG. 2d) settled into the chultun after abandonment. The similarity of the sherds to overlying material (Plat. 6F-1:LG. 1 and 2a) has already been noted; it may be pointed out here that the sherd content of Ch. 3F-6:LG. 2d falls between that of Plat. 6F-1:LG. 1 and 2a, and that bone scraps occur in the chultun and above.

TIME SPANS

What is known of the construction history is summed up in Tables 2.346–2.348. Chultun 6F-3 long predates Str. 6F-62. It probably began (Ch. 6F-3-5th) as a two-chambered chultun, to which another chamber was added on account of a water problem (Ch. 6F-3-4th-B). Following a reorganization of these chambers (Ch. 6F-3-4th-A), another chamber was added (Ch. 6F-3-3rd). Again because of a water problem, the existing orifice (Or. 3) and the chamber beneath were abandoned, and a new orifice and antechamber were provided (Ch. 6F-3-2nd). Because this failed to solve the water problem, the new orifice and antechamber were soon abandoned, and a third orifice (the one on the map) was constructed (Ch. 6F-3-1st-B). Later, there was modification of this orifice (Ch. 6F-3-1st-A), perhaps simply the result of experimentation.

All of this activity took place in locus TS. 20 through 8. The fill used for Ch. 6F-3-2nd and 1st-B (Locus TS. 12 and 10) was evidently drawn from a nearby midden full of Cauac sherds. This, the presence of Chuen material in other sources, and the total lack of any Manik material whatsoever (see Table 2.343), suggests that Ch. 6F-3-5th was built while Chuen ceramics were in vogue, but that Cauac ceramics came into production some time between locus TS. 19 and 13. They were still in use when Ch. 6F-3-1st-B was built. Given this dating, and given a nearby trash deposit, it follows that an unknown structure (or structures) was associated with Ch. 6F-3 (see Str. 2G-61 for one example of such a situation).

Cauac ceramics were still in use (Table 2.347) when Or. 1 was enlarged to produce Ch. 6F-3-1st-A (Locus TS. 8). Some time later the chultun was abandoned, probably along with abandonment of the structure or structures with which it was associated. This took place long before construction of Plat. 6F-1, the use of which is dated by Ik and/or Imix ceramics (Table 2.343:LG. 2a–c). Presumably, these date the use of Str. 6F-62 as well. This and the previously noted lack of Manik ceramics indicate that abandonment of the chultun took place in Preclassic

TABLE 2.344
Platform 6F-1: Artifacts by Lot Group

Study Category	Object	Lot Groups			
		1	2a	2b	2c
Pottery Vessels	Sherds per cubic meter (lbs)	1.34	2.38	2.40	3.18
Flaked Chert Artifacts	Point-retouched flake			1	
	Flake cores	3			
Ground, Pecked, and Polished Stone Artifacts	Mano	1			
Shell and Bone Artifacts	Bone, unidentifiable, unmodified	15			

TABLE 2.345
Chultun 6F-3: Artifacts by Lot Group

Study Category	Object	Lot Groups 1a	1b	1c	2a	2b	2c	2d
Pottery Vessels	Sherds per cubic meter (lbs)	3.78 to 66.93*	10.96	19.10	0	?	0	1.63
Other Pottery Artifacts	Unperforated shaped sherd	1						
Flaked Chert Artifacts	Flake cores			5				
	Elongate biface	1						
	Irregular, retouched flakes	2		1				
	Point-retouched flake	1						
	Used flakes	2		2				
	Unused flakes	7		3				
	Nodules	1	3					
Flaked Obsidian Artifacts	Flake	1						
Ground, Pecked, and Polished Stone Artifacts	Mano	1						
	Metate			1				
	Rubbing stones	2						
Shell and Bone Artifacts	Bone, animal, unworked	15						
	Bone, unidentifiable, unworked	7						200

*Quantity not recorded for all lots

TABLE 2.346
Platform 6F-1: Time Spans

Time Span	Architectural Development	Unit	Special Deposits: Burial	Descriptive Data	Ceramics in Vogue
1				Final abandonment of locus	
2				Reoccupation of the locus	Caban
3		2	218?	Abandonment and beginning ruin	
4		2	218?	Use	Imix
5	Plat. 6F-1	1		Construction, probably for Str. 6F-62	Ik

TABLE 2.347
Chultun 6F-3: Time Spans

Time Span	Architectural Development	Construction Stage	Unit	Descriptive Data	Lot Group		Ceramics in Vogue
1			5,6	Collapse of the seal for Or. 1, followed by partial filling of Chm. 1	2d	2c	
2			3,4, 11,12	Abandonment with the sealing of Or. 1, followed by accumulation of marl from the gradual disintegration of material from ceilings and walls	2a,b		Imix Ik Manik
3				Use			
4	Ch.6F-3-1st-A	None defined	1	Enlargement of Or. 1			
5				Use			
6	Ch.6F-3-1st-B	None defined	2,8	Opening between Chm. 1 and 2 sealed; Chm. 2 and 3 filled; Or. 1 constructed	1a		
7				Use			
8	Ch.6F-3-2nd	1	9	Chm. 4 partially filled; stone cover sealed in place over Or. 3	1c		
		2	10,15	Or. 2 and Chm. 2 constructed	1b		
		3	10,15	Chm. 3 constructed			
9				Use			Cauac
10	Ch.6F-3-3rd	1		Chm. 6 constructed			
11				Use			
12	Ch.6F-3-4th-A	None defined	7	Chm. 4 enlarged to open into Chm. 5; opening between Chm. 1 and 4 sealed			
13				Use			
14	Ch.6F-3-4th-B	1	14	Construction of Chm. 5			
15				Use			
16	Ch.6F-3-5th	1		Construction of Chm. 1			
		2	13	Construction of Or. 3 and part of Chm. 4 as an antechamber			Chuen

times. Locus TS. 6, therefore, is defined to cover this hiatus, prior to renewed activity (locus TS. 5).

Locus TS. 4 covers the period of use of Plat. 6F-1 and, presumably, Str. 6F-62. Since so little is known of this construction, there may have been several modifications. Abandonment (start of locus TS. 3) came prior to the appearance of Eznab ceramics, but there was a brief reoccupation (locus TS. 2) by users of Caban ceramics.

On the basis of the dates for the Tikal Ceramic Complexes, the Preclassic occupation at this locus began between 350 BC and AD 1, probably later rather than earlier. It ended by AD 250. Structure 6F-62 was built after AD 550, possibly even after AD 700. It was abandoned by AD 869. The reoccupation of TS. 2 occurred at some point after AD 950.

Group 7F-2

These structures are located on a marked knoll at 7F:S85 E245, 135 m S of the platform on which Str. 6F-27, the Temple of the Inscriptions, was built (at ca. AD 766). They are also 120 m SE of the Inscriptions Reservoir, and 100 m NE of Gp. 7F-1 (TR. 22). Other small-structure groups are located 40 m W, 65 m NW, 90 m NE, and 80 m E. South of the knoll are Ch. 7F-2 (18 m distant) and 7F-9 (unmapped; 22 m S and E of the group and 20 m E of Ch. 7F-2). Their proximity to the knoll, as well as their distance from any other known group, suggests that they were functionally related to Gp. 7F-2. In the case of Ch. 7F-9, such an interpretation seems reasonable (this discussed below), but it is not so clear in the case of Ch. 7F-2.

None of the mapped structures of Gp. 7F-2 have been excavated, but all are of sizes and shapes appropriate for square to rectangular house platforms (see TR. 11). Both chultuns were excavated in 1963 as Op. 66Y and Z by Puleston, who also excavated test trenches nearby. Another test trench was excavated (as Op. 103A) by Ch. 7F-9 in 1964, as part of Culbert's ceramic test pit programs. These test excavations revealed the presence of unmapped structures associated with Ch. 7F-2, but none in association with Ch. 7F-9. Hence, 7F-9 may have been used by the same people who made use of the mapped structures of Gp. 7F-2, although Ch. 7F-2 apparently was not.

STRUCTURE 7F-89-2ND

Little is known of this structure, as only a portion of its S wall and fill were excavated (Fig. 158, 159a). The wall (U. 1) rests on the same fill over which Plat. 7F-4:U. 1 was laid, a floor that turns up to the base of the structure wall. Fill N of the wall is identical with that beneath the plaza floor, so it is evident that the two constructions

TABLE 2.348
Correlation of Time Spans for Platform 6F-1 and Chultun 6F-3

Locus Time Span	Platform 6F-1 (Table 2.346)	Chultun 6F-3 (Table 2.347)
1	1	
2	2	
3	3	1
4	4	
5	5	
6		2
7		3
8		4
9		5
10		6
11		7
12		8
13		9
14		10
15		11
16		12
17		13
18		14
19		15
20		16

were contemporary. Of the wall, only two blocks of masonry were seen in excavation, but its position is indicated by the straight line of termination, with turnup, of Plat. 7F-4:U. 1 in line with that masonry. Evidently, the wall was largely removed when Str. 7F-89:U. 2 was laid. This also undoubtedly explains the lack of plaster floor running N from the top of Str. 7F-89:U. 1.

In the face of such slim evidence, it is impossible to reconstruct what Str. 7F-89 looked like. It could have been a square or rectangular platform of at least one, if not two levels. Although its S wall formed a straight line, one or more walls could have been straight or rounded. Only more excavation could settle these points.

STRUCTURE 7F-89-1ST

This version of 89 is represented solely by a floor, U. 2. Actually, the pavement could have been a new one for Plat. 7F-4, but its elevation is the same as the presumed tops of Str. 7F-89 and 90. This suggests that such a plaza floor would have eliminated both structures, in which case there would not have been much reason to have a plaza here. Moreover, no trace of the floor exists near Str. 7F-90. Finally, it can be interpreted as an addition to the front of 7F-89, analogous to that of Str. 7F-90 represented by Str. 7F-90:U. 3. In the last analysis, though, only further excavation could make the reconstruction offered here more than a hypothesis.

Unit 2 consists of a substantial floor remnant 0.10 m N of U. 1 (the front wall of 89-2nd), as well as several fragments over, and S of, U. 1. All are at the same elevation, about 0.20 m above that of Plat. 7F-4:U. 1. Its northern remnant may actually be the floor of 89-2nd, as its elevation is appropriate for this. When 89-1st was built, however, a portion of U. 1 was torn out where it did not matter, probably to use in new construction. This would have destroyed the original relationship of floor and wall. Following this, an addition was built onto the structure extending S into Plat 7F-4. The E wall of this may be represented by Str. 7F-89:U. 3, a rubble retaining wall built on Plat. 7F-4:U. 1. Preservation here was poor, but it looks as though this wall may have abutted the remaining masonry of Str. 7F-89:U. 1. Unit 3 appears not to have extended farther S than Ch. 7F-2, and the arrangement of rubble indicates that U. 3 could have turned a corner to run W immediately S of the chultun. No further wall remains were identifiable, but the absence of Str. 7F-89:U. 2 near 7F-90:U. 3 suggests that a W wall must have run N to abut U. 1 of 89 just W of the excavated area around Ch. 7F-2.

In support of this interpretation, no trace of the floor, U. 2, can be found E of U. 3 except for the portion N of U. 1. Nor can any be found S of Ch. 7F-2. The floor itself is close enough in elevation to the surviving top of U. 3 to be interpreted as pavement for a platform of which U. 3 was one wall. Suggested by all this is that a small platform was added onto the S side of Str. 7F-89, the floor of which sealed Ch. 7F-2 (see "Discussion," Ch. 7F-2).

STRUCTURE 7F-90-2ND

This structure is almost as poorly known as 89-2nd (Fig. 158). One of its walls, U. 1, was built as part of the same construction as Plat. 7F-4:U. 1, for the plaster of that pavement turns up onto the wall masonry and so served as its facing (Fig. 159b). North of U. 1, a test trench encountered another wall, U. 2, in line with U. 1. This and the identical elevation of U. 1 and 2 indicate that both are parts of a single wall. In the case of U. 2, the turnup of the plaza floor was not seen, undoubtedly because of poor preservation. It is therefore clear that this is the E face of a platform, tentatively labeled as Str. 7F-90-2nd. A search for the W wall of the structure was unproductive. As with Str. 7F-89, 90-2nd could have been square or rectangular, with or without one or more rounded end walls, and with one or more levels.

STRUCTURE 7F-90-1ST

East of U. 1 is another wall, U. 3, which was built on the surface of Plat. 7F-4:U. 1 (Fig. 159b). It is more closely oriented to magnetic N-S than is U. 1, but it turns a right angle E of U. 2 and runs W towards that exposure of the wall of 90-2nd. Unfortunately, there has been disturbance here, but the wall almost surely was built so as to abut U. 2. Clearly, U. 3 represents a major alteration of 7F-90, and so is designated as part of 90-1st. Just what this looked like is even more of a question than how 90-2nd appeared, since the alignment of the new addition was not the same as that of the original structure. At least some of this original structure must have remained in use as part of the remodeled version.

No traces of structure floors were found in the excavations. Presumably, such pavements once existed, since plaster was used for the plaza surfaces. Behind U. 1 is what almost surely is a burial (Bu. 219), running N-S. Its precise sequential position is not known.

PLATFORM 7F-4-2ND

Platform 7F-4 is the plaza area S of Str. 7F-89 and E of 7F-90 (Fig. 158). Its overall extent is not known, but it was provided with a good plaster pavement (U. 1) that was laid on fill 0.10–0.20 m thick over bedrock. The floor is now destroyed around the orifice of Ch. 7F-2, but it was probably in use with the chultun (see discussion of Ch. 7F-2). It clearly was laid at the time of construction of Str. 7F-89-2nd and 90-2nd, as already noted. Its plaster continues upward as the outer face of the E wall of 90-2nd, and it turns up to the base of the S wall of 7F-89-2nd, which was built on the same fill over which the plaza floor was laid.

PLATFORM 7F-4-1ST

Platform 7F-4 was modified on at least one occasion. Although this may have involved construction of a new floor, this seems doubtful (see discussion of Str. 7F-89-1st). More likely, the modification was brought about by additions to Str. 7F-89 and 90 that extended those structures out into the plaza, burying portions of Plat. 7F-4:U. 1. Some of the replastering noted on U. 1 may be associated with this modification.

CHULTUN 7F-2

DESCRIPTION

The single orifice of this chultun (Fig. 158 and Table 2.349) opens downward into a single steep-sided chamber (Fig. 159a). In shape, the chamber resembles an irregular cone, with a flat bottom. There is no evidence of plaster. A mass of rubble (U. 4) was found around the orifice of the chultun.

The chultun was filled to within 1.50 m of the top. On the floor was 0.30 m of gray-white soil (U. 1) packed with large sherds, artifacts, and small stones that average 0.10 by 0.04 m. The source of much of this material seems to have been a midden. Also within U. 1 were three large blocks of masonry. Above this was U. 2, a deposit of gray-white to brown-gray soil 0.60 m thick with few sherds and almost no artifacts. The fill (U. 3) above U. 2 was progressively darker in color towards the top. As with U. 2, it contained few sherds, but did contain some other artifacts.

DISCUSSION

It is almost certain that, upon abandonment, Ch. 7F-2 was sealed by a mass of masonry (just as was done with Or. 2 of Ch. 6E-7 in Gp. 6E-1, this report). This is indicated by the rubble still to be seen around the orifice (U. 4), as well as the large blocks of masonry at the bottom of the chultun (in U. 1). Some of these blocks actually fit pieces of U. 4, demonstrating the subsequent collapse into the chultun of the masonry seal. Moreover, some of the U. 4 masonry still overhangs the orifice slightly. Finally, the sherds and artifacts found in U. 1 are similar to those in the fill of Str. 7F-89:U. 2. The difference between U. 1 and the overlying U. 2 and 3 indicates that, following collapse of the seal, earth and forest detritus washed gradually into the chultun over the centuries. Such a process generally results in fill that is lighter at the bottom and darker at the top, as here, and which does not necessarily fill the whole chultun.

It is almost certain as well that the chultun was sealed when Str. 7F-89:U. 2 was laid. It could not have been ear-

TABLE 2.349
Chultun 7F-2: Average Dimensions (meters)

	Diameter	Height
Neck	0.65	1.00
Chamber	1.20	2.14

lier, for the rubble seal projects considerably above Plat. 7F-4:U. 1. It does not, however, project above the level of Str. 7F-89:U. 2. This indicates use of the chultun by the occupants of Str. 7F-89-2nd and 90-2nd. Hence, all three features could have been constructed at the same time.

A final point relates to the presence of a censer (PD. 262, discussed in section III) on the top of U. 1 (Fig. 159a:5). This could represent an offering that was dropped into the chultun after collapse of the seal. This is the view of Puleston, who regarded U. 2 as fill purposely placed to seal such an offering. Another possibility is that it was in the structure above the chultun when the seal collapsed.

CHULTUN 2F-9

DESCRIPTION

This hitherto unmapped chultun, with its orifice at 7F:S138 E297, was discovered by Puleston in 1963. It is one of the smallest that has been investigated at Tikal (Table 2.350), and as a consequence, it was difficult to excavate. A single, manhole-like orifice gives access to the chultun (not illustrated). The lip, which is not stepped, is slightly elevated relative to the surrounding bedrock, which would have protected the chultun from seepage of rainwater. Whether this elevation is natural or the result of some quarrying of peripheral bedrock is unknown. The stone cover was found in place over the orifice, though it was cracked into five pieces, the probable result of tree root growth. A sixth fragment was missing and could not be found. In shape, the stone is oval or slightly rectangular, rather than round. A notch cut 0.26 m deep into the SW side of the orifice may have served as an aid to lift the stone cover. The presence of this notch permitted some of the forest humus to drop into the chultun, leaving a hole about 0.10 m in diameter in the forest floor. It was this that led to discovery of the chultun.

Beneath the orifice, the neck flares downward to form Chm. 1. This antechamber is unusual, in that it is completely conical in shape, with no bowing out of the walls. An entrance, restricted on the sides but with no sill, gives access to the laterally placed Chm. 2. This is round in plan, and actually cuts slightly into the floor of Chm. 1. In section, it is dome-shaped, and is unusual in that the ceiling is not highest near the entrance.

The chultun was partly filled by dark brown topsoil, 1 m thick, which capped a deposit of gray soil. The latter was generally lighter in color towards the floor. Very few sherds and only a single artifact came from either the gray earth or the topsoil.

In 1964, a ceramic test trench was excavated just S of a 2-m square that had been excavated around the chultun orifice. The trench runs 6 m E and W of the orifice, and is 0.50 m wide. No architecture of any kind was found.

TABLE 2.350
Chultun 7F-9: Average Dimensions (meters)

Feature	Length	Width	Height	Diameter
Stone cover	0.56	0.48	0.10	---
Neck	---	---	---	0.44
Chamber 1	0.88	0.85	1.20	---
Chamber 2	1.60	1.48	0.88	---

DISCUSSION

It seems clear that this chultun was empty when abandoned by the Maya, with the stone cover in place. Over the centuries, all the material above U. 1 filtered in gradually via the notch in the lip of the orifice.

Overlying bedrock around the orifice of the chultun is a hard, packed layer of fine, yellowish-gray material (U. 1). Contained within this are some sherds. Unit 1 appears to be an informal occupation surface composed of material excavated when the chultun was constructed.

In the summer of 1965, Ch. 7F-9 was chosen as the site of an experiment to test the water-holding capabilities of chultuns (Puleston 1971). This was during the rainy season, at a time when the limestone bedrock was saturated with water. Some 400 gallons of water drawn from the Tikal Reservoir were carried by truck to this chultun and poured into it. The absorption of the water into the limestone was so rapid that little more than 50 gallons remained after 3.5 hours. By the end of the day all the water was gone. Without plaster lining, which clearly was not used in Tikal chultuns, these chambers could never have been used to hold water, as has sometimes been suggested.

SHERDS AND ARTIFACTS

Lot groups for Gp. 7F-2 are defined in Table 2.351, with material from them listed in Tables 2.352–2.354. The earliest material is in LG. 1 of Plat. 7F-4 and LG.

3 of Ch. 7F-2. All this derives from Plat. 7F-4, primarily from around the orifice of the chultun. It is probably a combination of fill for Plat. 7F-4-2nd and Str. 7F-89-1st, with perhaps some occupation debris included. Most likely it is structure fill, which in turn may consist of reused trash from Str. 7F-89-2nd and 7F-90-2nd. The sherds, which are fairly numerous, are exclusively from Manik vessels.

Most of the sherds in LG. 2 of Plat. 7F-4 also are from Manik vessels, though there is a scattering of later material that seems to represent intermittent littering by those who made use of the nearby Ch. 7F-9 (see below). The Manik material probably is a mixture of fill from Str. 7F-89 and 90 and Plat. 7F-4, with some later occupation debris from 89-1st and 90-1st.

The most likely source of material in U. 2 and 3 in Ch. 7F-2 (LG. 1 and 2) is the same as that for Plat. 7F-4:LG. 2. Hence, it is not surprising that the sherds are quite similar, especially in the case of Ch. 7F-2:LG. 1. Lot Group 2, on the other hand, could be purposeful fill dumped on the

TABLE 2.351
Group 7F-2: Lot Groups

Feature	Lot Group	Lot	Provenience	Ceramic Evaluation
Ch.7F-2 (Op.66Z)	1	3-7	U. 3	Manik; 1 possible Ik; 1 possible Ik or Imix
	2	8-11	U. 2	Manik; 1 possible Preclassic
	3	12,13	U. 1	Manik
Ch.7F-9	1	66Y/3-5	Fill	Ik and/or Imix; 1 Preclassic
	2	66Y/1,2; 103A/1-10	Surface	1 Manik; much Ik and probable Imix; 1 Caban
Plat.7F-4 (Op. 66Z)	1	2	Plat.7F-4: above U. 1 (includes fill of Str. 7F-89-1st)	Manik
	2	1,14	Surface	Much Manik; some probable Ik and/or Imix

censer that was placed on U. 3 (see PD. 262).

The material from Ch. 7F-9 is quite different from that around Plat. 7F-4, in that most of it is later. Clearly, this indicates use of Ch. 7F-9 after Plat. 7F-4 and associ-ated architecture. The abundance of sherds S, E, and W of the chultun suggests that the area served as a kind of dumping ground for material, most likely (but not surely) from Gp. 7F-2.

TABLE 2.352
Chultun 7F-2: Artifacts by Lot Group

Study Category	Object	Lot Group		
		1	2	3
Pottery Vessels	Sherds (not weighed)	Few	Few	Many
Other Pottery Artifacts	Figurine			1
	Censer			1
Flaked Chert Artifacts	Core			1
	Ovate biface	1		
	Elongate biface			1
	Unclassifiable biface			1
	Irregular, retouched flake			1
	Point-retouched flake			1
	Used flakes			4
	Unused flakes			11
	Nodules	1		1
Flaked Obsidian Artifacts	Prismatic blade			1
Ground, Pecked, and Polished Stone Artifacts	Hammer stone	1		
	Rubbing stones	1		4
Shell and Bone Artifacts	Bone, animal, unmodified			1
	Bone, unidentified, unmodified			1

TABLE 2.353
Chultun 7F-9: Artifacts by Lot Group

Study Category	Object	Lot Group	
		1	2
Pottery Vessels	Sherds per cubic meter (lbs)	Several	41.31*
Other Pottery Artifacts	Figurine		1
Flaked Chert Artifacts	Core		1
	Thin biface		1
	Used flake	1	
	Unused flake		1
	Nodules		2

*Calculated from the ceramic test (Op. 103A)

TABLE 2.354
Platform 7F-4: Artifacts by Lot Group

Study Category	Object	Lot Group	
		1	2
Pottery Vessels	Sherds per cubic meter (lbs)	?	?
Flaked Chert Artifacts	Ovate biface		1
	Unused flakes		2
Ground, Pecked, and Polished Stone Artifacts	Manos	2	
	Metate	1	

TIME SPANS

Since the unmapped structures near Ch. 7F-2 have only been tested, and none of the mapped structures have been excavated or tested, a reconstruction of events at this locus is, to say the least, tentative. Nonetheless, a few points are clear, and suggest the following reconstruction (see Tables 2.355–360). The earliest known construction here is that of Str. 7F-89-2nd and 90-2nd, with Plat. 7F-4-2nd (Gp. TS. 9). All of this architecture is securely tied together stratigraphically. Almost surely, Ch. 7F-2 was part of this construction. The chultun was abandoned and sealed, however, when Str. 7F-90, and probably 7F-89, were enlarged in Gp. TS. 7. Both Str. 7F-89 and 90, with Plat. 7F-4, were abandoned in Gp. TS. 5, probably about the time the seal of Ch. 7F-2 collapsed. With this event, some sort of offering may have been placed in the chultun (see PD. 262). All of this activity took place while Manik ceramics were in vogue, although abandonment could have been about the time when Ik ceramics appeared.

Whether this unmapped architecture represents the beginnings of Gp. 7F-2 is not known. Perhaps Str. 7F-89 and 90 were two of a number of structures, others of which now lie beneath the mapped structures of Gp. 7F-2. Or perhaps the locus of the group shifted northward with time. A third possibility, of course, is that Str. 7F-89 and 90 had nothing to do with Gp. 7F-2. More excavation would be needed to shed light on this, but a probable as-sociation between Ch. 7F-9 and the mapped structures of 7F-2, as discussed below, suggests that one of the first two alternatives is most likely.

A scattering of Ik and/or Imix sherds over the construction just discussed seems to indicate that it was no longer in use after Early Classic times. Such material is also found around Ch. 7F-9 in some quantity. This small, two-chambered chultun was abandoned empty, with its cover in place; but some of this Ik and/or Imix material had washed in around the cover. A single Manik sherd was found in proximity to this chultun.

These facts, the lack of any apparent structure ruins other than those on the map, and the general rarity of structures that have left no visible ruin mounds occupied in Ik and especially Imix times, combine to suggest that Ch. 7F-9 was used by the occupants of the mapped structures of Gp. 7F-2. The most likely (if unproven) source of the Ik and Imix sherds and associated artifacts is the same. On this basis, Gp. 7F-2 seems to have been abandoned by the time Eznab ceramics came into vogue. The inclusion of a Caban sherd in LG. 1 of Ch. 7F-9, however, which produced a relatively small sherd collection, suggests that there was a brief Postclassic occupation here.

To sum up, the locus of Gp. 7F-2 seems to have been occupied surely between AD 250 and 869, when Manik, Ik, and Imix ceramics were current, with a later brief reoccupation.

TABLE 2.355
Structure 7F-89: Time Spans

Time Span	Architectural Development	Unit	Descriptive Data	Lot Group	Ceramics in Vogue
1			Abandonment and collapse		----------
2			Use		
3	Str.7F-89-1st?	2,3	Addition of a platform to the S of the structure?	Ch.7F-2:3	Manik
4			Use		
5	Str.7F-89-2nd	1	Original construction		

TABLE 2.356
Structure 7F-90: Time Spans

Time Span	Architectural Development	Unit	Special Deposits: Burial	Descriptive Data	Lot Group	Ceramics in Vogue
1			219?	Abandonment and collapse		----------
2				Use		
3	Str.7F-90-1st	3	219?	Platform extended to E	None	Manik
4				Use		
5	Str.7F-90-2nd	1,2	219?	Original construction		

TABLE 2.357
Platform 7F-4: Time Spans

Time Span	Architectural Development	Unit	Descriptive Data	Lot Group	Ceramics in Vogue
1			Total abandonment of locus with forest growth		
2			Abandonment, with later intermittent activity		Imix
					Ik
3			Use	2	
4	Plat. 7F-4-1st		Modification by construction of Str. 7F-89-1st and 90-1st	1	Manik
5			Use		
6	Plat. 7F-4-2nd	1	Construction of plaza		

TABLE 2.358
Chultun 7F-2: Time Spans

Time Span	Architectural Development	Unit	Special Deposits: Problematical Deposit	Descriptive Data	Lot Group	Ceramics in Vogue
1		3		Filling of chultun following collapse of seal	1,2	
2		1,2	262	Collapse of rubble masonry seal, with possible censer offering (PD. 262)	3	
3		4		Chultun abandoned and sealed with rubble masonry		
4				Use		Manik
5	Ch. 7F-2			Construction of chultun		

TABLE 2.359
Chultun 7F-9: Time Spans

Time Span	Architectural Development	Construction Stage	Unit	Descriptive Data	Lot Group		Ceramics in Vogue
1				Final abandonment of locus, continued gradual deposition in chultun			
2				Probable brief reoccupation of locus			Caban
3				Abandonment, possible gradual deposition in chultun		1	
4				Use	2		Ik and/or Imix
5	Ch. 7F-9	1	1	Construction of Chm.2			
		2	1	Construction of Or. and Chm.1			

TABLE 2.360
Group 7F-2: Tentative Time Spans

Group Time Span	Str. 7F-89 Time Span (Table 2.355)	Str. 7F-90 Time Span (Table 2.356)	Ch. 7F-2 Time Span (Table 2.357)	Ch. 7F-9 Time Span (Table 2.358)	Plat. 7F-4 Time Span (Table 2.359)
1				1	
2				2	
3				3	1
4			1	4	
5	1	1	2	5	2
6	2	2			3
7	3	3	3		4
8	4	4	4		5
9	5	5	5		6

Group 7G-1

Group 7G-1 is located in Sq. 7G at S240 E16, or 110 m NE of Gp. 7F-3. Other groups are located 36 m NW, 84 m S, and 62 m to the NE. The terrain here slopes gently down towards the bajo, about 1.30 m to the E. As depicted on the site map (TR. 11), the group consists of three structures, 7G-30 through 32, arranged on the E, S, and W edges of a small plaza. All are comparable to known house ruins. Two chultuns, 7G-4, and the unmapped 7G-6, are located in the plaza. The only excavations conducted here are those of Puleston in and around Ch. 7G-4 and 6 (Op. 72C).

PLATFORM 7G-1

Limited excavations around the orifice of Ch. 7G-4 (Fig. 160) revealed the remains of two walls and two floors, the latter almost surely for a plaza. The walls are enigmatic; they could be parts of one or two structures, parts of a single raised terrace, or some such construction. Since so little is known about them, it seems best just to describe them without trying to draw conclusions.

Unit 1 is a wall that runs N-S for a distance of 2.23 m. Its S end is just W of the N edge of the chultun orifice. A floor, U. 2, turns up to its E face. This pavement lies about 0.30 m below the present ground surface, and is now poorly preserved. It could not be followed for any significant distance from U. 1.

Unit 3 is a wall that runs S from a point 0.53 m S of the orifice of Ch. 7G-4. It is parallel to U. 1, but its face is 0.20 m E of that of U. 1. The elevation of the two walls is essentially the same. No floor remnants were found near U. 3.

Units 4–6 are probably parts of a single pavement, for all are at the same elevation, roughly 0.10 m above U. 2. Unit 4 abuts the masonry blocks that sealed Ch. 7G-4. Just how it relates to U. 1 and 3 is not known. U. 5 covers the masonry that seals Ch. 7G-6.

Units 7 and 8 are masonry blocks that overlie U. 2 (in the case of U. 8) or fill at about the same elevation (in the case of U. 7). These may be no more than parts of fill for a later plaza surface.

In the face of such limited excavation, one cannot present a detailed account of the history of Plat. 7G-1. A tentative suggestion, though, is that at least three different plaza surfaces were constructed. The earliest (Plat. 7G-1-3rd) would be represented by U. 2, the next (2nd) by U. 4 and 5, and the last is inferred by the depth of soil above the latter. Generally, in small-structure groups, final plaza floors survive only in proximity to structures, where collapsed rubble and fill from the structure affords some protection for such surfaces. Just what U. 2 and 3

represent is not known, nor is it known whether the second plaza floor (U. 4) covered them. If it did, then the presence of floor remnants E and W of U. 1 and 3 makes sense; if not, it is hard to explain this fact, unless U. 2 and 3 are parts of two different structures with the plaza floor running between them.

CHULTUN 7G-4

DESCRIPTION

This chultun consists of a single chamber (Table 2.361) entered from above through a round, manhole-like orifice (Fig. 160). Below the orifice, the neck is an almost vertically walled shaft, which expands only slightly to form the chamber itself. The floor is unusual, for it slopes markedly (ca. 20°) to its deepest point on the NE. On the E side, 0.50 m above the lowest point of the floor, the wall was hollowed out to a depth of 0.60 m, forming a bench-like construction in bedrock. To enter and leave the chultun, nine sloping footholds were provided in the walls.

The chultun was partially filled with several different strata of material. At the base was U. 1, a stratum of yellowish-gray earth containing a small quantity of Manik sherds and some human skull fragments. Unit 1 is 0.30 m thick where the chultun is deepest, and includes part of a large masonry block that is 1.00 m long, 0.33 to 0.38 m wide, and 0.14 to 0.16 m thick. The upper portion of this block was buried in U. 2, a stratum of gray soil 0.30 m thick, full of midden-quality, early Imix sherds and some artifacts. Overlying this was 0.30 m of light, yellow-gray soil (U. 3), which contained a few Imix sherds, some Manik midden quality sherds, and PD. 263. On top of U. 3 was U. 4, a 0.90 m deposit containing small quantities of Imix sherds. Unit 4 was brownish gray in its deeper portion, becoming brownish black at the top. At the bottom, just above U. 3, was a large masonry block. This fits a piece of masonry that was found in situ by the orifice, between the two slabs that lie across the N and S edges of the orifice.

TABLE 2.361
Chultun 7G-4: Average Dimension (meters)

	Diameter	Height
Orifice	0.80	---
Chamber	1.20	3.00

DISCUSSION

It is difficult to reconstruct past events at this chultun. The following explanation was suggested by Puleston. Following a period of use, the chultun was closed off by placement of three large masonry slabs. These may have been used previously in lieu of a single stone cover for the chultun. These three slabs were not the same as were later used to seal the chultun, for the original one that later fell into the chultun (see below) is thicker than the later slabs. Eventually, one of the covering slabs fell into the chultun, where it was found by the excavators in U. 1, which could be fill that fell in with the slab.

Following collapse of the chultun seal, the orifice was left open. During this time, a small midden full of Imix sherds accumulated on top of the collapsed block and fill in the chultun. What happened to the two other original slabs is not known; perhaps they were taken to be used in some new construction.

At some point during Late Classic times, the Maya decided to close the chultun permanently. Although they dumped in rubbish (including PD. 263) from a nearby source, they chose not to fill the chamber to the top. Instead, three new slabs were positioned over the orifice, and small stone rubble was placed around the edges. Pavement for Plat. 7G-1 (U. 4) was then laid, abutting the masonry of this seal. Why this floor did not cover the chultun seal completely is a mystery. Surely, the chultun could not have been used in association with that floor, for removing the slabs would have damaged the edges of the pavement. Moreover, the chultun was about one-third filled with debris.

Eventually, probably after the group was abandoned, the chultun seal once again collapsed. In this case, part of the central stone slab fell in, while part of it remained in situ at the edge of the orifice. The part that fell in is the block above U. 3. Thereafter, fill and organic debris washed into the chultun over the centuries until removed by modern excavation.

The difficulty with the Puleston hypothesis is twofold. First, it requires that, after its original seal collapsed, the chultun was left open while there was a nearby occupation. Certainly, the source of the midden material in the chultun was not far distant, or the sherds would have been damaged to a greater degree. The most likely source of the material would be Gp. 7G-1 itself, for there was no point in carrying trash 55 m from the nearest other group; this trash could more easily have been disposed of just outside the group of origin. Moreover, Gp. 7G-1 is known to have had a Late Classic occupation. Why would its occupants have allowed an unused chultun to remain open, in the middle of the plaza, for people to fall into?

The second problem with the Puleston hypothesis is the presumed removal of two of the original stone slabs. If these were taken for use elsewhere, why leave the third one behind? It would have been no less useful than the other two.

An alternative explanation of the post-use history of the chultun is that U. 1–3 are all purposeful fill, put in

at the time of abandonment, following which the chultun was sealed with the three known masonry slabs. This way, the chultun would not have been left open as a hazard. The large masonry block at the bottom of the chultun could have been a piece of construction masonry available at the time of filling, and so it was dumped into the chultun. The differences between U. 1, 2, and 3 need indicate no more than that the fill was drawn from three different sources. In the last analysis, though, there is no more proof for this interpretation than for Puleston's hypothesis.

CHULTUN 7G-6

DESCRIPTION

The orifice of this newly discovered chultun is located 0.70 m NE of Ch. 7G-4 (Fig. 160a). It was excavated to a depth of only 0.40 m, sufficient only to make sure it was a chultun, so little can be said about it. Its orifice (Table 2.362) may best be described as a square with rounded corners and slightly rounded sides. The chultun was found completely filled, with gray to light brown earth containing a small quantity of sherds. It was sealed with a masonry block, the NW corner of which was broken off. On the surface of this masonry was plaster, 5 cm thick (Plat. 7G-1:U. 5). Its elevation is the same as that of Plat. 7G-1:U. 4.

TABLE 2.362
Chultun 7G-6: Average Dimensions (meters)

	Length	Width	Thickness
Orifice	0.63	0.58	---
Stone cover	0.74	0.71	0.24

DISCUSSION

There is little to say about this chultun, since data are scant. It probably was abandoned when Plat. 7G-1-2nd was constructed, unless Plat. 7G-1:U. 5 was not part of that plaza floor.

SHERDS AND ARTIFACTS

Virtually all the material from Gp. 7G-1 is fill (Table 2.363). The one exception may be LG. 2 of Ch. 7G-4. Since no other structures are closer than 36 m, it is likely that all fill (including PD. 263) was derived from trash associated with occupations in Gp. 7G-1. Certainly, Ch. 7G-4:LG. 2 was not transported any distance, or the sherds would have been damaged more than they are.

For material recovered from Gp. 7G-1 lot groups, see Tables 2.364–2.366.

TABLE 2.363
Group 7G-1: Lot Groups

Feature	Lot Group	Lot	Provenience	Ceramic Evaluation
Ch.7G-4 (Op.72C)	1	7	U. 1	Manik
	2	6	U. 2	Early Imix
	3	5	U. 3	Manik, possible Ik and/or Imix
	4	2-4	U. 4	Ik, probable Imix
Ch.7G-6 (Op.72C)	1	16,17	Chultun neck	?
Plat.7G-1 (Op.72C)	1	9,12,14	Below the elevation of U. 4-6	Manik, Ik and/or Imix
	2	8,10, 11,15	Above LG. 1	Manik, Ik, Imix
	3	1	Above and below U. 4-6	Probable Ik and Imix

TABLE 2.364
Chultun 7G-4: Artifacts by Lot Group

Study Category	Object	Lot Group			
		1	2	3	4
Pottery Vessels	Sherds per cubic meter (lbs)	1/10	11/6	3/2	2/10
Other Pottery Artifacts	Figurine			1	
	Censer		1		
Flaked Chert Artifacts	Elongate biface		1		
	Thin biface			1	
	Irregular, retouched flake		1		
	Used flake				1
Flaked Obsidian Artifacts	Prismatic blade				1
Ground, Pecked, and Polished Stone Artifacts	Metates		2		
	Rubbing stone		1		
Shell and Bone Artifacts	Shell, scarcely altered		1		
	Cut bone			3	
	Bone, unidentified, unworked	20			

TABLE 2.365
Chultun 7G-6: Artifacts by Lot Group

Study Category	Object	Lot Group 1
Pottery Vessels	Sherds	Lost

TABLE 2.366
Platform 7G-1: Artifacts by Lot Group

Study Category	Object	Lot Group		
		1	2	3
Pottery Vessels	Sherds per cubic meter (lbs)	?	5/8+	2
Flaked Chert Artifacts	Ovate biface		1	
	Unclassifiable biface		1	
	Used flake		1	
	Unused flake		1	
	Nodule		1	
Flaked Obsidian Artifacts	Prismatic blades		3	

TIME SPANS

On the basis of such limited excavations, little can be said about the group as a whole. Time spans have been defined only for Ch. 7G-4 itself (Table 2.367). There may have been three architectural developments for Plat. 7G-1, but this is far from certain. For the purposes of this report, the important thing is that the excavations produced ceramic samples, including midden-like material, which probably all derive from Gp. 7G-1. A period of occupation spanning the times when Manik, Ik, and Imix ceramics were in vogue is clearly indicated (Table 2.363). The group probably was abandoned after the appearance of late Imix ceramics, for early Imix ceramics were sealed in Ch. 7G-4, and the final floor of Plat. 7G-1 probably postdates even this event.

Group 7F-3

Group 7F-3 consists of the structures near which St. 25 was found. A brief description of the group is given in TR. 8 (p. 161). In 1957, Vivian L. Broman excavated an area 1.25 by 1.75 m to bedrock beneath where the stela had lain (TR. 3:82). Traces of plaster pavement were encountered, which suggests that the excavations penetrated into fill towards the E edge of the plaza for Gp. 7F-3. The few sherds from the excavation have not previously been published, and so they are here. The floor itself seems to have been laid sometime between AD 550 and 700, when Ik ceramics were in use. The number of Manik sherds, however, suggests that the group was first occupied in Early Classic times. A Late Classic occupation, when Imix ceramics were in production, is likely but unproven.

TABLE 2.367
Chultun 7G-4: Time Spans

Time Span	Architectural Development	Unit	Special Deposits: Problematical Deposit	Descriptive Data	Ceramics in Vogue
1		4		Natural filling of the chultun	
2				Collapse of the central slab of the chultun fill	
3				Period of disuse	
4		1-3	263	Chultun abandoned, partially filled and sealed	Imix
5				Use	Ik
6	Ch. 7G-4			Construction	Manik

10. Excavations in the Peripheral Squares of the Sixteen-Square Kilometer Map

Introduction

The only excavations undertaken in the outer squares of the 16 km² "Gregerson sheet" pertain to Sq. 1D, 1E, 3H, and 5H. Those in Sq. 1D and 1E are reported here, the others in TR. 21. It is not certain what percentage of the total structures or structure groups of this 7 km² area this represents. These outer squares were mapped by reconnaissance methods (TR. 11:2) before project personnel had much experience with such techniques. It is scarcely surprising, then, that in those areas investigated, the accuracy of the map is not up to the standard of the central nine square kilometers. Later, some of the peripheral squares were the subject of more detailed mapping by Becker and Puleston (TR. 13 and 21). These resulted in the discovery of 42% more structures in five peripheral squares (Table 2.368). Applying this figure to the 543 originally mapped structures in the remaining peripheral squares, the total probable number for all 28 peripheral squares should be on the order of 923.

Square 1D, as now known (TR. 13), includes some ten small-structure groups. Of these, eight were tested in 1967 by Fry as part of his ceramic test program running N from the center of Tikal. A ninth group, in the extreme NW part of Sq. 1E, was also tested. Material recovered in these tests is inventoried in the Appendix. The technique employed was described in TR. 24A. No extensive excavations were undertaken in Sq. 1D or 1E.

Group 1D-1

Group 1D-1 is located at 1D:S190 E185, just NE of an arm of bajo that extends to the S and W. Most, but not all, structures appear on the Gregerson sheet, although the group is shown there slightly farther N and W than is actually the case. Included are 19 structures, arranged around a number of plazas. On the N are six small, rectangular platforms, Str. 1D-27 through 32. All are comparable to the ruins of known house platforms elsewhere at Tikal. Their arrangement appears unusual, but they might be a series of three plazas, with structures on two sides of each, all built closely together. Such a plaza-structure arrangement appears often (see Gp. 4F-3, 5B-2, 5F-1, 6E-1, 7C-1, this report). In this particular case, Str. 1D-27 and 28 might define the N and E edges of one plaza, 1D-29 and 30 the N and W edges of a second, and 1D-31 and 32 the N and W edges of a third. Just to the E of this are the somewhat larger Str. 1D-33 and 36, on the N and W sides of a fourth and larger plaza, with the smaller rectangular Str. 1D-35 on the S and the square Str. 1D-34 on the E side. The latter is suggestive of a household shrine (TR. 21).

The long axis of Str. 1D-36 is continued to the S by the smaller rectangular 1D-37. This seems to mark the E side of a fifth plaza, with 1D-37 on its S edge and 1D-41 on the W. South of this plaza is a sixth, with Str. 1D-42, 44, and 39 on the W, S, and E sides, all apparently small rectangular platforms. A wall joining Str. 1D-41 and 43 suggests that these two plazas may have begun as one, to be separated later by Str. 1D-38.

A seventh plaza, raised on its S side, is positioned immediately E of the sixth; the small rectangular Str. 1D-45 is on its N edge. Two other very small square-to-rectangular structures, 1D-40 and 43, are located W and SW, respectively, of the sixth plaza. Overall, the situation is suggestive of a complex group of several households, complete with associated shrine and utility buildings.

The two test pits (Table 2.369) probably sample construction fill (most of 136C) and occupation debris (most of 136P). A Preclassic occupation somewhere in the group is likely; Early through Late Classic occupation, probably continuous, is almost certain (Table 2.370). Abandonment seems to have followed the appearance of Eznab ceramics.

TABLE 2.368
Numbers of Structures to be Added to the Outer Squares of the Sixteen-square Kilometer Site Map

Square	Number of structures originally mapped	Number of new structures discovered	Percentage increase
1D	28	28	100
4H	17	1	6
5A	13	0	0
5H	23	11	48
8D	26	5	19
Total	107	45	42

Group 1D-2

This group, located at 1D:S120 E370, is not depicted on the Gregerson sheet. Its two structures, 1D-17 and 18, are arranged on two sides of a plaza. This was probably S of Str. 1D-17 and W of 1D-18, as suggested by the absence of identifiable floors and the great abundance of debris in the test pit immediately E of Str. 1D-17. As mapped, the ruins appear to be those of small, square structures, although Fry in his field notes sketched 1D-17 as rectangular. This could have been a domestic structure, with 1D-18 possibly a household shrine (TR. 21).

The single test pit (Table 2.369) is primarily situated just outside the E end wall of Str. 1D-17. The numerous large utilitarian artifacts (see the Appendix), and the high sherd content (for example, 18.88 lbs per cubic meter in Lot 4 alone) combine to indicate that the sample consists of occupation debris. This was apparently disturbed for interment of Bu. 208 (see section III). The ceramics (Table 2.370) clearly indicate an occupation that began while Manik ceramics were in vogue. Abandonment surely postdates appearance of Imix, and may have followed the appearance of Eznab ceramics.

Group 1D-3

This group is located at 1D:S75 E260, about 1.50 m W of Gp. 1D-2. No structures are shown here on the Gregerson sheet, but some shown just to the N, where none in fact exist, is probably an erroneous depiction of Gp. 1D-3. Although four structures are included, 1D-11, 12, 14, and 15 on the four edges of a low platform, there is a diminutive fifth structure, 1D-13, on the N end of 1D-14, and a sixth structure, 1D-16, just S of 1D-15. All but 1D-13 and 16 are rectangular, and might be the ruins of houses. Structure 1D-13, in relation to 1D-14, suggests the small platforms added to the ends of Str. 4F-2, 4F-3, 4F-7, 4F-13, and 4F-14 in Gp. 4F-1 and 4F-2 (TR. 19), supporting the hypothesis that Gp. 1D-3 was residential. The presence of the small, shrinelike 1D-16 S of the group, though, seems peculiar.

The single test pit (Table 2.369) samples construction fill and occupation debris. The Manik sherds beneath two floors of the platform on which Str. 1D-11 through 15 were built indicate original construction in Early Classic times (Table 2.370). The above-floor debris indicates an occupation lasting through the time when Imix ceramics were in production. An E wall of 1D-12 rests on the uppermost floor of the group platform, which could indicate that the structure was built while Ik ceramics were in use.

Group 1D-4

Group 1D-4, not depicted on the site map, is located just SW of one that is. Its location is 1D:S440 E415, just E of the same bajo near which Gp. 1D-1 stands. Two of four rectangular mounds, Str. 1D-53 and 54, face each other from the N and S edges of a low, raised platform. The smaller rectangular 1D-56 is on the E side of the same platform, with the even smaller 1D-55 extending from its N and W towards the center of the platform. The overall size and configuration suggests a residential group, although the position of Str. 1D-55 seems peculiar.

The test pit (Table 2.369) samples fill of the platform on which the structures were built; hence the mixture of material in Lots 5–7 (Table 2.370). Some occupation debris is probably included in the surface lot. The ceramics indicate an occupation that began in Early Classic times (possibly late), and lasted through Late Classic times. Eznab ceramics may have made their appearance just prior to abandonment.

Group 1D-5

These structures are positioned 100 m N of Gp. 1D-4, at 1D:S310 E410. They are depicted on the Gregerson sheet, slightly N of their correct location, as a single, rectangular structure. Actually, there may be two structures: 1D-48 and 49. The latter is a small, rectangular ruin suitable for a house (and note the metate fragment from the test pit; see the Appendix). North and E of it, and parallel, is Str. 1D-48, which might possibly be no more than the raised western edge of a plaza associated with 1D-49.

The test pit (Table 2.369) samples a deposit that is a mixture of fill and occupation debris. The group could have been constructed in late Early Classic times or very shortly thereafter (Table 2.370). Certainly, the earliest of two pavements encountered postdates the appearance of Ik ceramics. There may, though, have been construction elsewhere prior to the laying of this floor, for a lack of nearby structures makes it dubious that all the Early Classic material was brought in from elsewhere. How much later the occupation continued is a matter of speculation. The only possible Eznab ceramics came from beneath the deepest floor, and so their identification is highly suspect. On the other hand, the certain occurrence of Ik and/or Imix material in two lots, and possibly in two others above floors, suggests occupation of the two floors while Ik ceramics were in vogue. Surely, though, the group was abandoned prior to the appearance of Eznab ceramics.

Group 1D-6

This group, depicted on the Gregerson sheet, although incorrectly, is located 100 m E of Gp. 1D-3, 50 m E of Gp. 1E-1, and 25 m NE of Gp. 1D-2 (1D:S30 E415). Actually, what is shown on the Gregerson sheet is probably Gp. 1D-2, incorrectly located. Group 1D-6 includes eight structures, of which 1D-20, 26, and 25 are arranged in an approximate line along the W edge of a plaza. Facing 1D-26 across the plaza is 1D-22, with 1D-21 at the N edge of the plaza. Facing this from the S is 1D-24. The smaller 1D-19 is located behind (W of) 1D-25, and Str. 1D-23 is just E and S of 1D-24. All these are rectangular, and of a size suitable for the foundations of houses and outbuildings (and note the spindle whorl from the test pit; see the Appendix). The largest are Str. 1D-21 through 23. This, and the overall layout, suggests that Str. 1D-19, 20, and 23 through 25 are later additions to the group. There is no way of knowing this, though, without excavation.

A single test pit (Table 2.369) straddles the W wall of the plaza S of Str. 1D-25, thereby sampling a mixture of occupation debris and fill. The wall itself seems to postdate the appearance of Ik ceramics (Table 2.370:Lot 6), but the consistent presence of Manik sherds in some quantity indicates an Early Classic occupation. Since Preclassic sherds occur in at least one lot, occupation probably began just prior to Early Classic times. Abandonment of the group was probably some time after the appearance of Imix ceramics, but before the appearance of Eznab ceramics.

Group 1D-7

Positioned at 1D:S90 E90, about 120 m E of Gp. 1D-3 on the other side of a seasonal stream, the group depicted on the Gregerson sheet in the NW corner of Sq. 1D represents the approximate location of this group, but is an incorrect representation. Three small, rectangular structures (1D-6 through 8) are located on the W, N, and E sides of a raised platform. The two smaller rectangular Str. 1D-9 and 10 project in from the S ends of 1D-6 and 8, dividing the supporting platform in half. Again, a domestic situation is suggested.

The test pit (actually two contiguous test pits; Table 2.369) samples construction fill, with perhaps a very small bit of occupation debris (Fig. 161). Sherds, though, were not especially numerous. The inclusion of Manik sherds in most lots suggests initial construction in Early Classic times (Table 2.370). The deepest two floors in the test pit, pavements of the platform on which the structures were built, might appear to date from this time (136H, Lot 5). But the likelihood is that Bu. 205, which these floors seal, postdates the appearance of Ik ceramics (Lot 7 and 8 of 136H, see also section III). The uppermost floor surely was laid while Ik ceramics were in use. The structure, which was based on that floor, could postdate appearance of Imix ceramics. Abandonment of the group could postdate the appearance of Eznab ceramics.

Group 1D-8

Group 1D-8, not shown on the Gregersn sheet, is located at 1D:S210 E0, about 100 m SW of Gp. 1D-7. The nineteen structures included are arranged around three plazas. On the northernmost, the substantial 1D-3 occupies the entire E edge. This appears to have been a small, range-type structure. On the N edge are Str. 1D-2 and 1C-10, two small rectangular platforms. A third, similar structure (1D-1) projects S from these towards the center of the plaza. Two other small, rectangular structures, 1D-4 and 1C-11, delimit the plaza on the S and W.

South and slightly W of the first plaza is a smaller one, with small rectangular platforms on the four sides (Str. 1C-12, 13, and 14 and 1D-5). Of these, 1C-12 has its NE corner in contact with the SW corner of 1D-4. Directly W of the second plaza is a third, the most complex of the three. Structure 1C-1, with 1C-2 and 9 on either side, is a substantial pyramidal structure on the N edge of this W plaza. Together, 1C-2 and 9 give the appearance of "wings" for this possible temple. Structures 1C-4 and 5 are two small rectangular platforms built on the raised E edge of the plaza. On the S edge are the rectangular 1C-6 and 15, although 15 could be a parapet rather than a structure. On the W edge of the plaza is 1C-7, a small, range-type structure, to which 1C-6 is attached. North of Str. 1C-7 is 1C-8, also on the W edge of the plaza. Finally, the small rectangular 1C-3 is located adjacent to the NE corner of 1C-2, off the plaza proper. Since most of the structures are comparable to known house ruins, this could be a residential assemblage. Consistent is the presence of a metate fragment from near Str. 1D-5 (see the Appendix).

The single test pit (Table 2.369) samples a mixture of fill and occupation debris. There surely was an occupation of some part of Gp. 1D-8 accompanied by Manik ceramics (Table 2.370), though the small, middle plaza of the group, where the test pit is located, most likely was built later. The bulk of the occupation here appears to be associated with Imix ceramics, but the one plaza floor encountered may postdate the appearance of Eznab pottery. Abandonment surely came after such ceramics had been in use for a while.

Group 1E-1

This group is located at 1E S60 E0, where no structures are shown on the Gregerson sheet. It consists of two structures, up to 4 m in height. The northernmost, 1E-2, appears to be square; the easternmost, 1E-3, is rectangular. The associated plaza probably extended S and a little W of Str. 1E-2; no floor was encountered in the test pit N of 1E-3 (E of Str. 1E-2), but one was encountered W of Str. 1E-2. The group was possibly residential; it shows a similarity to Gp. 1D-2.

The two test pits (Table 2.369) sampled a mixture of occupation debris and trash. Ceramic evaluations (Table 2.370) suggest a middle-to-late Early Classic date for the floor that was encountered, while many Ik sherds may have spilled from the two structures. The group was abandoned by the end of Late Classic times, probably sometime after the appearance of Imix ceramics.

TABLE 2.369
Location of Test Pits: Peripheral Squares

Group	Test Pit	Location
1D-1	136C/1	Posthole, SE corner of SE plaza
	136C/2-6	SE corner of plaza between Str. 1D-39 and 44
	136P/1	Posthole S of Str. 1D-40
	136P/2-7	By SE corner, Str. 1D-40
1D-2	146J/1	Posthole by test pit
	146J/2-9	Off E end of Str. 1D-17
1D-3	146K/1-4	Posthole test
	146K/5-10	Off E end of Str. 1D-12
1D-4	136A/1-4	Posthole tests around Str. 1D-55
	136A/5-7	In plaza off W end of Str. 1D-55
1D-5	136B/1-4	Posthole tests around Str. 1D-49
	136B/5-9	Off W side of Str. 1D-49
1D-6	136F/1	Posthole tests around periphery of group
	136F/2-7	SW corner of plaza off end of Str. 1D-24, 25
1D-7	136E/1-3	Posthole tests around periphery of group
	136E/4-7	Off E end, Str. 1D-7
	136H	Adjacent to 136E/4-7 on N
1D-8	136D/1,2	Postholes by Str. 1D-5
	136D/3-7	Off N end, Str. 1D-5
1E-1	146G/1-3	Posthole tests around Str. 1E-2
	146G/4-9	Off W end, Str. 1E-2
	146H/1	Posthole by test pit
	146H/2-6	Off N end, Str. 1D-3

TABLE 2.370 (Part 1)
Ceramic Evaluations: Peripheral Squares

Group	Lot	Provenience	Ceramics
1D-1	136C/1	Posthole test	Classic, possibly late
	136C/2	0-0.20 m S of Str. 1D-39	Some Manik; Ik; probable Imix
	136C/3	0.20-0.40 m	Ik and/or Imix; possible Manik
	163C/4	0.40-0.60 m	Imix, possible Ik; possible Preclassic (1); Manik; Eznab
	163C/5	0.60 m-bedrock	Probable Manik; possible Preclassic
	163C/6	Bedrock pit	Preclassic or Manik
	136P/1	Posthole test	Probably mainly Ik and/or Imix; some possible Manik
	136P/2	0-0.20 m over structure 1D-40	Classic; possibly Manik
	136P/3	0.20-0.25 m over structure 1D-40	Ik and/or Imix
	136P/4	0-0.20 m S of structure 1D-40	Manik; probable Imix; possible Ik
	136P/5	0.20-0.40 m below 136P/4	Manik; Ik; Eznab; possible Imix and 1 Preclassic
	136P/6	0.40-0.60 m below 136P/5	Mostly Manik; Ik; possible Imix
	136P/7	0.60 m-bedrock below 136P/6	Manik; Ik
1D-2	146J/1	N of Str. 1D-17	Ik and/or Imix; possible Manik
	146J/2,3	0-0.20 m E of Str. 1D-17	Manik; Ik; Imix
	146J/4	0.20-0.40 m	Manik; mainly Ik; Imix
	146J/5	0.40-0.60 m	Manik; possible Ik; Imix
	146J/6,7	Around Bu. 208	Manik; Ik; possible Imix; possible Eznab
	146J/8	Bu. 208	No data
	146J/9	0.60 m–bedrock	Manik; possible Ik and/or Imix
1D-3	146K/1	E of Str. 1D-12	Ik; possible Imix
	146K/2	N of Str. 1D-14	No data
	146K/3	Between Str. 1D-15 and 16	Probable Ik and/or Imix; possible Manik
	146K/4	W of Str. 1D-16	Manik; possible Ik and/or Imix
	146K/5	0-0.20 m E of Str. 1D-12	Manik; Ik; and possible Imix
	146K/6	0.20-0.45 m	Manik; Imix
	146K/7	0.45-0.55 m (floor)	Manik
	146K/8	0.55-0.80 m	Manik
	146K/9	0.80-1.05 m (floor)	Manik; possible Preclassic

TABLE 2.370 (Part 2)
Ceramic Evaluations: Peripheral Squares

Group	Lot	Provenience	Ceramics
	146K/10	1.05 m-bedrock	Probable Manik
1D-4	136A/1	E of Str. 1D-55	Possible Manik; probable Ik and/or Imix
	136A/2	S of Str. 1D-55	Manik; probable Ik and/or Imix
	136A/3	W of Str. 1D-55	Manik; probable Ik and/or Imix
	136A/4	E of Str. 1D-53	Manik; possible Ik and/or Imix
	136A/5	0-0.20 m W of Str. 1D-55	Some Manik; Ik; Imix; possible Eznab
	136A/6	0.20-0.40 m	Ik; Imix; possible Manik
	136A/7	0.40 m-bedrock	Probable Ik; possible Manik
1D-5	136B/1	N of Str. 1D-49	Ik and/or Imix; probable Manik
	136B/2	S of Str. 1D-49	Ik and/or Imix; probable Manik
	136B/3	W of Str. 1D-49	Manik; possible Ik and/or Imix
	136B/4	E of Str. 1D-49	Manik; possible Ik and/or Imix
	136B/5	0-0.20 m W of Str. 1D-49	Manik and Ik
	136B/6	0.20-0.28 m (floor)	Manik; Ik; possible Preclassic
	136B/7	0.28-0.44 m (floor)	Manik; possible Ik and Preclassic
	136B/8	0.44-0.64 m	Manik; Ik and/or Imix; possible Eznab
	136B/9	0.64 m-bedrock	Manik; possible Ik and/or Imix
1D-6	136F/1	Around periphery of group	Manik; Ik and/or Imix
	136F/2	0-0.20 m S of Str. 1D-25	Manik; possible Ik and/or Imix; 1 possible Preclassic
	136F/3	0.20-0.40 m	Manik; Ik; possible Imix
	136F/4	0.40-0.60 m	Manik; possible Imix
	136F/5	0.60-0.70 m (wall)	Preclassic; Manik; Ik and/or Imix
	136F/6	E of wall, 0.70-0.90 m	Manik; Ik
	136F/7	W of wall, 0.70 m-bedrock	Manik
1D-7	136E/1	E of Str. 1D-7	Ik; possible Manik and Imix
	136E/2	S of Str. 1D-6	Probable Imix or Eznab
	136E/3	SW corner of group	Manik; possible Ik and/or Imix
	136E/4	0-0.20 m, E of Str. 1D-7	Ik; possible Manik and Imix
	136E/5	0.20-0.40 m	Ik; possible Manik and Imix
	136E/6	0.40 m-bedrock	Manik; possible Ik

TABLE 2.370 (Part 3)
Ceramic Evaluations: Peripheral Squares

Group	Lot	Provenience	Ceramics
1D-7	136E/7	Fill, S part of Bu. 205	Manik; possible Ik and/or Imix
	136H/1	Surface, to top of structure wall and floor level to E and N of Str. 1D-7	Probable Eznab; Manik; Imix; possible Ik
	136H/2	Unsealed fill, NE corner of structure	Manik; Ik; possible Imix
	136H/3	Partially sealed fill of uppermost floor beneath structure	Ik; probable Manik
	136H/4	N of group platform from Lot 1 to level of Lot 6	Manik; Ik
	136H/5	Fill of second floor down beneath structure	Manik
	136H/6	Fill of third floor down	No data
	136H/7	Hard, packed gray stratum over bedrock	Manik; possible Ik and/or Imix
	136H/8	Fill, Bu. 205	Manik; possible Ik
1D-8	136D/1	Posthole test E of Str. 1C-14	Possible Manik and Ik and/or Imix
	136D/2	Posthole test N of Str. 1D-5	Eznab; possible Manik and Ik
	136D/3	0-0.25 m; N of Str. 1D-5	Manik; probable Imix
	136D/4	0.25-0.50 m (floor)	1 Manik; possible Ik; probable mainly Imix; possible Eznab
	136D/5	0.50-0.70 m (unsealed)	Manik; Imix; possible Ik and Eznab
	136D/6	0.50-0.70 m (sealed)	1 Manik; possible Ik; mainly Imix; possible Eznab
	136D/7	0.70 m-bedrock	Ik and/or Imix; possible Manik and Eznab
E-1	146G/1	S of Str. 1E-2	Classic; possibly Manik through Imix
	146G/2	W of Str. 1E-2	No data
	146G/3	Top of Str. 1E-2	No data
	146G/4	0-0.20 m W of Str. 1E-2	Manik; Ik; possible Imix
	146G/5	0.20-0.40 m	Manik; possible Ik and/or Imix
	146G/6	0.40-0.60 m	Probable Manik; possible Ik and/or Imix
	146G/7	0.60-0.80 m	Manik; probable Ik
	146G/8	0.80 m to floor	Classic; including probable Manik

TABLE 2.370 (Part 4)
Ceramic Evaluations: Peripheral Squares

Group	Lot	Provenience	Ceramics
E-1	146G/9	Below floor	Classic; including probable Manik
	146H/1	N of Str. 1E-3	No data
	146H/2	0-0.20 m	Possible Manik; probable Ik and/or Imix
	146H/3	0.20-0.40 m	Classic; including possible Manik; Ik and/or Imix
	146H/4	0.40-0.60 m	Classic; including probable Manik; Ik and/or Imix
	146H/5	0.60-0.80 m	Manik; possible Ik and/or Imix
	146H/6	0.80 m-bedrock	Probable Manik

Special Deposits

1. Introduction

Described in this section are the 47 burials and other special deposits recovered in the excavations reported here. Analysis is scheduled to follow in TR. 20B. Burials (see Table 3.1) are presented first, followed by twenty problematical deposits (see Table 3.2).

Three definitions pertain to the discussions that follow. By *primary burial* is meant interment of a whole body soon after death. A *two-stage burial*, by contrast, is one that follows a delay allowing for some alteration of the corpse following death. At the least, some decomposition has taken place; typically, however, something such as dismemberment and/or cremation has been done to the body prior to its final inhumation. Finally, the term *secondary burial* is reserved here for primary or two-stage burials that have been dug up or exposed accidentally and then redeposited by the Maya in some sort of grave.

Haviland examined all human skeletal material as it materialized from excavation. Procedures used in his analysis are discussed in detail in TR. 30 (TR. 19 is not concerned with the skeletal analysis).

2. Burials

BURIAL 45

LOCATION:

Gp. 4F-6, 1 m E of the N end of Str. 4F-26, or Sq. 4F:S96 E419 (TR. 11). 24B/1; see Fig. 164e for plan. Amorphous shape with no special construction, but covered by irregular masonry blocks. Burial measured 1.1 m N-S, 0.64 m E-W, just large enough to accommodate the body.

INDIVIDUAL AND ASSOCIATED MATERIAL:

Individual: Middle adult male. Body lay on left side, head to the S, resting on an inverted vessel (No. 3). Legs were flexed at the knees, perpendicular to the body, with feet together. The left arm extended over the very slightly contracted right arm, wrists apart. Primary burial.

Associated material: Three pottery vessels. No. 1, a Palmar Ceramic Group round-side bowl (TR. 25A:fig. 54d3), upright, E of the right shoulder. No. 2, a Mex Composite outflaring-side bowl (TR. 25A:fig. 54d1), upright by the right knee. No. 3, Palmar Ceramic Group slightly outcurving-side bowl (TR. 25A:fig. 54d2), inverted beneath the base of the skull. A tiny piece of Spondylus shell was found in the vicinity of the mouth, but not clearly in the mouth. A piece of chert flake over the skull undoubtedly was a fill item.

SKELETAL MATERIAL:

A complete skeleton was represented, though few bones could be salvaged. The skull, particularly, was badly crushed, although artificial frontal flattening was apparent. The individual was a bit below average stature for his time (for stature data see TR. 30). His dentition was complete, with moderate wear apparent except for heavily worn upper third molars. Anterior crowding was visible in the lower dentition. The upper canines and central incisors were notched in the distal corner of each (Type B4; Romero 1960:51), and the lower incisors had a single vertical groove in the center of each (Type A1; Romero 1950:51). Slight periodontal disease was apparent.

DISCUSSION:

Little can be said about this burial, except that its proximity to unexcavated Str. 4F-26 suggests an association with that structure. The burial, however, could have been put in place before, during, or after the period of structure use. The pottery vessels pertain to the Imix Ceramic Complex, suggesting use of Str. 4F-26 sometime

TABLE 3.1
Burials Discussed in This Report

Group	Burial	Location	Illustration
1D-2	208	Str. 1D-17	169c
1D-7	205	Str. 1D-7	169d
2G-1	49	Str. 2G-59	162a
	50	Str. 2G-59	162b
	52	Str. 2G-59	162d
	53	Str. 2G-59	162c
	54	Str. 2G-59	162e, 173c
	55	Str. 2G-59	163a, 173d
	56	Str. 2G-59	163c, 174a
	57	Str. 2G-59	163e, 174b
	58	Str. 2G-59	163b
	59	Str. 2G-59	163d, 174c,d
	60	Str. 2G-59	---
2G-2	63	Ch. 2G-10	164a
Str. 2G-61	62	Ch. 2G-2	164b
	64	Str. 2G-61	164c
3F-1	65	Str. 3F-24	165a, 177b
	66	Str. 3F-24	165b, 177c
	67	Str. 3F-25	165c
3F-2	68	Str. 3F-26	165f
	69	Str. 3F-26	165e
	70	Str. 3F-27	165d
Str. 4C-34	212	Str. 4C-34	167a,b
4F-3	61	Plat. 4F-6	164d, 179b
4F-6	45	Str. 4F-26	164e
4G-3	189	Str. 4G-7	164f
5D-1	169	Str. 5D-7	166a
	170	Str. 5D-7	166b
	171	Str. 5D-7	166c
5F-1	158	Plat. 5F-1	167c
6C-1	136	Str. 6C-47	166d
	146	Str. 6C-45	166e, 180b
6C-2	145	Str. 6C-57	166f
Str. 6C-60	143	Ch. 6C-10	---
6E-1	128	Str. 6E-Sub.1	168a, 182b,c
	129	Plat. 6E-1	168b
	130	Plat. 6E-1	168c
	131	Str. 6E-26	---
	138	Plat. 6E-1	168d
	151	Str. 6E-Sub.1	168f
	152	Str. 6E-26	168e, 182d, 183a
	153	Str. 6E-Sub.1	169a
	161	Plat. 6E-1	169b
6E-14	118	Plaza Test Pit	---
Str. 6F-62	218	Plat. 6F-1	---
7E-6	119	Plaza Test Pit	---
7F-2	219	Str. 7F-90	---

TABLE 3.2
Problematical Deposits Discussed in this Report

Group	Problematical Deposit	Location	Illustration
2G-1	64	Str. 2G-59	171b
3F-1	65	Ch. 3F-6	44a, 176d, 177a
3F-3	109	Str. 3F-12	172b, 177d
3G-1	214	Ch. 3G-5	---
Str. 4C-34	221	Str. 4C-34	171a,c
5B-2	110	Str. 5B-7	171d
Str. 5C-56	72	Ch. 5C-8	70a,b; 71a,b
	224	Ch. 5C-8	---
5D-1	124	Str. 5D-7	172c
	126	Str. 5D-7	172c
5F-1	108	Plat. 5F-1	172e
	130	Plat. 5F-1	104
	131	Ch. 5F-5	---
	140	Str. 5F-Sub.1	104
6C-1	101	Plat. 6C-1	172d, 180c
	275	Str. 6C-45	119
6C-5	231	Ch. 6C-11	170
7C-1	99	Str. 7C-4	172a, 183b
7F-2	262	Ch. 7F-2	159
7G-1	263	Ch. 7G-4	160

between AD 700 and 869; the dates for the Imix Complex.

SEQUENTIAL POSITION:

No time spans defined.

BURIAL 49

LOCATION:

Gp. 2G-1, 14.60 m N, 21.00 E of Datum 24C (Fig. 27); in front of, and slightly beneath, the S end of the surviving stairs for Str. 2G-59-2nd (Fig. 21–23). In fill on the front-rear axis of Str. 2G-59-1st, intruded slightly into 59-2nd and Plat. 2G-1:Fl. 2. 24C/69; see Fig. 162a for plan.

GRAVE:

Amorphous shape with no specially constructed walls, and roofed by two coverstones, measuring approximately 0.56 m in length, 0.36 m in width, and 0.15 m in thickness. These dipped slightly to the W. Burial measured 1.34 m N-S, 0.64 m E-W, just large enough to accommodate the body.

INDIVIDUAL AND ASSOCIATED MATERIAL:

Individual: Adult male. The body lay on its right side with head to the N, resting on an inverted vessel (No. 2). The legs were flexed at the knees, and perpendicular to the body, with the feet together. The right arm was flexed, with the hand by the chin; the other was slightly contracted with the hand by the pelvis. Primary burial.

Associated material: Three pottery vessels of the Imix Complex. No. 1, a fluted type cylinder (TR. 25A:fig. 55a1), was placed upright N of the head; No. 2, an out-curving-side bowl (TR. 25A:fig. 55a2) with a "kill hole" in its base, was inverted beneath head; No. 3, another out-curving-side bowl (TR. 25A:fig. 55a3), was placed upright by the pelvis.

SKELETAL MATERIAL:

Though poorly preserved, the burial was unquestionably primary. The individual was slightly below average stature for his time, but the long bones are nonetheless of rugged appearance. Although attrition was only moderate, a number of teeth were probably lost antemortem, including a lower lateral incisor, first premolars, first molars, and third molars. Missing uppers include a lateral incisor, two premolars, and all but one molar. Not only are the surviving teeth few in number, but decay is extensive on both coronal and root surfaces. Heavy calculus deposits are also evident. All in all, this individual shows poor dental health, and the extensive tooth loss need not indicate old age.

Although this individual underwent no cranial modification, at least five and probably six of his teeth had been altered. The two upper central incisors were notched in the distal corners (Type B7; Romero 1960:51), and the lowers were pointed (Type C4 or 7; Romero 1960:51).

DISCUSSION:

The sequential position of this burial is a problem. Located in the fill of Str. 2G-59-1st, it obviously postdates abandonment of 59-2nd. This means it could have been placed as early as TS. 3 (but no earlier), or as late as TS. 1. The problem arises from the protrusion of the coverstones of the burial above the level of the top of the riser to the lower level of the final platform. Although no floor surface was found, one presumably existed (see Fig. 23a). Three possibilities exist: (1) The floor was in reality about 0.10 m higher to the E than I have reconstructed it. This would require either a slope to the W, or a second course of masonry for the W wall of the structure. There is no evidence for this second course, but a slope of 0.10 m over a horizontal distance of 1.50 m is not great, and such slopes are known for small-structure floors. One example is the floor of the lower platform level of Str. 3F-25-1st (Fig. 43), the slope of which is almost twice that called for here if a lower platform floor for 59-1st sealed Bu. 49. (2) Root action may have distorted the true relation of the coverstones to the upper and lower walls of the two platform levels. They may now be slightly higher than they were when originally placed, and so the floor for Str. 2G-59-1st may have covered them. (3) The coverstones actually protruded above floor level, in which case the burial probably was put in place after abandonment of 59-1st.

Although complete assurance is out of the question, a combination of the first two possibilities seems most probable. This would place the burial in TS. 3 of Str. 2G-59. Furthermore, two lines of evidence serve to bolster this judgment. This is one of eight burials in Str. 2G-59 that postdate Bu. 54, 57, and 58, in the same structure (the others are Bu. 50, 52, 53, 55, 56, 59, and 60). Of these eight, four included three pottery vessels as associated materials (Bu. 49 is one of these). The others are Bu. 50, 52, and 56, all of which are located near Bu. 49. Hence, they seem to stand apart as a group from the other four. Two of them, Bu. 52 and 56, are surely assignable to TS. 3. Burial 50 may be assigned to the same time span. The other four—Bu. 53 and 60 surely, Bu. 55 and 59 possibly—seem to postdate TS. 3. All four are very much poorer

than Bu. 49, 50, 52, and 56, which might suggest that the fortunes of the occupants of Gp. 2G-1 were in decline by then. In any event, these considerations are consistent with contemporaneity between Bu. 49 and Bu. 52 and 56.

The second line of evidence relates back to Bu. 54 and 57, which were put in place in Str. 2G-59:TS. 5. Burial 54 was placed in a formal grave, while Bu. 57 was not. Of the four burials thought to have been placed in TS. 3, only Bu. 49 was provided with a formal grave. This suggests that it has the same relationship to Str. 2G-59-1st and 2nd that Bu. 54 has to 2nd and 3rd. Given this, it is interesting to note its position due W of Bu. 54, on the same axis. It is also interesting that Bu. 49 appears to have been placed earlier in the construction sequence of TS. 3 than the others, for Bu. 54 has this same relationship to 57 in TS. 5.

If the judgment that Bu. 49 was placed in TS. 3 is correct, the problem arises as to why three, if not four, adult males should have died at approximately the same time. This could suggest sacrifice, but there is no evidence for this. Another real possibility is that three men, perhaps not far apart in age, all contracted an illness that proved fatal (see also discussion of Bu. 57).

SEQUENTIAL POSITION:

Probably Str. 2G-59:TS. 3, intruded into 59-2nd (see Table 2.49).

BURIAL 50

LOCATION:

Gp. 2G-1, 14.90 m N, 22.40 m E of Datum 24C (Fig. 27); about 0.70 m E of Bu. 49, intruded into the front wall of Str. 2G-59-2nd, on the front-rear axis of 59-1st (Fig. 22, 23). 24C/70; see Fig. 162b.

GRAVE:

Amorphous shape with no walls, no roof. Burial measured 1.10 m N-S, 0.40 m E-W, just large enough to accommodate the body.

INDIVIDUAL AND ASSOCIATED MATERIAL:

Individual: Adult, probably male, the head N and partially inside Vessel No. 1. The arms were flexed at the elbows, hands beneath the chest but wrists apart. The legs were drawn against the abdomen in complete flexation, with feet together. The body lay prone but somewhat twisted. Primary burial.

Associated material: Three pottery vessels of the Imix Complex; No. 1 a Palmar Ceramic Group short cylinder (TR. 25A:fig. 55*b*2) was positioned N of, and partly over the head, resting on its side. Vessel No. 2, a Palmar Orange Polychrome cylinder (TR. 25A:fig. 55*b*3) was positioned over the neck and rested on its side. No. 3, a Mex Composite outflaring-side bowl (TR. 25A:fig. 55*b*1) was positioned over the feet and rested on its side.

Skeletal material: Owing to its position only 0.30 m below the surface of the mound, the skeleton was only fragmentary. There is no reason to doubt that a whole skeleton was originally present. Only 15 teeth were recovered, including 3 incisors, 2 canines, 4 premolars, and 6 molars. The mandible reveals antemortem loss of both lower first and third molars, and the other missing teeth were probably also lost before death. All remaining teeth show moderate wear, and there are heavy calculus deposits on the incisors. Periodontitis is moderate. Advanced age is suggested by tooth wear and antemortem loss of so many teeth. There was no cranial modification, and stature was average for the time.

DISCUSSION:

Burial 50 clearly was intruded into the front wall of Str. 2G-59-2nd, and so cannot predate TS. 3. Its proximity to the surface makes it impossible to determine whether it was intruded into 59-1st. It could have been, but it is equally possible that it was sealed beneath the floor of that structure. This seems likely, on the basis of considerations discussed in connection with Bu. 49. Its position high in the platform suggests that Bu. 50 was placed later in the sequence of construction of 59-1st than Bu. 49.

SEQUENTIAL POSITION:

Probably Str. 2G-59:TS. 3, intruded into Str. 2G-59-2nd (see Table 2.49).

BURIAL 52

LOCATION:

Gp. 2G-1, 13.40 m N, 22.24 m E of Datum 24C (Fig. 27); about 0.14 m S of Bu. 50, and intruded into the front wall of Str. 2G-59-2nd (Fig. 22). 24C/104; see Fig. 162d for plan.

GRAVE:

Amorphous shape with no walls or roof. Burial measured 1.45 m N-S, 0.44 m E-W, large enough for one body only.

INDIVIDUAL AND ASSOCIATED MATERIAL:

Individual: Mature male, probably of advanced age. The body was fully extended and supine, with the head N. Primary burial indicated.

Associated material: Three Imix pottery vessels; No. 1, fluted cylinder (TR. 25A:fig. 55*c*1) was placed semi-upright over the right shoulder. No. 2, a Palmar Ceramic

Group slightly outcurving-side bowl (TR. 25A:fig. 55*c*3), was placed upright over the right forearm. No. 3, a small cylinder (TR. 25A:fig. 55*c*2), was placed on its side above the feet.

SKELETAL MATERIAL:

Preservation was very poor, though a complete skeleton seems to have been present. The major long bones have a robust appearance characteristic of males, but stature was quite small by the standards for the time. Two teeth are all that was found: 1 canine and 1 incisor. The right mandible fragment (the best-preserved jaw fragment) reveals alveolar resorption indicative of loss of all molars on that side, so that other teeth quite likely were lost antemortem as well. This, and the extensive attrition of the remaining teeth, suggest a somewhat advanced age for this individual at death. The surviving left central incisor had been notched in the distal corner, somewhat like Romero's type B4 (Romero 1960:51), though rounded rather than squared off.

DISCUSSION:

The position of this burial, intruded into the front wall of Str. 2G-59-2nd, clearly indicates association with the final structure (1st). That it was so deep in the fill favors the interpretation that interment was made during TS. 3, when 1st was being built. A later date for interment, however, cannot be absolutely ruled out, although the possibility seems unlikely (see also discussion of Bu. 49). Possibly, the burial was placed after Bu. 49, but before Bu. 50 (see its discussion).

SEQUENTIAL POSITION:

Probably Str. 2G-59:TS. 3, intruded into Str. 2G-59-2nd (see Table 2.49).

BURIAL 53

LOCATION:

Gp. 2G-1, 11 m N, 22.98 m E of Datum 24C (Fig. 27); only 0.10 m beneath the surface of the mound covering Str. 2G-59. 24C/114; see Fig. 22 and Fig. 162c for plan.

GRAVE:

Amorphous shape, with no walls, no roof. Burial measured 1 m N-S, 0.33 m E-W, sufficient only for the one body.

INDIVIDUAL AND ASSOCIATED MATERIAL:

Individual: Age and sex unknown (see skeletal material). The body lay on its right side, with head N. The legs were partially flexed, but arm position is unknown. Primary burial probable.

Associated material: One weathered Imix cylinder (TR. 25A:fig. 55d) was placed on its side by the feet.

SKELETAL MATERIAL:

In spite of very poor preservation, a complete individual seems to be represented. The leg bones appear small and gracile as nearly as can be determined, and might be those of a female or young male. No teeth were found, and it cannot be determined if these were lost before or after death. From in situ observation, stature was close to the mean for females, but low even by the standards for males who lived between AD 550 and 869.

DISCUSSION:

The absence of any teeth in this burial raises the question as to whether they could have been extracted from the body after death as in Bu. 63 (discussed below). Unfortunately, this question cannot be answered in view of the poor preservation of the mandible and maxilla.

The proximity of Bu. 53 to the surface leaves little doubt that it was intrusive, postdating construction of the final structure, but by how much cannot be answered.

SEQUENTIAL POSITION:

Probably Str. 2G-59:TS. 1, postdating construction of Str. 2G-59-1st (see Table 2.49).

BURIAL 54

LOCATION:

Gp. 2G-1, 15.75 m N, 22.76 m E of Datum 24C (Fig. 27); in bedrock grave beneath fill of Str. 2G-59-2nd (Fig. 22). 24C/125; see Fig. 162e for plan; 173c for photo.

GRAVE:

The grave was cut from bedrock, measuring 1.21 m N-S, 0.46 m E-W, and 0.57 m in depth, sufficient for only one body. It was wider at the bottom than at the top, and both ends were rounded, the S end being slightly wider than the N. Overall shape was rectangular. A row of coverstones two courses high covered the burial (Fig. 23). The grave had been purposely filled with earth.

INDIVIDUAL AND ASSOCIATED MATERIAL:

Individual: Adult of unknown sex. The body lay on its left side, head N, and face up. The left arm was extended, the right flexed at the elbow. The legs were contracted, with the feet together. Primary burial indicated.

Associated material: Three pottery vessels of the Ik Complex; No. 1, a Sibal Buff Polychrome outflaring-side bowl (TR. 25A:fig. 52b3), sat upright N of the head in the W side of the grave. No. 2, a Sibal Polychrome outcurving-side bowl (TR. 25A:fig. 52b2), sat upright E of No. 1. No. 3, a Sibal Buff Polychrome barrel (TR. 25A:fig. 52b1), lay on its side near the feet.

SKELETAL MATERIAL:

Little remained of the skeleton but scraps. Bones seem to indicate an adult of exceptionally small size.

DISCUSSION:

This burial was clearly placed at the time of construction of Str. 2G-59-2nd, as no evidence for intrusion could be detected. This places it in TS. 5, by which time elements of the Imix Ceramic Complex were making their appearance. Yet, the burial contained Ik pottery. While the vessels may not have been quite old by the time they were placed in Bu. 54, they evidently were not procured new expressly to be placed in the grave. This matter is discussed further in TR. 20B. As noted elsewhere, Bu. 54 seems to be contemporary with Bu. 57 (see its discussion).

SEQUENTIAL POSITION:

Str. 2G-59:TS. 5, at the time of construction of Str. 2G-59-2nd (Table 2.49).

BURIAL 55

LOCATION:

Gp. 2G-1, 18.80 m N, 26.37 m E of Datum 24C (Fig. 27); intruded into the E platform (U. 1) of Str. 2G-59 (Fig. 22). 24C/127; for plan, see Fig. 163a; 173d for photo.

GRAVE:

The grave penetrated Str. 2G-49; U. 5 (Fig. 24) and was roughly walled on the E and W sides with large masonry blocks. Two coverstones, 0.49 m long, 0.36 m wide, and 0.18 m thick were placed above the burial, 0.50 m above U. 5. The burial measured 1.06 m N-S, 0.46 E-W, and was intentionally earth-filled. It was just large enough for the body.

INDIVIDUAL AND ASSOCIATED MATERIAL:

Individual: Subadult of unknown sex. The body was prone, with head to the N. The arms were extended with the right hand by the hip, the left hand by the knees. The legs were flexed at the knees and arranged perpendicular to the body. Primary burial; no associated materials.

SKELETAL MATERIAL:

There is better than average preservation here, although all the epiphyses have decayed. The skull reveals pronounced frontal flattening. The third molars were impacted, and there is crowding of both upper and lower teeth, with the upper right central incisor rotated out of position. This individual also had a Class I malocclusion. There are no other signs of pathology, and attrition is virtually non-existent.

DISCUSSION:

The problem with this burial pertains to its sequential position. Its intrusion into an old floor, U. 5, obviously places it as post TS. 9. The possibility exists that it post-dates abandonment of the final structure. Since the elevation of the final floor of the E platform is unknown, this cannot be said with certainty, but the elevation of the coverstones 0.20 m above the surviving level of the platform makes it likely that these protruded above any pavement.

SEQUENTIAL POSITION:

Probably Str. 2G-59:TS. 1, intruded into Str. 2G-59-1st, but this is uncertain (see Table 2.49).

BURIAL 56

LOCATION:

Gp. 2G-1, 16.44 m N, 21.10 m E of Datum 24C (Fig. 27), intruded into the front stairway of Str. 2G-59-2nd, 0.60 m N of Bu. 49 (Fig. 22). 24C/135; see Fig. 163c for plan; 174a for photo.

GRAVE:

No specially prepared grave is apparent. The Maya dug into the stairway of the existing structure, placed the body and associated material in position, and covered them over with fill for Str. 2G-59-1st. Grave measured 0.63 m N-S, 1.10 m E-W, sufficient only for the one body.

INDIVIDUAL AND ASSOCIATED MATERIAL:

Individual: Middle adult male. The legs were flexed and perpendicular to body; the arms were extended. The body lay on its left side with the head to the E. Primary burial.

Associated material: Two Imix pottery vessels and part of a third. No. 1, a tripod plate (Haviland 1963:fig. 97d), was upright by the right hip; No. 2, a weathered cylinder (TR. 25A:fig. 56a), was on its side W of No. 1; No. 3 (uncatalogued) consisted of rim sherds E of No. 1.

SKELETAL MATERIAL:

Sufficient remnants of an entire skeleton indicate a primary burial. The skull was badly crushed, but frontal flattening was evident. The maxillary teeth recovered are 4 molars, 2 premolars, 1 canine, 1 worn incisor, and the

roots of the first right molar and second molar. All teeth are present in the mandible except for one premolar, a canine, and all incisors. The wear on the molars is moderate. The individual was of slightly less than average stature.

DISCUSSION:

Extensive root action would have obliterated any traces of intrusive cuts in this area. Hence, in the absence of any other evidence, this burial could be construed as intrusive into Str. 2G-59-1st. A better interpretation is that it was intrusive into 59-2nd, but contemporaneous with the construction of 1st for the following reasons. First, its position deep within the fill of the final structure does not suggest intrusion into that structure. Second, a well-cut masonry block, found just N of the burial and in front of Str. 2G-Sub.1 (Fig. 21:5 and 173b) is the exact size required for the first riser stone of the stairway for 59-2nd, into which the burial was intruded. It appears that this stone was removed and placed out of the way by Sub.1, an action that could not have taken place after the construction of 59-1st.

As discussed in connection with Bu. 49, this interment seems to be contemporary with two, and probably three, others. In the sequence of construction of 59-1st, it probably was placed before Bu. 50 and 52, at the same time or just after Bu. 49.

The pottery vessels associated with Bu. 56 present a problem, as only two are whole and the third is fragmentary. This suggests that the surviving family wished to do right by the deceased by placing three vessels in the burial. Perhaps only two were available, so sherds from a broken vessel were substituted for the third.

SEQUENTIAL POSITION:

Str. 2G-59:TS. 3, intruded into Str. 2G-59-2nd (see Table 2.49).

BURIAL 57

LOCATION:

Gp. 2G-1, 12.90 m N, 23.60 m E of Datum 24C (Fig. 27); in the fill of Str. 2G-59-2nd, above U. 15 (Fig. 21, 22). 24C/137; for plan, see Fig. 163e; 174b for photo.

GRAVE:

No specially prepared grave was apparent. The burial was placed on a bare surface, and then covered by fill for 59-2nd. The grave measured 0.74 m N-S and 0.50 m E-W, just large enough to accommodate the body.

INDIVIDUAL AND ASSOCIATED MATERIAL:

Individual: Adult, possibly a male. The legs were flexed perpendicular to the body; the left arm was flexed, and the right arm was extended. The body lay on its right side with head to the N. Primary burial.

Associated material: A major wall fragment of a vessel (Haviland 1963:fig. 97f) was positioned W of the legs. A pottery bead was placed E of the legs (TR. 27B:Fig. 132*n*2).

SKELETAL MATERIAL:

There was very poor preservation, but a primary burial is indicated. Only 12 teeth were found: 1 upper and 3 lower molars; 2 upper and 1 lower premolar; 1 lower right canine; 1 lower right lateral incisor and upper right central incisor. All molars show wear; the premolars show moderate wear, and extensive root surface caries are evident on both molars and premolars. In all, advanced age seems indicated. The one surviving upper central incisor was notched in its distal corner (type B2; Romero 1960:51). The incisor also displays an enamel hypoplasia.

DISCUSSION:

The position of this burial beneath the heavy stone fill of the S portion of Str. 2G-59-2nd suggests it was contemporaneous with construction of 2nd. Thus, it was also contemporary with Bu. 54, though its position in the fill suggests that it was the second of the two interments. To speculate, perhaps the individuals were brothers of approximately the same age who happened to die at the same time. Or, perhaps these two individuals contracted a single disease, which proved fatal to both.

This burial was unusual in that it included a clay bead. The other grave object, the vessel fragment, suggests that the survivors wanted to provide burial pottery for the deceased, but a large sherd was the best they could do. Similar situations include Bu. 60 and 62 (and previously discussed Bu. 56).

SEQUENTIAL POSITION:

Str. 2G-59:TS. 5 contemporary with construction of Str. 2G-59-2nd (see Table 2.49).

BURIAL 58

LOCATION:

Gp. 2G-1, 10.56 m N, 22.45 m E of Datum 24C (Fig. 27); intruded through Str. 2G-59:U. 7, S of front wall of 59-2nd (Fig. 20–22). 24C/138; for plan, see Fig. 163b.

GRAVE:

The grave was rectangular in shape, but with no special construction or coverstones. Burial measured 1.30 m N-S, 0.78 m E-W, just large enough for the one body.

INDIVIDUAL AND ASSOCIATED MATERIAL:

Individual: Adult, of unknown sex. Position is largely unknown because of the scantiness of remains, but the head was N and partially inside Vessel 2. Grave size suggests that the body was flexed.

Associated material: Four Ik pottery vessels; No. 1, a Desquite Red-on-orange, lateral-ridge tripod plate (TR. 25A:fig. 42*b*3), upright at the N end of the grave. No. 2, a Veracal Orange, unusual everted-rim bowl (TR. 25A:fig. 42*b*4), on its side E of No. 1, partially over the head of the corpse. No. 3, a Desquite Red-on-orange bowl (TR. 25A:fig. 42*b*1), upright in the vicinity of the feet. No. 4, a Desquite Red-on-orange round-side bowl (TR. 25A:fig. 42*b*2), was S of No. 3.

SKELETAL MATERIAL:

Little may be said, since but few fragments remained. Probably a whole individual was interred, but only a vault fragment and femur shaft survived.

DISCUSSION:

Intruded through a floor (U. 7) of Str. 2G-59-4th, Bu. 58 can date no earlier than TS. 7, the time of construction of U. 13 (see Fig. 20). The ceramics prove this burial to be earlier than Bu. 49, 50, 52, and 54, one of which was surely associated with construction of 59-2nd. Since the burial was placed on the line of the front wall of 2nd, it cannot be associated with that structure, and was probably, therefore, associated with U. 13 of 3rd.

SEQUENTIAL POSITION:

Str. 2G-59:TS. 7, intruded into Str. 2G-59-4th (Table 2.49).

BURIAL 59

LOCATION:

Gp. 2G-1, 15.50 m N, 25.10 m E of Datum 24C (Fig. 27); 0.70 m E of the back wall of Str. 2G-59-1st and 2nd, at the base of the final N wall of the E platform (Fig. 22, 23). 24C/146; for plan, see Fig. 163d; 174c,d, for photos.

GRAVE:

Amorphous-shaped, with no special grave construction or coverstones. Burial measured 0.44 m N-S by 1.00 m E-W, just large enough for the one body.

INDIVIDUAL AND ASSOCIATED MATERIAL:

Individual: Adult male, lying on his right side with head W. The arms were flexed, wrists together and hands by chin. The legs were tightly flexed at the knee and arranged perpendicular to the body. The feet were together.

Associated material: None. Primary burial indicated.

SKELETAL MATERIAL:

The bones were fragile, and none survived in their entirety. Only 6 teeth: 2 heavily but unevenly worn, right lateral incisors; 3 heavily worn canines (both upper and lower right); 1 premolar; and the roots of 2 other teeth. The mandible shows alveolar resorption from the second right molar to the canine; there is no other surviving alveolar area. Probably all the missing teeth were lost antemortem. The individual appears to have been of average stature. There was no cranial modification.

DISCUSSION:

The location next to Str. 2G-59 renders the relation of this burial to the structure a problem. Its placement in proximity to both the E platform and the back of the final structure, as well as its position beneath the final outside occupation surface, suggests that it postdates final construction. The situation recalls Landa's statement that burials were sometimes placed behind houses (Tozzer 1941:130).

SEQUENTIAL POSITION:

Problematical (see discussion), but perhaps Str. 2G-59:TS. 1 (see Table 2.49).

BURIAL 60

LOCATION:

Gp. 2G-1, 18.40 m N, 20.68 m E of Datum 24C (Fig. 27), intruded into Str. 2G-59-1st (Fig. 22). 24C/143, no plan of the burial exists.

GRAVE:

Amorphous-shaped, with no special grave construction or coverstones. Burial measured 1.14 m N-S, 0.50 m E-W; just large enough for one body.

INDIVIDUAL AND ASSOCIATED MATERIAL:

Individual: Old adult, possibly male. The head was N and feet S. Preservation was too poor for further observations. Primary burial probable.

Associated material: Part of an Imix tripod plate (not illustrated) on floor of the burial.

SKELETAL MATERIAL:

Preservation was so poor that only bone scraps were found. One molar was preserved, showing very heavy wear, the cusp pattern all but obliterated. The long-bone fragments gave the impression of muscularity, suggesting the body of a male.

DISCUSSION:

Burial 60 compares with Bu. 57 and 62 (this report) in the inclusion of only a portion of a whole vessel, perhaps another example of the inability of the survivors to provide grave goods (see also Bu. 56).

SEQUENTIAL POSITION:

Str. 2G-59:TS. 1, intruded into Str. 2G-59-1st (Table 2.49).

BURIAL 61

LOCATION:

Gp. 4F-3, 15.10 m N, 24.04 m E of Datum 24A (Fig. 99); in fill just inside the NE corner of Plat. 4F-6 (Fig. 100). 24A/74; see Fig. 164d for plan; 179b for photo.

GRAVE:

No special grave construction or coverstones was apparent, and shape was amorphous. Burial measured 0.75 m N-S, 0.45 m E-W; just large enough to accommodate the one body.

INDIVIDUAL AND ASSOCIATED MATERIAL:

Individual: Subadult of unknown sex. The body lay on its right side, with head N. The arms were mostly extended, but it is not known if the wrists were together. The legs were flexed at the knee and arranged perpendicular to the body. Primary burial indicated.

Associated material: None.

SKELETAL MATERIAL:

Very little could be salvaged of the once complete skeleton. Five teeth were recovered: the upper right first premolar through second molar and the lower right first molar. They show very slight wear and the third molar was unerupted. There was no cranial modification.

DISCUSSION:

The burial may have been intruded into the plaza, but no evidence either for or against this was found. Lack of coverstones or special grave construction might favor intrusion.

SEQUENTIAL POSITION:

Problematical, possibly Plat. 4F-6: TS. 1, intruded into the plaza (see Table 2.210).

BURIAL 62

LOCATION:

Str. 2G-61 locus, 11.90 m W of Datum 24G (Fig. 34), on the floor of Ch. 2G-2:Chm. 2, in fill placed for construction of Str. 2G-61 (Fig. 39). 24H/9; see Fig. 164b for plan.

GRAVE:

Within the chultun proper, the body lay covered by purposely placed fill.

INDIVIDUAL AND ASSOCIATED MATERIAL:

Individual: Adult male. The legs were contracted, with a right angle formed by the lower leg and thigh. The arm bones were not in correct anatomical position, and the phalanges were scattered. The mandible was found below the right shoulder. The body itself lay on its right side, with the head N. A two-stage burial seems indicated by this situation.

Associated material: Three sherds from a large, coarse-ware vessel (not illustrated), one positioned N of the head, and two by the knees.

SKELETAL MATERIAL:

The skeleton was extremely fragile, but it all seems to have been present. Some teeth may have been taken from the body postmortem, a practice noted for Bu. 63. Missing were all lower molars; three lower and one upper (first left) premolars; two lower and one upper canine; all lower and both upper central incisors. Surviving teeth show marked attrition. Moderate periodontal disease is evident, as is a marked hypoplasia on the surviving canine. Indications are that this individual was slightly below the average stature for his time.

DISCUSSION:

At the time of construction of Str. 2G-61, the burial was placed in the chultun, which was then filled to permit construction above it. That the bones of the lower arms, the phalanges of the feet and hands, and the mandible were out of position is of interest, particularly since the legs and shoulders are correctly articulated. There are two possibilities: either the corpse was in this condition when it was placed in the chultun, or rodents disturbed the decomposing remains. Since there was no evidence of rodent activity, the former is likely. Indeed, since some bones were not articulated and others were, the probability is that Bu. 62 was a two-stage burial—that is, there was a process of unknown duration that significantly affected the human remains, which were then buried for the first time. Secondary burial can probably be ruled out, as organic remains decompose rapidly in the environment of Tikal, and if an old burial had accidentally been dug up, the bones probably would not have been articulated at all when reburied. The partial articulation of the corpse suggests that the period of time between death and interment was brief. Then the remains were buried, according to a definite pattern, in the chultun.

The inclusion of fragments of a pottery vessel suggests an analogy with the later Bu. 57 and 60 (discussed

above). As indicated for those burials, perhaps the inclusion of sherds resulted from the inability of the next of kin to afford complete vessels.

SEQUENTIAL POSITION:

Ch. 2G-2:TS. 1, prior to construction of Str. 2G-61 (see Table 2.72).

BURIAL 63

LOCATION:

Gp. 2G-2, 0.90 m N, 0.40 m W of Datum 24E (Fig. 33); in Chm. 5 of Ch. 2G-10 (Fig. 32). In fill placed for construction of Str. 2G-14. 24F/11; see Fig. 164a for plan.

GRAVE:

The burial rested on the floor of Chm. 5, which was sealed off from the rest of the chultun by a masonry slab, and then filled through Neck 3.

INDIVIDUAL AND ASSOCIATED MATERIAL:

Individual: Old adult female. The legs were tightly flexed, with the feet together. The arms were both extended, placed between the knees and abdomen, with the wrists together. The body was supine, with the head N. Primary burial indicated.

Associated material: None.

SKELETAL MATERIAL:

Preservation of this skeleton was exceptionally good, permitting many observations and measurements (for this data see TR. 30). Of the skull, the vault was largely complete; it is markedly brachycranic with a high forehead, and pseudocircular modification is indicated. Suture closure suggests an age of 30–35 years, but dentition suggests greater age. This may represent a case of abnormally retarded suture closure. No teeth were found, the lower second premolar and molars on the right, along with the lower left first and second molars having been lost antemortem. The other teeth were probably removed at death. Advanced periodontitis characterizes the posterior portion of the mandibular corpus.

Of particular note are the prominent deltoid tuberosites, more common among females than males at Tikal. Also apparent are squatting facets. Muscle attachments were not prominent on the bones of the lower limbs. Stature seems to have been slightly below the mean for females.

DISCUSSION:

This is a straightforward situation: the burial was contemporary with the filling of the chultun prior to the earliest construction at the locus of Str. 2G-14. The removal of all remaining teeth prior to burial is of interest, for this is the only sure example of such practice from the burials discussed here. In many other poorly preserved burials lacking teeth, however, postmortem removal of teeth is a possibility, even if impossible to prove.

SEQUENTIAL POSITION:

Str. 2G-14:TS. 9, prior to the earliest construction here (see Table 2.58).

BURIAL 64

LOCATION:

Str. 2G-61 locus, 8.70 m S, 12.76 W of Datum 24G; beneath S wall, Str. 2G-61 (Fig. 34). 24G/106; see Fig. 164c for plan.

GRAVE:

No specially constructed grave or coverstones apparent; amorphous shape. Burial measured 1.10 m N-S, 0.30 m E-W, sufficient only for the one body.

INDIVIDUAL AND ASSOCIATED MATERIAL:

Individual: An adult, of unknown sex. The body lay on its left side, with head S. The arms were flexed, with the hands near the face, possibly together. The legs were extended, but it was impossible to tell if the feet were together. Primary burial indicated.

Associated material: None.

SKELETAL MATERIAL:

The bones were in exceptionally poor condition, but there is no reason to doubt that an entire skeleton was represented. Advanced age is indicated by alveolar resorption in the area of the lower molars, premolars, and right canine. No teeth were found; perhaps all were lost antemortem. There was no cranial modification.

DISCUSSION:

No evidence was found for or against intrusion of this burial into the fill of the structure. Though inconclusive, the simplicity of the burial might argue for intrusion.

SEQUENTIAL POSITION:

Problematical, but probably Str. 2G-61:TS. 4 or 5, intruded into Str. 2G-61 (see Table 2.69).

BURIAL 65

LOCATION:

Gp. 3F-1, 7 m S, 6.60 m E of Datum 24R (Fig. 45), in fill of Str. 3F-24-3rd, on its front-rear axis (Fig. 41). 24R/16; see Fig. 165a for plan; 177b for photo.

GRAVE:

A pit, basically rectangular but with rounded ends, was cut into bedrock just for this burial. It was intentionally earth filled and roofed with five coverstones ranging from 0.34 to 0.63 m in length, 0.20 m to 0.30 m in width, and about 0.16 m thick. The entire grave measured 0.43 m N-S and 1.70 m E-W, sufficient only for one body.

INDIVIDUAL AND ASSOCIATED MATERIAL:

Individual: Adult of unknown sex. The body was fully extended, with feet together, supine, with the head to the E. Primary burial.

Associated material: None.

SKELETAL MATERIAL:

The poorly preserved bones were softer than the surrounding marl, hence only teeth could be salvaged. Only three were found: the first and second right upper premolars; and lower right second molar. All were moderately worn, and the molar displayed buccal root surface caries. The other teeth could have been lost antemortem, but this is not certain. That the individual was an adult is indicated by the size of the surrounding bone scraps, the wear on the teeth, and by an estimate in situ of a stature of about 150 cm. This is slightly below the mean for adult males who lived between AD 550 and 869, and a bit above the mean for females. There was no cranial modification.

DISCUSSION:

This interment was clearly contemporaneous with construction of Str. 3F-24-3rd. This is indicated by the position of the burial beneath a covering of distinctive marl fill for the front of the original platform, which had obviously not been cut into later. The burial may not have been initial, but rather associated with abandonment of an earlier structure represented by several postholes, U. 7 through 11 (Fig. 41).

Of interest is the absence of pottery vessels in this burial. Burials with similar graves often contain at least two vessels (e.g., Bu. 66 below).

SEQUENTIAL POSITION:

Str. 3F-24:TS. 7, prior to construction of Str. 3F-24-3rd (see Table 2.83).

BURIAL 66

LOCATION:

Gp. 3F-1, 4.20 m S, 8 m E of Datum 24R (Fig. 45), intruded into the fill of Str. 3F-24-3rd, on the front-rear axis (Fig. 41). 24R/17; see Fig. 165b for plan; 177c for photo.

GRAVE:

A pit 0.60 m deep, essentially rectangular in shape, was cut into bedrock especially to receive the burial. This was earth filled, and roofed by five well-dressed coverstones of uniform length (0.48 m) ranging in width from 0.26 to 0.40 m, and about 0.20 m thick. Grave measured 1.70 m N-S and 0.48 m E-W, just large enough for the one body.

INDIVIDUAL AND ASSOCIATED MATERIAL:

Individual: Adult, possibly a male. The body lay fully extended with feet together; supine, with the head to the N. Primary burial.

Associated material: Two Imix pottery vessels; No. 1, Palmar Orange Polychrome, slightly outcurving-side bowl (TR. 25A:fig. 56b3), was positioned upright E of the head. No. 2, a Mex Composite Cylinder (TR. 25A:fig. 56b1), rested on its side against the right leg (a Tinaja Red jar neck illustrated in TR. 25A:fig. 56b2 was *not* included in the burial).

SKELETAL MATERIAL:

As with Bu. 65, the remains were fragmentary and could not be saved. A complete skeleton was, however, represented. The bones were obviously those of an adult, possibly of advanced age, since no teeth were found (see "Discussion"). The size of the remaining bone scraps suggests the possibility that a male was represented, though this is a very tenuous conclusion. An in situ stature estimate of 150 cm falls slightly below the mean for males who lived between AD 550 and 869.

DISCUSSION:

There is little problem in assigning this burial to a specific time span. The destruction of Str. 3F-24:U. 3, 0.40 m N of U. 4, the position of the front wall of the upper platform level of 24-2nd, and the absence of the marl fill beneath the level of U. 3 to the S all indicate that Bu. 66 was intrusive into 24-3rd and preceded the laying of the upper floor (U. 5) of 2nd. Interment was therefore contemporaneous with construction of 2nd.

An unusual feature of this burial was the inclusion of only two vessels. Two-vessel Late Classic burials are rare elsewhere at Tikal (see TR. 25A).

The absence of teeth in this burial may indicate either that they were lost prior to death, or that they were extracted from the dead individual, a possibility already noted for Bu. 63. In the absence of well-preserved alveolar portions of the mandible and maxilla, this could not be determined for Bu. 66.

SEQUENTIAL POSITION:

Str. 3F-24:TS. 5; intruded into Str. 3F-24-3rd (see Table 2.83).

BURIAL 67

LOCATION:

Gp. 3F-1, 21.88 m S, 10.20 m E of Datum 24R (Fig. 45) in the fill of Str. 3F-25 (Fig. 42). 24R/30; Fig. 165c for plan.

GRAVE:

An amorphous-shaped grave, with no apparent walls or roof. The body lay on bedrock in the earth fill of the structure. Burial measured 0.40 m N-S and 0.80 m E-W, just large enough for the one body.

INDIVIDUAL AND ASSOCIATED MATERIAL:

Individual: Adult, male. Body was tightly flexed with wrists together, hands under chin. The legs were drawn up close to the abdomen. The body lay on its right side, with the head to the E. Primary burial.

Associated material: None.

SKELETAL MATERIAL:

The major long bones were all represented, but they were badly broken, and no measurements were possible. The burial was unquestionably primary. Heavy musculature was indicated in the lower extremities, while the arms were more gracile. This, and the estimated lengths for the long bones in situ suggest the male sex. There was moderate bowing of the femurs. Stature is estimated to have been about the mean for males who lived between AD 550 and 869.

All mandibular teeth were lost antemortem, and only four maxillary teeth survive. They are the right central and lateral incisors and the two right premolars. The second right premolar was largely rotted out. The lateral incisor had been notched to remove the right corner.

DISCUSSION:

Since all pavements in the vicinity of the burial had been destroyed, it was impossible to determine conclusively if the burial was a later intrusion or not. Its position beneath the front wall of the upper level of Str. 3F-25-1st suggests that it was intruded into the original structure at the time of construction of 1st.

SEQUENTIAL POSITION:

Probably Str. 3F-25:TS. 3 (see Table 2.84).

BURIAL 68

LOCATION:

Gp. 3F-2, 4.84 m S, 9.20 m E of Datum 24T-W (Fig. 52), partly beneath the SW corner of Str. 3F-26 (Fig. 46). 24T/24; see Fig. 165f for plan.

GRAVE:

A pit of irregular shape was dug into bedrock especially for the burial, and was roofed by four well-dressed coverstones ranging from 0.52 to 0.60 m in length, 0.27 to 0.36 m in width, and 0.09 to 0.14 m in thickness. These coverstones were placed at an angle and sealed with lime mortar. The burial measured 1.60 m N-S and 0.83 m E-W, a size just large enough to accommodate the one body. It was not intentionally filled.

INDIVIDUAL AND ASSOCIATED MATERIAL:

Individual: Adult, of unknown sex. The legs were flexed perpendicular to the body with the feet together. The arms were also flexed with the wrists apart and the right hand by the face. The body lay on its right side, with the head to the N resting on top of an inverted vessel (No. 2). Primary burial.

Associated material: Three Imix pottery vessels; No. 1 a Palmar Ceramic Group tripod plate (TR. 25A:fig. 56c2), was placed behind the head, upright; No. 2, a Palmar Ceramic Group slightly outcurving-side bowl (TR. 25A:fig. 56c3), was placed inverted beneath the head; No. 3, a Mex Composite cylinder (TR. 25A:fig. 56c1), was placed S of No. 1 on its side.

SKELETAL MATERIAL:

Very little osseous material was recovered from this burial, but there is no reason to doubt that it was primary. Surviving bone scraps indicate an adult. No teeth were found, which may indicate advanced age, or they may have been extracted at death (see "Discussion"). Stature was slightly above the mean for males who lived between AD 550 and 869 .

DISCUSSION:

The elaborateness of the grave is of interest, but there is no great difference from Bu. 54, 65, 66, and 70 (all this report). The interment must have preceded construction of Str. 3F-26:U. 9 (Fig. 46), since this was positioned just above a portion of two of the coverstones. By how much time it preceded this construction is not known, but it is possible (though doubtful) that the burial might even predate 26-3rd. More probably, it was contemporary with construction of 2nd.

The absence of teeth in this burial may indicate that they were lost prior to death, or that they were extracted from the dead individual, a possibility already noted for Bu. 63. In the absence of well-preserved alveolar portions of the mandible and maxilla, this could not be determined for Bu. 68.

SEQUENTIAL POSITION:

No later than Str. 3F-26:TS. 5, contemporary with construction of Str. 3F-26-2nd. Possibly earlier, but doubtful (see Table 2.94).

BURIAL 69

LOCATION:

Gp. 3F-2, 1.40 m S, 13.00 E of Datum 24T-W (Fig. 52), in fill of Str. 3F-26 (Fig. 46). 24T/20; see Fig. 165e for plan.

GRAVE:

An amorphous-shaped grave, with no specially constructed walls or coverstones. Burial measured 0.40 m N-S and 1.00 m E-W, just large enough for one body.

INDIVIDUAL AND ASSOCIATED MATERIAL:

Individual: Old adult, of unknown sex but perhaps male. The body lay on its left side, with head to the W. The arms were flexed, as were the legs. The feet were together. Primary burial.

Associated material: None. A miniature vessel illustrated in TR. 25A (fig. 97c) is mistakenly labeled as from Bu. 69, but is actually from LG. 1 of Str. 3F-26 (Table 2.90).

SKELETAL MATERIAL:

Little osseous material could be salvaged, although it seems clear that the full skeleton had been buried there. Three teeth were in place in the mandible: the right canine and premolars. The mandibular posterior teeth were certainly lost antemortem, and the others may have been as well. The only other surviving tooth was a right upper canine, notched in one corner. The loss of so many teeth, the extensive attrition on the few that remain, and root surface caries on these combine to suggest advanced age at death.

Long-bone scraps were moderately robust in appearance, and the ribs appeared to be particularly heavy and wide. The individual may have been a male, but this is a dubious identification in the absence of better data. On the other hand, stature appears to have been close to the female mean.

DISCUSSION:

This burial predates Str. 3F-26-2nd, since its fill was clearly disturbed. It seems to have been intruded into 26-3rd, as the floor of that structure was destroyed over the area for no other apparent reason. No evidence of the intrusion was noted in the fill, which contained ceramics identical to those sealed below the early floor. A possible explanation for this is that the Maya, in excavating the grave, probably piled the old fill by the edge of the pit, and then later threw it back in after the completion of the interment.

SEQUENTIAL POSITION:

Str. 3F-26:TS. 5, intruded into Str. 3F-26-3rd (see Table 2.94).

BURIAL 70

LOCATION:

Gp. 3F-2, 20.35 m S, 24.80 m E of Datum 24T-W (Fig. 52) in the fill of Plat. 3F-2, just W of Str. 3F-27, and oriented to the front-rear axis of that structure (Fig. 48a). As noted in its discussion, this part of Plat. 3F-2 may actually have been incorporated into Str. 3F-27 as a front room. 24W/8; see Fig. 165d for plan.

GRAVE:

A rectangular pit was dug into bedrock especially for the burial, 0.26 m deep, and roofed by two coverstones 0.64 and 0.74 m in length, 0.30 m and 0.32 m in width, and 0.13 and 0.16 m in thickness. The grave was intentionally earth filled. Burial measured 1.00 m N-S and 0.45 m E-W, just large enough to accommodate the one body.

INDIVIDUAL AND ASSOCIATED MATERIAL:

Individual: Presumed adult, sex unknown. The grave size suggests some flexion and the head was N. Burial probably primary.

Associated material: Four Imix pottery vessels; No. 1, a Palmar Ceramic Group cylinder (TR. 25A:fig. 56*d*1) was W of head, resting on its side. No. 2, a Palmar Ceramic Group slightly outcurving-side bowl (TR. 25A:fig. 56*d*2) was N of the head, upright above No. 3. No. 3, a Palmar Ceramic Group short cylinder (TR. 25A.fig. 56*d*3), was upright beneath No. 2. No. 4, a second Palmar Ceramic Group slightly outcurving-side bowl (TR. 25A:fig. 56*d*4), was inverted beneath the head with a small hole in its base. A small jade bead (Field No.:24W-25) was also included in the burial, and seems to have been placed in the mouth of the deceased.

SKELETAL MATERIAL:

Since so little was found, nothing meaningful can be said. Only a few scraps of the skull were recovered.

DISCUSSION:

The lack of osseous remains is a problem. This could be used to argue that a complete body was not interred, and that this is either a secondary burial or some sort of special deposit, not a burial at all. Primary burial is most likely, however, for the grave is of sufficient size to have accommodated an entire individual in a flexed position. It is much larger than necessary for the deposit of a skull alone with four vessels. Moreover, the skull and vessels are all together in a bunch at one end of the bedrock cut, suggesting that something else occupied the remaining space. That the "something" was a body is indicated by the position and orientation of the skull fragments, which are as they should be if they were part of a body interred in a flexed position. The paucity of surviving bone fragments seen here has also been seen in other primary burials (see especially Bu. 58, already discussed, or Bu. 30, in TR. 19:131-132). In the case of Bu. 70, the bedrock into which the grave was dug is non-porous, and may have acted to speed the decay of the bones by trapping water.

The presence of four vessels, and particularly the jade bead, suggests that the individual was someone of importance. Fewer grave objects are the rule in the majority of small-structure burials that contain Imix pottery, and the inclusion of objects of jade is all but unknown. Given some tendency to more lavish burial of males than females at Tikal (Haviland 1997:5–6), the subject of Bu. 70 may have been a male.

The position of the grave on the axis of the structure suggests that the burial was oriented to 3F-27, and postdated construction of Plat. 3F-2-2nd. Whether it was so placed when 27 was constructed, or later, could not be determined.

SEQUENTIAL POSITION:

Probably no earlier than Str. 3F-27:TS. 1 (see Table 2.95).

BURIAL 118

LOCATION:

Gp. 6E-14, in ceramic test pit through the plaza at a depth of 0.95 m. 35C/5; no plan of the burial is available.

GRAVE:

No reference is made in the excavator's notes to a prepared grave. Presumably, a pit was dug into the plaza fill sufficient to receive the body, or else the body was put in place on an exposed surface, fill was dumped over it, and the plaza then constructed. No measurement of the interment was made.

INDIVIDUAL AND ASSOCIATED MATERIAL:

Individual: Middle adult male. Body position was not recorded, except that it was oriented in an E-W direction.

Associated material: Two whole and one partial Imix pottery vessels (TR. 25A:fig. 76a): a probable Palmar Orange Polychrome slightly outcurving-side bowl; a weathered tripod plate; a rim fragment of a cylinder. Their arrangement in the burial was not recorded by the excavator.

SKELETAL MATERIAL:

A complete skeleton was present, of which most was salvaged for later study. Pseudocircular head modification is evident, and wormian bones were present. The latter are uncommon in skeletons from small domestic groups. Squatting facets, not uncommon in such skeletons, are present.

DISCUSSION:

The burial was clearly put in place when Imix ceramics were in vogue. As noted in section II, the excavations that produced this burial encountered two floors, the uppermost of which probably dates from Early Classic times. Burial 118 is higher in the fill than this floor, but still well below ground surface. Experience suggests that there probably was a final plaza floor at about the elevation of present ground surface. Such floors usually survive only in proximity to structures, where debris from structure collapse affords some protection. Without such protection, final plaza floors are usually totally destroyed. This particular burial is deeper than expected if the burial had been intruded through the final floor. Hence, it probably was placed at the time the final pavement of the plaza was laid. This does not mean that the burial was necessarily dedicatory to the final plaza. Rather, given a recent death, the most convenient spot for burial could have been in the fill for a new modification of the plaza.

SEQUENTIAL POSITION:

No time span defined; burial was interred sometime between AD 700 and 869, the dates for the Imix Ceramic Complex.

The presence of two complete and one partial pottery vessel brings to mind Bu. 56 from Gp. 2G-1, already discussed. This may be another case of a family that wished to do its best by the deceased, but lacked the resources to provide a full set of funerary pots (see also Bu. 60 and 62).

BURIAL 119

LOCATION:

Gp. 7E-6, in ceramic test pit through the plaza in front of Str. 7E-42, at a depth of 0.91 m. 360/7; no plan drawing.

GRAVE:

No reference is made in the excavator's notes to a specially prepared grave. Presumably, a pit was dug into the plaza fill sufficient to receive the body, or else the body was placed on an exposed surface, fill was dumped over it, and the plaza then constructed. No measurement of the interment was made.

INDIVIDUAL AND ASSOCIATED MATERIAL:

Individual: Young adult, perhaps a male. Body position was not recorded, except that the head was to the E, apparently face-up.

Associated material: None.

SKELETAL MATERIAL:

Although the excavator's notes suggest that a complete skeleton was present, little was salvaged. A non-robust individual is suggested with no artificial head modification. The absence of 6 incisors, 2 canines, 5 premolars and 9 molars may indicate extensive antemortem tooth loss.

DISCUSSION:

Elsewhere (see section II), a span of occupation for this group beginning in Early Classic times and lasting until between AD 700 and 869 is indicated. The fill in which the burial was placed contained only Manik sherds, but Ik sherds were found at a comparable level (36Q/5; see Table 2.341). Probably, the burial was put in place at the time Ik ceramics were in vogue.

SEQUENTIAL POSITION:

No time spans defined; probable burial between AD 550 and 700, the dates for the Ik Ceramic Complex.

BURIAL 128

LOCATION:

Gp. 6E-1, in the fill of Str. 6E-Sub.1 (Fig. 143), or Sq. 6E:S162.80 E63.20. 68I/26 and 27; see Fig. 168a for plan; 182b,c, for photos.

GRAVE:

The grave was roughly walled and roofed with five stone slabs. Two of these, on the W side, leaned against the burial; the others were horizontal. The burial measured 1.45 m NW-SE, 1.30 m NE-SW, and was purposely earth-filled. The entire grave was somewhat larger than necessary.

INDIVIDUAL AND ASSOCIATED MATERIAL:

Individual: Middle adult female. The remains were placed in an urn that was covered by a large pottery lid (TR. 25A:fig. 8b1). Therefore, this was not a primary burial. The bones were completely jumbled, with foot bones beneath the skull, a tooth inside one bone, and a general lack of articulation, with the possible exception of the mandible. The skull, right side up, was in the eastern portion of the urn, and faced W. A complete skeleton seems to be represented.

Associated material: Six pottery vessels of the Cauac Complex in addition to the urn and its lid: on the side W of the urn, a Sierra Red widely outflaring-side dish (TR. 25A:fig. 9a2); on its side S of urn, a Laguna Verde Incised: Usulatan-Style Variety, restricted-orifice medial-flange dish (TR. 25A:fig. 8b2); on their sides N of urn, a Sierra Red, medial-flange dish (TR. 25A:fig. 9a4) and Laguna Verde Incised: Usulatan Variety, restricted-orifice medial-flange dish (TR. 25A:fig. 9a1); beneath TR. 25A:fig. 9a2 were a Sierra Red medial-flange dish (TR. 25A:fig. 9a5) and a Morfin Unslipped, round-side dish (TR. 25A:fig. 9a3), placed right side up. All those vessels on their sides had their openings toward the urn.

The following objects were in the urn: 1 unworked bird bone (68I-10); 165 jade beads (68I-11); 1 jade flare (68I-12); 399 whole, 15 fragmentary shell beads (68I-13); 4 bone hasps perforated to sustain strands of beads (68I-14); some number of stingray spines (68I-15); 3 perforated clam shells (68I-16); 1 chert nodule (68I-19); unmodified mineral pigment, cinnabar (68I-17); and painted stucco (68I-18). The beads were distributed entirely at random. The holes seldom lined up, and they occurred everywhere—beneath the skull, beneath the limb bones, under vertebrae, under the pelvic bones, and even inside some long bones. The large jade bead was beneath the pelvic bones in the western portion of the urn. Near it were the three shells and the chert nodule. Stucco fragments were found everywhere, but one shell had a tiny piece of red stucco that adhered to it. The stingray spines were beneath the shells, and the other large jade beads were close by. The red pigment was distributed generally in the urn, and discolored most of the bones. The bone hasps were for stringing beads, and one of these may have been strung when it was put in the urn. A tubular bead was positioned as if pendent from the center of the bone hasp, while tabular beads were positioned as if pendent on either side. This pattern was absent in the case of the other bone hasps.

Skeletal Material:

Owing to the protection afforded by the urn and its cover, many bones of this individual survived despite great antiquity (see sequential position). All bones are paper thin, however. This caused some, such as the occipital and even teeth, to disintegrate partially despite application of a hardening agent. There is no reason to doubt that the complete (though dismembered) remains of single individual were placed in the urn.

The skull is most interesting, for it appears to indicate the early practice of pseudocircular head modification. This is shown by a slight transverse groove on the frontal, a compressed occipital, a slight depression above the sqamous suture with a slight bulge of the parietals, and a slight constriction of the parietals just above the mastoid processes. All of these features suggest that a band was tied tightly around the head. The excessive breadth of the

skull is unusual, for as Stewart (1953:296) has noted, this is normally not a feature of pseudocircular modification.

Several teeth were missing, including 5 molars, 2 premolars, 2 canines, 6 incisors. Alveolar resorption of surviving pieces of the mandible suggests antemortem loss. Advanced periodontal disease was also indicated. Of the remaining teeth, 1 molar, 1 premolar, the canine, and 3 incisors are extensively decayed. Attrition is marked, and a lower left third molar shows extensive root surface caries.

Little need be said with respect to the other bones of the body. The second cervical vertebra (axis) is markedly more robust than in the case of known Tikal females, and even some males. Stature, however, appears to have been on the small side.

Discussion:

The first problem to confront is whether this is a true burial or some sort of special offering. If a burial, it was either two-stage or secondary. Since a complete skeleton seems to have been present, secondary interment can probably be ruled out. In most such cases, some of the remains are generally missing, for one reason or another. Bones may be destroyed when exhumed, or choice long bones may be appropriated for other uses. The presence of the burial objects is another piece of evidence, for in a case of exhumation and reburial, such choice objects might not be replaced. Moreover, there is evidence that a few beads may still have been strung when placed in the urn. The non-damaged nature of the pottery suggests it had never been exhumed, for if it had been, some chipping or breakage quite likely would have resulted. Finally, there is the grave itself. Normally, one would not expect much more than an amorphous grave for a secondary burial. Admittedly, none of this is conclusive. It does not rule out secondary burial, but it does seem to favor a scenario in which the body of a recently deceased woman was dismembered so that her parts could be placed in the urn prior to its burial.

Burial 128 brings to mind certain aspects of North Acropolis Bu. 167 (TR. 14:230–233). Roughly contemporary, it has been dated to about AD 50 (see below). Three individuals, one infant and two adults, were placed together in a large chamber with Sk. A, an adult male, on the floor in an extended supine position. In one of two lidded vessels (similar to the urn of Bu. 128) placed on Sk. A were found the disarticulated remains of an adult female. Skeleton A wore bracelets that appear to have been comparable to some that must have been included in Bu. 128. In other words, despite the many jade beads, Bu. 128 seems representative of a much poorer interment than Bu. 167. Indeed, it is more comparable to what might have been one of the grave offerings for the richer "tomb." It is this that raises the question: was Bu. 128 a true burial or some kind of offering? Skeleton B of Bu. 167 was placed in its urn without other objects. The individual of Bu. 128 was placed in an urn with objects comparable to the funerary adornments of Sk. A of Bu. 167. Burial 128 was associated with a structure that is somewhat problematical as to function. While it is impossible to be sure, it does not appear to have been a religious structure, for it was not oriented in the manner of household shrines, as known from Early Classic and later times (see TR. 21). Nor can we be sure the dismembered woman in Bu. 167 was merely part of an "offering" placed with the body of the principal occupant (SK. A) of the "tomb." If the occupant of North Acropolis Bu. 85 was the founder of the later Tikal Dynasty, as some have proposed (Martin 2003:5–6), then all three individuals in Bu. 167 could have been members of a previous ruling family. Dated to about AD 75, Bu. 85 followed 167 by perhaps 25 years (TR. 14:233). When the man in Bu. 85 assumed power, he could have put to death any potential challengers to his rule.

Speculative though much of this is, there still seems to be no reason not to regard 128 as a burial. Remaining is consideration of its sequential position. The stratigraphy seems to indicate that Str. 6E-Sub.1-2nd was razed to the level at which a new floor for Plat. 6E-1 was to be laid (the floor for 9th), following which Sub.1-1st was built on the remains of the preceding structure. Burial 128 was included in the fill of this new structure, and there is no trace of an intrusive grave. Rather, it looks as if the burial was put in place, and the fill was then heaped up around and over it. Thus, Bu. 128 seems to have a terminal relationship to Sub.1-2nd, and an initial relationship to 1st.

Ceramic evidence is consistent with this. The burial ceramics are characteristic of the Cauac Complex, while the most recent sherds from the fill Sub.1-2nd, as well as from the fill of the associated floor of Plat. 6E-1-10th, are Chuen. The sherd samples are quite large, so they seem to confirm that the burial postdates Sub.1-2nd and Plat. 6E-1-10th.

A small sherd sample from the fills of Sub.1-1st and the associated Plat. 6E-1-9th:Fl. 1 also produced nothing more recent than Chuen material. This, though, does not rule out an association between the burial and their construction. Firstly, since the sherd sample was very small, chance alone might explain the failure to find one or two Cauac sherds. Secondly, the most logical source of fill for Str. 6E-Sub.1-1st and Plat. 6E-1-9th would have been trash from Str. 6E-Sub.1-2nd, along with fill from its demolition. Given this, it is even less likely that Cauac material would be found in these fills.

As collateral evidence, Plat. 6E-1-8th (the first known construction following that of Str. 6E-Sub.1-1st) was built after the appearance of Manik ceramics. This reinforces the ceramic dating of Plat. 6E-1-9th:Fl. 1 and Str. 6E-Sub.1-1st. Since Str. 6E-Sub.1, in some form, was

in use until after the appearance of Ik pottery, a Cauac occupation surface for Plat. 6E-1 must have been a reality, and the floor of 9th is the only candidate for such a surface.

SEQUENTIAL POSITION:

Str. 6E-Sub.1:TS. 3 (Table 2.333), preceding construction of Str. 6E-Sub.1-1st.

BURIAL 129

LOCATION:

Gp. 6E-1, intruded into Plat. 6E-1:U. 10 (Fig. 146), or Sq. 6E:S158.72 E62.80. 68G/18; see Fig. 168b for plan.

GRAVE:

An amorphous-shaped grave, with no specially constructed walls. Large, rough blocks, about 0.40 by 0.30 m, lay directly on the body S of the skull. The grave had not been completely earth-filled. Burial measured 1.15 m N-S, 0.50 m E-W, just sufficient to accommodate the body.

INDIVIDUAL AND ASSOCIATED MATERIAL:

Individual: Middle-to-old adult male. Supine position, head to the N with the face up and slightly to the E. The hands were folded low over the stomach, and the legs were slightly flexed at the hips, but tightly so at the knees.

Associated material: Shell fragments by the right elbow and foot seem to be items from structure fill. Otherwise, no associated material.

SKELETAL MATERIAL:

Despite poor preservation, primary burial is clearly indicated. All mandibular teeth were lost antemortem, and there was complete alveolar resorption. The maxilla was not preserved, but since no teeth were found, the upper dentition was probably lost antemortem also. There was no cranial modification.

The long bones are robust, but none survive in their entirety. The individual seems to have been of slightly greater than average stature for his time. Of particular note: although the skeleton of the right hand was relatively complete, only the bones of two fingers were found from the left hand.

DISCUSSION:

The sequential position of this burial is clear. A portion of Plat. 6E-1:U. 10, a light-colored fill associated with the floor of Plat. 6E-1-6th, was removed to provide the grave for the burial. This was then filled, an operation marked by Str. 6E-26:U. 2 (Fig. 151), a pause-line over the grave. Structure 6E-26-3rd was then constructed above the locus of the burial.

The condition of the hand bones constitutes a problem here. The lack of finger bones for the left hand suggests that these were lost during life. Preservation does not seem to have been a factor, for the bones of the right hand were all present.

SEQUENTIAL POSITION:

Str. 6E-26:TS. 13, intruded into strata that served as fill for Str. 6E-26-4th (see Table 2.330).

BURIAL 130

LOCATION:

Gp. 6E-1, N of Bu. 128 and S of Bu. 129 (Fig. 145), or Sq. 6E:S162.22 E63.16. Intruded into the fill of Str. 6E-Sub.1-1st. 68I/31; see Fig. 168c for plan.

GRAVE:

The grave was of amorphous shape, with no specially constructed walls or cover. Burial measured 0.93 m N-S, 0.44 m E-W.

INDIVIDUAL AND ASSOCIATED MATERIAL:

Individual: Middle adult female. The body lay on its right side, with the head in Vessel No. 1 and the face to the W. The knees were flexed, so the legs were about parallel to the thighs. The arms were flexed so that the hands were in the vicinity of the mandible.

Associated material: Two Ik pottery vessels. No. 1 a Saxche Orange polychrome lateral-ridged tripod plate (TR. 25A:fig. 44c2) was at the N end of the grave, right side up, and the head of the corpse rested within it. No. 2, a Saxche Orange Polychrome barrel (TR. 25A:fig. 44c1) was also right side up, and was immediately SW of No. 1.

SKELETAL MATERIAL:

Primary burial, but preservation in this case was extremely poor. The skull was badly fragmented, and beyond hope of reconstruction. In shape, it seemed to be dolichocranic with no modification. Since no teeth were found, they could have been lost antemortem, or they could have been taken from the body postmortem. The latter is perhaps more likely in view of the age at death of the individual, estimated from cranial suture closure. Or perhaps this is a case of retarded suture closure.

The lower limb bones are generally heavy and robust for a female at Tikal, although less so than for most males.

DISCUSSION:

The sequential position of this burial is a problem, for later activity in the area completely altered the stratigraphy. The Ik ceramics, however, associate the burial with either Plat. 6E-1-6th or 7th. Since the burial is within the area of Str. 6E-Sub.1-1st, it could pertain to that structure abandoned when Plat. 6E-1-6th:Fl. 1 was laid. The ceramics would be consistent with intrusion into the structure when both it and the floor of Plat. 6E-1-7th were abandoned, and the floor for Plat. 6E-1-6th was laid. It could not mark abandonment of the latter floor, for by then Imix ceramics were in vogue (unless the vessels were heirlooms). Nor could it mark abandonment of Str. 6E-Sub.1-1st; this would help explain the lack of any trace of floor for that structure, but other activities might just as well have been responsible (see discussion, Bu. 131).

SEQUENTIAL POSITION:

Plat. 6E-1:TS. 15 or 17, intruded into Str. 6E-Sub.1-1st (see Table 2.338).

BURIAL 131

LOCATION:

Gp. 6E-1, N of Bu. 130, S of Bu. 129 (Fig. 148) or Sq. 6E:S161.80 E63.60. 68I/32; there is no plan drawing.

GRAVE:

Amorphous-shaped grave, with no specially constructed walls or roof. Burial measured ca. 0.90 m N-S and 0.70 m E-W, sufficient for one individual.

INDIVIDUAL AND ASSOCIATED MATERIAL:

Individual: Adult, sex unknown. The head was to the N, and the legs appear to have been flexed. Poor preservation did not permit further observation.

Associated material: None.

SKELETAL MATERIAL:

The remains were very poorly preserved, and the fill that surrounded them was extremely hard. Unfortunately, the few bones that were salvaged were misplaced during processing. Field observation suggests primary burial of an adult.

DISCUSSION:

Like Bu. 130, this one was found in an area of extensive stratigraphic disturbance. The interment seems to have postdated Str. 6E-Sub.1-1st, as it lay in part over the surviving masonry for that structure. This means also that it projected above the level of the floor for Plat. 6E-1-6th. Perhaps, then, this burial was partially responsible for the floor destruction in this area. Since the stair masonry of Str. 6E-26-2nd was missing above the burial, it is possible that the burial was intruded into these stairs. This is particularly likely, as the riser stones seem to have been set on the surface of the floor of Plat. 6E-1-6th. Therefore, it is probable, but not conclusive, that the burial was intruded into Str. 6E-26-2nd-C, following which Plat. 6E-1-2nd:Fl. 1 was laid, eliminating the basal step of the structure. The three preceding platform floors were not seen in this area because the burial destroyed them.

SEQUENTIAL POSITION:

Probably Str. 6E-26:TS. 7, intruded into Str. 6E-26-2nd-C (see Table 2.330).

BURIAL 136

LOCATION:

Gp. 6C-1, 12.80 m S, 19.65 m E of Datum 67A (Fig. 115), intruded into bedrock beneath the stairs of Str. 6C-47 (Fig. 122). 76A/30; see Fig. 166d for plan.

GRAVE:

The grave was rectangular, in part cut from bedrock. Covering stones were absent, and the grave was purposely earth filled. Burial measured 1.00 m N-S, 0.50 m E-W, just sufficient for the one body.

INDIVIDUAL AND ASSOCIATED MATERIAL:

Individual: Adult, possibly male. The body was generally supine, with the head N and face up, but turned slightly to the E. The arms were flexed, with the hands in the mouth region. Preservation was so bad that little else may be said, except that the legs were probably flexed.

Associated material: Two tiny animal long bones found in the mouth (67A-85).

SKELETAL MATERIAL:

Almost nothing survived of this burial, although it appeared to have been primary. Only two teeth were found, even though the supporting bone structure suggests a reasonably complete dentition at death. The surviving teeth, a canine and a molar, show very heavy wear, and the molar has been chipped. Both teeth show root surface caries. Nothing more can be said about these remains.

DISCUSSION:

Although erosion was extensive, enough evidence survived to suggest, but not prove, that the burial was put in place when Str. 6C-47 was built. The grave was dug into bedrock itself, which would have been difficult to do after the structure had been built. It would have been a simple matter to dig the grave at the time when bedrock was being modified to help form the steps up to Str. 6C-47.

SEQUENTIAL POSITION:

Str. 6C-47:TS. 3 (see Table 2.258).

BURIAL 138

LOCATION:

Gp. 6E-1, between Str. 6E-Sub.1 and 6E-Sub.3 (Fig. 144), or Sq. 6E:S165.70 E64.48. 68I/33; see Fig. 168d for plan.

GRAVE:

Amorphous-shaped grave. A square stone block that measured 0.25 by 0.25 by 0.09 m lay above the body. The grave was purposely earth filled. Burial measured 0.28 m N-S, 0.44 m E-W. There is some question as to whether the grave was not actually somewhat larger (see discussion).

INDIVIDUAL AND ASSOCIATED MATERIAL:

Individual: Young child, sex unknown. The head was to the W, extending beyond the stone block cover. The body was supine. The legs were flexed, and the left arm was sufficiently bent so that the hand was in the pelvic region. The right arm was entirely decomposed.

Associated material: None.

SKELETAL MATERIAL:

The tiny bones were extremely fragile and therefore badly disintegrated. Preservation was impossible. Nonetheless, a complete individual was clearly represented. The deciduous dentition was fully erupted.

DISCUSSION:

This burial was located in a heavy deposit of Early Classic material between Str. 6E-Sub.1 and Sub.3 (Table 2.320, Plat. 6E-1:LG. 4b). As noted (in section II), this material was deposited in a pit intruded through the floor of Plat. 6E-1-8th. The most plausible explanation for this pit is that it was dug to receive the burial, in which case it was considerably larger than necessary. There is no reason to suppose that the burial postdated the floor of Plat. 6E-1-7th. If it did, a few Ik sherds might have been included in the grave fill, as such sherds were consistently found in the fill for this floor.

SEQUENTIAL POSITION:

Plat. 6E-1:TS. 18; intruded into Fl. 1 of Plat. 6E-1-8th (see Table 2.338).

BURIAL 143

LOCATION:

Str. 6C-60 locus, on the floor of Ch. 6C-10:Chm. 2, against the SW wall (Fig. 130c). 66E/6; there is no plan.

GRAVE:

The burial was placed on the floor of the chultun, where it was covered with purposely placed fill (see Bu. 62, 63 in this report for analogous situations).

INDIVIDUAL AND ASSOCIATED MATERIAL:

Individuals: Young adult female (Sk. A); humerus and femur of adult, possibly female (Sk. B). Skeleton A lay on its back, head to the NNE and resting on a small stone. The legs were spread apart, so that the thighs extended laterally perpendicular to the body. The lower legs, in turn, extended perpendicular to the thighs. The arms lay on either side of the head, with the hands close together (not necessarily touching) above the head. Primary burial indicated.

Skeleton B is represented only by an extra humerus and femur, which were not recognized by the excavator as being from a skeleton separate from that of Sk. A. They seem to have been placed beside Sk. A.

Associated material: Bone ring (66E-2), probably placed in the vicinity of the head, though its exact location was not recorded. Two unused chert flakes and 6 unmodified animal teeth are probably fill items, and are included in Ch. 6C-10:LG. 2 (Table 2.288).

SKELETAL MATERIAL:

Skeleton A is that of a female who was quite tall and robust by Tikal standards. There is no evidence for or against cranial modification, as the skull was poorly preserved. A number of teeth were missing: 2 lower and 1 upper incisor, both lower and 1 upper canine, 2 lower and 2 upper premolars, and an upper molar. The state of preservation of the supporting bone does not permit a positive statement as to whether or not they were lost before or after death, but it looks as though one of the lower premolars was lost no earlier than close to the time of death. That so many teeth are missing is noteworthy in view of the young adult age of the individual. Of the remaining teeth, the anteriors show heavy wear and polish, whereas the posteriors do not, but they do show small chips accidentally detached during life. The wear pattern, then, indicates use of the teeth during life for some purpose other than eating (i.e., as a "tool"), and perhaps this had something to do with the tooth loss.

The only other observation to be made about Sk. A is that the femora are slightly bowed. All that can be said of the humerus and femur of Sk. B is that they are from a smaller adult than Sk. A.

DISCUSSION:

The first problem to be confronted is the presence of the extra humerus and femur (Sk. B). Single humerus bones are occasionally found in structure fills (e.g., this report: PD. 101), and these might be just such bones that, coincidentally, were in the debris used to fill the chultun. In this regard, fragments of a skull, humerus, radius and ulna were found in the fill of the antechamber just off the floor in the SW corner (66E-3). Not known is whether they belong to Sk. B, for they seem to have been discarded in the field before they were ever seen by a specialist. Their presence, though, does lend support to the idea that the bones are incidental inclusions of no other significance. Further support for this comes from the strong possibility that the chultun fill was originally associated with Str. 6C-60, in which case a burial may have been disturbed when the fill was placed in the chultun.

Another possibility is that the bones of Sk. B were deliberately placed as some sort of burial offering. In favor of this, at least leg bones were occasionally removed from corpses before burial, and there is some evidence to support the idea that as least leg bones were occasionally used in some kinds of offerings (for discussion see TR. 30). It is possible, therefore, that the humerus and femur were originally saved from another body buried in the area, and were later included as accoutrements in Bu. 143.

While neither of these two possible explanations for the presence of Sk. B can be ruled out, the second does seem least likely.

The second problem concerns the position of the corpse. It is possible that, at the time of burial, the knees were up and together, only to fall to the sides as fill was thrown into the chultun. Or, if the legs were tied together, or rigor mortis had not yet worn off at the time of burial, the legs may not have collapsed until after filling was complete, following considerable decay of the corpse. This seems unlikely, though, if the corpse was already surrounded by earth. Another alternative is that the body was deliberately placed in the position in which it was found, a position not unlike one that might be adopted by a woman in the act of copulation. In favor of this, the position of the arms suggests that they were placed as found. While such an overall position is unusual for Tikal burials, so is the other possibility noted above. On balance, the corpse was probably positioned as found, but there is not sufficient evidence to rule out other possibilities.

A final problem concerns the sequential position of the burial. Chultun 6C-10 seems to have been purposely filled at the time of burial. This is thought to have taken place when the nearby Str. 6C-61 was abandoned, right after the appearance of Ik ceramics.

SEQUENTIAL POSITION:

Ch. 6C-10:TS. 2 (see Table. 2.293).

BURIAL 145

LOCATION:

Gp. 6C-2, 5.18 m N, 3.19 m E of Datum 70E (Fig. 124), on the front-rear axis of Str. 6C-57 (Fig. 125) 0.53 m below the mound surface. 70E/3; see Fig. 166f for plan.

GRAVE:

A round-to-oval shaped pit in the fill of Str. 6C-57, purposefully earth filled. Burial measured 0.30 m N-S, 0.27 m E-W, sufficient for the one body.

INDIVIDUAL AND ASSOCIATED MATERIAL:

Individual: Infant, sex unknown. All the skull pieces were placed with the outside surface up, which means that this was either a two-stage or secondary burial.

Associated material: None.

SKELETAL MATERIAL:

No meaningful observations were possible, because of poor preservation. It is not known if a complete skeleton is preserved.

DISCUSSION:

The first problem is whether this was a two-stage or secondary burial. Unfortunately, a meaningful choice between these alternatives cannot be made because of poor preservation.

The second problem is whether the burial is an initial one (put in place when Str. 6C-57 was built), or whether it was later intruded into the structure. While the evidence is not conclusive, it at least favors the latter hypothesis. Generally, one would expect an initial burial to be placed on or in the base surface on which construction took place, whereas an intrusive burial is likely to be higher in the fill. As shown in Fig. 125b, the latter is the case here.

SEQUENTIAL POSITION:

Str. 6C-57:TS. 1 or 2 (see Table 2.263).

BURIAL 146

LOCATION:

Gp. 6C-1, 7.62 m S, 5.80 m E of Datum 67A (Fig. 115), beneath Str. 6C-45-5th, intruded into the floors of 6th, 7th, and 8th (Fig. 117). 67A/45; Fig. 166e for plan; 180b for photo.

GRAVE:

Roughly rectangular, this grave penetrates the floors of Str. 6C-45-6th, 7th, and 8th. There were no specially constructed walls or roof. A few small blocks of masonry lay in the grave. Burial measured 1.30 m N-S, 0.70 m E-W, just sufficient for the body.

INDIVIDUAL AND ASSOCIATED MATERIAL:

Individual: Middle adult male. The body lay on its back, with head to the N and face to the W. The arms were extended at the sides. The legs were flexed, with tibia and fibula at a right angle to the body; the knees pointed to the W. The left leg was above the right.

Associated material: Three tiny animal bones (unidentified) that were found in the mouth area.

SKELETAL MATERIAL:

The complete skeleton of a single individual was present, although most bones were disintegrated to varying degrees. Of particular note is the extensive wear apparent on the teeth. Six incisors were found, all of which were worn down into the dentine, some quite unevenly. Three canines were also extensively worn, and 6 premolars were worn and chipped. Decay is apparent on 1 canine. The other teeth are missing. The individual appears to have been slightly over average stature, with no head modification.

DISCUSSION:

The situation here is reasonably clear: the burial was surely intruded into Str. 6C-45-6th, and was sealed by the floor of 6C-45-4th-C. Therefore, it is of Early Classic date. The burial was situated beneath the S end of Str. 6C-45-5th, for which no floor surface survived. It would have been difficult and unnecessary to intrude the burial into Str. 6C-45-6th if 5th was already in existence, however. Moreover, there was no clear evidence of intrusion into 5th. Rather, it appears that the burial was placed so as to be covered by that structure. Thus, it probably immediately preceded construction of 45-5th.

The small bones in the mouth of the deceased deserve special notice, as this is an unusual feature in Tikal burials. The only other known burial from Gp. 6C-1 (No. 136) also had animal bones in the mouth of the deceased.

SEQUENTIAL POSITION:

Str. 6C-45:TS. 15, intruded into 45-6th (see Table 2.256).

BURIAL 151

LOCATION:

Gp. 6E-1, intruded into the deep fill of Str. 6E-Sub.1-2nd (Fig. 146), or Sq. 6E:S163.70 E65.55. 68I/39–41; see Fig. 168f for plan and 183c,d for photos.

GRAVE:

An amorphous-shaped grave, with no specially con-structed walls, and covered by rubble in the form of large stones. It was purposely earth filled. Burial measured 1.50 m N-S, 0.50 m E-W, just sufficient for the three bodies.

INDIVIDUAL AND ASSOCIATED MATERIAL:

Three individuals: Sk. A, a young adult, probably male; Sk. B, an infant; Sk. C, a child, perhaps about the age of Sk. B. Skeleton A lay supine, head to the N with arms at the sides and hands in the pubic region. The legs were also extended. The body as a whole was very slight-ly tipped so that its left side was slightly higher than the right. The right foot was rotated to the inside.

Skeleton B lay with its head to the N, beneath the easternmost stones that covered the burial, near the left shoulder of the adult. The body was supine. The left arm was damaged, but this may have occurred after burial, as the bones were so extremely delicate.

Skeleton C lay immediately W of Sk. B, directly be-neath the adult. The position appeared to have been iden-tical to that for Sk. B.

Associated material: None.

SKELETAL MATERIAL:

Preservation here ranges from fair to poor, but com-plete skeletons were unquestionably present. The skull of the adult is in very poor shape, so little can be said about it. The mandible and maxilla are robust, and dental health seems to have been excellent. Attrition is generally slight, but the maxillary incisors and canines were all cut to points. The individual was slightly above average stature.

The bones of Sk. B were delicate and therefore largely disintegrated. None could be preserved. The deciduous teeth of this child were unerupted except for the incisors.

Unfortunately, Sk. C was disturbed by a very large tree root that had grown through it. Therefore, no parts of the skull or teeth were found. This child appears to have been of the same size as Sk. B, suggesting that they were of the same age. If so, they may well have been twins.

DISCUSSION:

The meaning of this collection of individuals is an enig-ma. Twins seem to be indicated by the juvenile remains. One might suspect a burial of twins with their mother, but the adult appears to have been a male. Was he perhaps their father? Perhaps, upon his death, his twins were sacrificed for his grave, for they certainly had not died at the time of birth. On the other hand, it is unlikely that the adult was a person of much importance, in view of the lack of grave goods, and so sacrifice seems improbable. Perhaps the ex-planation is that all three died from some disease.

The sequential position of this burial is not immedi-ately obvious. It was deep in the fill of Str. 6E-Sub.1-2nd, a Preclassic structure. Sherds from vessels of the Imix Com-plex were found in the grave fill, however, and so indicate a Late Classic intrusion. Thus the burial had to be subsequent to construction of Plat. 6E-1-6th:Fl. 1. The great depth of the burial suggests interment prior to much buildup of de-bris E of the location of Plat. 6E-1:U. 14 (Fig. 148). Oth-erwise, there would have been no need to dig down so far. The most likely time would have been when Plat. 6E-1-5th was constructed, or shortly thereafter. This was the first ar-chitectural development to be constructed after the start of Imix ceramic production. Burial 151 lay just outside of the location of the E wall for 5th, and would have been only some 0.40–0.50 m beneath the informal occupation surface associated with 5th. After this time, considerable debris ac-cumulated here, and burial at such a depth would have be-come increasingly improbable.

SEQUENTIAL POSITION:

Plat. 6E-1:TS. 13 (see Table 2.338).

BURIAL 152

LOCATION:

Gp. 6E-1, beneath the SW corner of the steps for Str. 6E-26-2nd and intruded into Plat. 6E-1-6th:Fl. 1 (Fig. 147), or Sq. 6E:S161.90 E562.60. 68G/20; Fig. 168e for plan; 182d and 183a,b, for photos.

GRAVE:

The grave was partially formed by the masonry of the stairway for Str. 6E-26-2nd and an intrusive cut into Plat. 6E-1-6th:Fl. 1. It was generally rectangular in shape, and was earth filled, with a large masonry block 0.46 by 0.23 by 0.13 m, placed over the bones. The block originally was well dressed, but one corner was considerably battered. This suggests secondary use, and it would not have been out of place in the wall of the preceding 26-3rd. Burial measured 0.56 m N-S by 0.66 m E-W, just sufficient for the remains.

INDIVIDUAL AND ASSOCIATED MATERIAL:

Individual: A young adult female. Clearly a secondary burial, as evidenced by the following facts: the occlusal surfaces of the upper and lower teeth were in the same plane; a phalanx was found where the palate should have been; pieces of skull were scattered at random; the ribs were not all present, nor were they articulated with verte-brae; the limb bones were not articulated; phalanges were few in number and were scattered around, some amongst the skull fragments.

Associated material: Four pottery vessels of the Manik Complex. No. 1, a round-side bowl with flat base (TR. 25A:fig. 35b4) was positioned W of the coverstone, on its side. No. 2, an Aguila Orange round-side bowl with ring base (TR. 25A:fig. 35b3), was inverted S of the coverstone. No. 3, a small Aguila Orange everted-rim tripod dish (TR. 25A:fig. 35b1) was inverted beneath No. 2. No. 4, a dish similar to No. 3 (TR. 25A:fig. 35b2), was upright, N of No. 1, and had been chipped prior to burial here.

SKELETAL MATERIAL:

This was a secondary burial, which accounts for the fragmentary nature of the remains (Fig. 183b). There seem to be two extra mandibular incisors that do not belong with the other teeth. The dentition on the lower right is intact and displays reasonably good dental health. The molars on the lower left, however, appear to have been lost (with periodontal abscesses) recently before death. Root surface caries are apparent on the upper left first molar and central incisor, as well as the lower right central incisor. The lower right first premolar shows coronal caries, slight periodontitis is indicated on the anterior teeth, and attrition generally is marked. The left lateral upper incisor exhibits lingual extension of its lateral border to form a barrel-shaped tooth.

The only other observation that may be made about this individual is that she seems to have been of exceptionally small stature.

DISCUSSION:

The sequential position of this burial is clear. At the time of construction of Str. 6E-26-2nd-D, Plat. 6E-1-6th:-Fl. 1 was cut into and the burial put in place. The stones for the SE corner of the stairs were then placed in the intrusive cut in the floor S and W of the burial itself, thereby forming walls for the grave.

Reasons have already been given for considering this a secondary burial. In addition, the burial vessels are Manik, although the burial penetrated a later floor beneath which Ik sherds were sealed. The question therefore arises as to the original place of interment of these remains. On this, one can only speculate. The most likely place of origin was Str. 6E-Sub.1-1st, which was occupied through the Early Classic period. At the time of the redeposition of the burial, the E retaining wall of Plat. 6E-1-5th, which ran past the locale of Str. 6E-Sub.1-1st, was torn out for a new wall. In this process, an older burial may have been disturbed, and then reinterred in new construction.

SEQUENTIAL POSITION:

Primary: probably Str. 6E-Sub.1:TS. 2. Secondary: Str. 6E-26:TS. 11 (see Tables 2.330 and 2.333).

BURIAL 153

LOCATION:

Gp. 6E-1, intruded into Str. 6E-Sub.1-2nd (Fig. 144), or Sq. 6E:S164.20 E65.08. 68I/42; see Fig. 169a for plan.

GRAVE:

Amorphous-shaped grave, covered by irregular stones. It was not purposely earth filled. The burial measured 1.20 m N-S, 0.47 m E-W, just sufficient for the one individual.

INDIVIDUAL AND ASSOCIATED MATERIAL:

Individual: Middle adult male. The body was supine, with the head N but turned to face W. The right arm was extended, while the left was bent at the elbow so the forearm rested on the abdomen. The knees were raised and slightly tipped to the W so that the left knee was above the right.

Associated material: None.

SKELETAL MATERIAL:

The ends of all the long bones had disintegrated, and the skull was in a poor state of preservation. Nevertheless, primary burial was clearly indicated. A single tooth (a canine) was the only one recovered. Presumably, the others were lost antemortem. There was no head modification.

DISCUSSION:

The sequential position of this burial is impossible to establish with certainty. It was clearly intruded into Str. 6E-Sub.1-2nd. Sherds among the covering stones suggest that the time of intrusion was Early Classic, while Str. 6E-Sub.1-1st was in use. More than this cannot be said.

SEQUENTIAL POSITION:

Probably Str. 6E-Sub.1:TS. 2 (see Table. 2.333).

BURIAL 158

LOCATION:

Gp. 5F-1, 2.15 S, 18.70 E of Datum 71F (Fig. 104), 2.26 m NE of Str. 5F-Sub.1, in the midden that fills Plat. 5F-1:U. 5 (Fig. 104). 71F/50; Fig. 167c for plan.

GRAVE:

Apparently, a pit was dug in the midden to the E of Str. 5F-Sub.1, which was then lined with rough-cut stones. Following the interment, the grave was filled and covered with midden material. The grave measured 0.67 m N-S and 0.68 m E-W; sufficient for the one body.

INDIVIDUAL AND ASSOCIATED MATERIAL:

Individual: Middle adult male. The body was buried in a flexed, seated position, facing E. The arms were extended inside the legs with the hands (clenched into fists) behind the ankles. Primary burial.

Associated material: One whole and two reconstructible pottery vessels of the Tzec Complex. In addition, PD. 108 might also pertain to this burial. A Polvero Black outcurving-side dish (TR. 25A:fig. 2a3) was inverted over the head. A large sherd from an Ahchab Red-on-buff cuspidor (TR. 25A:fig. 2a1) lay just E of the body, and another large sherd from an Ahchab Red-on-buff: Alapp Variety plate (TR. 25A:fig. 2a2) was 0.17 m S of the grave, and a patch of cinnabar was 0.17 m to the W.

SKELETAL MATERIAL:

The subject of this burial was an individual of slightly more than average stature, by Tikal Preclassic standards (. Despite great postmortem distortion of the skull, there is no evidence for artificial cranial modification. There had been no tooth loss, but a heavy buildup of calculus is apparent. About half of the lower right central incisor was broken off anciently. The teeth generally show moderate wear; a bit more on the anterior than other teeth. Interestingly, this individual had an open bite (Class I, Type 3 malocclusion).

DISCUSSION:

The sequential position of this burial is reasonably straightforward; it was put in place after a considerable amount of trash had accumulated E of Str. 5F-Sub.1. This was probably just prior to TS. 9 of Plat. 5F-1, by which time Chuen ceramics had come into production, for the burial is in the upper portion of the Tzec-related portion of the midden. Since the trash in which the burial was placed appears to have been discarded by those who made use of Sub.1-2nd, it is likely that the person interred was also one of those who made use of the structure. It is tempting to link this burial to some unknown renovation of Sub.1-2nd. The apparent association of the later part of the midden with Sub.1-1st, and the position of the burial high in the earlier part of the midden, suggests that the burial postdates the earliest version of Sub.1.

SEQUENTIAL POSITION:

Probably Plat. 5F-1:TS. 10 (see Table 2.221).

BURIAL 161

LOCATION:

Gp. 6E-1, intruded into Fl. 1 of Plat. 6E-1-3rd (see Fig. 148), or Sq. 6E:S162.42 E60.60. 68I/50; see Fig. 169b for plan.

GRAVE:

This consists of a hole (U. 25) cut through Plat. 6E-1-3rd:Fl. 1 that measured 0.30 m N-S, 0.20 m E-W. Essentially oval in shape, it was purposely filled.

INDIVIDUAL AND ASSOCIATED MATERIAL:

Individual: Young child, sex unknown. The burial faced S. If it was primary, then the legs and arms were tied behind the back, and the body was pushed into the small grave with the head up.

Associated material: None.

SKELETAL MATERIAL:

These bones were badly broken up, so little can be said. The maxilla contained 3 deciduous molars; 2 deciduous canines; and a deciduous incisor. The mandible contained a complete compliment of deciduous molars and canines. The fate of the incisors is a moot question. Perhaps they exfoliated for the permanent teeth. Although the first permanent molar was not yet erupted, it was imminent. The permanent incisors, formed in the crypts, were shovel-shaped. The laterals had vertical grooves on each that ran from two slight tics on the occlusal surface.

DISCUSSION:

The burial is peculiar in that the child was bundled up so tightly and shoved into so small a hole. There is the possibility that it was related to some sort of ceremony connected with several holes that were dug through the floor surfaces. This activity marked the start of construction of Plat. 6E-1-2nd.

SEQUENTIAL POSITION:

Plat. 6E-1:TS. 5, intruded into Plat. 6E-1-3rd (Table 2.338).

BURIAL 169

LOCATION:

Gp. 5D-1, 17.85 m S of Datum 76B (Fig. 98); beneath the front part of Str. 5D-7-1st, on the front-rear axis (Fig. 93). 76B/5; see Fig. 166a for plan.

GRAVE:

A chultun-like excavation into the natural marl. The entrance, square in plan, is about 0.60 m deep; an opening in its W wall leads to the deeper burial chamber. This is larger than required for burial, measuring 1.20 m N-S, 0.93 m E-W. The grave was purposely earth filled.

INDIVIDUAL AND ASSOCIATED MATERIAL:

Individual: Adult, probably male (see discussion). The body lay with its head to the S, on its left side, with the legs slightly flexed at the hips, tightly flexed at the knees. The arms were probably extended. Primary burial.

Associated material: Major portions of two Manik pottery vessels: No. 1, probably a Dos Arroyos Ceramic Group basal-flange dish, round-side variety (TR. 25A:fig. 37*a*1) was upright N of the knees; No. 2, possibly a Balanza Black unusual cylindrical tripod (TR. 25A:fig. 37*a*2) lay on its side E of No. 1.

SKELETAL MATERIAL:

There is little to say, since so little remains. The field drawing, however, shows sufficient skeletal parts to indicate that a whole body was probably represented.

DISCUSSION:

The bones could not be salvaged for inspection by a physical anthropologist, so an adequate diagnosis of sex could not be made. At Tikal, the diagnosed remains from burials such as these are usually those of males, so the odds favor it in this case.

The condition of the two fragments of the Dos Arroyos dish (Vessel No. 1) merits special comment, for they are differentially weathered. What is suggested is a vessel that had been in use for enough time to become broken prior to its inclusion in the burial. Even at that, at least one other piece of Vessel No. 1 was apparently lost prior to its inclusion. This seems suggestive of a death where the survivors could not afford much in the way of burial objects. The two broken vessels may be compared, for example, with the six vessels of the somewhat similar Bu. 35 (TR. 19:135 and TR. 25A:fig. 27c, 28a).

The dating of this burial presents a problem, for the earliest floor that survives (Plat. 5D-29:U. 7) postdates the appearance of Ik ceramics. The Manik vessels might be regarded as heirlooms placed in the grave at that time, on account of their broken condition. While this grave is peculiar in that it is the only such grave known at Tikal with its antechamber to the E, rather than the W, such chultun-like graves were not constructed elsewhere at Tikal after the appearance of Ik ceramics. Given the normal location of burials in chultun-like graves on the front-rear axis of associated structures (TR. 21), the best interpretation of this situation is that Bu. 169, in spite of its peculiarity, was placed on the front-rear axis of a structure (5D-7-6th) built above it, and that this predated the appearance of Ik ceramics. At a later time, this structure was completely demolished (for an analogous situation, see Str. 4F-8 and Bu. 35:TR. 19: 36–37, 135).

SEQUENTIAL POSITION:

Str. 5D-7:TS. 13, initial to Str. 5D-7-6th (see Table 2.191).

BURIAL 170

LOCATION:

Gp. 5D-1, 16.30 m S, 6.45 m W of Datum 76B (Fig. 98); 0.58 m W of the NW corner of Str. 5D-7-3rd (Fig. 93), intruded through Plat. 5D-29:U. 8. 76B/14; see Fig. 166b for plan.

GRAVE:

A roughly oval cut into the natural marl, 0.16 to 0.39 m deep. The grave was purposely filled with earth, which was covered by a stratum of medium-sized, unshaped stones (see Fig. 94). Burial measured 0.95 m E-W and 0.47 m N-S, sufficient only for the one body.

INDIVIDUAL AND ASSOCIATED MATERIAL:

Individual: Subadult female. The body lay on its right side with the right arm extended beneath the body. The left arm was flexed at the elbow and wrist, with the hand parallel to the body and in front of it. The legs were arranged more or less perpendicular to the body, with the knees tightly flexed and the heels over the right hand. The head was to the E, and faced N. Primary burial.

Associated material: None.

SKELETAL MATERIAL:

The bones of this skeleton were very badly preserved, to the extent that most foot and hand bones, vertebrae, ribs, scapulae, clavicles, ilia, and long bones had decayed. The position of the remnants indicates that a whole articulated skeleton was once here. Enough of the bones survived to permit diagnosis of sex with moderate, though not complete, confidence.

DISCUSSION:

The stratigraphy is clear; the grave was dug into Plat. 5D-29:U. 8, and covered by the fill of Plat. 5D-29:U. 10. The latter is continuous with the fill of Str. 5D-7-3rd. Although the burial is in line with Bu. 169, which may have been on the front-rear axis of its associated structure, Bu. 170 did not have an axial relationship to Str. 5D-7-3rd nor to the preceding 4th (see discussion of Bu. 171).

SEQUENTIAL POSITION:

Str. 5D-7:TS. 7 (see Table 2.191).

BURIAL 171

LOCATION:

Gp. 5D-1, 16.35 m S, 4.60 m W of Datum 76B (Fig. 98); beneath the rear portion of Str. 5D-7-4th (Fig. 93). 76B/17; see Fig. 166c for plan.

GRAVE:

The grave was dug into the natural marl to a depth of 0.60 to 0.90 m, with a shape that might be described as truncated-oval. It was purposely earth filled, and a large block of masonry was placed over the western portion of the grave (see Fig. 94). Burial measured 1.12 m N-S, 0.90 m E-W; essentially sufficient for the one body.

INDIVIDUAL AND ASSOCIATED MATERIAL:

Individual: Old adult male. The body lay on its back, though tipped slightly onto its left side, with head to the N. The legs were tightly flexed, and the arms were flexed at the elbows, with the right hand near the knees and the left near the right elbow. Primary burial.

Associated material: An irregularly shaped jade bead (Field No. 76B-7) may have been in the mouth.

SKELETAL MATERIAL:

This skeleton was exceedingly well preserved, so that age and sex diagnoses are firm. The individual was unusually tall for his time, and quite robust (including an occipital torus). His upper incisor teeth had been notched in their lateral corners, but there was no artificial modification of head form. Squatting facets could be noted on the tibiae, and his femora were bowed.

DISCUSSION:

Stratigraphically, there is no distinguishable break between the grave fill and that of Str. 5D-7-4th above. On this basis alone, the burial would be interpreted as contemporary with construction of that structure. The one problem is that the grave fill contained only Manik sherds. The overlying fill contained Ik and Imix, in addition to Manik sherds. Still, the stratigraphy seems clear, and placement of Bu. 171 when 7-4th was built would explain why the excavations found no surviving architecture for a Str. 5D-7-5th and 6th. So, it seems best to regard the lack of Ik or Imix sherds in the grave fill as purely coincidental.

It is not known if the burial was placed on the front-rear axis of Str. 5D-7-4th, which covered it, or 7-5th, which preceded it. It may have been on the axis of both, for it is due W of Bu. 169, which is assumed to have been on the axis of 7-6th. Moreover, the appearance of the ruin mound suggests that the axis of Str. 5D-7-1st falls almost on the line of Bu. 169 and 171. On the other hand, the N

end of 7-3rd was very close to the locus of these burials, so that its front-rear axis must have been a considerable distance to the S. Moreover, Bu. 170, which was interred when 3rd was built, is on the same line as Bu. 169 and 171. Consequently, it was not on the axis of the structure built at the time of interment. At some time, therefore, the front-rear axis of Str. 5D-7 was shifted to the S after demolition of 6th, but by the time of construction of 3rd. Later, it was shifted northward again.

Although it cannot be proved, the most likely time for the southward shift to have taken place was when 5th was built. For this, the westward-facing 6th was totally demolished, and replaced by the eastward-facing 5th. Such extensive demolition, coupled with a basic reorientation of the structure, could easily have included a change in location of the axis. Thus, Bu. 171 is regarded as non-axial, as was the succeeding Bu. 170.

The battered appearance of the otherwise highly polished jade bead deserves special comment. It suggests prior use before it was eventually placed with a burial.

SEQUENTIAL POSITION:

Str. 5D-7:TS. 9; intruded into Str. 5D-7-5th at the time of construction of 4th (see Table 2.191).

BURIAL 189

LOCATION:

Gp. 4G-3, at the bottom of ceramic test pit through the E end of Str. 4G-7. 103C/5; see Fig. 164f for plan; 179c for photo.

GRAVE:

The specially prepared grave was walled on either side by large, rectangular blocks of masonry. Over the grave were placed four other large, rectangular blocks; some of them laid nearly flat, and some nearly vertical. Over these were a number of smaller irregular stones. The grave was incidentally, rather than purposely, filled with earth. The grave measured 1.65 m N-S and 0.70 m E-W, sufficient only for the one body.

INDIVIDUAL AND ASSOCIATED MATERIAL:

Individual: Adult, sex unknown. The body lay on its left side, head to the N, facing E. Inverted beneath the head was pottery vessel No. 1 (see below). The legs were tightly flexed up against the abdomen. The arms, however, were extended, with the hands (together) in the pelvic region.

Associated material: Three Imix pottery vessels: No. 1, a Palmar Orange Polychrome tripod plate with the feet removed (TR. 25A:fig. 80d3) inverted beneath the head.

No. 2, a Mex Composite slightly outcurving-side bowl with worn feet (TR. 25A:fig. 80*d*2), upright immediately E and slightly N of No. 1. No. 3, a Palmar Orange Polychrome cylinder (TR. 25A:fig. 80*d*1), was upright just S of No. 2.

SKELETAL MATERIAL:

Photographs of this burial show an essentially complete skeleton. Apparently, none of the skeletal material reached the laboratory.

DISCUSSION:

The elaboration of this grave, and its placement deep beneath Str. 4G-7, combine to suggest that the interment is initial to some architectural development of that structure. This could also be terminal to some earlier architectural development, but the available data are insufficient to confirm this. Data do suggest an Imix occupation (between AD 700 and 869) of Gp. 4G-3.

SEQUENTIAL POSITION:

No time span defined (see discussion).

BURIAL 205

LOCATION:

Gp. 1D-7, 1.56 m deep in test pit, just under the W wall of Str. 1D-7, the northernmost structure in the group (Fig. 161). 136H/9; see Fig. 169d for plan.

GRAVE:

A roughly rectangular pit was dug slightly into the bedrock, and covered over with four very rough stones. The grave was purposely earth filled and measured 1.30 m N-S, 0.55 m E-W, sufficient for only one body.

INDIVIDUAL AND ASSOCIATED MATERIAL:

Individual: Middle adult male. The body was placed on its left side, head to the N, facing E, and a bit down. The legs were tightly flexed at the knees, and arranged more or less perpendicular to the body. The arms were extended, with the hands apparently together midway along the thighs. Primary burial.

Associated material: A notched pebble (TR. 27B:fig. 118l) near the knees probably is an incidental fill item unrelated to the burial.

SKELETAL MATERIAL:

Some time after death, the skull was crushed to one side, but nonetheless artificial modification is evident. Overall, the individual appears robust, with a stature probably close to the average for males who lived between

AD 550 and 869 (TR. 30). In keeping with a somewhat advanced age, a number of teeth are missing: 2 molars; 1 premolar; 2 canines; and 5 incisors (including the laterals).

DISCUSSION:

The excavations at this locus uncovered the remains of two, possibly three floors (the excavator's notes are not clear as to whether the lowermost "floor" was plaster, or a layer of packed earth). The known structure wall postdates the uppermost floor, which in turn is dated by Ik ceramics. It is the floor beneath this (the second one down) that seems to have sealed the burial (Fig. 161). Nothing later than Manik ceramics were sealed by this floor, but there were possible Ik or Imix sherds in the burial fill, and in a thin stratum of packed, gray earth that lies directly on bedrock. Given these facts, a reasonable interpretation is that none of the floors predate Ik ceramics, with the deepest perhaps being laid shortly after production of Ik ceramics began. Burial 205, therefore, probably was interred while Ik ceramics were in use. It predates the known architectural development of the structure above it, but there could be architectural developments as yet unknown nearby.

SEQUENTIAL POSITION:

No time spans defined (see discussion).

BURIAL 208

LOCATION:

Gp. 1D-2, 0.59 m deep in test pit, just E of Str. 1D-17, the northernmost structure in the group. 146J/8; see Fig. 169c for plan.

GRAVE:

Appears to consist of a pit dug into the earth, sufficient for the one body. Burial measured 0.90 m N-S, 0.35 m E-W.

INDIVIDUAL AND ASSOCIATED MATERIAL:

Individual: Old adult female. The body was placed on its right side, head to the N, facing W. The legs were tightly flexed; the arms were flexed with the right hand by the mouth, and the left hand near the middle of the right forearm. Primary burial.

Associated material: None.

SKELETAL MATERIAL:

The skeleton indicates a female of average stature by Tikal standards. In keeping with her advanced age, all teeth seem to have been lost antemortem. Probably, the molars were the first to go, for alveolar resorption is most complete in that area. The skull shows pseudocircular modification, and the femura are markedly bowed. A deep bicipital groove on the humeri is unusual, in that this is more frequent for Tikal males than females (see discussion in TR. 30).

DISCUSSION:

As noted in section II, the test pit penetrates what appears to be occupation debris. The three 0.20 m levels above the burial contained Manik, Ik, and Imix ceramics, although Manik sherds were most common from 0.40 to 0.60 m, and Ik from 0.20 to 0.40 m. What is suggested is normal stratigraphy that has been disturbed. The most logical source of that disturbance would have been the burial. Consistent is possible Eznab material near the burial itself. Thus, while it cannot be conclusively proven, it seems more likely than not that the burial was intruded in terminal Classic times.

SEQUENTIAL POSITION:

No time spans defined (see discussion).

BURIAL 212

LOCATION:

Str. 4C-34 locus, beneath what may be the S portion of Str. 4C-34 or a plaza just in front of it; Sq. 4C:S260 E500. 140A/2; see Fig. 167a,b, for plan and section.

GRAVE:

Amorphous shape with no specially constructed grave. Burial measured 1.28 m N-S, 0.60 m E-W, just large enough to accommodate the body and associated materials.

INDIVIDUAL AND ASSOCIATED MATERIAL:

Individual: Adult male. The body lay on its back, with the head to the N facing up and very slightly to the E. The upper arms were extended beside the body, with the forearms at about 90° to them, so that the hands rested on the abdomen. The wrists were together, and the hands extended beyond one another. The legs were arranged so as to be roughly perpendicular to the body. The knees, tightly flexed, were bent over to the E, and the heels were pulled up right beneath (S of) the pelvis. Primary burial.

Associated material: Three pottery vessels, probably of the late Imix Complex. No. 1, a Palmar Ceramic Group tripod plate with feet removed (TR. 25A:fig. 97*d*3) was placed upright, S of (and against) the legs. No. 2, a Palmar Ceramic Group Barrel (TR. 25A:fig. 97*d*2) was placed upright inside No. 1. No. 3, a Palmar Ceramic Group cylinder (TR. 25A:fig. 97*d*1) was placed upright immediately E (and against) No. 1.

SKELETAL MATERIAL:

The excavator's drawing clearly indicates that a complete skeleton was present, though little of it could be utilized in later analysis. Hence, meaningful statements are not possible, save that sex diagnosis is reasonably sure, and that all teeth were missing. Whether they were lost ante- or postmortem is not known.

DISCUSSION:

As will be indicated by the general burial discussion in TR. 20B, this burial is much like a number of Imix-related burials from residential situations. Unfortunately, excavation was not sufficient to show its precise relation to Str. 4C-34. The burial is sealed by a tamped surface (U. 1), which could be the remains of a lower surface for a multiple-level, rectangular platform. Conversely, it could be a plaza surface in front of the structure. Construction of Str. 4C-34:U. 1 in late Imix times is indicated. Manik sherds from the fill, however, suggest that Str. 4C-34 may have had a predecessor at this locus.

SEQUENTIAL POSITION:

No time spans defined (see discussion).

BURIAL 218

LOCATION:

Str. 6F-62 locus, in Plat. 6F-1, its E end directly S of Or. 1 of Ch. 6F-3 (Fig. 156a). 72D, partial excavation included in Lot 2; no plan was drawn.

GRAVE:

Rectangular grave excavated from bedrock, and covered by five well-cut, rectangular stone slabs. All were of the same size, approximately 0.52 by 0.28 m. Their thickness was not measured. The slabs lay at an approximate 45° angle, with their S edges partly in the bedrock cut and their N edges resting on fill, 0.25 to 0.30 m above bedrock. Evidently, the grave was purposely earth filled. The grave measured 1.52 m E-W and 0.46 m N-S, sufficient for only one body.

INDIVIDUAL AND ASSOCIATED MATERIAL:

Individual: Unknown, but probably an adult given the size of the grave. The body was not exposed by excavation, but based on a series of 12 burials reported here in formal roofed graves (Nos. 54, 55, 65, 66, 68, 70, 170, 171, and 205), and in TR. 19 (Nos. 20, 30, 42), the body was probably buried in an extended or partially extended position. The length of graves in such instances ranges from 1.20 to 1.85 m (average 1.62 m). This is compared to a range of 0.95 to 1.60 m (average 1.19 m) for formal walled and roofed graves with bodies in a flexed or partially flexed position.

Associated material: Unknown. Such graves frequently contain some objects placed with the deceased (TR. 20B). In the present instance, a large piece of a Preclassic florero-shaped jar (72D-1) was found beneath one of the two stone slabs that were removed at the E end of the burial. Given the abundance of large Preclassic sherds in the Op. 72D excavations, however, this may be a fill item rather than an intentionally placed burial object.

SKELETAL MATERIAL:

Except for removal of two stone slabs, the burial remains unexcavated. Therefore, nothing can be said of the skeleton.

DISCUSSION:

Although this feature was not excavated, and no skeletal material is known, its resemblance to the graves of a number of residential burials makes it reasonably clear that this, too, is a burial (see especially Bu. 54, 65, 66, 68, 70, 171, and 205, this report; Bu. 30 in TR. 19). These fall into the category of formal walled and roofed graves (TR. 19:142–145), which are known from Preclassic and later times. This particular one, however, has its closest affinities to Imix related formal walled and roofed graves. For this reason, the Preclassic jar sherd noted above is thought to be a fill item, rather than an intentionally placed burial object. As noted, this is consistent with a large quantity of "midden quality" Preclassic sherds in the excavations. Moreover, a date for this burial between AD 700 and 869 "makes sense," given a probable date of construction and use of Plat. 6F-1, and probably Str. 6F-62, in this time period. It also accords with the slight overlap of one of the coverstones of Or. 1 of Ch. 6F-3, which suggests the burial postdates the abandonment of the chultun. As to the precise relation of the burial to the plaza, it could be initial or intrusive. The tilted position of the slabs, which rest in fill on their high ends, suggests intrusion into existing plaza fill.

SEQUENTIAL POSITION:

Though not absolutely certain, probably TS. 4 or the very start of TS. 3 of Plat. 6F-1 (see Table 2.346).

BURIAL 219

LOCATION:

Gp. 7F-2, in Str. 7F-90, just inside (W) of the front wall (U. 1) of Str. 7F-90-2nd (Fig. 158). 66Z/unexcavated.

GRAVE:

Apparently rectangular grave, and covered by at least four well-cut, rectangular stone slabs. The grave was longest N-S, but its full length is not known. It appears to have been large enough for only one body.

INDIVIDUAL AND ASSOCIATED MATERIAL:

Individual: Unknown, but probably an adult buried in an extended or partially extended position (see, for example, Bu. 218).

Associated material: Unknown. Such graves often contain some objects placed with the deceased (TR. 20B).

SKELETAL MATERIAL:

Unknown (unexcavated).

DISCUSSION:

Although this feature was not excavated, and no skeletal material is known, its resemblance to the graves of a number of residential burials makes it reasonably clear that this, too, is a burial (see discussion of Bu. 218). Just how it relates to the architectural sequence of Str. 7F-90 is not known. It could have been placed at any time from original construction to final abandonment.

SEQUENTIAL POSITION:

At any time from TS. 5 through 1 of Str. 7F-90 (Table 2.356).

3. *Problematical Deposits*

PROBLEMATICAL DEPOSIT 64

LOCATION:

Gp. 2G-1, 15 m N and 23.35 m E of Datum 24C (Fig. 27), about 0.68 m E of Bu. 50 (see Fig. 22). In the fill of Str. 2G-59-2nd, on the front-rear axis of Str. 2G-59-1st. 24C/71; see Fig. 171b plan.

CONTENT AND ARRANGEMENT:

Incomplete adult human osseous remains, and one unusual grooved type, unusual outcurving-side vessel angling to base (TR. 25A:fig. 132a). The pottery vessel was placed N of a left temporal bone. Femur and tibia shafts extend S of the temporal, along with a few miscellaneous bone scraps.

DISCUSSION:

This would be placed in the burial series, except that the quantity and arrangement of the bones suggest that a complete skeleton was not represented. It does not seem that poor preservation alone was responsible for this, particularly in comparison with nearby Bu. 50 and 53 in the same structure. Those were much closer to the surface and, therefore, more vulnerable. Moreover, the femur shaft was much too close to the temporal bone to have been in correct anatomical position. A reasonable explanation for this deposit is that it is a secondary burial. A likely possibility is that an earlier interment was disturbed in the course of construction of Str. 2G-59-2nd. Since the structure seems to have been favored through time as a place to be buried, this could easily have happened when 59-3rd was extensively razed for replacement by 2nd.

Problematical Deposit 64 was located in the fill of 2nd, and so is placed in TS. 5. It probably was not intruded into 2nd.

SEQUENTIAL POSITION:

Str. 2G-59:TS. 5 (see Table 2.49).

PROBLEMATICAL DEPOSIT 65

LOCATION:

Gp. 3F-1, Ch. 3F-6, on the floor of Chm. 2. 24S/2, 3; see Fig. 44a for plan; 176d and 177a for photos.

CONTENT AND ARRANGEMENT:

Five pottery vessels: Vessel No. 1, unnamed red type, wide-mouth jar (TR. 25A:fig. 132*b*5); Vessel No. 2, unnamed black-on-red type, wide-mouth jar (TR. 25A:fig. 132*b*3); Vessel No. 3, unnamed type, round-side bowl (TR. 25A:132*b*1); Vessel No. 4, unnamed red type wide-mouth jar (TR. 25A:fig. 132*b*4); Vessel No. 5, unnamed black-on-red type wide mouth jar (TR. 25A:fig. 132*b*2).

ARRANGEMENT:

Vessel 1 lay on its side between Vessels 2 and 5. Vessel 2 was inverted by the S wall of the chultun, directly opposite the entrance and 9 cm S of Vessel 1. Vessel 3 was upright, 0.14 m W of Vessel 1. Vessel 4 was inverted, 0.22 m W of Vessel 1, and 0.06 m S of Vessel 3. Vessel 5 was upright, 3 cm N of Vessel 1, on a line with the entrance and Vessel 2.

DISCUSSION:

The two upright vessels were filled with earth, and contained a few tiny animal bones as well. The other vessels were empty. As noted in the discussion of Ch. 3F-6, the evidence indicated that the earth within the chultun washed in naturally after abandonment. It seems that this was responsible for filling the two vessels. The bones most likely were left by small, burrowing animals. Thus,

the vessels must have been left empty in a haphazard manner by their owner, prior to the filling of the chultun.

The vessels are unlike anything else found at Tikal, but designs hint at a Postclassic date (TR. 25A:fig. 132). Judging by form, they appear to be storage vessels. Because of this, and because of their seemingly haphazard arrangement, it is tempting to see them as left in an underground storage chamber, empty, but ready for use at any time. Then, for some unknown reason, their owner left. Such an hypothesis would be on firmer ground were it not for the apparently foreign origin of the vessels, and that the structures of Gp. 3F-1 were apparently in ruins when these vessels were placed in the chultun. The possibilities cannot be ruled out that the vessels represent some sort of votive offering, or that a traveler found this a convenient place to leave the vessels temporarily, and meant to retrieve them later.

SEQUENTIAL POSITION:

Ch. 3F-6:TS. 2 (Table 2.85).

PROBLEMATICAL DEPOSIT 72

LOCATION:

Str. 5C-56 locus, in Chm. 10 of Ch. 5C-8 (see Fig. 70a). Included in 26H/1–3; see Figs. 71a and b for sections.

CONTENT AND ARRANGEMENT:

Fragments from the skeleton of a single, young adult male, some of which were charred, were found in a deposit of apparent domestic refuse (Ch. 5C-8:U. 3–6, see Fig. 71). These bones, including an innominate, a number of skull fragments, and several pieces of long bones, were randomly scattered amongst other trash that included charcoal and remains of corn and beans.

DISCUSSION:

Chamber 10 was filled with material from the same source as that used for the rest of Ch. 5C-8 (see discussion in section II), as indicated by a number of interlot ceramic fits. A few human bones from other chambers (Cat. Nos. 26A-16/1; 26A-17/1; 26B-10/1; 26B-21/2; 26B-25/4; 26B-29/5; and 26B-40/10) almost surely relate to PD. 72 (see discussion of PD. 224).

It is quite possible that Chm. 10 was specially dug to receive PD. 72. It differs slightly in form from Chm. 7 and 9, which, like 10, open from the floor of Chm. 3. It even shows an intriguing, albeit faint, resemblance to the grave of Bu. 54 (compare Fig. 71 and 23a). Moreover, it is positioned in front of the entrance to a lateral chamber, as 7 and 9 are not. Finally, there is no sill around its entrance as there are for Chm. 7 and 9.

This deposit is difficult to interpret. One possibility is that it is a redeposited household burial. That such burials were sometimes reinterred is indicated by Bu. 152, in Gp. 6E-1 (this report). Supporting this possibility is the overall nature of the debris that fills the pit. The bulk of the artifacts are those that were basic essentials to all households (to be described in TR. 20B; in the interim see Haviland and Moholy-Nagy 1992:55). Five of the ten basic types are present: chert cores, used and unused flakes, prismatic blades (all used) and a metate fragment, 32 items in all. In addition, the thin biface, censer, and hammer stone (TR. 27B:fig. 98) are common household tools. A jade bead, and a celt (TR. 27B:fig. 100p) are items that sometimes are found around houses. These facts, coupled with the presence of ash, charcoal, and food remains (corn, beans, 44 animal bones, 15 other possible animal bones and a freshwater snail shell) strongly suggest household refuse. Unusual items are a perforated animal tooth; a bone-rasp fragment (TR. 27B:fig. 124c); 5 scarcely altered (pierced) Marginella shells (but note that they are not Spondylus); and an unmodified Strombus shell fragment, but such items are not totally foreign to household trash. Most of the animal bone and artifacts are burned—as might be expected in a household context. Finally, not all of the human bones are burned, nor do they resemble bones from cremations elsewhere in North America.

As discussed in section II, it appears that the Maya used the refuse, masonry, and fill of a house to fill Ch. 5C-8; given the usual placement of burials beneath and near houses, it is likely that a primary interment would have been disturbed in the process.

There are some problems with this interpretation. First, since chultuns were sometimes used as convenient spots for burial (e.g., this report, Ch. 2G-2, 2G-10, and 6C-10), it seems odd that the Maya would have dug a special pit in Ch. 5C-8 for a secondary interment. Nor is the partial burning of the bones normally seen in other secondary burials. Finally, Moholy-Nagy (pers. comm.) has pointed out that PD. 72 resembles PD. 22, 50, and 74, which she is inclined to see as terminal deposits of some kind. In favor of this are the burned human remains; their scattered arrangement in a pit full of burned household debris (particularly reminiscent of PD. 74); the presence of a stemmed thin biface of green obsidian in the pit (PD. 22, 50, and 74 all have stemmed thin bifaces, whereas all other Tikal burials lack these items altogether—the one exception being a deposit external to a chamber burial); and the fact that the celt is of an unusual light green (gem type) jade, a material found in the Teotihuacan-influenced Bu. 48, but not at all like the usual dark green to black jadeite celts sometimes found in household trash.

The burial-like PD. 22, 50, and 74 all date to late Early Classic times, after AD 378 (Iglesias 2003). There are sufficient Manik sherds in Ch. 5C-8 to indicate that it was filled in Early Classic times. The green obsidian thin biface, too, is likely an Early Classic item (Moholy-Nagy, pers. comm.). It seems clear, therefore, that PD. 72 was placed in Ch. 5C-8 in the Early Classic period. The few Ik sherds in the chultun appear to have washed in following abandonment of Str. 5C-56 (see discussion in section II).

In terms of the entire stratigraphy for the locus of Str. 5C-56, it seems that Str. 5C-56-2nd was built following deposition of PD. 72 and filling of the chultun. The problematical deposit also seems to be associated with demolition of Str. 5C-57. This is because the most likely source of the chultun fill consists of trash, fill, and masonry from the structure. Just before the material was placed in the pit (Chm. 10), the chultun was left open, allowing water-deposited clay to accumulate on the floor of Chm. 3 and 10. In Chm. 3, this clay ran up to, and abutted, a block of masonry in the entrance to Chm. 6. This is one of a number of blocks in the entrances to Chm. 4–6 that probably were robbed from Str. 5C-57, and which were positioned so that when the chultun was filled, it would not be necessary to fill these three chambers along with the rest. Hence, less material was required to do the job. Thus it appears that detritus from Str. 5C-57 was placed in the chultun immediately before, in conjunction with, and immediately after PD. 72.

Putting all these things together, it is possible that PD. 72 is a two-stage rather than a secondary burial. The objects included in PD. 72 suggest that the subject of this burial was of lower social status than the subjects of PD. 22, 50, and 74 (Moholy-Nagy, pers. comm.). In short, the individual may have lived in Str. 5C-57, which, architecturally, seems comparable to low-status residences (discussed in TR. 20B, section II). This structure, first occupied in very Late Preclassic times, appears to have been abandoned for good with this individual's death, whereupon it was totally demolished and used to fill the chultun.

Left unresolved is this question: did the man's death precipitate abandonment of the structure, or did abandonment call for his death as part of some sort of termination ritual? In fact, the alternatives are not mutually exclusive, as burials of heads of households commonly precipitated abandonment of houses, while at the same time perhaps serving as the focus of termination ceremonies (see TR. 19:150–151 and TR. 20B).

SEQUENTIAL POSITION:

Ch. 5C-8:TS. 1 (see Table 2.151).

PROBLEMATICAL DEPOSIT 99

LOCATION:

Gp. 7C-1, 2.50 m S of Str. 7C-4 in U. 4 (see Fig. 135), or 1.60 m E and 18.65 m S of Datum 67C (Fig. 133). 67C/10; see Fig. 172a for plan; 183e for photo.

CONTENT AND ARRANGEMENT:

67C-15a,b: shell, unworked? (Vermicularia spirata and ?); 67C-16: unmodified mineral (to be identified); 67C-17a–c: reconstructible Aguila Orange, outcurving-side Cache bowls (TR. 25A:fig. 142c1–3); 67C-18: specular hematite, mosaic element?

One of the cache bowls was placed upright in U. 4, a hole in bedrock, 0.15 m deep with a diameter of 0.28 m. Sherds of the other cache bowls were in, or just above, the first. One of them may have been inverted over the other in a lip-to-lip arrangement, but this is not clear. One cache bowl was fire-smudged on the inside. The other materials were mixed with the sherds, and part or all of this could be unrelated, belonging instead in LG. 3b of Str. 7C-4 (Table 2.296). Vermicularia shells, however, were used in Maya caches (Andrews 1969:7).

DISCUSSION:

The bowls are of a type common to Early Classic caches, and the material around and above this deposit (Str. 7C-4:LG. 3b; Table 2.296) is also pure Early Classic. Hence, this deposit predates any known structure of Gp. 7C-1 (Tables 2.296, 2.303). The fills of those structures also included considerable Early Classic materials. Clearly, PD. 99 predates TS. 3 of Str. 7C-4 (Table 2.301).

All of this indicates probable construction at the locus of Gp. 7C-1 in Early Classic times, which later must have been razed. Probably Str. 7C-4:U. 4 and Str. 7C-4:U. 3 (Fig. 135) also relate to that construction. A likely scenario is that when this construction was dismantled, PD. 99 itself was disturbed, with only the basal vessel remaining relatively unbroken, owing to its protected position in U. 4. Such an interpretation is suggested by the jumbled nature of the deposit.

If two of the containers of PD. 99 were placed in a lip-to-lip arrangement, as was likely, then it resembled Early Classic PD. 23, 24, and 25 from Gp. 4F-1 (TR. 19:155–156), and PD. 109 from Gp. 3F-1 (this report). If some or all of the other objects were placed inside such a container, then it calls to mind Late Classic Ca. 85 from Gp. 4F-1 (TR. 19:154–155). These resemblances suggest that PD. 99 was some sort of cached offering.

SEQUENTIAL POSITION:

Str. 7C-4:TS. 4 (Table 2.301).

PROBLEMATICAL DEPOSIT 101

LOCATION:

Gp. 6C-1, beneath the fill for Plat. 6C-1-2nd, immediately off the NE corner of Str. 6C-46-3rd (see Fig. 120b), or 3 m N, 14.60 m E of Datum 67A (Fig. 115). 67A/23; see Fig. 172d for plan; 180c for photo.

CONTENT AND ARRANGEMENT:

Large, decorated Manik sherds (uncatalogued), 4 animal bones and several human bone fragments (67A-22 as follows): 1 occipital; 1 frontal; 1 clavicle; 2 humerii; 1 ulna; 1 radius. There appears to be no purposeful arrangement of materials. The sherds and bone fragments lay together in a haphazard manner.

DISCUSSION:

This deposit could be either of two things: miscellaneous fill material or a secondary burial. In favor of the former is the scantiness of the material and lack of order that may be compared, for example, to PD. 64 or Bu. 152 (both this report) that almost surely are secondary burials. In addition, neither of the two known primary burials (136, 146) from Gp. 6C-1 included ceramics. The sherds, in terms of size and preservation, resemble those from middens; these could be from the deposits around an early version of Str. 6C-45 that were used for fill here. In support of this, there were some animal bone fragments, an unused chert flake and some burned limestone chunks in proximity to the deposit. Moreover, human bone fragments are not uncommon in occupation debris around small structures.

In favor of secondary burial is the lack of surrounding midden-like material. These large sherds and bones occur together and seem quite unlike the surrounding fill. This could be chance; some ancient Maya builder could have brought a basket full of trash from Str. 6C-45 to use as fill, but all subsequent fill was procured from another source. But the bone fragments are somewhat more substantial than usual for such material in occupation debris. The presence of a few animal bones, too, is suggestive, for animal bones were associated with the two known primary burials (136 and 146) from Gp. 6C-1. On balance, the interpretation that this was not a special deposit seems probable, even if secondary burial cannot be ruled out.

The sequential position of the deposit is not a problem; it was clearly included in the fill for Plat. 6C-1-2nd in the course of construction. This is when Str. 6C-45-4th-A was abandoned and 45-3rd built (Table 2.256 and 2.260). It is possible that when this took place, an existing burial was disturbed which then had to be reinterred. On the other hand, there is no evidence that the building platform of 45-4th-A was disturbed when 3rd was built.

Plat. 6C-1:TS. 5 (Table 2.259).

PROBLEMATICAL DEPOSIT 108

LOCATION:

Gp. 5F-1, in the Preclassic midden that fills the large pit in bedrock (Fig. 104; Plat. 5F-1:U. 5) NE of Str. 5F-Sub.1; just S of Bu. 158 (see Fig. 106b). Coordinates are 2.90 m S and 18.50 m E of Datum 71F. Included in 71F/56 and 57; see Fig. 172e for plan.

CONTENT AND ARRANGEMENT:

There is a discrepancy here between the excavator's notes and content illustrated in TR. 25A (fig. 142d and 143a). Fourteen vessels are illustrated, whereas the field drawing reproduced here shows only nine. A possible explanation is that TR. 25A illustrates some of the pottery from the midden in which PD. 108 was found. The nine Tzec vessels surely from the problematical deposit are as follows:

Vessel No. 1, 71F-90 (TR. 25A:fig. 143*a*3); Vessel No. 2, 71F-91 (TR. 25A:fig. 143*a*2); Vessel No. 3, 71F-92 (TR. 25A:fig. 143*a*6); Vessel No. 4, 71F-93 (TR. 25A:fig. 143*a*1); Vessel No. 5, 71F-94 (TR. 25A:fig. 142*d*6); Vessel No. 6, 71F-95 (TR. 25A:fig. 142*d*4); Vessel No. 7, 71F-96 (TR. 25A:fig. 143*a*5); Vessel No. 8, 71F-99 (TR. 25A:fig. 143*a*8); Vessel No. 9, 71F-98 (TR. 25A:fig. 143*a*7).

The arrangement of these vessels is sufficiently clear in Fig. 172e. Vessel Nos. 1–3, 5, 8, and 9 form a roughly E-W line, with No. 1 at the W, No. 8 at the E. Number 7 is S of No. 1, No. 4 is S of No. 3, and No. 6 is S of No. 5. These three vessels also form a line running E from No. 7 to No. 6. The precise location of a heavily worn human molar (71F-97) that was included in the deposit was not reported. Two chert blade cores illustrated in TR. 27B (fig. 58c,e), purportedly from PD. 108, are probably from the surrounding midden.

DISCUSSION:

According to the excavator, Sisson, the vessels were probably placed in the midden in random order. Yet their placement in the midden intact, or nearly so, argues against their being ordinary discards on a trash heap. There are no other whole vessels in the midden, save those in the nearby Bu. 158. These may have something to do with that burial, but there is no clear connection between them. In the absence of any other obvious suggestion, they could constitute some kind of offering. This suggestion might amount to grasping at straws, except that other evidence

to be discussed in TR. 20B helps to support this idea.

The sequential position of this deposit is clear: it was placed during the time that Tzec-related trash was accumulating NE of Str. 5F-Sub.1.

SEQUENTIAL POSITION:

Plat. 5F-1:TS. 10 (Table 2.221).

PROBLEMATICAL DEPOSIT 109

LOCATION:

Gp. 3F-3, in a bedrock pit beneath the front of the supplementary platform for Str. 3F-12-1st, on its front-rear axis and just in front of the wall (U. 1) for Str. 3F-12-2nd (see Fig. 53, 54). 67F/9; see Fig. 172b for plan; 177d for photo.

CONTENT AND ARRANGEMENT:

Two Aguila Orange, outflaring-side cache vessels: small variety (TR. 25A:fig. 143b), set lip-to-lip. No identifiable content.

DISCUSSION:

This deposit is virtually identical to Early Classic PD. 23–25 from Gp. 4F-1 (TR. 19:155–156). When found, these contained dirt, but could once have contained organic materials. This problematical deposit likewise contained dirt, but there were also four tiny pieces of carbon. Problematical Deposits 23–25 are thought to be dedicatory to Str. 4F-8, which probably was not itself a house. Problematical Deposit 109 probably was dedicatory to Str. 3F-12-2nd, as 1st-C was built after the appearance of Imix ceramics. Structure 3F-12-2nd was built in the late Early Classic or (at the very latest) just as Ik pottery was making its appearance, and there is no evidence for an earlier structure at the locus of PD. 109 itself.

Worth emphasizing is that 12-2nd is thought to have been a pole-and-thatch range-type structure, so that 1st-C was, in a sense, a more elaborate version of it. Structure 3F-12-1st-C, in turn, bears a striking similarity to Str. 4E-31 in Gp. 4F-1, on the axis of which was a cached offering that shows some resemblance to PD. 109 (Ca. 85; TR. 19:154–155). Structure 4E-31 is thought to have been a successor to the earlier Str. 4F-8.

The pit in which PD. 109 was placed may have been dug specifically for the purpose, or may already have been present. In favor of the latter option is abundant early sherd material within it (Table 2.100), suggestive of earlier activity. Moreover, the pit was larger than required for the problematical deposit, suggesting opportunistic use of an existing feature.

SEQUENTIAL POSITION:

Str. 3F-12:TS. 9 (Table 2.104).

PROBLEMATICAL DEPOSIT 110

LOCATION:

Gp. 5B-2, in the bottom of the deep quarry behind Str. 5B-7 (see Fig. 62:6), or 6.30 m S and 1.80 m W of Datum 67L (Fig. 64). 67L/25; see Fig. 171d for plan.

CONTENT AND ARRANGEMENT:

Skull and miscellaneous bones of a young child (67L-9). The bones were not placed in proper anatomical order. Skull fragments were found both E and W of the vertebrae and ribs. The mandible was next to a humerus fragment S and E of some of the skull fragments, and an isolated vertebra was S of these. One pelvic fragment was E of one skull fragment, right by the ribs; another pelvic fragment was 0.12 m N of this. Leg bones are scattered up to 0.20 m N and E of this.

DISCUSSION:

This almost surely is a secondary burial. The bones are all from one individual, but the skeleton is not complete, nor are the bones properly arranged.

The secondary burial obviously postdates the quarrying that produced the pit in which the bones were placed. The great quantity of middle Manik and earlier ceramics with other debris that filled the pit (Table 2.128:LG. 3a and 3b of Str. 5B-7) suggests that an occupation of this locus predating that of Gp. 5B-2 was disturbed when the quarrying took place, and that material from that occupation was used to fill the quarry. Such disturbance could well have uncovered a primary burial. Hence, the original interment of the remains now in PD. 110 probably took place in Early Classic times.

Just when the redeposition of the remains took place is not known. The quarrying took place after middle Manik ceramics were in production, but prior to construction of Str. 5B-7-2nd. By then, Imix ceramics were in use. Since the large sample of sherds from the quarry included not a single one from an Imix, Ik, or even a late Manik pot, the quarrying (and reburial) probably took place in Early Classic times. Accordingly, PD. 110 is assigned to TS. 9 of Str. 5B-7.

SEQUENTIAL POSITION:

Str. 5B-7:TS. 9 (Table 2.132).

PROBLEMATICAL DEPOSIT 124

LOCATION:

Gp. 5D-1, against the N wall of Str. 5D-7-3rd (Fig. 94, Str. 5D-7:U. 2), 0.28 m from the NW corner, 15.90 m S and 5.25 m W of Datum 76B (Fig. 98). The deposit rests on Str. 5D-7:U. 1, its top is below the level of Plat. 5D-29:U. 10, which stops just to the W, and it is covered by fill for the floor (U. 11) for Plat. 5D-29-3rd (see Fig. 94:U. 1, 10, and 11). 76B/13; see Fig. 172c for plan.

CONTENT AND ARRANGEMENT:

Two Manik outflaring-side cache vessels, small variety (TR. 25A:fig. 144e), placed lip-to-lip, with the smaller serving as a lid for the larger one.

DISCUSSION:

This deposit shows a close relationship to PD. 109, just discussed; it too could be some sort of cached offering. This possibility will be discussed in TR. 20B. Though filled only with dirt when found, there could once have been organic material, now decomposed, in the vessels.

Stratigraphically, the deposit must postdate Str. 5D-7-4th, but cannot postdate Plat. 5D-29-3rd. The U. 10 break in the floor for Plat. 5D-29-4th, just W of the deposit, suggests that it was intruded through that floor. There is no other apparent reason for this floor break. This means that the deposit was probably placed when Plat. 5D-29-3rd was built. This could, in turn, relate to construction of Str. 5D-7-2nd, and so the deposit must have been just behind that structure, possibly on its front-rear axis. Given all this, it may have had a dedicatory relationship to Str. 5D-7-2nd.

At odds with this reconstruction of events are the Manik vessels in an Imix context (Table 2.191). A possible clue may be their weathered condition; they could have been retrieved by the Maya when Early Classic Str. 5D-7-6th was demolished, and reused in an offering perhaps 200 years later. If so, one can only wonder at their survival over such a long period of time.

SEQUENTIAL POSITION:

Str. 5D-7:TS. 5 (Table 2.191), or Plat 5D-29:TS. 9 (Table 2.193).

PROBLEMATICAL DEPOSIT 126

LOCATION:

Gp. 5D-1, on the fill of Str. 5D-7-3rd, covered by fill for Plat. 5D-29:U. 11 and partly sealed by that floor (see

Fig. 94). This is 16.68 m S and 4.85 m W of Datum 76B (Fig. 98), or just SE of PD. 124 (see Fig. 172c). 76B/8.

CONTENT AND ARRANGEMENT:

Six lbs 9 oz of large Ik and probably Imix sherds with sharp breaks (76B-2); 1 chert pointed, retouched flake (76B-26); 1 unmodified chert flake; 1 obsidian prismatic blade; 1 large unmodified fragment of chert; all densely packed, but with no detectable purposeful pattern. The deposit was 0.10 m thick.

DISCUSSION:

This, clearly, is a small midden deposit. Its position on the structure fill, and the concentrated nature of this deposit, indicates that it probably did not accumulate in situ. Thus, it probably was brought from somewhere else, probably not far away or the sherds would have been broken and battered. As to why it should have been brought here, the most obvious suggestion is that, in the process of building up the fill for Plat. 5D-29-3rd, someone happened to fill a container from a midden, which then happened to be dumped on the old construction to be buried in the new construction. There are no indications of any other significance for this deposit.

SEQUENTIAL POSITION:

Plat. 5D-29:TS. 9 (Table 2.193).

PROBLEMATICAL DEPOSIT 130

LOCATION:

Gp. 5F-1, on Plat. 5F-1:U. 7, W of Str. 5F-Sub.1 and just S of the locus of Str. 5F-17; 7.20 m S and 3.90 m W of Datum 71F (see Fig. 104). Included in 71F/140.

CONTENT AND ARRANGEMENT:

Plaster, ash, small stones and other charred materials (unspecified, but including a whetstone; TR. 27B:fig. 97c), in a low mound (up to 0.11 m thick) with a diameter of 0.90 m. The mound is made up of a lens of the charred material, ash, and small stones to 6 cm in thickness that is covered by plaster up to 5 cm in thickness. The plaster is feathered to the plaster floor, U. 7, at the edge of the mound. The lens was thickest at the center, whereas the plaster tended to be thickest towards the edge and thinnest towards the center of the mound.

DISCUSSION:

This deposit looks very much as if the Maya built a fire on the floor (U. 7) of Plat. 5F-1-3rd. Then, after it was

through burning, they plastered over it. While this could have been done when the floor (U. 3) for Plat. 5F-1-2nd was about to be built, this does not seem likely. In the first place, there would seem to be no necessity to specially plaster over the remains of the fire, if it was to be buried immediately in fill beneath a brand new plaster floor. In the second, the careful feathering of the plaster to U. 7 would be quite unnecessary. The deposit probably dates to sometime within Plat. 5F-1:TS. 8.

The significance of this deposit is an enigma. Why should the Maya apparently "enshrine" the remains of a fire? It seems unlikely that this would have been done unless the fire had some special significance, possibly a ritual significance. Perhaps it is all that remains of objects burned in the course of some sort of ceremony.

SEQUENTIAL POSITION:

Plat. 5F-1:TS. 8 (Table 2.221).

PROBLEMATICAL DEPOSIT 131

LOCATION:

Gp. 5F-1, on the floor of Chm. 2, Ch. 5F-5 (see Fig. 104 for location). Included in 71F/165.

CONTENT AND ARRANGEMENT:

Fragments of human and animal bone (uncatalogued).

DISCUSSION:

The deposit probably dates from the time of abandonment of Ch. 5F-5-1st; otherwise the bones would have been reduced to very tiny fragments, as people entered and left Chm. 2 in the course of normal usage.

The significance of the deposit is uncertain. It could be some kind of special offering associated with abandonment of the chultun. Alternatively, its placement here may have been purely opportunistic; because the chultun was about to be abandoned, it was a convenient spot for the offering. This last option is more likely, for most chultuns when they were abandoned were not apparently treated to special offerings. They were, however, occasionally used as convenient burial spots. It is possible, though, that this deposit is no kind of offering at all, but rather is living debris that was disposed of here. As noted elsewhere, human bones are often included in such debris. This last possibility, though, gains no support by the presence of somewhat similar PD. 214 in Ch. 3G-5, beneath Str. 3G-1 (see below).

SEQUENTIAL POSITION:

Ch. 5F-5:TS. 1 (Table 2.220).

PROBLEMATICAL DEPOSIT 140

LOCATION:

Gp. 5F-1, just N of Str. 5F-Sub.1 (Fig. 104), above the level of Plat. 5F-1:U. 3, but below U. 1, 5.20 m S and 13.85 m E of Datum 71F. 71F/164.

CONTENT AND ARRANGEMENT:

71F-142a,b: marine shell pendants; 71F-143: freshwater clam pendant; 71F-uncat.: 20+ unidentifiable unworked bone; 71F-uncat: gray obsidian prismatic blade fragment. The excavator's notes do not report any arrangement, and so it is probable that the materials were found together with no detectable purposeful order.

DISCUSSION:

On stratigraphic grounds, this deposit must date to the time of construction of Plat. 5F-1-1st. This is when Str. 5F-Sub.1 was completely abandoned. This, and the location of the deposit by that structure suggest that it may be some kind of offering associated with its abandonment. It is worth noting that apparent non-dedicatory offerings beside houses were found in Gp. 4F-1 (TR. 19:PD. 46, 47, 211). Their content is quite different from this one, but they were household objects, and the shells used here may also have been ornaments owned by the householder.

SEQUENTIAL POSITION:

Plat. 5F-1:TS. 5 (Table 2.221).

PROBLEMATICAL DEPOSIT 214

LOCATION:

Gp. 3G-1, Chm. 2 and 3 of Ch. 3G-5, approximately on the centers of the floors (see Fig. 56, 58). In 72A:7 and 10.

CONTENT AND ARRANGEMENT:

Circa 400 bones of small mammals including possum (*Didelphis marsupialis*) and cotton tail rabbit (*Sivalegus floradaneus*). The bones were disarticulated, and surrounded by a deposit of black earth. The earth in turn was surrounded by midden material in the chultun (Table 2.111:LG. 2 of Ch. 3G-5).

DISCUSSION:

The dark soil around the bones suggests possible burial in a container of cloth or some other organic substance. It is unlikely that the soil represents simply the decomposition of the animals. Bones of animals that had died in chultuns are commonly found in the course of excavations, but not in association with a deposit of black earth. The disarticulated and incomplete nature of the skeletons suggests that they were placed here in that condition. They must have been so placed when the chultun was abandoned, or they probably would have been scattered and badly broken during use of the chultun.

Two possible explanations may be offered for this situation: (1) the bones represent a ritual related to abandonment of the chultun, construction of the structure above it, or perhaps some other event in Gp. 3G-1; or (2) the bones are part of the midden that was used to fill the chultun. Of these, the latter may probably be ruled out. The presence of the material near the center of each chamber points more to purposeful placement than to coincidence. It is also unlikely that the bones would have been bundled up, had they been ordinary midden material.

If the deposit is ceremonial, does it relate to abandonment of the chultun? The answer is probably no. While burials sometime occur in chultuns (Ch. 2G-2, 2G-10, and 6C-10, this report; or Ch. 7F-8, TR. 22), it appears that in these cases the chultuns were being abandoned anyway, and so made convenient graves. Other deposits sometimes occur in chultuns, such as PD. 231 (this report). This, however, has the appearance of a very unusual situation. The same is true of PD. 65 in Ch. 3F-6, PD. 72 in Ch. 5C-8 (both this report), or an elaborate ceremonial deposit in Ch. 5C-1, beneath the Tozzer Causeway (TR. 23H). Indeed, only PD. 131 seems analogous to this one; more often, chultuns seem to have been abandoned without ceremony (e.g., Ch. 2B-15; 2F-5; 2G-1; 2G-5; 2G-11; 3F-4; 3F-5; 4F-2; 4F-4; 4G-2; 5B-11; 5C-5; 5C-6; 6C-6; 6C-7; 6C-9; 6E-6; 6E-7; 7C-3, all this report).

Although the deposit could be dedicatory to Str. 3G-1-3rd, there is no indication that it was intended to be. The main reason for this is that the only such deposits known for domestic or domestic-related structures involved cache vessels set lip-to-lip (as will be discussed in TR. 20B). Another is that PD. 131, which may be analogous to this one, was placed in a chultun over which a structure was not built. What remains, therefore, is the possibility that PD. 214 is a non-dedicatory offering that relates to ceremonial activity carried out in Gp. 3G-1, but not directly related to Str. 3G-1. This subject is scheduled for discussion in TR. 20B.

SEQUENTIAL POSITION:

Ch. 3G-5:TS. 1 (Table 2.113).

PROBLEMATICAL DEPOSIT 221

LOCATION:

Str. 4C-34, beneath the fill (Fig. 171c), 3 m N of Bu.

212 (Fig. 167a) or Sq. 4c: ca. S250 E500. 140A/1; see Fig. 171a for plan.

CONTENT AND ARRANGEMENT:

Human posterior cranial fragment (140A-7) and two late Imix Palmar Orange Group slightly outcurving-side bowls (TR. 25A:fig. 153*d*1,2). One bowl was placed upright, with the human cranial fragment inside it with the inner surface of the bone up. The other bowl was upright immediately S of the first, with its rim touching that of the other vessel.

DISCUSSION:

The vessels were placed in the fill beneath Str. 4C-34:U. 2, which seals the deposit, immediately above bedrock. Since U. 2 is thought to relate to the earliest known version of 34, this structure must be dated by the late Imix ceramics of this deposit, which must have been placed at the time of construction. There may, though, have been an earlier structure nearby.

The significance of this deposit is unknown. An obvious possibility is that it is a secondary burial, with almost all of the skeleton and perhaps a tripod plate or other vessel missing. To speculate, perhaps a burial was disturbed in the course of some architectural alteration at the locus of Str. 4C-34, and it was convenient to rebury this much of it in the construction of Str. 4C-34.

SEQUENTIAL POSITION:

No time span defined (see "Discussion").

PROBLEMATICAL DEPOSIT 224

LOCATION:

Str. 5C-56 locus in fill of Ch. 5C-8 (see Fig. 70 and 71). Included in LG. 2 and 3 (Table 2.143).

CONTENT AND ARRANGEMENT:

See Table 2.149:LG. 2 and 3 for list of content. Illustrated in TR. 27B are a chert ovate biface (fig. 8a); chert elongate bifaces (fig. 15d and 19c); a thin biface probably of Ucareo obsidian (fig. 65n) above a needle with drilled eye (fig. 121q); a beveled long-bone end (fig. 125j); a miscellaneous-formed pottery object (fig. 148b); and fragments of a bone rasp that join one from PD. 72 (fig. 124c). Objects were found randomly distributed in fill of Chm. 2, 3, and 9.

DISCUSSION:

Defined in the laboratory on the basis of "exotic" objects of the sort found in burial-like deposits such as PD. 50, 72, and 74, this does not seem to be a special deposit.

As discussed elsewhere (section II), the chultun was purposely filled as a single operation following placement of PD. 72 (see its discussion). As indicated by the broken pieces of the rasp noted above, a few objects associated with PD. 72 were dropped in the chultun just before it was filled. Alternatively, the rasp and some of the other "exotics" were present by chance in the original source of the fill, and got mixed with the material in PD. 72.

SEQUENTIAL POSITION:

Ch. 5C-8:TS. 1 (Table 2.151).

PROBLEMATICAL DEPOSIT 231

LOCATION:

Gp. 6C-5, near or on the floor of Ch. 6C-11 in Chm. 1, 2, and 3. 66H/6, 7, 9, through 16; see Fig. 170 for plan.

CONTENT AND ARRANGEMENT:

The deposit consists of the following items: 66H-1, 7: adult male human skeleton, with extra adult mandible and femur; 66H-5: chert ovate biface, burned, with reworked ends (TR. 27B:fig. 4a); 66H-6, 16, 25: unmodified animal bone; 66H-9: unmodified stone; 66H-10, 24: centrally perforated bone discs (TR. 27B:fig. 122*r*1,2); 66H-11, 39: chert thin bifaces (TR. 27B:fig. 32f; 41j); 66H-12a,b: freshwater mussel shells; 66H-13a,b, 54: shell pendants; 66H-14: flat, rounded-end chert biface (TR. 27B:fig. 44b); 66H-15: green obsidian prismatic blade; 66H-17: Balanza black narrow-mouth jar with medium neck (TR. 25A:fig. 154a); 66H-18, 46: scarcely altered shells; 66H-19: miniature cup or candelero (TR. 25A:fig. 153*f*4; also TR. 27B:fig. 141t); 66H-20, 21: Maa Red-striated narrow-mouth jars with medium neck (TR. 25A:fig. 154b,d); 66H-22, 41: manos (TR. 27B:fig. 73c, 78l); 66H-23: metate (TR. 27B:fig. 73c, 82a); 66H-26-28, 42: obsidian thin bifaces (TR. 27B:fig. 64i, 66e,v, 67a); 66H-29: celt (TR. 27B:fig. 100b); 66H-30: unclassified ground stone artifacts; 66H-31, 44a,b: unmodified shells; 66H-32: pyrite mosaic element; 66H-33: unmodified pebble; 66H-34: grinding stone (TR. 27B:fig. 92c); 66H-35: squash seeds; 66H-36: jade flare; 66H-40: rubbing stone (TR. 27B:fig. 95h); 66H-43: cut shell fragment; 66H-38: rectangular/oval chert biface (TR. 27B:fig. 25a); 66H-45: shell tinkler; 66H-47: figurine (TR. 27B:-fig. 137l); 66H-48: Aguila Orange narrow-mouth jar with medium neck (TR. 25A:fig. 154e); 66H-49: Dos Arroyos Ceramic Group, narrow-mouth jar with medium neck (TR. 25A:fig. 154c); 66H-50: Aguila Red-orange round-side bowl with pedestal base (TR. 25A:fig. 153*f*1); 66H-51: Aguila Red-orange round-side bowl (TR. 25A:fig. 153*f*2); 66H-52: Urita gouged-incised cylinder tripod (TR. 25A:-fig. 153*f*3); 66H-53: sherd, Urita gouged-incised cylindrical tripod; uncatalogued obsidian prismatic blade.

Of the human skeleton, the skull was in the N end of Chm. 2, upside down with the face to the W and slightly S. The scapulae were placed in the NE part of Chm. 1, 1.20 m SE of the skull. Immediately SW of these the finger bones are located. A humerus lay a short distance S, its distal end 0.34 m S and slightly E of the scapula, its proximal end (broken) 0.08 m from the scapula. To the E of the humerus are a clavicle (one end near the proximal end of the humerus), a radius and ulna. The latter were roughly parallel to the humerus, about 0.10 m distant. About 0.25 m W and slightly S of the humerus, towards the center of Chm. 1, were portions of rib and vertebrae (Fig. 170:13). The distal end of one femur was 0.12 m SW of these, its proximal end SE, 0.30 m from pelvic remains against the E jamb of the entrance to Chm. 3. The mate to this femur lay in the entrance, its proximal end 0.15 m W of the pelvis, its distal end farther NW so that the bone lay parallel to its mate. Remains of a smaller, third femur lay between the proximal ends of these two bones. Fragments of fibulae lay around these bones, but the tibiae were in the NE part of Chm. 3 (0.30 m from the nearest femur). The foot bones were in the entrance to Chm. 3, 0.08 m from the proximal end of one femur, and 0.30 m from the nearest tibia.

The whole metate was placed upright towards the center of Chm. 2, and set down into U. 3 (Fig. 128d). Its NE corner was 0.26 m S of the skull. Near the W wall, 0.42 m from the metate, was the complete mano 66H-22 (also in U. 3). Together, the mano and metate form a set (TR. 27B:fig. 73c). Twenty centimeters S of the mano was the scarcely altered freshwater mussel shell 66H-18. On the top of the metate were one large and two small jar rims (66H-48, 20, and 21; Fig. 170:2, 4, and 5). The latter sat upright, the former lay on its side over the N half of the metate, its opening to the S. Between the two small jar necks was the upright miniature vessel (Fig. 170:10). A fourth large jar neck, 66H-17, sat upright 6 cm E of the metate (Fig. 170:1). Between this and the SE corner of the metate in U. 3, its point partly under the edge of the jar neck, lay a stemmed thin biface (TR. 27B:fig. 64i) of red and black streaked obsidian (pointing NE; see Fig. 170:9). Between the skull, the metate, and the jar neck 66H-17 is a large sherd (Fig. 170:6; 0.05 m from the skull), a perforated bone disc 66H-24 (0.20 m from the skull; Fig. 170:11 and TR. 27B:fig. 122*v*1), and the celt (0.25 m from the skull; Fig. 170:12). The latter is unique, being of a soft brown stone, rather than the usual green to black jadeite (TR. 27B:fig. 100b). Part of a thin biface (TR. 27B:fig. 67a) lay 0.16 m E of the perforated bone disc (Fig. 170:9), and a stemmed brown and black streaked obsidian blade (TR. 27B:fig. 66v) lay 0.04 m from the face (SW) of the skull (see also Fig. 170:9). Of

these, the two pieces of streaked obsidian were in U. 3. Eight slightly charred squash seeds also came from Chm. 2, but they may have been in U. 2, the later fill (they were found in the backdirt). Unfortunately, they mildewed before they could be identified as a species. Also from Chm. 2 are the flat, rounded-end chert biface; the green obsidian prismatic blade; the pyrite mosaic element; the jade flare fragment and grinding stone; the unmodified pebble 66H-33; the unclassifiable ground-stone artifact 66H-30; the unmodified *Pomacea flagellata* shell 66H-31; the unmodified animal bones 66H-16 (dog); and 25 (dog and possum); and sherds from the vessels 66H-49, 50, and 52 (see under Chm. 1); their precise location within the chamber is not given by the excavator.

In Chm. 1, a burned stone 66H-9 (Fig. 170:15) and several large sherds from vessels 66H-17, 20, 21, 48-53 were placed under or near the arm and shoulder remains (Fig. 170:3, 14). Of these, 66H-52 was N, while the pedestal bowl, possibly of foreign origin (TR. 25A:fig. 153/1) was S of the arm bones. The two shell pendants, 66H-13a,b (Fig. 170:16), were beneath the humerus, and an uncatalogued obsidian prismatic blade was beneath the ribs (Fig. 170:13). The two mussel shells, 66H-12a,b, were placed on either side of the two northernmost femora (Fig. 170:7). By the W jamb of the entrance to Chm. 3 was an almost complete stemmed thin biface of chert, 66H-11 (Fig. 170:20 and TR. 27B:fig. 32f), with cinnabar on its under-surface. Just E of this was the stemmed translucent gray obsidian thin biface base, 66H-42 (Fig. 170:9 and TR. 27B:fig. 66e), and 0.32 m to the W, was a water-worn quartzite pebble (uncatalogued), coated with cinnabar. Also from Chm. 1 is the second perforated bone disc, 66H-10 (TR. 27B:fig. 122*v*2), but its precise location is not given by the excavator.

In Chm. 3, numerous artifacts were found in U. 5. Of these, the mano 66H-41, the cut and drilled oliva shell tinker 66H-45, the cut or scarcely altered shell 66H-43 (cut marine univalve) or 46 (freshwater mussel), the shell pendant 66H-54, and carbon fragments were placed with the foot bones (Fig. 170:7, 8, 22, 23). To the SW were the two unmodified freshwater mussel shells, 66H-44a,b (Fig. 170:7) and the stemmed thin biface of chert (TR. 27B:fig. 41j). To the S was the cut or scarcely altered shell 66H-43 or 46 (Fig. 170:18). Near the tibiae are the rubbing stone 66H-40 (Fig. 170:18) and the rectangular-oval chert biface 66H-38. Also from Chm. 3 is the figurine, and sherds from Vessels 66H-17, 20, 21, and 48. Their precise positions are not recorded.

DISCUSSION:

There seems no doubt that the human remains represent a secondary burial. The bones are too widely spread apart for the skeleton to have been articulated when it was placed here, nor is there evidence for any natural disturbance (roof collapse or the like) that could have scattered the remains of an articulated skeleton. In addition, sherds from the pottery vessels were too widely dispersed to have been broken in situ.

The individual was an old adult male of exceptionally large stature (over 170 cm). In all respects, he is typical of those normally placed in the chamber burials ("tombs") of the Great Plaza-North Acropolis, rather than less elaborate graves in small-structure groups (TR. 30). The objects with the human remains were placed in the chultun at the same time, so they likely are redeposited from the same source as the bones. It is, therefore, noteworthy that they are quite unlike the materials from "ordinary" burials, but do have analogues in Early Classic chamber burials. For example, the important Bu. 48 included some utilitarian pottery similar to the large jars here, green obsidian prismatic blades, a mano and metate set, mosaic elements (not pyrite, but mosaic elements of this substance were in elite Bu. 160), jade flares, unmodified pebbles, abundant marine shells (including unmodified and scarcely altered shells), plant seeds, unmodified animal bones, red pigment and carbon. Not included in Bu. 48, but included in other Early Classic "tombs," are perforated bone discs (Bu. 22), shell pendants (Bu. 160), a rubbing stone (Bu. 22), and a used chert flake (Bu. 10; analogous to the flat, rounded-end chert biface of PD. 231?). The extra femur could be from a sacrificial victim.

Although one thin biface is known from a deposit exterior to a chamber burial (TR. 27B:17–18), they have not been found in other "tombs." They are not known from other burials either, although they were sometimes placed in other ritual deposits (TR. 27B:18). Four of the six in this problematical deposit are of obsidian, three of which surely and one probably were imported from Central Mexico (TR. 27B:28, 29). Moreover, the brownred streaked obsidian of two is exceedingly rare at Tikal (only eight examples are known), suggesting that they were special objects. The painting of one of the chert specimens, too, seems to mark it as special (TR. 27B:17). Stemmed thin bifaces (as these six are) are present in four burial-like problematical deposits (22, 50, 72, and 74) that seem to exhibit, to one degree or another, influence from Teotihuacan. In PD. 231, the bone discs, freshwater mussel shells, the mano and metate set, and the figurine and candelero are suggestive of such influence (Moholy-Nagy, pers. comm.; see also Iglesias 2003:181–182). Finally, none of the objects in PD. 231 (including the particular vessel forms) are normally found in household burials.

The best explanation of PD. 231 seems to be that it is redeposited from an Early Classic, Teotihuacan-influenced elite burial (such as Bu. 48, which PD. 231 most

closely resembles). Perhaps not all of the original burial goods made it as far as Ch. 6C-11. At Tikal, Teotihuacan influence in elite burials is most prominent between AD 378 and 480 (Iglesias 2003).

The materials from this deposit in Chm. 2 and 3 rest on, or in the tops of, U. 3 and 6 (Fig. 128d). These deposits apparently accumulated while the chultun was in use. Debris covering the skeleton and associated materials in all chambers seems to have entered the chultun around its cover, which had been sealed in place. Hence, the secondary burial clearly is related to abandonment of the chultun. Possibly abandonment was brought about by use of the chultun for the secondary burial. But since other chultuns containing burials seem to have been so utilized because they were abandoned, and so made convenient "graves," it is possible that PD. 231 represents similar opportunistic use of Ch. 6C-11. For reasons to be discussed in TR. 20B, however, the first possibility may be more likely, although this cannot be proven.

SEQUENTIAL POSITION:

Ch. 6C-11:TS. 3 (Table 2.278).

PROBLEMATICAL DEPOSIT 262

LOCATION:

Gp. 7F-2, in Ch. 7F-2, on U. 1, the deepest fill in Ch. 7F-2, beneath U. 2 (Fig. 159a:5). In 66Z/12.

CONTENT AND ARRANGEMENT:

Two nearly complete "hour glass" censer bowls, 66Z-15a and b, with part of one cover (see Coe 1965b:35). They lay, broken, where they had apparently fallen on the fill, U. 1.

DISCUSSION:

The fact that the censers were nearly complete, and that the pieces were all together in one place on U. 1 suggests that placement here was probably deliberate. As noted in section II, U. 1 derives from collapse of the seal over the chultun, probably when the nearby structures were abandoned. Hence placement of the censers must have occurred at this time. The difference between the fill (U. 2) immediately over the censers, and fill (U. 3) higher in the chultun, suggests that U. 2 was intentionally placed in the chultun to cover the censer.

It is worth noting that the censers were not complete when they were thrown into the chultun. This suggests that, if the deposition of the censers had ceremonial significance, it was some sort of ceremony that involved objects that had been in use for some time prior to their ultimate deposition.

SEQUENTIAL POSITION:

Ch. 7F-2:TS. 2 (Table 2.358).

PROBLEMATICAL DEPOSIT 263

LOCATION:

Gp. 7G-1, in the third stratum of fill of Ch. 7G-4 (Fig. 160b:U. 3).

CONTENT AND ARRANGEMENT:

Two pottery vessels: Vessel No. 1 (TR. 25A:fig. 155c2) was an Aguila Orange narrow-mouth jar with medium neck, in the upper third of U. 3, just E of the chultun orifice. Vessel No. 2 (TR. 25A:fig. 155c1), a larger Aguila Orange narrow-mouth jar with medium neck, was S of the orifice, in the very bottom of U. 3 on the surface of a lower stratum of fill (U. 2).

DISCUSSION:

The vessels were empty when placed in the chultun fill. As noted in the discussion of Ch. 7G-4, U. 3 was placed in the chultun when it was sealed unequivocally, at a time when Imix ceramics were in vogue. This may have been at the moment of abandonment, or sometime thereafter.

This raises the issue of identification of the vessels as Manik (TR. 25A:fig. 155c). In fact, their assignment to this complex was "based on stratigraphic position." Yet, the deposit in which they were found contained a few Imix, in addition to several Manik sherds. More telling, beneath this deposit was a small midden full of Imix sherds. Both vessels are utilitarian jars, and No. 1 is burned on the exterior. Vessel No. 2 is weathered, and one side of it is missing. These facts suggest that, if this deposit represents some kind of offering, it was one that involved ordinary household belongings. But if these were truly Manik pots, then it is probable that they, like the other Manik sherds in U. 3, were present in the original deposit from which this fill was drawn. If so, then PD. 263 has no special significance at all.

SEQUENTIAL POSITION:

Ch. 7G-4:TS. 4 (Table 2.367).

PROBLEMATICAL DEPOSIT 275

LOCATION:

Gp. 6C-1, in fill of Str. 6C-45, sealed beneath 45-3rd (see Table 2.251: LG. 1, 4b, and 5b of 6C-45). See Fig. 119 for section through this deposit.

CONTENT AND ARRANGEMENT:

Abundant Manik IIIA sherds of midden quality, as well as a great number and variety of other objects, as listed in Table 2.252 (LG. 1, 4b, and 5b). Artifacts illustrated in TR. 27B include thin bifaces of chert (fig. 30k,n, 31a–c, 35a); a cortical chert flake with short point (fig. 55t); thin bifaces of obsidian (fig. 64p, 65c, 66p,q, 67d,n); bone perforators (fig. 121c,h); bone disc (fig. 122t); deer phalanx (fig. 124i); beveled-end long bone (fig. 125a); centrally perforated worked sherd (fig. 132n4). Included were fragments of two human skeletons (one of them a male), ash, and charcoal, with none of the material deliberately arranged.

DISCUSSION:

The problematical deposit was defined in the laboratory on the basis of content that showed some similarity to burial-like problematical deposits such as PD. 50, 72, and 74. In this case, however, the similarity seems to be superficial. Unlike the others, there was no special repository here: no pit, no pot, or whatever. Nor was it the product of a single act. Instead, all the material was clearly discarded piecemeal over time, a result of use of the various architectural developments of Str. 6C-45 (see discussion in section II of lot groups for Gp. 6C-1). Moreover, this accumulating midden was occasionally disturbed (remixed) in connection with the various alterations of Str. 6C-45. In short, this seems to be a domestic midden that happens to include various "exotic" items as well as ordinary household refuse.

SEQUENTIAL POSITION:

Str. 6C-45:TS. 2C through 7 (Table 2.256).

Appendix
Test Pit Contents: Peripheral Squares

Group	Operation/Lot	Content
1D-1	136C/1	Sherds: 5 oz Unused chert flake 4 chert nodules
	136C/2	Sherds: 5 lbs 14 oz Chert ovate biface Retouched chert core Small, crude chert core Retouched chert flake 2 used chert flakes 8 unused chert flakes 29 chert nodule fragments and chips Obsidian prismatic blade
	136C/3	Sherds: 4 lbs Miscellaneous modeled pottery object Pottery figurine Chert core Chert flake with worked edge 16 unused chert flakes 24 chert nodules and fragments
	136C/4	Sherds: 5 lbs Pottery figurine Chert ovate biface Chert unclassifiable biface Chert core 3 retouched chert flakes Used chert flake 8 unused chert flakes 17 chert nodules and fragments 2 obsidian prismatic blades
	136C/5	Sherds: 4 oz Retouched chert flakes

Group	Operation/Lot	Content
		13 unused chert flakes
		7 chert nodules and fragments
		5 chert chips
	136C/6	Sherds: 5 oz
		Unused chert flake
		Chert nodule
	136P/1	Sherds: 9 oz
		Chert core
		4 used chert flakes
		7 unused chert flakes
		11 chert nodule fragments
		Polished chert tool fragment
	136P/2	1 sherd
		Eccentrically perforated pottery sherd
		Pottery figurine
		Irregular chert biface
		Chert core
		2 used chert flakes
		14 unused chert flakes
		7 chert nodule fragments
	136P/3	Sherds: 1 lb 1 oz
		Pottery figurine
		3 chert nodule fragments
	136P/4	Sherds: 6 lbs 6 oz
		Pottery pellet
		2 chert cores
		2 chert blades
		Retouched chert flake
		2 used chert flakes
		12 unusual chert flakes
		9 chert nodule fragments and chips
	136P/5	Sherds: 16 lbs 9 oz
		2 pottery censers
		Pottery perforated sherd
		3 chert cores
		Variably retouched chert flake
		Used chert flake
		16 unusual chert flakes
		9 chert nodule fragments
		1 quartzite mano
	136P/6	Sherds: 8 lbs
		Chert elongate biface

Group	Operation/Lot	Content
		Chert core
	136P/7	Sherds: 10 oz
		2 unused chert flakes
		2 chert nodules
	146J/1	Sherds: 1 lb 3 oz
		4 unused chert flakes
		1 used chert flake
	146J/2	Sherds: 3 lbs 20 oz
		Pottery figurine
		5 chert cores (2 retouched)
		Retouched chert scraper
		3 retouched chert flakes
		11 unusual chert flakes
		Obsidian prismatic blade
	146J/3	Sherds: 7 lbs 22 oz
		Pottery adorno
		Pottery perforated sherd
		Pottery partially perforated sherd
		11 chert cores (1 battered)
		Chert biface ovate
		Chert bifacial blade
		Variably retouched chert flake
		Pointed retouched chert flake
		24 retouched chert flakes
		24 unused chert flakes
		3 chert nodules
		2 obsidian prismatic blades
		Quartz pebble
	146J/4	Sherds: 8 lbs 8 oz
		2 pottery figurines
		5 chert cores
		Bifacial chert tool fragment
		4 retouched chert flakes
		2 used chert flakes
		17 unused chert flakes
		6 chert nodules
		Quartzite metate
		Chert hammer stone
		Unworked shell
	146J/5	Sherds: 2 lbs 6 oz
		3 chert cores
		Pointed retouched chert flake
		11 unused chert flakes
		Bone chip

Group	Operation/Lot	Content
	146J/6	Sherds: 1 lb 5 oz Chert core Used chert flake 5 unused chert flakes Chert nodules
	146J/7	Sherds: 10 oz 2 unused chert flakes
	146J/8	See Bu. 208
	146J/9	Sherds: 11 oz Variably retouched chert flakes 3 unused chert flakes
1D-3	146K/1	Sherds: 4 oz Chert blade
	146K/2	None
	146K/3	Sherds: 2 oz Unused chert flake
	146K/4	Sherds: 6 oz
	146K/5	Sherds: 3 lbs 9 oz Chert core Used chert flake 2 unused chert flakes
	146K/6	Sherds: 3 lbs 16 oz Chert biface tool fragment Retouched chert flake 2 unused chert flakes
	146K/7	Sherds: 4 lbs 23 oz Censer 2 chert elongate bifaces
	146K/8	Sherds: 6 oz 2 unused chert flakes
	146K/9	Sherds: 5 oz
	146K/10	Sherds: 1 oz
	136A/1	Sherds: 11 oz Chert nodule fragment
	136A/2	Sherds: 4 oz

Group	Operation/Lot	Content
		4 chert nodule fragments
	136A/3	Sherds: 9 oz
		Pottery figurine
		Chert core
		2 unused chert flakes
		6 chert nodule fragments
		Obsidian prismatic blade
	136A/4	Sherds: 1 oz
		Chert core
		Obsidian prismatic blade
	136A/5	Sherds: 17 lbs 29 oz
		Pottery figurine
		3 chert cores
		Chert rectangular/oval biface
		Variably retouched chert flake
		2 retouched chert flakes
		3 used chert flakes
		22 unused chert flakes
		8 chert chips
		94 chert nodules and fragments
		Obsidian prismatic blade
		Limestone spindle whorl
	136A/6	Sherds: 8 lbs 15 oz
		Pottery figurine
		Pottery colander
		2 chert cores
		Chert bifacial tool fragment
		Chert blade
		4 retouched chert flakes
		22 unused chert flakes
		15 chert nodules and fragments
		2 retouched obsidian prismatic blades
		3 used obsidian prismatic blades
		3 unused obsidian prismatic blades
	136A/7	Sherds: 1 lb 2 oz
		3 unused chert flakes
		Chert nodule fragment
	136B/1	Sherds: 5 oz
		Retouched chert flake
		6 unused chert flakes
	136B/2	Sherds: 1 oz
		Chert core

Group	Operation/Lot	Content
		Used chert flake
		Unused chert flake
	136B/3	Sherds: 7 oz
		2 unused chert flakes
		15 chert nodule fragments
	136B/4	Sherds: 6 oz
		3 unused chert flakes
		8 chert nodules and fragments
		1 land snail shell
	136B/5	Sherds: 5 lbs 18 oz
		Pottery figurine
		Retouched chert core
		Retouched chert flake
		7 used chert flakes
		22 unused chert flakes
		85 chert nodules and fragments
		Obsidian prismatic blade
		Metate
	136B/6	Sherds: 1 lb
		4 chert cores (1 used, 1 ground)
		4 used chert flakes
		3 unused chert flakes
		17 chert nodules and fragments
	136B/7	Sherds: 1 lb 8 oz
		4 chert cores (1 retouched, 1 used)
		Chert ovate biface
		Unclassifiable chert biface
		5 unused chert flakes
		29 chert nodules and fragments
		Granite metate
	136B/8	Sherds: 4 lbs 8 oz
		Miniature pottery vessel
		Pottery figurine
		Partially centrally perforated pottery sherd
		3 chert cores
		Variably retouched chert flake
		3 used chert flakes
		18 unused chert flakes
		33 chert nodules and fragments
	136B/9	Sherds: 6 oz
		Unused chert flake

Group	Operation/Lot	Content
1D-6	136F/1	Sherds: 11 oz Chert elongate biface Obsidian prismatic blade Obsidian flake
	136F/1A	Sherds: 3 oz
	136F/1B	Sherds: 2 oz
	136F/1C	Sherds: 11 oz Used chert flake Unused chert flake
	136F/2	Sherds: 1 lb 14 oz Used chert core Chert ovate biface 3 chert blades Pointed, retouched chert flake Variably retouched chert flake Retouched chert flake 8 used chert flakes 21 unused chert flakes 15 chert nodules and fragments 2 obsidian prismatic blades
	136F/3	Sherds: 7 lbs Chert core 2 chert retouched flakes 5 used chert flakes 13 unused chert flakes 2 chert nodule fragments Obsidian prismatic blade
	136F/4	Sherds: 3 lbs 9 oz Pottery figurine 3 unused chert flakes 8 chert nodules and fragments
	136F/5	Sherds: 1 lb 9 oz Unclassifiable chert biface Unused chert flake 3 chert nodule fragments
	136F/6	Sherds: 3 lbs 2 chert biface tools Used chert flake 10 unused chert flakes 5 chert nodule fragments 2 obsidian prismatic blades

Group	Operation/Lot	Content
	136F/7	Sherds: 13 oz Pottery spindle whorl 5 unused chert flakes Chert nodule
1D-7	136E/1	Sherds: 9 oz 2 used chert flakes
	136E/2	Sherds: 9 oz
	136E/3	Sherds: 1 lb 1 oz
	136E/4	Sherds: 5 lbs 10 oz Eccentrically perforated pottery sherd Used chert flake 7 unused chert flakes Obsidian prismatic blade Ground limestone object
	136E/5	Sherds: 3 lbs 8 oz 2 used chert blades Obsidian (green) prismatic blade
	136E/6	Sherds: 13 oz Censer ladle Used chert flake Unused chert flake Obsidian prismatic blade
	136E/7	Sherds: 6 oz Unused chert flake 3 human bone fragments (1 possibly drilled)
	136H/1	Sherds: 6 lbs 13 oz 2 chert cores (1 used) Chert ovate biface Chert elongate biface Chert unclassifiable biface 3 used chert flakes 2 unused chert flakes 10 chert nodule fragments Obsidian blade core 4 used obsidian prismatic blades Retouched obsidian prismatic blade 2 hematite nodules
	136H/2	Sherds: 1 lb

Group	Operation/Lot	Content
		Chert nodule
		Painted stucco fragment
	136H/3	Sherds: 2 lbs 2 oz
		Chert core
		Chert blade
		Unused chert flake
	136H/4	Sherds: 5 oz
		Obsidian prismatic blade
	136H/5	Sherds: 7 oz
		Used chert flake
	136H/6	Sherds: quantity not recorded
		2 unused chert flakes
		3 chert nodules and fragments
		Used obsidian prismatic blade
	136H/7	Sherds: 12 oz
		Unused chert flake
	136H/8	Sherds: 1 lb 2 oz
		3 unused chert flakes
		3 chert nodules
	136H/9	Bu. 205
1D-8	136D/1	Sherds: 13 oz
	136D/2	Sherds: 15 oz
		Chert ovate biface
		Used chert flake
		Granite metate
	136D/3	Sherds: 4 lbs 5 oz
		2 pottery figurines
		Unused chert flake
	136D/4	Sherds: 4 lbs 8 oz
		Pottery figurine
		2 chert cores
		Chert ovate biface
		3 used chert flakes
		2 unused chert flakes
	136D/5	Sherds: 7 lbs 14 oz
		2 pottery wall inserts
		2 pottery figurines
		Miscellaneous modeled pottery object

Group	Operation/Lot	Content
		Retouched chert flake
		Used chert flake
		5 unused chert flakes
		7 chert nodule fragments
		Obsidian core
	136D/6	Sherds: 8 lbs 12 oz
		Variably retouched chert flake
		Used chert flake
		9 unused chert flakes
		6 chert nodules and fragments
		Shell fan handle
	136D/7	Sherds: 1 lb 9 oz
		Unused chert flake
		Chert nodule fragment
1E-1	146G/1	Sherds: 3 oz
		3 chert cores
		Chert ovate biface
		67 unused chert flakes
		Retouched obsidian prismatic blade
	146G/2	Sherds: No data
	146G/3	Sherds: none
		5 unused chert flakes
	146G/4	Sherds: 9 oz
		5 chert cores
		Variably retouched chert flake
		Retouched chert flake
		10 unused chert flakes
	146G/5	Sherds: 12 oz
		Chert core
		Chert blade
		Unused chert flake
		Chert nodule
	146G/6	Sherds: 9 oz
	146G/7	Sherds: 2 lbs 1 oz
		Unused chert flake
	146G/8	Sherds: 13 oz
		Chert blade
		Unused chert flake

Group	Operation/Lot	Content
	146G/9	Sherds: 2 oz
	146H/1	Sherds: quantity not recorded Unused chert flake Chert nodule fragment
	146H/2	Sherds: 5 oz
	146H/3	Sherds: 4 oz
	146H/4	Sherds: 13 oz
	146H/5	Sherds: 13 oz 2 chert cores Chert blade Variably retouched chert flake 2 retouched chert flakes Used chert flake 4 unused chert flakes
	146H/6	Sherds: 2 oz Chert core, battered

References

Andrews, E. Wyllys
  1969 *The Archaeological Use and Distribution of Mollusca in the Maya Lowlands.* Tulane University, Middle American
    Research Institute, Publication 34.

Coe, William R.
  1965 Tikal: Ten Years of Study of a Maya Ruin in the Lowlands of Guatemala. *Expedition* 8(1):5–56.

Haviland, William A.
  1961 Excavation of Stela 27, in Tikal Report No. 8, Miscellaneous Investigations. In *Tikal Reports Numbers 1–11*,
    edited by E. M. Shook, W. R. Coe, V. L. Broman, and L. Satterthwaite, pp. 163–165. Philadelphia: The
    University Museum, University of Pennsylvania. Facsimile Reissue of Original Reports Published 1958–1961,
    1986.

  ———.
  1963 *Excavation of Small Structures in the Northeast Quadrant of Tikal, Guatemala.* Ph.D. dissertation, Department
    of Anthropology, University of Pennsylvania. Ann Arbor: University Microfilms International.

  ———.
  1997 The Rise and Fall of Sexual Inequality: Death and Gender at Tikal, Guatemala. *Ancient Mesoamerica* 8:1–12.

Haviland, William A., and Hattula Moholy-Nagy
  1992 Distinguishing the High and Mighty from the Hoi Polloi at Tikal, Guatemala. In *Mesoamerican Elites: An
    Archaeological Assessment*, edited by D. Z. Chase and A. F. Chase, pp. 50–60. Norman, OK: University of
    Oklahoma Press.

Iglesias Ponce de León, María Josefa
  2003 Problematical Deposits and the Problem of Interaction: The Material Culture of Tikal during the Early Classic
    Period. In *The Maya and Teotihuacan: Reinterpreting Early Classic Interaction*, edited by G. E. Braswell, pp. 167–
    198. Austin: University of Texas Press.

Laporte, Juan P.
  2003 Thirty Years Later: Some Results of Recent Investigation in Tikal. In *Tikal: Dynasties, Foreigners, and Affairs of
    State*, edited by J. A. Sabloff, pp. 281–318. Santa Fe, NM: School of American Research Press.

Martin, Simon
  2003 In the Line of the Founder: A View of Dynastic Politics of Tikal. In *Tikal: Dynasties, Foreigners, and Affairs of
    State*, edited by J. A. Sabloff, pp. 3–45. Santa Fe, NM: School of American Research Press.

Puleston, Dennis E.
    1971   An Experimental Approach to the Function of Classic Maya Chultuns. *American Antiquity* 36:322–335.

———.

    1974   Intersite Areas in the Vicinity of Tikal and Uaxactun. In *Mesoamerican Archaeology: New Approaches*, edited by
            N. Hammond, pp. 303–311. Austin: University of Texas Press.

Romero, Javier
    1960   Ultimas Hallazgos de Mutilaciones Dentarias en Mexico. *Sobretiro de los Anales del INAH*, Vol. 12:151–215.

Satterthwaite, Linton
    1952   Sweathouses. In *Piedras Negras Archaeology: Architecture*, Part 5, No. 3, pp. 1–91. Philadelphia: The University
            Museum, University of Pennsylvania.

Stewart, T. Dale
    1953   Skeletal Remains from Zaculeu, Guatemala. In *The Ruins of Zaculeu, Guatemala*, Vol. 1, by Richard B.
            Woodbury and Aubrey S. Trick, pp. 295–311. Boston: United Fruit Co.

Thompson, J. Eric S.
    1970   *Maya History and Religion*. Norman: University of Oklahoma Press.

Tozzer, Alfred M., ed. and trans.
    1941   *Landa's Relación de las Cosas de Yucatan, A Translation*. Papers of the Peabody Museum of Archaeology and
            Ethnology, Harvard University, Cambridge, Vol. 18.

Tikal Reports (see TR. 12):

TR. 3:
Satterthwaite, Linton
    1986   *The Problem of Abnormal Stela Placements at Tikal and Elsewhere*. Philadelphia: The University Museum,
            University of Pennsylvania.

TR. 4:
Satterthwaite, Linton
    1986   *Five Newly Discovered Carved Monuments at Tikal and New Data on Four Others*. Philadelphia: The University
            Museum, University of Pennsylvania.

TR. 8:
Satterthwaite, Linton, Vivian L. Broman, and William A. Haviland
    1986   *Miscellaneous Investigations: Excavation Near Fragment 1 of Stela 17, with Observations on Stela P34 and
            Miscellaneous Stone 25; Excavation of Stela 25, Fragment 1; Excavation of Stela 27; Excavation of Stela 28, Fragment
            1*. Philadelphia: The University Museum, University of Pennsylvania.

TR. 11:
Carr, Robert F., and James E. Hazard
    1986   *Map of the Ruins of Tikal, El Peten, Guatemala*. Facsimile Reissue of Original Reports Published 1958–1961.
            Philadelphia: The University Museum, University of Pennsylvania.

TR. 12:
Coe, William R., and William A. Haviland
    1982   *Introduction to the Archaeology of Tikal, Guatemala*. Philadelphia: The University Museum, University of
            Pennsylvania.

TR. 13:
Puleston, Dennis E.
1983   *The Settlement Survey of Tikal.* Philadelphia: The University Museum, University of Pennsylvania.

TR. 14:
Coe, William R.
1990   *Excavations in the Great Plaza, North Terrace and North Acropolis of Tikal, Vols. 1–4.* Philadelphia: The University Museum, University of Pennsylvania.

TR. 15:
Harrison, Peter D.
n.d.   *Excavations in the Central Acropolis of Tikal.*

TR. 18:
Jones, Christopher
n.d.   *Excavations in the Twin Pyramid Groups of Tikal.*

TR. 19:
Haviland, William A., with Marshall J. Becker, Ann Chowning, Keith A. Dixon, and Karl Heider
1985   *Excavations in Small Residential Groups of Tikal: Groups 4F-1 and 4F-2.* Philadelphia: The University Museum, University of Pennsylvania.

TR. 20B:
Haviland, William A.
2014   *Excavations in Residential Areas of Tikal: Non-elite Groups without Shrines: Analysis and Conclusions.*

TR. 21:
Becker, Marshall J., contributions by Christopher Jones
1999   *Excavations in Residential Areas of Tikal: Groups with Shrines.* Philadelphia: The University Museum, University of Pennsylvania.

TR. 22:
Haviland, William A.
n.d.   *Excavations in Residential Areas of Tikal: Group 7F-1.* [in prep.]

TR. 23A:
Loten, H. Stanley
2002   *Miscellaneous Investigations in Central Tikal.* Philadelphia: University of Pennsylvania Museum of Archaeology and Anthropology.

TR. 23G:
Puleston, Dennis E., and William R. Coe
n.d.   *Investigations of Group 6E-2 in Addition to Structures 6D-59 and 6F-51.* Philadelphia: University of Pennsylvania Museum of Archaeology and Anthropology.

TR. 23H:
Coe, William R., and Luis Luján M.
n.d.   *Investigations of Causeways.* Philadelphia: University of Pennsylvania Museum of Archaeology and Anthropology.

TR. 23I:
Dahlin, Bruce H.
n.d.   *Investigations of Reservoirs and Hydraulic Features.*

TR. 24A:
Fry, Robert E., and Dennis E. Puleston
    n.d.   *Excavations along the North and South Survey Strips.*

TR. 25A:
Culbert, T. Patrick
    1993   *The Ceramics of Tikal: Vessels from the Burials, Caches and Problematical Deposits.* Philadelphia: The University
            Museum, University of Pennsylvania.

TR. 27A:
Moholy-Nagy, Hattula, with William R. Coe
    2008   *The Artifacts of Tikal: Ornamental and Ceremonial Artifacts and Unworked Material.* Part A. Philadelphia:
            University of Pennsylvania Museum of Archaeology and Anthropology.

TR. 27B:
Moholy-Nagy, Hattula
    2003   *The Artifacts of Tikal: Utilitarian Artifacts and Unworked Material.* Part B. Philadelphia: University of
            Pennsylvania Museum of Archaeology and Anthropology.

TR. 30:
Monge, Janet and William A. Haviland
    n.d.   *The Skeletal Series of Tikal.* [in prep.]

TR. 32:
Puleston, Dennis E., and William A. Haviland
    n.d.   *The Chultuns of Tikal.*

TR. 33A:
Jones, Christopher, and Linton Satterthwaite
    1982   *The Monuments and Inscriptions of Tikal: The Carved Monuments.* Philadelphia: The University Museum,
            University of Pennsylvania.

TR. 37:
Moholy-Nagy, Hattula
    2012   *Historical Archaeology at Tikal, Guatemala.*

Illustrations

FIGURE 1

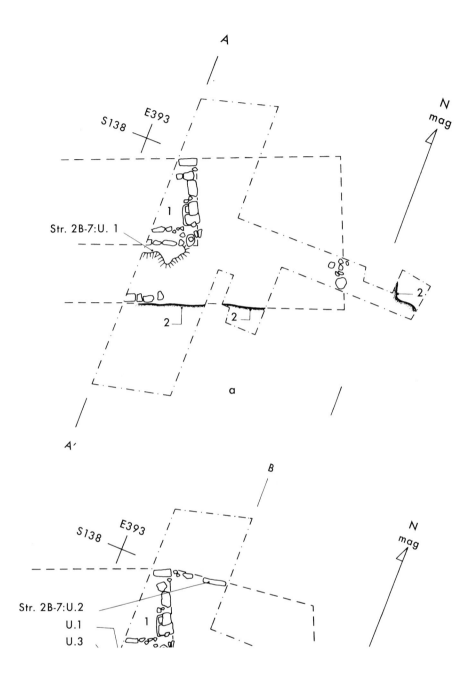

Str. 2B-7-2nd (a) and 1st (b): Plans.

Pertinent to Str. 2B-7: 1, Small platform built on fill of the main platform. Its wall, to which U. 1 turns up (Fig. 3a), was constructed of two lines of masonry with rubble hearting. Mound configuration suggests axial placement for this platform. *2*, Quarried bedrock; in front of the main platform, incorporated into the wall. Location of the E wall of the platform is indicated by badly ruined masonry. U. 1, Floor remnant that turns up to the base of small platform (1). Because a projection of this floor meets the top of the main platform wall (Fig. 3), U. 1 is assumed to have covered the main platform. U. 2, Rear wall for main platform of 1st on bedrock. Its top is 0.15 m above the level of U. 1 but about 0.25 m below the top of the small platform (1). U. 3, Wall that abuts the small platform (1) and rests on U. 1 as well as the top of the original S wall of the main platform. The top of U. 3 is at approximately the same elevation as U. 2, which suggests an E end platform higher than the surface of U. 1, but not as high as the small axially placed platform (1). For sections A-A' and B-B', see Fig. 3.

Str. 2B-Sub.1 (a) and Ch. 2B-15 (b): Plans.

Pertinent to Str. 2B-Sub.1: U. 4–7, Holes in bedrock that form a nearly straight line at intervals suggestive of posts for a structure wall unrelated to those of Str. 2B-7. U. 8–10, Apparent postholes in bedrock that form no meaningful pattern with U. 4–7 and 11. One possibility is that they relate to some sort of shelter built over Ch. 2B-15, but there is no verification for this. U. 11, Apparent posthole in bedrock so located that it could have supported a pole for the N wall of the same structure represented by U. 4–7. U. 12, Floor remnant, laid directly on bedrock, and later covered by fill for Str. 2B-7-2nd (Fig. 3). Its location between U. 5 and 11 suggests that it was pavement for a structure represented by these postholes. *Pertinent to Ch. 2B-15*: 3, Orifice. For sections A-A' and B-B', see Fig. 3.

FIGURE 2

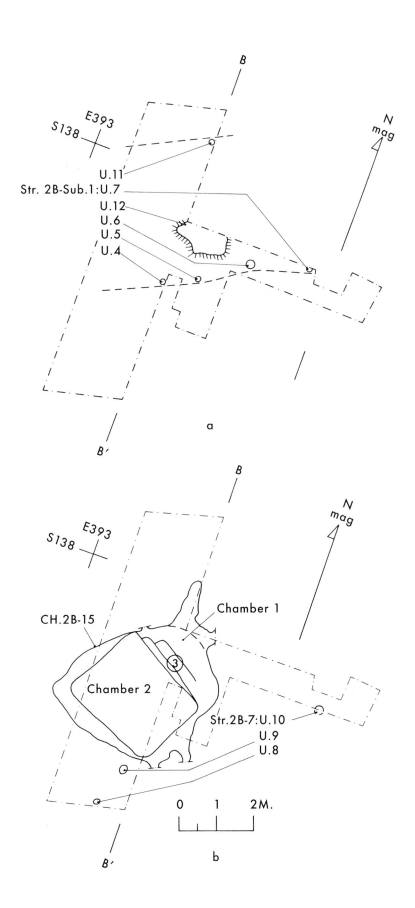

a

b

Str. 2B-7, 2B-Sub.1 (a, b) and Ch. 2B-15 (b): Sections A-A' and B-B', as located in Fig. 1 and 2.

Pertinent to Str. 2B-7: 1, Small platform (see Fig. 1:1). *2*, Quarried bedrock (see Fig. 1:2). U. 1, Pavement for the main platform (see Fig. 1). U. 2, N wall, Str. 2B-7-1st (see Fig. 1). U. 3, Wall for raised end section of Str. 2B-7-1st (see Fig. 1). The broken line from the top of U. 3 to the top of U. 2 is the reconstructed level of the floor for this portion of the structure; the broken line beneath is the elevation of U. 1 (see Fig. 1). The wall beneath U. 3 is now totally destroyed. U. 13, Mound of earth, very light in color near the top, darker near the bottom, which overlies U. 1 and 3; thought to be spoil from construction of Ch. 2B-15. *Pertinent to Ch. 2B-15: 3*, Orifice. Note suggestion of stepping on S edge (see Fig. 2:3). *4*, Step in Chm. 1, off-section. Where the section passes, this step has been worn away. *5*, White-colored earth, including well-preserved sherds and the stone cover for the chultun. *6*, Yellow-white earth, transitional in color between the very light (5) and the darker (7). Most of (5), and much of (6), seem to derive from ceiling collapse, the quantity of which suggests the reconstruction of the ceiling of Chm. 2 shown here in broken line. *7*, Dark earth, with higher organic content than (6), below it. *8*, Low cone of humus.

FIGURE 3

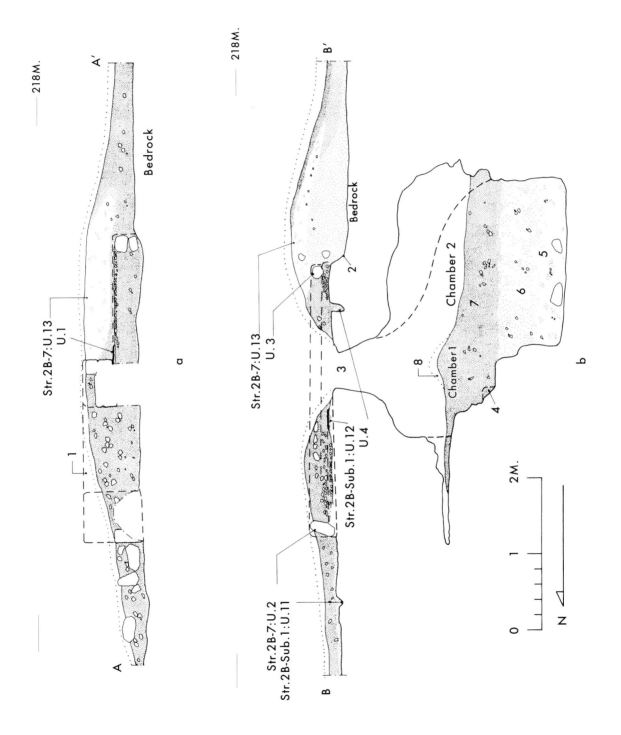

218M.

A'

Bedrock

Str.2B-7:U.13
U.1

1

a

A

218M.

B'

Bedrock

2

Str.2B-7:U.13
U.3

3

Str.2B-Sub.1:U.12
U.4

Chamber 1

Chamber 2

8

4

7

6

5

b

Str.2B-7:U.2
Str.2B-Sub.1:U.11

B

0   1   2M.

N

Str. 3D-8: Plan (a) and Section A-A' (b).

Pertinent to Str. 3D-8: 1, In situ masonry block for the front (E) wall. *2*, Disturbed masonry of the rear (W) wall. Wall height is reconstructed on the basis of floor reconstruction (see 6, below). *3*, In situ masonry, SE corner. *4*, Broken masonry, NE corner. *6*, Gray earth fill of structure, placed as CS. 2. At one time, this probably was covered by a floor (broken line) that ran from the top of the front wall (1) to the top of the rear wall (2). U. 1, Light-colored earth, thought to be the original ground at this locus. This is presumed to have been scraped and leveled to provide a base surface on which to build. U. 2, Packed, marly level that distinguished the operations of CS. 4 (preparation of a base surface) from those of CS. 2 (construction of the platform) and 3 (see U. 3, below). U. 3, Gray earth fill placed over U. 1 and 2 as CS. 3 to build up the level of Plat. 3D-5. The front wall of Str. 3D-8 was based on this, and probably a floor covered U. 3 E of Str. 3D-8. U. 4, Stony, light-colored soil, probably from disintegration of bedrock.

FIGURE 4

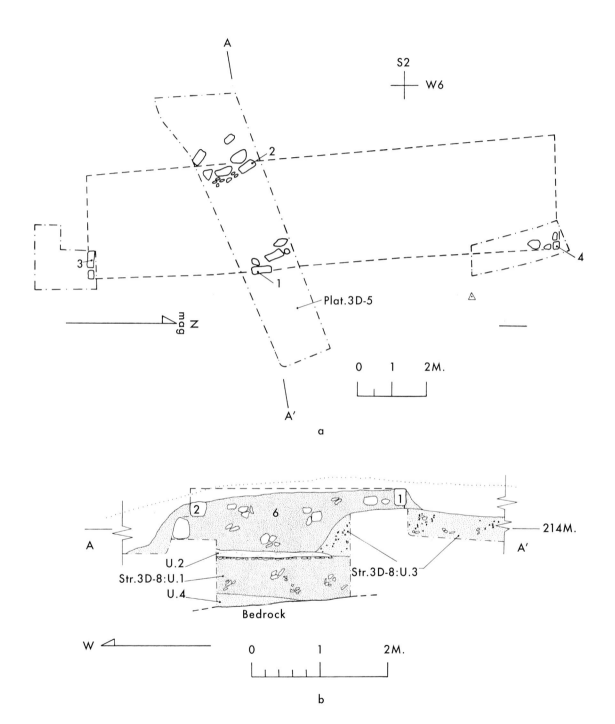

Str. 3D-9: Plan (a) and Section A-A' (b).

Pertinent to Str. 3D-9: 1, 2, S and N walls of the structure. The base of the N wall is in union with U. 1, a remnant of floor for Plat. 3D-5. Reconstructed maximum extent of these walls to the E and W is based on the configuration of the ruin mound. *3*, Earth and rubbish fill for Str. 3D-9-2nd. Poor preservation probably accounts for lack of a floor, but one probably ran from the top of the front to the top of the rear wall. A portion of this, reconstructed here, may have continued to serve Str. 3D-9-1st S of U. 3. U. 1, Remnant of a floor for Plat. 3D-5, in union with the base of the front wall of Str. 3D-9, which runs S from this wall. U. 3, Stones, apparently the remnant of fill for Str. 3D-9-1st. They overlie earth fill of Str. 3D-9-2nd, the top of which is at the same approximate elevation as the top of the S wall of the structure (1). These stones end, to the S, in a line parallel to the front wall. Apparently, a wall for an upper platform level was built here. U. 3 was followed far enough to the E to indicate that it probably ran the length of the structure. The reconstructed floor over this fill shown in the section is based on the surviving height of U. 3; it could have been higher, but not lower.

FIGURE 5

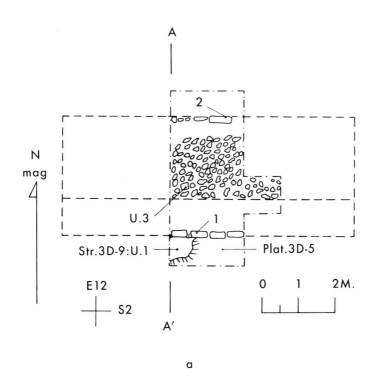

a

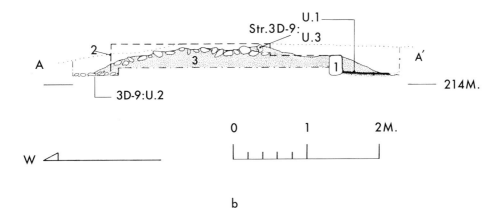

b

Str. 3D-10: Plan (a) and Section A-A' (b).

Pertinent to Str. 3D-10: 1, Bedrock quarried away to the N and E so as to produce vertical faces; marks the NE corner of Str. 3D-10, the masonry of which survives (badly ruined) just inside the corner. *2*, Broken masonry of the NW corner of Str. 3D-10. *3*, Rear wall masonry, Str. 3D-10. The masonry actually is set into the structure fill (U. 1), which therefore must have been dumped in place as the structure walls were built. Note the presence of two lines of stretchers, with a rubble core. *4*, Masonry from the same wall represented by U. 2 (see below). *5*, Front of hypothetical upper platform level, reconstructed on the basis of U. 5. U. 1, Combination of light gray earth and rubbish fill for CS. 3 of Str. 3D-10-2nd. U. 2, Front wall, built as CS. 3 of Str. 3D-10-2nd, upper platform level. Reconstructed height of U. 2 is based on the height of the rear structure wall (3) and U. 1 N of this. That the wall ran the length of the structure is indicated by 4 (above). U. 3, Light-colored earth fill for the lower platform level built against U. 2 as CS. 2. Presumably, this was covered by a floor that ran from the top of U. 4 and abutted U. 2. U. 4, Front wall of lower platform level, N of U. 2. The wall is based in part on bedrock and in part on a thin earth fill over bedrock, and was built as part of CS. 2. U. 5, Masonry block, possibly a remnant of an upper platform level (Str. 3D-10-1st) added to the original structure (Str. 3D-10-2nd). It rests on U. 1, and its height is matched by some rubble along the top of the S wall.

FIGURE 6

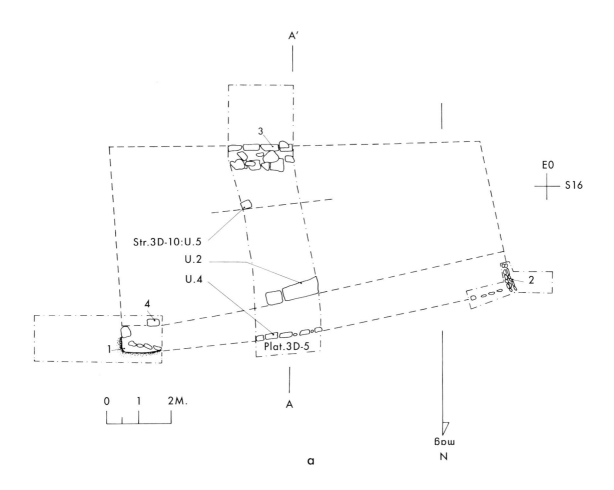

3

Str.3D-10:U.5

U.2

U.4

4

1

Plat.3D-5

E0
S16

2

0   1   2M.

A'

A

N
6ᴘɯ

a

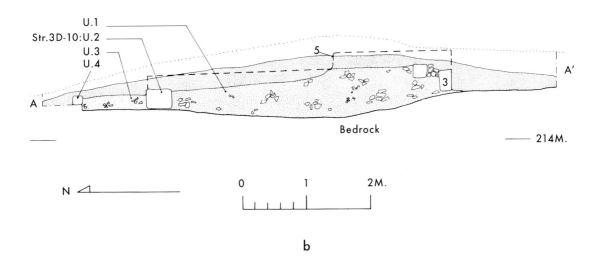

U.1

Str.3D-10:U.2

U.3
U.4

5

3

A

A'

Bedrock

214M.

N

0   1   2M.

b

FIGURE 7

GROUP 3D-3

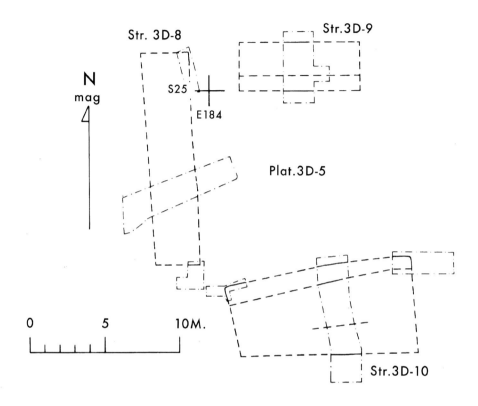

Gp. 3D-3: Plan as it appeared ca. Gp. TS. 2 (Table 2.20).

Figure 8 (facing page)
Gp. 3D-9: Plan and location of nearby test excavations. Shown are the group and hypothetical trails leading off to the NW and SW. The location of such trails is suggested by the pattern of sherd distributions in the test pits. Generally, sherd frequencies are highest in proximity to the broken-line trail reconstructions, dropping off to either side. This pattern could have been produced by habitual littering of people using trails as reconstructed here. Test pits are numbered 1 through 36. For section A-A', see Fig. 9.

FIGURE 8

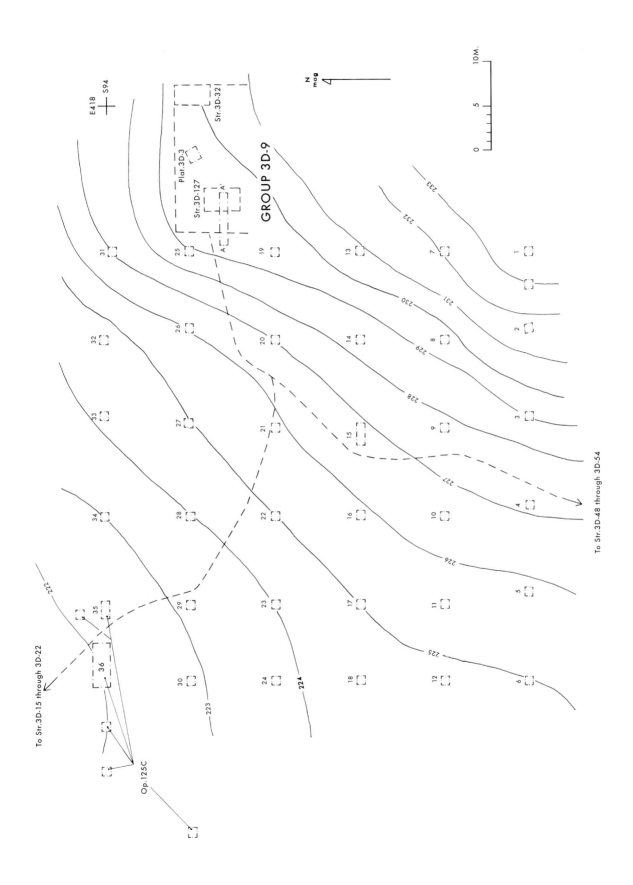

GROUP 3D-9

FIGURE 9

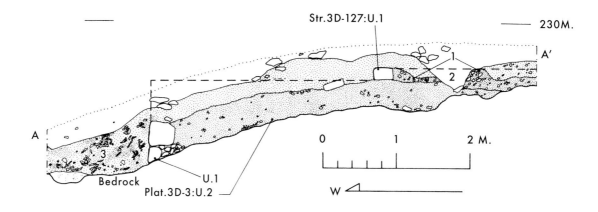

Pertinent to Str. 3D-127: 1, Structure fill composed of rock, earth, now badly disturbed. *2*, Pit dug into structure sometime following abandonment. U. 1, W wall of structure. The broken line that runs E from the top of the wall is a reconstruction of the structure floor, of which no trace now remains. *Pertinent to Plat. 3D-3: 3*, Post-construction material, consisting for the most part of midden W of Plat. 3D-3:U. 1, but blending with material to the E above Plat. 3D-3 and Str. 3D-127 that consists mostly of fill from erosion of architecture and the pit dug into the structure. U. 1, W wall of Plat. 3D-3, which rests on bedrock. Originally, the wall must have risen as high as the base of Str. 3D-127, but it has eroded down in the centuries following abandonment. U. 2, Fill for Plat. 3D-3, of blue-to-tan soil; overlies bedrock, is retained to the W by U. 1, and Str. 3D-127 was built upon it.

Figure 10 (facing page)
Gp. 2F-1: Plan and location of nearby test excavations. Shown are Plat. 2F-1-1st and Str. 2F-31-1st, although the two were not contemporary. The six previously mapped chultuns have been resurveyed, and their arrangement here supersedes that shown on the Encanto sheet of TR. 11. Note the two new chultuns, 2F-16 and 17. Chultun 2F-5, which appears near the bottom of the map, is discussed elsewhere. Test pits and trenches, other than those in Gp. 2F-1 itself, are numbered 1 through 8. Of these, numbers 1 and 2 are discussed in conjunction with Ch. 2F-5. For plans of Str. 2F-Sub.1, 2F-31, and Plat. 2F-1, see Fig. 11 and 13.

FIGURE 10

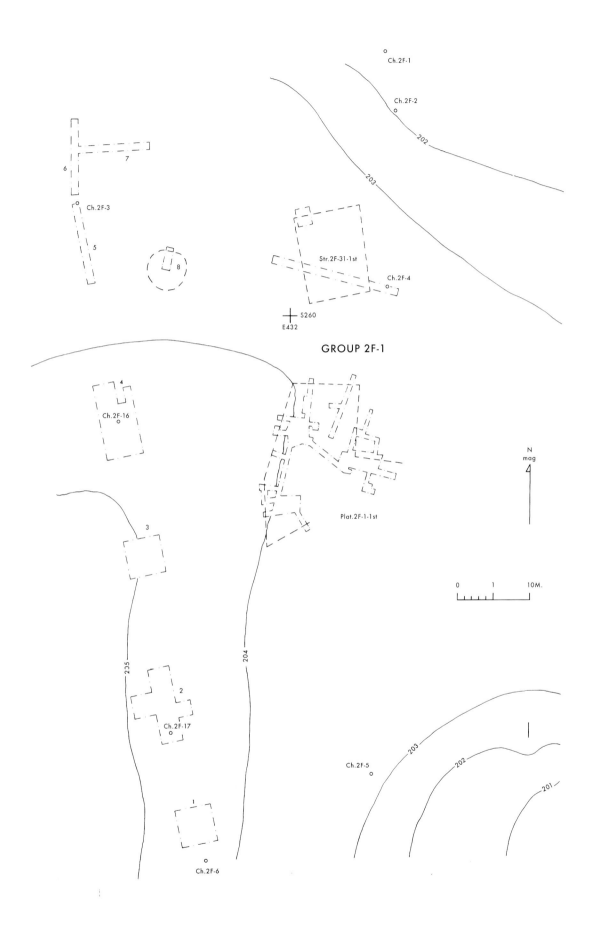

GROUP 2F-1

Plat. 2F-1: Plan.

Pertinent to Plat. 2F-1: 1, Hypothetical W wall of Str. 2F-30, on the basis of a projection N from the SW corner of Plat. 2F-1:U. 5. U. 2, 3, 4, Rubble walls, set on bedrock, which U. 1 (Fig. 12) abuts. They are interpreted as the walls for Plat. 2F-1-3rd, of which U. 2 and 4 continued to serve in later architectural developments. U. 5, Wall, based on bedrock, and abutted by U. 1. Its position relative to U. 1, 2, 3, and 4, and its apparent contemporaneity, indicate it likely is the S wall of a structure, 2F-30. U. 6, Wall of rubble and cut stone that rests on U. 1, W of Str. 2F-30 (1), and on bedrock to the E. In height, it is roughly equivalent to U. 2 and 4, and is interpreted as the N wall of Plat. 2F-1-2nd. U. 7, 8, 9, 10, Fills of small stones and rubble, placed on U. 1 and no higher than the level of U. 11. U. 11, floor remnants at the same general elevation as the tops of U. 2, 4, and 6. Projection of this surface covers U. 7, 8, 9, and 10. Interpreted as the floor for Plat. 2F-1-2nd, it must have covered U. 5. U. 12, 13, 14, 15, 16, Lines of stones that separate the various fills placed prior to the laying of U. 11. For section A-A', see Fig. 12.

FIGURE 11

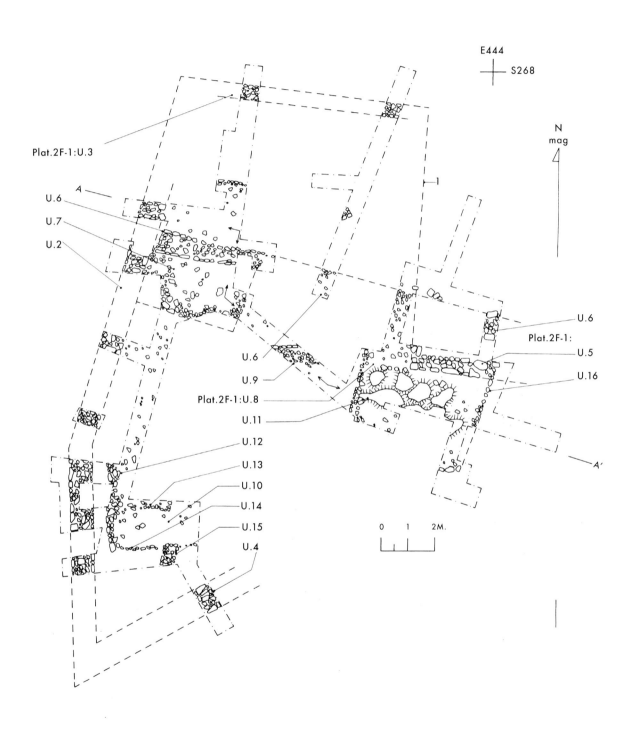

FIGURE 12

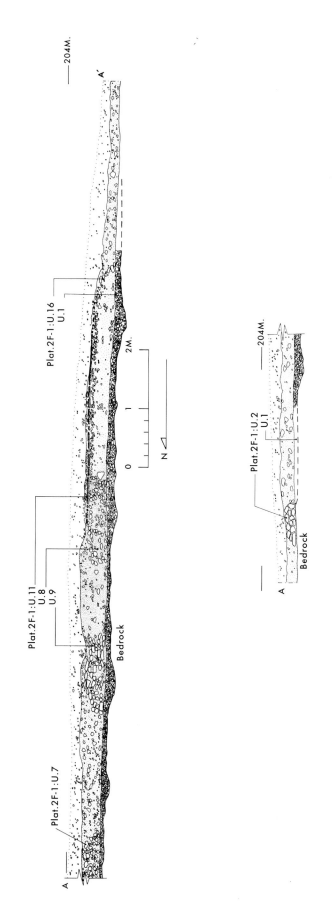

Plat. 2F-1: Section A-A', as located in Fig. 11.

Unit 1, Hard, packed stratum of stones that rests on bedrock and abuts U. 2, 3, 4, and 5; interpreted as the occupation surface for Plat. 2F-1-3rd. U. 2, Rubble wall for Plat. 2F-1-3rd (see Fig. 11). U. 7, 8, 9, Stone and rubble fill for Plat. 2F-1-2nd (see Fig. 11). Fill elsewhere is of light-colored earth, relatively stone-free. U. 11, Floor remnant, Plat. 2F-1-2nd (see Fig. 11). U. 16, Line of stones separating different fill operations (see Fig. 11).

FIGURE 13

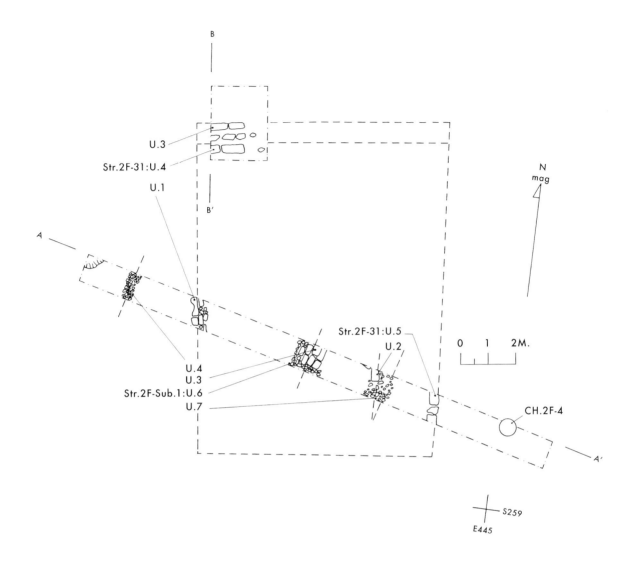

Str. 2F-31 and 2F-Sub.1: Plan.

Pertinent to Str. 2F-31: U. 1, W wall of 2nd, built on the floor of Str. 2F-Sub.1-1st. Its southward extent is not known, but location of U. 2 and 5 suggest it could not have been much shorter than shown, although it could have been longer. U. 2, E wall of 2nd, built in part on the E wall of Str. 2F-Sub.1-1st. U. 3, 4, Steps which, on the basis of their presence so close to the NW corner of the structure, probably ran the length of its N end. U. 5, E wall, Str. 2F-31-1st, constructed on Str. 2F-Sub.1:U. 9. Badly collapsed, much of its fill has spilled down into Ch. 2F-4. U. 5 surely could not have been significantly shorter than shown, but it could have run farther S. *Pertinent to Str. 2F-Sub.1: U. 3*, N doorjamb for a building that faced W (Str. 2F-Sub.1-2nd). Built on bedrock, it was later incorporated into a wall for an upper platform level for Str. 2F-Sub.1-1st. U. 4, wall of limestone rubble, built on U. 2 (Fig. 14), which retains fill to the E of earth (U. 5). It is interpreted as the W wall for a lower platform level for Str. 2F-Sub.1-1st. U. 6, Rubble added to convert U. 3 into a wall for an upper platform level, Str. 2F-Sub.1-1st. It is abutted by the fill (U. 5) E of U. 4; like U. 4, it rests on U. 2. U. 7, Wall of burned limestone rubble, placed where the earlier E wall of Str. 2F-Sub.1 probably stood; interpreted as the rear wall for Str. 2F-Sub.1-1st. For section A-A', see Fig. 14; section B-B', see Fig. 15.

FIGURE 14

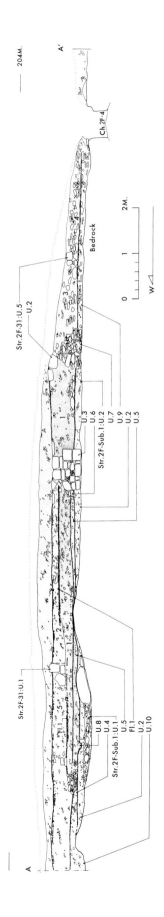

Str. 2F-31 and 2F-Sub.1: Section A-A', as located in Fig. 13.

Pertinent to Str. 2F-31: 2, Earth fill of CS. 2, Str. 2F-31-2nd. 3, Fill for 31-1st. U. 1, W wall of 31-1st and 2nd (see Fig. 13). U. 2, E wall of 2nd (see Fig. 13); occupation surface shown running between U. 1 and 2 is of packed, limy earth. U. 5, E wall of 1st (see Fig. 13). The occupation surface for this structure E of U. 2 has eroded away. *Pertinent to Str. 2F-Sub.1: 1,* Earth fill, placed for construction of Fl. 1 and CS. 2, Str. 2F-Sub.1-1st. U. 1, Stony stratum over bedrock, may predate all construction at this locus. U. 2, Packed, limy occupation surface for Sub.1-2nd; runs through the doorway of the structure. U. 3, N doorjamb of Sub.1-2nd (see Fig. 13), built as part of CS. 3. U. 5, Earth fill for CS. 3 of Sub.1-1st; runs E from U. 4 over U. 2 to abut U. 6. U. 6, Upper platform wall of Sub.1-1st (see Fig. 13); represents CS. 4. U. 7, E wall of Sub.1-1st (see Fig. 13); constructed as part of CS. 4. U. 8, Round hole in U. 2, probably a posthole. Evidence for or against a break in the overlying strata was destroyed, so it could relate to a building of perishable materials on the platform of Sub.1-1st. U. 9, Packed layer of earth and stones that abuts U. 7, probably the outside living surface when Sub.1-1st was in use. It was prevented from spilling into Ch. 2F-4 by rubble placed around the orifice. U. 10, Similar to U. 9, this stratum abuts the W face of U. 4. Fl. 1, plaster pavement for Str. 2F-Sub.1-1st. Note that it shows a turnup to a now missing wall E of U. 1, with another to the wall represented by U. 3 and 6. Apparently, the platform for Str. 2F-Sub.1-1st had three levels.

FIGURE 15

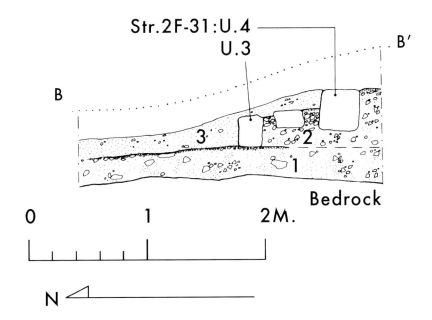

Str. 2F-31: Section B-B', as located in Fig. 13. *1*, Packed earth surface on which U. 3 and 4 rest. *2*, Fill behind U. 3 and 4, identical to that seen elsewhere for Str. 2F-31 (see Fig. 14:2). *3*, Probable washed-out fill of Str. 2F-31. U. 3, 4, Steps for Str. 2F-31 (see Fig. 13).

Figure 16 (facing page)

Str. 2G-56 and 2G-57: Plan.

Pertinent to Str. 2G-56: 1, 2, E (front) and W (rear) walls, which contain the fill of CS. 2. *5,* NW corner. *7,* Reconstruction of N wall, based on known location of NW corner (5) and point at which the wall abuts the rear of Str. 2G-57. U. 7, E (front) wall of upper platform level, consists of inner and outer faces, with a rubble core. It retains the fill of CS. 1. Excavation was sufficient to establish the wall probably ran the length of the structure. U. 9, Surviving portion of lower platform pavement E of U. 7. Badly preserved by U. 7, the two appear to be in union. U. 11, Rubble remains of the wall of a small platform constructed above the level of pavement for Str. 2G-56-B. A surviving fragment of that floor (Fig. 17a:U. 10) beneath the fill for U. 11 indicates that pavement ran beneath the wall, thus the platform was a later addition. U. 11, reconstructed on the basis of a few surviving veneer stones, apparently consisted of inner and outer faces with a rubble core. The S wall of U. 11 is reconstructed on the assumption of symmetry. *Pertinent to Str. 2G-57: 3,* E (front) wall for 2G-57-1st and 2nd. It rests on U. 1 and is in union with U. 5, a floor (not shown here) E of the structure. *4,* S wall, Str. 2G-57, abuts the E wall of 2G-56. *6,* NW corner. U. 2, Pavement, apparently surviving from the floor of Str. 2G-57-2nd. Its elevation is the same as that of the top of the E wall of the structure (3), and it runs beneath the E wall of the upper level of 57-1st (U. 6). U. 4, Apparently a burned floor remnant, on the ancient living level W of 57-1st, and at the same elevation as U. 2. U. 6, E (front) wall of upper platform level, based on U. 2. A line of rubble that continues N suggests that U. 6 runs the length of the structure. U. 7, W (rear) wall of 1st. A stone from its S end seems to have been removed when the front wall of Str. 2G-56 was built. The N wall of 56 abuts Str. 2G-57:U. 7. U. 8, A small platform that incorporated in its E wall the masonry of U. 6. The N and S walls rest on thin layers of fill over U. 2. The top of this platform was higher than the floor for the upper platform level of 2G-57. For sections A-A' and B-B', see Fig. 17. Coordinates are to datum shown in Fig. 27.

FIGURE 16

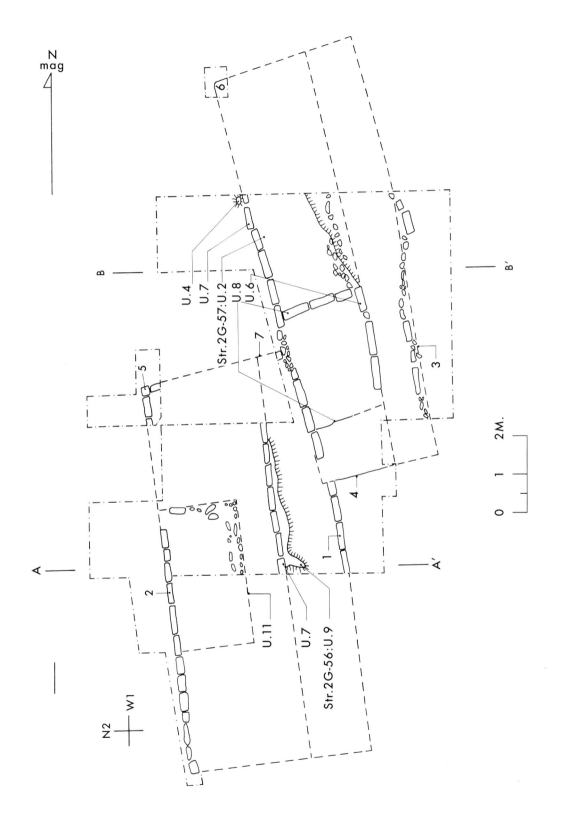

Str. 2G-56 and 57: Sections A-A' (*a*) and B-B' (*b*), as located in Fig. 16.

Pertinent to Str. 2G-56: 1, 2, Front and rear walls of structure (see Fig. 16:1, 2). 8, Reconstructed top of small, axially placed platform, on the basis of surviving height of U. 11. U. 1, Stratum of gray earth with large stone inclusions, but no sherds or artifacts. Evidently, bedrock here was never exposed. U. 2, Fill of CS. 4: compact gray earth with some stones, sherds and artifacts. U. 3 and 4, Packed, limy deposits that mark a pause in construction operations; structure walls rest on these. U. 5 and 6, Pause-lines similar to U. 3 and 4, separating the fills for CS. 3 and 2. The front and rear walls of the upper platform level rest on these. U. 7, Front wall, upper platform level (see Fig. 16). U. 8, Apparent inner face of the W (rear) wall of the upper platform level. It seems to have been constructed in the manner of U. 7, but the outer face and core have collapsed. Unit 8, with U. 7, retains the fill of CS. 2. U. 9, Floor for lower platform level (see Fig. 16). U. 10, Floor remnant beneath the fill for U. 11, at the correct elevation relative to U. 7 and 8 to be the pavement for the upper platform level, at one time sealing the fill of CS. 2. U. 11, Wall of small, axially placed platform (see Fig. 16). *Pertinent to Str. 2G-57: 3*, Front wall, 57-1st and 2nd (see Fig. 16:3). 9, Reconstructed floor of upper platform level, based on the height of U. 7. U. 1, Stratum of gray earth and small stones, on which the front wall (3) of Str. 2G-57 and U. 5 rest. U. 2, Floor for 57-2nd (see Fig. 16). U. 3, Line of stones beneath the W wall of 57-1st (U. 7) that might be the comparable wall for 57-2nd. Unit 2 ends by the top of U. 3, but it could have been chopped out for the placement of U. 3. U. 5, Plaza floor overlying U. 1, and in union with the base of the E wall (3) for Str. 2G-57. U. 6, E wall, upper platform level, off-section (see Fig. 16). U. 7, Rear wall, 2G-57-1st (Fig. 16).

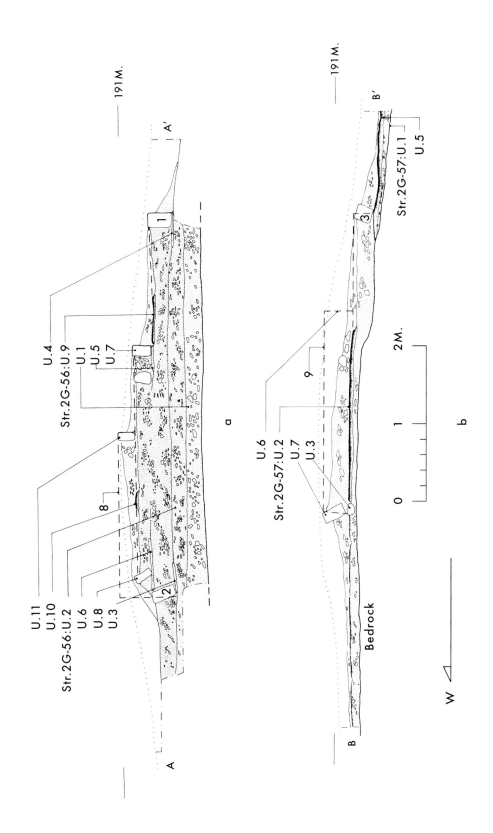

FIGURE 17

FIGURE 18

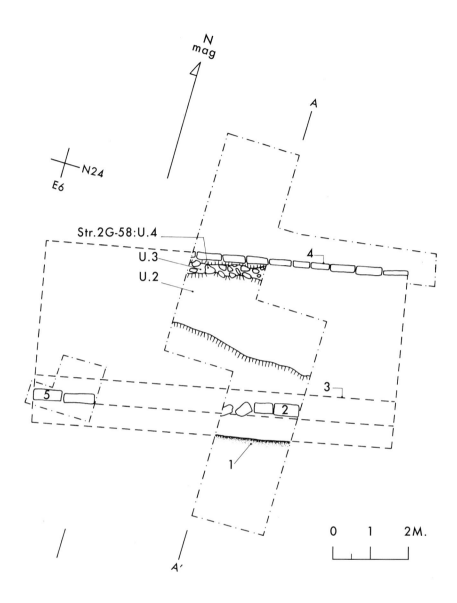

Str. 2G-58: Plan.

Pertinent to Str. 2G-58: 1, Riser to first platform level, here formed by cutting bedrock; it is reconstructed as running the length of the structure, only because the second riser does so. *2*, Riser to second platform level, reconstructed as running the length of the structure on the basis of a test at the W end (5). The wall rests on a thin layer of packed gray earth over bedrock. *3*, Riser to third platform level, reconstructed as running the length of the structure on the basis of data for the second riser. Its position is reconstructed on the basis of the location of U. 2, and the distance between the risers for the first and second platform levels. *4*, N (rear) wall of structure, based on the same stratum as the second riser (2). *5*, SW corner, second riser and W end wall. U. 2, Surviving portion of pavement for the upper platform level, 2G-58-3rd. U. 3, Remnant of a floor laid directly over U. 2. U. 4, Stone rubble based on U. 3, which could be a remnant of a rear base-wall, or an added upper platform level. For section A-A', see Fig. 19. Coordinates are to datum shown in Fig. 27.

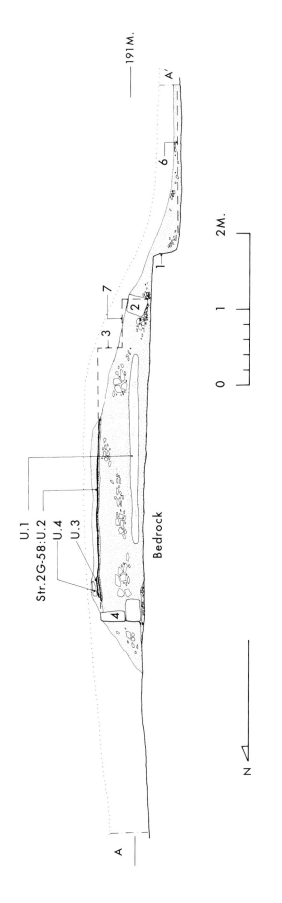

FIGURE 19

Str. 2G–58: Section A-A', as located in Fig. 18.

Pertinent to Str. 2G-58: 1, Riser of first platform level (see Fig. 18:1). *2,* Riser of second platform level (see Fig. 18:2). *3,* Riser of third platform level (see Fig. 18:3). *4,* Rear wall of structure (see Fig. 18:4). *6,* Reconstructed floor for Plat. 2G-1, on the basis of the elevation of the bedrock surface, height of the second and third risers (2 and 3), and elevation of Str. 2G-57:U. 5 (Fig. 17), which is within 3 cm of the reconstruction here. *7,* Reconstructed level of floor between second and third risers (2 and 3) based on a division in half of the height from the first to third platform levels. U. 1, Limy deposit from pause in fill operation between CS. 3 and 2 of 58-3rd. Fill for the former consists of packed gray earth; for the latter of darker earth retained by the second riser (2). U. 2, Floor for upper platform level of 58-3rd (see Fig. 18). U. 3, Floor for 58-2nd (see Fig. 18). U. 4, Stone rubble (see Fig. 18).

Str. 2G-59-3rd and earlier construction: Plan.

Pertinent to Str. 2G-59: 1, Location of outer walls, 59-1st (Fig. 22) for reference. U. 5, Floor of the E platform of 59-4th; it covers the westernmost stone of U. 3 (Fig. 24), and must have covered the others. To the N, U. 5 turns down over the rough masonry of a platform wall that rests on the same gray fill as U. 3, and to the W it turns up to U. 6. Burial 55 represents a later penetration of this floor. Beneath Bu. 55 is U. 2, the floor that preceded U. 5, and the earliest at this locus. U. 6, Masonry to which U. 5 turns up. Unit 7 meets the top of U. 6 to the W. U. 7, Floor that meets the top of U. 6; it may have covered U. 6 at one time. This is likely an early floor for Plat. 2G-1; eventually it was penetrated by Bu. 58. U. 10, N wall for the E platform of 59-3rd. To the W it rests on U. 5; to the E, it rests on earth fill just N of U. 5. U. 11 and 12, S and E walls for the E platform of 59-3rd. Unit 12 was built directly above U. 3, and was based directly on U. 5. Units 10, 11, and 12 retain a brown earth fill. U. 13, N-S wall based (like U. 12) on U. 5; it defines the western limit of the E platform for 59-3rd, as U. 10 and 11 end in line with it. U. 14, Wall joining U. 10 and 15. The S end abuts U. 10, and N end lies beneath the S wall of U. 15; it retains a tamped earth fill to the W. U. 15, Small platform based on the fill N of U. 10, the fill W of U. 14 and U. 9 (Fig. 23). U. 16, Pavement for U. 15; it abuts the N and W walls of the platform, but covers the S and E walls (see Fig. 23). U. 21 and 22, Two postholes in bedrock. For sections A-A' and B-B', see Fig. 23. For section C-C', see Fig. 24. Coordinates are to datum shown in Fig. 27.

FIGURE 20

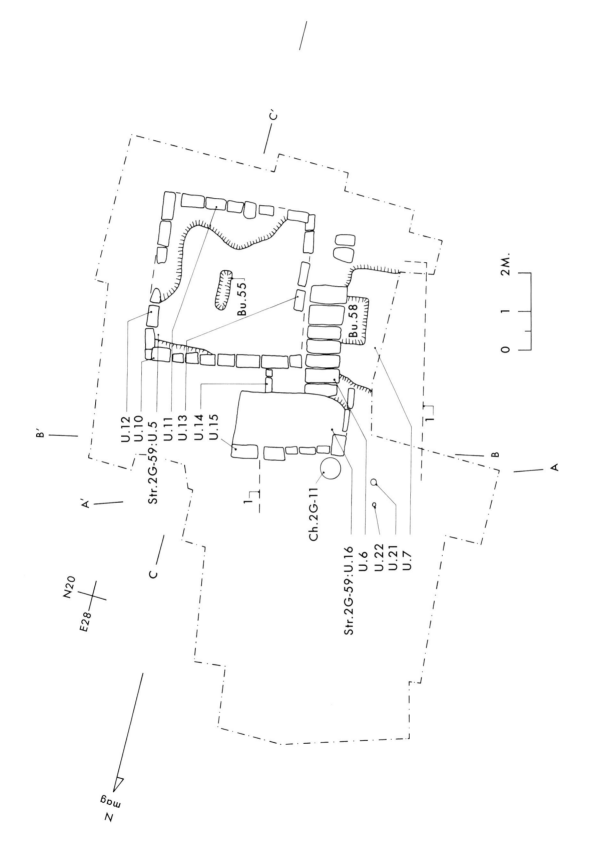

Str. 2G-59-2nd and 2G-Sub.1: Plan.

Pertinent to Str. 2G-59-2nd: 1, Location of outer wall, Str. 2G-59-1st, for reference. *2,* E (rear) wall, 59-2nd. To the N, this is based on a layer of thin gray fill over bedrock. Farther S, it rests on U. 16 (Fig, 20, 24), and must also have rested on the now destroyed surface of the E platform of 59-3rd. The southward projection of this wall is based on data for the front of this structure, and analogy with 59-1st. *3,* N wall, 59-2nd; rests on the same stratum as the rear wall (2) and Str. 2G-Sub.1. *4,* N stairs, 59-2nd; later Bu. 49 destroyed a small portion of its lowest step. The stairs are based on Fl. 2 of the plaza, with plaster patching forming a turnup. In the reconstruction of Str. 2G-59-2nd, it has been assumed that the S wall was positioned at the same location as the comparable wall for Str. 2G-59-1st, and that the front was symmetrical, thus requiring a S stairway similar to the N stairway (4). *5,* Block, apparently out of position, of the exact size to fit the space in the lowest riser of the N stairway (4) where Bu. 56 was later placed (Fig. 22 and 173b). This block could only have been removed and placed in its present position prior to construction of 59-1st. This is the basis of the conclusion that Bu. 56 marks abandonment of 59-2nd, and was not intruded at a later time. *6,* W wall of 59-2nd; based on earth fill, it incorporates the W wall of U. 15 (Fig. 23). It retains a mixed fill of brown earth and large stones. The N stairway (4) is built against this wall, and Fl. 2 of the plaza runs up to it. U. 15, See Fig, 20; shown here are the stones incorporated in Str. 2G-59-2nd. U. 17, 18, 19, and 20, Walls of the E platform of 59-2nd. Unit 17 rests upon the same gray fill on which U. 3 and the rear wall of Str. 59-2nd were built. U. 17 retains a fill of rubble. Units 18 and 19 are based on bedrock. Short U. 20 runs in line with the earlier U. 13. *Pertinent to Plat. 2G-1: Fl. 2,* Plaza floor in front of Str. 2G-59-2nd. It turns up to the W wall (6) of the structure, and the steps (4) were built on it, with secondary turnup. For sections *A-A'* and *B-B',* see Fig. 23. For section *C-C',* see Fig. 24. Coordinates are to datum shown in Fig. 27.

FIGURE 21

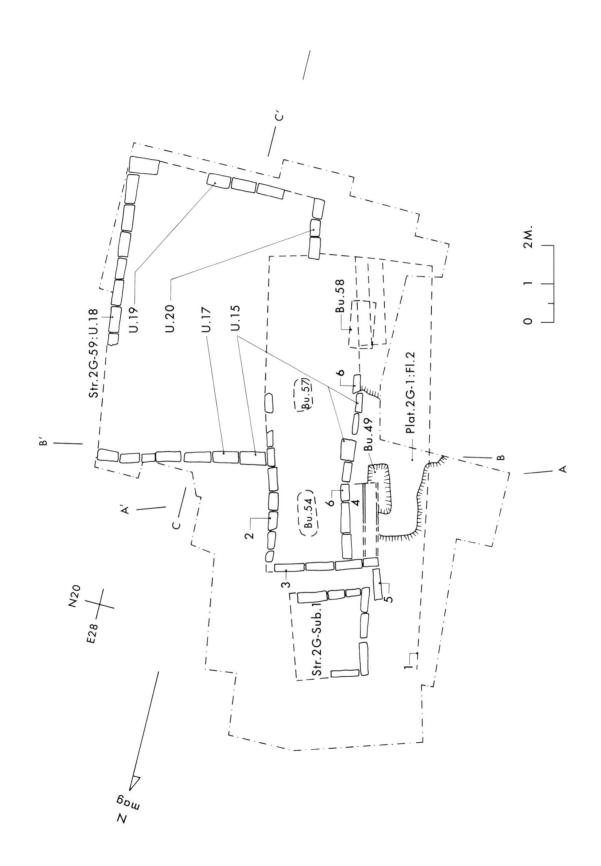

Str. 2G-59-1st: Plan.

Pertinent to Str: 2G-59: 2, NE corner, 59-2nd. Its rear wall was incorporated into that of 59-1st (see TR. 20B:fig. 1b, showing the juncture of these walls). *7*, S end of masonry added to that of 59-2nd to complete the E wall of 59-1st. *8*, Masonry of the N wall, Str. 2G-Sub.1, incorporated into 2G-59-1st. *9*, Masonry added to that of 2G-Sub.1 to complete the N wall of 59-1st. *10*, W (front) wall, 59-1st. Missing masonry N of the front-rear axis may have been robbed, since the blocks on either side are well preserved. *11*, S wall, 59-1st, in union with Fl. 1 of the plaza. *12*, W wall, upper platform level. Note the two cover stones for Bu. 49 just to the W; it is not known whether they were visible after their placement (see section III). U. 15, See Fig. 20 and 21; this one stone remained exposed after construction of 59-1st. U. 17, 18, 19, and 20, E platform walls (see Fig. 21). *Pertinent to Plat. 2G-1:Fl. 1*, Plaza floor in union with the S wall (11) of Str. 2G-59-1st. For sections A-A' and B-B', see Fig. 23. For section C-C', see Fig. 24. Coordinates are to datum shown in Fig. 27.

FIGURE 22

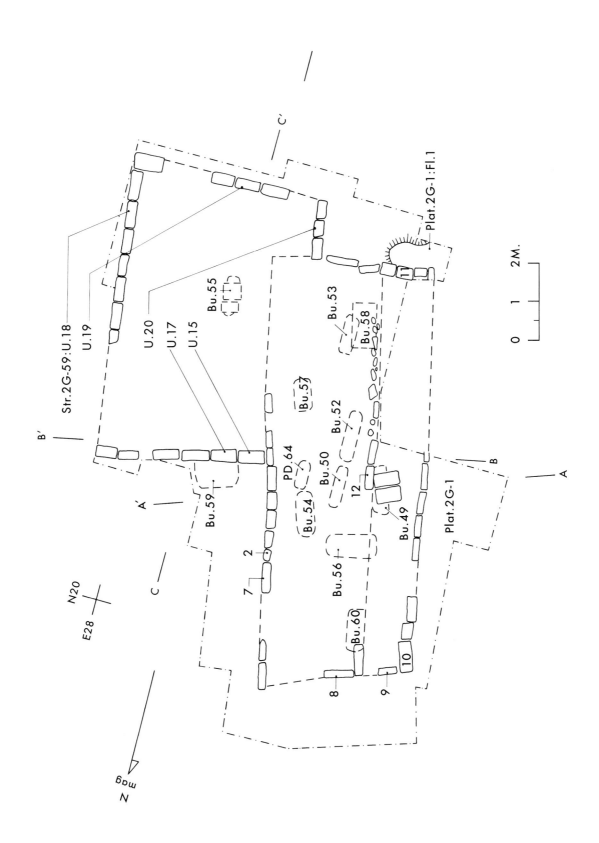

Str. 2G-59: Sections A-A' (*a*) and B-B' (*b*), as located in Fig. 20, 21 and 22.

Pertinent to Str. 2G-59: 2, Rear wall, 2G-59-2nd, reused in 2G-59-1st (see Fig. 20 and 22:2). *4,* N stairs, 2G-59-2nd (see Fig. 21:4). The top step correlates with the top of the stony fill to the E, hence the floor reconstruction for Str. 2G-59-2nd indicated by the lower broken line. *6,* Front wall, 2G-59-2nd (see Fig. 21:6). *10,* Front wall, 2G-59-1st (see Fig. 22:10). Note that the stones covering Bu. 49 project slightly above a hypothetical level floor running from the top of the front wall (10). If, though, the floor had a slope like that of the comparable floor of Str. 3F-25-1st (Fig. 43:U. 1), then Bu. 49 would have been sealed by the floor. *12,* W wall, upper platform level, 2G-59-1st (see Fig. 22:12). *15,* Masonry block fill for 2G-59-2nd. *16,* Fill N of U. 10 (Fig. 20). Paved after construction of U. 10, its surface is higher than U. 5 (Fig. 20). The surface of this fill probably was an informal occupation surface associated with 59-3rd. Now, fill for 59-2nd overlies it. U. 8 and 9, Small floor remnants identified in the trench through the front-rear axis of 2G-59 beneath Plat. 2G-1:Fl. 2. Their elevation is the same as U. 7 (Fig. 20), and probably they are parts of the same floor. U. 15 and 16, Walls and floor of the small platform associated with Str. 2G-59-3rd (see Fig. 20). *Pertinent to Ch. 2G-11: 13,* Possible stone cover. *14,* Packed, sterile gray earth. *Pertinent to Plat. 2G-1: Fl. 1,* Identified by the S wall of Str. 2G-59-1st (see Fig. 22:11). Fl. 2, Associated with Str. 2G-59-2nd. Off-section, this floor turns up to the W wall (6) of Str. 2G-59-2nd (see also Fig. 21:4).

FIGURE 23

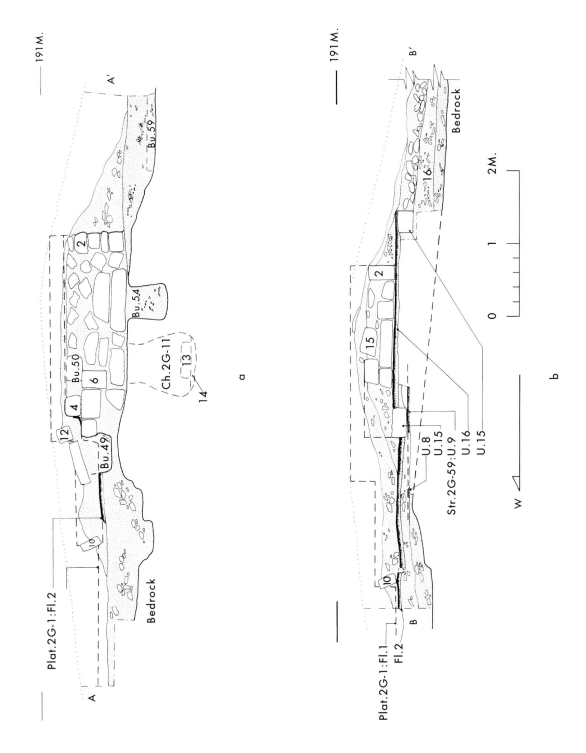

FIGURE 24

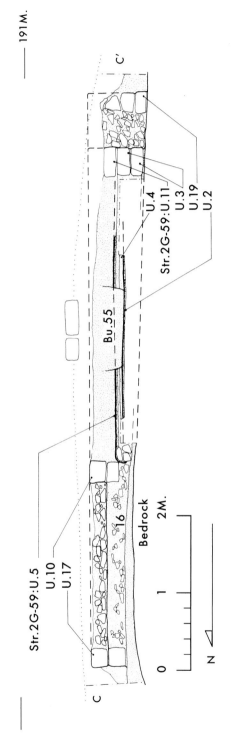

— 191 M.

Str. 2G-59:U.5
U.10
U.17

Bedrock

Str. 2G-59:U.11
U.4
U.3
U.19
U.2

Bu. 55

16

0   1   2 M.

N

Str. 2G-59: Section C-C', as located in Fig. 20, 21, and 22.

Pertinent to Str. 2G-59: 16, Fill N of U. 10 (see Fig. 23:16). U. 2, Floor for 59-5th (see Fig. 20:U. 5). U. 3, S wall of E platform, 59-4th, based on a very thin stratum of gray earth over bedrock. U. 4, Light-colored pause-line in fill for 59-4th. U. 5, E platform floor for 59-4th (see Fig. 20). U. 10 and 11, N and S walls for the E platform of 59-3rd (see Fig. 20). The height of U. 10 suggests the one-time presence of a floor as shown by the broken line between U. 10 and 11. U. 17 and 19, Walls for the E platform of 59-1st and 2nd (see Fig. 21, 22). The fill N of U. 10 (16) seems to have been cut away for placement of U. 17, and then a fill of rubble was dumped on top of it. The height of this rubble, as well as U. 17, suggests that the floor level remained the same as for 59-3rd.

FIGURE 25

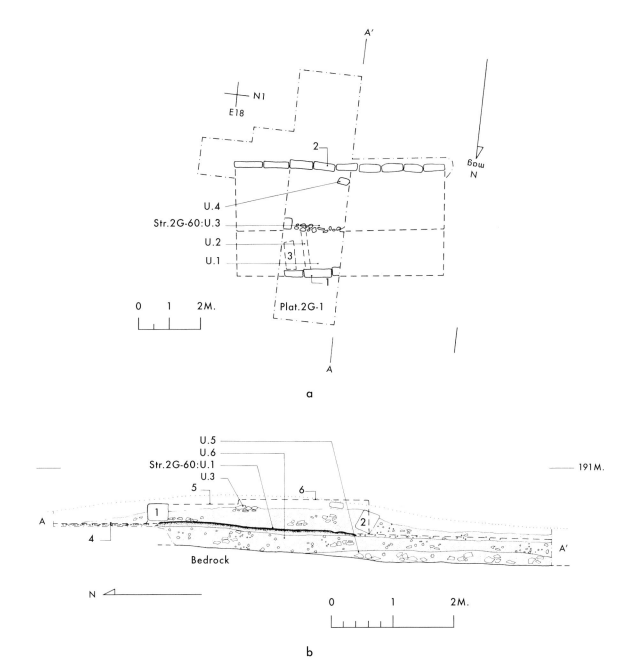

Str. 2G-60: Plan (*a*) and Section A-A' (*b*).
Pertinent to Str. 2G-60: 1, N (front) wall, 60-1st. *2*, S (rear) wall, based on U. 6. This, and the N wall, retains a fill of brown earth barely distinguishable from U. 6. *3*, Masonry block, significance unknown. *4*, Reconstructed plaza floor, based on existence of a level of compact pebbles at the same elevation as the base of the N wall (1). *5*, Reconstructed level of floor for lower platform level, based on height of N wall. *6*, Reconstructed level of summit floor, based on height of lower plat-form level and height of mound. U. 1, Floor that runs partially beneath the front wall of the structure. It turns up to U. 2; other relations are unknown. U. 2, Wall associated with otherwise unknown construction beneath Str. 2G-60; U. 1 turns up to it. U. 3, Line of rubble that is reconstructed as the front wall for an upper platform level, but which could be the front of a smaller platform. U. 4, Single stone, perhaps the only remnant of a rear counterpart for U. 3. U. 5, Light gray stratum that overlies bedrock, virtually devoid of sherds and artifacts; likely represents ancient undisturbed surface into which a few broken objects had been trampled. U. 6, Stratum of brown earth containing many sherds and artifacts; undoubtedly fill to raise this lower area to the level of the plaza. Units 1, 2, and Str. 2G-60 are all based on this stratum. Coordinates are to datum shown in Fig. 27.

FIGURE 26

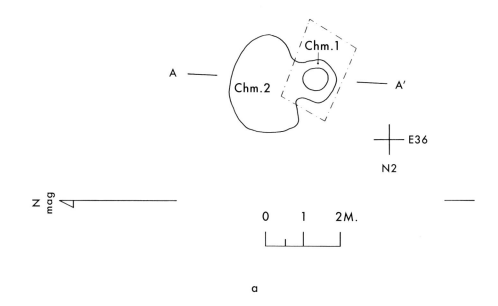

a

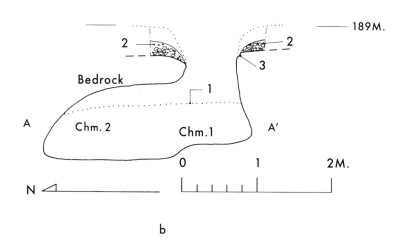

b

Ch. 2G-5: Plan (*a*) and Section A-A' (*b*).
Pertinent to Ch. 2G-5: *1*, Loose earth fill containing a few sherds and the broken stone cover. *2*, Stratum of gray earth and pebbles. *3*, Stepped lip, cut to receive the stone cover.

FIGURE 27

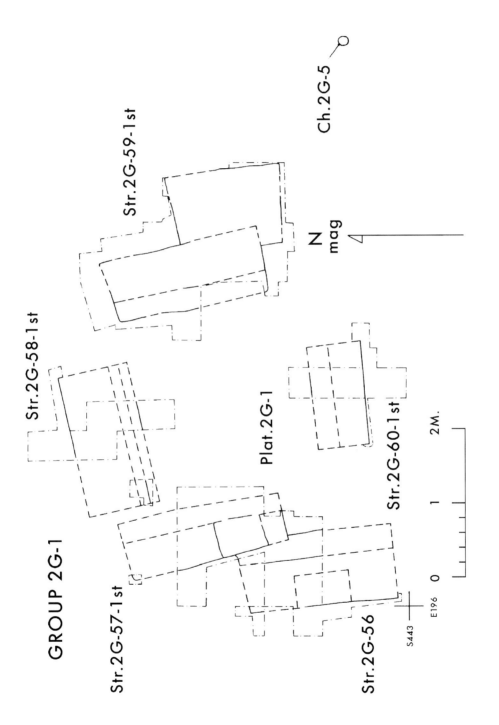

GROUP 2G-1

Str.2G-57-1st

Str.2G-58-1st

Str.2G-59-1st

Ch.2G-5

N mag

Plat.2G-1

Str.2G-60-1st

Str.2G-56

S443

E196

0 1 2M.

Gp. 2G-1 as it appeared ca. Gp. TS. 2 (Table 2.52).

FIGURE 28

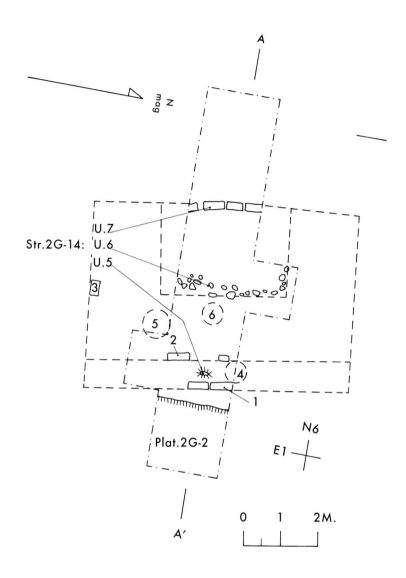

Str. 2G-14: Plan.

Pertinent to Str. 2G-14: 1, E (front) wall of 14-1st; rests on U. 2, the floor that can be seen immediately E of the wall (1). The fill W of this wall, and beneath the level of U. 5, is distinct from fill associated with U. 4 (Fig. 29). The N-S extent of this wall is reconstructed on the basis of the position of a stone of the S wall (3) and overall mound configuration. *2*, E (front) wall of upper platform level of 14-1st. Its forward position suggests that it runs the length of the structure, and is not the front wall of a small, axially placed platform. *3*, S end-wall masonry, visible from the surface without excavation. U. 5, Floor remnant, indicating one-time presence of pavement for the front of the lower platform level. U. 6, Rubble wall that indicates one-time presence of a small, axially placed platform. The height and position of U. 6 indicate that it replaced the platform associated with U. 3 (Fig. 29). U. 7, W (rear) wall, 14-1st. No change in the fill was noted at the base of U. 7, but one would expect that it was based on packed earth fill that continued W as an informal occupation surface. *Pertinent to Ch. 2G-10: 4*, Or. 2 (Fig. 32:2). *5*, Or. 3 (Fig. 32:3). *6*, Or. 1 (Fig. 32:1). For section A-A', see Fig. 29. Coordinates are to datum shown in Fig. 33.

FIGURE 29

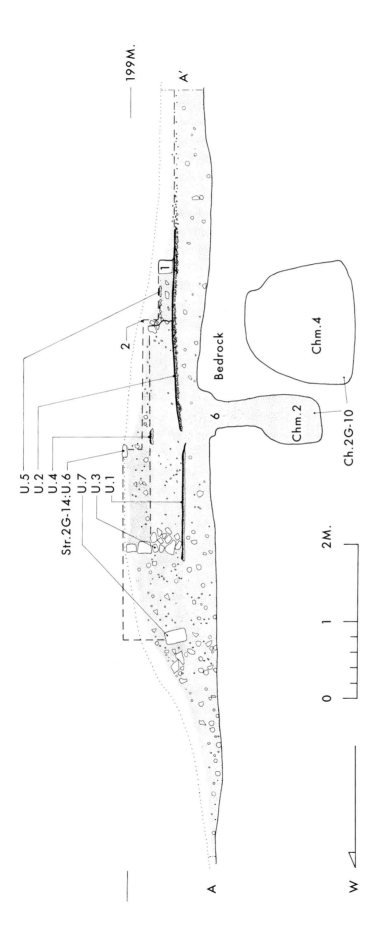

Str. 2G-14 and Ch. 2G-10: Section A-A', as located in Fig. 28.

Pertinent to Str. 2G-14: 1, Front wall, 2G-14-1st (see Fig. 28:1). 2, Front wall, upper platform level, 2G-14-1st, off-section (see Fig. 28:2). U. 1, Floor surface at the same approximate elevation as U. 2. U. 2, Floor surface at the same approximate elevation as U. 1, but laid on a foundation of small stones. The front wall (1) of 1st is based on this floor. U. 3, A wall that runs N-S, of which the lowest portion is composed of rubble. This is based on U. 1. The rubble portion, which reaches as high as U. 4, supports an upper portion of well-cut masonry. The masonry differences suggest that the two portions were constructed at different times. Since the fill E and W of the lower portion differs slightly, this may be the remains of the rear wall for 14-2nd. The upper masonry may relate to an early version of U. 6. U. 4, Floor remnant at the same elevation as the top of the rubble portion of U. 3, reinforcing the interpretation of that wall as a portion of 14-2nd. To the E, U. 4 is reconstructed as running as far as an apparent chop-line in its fill beneath the later wall (2). Presumably, this is where the front wall of 14-2nd stood, before it was later torn out. U. 5, Floor for 2G-14-1st (Fig. 28). U. 6, Remains of wall for small axially placed platform (see Fig. 28). U. 7, Rear wall, 2G-14-1st (see Fig. 28). *Pertinent to Ch. 2G-10:* 6, Or. 1 (Fig. 28:6, 32:1). Note stepped lip.

Str. 2G-15-3rd (*a*), 2nd (*b*), 1st (*c*) and 2G-Sub.2-2nd (*a*), 1st (*b*): Plans.

Pertinent to Str. 2G-15: 3, Masonry originally associated with 15-2nd (W end) that appears to have protruded beneath the W wall of 15-1st. This, its axial placement relative to the final structure, as well as the height of the latter, suggest continued use of this older masonry as part of a step to 15-1st. U. 1, NW corner of 3rd, built on Str. 2G-Sub.2:U. 7. U. 2, N, E, and W walls for 15-2nd, which includes in its fill the remains of 15-3rd. The walls rest on the same stratum as U. 3. U. 3, Plaster floor that abuts, and turns up to, U. 2 as well as to Str. 2G-Sub.2-1st. It lies on fill continuous with that of both constructions. U. 4, Floor surface that turns up to the base of the wall for 15-1st. *Pertinent to Str. 2G-Sub.2: 1*, Position of known walls for Sub.2-1st. The walls of Sub.2-2nd are unknown, as they were torn out for construction of Sub.2-1st. The surviving fill for Str. 2G-Sub.2nd and 3rd, however, the location of U. 4, and the known extent of surrounding floors combine to suggest that the walls of the successive architectural developments of Sub.2 did not differ greatly in size. U. 2, Plaster floor surface N of the structure, 3 cm thick. The floor ends at a stone by U. 4, and overlies fill continuous with that for Str. 2G-Sub.2-2nd and 3rd. U. 4, Hole in the stone fill for Str. 2G-Sub.2-2nd and 3rd, probably for support of a pole. U. 6 and 7, Floor surfaces S of the structure, 3 cm thick. U. 6, With its small stone foundation, was laid directly over an earlier floor, U. 5; Str. 2G-15-3rd was built directly on U. 7. Since both are at the same elevation, both are interpreted as remnants of the same floor. U. 8, Pavement at the same elevation as Str. 2G-15:U. 3 and thought to be a remnant of the same floor. For section A-A', see Fig. 31. Coordinates are to datum shown in Fig. 33.

FIGURE 30

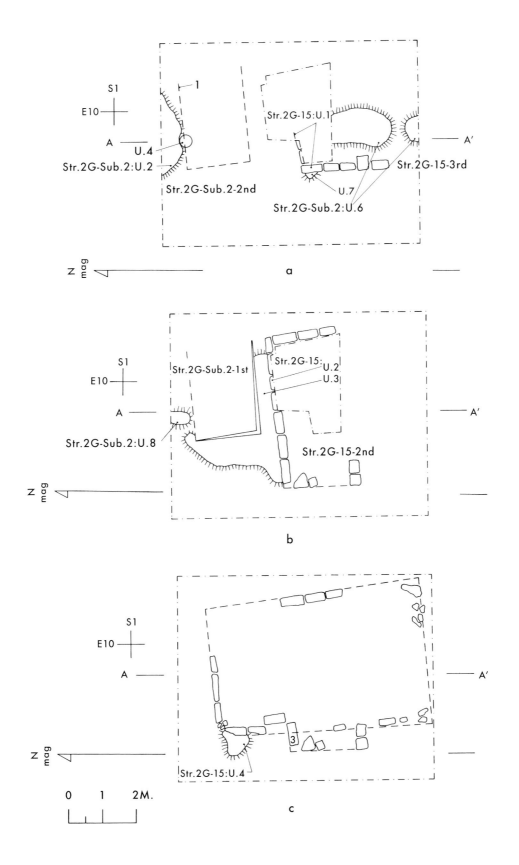

Str. 2G-15 and 2G-Sub.2: Section A-A', as located in Fig. 30.

Pertinent to Str: 2G-15: 4, N wall, 15-1st, badly broken (see Fig. 30). It is based on earth 8 cm above the elevation of 2G-Sub.2:U. 8 and it crossed the W wall of Sub.2-1st. The new plaza floor indicated in broken line above Str. 2G-Sub.2:U. 8 is reconstructed on the basis of Str. 2G-15:U. 4 (Fig. 30). *5,* Marl fill of 15-2nd. *6,* Reconstructed floor level, 15-1st, based on the surviving height of U. 2 that was included in the fill of the structure. *7,* S wall, 15-1st (Fig. 30), reconstructed on the basis of an E-W line of rubble. U. 1, Wall of 15-3rd (see Fig. 30). U. 2, Wall of 15-2nd (see Fig. 30). U. 3, Floor between Str. 2G-15-2nd and 2G-Sub.2-1st (see Fig. 30).

Pertinent to Str: 2G-Sub.2: 1, N wall, Sub.2-1st (Fig. 30), reconstructed on the basis of surviving extent of the W structure wall, and U. 8. 2, Reconstructed floor level, Sub.2-1st, based on the height of the S wall. U. 1, Floor, based on a foundation of small stones, within 2 cm of the elevation of U. 2. U. 2, Floor, based on a foundation of small stones, within 2 cm of the elevation of U. 1. U. 2 abuts a stone by U. 4 (see also Fig. 30). U. 3, Fill for Sub.2-2nd and 3rd, of packed rubble; it continues to the N beneath U. 2. To the S, it ends at the wall for Str. 2G-Sub.2-1st, where some of the fill could have been removed when that wall was constructed. U. 4, Posthole for Str. 2G-Sub.2-2nd and 3rd (see Fig. 30). U. 5, Floor laid on a foundation of small stones, 9 cm above U. 1. Other relations of this floor are unknown. U. 6, Floor laid above U. 5 (see Fig. 30). U. 8, Floor N of 2G-Sub.2-1st (see Fig. 30).

FIGURE 31

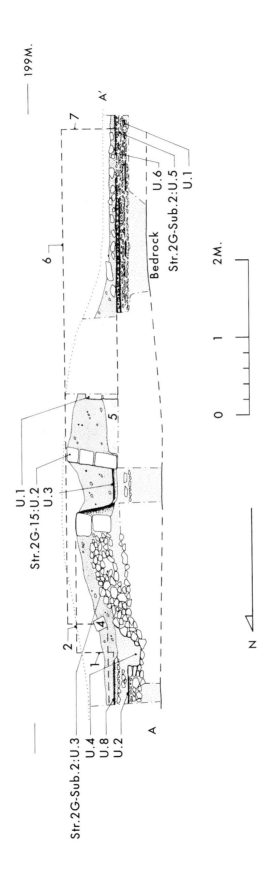

FIGURE 32

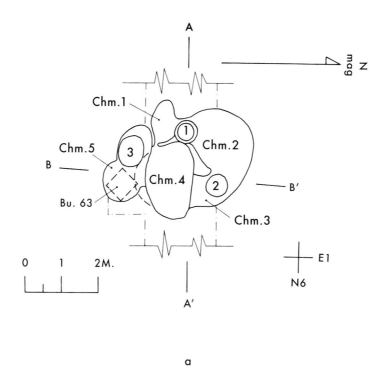

a

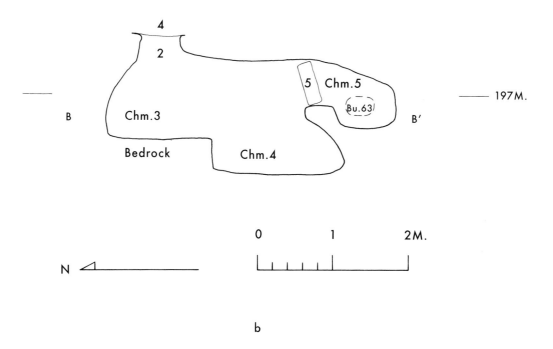

b

Ch. 2G-10: Plan (*a*) and Section B-B' (*b*).
Pertinent to Ch. 2G-10: 1, Or. 1 (see Fig. 28:6). The concentric circles denote a stepped lip, cut to receive a stone cover. *2*, Or. 2 (see Fig. 28:4). *3*, Or. 3 (see Fig. 28:5); more irregular in shape, and larger than the other two. *4*, Stone cover, in place in Or. 2. There has been no excavation above this. *5*, Masonry block, sealing Chm. 5 from Chm. 4. For section A-A', see Fig. 29. Coordinates are to datum shown in Fig. 33.

FIGURE 33

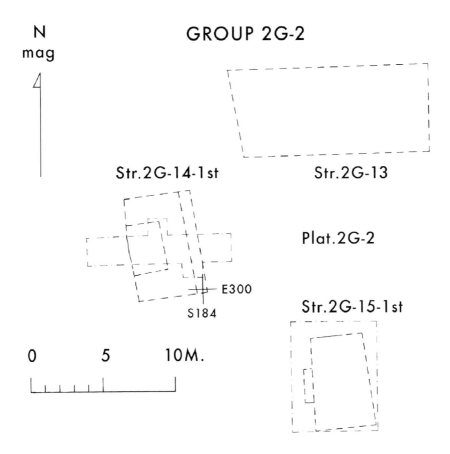

N
mag

GROUP 2G-2

Str.2G-14-1st

Str.2G-13

Plat.2G-2

E300

S184

Str.2G-15-1st

0   5   10M.

Gp. 2G-2 as it appeared ca. Gp. TS. 2 (Table 2.62).
Structure 2G-13 remains unexcavated; plotted here is its ruin mound.

Str. 2G-61, 62, and Qu. 2G-1 through 3: Plan.

Pertinent to Str. 2G-61: 1, N wall, based on a layer of gray earth over bedrock. Projection of this wall to the E is based on the location of the SE corner (see also Fig. 175c). 2, W wall, based on a layer of gray earth over bedrock. This follows the E face of Qu. 2G-2. Southward projection of the wall is based on the location of the SE corner (see also Fig. 175d). 3, Rubble remains of the SE corner. The rubble is based on gray earth, like the two walls above (1 and 2). This corner serves as a basis for the reconstruction of the S and E structure walls. 4, Reconstruction of the S wall (see 3, above). 5, Western bedrock face of Qu. 2G-1; note the proximity to the projected E wall of the structure. The quarry itself undercuts the wall, suggesting that Str. 2G-61 was in use when the quarry was formed. 7, Stone cover in place on Or. 1 of Ch. 2G-1 (see also Fig. 176a). 8, Or. 2 of Ch. 2G-1. 9, Or. 2 of Ch. 2G-2 (Ch. 2G-2 on the site map; see also Fig. 175b). This was buried beneath Str. 2G-61. 10, Or. 1 of Ch. 2G-2 (Ch. 2G-3 on the site map; see also Fig. 36). This was buried beneath Str. 2G-61. 11, Test pit, NE of structure. U. 1, Floor remnant at the correct elevation to be interpreted as pavement for an upper platform level. Projection of this floor to the N and W meets the top of the structure walls. U. 2, Floor remnant overlying the same stratum of fill as U. 1, and at the same general elevation, interpreted as part of the same floor. U. 1. U. 3, Floor remnant at the same elevation as U. 2, linked to it by a stratum of pebbles, and undoubtedly part of the same floor. U. 4, Floor remnant at a much lower elevation than U. 1–3, calling for reconstruction of Str. 2G-61 as a two-level platform. The hypothetical wall for the upper level, shown between U. 3 and 4, is based on the elevation of the structure fill. Here, it rises above the projected level of U. 4, so it could be no farther N. U. 5, Apparent step, based on gray fill in Qu. 2G-2, and built against the structure wall. Though it falls off-section, it is indicated in broken line in Fig. 36 to show its elevation relative to the structure. Pertinent to Str. 2G-62: U. 1–3, Postholes in bedrock, so arranged as to suggest a structure wall parallel to the W edge of Qu. 2G-2 (6). A fourth hole, U. 4 (not shown) is located 5.70 m SW of U. 3. This would be the proper position for the corner post of the W wall, if U. 3 held the northeastern corner post. Pertinent to Qu. 2G-2: 6, Bedrock faces of Qu. 2G-2. The E wall of the quarry conforms in part to the W wall of Str. 2G-61; its W wall (allowing for its irregularities) runs parallel to the E wall of Str. 2G-62. U. 2, Burned stones that rest on the surface of the quarry fill. For section A-A', see Fig. 35; for section B-B', see Fig. 36. Coordinates are to datum located at 2G:S392 E80.

FIGURE 34

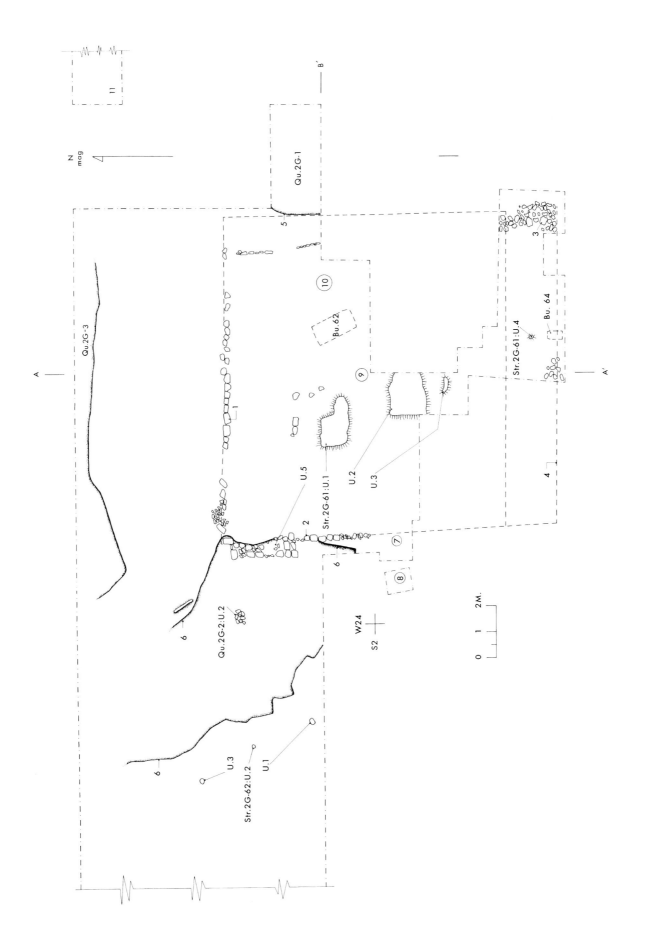

FIGURE 35

— 198M.

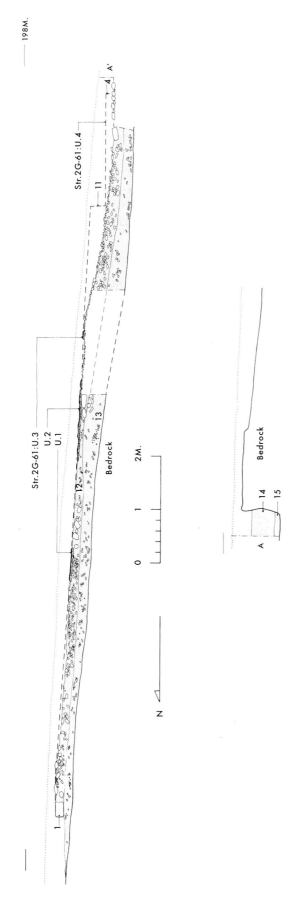

Str. 2G-61: Section A-A', as located in Fig. 34.

Pertinent to Str. 2G-61:1, N wall (see Fig. 34:1). *4*, Reconstructed S wall (see Fig. 34:4). *11*, Hypothetical step up from lower to upper platform level. The existence of two levels is indicated by the relative elevations of U. 3 and 4, but precise location of the step is unknown. The configuration of the fill indicates it could be no farther N than shown here. *12*, Structure fill; dark earth with numerous stones within. It overlies a gray stratum of earth, on which the structure walls also rest. *13*, Hard, packed gray stratum that overlies bedrock; included in it are numerous small stones. The N and W walls and the SE corner of the structure rest upon it, as does the structure fill. U. 1, 2, 3, Remnants of floor for the upper platform level (see Fig. 34). U. 4, Floor remnant (off-section), lower platform level (see Fig. 34). *Pertinent to Qu. 2G-3: 14*, Gray earth fill. *15*, Marl.

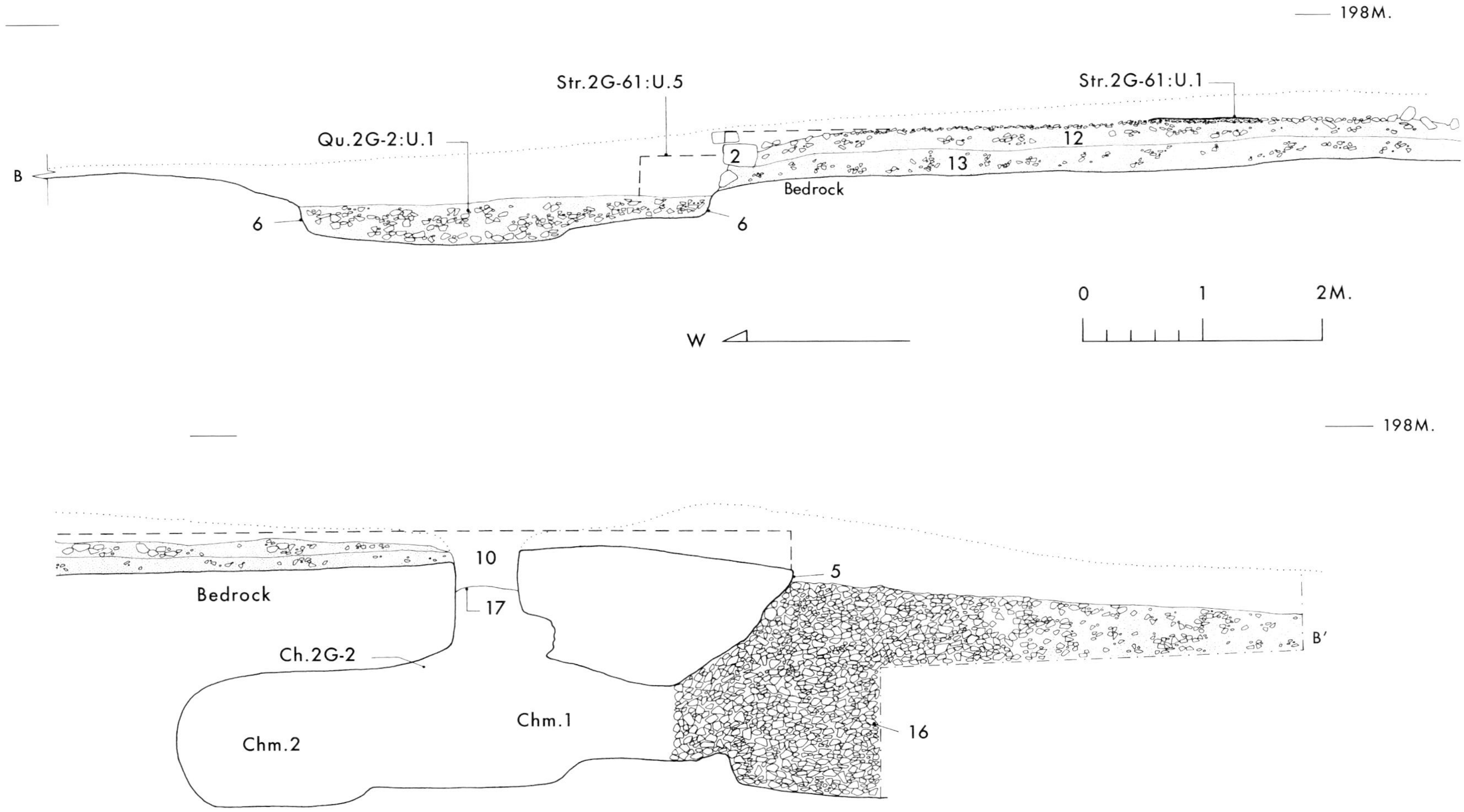

FIGURE 36

Str. 2G-61 and Ch. 2G-2: Section B-B', as located in Fig. 34.

Pertinent to Str. 2G-61: 2, W wall, Str. 2G-61 (see Fig. 34:2). *5*, W bedrock face of Qu. 2G-1, above which the E wall of the structure was built (see Fig. 34:5). *12*, Structure fill (see Fig. 35:12). *13*, Hard, packed gray stratum (see Fig. 35:13). U. 1, Remnant of floor for the upper platform (see Fig. 34, 35). U. 5, Step (off-section) W of Str. 2G-61 (see Fig. 34). *Pertinent to Ch. 2G-2: 10*, Or. 1 (see Fig. 34:10, Or. 1). *16*, Stone fill of Qu. 2G-1, which rests against the chultun fill (see also Fig. 39). *17*, Fill (see Fig. 39). *Pertinent to Qu. 2G-2: 6*, E and W bedrock faces of Qu. 2G-2 (see Fig. 34:6). U. 1, Compact gray earth with stones, on which U. 5 of Str. 2G-61 was built.

FIGURE 37

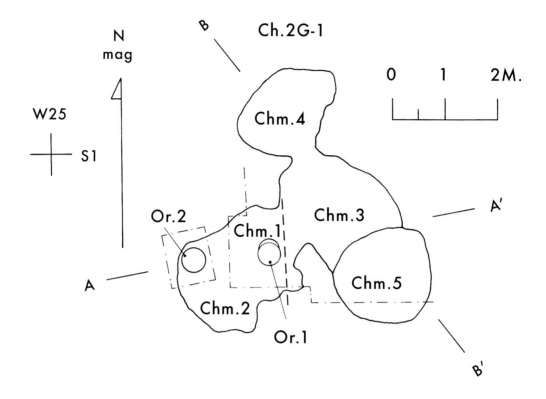

Ch. 2G-1: Plan.

Orifice 1 and 2 are shown in relation to Str. 2G-61 in Fig. 34 (7, 8). The stone cover is shown in place on Or. 1 (Fig. 176a); note the gap between the lid and orifice on the N, which was penetrated by a large tree root. This is the uphill side of the orifice, and just to the N was a considerable deposit of trash, including ceramics contemporary with several found in the chultun. Note also the proximity of the orifice to Str. 2G-61 (broken line on E). The wall here was completely destroyed, and some of the ceramics in the chultun are contemporary with those from the structure fill. For section A-A' and B-B', see Fig. 38.

FIGURE 38

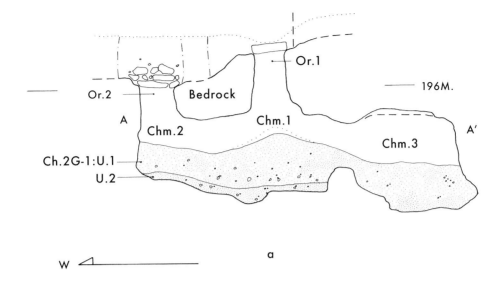

a

W

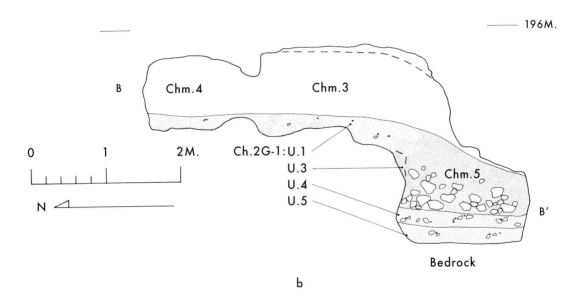

b

Ch. 2G-1: Sections A-A' (*a*) and B-B' (*b*), as located in Fig. 37.
Note the stone cover in place on Or. 1, and the stone rubble over Or. 2. Note also the proximity of Str. 2G-61 (broken line E of Or. 1), discussed in Fig. 37.
Pertinent to Ch. 2G-1: U. 1, Gray earth, highest beneath Or. 1 and 2. Note the low cone of humus above U. 1 beneath Or. 1. U. 2, Hard, packed gray earth, lighter in color than U. 1. U. 3, Dark gray earth that includes large numbers of stones, sherds, and three animal bone fragments. U. 4, silty deposit. U. 5, Gray earth, with carbon.

FIGURE 39

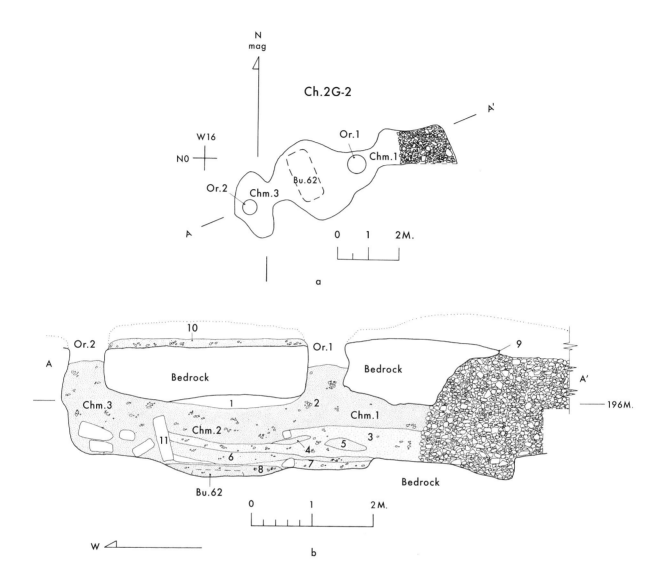

Ch. 2G-2: Plan (*a*) and Section A-A' (*b*).

Pertinent to Ch. 2G-2: 1, Unfilled portion of Chm. 2. *2*, Dark stratum of fill; although shown here as continuous from Chm. 3, the consistency does differ between the two. Probably, Chm. 3 was filled while the rest of the chultun remained in use. *3*, Stratum of light-colored earth. *4*, Lens of brown earth. *5*, Lens of brown earth. *6*, Stratum of brown earth. *7*, Stratum of light-colored earth. *8*, Stratum of dark-colored earth. *9*, W face of quarry. As shown in Fig. 34, the E wall of Str. 2G-61 is presumed to have stood directly above this. Small stones fill the quarry. *10*, Stratum of packed gray earth, with several small stones, which lies on bedrock. The walls and fill of Str. 2G-61 were built on this. *11*, Entrance block between Chm. 2 and 3. For relation of Or. 1 and 2 to other features at this locus, see Fig. 34.

FIGURE 40

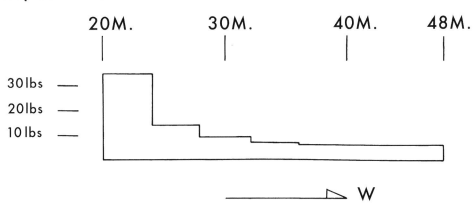

Sherds
Pound/cubic Meter

Schematic representation of sherd quantities W of Str. 2G-61.
Distances are from a stake 23 m E of the datum shown in Fig. 34.

Str. 3F-24: Plan (*a*) and Section A-A' (*b*).

Pertinent to Str. 3F-24: 1, E end wall, 24-1st, 2nd, and 3rd. *2*, Reconstructed floor for upper platform level of 1st, based on surviving height of U. 6. *3*, Informal occupation surface of packed, gray earth N of structure. *4*, Easternmost cover stone, Bu. 65. U. 1, S (front) wall based on bedrock. This wall served 1st, 2nd, and 3rd. It retains a fill of packed marl. U. 2, N (rear) wall, based on tamped earth that served as an informal occupation surface (3) N of the structure. The basal course of the wall probably served 3rd; upper courses were added for 2nd and 1st. U. 3, Remnants of floor for 3rd. Unit 4 rests on this, which may have continued to serve later versions of Str. 3F-24 S of U. 4. Projection of U. 3 to the S meets the top of U. 1. Evidently, the floor sealed the marl fill N of U. 1, and was penetrated at some time by Bu. 66. U. 4, Wall, based on U. 3, apparently the front of an upper platform level (for 24-2nd). It retains a brown earth fill to the N. U. 5, Floor remnant that seals Bu. 66, and which meets the top of U. 4. The brown earth fill beneath this floor runs to U. 2 on the N, thus U. 5 must have served as the floor for the upper platform level of 24-2nd. U. 6, Wall, based on U. 5. Since there is no break in this wall on the axis, it must be the front of a third platform level for 24-1st. U. 7–11, Apparent postholes, in bedrock. They may be associated with a hypothetical Str. 3F-24-4th. Coordinates are to datum shown in Fig. 45.

FIGURE 41

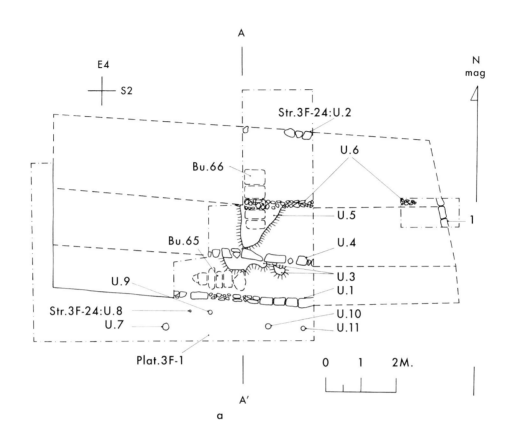

a

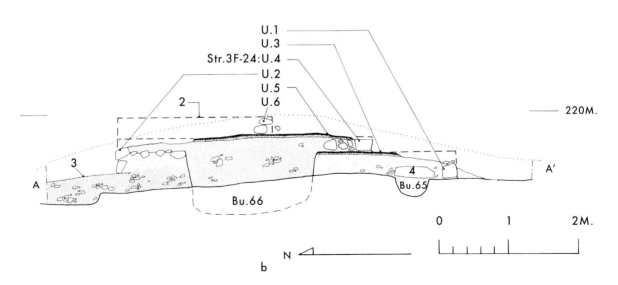

b

Str. 3F-25: Plan (*a*) and Isometric (*b*).

Pertinent to Str. 3F-25: 1, S (rear) wall of 1st and 2nd; rests on a stratum of gray-brown earth, and retains a brown earth fill to the N. U. 1, Floor remnant which, when projected, meets the tops of U. 3 and the S wall (1). It evidently was pavement for the one-level 25-2nd. U. 2, Floor remnant N of U. 3, in union with the base of that wall. U. 3, 4, N (front) wall of 1st and 2nd. Built on earth fill, it is in union with U. 2, a plaza floor to the N, and it retains the same brown earth fill to the S as that noted for the rear wall (1). See Fig. 176b for photo of NE corner. U. 5, N-S wall that abuts U. 4; its elevation is such as to indicate that it was a retaining wall for Plat. 3F-1. U. 6, Wall, based on U. 1, reconstructed as the front of an upper platform level of Str. 3F-25-1st. It retains a brown earth fill to the S, and U. 7 covers this brown fill. U. 7, Floor remnant at the same general elevation as the top of U. 6. Rubble S of U. 7 suggests that the rear wall (1) stood as high as U. 7; therefore, U. 7 is interpreted as a portion of pavement for an upper platform level. U. 8–10, Holes in bedrock, spaced at intervals relative to each other and structure walls to suggest that they held posts for a building of perishable materials. U. 11, Double hole in bedrock. Coordinates are to datum shown in Fig. 45.

FIGURE 42

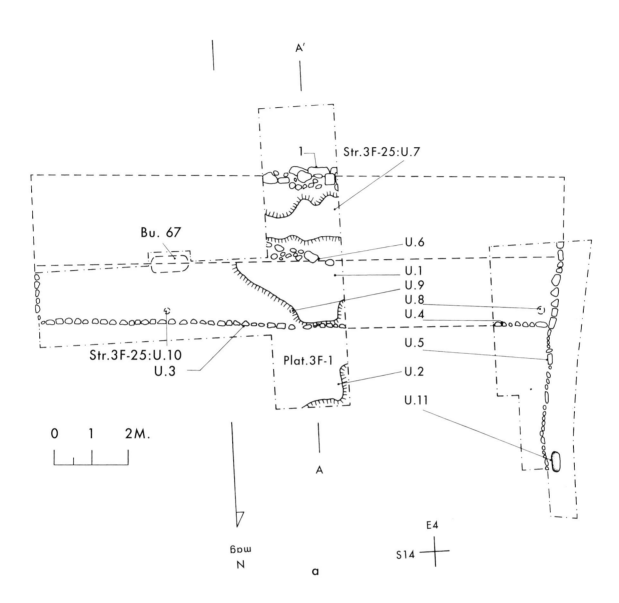

A'

1   Str.3F-25:U.7

Bu. 67

U.6

U.1

U.9

U.8

U.4

U.5

U.2

U.11

Str.3F-25:U.10

U.3

Plat.3F-1

0   1   2M.

6ɒɯ
N

A

E4

S14

a

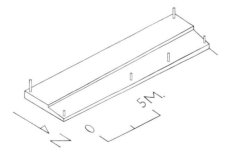

5M.

N

0

b

FIGURE 43

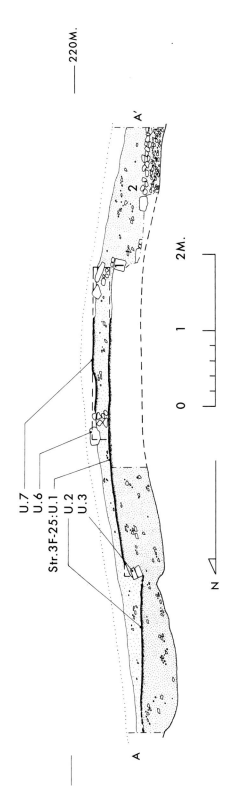

Str. 3F-25: Section A-A', as located in Fig. 42.

Pertinent to Str. 3F-25: 1, Rear wall of structure (see Fig. 42:1). *2*, Stratum of compact gray earth S of structure. Though it does not show clearly here, its surface is at the same elevation as the base of the rear structure wall (1), and probably was the ancient occupation surface. Beneath is a layer of earth and stones above bedrock. U. 1, Floor of 2nd (see Fig. 42). U. 2, Floor, Plat. 3F-1 (see Fig. 42). U. 3, Front structure wall (see Fig. 42). U. 6, Front wall, upper platform level (see Fig. 42). U. 7, Floor, upper platform level (see Fig. 42).

FIGURE 44

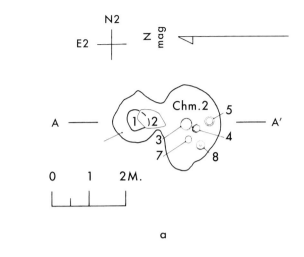

a

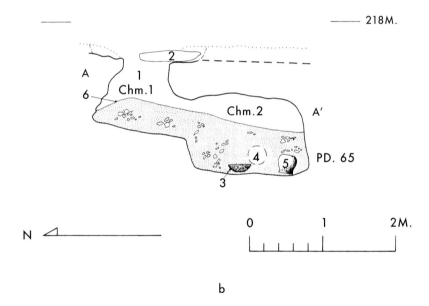

b

Ch. 3F-6: Plan (*a*) and Section A-A' (*b*).

Pertinent to Ch. 3F-6: 1, Orifice. Its irregular shape is from root destruction (see Fig. 176c). *2*, Stone cover, as found. *3*, Vessel 24S-7 (PD. 65). *4*, Vessel 24S-1 (PD. 65). *5*, Vessel 24S-2 (PD. 65). *6*, Loose, dark earth fill. *7*, Vessel 24S-5 (PD. 65). *8*, Vessel 24S-6 (PD. 65). For photos, see Fig. 176d and 177a. Coordinates are to datum shown in Fig. 45.

FIGURE 45

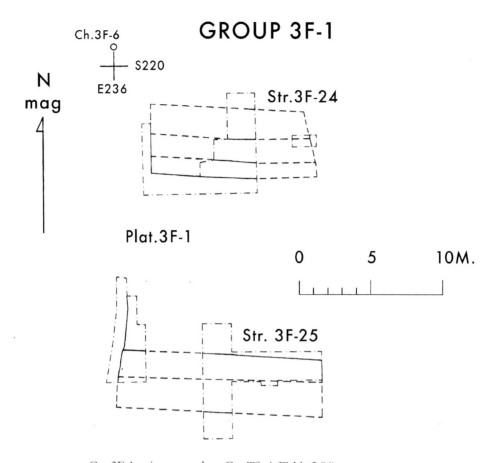

Gp. 3F-1 as it appeared ca. Gp. TS. 4 (Table 2.86).

Figure 46 (facing page)
Str. 3F-26: Plan.
Pertinent to Str. 3F-26: U. 2, Line of rubble indicating one-time existence of a retaining wall. The rubble is based on U. 1, and the top is at the same general elevation as U. 5. Length of the U. 2 wall is reconstructed from the known location of the SW corner of the structure, overall mound configuration, and a magnetic and resistivity survey conducted by R. E. Linnington. U. 3, Line of rubble indicating one-time existence of a wall. The E-W extent of U. 3 is unknown. Platform 3F-2:U. 12 turns up to U. 3. U. 4, Floor remnant that appears to turn up to U. 2. Its elevation indicates that it covered the top of U. 3 at one time. U. 5, Floor remnant that ends at U. 8 (Fig. 47) on the N; its elevation is the same as the top of U. 2. U. 7, outer face of the N wall, built on bedrock. Its length is reconstructed from the known location of the W structure wall, overall mound configuration, and a magnetic and resistivity survey conducted by R. E. Linnington. U. 9, W end wall. U. 10, Floor remnant, at the approximate elevation of U. 5 and probably part of the same floor. U. 11, Line of rubble indicating one-time existence of a retaining wall that was based on U. 5. It is reconstructed as running the length of the structure on the basis of U. 12. U. 12, Line of rubble parallel to U. 9, suggesting the one-time presence of a higher (second) platform level. To the S, U. 12 ends about where a westward projection of U. 11 meets the W end of the structure. U. 13, Line of rubble indicating one-time existence of a wall. Extent of the wall is unknown; it rests on earth overlying the projected level of the upper platform floor. U. 14-19, Postholes in bedrock. All but U. 19 may relate to Str. 3F-Sub.1. *Pertinent to Plat. 3F-2: U. 4*, Lowermost plaza floor S of Str. 3F-26. U. 12, Plaza floor that turns up to Str. 3F-26:U. 3. For section A-A', see Fig. 47. Coordinates are to datum shown in Fig. 52.

FIGURE 46

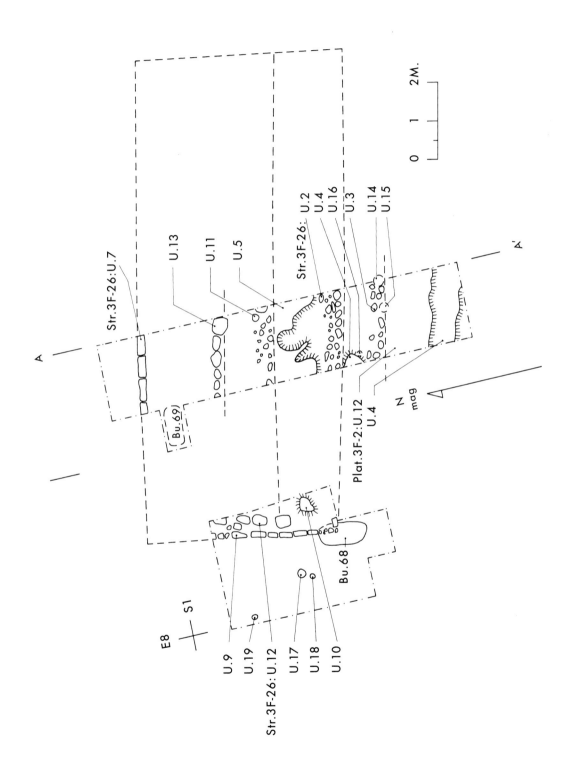

Str. 3F-26: Section A-A', as located in Fig. 46.

Pertinent to Str. 3F-26: 1, Projected level of U. 4 (see Fig. 46:11). *2*, Hypothetical level, floor for upper platform, based on the height of U. 11 and 12. U. 1, Floor that runs N from vertically cut bedrock face; defines Str. 3F-26-3rd. U. 2, Structure wall (see Fig. 46). U. 3, Wall, possibly for front step (see Fig. 46). U. 5, Floor that runs N from the top of U. 2 (see Fig. 46). U. 6, Inner face of the N (rear) wall. U. 7, Outer face of rear wall (see Fig. 46). U. 8, Limy deposit that marks a pause in fill operations; extends almost to the top of U. 6 from U. 5. It suggests that a wall once stood, where U. 5 ends, for an upper platform level (Str. 3F-26-2nd), but was later torn out and replaced by U. 11 (part of 26-1st). U. 11, Wall, upper platform level (see Fig. 46). U. 13, Possible late wall (see Fig. 46). U. 14, Posthole in bedrock. *Pertinent to Plat. 3F-2*: U. 4, Floor that predates Str. 3F-26:U. 3 (see Fig. 46). U. 12, Floor that turns up to Str. 3F-26:U. 3 (see Fig. 46).

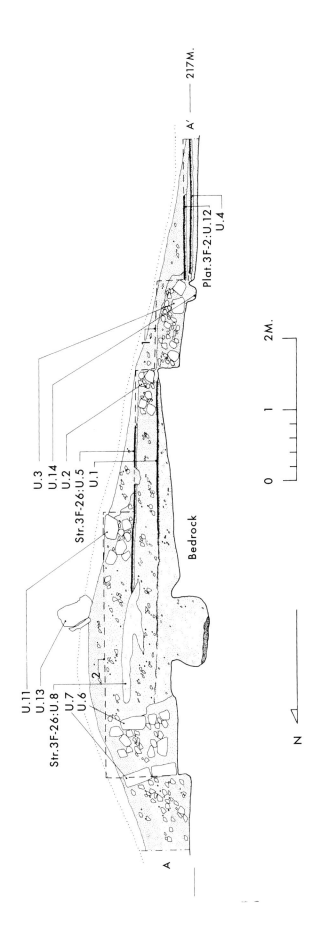

FIGURE 47

217 M.

A'

Plat.3F-2:U.12
U.4

U.3
U.14
U.2
Str.3F-26:U.5
U.1

Bedrock

2M.

1

0

U.11
U.13
Str.3F-26:U.8
U.7
U.6

2

A

N

Str. 3F-27: Plan (a) and Section A-A' (b).

Pertinent to Str. 3F-27: 2, Reconstruction of one-time extent of Str. 3F-27:U. 3, based on position of U. 1 and 2. U. 1, W wall; its length is reconstructed from overall mound configuration and a magnetic and resistivity survey conducted by Linnington. U. 2, E wall, to the base of which U. 4 turns up. Its length is reconstructed as for U. 2. U. 3, Floor remnant at the correct elevation to have served as a portion of the platform pavement associated with U. 1 and 2. U. 4, 5, 6, Three floor remnants at the same elevation and probably parts of a single pavement. U. 4 is in union with U. 2; other relations are unknown. The elevation of U. 4–6 is the same as Plat. 3F-2:U. 6 W of the structure.

Pertinent to Plat. 3F-2: 1, Projected level of U. 6. 3, Large masonry block fill immediately W of U. 7. U. 5, Floor remnant at the same elevation as the tops of the large fill masonry (3) and U. 7. U. 6, Floor remnant at the approximate elevation as the base of Str. 3F-27:U. 1. It may have been covered by the roof of Str. 3F-27 (see TR. 20B). U. 7, Wall that runs N-S beneath Str. 3F-27; its top is at the approximate elevation as U. 5. Coordinates are to datum shown in Fig. 52.

FIGURE 48

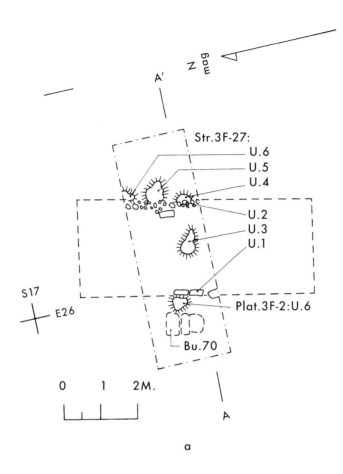

Str.3F-27:
U.6
U.5
U.4
U.2
U.3
U.1

S17

E26

Plat.3F-2:U.6

Bu.70

0   1   2M.

a

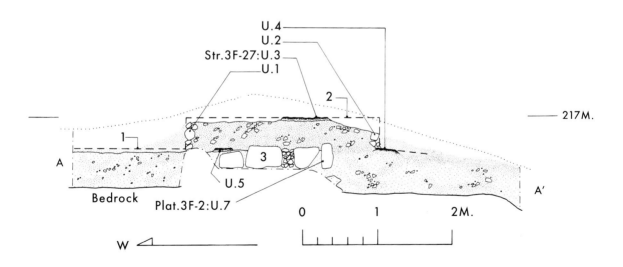

U.4
U.2
Str.3F-27:U.3
U.1

2

1

217M.

A

3

A'

Bedrock

U.5

Plat.3F-2:U.7

W

0   1   2M.

b

FIGURE 49

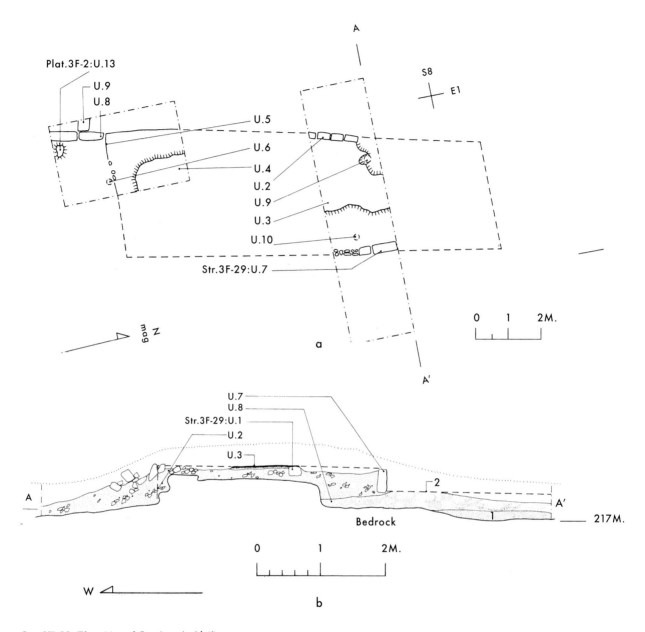

Str. 3F-29: Plan (*a*) and Section A-A' (*b*).

Pertinent to Str. 3F-29: U. 1, Wall, based on earth fill, parallel to U. 2 and 7. U. 3 meets the top of this wall, thought to be a part of 29-2nd. U. 2, W (rear) wall, based on bedrock; its top reaches the same general elevation as that of U. 3. Length of the wall is reconstructed on the basis of the known location of the SW corner, overall mound configuration, and a magnetic and resistivity survey conducted by Linnington. U. 3, Floor remnant that covers the top of U. 1. U. 4, Floor remnant near SW corner, at the approximate elevation of U. 3. U. 5, SW corner. The tops of the walls reach the approximate elevation of the top of U. 2. U. 6, Small hole in bedrock immediately S of U. 5. U. 7, E (front) wall, built on the surface of U. 8. The top of U. 7 is at the approximate elevation of U. 3. U. 8, Stratum of light marl over bedrock and (to the E) sterile earth. U. 9, 10, Holes in bedrock inside U. 1 and 2, thought to be postholes. *Pertinent to Plat. 3F-2: 1*, Stratum of earth beneath Str. 3F-29:U. 8, contains no sherds or artifacts. *2*, Reconstructed floor, based on elevation of the base of Str. 3F-29:U. 7, elevation of surface of Str. 7F-29:U. 8, and elevation of Plat. 3F-2:U. 13. U. 8, Wall that runs S, continuing the line of the rear structure wall. Its top is at the approximate elevation of Plat. 3F-2:U. 13. U. 9, Wall, at the same elevation as U. 8. It turns W from, and abuts, U. 8. U. 13, Floor remnant at the approximate elevation of the top of U. 8. Coordinates are to datum shown in Fig. 52.

FIGURE 50

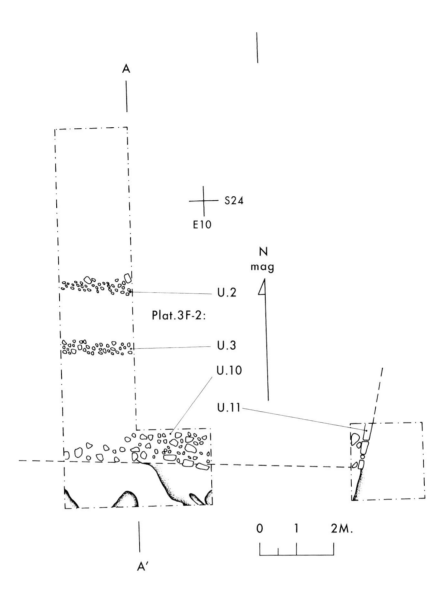

Plat. 3F-2: Plan of excavations at S edge.

Pertinent to Plat. 3F-2: U. 2, E-W line of rubble based on bedrock, with the top at the approximate elevation of U. 1 (Fig. 51). U. 3, E-W line of rubble with the top at the approximate elevation of U. 1 (Fig. 51) and 2. It rests on a stratum of earth fill. U. 10, E-W line of rubble, based on bedrock; reconstructed as the southernmost plaza wall (Plat. 3F-2-1st). U. 11, N-S line of masonry based on bedrock. The basis of reconstruction of this portion of the plaza is discussed in detail in text. A quarried face of bedrock continues the line of this wall to the S. For section A-A', see Fig. 51. Coordinates are to datum shown in Fig. 52.

FIGURE 51

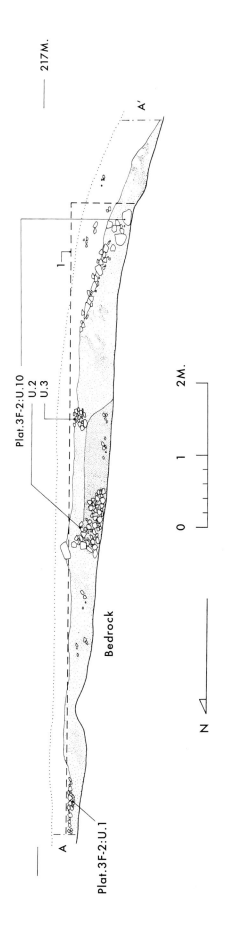

Plat. 3F-2: Section A-A', as located in Fig. 50.
Pertinent to Plat. 3F-2: 1, Reconstructed plaza floor level, from the elevation of U. 1, the heights of U. 2 and 3, and the elevation of fragments of plaza floor elsewhere in Gp. 3F-2. U. 1, Stratum of small stones at approximately the same elevation as U. 6 (Fig. 50). U. 2, Remains of wall (see Fig. 50). U. 3, Remains of wall (see Fig. 50). U. 10, Remains of wall (see Fig. 50).

FIGURE 52

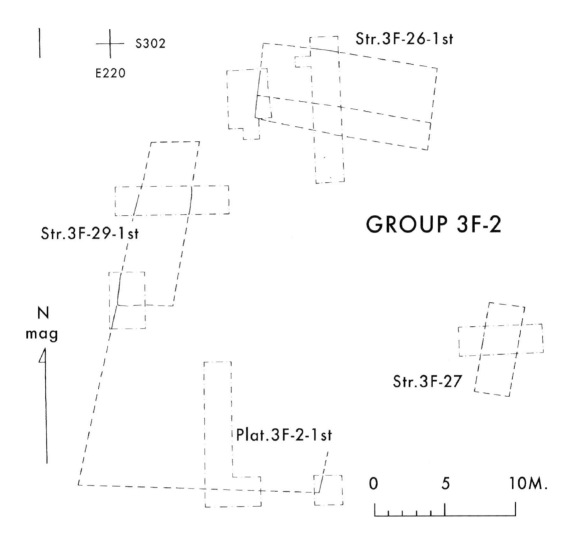

Gp. 3F-2 as it appeared ca. Gp. TS. 2 (Table 2.99).

Str. 3F-11, 12, 13, 14, and Plat. 3F-3: Plan.

Pertinent to Str. 3F-12: 3, Lowest stair riser. Its length is hypothetical, but in the somewhat similar Str. 4E-31 (TR. 19:fig. 2), the stairs stopped short of the ends of the platform. This, with the known wall of Str. 3F-13 and mound configuration of Str. 3F-11, suggest the reconstruction here. *4*, Upper stair riser, its position relative to the lowest riser reconstructed on the basis of stair measurements for the similar Str. 4E-31 (TR. 19:table 96) and 4E-50 (TR. 20B). *5*, Base of the E end wall. Knowledge of its location, with data for Rm. 1, is the basis for the reconstruction of the outer dimensions for the structure. Rooms 2 and 3 are reconstructed on the basis of analogy with Str. 4E-50 (Fig. 81) and 4E-31 (TR. 19:fig. 2). U. 1, Wall for 12-2nd, covered by U. 7, the floor in front of the building platform (see Fig. 54). U. 3, Front wall of building platform for 12-1st, which may also have served 2nd. Its top is slightly higher than the floor of Rm. 1, but at the same elevation as U. 2 (Fig. 54), a floor for 2nd. Unit 7 turns up to its base. U. 5, Rear wall of the supplementary platform; it rests on bedrock, with its top only slightly below the rear wall of the building platform. U. 6, Front wall of interior platform, Rm. 1. U. 9, Uppermost floor of interior platform in Rm. 1. U. 10, 11, Walls that divide the interior platform in Rm. 1 into three sections. They abut the rear room wall, and U. 9 turns up to them. U. 12, Hole (posthole?) in U. 9. U. 13, Wall beneath U. 7 that abuts U. 1. U. 14, 15, Rectangular holes on either side of the doorway of Rm. 1, 0.29 m above the room floor. Not shown are U. 16 and 17, round holes 1.06 m from the floor directly above U. 14 and 15. *Pertinent to Str. 3F-14: 1*, SE corner, based on U. 1 (Fig. 54:1). *2*, N wall, based on U. 1. No other masonry for this structure survives, suggesting that it was robbed at a later date for some unknown purpose. The missing walls are reconstructed here on the basis of the surviving masonry and the extent of structure fill. For section A-A', see Fig. 54; for section B-B', see Fig. 55.

FIGURE 53

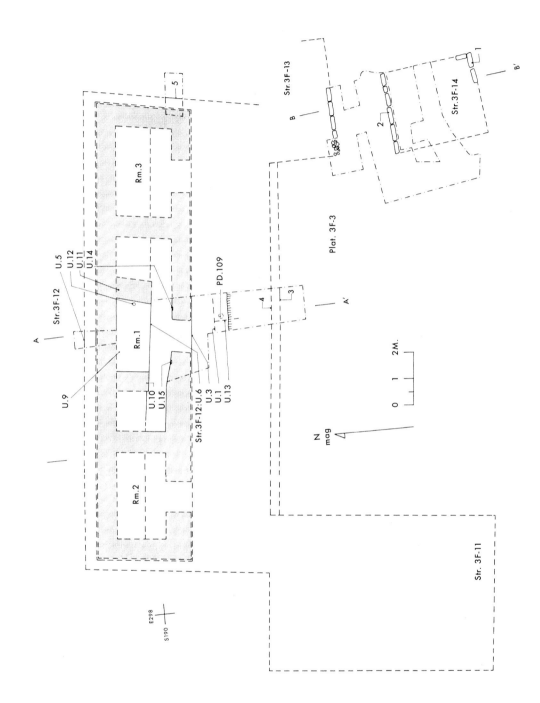

Str. 3F-12: Section A-A', as located in Fig. 53.

Pertinent to Str. 3F-12: 1, Fill of earth, stones, and cultural debris on which U. 2 is laid and which is partly retained by U. 1; thought to belong to 12-2nd. 2, Quarried bedrock face; may represent the rear wall for the platforms of 12-2nd and 1st-C. 3, Lower riser stone for steps (see Fig. 53:3). U. 1, Wall for 12-2nd (see Fig. 53). The fill to the N (1) differs in consistency from that to the S. U. 2, Floor for 12-2nd; lies on fill retained by U. 1 and 3. Note that its elevation is precisely that of the top of U. 3; the floor may once have run all the way to U. 3, later being chopped out when 1st-C was built. U. 3, Front wall of building platform (see Fig. 53). U. 4, Earliest floor of interior platform; defines 1st-C. U. 5, Final rear wall for supplementary platform (see Fig. 53). U. 6, Front wall of interior platform for 1st-A. The lowermost line of masonry may have served in 1st-B. U. 7, Floor of supplementary platform that turns up to U. 3 and abuts stones beneath it. Unit 7 is projected as running to an upper stair riser (see Fig. 53:4). U. 8, Second floor for interior platform; defines 1st-B. Since the floor is roughly the same elevation as the lower masonry of U. 6, that masonry may have served with this floor. U. 9, Uppermost floor for interior platform (see Fig. 53). U. 14, Rectangular hole in E wall near door (see Fig. 53). U. 16, Round hole in E wall near door directly above U. 14. A small, round hole opens into its base. Note that the reconstruction of building wall height, door height, and the vault are hypothetical. The vault and walls had collapsed, leaving only the masonry shown.

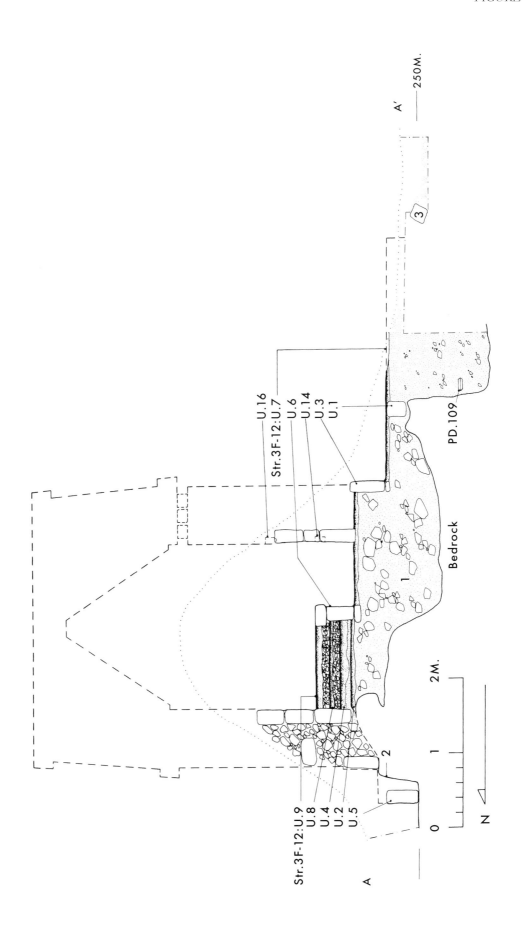

FIGURE 54

FIGURE 55

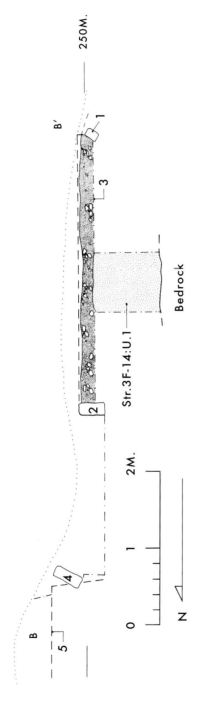

Str. 3F-13 and 3F-14: Section B-B', as located in Fig. 53.

Pertinent to Str. 3F-13: 4, S wall (see Fig. 53:4). Its length is reconstructed in Fig. 53 on the basis of overall mound configuration. The W wall must have abutted Str. 3F-12, and 3F-13 might actually have been a part of 3F-12. *5*, Reconstruction of the floor for Str. 3F-13, based on the height of its S wall (4). This is the same elevation as U. 7 of 3F-12, which may have continued over 3F-13 at one time. *Pertinent to Str. 3F-14: 1*, S wall (see Fig. 53:1). *2*, N wall (see Fig. 53:2). *3*, Excavation limit, at the base of the structure fill and the top of U. 1. Height of the fill within the walls suggests that there once may have been a floor as shown in broken line. U. 1, Sterile stratum that underlies the structure. The top of 1 must mark the original ground level here.

FIGURE 56

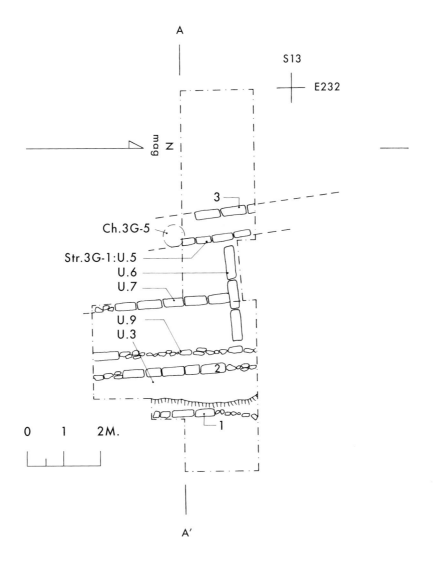

Str. 3G-1: Plan of architecture in trench through front-rear axis.

Pertinent to Str. 3G-1: 1, E (front) wall, 1st, 2nd, and 3rd, built on the fill of CS. 4 (Fig. 57:5). It retains a fill of light-colored earth and trash. On the basis of overall mound configuration, this wall is estimated to have been about 24 m long. *2*, E wall of an upper platform level for 3rd and reused in subsequent structures. It is based on, and retains the same fill behind the front structure wall (1). Overall configuration of the ruin-mound suggests that the upper platform ran the length of the structure. *3*, W (rear) wall of 1st and 2nd. It retains a fill quite different from that behind the E walls of 3rd (1 and 2). U. 3, Floor assigned to 3rd; runs from the top of the E structure wall (1) to the base of the wall for the upper platform level (2). Debris found lying on this floor testifies to its use up to the time the structure was abandoned. U. 5, Inner veneer masonry of the rear wall for 2nd, built on fill inside the lowest two courses of the outer veneer of the rear wall. The broken line in the plan marks the inner (W) face of the veneer. U. 6, Wall, built on U. 4 (Fig. 57), 0.20 m higher than U. 7. It may be the S wall of a small, interior platform that was part of 1st and 2nd. U. 7, Wall, built on U. 4 (Fig. 57), to which U. 8 (Fig. 57) turns up. The same height as U. 5, U. 7 is reconstructed as the front of a platform, the floor of which was not as high as that presumably associated with U. 6. Part of 2nd, it was not visible in 1st. U. 9, Wall, built on U. 4 (Fig. 57). This converted the older wall (2) into a step to an upper platform level, which included in its fill the older U. 7. For section A-A', see Fig. 57. Coordinates are to datum shown in Fig. 27.

FIGURE 57

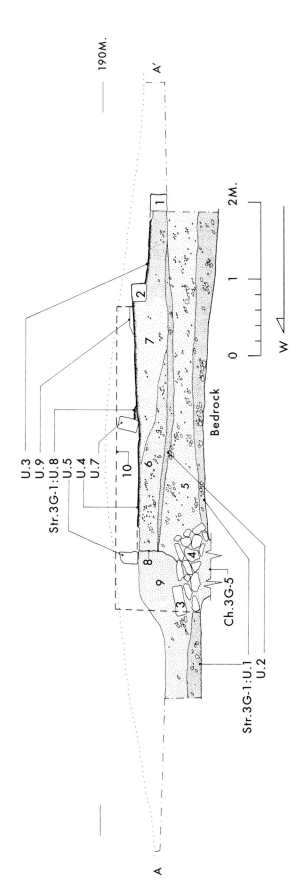

Str. 3G-1: Section A-A', as located in Fig. 56.

Pertinent to Str. 3G-1: 1, Front wall of 3rd through 1st (see Fig. 56:1). *2,* Front wall, upper platform level of 3rd; became the middle platform level of CS. 5 for Str. 3G-1-3rd (filling of the chultun). *5,* Light-colored fill of CS. 4 for 3rd, built up to plaza level. *6,* Dark earth and trash of CS. 3 for 3rd. *7,* Light-colored fill of CS. 2 for 3rd. This was placed at the time of construction of the front walls (1 and 2). *8,* Chop-line, from ripping out the rear wall of 3rd. Fill for the rear wall of 2nd rests against it. *9,* Fill for the rear wall of 2nd, much of which has spilled out to the W. *10,* Reconstructed floor for the upper level of 2nd (E to U. 7) and 1st (E to U. 9). Its elevation is based on the heights of U. 5, 7, and (off-section) U. 9. U. 1, Packed, gray stratum, the top of which may have been exposed when Ch. 3G-5 was in use. U. 2, Pause-line, marking the end of CS. 4 for 3rd. U. 3, Floor, lower platform level (see Fig. 56). U. 4, Floor that runs W from the top of the upper platform wall (2) of 3rd, almost to the W extent of the fill for that structure. Two walls, U. 6 and 7 (of Str. 3G-1-2nd) were built upon it. U. 5, Inner veneer of the rear wall for 2nd (see Fig. 56). U. 7, Front wall, upper platform level of 2nd (see Fig. 56). U. 8, Floor remnant on U. 4 that turns up to U. 7. U. 9, Front wall, upper platform level of 1st (see Fig. 56). The height of this is based on evidence off-section.

FIGURE 58

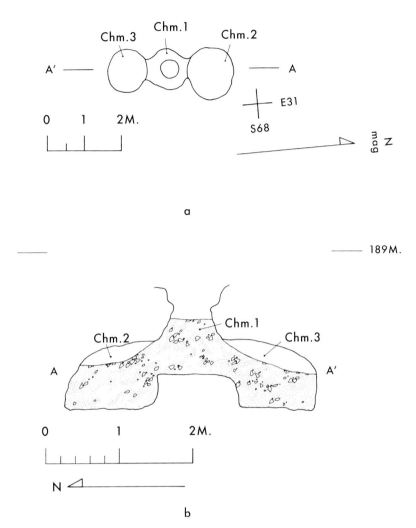

Ch. 3G-5: Plan (*a*) and Section A-A' (*b*).
Material in the upper part of the orifice and above is shown in Fig. 57. Note the deeply stepped lip. The fill of the chultun, light gray in color, includes some cultural material, and is quite uniform except for a skimming of dark earth on top in the air spaces. For location, see Fig. 56.

Ch. 2F-5: Plan (*a*) and Sections A-A' (*b*), B-B' (*c*), and C-C' (*d*).

Pertinent to Ch. 2F-5: 1, Orifice (see Fig. 10 for location). 2, Bedrock off-section, NE of U. 7. Note that small amounts of water entering the chultun would flow away from Chm. 2. U. 1, Humus and roots in the upper portion of Chm. 1. U. 2, Stratum of limestone chunks and light-colored earth, probably from minor ceiling collapse following slumping of U. 3. U. 3, Light-colored earth fill, thought to have been purposely dumped in through the orifice. With the passage of time, it would have slumped into deeper parts of the chultun. U. 4, Earth, containing minute carbon particles, overlies U. 5. It is thought to be water-borne material that accumulated prior to abandonment of the chultun. U. 5, Stratum of irregular stones, on which several large sherds were found; U. 5 is interpreted as material placed to facilitate drainage of water in the chultun. U. 6, Fine, silty soil on the floor of Chm. 5, beneath U. 5. U. 7, "Step," between Chm. 1 and 2. U. 8, Masonry sill, between Chm. 2 and 3. U. 9, Marl that covers a number of large pot sherds, thought to be material off the ceiling that collected prior to purposeful filling (U. 3).

FIGURE 59

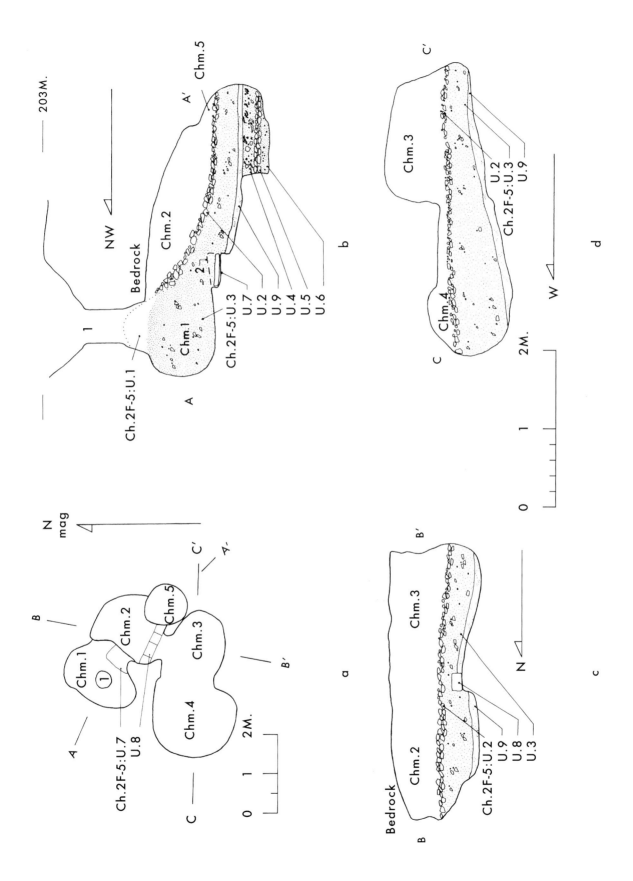

Ch. 3F-4: Plan (*a*) and Section A-A' (*b*); Ch. 3F-5, Plan (*c*) and Section A-A' (*d*).

Pertinent to Ch. 3F-4: 1, Orifice. Its location is 3F:S215 E266. Note that the E portion is severely damaged by erosion. *2*, Maximum known diameter. Note that earth fill almost completely fills the chultuns. *Pertinent to Ch. 3F-5: 1*, Orifice. Its location is 3F:S220 E265. *2*, Diameter near bottom. *3*, Point of maximum present diameter. *4*, Reconstruction of walls, based on off-section remains. U. 1, Pit in chultun floor. U. 2, Stratum of silt-like soil beneath earth fill.

FIGURE 60

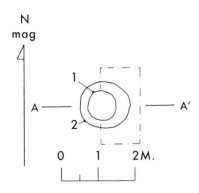

a

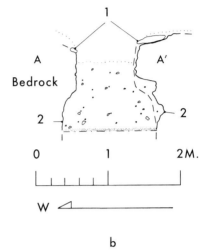

b

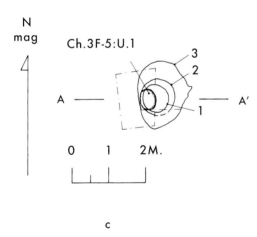

c

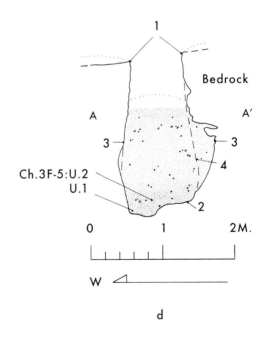

d

Str. 5B-6: Plan (a) and Section A-A' (*b*).

Pertinent to Str. 5B-6: 1, Rear (N) wall for 1st and 2nd. Now mostly collapsed, it must have been as high as the floor for 2nd and, later, the upper platform level. *2*, Front (S) wall for 1st and 2nd. This wall is based in a stony fill for CS. 4 that continued S beneath the floor of Plat. 5B-2. *3*, Front wall for an upper platform level, built on the floor for 2nd. That this is not the wall of a small, axially placed platform is suggested by the extent exposed in excavation, as well as mound configuration. *4*, Stony fill for 2nd; continues S beneath the floor of Plat. 5B-2. *5*, Reconstructed surface floor of upper platform level (Str. 5B-6-1st). U. 1, Gray earth over bedrock, retained in part on the N by the rear structure wall (1), and in part extending N beneath this wall. U. 1 may be part fill and part natural earth. U. 2, Layer of packed, marly material that represents a pause in the filling operations when the stony fill had reached the desired elevation for Plat. 5B-2; this separates CS. 3 from 2. U. 3, Floor of Plat. 5B-2, lies on fill continuous with that on which the front wall (2) of the structure is based, and turns up to this wall. Str. 5B-6-2nd:Fl. 1, pavement at the same approximate elevation as the top of the front structure wall (2), on which the upper platform level (3) was built. Fill for the floor is retained on the S by the front structure wall (2). Coordinates are to datum shown in Fig. 64.

FIGURE 61

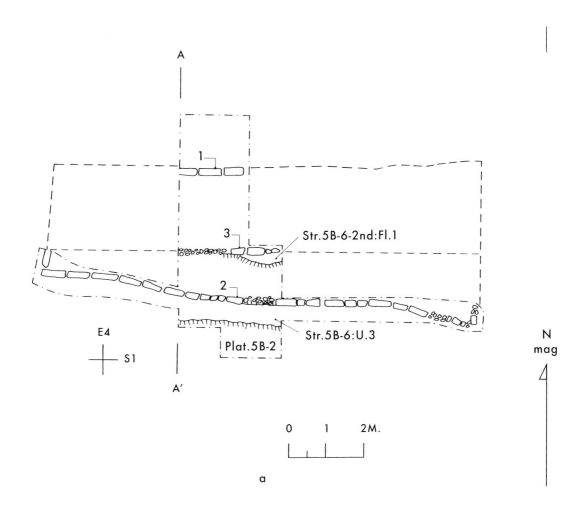

a

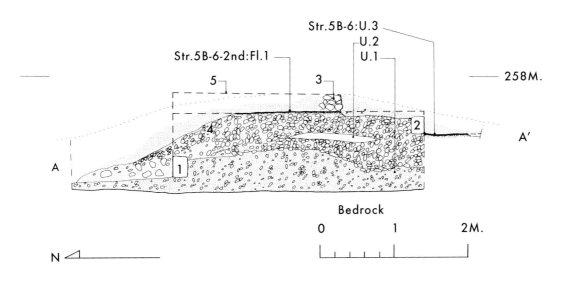

b

FIGURE 62

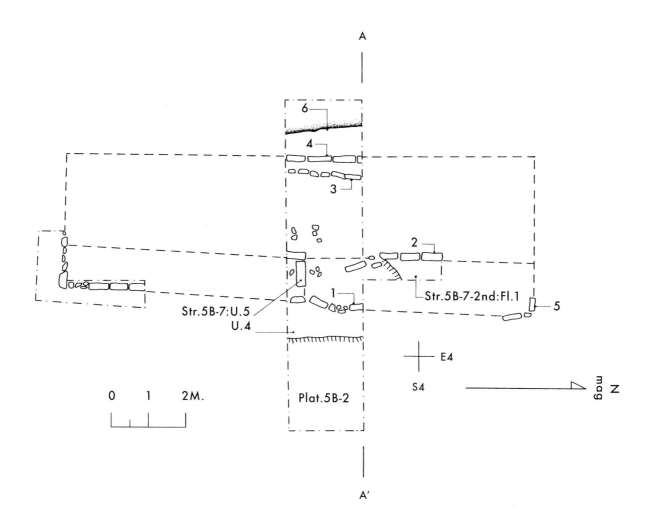

Str. 5B-7: Plan.

Pertinent to Str. 5B-7: 1, Front (E) wall for 1st and 2nd, based on fill that continues E from the structure beneath the floor of Plat. 5B-2. *2*, Front wall for an upper platform level, built on the floor for Str. 5B-7-2nd. This wall was excavated sufficiently to establish the probability that it is not part of a small, axially placed platform. *3*, Line of masonry, 0.34 m inside the back wall (4) that Fl. 1 of 2nd abuts. *4*, Rear (W) wall for 1st and 2nd; rests on bedrock. Now mostly collapsed, it probably was as high as the top of U. 3 and, later, the upper platform level. *5*, Masonry for the NE corner of the structure, visible on the surface without excavation. *6*, Quarried bedrock face behind the structure. U. 4, Floor of Plat. 5B-2; lies on fill continuous with that on which the front structure wall (1) is built. U. 5, Wall built on the level of Str. 5B-7-2nd:Fl. 1 that abuts the upper platform (2), and defines Str. 5B-7-1st-A. It may indicate an extension of the upper platform level over the entire S end of the structure, or it may be part of some sort of formal entry. Str. 5B-7-2nd:Fl. 1, Plaster floor remnant at the same elevation as the top of the front structure wall (1) that abuts a dwarf wall (3) at the rear and on which the upper platform level (2) was built. For section A-A', see Fig. 63. Coordinates are to datum shown in Fig. 64.

FIGURE 63

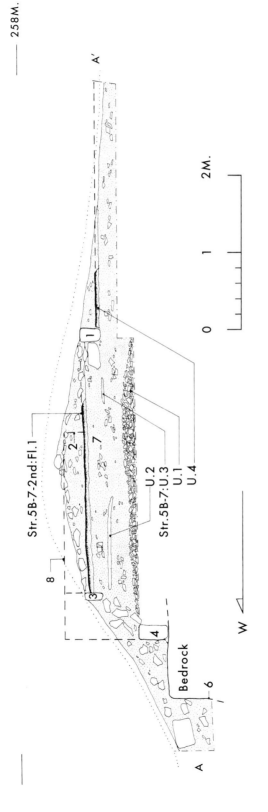

— 258M.

A'

2M.

0   1   2M.

W ◁

Str.5B-7-2nd:Fl.1

8

2

7

3

4

6

Bedrock

A

U.2
Str.5B-7:U.3
U.1
U.4

Str. 5B-7: Section A-A', as located in Fig. 62.

Pertinent to Str. 5B-7: 1, Front wall for 1st and 2nd (see Fig. 62:1). *2,* Front wall (off-section) for upper platform level (see Fig. 62:2). *3,* Inner face of rear dwarf-wall (see Fig. 62:6). *4,* Rear wall for 1st and 2nd (see Fig. 62:4). *6,* Quarried bedrock face (see Fig. 62:6). *7,* Gray earth fill for 2nd; it continues E beneath the floor of Plat. 5B-2, and was placed as CS. 3 and 2. *8,* Reconstructed floor of upper platform level (Str. 5B-7-1st-B). U. 1, Stony fill of CS. 4, similar to that used for CS. 2 and 3 of Str. 5B-6-2nd (see Fig. 61b:4). This fill is retained on the W by the lowest course of the rear structure wall (4). U. 2 and 3, packed, marly layers that represent a pause in fill operations when the appropriate elevation for Plat. 5B-2 had been reached. They define the break between CS. 3 and 2. U. 4, Floor for Plat. 5B-2 (see Fig. 62).

FIGURE 64

GROUP 5B-2

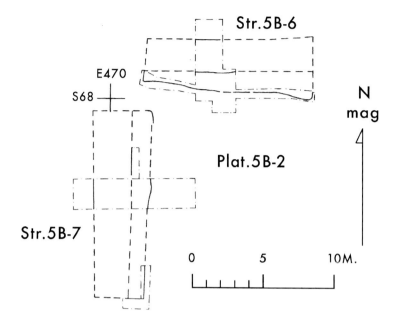

Gp. 5B-2 as it appeared ca. Gp. TS. 5 (Table 2.133).

Figure 65 (facing page)

Gp. 5C-3: Plan and location of nearby test excavations.

Shown is Plat. 5C-4-1st, on which two structures are thought to have been built. Numbers refer to test pits. For a detailed plan of Plat. 5C-4, see Fig. 66.

FIGURE 65

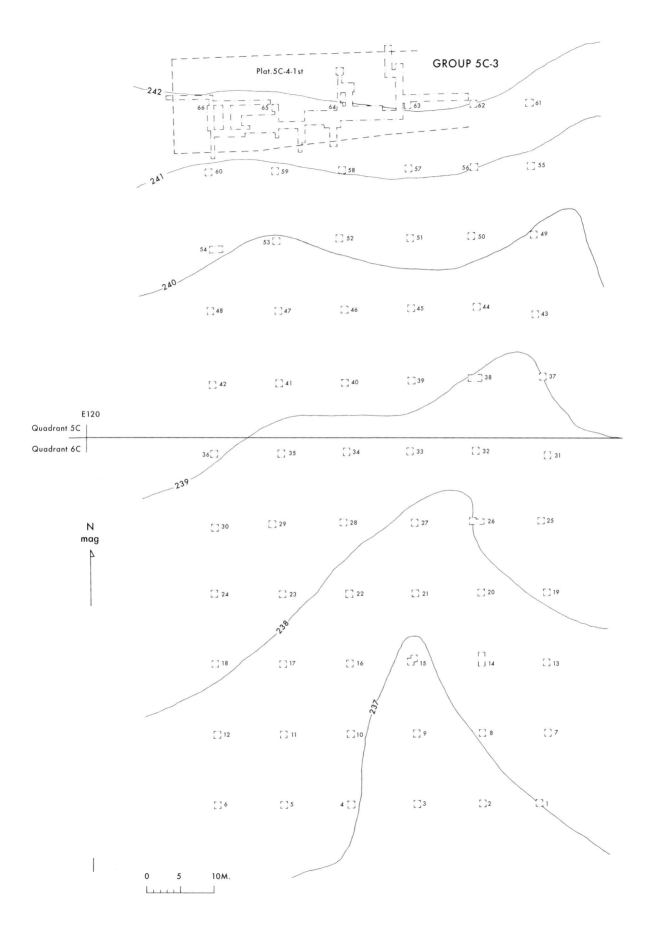

Plat. 5C-4: Plan.

Pertinent to Plat. 5C-4: 1, Quarried bedrock, to which Fl. 1 turns up. 62, Test pit 62 (see Fig. 65). U. 1, S wall for 2nd of rough-cut masonry based in a hard, red to tan earth fill (Fig. 67:U. 2) as high as the wall on its N side. U. 3, Line of stones, apparently a wall, which runs N from U. 1; may be associated with a structure built on the W end of Plat. 5C-4-2nd. U. 5, 6, S and W walls for 1st. U. 5 is based on fill of earth and small stones; with U. 6 it retains fill of brown earth. U. 7, Stones, perhaps the remains of a wall, around which Fl. 1 was laid. Positioned above U. 4 (Fig. 67), they may pertain to a modification of an earlier structure associated with Plat. 5C-4-1st. U. 8, Line of stones near the W end of 1st, based on Fl. 1. Possibly part of a structure, they suggest renovation of an earlier one represented by U. 3. Fl. 1, Floor for 1st, to the N, turns up to bedrock (see Fig. 67). It covers earlier U. 1, 3, and 4, and must have run to the top of U. 5. Coordinates are to Sq. 5C of the site map.

FIGURE 66

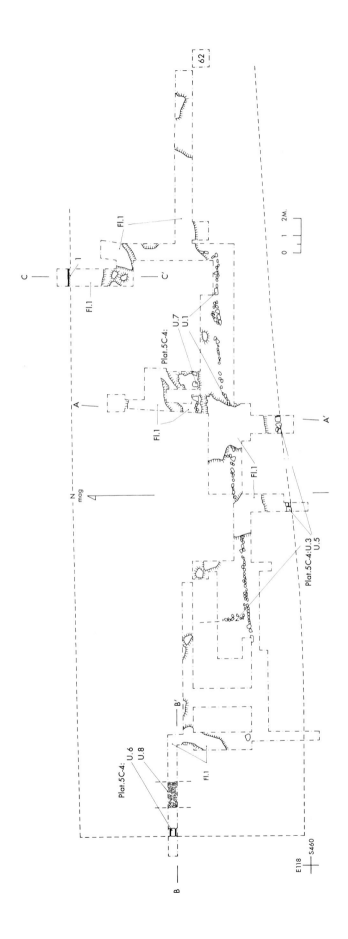

Plat. 5C-4: Sections A-A' (*a*), B-B' (*b*), and C-C' (*c*), as located in Fig. 66.

Pertinent to Plat. 5C-4: 1, Turnup of Fl. 1 to bedrock. *2*, Brown earth fill for 1st; rests on U. 2, against the S face of U. 1. Floor 1 was laid on it, running across U. 1 as well. *3*, Occupation debris, almost totally devoid of sherds and artifacts. U. 1, S wall for 2nd (see Fig. 66). U. 2, Loose, red-tan earth fill for 2nd; overlies bedrock, light tan-colored earth to the S, and hard, dark-colored silt on the N that rises as high as U. 2. Unit 1 rests on U. 2, which rises N of U. 1 to the same elevation as the top of that wall, indicating contemporaneity of the two. U. 4, Masonry mass in U. 2 (see Fig. 66). U. 5, S wall for 1st (see Fig. 66); evidently, U. 2 was cut for placement of its masonry. Given the relative elevations of Fl. 1 and its fill to the N, U. 5 must have consisted of two courses. U. 6, W end wall of 1st (see Fig. 66). U. 7, Possible wall, around which Fl. 1 was laid (see Fig. 66). U. 8, Line of stones on Fl. 1 (see Fig. 66). Fl. 1, pavement for 1st (see Fig. 66).

FIGURE 67

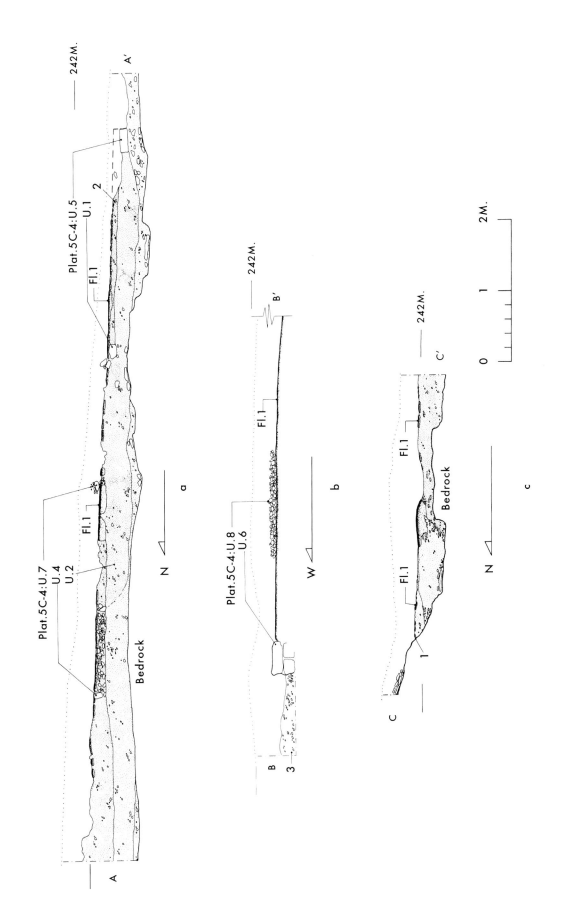

242M.

A'

Plat.5C-4:U.5

U.1

Fl.1

2

Plat.5C-4:U.7

U.4

U.2

Fl.1

Bedrock

N

a

A

242M.

B'

Fl.1

Plat.5C-4:U.8

U.6

W

b

B

3

242M.

C'

Fl.1

Bedrock

Fl.1

1

N

c

C

2M.

0   1   2

Str. 5C-56 and 5C-57: Plan.

Pertinent to Str. 5C-56: 1, Extension of U. 1 to the W as part of 1st. U. 1, S wall for 2nd, built on a thin layer of fill over bedrock. To the S, Plat. 5C-6:U. 1 is in union with the wall. U. 2, Probable end wall for 2nd and 1st; it and U. 1 retains the same fill. U. 3, N wall for 2nd and 1st. U. 4, S wall for 1st; based on Plat. 5C-6:U. 4 and Plat. 5C-6:U. 5, turns up to its S face. U. 5, End wall for 1st. U. 6, Posthole in bedrock N of 56, seemingly unrelated to other postholes in the vicinity. *Pertinent to Str. 5C-57: 2*, Reconstructed E end from an arrangement of U. 1–5. U. 1–5, Postholes in bedrock that, by their alignment and regular spacing, suggest the E end of a structure. Absence of further postholes to the W may be explained by lack of necessity to dig into bedrock, lower here than to the E. Or, bedrock may have been quarried away at a later date. U. 6–14, Postholes in bedrock that show no discernible pattern. Some may relate to Str. 5C-57; some may relate to a shelter over Ch. 5C-5. *Pertinent to Plat. 5C-6:* U. 1, Original floor, in union with U. 1 of Str. 5C-56. U. 2, Grading floor laid on U. 1 S of Str. 5C-56. U. 5, Floor laid over U. 3 (following removal of U. 4) that turns up to Str. 5C-56:U. 4. For section A-A', see Fig. 69. Coordinates are to Sq. 5C of the site map.

FIGURE 68

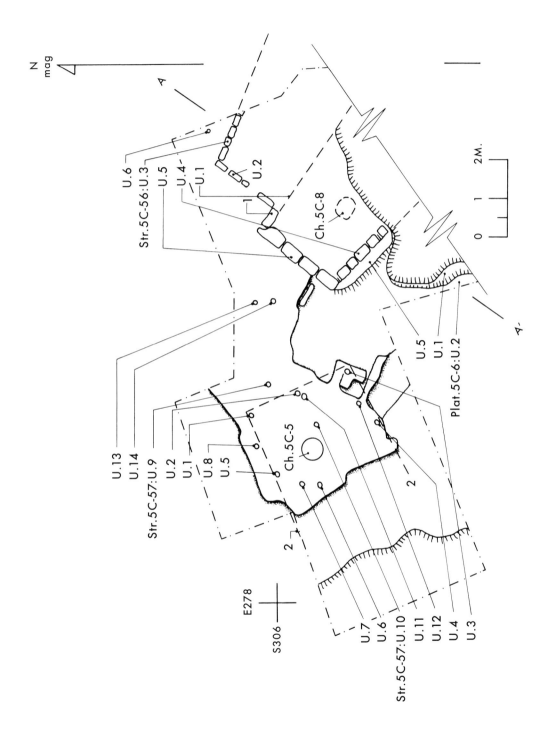

N mag

A

Str.5C-56:U.3
U.6
U.5
U.4
U.1
U.2

Ch.5C-8

U.5
U.1
Plat.5C-6:U.2

A-

0   1   2M.

U.13
U.14
Str.5C-57:U.9
U.2
U.1
U.8
U.5

Ch.5C-5

E278
S306

2
2

Str.5C-57:U.10
U.7
U.6
U.11
U.12
U.4
U.3

Str. 5C-56: Section A-A' (*a*), as located in Fig. 68; Ch. 5C-5: Plan (*b*) and Section A-A' (*c*).

Pertinent to Str. 5C-56: 3, Reconstructed floor for 2nd, from the height of U. 1. *4*, Reconstructed floor for 1st, from height of U. 1 and 5. Note that U. 4 must have consisted of more than one course of masonry. U. 1, S wall of 2nd (see Fig. 68:3). U. 3 and 4, N and S walls of 1st and 2nd (see Fig. 68). Note stony fill between U. 1 and 4. *Pertinent to Plat. 5C-6: 5*, Earth and pebble fill for U. 1. *6*, Fill for U. 2, similar to that for U. 3, similar to that for U. 1 and 2. U. 1, Original floor (see Fig. 68). U. 3, Second grading floor. U. 4, Third grading floor, later removed S of Str. 5C-56-1st. U. 5, Final floor, turns up to Str. 5C-56-1st (see Fig. 68). *Pertinent to Ch. 5C-5:* Orifice (see Fig. 68), opens into Chm. 1. In Chm. 3, the floor is shown in solid line; maximum extent of the chamber (above the floor) in broken line. Not shown is the fill, consisting of loose earth and lime that has flaked off the ceiling. This fill sloped downward into Chm. 1 and 2 from below the orifice. At the time of excavation, the chultun orifice was enlarged from the original (broken line) as shown here.

FIGURE 69

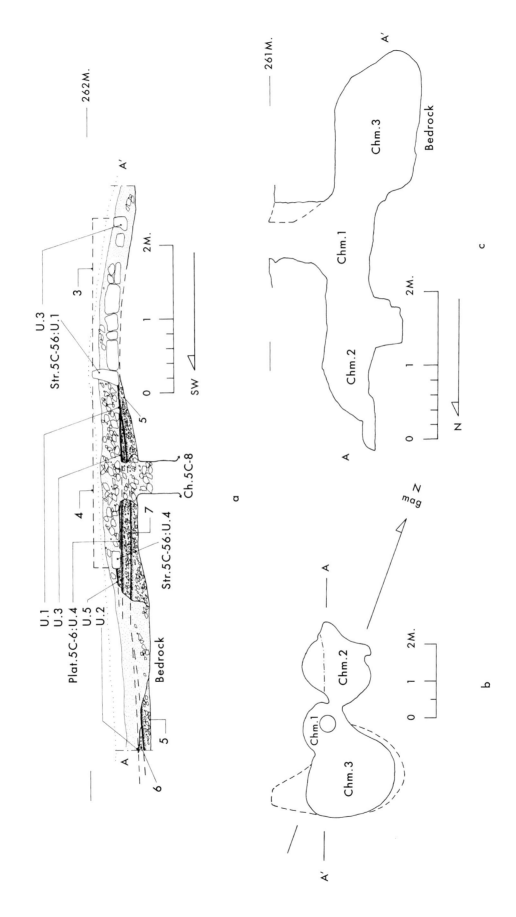

FIGURE 70

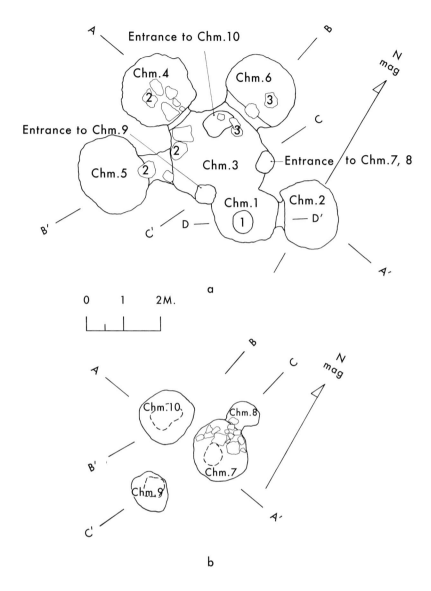

Ch. 5C-8: Plan of upper (*a*) and lower (*b*) chambers.

1, Orifice (see also Fig. 68, 69). *2, 3*, Masonry that may have served to block the entrances to Chm. 4, 5, and 6. The entrances to the lower chambers are shown in solid line in "a" and in broken line in "b." For sections, see Fig. 71. For photo from Ch. 1 into Ch. 3, with openings to Chm. 4 and 6, see Fig. 178a.

Figure 71 (facing page)
Ch. 5C-8: Sections A-A' (*a*), B-B' (b), C-C' (*c*), and D-D' (*d*), as located in Fig. 70.
Pertinent to Ch. 5C-8: 2, Masonry blocks. Those in Chm. 4 may once have blocked its entrance, later to be pushed in by pressure of fill from Chm. 3. The block in Chm. 5 may also have been pushed from position in the entrance (see also Fig. 70). The fills of Chm. 4 and 5 are quite similar (see 5, below). *3*, Masonry blocks in Chm. 6, perhaps analogous to those in Chm. 4 and 5. The fill of Chm. 6, virtually devoid of sherds and artifacts, consists of thin layers of white lime and gray soil, with stones. This could derive from construction of Chm. 10, with admixture of bat dung. *4*, Stone masonry blocking Chm. 8, may be analogous to that in Chm. 4. Fill of Chm. 8 is of midden-like material, not dissimilar to the overlying midden-like material in Chm. 3, 7, and 9. *5*, Deposit of earth, stones, charcoal, sherds, animal bones, and human bones. U. 1, Brown earth. U. 2, Banded layers of water-deposited clay. U. 3, Brown earth, fill of burned bone and charcoal (including PD. 72). U. 4, Yellow, sandy soil. U. 5, Loose, stony, brown earth. U. 6, Lime. U. 7, Water-deposited clay, similar to U. 2. Over this is midden-like material, continuous with that in Chm. 1, 2, 7, and 9, and not dissimilar to that in Chm. 4, 5, and 8. Note the break in the E portion of Chm. 2; this was caused by modern quarrying for the Tikal Project, resulting in discovery of this chultun. *Pertinent to Plat. 5C-6*: U. 1, First floor (Fig. 68). U. 3, Second grading floor (Fig. 69). U. 4, Third grading floor (Fig. 69). Note the air space in the neck above Chm. 1, beneath the wedged-in masonry in the orifice. This suggests that fill in the chultun has slumped, spilling into deeper chambers.

FIGURE 71

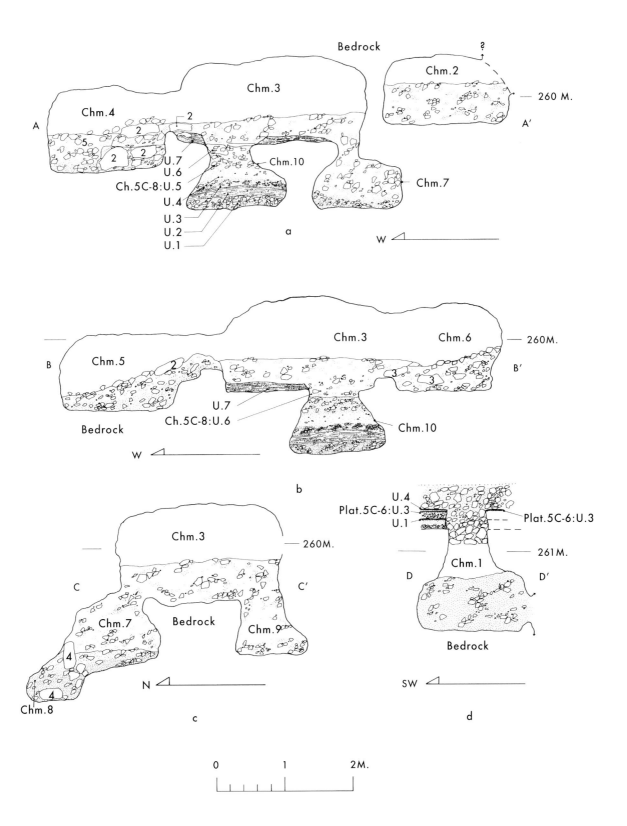

FIGURE 72

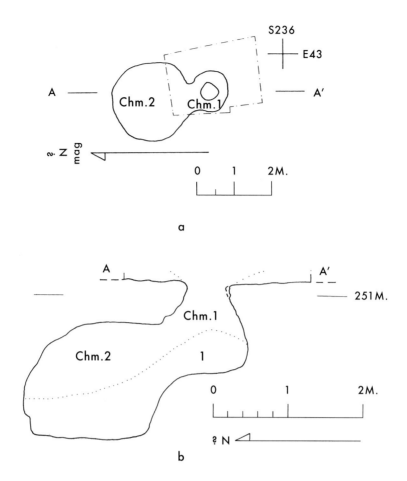

Ch. 5B-11: Plan (*a*) and Section A-A' (*b*).
The chultun was partly filled with loose humus (1). Note the shallowness of Chm. 1 and the lack of a sill between chambers. The precise orientation of the chultun was, unfortunately, not recorded. Coordinates are to Sq. 5B of the site map.

FIGURE 73

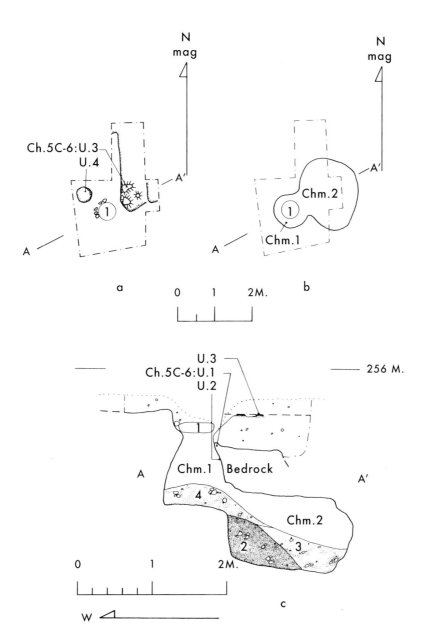

Ch. 5C-6: Plan of surface features (*a*), Chultun (*b*), and Section A-A' (*c*).
Pertinent to Ch. 5C-6: 1, Orifice, Ch. 5C-6: Location 5C:S330 E90. Note the small stones wedged between the stone cover and the edge of the orifice. Note too the unusual depth of the orifice to the W, and the lack of deep bedrock in the quarried area to the E. *2*, Black earth, with few sherds. *3*, Light-colored earth, packed with sherds. *4*, Humus and ceiling collapse. U. 1, Hump in bedrock; could have served with the quarry to the E to facilitate drainage of water away from the chultun. U. 2, Area where bedrock may have broken off beneath the lip of the chultun, one possible explanation for its abandonment. U. 3, Floor overlying fill in quarried area. Its elevation is the same as bedrock at all but the E side of the orifice. U. 4, Circular pit in bedrock, 0.10–0.15 m deep, similar to other such pits by Ch. 6C-7 (Fig. 126).

FIGURE 74

Str. 4E-14: Plan.

Pertinent to Str. 4E-14: 1, W (rear) wall, now partly collapsed, based on marl. U. 8 (Fig. 75), on which MS. 57-62 rest, abuts it. Its length is reconstructed from overall mound configuration. For elevation, see TR. 20B. U. 3, Rubble remnant of E (front) wall. The basis for length reconstruction is the same as for the rear wall. U. 4, Retaining wall, based on U. 2 (Fig. 75). On the basis of the mound configuration, this ran the length of the structure. U. 6, Floor remnant, at the approximate elevation of the tops of U. 4 and 5 (Fig. 75), and therefore reconstructed as pavement for an upper platform level. U. 7, Floor remnant based on U. 2 E of U. 4, which turns up to the latter. Its elevation is the same as the top of U. 3, to which it probably ran. For Section A-A', see Fig. 75; for photo of MS. 61 and 57 with rear wall of 4E-14 in background, see Fig. 178b. Co-ordinates are to datum shown in Fig. 80.

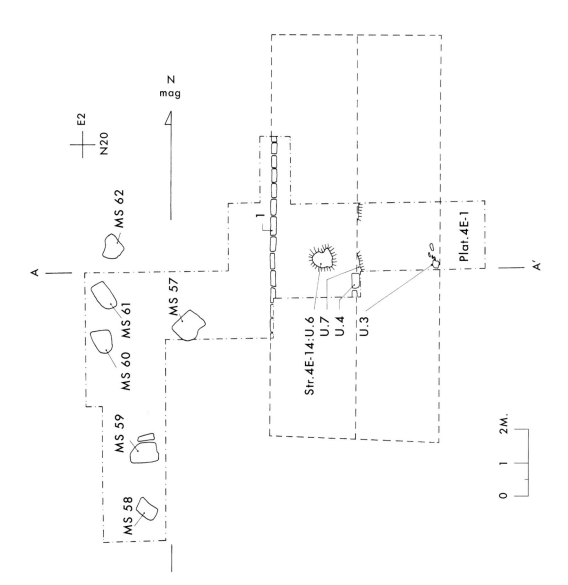

FIGURE 75

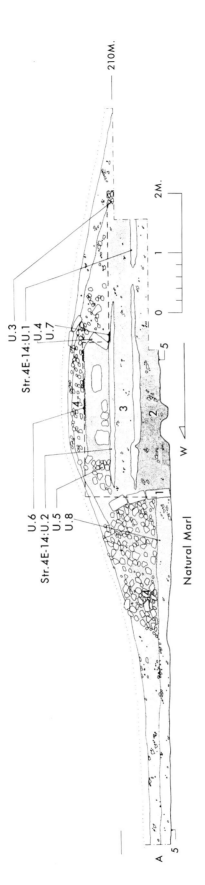

210M.

2 M.

U. 3
Str. 4E-14: U. 1
U. 4
U. 7

U. 6
Str. 4E-14: U. 2
U. 5
U. 8

Natural Marl

A
5

Str. 4E-14: Section A-A', as located in Fig. 74.

Pertinent to 4E-14: 1, Rear structure wall (see Fig. 74). *2*, Earth fill of CS. 4, partially sealed by U. 1. *3*, Earth fill of CS. 3; overlies U. 1 and is partially sealed by U. 2. To the E, it is retained by U. 3. *4*, Debris from structure collapse. Its quantity suggests that the two-level platform of 14 supported a building with masonry dwarf walls akin to those of Str. 4E-16 (Fig. 77, 78). *5*, Surface of marl, devoid of cultural material and apparently natural. U. 1, Pause-line in fill operations between CS. 3 and 4. The top of this is close to that of the second course of masonry in the rear wall. U. 2, Stratum similar to U. 1, separating the fills of CS. 2 and 3. Note that its surface is close to the elevation of the top of the third course of masonry in the rear wall. U. 3, Front structure wall (see Fig. 74). U. 4, Front wall, upper platform level (see Fig. 74). U. 5, Rubble fill-retaining wall, based on U. 2. Units 4 and 5 retain the earth fill of CS. 2. U. 6, Upper platform floor (see Fig. 74). U. 7, Lower platform floor (see Fig. 74). U. 8, Stratum of compact earth that overlies marl (5). Rubble from structure collapse (4) lies on U. 8, as do MS. 57–62 (see Fig. 178b).

FIGURE 76

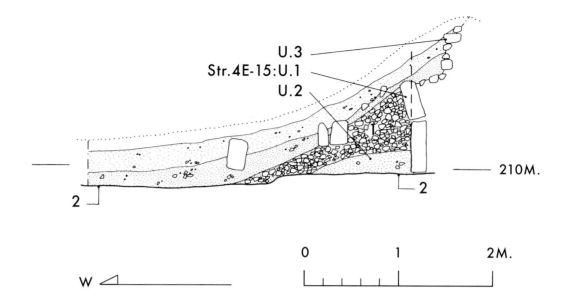

Str. 4E-15: Section through debris west of structure, as located in Fig. 80.

Pertinent to Str. 4F-15: 1, Rubble from structure collapse, analogous to that behind Str. 4E-14 (Fig. 75:4). *2*, Surface of natural marl (see Fig. 75:5). U. 1, W wall of structure, based on marl. U. 2, Midden-like stratum overlying marl that abuts U. 1. U. 3, Vertical arrangement of rubble, suggestive of a fill-retaining wall (analogous to Str. 4E-14:U. 5:Fig. 75).

Figure 77 (facing page)

Str. 4E-16: Plan.

Pertinent to Str. 4E-16: 1, Dividing wall between Rm. 1 and 4, constructed of two veneers with a rubble core. Units 4 and 19 turn up to this wall. *2*, Dividing wall between Rm. 2 and 3. Although not excavated, the veneer stones for Rm. 2 were visible after the mound was cleared of detritus. *3, 4*, Reconstructed walls between Rm. 1 and 2 and Rm. 4 and 5, from rises on the mound similar to those noted for the walls between Rm. 1 and 4 and 2 and 3. *5*, NW corner, building platform. The elevation of its top is the same as the broken line in Fig. 78 (6) that runs N from the top of U. 2. For elevation, see TR. 20B. U. 2, Retaining wall, its base at the same elevation as the top of U. 1 (Fig. 78 and represented here by the broken line to the N). Its length is reconstructed on the assumption of basic symmetry of the structure, the known room walls, and the known NW corner. U. 3, 4, Floor remnants that partially seal earth fill contained between U. 2 and the lowest course of the rear wall. They are at the same elevation as two pause-lines (8, and U. 8 in Fig. 78), and turn up to U. 15, as well as U. 12 and its counterpart W of the doorway of Rm. 1. U. 6, Inner veneer of the S (rear) wall. It is based on fill, and U. 5 (Fig. 78) turns up to its base. U. 7, Outer veneer of the S (rear) wall, based on a pause-line (Fig. 78:7). Its length is assumed the same as U. 2. U. 10, Stone, correctly positioned to be interpreted as part of the N step to 16-1st. Length of U. 10 is reconstructed on the basis of the NW corner and assumed symmetry. U. 11, NW corner, step for 16-1st. The elevation of its top is the same as the broken line in Fig. 78 that runs from the top of U. 10 to the top of U. 1. U. 12, Stone of inner face, N building wall. Unit 3 turns up to its base. U. 14, Floor for interior platform in the rear of Rm. 1. U. 15, 16, Front walls of interior platforms in the rear of Rm. 1 and 4. These abut the room end walls, and the room floors turn up to them. U. 17, 18, Interior platforms added to the ends of Rm. 1. Based in part on U. 14, they abut the front and rear building walls and U. 15. U. 19, Floor in Rm. 4 at the same elevation as U. 3, 4, and 5 in Rm. 1. It turns up to the building walls and U. 16. For section A-A', see Fig. 78. Coordinates are to datum shown in Fig. 80.

FIGURE 77

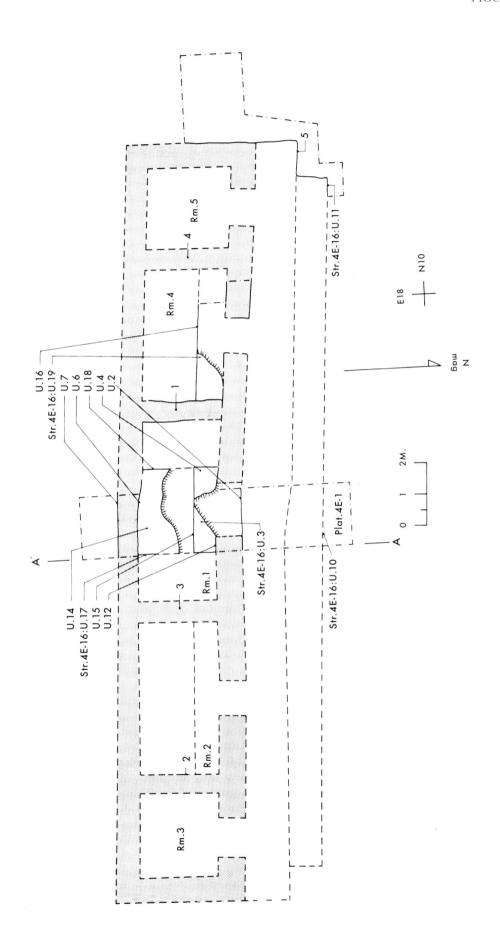

FIGURE 78

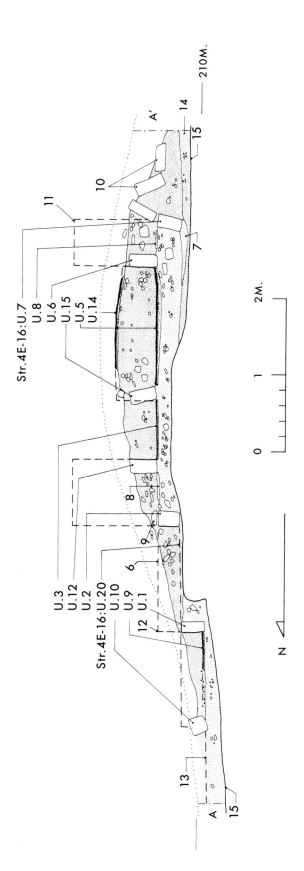

Str. 4E-16: Section A-A', as located in Fig. 77.

Pertinent to Str. 4E-16: 6, Reconstructed floor level for front platform of 1st. The validity for this is indicated by the elevation of U. 11 (Fig. 77). *7,* Pause-line, on which the outer veneer of the back wall rests. *8,* Pause-line between the inner and outer faces of the N building wall. Note that elevation is the same as the comparable pause-line (U. 8) in the rear wall. *9,* Surviving stub of the outer veneer of the building wall, based on U. 2. The total height of the front wall is reconstructed from data on the rear wall. *10, 11,* Stones fallen from the rear wall, the dimensions of which indicate a total masonry wall height as shown. *12,* Reconstructed front wall of building platform of 1st, from the elevation, position, and projection of the NW corner of the platform. *13,* Reconstructed plaza floor, from the position of the base of U. 10. Elevation is the same as for U. 9. *14,* Compact gray earth that overlies marl. *15,* Natural marl (see Fig. 75:5, 76:2, 79:4). U. 1, Retaining wall, to which U. 9 turns up. Its top is at the same elevation as U. 20. U. 2, Retaining wall (see Fig. 77). U. 3, Room floor (see Fig. 77). U. 5, Floor at the same elevation as U. 3 and 4, over which an interior platform was built. U. 5 turns up to the rear wall. U. 6, 7, Veneer of rear wall (see Fig. 77). U. 8, Pause-line between U. 6 and 7. Note its elevation, basically the same as the base of the inner wall veneer, and the top of the first course of the outer veneer. U. 9, floor remnant that turns up to the base of U. 1. U. 10, Stair riser (see Fig. 77). The reconstructed floor for this step is based on the elevation of U. 11 (see Fig. 77). U. 12, Inner veneer, N building wall (see Fig. 77). U. 14, 15, Floor and wall of interior platform (see Fig. 77). U. 20, Remnant of the floor over the lower platform level of 16-2nd (off-section). It turns up to the base of U. 2, and must have run to the top of U. 1.

FIGURE 79

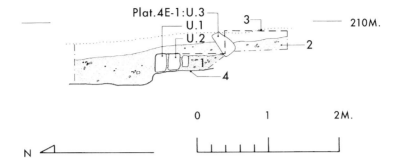

Plat. 4E-1: Section through N wall.

Pertinent to Plat. 4E-1: 1, Gray-brown earth fill. The broken line above is a hypothetical floor level based on the height of U. 1 and 2. *2*, Yellow earth fill. *3*, Reconstructed floor for the plaza, based on the height of U. 3. *4*, Natural marl (see Fig. 75:5, 76:2). U. 1, E-W wall, built on marl. U. 2, E-W wall of crude masonry that retains the gray-brown earth (1). U. 3, E-W wall, based on the gray-brown fill (1), its base at the same approximate elevation as the tops of U. 1 and 2.

FIGURE 80

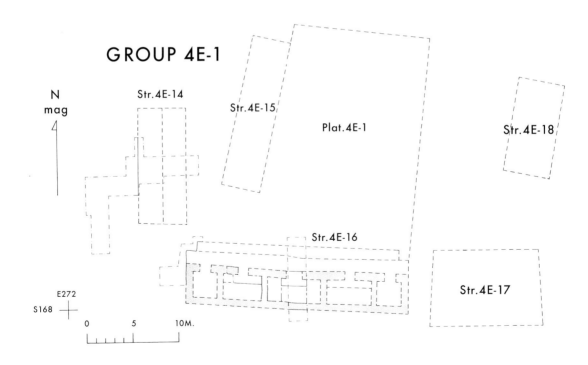

Gp. 4E-1 as it appeared ca. Gp. TS. 4 (Table 2.173).

Str. 4E-50: Plan.

Pertinent to Str. 4E-50: 1, Reconstructed stairway. Given the close resemblance of this structure to 4E-31 (TR. 19:fig. 2), the stairs here are reconstructed by analogy with it (see also Fig. 82:11). *2,* E (front) wall, upper level of building platform. Unit 13 is in union with this wall, and U. 12 covers it in the doorway to Rm. 1. The wall is based on U. 7 (Fig. 82). Its length is reconstructed from the known location of the S end wall (10), and assumption (consistent with the mound configuration) of structural symmetry. *3,* W (back) wall of building platform. The basis for its length reconstruction is the same as for the front wall of the upper level of the building platform (2). *5,* Reconstruction of rear building wall, assuming a plinth comparable to that in front. The location of the inner face of the rear wall is indicated by turnup of U. 14 and 15; wall height is unknown. *6,* Front wall, based on U. 9 (Fig. 82) and the front wall of the building platform (2). Wall height is unknown. See also Fig. 82. *7, 8,* Shelves in U. 16 and 17. *9,* Wall between Rm. 1 and 3; abuts the E wall and the interior platform, and must postdate these (by a few hours or several years). Assumed is that the wall between Rm. 1 and 2 is equivalent in location and construction. *10,* S end wall; assumed is that the N end wall was an equal distance from the front-rear axis. U. 12, Floor of Rm. 1. Based on U. 9 (Fig. 82), it is in union with the front room wall and that of the interior platform. U. 13, Floor, laid over a small-stone foundation, and in union with the front of an upper building platform level. At its western extent U. 13 lies on U. 7 (Fig. 82). Unit 13 obviously is part of a floor for the front of the lower building platform level. U. 15, Final floor of the interior platform, Rm. 1. It was laid on U. 14 (Fig. 82), and turns up to the room walls, as well as U. 16 and 17. U. 16 and 17, Platform dividing walls, in union with U. 14 and to which U. 15 turns up. These walls survive to a height 0.32 m above the surviving height of the front building wall. U. 18, Pit in bedrock. U. 19, Floor close to the elevation of U. 14 and 15, and undoubtedly part of the floor of an interior platform in Rm. 2. Assuming symmetry, a similar platform is predicted for Rm. 3, and is verified by abutment of the wall between Rm. 1 and 3 (9) against the interior platform of Rm. 1, which seems to continue N. For Section A–A', see Fig. 82; for photo of N end of Rm. 1, see Fig. 178c. Coordinates are to datum shown in Fig. 88.

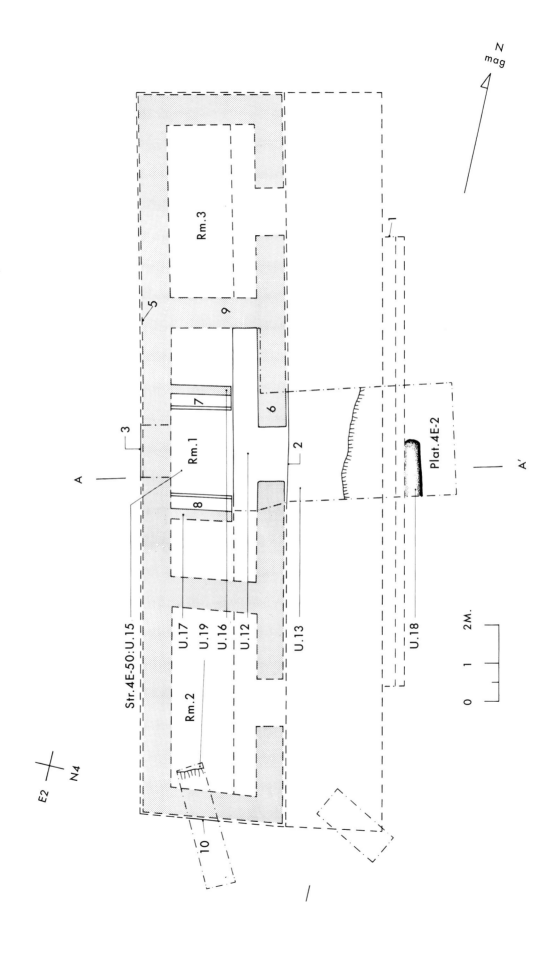

FIGURE 81

Str. 4E-50: Section A-A', as located in Fig. 81.

Pertinent to Str. 4E-50: 1, Reconstructed steps (see Fig. 81). *2*, Front wall, upper level of building platform (see Fig. 81). *3*, Rear wall of building platform (Fig. 81). *4*, Front wall of the interior platform in Rm. 1, in union with U. 12. The wall is abutted by the N end wall of the room (see Fig. 81:9). *5, 6*, Building walls (see Fig. 81). Badly collapsed, no spring or vault stones were in place, so vault reconstruction and doorway height are hypothetical. *11*, Reconstructed position of fallen riser stone. The first stair riser for some of its extent seems to have been quarried bedrock, but here bedrock is too far W. *12*, Point W of which the hard bedrock crust has been quarried away to the soft underlying marl. *13*, Fill of dark earth for CS. 3. *14*, Fill of gray earth and stone beneath the front of the building platform. *15, 16*, Fill of the upper building platform level, sealed by U. 9; 15 is gray earth, 16 is darker earth. U. 1 and 2, Fill strata, composed largely of pebbles (U. 1) or earth with few stones (U. 2). U. 3, 4, Pause-lines at the same elevation as the top of U. 5, 6, 7, Pause-lines that overlie fill for CS. 3. U. 8, Pause-line. U. 9, Pause-line that seals the fill of the upper building platform level. U. 10, Pause-line in the fill of the interior platform; seals a light earth below and underlies a light fill that is sealed by U. 11. U. 11, Pause-line that seals the fill of the interior platform and forms the foundation for U. 14. U. 12, 13, Building platform floors (see Fig. 81). U. 14, 15, original and final floor of interior platform (see Fig. 81). U. 18, Pit in bedrock (see Fig. 81).

FIGURE 82

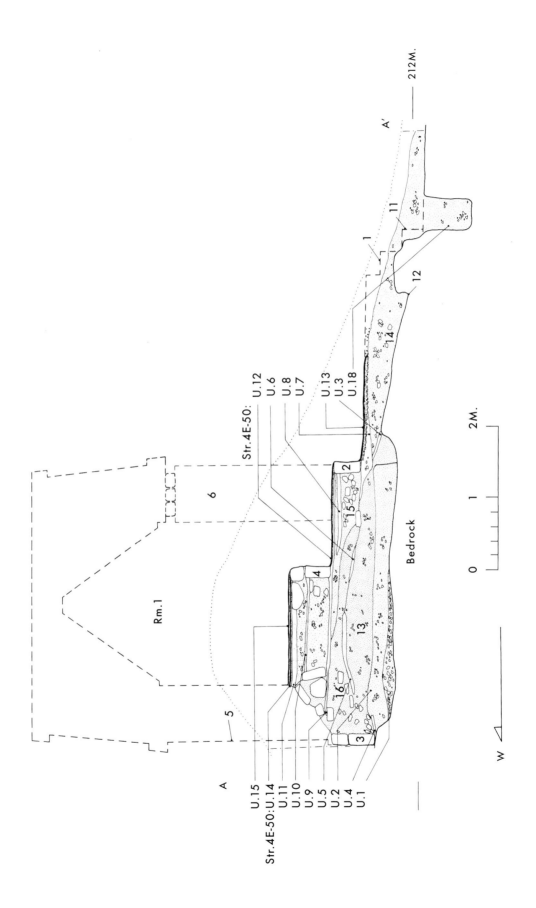

FIGURE 83

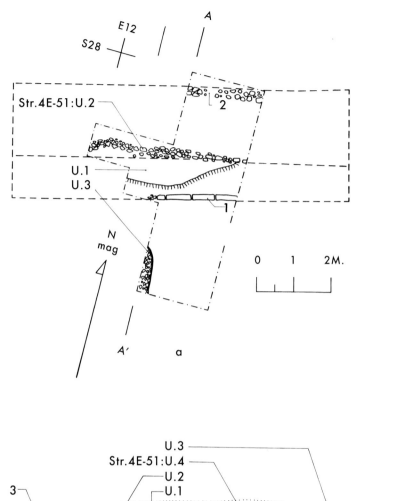

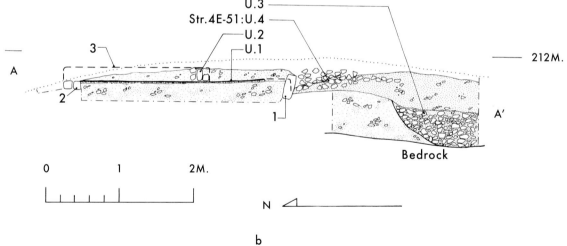

Str. 4E-51: Plan (*a*) and Section A-A' (*b*).

Pertinent to Str. 4E-51: 1, S (front) wall of structure. Its length is reconstructed from mound configuration. The wall is based on earth indistinguishable from the structure fill. *2*, N (rear) wall of structure. Its length is reconstructed on the same basis as that of the S wall (1). *3*, Hypothetical floor for upper platform level, from surviving height of U. 2. U. 1, Floor that runs from the N wall (2) to a point near the S wall, with an elevation close to that of the top of that wall. Unit 2 was built on this floor. U. 2, Wall, based on U. 1, its excavation sufficient to indicate that it probably ran the length of the structure. Lack of a break indicates that it is a platform wall, rather than freestanding. U. 3, Pit, filled with burned stones. U. 4, Rubble above the occupation surface S of the structure. Coordinates are to datum shown in Fig. 88.

FIGURE 84

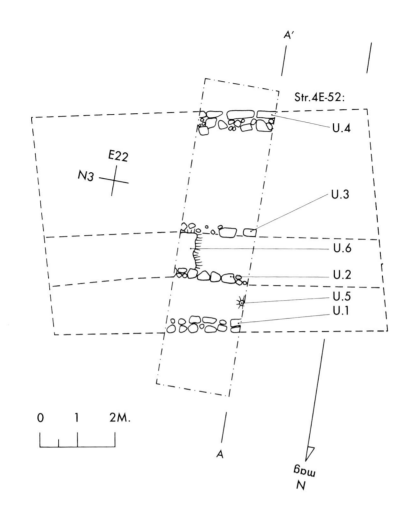

Str. 4E-52: Plan.

Pertinent to Str. 4E-52: U. 1, N (front) wall, built on a grainy gray fill. Reconstructed length is from overall mound configuration. U. 2, Wall for second platform level, built on a pebble fill behind U. 1. From mound configuration and the presence of yet another wall (U. 3), U. 2 is reconstructed as running the length of the structure. U. 3, Wall built on brown earth, probably for an upper platform as there is no break in the wall. Mound configuration, which may not be reliable here, suggests the wall ran the length of the structure. The other possibility is that U. 3 is the front of a small, axially placed platform. U. 4, S (rear) wall, built on grainy, gray fill. Mound configuration suggests it probably was the same length as U. 1. U. 5, Floor remnant laid on a pebble fill S of U. 1, at the correct elevation to have run from the top of U. 1 to the base of U. 2. U. 6, Floor runs from the top of U. 2 to the base of U. 3. For section A-A', see Fig. 85. Coordinates are to datum shown in Fig. 88.

FIGURE 85

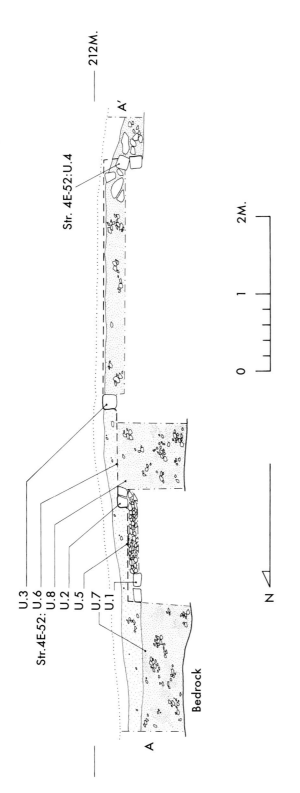

Str. 4E-52: Section A-A', as located in Fig. 84.

Pertinent to Str: 4E-52: U. 1, Front wall (see Fig. 84). U. 2, Front wall, upper platform level (see Fig. 84). U. 3, Front wall, second platform level (see Fig. 84). U. 3, Front wall, once ran S from the top of U. 3. U. 5, Lower platform floor (see Fig. 84). Its height is reconstructed on the assumption that a floor once ran S from the top of U. 3. U. 5, Lower platform floor (see Fig. 84). U. 6, Floor for second platform level, off-section (see Fig. 84). U. 7, 8, Two exposures of grainy, gray fill.

FIGURE 86

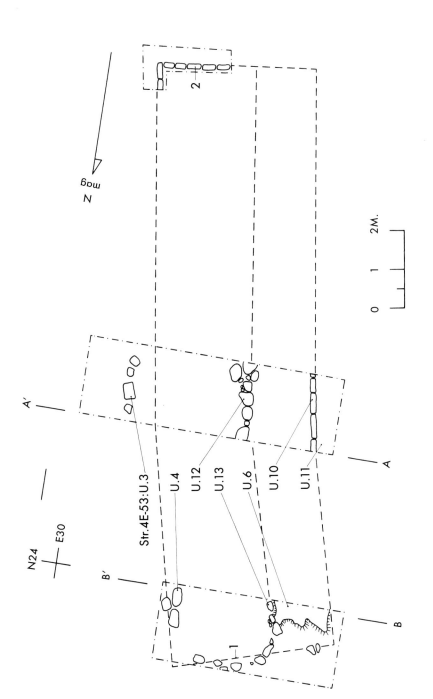

N24
E30

Str.4E-53:U.3

A'

B'

U.4
U.12
U.13
U.6
U.10
U.11

A

B

N
mag

0   1   2 M.

Str. 4E-53: Plan.

Pertinent to Str. 4E-53: 1, N end wall, indicated by a line of rubble. *2*, SE corner. U. 3, Masonry apparently fallen from place. Its original position has been reconstructed in Fig. 87 from the maximum eastward extent of U. 8. U. 4, Masonry positioned to suggest that it is a part of the same wall as U. 3. These two units, plotted in relation to the SE corner (2) are interpreted as parts of the rear structure wall. U. 6, Floor, a few centimeters above U. 5 (Fig. 87) that must have abutted U. 2 (Fig. 87). U. 10, W (front) wall, built on U. 7 (Fig. 87), in union with U. 11. The length of U. 10 is reconstructed from the known locations of the N end wall (1) and the SE corner (2). U. 11, Floor W of structure in union with U. 10. U. 12, Wall, its base at the same elevation as the top of U. 10, and built on earth fill. U. 13, Wall in same position relative to U. 2 (Fig. 87) as U. 12 is to U. 1 (Fig. 87). Both apparently are parts of a single wall that must have run the length of the structure. For sections A-A' and B-B', see Fig. 87. Coordinates are to datum shown in Fig. 88.

Str. 4E-53: Sections A-A' (*a*), B-B' (*b*), as located in Fig. 86, and at base of slope 6 m E of Str. 4E-53 (*c*).
Pertinent to Str. 4E-53: 3, Yellow-brown earth fill that has spilled from the structure in back. *4,* Light-brown earth. *5,* Orange earth beneath structure fill (3). *6, 8,* Reconstructed floor, lower platform of 1st, from the relative elevations of U. 10 and 12. *7, 9,* Reconstructed floor, upper platform level, from height of U. 12. U. 1, Wall, in union with U. 7, its top covered by U. 8. U. 2, Wall in the correct position to be part of the same wall as U. 1. Unit 5 abuts this wall, U. 9 covers its top. U. 3, 4, Rear wall of 1st (see Fig. 86). U. 5, Floor that abuts U. 2, close to the elevation of U. 7. U. 6, Floor that must have abutted U. 2 (see Fig. 86). U. 7, Floor that runs beneath U. 10 and is in union with U. 1. U. 8, Floor that runs E from the top of U. 1. U. 9, Floor related to U. 2 as U. 8 is to U. 1. U. 10, Front of 1st (see Fig. 86). U. 11, Plaza floor W of 1st (see Fig. 86). U. 12, Wall for upper platform level of 1st. U. 13, Wall for upper platform level of 1st (see Fig. 86). *Pertinent to trench 6 m E of Str. 4E-53: 1,* Stratum of dark brown earth. *2,* Stratum of yellow-brown earth (like Fig. 87:3). *3,* Hard, marl.

FIGURE 87

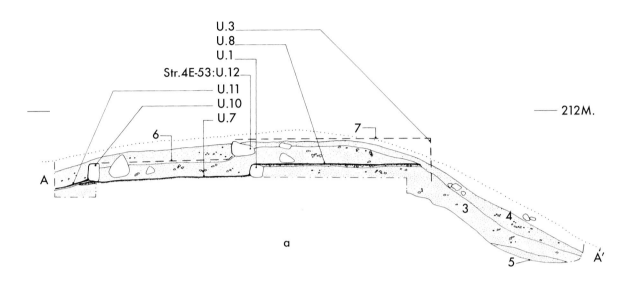

U.3
U.8
U.1
Str.4E-53:U.12
U.11
U.10
U.7
6
7
212M.

A

3
4
5
A'

a

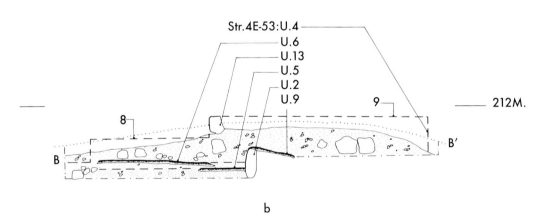

Str.4E-53:U.4
U.6
U.13
U.5
U.2
U.9
8
9
212M.

B
B'

b

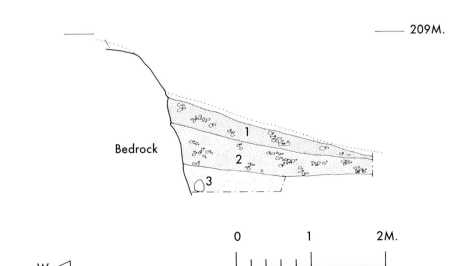

209M.

Bedrock
1
2
3

0   1   2M.

W

c

FIGURE 88

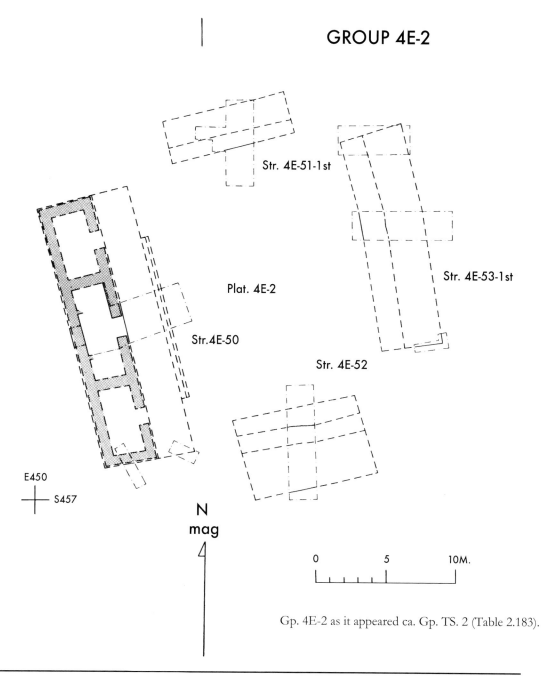

GROUP 4E-2

Str. 4E-51-1st

Str. 4E-53-1st

Plat. 4E-2

Str.4E-50

Str. 4E-52

E450

S457

N
mag

0   5   10M.

Gp. 4E-2 as it appeared ca. Gp. TS. 2 (Table 2.183).

Figure 89 (facing page)
Str. 5D-6-3rd: Plan.
Pertinent to Str. 5D-6: U. 1, E wall, upper platform level, based on fill above Plat. 5D-30:U. 1. Plat. 5D-29:U. 9 is in union with the base of the wall. To the W, the wall retains a fill of light-colored earth and rubble. The length of U. 1 is reconstructed from mound configuration. U. 2, W wall, upper platform level; retains the same fill as U. 1, and its length is also reconstructed from mound configuration. U. 3, Floor remnant, close to the elevation of the tops of U. 1 and 2. The floor is very hard, with a small, blue-stone aggregate; traces of burning are apparent on its surface. U. 4, W wall (front), lower platform level. Its length is reconstructed from mound configuration. U. 5, 6, Steps up from Plat. 5D-30 to the lower level of Str. 5D-6-3rd. U. 5 is based on a dark earth fill; U. 6 on a higher earth fill behind U. 5. The length of the stairway is unknown; by analogy with Str. 4E-16 (in Gp. 4E-1, this report) and Str. 4E-31 (TR. 19:fig. 2 and table 96), its length relative to the structure is estimated as shown. *Pertinent to Plat. 5D-29*: U. 9. Floor remnant, in union with the base of Str. 5D-6:U. 1. For section A-A', see Fig. 92. Coordinates are to those shown in Fig. 98.

FIGURE 89

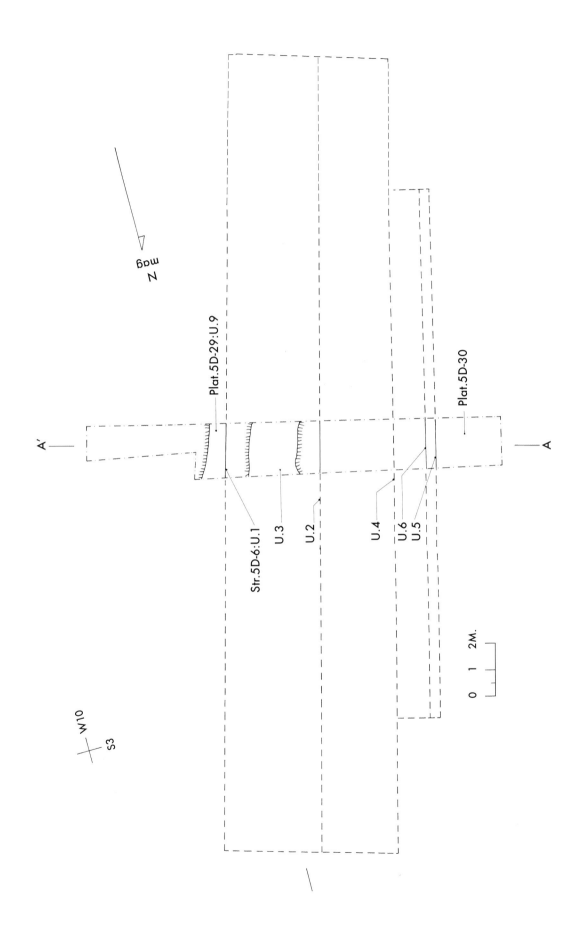

Str. 5D-6-2nd: Plan.

Pertinent to Str. 5D-2-2nd: U. 2, W (front) wall, upper platform level, originally part of 3rd (see Fig. 89). U. 4, W (front) wall, lower platform level, originally part of 3rd (see Fig. 89). U. 5, 6, Steps, originally part of 3rd (see Fig. 89). U. 7, E (rear) wall, upper platform level, built to replace U. 1 (Fig. 89). It was built above Plat. 5D-29:U. 9 (Fig. 89), and retained a fill of rubble and dark earth beneath U. 8. U. 8, Floor that runs over the top of U. 7 and is continuous with plaster on the E face of that wall; probably a remnant of pavement for the upper platform level. U. 9, Major floor patch on U. 3 (Fig. 89), thought to be part of 2nd. For section A-A', see Fig. 92. Coordinates are to those shown in Fig. 98.

FIGURE 90

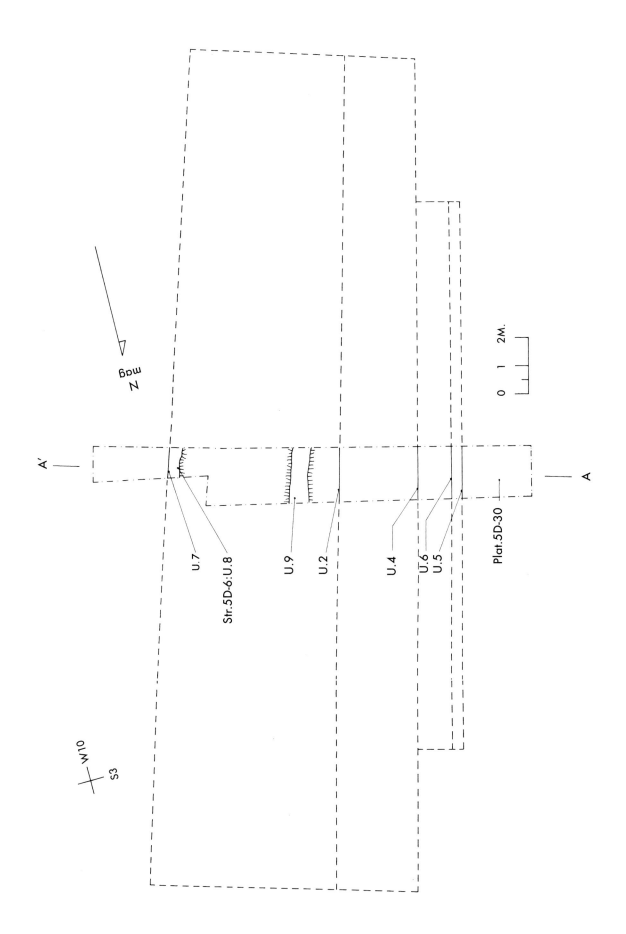

Str. 5D-6-1st: Plan.

Pertinent to Str. 5D-6: 9, Hypothetical dwarf wall; its existence seems required to account for numerous masonry blocks found E of U. 1, as well as a large amount of debris on the platform itself. U. 1, Rear wall, upper platform level, originally constructed for 3rd, buried in the fill of 2nd, and resurrected for 1st (see Fig. 89, 90). U. 2, Front wall, upper platform level, originally part of 3rd (see Fig. 89, 90). U. 4, Front wall, lower platform level, originally part of 3rd (see Fig. 89, 90). U. 5, 6, Front steps, originally part of 3rd (see Fig. 89, 90). U. 9, Major floor patch on the upper platform level, part of 2nd or 1st.

Pertinent to Plat. 5D-29: 1, Stairs that lead down from Plat. 5D-29 to 30. Construction is thought to be contemporary with the laying of U. 16 (Fig. 93) and hence part of 29-1st. They were built against U. 17, a wall that served 29-2nd and 3rd. Length of the stairs is reconstructed from mound configuration of Str. 5D-6 and projection of the N wall of Plat. 5D-29 as seen behind Str. 5D-8 (Fig. 95). U. 9, Floor remnant, thought to have been laid as part of 5th. It is in union with the base of Str. 5D-6:U. 1, and Plat. 5D-29:U. 12 was built on another remnant of this pavement. U. 12, Lower riser of two steps up to Plat. 5D-29-3rd. Built on U. 9, it was placed against a surviving bit of fill for Str. 5D-6-2nd just to the E. U. 13, Second riser of two steps up to Plat. 5D-29-3rd. Now poorly preserved, this riser was built on Str. 5D-6:U. 8 (Fig. 89), and was of about the same height as U. 12. To the E, this riser retains a fill of earth, stone, and bits of masonry, all of which rests on Plat. 5D-30:U. 1 (Fig. 92). The top of this fill is close to the elevation of Plat. 5D-29:U. 11, the floor for Plat. 5D-29-3rd behind Str. 5D-7 (Fig. 94). U. 17, Wall that predates construction of the stairway (1) N of Str. 5D-6. A projection of this wall to the S meets a projection to the N of U. 13. Hence, both are probably parts of the same wall. For section, A-A', see Fig. 92; for section B-B', see Fig. 97a. Coordinates are to those shown in Fig. 98.

FIGURE 91

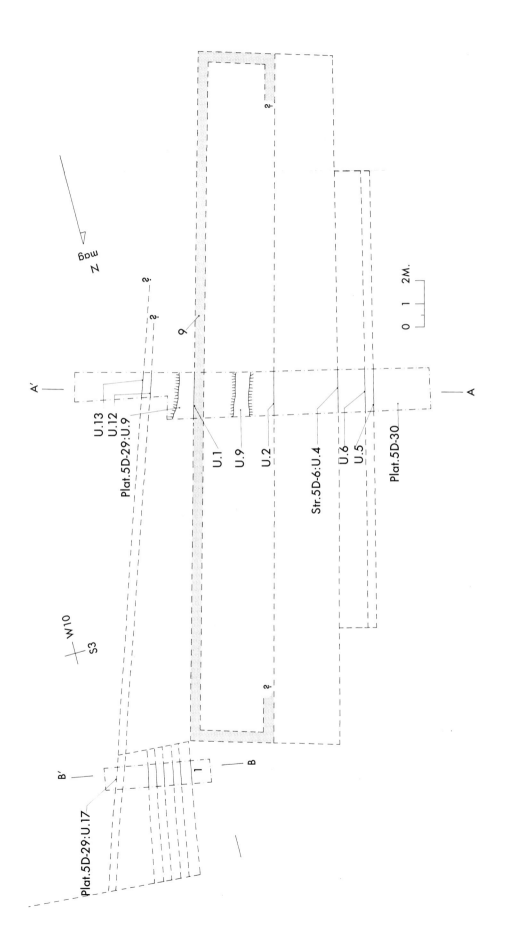

FIGURE 92

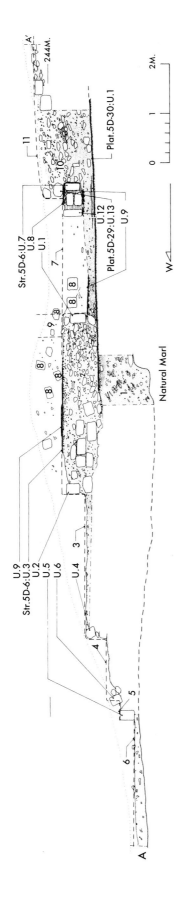

Str. 5D-6: Section A-A', as located in Fig. 89, 90, and 91.

Pertinent to Str. 5D-6: 2, Fill of 3rd: light-colored earth and rubble. *3*, Reconstructed floor over the lower platform level. No trace of such a floor was found, but since the upper portion of the structure was floored, this probably was also. Its elevation is estimated from the height of U. 4 and its fill. *4*, Reconstructed floor of the second step. Such a floor is suggested by the presence of plaster floors elsewhere; its elevation is indicated by the height of U. 6 and its fill relative to the base of U. 4. *5*, Presumed tread of the lowest step, from the relative positions of U. 5 and 6. *7*, Reconstructed floor of 2nd from a projection of U. 8 to U. 3. *8*, Masonry blocks, thought to be debris from a dwarf wall (9) that stood on the rear of 1st. U. 1, Rear wall, 1st and 3rd (see Fig. 89 and 91). U. 2, Front wall, upper platform level of 1st, 2nd, and 3rd (see Fig. 89, 90, 91). U. 3, Floor for upper platform level of 3rd (see Fig. 89). U. 4, Front wall of 1st, 2nd, and 3rd (see Fig. 89–91). U. 5, 6, Steps of 1st, 2nd, and 3rd (see Fig. 89–91). U. 7, Rear wall of 2nd (see Fig. 90). U. 8, Floor for upper platform level of 2nd (see Fig. 90). U. 9, Major floor patch (see Fig. 90). *Pertinent to Plat. 5D-29: 10*, Rubble fill, thought to relate to 3rd. *11*, Projection westward of U. 11, a floor remnant of 3rd behind Str. 5D-7 (see Fig. 94). This correlates well with the top of the rubble fill (10) thought to relate to Plat. 5D-29-3rd, as well as the top of U. 13. U. 9, Floor remnant, thought to be part of 5th (see Fig. 89). U. 12, 13, Risers of stairs thought to relate to 3rd (see Fig. 91). *Pertinent to Plat. 5D-30: 1*, Fill of hard, packed, medium-brown earth rich in Manik sherds. They suggest that Plat. 5D-30-2nd, for which this is the fill, may have been associated with Str. 5D-7-6th. *6*, Hypothetical floor for 1st, its existence suggested by the use of plaster surfaces in the associated Str. 5D-6. Elevation of the floor is suggested by the height of the plaza fill and the position of the base of Str. 5D-6:U. 5. U. 1, Floor of 2nd.

FIGURE 93

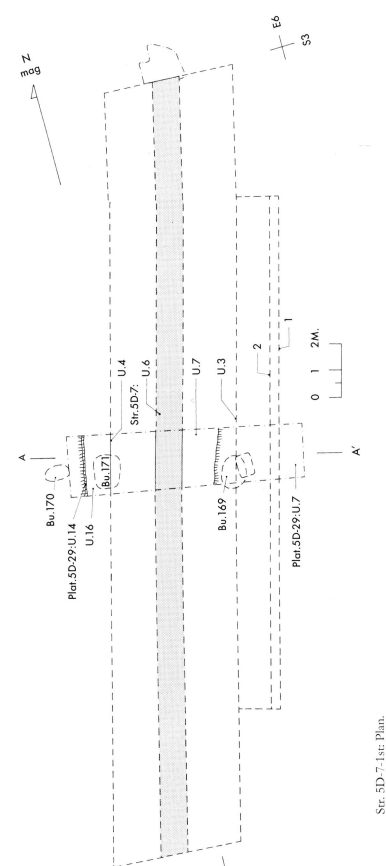

Str. 5D-7-1st: Plan.

Pertinent to Str. 5D-7: 1, 2, Risers for steps giving access to 1st. The basal riser rests on Plat. 5D-29:U. 7, the second on fill. Remains of a floor (U. 5, not shown here) show that plaster pavement ran from the top of the second riser and turned up to U. 3. Length of the stairway is not known; it is reconstructed here in the same way as the stairway for Str. 5D-6 (see Fig. 89). U. 3, E fill-retaining wall for CS. 4. The stairway (1, 2) was built against this wall that served as the front of the structure platform. The wall rests in part on the core fill, and in part on fill for Plat. 5D-29:U. 7. Length of U. 3 is reconstructed from mound configuration and the known location of the N end of U. 6. U. 4, W (rear) wall, built on Plat. 5D-29:U. 11, the floor for Plat. 5D-29-3rd (see Fig. 92 for the other components of this platform). Plat. 5D-29:U. 14 turns up to the base of the wall. U. 6, Wall, built as CS. 2; U. 7 is in union with its base that rests on the fill of CS. 4. Finished faces on both sides of the wall show that it was freestanding, but with no axial doorway. The wall surely ran to the N, and probably S, ends of the structure. It is thought that U. 6 is analogous to Str. 4F-21:U. 2 (Fig. 100), and off-axis doorways must have been provided. U. 7, Remnant of a floor in union with the base of U. 6 and close to the elevation of the top of U. 3. It is interpreted as the platform floor for Str. 5D-7-1st. *Pertinent to Plat. 5D-29:* U. 7, Plaster floor, thought to have been laid as part of 6th. It runs beneath the steps of Str. 5D-7-1st, and is at precisely the same elevation as U. 1 S of Str. 5D-8 (Fig. 96). U. 14, Floor remnant that overlies U. 11, and turns up to the base of the wall for Str. 5D-7-1st. This floor, which defines Plat. 5D-29-2nd, is thought to be represented by U. 15 at Str. 5D-8 (Fig. 95). U. 16, Remnant of the floor for 1st that abuts the back wall of Str. 5D-7-1st. Its elevation, 0.12 m above U. 14, suggests a major alteration (Plat. 5D-29-1st), of which the stairway N of Str. 5D-6 (Fig. 91:1) may have been a part. For section A-A', see Fig. 94. Coordinates are to those shown in Fig. 98.

Str. 5D-7: Section A-A', as located in Fig. 93.

Pertinent to Str. 5D-7: 1, Fill, thought to belong to 4th. Continuous with that of Bu. 171, it consists of brown earth and cultural debris that includes Imix sherds. *2*, Fill, thought to belong to 3rd. Consisting of earth and cultural debris, it buries the remains of 4th and continues to the W beneath Plat. 5D-29:U. 8. Note that it continues down in the cut for Bu. 170 through Plat. 5D-29:U. 8. *4*, Fill for 1st:CS. 4. Consisting of rubble, earth, and cultural debris, it is retained on the E by U. 3. *5*, Fill for 1st:CS. 3. Consisting of rubble, earth, and cultural debris, it abuts U. 3 and is retained by two stair risers on the E (see Fig. 93:1 and 2). U. 1, Rear fill-retaining wall, thought to belong to 4th. Apparently, a finished wall that once stood here was later ripped out. U. 2, Wall thought to belong to 3rd. Just N of the section line, it turns a right angle to run E. A floor (Plat. 5D-29:U. 10) is in union with the wall base on the W. Both floor and wall are based on fill (2) higher E and S of the walls. U. 3, E fill-retaining wall of 1st:CS. 4 (see Fig. 93). Note that the upper part probably served as the front of the main platform, as reconstructed here. U. 4, Rear wall of 1st (see Fig. 93). Its height is reconstructed from the known height for the front platform floor (U. 7), and of rubble W of U. 6. U. 5, Badly preserved remains of a broad stair tread E of the main platform of 1st; seems to have run E from the top of the second stair riser (Fig. 93:2) to turn up to U. 3. U. 6, Apparent dwarf-wall (see Fig. 93). U. 7, Platform floor (see Fig. 93). U. 8, Hollowed-out area in the natural marl, possibly a chultun. *Pertinent to Plat. 5D-29: 3*, Fill for 3rd and 2nd of dark earth, it overlies the remains of Str. 5D-7-3rd. 6, Fill, thought to belong to 6th, it continues beyond the W end of U. 7, sealing the entrance to the grave for Bu. 169. U. 7, Floor, thought to belong to 6th (see Fig. 93). U. 8, Floor remnant, laid directly on fill continuous with that of Str. 5D-7-4th (1). It shows a turnup 0.10 m W of Str. 5D-7:U. 1; apparently there was a veneer here that later was ripped out. Possibly, Plat. 5D-29:U. 9 is part of this same floor (see Fig. 89, 92), probably of 5th. U. 10, Floor, probably of 4th, laid directly on fill continuous with that of Str. 5D-7-3rd, and in union with the base of Str. 5D-7:U. 2. U. 11, Floor remnant, probably of 3rd. The rear wall of Str. 5D-7-1st was built on its surface, which may have run W to the top of U. 13. U. 14, Floor remnant of 2nd (see Fig. 93). U. 16, Floor remnant of 1st (see Fig. 93).

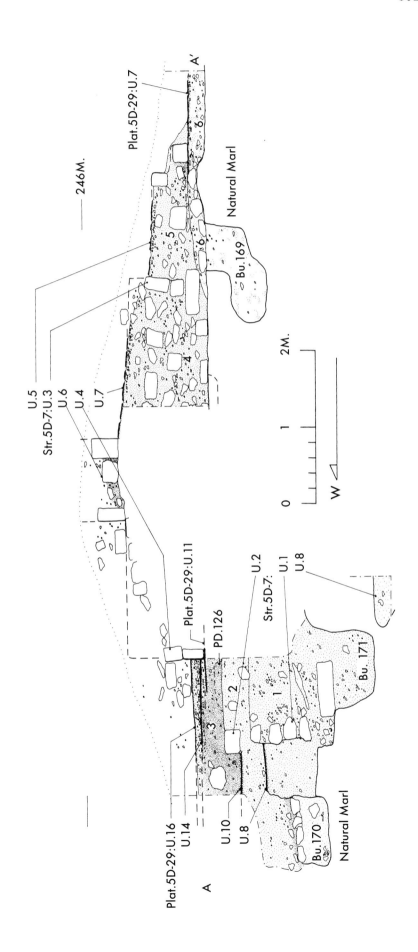

FIGURE 94

Str. 5D-8: Plan.

Pertinent to Str. 5D-8: 1, Step built on Plat. 5D-29:U. 1, with Plat. 5D-29:U. 15 turning up to its base. The step probably did not run the length of the structure, by analogy with Str. 4E-16 and 4E-31 (see Fig. 77 and TR. 19:fig. 2 and table 96). 2, S wall of the front platform, its base (where excavated) rests on the dark earth fill of CS. 4 that was placed behind the stair riser (1). Length of the wall is reconstructed from the known length of the building platform. U. 3, Two-course wall, built on dark earth fill of CS. 4, which served as the front for an upper building platform level. A floor (U. 5) is in union with the base of U. 3 to the S. U. 4, Rear wall of the building platform, based on fill of Plat. 5D-29-6th. With U. 3, it retains a dark earth fill dumped over that of CS. 5. U. 5, Remnant of a floor laid over the fill of CS. 4 in union with the base of U. 3. The floor is at the proper elevation to have terminated on top of the masonry that served as the upper stair riser (2). U. 7, 8, Faces of interior platforms in the rear of Rm. 1 and 2. Assumed is that Rm. 3 also contained a comparable platform. Built on the original building floor (U. 6 in Rm. 1), their construction defines 5D-8-B. The fill retained by U. 7 is a rede- posited midden. U. 10, Final floor in Rm. 1, laid on U. 9 that in turn overlies the original room floor (U. 6), and turns up to U. 7. U. 10 defines 5D-8-A. *Pertinent to Plat. 5D-29:* U. 5, Base of the N retaining wall, built as part of 6th. To the S, it retains a fill of brown earth (U. 2; Fig. 96), on which U. 1 (Fig. 96) was laid. U. 1, then, must have run N to the top of U. 5, which has since been badly eroded. N of U. 5 is a layer of compact earth and pebbles at the same elevation as the wall base, U. 6. This probably was an informal surface while Gp. 5D-1 was in use. U. 15, 18, 19, Floor remnants around Str. 5D-8, probably remnants of surface for Plat. 5D-29-2nd. U. 15 overlies U. 1 and turns up to the step (1) of Str. 5D-8. U. 18 has the same elevation as U. 15, but U. 19 is a bit lower and could be part of an earlier floor. For section A-A', see Fig. 96. Coordinates are to those shown in Fig. 98.

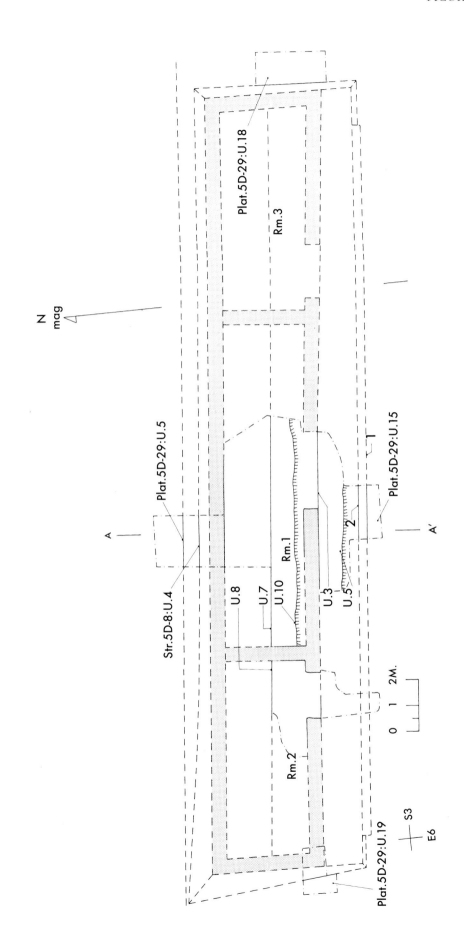

FIGURE 95

Figure 96

Str. 5D-8: Section A-A', as located in Fig. 95.

Pertinent to Str. 5D-8: 2, Core of earth and rubble fill for CS. 5 of 8-C. *3*, Dark earth fill for step and front platform of 8-C, built as CS. 4. It abuts U. 2 that retains the fill (2) of CS. 5. *4*, Dark fill for CS. 3 of 8-C, retained on the N by U. 4, on the S by U. 3. *5*, Midden-like fill for U. 7, part of 8-B. *6*, Front building wall, built as CS. 2 of 8-C. Its one-time height is not known, but the small quantity of debris suggests walls similar to those of Str. 4E-16 (see Fig. 78). *7*, Reconstructed level of the interior platform (U. 7) in Rm. 1, from off-section remains. U. 1, 2, N and S retaining walls for fill (2) of Str. 5D-8:CS. 5. U. 3, Front wall, upper building platform level; retains the fill (4) of CS. 3 and is based on fill (3) of CS. 4. U. 4, Rear wall of the building platform (see Fig. 95). U. 6, Floor of Rm. 1, Str. 5D-8:C. The floor is in union with the building walls (off-section). Unit 7, Front wall, interior platform (see Fig. 95). U. 9, Floor of Rm. 1, Str. 5D-8-D. Laid on U. 6, it turns up to the base of U. 7. U. 10, Floor of Rm. 1, Str. 5D-8-A (see Fig. 95). *Pertinent to Plat. 5D-29: 1*, Top of fill for 6th, on which Str. 5D-8-C was built. U. 1, Plaster floor for 6th. U. 2, Brown earth fill for 6th, on which U. 1 was laid. Easily distinguishable from U. 3, it contains Ik sherds. U. 3, 4, Earth fill, clearly distinguishable from U. 2; contains nothing more recent than Manik sherds. U. 5, E-W wall that retains U. 2 on the S (see Fig. 95). This was the N edge of 6th, and later it must have continued in use behind Str. 5D-8, as reconstructed here. U. 6, Compact earth and pebbles that probably was an exposed surface when the group was in use. U. 15, Floor remnant of 2nd (see Fig. 95).

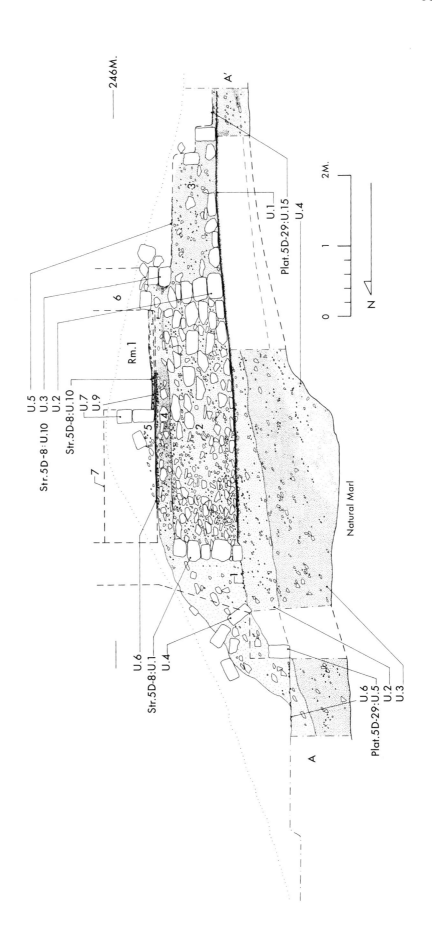

FIGURE 96

246M.

A'

3

U.1

Plat.5D-29:U.15
U.4

2M.

N

0   1

6

Rm.1

U.5
U.3
U.2
Str.5D-8:U.10

U.7
U.9

Str.5D-8:U.10

4

5

2

7

Natural Marl

U.6

Str.5D-8:U.1
U.4

A

U.6
Plat.5D-29:U.5
U.2
U.3

Plat. 5D-29: Section B-B' (*a*), as located in Fig. 91; St. P36 reconstructed (*b*), and fragments as found (*c*), as located in Fig. 98; St. P36: Section A-A' (*d*).

Pertinent to Str. 5D-29: 1, Reconstructed floor level of 1st. If the stairs were built against U. 17 (Fig. 91), then the floor of 1st could have been no lower than this. The reconstruction fits well with a reconstruction of the two upper steps, based on a projection of the risers and treads of the known steps below them. The supposed elevation of this floor is 0.20 m above U. 16 some 18 m to the S, thought to be contemporary. *2*, Apparent elevation of the floor of Plat. 5D-30 N of Str. 5D-6. U. 17, W wall of Plat. 5D-29-3rd and 2nd (see Fig. 91).

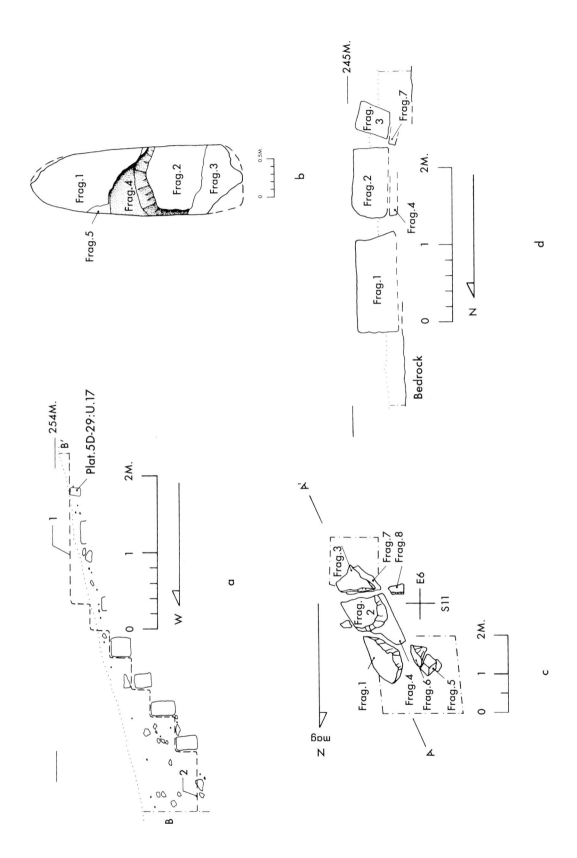

FIGURE 97

FIGURE 98

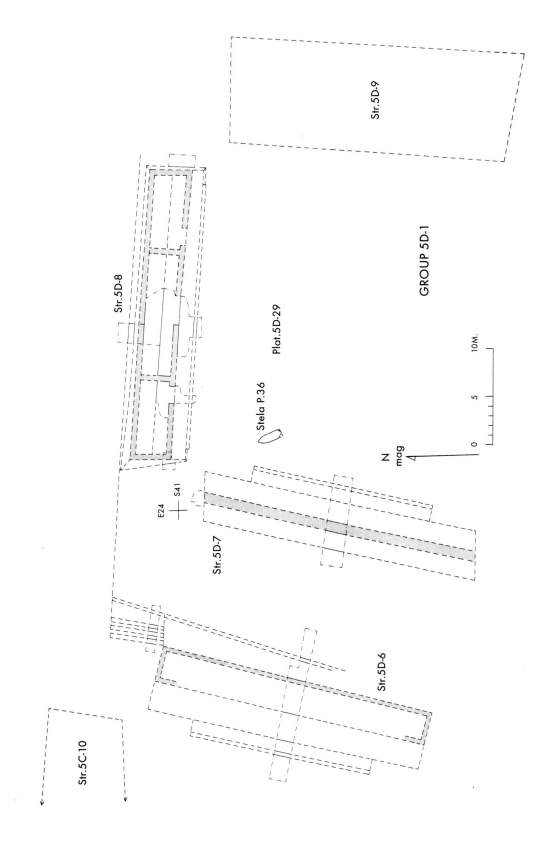

Gp. 5D-1 as it appeared ca. Gp. TS. 2 (Table 2.195).

FIGURE 99

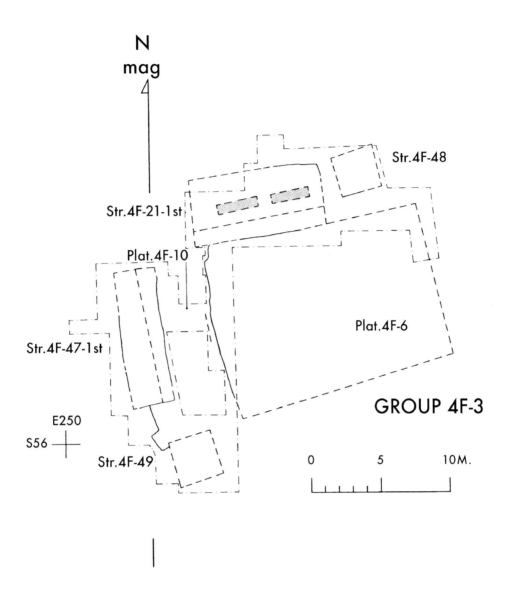

N
mag

Str.4F-48

Str.4F-21-1st

Plat.4F-10

Plat.4F-6

Str.4F-47-1st

GROUP 4F-3

E250

S56

Str.4F-49

0   5   10M.

Gp. 4F-3 as it appeared in Gp. TS. 2 (Table 2.211).

Str. 4F-21 and 4F-48: Plan.

Pertinent to Str. 4F-21: 2, S (front) wall, probably originally a part of 4F-21-2nd, as a projection of U. 4 meets its top. Wall length is known on the basis of the ruined remains of the two structure end walls. Note how, at the W end, quarried bedrock conforms to the line of the wall. 3, Rear wall of 4F-21-1st, which retains a fill of brown earth with some stones mixed in. Its length is reconstructed on the basis of the known location of the structure end walls. U. 1, wall based on U. 4 that runs the length of the structure. Elevation of U. 3 is the same as the wall top. U. 2, freestanding masonry walls built on the fill for the upper platform level. U. 3 turns up to the N faces of U. 2. U. 3, Remnant of an upper platform floor that turns up to U. 2, and which must have run to the tops of U. 1 and the rear structure wall (3). Elevation is the same as the tops of these walls. U. 4, Floor that runs N beneath U. 1, and covers the top of the rear wall of Str. 4F-21-2nd (Fig. 101:1a). A southward projection of this floor comes close to the top of the front structure wall (2), suggesting that the latter was built as part of 4F-21-2nd, and that it and the front portion of U. 4 continued to serve 21-1st. *Pertinent to Str. 4F-48: 5*, Walls, visible for the most part as lines of rubble. Three relatively undamaged masonry blocks survive in the S wall. All walls are based on Str. 4F-21:U. 6 (Fig. 101b). U. 1, Hole in bedrock, probably a posthole. *Pertinent to Plat. 4F-6: 4*, Reconstructed N edge, based on relative locations of the S wall of Str. 4F-21 and Plat. 4F-6:U. 1. Note that the W part of this plaza is sunken in relation to the terrain to the W, and its NW corner is formed by quarried bedrock. U. 1, Rubble remains of the NE corner of the plaza. Here, the plaza is elevated relative to the surrounding terrain. For sections A-A' and B-B', see Fig. 101. For photos of the E half of Str. 4F-21, see Fig. 178d; 179a for Str. 4F-48. Coordinates are to datum shown in Fig. 99.

FIGURE 100

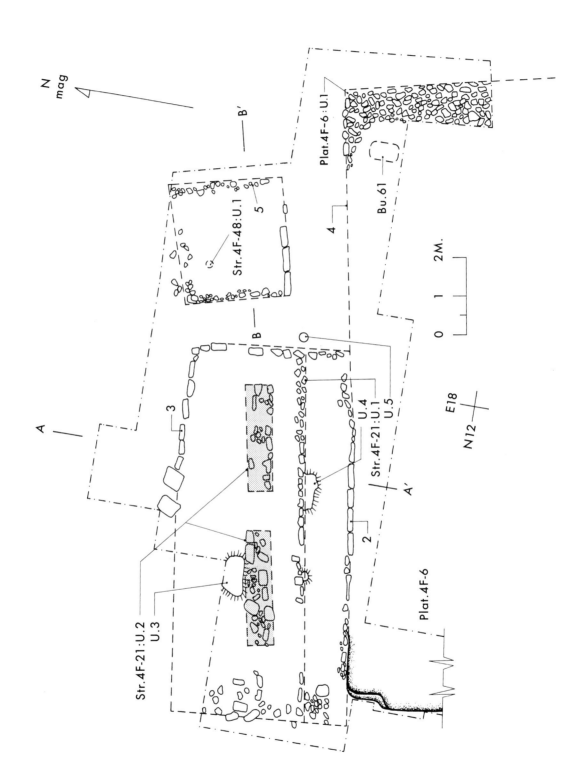

Str. 4F-21 and 48: Sections A-A' (*a*) and B-B' (*b*), as located in Fig. 100.

Pertinent to Str. 4F-21: 1, N (rear) wall, Str. 4F-21-2nd, based on U. 6, with its top covered by U. 4. *2*, S wall of 4F-21-1st and 2nd (see Fig. 100). *3*, Rear wall of 4F-21-1st (see Fig. 100). U. 1, Upper platform wall (see Fig. 100); badly ruined. U. 2, Freestanding masonry wall (see Fig. 100); badly ruined, its original height unknown. U. 3, Floor (off-section) for upper platform level of 1st (see Fig. 100). U. 4, Floor of 21-2nd (see Fig. 100). U. 6, Compact gray earth on which the walls of 21-1st and 2nd, as well as Str. 4F-48, are based. *Pertinent to Str. 4F-48: 5*, Walls of 4F-48 (see Fig. 100). *6*, Reconstructed floor, based on the height of the best-preserved masonry in the S wall and the height of stony fill within the walls. For photo, see Fig. 179a.

FIGURE 101

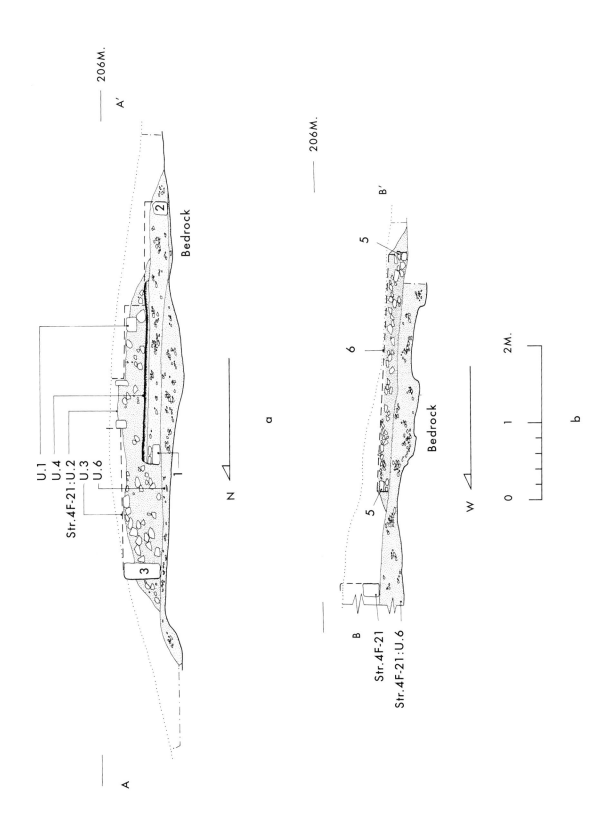

Str. 4F-47 and 4F-49: Plan.

Pertinent to Str. 4F-47: 4, E (front) wall, 4F-47-1st; wall is based on Plat. 4F-10:Fl. 1, and Plat. 4F-10:U. 1 turns up to its base. 6, W (rear) wall, 4F-47, based on U. 6. U. 2, 3, Areas of small stone fill (only the outer portion is shown here) above the level of U. 4, on either side of it. They are interpreted as remnants of two small platforms. U. 4, Floor remnant, at same elevation as tops of E and W structure walls, as reconstructed (Fig. 103). The N and S limits of U. 4 conform to U. 2 and 3. At one point, U. 4 was seen for a short distance along the front of U. 3. U. 5, A line of rubble, based on U. 4, which joints the E faces of U. 2 and 3, interpreted as a wall that converted the two small platforms into a single upper platform level (Str. 4F-47-1st). U. 7-10, Holes in bedrock, located in the corners of Str. 4F-47-1st. Almost surely, these supported corner posts for a building of perishable materials. *Pertinent to Str. 4F-49: 7*, Shallow quarry W of structure that contained a concentration of sherds and artifacts (Table 2.199 and 2.203:LG. 2b of Str. 4F-49). U. 1, 2, Holes in bedrock in the approximate NE and NW corners (as indicated by rubble fill, the quarried wall to the W, and Plat. 4F-10:U. 3 to the N); the walls of the structure are in even worse condition than those of Str. 4F-48 (see Fig. 100:5). The other two corners were not excavated to bedrock; there may be postholes there. Almost surely, these supported corner posts for a small building of perishable materials. *Pertinent to Plat. 4F-10: 1*, E terrace wall; its N portion is formed by quarried bedrock, which turns E to merge with the front wall of Str. 4F-21 (see Fig. 100:2, 4). The S portion consists of U. 2, a masonry wall. 2, Hypothetical step up to Plat 4F-10; seems required by the 0.70 m height of Fl. 1 above the level of Plat. 4F-6 (see Fig. 103). Its location is suggested by a stratum of gray earth that continues E from beneath Fl. 1, and ends at about this point. 3, Olla neck inserted through Plat. 4F-10:U. 3. 8, Hypothetical end of U. 2 (see 1, above). Extent of U. 3 shows that Plat. 4F-10 reached at least this far S; it may have extended farther. Fl. 1, On which the front wall (4) of Str. 4F-47-1st rests; pavement turns up at its W extent on a line with Str. 4F-47:U. 1 (Fig. 103). U. 3, pavement at the same elevation as Fl. 1, which turns up to U. 4 and the S wall of Str. 4F-47; probably, remnant of Fl. 1. U. 4, A wall linking Str. 4F-47 and 49. Unit 3 turns up to its base; to the W, wall retains a compact gray earth. For section A-A', see Fig. 103. Coordinates are to datum shown in Fig. 99.

FIGURE 102

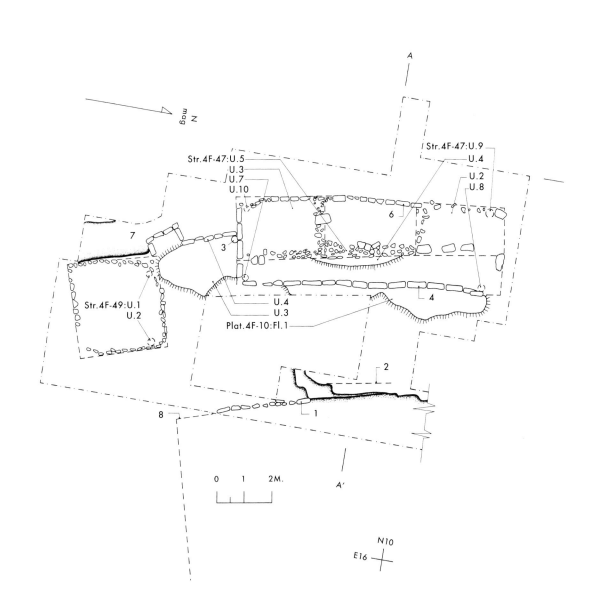

Str. 4F-47: Section A-A', as located in Fig. 102.

Pertinent to Str. 4F-47: 4, Front wall of 47-1st (see Fig. 102). *6,* Rear wall of 1st and 2nd (see Fig. 102). *9,* Reconstructed floor for the upper platform level of 47-1st, based on the height of the fills for U. 2 and 3 (Fig. 102). U. 1, base of a wall, based on U. 6; off-section, Fl. 1 of Plat. 4F-10 turns up along the line of U. 1, suggesting that the wall at one time stood higher. Thus U. 1 is interpreted as the remains of the front wall for Str. 4F-47-2nd. U. 4, floor for Str. 4F-47-2nd (see Fig. 102). U. 5, front wall for an upper platform level of 47-1st (see Fig. 102). U. 6, compact gray earth overlies bedrock on which U. 1 and the rear structure wall *were* built; stratum extends to the S, where it is exposed W of Str. 4F-47 and Plat. 4F-10:U. 4. *Pertinent to Plat. 4F-10: 2,* Hypothetical step up to the level of Fl. 1 (see Fig. 102:2). *10,* Probable floor level E of Plat. 4F-10, based on a soil change at this elevation. U. 1, patch on Fl. 1 turns up to the wall (4) of 47-1st; evidently, Fl. 1 continued to serve E of this structure.

FIGURE 103

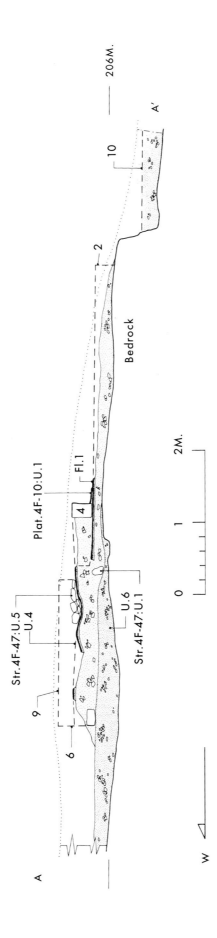

Group 5F-1: Plan.

Pertinent to Str. 5F-17: U. 1, front structure wall. Mound configuration suggests the reconstructed length shown here. Pertinent to Str. 5F-18: *2*, Estimated location of the final structure wall, based upon the presence of U. 3 in only one of the two test pits and overall mound configuration. U. 1, E-W wall built on Plat. 5F-1:U. 2, and as high as U. 3. U. 3, Badly preserved floor, seen in the N, but not the S, test pit. It runs S from near the top of U. 1, to a point somewhere between the two test pits. Thus, its S extent seems to correlate with the edge of the visible ruin mound, and it is interpreted as a later extension of the original 5F-18. *Pertinent to Str. 5F-Sub.1*: E wall based on bedrock; the N end of this probably represents the NE corner because of apparently collapsed masonry where the N wall is reconstructed. On this basis, one may assume that the S end of the wall represents the SE corner. The location of the W wall is unknown. *Pertinent to Str. 5F-Sub.2*: Part of the W wall, based on Plat. 5F-1:U. 3 (Fig. 106). Nothing more is known of the structure. Pertinent to Ch. 5F-5: Location of the orifice. *Pertinent to Plat 5F-1:1*, Estimated location of the final E wall, based on the presence of apparent wall remains in the easternmost trench, and the presence of an "Imix midden" in the trench just E of this line. U. 4, Shallow basin in U. 3, filled with burned cobbles and fine charcoal; possibly a hearth. U. 5, Large deep pit (quarry?), filled by a Preclassic midden. U. 6, Pit in bedrock that was filled with a densely packed fine, ashy soil, with a few stones and many sherds. Shown here is the top of a smaller pit in the floor of the larger one, the fill of which was capped by stones. For sections A-A', B-B', C-C', and D-D', see Fig. 105-107.

FIGURE 104

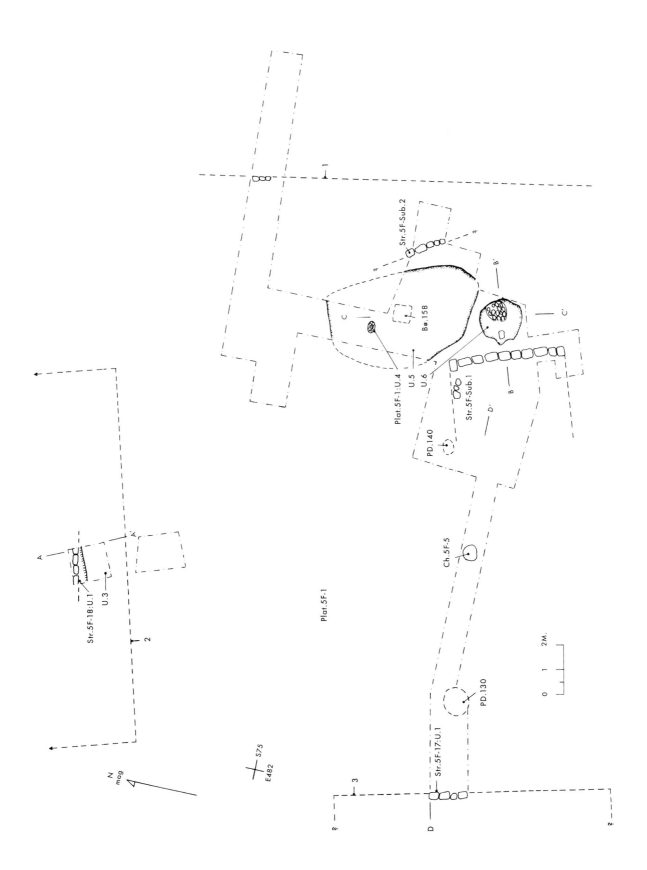

FIGURE 105

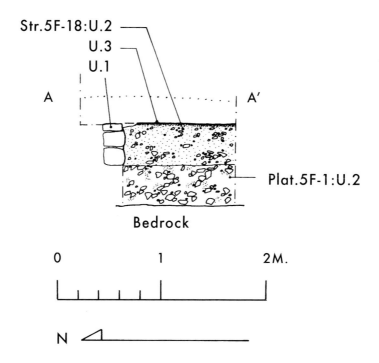

Str. 5F-18: Section A-A', as located in Fig. 104.
Pertinent to Str. 5F-18: U. 1, early wall of Str. 5F-18 (see Fig. 104). U. 2, Light brown earth fill for later version of Str. 5F-18. U. 3, floor for expanded Str. 5F-18 (see Fig. 104). *Pertinent to Plat. 5F-1*: U. 2, white fill that contains sherds identical to those beneath Plat. 5F-1:U. 1 (see Fig. 106, 107).

FIGURE 106

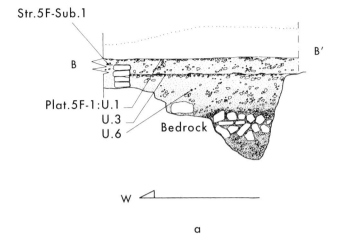

a

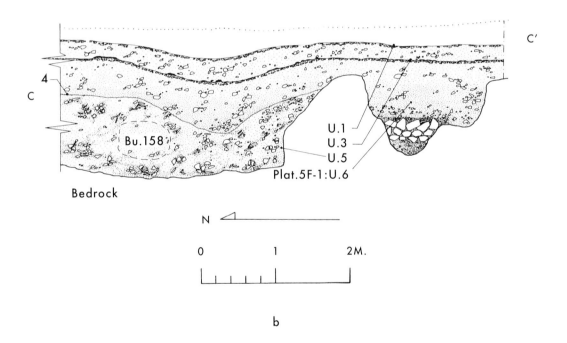

b

Str. 5F-Sub.1 and Plat. 5F-1: Sections B-B' (a) and C-C' (b), as located in Fig. 104.
Pertinent to Plat. 5F-1: 4, Top of the Middle Preclassic (Tzec) midden in U. 5. U. 1, Thin stratum of small stones thought to be the remains of a Late Classic floor. This covered the remains of both Str. 4F-Sub.1 and Sub.2. U. 3, Irregular occupation surface, consisting in part of bedrock (off-section). Where the surface of bedrock is low, as here, it consists of small stones that bear traces of plaster, above which roots grow horizontally. Unit 3 abuts Str. 5F-Sub.1, and Str. 5F-Sub.2 was built on it. The basin for U. 4 (Fig. 104) penetrates U. 3, 0.40 m W of the N end of section C-C'. U. 5, Large quarry(?) NE of Str. 5F-Sub.1 (see Fig. 104). U. 6, Small pit in bedrock E of Str. 5F-Sub.1 (see Fig. 104).

FIGURE 107

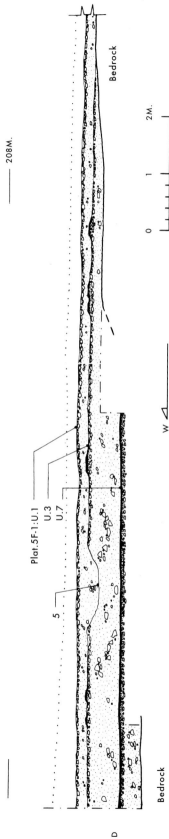

Figure 107

Plat. 5F-1: Section D-D', as located in Fig. 104. (This section is a reconstruction from descriptions and measurements in the excavator's field notes.)

Pertinent to Plat. 5F-1-5, Pit that penetrates U. 3, purposely dug or the result of a tree-fall. U. 1, Remains of Late Classic floor (see Fig. 106). U. 3, Remains of floor that abuts Str. 5F-Sub.1 (see Fig. 106). U. 7, Deep floor that overlies fill similar to that of Str. 5F-Sub.1. Given the contemporaneity of sherds from the fills, the placement of fill for both on bare bedrock, and the bedrock profile shown here, U. 7 probably feathered into bedrock, forming the occupation surface W of Str. 5F-Sub.1.

FIGURE 108

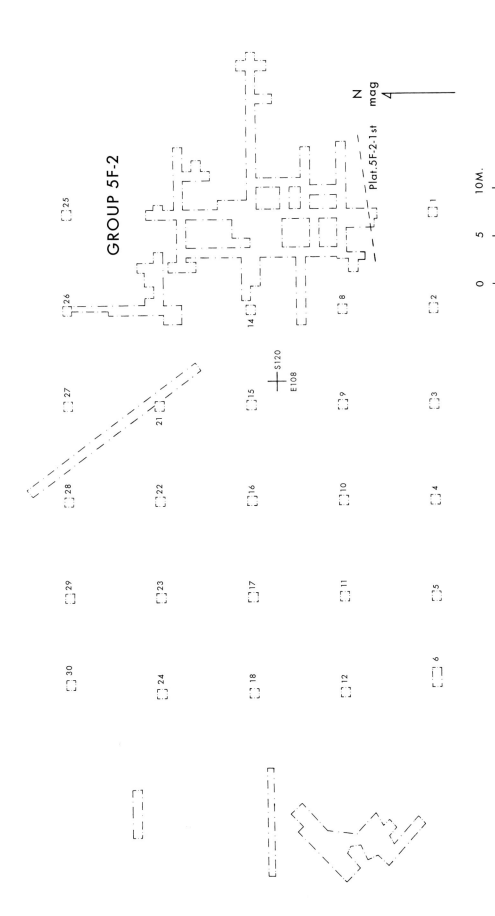

Location of Gp. 5F-2 and test pits.
Numbers 1–30 refer to the test pits (numbers 7, 13, 19, 20 are missing, on account of their inclusion within the excavated area). Of these test pits, only those E of a line passing through Test Pits 5, 12, 16, 21, and just W of 27 are relevant to the present report; the rest pertain to a consideration of Tikal hydraulics (TR. 23I). For plan of Gp. 5F-2, see Fig. 109.

Gp. 5F-2: Plan.

Pertinent to Str. 5F-42: 1, NE corner, 5F-42-2nd and 3rd. Depicted here is the lowermost course of wall masonry; the uppermost course is reduced to rubble, set back relative to the lower course. Note the curved portion of the wall W of the corner. The wall rests on a thin stratum of pebbles over sterile clay. *2*, NE corner of 5F-42-1st. This is marked by a line of rubble that abuts the NE corner of 5F-42-2nd (1), and which seems to turn an approximate right angle to run S, about where expected if it is part of the same wall as U. 6 (3, below). *3*, U. 6, a wall seen only in the trench (B-B') built directly on the E wall of Str. 5F-Sub.3. From the top of U. 6, a floor (U. 7) runs W to join U. 4. These stratigraphic associations, plus an alignment for U. 6 that suggests it met the presumed NE corner of 5F-42-1st (2), implying that U. 6 is the E wall for 5F-42-1st. U. 1, N-S wall, based on Plat. 5F-2:U. 1; to the W, it retains a fill of earth and stones. These, and the alignment of the wall relative to the NE corner of Str. 5F-42 (1), suggest that this is the E wall of Str. 5F-42-2nd. U. 2, N-S wall based on Plat. 5F-2:U. 1; it retains the same fill as that retained by U. 1, and so is interpreted as the W wall for Str. 5F-42-2nd. It probably also served Str. 5F-42-1st. U. 3, E-W wall, with the same stratigraphic relationships as U. 1 and 2; it is interpreted as the S wall for 5F-42-2nd. U. 5, small, rubble-filled platform, built on Plat. 5F-2:U. 1. It abuts the wall of Str. 5F-42-2nd, and was later buried by fill for 42-1st; it must have therefore been part of 42-2nd. *Pertinent to Str. 5F-43: 4*, Lines of rubble that mark the S, E, and W walls of 5F-43. They were built on U. 1, thought to be an earlier occupation surface that abuts Str. 5F-Sub.3 and which overlies Plat. 5F-2:U. 1. The walls contain a fill of earth, topped by small stones. The latter suggest the one-time presence of a floor slightly below the top of the structure walls. *Pertinent to Str. 5F-44: 19*, Structure walls, based on earth fill (U. 1) that runs to the base of the wall of Str. 5F-42-2nd, and covers the wall of 42-3rd (see Fig. 111). The structure is reconstructed from the known locations of three corners. *Pertinent to Str. 5F-45: 5–7*, SE, SW, and NW corners of 45-2nd. The walls for this structure rest on sterile clay and contain a fill of earth, stones, and trash. Platform 5F-2:U. 1 runs up the E wall of the structure. *9*, Wall, thought to represent part of 5F-45-1st. The N end of this wall presumably represents the NE corner of a structure somewhat larger than 45-2nd. The absence of a N wall is assumed to be the result of the subsequent excavation of a pit. A wall that runs W from the NW corner (7) of 45-2nd may also be related to 45-1st. *Pertinent to Str. 5F-46: 10*, Walls 46-2nd; the E and S walls were later partially covered by new construction (U. 2). The N wall is based in part on Plat. 5F-2:U. 1 and an extension of its fill to the S; the other walls are based on natural clay, and Plat. 5F-2:U. 1 runs up to the E wall. Contained by the walls is a fill of earth, stones and cultural materials. U. 1, Small platform, built on the NW corner of 46-2nd. Since no floor runs beneath its small stone fill, it is interpreted as part of 2nd. The E-W dimension of U. 1 is known from its N wall. U. 2, Small stone rubble, with traces of plaster that covers construction associated with 46-2nd (10). A SW corner is evident and the rubble seems to form regular lines; what it seems to represent is an enlargement of the original 5F-46, but with an inset in the NW corner. Unit 1 was incorporated in the fill of the enlarged structure (see also Fig. 110). *Pertinent to Str. 5F-47*: U. 2, Freestanding dwarf wall built on U. 1, a stratum of dark-colored earth. The wall is composed in part of well-cut masonry and in part of rubble plastered on its inner and outer faces. U. 3, Remnant of a plaster floor, laid on U. 1. Small fragments to the E indicate that the floor abutted U. 2. U. 4, Mass of rubble on U. 1, opposite the S end of U. 2; possibly relates to a badly destroyed S wall. U. 5, Round hole, apparently for a wooden post just S of U. 2; suggests that 5F-47 was composed in part of a building of perishable materials. *Pertinent to Str. 5F-Sub.3*: Portions of the E, W, and S walls. The N-S length of the structure is not known, but the E-W dimension implies that it was not large. Platform 5F-2:U. 1 abuts the walls, which rest mostly on natural clay. The walls contain a stone fill. Structure 5F-Sub.3 was eventually buried in the fill for Str. 5F-42-1st. *Pertinent to the Plat. 5F-2*: U. 1 plaster floor, which runs E from the top of U. 3, and overlies white marl retained by U. 3. This pavement is associated with Str. 5F-42-3rd, 5F-45-2nd, 5F-46-2nd, and Str. 5F-Sub.3. Between Str. 5F-45 and 5F-46, the floor ends at Plat. 5F-2:U. 7. U. 2, 3, Lower and upper courses of the W platform wall, based on natural clay; they retain white marl over which U. 1 was laid. To the W, Str. 5F-44:U. 1 abuts the wall. Unit 2 continues to the N as part of the E wall of Str. 5F-42-3rd. Unit 3, however, turns at right angle to run E, apparently where the S end of Str. 5F-42-3rd stood. Other corners turned by U. 3 suggest that the structure had a central outset on the S. Eventually, the E-W portion of U. 3 was covered by Str. 5F-42-2nd. U. 7, Wall that runs S from the SE corner of Str. 5F-45-2nd and then turns to abut the W wall of Str. 5F-46-2nd. On the N and E, Plat. 5F-2:U. 1 ends at this wall. U. 8, Line of rubble that runs in part beneath the S end of Str. 5F-46-1st. It is interpreted as a S wall for Plat. 5F-2 that postdates U. 7, but predates Str. 5F-46-1st. Also shown are Test Pits 8, 14, 25, 26 (see Fig. 108). Feature 1 (apparently a masonry wall, perhaps for a structure E of Str. 5F-42); and Feature 2 (possible wall, similar in appearance to Str. 5F-46:U. 2; could be part of a structure E of Str. 5F-42). For sections A-A', B-B', C-C', and D-D', see Fig. 110–112.

FIGURE 109

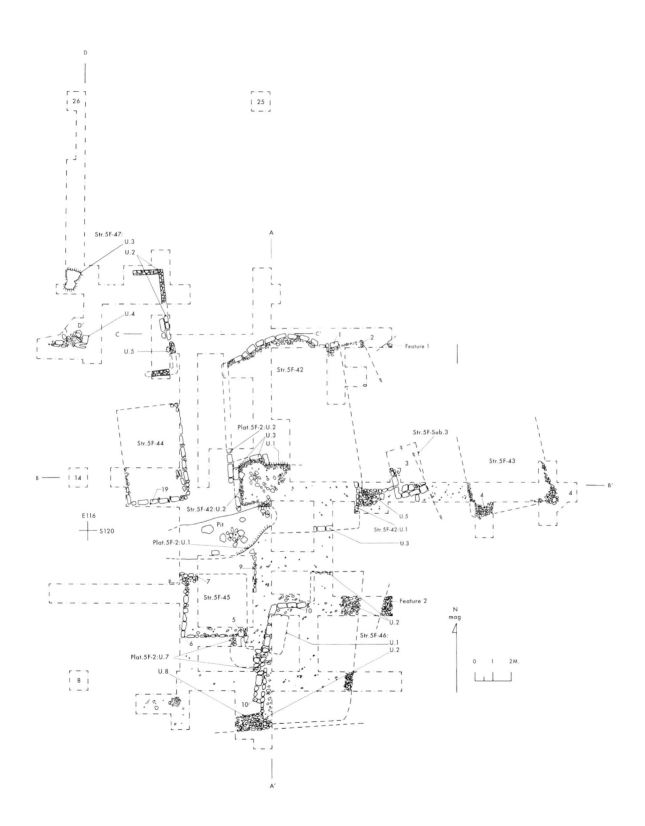

Gp. 5F-2: Section A-A', as located in Fig. 109.

Pertinent to Str. 5F-42: *11*, N wall, 5F-42-1st, 2nd, and 3rd (see also Fig. 109:1 and 2), based on a thin stratum of pebbles and mud that overlies sterile clay. Retained by the wall to the S is fill of marl and limestone (see *12*, below). *12*, Top of the fill for 42-3rd; irregularity of its surface is best explained as the result of partial demolition of the structure prior to construction of 42-2nd. *13*, Small stone fill for 42-2nd, which was placed on an early floor for Plat. 5F-2 (U. 1), and was covered by a floor, U. 4. This floor covers fill to the N (15) that in part covers this small stone fill; hence the latter represents the first known filling operation in the construction of 42-2nd. *15*, Brown earth fill for 42-2nd, representing the second known filling operation in the construction of this structure. It overlies the fill for 42-3rd and a small stone fill (13) for Str. 42-2nd. U. 3, S wall, 42-2nd (see also Fig. 109); it rests on the same surface of Plat. 5F-2 as the fill (13) for Str. 5F-42-2nd, and its top is at the same general elevation as U. 4. Note how part of the wall has been destroyed by a pit intruded through U. 4 and its fill. U. 4, Floor for 42-2nd, later disturbed by the digging of a pit. The floor may also have been incorporated into that of Str. 42-1st. *Pertinent to Str. 5F-46:* *10*, Walls for 46-2nd (see Fig. 109). *16*, S extent of 46-1st; here, the stony fill of the structure cannot be distinguished from the wall, probably because of severe damage from natural forces following abandonment. Note that the fill rests directly on that for 46-2nd, and abuts the walls of U. 1. U. 1, Small platform on 46-2nd (see Fig. 109). U. 2, wall for 46-1st (see Fig. 109). Note here the plaster on the exposed face, which turns over the top to meet the top of the old U. 1. *Pertinent to Str. 5F-47:* U. 1 (see Fig. 112). *Pertinent to Plat. 5F-2:* U. 1, Earliest platform floor, laid on a fill of compact, light-colored earth (see Fig. 109). Note that the floor itself runs slightly beneath the N wall of Str. 5F-46-2nd (10), and that its fill continues farther S beneath that structure. Note also the disturbance N of Str. 5F-46, where a pit was intruded into Str. 5F-42-2nd, which was built in part on U. 1. Suspected is that the S wall of Str. 5F-42-3rd stood about where U. 1 ends on the N, for the surviving fill for this structure (12) abuts the fill of U. 1 here. U. 4, Floor laid on an earth fill over U. 1 that abuts the N wall of Str. 5F-46-2nd (10) and the top of the S wall of Str. 5F-42-2nd (Str. 5F-42:U. 3). U. 5, Floor, laid directly over U. 4, with the same stratigraphic relationships as U. 4. U. 6, A grading floor, laid over the S portion of U. 5 to turn up to Str. 5F-46-1st (Str. 5F-46:U. 2). U. 8, Rubble wall marking the southern limit of some version of Plat. 5F-2 (see Fig. 109). Also shown *17*, Silt-clay that overlies sterile clay. *18*, Pebbles and sand that overlie sterile clay near Str. 5F-42 and the silt-clay (17) to the N.

FIGURE 110

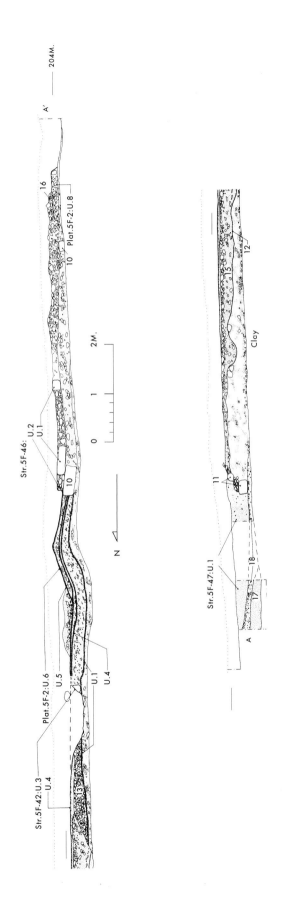

Gp. 5F-2: Section B-B', as located in Fig. 109.

Pertinent to Str. 5F-42: 13, Fill of 42-2nd (see Fig. 110). U. 1, E wall of 42-2nd (see Fig. 109). Here, some of the fill W of the wall has spilled over slightly to the E. U. 2, W wall of 42-1st and 2nd (see Fig. 109). U. 4, Floor of 42-2nd (see Fig. 110). U. 6, Wall, now badly ruined, for 42-1st (see Fig. 109:3). U. 7, Floor of 42-1st; may have joined U. 4, which continued in use with U. 7. *Pertinent to Str. 5F-43: 4*, E and W walls (see Fig. 109). U. 1, Stratum of packed earth that overlies Plat. 5F-2:U. 1 and abuts Str. 5F-Sub.3; Str. 5F-43 was built on this stratum, which seems to have served as an unpaved occupation surface outside the structure. *Pertinent to Str. 5F-44: 19*, E and W walls of the structure (see Fig. 109); they contain a fill of stony earth and cultural debris. *20*, Stratum of silt and stone, which appears to have served as the structure floor. U. 1, Fill of compact, light gray earth, part of which may have been purposely placed just prior to construction of 5F-44. It abuts the W wall of Plat. 5F-2 just at the base of the W wall for Str. 5F-42-2nd. It is continuous with Str. 5F-47:U. 1 (see Fig. 110). *Pertinent to Str. 5F-Sub.3*: Walls and fill. The structure was later buried in the fill of Str. 5F-42-1st. *Pertinent to Plat. 5F-2*: U. 1 (see Fig. 109); U. 2 (see Fig. 109); U. 3 (see Fig. 109). Also shown: *21*, Brown, claylike earth and debris. This probably derives in part from trash discarded by the occupants of Str. 5F-42 and 44, augmented by fill that has eroded since abandonment. *22*, Brown earth and debris, probably largely from structure collapse.

FIGURE 111

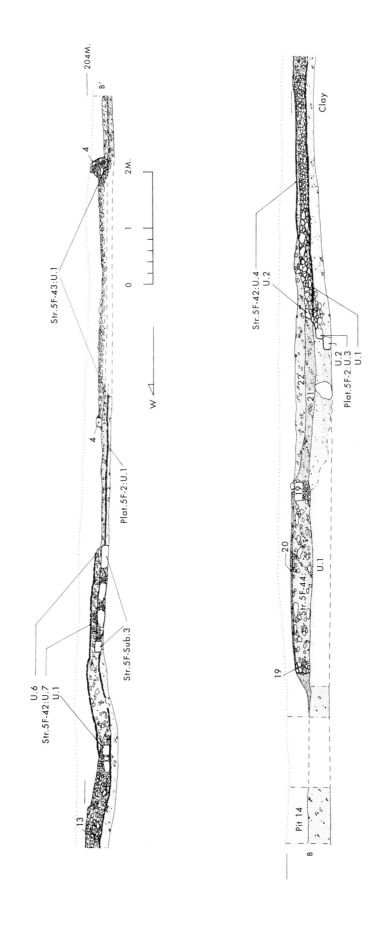

FIGURE 112

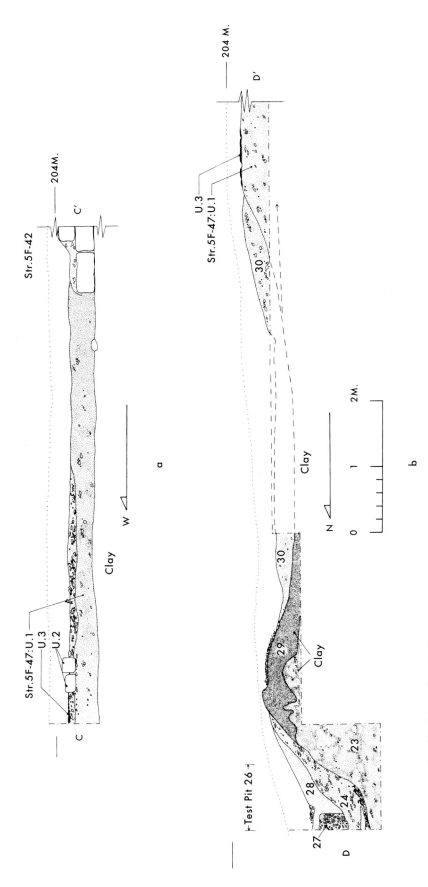

Str. 5F-47: Section C-C' (*a*) and D-D' (*b*), as located in Fig. 109.

Pertinent to Str. 5F-47: U. 1, Dark tan earth, continuous with Str. 5F-44:U. 1 (Fig. 111). The floor and walls of 5F-47 were built upon it, and it in turn overlies the stratum on which Str. 5F-42-3rd was built. It abuts the walls of Str. 5F-42. East of U. 2, a rich deposit of sherds overlies U. 1. The packed, relatively level surface of U. 1 suggests that it served as an outside occupation surface; it is thought to have built up over time while Str. 5F-42 was in use. U. 2, E structure wall (see Fig. 109). The deposit against the E face of the wall, over U. 1, is a small midden. U. 3, Structure floor (see Fig. 109). *Pertinent to Test Pit 26: 23,* Mottled gray clay, with cultural material in the top 0.10 m only. *24,* Mixture of clay, small stones and cultural material; a bed of large, soft sherds lay in the lowest part of the stratum. *27,* Sand and gravel. *28,* Light-colored deposit of sand, silt, and cultural material. *29,* Sterile black earth. *30,* Sandy, gray-brown earth.

FIGURE 113

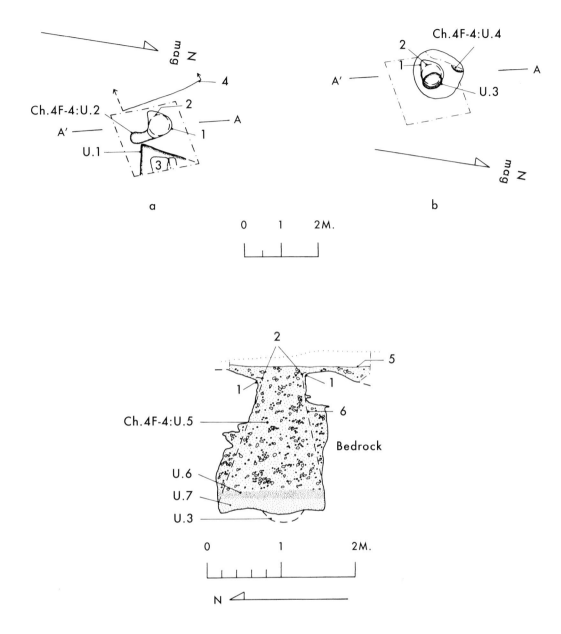

Ch. 4F-4: Plans (*a, b*) and Section A-A' (*c*).

Pertinent to Ch. 4F-4: 1, Orifice as it presently exists following extensive erosion. Its location is 4F:S60 E425 on the site map (TR. 11). *2,* Reconstruction of the orifice as originally constructed. *3,* Possible burial in quarried area; two irregularly cut stones appear to cover a deeper cut in bedrock. *4,* Modern outbuilding. *5,* Hard-packed stratum of gray colored earth over bedrock. *6,* Chultun wall, as originally constructed, seen off-section. U. 1, Quarried area E of chultun. U. 2, Trough cut in bedrock, ending on the S in a round hole. U. 3, Round hole in the floor of the chultun. U. 5, Light brown pebbly soil, with many sherds, which fills the chultun; its quantity and consistency are suggestive of purposeful fill. U. 6, Stratum of dark brown soil, about 0.10 m thick, over U. 7; its composition suggests that this was once humus. U. 7, Stratum of fine, gray silt about 0.15 m thick over the chultun floor; composition suggest a deposit that accumulated gradually while the chultun was in use.

Ch. 4F-2: Plan (*a*), Wall Elevation (*b*), and Section A-A' (*c*).

Pertinent to Ch. 4F-2: 1, Orifice; note stepped lip on the NW side (Fig. 114c). Its location is 4F:S283 E215. *2*, Stone cover, as found (Fig. 114c), and removed for excavation (Fig. 114a). *3*, Reconstructed original wall and ceiling of Chm. 2, based on the break from floor to wall, the quantity of debris from collapse, and analogy with other chultuns. *4*, Present maximum extent of Chm. 2 following extensive collapse of ceiling and walls. *5*, Base of area that has collapsed. *6*, Shallow hole in the floor of the chultun; 0.04 m deep on the N, 0.11 m deep on the S. U. 1, Cuplike hole in bedrock; note that, towards its base, the sides of the hole turn inward, suggesting the reconstruction shown here. Apparently, U. 1 was a posthole that opened into the chultun only after the ceiling collapse in Chm. 2. U. 2, Masonry wall, which forms a sill between Chm. 1 and 2 (for elevation, see Fig. 114b). Built on U. 3, U. 4 abuts its face. Since both U. 3 and 4 seem to represent occupation debris, U. 2 is interpreted as the distinguishing feature between Ch. 4F-2-A and B. A dip in the central portion could be the result of the sill being worn down through use. U. 3, Stratum of packed, gray earth, thought to be material that accumulated while the chultun was in use, before construction of U. 2. U. 4, Stratum of brownish-gray material that abuts U. 2; it, too, is thought to be material that accumulated while the chultun was in use, in this case after construction of U. 2. U. 4-8, Alternating strata of gray and brown earth, thickest against U. 2. The dark layers match the interstices of the U. 2 masonry. These strata probably represent post-abandonment debris. U. 9, Whitish-gray material that extends over the floor of Chm. 1, and which slopes downward from SE to NW. Rich in artifactual material, it appears to be midden debris that was dumped into Chm. 1, but which settled with time into Chm. 2. U. 10, Lens of dark earth, rich in artifacts; it seems to be some of the same midden material as U. 9, mixed with water-borne sediments. U. 11, Gray material, deepest beneath U. 1 and nonexistent in Chm. 1. It is thought to derive from collapse of the ceiling, which was caused by pressure from a post that stood in U. 1. U. 12, Dark brown soil, most of which appears to have washed into the chultun through U. 1.

FIGURE 114

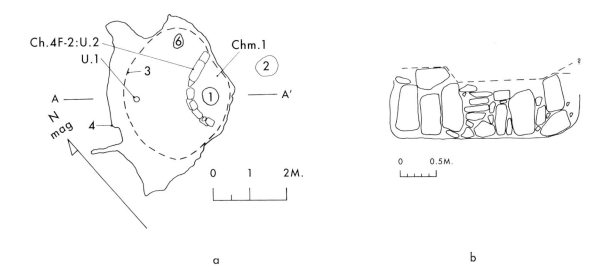

a

b

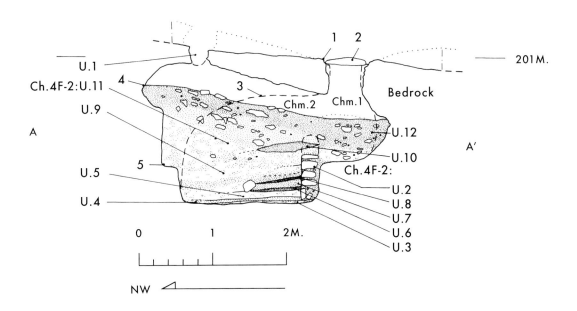

c

FIGURE 115

GROUP 6C-1

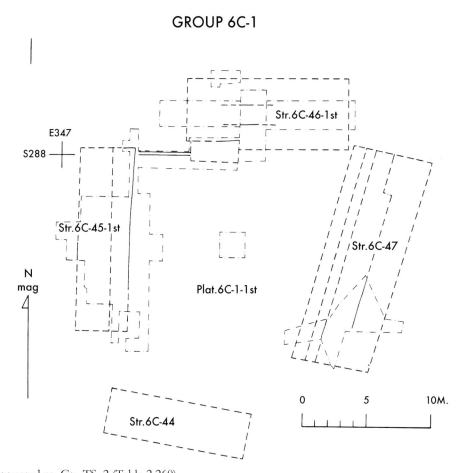

Gp. 6C-1 as it appeared ca. Gp. TS. 2 (Table 2.260).
Structure 6C-44 remains unexcavated; plotted here is its ruin mound. For detailed plans of the other structures, see Fig. 116–118, 120, 122.

Figure 116 (facing page)
Str. 6C-45-8th-A, B, and C (*a*) and Str. 6C-45-6th and 7th (*b*): Plans.
Pertinent to Str. 6C-45: 1, Walls of Str. 8th, built on bedrock, containing an earlier midden. The reconstructed parts of the wall are based on projections from the excavated portions. The N and E walls show that the structure had two square and two rounded corners; part of this wall continued to serve 45-7th and 6th. *2*, N wall of 7th and 6th, which abuts the N end of 8th. Assumed is that a comparable S wall was added to produce a generally apsidal structure. The new N wall is a single course of masonry based on a midden that had accumulated against the N end of 8th. U. 1, Apparent posthole in the floor of 8th. U. 4, Wall apparently for an interior platform. Built on the floor of 8th, Fl. 1 of 7th turns up to its base. U. 5–10, apparent postholes through the floor of 7th. They form no recognizable pattern, and functions of the indicated posts are unknown. U. 11, Wall, interpreted as the N face for a raised S level of 6th, built on the floor of 7th, against the fill of U. 4. There is no apparent break in U. 11, as would be expected in a freestanding wall, and its top is some 0.15 m above that of U. 4. Not shown here is U. 12, a grading floor laid directly on Fl. 1 of 7th that turns up to the N face of U. 11. Fl. 1 of 8th is laid over an earlier midden that served as fill for the structure. It apparently ran over the tops of structure walls to their outer faces. Note that there are no postholes in this floor near its eastern and northern extent; either the structure did not consist in part of a building of perishable materials, or posts for such a building rested on the floor or just outside the platform walls. The floor was renovated on at least two occasions (U. 2 and 3, Table 2.256). Later, a burial was intruded through it. Fl. 1 of 7th is laid directly on the pavements for 8th-A. Thicker to the S than the N, part of the older floor may have continued in use in the N part of the structure. The floor turns up to U. 4, and U. 11 rests upon it; Bu. 146 is a later intrusion. For section A-A', see Fig. 119. Coordinates are to datum shown in Fig. 115.

FIGURE 116

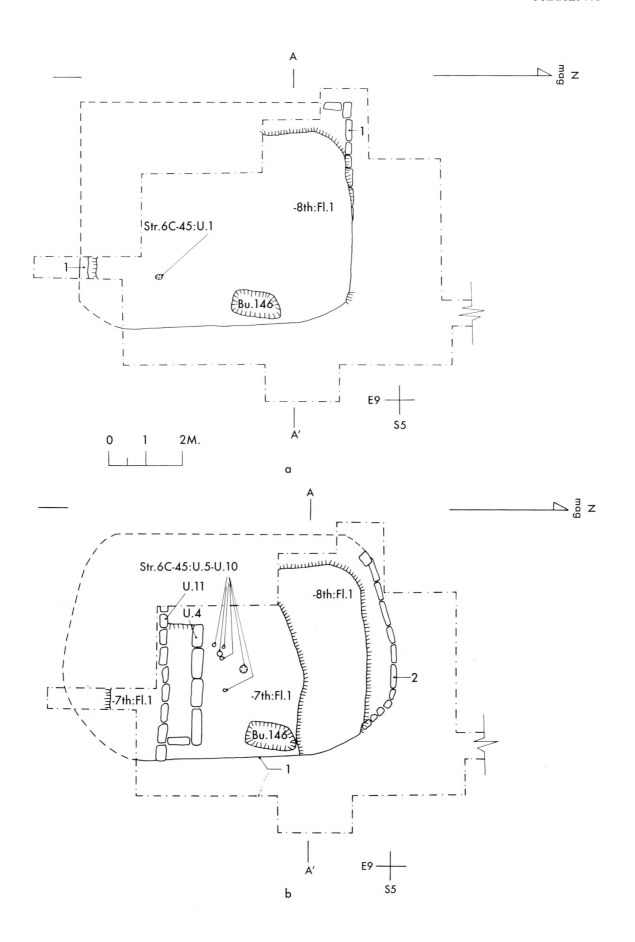

a

b

Str. 6C-45-5th (*a*) and Str. 6C-45-4th-A, B, and C (*b*): Plans.

Pertinent to Str. 6C-45-5th: Structure walls and Bu. 146 beneath its fill. Both in size and shape, the structure marks a radical departure from preceding ones at this locus. For photo of W wall masonry, see Fig. 179d. Pertinent to Str. 6C-45-4th: *3*, Walls for 4th. These rest on fill placed round the preceding 45-5th, as well as on a midden W of that structure. Much of that midden was retained as fill for the new structure; added to it was earth and debris. U. 11, Originally the wall for an upper level of 6th; this was renewed with the addition of an upper course of masonry, to which Fl. 2 of 4th turns up on the N. The same floor runs S from the top of the renewed U. 11 as an upper level platform. U. 15, Apparent posthole in Fl. 2 of 4th. U. 16, Grading floor laid on Fl. 2 over the structure N of U. 11. This floor is the only architecture referable to 4th-B. U. 17, Hole, apparently dug through the floors of 4th-A and C, S of U. 11. It was filled with burned stones and sherds. Fl. 1 for 4th-A is laid directly on Fl. 2 and U. 16. Fl. 2 for 4th-C is laid directly on the earth fill for the structure. It may have abutted the E wall so that the latter formed a low sill. Fl. 2 turns up to the face of the upper course of U. 11 on the N, then runs S from the top of U. 11. *Pertinent to Plat. 6C-1*: U. 1, Pavement that abuts the front wall (3) of Str. 6C-45-4th-C. It lies directly on the same fill on which the wall is based. Unit 1 is assigned to Plat. 6C-1-4th. U. 2, Plaster floor, laid over the older U. 1. This pavement is thought to be contemporary with Str. 6C-45-4th-A. For section A-A', see Fig. 119; for photo of N end, see Fig. 180a. Coordinates are to datum shown in Fig. 115.

FIGURE 117

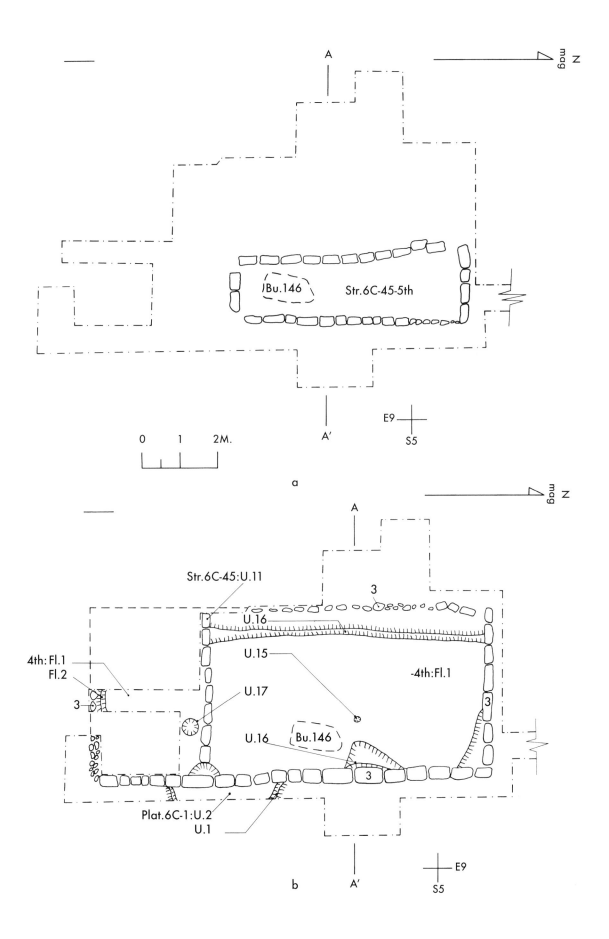

Str. 6C-45-3rd (*a*) and Str. 6C-45-2nd and 1st (*b*): Plans.

Pertinent to Str. 6C-45: 3, Walls, built for 4th-C and reused in 3rd. *4–6*, Portions of the E, W, and S walls for 2nd and 1st, which are the basis for the reconstruction shown here. The E wall (4) rests in part on the floor of 3rd, while the W wall (5) rests on a few centimeters of fill above the floor for 8th. Fill within the walls includes the earlier architecture and some trash, to which was added earth and additional cultural debris. *7*, Rubble remains of a masonry wall that evidently ran the length of 1st. This, and the lack of any break, indicate that it probably is the E wall of an upper platform level. Based on the floor of 2nd, it is the only surviving architecture that relates exclusively to 1st. Its fill probably was the rubble that can be seen on section (Fig. 119) to run down the W face of the ruin mound. U. 18, E wall for an upper platform level of 3rd. The floor of 3rd is in union with the base of U. 18 to the E, but continues W from the top of the wall. It is not known if U. 18 ran the length of the structure; as shown, it ends at a pile of rubble. The rubble could be from later ripping out of U. 18 S of this point, or from ripping out of a wall that ran from the S end of U. 18 to the rear wall of the structure. U. 19, 20, Apparent postholes in the floor of 3rd. They probably relate to 2nd and 1st, the front wall of which was just E of these holes. In this case, the posts for a building of pole-and-thatch would have been set to a depth of 0.36 m below the structure floor. Fl. 1 of 3rd, Pavement laid on earth fill above Fl. 1 of 4th. It runs from the top of the E structure wall to the base of U. 18, with which it is in union, and continues W from the top of U. 18. *Pertinent to Plat. 6C-1*: U. 3, Plaster floor, laid over the older U. 2 (see Fig. 119). It is thought to be contemporary with Str. 6C-45-3rd, and constitutes part of Plat. 6C-1-2nd. U. 9, Plaster floor, laid directly on earth fill that covers the older U. 3. The floor covers the old E wall of Str. 6C-45-3rd and is in union with the base of the front wall (4) of 45-2nd, as well as U. 10 (see below). This floor, with U. 10, defines Plat. 6C-1-1st. U. 10, Wall of masonry identical to that used for 45-2nd and 6C-46-2nd. Unit 9 is in union with the base of this wall, which must have abutted 45-2nd and U. 1 of Str. 6C-46 (see Fig. 120). For section A-A', see Fig. 119. Coordinates are to datum shown in Fig. 115.

FIGURE 118

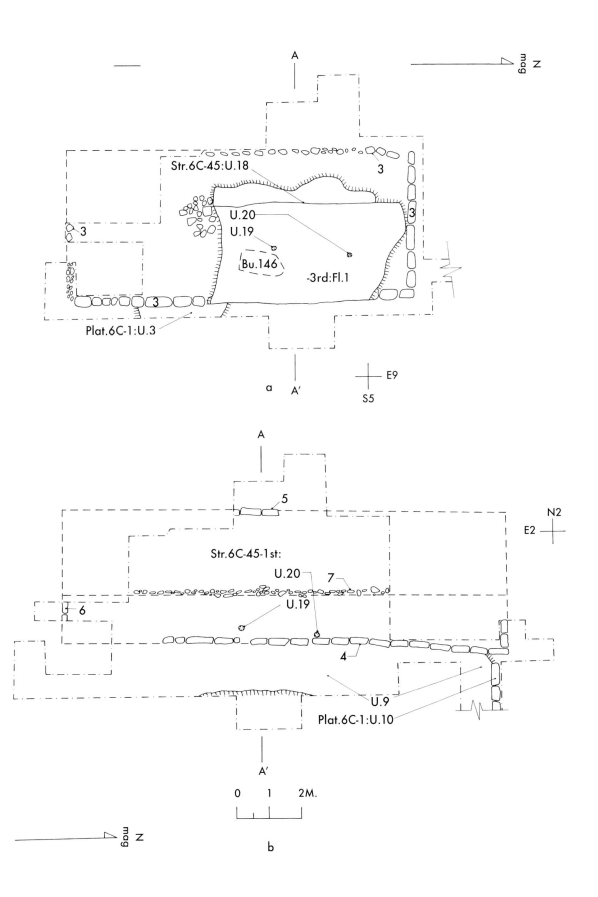

Str.6C-45:U.18

3

3

3

U.20

U.19

Bu.146

-3rd:Fl.1

Plat.6C-1:U.3

A

A'

mag N

E9

S5

a

A

5

Str.6C-45-1st:

U.20

7

6

U.19

4

U.9

Plat.6C-1:U.10

N2

E2

A'

0   1   2M.

mag N

b

Str. 6C-45: Section A-A', as located in Fig. 116, 117, and 118.

Pertinent to Str. 6C-45: 1, E wall of 45-8th and 7th (see Fig. 116). *3*, E and W walls for 2nd and 1st (see Fig. 118). *4, 5*, E and W walls for 4th and 3rd (see Fig. 117, 118). *4, 5*, E and W walls for 2nd and 1st (see Fig. 118). The height of the W wall is reconstructed from the apparent height of the wall (7) for the upper platform level of 1st (see Fig. 118). *8*, Midden, full of the late Manik ceramics, incorporated as fill in 8th-C. *9*, E and W walls of 5th. Assumed is that pavement (broken line) was laid over the earth fill of this structure. *10*, Extensive Early Classic midden, consisting of debris apparently thrown off the back of 5th. It was later incorporated in the fill of 4th-C. *11*, Dark earth fill for 45-2nd. *12*, Rubble fill for the upper platform level of 1st. *13*, Hypothetical pavement for the upper platform level of 1st, based on the known height of the E wall (7). The steep slope down to the W accounts for the lack of surviving traces of such a floor. U. 13, Thin, packed stratum of marl, apparently an occupation surface W of 5th. Over this was dumped trash (10) from 5th. U. 16, Grading floor of 4th-B (see Fig. 117). U. 18, E wall, upper platform level of 3rd. Fl. 1 of 8th (see Fig. 116). Fl. 1 of 4th (see Fig. 117). Fl. 1 of 3rd (Fig. 118). Fl. 1 of 2nd appears to have abutted the front wall of the structure, with this forming a low sill. The upper platform level of 45-1st was built on this floor, which may have continued in use to the E. *Pertinent to Plat. 6C-1: 14*, Hypothetical plaza floor E of Str. 6C-45-4th. Presently, there is no apparent distinction in the fill above and below this elevation. U. 1, Floor for Plat. 6C-1-4th, off-section (see Fig. 117). U. 2, Floor for Plat. 6C-1-3rd, off-section (see Fig. 118). U. 3, Floor for Plat. 6C-1-2nd, off-section (see Fig. 117). U. 9, Floor for Plat. 6C-1-1st (see Fig. 118).

FIGURE 119

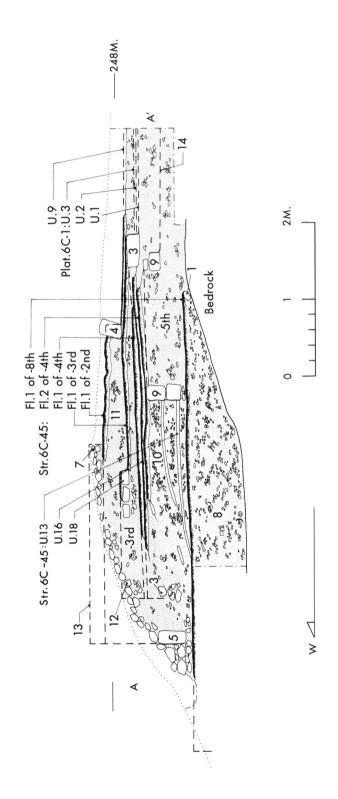

Str. 6C-46-1st and 2nd (*a*) and Str. 6C-46-3rd (*b*): Plans.

Pertinent to Str. 6C-46-1st and 2nd: 1, N (rear) wall for 1st, built on earth fill 0.90 m N of the comparable wall for 2nd, retaining an earth fill. Its length is reconstructed on the basis of the known length of 46-2nd, and mound configuration. *2*, Rubble remains of the S (front) wall for 1st and 2nd. The wall rests on fill retained by the N (rear) wall of 2nd, which continues S beneath the level of the plaza floor. The wall abuts U. 1 to the W, but presumably ran to the E end of the structure. *3*, S (front) wall for an upper platform of 2nd, which became a middle platform level of 1st. *4*, S (front) wall for an upper platform level of 1st. It rests directly on the floor for 2nd. U. 1, An enigmatic feature that appears to have been a small platform, around which the lower platform level of 46-2nd was built. Plat. 6C-1:U. 10 seems to abut it on the W. Str. 6C-46-2nd:Fl. 1, Remnant of pavement for 46-2nd, portions of which may have continued in use with 1st. The S portion of the floor was laid on a light-colored fill retained by the front structure wall (2), at about the same elevation as the top of that wall. It is in union with the base of the wall (3) for the second platform level. The N portion of the floor was laid on the fill retained by the N wall of 2nd, and runs S from the top of that wall at the same elevation as the front wall (3) for this platform. *Pertinent to Str. 6C-46-3rd*: E end wall. Based on compact gray earth, it retains a fill of gray earth with a high content of sherds and artifacts on the W. Plat. 6C-1:U. 7 turns up to the wall on the E. Nothing more is known of 46-3rd. *Pertinent to Plat. 6C-1*: U. 7, Plaza floor that turns up to Str. 6C-46-3rd and terminates on the N at the top of U. 8. It is thought to be part of the same floor as U. 3 (see Fig. 118), a part of Plat. 6C-1-2nd. U. 8, E-W wall that apparently marks the N edge of Plat. 6C-1-2nd. Unit 7 ends at the top of this wall on the S. U. 9, Floor for Plat. 6C-1-1st (see Fig. 118b). U. 10, N wall, Plat. 6C-1-1st (see Fig. 118b). For section A-A', see Fig. 121. Coordinates are to datum shown in Fig. 115.

FIGURE 120

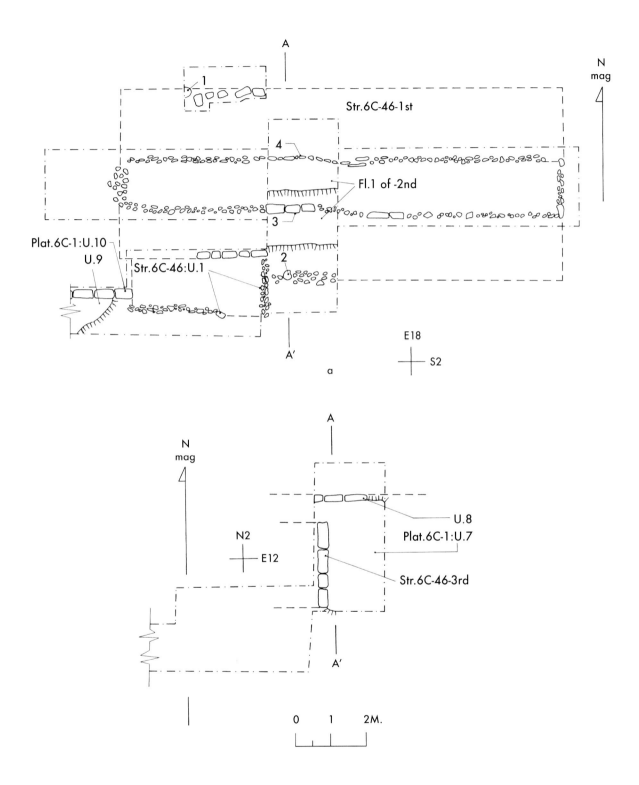

FIGURE 121

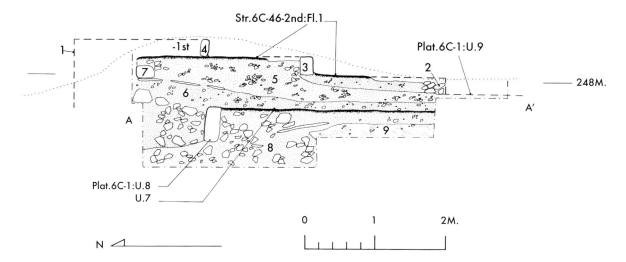

Str. 6C-46: Section A-A'.

Pertinent to Str. 6C-46: 1, Reconstruction of the rear wall of 1st. Its position is based on off-section remains (Fig. 120a:1); height is reconstructed on the basis of the height of the front wall (4) for the upper platform level. *2*, Front wall of 2nd and 1st (see Fig. 120a:2). *3*, Front wall, second platform level of 2nd and 1st (see Fig. 120a:3). Its relation to the fill retained by the front wall (2) indicates that both walls were constructed at about the same time (CS. 2 of 46-2nd). *4*, Front wall, upper platform level of 1st (see Fig. 120a:4). Assumed is that a plaster floor ran N from the top of this wall. Absence of traces of such a floor is understandable in view of the marked slope down to the N. *5*, Gray earth fill of 2nd: CS. 3. Its high sherd and artifact content suggests reuse of trash associated with 3rd. This fill continues S beneath the front wall of 2nd, suggesting that the plaza surface was raised at the same time the structure was built. *6*, Dark gray fill placed as CS. 4 for 2nd. It provided a level surface on which to build. *7*, N (rear) wall of 2nd, built as part of CS. 3. Fl. 1 of 2nd (see Fig. 120). *Pertinent to Plat. 6C-1: 8*, Earth and rubble fill for 2nd. *9*, Sterile, light-colored earth. U. 7, Floor for 2nd (see Fig. 120). U. 8, N retaining wall of 2nd (see Fig. 120).

Figure 122 (facing page)
Str. 6C-47: Plan.

Pertinent to Str. 6C-47: 1, Riser stones for lowest step. The masonry, similar to that used in Str. 6C-45-2nd and 46-2nd, rests on an earth fill a few centimeters W of a sharp rise in bedrock. The precise length of this riser is unknown, but its presence, so close to the S end of the ruin mound, suggests that it ran the length of the structure, as shown here. *2*, Second stair riser, formed in part by quarried bedrock. As with the basal riser, this is assumed to have run the length of the structure. *3*, Third stair riser, built of masonry similar to that used for the basal one. It is based on earth fill above the bedrock, and must have run the length of the structure since it formed the front of a lower platform level for the structure itself. *4*, Masonry wall for what probably was an upper platform level. To the W, a floor (U. 1) meets its base; to the E the wall retains an earth fill. The S end of the wall was identified in the excavations; the rest is reconstructed on the basis of mound configuration, and the assumption that the structure was symmetrical. U. 1, Floor remnant for a lower platform level, laid on the fill retained by the uppermost riser (3). It turns up to the base of the W wall (4) for the upper platform level. U. 2, Wall, very much lower than the rear structure wall, which runs E from that wall. Its purpose is unknown; perhaps this wall was part of a low platform at the rear of the structure (analogous to such a feature on Str. 2G-59-1st and 2nd; Fig. 21, 22), and it appears to have been built at the same time as the rear of the structure. For section A-A', see Fig. 123. Coordinates are to datum shown in Fig. 115.

FIGURE 122

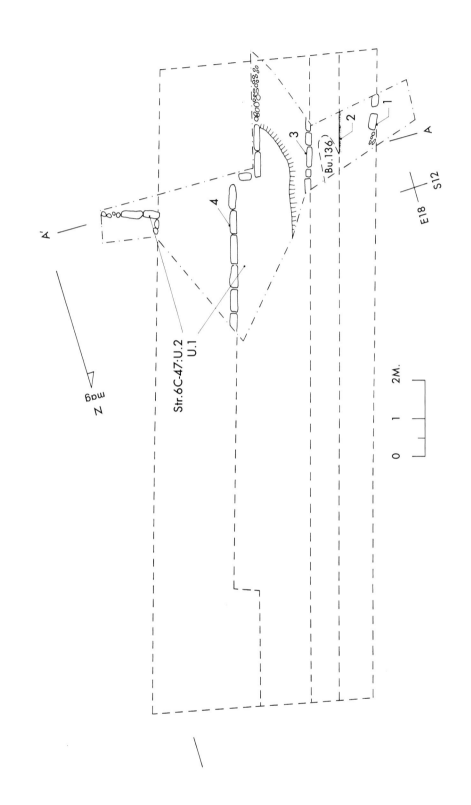

FIGURE 123

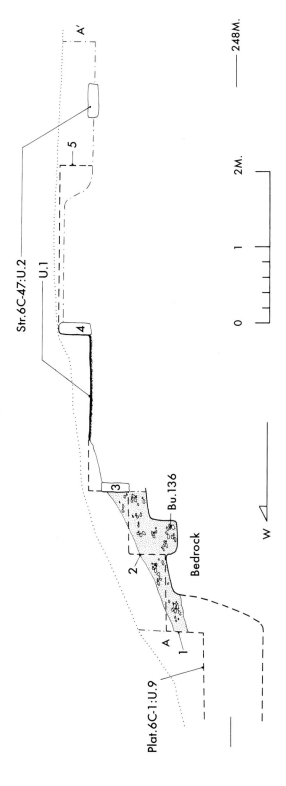

Str. 6C-47: Section A-A', as located in Fig. 122.

Pertinent to Str. 6C-47: 1, Lowest stair riser (see Fig. 122:1); its height is reconstructed on the basis of the known height of the uppermost riser (3). A plaster tread is assumed E of the riser, as the structure itself had a plaster floor. *2*, Second stair riser (see Fig. 122:2). Its height is reconstructed on the basis of the position of the base of the uppermost riser (3) and the surface of bedrock. As with the lowest riser (1), a plaster tread is assumed E of this riser. *3*, Uppermost stair riser (see Fig. 122:3). *4*, Front wall, upper platform level. Since there was a plaster floor W of this wall, a similar floor is assumed to have run E from its top as reconstructed here. *5*, Rear structure wall, from off-section remains. U. 1, Floor, lower platform level (see Fig. 122). It is assumed to have run to the top of a now-destroyed upper portion of the uppermost stair riser (3). U. 2, Low wall E of the structure (see Fig. 122). *Pertinent to Plat. 6C-1:* U. 9, Reconstructed surface of Plat. 6C-1-1st, no trace of which was found here. The reconstruction is based on the supposed height of the lowest stair riser (1) for Str. 6C-47, which is within 0.14 m of the elevation of U. 9, near Str. 6C-45, across the plaza. Apparently, the lowest riser masonry (1) was abutted by this plaza floor ca. 0.18 m above the base of the masonry. Hence, the structure could well predate Plat. 6C-1-1st.

FIGURE 124

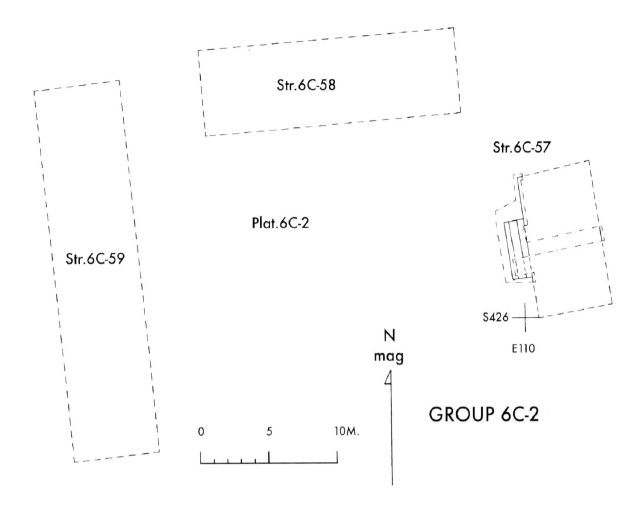

Str.6C-58

Str.6C-57

Plat.6C-2

Str.6C-59

S426

E110

N
mag

GROUP 6C-2

0   5   10M.

Gp. 6C-2 as it appeared when Str. 6C-57 was in use. Structures 6C-58 and 59 have not been excavated; their outlines are reconstructed from mound configurations.

FIGURE 125

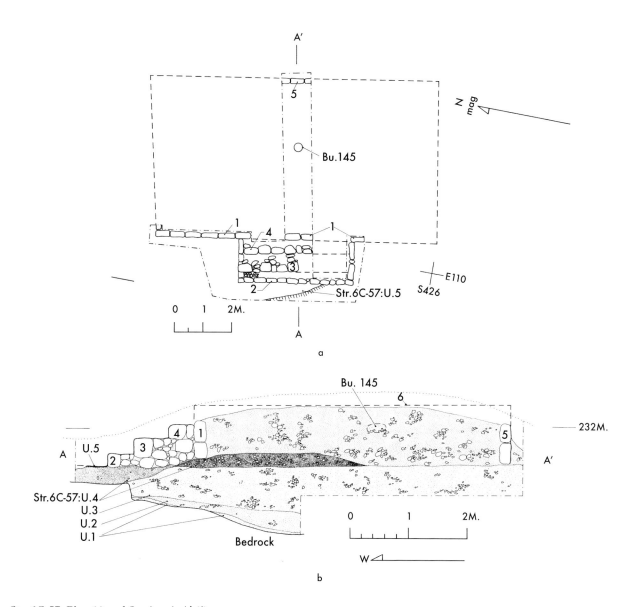

Str. 6C-57: Plan (*a*) and Section A-A' (*b*).

Pertinent to Str. 6C-57: 1, Portions of the front wall. The SW corner is assumed to be the same distance S of the front stairway as the NW corner is to the N of it, an interpretation consistent with mound configuration. The wall was built as CS. 3. *2, 3, 4*, Risers for the front stairway. These, with the stone stair fill, are based on the same stratum as the front wall (1) and abut that wall. Hence, they represent a later construction stage (CS. 2) than the wall itself. *5*, Rear wall. With the front wall (1), it contains a fill of stony brown earth. Reconstructed length of the wall is based on that of the front wall. Its construction was part of Stage 3. *6*, Reconstructed pavement. Though no traces for such a floor remain at present, most such structures had them. The elevation of this one is reconstructed on the basis of the known stair-riser height and surviving height of the structure fill. U. 1, 2, Sterile strata that overlie bedrock. U. 3, Fill placed as CS. 4, as part of the preparation of a surface on which to build. It consists of gray soil. U. 4, Packed gray-black earth, part of the fill of CS. 4. U. 5, Plaza floor, laid directly on fill (U. 4) placed as CS. 4, in union with the base of the lowest stair riser (2).

FIGURE 126

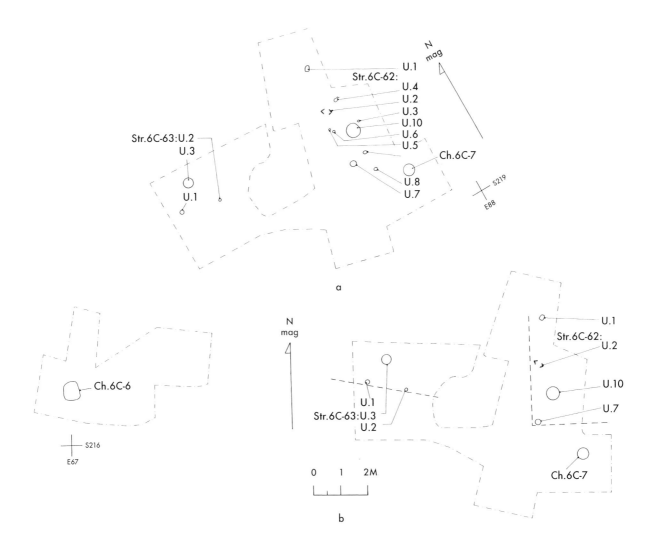

Str. 6C-62 and 6C-63: Plans. Postholes alone (*a*) and probable structure outlines (*b*).

Pertinent to Str. 6C-62: U. 1, 2, Square holes in bedrock, apparently postholes. Their comparable size and alignment suggest that they mark a structure wall, thought to be its W wall. U. 3–6, Round holes in bedrock, apparently postholes. U. 4, 5, and 6, with U. 7 and 8, may mark a rounded end wall for an architectural development different from the one represented by U. 1 and 2. Alternatively, some or all of these, with U. 3, may relate to minor architectural details of the structure represented by U. 1 and 2. U. 7, Round hole in bedrock, probably a posthole, in line with U. 1 and 2. Its alignment with U. 1 and 2, its comparable size (but not shape), its spacing from U. 2, and lack of further holes to the S and W suggest that it served as the SW corner post for Str. 6C-62. The possibility exists that it served two architectural developments. U. 8, 9, Round holes, probably postholes. Unit 8, with U. 4–6, and 7, may have been part of the wall noted above. Unit 9 probably relates to a minor architectural detail. U. 10, Basin cut in bedrock, also shown on the Perdido sheet of the Tikal site map (TR. 11). *Pertinent to Str. 6C-63*: U. 1, 2, Round holes in bedrock, probably holes for posts of a S structure wall. U. 3, Basin cut in bedrock, similar to Str. 6C-62:U. 10. Since the latter is positioned inside a presumed structure wall, U. 3 is interpreted as inside the wall represented by U. 1 and 2.

Ch. 6C-6, as located in Fig. 126b: Plans (*a, b*) and Section A-A'(*c*).

Pertinent to Ch. 6C-6: 1, Stone cover in place. *2*, Fine gray silt stratum. *3*, Limestone chunks and light-colored soil. *4*, Brown topsoil. *5*, Purposely placed fill of Chm. 4. U. 1, Masonry entrance block that prevented the fill of Chm. 4 from spilling out into the rest of the chultun. U. 2, Small hole in surface of bedrock, probably a posthole. U. 3, 4, Linear cuts in surface of bedrock. U. 5, 6, Basin-like cuts in surface of bedrock, 0.20 and 0.40 m deep respectively.

FIGURE 127

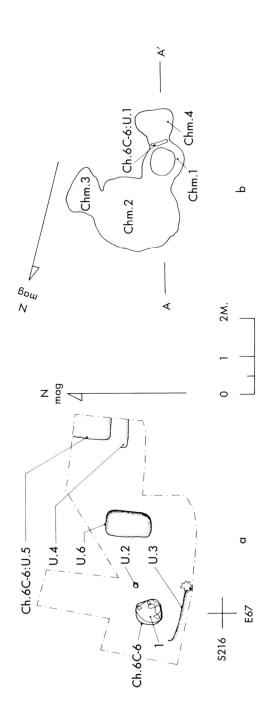

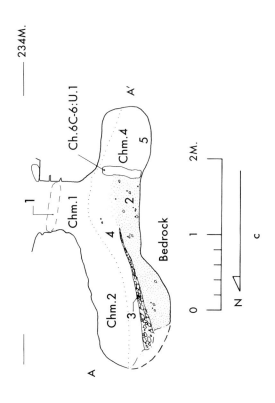

Ch. 6C-7 (*a*) and 6C-11 (*c*): Plans and Sections A-A' (*b*, *d*).

Pertinent to Ch. 6C-7: 1, Orifice, shown in Fig. 126b relative to Str. 6C-62. *2*, Burrow, probably made by an animal, the bones of which were found in the chultun. *3*, Gray soil and limestone. *4*, Lens of dark brown soil, probably old topsoil. *5*, Brownish-gray soil, the partial result of ceiling collapse. *6*, Dark brown topsoil. Pertinent to Ch. 6C-11: 1, Square stone, now broken, in place over the orifice. 2, Stones, some burned, packed around the end of the stone cover. 3, Mano fragment, included among stones (2) packed around cover. 4, Crumbled, rectangular stone packed against stone cover. 5, Portions of orifice not covered by stone cover. 6, Walls of neck at center, off-section. U. 1, 2, 4, 5, Loose, dark fill, covering PD. 231. U. 3, Compact earth, flecked with white. Artifacts of PD. 231 occur only in the top of this deposit and above. U. 6, Packed earth, perhaps in part the "sweepings" of Chm. 1 and in part water-born sediments (note the lack of a sill between the chambers). Materials associated with PD. 231 occur on or above this stratum.

FIGURE 128

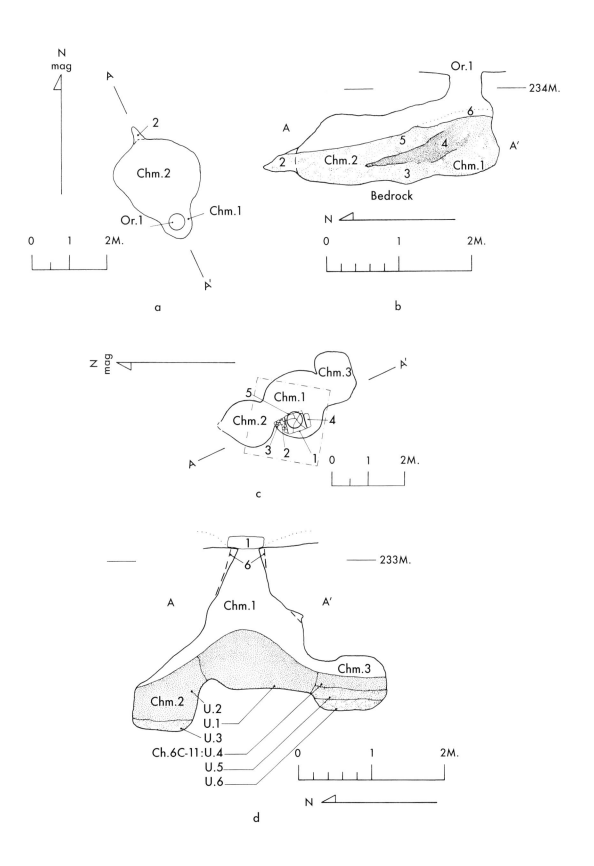

Str. 6C-60, 6C-61, and Sub.1; Ch. 6C-9: Plan.

Pertinent to Str. 6C-60: U. 1–4, Round holes in bedrock, in which posts presumably stood. They form a line roughly N-S, suggesting that posts were part of a building wall. The larger size of U. 4, and lack of further holes to the N, suggests that U. 4 held a corner post. U. 5, Apparent posthole in bedrock. Its position relative to U. 1–4 suggests that it relates to the N wall of a building. Note, too, that such a wall would be roughly parallel to U. 6. U. 6, Line of stone rubble N of, and parallel to, the presumed N wall of Str. 6C-60. Set in a low area of bedrock, it may be all that remains of a N dwarf wall or platform wall of Str. 6C-60. *Pertinent to Str. 6C-61: 1*, Estimated location of the W wall, based on the location of U. 5. Possibly, the wall was a few centimeters to the W. *2*, Estimated location of the N wall, based on the location of U. 5. This wall, too, may have been a few centimeters to the N; its eastward extent is based on the maximum eastward extent of U. 3. *3*, Location of mano (see text). U. 1, Portion of S structure wall, based in part on U. 6. U. 2, Portion of E structure wall. U. 3, Portion of S structure wall, which is sufficiently preserved to show that its S side alone was dressed. U. 4, Square hole in bedrock, probably for a post of the E wall. U. 5, Quarried bedrock "steps," so positioned as to suggest association with the NW corner of the structure. *Pertinent to Str. 6C-Sub.1*: U. 1, 3, 9, Three apparent postholes in bedrock, all similar in diameter and spaced about 3 m from one another. Although they do not form a perfectly straight line, they are close enough to such an alignment so that their size and spacing may be taken to indicate that they held three main posts for a building wall. Lack of other postholes N of U. 9 suggests that this marks one corner of the building; U. 3 is interpreted as another corner on the basis of other evidence (see U. 5, below). U. 2, 4, Small holes in bedrock, next to larger posts for the E wall of 6C-Sub.1. This pattern of large and small postholes together has been seen elsewhere at Tikal (TR. 19:fig. 5). U. 5, Apparent posthole in bedrock, similar in diameter to U. 1, 3, and 9. Its position relative to those postholes indicates that it probably supported a main post for the S wall of 6C-Sub.1. U. 6–8, Apparent postholes of a size comparable to U. 2 and 4, or Str. 6C-60:U. 1, 2, and 3. They cannot be conclusively linked to either structure, and their significance is unknown. Since they seem to arc around the SE corner of 6C-Sub.1, they are thought to relate to it. U. 9, see U. 1, 3, above. Also shown: *1–3*, Quarried bedrock, beneath the locus of Str. 6C-60. The quarrying suggests production of blocks of the sort used for Classic Period construction at Tikal. *4*, Quarried basin, about 0.30 m deep; a vertical groove on its W edge suggests that masonry blocks may have been quarried here. *5*, Quarried basin, about 0.70 m deep. It differs from the basin noted above (4) in that the sides are not vertical, nor are there any clear corners to it. Str. 6C-61:U. 7, Quarry 6 cm deep. Str. 6C-61:U. 8, Quarry, 0.10 m deep. For sections A-A' and B-B', see Fig. 130a,b; for section C-C', see Fig. 131. Coordinates are to Sq. 6C of the site map (TR. 11).

FIGURE 129

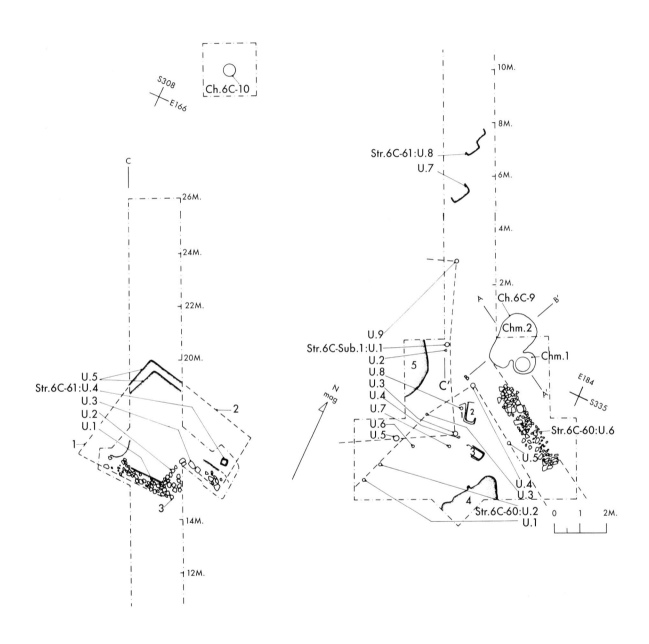

Ch. 6C-9: Sections A-A' (*a*) and B-B' (*b*) as located in Fig. 129; Ch. 6C-10, as located in Fig. 129: Plan (*c*) and Section A-A' (*d*). *Pertinent to Ch. 6C-9: 1*, Dark brown earth with few sherds or artifacts, which may have washed into the chultun after it was filled. *2*, Gray-brown earth full of sherds, chert flakes, obsidian fragments, and large biface fragments. It appears to be midden material that was purposely placed in the chultun. *3*, Sill, runs the length of the chultun floor. *4*, Maximum depth of the chultun, beside the sill (3). On the floor is a thin stratum of material distinguishable from the main fill (2) in that it contains only a few sherds. It may represent material that accumulated while the chultun was in use. *Pertinent to Ch. 6C-10: 1*, Stone slab, which may have served as a stone cover. *2*, Sill between Chm. 1 and 2. Note also the associated restrictions on the sides of this entrance. *3*, Shelflike feature, 0.25 m above floor level; it probably is the result of activity of burrowing animals. *4*, Chultun fill, interpreted as purposely placed material. Lack of material in the neck is probably the result of the fill having later settled into Chm. 2.

FIGURE 130

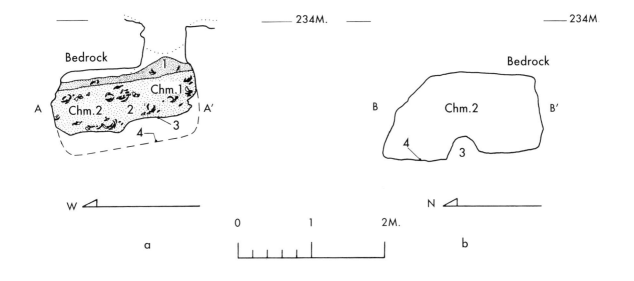

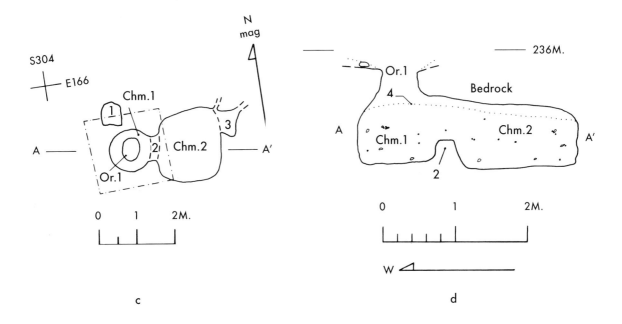

FIGURE 131

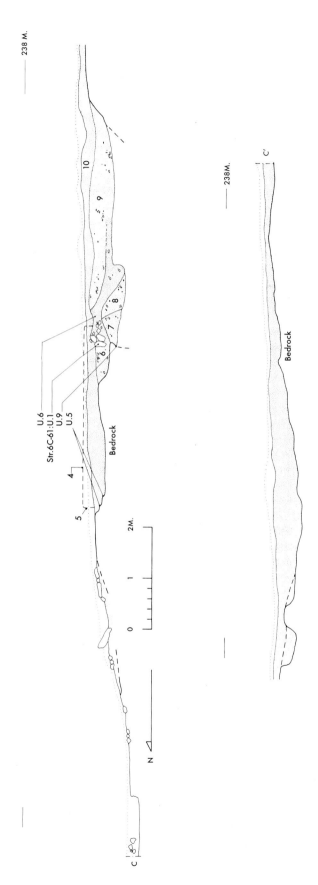

Str. 6C-61: Section C-C', as located in Fig. 129.

4, Estimated elevation of the platform surface. It is based on the assumption that U. 1, before it was reduced to rubble, stood at least 0.10 m higher than it does presently. *5*, Estimated W wall, 6C-61, based on the location of U. 5. Such a wall seems required by the estimated height of the structure. The configuration of U. 5 suggests that the wall was positioned as shown here, or ca. 0.20 m farther to the right. *6*, Gray-brown earth, thought to be a remnant of the structure fill. It is retained by U. 1. *7*, Gray fill in the U. 9 quarry, overlain by U. 6 and another fill layer (8). *8*, Light brown fill of the U. 9 quarry, overlain by U. 6. *9*, Light brown earth that overlies U. 6 near the structure. *10*, Brown soil beneath the humus. U. 1, Portion of S structure wall (see also Fig. 129). Its relation to U. 6 can best be described as union; some of U. 6 lies beneath the wall, and some lies against the S face of the wall (see U. 6, below). U. 5, Quarried bedrock "steps" (see also Fig. 129). U. 6, Hard, packed gray stratum that overlies fill in a quarried area beneath U. 9. The poor condition of the structure wall here (U. 1) and the appearance of U. 6 and the two fill layers (7, 8) below combined to suggest that there has been upheaval here by tree roots. Probably, U. 6 was laid on the quarry fill, and the wall was built on U. 6. The latter served as an informal occupation surface S and E of the structure. U. 9, Quarried area, of unknown depth, SE of 6C-61.

FIGURE 132

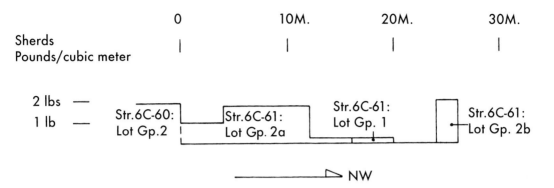

Schematic representation of sherd quantities (pounds per cubic meter) NW of Ch. 6C-9 (see Fig. 129 for plan of excavation). Ceramic evaluations, in Table 2.283, indicate a change at approximately 0 m NW; material SE of this point is high in Pre-classic sherds and low in Early Classic sherds; that to the NW is high in Manik, with few Preclassic sherds. This change correlates with the point of lowest sherd frequencies. The obvious conclusion is that the material to the SE was discarded by the occupants of Str. 6C-60, that to the NW by the occupants of Str. 6C-61. Moving NW, sherd frequencies are depicted as extraordinarily low, between 12 and 15 m. This is an exaggerated picture, because this portion of LG. 2a includes parts of strata beneath occupation debris, in which there are few sherds per cubic meter, as well as some fill from Str. 6C-61, in which sherd frequencies are depicted as between 16 and 20 m. The field data indicate the material collected between 12 m and the structure is midden-like: large sherds, with fairly sharp breaks and in some quantity. Northwest of Str. 6C-61, quantities again increase, as might be expected (24 to 26 m). This material was not dated, but should be equivalent to material between 0–15 m.

GROUP 7C-1

FIGURE 133

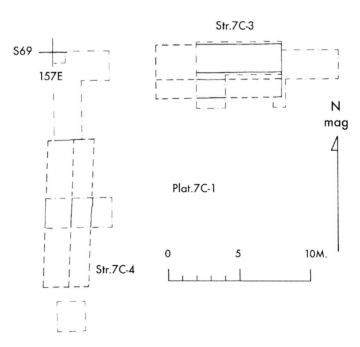

Gp. 7C-1 as it appeared ca. Gp. TS. 2 (Table 2.303).
For detailed plans of the structures, see Fig. 134 and 135. See also Fig. 136 for Ch. 7C-3.

Str. 7C-3: Plan (*a*) and Section A-A' (*b*).

Pertinent to Str. 7C-3: 1, S (front) wall, which served both 2nd and 1st. The wall is reconstructed here on the basis of the known locations of the W wall (2) and SE corner. It was built as part of CS. 2. *2*, Masonry of the W end wall, visible above the surface of the ruin mound. *3*, N (rear) wall, which served both 2nd and 1st. The wall is reconstructed on the basis of known locations of the W wall (2) and NE corner. It was built as part of CS. *4*, partly on bedrock and partly on a thin deposit of soil. 4, Front wall of an upper platform level for 1st. Placed on Fl. 1 of 2nd, Fl. 1 of 1st turns up to its base. Built of two veneers with a rubble hearting, it probably ran all the way to the W end of the structure, as it does to the E. *5*, Gray fill that was dumped inside the rear wall of 2nd as this was constructed. It apparently helped stabilize the wall until construction could proceed. *6*, Light brown fill. Since this continues S of the structure, the plaza must have been built up at the same time as the structure itself. This fill, along with that against the rear wall (5), was placed as part of CS. 4. *7*, Brown fill for CS. 3. Like that of CS. 4, it continues S in the plaza area. *8*, Brown fill for CS. 2, placed within the walls of 2nd, on which the structure floor was laid. *9*, Earth and debris fill for 1st. Note the rubble N of this fill, probably all that remains of masonry added to the rear wall (3) to increase its height. *10*, Reconstructed level for the pavement of the upper platform level of 1st. Since a plaster floor was laid for the lower level of this structure, it is reasonable to suppose that one was laid for the upper level, even though traces of this no longer exist. The reconstruction is based on the height of the fill (9) and the front wall (4). U. 1, Packed white stratum that marks the end of CS. 4 for 2nd. U. 2, Light colored, pebbly stratum that marks the end of CS. 3 for 2nd. U. 3, Plaster floor for the plaza S of 7C-3, and in union with the wall of 7C-3-2nd. U. 4, Barely detectable hole through Str. 7C-3-2nd:Fl. 1, apparently for a corner post of a building of perishable materials. Str. 7C-3-2nd:Fl. 1, pavement that runs from the top of the front wall (1) to the top of the second course of the rear wall (3), and which is penetrated by U. 4. It was laid directly on earth fill, and an upper platform level (4) was later built on it. Fl. 1 of 1st, plaster floor remnant, laid directly on the floor for 2nd and which turns up to the base of the S face of the upper platform level (4) for 1st. It must have run all the way over the top of the front wall (1) when laid originally. Coordinates are to datum shown in Fig. 133.

FIGURE 134

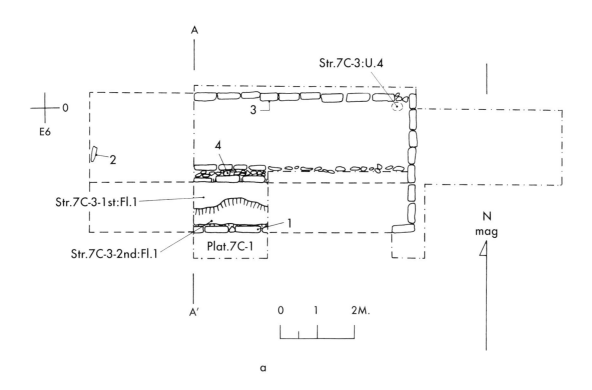

a

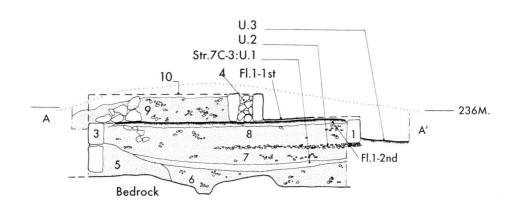

b

Str. 7C-4: Plan (*a*) and Section A-A' (*b*).

Pertinent to Str. 7C-4: 1, E (front) wall, built as part of CS. 3. West of the wall is a light-colored fill; to the E a plaza floor is in union with the wall base. Wall length is reconstructed from the known location of the N end wall (2) and the assumed location of the S end wall (5). *2*, N end wall, built as part of CS. 3. The wall is based on bedrock, and its length is reconstructed from the known locations of the E (1) and W (4) walls. *3*, E wall for an upper platform level, built as part of CS. 2. To the W is a fill of earth and debris almost as high as the wall; to the E a floor remnant is in union with the wall base. That the wall ran the length of the structure is indicated by mound configuration as well as the height of the N end wall (2). *4*, W (rear) wall, built as part of CS. 2. It is based on the fill retained by the E wall (1), and rises nearly to the height of the E wall (3) for the upper platform level. *5*, Approximate location of the S end wall, on the basis of mound configuration. *6*, Reconstructed pavement for the upper platform level. Though no trace of such a floor can now be found, the presence of plaster surfaces for the lower platform level and the plaza in front suggest that it once existed. Its height is reconstructed on the basis of the height of the front wall of the upper level (3). U. 1, Light-colored fill of CS. 3. This continues W behind the structure, and the rear wall was built upon it. Apparently, its surface served as an informal occupation surface behind the structure. U. 2, Plaster floor for Plat. 7C-1, in union with the base of the E wall (1) of the structure. The floor was laid directly on bedrock. U. 3, Small round hole in bedrock 0.10 m deep. Possibly, it is a posthole for a small structure constructed entirely of perishable materials built S of Str. 7C-4, analogous to Str. 4F-49 (Fig. 102) or Str. 6E-163 (Fig. 149). More excavation would be needed to verify this. U. 4, Round hole in bedrock, in which PD. 99 was placed. Fl. 1, Remnant of a floor laid on fill behind the E structure wall (1), in union with the base of the E wall of the upper platform level (3), and at the same general elevation as the top of the E structure wall (1). Presumably, the floor ran to the top of the latter wall. Coordinates are to datum shown in Fig. 133.

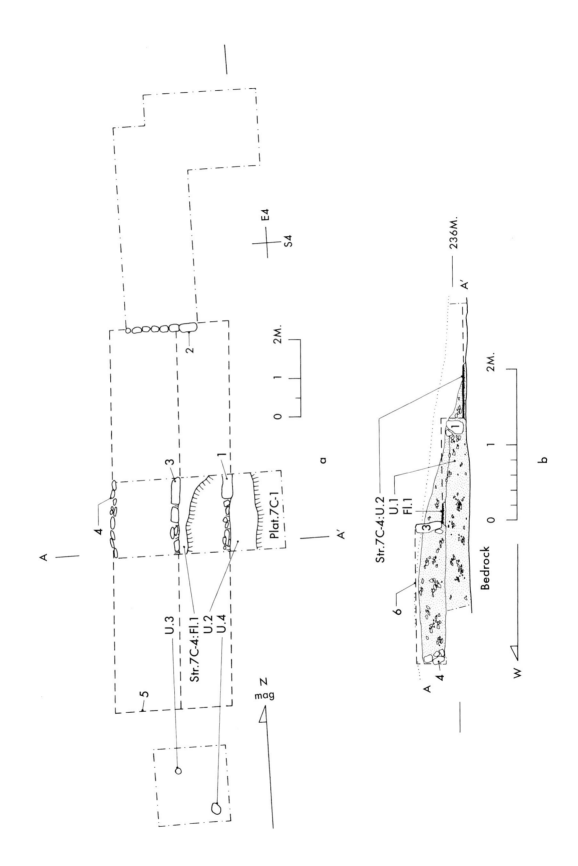

FIGURE 135

FIGURE 136

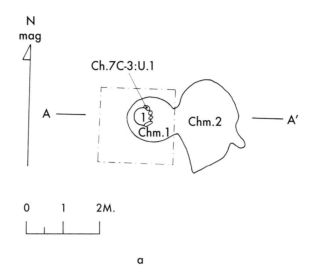

a

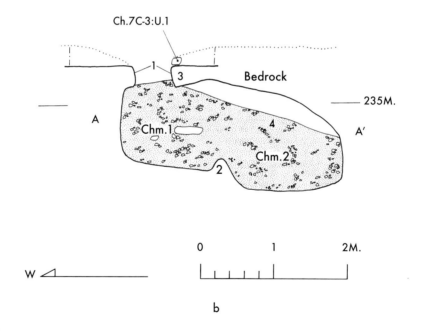

b

Ch. 7C-3: Plan (*a*) and Section A-A' (*b*).

Pertinent to Ch. 7C-3: 1, Orifice. Its coordinates 7C:S95 E190. *2*, Sill between the antechamber and inner chamber. *3*, Upper restriction between the antechamber and inner chamber. Restrictions on either side run from this to the sill (2), so that the entrance to Chm. 2 resembles a tilted hatchway. *4*, Fill of loose brown earth, a few stones, and some cultural material. The consistency, color, and arrangement of the fill indicate that it washed in after the chultun was abandoned. U. 1, Partial ring of rubble, apparently to prevent earth from spilling into the orifice. Some of the larger stones in the chultun fill may once have been part of this ring.

FIGURE 137

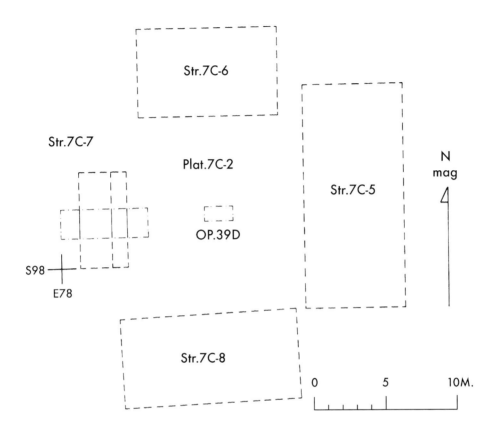

GROUP 7C-2

Gp. 7C-2, as it appeared when Str. 7C-7-1st was in use.
Structures 7C-5, 6, and 8 have not been excavated; their outlines are reconstructed on the basis of mound configuration. The location of the test pit in the plaza is approximate. For detailed plan of Str. 7C-7, see Fig. 138.

Str. 7C-7: Plan (*a*) and Section A-A' (*b*).

Pertinent to Str. 7C-7: 1, E (front) wall for 2nd, which later served 1st. The length of the wall is reconstructed on the basis of mound configuration. Note in section the elevation of the top of the wall relative to Str. 7C-7-2nd:Fl. 1; it suggests the one-time presence of a low sill. *2*, W (rear) wall for 2nd and 1st; its length is reconstructed on the basis of mound configuration. *3*, Wall, built on Fl. 1 of 2nd. Since there is no evidence for an axial opening, it is interpreted as the front wall for an upper platform level of 1st. Considering the extent of the slope to the W, the amount of fill behind the wall is sufficient to support the interpretation that the wall was not freestanding. The wall is reconstructed as running the length of the structure on the basis of mound configuration. *4*, Dark earth and pebble fill for 2nd; it overlies an early floor of Plat. 7C-2 and continues E beneath the structure wall (1) and Plat. 7C-2:U. 4. *5*, Stone fill for the upper platform level of 1st. Now badly destroyed, there is sufficient distinctive fill to indicate that the wall (3) was the face of a platform, rather than freestanding. Assumed is that the rear structure wall was raised to a height comparable to (3), and that a floor ran between them, as reconstructed here. Str. 7C-7-2nd:Fl. 1, Remnant of a floor that runs beneath the upper platform wall (3), at about the same elevation as the top of the front and rear walls (1 and 2). The portion of this floor E of the upper platform level may have continued in use with 1st. *Pertinent to Plat. 7C-2*: U. 1, Stratum of brown soil that overlies bedrock, interpreted as a natural deposit that predates Plat. 7C-2. U. 2, Gray soil and pebbles, probably deliberately placed fill for 2nd. U. 3, Floor for 2nd. Its continuation W of the excavation implies that Gp. 7C-2 was in use for an unknown period of time before Str. 7C-7-2nd was built. The floor shows traces of burning. U. 4, Plaza floor E of Str. 7C-7; abuts and turns up to the front wall of Str. 7C-7-2nd and 1st. Fill beneath the floor is continuous with that of Str. 7C-7-2nd.

FIGURE 138

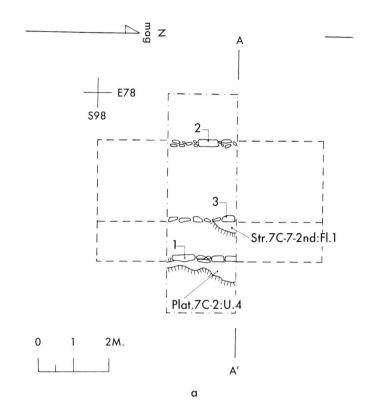

mag
N

E78
S98

A

2

3

Str.7C-7-2nd:Fl.1

1

Plat.7C-2:U.4

0   1   2M.

A'

a

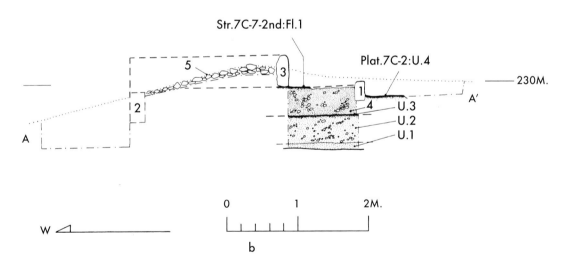

Str.7C-7-2nd:Fl.1

Plat.7C-2:U.4

5

3

230M.

2

1

4   U.3

U.2

U.1

A

A'

0   1   2M.

W

b

Str. 7C-62: Plan of excavations.

Pertinent to Str. 7C-62: 1, N and S extent of a midden, which rests on U. 1. The latter is a packed, gray-colored stratum that overlies bedrock, and is thought to represent an ancient ground surface, into which some artifactual material was trampled. As such, it resembles the strata of hard, packed gray material frequently seen behind small masonry structures (see Fig. 41b:3). The N extent of the midden correlates with the S extent of U. 3, which could be an artificially built-up surface. Hence, the midden could be trash discarded by the occupants of a structure of which U. 3 was the floor. U. 2, Round hole that penetrates U. 1 (see above) to bedrock, a depth of 0.30 m. Apparently a posthole, it is thought to relate to some version of the structure of which U. 3 (see above) was also a part. It could not be determined if the midden (1) covered U. 2, or whether the trash built up around a post that was set in the hole.

FIGURE 139

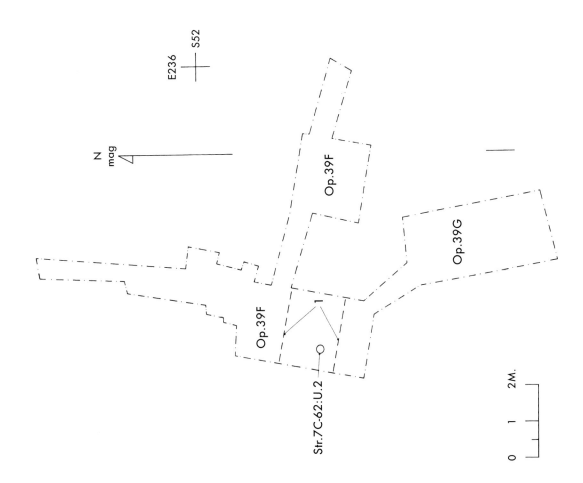

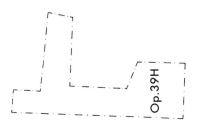

FIGURE 140

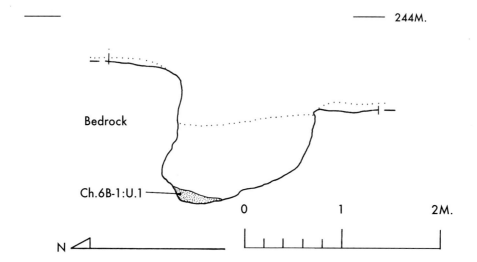

―――― 244M.

Bedrock

Ch.6B-1:U.1

0   1   2M.

N

"Ch. 6B-1": Section.

The "chultun" actually is a pit, roughly rectangular in shape (there is no plan drawing). The section here passes through the longest dimension. Unit 1 is packed, gray earth. Devoid of all cultural material, it probably represents limestone dust, tramped down before the pit was filled. Above this is humus-like earth.

FIGURE 141

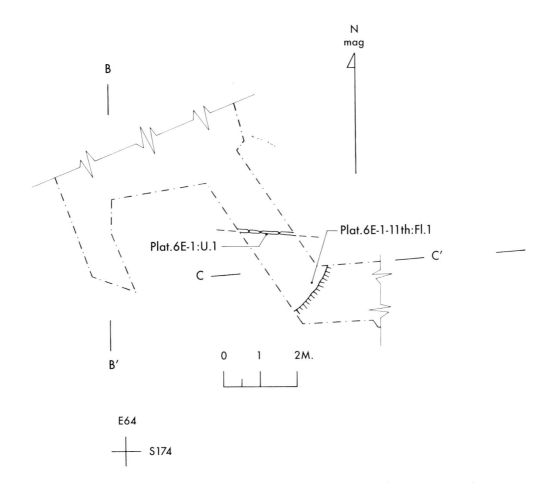

Gp. 6E-1: Plan of architecture in use in Gp. TS. 26 (Table 2.339).
Pertinent to Plat. 6E-1-11th: U. 1, Wall, part of Plat. 6E-1:11th; Fl. 1 abuts its S face 0.10 m below the top of the wall. North of U. 1 is fill of packed, light-colored earth and pebbles 0.20 m thick, its top level with that of U. 1. This fill extends 3.20 m N. Fl. 1, Hard plaster pavement that abuts U. 1, and rests on the same fill as U. 1. Consists of stone, earth, and abundant sherds. For sections B-B' and C-C', see Fig. 151, 152.

Str. 6E-Sub.1-2nd: Isometric reconstruction (*a*): Plan of Gp. 6E-1 architecture in use in Gp. TS. 24 (Table 2.339) (*b*).

Pertinent to Str: 6E-Sub.1: 1, Cut, for Bu. 153 (Fig. 144). *2*, Masonry step for 6E-Sub.1-2nd, built on the same fill as the structure walls and Fl. 1 of Plat. 6E-1-10th. The floor abuts the base of the step, which was built against the structure wall. Height of the step is unknown; eventually it was cut down almost to floor level. *3*, Cut probably made in Gp. TS. 20 (Table 2.339), for Bu. 138 (Fig. 144). *4*, Reconstructed N wall, 6E-Sub.1-2nd, based on the maximum northward extent of the structure fill (Fig. 151) and position of the apparent NW corner masonry. Eastward extent of the wall is indicated by a projection from the surviving E wall masonry. *Pertinent to Ch. 6E-6:* Or. 1, Thought to be the only orifice for 6E-6-2nd. *Pertinent to Plat. 6E-1-10th:* U. 2, One-course wall built on black earth that is higher S of the wall than on the N. This is the same fill over which Fl. 1 of Plat. 6E-1-10th was laid and on which Str. 6E-Sub.1-2nd was built. The top of U. 2 is at the same general elevation as the floor, and so the wall is interpreted as the N one of Plat. 6E-1-10th. It must have extended as far W as the floor does; how much farther is unknown. Its eastern extent is reconstructed on the basis of a projection N of U. 3. U. 3, Two-course wall, rests on a stratum of hard, packed earth. It is interpreted as the E wall for Plat. 6E-1-10th, on the basis of its relation to U. 4. U. 4, Packed, white material that runs W from the top of U. 3. It is the same thickness as Fl. 1 of Plat. 6E-1-10th and, taking the dip eastward of both surfaces into consideration, a projection of U. 4 westward meets Fl. 1. Hence, U. 4 is interpreted as a remnant of that pavement. Fl. 1, Thick, plaster pavement that abuts the surviving wall and step of Str. 6E-Sub.1-2nd.

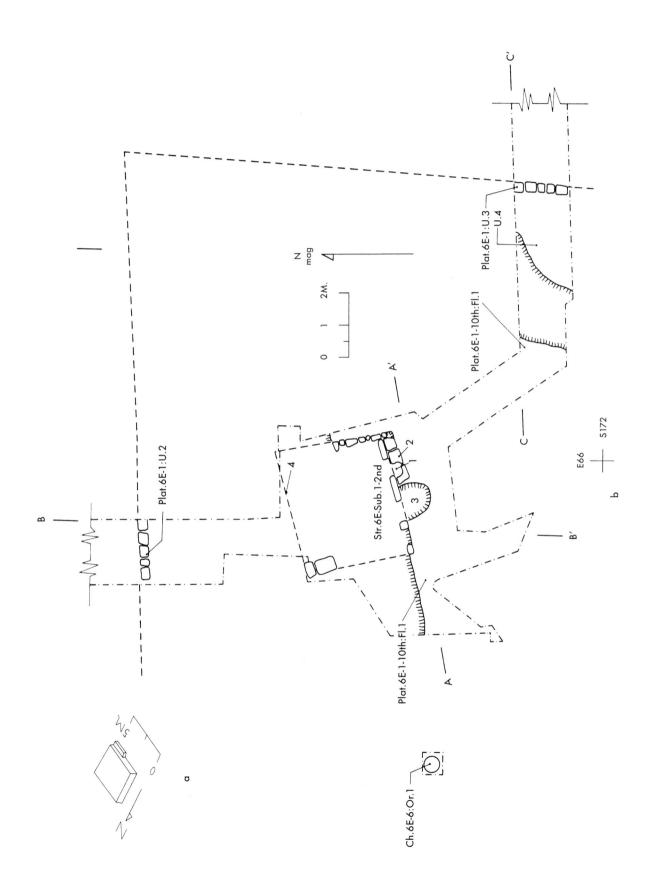

FIGURE 142

Gp. 6E-1: Plan of architecture in use in Gp. TS. 22 (Table 2.339).

Pertinent to Str. 6E-Sub.1: 5, Walls of Sub.1-1st, the only actual remnants of which are the two stone slabs shown. These are just S of the reconstructed location of the N wall of Sub.1-1st, in a slightly different alignment close to that of Str. 6E-Sub.2. The reconstruction is based on these facts, the assumption that the structure was about the same size and shape as its predecessor, and the line of termination of Plat. 6E-1-7th:Fl. 1 (Fig. 144), which at one time abutted the structure. *Pertinent to Str. 6E-Sub.2: 6*, E wall, which retains a dark earth fill to the W; to the E, it is abutted near its base by Fl. 1 of Plat. 6E-1-9th. Its maximum southward extent is not known, but its northward extent is clearly indicated by Fl. 1 of Plat. 6E-1-9th, which runs westward N of the wall, terminating in a straight E-W line where the N structure wall was later ripped out. 7, Reconstructed N wall; its position is indicated by the straight break of Fl. 1 of Plat. 6E-1-9th W of the N end of the E wall (6). Actual length of the N wall is not known; here it has been drawn as long as the known portion of the E wall. This is N of Or. 1 of Ch. 6E-6 (shown in Fig. 142), suggesting that this orifice was closed when Str. 6E-Sub.2 was built. *Pertinent to Ch. 6E-6: Or. 2*, Thought to have been constructed when Or. 1 was closed (see 7, above). Note the masonry of the shaft above the actual opening in bedrock. *Pertinent to Ch. 6E-7: Or. 1*, The original one for Ch. 6E-7-2nd. *Pertinent to Plat. 6E-1-9th:* U. 3, E wall, Plat. 6E-1-10th (Fig. 142). Though not proven, it is likely that the height of this wall was increased to serve Plat. 6E-1-9th as well. U. 5, plaster floor remnant, with an elevation 0.17 m below that of Fl. 1, an insignificant difference in view of the distance between the floor exposures. Unit 5 cannot be related to Plat. 6E-1-10th and its elevation is too low for it to be interpreted as part of the floor for Plat. 6E-1-8th. Thus, it is seen as a remnant of Plat. 6E-1-9th:Fl. 1. U. 6, Informal floor surface of packed, light-colored earth that abuts the E face of U. 3, which it probably postdates. Sherds in the fill of U. 6 suggest that the surface dates from Preclassic times. Since Plat. 6E-1-9th is the last Preclassic version of the platform, it is probable that U. 6 relates to it. Fl. 1, plaster pavement that abuts and turns up to the wall of Str. 6E-Sub.2 close to its base. It probably also abutted the wall of Str. 6E-Sub.1-1st, for surviving masonry of that structure projects 0.40 m above the elevation of Fl. 1. For sections *A-A'*, *B-B'*, and *C-C'*, see Fig. 150, 151, and 152.

FIGURE 143

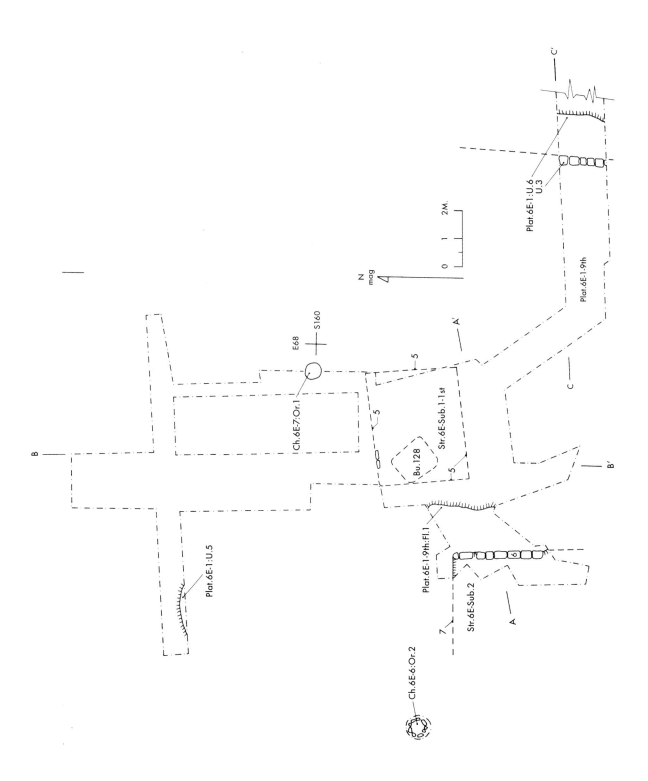

Gp. 6E-1: Plan of architecture in use in Gp. TS. 20 and 18 (Table 2.339).

Pertinent to Str. 6E-Sub.1: 5, Walls for Str. 6E-Sub.1-1st (see Fig. 143:5). *Pertinent to Str. 6E-Sub.2: 6, 7*, E and N walls (see Fig. 143:6, 7). *Pertinent to Str. 6E-Sub.3: 8*, Walls; the only actual masonry is the single stone shown, which is set slightly into the contemporary floor of Plat. 6E-1-8th. The masonry is part of an E wall, shown by a substantial midden to the E. It is doubtful if the N wall was significantly closer to Str. 6E-Sub.1 than shown here. *Pertinent to Ch. 6E-6*: Or. 2 (see Fig. 143); its masonry shaft is thought to have been extended upward when Fl. 1 of Plat. 6E-1-7th was laid. Pertinent to Ch. 6E-7: Or. 1 (see Fig. 143). *Pertinent to Plat. 6E-1*: U. 3, Wall associated with Plat. 6E-1-10th and 9th (see Fig. 142, 143). It may have continued as the edge of a low platform level for Plat. 6E-1-8th, but it was eventually covered by refuse apparently discarded from Str. 6E-Sub.3. U. 7, Packed informal occupation surface above U. 6; the only feature here that could possibly relate to Plat. 6E-1-8th. U. 8, Wall interpreted as the S face of Plat. 6E-1-8th, based on the presence of apparently Early Classic fill N of it, and Early Classic trash at its base to the S. Later rubbish above the Early Classic trash suggests that the wall also served 7th and later versions of Plat. 6E-1. Plat. 6E-1-8th:Fl. 1, a packed, light-colored stratum that served as floor for Plat. 6E-1-8th. It runs beneath the walls of Str. 6E-Sub.3 in standard Early Classic fashion. Plat. 6E-1-7th:Fl. 1, plaster pavement, with an exceptionally thick body, which abuts the surviving wall of Str. 6E-Sub.2, 9 cm below the top of the wall. It probably abutted the walls of Str. 6E-Sub.1-1st a comparable distance below their top. The surface of this floor is at almost the same elevation as that of Fl. 1 of 8th. Therefore, it is interpreted as a replacement for the latter, except where it was covered by Str. 6E-Sub.3. For sections A-A', B-B', and C-C', see Fig. 150, 151, and 152.

FIGURE 144

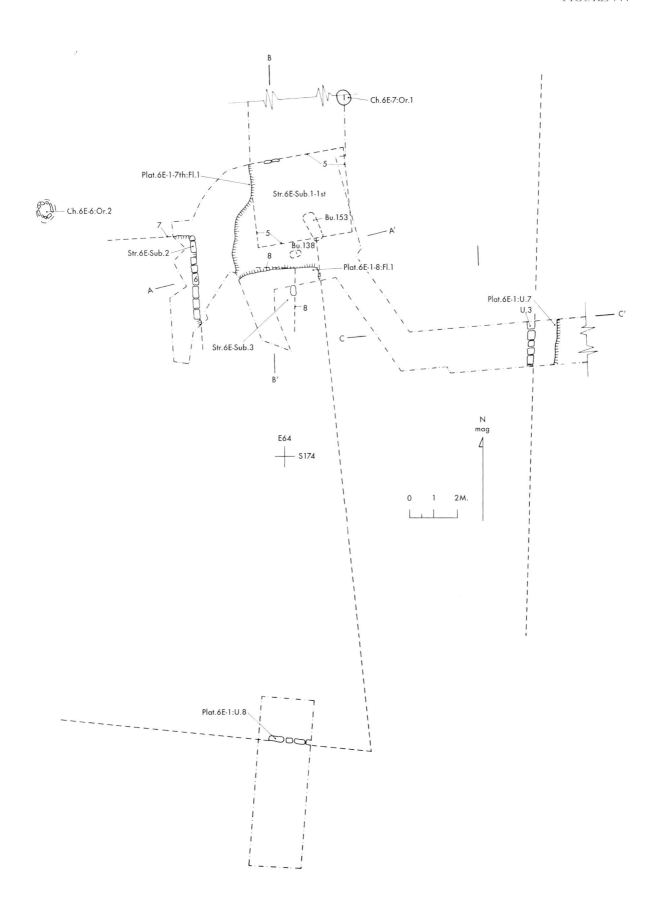

Gp. 6E-1: Plan of architecture in use in Gp. TS. 16 (Table 2.339).

Pertinent to Str. 6E-25: 9, W wall that served the later Str. 6E-25-1st. Since the known wall (U. 1) of 25-2nd corresponds so closely with the comparable wall of 25-1st, it is thought that the rear wall served Str. 2nd as well as 1st. U. 1, E (front) wall of 2nd. Its base is at the same general elevation as the floor of Plat. 6E-1-6th and the two are thought to be contemporary, later activity having destroyed positive evidence for this. Since U. 1 in its known portion conforms so closely to the comparable wall of 25-1st, it is reconstructed to an equivalent length. Pertinent to Str. 6E-26: 10, Approximate location of S (front) wall of 26-4th. The basis for this reconstruction is the straight-line termination of Plat 6E-1-6th:Fl. 1 that indicates that structure walls have been ripped out. The size of the structure is not known, but the walls reconstructed suggest a structure much like 26-3rd, though not as wide. Midden debris to the E suggests that this end of the structure did not extend significantly E of Plat. 6E-1. *Pertinent to Str. 6E-Sub.3: 8*, Walls (see Fig. 144:8). That this structure continued in use is suggested by the elevation of Plat. 6E-1-6th:Fl. 1, which is below that of the top of the surviving wall masonry. *Pertinent to Ch. 6E-6*: Or. 2 (see Fig. 143). Originally, Plat. 6E-1-6th:Fl. 1 seems to have sealed this orifice. This pavement overlies the top of the masonry shaft by the same amount as it does the floor of Plat. 6E-1-7th farther E. Later, as the chultun fill settled, the floors above it broke up as shown here. *Pertinent to Ch. 6E-7*: Or. 2, Its location in an area once covered by Str. 6E-Sub.1, rules out its construction before Gp. TS. 17, for Str. 6E-Sub.1 was still in use. The older Or. 1 (Fig. 144) seems to have been closed off because it was too close to the new Str. 6E-26-4th. *Pertinent to Plat. 6E-1-6th: 11*, Maximum northward extent of U. 10, the light-colored fill on which Fl. 1 was laid to the S. The walls of Str. 6E-26-4th were built on this, and it is likely that both the structure and platform extended no farther N than this point. *12*, Hypothetical location of the E platform wall; the position of Ch. 6E-7:Or. 2 indicates that it could have been no farther E. Moreover, the same wall may have served Plat. 6E-1-5th, which was positioned as shown here, perhaps running straight N to meet the N platform retaining wall (11). The southward extent of this wall is reconstructed on the basis of the known location of U. 8. *13*, Hypothetical location of the W platform wall. Since the N wall always seems to have incorporated the comparable wall of Str. 6E-26 (Fig. 146–149), it is assumed that the W wall of the platform and Str. 6E-25 were similarly constructed. The length of the wall is based on the known location of U. 8 and the presumed position of the N wall (11). U. 8, S platform wall, originally constructed for 8th (Fig. 144). Lack of any more recent identifiable wall suggests it continued to serve Plat. 6E-1-6th and subsequent architectural developments. U. 9, Apparent posthole, perhaps related to Str. 6E-26-4th. U. 15, Hole though Fl. 1, dug in Gp. TS. 7 (see Fig. 146). U. 22–29, Holes through Fl. 1, dug in Gp. TS. 7 (see Fig. 148). Fl. 1 of 6th, Plaster surface that must at one time have abutted the front wall of Str. 6E-25-2nd, since the base of that wall is slightly below the elevation of the floor (see Fig. 150). On the N, Fl. 1 breaks up in relatively straight lines even though its fill, U. 10 (see 11, above) continues. This suggests that the walls of an associated structure, 6E-26-4th, have been ripped out here (10, above). The overall extent of Fl. 1 is not known, but since it seems to have continued to serve Plat. 6E-1-5th, it probably terminated at the same E wall (see 12, above). For sections A-A', B-B', and C-C', see Fig. 150, 151, and 152.

FIGURE 145

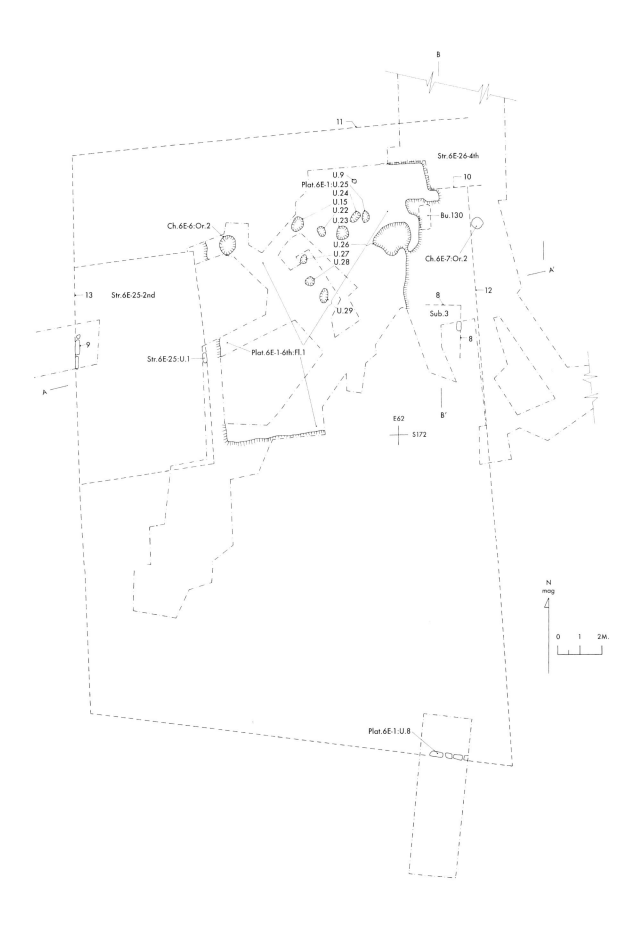

Gp. 6E-1: Plan of architecture in use in Gp. TS. 14 (Table 2.339).

Pertinent to Str. 6E-25: 9, Rear wall of 2nd (Fig. 145:9). U. 1, Front wall of 2nd (see Fig. 145). *Pertinent to Str. 6E-26*: U. 1, single-course masonry wall, resting in part on Plat. 6E-1-6th:Fl. 1 and in part on thin fill over Plat. 6E-1:U. 10. Unit 1 apparently served as part of the front of 6E-26-3rd. The last 1 m of this front wall to the E, like the entire E wall, rests on midden debris (see Fig. 181d for photo) associated with 26-4th, and was built of multiple courses to bring it up to the level of U. 1 (see Fig. 181b for photo). U. 3, Plaster pavement, laid on earth fill, running N from the top of U. 1. It represents a remnant of the floor for Str. 26-3rd. U. 4, Wall built on the floor of Plat. 6E-1-6th. It runs N from the W end of U. 1, and represents the E wall of a large inset at the SW corner of 26-3rd. U. 5, Rubble remains of the front wall of 26-3rd W of U. 4. It terminates at the rubble remains of the W wall that served 3rd and succeeding architectural developments. U. 6, Plaster floor N of U. 3 and laid at the same elevation. It, too, is probably a remnant of pavement for 26-3rd. The regularity of the break between U. 3 and 6 suggests that there may once have been a longitudinal, freestanding wall here. *Pertinent to Str. 6E-Sub.3: 8*, Walls (see Fig. 144:8). *Pertinent to Ch. 6E-6*: Or. 2 (see Fig. 143). *Pertinent to Ch. 6E-7*: Or. 2 (see Fig. 145). *Pertinent to Plat. 6E-1: 12*, E wall, probably constructed as part of 6th, but it certainly served 5th. It was later torn out, as indicated by a rip-line 1 m W of the SE corner of Str. 6E-26-3rd (at the E end of 6E-26:U. 1; see Fig. 181b). Assumed is that this E wall ran as far S as the wall of which U. 8 was a part. *13*, W wall, Plat. 6E-1 (see Fig. 145). *14*, N wall of 5th; to the E, this and the rear wall of Str. 6E-26-3rd were one and the same. It was based in part on Plat. 6E-1:U. 5 (see Fig. 143), and continued to serve subsequent architectural developments of the platform. U. 8, S wall, Plat. 6E-1 (see Fig. 145). U. 15, Hole through Plat. 6E-1-6th:Fl. 1 that may have been dug through later Fl. 1 of 3rd. U. 22–29, Holes through Plat. 6E-1-6th:Fl. 1 dug in Gp. TS. 7 (see Fig. 145). Fl. 1 of 6th, Pavement that presumably continued in use with Plat. 6E-1-5th. There must have been some patching around the new Str. 6E-26-3rd, but later alterations are probably responsible for destruction of the evidence. The floor also would have to be extended to the new N wall (14), but this was not investigated. For section A-A' and B-B', see Fig. 150 and 151.

FIGURE 146

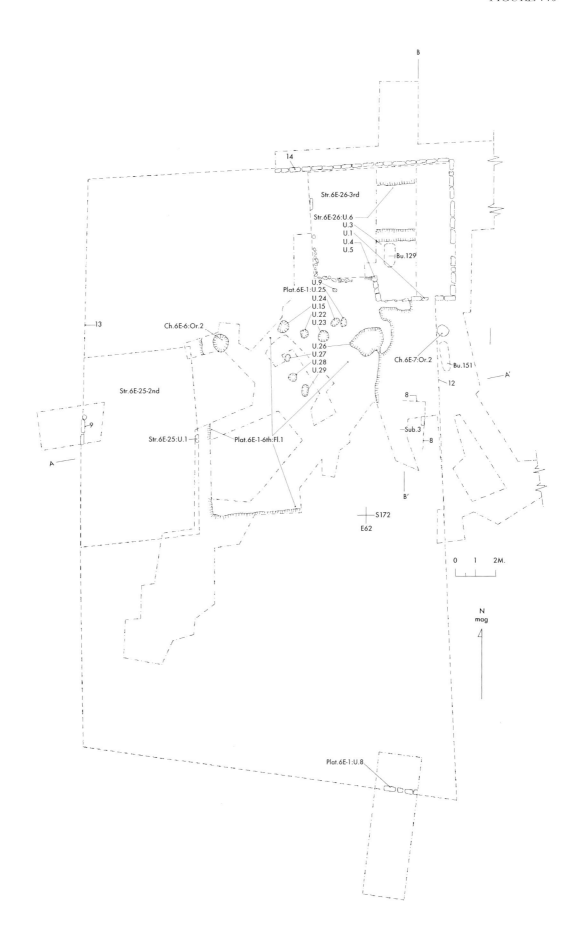

Gp. 6E-1: Plan of architecture in use in Gp. TS. 12, 10, and 8 (Table 2.399).

Pertinent to Str. 6E-25: 9, Rear wall of 2nd (see Fig. 145:9). U. 1, Front wall of 2nd (see Fig. 145). *Pertinent to Str. 6E-26: 15*, Front walls for the building platform of 2nd-D. These increased the height of the structure. *17*, Front wall for an upper platform level. The same brown earth fill beneath the wall rises as high as the masonry N of the wall. U. 8 turns up to the wall base on the S. *18*, Reconstructed position of the rear of the platform surface, based on a projection upwards of the batter of the surviving portion of the rear wall to the same elevation as the top of the front wall for the upper platform level (17). Apparently, the N, E, and W walls of 26-3rd were increased in height to serve 2nd-D. *19, 20*, Riser stones for two steps constructed against the S wall of 2nd-D. The masonry of the SW corner of the stairs was intruded into Fl. 1 of Plat. 6E-1-6th, and U. 13 of Plat. 6E-1-4th turns up to them. These stones also form the W and S sides of the grave for Bu. 152 (see Fig. 182d for photo). The E end of the steps is formed in part by Plat. 6E-1:U. 12. The absence of so much masonry from the lowest riser probably was caused by later intrusion of Bu. 131 (Fig. 148). 21, Hypothetical position of a front building wall. Such a wall would be more likely to have been straight, rather than following strictly the front wall (15). U. 8, Plaster floor remnant, laid on fill retained by the structure walls (15, 18), and which turns up to the front wall for the upper platform level (17). Presumably, this pavement once extended all the way to the top of the front wall (15). *Pertinent to Str. 6E-Sub.3: 8*, Walls (see Fig. 144:8). Apparently, this structure continued in use, and Plat. 6E-1:U. 12 is laid out in such a way as to suggest that it deliberately avoided the structure. *Pertinent to Plat. 6E-1-4th: 13*, W wall (see Fig. 145:13). *14*, N wall (see Fig. 146:14). U. 8, S wall (see Fig. 145). U. 12, One-course wall built on packed earth fill that blends to the E with a deep midden associated with occupation of Str. 6E-26-3rd. The top of the wall is at the same approximate elevation as Fl. 1 of Plat. 6E-1-4th. Suspected is that, after its swing to the W, possibly to avoid Str. 6E-Sub.3, it again swung S, running W of that structure. Hard evidence for this, however, is absent. U. 13, Plaster floor remnant at the same elevation, and in the same stratigraphic relationship to the floor of Plat. 6E-1-6th as Fl. 1 of Plat. 6E-1-4th. Presumably, it is a remnant of the same pavement. It turns up to the lowest step (19) of Str. 6E-26-2nd-D. Fl. 1, Pavement at the same general elevation as the top of U. 12. Laid directly on Plat. 6E-1-6th:Fl. 1, it probably is the floor for Plat. 6E-1-4th. It must once have covered the area E of U. 12, running up to Str. 6E-25-2nd and 6E-26-2nd-D. For sections A-A' and B-B', see Fig. 150 and 151.

FIGURE 147

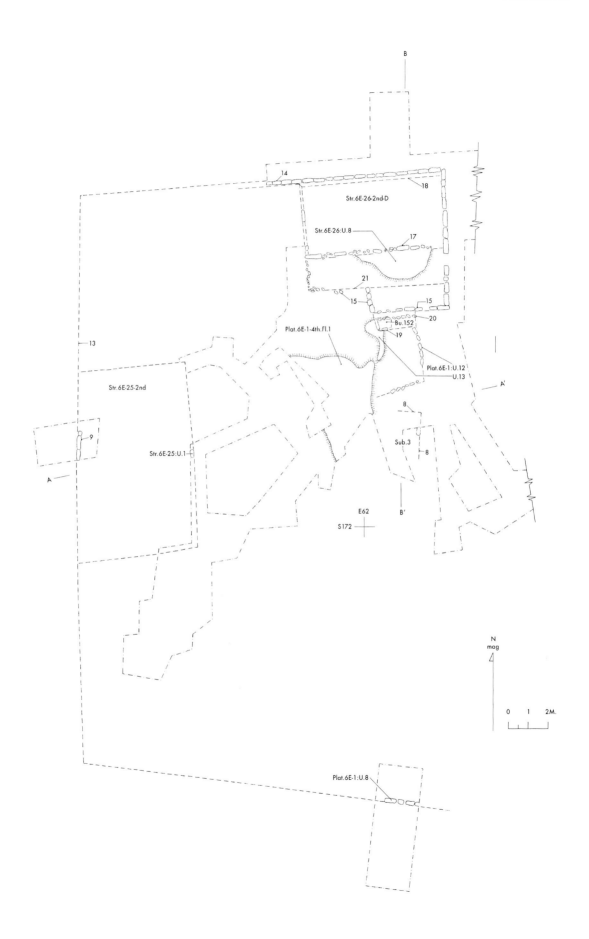

Gp. 6E-1: Plan of architecture in use in Gp. TS. 6 (Table 2.339).

Pertinent to Str. 6E-25: 9, Rear wall, thought to have served both 25-1st and 2nd (see Fig. 145:9). *22*, Wall, SE part of 25-1st, of one course; it rests on earth fill 0.15 m above the corresponding wall of 25-2nd (U. 1). Fl. 1 of Plat. 6E-1-2nd abuts the base of the wall. *23*, Masonry block in line with the known portion of the front wall (22) of 25-1st, and at the correct elevation to be interpreted as part of it. Since no further masonry continues to the N, this must be the NE corner, as also suggested by the mound configuration. *24*, Hypothetical front wall for an upper platform level of 1st. The existence of such a level is suggested by the mound configuration, but has not been verified. *Pertinent to Str. 6E-26: 15*, Front wall, built originally for 2nd-D (see Fig. 147:15). *17*, Front wall, upper platform level, built originally for 2nd-D (see Fig. 147:17). *18*, Rear of platform top (see Fig. 147:18). *20*, Single step to 2nd-B that originated as the second step up to 2nd-D (Fig. 147:20). Both steps were extended 0.60 m to the E for 2nd-C, and as 2nd-B, the lowest step (Fig. 147:19) was covered by a new, higher floor for Plat. 6E-1. 21, Hypothetical building wall (see Fig. 147:21). U. 8, Pavement on lower platform level (see Fig. 147). *Pertinent to Str. 163: 25*, Reconstructed walls; the N and part of the E walls are marked by some surviving masonry and the straight-line termination of Plat. 6E-1:U. 19. The length of the N wall, and the position of the structure relative to Str. 6E-25, suggest that 163 was very much like Str. 162 (Fig. 149), hence the reconstruction shown here. *Pertinent to Ch. 6E-6: Or. 2* (see Fig. 145). *Pertinent to Plat. 6E-1: 13*, W wall (see Fig. 145:13). *14*, N wall (see Fig. 146:14). U. 8, S wall (see Fig. 145). U. 14, E wall of 3rd, which continued to serve 2nd. The single course of masonry rests on deposits of trash; the N end was bonded to the wall of Str. 6E-26 (where the wall of Plat. 6E-1-5th once stood), and provided a new E wall to the steps to Str. 6E-26-2nd (see 20, above). The wall is presumed to have run all the way to the old S wall marked by U. 8. U. 15, Circular pit dug through the floor of Plat. 6E-1-3rd to bedrock. Though not proven, a possibility is that a chultun was planned here, but bedrock was so far beneath the platform surface that the project was abandoned. U. 16, Patch on the floor for Plat. 6E-1-3rd that defines 3rd-A. Only 3 cm thick, its edges taper to meet the surface of the main floor almost invisibly. U. 17, Narrow stairway, built against U. 14 for Plat. 6E-1-2nd (see Fig. 181a for photo). It was constructed on the exposed surface of a midden that slopes down to the E. U. 18, Wall, built of two veneers with rubble hearting that abuts the front wall of Str. 6E-25-1st. Its N face was intruded all the way into Plat. 6E-1-6th:Fl. 1. The S veneer is more carefully dressed than that on the N, and continues the line of the S end of Str. 6E-25. U. 19, Plaster pavement, turns up to this veneer near its base, and the top of the veneer is at about the same elevation as U. 17 and Plat. 6E-1-2nd:Fl. 1. Apparently, U. 18 served as a retaining wall for a higher surface for Plat. 6E-1-2nd on the N than on the S. U. 19, Plaster floor that turns up to Str. 6E-25-1st, Str. 6E-163, and Plat. 6E-1:U. 18. Assumed is that this floor was laid all the way to the top of the wall represented by U. 8. U. 20, Small remnant of pavement at the same general elevation as Plat. 6E-1-2nd:Fl. 1. It is interpreted as a part of that floor, and is of similar composition. U. 21, Floor remnant that turns up to the walls of Str. 6E-26-2nd-B. Its elevation is consistent with its interpretation as a remnant of Plat. 6E-1-2nd:Fl. 1. It is also of similar composition. U. 22–29, Holes dug through Fl. 1 of Plat. 6E-1-3rd prior to the laying of Fl. 1 of 2nd. All are deep enough to penetrate the floor of 6th. U. 23 and 26 contain rubble and masonry; U. 25 a burial. The others are empty except for earth. The significance of the holes is unknown. Fl. 1 of 3rd, Pavement laid for Plat. 6E-1-3rd-B. Its elevation is virtually the same as that of the top of U. 14, at the top of which the floor probably once terminated. It abuts the front wall (U. 1) of Str. 6E-25-2nd, and must have abutted Str. 6E-26-1st-C, on the basis of its presumed association with U. 14. This association also means that Str. 6E-Sub.3 was covered by this pavement. The break around the orifice of Ch. 6E-6 is probably the result of chultun fill settling, for the floor is several centimeters above the top of the shaft. Plat. 6E-1-2nd:Fl. 1, Pavement similar in composition to U. 20 and 21, and at the same general elevation. It turns up to the front wall (22) of Str. 6E-25-1st, and a projection of its surface through U. 20 suggests that it ran to the top of U. 17. Evidently the height of U. 14 was increased slightly for Plat. 6E-1-2nd. To the S, Fl. 1 must once have run to the top of U. 18, as both are at the same general elevation. For sections A-A' and B-B', see Fig. 150 and 151.

FIGURE 148

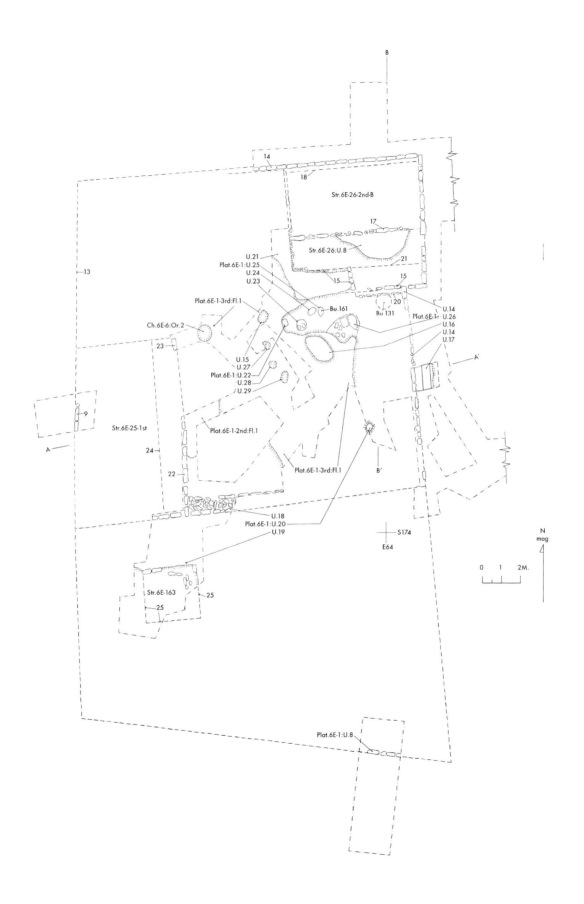

Gp. 6E-1: Plan of architecture in use in Gp. TS. 2.

Pertinent to Str. 6E-25: 9, Rear wall of 1st (Fig. 148:9). *22, 23*, Front wall of 1st (see Fig. 148:22, 23). *24*, Front wall, upper platform level of 1st (see Fig. 148:24). *Pertinent to Str. 6E-26: 15*, Front wall, built originally for 2nd-D (see Fig. 147:15). The sections shown here continued to serve 2nd-A, with only the southernmost serving 1st. *17*, Front wall, upper platform, built originally for 2nd-D (see Fig. 147:17). It continued in use for 1st. *18*, Rear of platform top (see Fig. 147:18). *20*, Single step for 2nd-B (see Fig. 148:20), which continued in use for 2nd-A and 1st. Unit 9, E wall of inset, built for 2nd-A on Plat. 6E-1 and Plat 6E-1:U. 31 turns up to its base. It is thought that the front building wall for 26-2nd-A remained where it was for 2nd-B (see Fig. 148:21). U. 9, and the part of the front wall (15) W of it, were eliminated in 26-1st. U. 10, Walls for 26-1st (based on Plat. 6E-1:U. 31), which eliminated the older corner inset. U. 11, Remnant of pavement laid directly on U. 8, which turns up to the wall (17) of the upper platform level. It probably relates to 1st, as elimination of the corner inset as indicated by U. 10 seems to require a new floor for this portion of the platform. *Pertinent to Str. 6E-162: 26*, Structure walls. The length of the W and E walls are known, and is the basis of the reconstruction shown here. The walls were built directly on midden material and U. 32 of Plat. 6E-1 indicates that a floor turned up to them. *27*, Fragments of a single metate as found in situ. They lay at the same elevation as Fl. 1. The metate was probably left on the floor when the structure was abandoned. Fl. 1, Pavement at the same general elevation as the top of the structure walls. This must have covered the entire structure platform. *Pertinent to Str. 6E-163: 25*, Reconstructed walls (see Fig. 148:25). *Pertinent to Plat. 6E-1: 13*, W wall (see Fig. 145:13). *14*, N wall (see Fig. 146:14). *28*, NE corner of 1st. Incorporated in its fill is a midden E of Str. 6E-26, on which Str. 6E-162 was built. The E wall of Plat. 6E-1-1st is reconstructed from a projection S of the line of wall seen here. U. 8, S wall (see Fig. 145). U. 14, Masonry block of the E wall for Plat. 6E-1-3rd and 2nd, utilized for 1st (see Fig. 148). U. 18, S wall, upper level of 2nd, which continued in use as part of 1st (see Fig. 148). U. 19, Floor S of U. 18 (see Fig. 148). This apparently continued in use with Plat. 6E-1-1st. U. 20, Remnant of the floor for 2nd, which continued in use for Plat. 6E-1-1st (see Fig. 148). U. 30, Line of rubble, apparently the remains of an E-W wall. It seems to have served as did U. 18 E of U. 14, as part of Plat. 6E-1-1st. U. 31, Plaster surface that closely overlies U. 21 (see Fig. 148). It turns up to the walls of Str. 6E-26-2nd-A (15 and U. 9), and is thought to be a grading floor on Plat. 6E-1-2nd:Fl. 1 associated with the modification that produced Str. 6E-26-2nd-A. The walls (U. 10) of Str. 6E-26-1st were built on this pavement. U. 32, Plaster floor remnant that appears to turn up to the S wall of Str. 6E-162. Laid directly on the midden E of Str. 6E-26, it is likely a remnant of a floor that was added on the E edge of Plat. 6E-1 2nd:Fl. 1 when Plat. 6E-1-1st was built. U. 33, Olla neck, built into U. 32 and later covered by the corner of Str. 6E-26-1st. U. 34, Masonry wall, apparently located E of the edge of Plat. 6E-1-1st and of seemingly different masonry than the wall (28) for that platform. It may be part of a stairway that replaced the preceding U. 17 (Fig. 148). U. 35, Informal "floor" E of U. 34, consisting of packed, gray-colored earth. Plat. 6E-1-2nd:Fl. 1. Floor for 2nd, probably reused in 1st (see Fig. 148). For sections A-A', B-B', and C-C', see Fig. 150, 151, and 152.

FIGURE 149

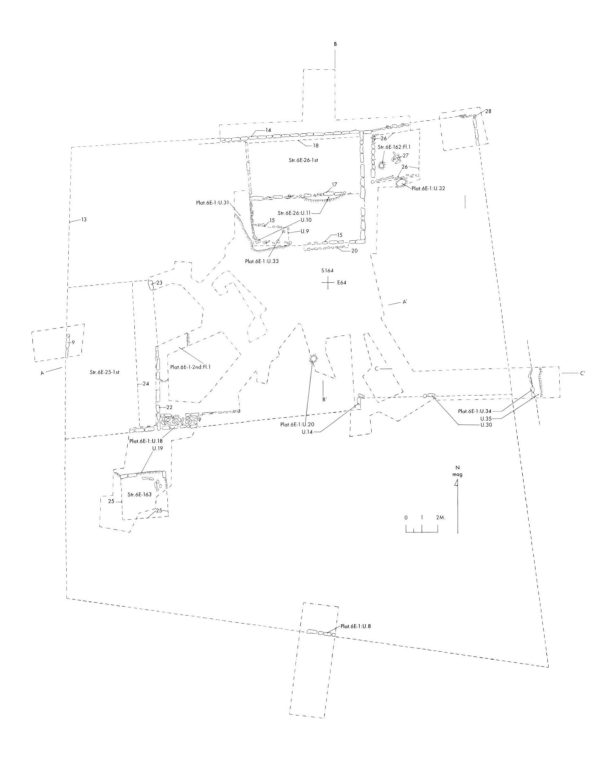

Gp. 6E-1: Section A-A', as located in Fig. 142-149.

Pertinent to Str. 6E-25: 9, Rear wall for 1st, and probably 2nd, off-section (see Fig. 148:9). The wall base as shown here is known from excavation; the elevation of the top is a reconstruction based on the height of the ruin mound. *22,* Front wall of 1st (see Fig. 148:22). *24,* Hypothetical wall, upper platform level of 1st (see Fig. 148:24). U. 1, Front wall of 2nd (see Fig. 145). *Pertinent to Str. 6E-Sub.2: 6,* E wall (see Fig. 143:6). Note how the structure was eliminated with the laying of Plat. 6E-1-6th:Fl. 1. Pertinent to Plat. 6E-1: 3, Pit, filled with Early Classic debris, in which Bu. 138 was placed. 29, Fill for 10th (see Fig. 151:29). *30,* Rocky fill, thought to be recycled from Str. 6E-Sub.3 (see Fig. 151:30). U. 14, E wall, constructed for 3rd-B (see Fig. 148); a projection from Plat. 6E-1-3rd:Fl. 1 nicely meets the top of U. 14. U. 17, Stairway built on the E side of 2nd (see Fig. 148). Elevation of the top of its masonry is closer to that of Plat. 6E-1-2nd:Fl. 1 than Plat. 6E-1-3rd:Fl. 1. The bottom step is reconstructed from the known stair tread. Fl. 1 of 10th (see Fig. 142). Fl. 1 of 9th (see Fig. 143). Fl. 1 of 8th (see Fig. 144), from off-section remains. It probably was destroyed here when the next platform floor was laid. Fl. 1 of 7th (see Fig. 144). The body of this floor, which is exceptionally thick, rests on the surface of Fl. 1 of 9th. This suggests removal of the floor for Plat. 6E-1-8th when this next pavement was laid. Fl. 1 of 6th (see Fig. 145). Note that Str. 6E-Sub.2 was abandoned when this floor was laid. The elevation of this pavement relative to Str. 6E-25:U. 1 suggests that it once extended all the way to this wall, as reconstructed here. Fl. 1 of 4th (see Fig. 147). The reason for its western termination far from Str. 6E-25 is not known. Fl. 1 of 3rd (see Fig. 148). An eastward projection of this surface meets the top of U. 14. Fl. 1 of 2nd (see Fig. 148). An eastward projection of this surface comes close to the top of U. 14. Fl. 1 of 1st, hypothetical eastward extension of Plat. 6E-1-2nd. Fl. 1 of which Plat 6E-1:U. 32 (Fig. 149) is thought to be a remnant.

FIGURE 150

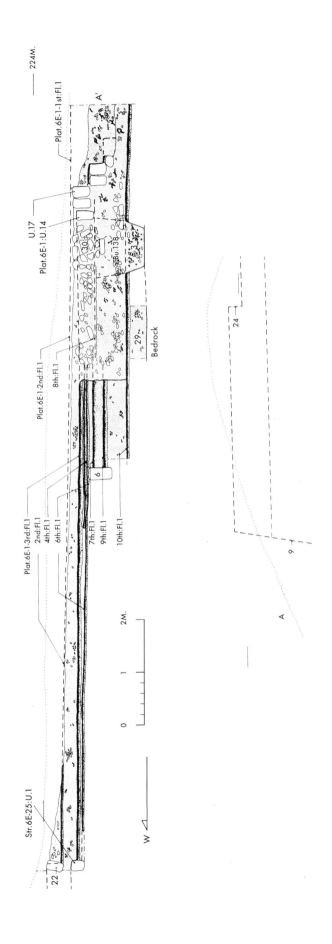

Gp. 6E-1: Section B-B', as located in Fig. 142–149.

Pertinent to Str. 6E-26: 14, Rear wall of 3rd, 2nd, and 1st, also the N wall for Plat. 6E-1-5th through 1st (see Fig. 146:14). *15*, Front wall of 2nd and 1st (see Fig. 149:15). Its height is reconstructed on the basis of the relative elevation of U. 8. *17*, Front wall, upper platform level of 2nd and 1st (see Fig. 149:17). *18*, Reconstructed top of the rear wall of 2nd and 1st, based on the height of the upper platform level (17) and the batter of existing wall masonry (14). A pavement is presumed to have run as shown in broken line. Note the surviving height of fill (32) N of the upper platform wall (17). *19, 20*, Steps, built for 2nd-D (see Fig. 147:19, 20). Their height is reconstructed from masonry off-section. Assumed is that there were plaster treads, as floors for the structure and Plat. 6E-1 were plaster. Note how the lowest step (19) was eliminated by the laying of Plat. 6E-1-2nd:Fl. 1. *31*, Light-colored earth, containing cultural debris, retained by the walls (14 and U. 1) of 26-3rd. This fill was placed as CS. 2. *32*, Earth fill for CS. 4 of 2nd-D. *33*, Midden behind 3rd, 2nd, and 1st (Table 2.320: Str. 6E-26:LG. 2e and 2f). U. 1, Front wall of 3rd (see Fig. 146). U. 2, Pause-line, marking the end of filling operations for Bu. 129 (CS. 3 for 26-3rd). U. 3, 6, Plaster floors for 3rd (see Fig. 146). There may once have been a freestanding wall between U. 3 and 6. U. 7, Pause-line, marking the end of fill operations for 26-3rd:CS. 2. U. 8, Plaster floor for 2nd-D (see Fig. 147). U. 11, Plaster floor for 1st (see Fig. 149). *Pertinent to Str. 6E-Sub.1: 4*, Walls of 2nd (see Fig. 142:4). Their reconstructed height is based on the presence of a step to gain access to the structure. Surviving fill consists of earth, some cultural material, and numerous stones. *5*, Walls of 1st (see Fig. 143:5). Fill for this structure is quite distinct from that for 2nd. Note how the base of the surviving wall masonry is set slightly below the elevation of Plat. 6E-1-9th:Fl. 1, and how the structure was eliminated with the laying of Plat. 6E-1-6th:Fl. 1. *Pertinent to Str. 6E-Sub.3: 8*, Hypothetical N wall (see Fig. 146:8). Its height and that of the structure are reconstructed from surviving masonry of the E wall. Note how the structure was eliminated with the laying of Plat. 6E-1-3rd:Fl. 1. *30*, Rocky earth, thought to be disturbed fill for Sub.3, suggested by its localization in the area of Sub.3. The vertical and horizontal distribution of this material beyond the structure is minimal, and is explicable on the basis of the eventual demolition of the structure (see also Fig. 150:30). *Pertinent to Plat. 6E-1: 11*, Reconstructed N wall for 6th (see Fig. 145:11). The N wall for Str. 6E-26-4th is thought to have been located directly above this. Later, Bu. 129 was intruded into Plat. 6E-1-6th. *29*, Fill for 10th; dark earth with a high organic content. North of Str. 6E-Sub.1-2nd, it is presumed to have risen as high as U. 2, as shown in broken line (see also Fig. 150:29). U. 2, N wall of 10th (see Fig. 142). U. 10, Fill for the N portion of 6th, this consisting of marl-like earth, with a stony deposit just N of Str. 6E-Sub.1. A rip-line beneath the wall (5) of 6E-Sub.1-1st indicates that earlier construction was torn out here, including the surface of Plat. 6E-1-10th (see 29), following which this material was dumped against what survived of Str. 6E-Sub.1. U. 12, Rubble remnant of retaining wall for 4th (Fig. 147). Fl. 1 of 10th (see Fig. 142). Fl. 1 of 9th (see Fig. 143), from off-section remains. The relative elevation of this floor to the base of the surviving wall masonry (5) of Str. 6E-Sub.1-1st, as well as to the top of the partially razed Str. 6E-Sub.1-2nd, indicates that the floor must have abutted the structure walls, and that floor and walls were contemporary. Fl. 1 of 8th (see Fig. 144), clearly laid after destruction of the floor for Plat. 6E-1-9th. Later, it seems to have been torn up except where protected by Str. 6E-Sub.3. As is common with Early Classic floors, this one runs beneath the contemporary Str. 6E-Sub.3. Fl. 1 of 7th (see Fig. 144) from off-section remains. Fl. 1 of 6th (see Fig. 145), from off-section remains. Note that Str. 6E-Sub.1-1st, but not 6E-Sub.3, probably was abandoned with the laying of this floor. Fl. 1 of 4th (see Fig. 147), from off-section remains. Fl. 1 of 3rd (see Fig. 148), from off-section remains. Note that Str. 6E-Sub.3 probably was abandoned with the laying of this floor. Fl. 1 of 2nd (see Fig. 148), from off-section remains. Unit 20 probably was part of this floor; note also that the floor eliminated the bottom step (19) for Str. 6E-26.

FIGURE 151

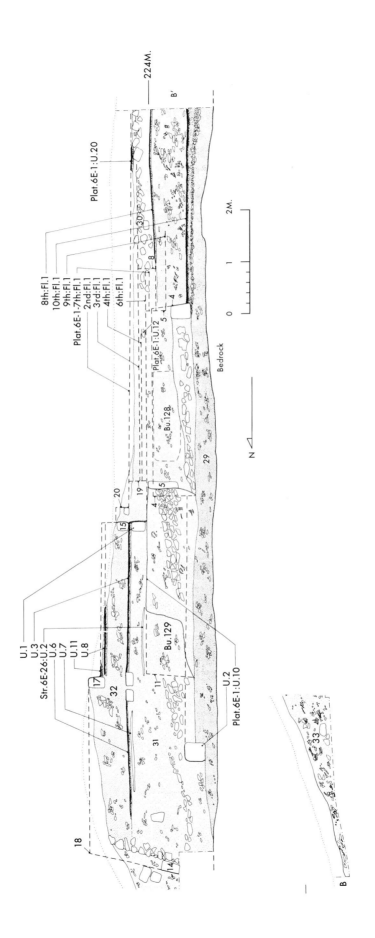

Gp. 6E-1: Section C-C', as located in Fig. 141–145 and 149.

Pertinent to Plat. 6E-1: U. 3, E wall for 10th (see Fig. 142); seems to retain the same dark earth on which U. 4 is laid, suggesting that U. 4 extended to the top of the wall. U. 4, Remains of a floor, thought to be Fl. 1 of 10th (see Fig. 142). U. 6, Informal occupation surface E of 9th (see Fig. 143). Beneath it is light-colored earth. U. 7, Informal occupation surface E of 8th (see Fig. 144). U. 34, Wall (off-section), thought to relate to an E stairway up to Plat. 6E-1-1st (see Fig. 149). U. 35, Informal occupation surface E of 1st (see Fig. 149). Fl. 1 of 11th (see Fig. 143). Fl. 1 of 10th (see Fig. 142). Fl. 1 of 9th (see Fig. 143). Its reconstruction is a projection from remains farther E, which are thought to have extended to a heightened version of U. 3. Fl. 1 of 1st (see Fig. 150). It is not know how far E this extended, but as shown here it extends to a point in line with the NE corner (Fig. 149:28) of Plat. 6E-1-1st. This does not accord with the interpretation of U. 34 as part of a stairway up to Plat. 6E-1-1st, so either the floor did not extend this far, or U. 34 is incorrectly interpreted.

FIGURE 152

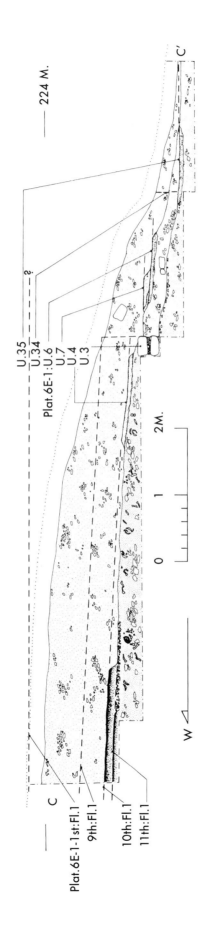

Ch. 6E-6: Plan (a) and Section A-A' (b), as located in Fig. 142–146 and 148.

Pertinent to Ch. 6E-6: 1, Stepped lip, unusual for its depth below the surface of bedrock. *2*, Edge of the deep portion of Chm.2, interpreted as the remains of the wall for a single lateral chamber of Ch. 6E-6-2nd. This was later altered so as to be incorporated into the larger Chm. 2, one of two lateral chambers, of Ch. 6E-6-1st. *3*, Sill in the constricted entrance between Chm. 1 and 2. Note the matching restriction on the ceiling of the entrance (section A-A'). *4*, Shaft masonry above Or. 2, the opening of Ch. 6E-6-1st. The three lowest courses of masonry are thought to relate to Plat. 6E-1-9th:Fl. 1. The shaft in its final form is seen to relate to the floor of Plat. 6E-1-7th, as the top of the shaft is the same distance below the floor for Plat. 6E-1-6th as is the floor of Plat. 6E-1-7th farther E. *5*, Stone rubble, placed in Or. 2 to support the fill for Plat. 6E-1-6th:Fl. 1. *6*, Loose earth, thought to have seeped in through the rubble (5) that seals Or. 2. *7*, Packed, gray earth that probably accumulated while the chultun was in use. *8*, Rubble that blocks the entrance between Chm. 1 and 2, retaining the earth and rubble fill in Chm. 1 and Neck 1. The fill is thought to have been placed when the shallow portion of Chm. 2, Chm. 3, and Or. 2 were constructed as Ch. 6E-6-1st. U. 1, Masonry blocks in Chm. 2, one of which may once have served as a stone cover for one of the orifices. *Pertinent to Plat. 6E-1*: Fl. 1 of 7th (see Fig. 144), reconstructed on the basis of the stratigraphic position of this floor farther E to Fl. 1 of 6th. Fl. 1 of 6th (see Fig. 145). Fl. 1 of 3rd (see Fig. 148).

FIGURE 153

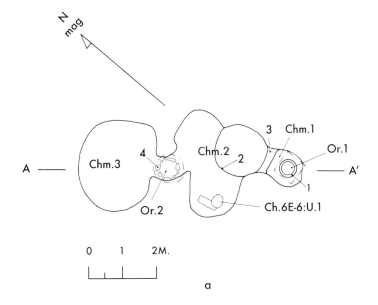

a

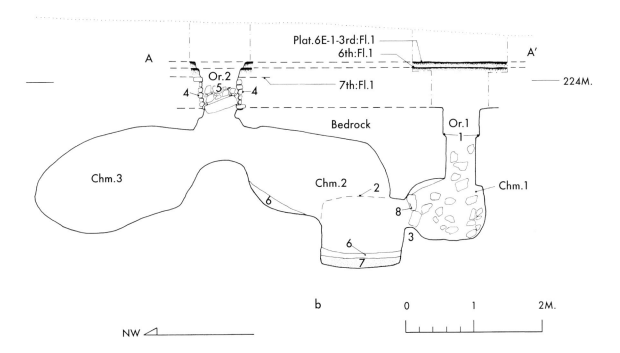

b

FIGURE 154

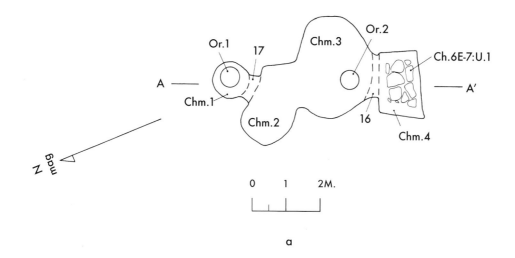

a

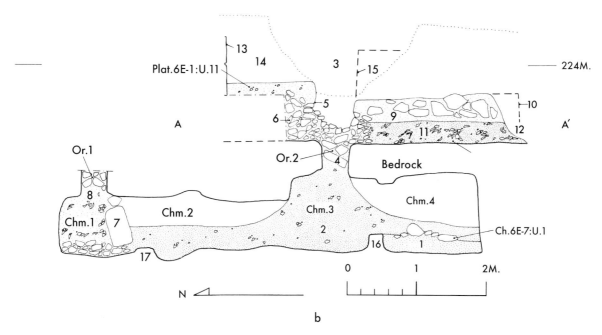

b

Ch. 6E-7: Plan (a) and Section A-A' (b), as located in Fig. 143–146.

Pertinent to Ch. 6E-7: 1, Compact, light-colored earth fill on which U. 1 was based. *2*, Loose earth, apparently derived from the slumping fill above Or. 2. *3*, Pit, resulting from the slump of fill into Or. 2. *4*, Rubble placed in Or. 2 to support overlying fill. *5*, Break in stratigraphy owing to slump of fill into chultun. *6*, Rubble, thought to have been placed to hold back fill around Or. 2. It cannot now be distinguished from the rubble in the orifice. *7*, Large masonry block that retained the fill (8) of Chm. 1, and against which the fill (2) of Chm. 2 eventually accumulated. *8*, Compact fill of earth, rubble, and trash purposely placed in Chm. 1 and Or. 1 in connection with the alterations that produced Ch. 6E-7-1st-B. *16*, Sill in the constricted entrance between Chm. 3 and 4. Note that it is matched by a restriction in the ceiling. *17*, Low sill between Chm. 1 and 2. The sides of this entrance are slightly restricted, but note the lack of a restriction on the ceiling. U. 1, Rectangular arrangement of rubble in Chm. 4, which rests on a fill of compact, light-colored earth. *Pertinent to Str. 6E-26: 13*, Surviving SE corner masonry of 3rd, 2nd, and 1st. *14*, Midden associated with 3rd, 2nd, and 1st. Pertinent to Str. 6E-Sub.1-2nd: *9*, Fill (see Fig. 151:4). Pertinent to Plat. 6E-1: *11*, Dark earth fill for 10th (see Fig. 151:29). *12*, Intrusive pit associated with Bu. 138 (see Fig. 150:3). *15*, Location of the E retaining wall for 5th (see Fig. 146:12). U. 11, Compact, light-colored earth that abuts Str. 6E-26-3rd (13). This deposit was prevented from falling into Or. 2 initially by masonry (6), but continued to build up E of Plat. 6E-1 after the chultun orifice was closed off.

FIGURE 155

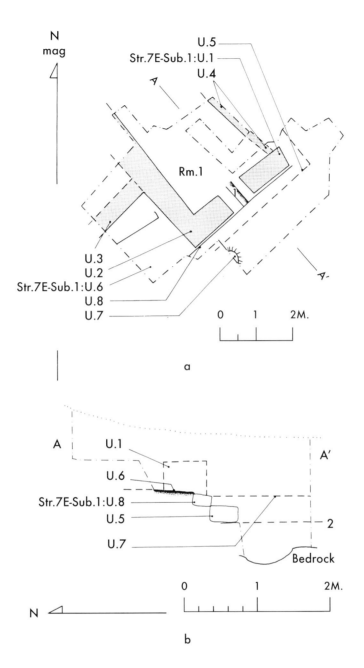

Str. 7E-Sub.1: Plan (*a*) and Section A-A' (*b*).

Pertinent to Str. 7F-Sub.1: 1, Channel 2 cm deep in the room floor, which slopes to the outside, evidently for drainage. *2*, Estimated height of the original plaza surface in front of the structure (see U. 5). U. 1, 2, 4, Freestanding building walls. Note the peculiar contrast in thickness between U. 4 and U. 1 and 2. In this, the building may be like the sweathouse of Str. J-17 at Piedras Negras. Original height of the walls is unknown. U. 3, Wall that abuts U. 2, could be either a freestanding wall, or the front wall of a platform. U. 5, Wall for a supplementary platform. Its height is not known, but the lack of known steps suggests that it may have been on the order of 0.20 m. U. 6, Plaster floor that runs N from the top of U. 8, both inside and outside Rm. 1. Note the slope of the floor to the periphery of the building (section A-A'). U. 7, Plaster floor remnant S of U. 8 at the same elevation as U. 6. Either the plaza in front of the structure was at some time raised to the same level as the building floor, or else the platform on which the building stood was considerably enlarged. U. 8, Front wall of the building platform. The excavator did not record what happens to this wall at the SE corner of the structure.

FIGURE 156

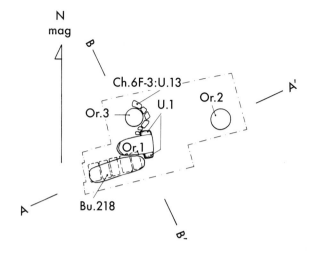

a

Ch. 6F-3: Surface excavations (*a*) and Plan (*b*).

Pertinent to Ch. 6F-3: U. 1, Notch cut in bedrock, probably to hold a large stone slab across the E end of Or. 1 (the slab is now missing). U. 2, Masonry and plaster wall, built on the sill (U. 15) between Chm. 2 and 3 and Chm.1. The E side of U. 2 was plastered part way up, and retained the fill (U. 8) in Chm. 2 and 3. U. 13, Stones around Or. 3 to retain surrounding fill. Based on bedrock, their tops are 0.14 m higher. Not shown are: (1) Ceramic test trench 0.50 m wide and 6 m long that runs N from these excavations. A similar trench runs from a point approximately 6 m W of these excavations. (2) Opening between Chm. 1 and 4, which was closed by a wall (U. 7) similar to U. 2. This appears on section in Fig. 157b, but its width was not recorded. For section A-A', B-B', and C-C', see Fig. 157.

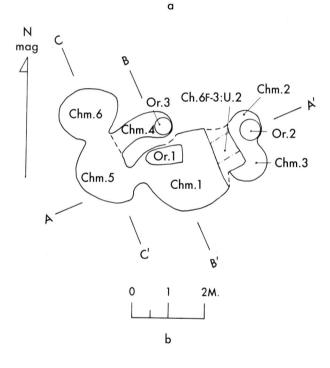

b

Figure 157 (facing page)

Ch. 6F-3: Sections A-A' (a), B-B' (b), and C-C' (c), as located in Fig. 156.

Pertinent to Ch. 6F-3: 1, Or. 1, off-section. U. 1, Notch in bedrock (see Fig. 156). U. 2, Wall in entrance between Chm. 1 and 2 (see Fig. 156b). U. 3, Grayish-white deposit on the floor of Chm. 1; contains some small stones, but is not packed hard. U. 4, Layer of fine yellowish-gray marl that abuts U. 2 and is devoid of stones, sherds, and artifacts. U. 5, Layer of gray soil, deepest under Or. 1, and abuts U. 2. Contains small stones and a few sherds and artifacts. U. 6, Dark brown soil deepest beneath Or. 1, abuts U. 2 and 7 and contains a few sherds and artifacts. U. 7, Plaster and masonry wall that closed an opening between Chm. 1 and 4. U. 8, Brownish- to light-gray deposit loaded with sherds and artifacts, retained by U. 2. U. 9, Grainy, grayish-white earth with about 4 pounds of Cauac sherds of midden quality. U. 10, Dark brown earth with ca. 3 pounds of Cauac sherds of midden quality. U. 11, 12, Strata of fine-textured, white earth, not packed and devoid of cultural material. *Pertinent to Plat. 6F-1*: U. 1, Gray earth, filled with stones. The top of this stratum may have been covered with plaster to provide a plaza in front of Str. 6F-62. U. 2, Dark brown earth above the probable plaza.

FIGURE 157

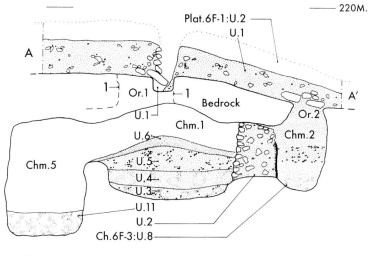

a

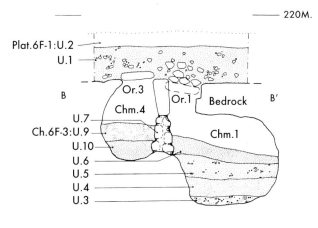

b

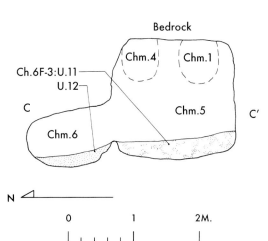

c

FIGURE 158

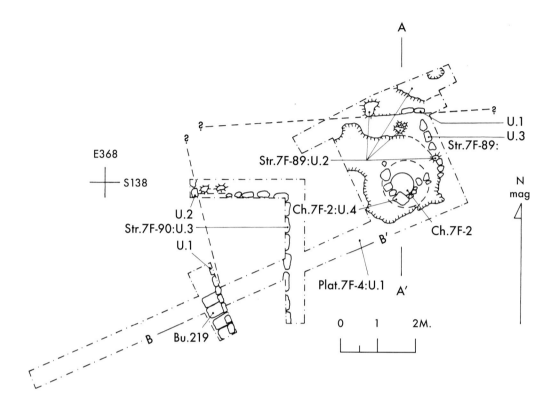

Str. 7F-89, 90, and Ch. 7F-2: Plan.

Pertinent to Str. 7F-89: U. 1, S wall of 2nd. Platform 7F-4:U. 1 turns up to its base, and both floor and wall are based in the same fill. Where the wall masonry is missing, the turnup of Plat. 7F-4:U. 1 indicates its one-time presence. Total length of the wall is unknown. U. 2, Floor, close to the elevation of the top of U. 1 as it now survives. The large remnant of the floor N of the surviving masonry of U. 1 may have been part of the pavement for 2nd; the other portions are thought to relate to a platform added on to the S (89-1st). Unit 2 apparently once sealed Ch. 7F-2. U. 3, Wall, thought to relate to 89-1st. It may have abutted U. 1, and may have turned a corner to extend W at its S end. The elevation of its top is near that of U. 2, traces of which occur W, but not E, of the wall. Unit 3 was built on Plat. 7F-4:U. 1. *Pertinent to Str. 7F-90*: U. 1, E wall of 2nd; Plat. 7F-4:U. 1 turns up onto the face of this wall. U. 2, Wall, probably part of the E wall of 2nd; its elevation and alignment are identical to U. 1. U. 3, Wall, built on Plat. 7F-4:U. 1, which probably abutted U. 2. This modification defines 90-1st. *Pertinent to Ch. 7F-2*: U. 4, Rubble surrounding the orifice, all that remains of a masonry and rubble seal. It projects above the surface of Plat. 7F-4:U. 1. Note the extension of the rubble towards Str. 7F-89:U. 3; perhaps the rubble was incorporated into a S wall for 7F-89-1st. *Pertinent to Plat. 7F-4*: U. 1, Floor that turns up to Str. 7F-89:U. 1 and 7F-90:U. 1, and on which Str. 7F-89:U. 3 and 7F-90:U. 3 were built. For sections A-A' and B-B', see Fig. 159.

FIGURE 159

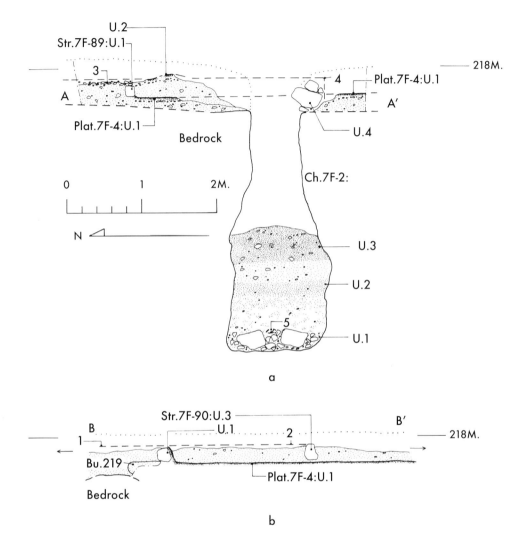

Str. 7F-89, 90, and Ch. 7F-2: Sections A-A' (*a*) and B-B' (*b*), as located in Fig. 158.

Pertinent to Str. 7F-89: 3, Layer of small stones, possibly disintegrated floor foundation for 2nd. Note its position just below the surface of Str. 7F-89:U. 2, part of which may have served as floor for 89-2nd. *4*, Hypothetical S wall of 1st (see Fig. 158, Ch. 7F-2:U. 4). U. 1, S wall of 2nd (see Fig. 158). U. 2, Floor of 1st (see Fig. 158). *Pertinent to Str. 7F-90: 1*, Reconstructed floor level of 2nd. *2*, Reconstructed floor level of 1st. U. 1, E wall of 2nd (see Fig. 158). U. 3, E wall of 1st (see Fig. 158). *Pertinent to Ch. 7F-2: 5*, Censer (Coe 1965:35), possibly thrown in as an offering on U. 1 (PD. 262). U. 1, Masonry and midden debris from collapse of rubble seal in the chultun orifice. Some of the masonry is similar to masonry from U. 4. U. 2, Gray-white to darker gray fill, possibly purposely placed to cover the censer (5). U. 3, Darker brown fill, more recent natural accumulation of forest detritus. U. 4, Rubble masonry remains of chultun seal (see Fig. 158). Note its projection above Plat. 7F-4:U. 1. *Pertinent to Plat. 7F-4:* U. 1, Plaza floor (see Fig. 158).

Plat. 7G-1 and Ch. 7G-4, 6: Plan (*a*) and Section A-A' (*b*).

Pertinent to Plat. 7G-1: U. 1, Wall, perhaps for a structure or terrace; Plat. 7G-1:U. 2 turns up to its E face (see also U. 6). U. 2, Lowermost plaza floor, which turns up to the E face of U. 1. U. 3, Wall, perhaps for a structure of which U. 1 was a part, or a second structure or a terrace. Its elevation is the same as that of U. 1 (see also U. 6). U. 4, Floor 0.10 m above the elevation of U. 2; abuts the masonry blocks (2) that sealed Ch. 7G-4 (see also U. 6). U. 5, Plaster on the stone cover for Ch. 7G-6; its elevation is the same as that of U. 4, so it could be part of the same floor. Or, it could be plaster on a piece of masonry reused from some other context. U. 6, Floor remnant at the same elevation as U. 4, and probably part of the same pavement. Either this covered U. 1 and 3, or else U. 1 and 3 are parts of different constructions between which this floor ran. U. 7, 8, Masonry blocks that overlie U. 2 or its reconstructed level. *Pertinent to Ch. 7G-4: 1*, Maximum breadth of the chultun. *2*, Stone slabs that sealed the chultun. Note that the center slab is broken; its W end is in situ, but the bulk of the block is in the chultun, on U. 3. *3*, PD. 263, Vessel 7C-1. *4*, PD. 263, Vessel 7C-2. *5*, Masonry slab, possibly one of a series of three that predate those that eventually sealed the chultun. *6*, Steps, cut into the walls of the chultun. *7*, Bedrock "bench," cut into the E wall of the chultun. U. 1, Yellow-gray soil, containing some Manik sherds and human skull fragments. U. 2, Gray soil full of midden-quality early Imix sherds and some artifacts. U. 3, Light, yellow-gray soil, with Imix sherds, some Manik sherds of midden quality, and PD. 263. U. 4, Dark-to-light brown soil, thought to have washed into the chultun following partial collapse of its seal. *Pertinent to Ch. 7G-6: 8*, Stone cover; its NW corner is broken off.

FIGURE 160

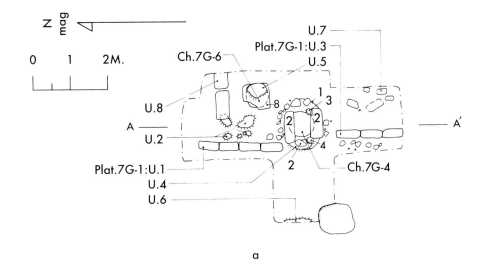

a

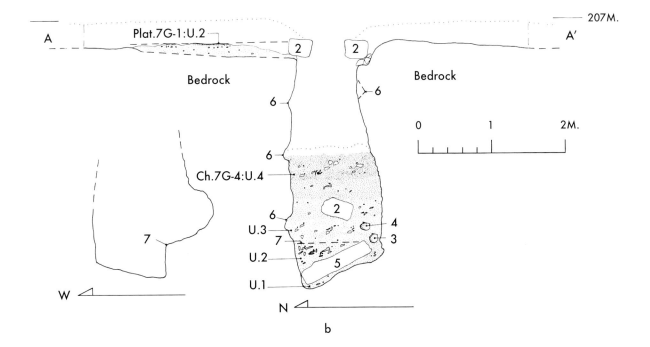

b

FIGURE 161

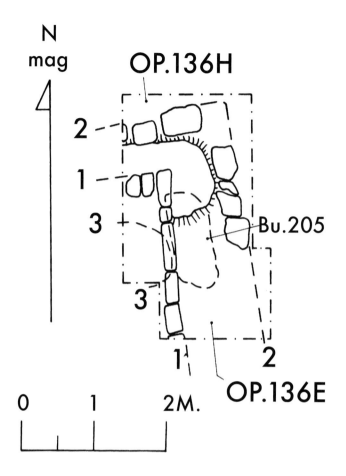

Plan of test pit, Gp. 1D-7.

1, NE corner, Str. 1D-7. The wall rests on the remains of a floor (3) for the group platform. *2*, NE corner of the group platform. The floor shown inside this wall is pavement for the platform that predates the floor (3) on which Str. 1D-7 was built. *3*, Floor for the group platform on which Str. 1D-7 was built; it overlies another, shown here N and E of Str. 1D-7. Its fill is brown to gray soil, with chunks of limestone.

Figure 162 (facing page)

Burials from Gp. 2G-1 (*a–e*), as located in Fig. 21 and 22.

a, Bu. 49. *1-3*, Pottery vessels; *4*, Skull. Not shown are two stone slabs that covered the burial (see Fig. 22). *b*, Bu. 50. *1–3*, Pottery vessels. *c*, Bu. 53. *1*, Pottery vessel; *2*, Skull fragments. *d*, Bu. 52. *1–3*, Pottery vessels; *4*, Skull fragments. *e*, Bu. 54. *1–3*, Pottery vessels.

FIGURE 162

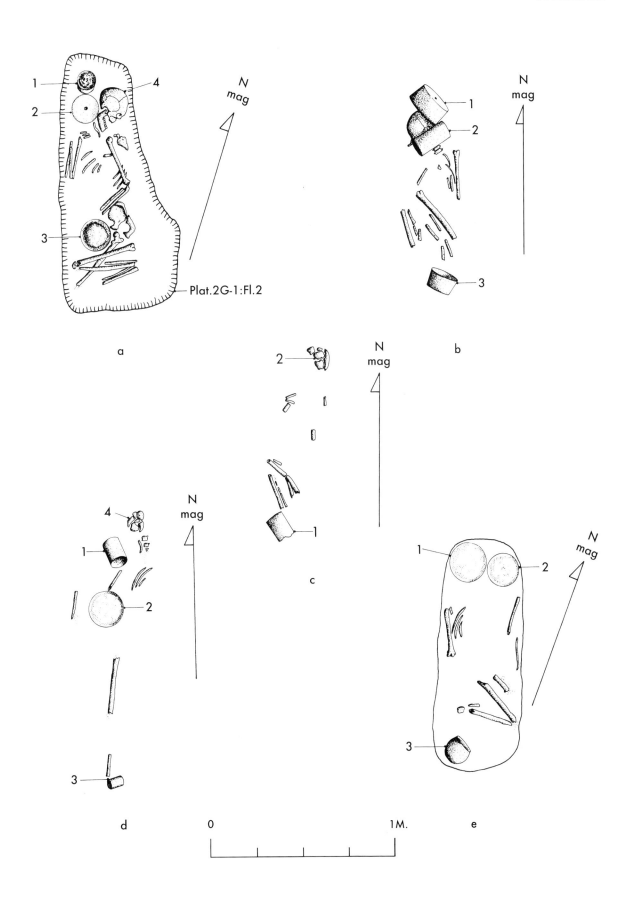

Plat.2G-1:Fl.2

a

b

c

d

e

0   1M.

Burials from Gp. 2G-1, as located in Fig. 20-22.

a, Bu. 55. 1, N stone of W wall of grave; 2, N stone of E wall of grave. Not shown are two stone slabs that covered the burial (see Fig. 22). *b*, Bu. 58. *1–4*, Pottery vessels. *5*, Femur. *c*, Bu. 56. *1*, *2*, Complete pottery vessels; *3*, Rim sherds. *d*, Bu. 59. *e*, Bu. 57. *1*, Pottery vessel; *2*, Clay bead; *3*, Skull fragment.

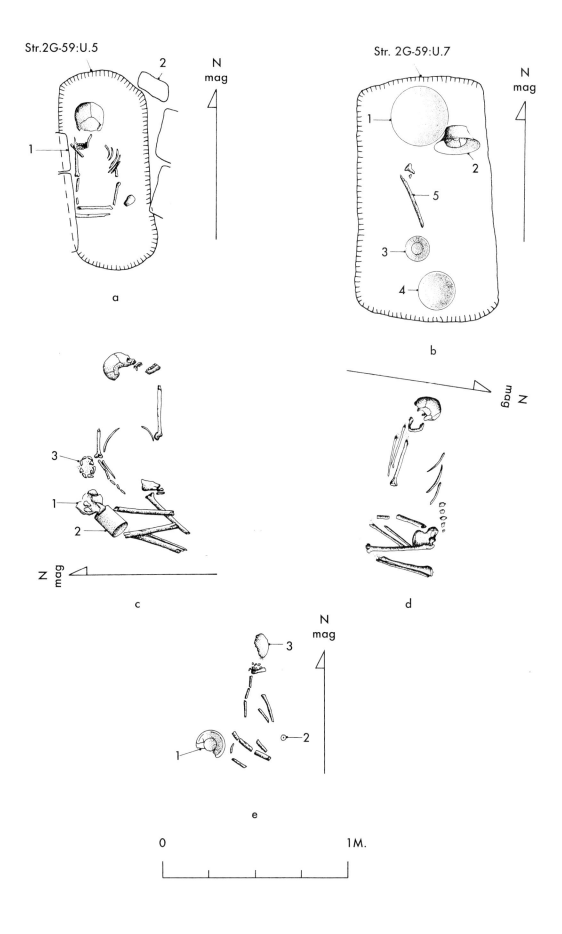

FIGURE 163

Str.2G-59:U.5

Str. 2G-59:U.7

a

b

c

d

e

0   1M.

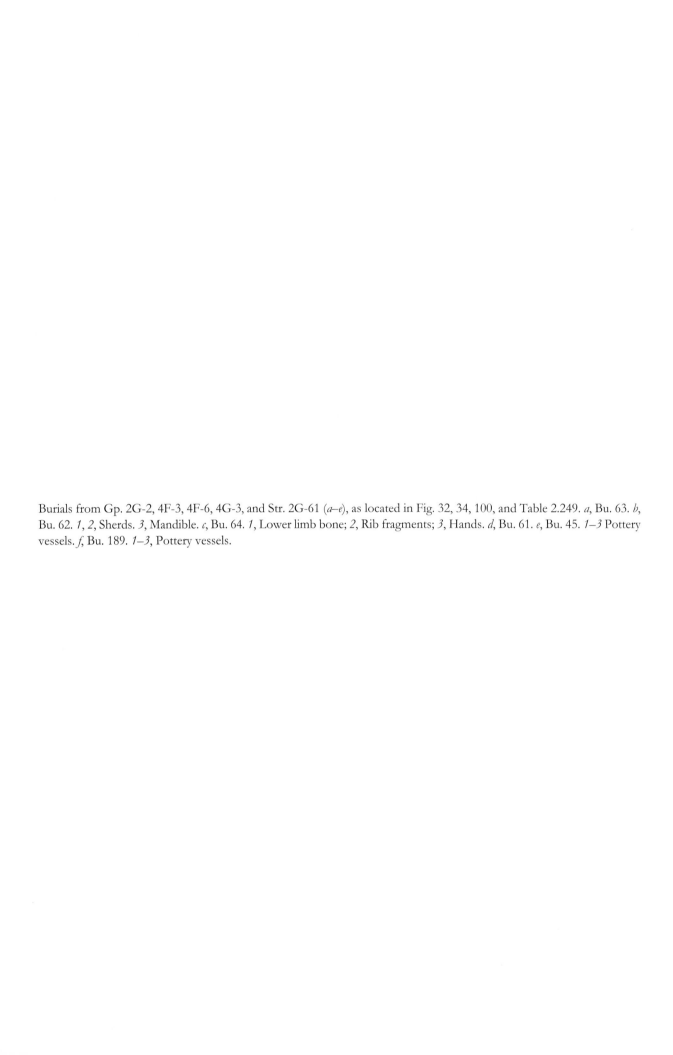

Burials from Gp. 2G-2, 4F-3, 4F-6, 4G-3, and Str. 2G-61 (*a–e*), as located in Fig. 32, 34, 100, and Table 2.249. *a*, Bu. 63. *b*, Bu. 62. *1*, *2*, Sherds. *3*, Mandible. *c*, Bu. 64. *1*, Lower limb bone; *2*, Rib fragments; *3*, Hands. *d*, Bu. 61. *e*, Bu. 45. *1–3* Pottery vessels. *f*, Bu. 189. *1–3*, Pottery vessels.

FIGURE 164

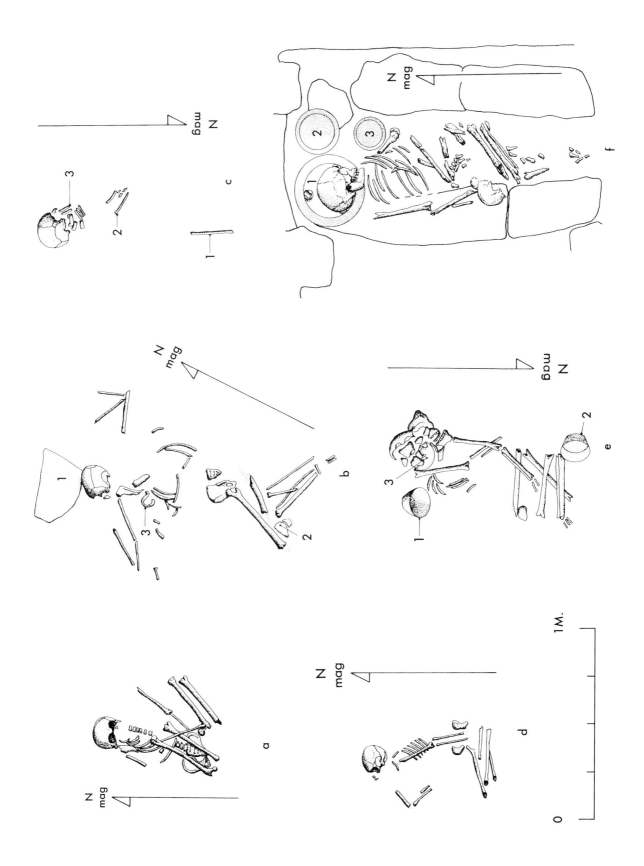

FIGURE 165

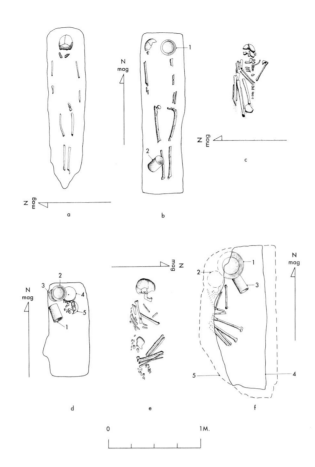

Burials from Gp. 3F-1 and 3F-2 (*a–f*), as located in Fig. 41, 42, 46, and 48a.
a, Bu. 65. Not shown are five stone slabs that covered the burial (see Fig. 41a). *b*, Bu. 66. *1*, *2*, Pottery vessels. Not shown are five stone slabs that covered the burial (see Fig. 41a). *c*, Bu. 67. *d*, Bu. 70. *1–4*, Pottery vessels; *5*, Skull. Not shown are three stone slabs that covered the burial (see Fig. 48a). *e*, Bu. 69. *f*, Bu. 68. *1–3*, Pottery vessels; *4*, Top of grave; *5*, Floor of grave.

Figure 166 (facing page)
Burials from Gp. 5D-1, 6C-1, and 6C-2 (*a–f*), as located in Fig. 93, 117, 122, and 125.
a, Bu. 169. *1*, *2*, Pottery vessels; *3*, Entrance; *4*, Burial chamber. *b*, Bu. 170; *c*, Bu. 171; *d*, Bu. 136; *e*, Bu. 146; *f*, Bu. 145.

FIGURE 166

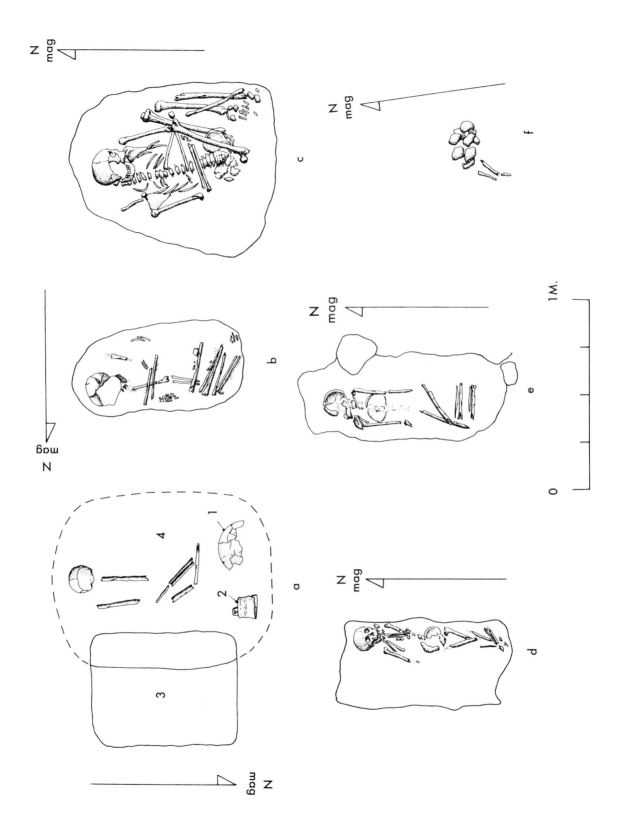

Burials from Gp. 5F-1 and Str. 4C-34 (*a–c*), as located in Fig. 104 and Table 2.161. *a, b*, Bu. 212 plan and section. *1–3*, Pottery vessels; *4*, Skull. *c*, Bu. 158. "A" shows the skeleton after removal of the pottery and some stones (shown in B). *1–3*, Pottery vessels; *4*, Cinnabar.

FIGURE 167

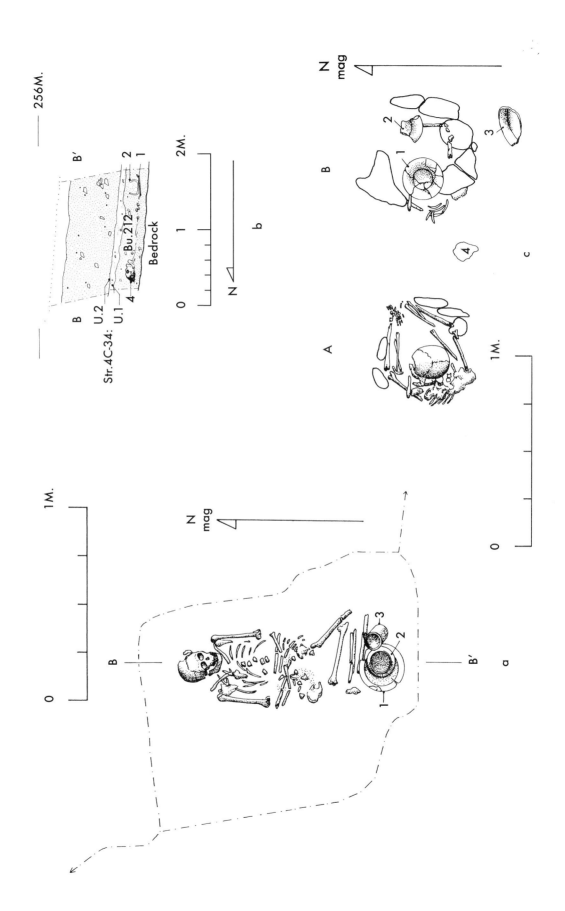

Burials from Gp. 6E-1 (*a–f*), as located in Fig. 143–147.
a, Bu. 128. *1–5*, Pottery vessels. The urn that contained the body is beneath 2. *b*, Bu. 129. *1*, Shell fragments; *2*, Sherd. *c*, Bu. 130. *1*, *2*, Pottery vessels. *d*, Bu. 138. *e*, Bu. 152. *1–4*, Pottery vessels; *5*, Front of the stairs for Str. 6E-26-2nd. *f*, Bu. 151.

FIGURE 168

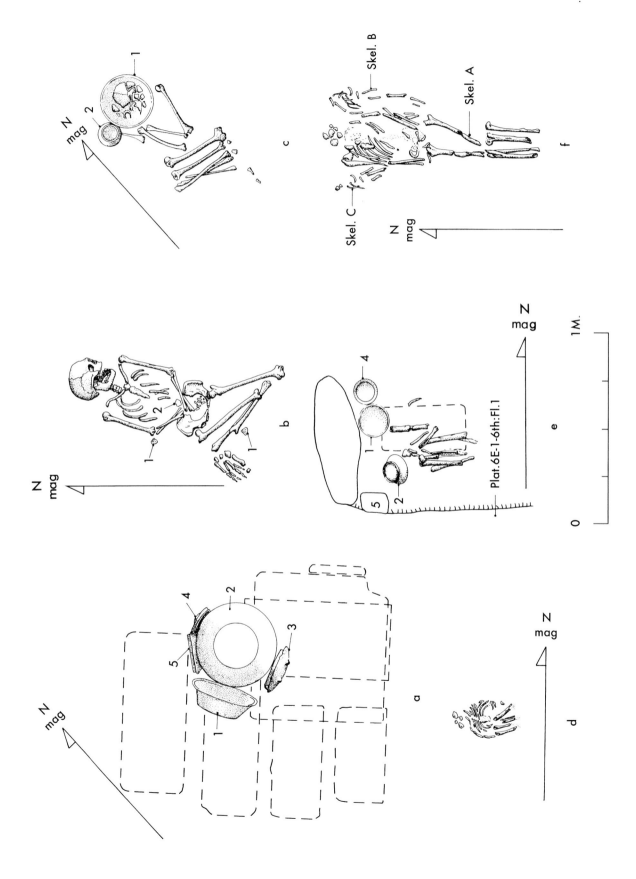

Burials from Gp. 6E-1 (*a*,*b*), 1D-2 (*c*), and 1D-7 (*d*), as located in Fig. 144, 148, 161, and Table 2.368. *a*, Bu. 153. *b*, Bu. 161. *c*, Bu. 208. *d*, Bu. 205.

FIGURE 169

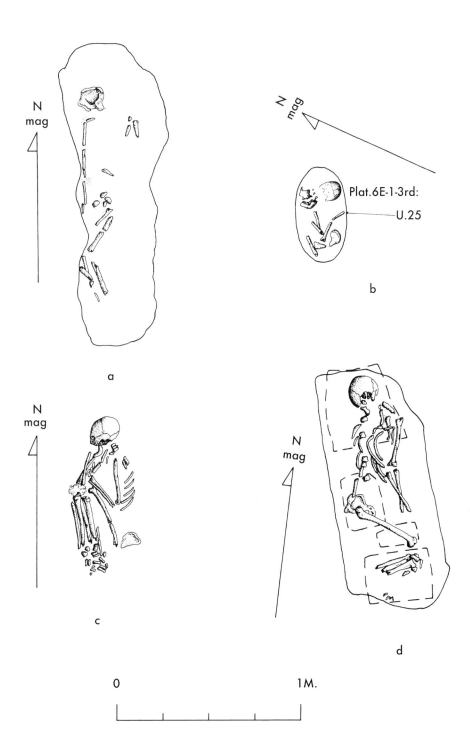

N
mag

b

Plat.6E-1-3rd:

U.25

a

N
mag

N
mag

c

d

0   1M.

PD. 231 in Ch. 6C-11.

1, Jar neck 66H-17; *2*, Jar neck 66H-48; *3*, Sherd from 66H-52; *4*, Jar neck 66H-21; *5*, Jar neck 66H-20; *6*, Large sherd from 66H-49 or 50; *7*, Objects of shell 66H-12a, b (Chm. 1), 66H-43 or 46 (entrance to Chm. 3), 66H-44a,b (Chm. 3); *8*, Complete manos 66H-22 (Chm. 2) and 66H-41 (Chm. 3), rubbing stone 66H-40 (Chm. 3); *9*, Obsidian thin bifaces 66H-26, 27, and 28 (Chm. 1), 66H-42 (Chm. 3); *10*, Miniature cup or candelero 66H-19; *11*, Centrally perforated bone disc 66H-24; *12*, Celt 66H-29; *13*, Rib cage overlying uncatalogued obsidian prismatic blade; *14*, Sherds from 66H-17, 20, 21, 48-51, 53; *15*, Burned stone (uncatalogued); *16*, Shell pendants 66H-13a,b; *17*, rectangular/oval chert biface; *18*, cut or scarcely altered shell 66H-43 or 46; *19*, Quartzite beach pebble with cinnabar 66H-9; *20*, Chert thin biface with cinnabar 66H-11; *21*, Chert thin biface 66H-39; *22*, Shell pendant 66H-54; *23*, Oliva shell tinkler 66H-45. For complete description, see text.

FIGURE 170

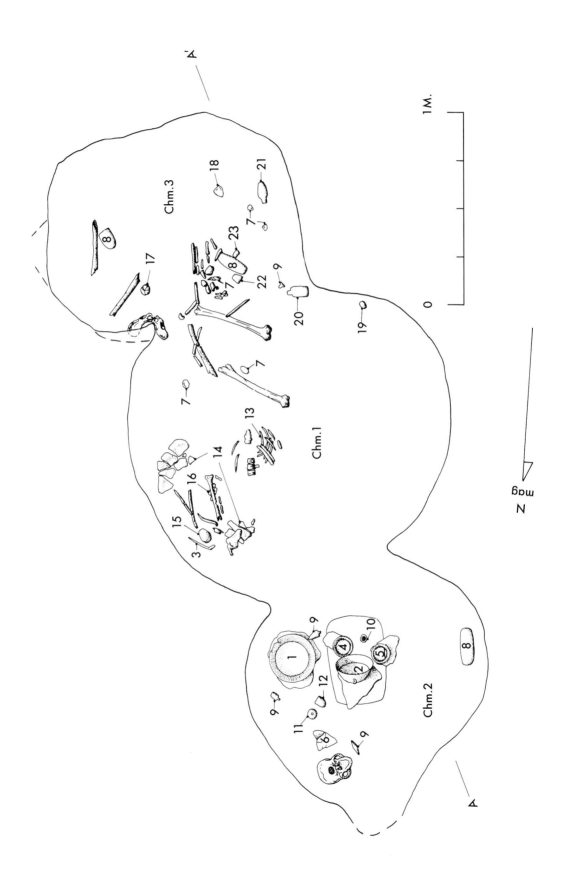

Probable secondary or disturbed burials (*a–d*), as located in Fig. 171c, 27, and 62.
a, c, PD. 221. *1, 2*, Pottery vessels. *b*, PD. 64. *1*, Pottery vessel; *2*, Teeth and left temporal fragment; *3*, Femur; *4*, Tibia fragment. *d*, PD. 110. *1*, Skull fragments; *2*, Vertebrae; *3*, Humerus; *4*, Ribs; *5*, Pelvic fragments; *6*, Mandible; *7*, Quarried bedrock; *8*, S and W extent of deposit.

FIGURE 171

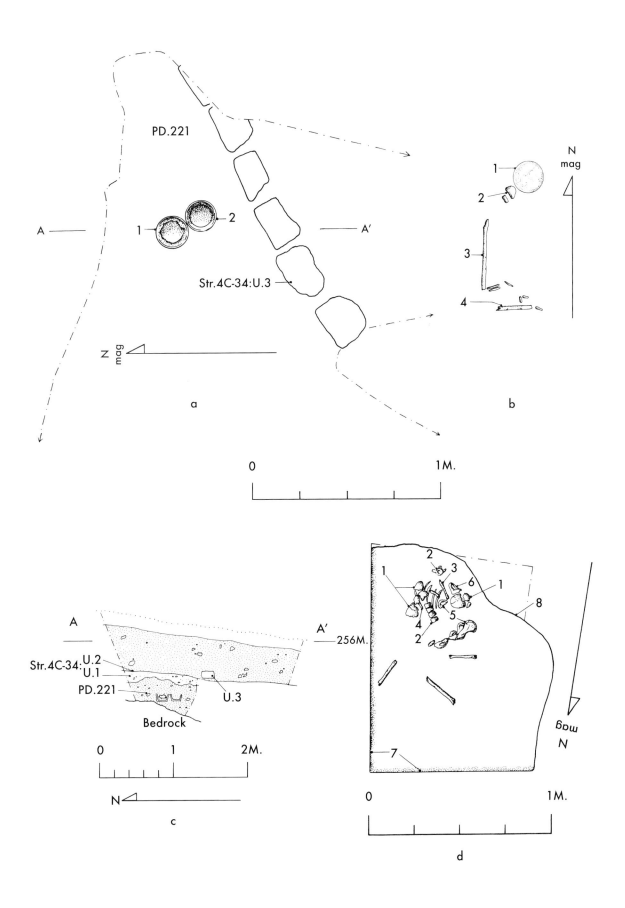

PD.221

1 2

A —— —— A'

Str.4C-34:U.3

N mag

0 1M.

a

N mag

1
2
3
4

b

A A'
256M.

Str.4C-34: U.2
U.1
PD.221
U.3
Bedrock

0 1 2M.

N

c

2
1 3
6 1
8
4 5
2
7

N mag

0 1M.

d

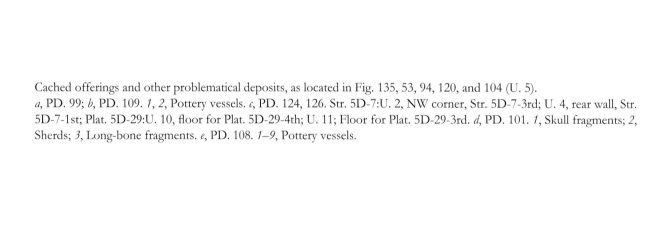

Cached offerings and other problematical deposits, as located in Fig. 135, 53, 94, 120, and 104 (U. 5).
a, PD. 99; *b*, PD. 109. *1*, *2*, Pottery vessels. *c*, PD. 124, 126. Str. 5D-7:U. 2, NW corner, Str. 5D-7-3rd; U. 4, rear wall, Str. 5D-7-1st; Plat. 5D-29:U. 10, floor for Plat. 5D-29-4th; U. 11; Floor for Plat. 5D-29-3rd. *d*, PD. 101. *1*, Skull fragments; *2*, Sherds; *3*, Long-bone fragments. *e*, PD. 108. *1–9*, Pottery vessels.

FIGURE 172

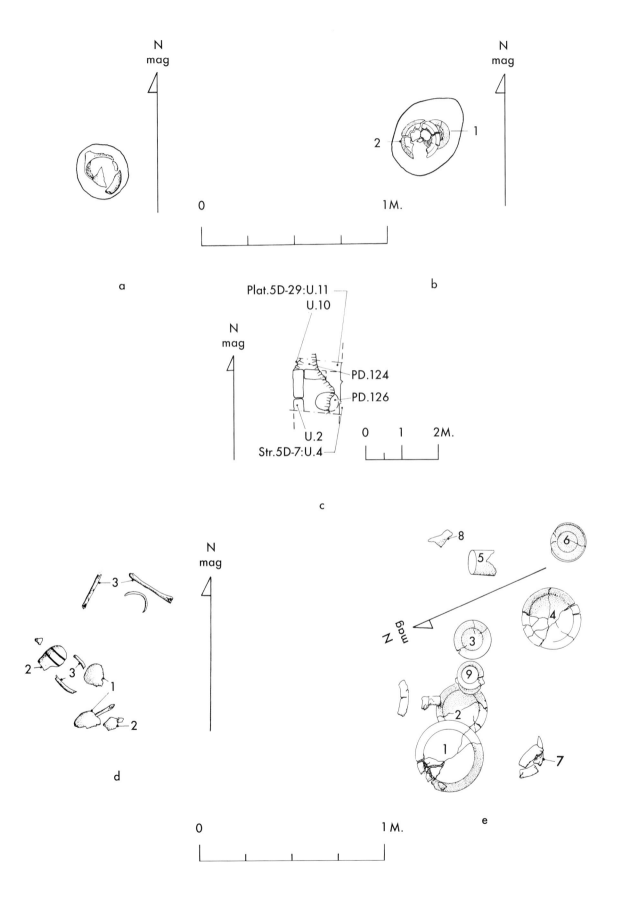

a

b

N
mag

0   1M.

Plat.5D-29:U.11
U.10

N
mag

PD.124

PD.126

U.2
Str.5D-7:U.4

0   1   2M.

c

N
mag

3

2

3

1

2

d

0   1M.

8

5

6

4

N
mag

3

9

2

1

7

e

FIGURE 173

a

b

c

d

a. Str. 2G-59, from U. 18, looking N at U. 15 (see Fig. 20, 21). The masonry remaining on U. 16 (Fig. 20) is a remnant of the rear wall of Str. 2G-59-2nd (Fig. 21:2). The trench penetrates to bedrock. Overlying earth fill (Fig. 23, 24:16) is stone fill between U. 10 and 17 (Fig. 20, 21). A portion of U. 10 is visible to the left, U. 17 to the right. Unit 14 (Fig. 20) may be seen between U. 10 and 15. *b*. NW corner, Str. 2G-59-2nd, showing in situ the masonry block (Fig. 21:5) that apparently was removed from the stairway to provide room for Bu. 56. The arrow is on Plat. 2G-1:Fl. 2 (Fig. 23), about where the feet of the subject of Bu. 56 were located. The SW corner of Str. 2G-Sub.1 is visible to the left. *c*. Bu. 54 from Str. 2G-59. See Fig. 162e. *d*. Bu. 55 from Str. 2G-59. See Fig. 163a.

FIGURE 174

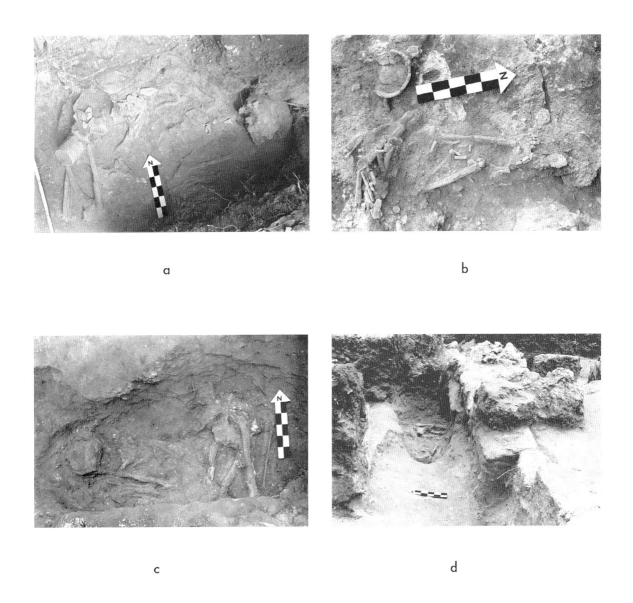

a

b

c

d

a. Bu. 56 from Str. 2G-59. See Fig. 163c. *b.* Bu. 57, from Str. 2G-59. See Fig. 163e. *c.* Bu. 59 from Str. 2G-59. See Fig. 163d. *d.* Bu. 59 from Str. 2G-59: View from the W. On the right is U. 17. See Fig. 22, 163d.

FIGURE 175

a

b

c

d

a. View of the location of Str. 2G-61, before excavation. Note the lack of any visible sign that a structure once stood here. *b.* Or. 1 of Ch. 2G-2, before excavation (see Fig. 34:10). Note the almost complete filling. *c.* Outer face of the N wall of Str. 2G-61 (see Fig. 34:1). *d.* W wall of Str. 2G-61, looking S. The S end of U. 5 (Fig. 34) is visible in the foreground, the stone cover of Ch. 2G-1 (Fig. 34:7 and 175a) in the distance.

FIGURE 176

a

b

c

d

a. Orifice 1 of Ch. 2G-1 (Fig. 34:7) after clearing of bedrock, with the stone cover in place. Shown here is the stepped lip, and displacement of the lid by a tree root. *b*. View looking S at the NE corner of Str. 3F-25 (fill inside has been removed; see Fig. 42). *c*. Orifice of Ch. 3F-6 in Gp. 3F-1. See Fig. 44, 45. *d*. PD. 65 in Ch. 3F-6. See Fig. 44.

FIGURE 177

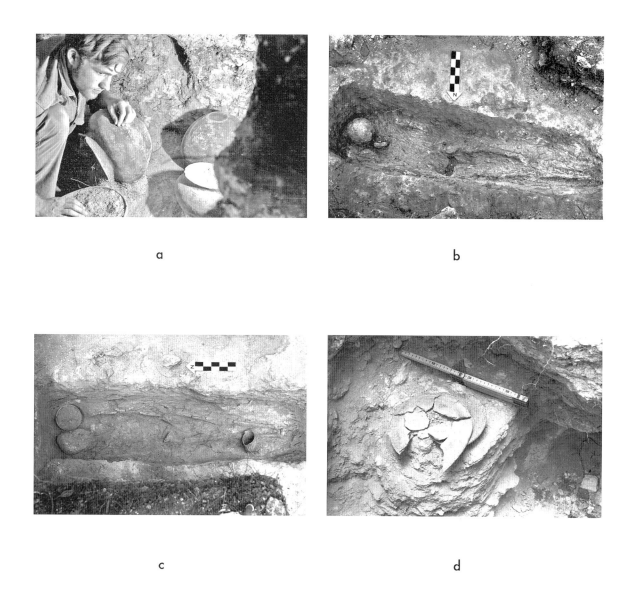

a
b

c
d

a. Vessels of PD. 65 from Ch. 3F-6 in situ with the late Dennis Puleston. *b*. Bu. 65 from Gp. 3F-1. See Fig. 165a. *c*. Bu. 66 from Gp. 3F-1 (see Fig. 165b). *d*. PD. 109 from Str. 3F-12 in Gp. 3F-3. See Fig. 172b.

FIGURE 178

a

b

c

d

a. Ch. 5C-8 beneath Str. 5C-56: View W into Chm. 3 from Chm. 1 (see Fig. 70). In the W wall are the openings to Chm. 4 (left) and 6 (right). *b*. View from the western edge of trench (Fig. 74), looking towards Str. 4E-14 in Gp. 4E-1. In the foreground is MS. 61; MS. 57 is in background. Both rest on Str. 4E-14:U. 8 (Fig. 75). Marl is exposed in the trench. *c*. Str. 4E-50 in Gp. 5E-2: View of the inner face of the front wall N of the doorway in Rm. 1 with characteristic rectangular blocks typical of Late Classic masonry. The arrow is on the floor of the interior platform, pointing N to U. 16 (see Fig. 81), a dividing wall. Between wall and interior platform is the room floor, running N to the partition between Rm. 1 and 3. *d*. Str. 4F-21 in Gp. 4F-3: View of the eastern half. The arrow lies on the rubble remnant of the front wall (U. 1) of the upper platform level. Behind U. 1 is U. 2, a dwarf wall (see Fig. 100).

FIGURE 179

a. Str. 4F-48 in Gp. 4F-3: A small square structure off the E end of 4F-21. *b.* Bu. 61 in Gp. 4F-3 (see Fig. 164d). *c.* Bu. 189 in Gp. 4G-3 (see Fig. 164f). *d.* Masonry of W wall, Str. 6C-45-5th in Gp. 6C-1 (see Fig. 117a).

FIGURE 180

a

b

c

d

a. N end of Str. 6C-45-3rd in Gp. 6C-1 (see Fig. 118a). Edward Crocker is on the floor of 3rd; in front of him is the front wall for 2nd and 1st (see Fig. 118b). *b*. Bu. 146 in Str. 6C-45 (see Fig. 166e). *c*. PD. 101 in Gp. 6C-1 (see Fig. 172d). *d*. Gp. 6E-1: The first day of excavations (June 1963). View is looking W over Plat. 6E-1, S of Str. 6E-26.

FIGURE 181

a

b

c

d

a. Plat. 6E-1: Narrow stairs constructed against the E wall of Plat. 6E-1 in TS. 5 (Fig. 148). The view is from the S looking N towards Str. 6E-26. *b*. E end of S (front) wall of Str. 6E-26-3rd in Gp. 6E-1, to SE corner. Shown is where its W end abutted a battered E wall of Plat. 6E-1-5th (Fig. 146). This was torn out for construction of Plat. 6E-1-4th and Str. 6E-26-2nd-D (Fig. 147). *c*. Small, square Str. 6E-162, off the E end of 6E-26 (Fig. 149); view from the N looking S. Shown are fragments of a single metate on its floor. The trowel rests on the floor of Plat. 5E-1, near a spot where fragments of burned material were found. *d*. View from above of midden E of Str. 6E-26-4th (Table 2.320:LG. 2a). Sherds are all from Imix vessels.

FIGURE 182

a. Masonry shaft above Or. 2 of Ch. 6E-6 in Gp. 6E-1 (see Fig. 143, 144). *b.* Bu. 128 in Gp. 6E-1 before removal of stones covering the grave (meter stick oriented N-S). *c.* Bu. 128 in Gp. 6E-1 after removal of covering stones. View is from S looking N (see Fig. 168a). *d.* Bu. 152 in Gp. 6E-1 before removal of covering stone and Vessel No. 2 (see Fig. 168e).

a. Bu. 152 in Gp. 6E-1 after removal of Vessel No. 2; Vessel No. 1 now visible (see Fig. 168e). *b*. Bu. 152 in Gp. 6E-1 after removal of covering stone and pottery vessels (see Fig. 168e). *c*. Bu. 151 in Gp. 6E-1 before removal of covering stones. *d*. Bu. 151 in Gp. 6E-1 after removal of covering stones (scale lies E of SK. A; see Fig. 168f). *e*. PD. 99 in Gp. 7C-1 (see Fig. 172a).

FIGURE 183

a

b

c

d

e